JANE'S FIGHTING SHIPS
OF WORLD WAR II

JANE'S FIGHTING SHIPS
OF WORLD WAR II

FOREWORD BY ANTONY PRESTON

CRESCENT BOOKS
NEW YORK • AVENEL, NEW JERSEY

Jane's Fighting Ships of WW II
Originally published by Jane's Publishing Company
1946/7

This 1994 edition published by Crescent Books,
distributed by Outlet Book Company, Inc., a Random House Company,
40 Engelhard Avenue, Avenel, New Jersey 07001.

Reprinted 1989, 1992, 1994

By arrangement with the proprietor

Printed in Singapore

ISBN 0 517 67963 9

8 7 6 5 4 3

PUBLISHER'S NOTE

This volume is reproduced from the 1945/6 edition of *Jane's All The World's Aircraft*, which was the first wholly uncensored issue of the famous book to appear following the opening of hostilities in 1939. The publication of this original volume was delayed following the emergence of numerous, until then, confidential reports from the Allied nations and indeed from Germany and Japan. Much of this newly released information was incorporated by the original editor. This volume has been specifically reformatted and the amendments and additions to the original edition have been incorporated into the text at the appropriate place. It should be remembered that this volume represents what was known at the time, and therefore follows the contemporary official reports, although new facts about the Second World War have inevitably since emerged. This edition does nevertheless represent the best compendium of information on the airforces of the world at the time of first publication.

RANDOM HOUSE

New York • Toronto • London • Sydney • Auckland

CONTENTS

FOREWORD

Antony Preston

How *Jane's Fighting Ships* has changed in forty years. This reprint brings back vivid memories of a world which has totally vanished, a time when the Royal Navy, even if overshadowed by the U.S. Navy, was still capable of meeting world-wide commitments, a time when the Soviet Navy was a collection of First World War veterans and ex-German prizes, giving little sign of its future greatness.

As the largest navies in the world, the U.S.N. and R.N. had largely pioneered the revolution in naval warfare, but paradoxically they were entering a period of greater uncertainty than either had known for a century. They had to absorb all the lessons of the late war, particularly the pressing tactical and strategic problems posed by nuclear weapons. Instead of being left to a leisurely decade of recuperation and conservation, the leading navies found their very existence challenged by new technology. The major navies of 1946 both lay under the shadow of the Bomb, and can be forgiven for taking time to come to terms with it.

What was not realised by the public, or indeed by many sailors, was the extent to which the post-war reserve fleets were rendered obsolescent by the rapid advance of technology. As in previous generations, there was a temptation to keep worn-out veterans in reserve to boost numbers and to reassure public opinion – but the truth was that many ships listed as operational in 1946 were unfit for front-line service. Yet the uncertainty about future naval warfare and the desperate need to rebuild a post-war civilian economy ruled out any large-scale replacement programmes. This was particularly true for the Royal Navy, whose ships had seen strenuous war service.

The advent of electronics was to transform the very nature of warship design. Already it was recognised that a warship's weaponry functioned much more efficiently if fire control and sensor data was processed through a Combat Information Center (CIC) or its British equivalent, the Action Information Organisation (AIO). The computer, with its need for internal volume, would encroach upon the space allocated to 'pure' weaponry; but despite complaints of 'toothless tigers', the next generation of warships would have vastly greater destructive power. Warship hulls would become 'volume-critical' rather than 'weight-critical', as armour rapidly went out of fashion. In the process all warship types would be transformed internally and externally.

The reader will look in vain for any sign of the future expansion of the Soviet Navy. Intelligence about the pre-war Soviet Navy had been very sketchy, and little useful information had emerged in 1941-5, despite the considerable technical help given by the Allies. What had been picked up was a hint of Stalin's pre-war plans for large battleships and cruisers, and the alacrity with which German shipyards had been plundered for useful expertise on U-boats.

Some of the data looks threadbare compared to what is available today; it must be remembered that this was the *first* attempt at unravelling what had happened between 1939 and 1945. Censorship accounted for much of the ignorance about the fates of obscure warships, but the official lists of warship and merchant ship losses published in 1947 contained many inaccuracies. The information published in *Fighting Ships* started a whole horde of ship-enthusiasts on a hunt for facts and figures which continues to this day.

In a less obvious sense this edition marks a watershed for *Fighting Ships*. It was changing from being a popular book on navies (which also happened to serve professional sailors as a useful recognition guide) to a weighty reference book crammed with facts and figures, used by civilian and uniformed professionals. Before long the price alone would put it beyond the reach of schoolboys, and the mass of technical facts and figures would deter all but the most serious students of naval affairs.

The old landscape format (in which this volume was originally published) was to last to the end of the 1950s, when it was exchanged for the present portrait shape. This was, we must assume, dictated by objections from booksellers, who have never liked awkward shapes, but who can deny that big photographs of ships look much better in landscape views? The joy of reading the old-style *Jane's* lies in the large, well-produced photographs. The line-drawings were never as good as those in *Weyer's*, and reproduction was sometimes better in *Flottes de Combat*, but nobody could beat *Jane's* on size.

Hindsight shows both the advantages and disadvantages of annual reference books. Ships lost, sunk or scrapped between editions are often lost 'between the cracks', and no editor can afford time or space to update information about ships which have been deleted in previous editions. There is also a tendency to leave information unchanged, long after it has ceased to be relevant. What is also fascinating is to see the extent to which official 'disinformation' encouraged *Jane's* to publish misleading information.

Reading this reprint of *Jane's Fighting Ships* will remind many what navies used to be like, but I hope it will also create a picture of world naval power as it was at the end of that titanic struggle, the Second World War. These were not only the survivors of fleets which had sustained huge losses but also the inanimate heroines of battles which brave seamen had fought.

INTRODUCTION
TO THE ORIGINAL EDITION

ALTHOUGH the second World War may be over, its after-effects could still be felt during the preparation of the present edition of *Fighting Ships*. Apart from the delay due to the coal crisis, paper supplies, printing, binding and the production of blocks all presented difficulties that were unknown in 1939. Per contra, the principal benefit accompanying the return of peace has been a welcome improvement in the quantity and quality of photographs available. This has done much to facilitate the replacement of the somewhat inferior prints of certain British and Allied ships which were the best that could be obtained under war conditions. In the present issue, indeed, nearly 600 fresh illustrations have been provided, with textual revisions on a corresponding scale.

Dispersal of war-built tonnage continues with small sign of abatement. Hundreds of the escort vessels and minesweepers which were a material factor in Allied victory at sea have been sold at bargain prices, with little or no restriction on their future employment. Naturally, other navies have not been slow to seize this opportunity of renewing their strength in such craft at moderate cost. Surplus ships of the British and United States fleets, such as destroyer-escorts, frigates, corvettes and minesweepers, are now to be found under the flags of Belgium, Brazil, Chile, China, Denmark, the Dominican Republic, Egypt, France, Greece, Honduras, the Netherlands, Norway, Peru, Russia, Siam, Turkey and Venezuela, involving numerous alterations in the text.

Nor is this the end of the process. By the time this volume appears, it is possible that an announcement will have been made regarding the allocation of ex-Italian warships, comprising three battleships, five cruisers, seven destroyers, six torpedo boats, eight submarines, a sloop, sixty-five minor war vessels and seventy-one auxiliaries, as listed in the Appendix. Under the Peace Treaty, this formidable fleet was placed at the disposal of the British, United States, French and Soviet Governments. How it is to be divided has still to be explained, but it seems probable that some of the smaller Allied Powers, notably Greece, may come in for a share of the spoil.

Distribution has also to be made of nearly 250 destroyers and smaller craft of the Japanese fleet, a matter in which China is known to be closely interested. All the surviving ships of larger size, with the submarines, were to be sunk or scrapped under the terms of surrender.

From various quarters there have been requests that a complete list of war losses, brought up to date, should be included in this issue. As this would have occupied more space than could reasonably have been afforded, a full supplement to the War Loss Section of the 1944–45 edition has been compiled instead, and will be found to give all available information. Other items in the Appendix are an analysis of U-boat losses, showing as far as known exactly what became of every vessel, and some useful notes on enemy war construction.

During the past twelve months publicity has been given to a number of novel weapons, none of which has yet made its début at sea. Still, there is no doubt that the temporary suspension of work on the U.S.S. *Kentucky* and *Hawaii* may be ascribed to the intention to incorporate rockets in their armaments. In a year or two, therefore, the rocket will have graduated as the main weapon of the capital ship, amounting to nothing less than a revolution in naval ordnance. Moreover, from official utterances it would seem that the United States Navy looks to guided missiles of exceptional accuracy and range to counter attacks by aircraft carrying atom-bombs.

In the opinion of the Admiralty, "the implications of atomic energy, in the long view of the situation, are by no means limited to defensive aspects, and may lead to an enhancement of naval power in a highly modified form and with wide offensive and defensive commitments. The atomically propelled warship would have no immediate refuelling problems, and the period for which it could stay at sea would be limited only by other and generally less urgent problems, a vital factor if the ship proved less vulnerable than the harbour."

So far the only indication of any novel departure in propulsion is the announcement by the First Lord of the Admiralty in March, 1947, that two new destroyers—the only ships to be laid down in the current year—"will introduce some important changes in naval shipbuilding and marine engineering." How far this can be related to another official statement, referring to experiments in progress with gas turbine propulsion, remains to be seen.

In the British section, a selection of photographs of H.M.S. *Vanguard*, together with an elevation drawing and plan, will give a good idea of her general appearance externally. Her profile is unique so far as the Royal Navy is concerned, though she might easily be mistaken for an American ship. Her late commanding officer, Rear-Admiral Agnew, has expressed the opinion that she will be the last of her type to be built. While one remembers similar views being expressed about new battleships in the past, there is plenty of support for the belief in the aircraft carrier as the capital ship of the future.

Now that their armaments have been landed, the present may be regarded as the final appearance in *Fighting Ships* of the battleships *Ramillies*, *Resolution* and *Revenge*; and though their sister ship, the *Royal Sovereign*, is due to be returned to the Royal Navy by the Soviet Government as soon as the division of the surrendered Italian ships is complete, it is improbable that she will be retained on the effective list.

Very little progress has been made towards the completion of the twelve new aircraft carriers left in hand at the end of the war, beyond the launching of the *Albion* and *Centaur*. Some of these ships have been towed away from their building yards to be laid up for the time being and completed at some future date, still to be determined.

A similar state of affairs exists with regard to the four cruisers that remain under construction, though there had been every expectation that the *Defence*, launched in September, 1944, would have been delivered by this time, as she was well advanced. It is to be hoped that she will not repeat the unfortunate experience of H.M.S. *Emerald* after the first World War: she was launched in May, 1920, but was not completed until January, 1926.

Almost all the twenty-four destroyers of the "Battle" class have now passed into service. Criticism of their armament has been met in the third flotilla of eight ships, each of which mounts a fifth 4.5-inch in "Q" position, immediately abaft the funnel. It is possible that the other sixteen ships may be given this extra gun as they become due for refit. Apart from this question, they are considered very fine ships.

Apparently the "Daring" type, none of which appears to be far advanced, are slightly enlarged "Battles" in their main features, though it seems probable that the First Lord's remarks (referred to above) may apply to two of the class. The four destroyers of the "Weapon" class are nearing completion.

Sixteen submarines of the new "A" class appear to have a hull form differing from the saddle-tank type which preceded them. All are of welded construction, and embody to some extent improvements based on examination of surrendered U-boats.

A vessel of entirely novel type is H.M.S. *Boxer*, seagoing radar training ship; apart from having four masts, she is a mass of radio equipment. Far smaller, but equally interesting, are the tiny river gunboats *Pamela* and *Una*, which did excellent service under the White Ensign in the Burma campaign. *Fighting Ships* is fortunate in having secured, through the kindness of Rear-Admiral Viscount Mountbatten of Burma and General Sir William Slim, exclusive pictures of these gallant little craft.

In Dominion Navies considerable reductions have taken place. The Royal Australian Navy has ordered two destroyers of the "Battle" class to be built in Commonwealth yards, instead of the "Tribals" originally contemplated. Four frigates which were on order have been cancelled. Eight of the so-called corvettes (officially they were designed as fleet minesweepers) of the *Bathurst* class have been sold to the Netherlands and five to Turkey. Two others have been converted into surveying vessels.

The Royal Canadian Navy has one "Tribal" destroyer completing and another one building. Nearly all the older destroyers have been scrapped, and of the large force of escort vessels, etc., that were in service at the end of the war, only eighteen frigates and eleven minesweepers remain, together with a couple of corvettes, which have been re-equipped as a controlled minelayer and a surveying and meteorological vessel, respectively.

The Royal Indian Navy is proposing to acquire three cruisers of the *Leander* class during 1947–48, having already disposed of its older sloops and most of its trawlers. The Royal New Zealand Navy has also reduced its trawler force, and has been lent two modern cruisers, H.M.S. *Bellona* and *Black Prince*. The South African Naval Forces have dispensed with the flotillas of whalers which were employed on minesweeping and patrol duties during the war.

Though an extensive scrapping programme has been instituted, the United States Navy still takes first place in the number of its ships, a high proportion having been placed in reserve owing to manning difficulties. At the moment the United States maintains only two battleships in commission, the *Iowa* in the Pacific Fleet and the *Missouri* in the Atlantic Fleet. Reference has already been made to the projected arming of the battleship *Kentucky* and battle cruiser *Hawaii* with rockets or "guided missiles," which according to Vice-Admiral E. L. Cochrane, Chief of the Bureau of Ships, will lead "to a revolution in their striking power."

Battleships discarded are the *Arkansas*, *New York*, *Texas*, *Nevada* and *Pennsylvania*. The *Mississippi* is being reconstructed for duty as a gunnery training ship, and her sister ships, the *Idaho* and *New Mexico*, will be stricken from the effective list at an early date. This will reduce the effective list of battleships to fifteen, with another building.

Three well-known fleet aircraft carriers of the U.S. Navy,

the *Saratoga*, *Enterprise* and *Ranger*, have disappeared. The former was expended in the course of the atom-bomb experiments at Bikini, while the two latter have been stricken from the effective list.

Though both the new light carriers, *Saipan* and *Wright*, are in commission, it has not yet been possible to obtain a satisfactory photograph. It is plain, however, that they are an enlargement of the *Independence* design, differing little from that type in appearance and general characteristics.

For the latest American cruisers, both heavy and light, a modified design has been adopted, with a single and somewhat stouter funnel replacing the two uptakes which characterise the ships of the *Baltimore* and *Cleveland* classes. At the same time the superstructure has been simplified.

In the 17,000-ton heavy cruisers of the *Des Moines* class, the whole of the armament, including nine 8-inch guns, will be fully automatic, a remarkable development in ordnance.

In the last three 6,000-ton cruisers of the *San Diego* class, "B" and "X" turrets, each containing a pair of 5-inch guns, have been installed a deck lower than in the six earlier ships of the series, doubtless with the object of improving stability. For the same reason, the eight torpedo tubes carried by the older ships have been omitted from the later ones.

There is little doubt that in the U.S. Navy during the war, as in the British fleet, there was a very natural tendency to overload ships with the object of increasing their offensive qualities. Another instance of this may be seen in the destroyers of the *Gearing* class, with six 5-inch guns in twin turrets, two forward and one aft. There are reports that the heavy weight thus imposed on the forecastle has caused cracks to develop in the hulls of some ships in the way of the forward turrets. This may possibly be the reason for the suspension of the construction of the last eleven units of the class in June, 1946.

After various contradictory reports had appeared, it has now been announced that a considerable number of U.S. submarines are to be fitted with the *schnorkel* type of breathing tube. Moreover, in the estimates approved by Congress early in 1947 provision is made for the construction of two new submarines of 2,000 tons to embody, in the words of the Navy Department, "many novel features of marine engineering and naval architecture peculiar to this type of vessel," including certain principles first developed in German submarines.

With the exception of four retained for training purposes, all the hundreds of motor torpedo boats constructed during the war have been discarded. It is the considered view of the Navy Department that in the Pacific War these vessels failed to justify expectations, whereas the submarine in comparison yielded a high dividend.

A high proportion of the numerous auxiliaries in service during the war reverted to mercantile employment during 1946, resulting in an appreciable reduction in the number of pages of *Fighting Ships* devoted to these categories.

In the French Navy, the principal addition is the aircraft carrier *Colossus*, lent by this country for five years and temporarily renamed *Arromanches*. This acquisition will enable training in naval aviation to be conducted on up-to-date lines. Of two captured U-boats taken over from the Royal Navy for experimental purposes, one was unfortunately lost, leaving only the *U* 2518. Generally speaking, French naval activity appears to be hampered by the paucity of funds voted under this head since the war ended.

In spite of the loss of over 50 per cent of its remaining strength under the terms of the Peace Treaty, the Italian Navy still ranks either fourth or fifth in importance, according to the view taken of the position occupied by the Soviet Navy. For some time to come the nucleus of the Italian fleet will be represented by two battleships, four cruisers, twenty torpedo craft and an equal number of corvettes. Whether the British trawlers and motor minesweepers lent for purposes of mine clearance will ultimately be added is presumably a matter for negotiation. Up to the time of going to press, no definite information had been released concerning the distribution of the ships surrendered by Italy.

Information concerning the Russian fleet continues to be scanty. It is difficult to credit the report that the 35,000-ton battleship laid down at Leningrad in 1939 has reached the launching stage, since it seems improbable that sufficient material for her construction can have been made available. The battleship *Arkhangelsk* (ex-H.M.S. *Royal Sovereign*), the cruiser *Murmansk* (ex-U.S.S. *Milwaukee*), and a large number of destroyers, submarines, frigates, minesweepers and smaller craft are due to be returned to the British and U.S. Navies during 1947. On the other hand, a large proportion of the Finnish fleet is reported to have been annexed, and the Russian share of the German naval prizes was a substantial one.

Work has been resumed on the hulls of the Netherlands cruisers *Eendracht* and *Zeven Provincien*, of which the former was launched towards the end of the war. Further additions to the fleet are in prospect, including the depot ship *Vulkaan* (ex-H.M.S. *Beachy Head*), taken over in April, 1947. The escort carrier *Karel Doorman* (ex-H.M.S. *Nairana*) is to be exchanged for one of the light fleet type in 1948.

Norway has acquired from the Royal Navy four new destroyers of the latest "C" design together with three more submarines, three corvettes and two fleet minesweepers. Some of these were previously on loan. Norwegian naval training is at present somewhat handicapped for lack of a cruiser capable of undertaking distant cruises with an adequate number of cadets or young seamen on board, but this will be remedied by the pending transfer of H.M.S. *Arethusa*.

Sweden's fine new cruiser, the *Tre Kronor*, has gone into commission, and the sister ship *Göta Lejon* should not be long in following. The new destroyers *Öland* and *Uppland* have both been launched. Denmark is busy refitting the remnants of her pre-war navy, and training personnel to man two destroyers and six torpedo boats which are nearing completion. Three submarines have been chartered from the Royal Navy. From the same source additional destroyers, submarines and smaller craft have been lent to the Royal Hellenic Navy.

Both Belgium's sloops have been recovered from German hands, more or less intact. Very little has been done towards creating a new Polish fleet. Apart from the destroyers *Blyskawica* and *Burza*, which have returned from British waters, the surface units added are all very small. Portugal has acquired a British minesweeper for conversion into a surveying vessel.

In South America, a lead has been given to naval renascence by the new Argentine programme, authorising the acquisition of an aircraft carrier, a cruiser, four destroyers, three submarines, ten patrol craft and a supply ship. Some fresh tonnage, including three frigates, three corvettes, two transports and a number of landing craft, has already been added to the Chilean Navy. Peru has purchased two frigates, and Venezuela six corvettes.

In spite of the loss of the corvette *Fu Po* through an unlucky collision, the Chinese programme of expansion is going ahead steadily. Of the long list of ships to be acquired from the British and United States Navies, the largest is the cruiser *Aurora*. A certain degree of delay is inevitable while personnel are trained to man these ships and operate their armaments.

It remains to express many thanks to the various Admiralties, Navy Departments, Naval Boards, Ministries of Marine, Ministries of Defence and Naval Staffs who have officially contributed to the revision of the contents of this volume. The courtesy and consideration shown by their Naval Attachés and representatives in London is particularly appreciated, in which connection the names must be mentioned of Rear-Admiral A. Sala, D.S.O., and Commander P. Poncet, of the French Navy; Rear-Admiral Spencer S. Lewis, United States Navy; Commodore J. E. Jacobsen, Royal Norwegian Navy; Commodore E. Gester, Royal Swedish Navy; Commodore Adrian M. Hope, O.B.E., Royal Canadian Navy; Captain Natal Arnaud, Brazilian Navy; Captain Y. T. Chow, Captain N. Soong, and Lieutenant-Commander H. Y. Chen, Chinese Navy; Captain J. B. de Meester, Royal Netherland Navy; Captain E. Georgacopoulos, Royal Hellenic Navy; Captain T. E. Hartung, Argentine Navy; Captain E. J. C. Qvistgaard, Royal Danish Navy; Captain A. Ulusan, Turkish Navy; Commander H. Cubillos, Chilean Navy; Commander the Duke of Luna, Spanish Navy; Commander J. Conceiçao da Rocha, Portuguese Navy; Lieutenant-Commander Geoffrey S. Rawson, Royal Australian Navy; Lieutenant-Commander J. H. Orozco Silva, Mexican Navy; the Dominican Chargé d'Affaires; the Secretary of the Icelandic Legation; Mr. E. A. Broadbridge, of the New Zealand Naval Affairs Office; and Captain Ernesto Giurlo, Director of *Rivista Marittima*.

A record number of private individuals, some of whom prefer to remain anonymous, have contributed information, corrections and photographs to this edition, including the following: Ing. L. Accorsi; Mr. J. C. R. Agius; M. P. Banet-Rivet; Mr. L. F. Barham; Mr. John Bartlett; Mr. A. C. Bicknell; Mr. A. S. Bines; Mr. R. V. B. Blackman; Mr. A. John Brown; Mr. D. K. Brown; Mr. Gordon Brown; Mr. R. L. Cheesman; The Rev. R. D. Clarke, O.P.; Mr. R. J. Coleman; Lieutenant-Commander W. S. Crocker, R.N.V.R.; Mr. Michael Crowdy; Mr. William H. Davis; Mr. George Dott; Mr. Lunn Easton; Mr. Philip Ellis; the Hon. D. H. Erskine; Messrs. Evans, Deakin & Co. Ltd.; Mr. James C. Fahey, Editor of *Ships and Aircraft of the U.S. Fleet*; Lieutenant Aldo Fraccaroli; Mr. A. N. M. Garry; Mr. R. H. Gibson; Mr. Harvey Gilston; Mr. J. W. N. Glover; Mr. Alvin Grobmeier; Mr. R. Lloyd Gwilt; Hr. Torsten Hallonblad; Mr. E. H. Hanson; Mr. D. Head; Mr. S. C. Heal; Mr. Martin E. Holbrook; Mr. John Holton; Mr. G. M. Hudson; Messrs. Roger Kafka and Roy L. Pepperburg, joint Editors of *Warships of the World*; Mr. J. W. Kennedy; Mr. J. Launer of *Sea Power*; Mr. F. W. Lawrence; Mr. J. R. Lindgren; Mr. H. J. Logan; Dr. J. Luns; Mr. Joseph Lyster; Mr. A. J. McGinness; Lieutenant A. Murray McGregor, S.A.N.F.; Commander A. J. McHattie, D.S.C., R.D., R.N.R.; Lieutenant (E) Graeme Maclennan, R.N.; Primeiro Tenente Aluino Martins da Silva; Mr. Alan Meikle; M. Jurg Meister; Mr. Derek Mercer; Mr. Donald Monro; Admiral P. W. Nelles, C.B., R.C.N. (retired); Mr. Barrie E. Newton; Mr. M. J. O'Brien; Lieutenant-Commander (S) George E. Owen, R.A.N.R.; Lieutenant (S) J. H. H. Paterson, M.B.E., R.A.N.R.; Mr. R. Perkins; Mr. W. E. Peto; Lieutenant Robert A. Primrose, R.N.V.R.; Mr. Cyril W. E. Richardson; Mr. T. Robins; Lieutenant Douglas H. Robinson, U.S.N.M.C.; Mr. Walton L. Robinson; Mr. Frank J. Rogers; Mr. Stephen C. Rowan, Jr.; Mr. W. M. Russell; Lieutenant (L) J. P. Shelley; R.N.Z.N.V.R.; Mr. Raymond E. Smith; Mr. Graeme Somner; Commander R. Steen Steensen; Captain T. Stoklasa, P.N.; Mr. D. S. Taulbut; Mr. Matthew Thomlinson; Mr. Derisley Trimingham; Redaktör K.-E. Westerlund; Mr. G. C. O. Wilkinson; Mr. T. K. Williams; Group Captain K. G. Winicki; Mr. Geoffrey Wood; and Mr. David Woodward.

Especial thanks are due to M. Henri Le Masson, Editor of *Flottes de Combat*, for his readiness to share information which has reached him; to Captain T. D. Manning, V.D., R.N.V.R., for much aid in the collection of fresh photographs, and the revision of historical data on British warship names; and to Mr. Maurice Prendergast, who in spite of indifferent health has never failed to send along useful items that have come to his knowledge from various sources.

Those who may notice apparent errors, omissions or discrepancies, or who have information to impart, are asked to write as soon as possible to the Editor, care of Messrs. Sampson Low, Marston & Co. Ltd., at 43, Ludgate Hill, London, E.C.4, England. It should be added that while Press pictures of warships are seldom suitable for reproduction, the details which they disclose often prove of value for reference.

BRITISH NAVY

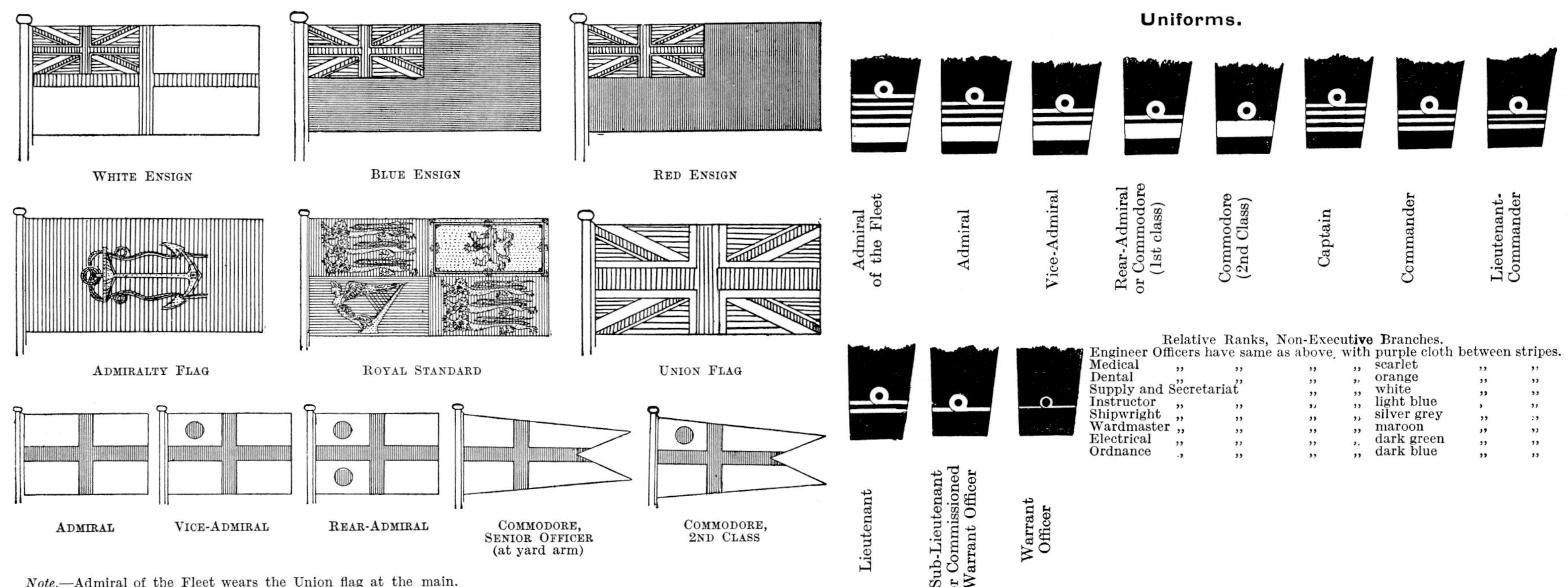

Note.—Admiral of the Fleet wears the Union flag at the main.

Board of Admiralty.

First Lord: The Right Hon. Viscount Hall.
First Sea Lord and Chief of Naval Staff: Admiral Sir John Cunningham, G.C.B., M.V.O.
Second Sea Lord and Chief of Naval Personnel: Admiral Sir Arthur Power, G.B.E., K.C.B., C.V.O.
Third Sea Lord and Controller: Vice-Admiral C. S. Daniel, C.B., C.B.E., D.S.O.
Fourth Sea Lord and Chief of Supplies and Transport: Vice-Admiral Sir Douglas Fisher, K.C.B., K.B.E.
Fifth Sea Lord and Deputy Chief of the Naval Staff (Air): Vice-Admiral Sir Philip Vian, K.C.B., K.B.E., D.S.O.
Vice Chief of the Naval Staff: Vice-Admiral Sir Rhoderick McGrigor, K.C.B., D.S.O.
Assistant Chief of the Naval Staff: Rear-Admiral G. N. Oliver, C.B., D.S.O.
Financial Secretary: John Dugdale, Esq., M.P.
Civil Lord: W. J. Edwards, Esq., M.P.
Permanent Secretary: J. G. Lang, Esq., C.B.

Some principal Admiralty officials (not on the Board):
Vice-Controller: Vice-Admiral H. C. Phillips, C.B.
Vice-Controller (Air): Rear-Admiral (acting) M. S. Slattery, C.B.
Engineer-in-Chief of the Fleet: Vice-Admiral (E) D. C. Ford, C.B., C.B.E.
Director of Naval Construction: Sir Charles Lillicrap, K.C.B., M.B.E.
Admiralty Representative on Military Staff Committee of Security Council, U.N.O.: Admiral Sir Henry Moore, G.C.B.

Colour of Ships. *(In peace time.)*

Warships in Home waters, dark grey; in Mediterranean, China, East Indies, America and West Indies, light grey, except submarines, very dark grey in Home waters, dark blue in Mediterranean and dark olive-green on China Station. Vessels on America and West Indies, New Zealand and Africa Stations, grey all over. All Destroyers (except Leaders) have their Pendant Numbers on bows and across sterns and Flotilla Numbers on funnels. Submarines have their Pendant Numbers painted on sides of Conning Tower.

Navy Estimates and Personnel.

(1946) £275,075,000 (including £20,000,000 Supplementary). Personnel: 492,800.
(1947) £196,700,000. Personnel: 192,665.

Mercantile Marine.

Total for whole of British Empire, at Sept. 30, 1945, *ca.* 15,100,000 tons gross.

ABBREVIATIONS USED IN FOLLOWING PAGES

AA. Anti-aircraft guns.
B.H.P. Brake horse power.
Boilers: D.E., double-ended.
,, S.E., single-ended.
cm. Centimetres.
C.T. Conning tower.
D.C.T. Depth charge thrower.
D.P. Dual purpose guns.
Dir. Con. Director controlled.
H.T. High tensile steel.
I.H.P. Indicated horse power.
K.C. Krupp cemented steel.
Length pp., between perpendiculars.
,, o.a., over all.
,, w.l., waterline.
M.G. Machine guns.
mm. Millimetres.
P. and S. Port and Starboard.
pdr. Pounder.
Q.D. Quarterdeck.
S.H.P. Shaft horse power.
S.L. Searchlight.
T.M. Thames Measurement (applying only to yachts).
T.T. Torpedo tubes.
W.T. Watertight.

KEY TO DIAGRAM OPPOSITE.

A, A, A. Primary armament.
B, B. Barbettes for 4—14 inch guns on centre line.
C. Barbette for twin 14 inch guns on centre line.
D, D, D, D. Secondary armament of dual purpose 5·25 inch guns (twin mounts, port and starboard).
E, E. Multiple pompoms on gun turrets.
F, F. Multiple pompoms on gun superstructure (port and starboard).

1. Jackstaff.
2. Forecastle (FX).
3. Breakwater.
4. "A" turret.
5. Range-finder (R.F.).
6. "B" turret.
7. Control tower and bridge structure.
8. Conning tower (C.T.).
9. Bridge.
10. Navigating bridge.
11. Main director tower.
12. Searchlights (S.L.), P. and S.
13. Twin director towers for secondary armament.
14. Foretop.
15. Tower.
16. Foretopmast.
17. Foreyards.
18. Tripod foremast.
19. Syren brackets.
20. Safety valve uptakes.
21. Caging.
22. Funnel cap.
23. Searchlights (S.L.), P. and S.
24. Cranes (P. and S.).
25. Crane housing.
26. Searchlights (S.L.), P. and S.
27. Wireless aerial.
28. Wireless cabin.

BRITISH NAVAL ORDNANCE.

NOTE.—All details unofficial, but believed to be approximately correct.

Calibre. ins.	Mark	Length of Bore in Calibres.	Weight of piece without B.M.	Weight of Projectile.	M.V.	M.E.	Weight of Full Charge.	REMARKS.
			tons cwts. qrs.	lbs.	f. s.	f. t.	lbs.	
								HEAVY B.L.
16	I	45	103 10 –	2461	2953	..	640	"Nelson" and "Rodney."
15	I	42	97 3 –	1920	2450	84,070	428	Mounted in "Vanguard," "Queen Elizabeth" and "Revenge" classes, "Renown" and monitors.
14			80 – –	1560				Mounted in "King George V" class.
								MEDIUM B.L.
8	I	50	16 10 –	256	3150	17,615	..	"Kent" and "London" classes, "Norfolk" and "Shropshire."
6	XVIII XVI XII XI	50 50 45 50	8 9 2 7 19 1 6 14 2 8 8 2	100 100 100 100	2800 3100 2750 2937	.. 6665 .. 5990	28$\frac{5}{8}$ 33 27$\frac{1}{8}$ 32$\frac{1}{12}$	Cruisers and Secondary Armament Battleships and Battle Cruisers.
5·25				85				Dual purpose. "Vanguard," "King George V" class, "Dido" class.
4.7	XII, etc. II I	 40 45	 3 1 – 3 1 –	 48.5 50	 2560 3000	 2205 2800	 .. 11$\frac{3}{8}$	Destroyers, down to and including "Wager" Class. **AA.** mounted in "Nelson." Semi-Automatic. Mounted in Destroyers and Sloops.
								LIGHT B.L.
4.5								Dual purpose. "Queen Elizabeth," "Valiant," "Renown," Aircraft Carriers, Depot Ships and Destroyers.

Calibre. ins.	Mark.	Length of Bore in Calibres.	Weight of piece without B.M.	Weight of Projectile.	M.V.	M.E.	Weight of Full Charge.	REMARKS.
			tons cwts. qrs.	lbs.	f. s.	f. t.	lbs.	
								LIGHT Q.F.
4	XVI XII VII	 40 40.5	 1 6 0 1 4 4	35 31 31	 2100 2750	 .. 1970	 5$\frac{1}{6}$ 5$\frac{7}{8}$	Semi-automatic. Do. Fixed ammunition. AA. mounting. Capital Ships, Cruisers, Sloops, Frigates, Corvettes, Submarines, Minesweepers. Do. do. do. do.
3	I	45	1 0 0	{16 12$\frac{1}{2}$}	2500	..	{2$\frac{1}{6}$ 2$\frac{1}{2}$}	Semi-Automatic. Fixed ammunition. AA. mounting. Submarines, Minesweepers.
	II I	39.37 39.37	1 3 1 3	2 2	2000 2000	55.5 55.5	3 3	Automatic. AA. mounting. Aircraft Carriers, Cruisers, Destroyers, etc. (in groups of 4 or 8).
								ANTI-SUBMARINE HOWITZERS, B.L. (D.C.T.)
							lbs.	
11 7.5	I I	8.5 8.5	1 14 2 6 0	200 100	.. 390	.. 105.5	.. 1$\frac{1}{4}$	
								LIGHT ANTI-AIRCRAFT AND MACHINE GUNS.
								These include Bofors 40 mm., 2 pdr., mounted singly, in pairs, or in groups of four or six; Oerlikon 20 mm.; Bofors 20 mm., sometimes mounted in pairs; Vickers ·5 inch machine guns, in quadruple, twin or single mounts; Hotchkiss ·303 inch; Lewis ·303 inch; and Savage ·303 inch.

29. Twin after director towers for secondary armament.
30. Maintopmast.
31. Mainyard.
32. Maintop.
33. Tripod mainmast.
34. Ensign.
35. Gaff.
36. Tower.
37. After main director tower.
38. Range-finder (R.F.).
39. "X" turret.
40. Quarterdeck (Q.D.).
41. AA. guns in separate emplacements (vary in number).
42. Ensign staff.
43. Stern.
44. Officers' quarters.
45. Level of main deck.
46. Carley floats, P. and S. (vary in number and positions).
47. Boat boom (stowed).
48. Sundry boats.
49. Athwartships fixed catapult (since removed).
50. Carley floats, P. and S. (vary in number and positions).
51. Flag deck.
52. Boat boom (stowed).
53. Forward shelter deck.
54. Boat.
55. Armour belt.
56. De-gaussing cable (fixed externally in *King George V* only).
57. Anchor in hawsepipe.
58. Bow.

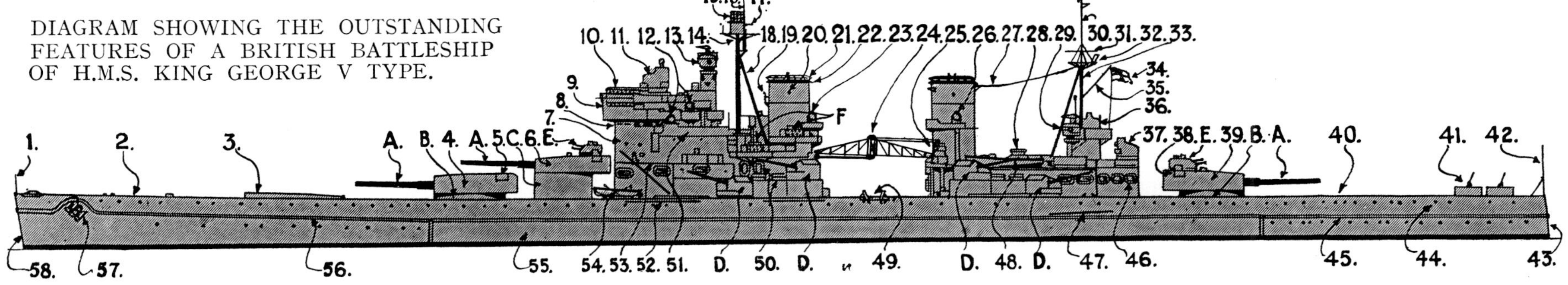

DIAGRAM SHOWING THE OUTSTANDING FEATURES OF A BRITISH BATTLESHIP OF H.M.S. KING GEORGE V TYPE.

Torpedoes.

No official details are available of the latest marks of torpedoes. Standard torpedo used is still the 21 inch heater type, though the *Nelson* and *Rodney* carry 24·5 inch torpedoes, which are discharged to port and starboard from submerged tubes forward. Increased size of latter type gives greater range and heavier explosive charge, but the extra weight and dimensions add to the difficulties of picking up and handling. On the other hand, the change of mounting to a position well forward of beam obviates the necessity for a bar to protect the torpedo while leaving the tube. All other tubes in ships of recent date are of the above-water pattern, each mounting carrying four or five tubes in destroyers. Few modifications of the internal mechanism of torpedoes have been divulged, but running results are reported to show greatly increased efficiency and reliability.

18 inch torpedoes are used by naval torpedo bombers and in motor torpedo boats.

Mines.

Both contact and non-contact types are in use, the latter category covering acoustic, magnetic and controlled mines.

Anti-Submarine Weapons.

These include the "hedgehog," a salvo of 24 depth charges each containing 32 lb. of explosive fired ahead of a ship from a spigot mortar, the propellant being contained in the projectile; and the "squid," a three-barrelled mortar firing a pattern of large depth charges ahead of a ship with great accuracy.

These charges could be set to explode at any depth, and employed a new explosive known as "minol," capable of cracking the pressure hull of a submarine at 25 feet.

Searchlights.

Most capital ships and cruisers now carry only two 20 inch for signalling. Ship's supply voltage is reduced by resistances to that required by the arc. The arcs are mounted before parabolic mirrors. Carbons feed in automatically and are rotated constantly. The crater is kept at the correct focal distance from the mirror by a "third electrode", thus ensuring a parallel beam. A carbon with a wiper action is used for striking the arc. Under normal conditions, no attention is required while burning until new carbons are needed. The barrels in which the lamp is mounted are fitted with iris shutters, and the light is controlled from the forebridge.

British Warship Builders.

In addition to the firms detailed below, the following shipyards have recently undertaken Admiralty orders for warships and/or Royal Fleet Auxiliaries: Ailsa Shipbuilding Co., Ltd., Troon; Caledon Shipbuilding & Engineering Co., Ltd., Dundee; Wm. Gray & Co., Ltd., West Hartlepool; Furness Shipbuilding Co., Ltd., Haverton Hill on Tees; Henry Robb, Ltd., Leith; Philip & Son, Ltd., Dartmouth; Ardrossan Dockyard Co., Ltd., Ardrossa; Lytham Shipbuilding Co., Ltd., Lytham; Blyth Shipbuilding and Dry Dock Co., Ltd.; Goole Shipbuilding & Repair Co., Ltd.; Wm. Simons & Co., Ltd., Renfrew; Lobnitz & Co., Ltd., Renfrew; Hall, Russell & Co., Ltd., Aberdeen; Charles Hill & Sons, Bristol; John Lewis & Sons, Aberdeen; Fleming & Ferguson, Ltd., Paisley; Smith's Dock Co., Ltd., South Bank-on-Tees; Vosper, Ltd., Portsmouth; British Power Boat Co., Ltd., Hythe, Southampton; Barclay, Curle & Co., Ltd., Whiteinch, Glasgow; Wm. Hamilton & Co., Ltd., Port Glasgow; Ferguson Bros. Ltd., Port Glasgow; A. & J. Inglis, Ltd., Glasgow; Grangemouth Dockyard Co., Ltd.; Cochrane & Sons, Ltd., Selby; Cook, Welton & Gemmell, Beverley; Geo. Brown & Co. (Marine) Ltd., Greenock; John Crown & Sons, Ltd., Sunderland; Wm. Pickersgill & Sons, Ltd., Sunderland; Burntisland S.B. Co., Ltd.; James Pollock, Sons & Co., Ltd., Faversham.

Note.—The headings give the abbreviated titles by which builders are mentioned on later Ship Pages. With a few exceptions, all details given below were kindly approved or furnished by the firms mentioned.

Cammell Laird.

CAMMELL, LAIRD & CO., LTD. (BIRKENHEAD AND TRANMERE). Area of yard, 108 acres. Six slips (longest 1000 ft.), six small slips. Seven graving docks, five small and No. 6, 708 × 80 ft.; No. 7, 861 × 90 ft. Outer basin, 14½ acres; inner basin, 2¾ acres. Annual capacity, 100,000 tons *gross* and 400,000 H.P. output. Establishment consists of North Yard, where vessels up to 500 feet in length can be constructed, and the South Yard, in which are slips suitable for vessels between 600 and 900 feet in length. Builders of heavy armoured ships, cruisers, flotilla leaders, destroyers, submarines, &c., as well as of merchant vessels of all classes. Equipment of yard thoroughly up-to-date.

Clydebank.

JOHN BROWN & CO., LTD. (SHIPBUILDING & ENGINEERING WORKS, CLYDEBANK, GLASGOW). Area, 80 acres. River frontage, 1050 yards. Building berths: Five of 1,000 to 600 ft. in length, and three 600 to 450 ft. in length. Building berths are commanded by derricks, tower and gantry cranes; two of berths are covered. Tidal basin: 5¼ acres in area, 35 ft. depth, L.W.O.S.T., with two entrances of 190 and 220 ft. width respectively. Basin commanded by two 150-ton cranes; also four wharf cranes of 5 to 30 tons capacity. Builders of war and mercantile vessels of all types and the largest dimensions, inclusive of machinery and equipment. Steam engines of reciprocating type, Parsons and Brown-Curtis turbine types; and Diesel oil engines.

Denny.

WM. DENNY & BROS., LTD. (LEVEN SHIPYARD, DUMBARTON). Area: 60 acres. Building berths up to 550 ft. in length. Two wet basins, one 475 ft., one 910 ft. Numerous cranes with lifts up to 110 tons. Destroyers, torpedo boats, escort vessels, surveying vessels, submarines and mercantile vessels built, with necessary machinery, &c.

Fairfield.

THE FAIRFIELD SHIPBUILDING & ENGINEERING CO., LTD. (GOVAN, GLASGOW). Area: 80 acres. Water front: 3,000 ft. 6 slips to build ships up to 1,000 ft. in length. Dock: 5½ acres with 270 ft. entrance. 250-ton crane. Wet basin: 900 ft. long. Naval and mercantile ships, engines, boilers, &c., of all types.

Harland & Wolff.

HARLAND & WOLFF, LIMITED. Shipbuilding, shiprepairing and engineering works at Belfast: 19 slips fully equipped to build the largest types of naval and mercantile vessels: 5 graving Docks in close proximity to the works. Shipyard and shiprepairing works at Govan, Glasgow: 7 large slips and graving dock adjoining. Up-to-date engineering works at Finnieston, Glasgow. Engineering and ordnance works at Scotstoun, Glasgow. Large iron foundry at Govan, Glasgow: castings up to 100 tons. Modern and fully equipped ship and machinery repair works at London, Liverpool and Southampton. Shipyard for small craft and general engineering works at North Woolwich, London.

Hawthorn Leslie.

R. & W. HAWTHORN, LESLIE & CO., LTD. (HEBBURN SHIPYARD, HEBBURN-ON-TYNE). Nine building berths. Capacity: Vessels up to 700 ft. Dry dock: 502 ft. 9 in. × 66 ft. wide at entrance. Builders of cruisers, destroyers, minelayers and other warship types. Passenger and cargo liners, oil tankers. Warship machinery up to highest powers constructed at Engine Works, St. Peter's, Newcastle-on-Tyne, also steam and diesel machinery for merchant vessels.

Scotts'.

SCOTTS' SHIPBUILDING & ENGINEERING CO., LTD. (GREENOCK). Slips for eight large vessels; fitting-out basin; graving dock. Build cruisers, destroyers, submarines, etc. Makers of heavy oil engines.

Stephen.

ALEX. STEPHEN & SONS, LTD. (LINTHOUSE, GOVAN, GLASGOW). Build cruisers, destroyers and torpedo craft; also mail, passenger and cargo steamers. Machinery: all types, 200,000 H.P. output per annum. Boilers: Scotch, cylindrical and all water-tube types. Six building berths for construction of ships up to 700 ft. long. Water front: 1,500 ft. Area of yard: 52 acres. Repairs of all classes to hulls and machinery.

Swan Hunter.

SWAN, HUNTER & WIGHAM RICHARDSON, LTD. (WALLSEND-ON-TYNE). Fifteen building berths up to 1,000 ft. in length, served by overhead electric cranes. Four of the largest berths covered in. Annual gross shipbuilding capacity, 150,000 tons. Engine works: 100,000 H.P. output per year.

The dry dock department includes a large repairing yard with three graving docks. Engine works build marine oil engines, marine steam turbines, Bauer-Wach exhaust turbines, and reciprocating steam engines. Total area of works: 80 acres. Water frontage: 4,000 ft.

Allied firms are the Wallsend Slipway & Engineering Co., Ltd., Wallsend; Barclay, Curle & Co., Ltd., of Whiteinch, Glasgow, Govan and Elderslie.

Thornycroft.

JOHN I. THORNYCROFT & CO., LTD. (WOOLSTON, SOUTHAMPTON). Builders of river gunboats, destroyers, light cruisers, merchant vessels up to 400 ft. Thirteen building berths, including three covered in. One hauling-up slip for ships up to 170 ft. long. Water frontage: 2,000 ft. opposite Southampton Docks. Specialities: Turbines, water-tube boilers, oil fuel gear. Workshops in Southampton Docks, adjacent to fitting-out dock for hull and machinery repairs. Total floor area: 25,000 sq. ft. Motor torpedo boats built at Hampton-on-Thames.

Vickers-Armstrongs.

(NAVAL CONSTRUCTION WORKS, BARROW-IN-FURNESS). Area of works: 144 acres. Thirteen building berths, of length respectively 800 ft.; 750 ft.; 680 ft.; two of 620 ft.; two of 580 ft.; two of 550 ft.; 530 ft.; 500 ft.; 410 ft.; 380 ft.—the last two being entirely under cover. Water frontage about 1,200 yards plus fitting-out quays about 1,100 yards. Building berths fitted with modern tower cranes and covered berths with gantry cranes. Fitting out berths equipped with one 250-ton and one 150-ton giant hammer-head cranes, 30-ton electric jib crane, 30-ton travelling hammer-head crane, 7½-ton cantilever crane, steam derrick and travelling cranes, etc. Floating dock, 420 × 59½ ft., to lift 5,200 tons. Graving dock, 500 × 60 × 22 ft. Extensive shops fully equipped with the most modern machinery for the construction of steam and internal combustion engines, boilers, electrical equipment, gun mountings, and every kind of naval and mercantile engineering work.

(NAVAL YARD, HIGH WALKER, NEWCASTLE-ON-TYNE). Area 83 acres. Opened 1913, equipped for the construction of both Warships and Mercantile Vessels. 10 Building Berths of lengths respectively 1,000 feet, 900 feet, 800 feet, two of 620 feet, five from 450 feet to 550 feet. Water frontage about 700 yards plus fitting-out quay about 800 yards. Building Berths fitted with modern Tower Cranes and fitting-out berth equipped with giant 250-ton Hammer Head Crane in addition to 30, 10, and 5-ton Travelling Cranes. Extensive Workshops fully equipped with the most modern machinery for Naval or Mercantile Ship construction, etc.

Also own the repairing establishment known as Palmers' Hebburn Co., Ltd., which includes the biggest graving dock on the N.E. coast. Agencies all over the world.

White.

J. SAMUEL WHITE & CO. LTD. (COWES). The oldest shipyard on the Admiralty list. Vessels up to 400 ft. in length, including light cruisers, flotilla leaders, destroyers, submarines, escort vessels, gunboats, patrol boats, high class passenger and cargo vessels, cross channel steamers, special service vessels, special craft for re-erection abroad, yachts, motor torpedo boats, pinnaces, and other small naval craft, high speed craft of all types. Seven building berths. Engine works for reciprocating engines and turbine engines of highest powers. Water-tube boilers (land and marine), "J. Samuel White" Diesel marine engines, "J. Samuel White" Diesel generating sets for marine service, "J. Samuel White" patent oil fuel installations for marine and land service, "Clinsol" clean-in-service strainers. Hammerhead 80-ton crane at fitting out quay.

Yarrow.

YARROW & CO., LTD. (SCOTSTOUN, GLASGOW). Area of yard: 16 acres. Water frontage: 750 ft. Six building berths, for ships up to 400 ft. long. Wet basin for fitting-out, 350 × 85 ft., served by 50-ton crane. Specialities are destroyers, fast yachts, vessels for shallow river navigation, both of stern-wheel type and of type propelled by screws working in tunnels, Yarrow water-tube boilers and Yarrow superheater, both for land and marine use. Also vessels propelled by internal-combustion motors.

NAMES OF EXISTING SHIPS OF THE ROYAL NAVY (including those of Dominion Navies), showing the number of ships which have borne each name and the date of its original adoption by the Royal Navy, but excluding those ships which are the first to bear their present names.

(Compiled by Captain **T. D. Manning**, V.D., R.N.V.R., **from the records of the late Commander J. A. Rupert-Jones, R.D., R.N.R.**)

Acheron (7th), 1799
Achilles (8th), 1744
Actæon (6th), 1757
Acute (4th), 1798
Adamant (3rd), 1779
Adelaide (7th), 1803
Agincourt (5th), 1796
Ajax (7th), 1767
Alacrity (8th), 1806
Albacore (7th), 1781
Albion (8th), 1763
Alcide (3rd), 1755
Alderney (4th), 1740
Alert (21st), 1753
Allegiance (2nd), 1779
Alliance (3rd), 1795
Amethyst (7th), 1793
Amphion (7th), 1780
Anchorite (2nd), 1916
Anson (7th), 1736
Anthony (2nd), 1417
Apollo (8th), 1747
Arabis (3rd), 1915
Arbutus (3rd), 1917
Arethusa (7th), 1759
Argonaut (3rd), 1782
Ariadne (9th), 1776
Ark Royal (4th), 1587
Armada (2nd), 1810
Athabaskan (2nd), 1941
Atherstone (2nd), 1915
Aurora (8th), 1758
Australia (3rd), 1886

Bacchus (6th), 1806
Barfleur (4th), 1697
Barnstone (2nd), 1937
Barrosa (4th), 1812
Bathurst (2nd), 1821
Bayfield (3rd), 1895
Beaufort (2nd), 1919
Bellerophon (5th), 1786
Bellona (9th), 1747
Belvoir (2nd), 1917
Bendigo (2nd), 1918
Bermuda (7th), 1759
Berwick (10th), 1679
Bicester (2nd), 1917
Birchol (2nd), 1917
Birmingham (2nd), 1912
Black Prince (5th), 1650
Blake (3rd), 1808
Bloodhound (4th), 1801
Bonaventure (10th), 1489
Brave (6th), 1796
Bridlington (3rd), 1918
Brine (2nd), 1918
Briton (4th), 1813
Brixham (2nd), 1919
Bullfinch (4th), 1856
Bulwark (6th), 1782
Bustler (5th), 1780

Cadmus (4th), 1808
Cæsar (4th), 1793
Calpe (2nd), 1800
Calypso (9th), 1783
Cambrian (5th), 1797
Camellia (2nd), 1915
Campania (2nd), 1914
Camperdown (5th), 1797
Canso (2nd), 1813
Carnatic (3rd), 1783
Carron (5th), 1813
Carysfort (5th), 1767
Cassandra (3rd), 1805
Cattistock (2nd), 1917
Celandine (2nd), 1916
Centaur (6th), 1746
Ceylon (2nd), 1805
Challenger (8th), 1806
Chameleon (9th), 1780
Champion (8th), 1779
Charity (3rd), 1242
Charlottetown (2nd), 1940
Charon (5th), 1778
Cheerful (6th), 1806
Chelmer (2nd), 1904
Cherwell (2nd), 1903
Childers (5th), 1778
Circe (5th), 1785
Cleopatra (5th), 1779
Cleveland (4th), 1671
Cockatrice (9th), 1781
Cockchafer (4th), 1795
Columbine (5th), 1806
Concord (8th), 1646
Constance (6th), 1797
Coquette (7th), 1780
Cossack (6th), 1805
Cotswold (2nd), 1917
Cottesmore (2nd), 1917
Courier (5th), 1778
Cowslip (2nd), 1917
Crane (7th), 1590
Crescent (11th), 1588
Crispin (2nd), 1940
Croome (2nd), 1917
Crusader (3rd), 1909
Cumberland (9th), 1695
Cygnet (18th), 1585

Dahlia (3rd), 1915
Dainty (5th), 1589
Daring (8th), 1804
Dart (11th), 1796
Defence (10th), 1741
Devonshire (7th), 1692
Dexterous (2nd), 1805
Diadem (5th), 1782
Diamond (13th), 1652
Dido (5th), 1784
Disdain (2nd), 1585
Dragon (17th), 1512
Druid (6th), 1760
Duchess (5th), 1652
Duke of York (7th), 1762
Dunkirk (4th), 1660
Dwarf (6th), 1826

Eagle (21st), 1592
Eglinton (2nd), 1916
Elfin (3rd), 1849
Emerald (9th), 1762
Eridge (2nd), 1916
Erne (5th), 1813
Espiegle (8th), 1793
Ettrick (2nd), 1903
Euryalus (5th), 1803
Excellent (8th), 1787
Exe (2nd), 1903
Exmoor (2nd), 1939
Falmouth (12th), 1652
Fame (11th), 1763
Fancy (4th), 1806
Fantome (5th), 1809
Fierce (2nd), 1807
Flamingo (2nd), 1876
Fleetwood (2nd), 1918
Fly (24th), 1648
Flying Fish (14th), 1778
Formidable (4th), 1777
Forth (4th), 1812
Franklin (2nd), 1916

Garth (2nd), 1917
Glasgow (8th), 1707
Glory (11th), 1747
Grenville (3rd), 1764
Griffin (16th), 1656
Griper (7th), 1797
Growler (8th), 1796
Guardian (2nd), 1783

Hambledon (2nd), 1917
Hare (8th), 1545
Harrier (9th), 1804
Hart (12th), 1546
Hawkesbury (2nd), 1943
Hazard (8th), 1711
Helmsdale (2nd), 1918
Hercules (7th), 1759
Hermes (9th), 1796
Hibiscus (2nd), 1917
Hind (20th), 1545
Hindustan (5th), 1795
Hobart (2nd), 1794
Hogue (3rd), 1811
Holderness (2nd), 1916
Holly (5th), 1808
Hotspur (5th), 1810
Hound (15th), 1652
Howe (5th), 1805
Huron (2nd), 1813
Hyderabad (2nd), 1917
Hydra (6th), 1778

Illustrious (4th), 1789
Implacable (3rd), 1805
Indefatigable (6th), 1784
Indomitable (2nd), 1907
Investigator (9th), 1798
Iroquois (2nd), 1918

Jamaica (6th), 1710
Jaseur (6th), 1807
Jason (11th), 1673
Jaunty (2nd), 1918
Javelin (3rd), 1914
Jed (2nd), 1904
Jewel (2nd), 1809
Jumna (4th), 1848

Kale (2nd), 1905
Kangaroo (7th), 1795
Katoomba (2nd), 1889
Kempenfelt (3rd), 1915
Kent (9th), 1652
King George V (2nd), 1911
Kingfisher (14th), 1675

Laburnum (2nd), 1915
Laertes (3rd), 1913
Lasso (2nd), 1915
Laurel (13th), 1651
Leander (6th), 1780
Leith (3rd), 1782
Lennox (4th), 1678
Leviathan (4th), 1750
Levis (2nd), 1940
Liberty (9th), 1649
Lilac (2nd), 1915
Linnet (11th), 1797
Lioness (2nd), 1779
Liverpool (10th), 1741
Llewellyn (3rd), 1847
Locust (4th), 1801
London (10th), 1636
Lookout (2nd), 1913
Loyal (2nd), 1913
Lyme Regis (2nd), 1941
Lysander (2nd), 1913

Madras (4th), 1795
Mænad (2nd), 1915
Magicienne (5th), 1781
Magnet (8th), 1807
Magnificent (4th), 1766
Magpie (7th), 1806
Maidstone (8th), 1654
Maine (2nd), 1908
Majestic (4th), 1785
Mallow (2nd), 1915
Mameluke (3rd), 1812
Mandate (2nd), 1915
Manxman (2nd), 1915
Marguerite (3rd), 1915
Mariner (4th), 1801
Marmion (3rd), 1915
Marne (2nd), 1915
Marvel (2nd), 1915
Mary Rose (7th), 1509
Matchless (2nd), 1914
Mediator (4th), 1745
Melita (3rd), 1885
Mermaid (13th), 1651
Meteor (9th), 1797
Meynell (2nd), 1917
Michael (4th), 1350
Mildura (2nd), 1889
Milford (8th), 1660
Milne (2nd), 1914
Mimosa (2nd), 1915
Minstrel (4th), 1807
Modeste (6th), 1759
Moon (4th), 1552
Musketeer (2nd), 1915
Mutine (10th), 1779
Myngs (2nd), 1914
Myrmidon (7th), 1781
Mystic (2nd), 1916

Napier (2nd), 1915
Narbada (2nd), 1847
Nasturtium (2nd), 1915
Nelson (8th), 1799
Nereide (4th), 1797
Nerissa (3rd), 1916
Ness (2nd), 1904
Newcastle (7th), 1764
Nigella (2nd), 1915
Niger (7th), 1759
Nightingale (10th), 1651
Nimble (11th), 1778
Nith (2nd), 1905
Nizam (2nd), 1916
Noble (3rd), 1915
Nonsuch (11th), 1603
Norfolk (4th), 1693
Norman (2nd), 1916
Nubian (3rd), 1903

Oakley (3rd), 1917
Obdurate (2nd), 1916
Obedient (2nd), 1916
Ocean (5th), 1761
Octavia (3rd), 1849
Olive (2nd), 1914
Onslow (2nd), 1916
Onyx (7th), 1808
Opportune (2nd), 1916
Opossum (5th), 1808
Orcadia (2nd), 1916
Orestes (7th), 1781
Orion (6th), 1787
Orwell (3rd), 1866
Ossory (3rd), 1682

Peacock (6th), 1651
Pelican (21st), 1577
Pelorus (4th), 1808
Perseus (6th), 1776
Petard (2nd), 1916
Pheasant (7th), 1761
Phoebe (6th), 1795
Pickle (7th), 1804
Pincher (7th), 1794
Pioneer (10th), 1804
Plantagenet (2nd), 1801
Plover (12th), 1652
Plucky (4th), 1856
Pluto (5th), 1758
Poole (3rd), 1696
Powerful (4th), 1783
Prompt (6th), 1793
Prosperous (7th), 1598
Protector (5th), 1755
Providence (16th), 1637
Prudent (5th), 1768
Pytchley (2nd), 1917

Queenborough (5th), 1671

Racehorse (10th), 1759
Raider (2nd), 1916
Rajputana (2nd), 1939
Ramillies (5th), 1706
Rapid (9th), 1804
Rattlesnake (9th), 1777
Ready (5th), 1798
Recruit (7th), 1806
Redoubt (3rd), 1793
Redpole (5th), 1808
Redwing (9th), 1806
Relentless (2nd), 1916
Renown (10th), 1651
Resolution (17th), 1667
Resource (3rd), 1778
Revenge (10th), 1575
Rifleman (6th), 1804
Rinaldo (6th), 1808
Ringdove (7th), 1806
Rochester (4th), 1693
Rocket (8th), 1804
Rodney (7th), 1759
Roebuck (13th), 1636
Romney (5th), 1694
Romola (2nd), 1916
Rosalind (2nd), 1916
Rosamund (3rd), 1806
Rosario (6th), 1797
Rother (2nd), 1904
Rowena (2nd), 1916
Royalist (8th), 1797
Rye (4th), 1696

St. John (3rd), 1695
St. Martin (2nd), 1691
Sandwich (10th), 1679
Satyr (2nd), 1916
Saucy (2nd), 1918
Savage (9th), 1748
Saxifrage (2nd), 1918
Scarborough (8th), 1691
Sceptre (4th), 1781
Scorpion (11th), 1746
Scotsman (3rd), 1901
Scott (3rd), 1915
Scylla (4th), 1809
Seabear (2nd), 1918
Seagull (9th), 1795
Sealion (2nd), 1918
Seamew (4th), 1857
Seanymph (2nd), 1782
Seawolf (2nd), 1918
Sentinel (3rd), 1804
Seraph (2nd), 1918
Serene (2nd), 1917
Sharpshooter (5th), 1805
Sibyl (9th), 1774
Sidon (2nd), 1846
Signet (3rd), 1666
Sirdar (2nd), 1918
Sirius (7th), 1786
Skipjack (6th), 1807
Snipe (6th), 1801
Solebay (7th), 1694
Southdown (2nd), 1916
Spanker (4th), 1794
Sparrow (8th), 1653
Speedwell (26th), 1559
Speedy (7th), 1782
Spey (6th), 1814
Spindrift (2nd), 1918
Spiraea (2nd), 1917
Spiteful (6th), 1794
Starling (8th), 1801
Stork (9th), 1652
Stormcloud (2nd), 1919
Sturdy (3rd), 1912
Suffolk (7th), 1680
Superb (10th), 1710
Surprise (16th), 1745
Sussex (4th), 1652
Sutlej (3rd), 1855
Swale (2nd), 1905
Swan (24th), 1420
Swiftsure (9th), 1573
Sylvia (6th), 1806
Syringa (2nd), 1917

Tactician (2nd), 1918
Tartar (14th), 1702
Tay (3rd), 1814
Teazer (7th), 1794
Tenacious (2nd), 1917
Termagant (7th), 1781
Terpsichore (5th), 1760
Terrible (8th), 1694
Teviot (2nd), 1903
Theseus (3rd), 1786
Thisbe (4th), 1783
Thrasher (4th), 1804
Tiger (12th), 1546
Trafalgar (4th), 1820
Transvaal (2nd), 1939
Troubridge (2nd), 1805
Truculent (2nd), 1917
Truelove (6th), 1650
Tulip (5th), 1653
Tumult (2nd), 1918
Tuscan (3rd), 1808
Tyne (4th), 1814
Tyrian (6th), 1808

Ulster (2nd), 1916
Ulysses (4th), 1779
Una (1st and 2nd), 1942
Undaunted (9th), 1794
Undine (6th), 1846
Unicorn (10th), 1544
Urania (2nd), 1797
Urchin (4th), 1797
Ursa (2nd), 1917

Valiant (7th), 1759
Vanguard (8th), 1586
Venerable (4th), 1784
Vengeance (7th), 1759
Venus (10th), 1758
Vernon (6th), 1782
Verulam (2nd), 1917
Victoria and Albert (3rd), 1842
Victorious (5th), 1785
Vigilant (16th), 1745
Vindex (2nd), 1915
Violet (8th), 1588
Virago (4th), 1805
Volage (6th), 1798
Vulcan (11th), 1691

Wager (4th), 1739
Wakeful (2nd), 1917
Warrego (2nd), 1911
Waterwitch (5th), 1834
Wave (4th), 1855
Waveney (2nd), 1903
Wear (3rd), 1904
Weazel (12th), 1704
Welcome (3rd), 1644
Welfare (3rd), 1350
Wessex (2nd), 1917
Whelp (12th), 1590
Whirlwind (2nd), 1917
Wizard (5th), 1804
Woodcock (5th), 1806
Woolwich (9th), 1677
Wrangler (6th), 1797
Wren (4th), 1653

Zealous (5th), 1785
Zebra (7th), 1777
Zenith (2nd), 1918
Zephyr (9th), 1756
Zest (2nd), 1919
Zetland (2nd), 1917

BRITISH NAVY

LIST OF PENDANT NUMBERS

(Furnished officially to "Fighting Ships" in 1946.)

D Flag Superior:

D 15 Vindex.
D 35 Pegasus.
D 44 Conrad.
D 47 Adelaide.
D 48 Campania.
D 49 Argus.
D 51 Perseus.
D 56 Penguin.
D 57 Fidelity.
D 58 Cardiff.
D 63 Hobart.
D 66 Emerald.
D 67 Carlisle.
D 74 Delhi.
D 76 Pioneer.
D 81 Frobisher.
D 84 Australia.
D 86 Hawkins.
D 89 Colombo.
D 95 Hermes.

G Flag Superior:

G 00 Jervis.
G 04 Onslaught.
G 11 Quadrant.
G 14 Milne.
G 15 Loyal.
G 17 Onslow.
G 18 Battleaxe.
G 20 Savage.
G 24 Huron, R.C.N.
G 25 Nepal.
G 29 Offa.
G 31 Broadsword.
G 32 Lookout.
G 35 Marne.
G 36 Nubian.
G 37 Kelvin.
G 38 Nizam.
G 39 Obdurate.
G 43 Tartar.
G 48 Obedient.
G 49 Norman.
G 50 Kimberley.
G 51 Ashanti.
G 52 Matchless.
G 56 Petard.
G 61 Javelin.
G 62 Quality.
G 63 Haida, R.C.N.
G 64 Scorpion.
G 65 Noble.
G 69 Paladin.
G 70 Queenborough
G 73 Meteor.
G 75 Eskimo.
G 77 Penn.
G 80 Opportune.
G 81 Quiberon.
G 86 Musketeer.
G 89 Iroquois, R.C.N.
G 92 Quickmatch.
G 93 Porcupine.
G 96 Crossbow.
G 97 Napier.
G 98 Orwell.

H Flag Superior:

H 01 Hotspur.
H 09 Rotherham.
H 11 Racehorse.
H 15 Raider.
H 32 Rapid.
H 41 Redoubt.
H 61 Gatineau, R.C.N.
H 69 Qu'appelle, R.C.N.
H 78 Fame.
H 85 Relentless.
H 92 Rocket.
H 95 Roebuck.

I Flag Superior:

I 06 Agincourt.
I 09 Dunkirk.
I 15 Daring.
I 16 Jutland.
I 17 Alamein.
I 22 Aisne.
I 30 Arunta, R.A.N.
I 43 Matapan.
I 44 Warramunga, R.A.N.
I 65 Barrosa.
I 91 Bataan, R.A.N.
I 97 Corunna.

J Flag Superior:

J 02 Hazard.
J 07 Beaumaris.
J 08 Bayfield.
J 09 Deepwater.
J 10 Alecto.
J 14 Boston.
J 15 Blyth.
J 17 Speedy.
J 19 Rothesay.
J 21 Canso.
J 30 White Bear.
J 31 Stornoway.
J 32 Tedworth.
J 34 Tenby.
J 36 Rhyl.
J 47 Sidmouth.
J 50 Bridport.
J 53 Dunbar.
J 55 Malwa, R.I.N.
J 59 Peterhead.
J 65 Bridlington.
J 68 Sharpshooter.
J 69 Ingonish.
J 71 Harrier.
J 76 Rye.
J 77 Romney.
J 79 Scott.
J 81 Investigator, R.I.N.
J 84 Franklin.
J 85 Seagull.
J 87 Speedwell.
J 95 Ilfracombe.
J 97 Polruan.
J 98 Challenger.
J 99 Jason.
J 101 Albacore.
J 105 Brixham.
J 106 Acute.
J 110 Oriole.
J 116 Bude.
J 117 Parrsborough.
J 119 Fort York.
J 121 Whitehaven.
J 123 Seaham.
J 124 Fraserburgh.
J 127 Eastbourne.
J 129 Deccan, R.I.N.
J 131 Ardrossan.
J 138 Qualicum.
J 139 Wedgeport.
J 143 Bootle.
J 147 Poole.
J 153 Whyalla, R.A.N.
J 155 Kathiawar, R.I.N.
J 158 Bathurst, R.A.N.
J 164 Kumaon, R.I.N.
J 166 Quinte, R.C.N.
J 167 Goulburn, R.A.N.
J 173 Dornoch.
J 175 Cessnock, R.A.N.
J 180 Rohilkhand, R.I.N.
J 182 Baluchistan, R.I.N.
J 184 Ballarat, R.A.N.
J 187 Bendigo, R.A.N.
J 190 Khyber, R.I.N.
J 195 Maryborough, R.A.N.
J 197 Rajputana, R.I.N.
J 199 Carnatic, R.I.N.
J 200 Orissa, R.I.N.
J 202 Warrnambool, R.A.N.
J 203 Rockhampton, R.A.N.
J 204 Katoomba, R.A.N.
J 205 Townsville, R.A.N.
J 206 Lithgow, R.A.N.
J 207 Mildura, R.A.N.
J 212 Shippigan.
J 214 Circe.
J 216 Espiègle.
J 218 Kapunda, R.A.N.
J 219 Rosario.
J 220 Tadoussac.
J 221 Onyx.
J 223 Ready.
J 224 Fantome.
J 225 Rinaldo.
J 226 Spanker.
J 227 Mutine.
J 228 Konkan, R.I.N.
J 229 Cockatrice.
J 230 Cadmus.
J 231 Bundaberg, R.A.N.
J 232 Deloraine, R.A.N.
J 233 Inverell, R.A.N.
J 234 Latrobe, R.A.N.
J 235 Horsham, R.A.N.
J 236 Glenelg, R.A.N.
J 237 Madras, R.I.N.
J 238 Gympie, R.A.N.
J 241 Bunbury, R.A.N.
J 242 Colac, R.A.N.
J 243 Bengal, R.I.N.
J 244 Castlemaine, R.A.N.
J 245 Oudh, R.I.N.
J 246 Fremantle, R.A.N.
J 247 Bihar, R.I.N.
J 248 Shepparton, R.A.N.
J 249 Bombay, R.I.N.
J 251 Dubbo, R.A.N.
J 252 Echuca, R.A.N.
J 275 Hydra.
J 276 Lennox.
J 277 Orestes.
J 278 Llewellyn, R.C.N.
J 279 Lloyd George, R.C.N.
J 285 Bowen, R.A.N.
J 287 Berar, R.I.N.
J 289 Melita.
J 290 Octavia.
J 291 Pelorus.
J 293 Pickle.
J 294 Pincher.
J 295 Plucky.
J 297 Rattlesnake.
J 298 Recruit.
J 299 Rifleman.
J 300 Skipjack.
J 302 Thisbe.
J 303 Truelove.
J 304 Waterwitch.
J 305 Brave.
J 306 Fly.
J 307 Hound.
J 308 Fancy.
J 315 Wagga, R.A.N.
J 316 Cootamundra, R.A.N.
J 319 Lyme Regis.
J 322 Assam, R.I.N.
J 323 Benalla, R.A.N.
J 324 Gladstone, R.A.N.
J 325 Providence.
J 326 Kapuskasing, R.C.N.
J 329 Moon.
J 330 Oshawa, R.C.N.
J 331 Portage, R.C.N.
J 332 St. Boniface, R.C.N.
J 333 Seabear.
J 334 Sault Ste. Marie, R.C.N.
J 335 Maenad.
J 336 Wallaceburg, R.C.N.
J 337 Winnipeg, R.C.N.
J 338 Strenuous.
J 344 Border Cities, R.C.N.
J 348 Stawell, R.A.N.
J 349 Courier.
J 350 Coquette.
J 351 Cowra, R.A.N.
J 353 Kiama, R.A.N.
J 354 Serene.
J 355 Rockcliffe, R.C.N.
J 356 Welfare.
J 360 Mary Rose.
J 361 Parkes, R.A.N.
J 362 Junee, R.A.N.
J 363 Strahan, R.A.N.
J 367 Stormcloud.
J 370 Flying-Fish.
J 376 Golden Fleece.
J 377 Lioness.
J 378 Prompt.
J 379 Lysander.
J 380 Mariner.
J 381 Marmion.
J 382 Sylvia.
J 383 Tanganyika.
J 384 Rowena.
J 385 Wave.
J 386 Welcome.
J 387 Chameleon.
J 388 Cheerful.
J 389 Hare.
J 390 Jewel.
J 391 Liberty.
J 396 Fort Francis, R.C.N.
J 397 New Liskeard, R.C.N.
J 422 Imersay.
J 424 Sandray.
J 426 Shillay.
J 427 Sursay.

K Flag Superior:

K 04 Saxifrage.
K 08 Spiraea.
K 10 Natal, S.A.N.F.
K 19 Nigella.
K 21 Dart.
K 23 Jasmine.
K 29 Tulip.
K 31 Camellia.
K 34 Ararat, R.A.N.
K 35 Violet.
K 51 Rockrose.
K 54 Marguerite.
K 59 Dahlia.
K 75 Celandine.
K 92 Exe.
K 94 Columbine.
K 107 Nasturtium.
K 132 Vetch.
K 144 Meadowsweet.
K 181 Sackville, R.C.N.
K 182 Bittersweet.
K 194 Fennel.
K 196 Cowslip.
K 207 Monkshood.
K 212 Hyderabad.
K 215 Nith.
K 217 Swale.
K 219 Ness.
K 221 Chelmer.
K 222 Teviot.
K 224 Rother.
K 230 Wear.
K 232 Tay.
K 235 Jed.
K 238 Woodstock, R.C.N.
K 239 Neza, R.I.N.
K 241 Kale.
K 243 Kukri, R.I.N.
K 244 Charlottetown, R.C.N.
K 246 Spey.
K 248 Waveney.
K 252 Helford.
K 253 Helmsdale.
K 254 Ettrick.
K 255 Ballinderry.
K 256 Tir, R.I.N.
K 257 Derg.
K 262 Tamar.
K 265 Dhanush, R.I.N.
K 266 Fal.
K 269 Meon.
K 270 Nene.
K 271 Plym.
K 272 Tavy.
K 274 Betony.
K 293 Tees.
K 294 Towy.
K 295 Usk.
K 306 Assam, R.I.N.
K 319 Montreal, R.C.N.
K 321 New Waterford, R.C.N.
K 323 Springhill, R.C.N.
K 326 Port Colborne, R.C.N.
K 328 Swansea, R.C.N.
K 331 Wentworth, R.C.N.
K 337 Kirkland Lake, R.C.N.
K 343 Burnet.
K 354 Gascoyne, R.A.N.
K 355 Hadleigh Castle.
K 356 Odzani.
K 362 Portchester Castle.
K 363 Hawkesbury, R.A.N.
K 364 Lachlan, R.A.N.
K 365 Lochy.
K 367 Taff.
K 371 Wye.
K 372 Rushen Castle.
K 375 Barcoo, R.A.N.
K 376 Burdekin, R.A.N.
K 377 Diamantina, R.A.N.
K 379 Carisbrooke Castle.
K 383 Flint Castle.
K 384 Leeds Castle.
K 385 Arabis, R.N.Z.N.
K 386 Amberley Castle.
K 387 Berkeley Castle.
K 388 Dumbarton Castle.
K 389 Knaresborough Castle.
K 390 Loch Fada.
K 391 Loch Killin.
K 392 Shamsher, R.I.N.
K 395 Mahratta, R.I.N.
K 397 Launceston Castle.
K 399 Tintagel Castle.
K 400 Levis, R.C.N.
K 403 Arbutus, R.N.Z.N.
K 405 Alnwick Castle.
K 406 Barwon, R.A.N.
K 407 Beaconhill, R.C.N.
K 408 Culgoa, R.A.N.
K 409 Capilano, R.C.N.
K 412 Bamborough Castle.
K 413 Farnham Castle.
K 417 Halladale.
K 420 Kenilworth Castle.
K 421 Loch Shin.
K 422 Loch Eck.
K 423 Largo Bay.
K 424 Loch Achanalt.
K 425 Loch Dunvegan.
K 426 Loch Achray.
K 427 Luce Bay.
K 428 Loch Alvie.
K 429 Loch Fyne.
K 431 Loch Tarbert.
K 432 Good Hope, S.A.N.F.
K 433 Loch Insh.
K 434 Loch Quoich.
K 435 Enard Bay.
K 436 Surprise.
K 437 Loch Lomond.
K 438 Derby Haven.
K 442 Murchison, R.A.N.
K 448 Orkney, R.C.N.
K 449 Pevensey Castle.
K 454 St. Stephen, R.C.N.
K 456 St. John, R.C.N.
K 517 Loch Morlich.
K 519 Lasalle.
K 523 Dovey.
K 526 Awe.
K 529 Hedingham Castle.
K 530 Oakham Castle.
K 532 Macquarie, R.A.N.
K 535 Shoalhaven, R.A.N.
K 600 St. Bride's Bay.
K 602 Transvaal, S.A.N.F.
K 603 Loch Arkaig.
K 604 Start Bay.
K 605 Tremadoc Bay.
K 606 Bigbury Bay.
K 608 Padstow Bay.
K 609 Loch Craggie.
K 611 Dampier.
K 615 Widemouth Bay.
K 616 Wigtown Bay.
K 619 Loch Glendhu.
K 620 Loch Gorm.
K 622 Burghead Bay.
K 625 Loch Katrine.
K 627 Mounts Bay.
K 628 Loch Killisport.
K 630 Cardigan Bay.
K 633 Whitsand Bay.
K 634 St. Austell Bay.
K 636 Carnarvon Bay.
K 638 Pegwell Bay.
K 639 Loch More.
K 640 Thurso Bay.
K 644 Cawsand Bay.
K 645 Loch Ruthven.
K 647 Alert.
K 648 Loch Scavaig.
K 650 Porlock Bay.
K 651 Veryan Bay.
K 654 Woodbridge Haven.
K 655 Loch Tralaig.
K 658 Loch Veyatie.
K 661 Antigonish, R.C.N.
K 668 La Hulloise, R.C.N.
K 677 Royalmount, R.C.N.
K 689 Allington Castle.
K 690 Caistor Castle.
K 691 Lancaster Castle.
K 692 Oxford Castle.
K 693 Morpeth Castle.
K 698 Condamine, R.A.N.

L Flag Superior:

L 05 Atherstone.
L 06 Avon Vale.
L 09 Easton.
L 12 Albrighton.
L 14 Beaufort.
L 15 Eggesford.
L 16 Stevenstone.
L 18 Talybont.
L 20 Garth.
L 24 Blencathra.
L 25 Southdown.
L 26 Slazak.
L 30 Blankney.
L 31 Chiddingfold.
L 32 Belvoir.
L 34 Bicester.
L 35 Cattistock.
L 37 Hambledon.
L 42 Brocklesby.
L 43 Blackmore.
L 45 Whaddon.
L 46 Cleveland.
L 48 Holderness.
L 50 Bleasdale.
L 52 Cowdray.
L 54 Cotswold.
L 58 Quantock.
L 59 Zetland.
L 60 Mendip.
L 61 Exmoor.
L 62 Croome.
L 68 Eridge.
L 70 Farndale.
L 71 Calpe.
L 73 Melbreak.
L 74 Middleton.
L 75 Haydon.
L 76 Brecon.
L 78 Cottesmore.
L 79 Brissenden.
L 82 Meynell.
L 83 Derwent.
L 86 Wensleydale.
L 87 Eglinton.
L 88 Lamerton.
L 90 Ledbury.
L 92 Pytchley.
L 97 Aberdeen.
L 98 Oakley.
L 99 Tetcott.
L 100 Liddesdale.
L 115 Krakowiak.
L 122 Wheatland.
L 128 Wilton.

M Flag Superior:

M 01 Apollo.
M 03 Whitethroat, R.C.N.
M 15 Blackbird.
M 19 Miner I
M 22 Dabchick.
M 25 Stonechat.
M 26 Plover.
M 31 Redshank.
M 34 Miner II
M 53 Miner III.
M 65 Ariadne.
M 68 Miner IV
M 69 Linnet.
M 70 Manxman.
M 74 Miner V.
M 77 Ringdove.
M 88 Miner VII.
M 94 Miner VI.

N Flag Superior:

N 47 Seawolf.
N 72 Sealion.
N 87 Una.

P Flag Superior:

P 18 Vagabond.
P 34 Ultimatum.
P 37 Unbending.
P 52 P52 (ex-*Sokol*)
P 61 Varangian.
P 62 Uther.
P 63 Unswerving.
P 67 P67 (ex-*Curie*).
P 72 Vampire.
P 73 Vox.
P 74 Vigorous.
P 75 Virtue.
P 76 Visigoth.
P 77 Vivid.
P 78 Voracious.
P 81 Varne.
P 82 Upshot.
P 83 Urtica.
P 84 Vineyard.
P 86 Vengeful.
P 87 Vortex.
P 214 Satyr.
P 215 Sceptre.
P 216 Seadog.
P 217 Sibyl.
P 223 Seanymph.
P 226 Sirdar.
P 227 Spiteful.
P 229 Sportsman.
P 231 Stoic.
P 233 Storm.
P 236 Spark.
P 237 Scythian.
P 239 Surf.
P 242 Shalimar.
P 243 Scotsman.
P 244 Sea Devil.
P 245 Spirit.
P 246 Statesman.
P 248 Sturdy.
P 249 Stygian.
P 251 Subtle.
P 252 Supreme.
P 253 Sea Scout.
P 254 Selene.
P 255 Seneschal.
P 256 Sentinel
P 257 Saga.
P 258 Scorcher.
P 259 Sidon.
P 261 Sleuth.
P 262 Solent.
P 263 Spearhead.
P 264 Springer.
P 265 Spur.
P 266 Sanguine.
P 312 Trespasser.
P 314 Tactician.
P 315 Truculent.
P 316 Templar.
P 317 Tallyho.
P 318 Tantalus.
P 319 Tantivy.
P 321 Telemachus.
P 324 Thorough.
P 325 Thule.
P 326 Tudor.
P 327 Tireless.
P 328 Token.
P 329 Tradewind.
P 331 Trenchant.
P 332 Tiptoe.
P 333 Trump.
P 334 Taciturn.
P 335 Tapir.
P 338 Teredo.
P 339 Taurus.
P 342 Tabard.
P 352 Totem.
P 353 Truncheon.
P 354 Turpin.
P 355 Thermopylae.
P 411 Acheron.
P 415 Alcide.
P 416 Alderney.
P 417 Alliance.
P 418 Ambush.
P 419 Auriga.
P 421 Affray.
P 422 Anchorite.
P 423 Andrew.
P 426 Aurochs.
P 427 Æneas.
P 439 Amphion.
P 441 Alaric.
P 447 Astute.
P 456 Artful.

R Flag Superior:

R 00 Troubridge.
R 01 Caprice.
R 02 Zest.
R 03 Kempenfelt.
R 04 Cayuga, R.C.N.
R 05 Urania.
R 06 Myngs.
R 07 Cæsar.
R 09 Cadiz.
R 10 Micmac, R.C.N.
R 11 Tumult.

R 12 Contest.
R 14 Armada.
R 15 Cavendish.
R 16 Crescent, R.C.N.
R 17 Algonquin, R.C.N.
R 18 St. Kitts.
R 19 Zephyr.
R 20 Crusader, R.C.N.
R 21 Chivalrous.
R 22 Ursa.
R 23 Teazer.
R 25 Carysfort.
R 26 Comet.
R 28 Verulam.
R 29 Charity.
R 30 Carron.
R 31 Vigo.
R 32 Camperdown.
R 33 Terpsichore.
R 34 Cockade.
R 36 Chieftain.
R 37 Whelp.
R 39 Zealous.
R 40 Nonsuch
R 41 Volage.
R 42 Undine.
R 43 Comus.
R 44 Lagos.
R 45 Tenacious.
R 47 Gabbard.
R 48 Wrangler.
R 50 Venus.
R 51 Chevron.
R 52 Chaplet.
R 53 Undaunted.
R 54 Zodiac.
R 55 Finisterre.
R 56 Tuscan.
R 57 Cossack.
R 59 Wakeful.
R 60 Sluys.
R 61 Chequers.
R 62 Cassandra.
R 63 Concord.
R 64 Sioux, R.C.N.
R 65 St. James.
R 66 Zambesi
R 67 Tyrian.
R 68 Crispin.
R 69 Ulysses.
R 70 Solebay.
R 71 Constance.
R 72 Wizard.
R 73 Cavalier.
R 74 Hogue.
R 75 Virago.
R 76 Consort.
R 77 Trafalgar.
R 78 Wessex.
R 79 Athabaskan.
R 80 Barfleur.
R 81 Zebra.
R 82 Creole.
R 83 Ulster.
R 84 Saintes.
R 85 Cambrian.
R 87 Whirlwind.
R 89 Termagant.
R 90 Cheviot.
R 91 Childers.
R 92 Z 10.
R 93 Vigilant.
R 95 Zenith.
R 96 Nootka, R.C.N.
R 97 Grenville.
R 98 Wager.
R 99 Urchin.

T Flag Superior:

T 12 Rampur, R.I.N.
T 19 Holly.
T 25 Elfin.
T 26 Lilac.
T 28 Locust.
T 36 Redwing.
T 43 Seamew.
T 47 Excellent.
T 51 Vulcan
T 57 Aphis.
T 59 Scarab.
T 68 Basset.
T 72 Cockchafer.
T 82 Nightingale.
T 89 Guardian.
T 92 Dwarf.
T 98 Protector.
T 102 Kiwi, R.N.Z.N.
T 103 Walnut.
T 126 Olive.
T 155 Inchkeith, R.N.Z.N.
T 160 Sanda, R.N.Z.N.
T 163 Skye.
T 174 Killegray, R.N.Z.N.
T 175 Scarba, R.N.Z.N.
T 179 Switha (DV 18).
T 180 Tiree (DV 19).
T 181 Trondra (DV 20).
T 202 Fetlar (DV 8).
T 207 Coll (DV 6).
T 208 Damsay.
T 229 Sir Tristram.
T 234 Tui, R.N.Z.N.
T 237 Scalpay (DV 15).
T 247 Neave (DV 14).
T 258 Nasik, R.I.N.
T 261 Amritsar, R.I.N.
T 267 Lucknow, R.I.N.
T 272 Lundy (DV 12).
T 273 Bardsey (DV 13).
T 288 Gateshead.
T 291 Graemsay (DV 10).
T 294 Bern (DV 4).
T 297 Earraid (DV 7).
T 315 Cochin, R.I.N.
T 339 Calcutta, R.I.N.
T 340 Hautapu, R.N.Z.N.
T 341 Annet (DV 2).
T 342 Foulness.
T 350 Bryher.
T 354 Flatholm (DV 9).
T 356 Steepholm (DV 17).
T 359 Caldy (DV 5).
T 361 Lindisfarne (DV 11).
T 375 Oronsay.
T 381 Skomer.
T 387 Gorregan.
T 392 Hermetray.
T 399 Hinau, R.N.Z.N.
T 401 Manuka, R.N.Z.N.
T 402 Rimu, R.N.Z.N.

U Flag Superior:

U 03 Erne.
U 07 Actæon.
U 10 Cauvery, R.I.N.
U 12 Sandwich.
U 16 Amethyst.
U 18 Flamingo.
U 20 Snipe.
U 21 Jumna, R.I.N.
U 23 Crane.
U 25 Scarborough.
U 28 Wren.
U 29 Whimbrel.
U 30 Mermaid.
U 33 Opossum.
U 34 Falmouth.
U 36 Leith.
U 38 Cygnet.
U 39 Hind.
U 40 Narbada, R.I.N.
U 42 Modeste.
U 45 Wild Goose.
U 46 Kistna, R.I.N.
U 47 Fleetwood.
U 49 Pheasant.
U 50 Rochester.
U 51 Milford.
U 52 Godavari, R.I.N.
U 57 Black Swan.
U 58 Hart.
U 60 Alacrity.
U 64 Nereide.
U 66 Starling.
U 69 Redpole.
U 71 Sparrow.
U 73 Warrego, R.A.N.
U 74 Swan, R.A.N.
U 80 Hindustan, R.I.N.
U 81 Stork.
U 82 Magpie.
U 86 Pelican.
U 90 Woodcock.
U 95 Sutlej, R.I.N.
U 96 Peacock.

Silhouettes—Capital Ships

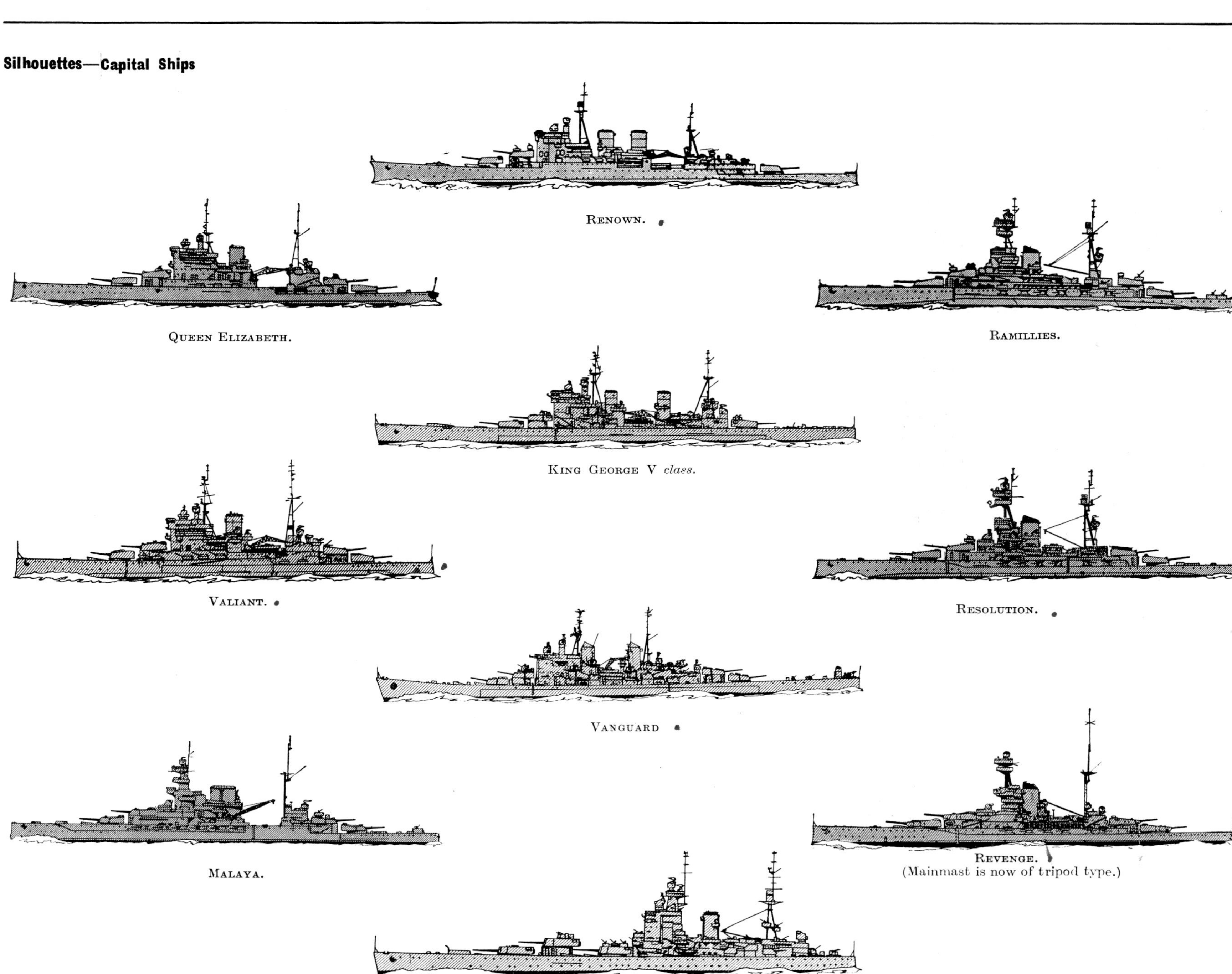

Renown.

Queen Elizabeth.

Ramillies.

King George V *class.*

Valiant.

Resolution.

Vanguard

Malaya.

Revenge.
(Mainmast is now of tripod type.)

Nelson.
(Rodney similar, but with slightly different foretop.)

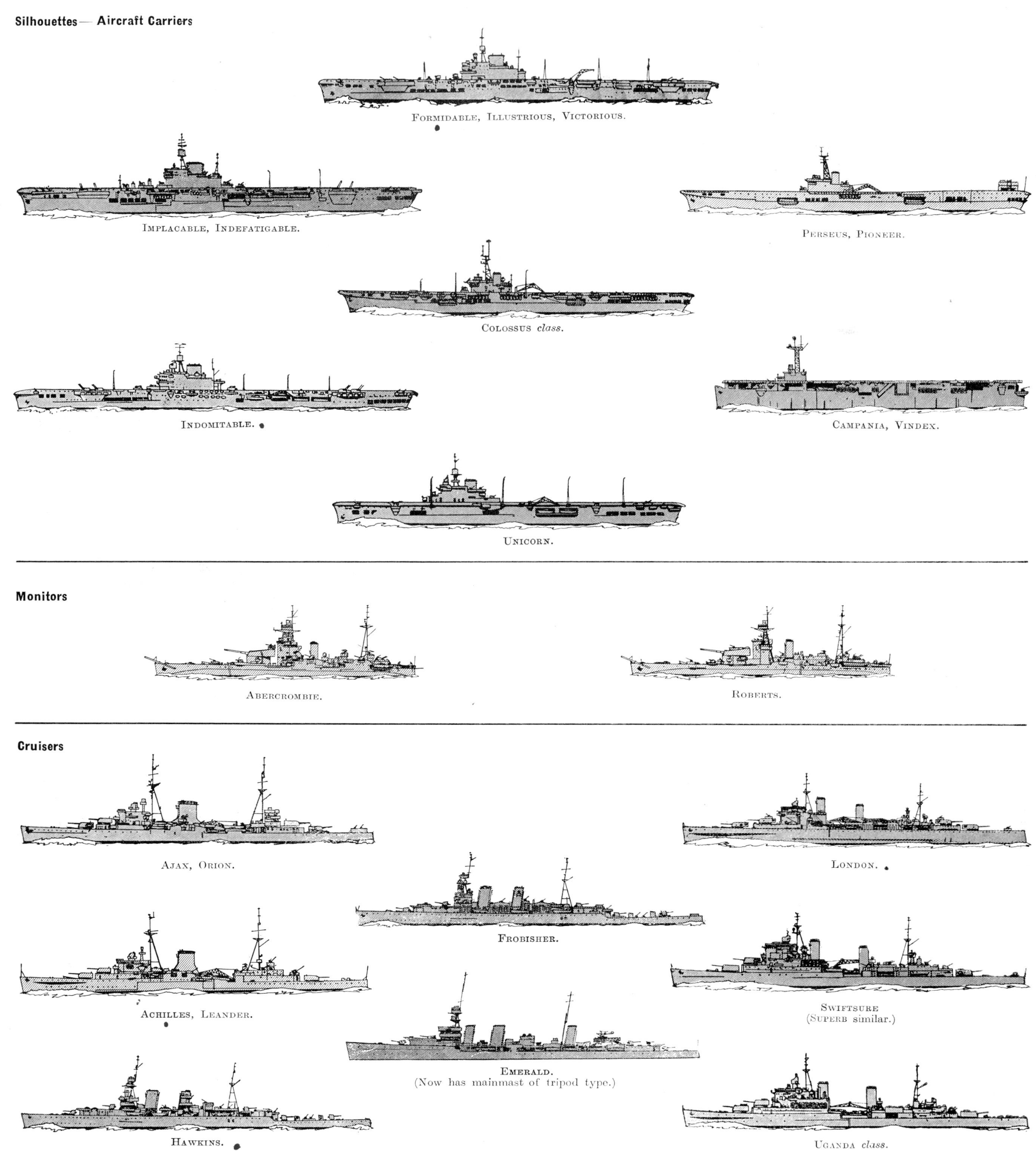

FORMIDABLE, ILLUSTRIOUS, VICTORIOUS.

IMPLACABLE, INDEFATIGABLE.

PERSEUS, PIONEER.

COLOSSUS *class.*

INDOMITABLE.

CAMPANIA, VINDEX.

UNICORN.

ABERCROMBIE.

ROBERTS.

AJAX, ORION.

LONDON.

FROBISHER.

ACHILLES, LEANDER.

SWIFTSURE
(SUPERB similar.)

EMERALD.
(Now has mainmast of tripod type.)

HAWKINS.

UGANDA *class.*

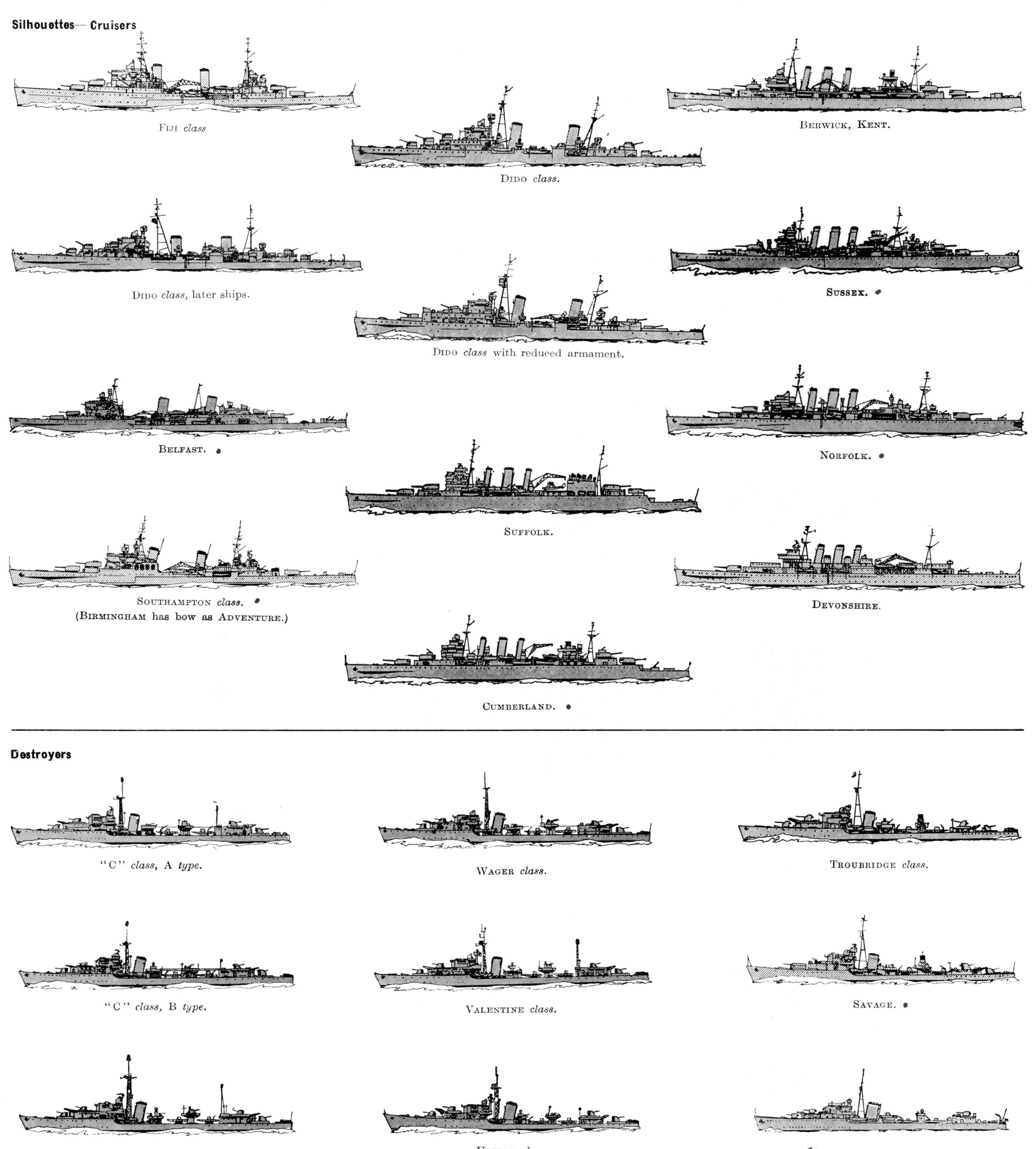
Silhouettes—Cruisers
Fiji class
Dido class.
Berwick, Kent.
Dido class, later ships.
Sussex.
Dido class with reduced armament.
Belfast.
Norfolk.
Suffolk.
Southampton class.
(Birmingham has bow as Adventure.)
Devonshire.
Cumberland.
Destroyers
"C" class, A type.
Wager class.
Troubridge class.
"C" class, B type.
Valentine class.
Savage.
Zambesi class.
Ulster class.
Javelin class.

Silhouettes—Destroyers

JERVIS.

"BATTLE" *class.*

"HUNT" *class,* No. 1 *type.*

"HUNT" *class,* No. 2 *type.*

"HUNT" *class,* No. 3 *type.*
(Individual ships vary.)

"HUNT" *class,* No. 4 *type.*

LAFOREY *class.*

MILNE *class.*

ONSLOW *class.*

ONSLOW *class* with reduced armament.

ROTHERHAM *class.*

FAME.

HOTSPUR.

"TRIBAL" *class.*

Minelayers

MANXMAN

APOLLO, ARIADNE.

Sloops

Modified BLACK SWAN *class*

PELICAN.

SANDWICH.

BLACK SWAN *class.*

STORK.

MILFORD, SCARBOROUGH
(Also ROCHESTER, with deckhouse aft.)

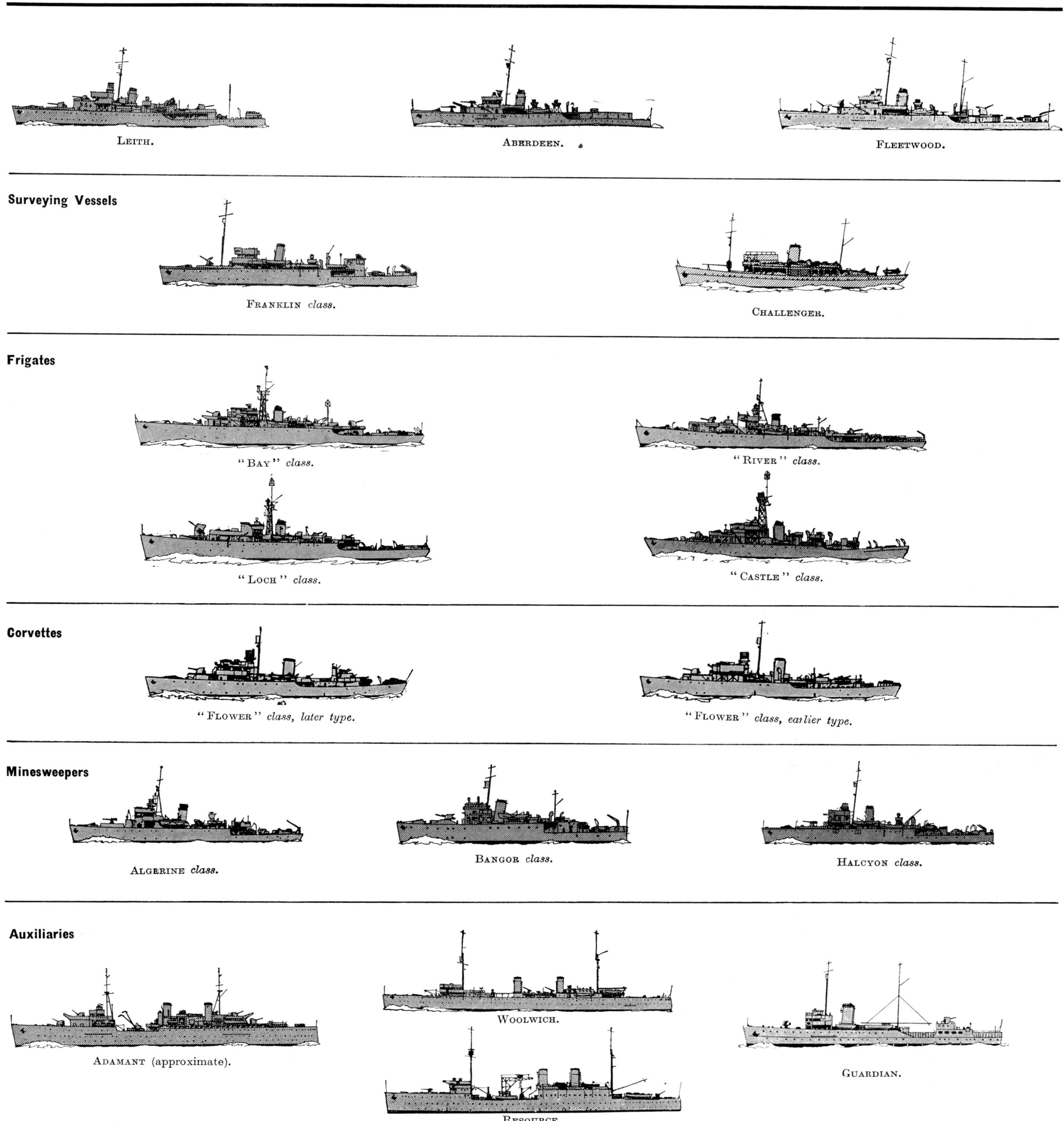

LEITH.

ABERDEEN.

FLEETWOOD.

Surveying Vessels

FRANKLIN *class.*

CHALLENGER.

Frigates

"BAY" *class.*

"RIVER" *class.*

"LOCH" *class.*

"CASTLE" *class.*

Corvettes

"FLOWER" *class, later type.*

"FLOWER" *class, earlier type.*

Minesweepers

ALGERINE *class.*

BANGOR *class.*

HALCYON *class.*

Auxiliaries

WOOLWICH.

ADAMANT (approximate).

GUARDIAN.

RESOURCE.

TYNE.

MAIDSTONE. FORTH.

PROTECTOR.

Silhouettes—Trawlers, etc.

RINGDOVE.
(LINNET has lower cowl.)

"ISLES" *class.*
("DANCE" *class* similar.)

BASSET

MERSEY *type.*

"TREE" *type.*
(Vary in details.)

VULCAN.

GREY GOOSE *class.*

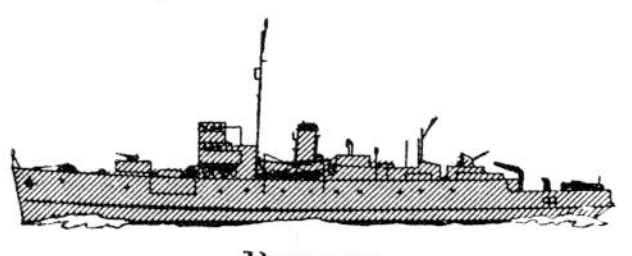

PLOVER.

MINER *class.*

MOTOR MINESWEEPERS.

Submarines

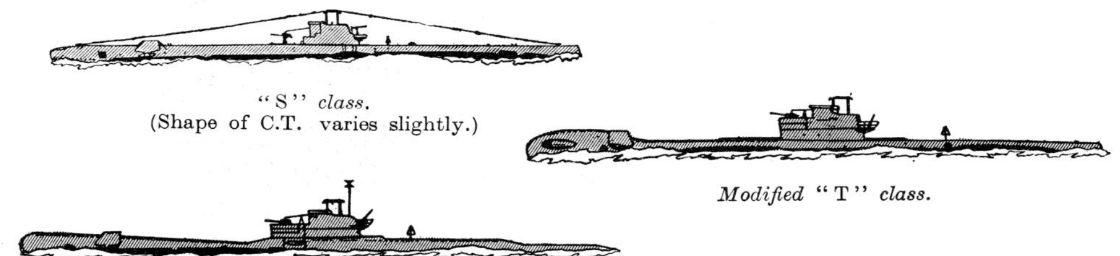

"S" *class.*
(Shape of C.T. varies slightly.)

Modified "T" *class.*

"T" *class.*

"U" *class.*

"V" *class.*

Battleship

VANGUARD (November 30, 1944)

Displacement: 42,500 tons *standard* (about 50,000 tons *full load*). Complement (war): 2,000.
Length: (*o.a.*) 814 feet 4 ins. Beam: 107 feet 6 ins. Draught: Not reported.

Guns:
8—15 inch, 42 cal.
16—5·25 inch, D.P.
4—3 pdr.
71—40 mm. AA. (Bofors).

Armour:
Protection believed to be fully equal to that of contemporary battleships of other navies.

1946, *Keystone.*

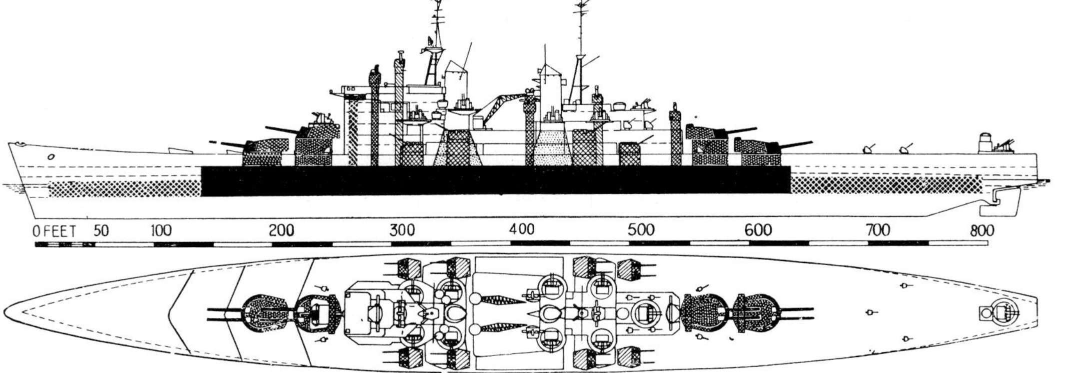

Battleship

Machinery: Parsons single reduction geared turbines. 4 shafts. S.H.P.: 130,000 = 29 kts. or more. Boilers: 8 Admiralty 3-drum type.

General Notes.—Authorised under War Estimates, and designed by Sir Stanley Goodall. Ordered March 14, 1941; laid down at Clydebank October 2, 1941, and completed in April, 1946. Cost £9,000,000, exclusive of 15-inch guns and mountings.

Gunnery Notes.—Latest system of radar control is installed. The 15-inch guns are those first mounted in H.M.S. *Courageous* and *Glorious* in 1917, and later removed from those ships to be added to reserve of weapons of that calibre maintained for *Hood*, *Queen Elizabeth* and *Royal Sovereign* types.

Engineering Notes.—Engine-rooms and boiler-rooms are arranged in four self-contained units. Oil-burning system is on novel lines. Damage control arrangements claimed to be the most thorough ever installed in H.M. ships.

1946, *Wright & Logan.*

1946, *P.A.—Reuters.*

VANGUARD. 1946, *Central Press.*

VANGUARD. 1946, *Central Press.*

Battleships

(King George V Class—4 Ships)

KING GEORGE V (Feb. 21, 1939), **DUKE OF YORK** (ex-*Anson*, Feb. 28, 1940), **ANSON** (ex-*Jellicoe*, Feb. 24, 1940), **HOWE** (ex-*Beatty*, April 9, 1940).

Standard displacement: 35,000 tons (*full load* averages about 44,650 tons).

Complement: Peace, 1,553–1,558; War, 1,900.

Length: (*pp.*) 739 feet 8 inches, (*o.a.*) 745 feet. Beam: 103 feet. Draught: 27 feet 8 inches (*mean*).

Duke of York. 1947, *Wright & Logan.*

Est.	Name	Builder	Machinery	Laid down	Completed
1936	*King George V*	Vickers-Armstrongs (Tyne)	V.-A., (Barrow)	Jan. 1, 1937	11/12/40
1937	*Duke of York*	Clydebank	Clydebank	May 5, 1937	4/11/41
1937	*Anson*	Swan Hunter	Wallsend Co.	July 20, 1937	22/6/42
1937	*Howe*	Fairfield	Fairfield	June 1, 1937	29/8/42

PRINCE OF WALES (1939). 35,000 tons.
Torpedoed by Japanese naval aircraft in S. China Sea, December 10, 1941.

Guns: **10**—**14** inch.
16—5·25 inch, D.P.
64 to **88**—2 pdr. pompoms. } AA.
8—40 mm. Bofors. } AA.
25 to **38**—20 mm. Oerlikon. } AA.
(No torpedo tubes).

Armour:
Officially stated that design incorporates enhanced defence against air attack, including an improved distribution of deck and side armour, more elaborate sub-division, and an improved system of under-water protection.
Unofficial reports give weight of armour as over 14,000 tons, and water-line thickness as 16 inches.

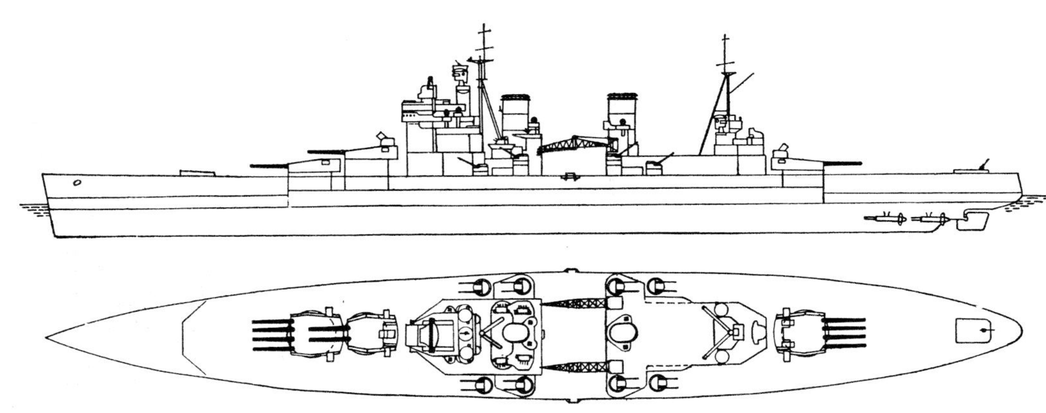

Machinery: Parsons single reduction geared turbines. 4 shafts. S.H.P.: 110,000 = 27 kts. (have actually developed 125,000 = 28·5 kts. in emergency). Boilers: 8 Admiralty 3-drum type. Oil fuel.

General Notes.—Name of second ship was changed December, 1938, and those of third and fourth ships in February, 1940. A fifth ship (*Prince of Wales*, built by Cammell Laird & Co.) was lost in Dec. 1941. Superstructure, abaft bridge, designed as hangar, is now used as a cinema.

Engineering Notes.—Improvements in boiler design have reduced boiler weights by about 15 per cent as compared with *Nelson* and *Rodney*. On trials these ships exceeded 28 kts. easily with about 112,000 S.H.P.

Gunnery Notes.—**14 inch guns are a new model, with an effective range greater than the 15 inch mounted in earlier ships, as measured by the perforation of any given thickness of armour. From photographs, elevation of 14 inch guns would appear to be at least 40°. Inclusive cost of armament (including fire control installation costing £213,000) has been officially stated as £2,900,000.**

Armour Notes.—Turret weights are 1,500 tons for quadruple 14 inch; 900 tons twin 14 inch; 80 tons 5·25 inch.

Howe. 1946, *Wright & Logan.*

Howe. 1946, *Dominion Press.*

HOWE 1946, *Wright & Logan.*

KING GEORGE V.

NELSON (September 3rd, 1925), **RODNEY** (December 17th, 1925).
Displacement, 33,950 tons (*Nelson*), 33,900 tons (*Rodney*), (*full load*, about 38,000 tons).
Length, (*pp.*) 660 feet, (*w.l.*) 702 feet, (*o.a.*) 710 feet. Beam, 106 feet. *Mean* draught, 30 feet
Complement, as flagship, 1361; as private ship, 1314. In wartime, 1640.

Guns:
- 9—16 inch.
- 12—6 inch.
- 6—4.7 inch A.A. in *Nelson;*
- 8—4 inch AA. in *Rodney.*
- 16—40 mm. AA.
- 48—2 pdr. pompoms
- 61—20 mm. A.A.

Torpedo tubes (*submerged*)
2—24.5 inch.

Armour:
Is largely concentrated over guns and magazines in fore part of ship. Internal bulge protection.
- 14" Belt ......
- 16"—9" Turrets
- 15" Barbettes.
- 6¼" Deck ....

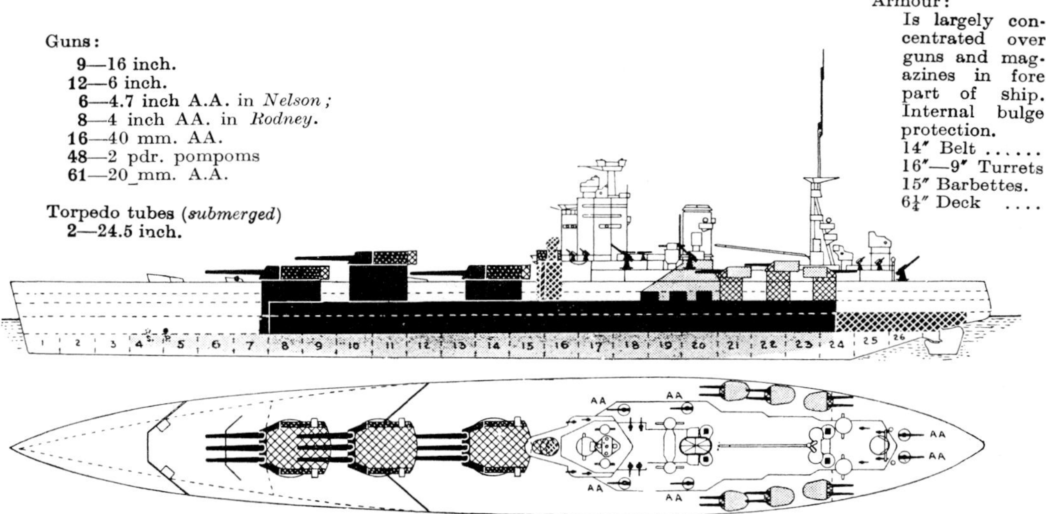

Machinery: Brown-Curtis geared turbines. 2 shafts. Boilers: 8 Admiralty 3-drum type (with superheaters). Designed H.P. 45,000=23 kts. Oil fuel: 4,000 tons. Consumption: full speed, 16 tons per hour; cruising speed, 2·7 tons per hour.

NELSON. 1946, *Wright & Logan.*

Battleships

Name	Builder	Machinery	Laid down	Completed	Trials	Boilers
Nelson	Armstrong	Wallsend Co.	Dec. 28, 1922	June, 1927	46,000 = 23·5	Admiralty 3-drum
Rodney	Cammell Laird	Cammell Laird		Aug. 1927	= 23·8	

General Notes.—Both laid down under 1922-23 Estimates, the last battleships designed by Sir E. Tennyson D'Eyncourt while D.N.C. They are reduced editions of the 48,000 ton battle-cruisers ordered in 1921 and cancelled under the Washington Treaty, in which 16 inch guns were to have been mounted in triple turrets. Designed to Treaty limits which could not be exceeded, and yet must be approached as closely as possible, weight estimation and economy was a far more important factor than in previous designs. The grouping of the main armament forward allows for a minimum length of armoured citadel with maximum protection to hull and magazines, and is considered fully to compensate for the loss of fire astern. The design is therefore peculiar, in that it is governed more by constructional than tactical principles. By placing the boiler room abaft the engine rooms smoke interference with the control positions is obviated. The bridge structure carries 16 inch, 6 inch and 4·7 inch directors, admiral's bridge, torpedo controls, signalling and navigating bridges, sea cabins and offices. Part of the material used in these two ships was originally ordered for two battle cruisers, the construction of which was abandoned in 1919.

High freeboard of these ships has proved its value in heavy weather, which makes little difference to their efficiency as compared with earlier designs. A number of scuttles which had been plated over in *Nelson* were reopened before she proceeded to E. Indies in 1944. *Rodney* placed in reserve, 1946, pending refit.

Cost.–Nelson £7,504,055 ; *Rodney* £7,617,799. Cost of guns and turret armour approx. £3,000,000 ; engines, £490,000. Steering gear is of novel design and rudder can be swung over in 30 secs. at full speed. Accommodation is on generous lines and all living spaces have natural lighting and ventilation.

Gunnery Notes.—The first British warships to mount 16-inch guns. Arcs of fire of the 3 turrets reported to be 298, 330 and 250 degrees respectively. Elevation is 40° and range 35,000 yards. Cost of firing a triple salvo is £700. 6-inch guns have 60° elevation and can be used as AA. They are the first power worked 6-inch in the Service. Special measures have been taken to protect personnel and instruments from the blast of the after 16-inch guns when fired abaft the beam at full elevation.

Armour.—Citadel belt extends from first 16 inch to aftermost 6 inch turret, with thick armour deck over same area with specially designed hatches. Underwater protection is most efficient and the usual external bulges have been replaced by an alternative system of hull construction developed from a long series of experiments.

War Service.—*Nelson* was mined in Dec. 1939 ; torpedoed in Sept. 1941 ; and again mined in June 1944. *Rodney* was with *King George V* in action with *Bismarck* in May 1941, when last-named ship was sunk.

(Queen Elizabeth Class)

QUEEN ELIZABETH (16th Oct., 1913), **VALIANT** (4th Nov., 1914), **WARSPITE** (26th Nov., 1913)

Displacement, 32,700 and 31,520 tons, respectively (37,000 tons *full load*).

Complement, 1124-1184. Both fitted as flagships.

Length (*pp.*), 600 feet; (*o.a.*) 643¾ and 639¾ ft. respectively. (*w.l.*) 634½ feet. Beam, 104 feet. *Mean* draught, 30⅔ feet; *Max.* „ 33½ „

Note.—Elevation given here represents *Warspite*, since scrapped.

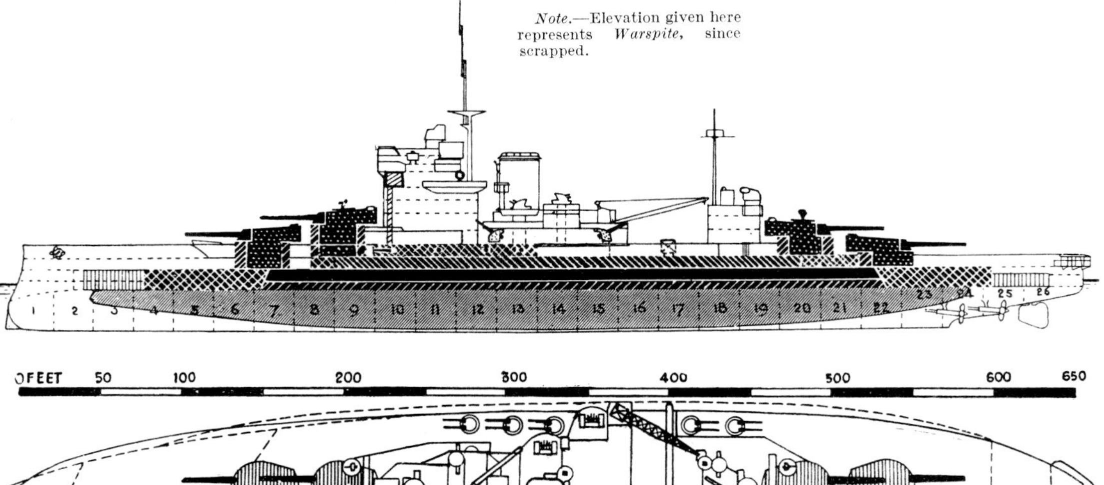

Guns:
8—15 inch, 42 cal.
20—4.5 inch AA.
Numerous 40 mm. and 20 mm. A.A.

Armour:
Originally as for *Malaya* (vide a later page) but has been modified extensively as a result of reconstruction. All are fitted with bulges.

Queen Elizabeth. *Added* 1944, *Lieut. D. Trimingham, R.N.V.R.*

Machinery: Parsons geared turbines. 4 shafts. Boilers: Admiralty 3-drum type. Designed H.P.: 80,000 as reconstructed = 24 kts. Oil fuel: 650 tons *normal*, 3,400 tons *max*. Radius of action: *about* 4,400 miles.

Name.	Builder.	Machinery.	Laid down.	Completed.	Trials.	Boilers.
Queen Elizabeth	Portsmouth	Wallsend	21/10/12	Jan., '15	75,130 =	Admiralty Type
Valiant	Fairfield	Fairfield	31/1/13	Feb., '16	71,112 =	
Malaya	Armstrong	Wallsend	Oct. '13	Feb., '16	76,074 =	24 Babcock

Queen Elizabeth. 1941.

(*The notes on these ships will be found on following page*)

Valiant. 1946, *P. A. Vicary.*

Battleship

(Queen Elizabeth Class)

MALAYA (18th Mar., 1915).

Displacement, 31,100 tons (*about* 35,000 tons *full load*). Complement, 1124-1184. Fitted as flagship.

Length (*pp.*), 600 feet; (*o.a.*) 639¾ ft. (*w.l.*) 634½ feet. Beam, 104 feet. *Mean* draught, 30⅔ feet. *Max.* „ 33½ „

Guns:
- 8—15 inch, 42 cal.
- 12—4 inch AA.
- 24—2 pdr. pompoms.
- 17—20 mm. AA.

Armour (H.T.):

Deck.
- 1″ Fo'xle (over battery).
- 2″—1¼″ Upper ....
- 1¼″ Main fwd. & aft. ..
- 1″ Middle ....
- 3″ (ends) } Lower.
- 1 (amidships) } Lower.

Special Protec.
- 2″—1″ Torp. pro. b'lkh'ds between end barbettes.

Vertical

Armour (K.C.): This protection has been modified and improved.)
- 13″ on waterline .. } Side
- 6″—4″ over w.l. .. } Side
- 6″—4″ (ends) .... } Side
- 6″, 4″ Bulkheads (f. & a.)
- 6″ Battery ....
- 10″—7″ Barbettes ......
- 11″ Gunhouses ....
- 6″—3″ C.T. base ......
- 14″ C.T. (6″—2″ Hood) ..
- 4″ Fore com. tube ....
- 6″ Torpedo C.T. ....

Malaya. 1942, *Official.*

Malaya. *Added* 1943, *Lieut. D. Trimingham R.N.V.R.*

BARHAM (1914). 31,100 tons.
Torpedoed by a German submarine in Eastern Mediterranean, November 25, 1941.

Note to Plan.—6-inch guns have been removed, and 4-inch AA. guns are now paired.

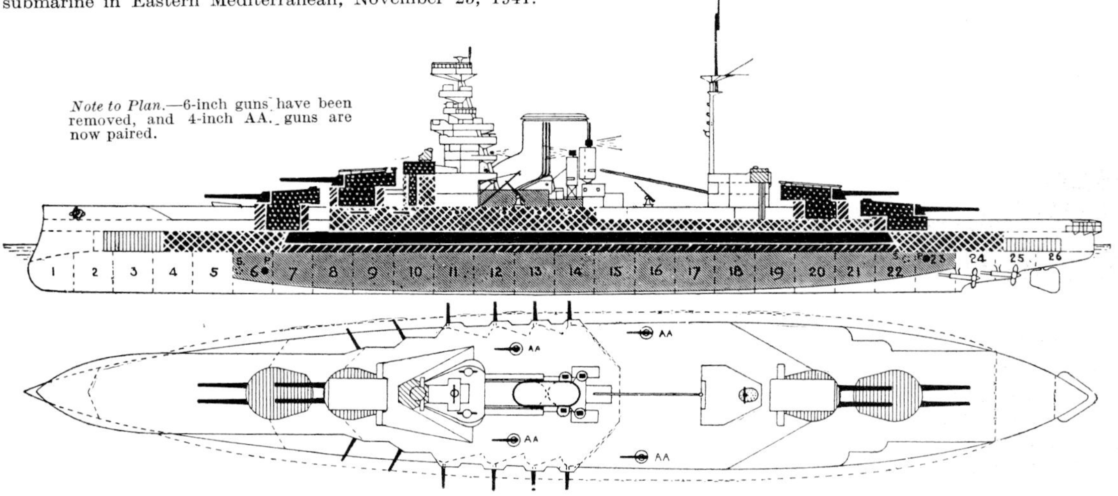

Machinery: Parsons geared turbine. 4 shafts. Designed H.P.: 75,000 = 24 kts. Oil fuel: 650 tons *normal*, 3,400 tons *max.* Radius of action: *about* 4,400 miles.

Gunnery Notes.—15 inch guns and mountings designed for 20° elevation (increased to 30° when reconstructed).

Engineering Notes.—These ships steam splendidly, and can maintain a high average speed for long periods.

Appearance Notes.—As rebuilt, these 3 ships differ completely from former appearance. ***Malaya*** has funnel encased by platforms.

Present Employment.—*Malaya* was recently accommodation ship, attached to torpedo school, Portsmouth. Future employment uncertain.

General Notes.—First two begun under 1912 Estimates. Designed by Sir Philip Watts. *Malaya*, extra ship, gift of Federated Malay States. Cost, nearly £3,000,000 per ship. (*Q.E.*, £3,014,103; *Malaya*, £2,945,709.) *Q. Elizabeth* alone has a stern walk. Reconstruction of this class, between 1925 and 1933, involved an expenditure of about £11,000,000 per ship; it included the remodelling of control top and bridgework and the trunking of the fore-funnel into the second. Two torpedo tubes were removed. In 1934 *Malaya* was taken in hand for further reconstruction of an extensive character involving the provision of new turbines, additional protection, and augmented AA. armament, with other modernisation affecting about 60 per cent of ship's structure. Cost of alterations, £976,963. *Valiant* and *Queen Elizabeth* have undergone much more extensive reconstruction, involving great improvement in watertight subdivision, replacement of propelling machinery and general modernisation throughout. *Valiant* was re-engined by Fairfield, *Q.E.* by Parsons. A fourth ship of this class (*Barham*) was lost in Nov., 1941, and *Warspite* was sold for scrapping in 1946.

For data describing first 2 units of this class, see preceding page.

Battle Cruiser

RENOWN (March 4, 1916).

Displacement: 30,750 tons (37,000 tons *full load*). Complement: 1,181/1,205.
Length: (*pp.*) 750 feet; (*w.l.*), 787¾ feet; (*o.a.*) 794 feet 1½ in. Beam: 102⅔ feet.
Draught: 26⅔ feet (*mean*), 30¼ feet (*max.*).
Fitted as flagship.

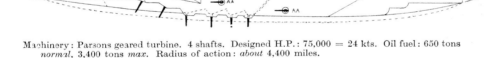

Renown. 1945, *Flight Lieut. P. A. Vicary.*

Guns:
- 6—15 inch, 42 cal.
- 8—4·5 inch (dual purpose)
- 24—2 pdr. pompoms.
- 64—20 mm. AA.

Armour:
Understood that protection was considerably increased during 1936–39 reconstruction.

Battleships

Note to Plan.—Mainmast is now a tripod. 12 of the 4·5-inch guns shown were removed when fire-control arrangements were brought up to date in 1946.

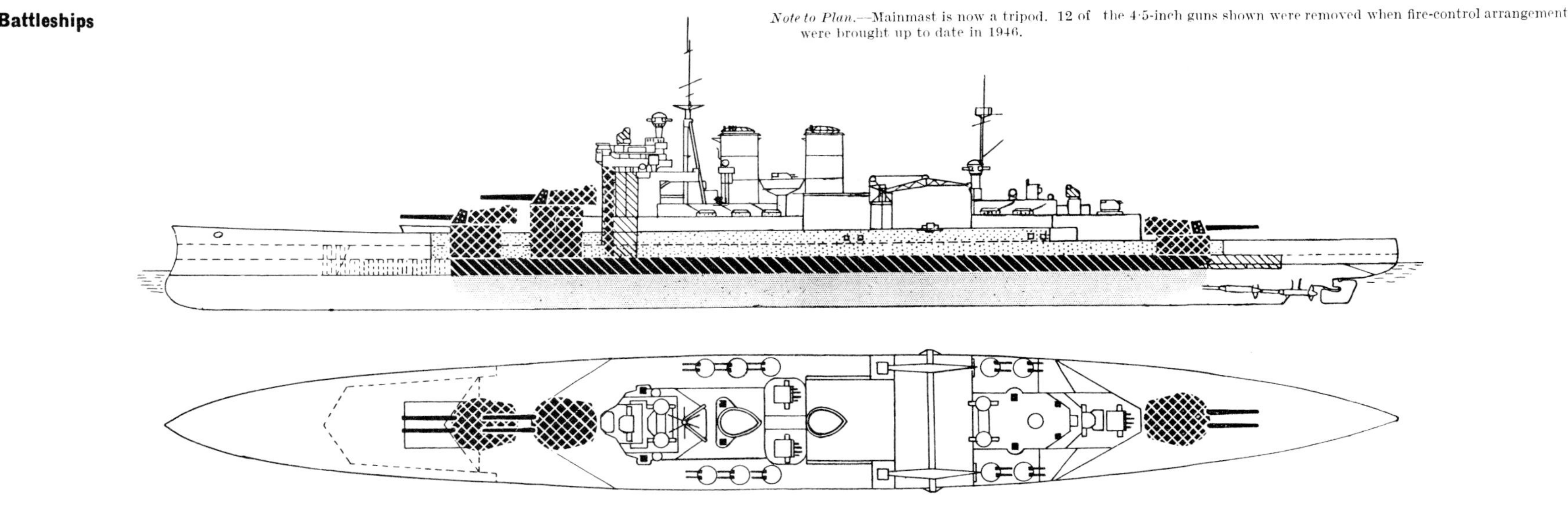

Name.	*Builder.*	*Machinery.*	*Begun.*	*Completed.*	*First Trials.*
Renown	Fairfield	Cammell Laird	Jan. 25, 1915 (to B.C. design)	Sept., 1916	126,300 = 32·68

Machinery: Parsons geared turbines. 4 shafts. Boilers: 8 Admiralty 3-drum type (300 lb. working pressure). S.H.P.: 120,000 = 29 kts. Oil fuel: 1,000 tons *normal*, 4,289 tons *max.* Radius of action, *about* 3,650 miles.

General Notes.—This ship was provided for under 1914 Navy Estimates, as a battleship. After Falkland Islands battle she was re-designed as a battle cruiser. Cost, £3,117,204. Refits: 1919–20, £100,738; 1921–22, £175,518; 1924–26, £979,927; 1936–39 (complete reconstruction and re-engining), £3,088,008. Sister ship, *Repulse*, was lost in Dec., 1941.

RENOWN. 1945, *Flight Lieut. P. A. Vicary.*

REPULSE (8th January, 1916).

Standard displacement, 32,000 tons (36,800—37,400 *full load*). Complement, 1181/1205

Length { (*p.p.*) 750 feet. { *o.a.* 794 feet 2½ in. *Repulse* } / (*w.l.*) 787¾ feet. { *o.a.* 794 feet 1½ in. *Renown* } Beam 102⅔ feet† Draught { *Repulse* — feet (*mean*), 31¾ feet (*max.*) / *Renown* 26⅔ feet (*mean*), 30¼ feet (*max.*)

Both fitted as flagships. †Outside bulges.

Guns:
- 6—15 inch, 42 cal. } **Dir.**
- 15—4 inch, 40 cal. } **Con.**
- 4—4 inch AA.
- 4—3 pdr.
- 1—12 pdr. Field
- 5 M.G.
- 10 Lewis

Torpedo tubes (21 inch):*
- 2 *submerged* (both ships)
- 8 *above water* in pairs (*Repulse*)

*See Torpedo Notes.

For illustrations, vide following page.

Notes to plan:

Now have range-finders mounted on turrets and additional control top at foremast head.

Renown is without main deck 6" side armour.

(See Armour Notes.)

Armour (K.C.):

Vertical.
- 9"—6" Side (amidships) } Lower belt
- 6"—4" Side (within bow) } Lower belt
- 3" (stern) } Lower belt
- 4" Fore b'lkhead } Lower belt
- 3" After b'lkh'd } Lower belt
- 1½" Upper belt ....
- 7"—4" Barbettes .....
- 11"—7" Gunhouses.....
- 1½" Funnel uptakes ...
- 2" C.T. base (3" tube within)............
- 10" C.T. ....
- 6" Sighting hood over C.T. ....
- 3" Torpedo C.T. ......

Armour (H.T.):

Decks
- 1½"—½" Fo'xle........
- 7/16"—1½" Upper ....
- 3"—¾" Main (2" slopes
- 2½" Bow } Lower
- 3½"—3" Stern } Lower

Crowns
- —" Barbettes ....
- 3" C.T. and hood .....
- 1½" Torpedo C.T. .....

Special protection:
- Modified bulges.......

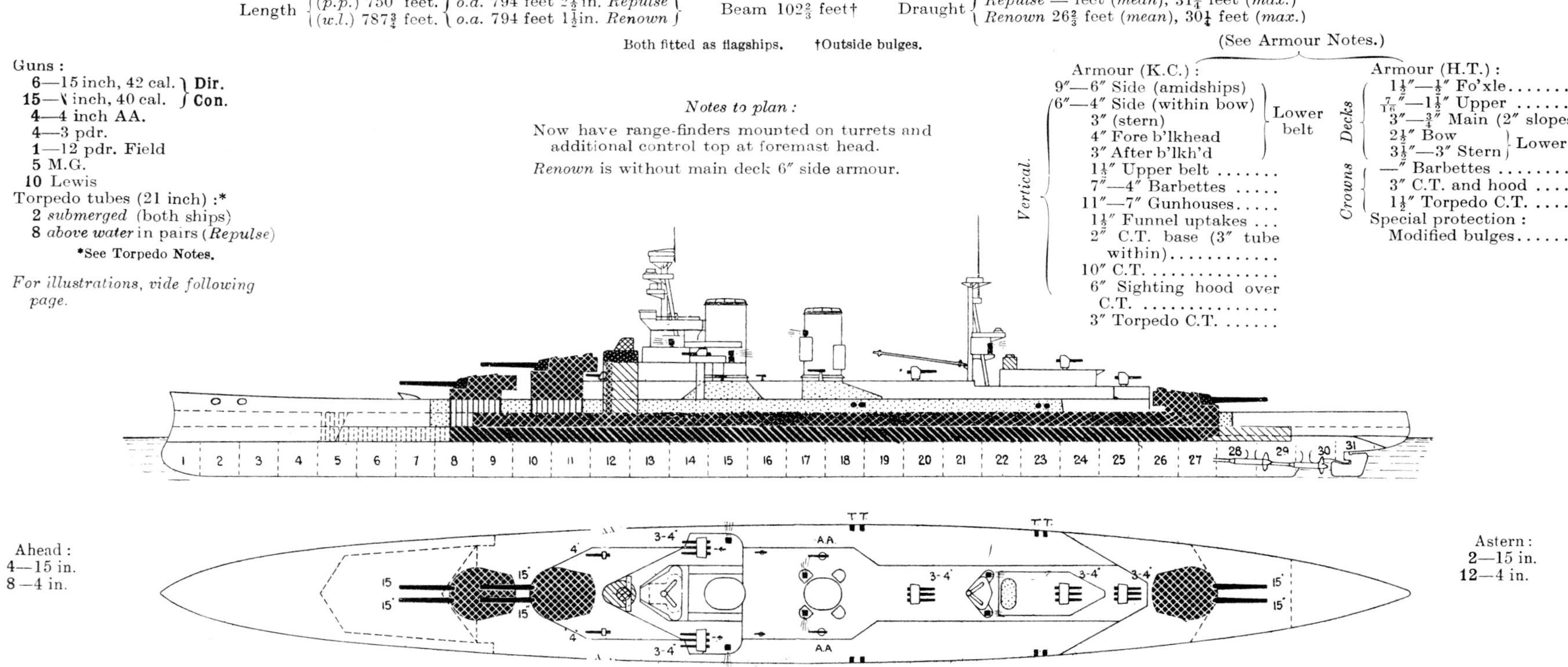

Ahead:
4—15 in.
8—4 in.

Astern:
2—15 in.
12—4 in.

Broadside: 6—15 in., 13—4 in., 4—21 in. tubes.

Machinery: Brown-Curtis (direct drive) turbines. 4 screws. Boilers: 42 Babcock & Wilcox. Designed H.P. not exactly specified, but expected to be 110,000 to 120,000 S.H.P. for 30 kts. In service, S.H.P. 112,000 = about 31.5 kts. Fuel (oil only): 1000 tons *normal*; *Repulse* 4243 tons *maximum*; *Renown* 4289 tons *maximum*. Radius of action, *about* 3650 miles. Tactical diameter: 4⅓ times length.

Name	*Builder*	*Machinery*	*Begun**	*Completed*	*Trials: H.P. kts.*
Repulse	Clydebank	Clydebank	Jan.25,'15	Aug.,1916	119,025 = 31.7*

*To Battle Cruiser design. *30 kts. on Arran mile after being re-armoured.

Gunnery Notes.—15-inch have range only limited by maximum visibility and Director tower is under control tower on foremast. 4 inch triples have 2 director towers, and all guns can be worked from either tower or half the 4-inch from one tower. If towers are destroyed, 4-inch can work independently. 4-inch triples are clumsy and not liked. They are not mounted in one sleeve; have separate breech mechanism: gun crew of 23 to each triple. It is said that first salvo fired by forward 15-inch of *Renown* did considerable damage forward, and she had to be docked for repairs.

Torpedo Notes.—*Repulse*, on 1919 re-fit, had 8 *above water* tubes in 4 twin mountings fitted on main deck above sections 19 and 23.

Armour Notes.—Armouring adapted from *Invincible* and *Indefatigable* classes. On re-fit 1919-20, *Repulse* re-armoured on w.l. with 9″ K.C. and 6″ K.C. between main and upper decks, extending over sections 8-27 on plans. Belt, *about* 9 ft. deep.

Engineering Notes.—Turbines similar to *Tiger*. For full description, *v.* "Engineering," April 11th, 1919. Boilers: 250 lbs. per sq. in. Heating surface: 157,206 sq. ft. Consumption at full speed: *about* 1400 tons oil fuel per day; at economical speed, *about* 180 tons per day.

Notes.—Provided for by 1914-15 Navy Estimates; first designed as slightly modified *Royal Sovereigns*, contracted for on that basis, and begun 1914, but building was not pushed on actively after the outbreak of War. After the Falklands Battle it was decided that these two ships should be re-designed as Battle Cruisers. Outline design was prepared in ten days, and builders received sufficient details by January 21st, 1915, to begin building, but full designs were not finished and approved till April, 1915. Intended that they should be completely built in fifteen months, but this time was somewhat exceeded. Both ships have turned out remarkably well and reflect great credit on their designers and builders. Internally, they are most spacious, but it has been stated that their guns "shake them up" considerably. Costs: *Repulse*, £2,627,401; *Renown*, £3,111,266; but former total is not inclusive of all charges, and is liable to revision. Refits: *Renown* (1919-20), £100,738, (1921-22) £175,518. *Repulse* (1918-22), £860,684; which is equivalent to the cost of a new *Carlisle* type Light Cruiser. *Renown* re-constructed, 1923-26, with addition of conspicuous bulge; bridge built up abaft fore tripod, as in *Revenge*; heavy upper control top on foremast and short topmast removed; gaff on main at heel of topmast.

REPULSE. 1925 *Photo, Abrahams, Weymouth.*

HOOD* (J. Brown & Co., Clydebank. Begun 1st Sept., 1916, Launched 22nd August, 1918, completed 5th March, 1920.)

Standard displacement, 42,100 tons (46,200 tons *full load*). Complement, 1341.

Length { *p.p.* 810 ft. / *o.a.* 860 ft. 7 in. } Beam { *w.l.* / *outside bulges* 105 ft. 2½ in. } Draught { *mean* 28½ ft. / *max.* 31½ ft. }

*Fitted as Flagship.

Guns:
- 8—15 inch, 42 cal. } **Dir. Con.**
- 12—5·5 inch, 50 cal. } **Dir. Con.**
- 2—4·7 inch AA.
- 4—4 inch (anti-aircraft.)
- 4—3 pdr.
- 1—12 pdr. Field.
- 5 M.G. and Multiple AA.
- 10 Lewis.

Torpedo tubes (21 inch)
- 2 *submerged* (P. & S.)
- 4 *above water* in pairs.

Aircraft:
- 1—Fairey III F.

Notes to Plan.—Combined thicknesses of side armour and conning tower shown by dark patch in section 11. Now carries flagstaffs on both masts, with gaff on main.

Armour (K.C.):

Vertical.
- 3″ Side (submerged) ..
- 12″, 7″, 5″ Side (amidships) ....
- 6″—5″ Side (forward)..
- 6″ Side (aft)..........
- 5″ 4″ Bulkh'ds (f. & a.)
- 12″— ″ Barbettes ....
- 15″ Face } Turrets
- 12″—11″ Sides } Turrets
- 12″ & 9″ C.T. ....
- 6″ C.T. Base ....
- 6″ Director tower ....
- 4″—3″ Torp. control tower ....
- —″ P. & S. R.F. towers (5.5″) ....
- —″ Funnel uptakes ...
- 1″ (H.T.) Shields to 5.5″ guns ....

Armour (H.T.):

Decks.
- 2″ Forecastle ....
- 1″ U.D. amidships ....
- 1½″—3″ Main deck ...
- 3″ M.D. over magazines
- 1½″—1″ L.D. forward
- 3″—1″ L.D. aft ......

Crowns.
- 3″ Director tower ....
- 5″ C.T. ....
- 3″ Torpedo control T.
- 5″ Turrets ....

Special protection (H.T.):
1½″ and ¾″ Torp. pro. b'lk'd over magazines, boiler and engine rooms, bulges and buoyancy spaces.

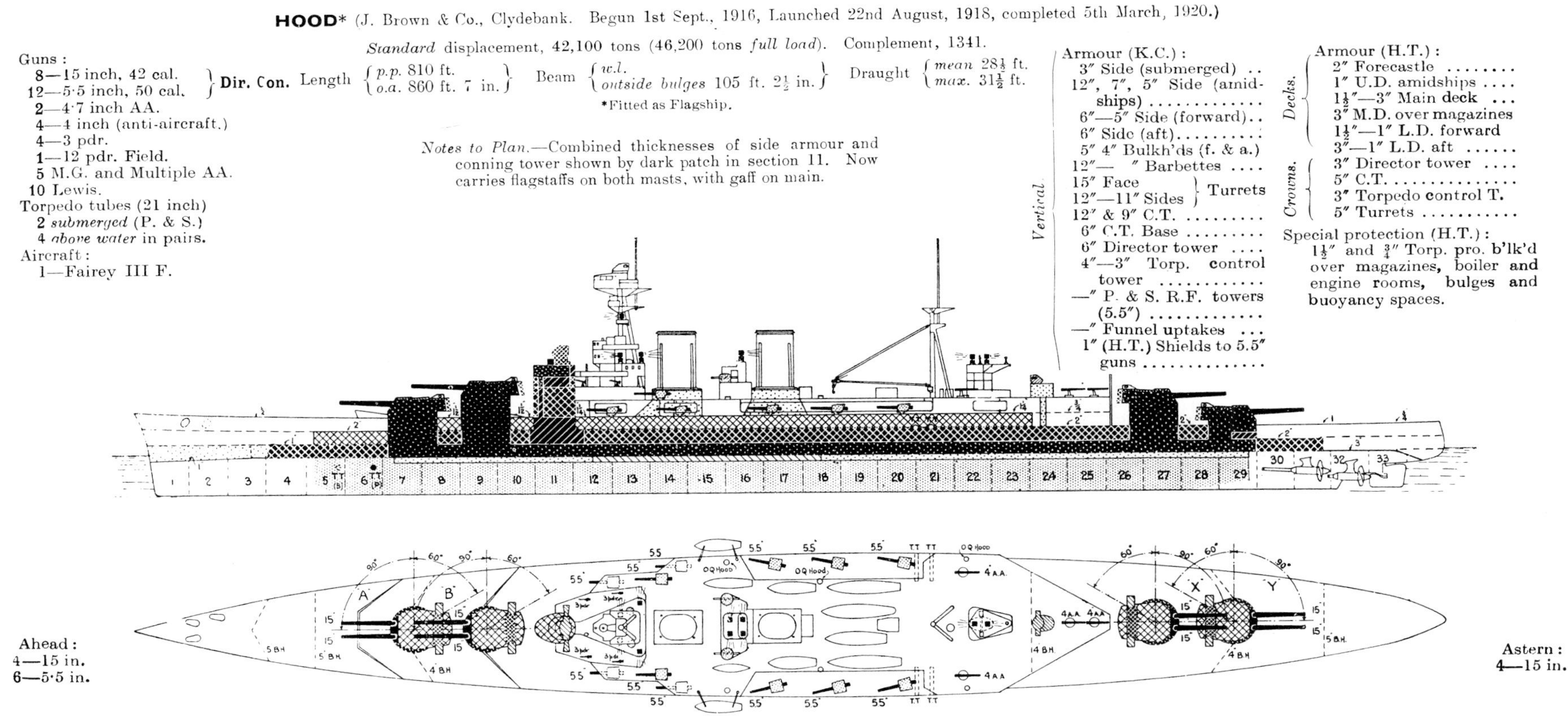

Ahead:
4—15 in.
6—5·5 in.

Astern:
4—15 in.

Broadside: **8—15 in., 6—5·5 in., 3—21 in. tubes.**

Machinery (by Builders): Brown-Curtis (geared) turbines. 4 screws. Boilers: 24 Yarrow (small tube). Designed S.H.P. 144,000 = 31 kts. Fuel: Oil only. 1200 tons *normal*, 4,000 tons *maximum*.

Battleships

HOOD. 1931 *Photo, Kestin.*

Gunnery Notes.—Barbette heights over l.w.l.: A, 32 ft.; B, 42 ft.; X, 31¾ ft.; Y, 21¾ ft. All turrets bear 150° on each beam. Designed to mount 16—5.5 inch, but the four after guns were removed before completion. Elevation of 15 inch guns, 30°. 8—36 inch controlled, and 4—24 inch signalling S.L. Stem attachment for PVs. of new design. guns, mountings, barbettes and ammunition = 5300 tons.

Armour Notes.—Vertical side armour is backed by strong 2″—1″ H.T. plating, not included in thicknesses given. Area of 12″ armour at w.l., 562 ft. long by 9½ ft. deep. Gun houses, new type with flat crowns, small square sighting ports cut low in face for laying over open sights. On roofs, armoured cases slightly wider than R.F. to allow R.F. to be traversed for fine adjustments. Barbettes, 6″—5″ as they descend through decks. C.T. is an enormous, elaborate, most expensive and ponderous structure; in upper stages, it consists of two shells, 12″ outer, 9″ inner, with narrow passage between. The slope inboard of hull side detracts from effects of plunging fire by virtual increase of armour thickness. A perpendicular, dropped from top sides, just meets outer edges of bulges, which are of the improved "D'Eyncourt-Hopkinson" type. Total weight of armour and protection, 13,800 tons.

Engineering Notes.—During world cruise, economical speed worked out at 288 miles in 24 hours on 180 tons of oil.

Trials (unofficial figures).—At 42,200 tons, 151,000 S.H.P. = 32.07 kts. (run in bad weather, wind force 6 Beaufort scale) on Arran mile. At 44,600 tons, 31.89 kts. *mean* attained. On ⅔ power, 25 kts. easily secured. Total weight of machinery (with water in boilers to working level) = 5,350 tons.

Original Design.— The original 1915 Design embodied same length and beam, but draughts were 25½ feet ***normal*** = 36,300 tons, and 29 feet deep. Speed: 32 kts. Belt 8″, barbettes 9″, much thinner deck armour, and only 2—21 inch *submerged* T. T. Four ships ordered to this design April, 1916. In the design produced after Jutland (not approved till 1917), 5,000 tons extra protection was worked in. By use of small-tube boilers, 24,000 S.H.P. gained on *same* machinery weights as for *Renown* class.

Notes.— Begun under Emergency War Programme. Originally, there were four ships in this class, ***Anson, Hood,*** *Howe, Rodney*. They were begun in the autumn of 1916, to meet the German Battle Cruisers, *Graf Spee, Mackensen, Ersatz Freya* and *Ersatz "A,"* which were laid down in 1916. Contractors were: ***Anson*** (Armstrong), ***Howe*** (Cammell Laird), *Rodney* (Fairfield), *Hood* (Brown). The enemy having ceased work on all his large ships, in 1917, ***Anson, Howe*** and *Rodney* were stopped in March, 1917, and dismantled to clear slips after the Armistice, but not before £860,000 had been expended on them. These ships were redesigned to meet the lessons of Jutland. In ***Hood,*** the outstanding feature is the huge areas covered by heavy armour, strong framing, &c.—in fact, the general scheme of protection is most comprehensive. Cost, *about* £6,025,000 = £145 per ton. Annual upkeep, £427,270. Due for replacement, 1941. General refit, 1929-30.

(ROYAL SOVEREIGN CLASS.)—All fitted as Flagships.

ROYAL SOVEREIGN (29th April, 1915), **ROYAL OAK** (17th Nov., 1914), **RESOLUTION** (14th Jan., 1916), **RAMILLIES** (12th Sept., 1916), **REVENGE** (29th May, 1915).

Standard displacement, 29,150 tons (about 33,500 tons *full load*). Complement, 1009-1146.

Length (*p.p.*) 580 feet, (*w.l.*) 614½ feet, (*o.a.*) 620½ feet.† Beam, about 102½ feet.* *Mean* draught, 28½ feet.

*With bulge protection. †*Revenge* 624½ feet (*o.a.*)

Name	*Builder*	*Machinery*	*Laid down*	*Com-pleted*	*Trials*:—	*Boilers*
Royal Sovereign	Portsmouth Y.	Parsons	Jan.'14	May, '16	41,115 = 21·6	18 Babcock
Royal Oak	Devonport Y.	Hawthorn	Jan.'14	May, '16	40,360 =	18 Yarrow
Resolution	Palmer	Palmer	Nov.'13	Dec., '16	41,406 =	18 Yarrow
Ramillies	Beardmore*	Beardmore	Nov.'13	Sept. '17	42,356 = 21·5	18 Babcock
Revenge	Vickers	Vickers	Dec.'13	Mar., '16	42,962 = 21·9	18 Babcock

*Towed to Liverpool and completed by Cammel Laird & Co.

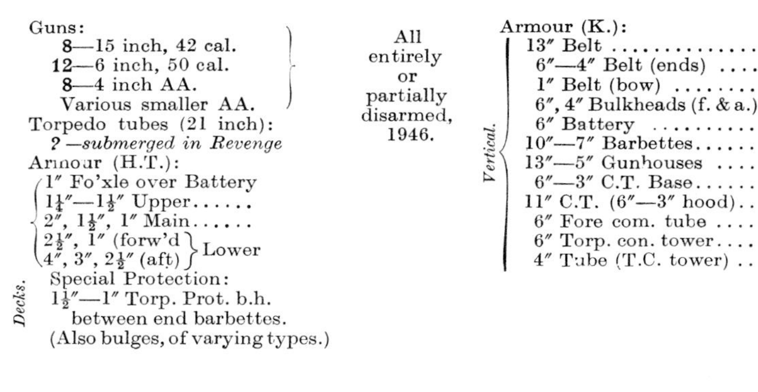

Guns:
8—15 inch, 42 cal.
12—6 inch, 50 cal.
8—4 inch AA.
Various smaller AA.
Torpedo tubes (21 inch):
?—submerged in Revenge
Armour (H.T.):
Decks.
1″ Fo'xle over Battery
1¼″—1½″ Upper......
2″, 1½″, 1″ Main......
2½″, 1″ (forw'd) } Lower
4″, 3″, 2½″ (aft) } Lower
Special Protection:
1½″—1″ Torp. Prot. b.h. between end barbettes.
(Also bulges, of varying types.)

All entirely or partially disarmed, 1946.

Armour (K.):
Vertical.
13″ Belt ....
6″—4″ Belt (ends) ....
1″ Belt (bow) ....
6″, 4″ Bulkheads (f. & a.)
6″ Battery ....
10″—7″ Barbettes......
13″—5″ Gunhouses ....
6″—3″ C.T. Base......
11″ C.T. (6″—3″ hood)..
6″ Fore com. tube ....
6″ Torp. con. tower....
4″ Tube (T.C. tower) ..

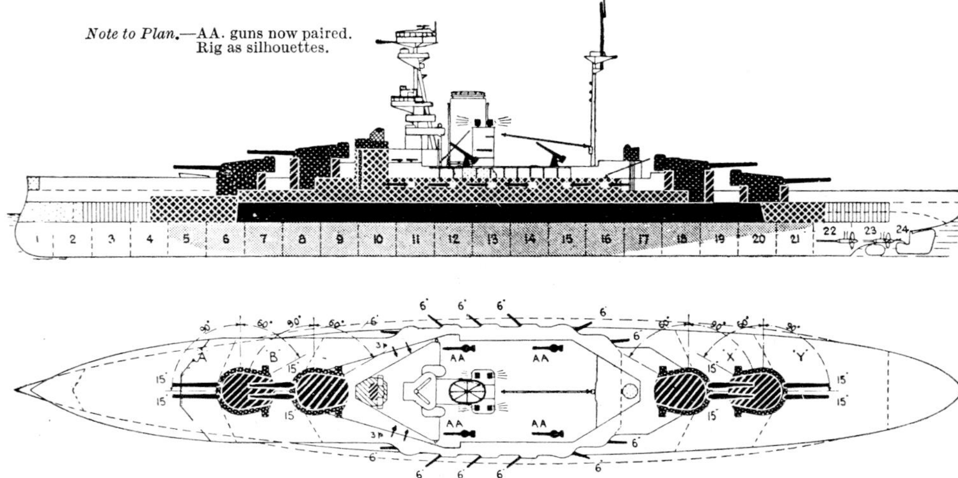

Note to Plan.—AA. guns now paired. Rig as silhouettes.

Machinery: Parsons turbines, 4 shafts. Designed H.P.: 40,000 = 21 knots *with* bulges (*now less*). Boilers: (see Table). Oil fuel: *normal*, 900 tons; *maximum*, 3,230 tons.

RESOLUTION. 1943, *Official.*

Battleships

RAMILLIES. (REVENGE similar, see notes.) 1944, *Official.*

Present Employment.—*Ramillies* is a training ship at Portsmouth, while *Revenge* and *Resolution* (disarmed) together constitute stokers' training establishment *Imperieuse* at Devonport.

Appearance Notes.—*Revenge* differs in having sternwalk and extra heavy forebridge. Details of bridge vary in each ship

Gunnery Notes.—6 inch batteries are wet in head seas, but dwarf walls in battery retain water and it is rapidly drained away. 4 inch AA. mounted in place of former 3 inch AA. in 1924–25. Two superstructure 6 inch removed in 1927–28.

Armour Notes.—Thicknesses much as *Queen Elizabeth* class, but armour differently distributed. Barbettes 6″—4″ as they decend behind belt. Gunhouses, 13″ face, 11″ sides and rear; crowns 5″. In these ships 2″ protective deck has a high 2″ slope behind belt, so that flat part of protection can be put on main deck and at top of belt, instead of a deck lower. Internal protection is very good, and with protective bulges, defence against underwater attack is very strong. All refitted with bulges, which in *Ramillies* were the first to be fitted to any battleship; they extended almost to level of battery, but have since been replaced.

Engineering Notes.—Designed to burn coal, but while building "all oil fuel" was adopted, so that 23 kts. would be secured with the resulting increase of H.P. Addition of bulges has brought speed down again to about 22 kts. Main turbines are direct drive, cruising turbines geared.

General Notes.—Begun under 1913–14 Estimates. *Ramillies* injured herself at launch and was delayed in completion. They are fine ships, but suffer rather from reduced freeboard. Searchlights on mainmast removed 1922. Refits: *Ramillies* and *Resolution*, 1926–27; *Revenge*, 1928; *Resolution*, 1930; *Revenge*, 1936–37; *Resolution*, 1937–38; *Ramillies*, 1938–39. *Royal Oak*, of this class, sunk Oct. 14, 1939. *Royal Sovereign* transferred to Soviet Navy in 1944.

Cost.—Averaged about £2,500,000.

Fleet Aircraft Carriers

(ARK ROYAL CLASS—2 Ships.)

ARK ROYAL, EAGLE (ex-*Audacious*, March 19, 1946).

Displacement: 33,000 tons. Dimensions not reported, but length believed to exceed 850 feet.

Guns:	Aircraft:	Armour:
16—4·5 inch, etc.	Probably 100 or more.	Not reported.

Machinery: Parsons geared turbines. 4 shafts. S.H.P. 150,000 = 32 kts. Boilers: 8 Admiralty 3-drum type.

Name.	*Builder and Machinery.*	*Begun.*	*Completed.*
Ark Royal	Cammell Laird.	1943.	
Eagle	Harland & Wolff.	1942.	

Notes.—These two ships will be the largest British aircraft carriers ever built. They are stated to be 90 per cent welded construction. Two more of this type, *Africa* and *Eagle*, were cancelled. Latter had been ordered from Vickers-Armstrongs (Tyne). Three much larger carriers, to have been named *Gibraltar, Malta* and *New Zealand*, were also cancelled.

(HERMES CLASS—4 Ships).

ALBION (May 6, 1947), BULWARK, CENTAUR (April 22, 1947), HERMES (ex-*Elephant*).

Displacement: 18,300 tons. Length: 737 feet. Beam: 90 feet. Draught not reported.

Guns:	Aircraft:	Armour:
8—4·5 inch	Probably 50 or more.	Not reported.
Over **40**—40 mm. AA.		

Machinery: Parsons geared turbines. 2 shafts. Speed believed to approach 30 kts. Boilers: Admiralty 3-drum type.

Name	*Builders*	*Begun*	*Completed*
Albion	Swan Hunter	1944	
Bulwark	Harland & Wolff	1944	
Centaur	do.	1944	
Hermes	Vickers-Armstrongs (Barrow)	30/6/44	

Notes.—These ships are believed to be enlarged *Majestics*. Of eight ships originally ordered, *Arrogant, Monmouth* and *Polyphemus* have been cancelled, together with the original *Hermes*.

(IMPLACABLE CLASS.)

Fleet Aircraft Carriers

IMPLACABLE (Dec. 10, 1942), INDEFATIGABLE (Dec. 8, 1942).

Displacement 23,000 tons (32,000 tons *full load*). Complement: *ca.* 2,000.
Length: (*o.a.*) 766 feet 2 in. and 766 feet 5 in., respectively.
Beam: 95 feet 9 in. Draught: 29 feet 4 in.

Guns:	Aircraft:	Armour:
16—4·5 inch dual purpose. **77** to **79**—40 mm., 20 mm. and 2 pdr. pompoms.	Over 60.	Not reported.

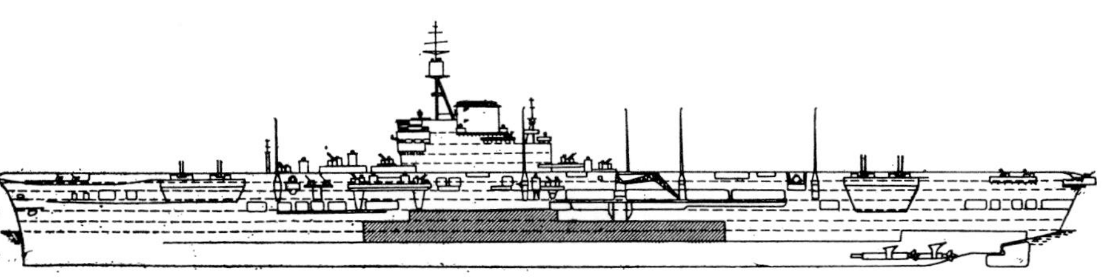

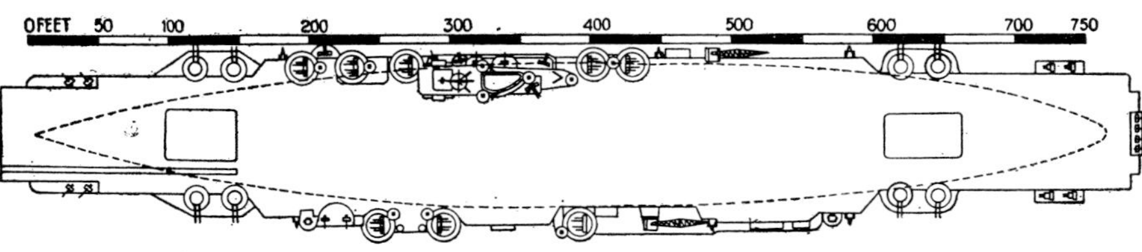

Machinery: Parsons single reduction geared turbines. 4 shafts. Speed: 32 kts. Boilers: 8 Admiralty 3-drum type.

Est.	*Name.*	*Builder and Machinery.*	*Ordered.*	*Begun.*	*Completed.*
1938	*Implacable.*	Fairfield.	11/10/38	21/2/39	28/8/44
1939	*Indefatigable.*	Clydebank.	19/6/39	3/11/39	3/5/44

Note.—To distinguish between them, observe that boats of *Indefatigable* are stowed one deck higher than in *Implacable*.

IMPLACABLE. 1944, *Official.*

INDEFATIGABLE. 1946, *Wright & Logan.*

Fleet Aircraft Carriers

INDEFATIGABLE. 1946, *Wright & Logan.*

INDEFATIGABLE. 1944, *Official.*

INDOMITABLE (March 26, 1940).

Displacement: 23,000 tons (29,730 tons *full load*). Complement: 1,600.
Length: (*o.a.*) 753 feet 11 in. Beam: 95 feet 9 in.
Draught: 22 feet 4 in. *mean*; 29 feet 5 in. *max*.

Guns:
16—4·5 inch (dual purpose).
Numerous 40 mm. AA. and 20 mm. AA.

Aircraft:
Over 60.

Armour:
Not reported.

Machinery: Parsons geared turbines. 3 shafts. S.H.P.: 110,000 = 31 kts. Boilers: 6 of 3-drum type.

Est.	*Name*	*Builder & Machinery*	*Ordered*	*Begun*	*Completed*
1937	*Indomitable*	Vickers-Armstrongs, Barrow	6/7/37	10/11/37	1/10/41

(*Plan does not differ widely from that of ILLUSTRIOUS class.*)

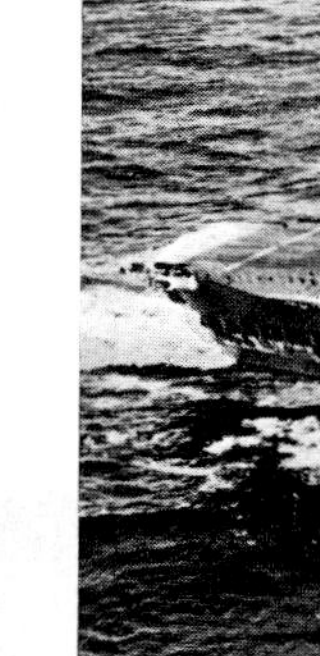

INDOMITABLE. 1944, *Official.*

INDOMITABLE. 1944, *Official.*

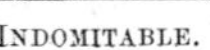

INDOMITABLE. 1946, *Wright & Logan.*

INDOMITABLE. 1944, *Official.*

(ILLUSTRIOUS CLASS—3 Ships.)

ILLUSTRIOUS (April 5, 1939), VICTORIOUS (Sept. 14, 1939), FORMIDABLE (August 17, 1939).

Displacement: 23,000 tons. Complement: 1,600.
Length: 753 feet. Beam: 95 feet. Draught: 24 feet.

Guns:
16—4·5 inch (dual purpose).
Numerous 40 mm. AA. and 20 mm. AA.

Aircraft:
Over 60.

Armour:
Not disclosed, but includes armoured flight deck.

Machinery: Parsons geared turbines. 3 shafts. S.H.P.: 110,000 = 31 knots. Boilers: 6 of 3-drum type.

Est.	*Name*	*Builder*	*Machinery*	*Ordered*	*Begun*	*Completed*
1936	*Illustrious*	V.-A., Barrow	Vickers-Armstrongs	13/1/37	27/4/37	21/5/40
1936	*Victorious*	V.-A., Tyne	Wallsend Slipway	13/1/37	4/5/37	15/5/41
1937	*Formidable*	Harland & Wolff	Harland & Wolff	19/3/37	17/6/37	24/11/40

FORMIDABLE. 1946, *Wright & Logan.*

Fleet Aircraft Carriers

VICTORIOUS. 1946, *Wright & Logan.*

ILLUSTRIOUS. 1942, *Official.*

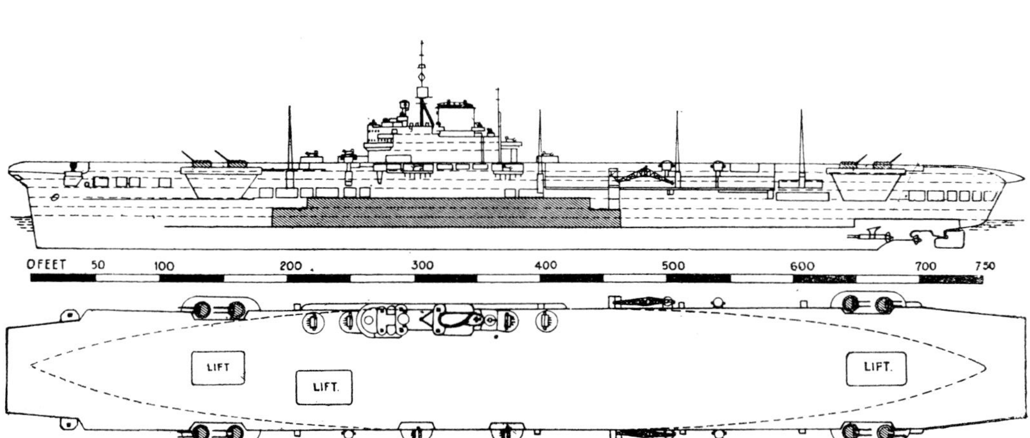

VICTORIOUS. 1946, *Wright & Logan.*

Light Fleet Aircraft Carriers

(COLOSSUS CLASS—6 Ships.)

GLORY (Nov. 27, 1943), **OCEAN** (July 8, 1944), **THESEUS** (July 6, 1944), **TRIUMPH** (Oct. 2, 1944), **VENERABLE** (Dec. 30, 1943), **VENGEANCE** (Feb. 23, 1944). (A seventh ship—**COLOSSUS**—is lent to French Navy for 5 years.)

Displacement: 13,190 tons (except *Theseus* and *Triumph*, 13,350 tons).

Complement: Peace, 840 to 854, excluding Air Squadron personnel.

(MAJESTIC CLASS—5 Ships.)

HERCULES (Sept. 22, 1945), **LEVIATHAN** (June 7, 1945), **MAJESTIC** (Feb. 28, 1945), **POWERFUL** (Jan. 30 1945), **TERRIBLE** (Sept. 30, 1944).

Displacement: 14,000 tons (over 18,000 tons *full load*). Complement: 1,400.

Length: (*pp.*) 630 feet; (*o.a.*) 693 feet 2 in. to 695 feet. Beam: 112½ feet (across flight deck). Draught: 21 feet 4 in. (*mean*), 23 feet 5 in. to 23 feet 7 in. (*max.*).

Guns (*Colossus* type):
4—3 pdr.
24—2 pdr. pompoms
19—40 mm. AA.
(*Majestic* type):
4—3 pdr.
30—40 mm. AA.

Aircraft:
39 to 44.

Armour:
Not reported.

VENERABLE. 1945, *Official.*

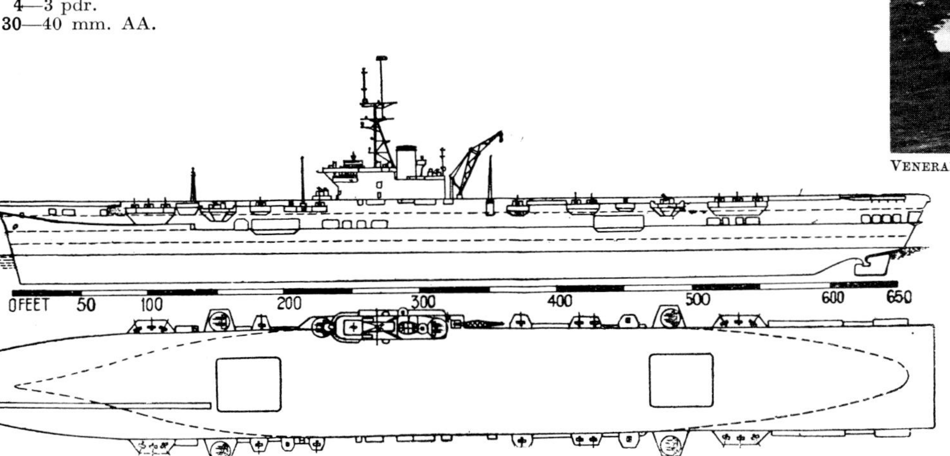

LEVIATHAN, while laid up awaiting completion, is to be given preservative coating on American system to prevent corrosion.

Name.	*Builder.*	*Begun.*	*Completed.*
Glory	Harland & Wolff	28/8/42	2/4/45
Ocean	Stephen	8/11/42	30/6/45
Theseus	Fairfield	42	9/1/46
Triumph	Hawthorn Leslie	42	9/4/46
Venerable	Cammell Laird	3/12/42	17/1/45
Vengeance	Swan Hunter	16/11/42	15/1/45
Hercules	Vickers-Armstrongs, Tyne	14/10/43	
Leviathan	Swan Hunter	43	
Majestic	Vickers-Armstrongs, Barrow	13/4/43	
Powerful	Harland & Wolff	43	
Terrible	Devonport	42	

Machinery: Parsons geared turbines. 2 shafts. S.H.P. 40,000=25 kts. Boilers: 4 Admiralty 3-drum type (400 lb. working pressure, 700° maximum superheat).

Light Fleet Aircraft Carriers

General Notes. — Differences between *Colossus* and *Majestic* classes are not appreciable externally and are confined to internal accommodation on mess decks, which is of improved type in latter. All are insulated for tropical service and partially air-conditioned. Besides *Colossus* being lent to France, as stated above, two (*Magnificent* and *Warrior*) have been transferred to R. Canadian Navy; and two were completed as maintenance aircraft carriers *Perseus* and *Pioneer*, recorded on later page.

Constructional Notes.—In some of these ships, flight deck is reported to have been strengthened to take aircraft of over 8 tons in weight. Sponsons can be dismantled to the extent of 3½ feet on either side if necessary to allow for passage through Panama Canal.

Engineering Notes.—Engine-rooms and boiler-rooms are arranged *en echelon*. In *Theseus*, one propeller is four-bladed and one three-bladed, in order to minimise vibration.

THESEUS. 1946, *Wright & Logan.*

GLORY. 1945, *Official.*

OCEAN. 1946, *London Studio.*

OCEAN. 1946, *London Studio.*

TRIUMPH. 1946, *Wright & Logan.*

THESEUS. 1946, *Wright & Logan.*

ARK ROYAL 1941. *Official.*

ARK ROYAL (1937). 22,000 tons.
Torpedoed by German submarine 150 miles E. of Gibraltar and subsequently foundered while in tow, November 14, 1941.

ARK ROYAL (13th April, 1937)

Normal displacement, 22,000 tons (about 27,720 tons full load)

Complement, 1580

Length (*p.p.*) 685 feet, (*o.a*) 800 feet. Beam, 94¾ feet

Draught 27¾ feet

Armour:	Guns:	Aircraft:
4½ Belt	16 – 4.5 inch HA	60
3″–2½″ bulkheads	32–2pdr	

Machinery 3-shaft Parsons geared turbines, 6 Admiralty 3-drum boilers, 102,000shp = 31 kts. Fuel oil, 4,620 tons.

(Courageous Class—2 Ships).

COURAGEOUS (5th February, 1916), **GLORIOUS** (20th April, 1916). (Late Cruisers.)

Normal displacement, *about* 18,600 tons (*about* 22,700 tons *full load*). Complement, 748 (with flying personnel included, *about* 1100).

Length { *p.p.* 735 ft. / *o.a.* 786¼ ft. } Beam (outside bulges), 81 ft. Draughts { *mean* 22¼ ft. / *max.* 26 ft.

Courageous. 1928 *Photo, Abrahams & Sons.*

Armour :
- 3″ Belt (amidships) ...
- 2″ Belt (forward) ....
- 2″ (H.T.) Fore bulkhead
- 3″—1″ (H.T.) After Bulkhead ....
- 1½″ Side over belt.....
- 1″ Upper deck.......
- 1½″ Lower (stern, flat)
- 3″ Lower (stern, over rudder) ....
- 2″ Lower (on slopes) ..
- Torpedo protection (H.T.) : Modified bulges 25 ft. deep ....
- ¾″ Inner screen to boiler and engine room vents.

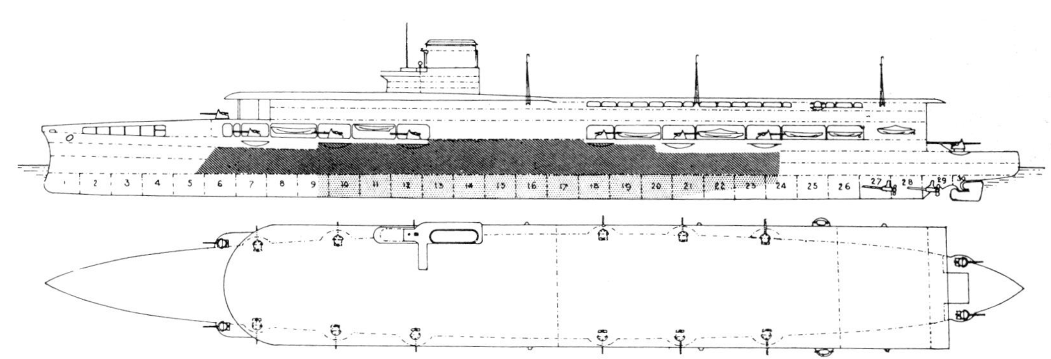

Guns :
- **16**—4·7 inch HA. and LA.
- **4**—3 pdr.
- **50** Smaller.

Flights carried :
- 2 Fighter (Flycatcher)
- 2 Spotter Reconnaissance (Fairey III F)
- 2 Torpedo (Dart)

Machinery : Parsons (all-geared) turbines. 4 screws. Boilers : 18 Yarrow (small tube). Designed H.P. 90,000 = *about* 31 kts. Fuel (oil only) : *normal,* 750 tons ; *maximum,* 3250 tons.

Armour Notes.—General scheme of armouring on Cruiser lines, the 3″ belt being built up of 2″ plating on 1″ shell plating. Decks round magazines thickened during completion.

Engineering Notes.—General arrangement of machinery as in Cruiser *Champion.* 4-shaft geared turbines and double helical gearing. Have done 32 kts. in service.

General Notes.—Emergency War Programme ships. Original cruiser design formulated by Lord Fisher in 1915, with a view to Baltic operations—hence the shallow draught. The lines are remarkably fine. On *trials, Courageous* met heavy weather and was driven into a head sea, straining her hull forward. Doubling plates were added here, and subsequent trials showed the defect had been overcome. *Glorious* strengthened in the same way a year later as a precautionary measure. No figures are available as to cost, but they are said to have run to three millions apiece. *Furious,* of slightly modified design, was converted while building into an Aircraft Carrier. *Courageous* and *Glorious* taken in hand for similar conversion at Devonport (June, 1924 and Feb., 1924 respectively). Work on *Glorious* was started at Rosyth, but on that yard being closed she was towed to Devonport for completion. *Courageous* completed March, 1928, her conversion having cost £2,025,800. *Glorious* completed January 1930.

Name	*Builder*	*Machinery*	*Begun*	*Completed*	*Trials*
Courageous	Armstrong	Parsons	May, 1915	Jan., 1917	93,780 = 31·58
Glorious	Harland & Wolff, Belfast	Harland & Wolff	Mar., 1915	Jan., 1917	91,165 = 31·6

Courageous. 1936, *Cribb.*

COURAGEOUS (1916). 22,500 tons.
Torpedoed by German submarine, September 17, 1939.

Glorious. 1935, *Cribb (added 1936).*

GLORIOUS (1916). 22,500 tons.
Sunk in action with German battleships *Scharnhorst* and *Gneisenau,* off North Norway, June 8, 1940.

Aircraft Carrier

1926 *Photo, Cribb, Southsea.*

1926 *Photo, Cribb, Southsea.*

FURIOUS (15 August, 1916). Late Cruiser.

Normal Displacement, *about* 19,100 tons, (about 22,450 tons *full load*). Complement, 748. †

Length, (*p.p.*) 735 feet, (*o.a.*) $786\frac{1}{4}$ feet. *Beam, $89\frac{3}{4}$ feet. Draught, { *mean* $21\frac{2}{3}$ feet. *max.* 25 feet.

*Outside bulges.

Guns (**Dir. Con.**):
- **10**—5·5 inch, 50 cal.
- **6**—4 inch AA.
- **54** Smaller.

Flights carried:
- 1 Fighter (Flycatcher).
- 3 Spotter Reconnaissance. (2 flights Fairey III F, 1 flight Blackburn).
- 2 Torpedo (1 Dart, 1 Ripon II).

Note to Plan.

Quarter deck to be raised one deck during present refit, 1931.

Armour:
- 3″ Belt (amidships)...............
- 2″ Belt (bow)......................
- 3″—2″ Bulkheads F. & A.........
- 1″ Decks (H.T at stern)...........
- 3″—$1\frac{1}{2}$″ Decks (H.T. at stern)..

Anti-Torp. Pro.
- Shallow bulges ....
- 1″ H.T. vertical. ....

†With flying personnel added, complement is about 1100.

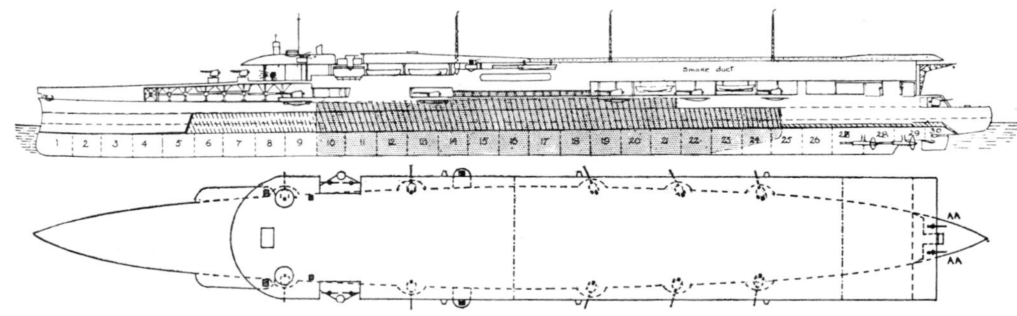

Machinery (by Wallsend Co.): Brown-Curtis (all geared) Turbines. 4 screws. Boilers: 18 Yarrow. Designed S.H.P. 90,000 = 31 kts. *Trials*: 90,820 = kts. Fuel (oil only): 4010 tons.

Armour Notes.—3″ Belt consists of 2″ plating over 1″ shell plating, as in Light Cruisers.

General Notes.—Built under Emergency War Programme, by Armstrong Whitworth. Begun June, 1915; completed July, 1917: re-built November, 1917, March, 1918. Designed as a modified *Courageous* but altered to Aircraft Carrier. Since conversion, she is said to be rather light, and is good now for 32-33 kts. Including cost of alterations, this ship is said to have absorbed over six million pounds. Underwent re-fit and alteration at H.M. Dockyards, Rosyth and Devonport, 1921-25, after which her appearance was completely altered, the funnel and mast being removed and a new hangar built forward. Smoke is discharged from vents at after end of hangar, or alternatively through flight deck, which measures 700×80 feet. Height of flight deck from water line is 75 feet. There are 2 hydraulic lifts from hangars to flight deck.

1926 *Photo. Cribb, Southsea.*

Furious. 1925 *Photo, Abrahams, Devonport.*

Aircraft Carrier

EAGLE (8th June, 1918), late Battleship.

Normal displacement, 22,600 (*deep load*, 26,200) tons. Complement, 748.

Length { (*p.p.*) 625 feet, (*o.a.*) 667 „ } Beam { 92¾, 105⅙ (*max.*) } feet.* Draught { 24 feet *mean.*, 27 feet *max.* }

* 100 feet, flight deck.

Guns:
- **9**—6 inch, 50 cal. (**Dir. Con.**)
- **5**—4 inch AA.
- **36** Smaller.

Flights carried:
- 1 Spotter Reconnaissance (Fairey III F).
- 1 Fighter (Flycatcher).
- 1 Torpedo (Dart).

Armour:
- ..." Side (amidships)......
- ..." Deck ....

Special protection:
Bulges over about four-fifths of length, projecting about 6 feet from side.

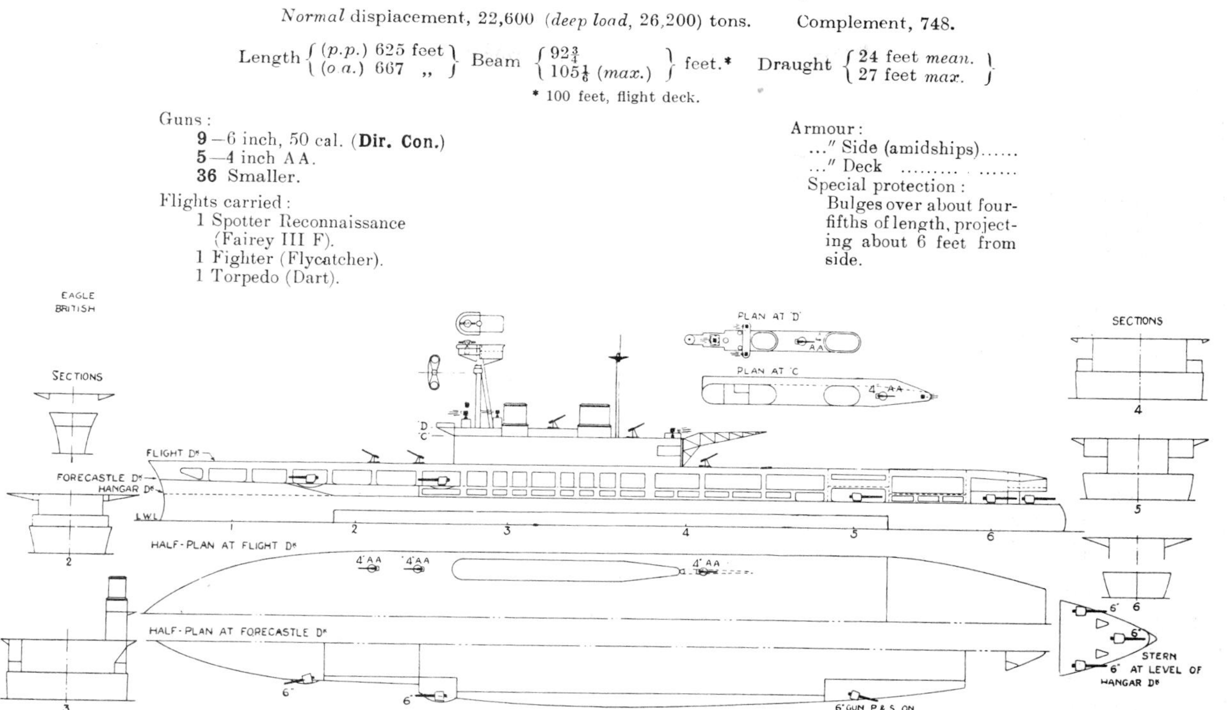

Machinery: Brown-Curtis (A.G.) turbines, by J. Brown & Co., Clydebank. Designed S.H.P. 50,000 = 24 kts. (No details available of trials). Boilers: 32 Yarrow small tube (oil burning). Fuel: *Normal*, 2500 tons; *maximum*, 3750 tons *oil fuel.*

General Notes—Designed and begun by Armstrong Whitworth, February, 1913, for Chile, as *Almirante Cochrane*, a Dreadnought Battleship and sister to Chilean *Almirante Latorre.* All work on this ship ceased in August, 1914, and she lay on her slip until 1917, when her purchase was negotiated with the Chilean Government. Her design was modified to an Aircraft Carrier by Sir E. H. Tennyson d'Eyncourt. Commissioned for ship and flying trials with one funnel and no masts, 13th April, 1920. As a result of trials made off Scilly Islands, put in hand at H.M. Dockyard, Portsmouth, for modifications, November, 1920. Finally completed in 1923. Bought from Chile for £1,334,358, sums subsequently expended have raised total cost to £4.617,636 (Statement by First Lord, April 1927).

Bow view. 1924 *Photo, Abrahams, Devonport.*

EAGLE (1918). 22,600 tons.
Torpedoed by enemy submarine in Western Mediterranean, August 11, 1942.

EAGLE. 1927 *Photo, Cassar.*

EAGLE 1931 *Photo, R. Perkins, Esq.*

Aircraft Carrier

HERMES (11th September, 1919).

Displacement, 10,950 tons *normal*. Complement, 664.

Length { *p.p.* 548 feet, *o.a.* 598 ,, } Beam { *w.l.*, outside bulges, 70 feet, over flight deck, 90 feet } Draught { *mean* 18¾ feet, *max.* — ,, }

Guns:
6—5·5 inch, 50 cal. (**Dir. Con.**)
3—4 inch AA.
26 Smaller.

Flights carried:
1 Fighter (9 Flycatchers in all).
1 Spotter Reconnaissance.
6 Fairey III F.

Armour:
Not known—probably of Light Cruiser type.
Anti-Torp. Pro. Bulges.

Name	Builder	Machinery	Ordered	Begun	Completed	Trials
Hermes	Armstrong Whitworth Devonport D.Y.*	Parsons	July, '17	15 Jan., '18	1923	

* Towed here for completion, January, 1920.

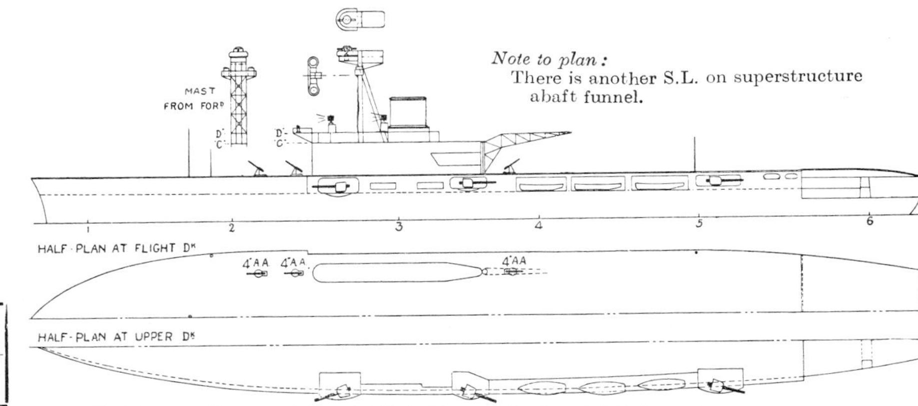

Note to plan: There is another S.L. on superstructure abaft funnel.

Machinery: Parsons (all geared) turbines. Designed S.H.P. 40,000=25 kts. 2 screws. Boilers: Yarrow or Babcock. Fuel (oil only): 1000 tons *normal*. 2000 tons *max.*

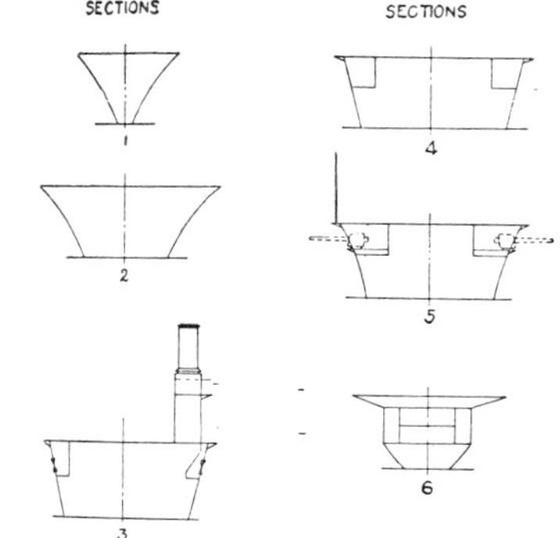

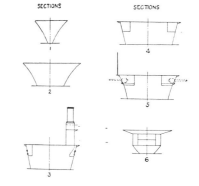

General Notes.—Begun under Emergency War Programme. First vessel specially designed by Admiralty as an **Aircraft Carrier.** Is a splendid sea boat, very steady, with remarkably little rolling propensity.

To carry 20 sea or aeroplanes. Special ventilation system to lessen danger of fire from petrol fumes, and new types of gear for handling, landing and flying-off aircraft. Hangar aft, with electric lift from quarterdeck to flight deck, 'planes being wheeled out from hangar on to lift through an opening normally closed by shutters. Transporter cranes fitted forward and aft.

HERMES (1919). 10,850 tons.
Sunk in action with Japanese aircraft 70 miles S. of Trincomali, April 9, 1942.

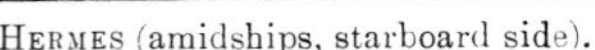

HERMES (amidships, starboard side).

HERMES (port quarter).

All Photos, Abrahams, Devonport

Aircraft Carrier

ARGUS (2nd Dec., 1917). Late Liner.

Normal displacement, 14,450 tons. Complement, 373.

Length, (*p.p.*) 535 feet (*w.l.*) 560 feet (*o.a.*) 565 feet.

Beam, 68 feet (excluding bulges).

Draught, 21 feet, *mean*.

Guns:
- **6**—4 inch AA.
- **4**—3 pdr.
- **4** M.G.
- **10** Lewis.

Flights carried:
- 1 Fighter (Flycatcher).
- 2 Spotter Reconnaissance (1 flight Fairey III F, 1 flight Blackburn).

Armour: *Nil.* (Bulges—see *General Notes.*)

ARGUS. 1929 *Photo, R. Perkins, Esq.*

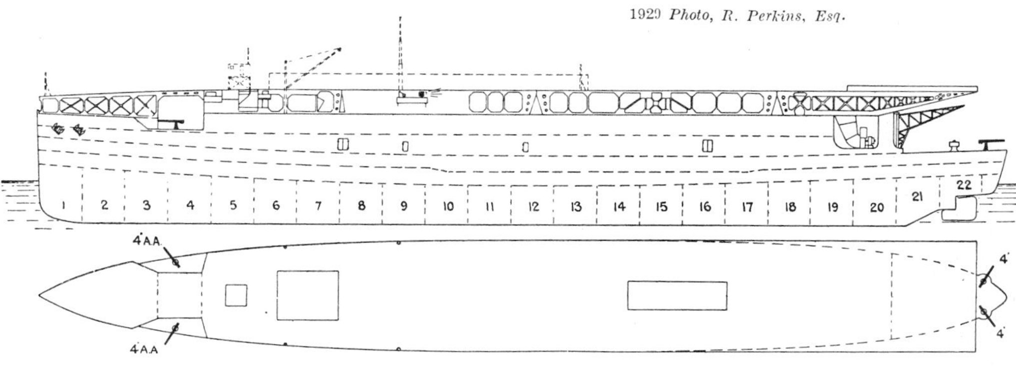

General Notes.—Begun 1914, by Beardmore, for Italian Lloyd Sabaudo Line, as S.S. *Conte Rosso*. All work on her ceased in 1914. She was purchased in 1916 and converted to Aircraft Carrier. Completed September, 1918. Refitted 1925-26, and Bulges fitted, extending from Section 4 to Section 19.

ARGUS. 1927 *Photo, Cribb, Southsea.*

Machinery (by builders): Parsons turbines. 4 screws. Designed S.H.P. 20,000 = 20·2 kts. Can make 20·75 kts. for short periods, but 20 kts. is usually best speed under ordinary conditions. Boilers: 12 cylindrical (6 D.E. and 6 S.E.), with Howdens forced draught. Fuel: 2000 tons oil.

Capacity, &c.—Hangar is 350 ft. long by 68 ft. wide (*over all*) and 48 ft. clear width, 20 ft. clear height. It is divided into four sections by fire-proof screens, and can accommodate 20 aeroplanes of sea and land types.

Stores, &c.—Torpedoes are carried for torpedo-dropping aeroplanes; aero-bombs, spare parts, wings, propellers, &c. Full equipment is carried for maintenance and repair of aircraft. There are large carpenters' and engineers' workshops, for executing rapid repairs.

Handling Gear.—Two electrically controlled lifts for raising aircraft from hangar to flight deck. Forward lift, 30 ft. × 36 ft. After lift, 60 ft. × 18 ft. When forward lift is at flight deck level, two roller platforms slide to the sides and uncover well opening. When lift descends, the platforms are closed together and give a 20-ft. platform for flying off. When a deck load of aeroplanes is carried, wind-breaking palisades can be raised simultaneously to 14 ft. above flying deck. Two derricks with electric winches amidships on flight deck and two electric cranes at stern on hangar deck level; all to pick up aeroplanes from the water.

Engineering Notes.—At the time designs were got out, a ¼-inch scale model was prepared for testing in the air tunnel at the National Physical Laboratory, Teddington, to solve various structural problems and to test eddy-making effects of hull. It was found that the emission of hot furnace gases from the usual type of funnels created such serious air disturbances, safe landings would be very difficult. Accordingly, horizontal smoke-ducts with big expelling fans were fitted, to deliver all furnace gases and smoke out abaft hangar, or alternatively through flight deck. Designed for 18 kts., but modifications during conversion raised speed by 2 kts. Mean H.P. on trial, 21,376 = 20·5 knots.

Escort Aircraft Carriers

CAMPANIA. 1944.

(RULER CLASS—14 Ships.)

AMEER (April 19, 1943), **ATHELING, BEGUM, EMPEROR, EMPRESS, KHEDIVE, NABOB, PREMIER, QUEEN, RAJAH, RANEE, RULER, SHAH, THANE.** Built by Kaiser Co., Inc., at Vancouver, Wash. According to American Press reports, are similar to U.S. Escort Carriers of *Casablanca* Class, described on a later page. Displacement of latter reported to approach 9,000 tons. Dimensions: 487 (*pp.*), 514 (*o.a.*) × 80 × —feet.

(ARCHER CLASS—23 Ships.)

ARBITER, ARCHER (ex-*Mormacland*, Dec. 14, 1939), **ATTACKER** (Sept. 27, 1941), **BATTLER** (April 4, 1942), **BITER** (ex-*Mormactern*, July 15, 1939), **CHASER** (June 19, 1942), **FENCER** (April 4, 1942), **HUNTER** (1942), **PATROLLER, PUNCHER, PURSUER** (July 18, 1942), **RAVAGER** (July 16, 1942), **REAPER, SEARCHER** (June 18, 1942), **SLINGER** (1942), **SMITER** (1942), **SPEAKER** (1942), **STALKER** (March 5, 1942), **STRIKER** (May 7, 1942), **TRACKER** (March 7, 1942), **TRAILER** (May 22, 1942), **TROUNCER** (1942), **TRUMPETER** (1942).

Displacement: 14,500 tons (*full load?*). Believed to be generally similar to U.S.S. *Charger*, described and illustrated under U.S. Navy section. All are ex-mercantile hulls, with original dimensions: 465 (*pp.*), 492 (*o.a.*) × 69½ × 28¼ feet. Guns: Photographs show varying numbers of 4 inch AA., 40 mm. Bofors, 20 mm. Oerlikon and M.G. *Battler* has Westinghouse geared turbines and Foster-Wheeler water-tube boilers, but some of the class are propelled by Diesels. Internally, these ships contain scarcely any wood, the bunks, lockers, chairs and tables being made of steel; but unlike British-built carriers, the 450 ft. flight deck is planked. *Avenger*, of this type, has been lost.

Builders: *Archer, Biter, Ravager, Searcher, Tracker*, Seattle-Tacoma S.B. Corporation, Tacoma; *Battler, Chaser, Pursuer, Trailer*, Ingall's S.B. Corporation, Pascagoula, Miss.; *Attacker, Fencer, Stalker, Striker*, Western Pipe & Steel Co., San Francisco. (*Trailer* may have been renamed.)

Escort Aircraft Carriers

VINDEX (May 4, 1943). Standard displacement: 13,455 tons (*full load*, 16,830 tons). Dimensions: 524 × 68 × 25¾ feet.
Guns: **2**—4 inch, **16**—2 pdr. pompoms, **8**—40 mm. AA., **16**—20 mm. AA. Aircraft: 20. Machinery: Diesel. 2 shafts. Complement: 700. Converted from mercantile hull laid down for Dominion Line.

VINDEX. 1944, *Official*.

NAIRANA. No particulars released, but believed to be bigger than foregoing.

ACTIVITY. Ex-merchant vessel; no particulars received, but design believed to be contemporary with that of *Audacity* (lost).

PRETORIA CASTLE (Harland & Wolff, 1938). Ex-passenger liner of 17,392 tons *gross*. Dimensions (originally): 540 (*pp.*), 560 (*o.a.*) × 72 × 28 feet. Machinery: Diesel. 2 shafts. B.H.P. 9,500 = 17 kts. Fuel: 2,170 tons. Employed as a training carrier and for experimental work. (*Photo in Addenda.*)

Cruisers

BELLEROPHON.

No particulars of this cruiser have been released, but it is understood that she was to have been the first ship of a new class, decidedly larger than the *Tiger* type. Laid down in 1944, work appears to have proceeded but slowly, and is now at a standstill, but construction has not so far been cancelled.

(TIGER CLASS—4 SHIPS)

BLAKE (ex-*Tiger*, ex-*Blake*, Dec. 20, 1945), **DEFENCE** (Sept. 2, 1944), **SUPERB** (Aug. 31, 1943), **TIGER** (ex-*Bellerophon*, Oct. 25, 1945).

Displacement: 8,000 tons.
Complement: Peace, 796; War, 1,000.
Length: (*o.a.*) 555 feet 6 in. Beam: 64 feet.
Draught: 21 feet 3 in. (*max.*).

Guns:
9—6 inch
10—4 inch AA.
18—2 pdr. pompoms
8—40 mm. AA.
10—20 mm. AA.

Armour:
Not reported.

Torpedo tubes:
6—21 inch.

SUPERB. 1946, *Wright & Logan*.

SUPERB. 1946, *Wright & Logan*.

SUPERB. 1946, *Wright & Logan*.

Name	*Builder*	*Begun*	*Completed*
Blake	Fairfield	1944	
Defence	Scotts	1943	1946
Tiger	Clydebank	6/43	1946
Superb	Swan Hunter	23/6/42	7/45

Note.—*Hawke*, of this class, laid down at Portsmouth in August, 1944, was cancelled. Work on construction of *Defence* suspended for 12 months from July, 1946; this probably applies also to *Blake* and *Tiger*.

Machinery: Parsons geared turbines. 4 shafts. S.H.P.: 72,500 = 31·5 kts. Boilers: 4 Admiralty 3-drum type.

(*Plan as shown under "Swiftsure" on following page.*)

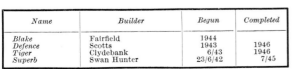

Cruisers

SWIFTSURE (Feb. 4, 1943)

Displacement: 8,000 tons. Complement: Peace, 730; War, 960.
Length: (*o.a.*) 555 feet 6 in. Beam: 63 feet. Draught: 20 feet (*mean*)

Guns:
9—6 inch.
10—4 inch AA.
16—2 pdr. pompoms
13—40 mm. AA.
Torpedo tubes:
6—21 inch.

Armour:
Similar to *Uganda* class.

Note to Plan.—This represents *Tiger* type, from which *Swiftsure* differs only slightly, as inset.

SWIFTSURE ONLY

0FEET 50 100 200 300 400 500 550

SWIFTSURE. 1946, *Wright & Logan.*

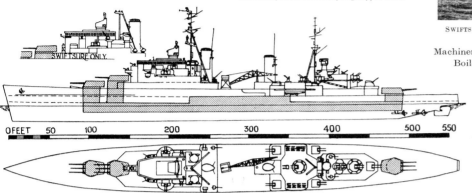

Machinery: Parsons single reduction geared turbines. 4 shafts. S.H.P.: 72,500=31·5 kts. Boilers: 4 Admiralty 3-drum type.

Name	*Builders*	*Begun*	*Completed*
Swiftsure	Vickers-Armstrongs, Tyne	22/9/41	22/6/44

Notes.—This ship seems to be a slightly modified *Uganda*. Another of same type, *Ontario* (ex-*Minotaur*), will be found under R. Canadian Navy.

(Uganda Class—2 Ships.)

CEYLON (July 30, 1942), NEWFOUNDLAND (Dec. 19, 1941).

Displacement: 8,000 tons. Complement: Peace, 730; War, 950. Length: (*pp.*) 549 feet; (*o.a.*) 555½ feet. Beam: 62 feet. Draught: 16½ feet (*mean*).

Guns:
9—6 inch.
10—4 inch AA.
Numerous 40 mm. and 20 mm. AA.
Torpedo tubes:
6—21 inch.

Armour:
Similar to *Fiji* class.

Note to Plan.—Stern is of transom type, as in *Fiji* class.

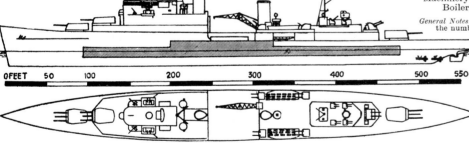

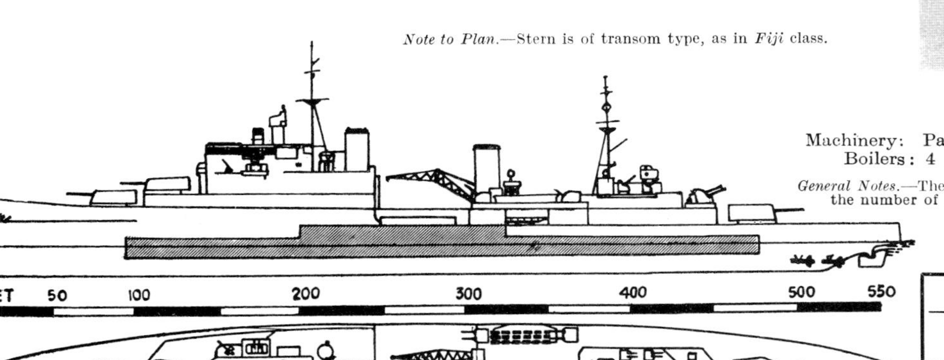

CEYLON. 1946, *London Studio.*

Machinery: Parsons single reduction geared turbines. 4 shafts. S.H.P. 72,500 = 31·5 kts. Boilers: 4 Admiralty 3-drum type.

General Notes.—These ships are a modification of original *Fiji* design, one 6-inch turret having been suppressed, and the number of light AA. guns augmented. *Uganda* transferred to R. Canadian Navy.

Est.	*Name*	*Builder*	*Machinery*	*Ordered*	*Begun*	*Completed*
1938	*Ceylon*	Stephen	Stephen	1939	1939	13/7/43
1939	*Newfoundland*	Swan Hunter	Wallsend	1939	1939	31/12/42

(Fiji Class—6 Ships)

Note to Plan.—Only one crane amidships. "X" turret replaced by AA. mounting in some ships. Transom stern as seen in photo.

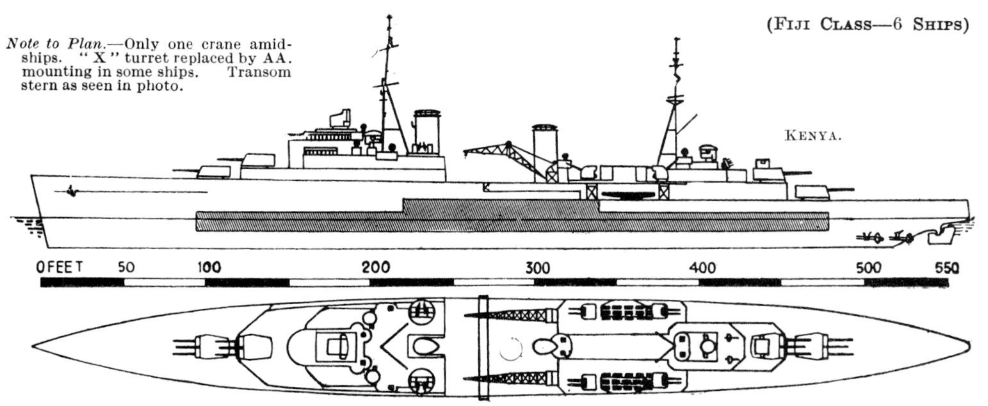

BERMUDA (Sept. 11, 1941), GAMBIA (Nov. 30, 1940), JAMAICA (Nov. 16, 1940), KENYA (Aug. 18, 1939), MAURITIUS (July 19, 1939), NIGERIA (July 18, 1939).

Displacement: 8,000 tons. Complement: 980.
Length: (*pp.*) 549 feet; (*o.a.*) 555½ feet. Beam: 62 feet.
Draught: 16½ feet (*mean*).

Guns:
9 or **12**—6 inch.
8—4 inch AA.
16 to **41**—2 pdr. pompoms or 40 mm. AA.
Torpedo tubes:
6—21 inch.

Armour:
Similar to *Belfast* with minor differences.

Cruisers

NIGERIA. 1946, *London Studio.*

Machinery: Parsons geared turbines. 4 shafts. S.H.P. 72,500 = 31·5 kts. Boilers: 4 Admiralty 3-drum type.

Est.	*Name*	*Builder*	*Machinery*	*Ordered*	*Begun*	*Completed*
1937	***Kenya***	Stephen	Stephen	Dec., 1937	18/6/38	28/8/40
1937	***Mauritius***	Swan Hunter	Wallsend Slipway	Dec., 1937	31/3/38	14/12/40
1937	***Nigeria***	V.-A., Tyne	Parsons	Dec., 1937	8/2/38	20/9/40
1938	*Gambia*	Swan Hunter	Wallsend Slipway	1939	24/7/39	21/2/42
1938	***Jamaica***	V.-A., Barrow	V.-A., Barrow	1939	28/4/39	29/6/42
1939	*Bermuda*	Clydebank	Clydebank	1939	1939	5/8/42

General Notes.—These ships are a logical development from *Newcastle* and *Belfast* designs, and are reported to have proved highly successful in service. Two others, *Fiji* and *Trinidad*, have been lost in action. *Gambia* refitted 1946.

1946, *Wright & Logan.*

(DIDO CLASS—4 LATER SHIPS)

BELLONA (Sept. 29, 1942), **BLACK PRINCE** (Aug. 27, 1942), **DIADEM** (Aug. 26, 1942), **ROYALIST** (May 30, 1942).

Displacement: 5,700 to 5,770 tons. (7,400 tons *full load.*)
Complement (peace): 535–551.

Length: (*o.a.*) 512 feet. Beam: 50 feet 6 in.
Draught: 15 feet (*mean*), 18 feet 7 in. (*max.*)

Guns:
8—5·25 inch d.p.
Numerous 40 mm. and 20 mm. AA.

Armour:
As in *Dido* class.

Torpedo tubes:
6—21 inch (tripled).

DIADEM. 1944, *Official.*

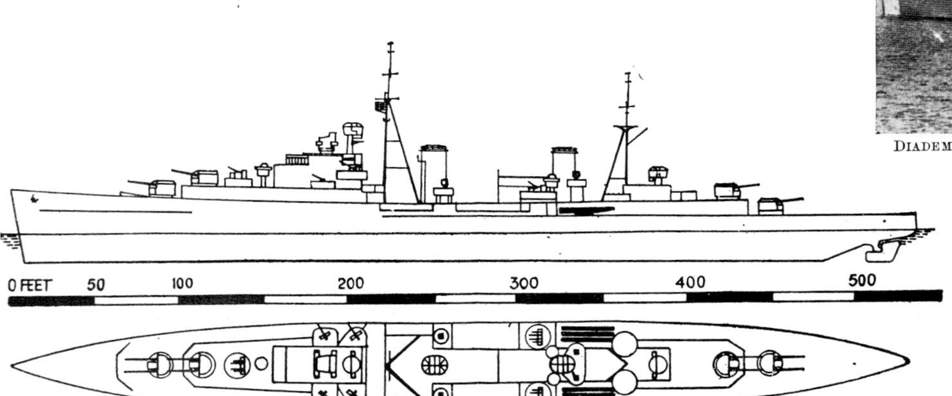

Machinery: Parsons single reduction geared turbines. 4 shafts. S.H.P.: 62,000 = 33 kts. Boilers: 4 Admiralty 3-drum type.

Special Note.

Bellona and *Black Prince* are on loan to Royal New Zealand Navy.

Est.	*Name.*	*Builder and Machinery.*	*Begun.*	*Completed.*
War	*Bellona*	Fairfield	11/39	10/43
War	*Black Prince*	Harland & Wolff	1/12/39	20/11/43
War	*Diadem*	Hawthorn	15/12/39	6/1/44
War	*Royalist*	Scotts	1939	25/8/43

Cruisers

ROYALIST. 1946, *Wright & Logan.*

Notes.—These 4 ships are easily distinguishable from earlier units of *Dido* class by absence of rake to masts and funnels. War loss: *Spartan.*

(DIDO CLASS—First 7 ships).

DIDO (July 18, 1939), **EURYALUS** (June 6, 1939), **PHOEBE** (March 25, 1939), **SIRIUS** (Sept. 18, 1940), **CLEOPATRA** (March 27, 1940), **SCYLLA** (July 24, 1940), **ARGONAUT** (Sept. 6, 1941).

Displacement: 5,450 tons. Complement (peace): 530–556.
Length: (*pp.*) 506 feet; (*o.a.*) 512 feet. Beam: 51½ feet.
Draught: 14 feet (*mean*); 17 feet 10 in. (*max.*).

Guns:
10—5·25 inch D.P.
(Several, including *Argonaut*, *Phoebe*, *Scylla*, now have only **8**—5·25 inch.)
26 to **28**—40 mm. and 20 mm. AA.
Torpedo tubes:
6—21 inch (tripled)

Armour: Similar to *Arethusa* class.

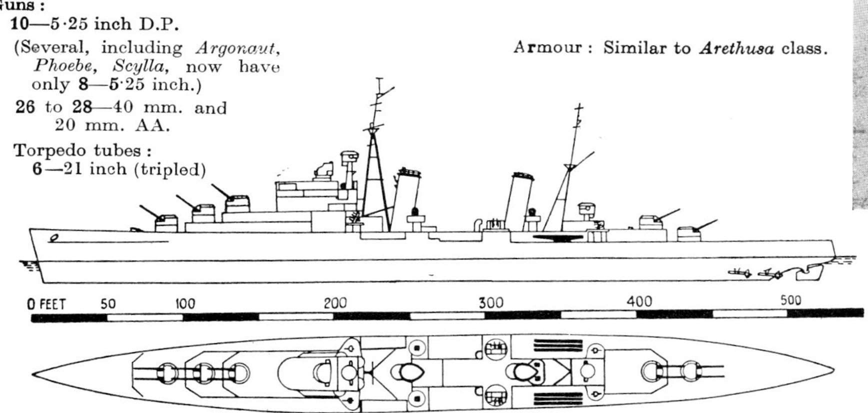

SIRIUS. 1946, *Wright & Logan.*

Machinery: Parsons single reduction geared turbines. 4 shafts. S.H.P.: 62,000 = 33 kts.
Boilers: 4 Admiralty 3-drum type, working pressure 400 lb.

Est.	*Name*	*Builder*	*Machinery*	*Ordered*	*Begun*	*Completed*
1936	*Dido*	Cammell Laird	Cammell Laird	21/8/37	20/10/37	1940
	Euryalus	Chatham	Hawthorn		21/10/37	
	Phoebe	Fairfield	Fairfield		2/9/37	
	Sirius	Portsmouth	Scotts		6/4/38	1942
1938	*Cleopatra*	Hawthorn	Hawthorn	18/8/38	5/1/39	20/11/41
	Scylla	Scotts	Scotts		19/4/39	1941
1939	*Argonaut*	Cammell Laird	Cammell Laird		1939	1942

War losses: *Bonaventure, Charybdis, Hermione, Naiad.* In 1943 *Argonaut* was so extensively damaged by torpedoes that she had to be one-third rebuilt at Philadelphia.

CLEOPATRA. 1946, *Wright & Logan.*

(Improved SOUTHAMPTON design)

BELFAST (March 17, 1938.)

Displacement: 10,000 tons.

Length: (*pp.*) 579 ft.; (*o.a.*) 613 ft. 6 in. Beam: 63 ft. 4 in. (since increased).
Draught: 17 ft. 3 in.

Guns:
12—6 inch.
8—4 inch AA.
46—2 pdr. pompoms and 20 mm. AA.

Torpedo tubes:
6—21 inch (tripled).

Armour:
3″—4½″ side. Otherwise similar to *Southampton* type, but extends over entire length of citadel. Protective deck right across ship's breadth above magazines.

BELFAST. 1944, *Official.*

Machinery: Parsons geared turbines. 4 shafts. S.H.P.: 80,000 = 32 kts.
Boilers: 8 Admiralty 3-drum.

Notes.—Built by Harland & Wolff under 1936 Estimates. Laid down December 10, 1936, and completed 3/8/1939. Reported to be designed to withstand 8 inch shell fire. Internal subdivision is exceptionally complete. Was practically rebuilt after being heavily damaged by a mine in early months of war. Sister ship *Edinburgh* lost in action.

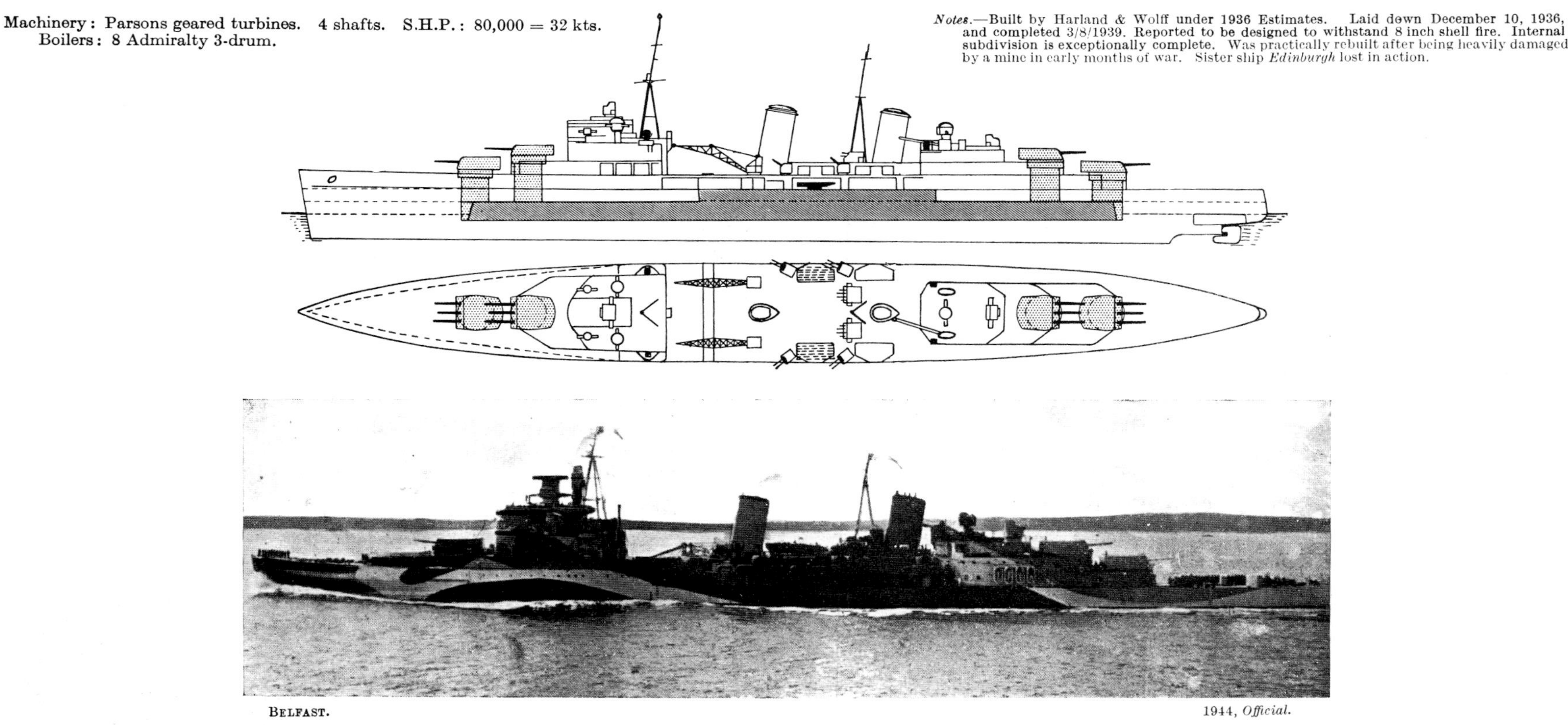

BELFAST. 1944, *Official.*

(SOUTHAMPTON CLASS—5 SHIPS).

NEWCASTLE (ex-*Minotaur*) (Jan. 23, 1936). **SHEFFIELD** (July 23, 1936).
BIRMINGHAM (Sept. 1, 1936). **GLASGOW** (June 20, 1936).
LIVERPOOL (March 24, 1937).

Displacement: 9,100 tons (*Liverpool* 9,400 tons). (Over 12,000 tons *full load.*)
Complement, (peace): 809–833. Length: (*pp.*) 558, (*w.l.*) 584 ft., (*o.a.*) 591 ft. 6 in.
Beam: 61 ft. 8 in., except *Liverpool*, 62 ft. 4 in.
Draught: 17 ft. (*mean*), except *Liverpool*, 17 ft. 5 in. All are 20 ft. (*maximum*).

Guns:
- **9—6 inch**
- **8—4 inch AA.**
- **16**—2 pdr. pompoms.
- **22—40 mm. AA.**
- **15—20 mm. AA.**

Tubes:
- **6—21 inch (tripled).**

Armour:
- 1"—2" Turrets.
- 4"—3" Side.
- 4" C.T.

Note to Plan.—All now have 2 quadruple Bofors mountings in place of "X" turret, and mount light AA. amidships.

Machinery: Parsons geared turbines. 4 shafts. S.H.P.: 75,000 = 32 kts. (*Liverpool:* 82,500 = 32·3 kts.). Boilers: 8 Admiralty 3-drum. Oil fuel: 1,970 tons.

Est.	Name	Builder	Machinery	Ordered	Begun	Completed
1933	*Newcastle*	V-A., Tyne	V-A., Barrow	1/6/34	4/10/34	5/3/37
1934	*Sheffield*	Do.	Do.	17/12/34	31/1/35	25/8/37
1934	*Glasgow*	Scotts	Scotts	17/12/34	16/4/35	8/9/37
1934	*Birmingham*	Devonport	Clydebank	1/3/35	18/7/35	18/11/37
1935	*Liverpool*	Fairfield	Fairfield	3/35	17/2/36	25/10/38

Notes.—Centre gun of each turret is mounted slightly further back than other two. Protection is somewhat better than in previous classes. Bridge structure extends a considerable distance aft, enveloping fore funnel. In *Sheffield, Newcastle*, and possibly other ships, special ventilating trunks have been installed, with openings on either side of hull at break of deck level abreast of "B" turret. War losses: *Gloucester, Manchester, Southampton.*

SHEFFIELD. 1946, *Wright & Logan.*

Cruisers

NEWCASTLE. 1945, *P. A. Vicary.*

BIRMINGHAM. (Observe bow.) 1946, *Wright & Logan.*

(ARETHUSA CLASS—2 SHIPS.)

ARETHUSA (March 6th, 1934). **AURORA** (August 20th, 1936).

Displacement: 5,220 and 5,270 tons, respectively.

Complement: 450.

Length: (*pp.*) 480 ft., (*w.l.*) 500 ft. Beam: 51 ft.

Draught: 13 ft. 10 in. (*mean*).

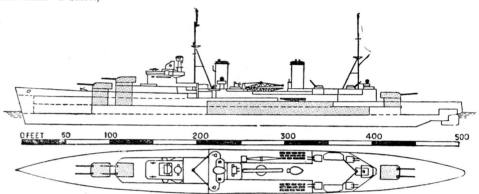

Guns:
6—6 inch.
8—4 inch AA.
Numerous 40 mm. and 20 mm. AA.

Torpedo tubes:
6—21 inch in triple mounts.

Armour:
1″ turrets.
2″ side.

Est.	Name	Builder	Machinery	Ordered	Begun	Completed
1931	*Arethusa*	Chatham	Parsons	1/9/32	25/1/33	Feb., 1935
1934	*Aurora*	Portsmouth	Wallsend	1/3/35	23/7/35	Nov., 1937

Special Note. ARETHUSA is to be lent to Norway for four years. *Aurora* is being lent to the Chinese Navy, early in 1947

Machinery: Parsons geared turbines. 4 shafts. S.H.P. 64,000=32·25 knots. Boilers: 4 Admiralty 3-drum type. Oil: 1,200 tons. Radius reported to be 12,000 miles at economical speed.

General Notes.—Displacement of this class is the minimum for oceangoing efficiency, and the armament is adequate to deal with raiders of armed mercantile type. Funnels are streamlined in order to take air current clear of aircraft between them. War losses: *Galatea, Penelope.*

Constructional Notes.—Weight reduction has been secured in these ships by the extensive use of electric welding for hull and internal subdivision, as well as by the employment of aluminium-covered plywood for cabin bulkheads and other light partitions, etc.

Engineering Notes.—A fluid flywheel enables power to be almost instantaneously switched over from main engines to cruising turbines. A reversion to two funnels is caused by the spacing of the boiler and engine rooms in two units, which obviates wholesale flooding of the boiler-rooms. Boiler temperature (with 300° superheat) is 650°.

Cost.—*Arethusa*, £1,251,161; *Aurora* £1,252,915.

ARETHUSA. 1942, *Official.*

AURORA. 1946, *Wright & Logan.*

(LEANDER CLASS—4 Ships.)

LEANDER (September 24, 1931).
ORION (Nov. 24, 1932).
ACHILLES (Sept. 1, 1932).
AJAX (March 1, 1934).

Displacement: *Leander*, 7,270 tons; *Orion*, 7,215 tons; *Achilles*, 7,030 tons; *Ajax*, 6,985 tons. Complement (peace): 646–680.

Length (*pp.*) 530 feet; (*o.a.*) 554½ feet. Beam, 55ft. 2in. Draught (*mean*) 16 feet. *Ajax*, 522 (*pp.*) × 55⅔ × 15½ feet (*mean*).

Machinery: Parsons I.R. geared turbines. 4 shafts. Designed S.H.P. 72,000=32·5 kts. (made with designed H.P. on trials). Boilers: 4 Admiralty 3-drum type. Oil: 1,800 tons.

General Notes.—This class represents a return to moderate dimensions, compared with preceding ships of the 10,000-ton Treaty type. The 6-inch guns were the first of an entirely new model produced by the "auto-frettage" system instead of being wire wound. Forecastle plating extended aft and boats raised a deck after trials. Cost £1,500,000 to £1,600,000 apiece (*Ajax*, £1,480,097). A fifth ship of this type, *Neptune*, became a war loss.

Est.	Name	Builder	Machinery	Ordered	Begun	Completed
1929	*Leander*	Devonport	Vickers-Armstrongs	18/2/30	8/9/30	23/3/33
1930	{ *Orion*	Do.	Do.	26/3/31	26/9/31	16/1/34
	{ *Achilles*	Cammell Laird	Cammell Laird	3/31	11/6/31	10/10/33
1931	*Ajax*	Vickers-Armstrongs	Vickers-Armstrongs	1/10/32	7/2/33	3/6/35

Guns:
- 6 or 8—6 inch
- 8—4 inch AA.
- 8—2 pdr. pompoms.
- 16—40 mm. AA.

Armour:
- 2″—4″ Side amidships.
- 1″ Turrets.
- 1″ Bridge.
- 2″ Deck.

Torpedo tubes:
- 8—21 inch (quadrupled).

Special Note.

Ajax, *Leander* and *Achilles* will be transferred to Royal Indian Navy in 1947–48.

Note to Plan.—Crane is actually mounted on centre line, not as shown below, and AA. guns are paired. Catapult has been discarded, and tripod masts stepped in all. In *Achilles* and *Leander*, "X" turret has been replaced by two anti-aircraft mountings.

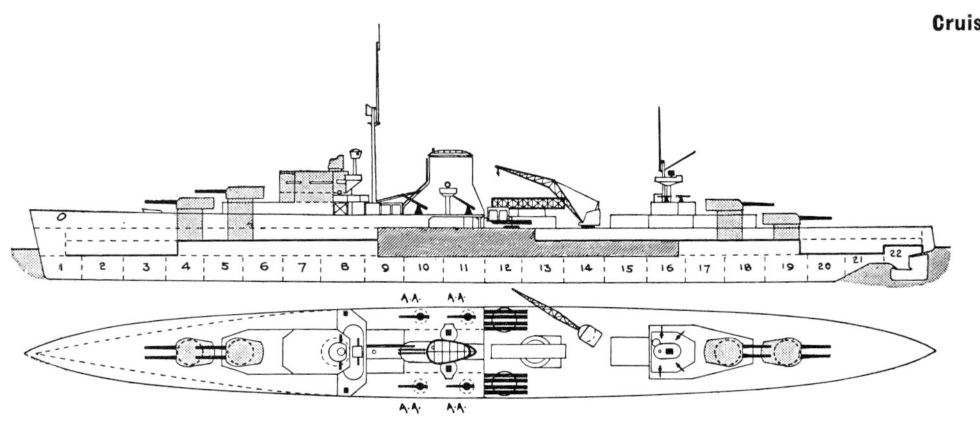

LEANDER. 1946, *London Studio.*

AJAX. 1942, *Official.*

DEVONSHIRE (Oct. 22, 1927), **SUSSEX** (Feb. 22, 1928).

Displacement: 9,850 and 9,830 tons respectively. Complement (peace): 852.

Length: (*pp.*) 595, (*o.a.*) 633 feet. Beam: 66 feet. Draught: 17 feet (*mean*).

NORFOLK (December 12, 1928).

Displacement, 9,925 tons.

Length: (*pp.*) 590, (*o.a.*) 630 feet. Beam, 66 feet. Draught, 17 feet (*mean*).

Complement (peace): 819.

Guns (except *Devonshire*—see Notes):
- 6—8 inch, 50 cal.
- 8—4 inch AA.
- 12—2 pdr. pompoms, etc.

Torpedo tubes:
- 8—21-inch (quadrupled).

Armour:
- 4″ Deck.
- 2″–1½″ Gunhouses.
- 3″ C.T.

Machinery: Parsons geared turbines. 4 shafts. Designed S.H.P. 80,000 = 32·25 kts. Oil fuel: 3200 tons. Boilers: 8 Admiralty 3-drum type.

DEVONSHIRE. ("B", "X" and "Y" turrets are being removed.) 1943, *Official.*

Cruisers

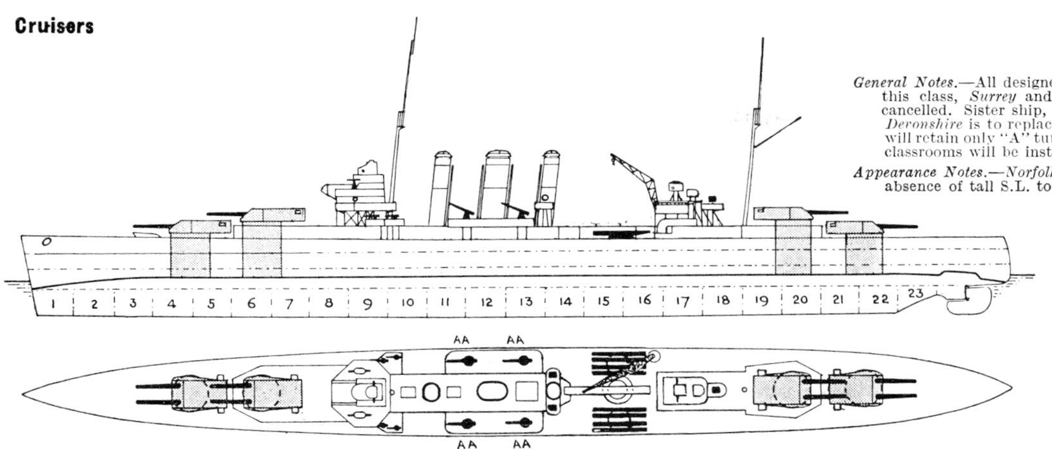

Note to Plan.—Crane is actually mounted forward of T.T. AA. armament has been augmented, guns shown being paired. Now have tripod masts. "X" turret has been replaced by AA. mounting.

General Notes.—All designed by Sir William Berry and built under 1925 and 1926 Estimates. Two other ships of this class, *Surrey* and *Northumberland*, were provided for under the 1926 Estimates, but were subsequently cancelled. Sister ship, *Dorsetshire*, lost in April, 1942. Another, *Shropshire*, transferred to R. Australian Navy. *Devonshire* is to replace *Frobisher* as seagoing training ship for cadets in April, 1947. Of her main armament she will retain only "A" turret, ship being stripped and rebuilt from after-funnel to stern. Navigational and instructional classrooms will be installed.

Appearance Notes.—*Norfolk* can be distinguished from others by lower bridge, also by sternwalk; and from *Kent* by absence of tall S.L. tower forward of mainmast.

Name	*Builder*	*Machinery*	*Begun*	*Completed*
Devonshire	Devonport	Vickers	16/3/26	19/3/29
Sussex	Hawthorn	Hawthorn	1/2/27	26/3/29
Norfolk	Fairfield	Fairfield	7/27	6/30

SUSSEX. 1943, *Official.*

NORFOLK. 1943, *Official.*

LONDON (Portsmouth Dockyard, Sept. 14, 1927).

Displacement: over 10,000 tons. **Complement** (peace): 789.

Length {*pp.* 595 feet / *o.a.* 633 feet} **Beam**, 66 feet. **Draught**, 17 feet (*mean*).

Guns:
8—8 inch, 50 cal.
8—4 inch AA.
16—2 pdr. pompoms, etc.

Torpedo tubes:
8—21 inch (quadrupled).

Armour:
3″—5″ Side (8 feet deep).
4″—Deck.
2″—1½″ Gunhouses
3″—C.T.

Machinery: Parsons geared turbines. 4 shafts. Designed S.H.P. 80,000 = 32·25 kts. Oil fuel: 3200 tons. Boilers: 8 Admiralty 3-drum type.

LONDON. 1946, *London Studio.*

LONDON. 1946, *London Studio.*

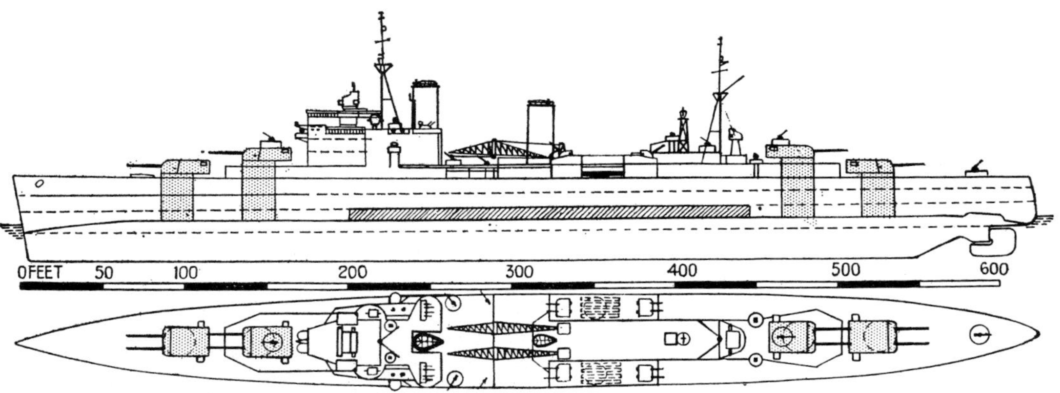

General Notes.—*London* was designed by Sir William J. Berry, and ordered under 1925 Estimates. Laid down Feb. 22, 1926, and completed Feb. 5, 1929. Was originally of same appearance as *Devonshire* and *Sussex*, but as reconstructed bears no resemblance to either. She might be mistaken for a ship of *Fiji* type at a distance, but can be distinguished by tall S.L. platform before mainmast. Refitted for further service, 1946.

(Kent Class—4 Ships.)

BERWICK (March 30th, 1926), **CUMBERLAND** (March 16th, 1926), **KENT** (March 16th, 1926), **SUFFOLK** (Feb. 16th, 1926).

Displacement: 10,000 tons, as refitted.

Complement, 679 (710 as flagship).

Length (*pp.*) 590 feet, (*o.a.*) 630 feet. Beam, 68¼ feet. Draught, 16½ feet (*mean*).

Guns:
8—8 inch, 50 cal.
8—4 inch AA.
16—2 pdr. pompoms, etc.

Torpedo tubes:
(Removed)

Armour:
3″–5″ Side at w.l.
4″ Deck over vitals
2″—1½″ Gunhouses
3″ C.T. ....
Bulges ....

Cumberland. (Suffolk similar, but fore tripod legs shorter.) — 1945, *Associated Press.*

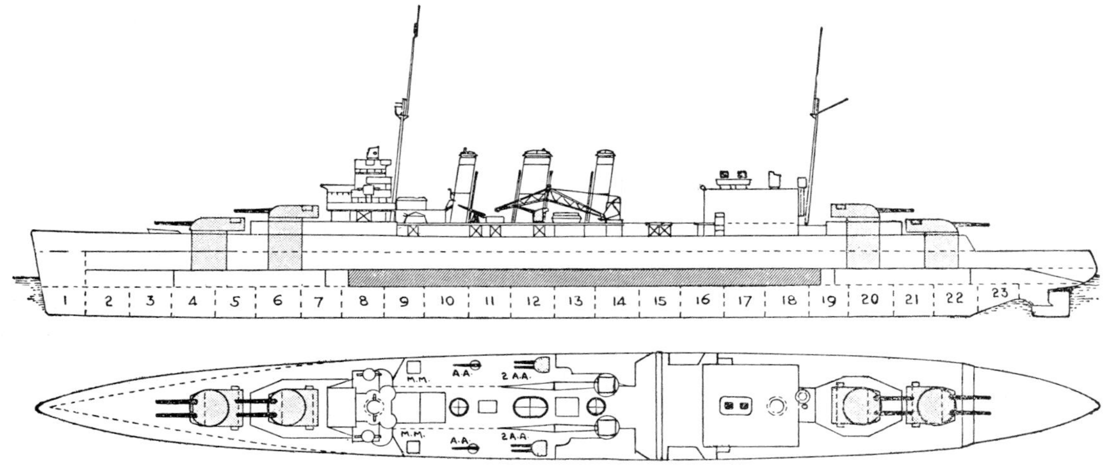

Note to Plan.—This represents *Cumberland* and *Suffolk;* others vary as in photos, and plan of *Australia*, on a later page. All have tripod masts.

Machinery: Geared turbines (see table). 4 shafts. Designed S.H.P. 80,000 = 31·5 kts. Boilers: 8 Admiralty 3-drum type, with superheaters (250 lb. working pressure). Oil fuel: 3400 tons. Radius at full speed, 2300 miles; at economical speed (11—14 kts.), 10,400 miles.

General Notes.—Built under 1924–25 Estimates; designed by Sir Eustace Tennyson d'Eyncourt. Although on paper these ships appear to be inferior to contemporary cruisers of other navies they are superior in sea-going qualities and have accommodation and habitability which is not equalled elsewhere. In addition, a considerable amount of weight has been expended in structural strength and internal protection. No attempt has been made to attain the high speeds recorded by the *Tourville* type, the ideal aimed at being the ability to sustain the designed speed indefinitely and in all weathers, without exceeding the normal H.P. Actually over 34 knots has been maintained in service without in any way pressing the boilers. *Suffolk* has the distinction of being the first warship ever to be fitted with a standard operational radar set. A ship of this class, *Australia*, will be found in the Royal Australian Navy. Two others, *Canberra* and *Cornwall*, were lost in action. Average cost was £1,970,000.

Gunnery Notes.—Exceptional elevation has been given to 8-inch guns, more than 65° having been observed. By means of an improved ammunition supply a rate of fire of four rounds per gun per minute can be maintained under director control. 8-inch broadside weighs 2,048 lbs. Total cost of armament £700,000; of firing a single broadside £408.

Armour Notes.—No side armour was included in original design, protection being afforded by a 3″—1½″ deck. External bulges are fitted and the internal subdivision is particularly well planned.

Appearance Notes.—All this class were reconstructed during 1935–38, alterations including increased armour protection and modernisation of the anti-aircraft armament. To compensate for the additional weight so imposed, the *Cumberland* and *Suffolk* were cut down by one deck aft, as shown in plan. This was not done in the *Berwick*. S.L. positions differ from *Devonshire*, *Sussex* and H.M.A.S. *Shropshire*. *Berwick*, *Cumberland* and *Suffolk* no longer possess in its entirety the large after superstructure so conspicuous in plan.

Berwick. — 1946, *Wright & Logan.*

Name	*Builder*	*Machinery*	*Ordered*	*Begun*	*Completed*	*Trials*	*Turbines*
Berwick	Fairfield	Fairfield	1924	15/9/24	2/2/28	81,700 = 32·5 (average of results)	Brown-Curtis
Cumberland	Vickers	Vickers		18/10/24	1/28		Parsons
Kent	Chatham Y.	Hawthorn		15/11/24	25/6/28		Parsons
Suffolk	Portsmouth Y.	Parsons		30/9/24	7/2/28		Parsons

EMERALD (19th May, 1920).
ENTERPRISE (23rd December, 1919).

Displacement, 7,550. (*Full load,* over 9,000 tons.)

Complement, 572.

Length {*pp.* 535 feet, *o.a.* 570 feet} Beam 54½ feet.

Draught {*mean* 16½ feet. *max.* feet.}

Guns:
7—6 inch, 50 cal.
5—4 inch AA.
Numerous smaller AA.

Torpedo tubes (21 inch):
16, quadrupled, *above water.*

Armour (H.T.):
3″ Side (amidships).
2½″—1½″ Side (bow).
2″ Side (stern).
1″ Upper Deck (amidships)
1″ Deck (over rudder).

Emerald. (Now has tripod mainmast.) — 1934 *Official Photo.*

Cruiser

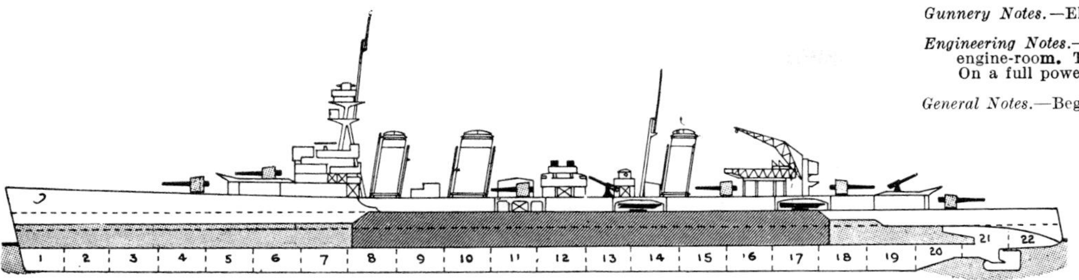

Gunnery Notes.—Elevation of 6-inch, up to 40°. Heavy Director on foremast. R.F. on forward bridge.

Engineering Notes.—8 boilers in 4 w.t. compartments, part forward of amidships magazines and part abaft forward engine-room. This arrangement of boiler rooms is responsible for the somewhat unusual spacing of the funnels. On a full power trial in 1939, *Emerald* is reported to have exceeded 32 knots.

General Notes.—Begun under Emergency War Programme. Expected soon to be scrapped.

Note to Plan.—4-inch AA. guns amidships should be shown as pairs. Mainmast now of tripod type.

Appearance Notes—Main differences are indicated in plan.

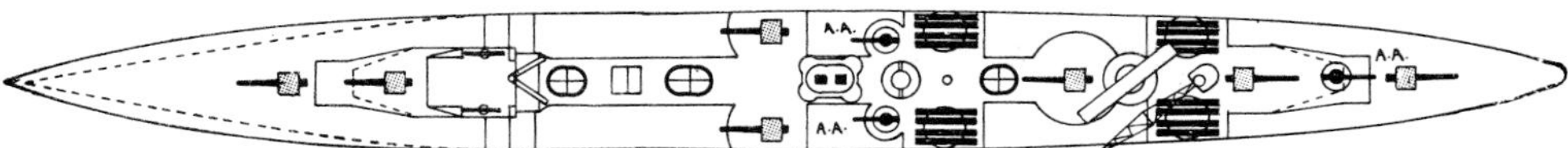

Machinery: Turbines, 4 sets Brown-Curtis (geared). 4 shafts. Designed S.H.P. 80,000 = 32 kts. Boilers: 8 Yarrow small tube. Fuel (oil only): *normal*, 650 tons; *maximum*, 1,746 tons.

Name	*Builder*	*Machinery*	*Ordered*	*Begun*	*Completed*	*Trials: H.P. kts.*	*Turbines*
Emerald	*Armstrong	Wallsend	7/3/18	Sept. 23/18	Jan. 14/26	80450 = 32·9	Brown-Curtis

*Towed to Chatham D.Y. for completion.

(Hawkins Class—2 Ships.)

Note to Plan.—This represents *Hawkins*. *Frobisher* has had armament reduced.

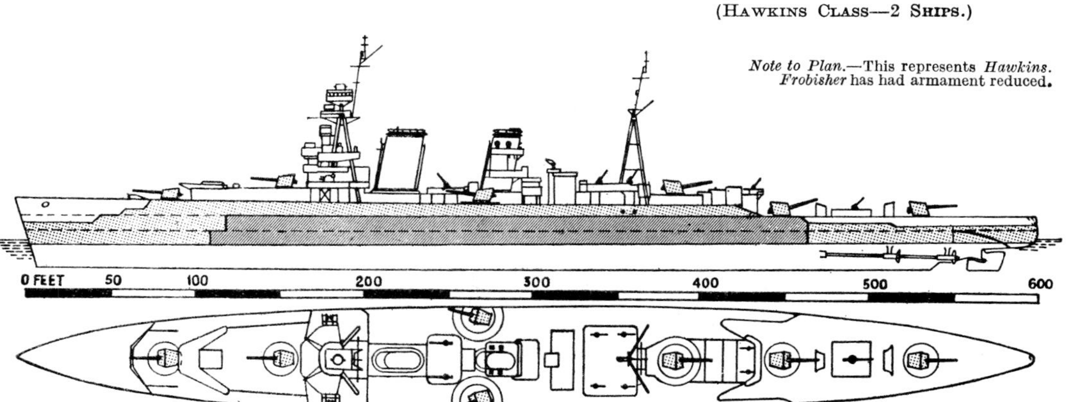

FROBISHER (20th March, 1920), **HAWKINS** (1st Oct., 1917).

Both fitted as Flagships.

Displacement, 9,860 and 9,800 tons, respectively.

Complement, 712/749.

Length { *pp.* 565 feet; *o.a.* 605 „ }

Beam { *w.l.* 58* feet; outside bulges 65 „ }

Draught { *mean* 17¼ feet; *max.* 20½ „ }

*Approximate.

Guns:
7—7·5 inch, 50 cal.
(*Frobisher*, 4, of 45 cal.)
9—4 inch AA.
Many smaller.

Torpedo tubes (21 inch):
4 *above water*.

Armour (H.T. or Nickel):
3″—2″ Side (amidships)
2½″—1½″ Side (bow) ..
2½″—2¼″ Side (stern)
1″ Upper deck (amids.)
1½″—1″ Deck over rudder (Hadfield) ..
3″ C.T. ....
Anti-Torpedo Protection:
Bulges, 5 ft. deep ...
Unpierced Bulkheads, below lower deck ...

Machinery: Turbines, Brown-Curtis or Parsons (geared cruising). Designed S.H.P. in *Hawkins*, 55,000 = 29·5 kts. *Frobisher*, 65,000 = 30·5 kts. 4 shafts. Boilers: Yarrow (small tube). Fuel: as completed, 1,000 tons oil *normal*, 2,150 *maximum*. *Hawkins*, as re-constructed, 2,600 tons *maximum*. (Ships were originally intended to burn coal.)

Note.—*Raleigh*, of same type, was lost in August, 1922. *Effingham* wrecked in May, 1940. *Vindictive* was demilitarised in 1936–37 and has since been scrapped. *Frobisher* is employed as Cadets' Seagoing Training Ship, but is likely to be relegated to harbour service when relieved by *Devonshire*. *Hawkins* may soon be scrapped.

Name	*Builder*	*Machinery*	*Begun*	*Completed*	*Turbines*
Frobisher	Devonport D.Y.	Wallsend	2 Aug., '16	20 Sept. '24	Brown-Curtis
Hawkins	Chatham D.Y.	Parsons	June, '16	July 25, '19	Parsons

Frobisher. 1944, *Official*.

Hawkins. 1944, *Official*.

Hawkins. 1942, *Official*.

Cruisers

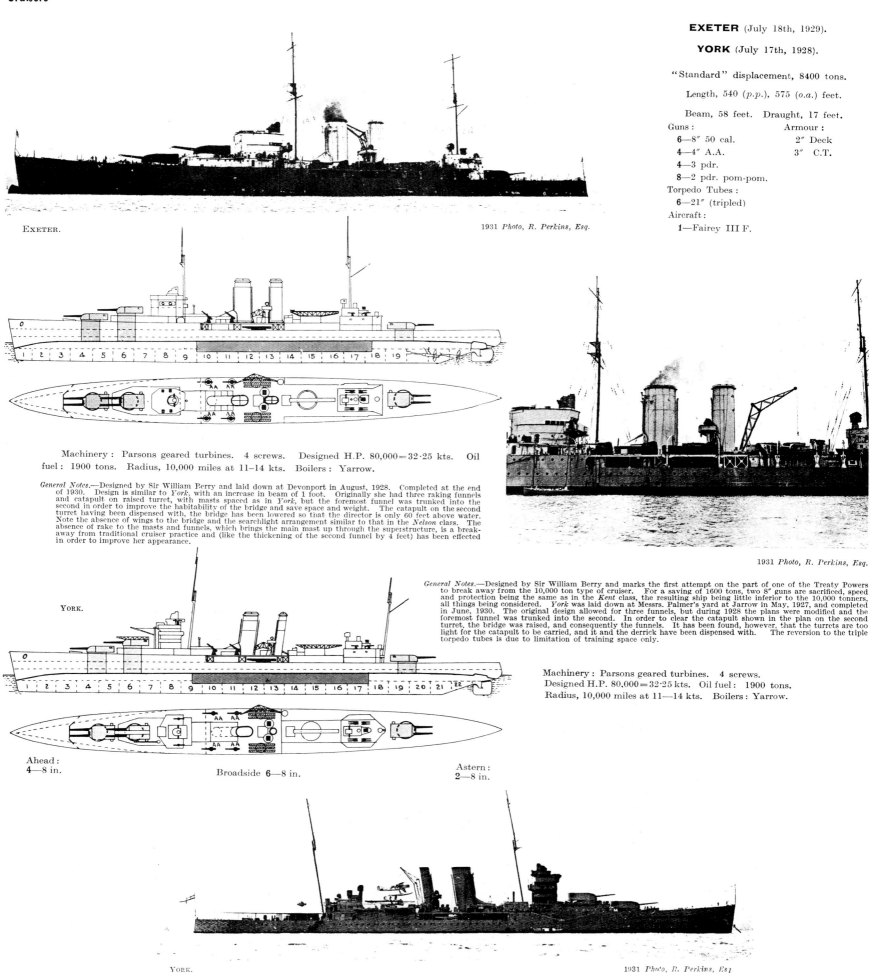

EXETER (July 18th, 1929).

YORK (July 17th, 1928).

"Standard" displacement, 8400 tons.

Length, 540 (*p.p.*), 575 (*o.a.*) feet.

Beam, 58 feet. Draught, 17 feet.

Guns:	Armour:
6—8″ 50 cal.	2″ Deck
4—4″ A.A.	3″ C.T.
4—3 pdr.	
8—2 pdr. pom-pom.	

Torpedo Tubes:
6—21″ (tripled)

Aircraft:
1—Fairey III F.

EXETER. 1931 *Photo, R. Perkins, Esq.*

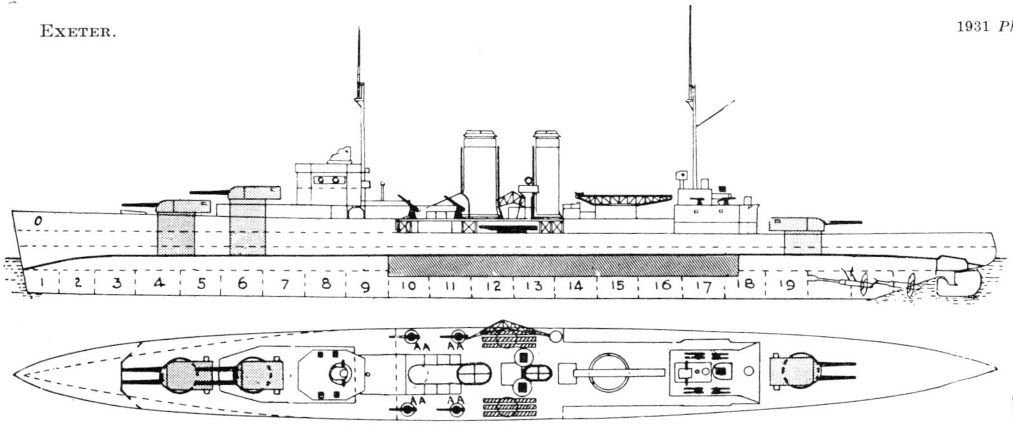

Machinery: Parsons geared turbines. 4 screws. Designed H.P. 80,000=32·25 kts. Oil fuel: 1900 tons. Radius, 10,000 miles at 11–14 kts. Boilers: Yarrow.

General Notes.—Designed by Sir William Berry and laid down at Devonport in August, 1928. Completed at the end of 1930. Design is similar to *York*, with an increase in beam of 1 foot. Originally she had three raking funnels and catapult on raised turret, with masts spaced as in *York*, but the foremost funnel was trunked into the second in order to improve the habitability of the bridge and save space and weight. The catapult on the second turret having been dispensed with, the bridge has been lowered so that the director is only 60 feet above water. Note the absence of wings to the bridge and the searchlight arrangement similar to that in the *Nelson* class. The absence of rake to the masts and funnels, which brings the main mast up through the superstructure, is a break-away from traditional cruiser practice and (like the thickening of the second funnel by 4 feet) has been effected in order to improve her appearance.

1931 *Photo, R. Perkins, Esq.*

General Notes.—Designed by Sir William Berry and marks the first attempt on the part of one of the Treaty Powers to break away from the 10,000 ton type of cruiser. For a saving of 1600 tons, two 8″ guns are sacrificed, speed and protection being the same as in the *Kent* class, the resulting ship being little inferior to the 10,000 tonners, all things being considered. *York* was laid down at Messrs. Palmer's yard at Jarrow in May, 1927, and completed in June, 1930. The original design allowed for three funnels, but during 1928 the plans were modified and the foremost funnel was trunked into the second. In order to clear the catapult shown in the plan on the second turret, the bridge was raised, and consequently the funnels. It has been found, however, that the turrets are too light for the catapult to be carried, and it and the derrick have been dispensed with. The reversion to the triple torpedo tubes is due to limitation of training space only.

YORK.

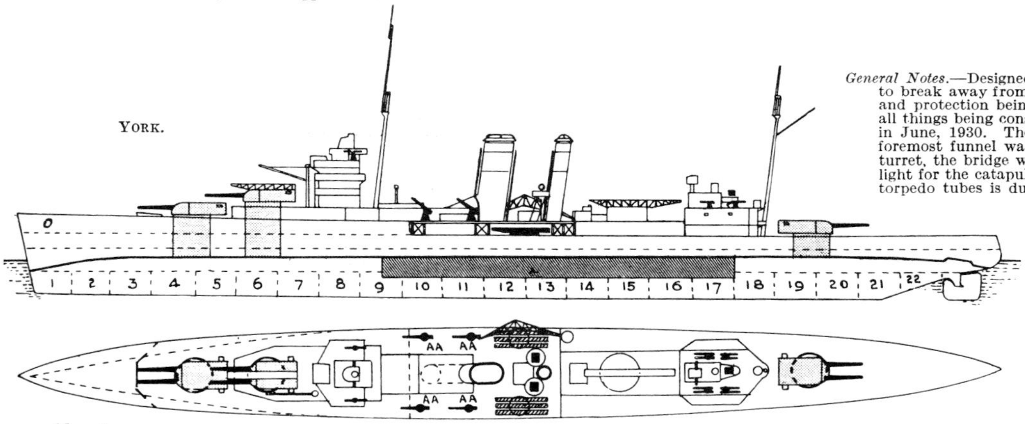

Machinery: Parsons geared turbines. 4 screws. Designed H.P. 80,000=32·25 kts. Oil fuel: 1900 tons. Radius, 10,000 miles at 11—14 kts. Boilers: Yarrow.

Ahead: **4**—8 in.

Broadside **6**—8 in.

Astern: **2**—8 in.

YORK. 1931 *Photo, R. Perkins, Esq.*

DESPATCH (24th Sept., 1919), **DIOMEDE** (29th April, 1919),
DELHI (23rd Aug., 1918),
DURBAN (29th May, 1919), **DANAE** (26th Jan., 1918),
DAUNTLESS (10th April, 1918).

Displacement, 4,850 tons.

Length (*p.p.* 445 feet, *w.l.* 465½ ,, *o.a.* 472½ ,,) Beam, 46½ ft. Draught (*mean* 14¼ ft., *max.* 16½ ft.)

Complements of all, 450/469. All except first two fitted as Flagships

Guns:
6—6 inch, 50 cal.
3—4 inch AA.
4—3 pdr.
11 to 13 smaller.
Torpedo tubes (21 inch):
12 in 4 triple deck mountings.

Armour (H.T.):
3″ Side (amidships) ...
2″, 1¾″, 1½″ Side (bow and stern) ....
1″ Upper deck (amids.)
1″ Deck over rudder ..
(Hull and armour, 2940 tons.)

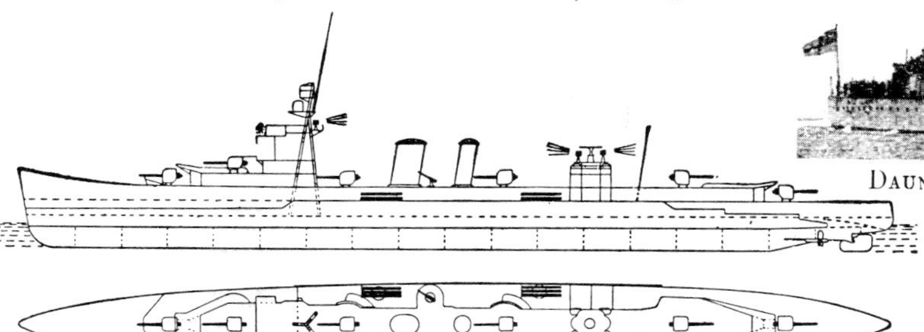

DAUNTLESS. 1928 *Photo, Cribb.*

Machinery: Turbines (all-geared), Brown-Curtis or Parsons types. Designed S.H.P. 40,000 = 29 kts. 2 shafts. Boilers: 6 Yarrow (small tube). Oil fuel only: *normal*, 300 tons; *maximum*, 1,050 tons. Machinery and engineering stores = 945 tons.

Name	*Builder*	*Machinery*	*Ordered*	*Begun*	*Completed*	*Trials: H.P. kts.*	*Turbines*
Diomede *Despatch*	Vickers* Fairfield*	Vickers Fairfield	Mar., 1918 Mar., 1918	June, 1918 July, 1918	24 Apr, 1922 2 June, 1922		Parsons Brown-Curtis
Delhi *Durban*	Armstrong Scotts*	Wallsend Scotts	Sept., 1917 Sept., 1917	29 Oct., '17 Jan., 1918	June, 1919 1 Sept. 1921	41,381 = 28·5† 41,026 =	Brown-Curtis Brown-Curtis
Danae *Dauntless*	Armstrong Palmer	Wallsend Palmer	Sept., 1916 Sept., 1916	Dec., 1916 Jan., 1917	July, 1918 Dec., 1918	40,463 = 42,808 =	Brown Curtis Parsons

*Towed to following Dockyards for completion: *Despatch* to Chatham, *Durban* to Devonport, *Diomede* to Portsmouth.
† With PVs. out, and on deep draught.

Notes.—Emergency War Programme ships. Design generally as *Ceres* class, but lengthened *about* 20 feet, to add a sixth 6-inch between foremast and first funnel; also triple tubes. Cost of *Delhi*, £840,182. *Diomede* served in New Zealand Division for over ten years. *Dauntless* badly damaged by grounding off Halifax, Nova Scotia, July 1928, and completely refitted 1929–30. *Dragon*, of this class, transferred to Polish Navy Jan. 1943. *Dunedin* became a war loss.

Cancelled Ships.—Dædalus, Daring, Desperate, Dryad (all ordered March 1918).

DAUNTLESS. (DANAE similar.) DIOMEDE has her forward forecastle 6 inch in gunhouse. 1942, *Official.*

DURBAN, DELHI, DESPATCH.
(Note revolving aeroplane platform and trawler bows.) *Photo added* 1925.

(Carlisle Class—5 Ships.)

CAIRO* (19th Nov., 1918), **CALCUTTA*** (9th July, 1918), **CARLISLE*** (9th July, 1918), **CAPETOWN*** (28th June, 1919), **COLOMBO*** (18th Dec., 1918).

(Ceres Class—5 Ships.)

CARDIFF* (ex *Caprice*, 12th April, 1917), **CERES** (24th March, 1917), **COVENTRY*** (ex *Corsair*, 6th July, 1917), **CURACOA*** (5th May, 1917), **CURLEW** (5th July, 1917).

Displacement, 4190 tons. Complement, 400/437.

Length { *p.p.* 425 feet / *o.a.* 450 „ } Beam, 43½ feet. Draught { *mean* 14 feet 1 inch. / *max.* 16¼ „

Guns:
- 5—6 inch, 50 cal. (**Dir. Con.**)
- 2—3 inch AA.
- 4—3 pdr. (Some mount 2 only).
- 2—2 pdr. pom-pom.
- 2 M.G.
- 8 Lewis.

Torpedo tubes (21 inch):
- 8 *above water*, in 4 *double* mountings.

*Fitted as Flagships.

Armour (H.T.):
- 3″ Side (amidships) . . .
- 2¼″—1½″ Side (bow) . .
- 2″ Side (stern) . . . .
- 1″ Upper deck (amids.)
- 1″ Deck over rudder . .
- (Harvey or Hadfield)
- 3″ C.T. . . . .
- — Tube . . . .

Colombo. 1926 *Photo, Grand Studio, Malta.*

Carlisle and *Capetown* originally had a hangar forward, but this has been removed and replaced by standard bridge work. *Curacoa* and several others now carry maintopmasts.

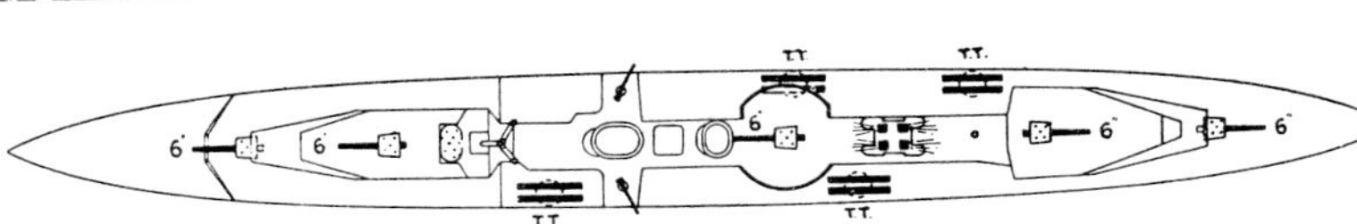

Ahead: 2—6 in. Broadside: 5—6 in., 4—21 in. tubes. Astern: 2—6 in.

Name	Builder	Machinery	Begun	Completed	Trials H.P. kts.	Turbines
Cardiff	Fairfield	Fairfield	July, 1916	July, 1917	41,450 = 28·96	B.-Curtis A.G.
Ceres	Clydebank	Clydebank	Apl.26,'16	June, 1917	39,425 = 29·1	B.-Curtis A.G.
Coventry	Swan, Hunter	Wallsend	Aug., 1916	Feb., 1918	39,967 =	B.-Curtis A.G.
Curacoa	Pembroke D.Y.	Harland & Wolff	July, 1916	Feb., 1918	40,428 =	B.-Curtis A.G.
Curlew	Vickers	Vickers	Aug., 1916	Dec., 1917	40,240 = 28·07	Parsons A.G.
Cairo	Cammell Laird	Cammell Laird	28 Nov.,'17	24 Sep.'19		Parsons
Calcutta	Vickers	Vickers	Oct., 1917	21 Aug.,'19		Parsons
Carlisle	Fairfield	Fairfield	Oct., 1917	11 Nov.'18	40,930 = 28·45	B.-Curtis
Capetown	Cammell Laird*	Cammell Laird	23 Feb.,'18	Feb., '22		Parsons
Colombo	Fairfield	Fairfield	Dec., 1917	June, '19		B.-Curtis

*Towed to Pembroke D.Y. for completion.

Machinery: Turbines (all-geared), see Table. 2 screws in all. Designed S.H.P. 40,000 = 29 kts. Boilers: Yarrow. Fuel (oil only): 300 tons, *normal*; *maximum*, 950 tons.

General Notes.—*Cardiff* class Emergency War Programme ships, ordered April, 1916. Very wet forward, to remedy which defect the later *Carlisle* and *Dragon* classes were given "trawler" bows. Heavy type Director on foremast. *Cairo* class Emergency War Programme ships, ordered June-July, 1917, that is *after* the first three units of "D Class" (*Danae, Dragon, Dauntless*) were ordered. In these ships "trawler" bows were added, to remedy defects shown by *Ceres* and *Calypso* classes. Conning tower also abolished. Heavy director on foremast. *Curacoa* was mined in 1919, and refitted 1919-20. Recent refits: *Carlisle, Coventry, Curacoa, Curlew*, 1928-29; *Cardiff, Ceres, Colombo*, 1929-30.

To distinguish: From *Dragon* and "*D*" Cruisers.—No 6 inch between foremast and first funnel. The same point separates this class from the *Caledon* class.

Curacoa (and others of *Ceres* class). 1926 *Photo, S. T. Abrahams, Weymouth.*

(Caledon Class—3 Ships.)

CALEDON* (25th Nov., 1916), **CALYPSO** (24th Jan., 1917), **CARADOC** (23rd Dec., 1916).

Displacement, 4120 tons. Complement, 400/437.

Length { *p.p.* 425 feet / *o.a.* 450 „ } Beam, 42¾ feet. Draught { *mean* 14 ft. 1 in. / *max.* 16¼ feet.

* Fitted as Flagship.

Guns:
- 5—6 inch, 50 cal. (**Dir. Con.**)
- 2—3 inch AA.
- 4—3 pdr.
- 2—2 pdr. pom-pom.
- 2 M.G.
- 8 Lewis.

Torpedo tube (21 inch):
- 8 *above water*, in 4 double mountings.

Armour (H.T.):
- 3″ Side (amidships) . . .
- 2¼″—1¼″ Side (bow) . .
- 2¼″—2″ Side (stern) . .
- 1″ Upper deck (amids.)
- 1″ Deck over rudder . .
- (Harvey or Hadfield)
- 6″ C.T. . . . .
- 4″ Tube . . . .

Name	Builder	Machinery	Begun	Completed	Trials: H.P. kts.
Caledon	Cammell Laird	Cammell Laird	Mar.17,'16	Mar., '17	47,887 =
Calypso	Hawthorn Leslie	Hawthorn Leslie	Feb.7,'16	June 21,'17	43,312 =
Caradoc	Scott S.B. Co.	Scotts	Feb., '16	June, '17	41,196 =

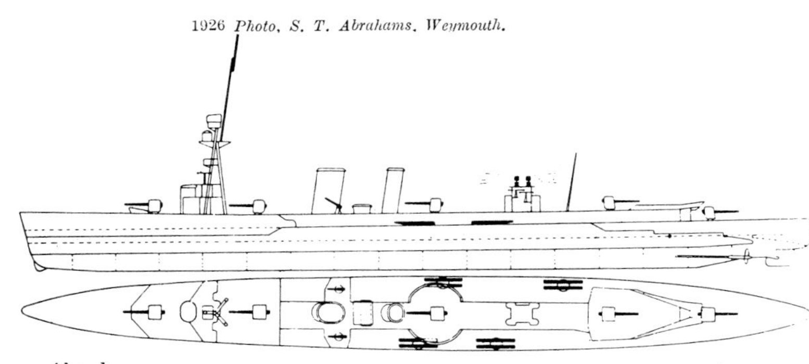

Ahead: 1—6 in. Broadside: 5—6 in., 4—21 in. tubes. Astern: 2—6 in.

Machinery: Turbines (all-geared), Parsons. 2 screws. Designed S.H.P. 40,000 = 29 kts. Boilers: 8 Yarrow. Fuel (oil only): *normal*, 300 tons; *maximum*, 935 tons.

Gunnery Notes.—Mark of 6-inch gun introduced in this class and mounted in later Cruisers has about 40° elevation. Heavy type Director.

Obsolete Cruisers.

DELHI. 1944, *Official.*

All laid up, awaiting sale.

CARLISLE. 1943, *Official.*

DELHI (Aug. 23, 1918). Displacement: 4,850 tons. Guns: **5**—5 inch, 38 cal., D.P., etc.

CARLISLE (July 9, 1918), **COLOMBO** (Dec. 18, 1918). Displacement: 4,200 tons. Guns: **8**—4 inch AA., etc.

Note.—Delhi is to be fitted out as stationary drillship for R.N.V.R.

Minelayers

(MANXMAN CLASS—3 SHIPS.)

APOLLO (April 5, 1943), **ARIADNE** (Feb. 16, 1943), **MANXMAN** (Sept. 5, 1940).

Displacement: 2,650 tons. Complement (peace): 242–246. Dimensions: 410 × 39¾ × 11⅛ feet. Guns: **4**—4 inch D.P., **10**—40 mm. AA. (*Manxman*, **8**—4 inch D.P., **4**—2 pdr. pompoms, **12**—20 mm. AA.) Mines: 100. Machinery: Parsons geared turbines. 2 shafts. S.H.P.: 72,000 = 40 kts. *max.* Boilers: **4** Admiralty 3-drum type.

Name.	*Builders & Machinery.*	*Begun.*	*Completed.*
Apollo	Hawthorn Leslie	10/10/41	12/2/44
Ariadne	Stephen	1941	10/9/43
Manxman	do.	April, 1939	7/6/41

ARIADNE. 1946, *P. A. Vicary.*

MANXMAN. *Added* 1944, *Official.*

Notes.–Manxman built under 1938 Estimates; others are war construction. Former ship was torpedoed by an enemy submarine and badly damaged, November, 1942. War losses of this type: *Abdiel, Latona, Welshman*, all 1938 Programme.

Destroyers

New Construction (1947 Estimates).

It is announced that 2 new destroyers will be laid down, embodying novel features in ship and engine design.

8 Daring Class.

1 *Clydebank:* ***Diamond.*** 1 *Stephen:* ***Dogstar.*** 1 *Thornycroft:* ***Duchess.*** 2 *Yarrow:* ***Dragon,***
1 *Fairfield:* ***Disdain*** (ex-*Ypres*). 1 *Swan Hunter:* ***Daring.*** 1 *White:* ***Dainty.*** ***Druid.***

Displacement: 2,610 tons. Dimensions: 390 (*o.a.*) × 43 × 12¾ feet. Guns: **6**—4·5 inch D.P., **10**—40 mm. AA. Tubes: **10**—21 inch. Machinery: Parsons geared turbines. 2 shafts. S.H.P. and speed not reported.

Notes.—These ships would appear to be an expansion of "Battle" design with increased armament. Whether all will be completed remains doubtful. Other units of class ordered under War Construction programme but since cancelled were: *Danae, Decoy, Delight, Demon, Dervish, Desire, Desperate, Doughty.*

4 "Weapon" Class.

1 *Thornycroft:* ***Crossbow*** (Dec. 20, 1945).

1 *White:* ***Scorpion*** (ex-*Tomahawk*, ex-*Centaur*, Aug. 15, 1946).

2 *Yarrow:* ***Battleaxe*** (June 12, 1945), ***Broadsword*** (Feb. 4, 1946).

Displacement: 1,980 tons. Dimensions: 365 (*o.a.*) × 38 × 12¼ feet. Guns: **6**—4 inch d.p. (in twin mounts), several smaller. Tubes: **10**—21 inch (quintupled). Machinery: Parsons geared turbines, arranged *en echelon.* 2 shafts. S.H.P.: 40,000 = 34 kts. Boilers: 2 Foster-Wheeler, with controlled superheat.

Notes.—This type appears to be an enlargement of *Brecon* design. Both Yarrow units are fitted as Leaders. Cancelled ships of class were *Carronade* (Scotts), *Culverin* (Thornycroft), *Cutlass* and *Dagger* (Yarrow), *Claymore* and *Dirk* (Scotts), *Halberd*, *Howitzer* (Thornycroft), *Longbow* (Thornycroft), *Musket* (White), *Poniard*, *Rifle* (Denny), *Spear* (Denny), *Sword* (ex-*Celt*) (White), *Grenade*, *Lance* and *Rapier*. Of these, *Carronade* and *Cutlass*, if not others, were actually launched before construction was abandoned.

SCORPION 1947, *A. John Brown, Esq.*

Observe novel funnel arrangement.

Destroyers

3 Ex-German Types

NONSUCH. 1948.

Nonsuch (ex-German *Z* 38, Nov. 11, 1941). Displacement: 2,650 tons (3,546 tons *full load*). Complement: 285. Dimensions: $388\frac{3}{4}$ (*pp.*), $403\frac{1}{2}$ (*o.a.*) × $38\frac{1}{3}$ × $9\frac{1}{2}$ feet (*light*). Guns: **5**—5·9 inch, **6**—37 mm. AA., **16**—20 mm. AA. Tubes: **8**—21 inch. Fitted for minelaying. Machinery: Geared turbines. 2 shafts. S.H.P.: 70,000 = 35·5 kts. Boilers: 6 Wagner (1,250 lb. working pressure). Fuel: 800 tons.

Z 10 (ex-*Hans Lody*, 1936), ***Z 4*** (ex-*Richard Beitzen*, 1935). Displacement: 1,625 tons. Dimensions: 374 (*pp.*), 381 (*o.a.*) × $37\frac{3}{4}$ × $9\frac{1}{3}$ feet (*light*). Guns: **5**—5 inch, **8**—37 mm. AA., **12**—20 mm. AA. Tubes: **8**—21 inch. Machinery: Geared turbines. 2 shafts. S.H.P.: 50,000 = 36 kts. Boilers: 6 Wagner.

24 "Battle" Class.

4 *Cammell Laird:* ***Gravelines*** (Nov. 30, 1944), ***Hogue*** (April 21, 1944), ***Lagos*** (Aug. 4, 1944), ***Sluys*** (Feb. 28, 1945).

2 *Clydebank:* ***Barrosa*** (Jan., 1945), ***Matapan*** (April 30, 1945).

5 *Fairfield:* ***Cadiz*** (Sept. 18, 1944), ***Camperdown*** (Feb. 8, 1944), ***Finisterre*** (June 22, 1944), ***St. James*** (June 7, 1945), ***Vigo*** (Sept. 27, 1945).

5 *Hawthorn Leslie:* ***Agincourt*** (Jan., 1945), ***Alamein*** (May 28, 1945), ***Armada*** (Dec. 9, 1943), ***Saintes*** (July 19, 1944), ***Solebay*** (Feb. 22, 1944).

2 *Stephen:* ***Dunkirk*** (Aug. 27, 1945), ***Jutland*** (ex-*Malplaquet*, Feb. 20, 1946).

5 *Swan Hunter:* ***Barfleur*** (Nov. 1, 1943), ***Corunna*** (May 29, 1945), ***Gabbard*** (March 16, 1945), ***St. Kitts, Trafalgar*** (Jan. 12, 1944).

1 *Vickers-Armstrongs* (*Tyne*)*:* ***Aisne*** (May 12, 1945).

Displacement: 2,315 tons. (Leaders, 2,325 tons). Dimensions: 379 (*o.a.*) × $40\frac{1}{4}$ × $12\frac{3}{4}$ feet (*mean*), $17\frac{1}{2}$ feet (*max.*). Guns: **4**—4·5 inch d.p. (twin mounts, forward), **12** to **14**—40 mm. AA. **2** D.C.T. But last 8 ships, *Agincourt, Aisne, Alamein, Barrosa, Corunna, Dunkirk, Jutland, Matapan*, all have: **5**—4·5 inch, **8**—40 mm. AA., **2** D.C.T. The extra 4·5 inch is mounted in "Q" position. Tubes: **10**—21 inch (quintupled), except some early units with 8. Machinery: Parsons geared turbines. 2 shafts. S.H.P.: 50,000 = 34 kts. Boilers: 3 Admiralty 3-drum type. Complement: 250 (peace), 337 (war).

Notes.—These destroyers were designed with a view to operations in the Pacific. Sixteen were cancelled before completion, including original *Jutland, Mons, Poictiers* (all ordered from Hawthorn Leslie), *Namur, Navarino, San Domingo* (all Cammell Laird), *Talavera, Trincomalee* (both Clydebank), *Belleisle, Omdurman, Waterloo* (all Fairfield), *St. Lucia* (Stephen), *Oudenarde, River Plate* (both Swan Hunter), *Albuera* (Vickers-Armstrongs), and *Vimiera*. At least 5 of them had been launched before cancellation. *Agincourt, Alamein, Armada, Barfleur, Jutland, Solebay* and *Trafalgar* reported to be fitted as Leaders.

SAINTES. 1946, *courtesy Messrs. Hawthorn Leslie.*

SOLEBAY. 1946, *London Studio.*

BARROSA 1947, *Wright & Logan.*

26 "C" Class.

2 *Clydebank:* ***Cæsar*** (ex-*Ranger*, Feb. 14, 1944), ***Cavendish*** (ex-*Sibyl*, April 12, 1944). (Ldr.)

2 *Denny:* ***Childers*** (Feb. 27, 1945). (Leader), ***Chivalrous*** (June 22, 1945).

4 *Scotts:* ***Cambrian*** (ex-*Spitfire*, Dec. 10, 1943), ***Carron*** (ex-*Strenuous*, March 28, 1944), ***Chequers*** (Oct. 30, 1944), ***Chieftain*** (Feb. 26, 1945).

3 *Stephen:* ***Cheviot*** (May 2, 1944), ***Chevron*** (Feb. 23, 1944), ***Consort*** (Oct. 19, 1944).

4 *Thornycroft:* ***Chaplet*** (July 18, 1944), ***Charity*** (Nov. 30, 1944), ***Comus*** (March 14, 1945), ***Concord*** (ex-*Corso*, July 14, 1945).

2 *Vickers-Armstrongs* (*Tyne*)*:* ***Constance*** (Aug. 22, 1944), ***Cossack*** (May 10, 1944).

5 *White:* ***Carysfort*** (July 25, 1944), ***Cavalier*** (April 7, 1944), ***Contest*** (Dec. 16, 1944), ***Crispin*** (ex-*Craccher*, June 23, 1945), ***Creole*** (Nov. 22, 1945).

4 *Yarrow:* ***Caprice*** (ex-*Swallow*, Sept. 16, 1943), ***Cassandra*** (ex-*Tourmaline*, Nov. 29, 1943), ***Cockade*** (March 7, 1944), ***Comet*** (June 22, 1944).

Displacement: 1,710 tons. Dimensions: $362\frac{3}{4}$ × $35\frac{2}{3}$ × 10 feet (*mean*), 16 feet (*max.*). Guns: **4**—4·5 inch d.p., **4**—40 mm. AA., **2** to **6**—20 mm. AA. Tubes: **4**—21 inch (quadrupled), except *Caesar* group, **8**. Machinery: Parsons geared turbines. 2 shafts. S.H.P.: 40,000 = 34 kts. (38 kts. reached in service). Boilers: 2 Admiralty 3-drum type. Complement: 186 (Leaders 222).

Notes.—These destroyers were built as 4 flotillas, i.e., *Cæsar, Chequers, Cossack* and *Crescent* groups. Otherwise, there appears to be little difference between this class and those immediately preceding it, except that the more recent of above destroyers are of all-welded construction. Two of this class, *Crescent* and *Crusader* will be found in R. Canadian Navy, and four more were sold to Norway. *Cavendish* and *Childers* probably displace 1,730 tons.

CHAPLET. 1946, *London Studio.*

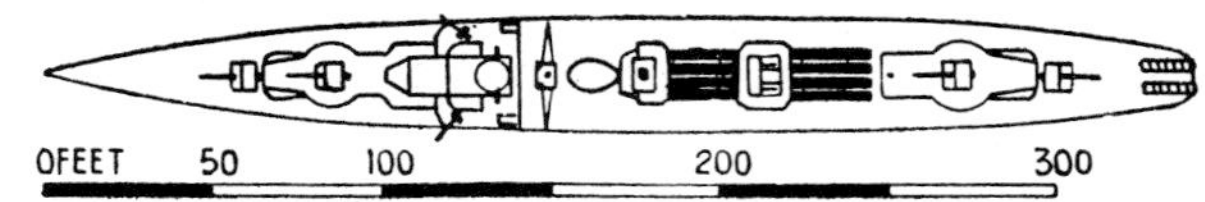

8 Zambesi Class.

2 *Cammell Laird:* **Zambesi** (Nov. 21, 1943), **Zealous** (Feb. 28, 1944).

2 *Denny:* **Zebra** (ex-*Wakeful*, March 8, 1944), **Zenith** (ex-*Wessex*, June 6, 1944).

2 *Thornycroft:* **Zest** (Oct. 14, 1943), **Zodiac** (March 11, 1944).

2 *Vickers-Armstrongs (Tyne):* **Myngs** (May 31, 1943), (Ldr.), **Zephyr** (July 15, 1943).

Displacement: 1,710 tons (*Myngs, Zephyr*, 1,730 tons). Guns: 4—4·5 inch d.p., 6—40 mm. AA., 4 D.C.T. (but *Myngs* has 4—4·5 inch, 2—2 pdr., 3—40 mm., 2—20 mm.). Dimensions and other particulars similar to "C" class. (Machinery of last pair by Parsons).

ZODIAC. 1944, *courtesy Messrs. Thornycroft.*

8 Ulster Class.

2 *Cammell Laird:* **Ulysses** (April 22, 1943), **Undaunted** (July 19, 1943).
2 *Swan Hunter:* **Grenville** (Oct. 12, 1942), (Leader), **Ulster** (Nov. 9, 1942).
2 *Thornycroft:* **Undine** (June 1, 1943), **Ursa** (July 22, 1943).
2 *Vickers-Armstrongs (Barrow):* **Urania** (May 19, 1943), **Urchin** (March 8, 1943).
Particulars similar to *Valentine* class, but *Grenville's* displacement is 1,730 tons.

UNDINE. 1944, *courtesy Messrs. Thornycroft*

8 Wager Class.

2 *Clydebank:* **Kempenfelt** (ex-*Valentine*, May 8, 1943), (Leader), **Wager** (Nov. 1, 1943).

2 *Fairfield:* **Wakeful** (ex-*Zebra*, June 30, 1943), **Wessex** (ex-*Zenith*, Sept. 2, 1943).

2 *Hawthorn:* **Whelp** (June 3, 1943), **Whirlwind** (Aug. 30, 1943).

2 *Vickers-Armstrongs (Barrow):* **Wizard** (Sept. 29, 1943), **Wrangler** (Dec. 30, 1943).

Displacement: 1,710 tons (*Kempenfelt*, 1,730 tons). Guns: 4—4·7 inch, 4—40 mm. AA., 4—20 mm. AA., 4 D.C.T. (Some may have 2 pdr. in place of 40 mm.) Other particulars similar to "C" and "Z" classes.

WESSEX. 1944, *Official.*

5 Valentine Class.

2 *Fairfield:* **Venus** (Feb. 23, 1943), **Verulam** (April 22, 1943).
2 *Swan Hunter:* **Vigilant** (Oct. 18, 1943), **Virago** (Feb. 4, 1943).
1 *White:* **Volage** (Dec. 15, 1943).

Displacement: 1,710 tons. Dimensions: 339½ (*pp.*), 362¾ (*o.a.*) × 35¾ × 10 feet (*mean*), 16 feet (*max.*). Guns: 4—4·7 inch, 4—40 mm. AA., 2 to 4—20 mm. AA. Tubes: 8—21 inch (quadrupled). Machinery: Parsons geared turbines. 2 shafts. S.H.P.: 40,000 = 34 kts. Boilers: 2 Admiralty 3-drum type.

Note.—Two of this group, *Valentine* and *Vixen*, were transferred to R. Canadian Navy and renamed. A third, the flotilla leader *Hardy* (Clydebank), has been lost. *Volage* had bow blown off by a mine explosion in 1946. It has been stated officially that, to insulate living spaces from cold in high latitudes, deckheads in these vessels have been sprayed with an asbestos coating.

VOLAGE. 1946

8 Troubridge Class.

2 *Cammell Laird:* **Teazer** (Jan. 7, 1943), **Tenacious** (March 24, 1943).

2 *Clydebank:* **Troubridge** (Sept. 23, 1942) (Leader), **Tumult** (Nov. 9, 1942).

2 *Denny:* **Termagant** (March 22, 1943), **Terpsichore** (June 17, 1943).

2 *Swan Hunter:* **Tuscan** (May 28, 1942), **Tyrian** (July 27, 1942).

Displacement 1,710 tons (*Troubridge*, 1,730 tons). Guns: 4—4·7 inch, 4—2 pdr. pompoms, 4—20 mm. AA. Other particulars similar to *Ulster* and *Valentine* types.

TERMAGANT. 1946, *Wright & Logan.*

SAVAGE. 1946, *Wright & Logan.*

1 *Hawthorn:* **Savage** (Sept. 24, 1942).

Displacement: 1,796 tons. Guns: 4—4·5 inch d.p., 6—40 mm. AA.

Notes.—*Savage* and ships of 5 later groups have been described officially as a "utility" type, priority being given in the design to war requirements above all other considerations. *Shark* (Scotts, since lost) and *Success* (White) both transferred to R. Norwegian Navy; *Scorpion*, *Scourge* and *Serapis* to R. Netherland Navy. *Swift* (White) has been lost; and *Saumarez* was so badly damaged by a mine in 1946 that she was not worth repairing. As will be observed from photo, *Savage* is fitted with a twin turret forward, prototype of those in "Battle" class.

Destroyers

8 Rotherham Class.

2 *Cammell Laird:* ***Raider*** (April 1, 1942), ***Rapid*** (July 16, 1942).

4 *Clydebank:* ***Racehorse*** (June 1, 1942), ***Rotherham*** (March 21, 1942) (Leader), ***Redoubt*** (May 2, 1942), ***Relentless*** (July 15, 1942).

2 *Scotts:* ***Rocket*** (Oct. 28, 1942), ***Roebuck*** (Dec. 10, 1942).

Displacement: 1,705 tons (*Rotherham*, 1,750 tons). Dimensions: 358¼ × 35⅔ × 9½ feet (*mean*), 16 feet (*max.*). Guns: **4**—4·7 inch, **4**—2 pdr. pompoms, **8**—20 mm. AA. Tubes: **8**—21 inch. Machinery: Parsons geared turbines. 2 shafts. S.H.P.: 40,000 = 34 kts. Boilers: 2 Admiralty 3-drum type.

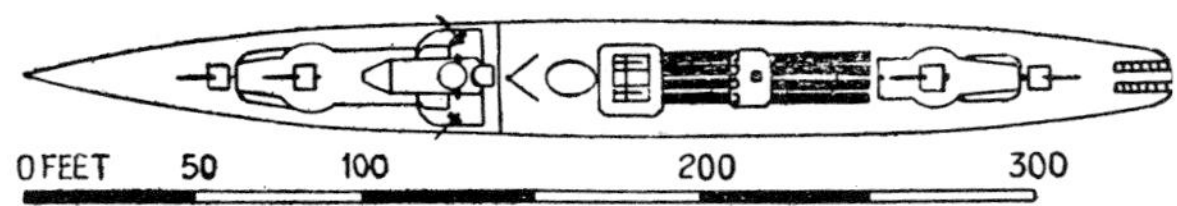

Rotherham and *Onslow* types.

Note.—5 destroyers similar to above (*Quadrant, Quality, Queenborough, Quiberon* and *Quickmatch*) have been transferred to R. Australian Navy, and a sixth (*Quilliam*) to R. Netherland Navy.

ROTHERHAM. 1946, *Wright & Logan.*

10 Onslow Class.

ONSLAUGHT. 1946, *Wright & Logan.*

2 *Clydebank:* ***Onslow*** (ex-*Pakenham*, March 31, 1941), ***Paladin*** (June 11, 1941).
2 *Denny:* ***Obdurate*** (Feb. 19, 1942), ***Obedient*** (April 30, 1942).
2 *Fairfield:* ***Offa*** (March 11, 1941), ***Onslaught*** (ex-*Pathfinder*, Oct. 9, 1941).
2 *Thornycroft:* ***Opportune*** (Jan. 21, 1942), ***Orwell*** (April 2, 1942).
2 *Vickers-Armstrongs (Tyne):* ***Penn*** (Feb. 12, 1941), ***Petard*** (ex-*Persistent*, March 27, 1941).

Displacement: 1,540 tons. Dimensions: 338½ (*pp.*), 345 (*o.a.*) × 35 × 9 feet (*mean*), 15⅝ feet (*max.*). Guns: **4**—4 inch Mark V (*Offa, Onslaught, Opportune, Penn*, only **2**—4 inch), **4**—2 pdr., **8**—20 mm. AA. Tubes: **8**—21 inch (removed from some). Machinery: Parsons geared turbines. 2 shafts. S.H.P.: 40,000 = 34 kts. Boilers: 2 Admiralty 3-drum type.

Notes.—These were the first destroyers built under War Construction programmes. Machinery of *Penn, Petard* and *Porcupine* was supplied from Barrow. *Oribi* transferred to Turkish Navy. *Pathfinder, Porcupine* scrapped, and others may follow. War losses of this class were *Pakenham* (ex-*Onslow*), Hawthorn; *Panther*, Vickers-Armstrongs; and *Partridge*, Fairfield.

Name	*Begun*	*Completed*	*Name*	*Begun*	*Completed*
Opportune	28/3/40	14/8/42	*Penn*	26/12/39	23/2/42
Orwell	16/5/40	7/10/42	*Petard*	26/12/39	14/6/42

OBDURATE. 1946, *Wright & Logan.*

7 Laforey Class.

3 *Scotts:* ***Lookout*** (Nov. 4, 1940), ***Loyal*** (Oct. 8, 1941), ***Milne*** (Dec. 31, 1941) (Ldr.).
1 *Vickers-Armstrongs (Tyne):* ***Marne*** (Oct. 31, 1940).
2 *Stephen:* ***Matchless*** (Sept. 4, 1941), ***Meteor*** (Nov. 3, 1941).
1 *Fairfield:* ***Musketeer*** (Dec. 2, 1941).

Displacement: 1,920 tons (*Milne*, 1,935 tons). Dimensions: 354 (*pp.*), 362½ (*o.a.*) × 36¾ × 10 feet (*mean*), 16¾ feet (*max.*). Guns: **6**—4·7 inch, **10** to **14**—20 mm. AA. Tubes: **8**—21 inch. Machinery: Parsons geared turbines. 2 shafts. S.H.P.: 48,000 = 36·5 kts. Boilers: 2 Admiralty 3-drum type. Ordered under 1937 and 1939 Estimates, *Lookout* and *Loyal* having been laid down Nov., 1938, and others in 1939. War losses: *Gurkha* (ex-*Larne*), *Laforey, Lance, Legion, Lightning, Lively, Mahratta, Martin* (another was Polish *Orkan*, ex-*Myrmidon*).

Notes.—Individual ships vary in details. Later units are insulated for service in high latitudes. *Marne* begun 28/10/39 and completed 2/12/41. *Loyal* now serving as accommodation ship.

MILNE. 1943 *Official.*

MATCHLESS. 1946, *Wright & Logan.*

49 "Hunt" Class.

2 "Brecon" (No. 4) Type.

2 *Thornycroft:* ***Brecon*** (June 27, 1942), ***Brissenden*** (Sept. 15, 1942).

Displacement: 1,175 tons. Dimensions: 296 × 33¼ × 9 feet. Guns: **6**—4 inch AA., **4**—2 pdr., **6** to **8**—20 mm. AA. Tubes: **3**—21 inch. Machinery: Parsons geared turbines. 2 shafts. S.H.P.: 19,000 = 25 kts. Boilers: 2 Admiralty 3-drum type. Complement: 170.

Note.—Designed for Arctic service, with double deck fore and aft, and extra beam.

Nos. 2 and 4 types (3 tubes in latter).

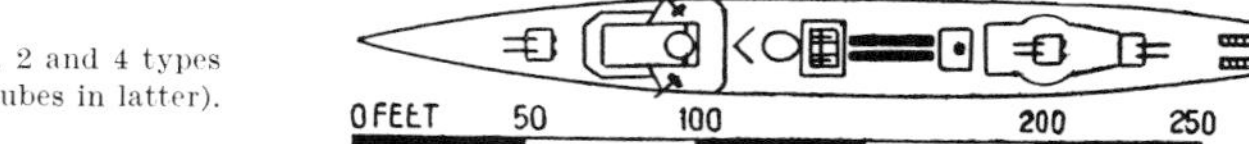

8 "Albrighton" (No. 3) Type.

1 *Cammell Laird:* **Belvoir** (Nov. 18, 1941).
1 *Clydebank:* **Albrighton** (Oct. 11, 1941).
2 *Vickers-Armstrongs (Tyne):* **Bleasdale** (July 23, 1941), **Haydon** (April 2, 1942).
4 *White:* **Easton** (July 11, 1942), **Eggesford** (Sept. 12, 1942), **Stevenstone** (Nov. 23, 1942), **Talybont** (Feb. 3, 1943).

Displacement: 1,050 tons (1,490 tons *full load*). Dimensions: 264¼ (*pp.*), 280 (*o.a.*) × 31½ × 7⅝ feet (*mean*). Guns: **4**—4 inch AA., 1—2 pdr. pompom, **2**—20 mm. AA. Tubes: **2**—21 inch. Machinery: Parsons geared turbines. 2 shafts. S.H.P.: 19,000 = 27 kts. Boilers: 2 Admiralty 3-drum type. Oil fuel: 280 tons. Complement: 168.

BRECON. 1943, *courtesy Messrs. Thornycroft.*

22 "Blankney" (No. 2) Type.

1 *Cammell Laird:* **Beaufort** (April 15, 1941).
2 *Clydebank:* **Avon Vale** (Oct. 23, 1940), **Blankney** (Dec. 19, 1940).
2 *Hawthorn:* **Bedale** (ex-*Slazak*, ex-*Bedale*, July 23, 1941), **Bicester** (Sept. 5, 1941).
2 *Scotts:* **Chiddingfold** (March 10, 1941), **Cowdray** (May 12, 1941).
2 *Stephen:* **Blackmore** (Dec. 2, 1941), **Croome** (Jan. 30, 1941).
5 *Swan Hunter:* **Calpe** (April 28, 1941), **Eridge** (Aug. 20, 1940). **Exmoor** (ex-*Burton*, March 12, 1941), **Farndale** (Sept. 2, 1940), **Lamerton** (Dec. 14, 1940).
1 *Thornycroft:* **Leabury** (Sept. 27, 1941).
1 *Vickers-Armstrongs (Tyne):* **Middleton** (May 12, 1941).
2 *White:* **Silverton** (ex-*Krakowiak*, ex-*Silverton*, Dec. 4, 1940), **Tetcott** (Aug. 12, 1941).
4 *Yarrow:* **Oakley** (ex-*Tickham*, Jan. 15, 1942), **Wheatland** (June 7, 1941). **Wilton** (Oct. 17, 1941), **Zetland** (March 6, 1942).

Nos. 1 and 3 types.

BELVOIR. 1946, *Wright & Logan.*

Displacement: 1,050 tons (1,490 tons *full load*). Dimensions: 264¼ (*pp.*), 280 (*o.a.*) × 31½ × 7⅝ feet (*mean*). Guns: **6**—4 inch AA., **1**—2 pdr. pompom, **2**—20 mm. AA. No tubes. Machinery: Parsons geared turbines. 2 shafts. S.H.P.: 19,000 = 27 kts. Boilers: 2 Admiralty 3-drum type. Oil fuel: 280 tons. Complement: 146.

17 "Atherstone" (No. 1) Type.

2 *Cammell Laird:* **Atherstone** (Dec. 12, 1939), **Brocklesby** (Sept. 30, 1940).
1 *Clydebank:* **Garth** (Dec. 12, 1939).
2 *Scotts:* **Pytchley** (Feb. 13, 1940), **Quantock** (April 22, 1940).
1 *Stephen:* **Whaddon** (July 16, 1940).
4 *Swan Hunter:* **Hambledon** (Dec. 12, 1939), **Holderness** (Feb. 8, 1940), **Mendip** (April 9, 1940), **Meynell** (June 7, 1940).
2 *Vickers-Armstrongs (Tyne):* **Eglinton** (Dec. 28, 1939), **Liddesdale** (Aug. 19, 1940).
1 *White:* **Southdown** (July 5, 1940).
4 *Yarrow:* **Cattistock** (Feb. 22, 1940), **Cleveland** (April 24, 1940), **Cotswold** (July 18, 1940), **Cottesmore** (Sept. 5, 1940).

Mostly laid down 1939, under Programme for that year, and completed 1940.

Displacement: 1,000 tons. Dimensions: 272⅓ (*pp.*), 280 (*o.a.*) × 29 × 7¾ feet. Guns: **4**—4 inch AA., **2**—20 mm. AA. (Some have **1**—2 pdr. besides.) No tubes. Machinery: Parsons geared turbines (by Wallsend Slipway in Swan Hunter units). 2 shafts. S.H.P.: 19,000 = 27·5 kts. Boilers: 2 Admiralty 3-drum type. Complement: 146.

Notes.—Designed for escort duties. Sundry units have been transferred to the R. Norwegian, R. Hellenic and French Navies. War losses comprise *Airedale* (Clydebank), *Aldenham*, *Berkeley* (both Cammell Laird), *Blean* (Hawthorn Leslie), *Dulverton*, *Exmoor* (Vickers-Armstrongs, Tyne), *Grove* (Swan Hunter), *Heythrop*, *Holcombe*, *Hurworth* (Vickers-Armstrongs, Tyne), *Limbourne*, *Penylan* (Vickers-Armstrongs), *Puckeridge*, *Quorn*, *Southwold* (all 3 White), *Tynedale* (Stephen), besides French *La Combattante*, Norwegian *Eskdale* (Cammell Laird), and Polish *Kujawiak* (Vickers-Armstrongs, Tyne). Others have been scrapped, and *Eridge* is used as accommodation ship. *Zetland* is being assigned to Solent Division R.N.V.R. as drillship.

EASTON. 1946, *Wright & Logan.*

Flotilla Leaders and Destroyers

9 Javelin Class

Appearance Note.—Most of this class now have lattice mast.

JERVIS. 1944, *Official.*

KELVIN. *Added* 1944, *Official.*

3 *Clydebank:* **Javelin** (ex-*Kashmir*), **Nizam, Noble** (ex-*Piorun*, ex-*Nerissa*).
2 *Fairfield:* **Kelvin, Napier.**
1 *Hawthorn:* **Jervis** (LEADER).
3 *Thornycroft:* **Kimberley, Nepal** (ex-*Norseman*), **Norman.**

Displacement: 1,760 tons. Complement: 220 (*Jervis*, 233). Dimensions: 348 × 35 × 9 feet. Guns: **6**—4·7 inch, **4**—40 mm. AA., **6**—20 mm. AA. Tubes: **10**—21 inch. Machinery: Parsons geared turbines. 2 shafts. S.H.P.: 40,000 = 36 kts. Boilers: 2 Admiralty 3-drum type.

Est.	*Name*	*Begun*	*Launch*	*Compl.*	*Est.*	*Name*	*Begun*	*Launch*	*Compl.*
1936	*Jervis*	26/8/37	9/9/38	5/8/39	1938	*Napier*	1939	22/5/40	1941
1937	*Javelin*	11/10/37	21/12/38	10/6/39		*Nepal*	9/9/39	4/12/41	29/5/42
	Kelvin	5/10/37	19/1/39	/39		*Nizam*	1939	4/7/40	1941
	Kimberley	1/38	1/6/39	1939		*Norman*	27/7/39	30/10/40	29/9/41
						Noble	1939	1940	1941

Notes.—Two ships of this class were transferred to R. Netherland Navy. War losses: *Jackal*, *Jaguar*, *Janus*, *Jersey*, *Juno*, *Jupiter*, *Kandahar*, *Kashmir*, *Kelly*, *Khartoum*, *Kingston*, *Kipling*, *Nestor*. Ex-Leader *Napier* is now used for anti-submarine training. *Noble* served under Polish flag during war.

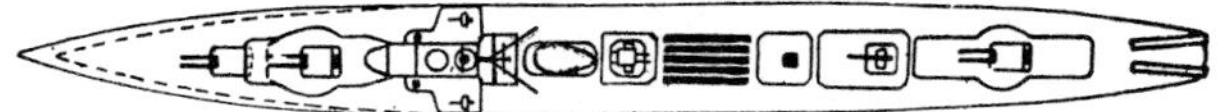

JAVELIN *class.*

Destroyers

4 "Tribal" Class

NUBIAN. 1947, *P. A. Vicary*

NUBIAN. 1947, *P. A. Vicary*

Note to Plan.—4 inch guns are in "X" position.

1 *Vickers-Armstrongs (Tyne)*: **Eskimo.**
1 *Thornycroft*: **Nubian.**
1 *Denny*: **Ashanti.**
1 *Swan Hunter*: **Tartar** (Leader).

Displacement: 1,870 tons. Complement: 190 (as Leader 219, or as Captain D., 226). Dimensions: $355\frac{1}{2} \times 36\frac{1}{2} \times$ 9 feet. Guns: **6**—4·7 inch, **2**—4 inch AA., **14** smaller. Tubes: **4**—21 inch. Machinery: Parsons geared turbines (by Parsons Co. in *Eskimo*; by Wallsend Co. in *Tartar*). 2 shafts. S.H.P.: 44,000 = 36·5 kts. Boilers: 3 Admiralty 3-drum type. Cost averages £467,000 apiece.

Notes.—*Tartar*, though fitted as Leader, does not differ in appearance from others. *Ashanti* has lattice mast. *Eskimo* now has deckhouse aft and no tubes. War losses: *Afridi, Bedouin, Cossack, Gurkha, Maori, Mashona, Matabele, Mohawk, Punjabi, Sikh, Somali, Zulu.*

Est.	*Name*	*Begun*	*Launch*	*Compl.*
1935	*Nubian*	10/8/36	21/12/37	6/12/38

Est.	*Name*	*Begun*	*Launch*	*Compl.*
1936	*Ashanti*	23/11/36	5/11/37	21/12/38
	Eskimo	5/8/36	3/9/37	30/12/38
	Tartar	26/8/36	21/10/37	10/3/39

HOTSPUR. 1944, *Official.*

Programme 1934 } 1 *Scotts*: **Hotspur.** Displacement: 1,340 tons.

Complement: 145. Dimensions: 312 (*pp.*), 320 (*w.l.*), 323 (*o.a.*) $\times$ 33 $\times$ $8\frac{1}{2}$ feet (*mean*). Guns: **3**—4·7 inch, **1**—3 inch AA., **6** smaller. Tubes: **4**—21 inch. Machinery: Parsons geared turbines. 2 shafts. S.H.P.: 34,000 = 36 kts. Boilers: 3 Admiralty 3-drum type. Oil fuel: 455 tons.

Name		*Begun*	*Launch*	*Comp.*
Hotspur	..	27/2/35	23/3/36	29/12/36

Notes.—First three of "H" type listed above were acquired from Brazilian Navy in 1939. *Hesperus* renamed for second time Feb. 27, 1940. On May 7–8, 1941, *Hurricane* sank in shallow water owing to damage received in action with enemy aircraft at Liverpool, but was salved and refitted, resuming service in Jan. 1942. In 1943 she became a total war loss; others were *Hardy* (Ldr.), *Harvester, Hasty, Havant, Havock, Hereward, Hostile, Hunter, Hyperion,*

FAME. 1946.

Programme 1932 } 1 *Vickers-Armstrongs (Barrow)*: **Fame.**

Displacement: 1,350 tons.
Complement: 145.
Guns: **4**—4·7 inch.
1—3 inch AA.
6 smaller.
Tubes: **4**—21 inch.
2 D.C. Throwers.

Dimensions: $318\frac{1}{4}$ (*pp.*), 326 (*w.l.*), 329 (*o.a.*) $\times 33\frac{1}{4} \times 8\frac{1}{2}$ feet (*mean*).
Parsons geared turbines (by Parsons Co.) S.H.P.: 36,000 = 36 kts.
Boilers: 3 Admiralty 3-drum type, working at 300 lbs. pressure with 200° superheat.
Oil fuel: 480 tons.

General Notes.—Other ships of this type are serving in R. Canadian Navy and R. Hellenic Navy. War losses: *Fearless, Firedrake, Foresight, Eclipse, Electra, Encounter, Escort, Esk, Exmouth* (Ldr.). *Fame* now used for *A/S* Training.

Engineering Notes.—Average speed on trials with designed horse power was 36·7 kts. Radius at 15 kts., 6,000 miles.

Name	*Begun*	*Launch*	*Completed*
Fame	5/7/33	28/6/34	26/4/35

"Isis" Class

IMPULSIVE. 1942, *Official.*

Programme 1935
2 *Clydebank*: **Icarus, Ilex**
1 *White*: **Impulsive**
1 *Yarrow*: **Isis**

War Programme. 2 *Vickers-Armstrongs (Barrow)*: **Inconstant, Ithuriel.**

Displacement: 1,370 tons. Complement: 145. Dimensions: 312 (*pp.*), 320 (*w.l.*) $\times$ 33 $\times$ $8\frac{1}{2}$ feet (*mean*). Guns: **4**—4·7 inch, **6** smaller. Tubes: **5**—21 inch. Machinery: Parsons geared turbines. S.H.P.: 34,000 = 36 kts. Boilers: 3 Admiralty 3-drum type, working pressure 350 lbs. Cost averages just over £320,000 apiece.

Note.—All this class are fitted for minelaying. War losses: *Imogen, Imperial, Intrepid, Ivanhoe.*

Name	*Begun*	*Launched*	*Completed*	*Name*	*Begun*	*Launched*	*Completed*
Icarus	3/36	26/11/36	3/5/37	*Impulsive*	3/36	1/3/37	29/1/38
Ilex	3/36	28/1/37	7/7/37	*Isis*	2/36	12/11/36	2/6/37

MM(4) 5-T.T.
MM(4) 5-T.T.

"I" *class.* (After group of T.T. now replaced by A.A. gun.)

"Gallant" Class

Programme 1933 } 1 *Stephen:* **Gallant.** Displacement: 1,335 tons.

Complement: 145. Dimensions: 312 (*pp.*), 320 (*w.l.*), 323 (*o.a.*) × 33 × 8½ feet (*mean*). Guns: **4**—4·7 inch, **1**—3 inch AA., **6** smaller. Tubes: **4**—21 inch. Machinery: Parsons geared turbines. S.H.P. 34,000 = 36 kts. Boilers: 3 Admiralty 3-drum type. Oil fuel: 455 tons. Cost averages just over £300,000 apiece.

Name	*Begun*	*Launch*	*Comp.*
Gallant	15/9/34	26/9/35	25/2/36

Gipsy, Glowworm, Grafton, Grenade, Grenville (Ldr.), *Greyhound.* Two others transferred to R. Canadian Navy.

Observe replacement of after torpedo tubes by a 3-inch AA. gun. 1941, *Official.*

1 Admiralty Type Leader.

FAULKNOR. (This type of mainmast has been fitted to a number of other destroyers recently.) 1942, *Official.*

1 *Yarrow:* **Faulknor.**

Displacement: 1,460 tons. Complement: 175. Dimensions: 322 (*pp.*), 340 (*w.l.*) × 33¾ × 8[illegible] feet (*mean*). Guns: **5**—4·7 inch, **6** smaller. Tubes: **4**—21 inch (quadrupled). Machinery: Parsons geared turbines. S.H.P.: 38,000 = 36·75 kts. Boilers: 4 Admiralty 3-drum type, 300 lbs. working pressure. Oil fuel: 490 tons. Cost: £330,239.

Est.	*Name*	*Begun*	*Launch*	*Comp.*
1932	*Faulknor*	31/7/33	12/6/34	24/5/35

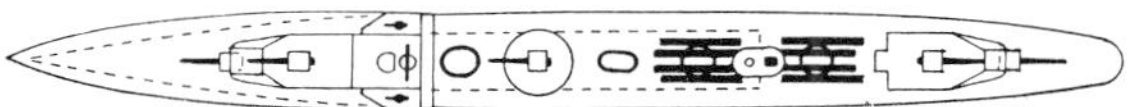

FAULKNOR.

"Escapade" Class.

FORESTER. 1943, *Official.*

Plan of "E," "F," "G" and "H" classes.

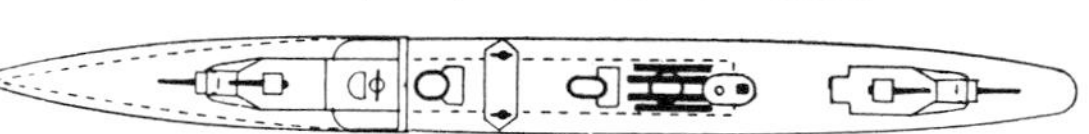

Programme 1932 { 2 *White.* **Forester, Fury.** 1 *Vickers-Armstrongs (Barrow):* **Fame.**

Programme 1931 1 *Scotts.* **Escapade.**

Displacement: *Escapade*, 1,375 tons, others, 1,350 tons.
Complement: 145.
Guns: **4**—4·7 inch. **1**—3 inch AA. **6** smaller.
Tubes: **4**—21 inch.
2 D.C. Throwers.

Dimensions: 318¼ (*p.p.*), 326 (*w.l.*), 329 (*o.a.*) × 33¼ × 8½ feet (*mean*).
Parsons geared Turbines (by Parsons Co. in *Fame;* and by Builders in others). S.H.P.: 36,000 = 36 kts.
Boilers: 3 Admiralty 3-drum type, working at 300 lbs. pressure with 200° superheat.
Oil fuel: 480 tons.

General Note.—Average cost approaches £300,000 apiece. Annual maintenance (direct expenditure), £41,000. Other ships of this type are serving in R. Canadian Navy and R. Hellenic Navy. War losses: *Fearless, Firedrake, Foresight, Eclipse, Electra, Encounter, Escort, Esk, Exmouth* (Ldr.).

Engineering Notes.—Average speed of class on trials with designed horse power was 36·7 kts. Some reported to have reached 38 kts. Radius at 15 kts., 6,000 miles.

Name	*Begun*	*Launch*	*Completed*	*Name*	*Begun*	*Launch*	*Completed*
Forester	15/5/33	28/6/34	29/3/35	*Fame*	5/7/33	28/6/34	26/4/35
Fury	19/5/33	10/9/34	18/5/35	*Escapade*	30/3/33	30/1/34	3/9/34

2 Admiralty Type Leaders.

1 *Portsmouth Dockyard:* **Duncan.**

Displacement: 1,400 tons. Dimensions: 317¾ (*pp.*), 326 (*w.l.*) × 33 × 8⅔ feet (*mean*). Guns: **4**—4·7 inch, **6** smaller. Tubes: **4**—21 inch (quadrupled). Machinery: Parsons geared turbines. S.H.P.: 36,000 = 35·75 kts. Boilers: Admiralty 3-drum type, 300 lbs. working pressure. Oil fuel: 470 tons. Complement: 175. Cost £302,904.

Est.	*Name*	*Begun*	*Launch*	*Comp.*
1930	*Duncan*	3/9/31	7/7/32	5/4/33

1942, *Official.*

Destroyers

CODRINGTON. 1930 *Photo, Abrahams, Devonport.*

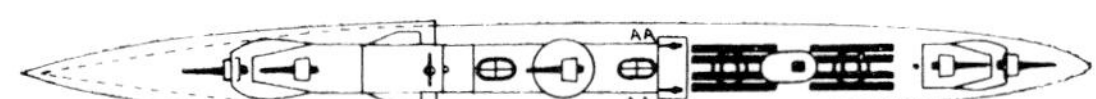

Codrington. Built by Swan Hunter. Laid down, 1928; launched, August 7, 1929. Completed. June, 1930. Displacement: 1540 tons standard. 2000 tons full load. Dimensions: 332 × 33¾ × 12¼ feet (*max.*), 9 feet (*mean*). Guns: 5—4·7 inch, 6 smaller. Tubes: 8—21 inch on quadruple mounts. Machinery: Parsons geared turbines. 2 shafts. Designed S.H.P.: 39,000 = 35 kts. Boilers: 4 Admiralty 3-drum, working pressure 300 lbs., with superheaters. Oil fuel: 500 tons. Complement: 185.

2 "A" Type.

AMAZON.

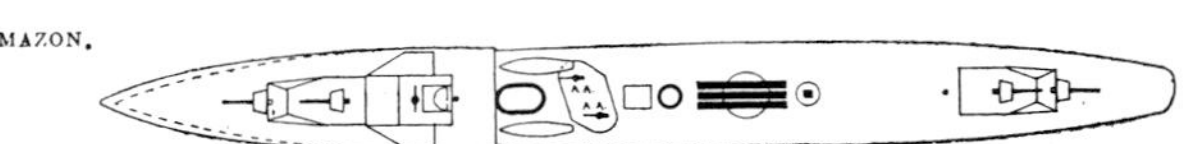

Appearance Note.—Forecastle continues well abaft bridge in these 2 ships, distinguishing them from other classes.

1 *Thornycroft*: ***Amazon*** (Jan. 27th, 1926). Displacement: 1350 tons. Dimensions: 311¾ (*pp.*) × 31½ × 9½ feet (*mean* draught).

1 *Yarrow*: ***Ambuscade*** (Jan. 15th, 1926). Displacement: 1170 tons. Dimensions: 307 (*pp.*) × 31 × 8¼ feet (*mean* draught).

AMAZON. 1935, *R. Perkins.*

AMBUSCADE. 1942, *Official.*

Guns: 4—4·7 inch, 1—3 inch AA., 6 smaller. Tubes: 3—21 inch in triple mounting. Machinery: Brown-Curtis turbines (all-geared type) H.P. and cruising; Parsons L.P. Boilers: Admiralty 3-drum type, by Builders. Designed S.H.P.: 39,500 (*Amazon*), 33,000 (*Ambuscade*) = 37 kts. (made on trials). Superheated steam. Oil: *Amazon*, 433 tons; *Ambuscade*, 385 tons. Complement: 138.

Notes.—Built under 1924-25 Estimates. All-steel bridges, higher freeboard and improved cabin accommodation are features of this and later types, which possess a larger radius of action than preceding classes. If necessary, induced ventilation can be supplied throughout the vessel, with a view to possible service in Tropics. *Ambuscade* laid down December 8th, 1924; *Amazon* in January, 1925. Both completed Sept., 1926. Cost: *Amazon*, £319,455; *Ambuscade*, £326,616.

11 Admiralty "Modified W."

1 *Swan Hunter*: ***Whitshed.***
4 *White*: ***Witherington, Wivern, Wolverine, Worcester.*** (Last ship completed by Portsmouth D.Y.)

To distinguish.—Proportions of funnels reversed compared with other V's and W's. These ships have *thick* fore funnel and *thin* after funnel. 2 pdr. pom-poms *en echelon* between funnels. White ships have plain S.L. tower without compass platform on fore side. *Witherington* and *Wivern*, only, have oval after funnel, built in sideways.

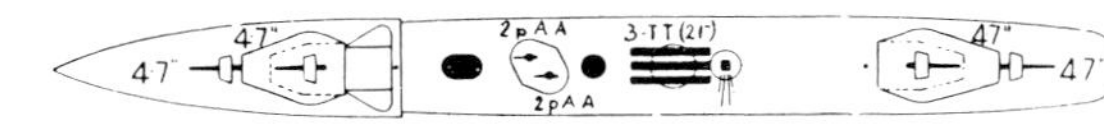

WHITSHED. FIVE, APPEARANCE AS ABOVE PHOTO:— 1943, *Official.*

VENOMOUS (VOLUNTEER, and possibly others, have had forefunnel removed). *Added*, 1943.

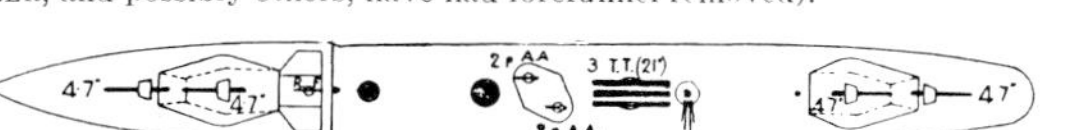

SIX, APPEARANCE AS ABOVE PHOTO:—

1 *Beardmore*: ***Vansittart.*** 2 *Clydebank*: ***Venomous*** (ex *Venom*), ***Verity.*** 1 *Denny*: ***Volunteer.***
1 *Fairfield*: ***Wanderer.*** 1 *Swan Hunter*: ***Whitehall.*** (Completed by Chatham D.Y.)

To distinguish.—Difficult to distinguish from V's and Admiralty W's, before latter were rearmed. Only *Venomous* and *Verity* have compass platform forward of S.L. tower.

Particulars of both Types.

Displacement: 1120 tons (1500 tons *full load*). Dimensions: 300 (*p.p.*), 312 (*o.a.*) × 29½ × 10[illegible] feet (*mean*) draught. Guns: 3—4·7 inch, 1—3 inch AA., 2—2 pdr. pom-poms, 1 M.G., 4 Lewis. Tubes: 3—21 inch, in triple mounting. Machinery: Turbines (all-geared type)—all Brown-Curtis, but *Whitehall*, Parsons. Designed S.H.P. 27,000 = 31 kts. 2 screws. Boilers: Yarrow, except White boats with White-Forster. Oil: 374-353/324-318 tons; *Whitehall*, 368/318. Complement, 134.

Notes.—Begun under War Emergency Programme, 1918, cost of completion coming under post-war Estimates.

	Begun.	Launch	Comp.		Begun.	Launch.	Comp.
Whitshed	6/18	31/1/19	11/7/19	*Venomous*	31/5/18	21/12/18	6/19
Witherington ..	27/9/18	16/4/19	10/10/19	*Verity*	17/5/18	19/3/19	17/9/19
Wivern	19/8/18	16/4/19	23/12/19	*Volunteer*	16/4/18	17/4/19	7/11/19
Wolverine	8/10/18	17/7/19	27/7/20	*Wanderer*	1918	1/5/19	18/9/19
Worcester	20/12/18	24/10/19	20/9/22	*Whitehall*	6/18	11/9/19	9/7/24
Vansittart	1/7/18	17/4/19	5/11/19				

2 Thornycroft "Modified W" Type.

WISHART. 1942, *Lieut.-Com. W. A. Fuller, R.N.V.R.*

2 *Thornycroft*: **Wishart, Witch.** Displacement: 1140 tons (1550 *full load*). Dimensions: 300 (*p.p.*), 312 (*o.a.*) × 30 ft. 7 ins. × 10 ft. 11 ins. Guns: 4—4·7 inch (DIR. CON.), 2—2 pdr. pom-poms, some smaller. Torpedo tubes: 3—21 inch. Machinery: Brown-Curtis turbines (all-geared type). 2 shafts. Boilers: 3 Thornycroft. Designed S.H.P.: 30,000 = 32 kts. Oil fuel: 374/322 tons. Complement: 134.

General Notes.—Begun under Emergency War Programme. Differ from Admiralty "Modified W's" in dimensions, H.P., speed and a few other details. *Witch* completed by Devonport D.Y.

To distinguish.—Big, flat-sided fore funnel, set well aft of bridges, both funnels nearly equal in height. Hull stands high out of water. (Plans generally as for *Wolverine* in preceding column.)

	Begun.	Launch.	Comp.
Wishart ..	6/18	18/7/19	6/20
Witch	6/18	11/11/19	3/24

2 Thornycroft "V."

2 *Thornycroft*: **Viceroy, Viscount.**

Displacement: 1,120 tons. Dimensions: 300 (*pp.*), 312 × 30½ × 7¾ feet (*mean* draught). Guns: 4—4 inch, several smaller. Tubes: 3—21 inch in triple mounting. Machinery: Brown-Curtis geared turbines. 2 shafts. S.H.P.: 30,000 = 31 kts. Boilers: 3 Thornycroft. Oil fuel: 374/322 tons. Complement: 134.

	Begun.	Launch.	Completed.
Viceroy	12/16	17/11/17	1/18
Viscount	12/16	29/12/17	3/18

1 Thornycroft Leader.

KEPPEL. 1942, *Official.*

1 *Thornycroft*: **Keppel.** Displacement: 1,480 tons. Dimensions: 318¼ (*pp.*), 329 (*o.a.*) × 31 ft. 9 in. × 12½ feet (*mean*), 14¾ (*max.*) draught. Guns: 4—4·7 inch, 1—3 inch AA., several smaller. Tubes: 6—21 inch in triple deck mounting. Machinery: Brown-Curtis all geared turbines. Designed S.H.P.: 40,000 = 31 kts. 2 shafts. Boilers: Thornycroft. Oil: 500/250 tons. Complement: 183.

General Notes.—Built under War Emergency Programme. Appearance almost exactly same as *Campbell* class, but for the usual big, flat-sided Thornycroft funnels. *Keppel* was completed at Portsmouth and Pembroke. *Cancelled* 1918: *Saunders, Spragge, Barrington, Hughes.* Scrapped: *Shakespeare, Spenser. Broke* lost in 1942. *Wallace*, of this type, rearmed for escort duties, 1939, will be found in a later column. First cost: over £400,000 per ship.

5 Campbell Class (Leaders).

DOUGLAS. 1942, *Official.*

4 *Cammell Laird*: **Campbell, Douglas, Mackay** (ex *Claverhouse*), **Malcolm.**
1 *Hawthorn Leslie*: **Montrose.**

Note.—*Stuart*, of this class, transferred to R.A.N. *Bruce* scrapped. *Scott* lost, 1918.

Displacement: 1530 tons. Dimensions: 320 (*p.p.*), 332½ (*o.a.*) × 31¾ × 12¼ feet (*max.*), 9¼ feet (*mean*) draught. Guns: 4—4·7 inch, 1—3 inch AA., with several smaller. Tubes: 3—21 inch, in triple mounting. Machinery: Parsons (all-geared) turbines in Cammell-Laird ships; Brown-Curtis in *Montrose*. Designed S.H.P.: 40,000 = 31 kts. Boilers: Yarrow. Oil fuel: 504/401 tons. Complement: 183.

Name.	Begun.	Launch.	Comp.	Name.	Begun.	Launch.	Comp.
Keppel	11/18	16/9/20	15/4/25	*Mackay*	5/3/18	21/12/18	6/19
Campbell	10/11/17	21/9/18	21/12/18	*Malcolm*	27/3/18	29/5/19	14/12/19
Douglas	30/6/17	8/6/18	30/8/18	*Montrose*	4/10/17	10/6/18	14/9/18

1942, *Official.*

Wallace (Thornycroft, Oct. 26, 1918). Displacement: 1,250 tons. Dimensions: 318¼ (*pp.*), 329 (*o.a.*) × 31¾ × 12¼ (*mean*), 14¾ feet (*max.*) draught. Guns: 4—4 inch H.A., 2 multi-M.G., etc. Machinery: Brown-Curtis geared turbines. S.H.P.: 20,000 = 28 kts. Boilers: Thornycroft. Oil fuel: 550 tons (*max.* stowage).

Note:—Was originally (and may still be) fitted as Leader.

WOLSEY. 1942, *Official.*

2 *Thornycroft*: **Wolsey** (March 16, 1918), **Woolston** (Jan. 27, 1918). Displacement: 920 tons. Dimensions: 300 (*pp.*), 312 (*o.a.*) × 30½ × 10¾ feet (*mean* draught). Guns: 4—4 inch H.A., 2 multi-M.G., etc. Machinery: Brown-Curtis geared turbines. S.H.P.: 18,000 = 28 kts. Boilers: 2 Thornycroft. Oil fuel: 374 tons.

VERDUN. 1943, *Official.*

(Additional illustrations on following page.)

3 *Doxford*: **Vega** (Sept. 1, 1917), **Velox** (Nov. 17, 1917), **Walpole** (Feb. 12, 1918).
3 *Beardmore*: **Vanessa** (March 16, 1918), **Vanity** (May 3, 1918), **Vimy** (ex-*Vancouver*) (Dec. 28, 1917).
1 *Fairfield*: **Wolfhound** (March 14, 1918).
2 *White*: **Winchester** (Feb. 1, 1918), **Winchelsea** (Dec. 15, 1917).
2 *Scotts*: **Westminster** (Feb. 24, 1918), **Windsor.**
1 *Swan Hunter*: **Wrestler** (Feb. 25, 1918).
3 *Denny*: **Valorous** (May 8, 1917), **Walker** (Nov. 29, 1917), **Westcott** (Feb. 14, 1918).
2 *Yarrow*: **Vivien** (Feb. 16, 1918), **Vivacious** (Nov. 3, 1917).
3 *Clydebank*: **Vanoc** (June 14, 1917), **Vanquisher** (Aug. 18, 1917), **Watchman** (Dec. 2, 1917).
2 *Hawthorn Leslie*: **Verdun** (Aug. 21, 1917), **Versatile** (Oct. 31, 1917).
2 *Stephen*: **Vesper** (Dec. 15, 1917), **Vidette** (Feb. 28, 1918).

Displacement (as refitted): 900 tons. Dimensions: 300 (*pp.*), 312 (*o.a.*) × 29½ × 10¾ feet (*mean*). Guns: 4—4 inch H.A., several smaller. Machinery: Brown-Curtis geared turbines in all except *Vega, Wrestler*, which have Parsons. S.H.P.: 18,000 = 28 kts. Boilers: 28 Yarrow in all except *Winchester* and *Winchelsea*, with White-Forster. Oil fuel: 360-370 tons.

War losses, "W" and "V" types: *Valentine, Venetia, Veteran, Vimiera, Vortigern, Wakeful, Warwick, Whirlwind, Wessex, Whitley, Wild Swan, Wren, Wryneck.*

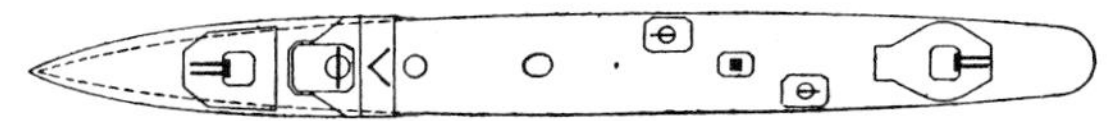

Destroyers

7 Admiralty "S" Class.
(Mostly fitted for minelaying).

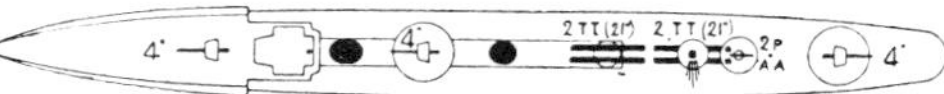

SCIMITAR. 1942, *Official.*

3 *Stephen:* **Sabre** (Sept. 23, 1918), **Saladin** (Feb. 17, 1919), **Sardonyx** (May 27, 1919).
2 *Clydebank:* **Scimitar** (Feb. 27, 1918), **Scout** (April 27, 1918).
1 *Doxford:* **Shikari** (July 14, 1919).
1 *Hawthorn Leslie:* **Tenedos** (Oct. 21, 1918).

Displacement: 905 tons. Dimensions: 265 (*pp.*), 276 (*o.a.*) × $26\frac{3}{4}$ × $10\frac{1}{8}$ feet (*mean*) draught. Guns: 2—4 inch, 1—3 inch AA., several smaller. Tubes: 2—21 inch in pair. Nearly all now fitted for minelaying. Machinery: Brown-Curtis turbines (all-geared type). Designed S.H.P.: 27,000 = 31 kts. 2 shafts. 3 Yarrow boilers. Oil: 301/254 tons. Complement: 98.

General Notes.—Emergency War Programme, 1918; but cost of completion of about 45 ships included in post-war Estimates. *Shikari* was completed by Chatham D.Y., 1922. Rest completed 1918–19. War losses: *Stronghold, Sturdy, Thanet, Thracian.*

1 Admiralty "R."

SKATE. 1942, *Official.*

1 *Clydebank:* **Skate** (Jan. 11, 1917).

Displacement: 900 tons. Length (*p.p.*), 265 feet (*o.a.* 276 feet). Beam, $26\frac{3}{4}$ feet. *Mean* draught, $10\frac{3}{4}$ feet. *Max.* draught, 15 feet. Guns: **3**—4 inch, **1**—2 pdr. pom-pom, **1** M.G., **4** Lewis. Torpedo tubes: **4**—21 inch in pairs. (Present armament uncertain). Machinery: Brown-Curtis A.G. turbines. Designed S.H.P. 27,000 = 31 kts. 2 shafts. Boilers: 3 Modified Yarrow. Oil fuel: 301–285 tons. Complement, 98.

3 Leeds Class

LEEDS (LUDLOW similar.) 1943, *Official.*

("TOWN" CLASSES—35 SHIPS OF "FLUSH DECK" DESIGN.)

These are ex-U.S. destroyers transferred to the Royal Navy under the Anglo-American Agreement of September 2, 1940. All are four-funnelled vessels with the exception of *Leeds* and *Ludlow*, which have only three funnels. *Churchill* is understood to be fitted as Leader. Two of these ships (*Lincoln* and *St. Albans*) are manned by the Royal Norwegian Navy, where they are now listed. Seven others are in R. Canadian Navy.

14 Burnham Class

BURWELL. (*Bradford* and *Clare* have only 2 funnels.) 1942, *Official.*

Bradford (ex-*McLanahan*) (Sept 22, 1918). **Broadway** (ex-*Hunt*) (Feb. 14, 1920). **Burnham** (ex-*Aulick*), (April 11, 1919). **Burwell** (ex-*Laub*) (Aug. 25, 1918). **Buxton** (ex-*Edwards*)(Oct. 10, 1918). **Cameron** (ex-*Welles*) (May 8, 1919). **Chesterfield** (ex-*Welborn C. Wood*) (March 6, 1920). **Churchill** (ex-*Herndon*) (May 31, 1919). **Clare** (ex-*Abel P. Upshur*) (Feb. 14, 1920). **Ramsey** (ex-*Meade*) (May 24, 1919). **Reading** (ex-*Bailey*) (Feb. 5, 1919). **Ripley** (ex-*Shubrick*) (Dec. 31, 1918). **Rockingham** (ex-*Swasey*) (May 7, 1919). **Sherwood** (ex-*Rodgers*, ex-*Kalk*) (April 26, 1919).

Displacement: 1,190 tons. Dimensions: 311 (*w.l.*) × $30\frac{2}{3}$ × $9\frac{1}{4}$ feet (*mean* draught). Machinery: Curtis or Westinghouse geared turbines, 2 shafts. Boilers: 4 White-Forster or Yarrow. S.H.P. 27,000 = 35 kts. Oil fuel: 375 tons.

10 Montgomery Class

Caldwell (ex-*Hale*) (May 29, 1919). **Castleton** (ex-*Aaron Ward*) (April 10, 1919). **Chelsea** (ex-*Crowninshield*) (July 24, 1919). **Lancaster** (ex-*Philip*) (July 25, 1918). **Leamington** (ex-*Twiggs*) (Sept. 28, 1918). **Mansfield** (ex-*Evans*) (Oct. 30, 1918). **Montgomery** (ex-*Wickes*) (June 25, 1918). **Richmond** (ex-*Fairfax*) (Dec. 15, 1917). **Salisbury** (ex-*Claxton*) (Jan. 15, 1919). **Wells** (ex-*Tillman*) (July 7, 1919).

Displacement: 1,090 tons. Dimensions: 309 (*w.l.*) × $30\frac{1}{2}$ × $8\frac{2}{3}$ feet (*mean*). Machinery: Parsons geared turbines. 2 shafts. S.H.P. 24,200 = 35 kts. Boilers: 4 Thornycroft, White-Forster or Normand. Oil fuel: 375 tons.

8 Newport Class

BRIGHTON. 1942, *Official.*

Brighton (ex-*Cowell*) (Nov. 23, 1918). **Charlestown** (ex-*Abbot*) (July 4, 1918). **Georgetown** (ex-*Maddox*) (Oct. 27, 1918). **Newark** (ex-*Ringgold*) (April 14, 1918). **Newmarket** (ex-*Robinson*) (March 28, 1918). **Newport** (ex-*Sigourney*) (Dec. 16, 1917). **Roxborough** (ex-*Foote*) (Dec. 14, 1918). **St. Mary's** (ex-*Doran*, ex-*Bagley*) (Oct. 19, 1918).

Displacement: 1,060 tons. Dimensions: 309 (*w.l.*) × $30\frac{1}{2}$ × $8\frac{1}{2}$ feet (*mean*). Machinery: Parsons or Curtis geared turbines. 2 shafts. S.H.P. 24,200 = 35 kts. Boilers: 4 Thornycroft, Yarrow or Normand. Oil fuel: 300 tons.

NEWARK. (Described in preceding column.) 1942, *Official.*

Leeds (ex-*Conner*) (Aug. 21, 1917). **Ludlow** (ex-*Stockton*) (July 17, 1917). **Lewes** (ex-*Conway*, ex-*Craven*) (June 29, 1918).

Displacement: 1,020 tons. Dimensions: 308 (*w.l.*) × $30\frac{2}{3}$ × $7\frac{1}{2}$ feet (*mean* draught). Machinery: Parsons turbines (geared only in *Lewes*). 3 shafts, except *Lewes*, 2. S.H.P.: 18,000 = 30 kts. Boilers: 4 White-Forster, except *Lewes*, 4 Thornycroft. Oil fuel: 290 tons.

Notes—All these ships are named after towns and villages common to the United Kingdom and the United States, and in some instances common to Newfoundland or the West Indies as well. When acquired all were armed with **4**—4 inch, 50 cal., **2**—·50 inch AA. and **12**—21 inch torpedo tubes (tripled), but this armament is understood to have been modified. *Bradford* and *Clare*, for example, have been rearmed for escort duties. Illustrations show only 6 tubes. War losses comprise *Belmont, Beverley, Broadwater, Campbeltown, Stanley*, as well as *Bath*, manned by R. Norwegian Navy.

Submarines

3 *Cammell Laird:* **Æneas** (Oct. 25, 1945), **Affray** (April 12, 1944), **Alaric** (Feb. 20, 19..

2 *Scotts:* **Artemis, Artful.**

10 *Vickers-Armstrongs (Barrow):* **Alcide** (April 12, 1945), **Alderney** (June 25, 1945), **Alliance** (July 28, 1945), **Ambush** (Sept. 24, 1945), **Amphion** (ex-*Anchorite*, Aug. 31, 1944), **Anchorite** (ex-*Amphion*, Jan. 22, 1946), **Andrew** (April 6, 1946), **Astute** (Jan. 30, 1945), **Auriga** (March 29, 1945), **Aurochs** (July 28, 1945).

1 *Chatham Dockyard:* **Acheron** (March 25, 1947).

Displacement: 1,120/1,620 tons. Dimensions: $279\frac{1}{4}$ (*pp.*), $281\frac{2}{3}$ (*o.a.*) × $22\frac{1}{4}$ × 17 feet. Guns: **1**—4 inch d.p., **1**—20 mm. AA., **3** M.G. Tubes: **10**—21 inch (4 external). 20 torpedoes carried. Machinery: Diesels and electric motors. H.P.: 4,300/1,250 = 19/8 kts. Fuel: 159 tons. Complement: 60.

Notes.—These submarines are understood to have been designed for service in the Pacific, and have a different hull form from "T" type. Construction is all-welded, and some are reported to have been painted a deep shade of sea-green, possibly for experimental purposes. Following 30 units were cancelled, though some had actually been launched: *Abelard, Acasta, Ace, Achates, Adept, Admirable, Adversary, Agate, Aggressor, Agile, Aladdin, Alcestis, Andromache, Answer, Antaeus, Antagonist, Anzac, Aphrodite, Approach, Arcadian, Ardent, Argosy, Asgard, Asperity, Assurance, Astarte, Atlantis, Austere, Awake, Aztec.*

16 "A" Class.

ASTUTE. 1946, *Wright & Logan.*

26 "T" Class.

4 *Chatham Dockyard:* **Thermopylae, Tradewind, Trenchant, Turpin.**

4 *Devonport Dockyard:* **Thule, Totem, Truncheon, Tudor.**

2 *Portsmouth Dockyard:* **Tireless, Token.**

1 *Scotts:* **Tabard.**

15 *Vickers-Armstrongs (Barrow):* **Taciturn, Tactician, Tallyho, Tantalus, Tantivy, Tapir, Taurus, Telemachus, Templar, Teredo, Thorough, Tiptoe, Trespasser, Truculent, Trump.**

Displacement: 1,090/1,575 tons. Complement: 59. Dimensions: 265 (*pp.*), 273½ (*o.a.*) × 26½ × 12 feet. Guns: **1**—4 inch d.p., **1**—20 mm. AA., **3** M.G. Tubes: **9** to **11**—21 inch (5 external). 17 torpedoes carried. H.P.: 2,500/1,450 = 15·25/9 kts. Fuel: 132/210 tons.

Notes.—Officially described as "Patrol type" submarines, for general service. Saddle-tank design, with endurance equal to a 42-day patrol. War losses: *Talisman* (Cammell Laird), *Tarpon, Tempest, Tetrarch, Thistle, Thorn, Thunderbolt* (Cammell Laird), *Tigris* (Chatham), *Traveller* (Scotts), *Triad, Triton, Triumph* (all 3 V.-A.), *Turbulent, P* 311 (both Vickers-Armstrongs), *Trooper*. Cancelled: *Talent* (ex-*Tasman*), *Theban, Thor, Threat, Tiara*. Others scrapped.

TRUCULENT. 1946, *Wright & Logan.*

Name	Begun	Launch	Completed	Name	Begun	Launch	Completed
Tabard	/44	21/11/45	46	*Tantivy*	4/7/42	6/4/43	26/7/43
Trespasser	8/9/41	29/5/42	25/9/42	*Telemachus*	25/8/42	19/6/43	25/10/43
Taurus	30/9/41	27/6/42	3/11/42	*Thorough*	26/10/42	30/10/43	29/2/44
Tactician	13/11/41	29/7/42	29/11/42	*Tiptoe*	10/11/42	25/2/44	13/6/44
Truculent	4/12/41	12/9/42	31/12/42	*Trump*	31/12/42	25/3/44	9/7/44
Templar	28/12/41	26/10/42	15/2/43	*Taciturn*	9/3/43	7/6/44	7/10/44
Tallyho	25/3/42	23/12/42	11/4/43	*Tapir*	29/3/43	21/8/44	30/12/44
Tantalus	6/6/42	24/2/43	2/6/43	*Teredo*	17/4/44	27/4/45	5/4/46

THULE *Added* 1946.

39 "S" Class.

Note.—*Seadog, Seanymph, Shalimar, Stoic, Stygian, Supreme* may be discarded in near future.

SCEPTRE. (3 inch gun.) 1943, *Official.*

SIDON. (4 inch gun.) 1946, *Wright & Logan*

Name	Begun	Launch	Completed
Sealion	16/5/33	16/3/34	21/12/34
Seawolf	25/8/34	28/11/35	12/3/36
Seraph	16/8/40	25/10/41	10/6/42
Sea Rover	42	18/2/43	7/7/43
Sirdar	42	26/3/43	18/9/43

2 *Chatham Dockyard:* **Shalimar, Sportsman** (ex-*P* 229).

24 *Cammell Laird:* **Saga, Sanguine, Scorcher, Seadog** (ex-*P* 216), **Sealion, Seanymph** (ex-*P* 223), **Sea Scout, Selene, Sibyl** (ex-*P*217), **Sidon, Sleuth, Solent, Spearhead, Spirit, Springer, Spur, Statesman, Stoic, Storm, Sturdy, Stygian, Subtle, Supreme, Surf.**

12 *Scotts:* **Satyr** (ex-*P* 214), **Sceptre, Scotsman, Scythian, Sea Devil, Sea Rover, Seawolf, Seneschal, Sentinel, Sirdar, Spark, Spiteful.**

1 *Vickers-Armstrongs (Barrow):* **Seraph** (ex-*P* 219).

Displacement: 715/1,000 tons, except *Sealion* and *Seawolf*, 670/960 tons. Complement: 44. Dimensions: 193 to 202½ (*pp.*), 217 (*o.a.*) × 23¾ × 10½ feet (*mean*). Guns: **1**—3 inch, **1**—20 mm. AA., **3** M.G. (In later units a 4 inch replaces the 3 inch.) Tubes: **6**—21 inch (bow), and **1** external. 13 torpedoes carried. H.P.: 1,900/1,300 = 14·5/10 kts. Fuel: 44 tons.

Notes.—Reputed to be very handy craft, capable of making a "crash-dive" in 30 seconds. Earlier units had 7 tubes, including one external at stern. Later units have slightly higher freeboard forward. *Sea Rover* and *Sirdar* were completed at Barrow. *Sceptre, Seraph, Solent* all reported to have been modified for experimental purposes. War losses: *Safari* (Cammell Laird), *Sahib, Salmon, Saracen, Seahorse, Shark, Sickle, Simoom, Snapper, Spearfish, Splendid, Starfish, Sterlet, Stonehenge* (Cammell Laird), *Stratagem, Swordfish, Syrtis, P* 222 (Vickers-Armstrongs). In addition, *Sunfish* was lost after transfer to Soviet Navy. Cancelled units: *Sea Robin, Sprightly, Surface, Surge* (all Cammell Laird).

SLEUTH 1947, *Wright & Logan.*

Submarines

8 Ex-German Types

U 3017. 1945, *Michael Crowdy, Esq.*

U 1171. 1945, *J. W. Kennedy, Esq.*

Ex-German U 190, 712, 953, 1108, 1171, 1407, 2348, 3017 are still in service, being used for experimental purposes; but it is not intended to retain them permanently.

Midget Types

1946, *Wright & Logan.*

XE 1-12 were in service when war ended.
Displacement: 30/34 tons. Dimensions: 53 × 5¾ × — feet. One Gardner engine and one electric motor. H.P. 42/30 = 6·5/6 kts. Complement: 3. Those with prefix XT are understood to be training vessels.

11 "V" Class.

VORACIOUS. 1944, *Official.*

7 *Vickers-Armstrongs (Barrow)*: **P 67** (ex-*Curie*, ex-*Vox*), **Urtica, Vampire, Vigorous, Virtue, Visigoth, Vox.**

4 *Vickers-Armstrongs (Tyne)*: **Vagabond, Varne, Vivid, Voracious.**

Displacement: 545/740 tons. Dimensions: 200 × 16 × 14¾ feet. Guns: **1**—3 inch or 4 inch, **2**—20 mm. AA. (Some may mount **3**—40 mm. AA. as entire gun armament.) Tubes: **4**—21 inch (bow). 8 torpedoes carried. Machinery: 2 Davey Paxman Diesels, 2 electric motors. B.H.P.: 800/760 = 13/10 kts. Oil fuel: 56 tons.

Notes.—This type is a modification of "U" design, remarks concerning which apply also to these vessels. One has been lent to French Navy, and another is on charter to R. Danish Navy. War loss: *Vandal.* Cancelled: *Vantage, Vehement, Venom, Verve, Veto, Virile, Visitant.*

Name	*Begun*	*Launch*	*Completed*
P 67	29/4/42	23/1/43	2/5/43
Vampire	9/11/42	20/7/43	13/11/43
Vox	19/12/42	28/9/43	20/12/43
Virtue	17/2/43	29/11/43	29/2/44
Urtica	27/4/43	23/3/44	20/6/44
Vivid	27/10/42	15/9/43	19/1/44
Voracious	27/10/42	11/11/43	13/4/44
Varne	29/10/42	24/2/44	29/7/44
Vigorous	14/12/42	15/10/43	13/1/44
Visigoth	15/2/43	30/11/43	9/3/44
Vagabond	4/5/43	19/9/44	27/2/45

VARANGIAN. 1946, *Lieut. R. L. Cheesman, R.N.V.R.*

7 "U" Class.

Note.—Most of these are expected to be discarded in near future.

UNA. 1943, *Official.*

Name	*Begun*	*Launch*	*Completed*
Ultimatum	19/6/40	11/2/41	29/7/41
Unbending	30/8/40	12/5/41	5/11/41
Upshot	3/5/43	24/2/44	15/5/44
Uther	31/1/42	6/4/43	15/8/43
Unswerving	17/2/42	2/6/43	3/10/43
Varangian	23/12/41	4/3/43	10/7/43

1 *Chatham Dockyard*: **Una.**

3 *Vickers-Armstrongs (Barrow)*: **Ultimatum** (ex-*P* 34), **Unbending** (ex-*P* 37), **Upshot.**

3 *Vickers-Armstrongs (Tyne)*: **Unswerving, Uther, Varangian.**

Displacement: 540/730 tons. Complement: 31. Dimensions: 197 × 16 × 14¾ feet. Guns: **1**—3 inch, **3** M.G. Tubes: **4**—21 inch (bow). 8 torpedoes carried. Machinery: 2 Davey Paxman Diesels, 2 electric motors. B.H.P.: 615/825 = 11/9 kts. Oil fuel: 50 tons.

Notes.—A simple type, useful for A/S training and capable of being produced rapidly in large numbers. Several have been transferred to Allied Navies. Most of main ballast tank capacity is inside pressure hull. Propulsion differs from other types, there being no direct Diesel drive. Diesels drive electric generators, which charge batteries; there is therefore no great disparity in surface and submerged speeds. Three units lent to Soviet Navy, one chartered by R. Danish Navy.

War losses: *Umpire* (Chatham), *Unbeaten, Undaunted, Undine, Union, Unique, Unity, Upholder, Urge, Usk, Usurper, Utmost, Vandal, P32, P33, P36, P38, P39, P48* (all V.-A.). Cancelled: *Ulex, Unbridled, Upas, Upward, Utopia.*

Figure given for draught of submarines of "U" and "V" classes, 14¾ feet, should be 12¾ feet.

Submarines

Note.—The Italian submarine *Galileo Galilei* was captured at Aden in June 1940, and at submarine *U 570* was also made a prize.

Trident Class.

TAKU. 1943, *Official.*

1 *Chatham Dockyard :* **Torbay.**
2 *Vickers-Armstrongs :* **Truant, Trusty.**
3 *Cammell Laird :* **Trident, Taku, Thrasher.**
2 *Scotts :* **Tribune, Tuna.**
9 *Builders not reported :* **Tactician, Tallyho, Tantivy, Thorough, Tradewind, Trespasser, Truculent, Tudor, Typhoon.**

Displacement : 1,090/1,575 tons. Complement : 53. Dimensions : 265 (*pp.*), 275 (*o.a.*) × 26½ × 12 feet. Guns : **1**—4 inch, **2** smaller. Tubes : **10**—21 inch. H.P. : 2,500/1,450 = 15·25/9 kts. Fuel : 210 tons.

Notes.—Officially described as "Patrol type" submarines, for general service. A return to moderate dimensions is the outstanding feature. Cost averages just under £350,000. War losses : *Talisman, Tarpon, Tempest, Tetrarch, Thistle, Thorn, Thunderbolt* (Cammell Laird), *Tigris, Traveller* (Scotts), *Triad, Triton, Triumph, Trooper, Turbulent* (Vickers-Armstrongs).

Est.	*Name*	*Begun*	*Launch*	*Completed*
1936	*Tribune*	3/3/37	8/12/38	39
	Trident	12/1/37	7/12/38	39
1937	*Taku*	18/11/37	20/5/39	40
	Truant	24/3/38	5/5/39	40
	Tuna	13/6/38		40
1938	*Torbay*	21/11/38		40

UNSHAKEN. (Described in next column.) 1943, *Official.*

Ursula Class.

URSULA. *Added* 1940, *courtesy Vickers-Armstrongs, Ltd.*

UNA. 1943, *Official.*

5 *Vickers-Armstrongs :* **Ursula, Umbra** (ex-*P35*), **Unity, Unbroken** (ex-*P42*), **Unseen** (ex-*P51*).
14 *Builders not reported :* **Ullswater, Ultimatum** (ex-*P34*), **Una, Unbending** (ex-*P37*), **Unison** (ex-*P43*), **United** (ex-*P44*), **Universal** (ex-*P57*), **Unrivalled** (ex-*P45*), **Unruffled** (ex-*P46*), **Unruly** (ex-*P49*), **Unshaken** (ex-*P54*), **Unsparing** (ex-*P55*), **Upright, Uproar** (ex-*P31*).

Displacement : 540/730 tons. Complement : 27. Dimensions : 180 × 16 × 12¾ feet. Armament : 6—21 inch tubes, 1—3 inch gun. B.H.P. : 615/825 = 11·25/10 kts.

Programme	*Name*	*Begun*	*Launched*	*Completed*
1936	*Ursula*	19/2/37	16/2/38	22/12/38

Notes.—Earlier units cost slightly over £200,000 apiece. Majority built under War Construction programmes. *Umbra* first commissioned Aug. 27, 1941. War losses : *Unbeaten* (Vickers-Armstrongs), *Undaunted, Undine, Union, Unique* (V.-A.), *Upholder* (V.-A.), *Urge* (V.-A.), *Usk, Usurper, Utmost* (V.-A.), *P 48, P 38, P 33, P 32.*

2 Severn Class

SEVERN. 1935, *R. Perkins.*

2 *Vickers-Armstrongs :* **Severn, Clyde.**
Displacement : 1,850/2,723 tons. Complement : 60.
Dimensions : 325 × 28 × 13½ feet. *Clyde,* 325 × 28⅛ × 13¾ feet. (Both 345 feet *o.a.*)
Guns : **1**—4 inch, **2** M.G. Tubes : **6**—21 inch (bow).
Diesels, B.H.P. : 10,000 = 22·25 kts. on surface. Electric motors, H.P. : 2,500 = 10 kts. *submerged.* Fuel : 210 tons.

Notes.—These were the first Diesel-driven submarines to exceed 21 kts. Cost : *Clyde,* £459,886. *Severn,* just over £500,000. *Thames,* of this type, was lost early in the war.

Est.	*Name*	*Begun*	*Launch*	*Completed*
1931	*Severn*	27/3/33	16/1/34	2/35
1932	*Clyde*	15/5/33	15/3/34	4/35

2 Porpoise Class (Minelayers.)

PORPOISE. 1935, *R. Perkins.*

2 *Vickers-Armstrongs :* **Porpoise, Rorqual.**
Displacement : 1,520/2,157 tons, except *Porpoise,* 1,500/2,053 tons. Complement, 55.
Dimensions : 271½ × 25½ × 15 feet (*Porpoise,* 267 × 29⅚ × 13¾ feet) (*mean*). (Both 289 feet *o.a.*)
Guns : **1**—4 inch, **2** M.G. Tubes : **6**—21 inch (bow).
Diesels of B.H.P. 3,300 = 15·75 kts. surface. (*Porpoise,* 15 kts.).
Electric motors, H.P. 1,630 = 8·75 kts. submerged.
Fuel : 136 tons.

Notes.—Very successful ships. Cost : *Rorqual,* £350,639. War losses : *Cachalot, Grampus, Narwhal, Seal.*

Est.	*Name*	*Begun*	*Launch*	*Completed*
1930	*Porpoise*	22/9/31	30/8/32	25/4/33
1934	*Rorqual*	1/5/35	21/7/36	10/2/37

Sealion Class (Improved Sturgeon design).

SCEPTRE. 1943, *Official.*

1 *Chatham Dockyard :* **Sunfish.**
1 *Cammell Laird :* **Sealion.**
1 *Scotts :* **Seawolf.**
12 *Builders not reported :* **Safari** (ex-*P211*), **Sceptre** (ex-*P215*), **Seadog** (ex-*P216*), **Seanymph** (ex-*P223*), **Seraph** (ex-*P219*), **Shakespeare** (ex-*P221*), **Sibyl** (ex-*P217*), **Sickle** (ex-*P224*), **Sportsman** (ex-*P229*), **Storm, Stratagem, Stubborn.**

Displacement : 670/960 tons. Complement : 40.
Dimensions : 193 (*pp.*), 202½ (*w.l.*) × 24 × 10½ feet (*mean*).
Guns : **1**—3 inch, **1** M.G. Tubes : **6**—21 inch (bow).
H.P. : 1,550/1,300 = 13·75/10 kts., except *Sunfish,* 1,900/1,300 = 15/10 kts. Fuel : 40 tons.

Notes.—Reputed to be very handy craft, capable of making a "crash-dive" in 30 seconds. Cost ranges between £230,000 and £245,000. Annual maintenance (direct expenditure only), £23,200. War losses : *Sahib, Salmon, Saracen, Shark, Simoom, Snapper, Spearfish, Splendid, Sterlet, Stonehenge, Syrtis, P 222* (Vickers-Armstrongs).

Appearance Notes.—For differences, see silhouettes. Later units have slightly higher freeboard at bow.

SEAWOLF. 1941, *Central Press.*

1 *Chatham Dockyard :* **Sturgeon.**
Displacement : 640/927 tons. Complement : 40.
Dimensions : 187 (*pp.*), 200¾ (*w.l.*) × 23½ × 10⅓ feet (*mean*).
Guns : **1**—3 inch, **1** M.G. Tubes : **6**—21 inch (bow).
H.P. : 1550/1300 = 13·75/10 kts. Fuel : 44 tons.

War losses : *Seahorse, Starfish, Swordfish.*

Est.	*Name*	*Begun*	*Launch*	*Completed*
1929	*Sturgeon*	3/1/31	8/1/32	15/12/32
1931	*Sealion*	16/5/33	16/3/34	21/12/34
1933	*Seawolf*	25/8/34	28/11/35	12/3/36
1934	*Sunfish*	22/7/35	30/9/36	13/3/37

Submarines

Proteus Class

ROVER. 1935, *Wright & Logan.*

3 *Vickers-Armstrongs:* **Rover** (June 11, 1930), **Proteus** (July 23, 1929), **Pandora** (ex-*Python*) (Aug. 22, 1929).

Displacement: 1475/2040 tons (*Rover*, 1475/2030 tons). Armament: **1**—4 inch gun, **2** M.G., **8**—21 inch tubes. Fuel: 159 tons (*Rover*, 156 tons). Complement, 50. Dimensions: 260 (*pp.*), 290 (*o.a.*) × 28 × 13⅜ ft. (*mean*). Designed H.P. $\frac{4400}{1350} = \frac{17\cdot5}{9}$ kts. (*Rover*, H.P. 4400/1320).

General Notes.—*Pandora* and *Proteus* laid down 1928 under 1927 Estimates *Rover* in 1929 under those for 1928. Generally resemble *Oberon* class, with slightly greater length and other improvements. Completed during 1930 (first two) and in Jan. 1931 (*Rover*). *Poseidon* lost in collision June 9th, 1931. War losses: *Rainbow, Regent, Regulus, Parthian, Perseus, Phoenix.*

4 Oberon Class.

Appearance Notes.—Three differing types of "O" series can be distinguished by shape of bows. *Oberon* has bow and C.T. screen as shown in photo. *Otway* is the only unit of this class with net cutters at bows.

OBERON. 1936, *Wright & Logan.*

1 *Chatham Dockyard:* **Oberon** (ex-*O* 1, Sept. 24th, 1926). Displacement 1311/1831 tons. Dimensions: 270 (*o.a.*) × 28 × 13¼ feet (mean). H.P.: 2,950/1,350 = 15/9 kts. Fuel: 185 tons.

1 *Vickers-Armstrongs:* **Otway** (ex-*AO* 2, Sept. 7, 1926). Completed in 1927. Displacement: 1,349/1,872 tons. Dimensions: 275 (*o.a.*) × 27¾ × 13½ feet (*mean*). H.P.: $\frac{3000}{1350} = \frac{15\cdot5}{9 \text{ kts.}}$ Fuel: 195 tons.

Following details are common to both above vessels: Complement: 54. Guns: **1**—4 inch, **2** M.G. Tubes: **8**—21 inch (6 bow, 2 stern).

2 *Vickers-Armstrongs:* **Osiris** (May 19th, 1928), **Otus** (Aug. 31st, 1928).

Displacement: 1475/2038 tons. Dimensions: 260 (*pp.*), 283½ (*o.a.*) × 28 × 13½ feet draught. Guns: **1**—4 inch, **2** M.G. Tubes: **8**—21 inch (6 bow, 2 stern). Designed H.P. 4400/1320 = 17·5/9 kts. Oil fuel: 200 tons. Complement, 50.

Notes.—*Oberon* laid down in March, 1924, under 1923 Estimates, and completed in Sept. 1926. *Otway* completed in June, 1927, for the Royal Australian Navy and presented to the Royal Navy in 1931. *Osiris* and *Otus* built under 1926 Estimates. War losses: *Odin, Olympus, Orpheus, Oswald, Oxley.*

OTWAY 1935, *R. Perkins.*

Midget Type.

X TYPE. 1943, *Official.*

All are distinguished by numerals prefaced by the letter X, and appear to be about 40 feet in length. Complement at least 3.

War losses: *X* 6, *X* 7 and another.

3 "L" Class.

L 23. 1938, *Wright & Logan.*

3 *Vickers* (Completed by Dockyards): **L 23, L 26, L 27,** (1918–19).

Admiralty saddle-tank type. Displacement: 760/1,080 tons. Dimensions: 229 (*pp.*), 238½ (*o.a.*) × 23½ × 13¾ feet. Complement: 39. Armament: **1**—4 inch, **1** M.G., and **4**—21 inch tubes. Machinery: 2 sets 12-cylinder solid injection Vickers type Diesels. H.P.: 2,400/1,600 = 17·5/10·5 kts. Fuel: 70 tons.

Notes.—All begun under Emergency War Programme, 1916. Breastwork revolves with gun. *L* 10 War loss. *L* 24 rammed off Portland, January, 1924. *L* 9 foundered in 1923, but was salved; since sold. Above 3 submarines are the sole survivors of a once very numerous class, with the exception of *L* 55 in Soviet Navy.

P 552. No particulars published.

P 512. *Added* 1943.

P 511 (ex-*R*3) (Jan. 18, 1919). Transferred from U.S. Navy in Nov., 1941. Electric Boat Co. design. Displacement: 530/680 tons. Dimensions: 179 (*w.l.*), 186 (*o.a.*) × 17½ × 13⅔ feet (*mean*). Armament: **1**—3 inch gun, **4**—21 inch tubes. Machinery: 2 sets 6-cylinder 4-cycle Nelseco Diesels and 2 Electric Dynamic Co. Motors. B.H.P.: 880/934 = 13·5/10 kts. Complement, 27.

P 512. No particulars published, but also appears to be of American type.

Note—Following submarines with "*P*" prefix, of unstated types, have been lost during the War: *P* 615 (Vickers-Armstrongs), *P* 311.

7 "H" Class.

H 33. 1939, *Wright & Logan.*

H 33, 34 are only ones of class with flat-topped C.T.; *H* 43, 44 have right-angled after screen to C.T., instead of curved as in others.

2 *Vickers:* **H 28, H 32** (both 1918).
2 *Armstrong Whitworth:* **H 43, H 44** (both 1919).
2 *Cammell Laird:* **H 33, H 34** (both 1918).
1 *Beardmore:* **H 50** (1919).

Single-hull "Holland" (Electric Boat Co.) type modified by Admiralty. Displacement, 410/500 tons. Dimensions: 164½ (*p.p.*), 170 (*o.a.*) × 15¾ × 12½ feet. Tubes: **4**—21 inch bow. Machinery: 2 sets of Diesel engines, 8 cylinder, 4-cycle, air injection "H" type, each developing 240 B.H.P. at 375 r.p.m., and built by Vickers, North British Diesel Co., Ruston & Hornsby, &c. Oil: 16 tons. H.P. 480/320 = 13/10·5 kts. **1** M.G. Complement, 22. (All used for training.)

Notes.—All built under 1914–1918 War Emergency Programme. First vessel was delivered in January, 1918, and *H* 44 last, in March, 1920. *H* 29 sank in dock at Devonport, August, 1926, and disposed of in consequence. *H* 42 lost 1922; *H* 47 sunk by collision with *L* 12, July, 1929. *H* 21, *H* 22, *H* 23, *H* 24, *H* 25, *H* 26, *H* 27, *H* 30, *H* 41, *H* 48, *H* 51, *H* 52 all scrapped. War losses: *H* 49, *H* 31.

18 Modified Black Swan Class.

MODESTE. 1946, *Wright & Logan.*

1 *Cammell Laird:* **CYGNET** (July 28, 1942).
2 *Chatham Dockyard:* **MODESTE, NEREIDE** (both Jan. 29, 1944).
7 *Denny:* **ALACRITY** (Sept. 1, 1944), **CRANE** (Nov. 11, 1942), **HIND** (Sept. 30, 1943), **MERMAID** (Nov. 11, 1943), **OPOSSUM** (Nov. 30, 1944), **SNIPE, SPARROW.**
1 *Fairfield:* **STARLING** (Oct. 14, 1942).
2 *Stephen:* **AMETHYST** (May 7, 1943), **HART** (July 7, 1943).
3 *Thornycroft:* **ACTAEON** (July 25, 1945), **MAGPIE** (March 24, 1943), **PEACOCK** (Dec. 11, 1943).
2 *Yarrow:* **PHEASANT** (Dec. 21, 1942), **REDPOLE** (Feb. 25, 1943).

Displacement: 1,430 to 1,490 tons (actual), 1,350 tons (designed). Dimensions: $299\frac{1}{2} \times 38 \times 8\frac{3}{4}$ feet. Guns: **6**—4 inch d.p., **8**—2 pdr. pompoms, etc. Exceptionally complete Asdic equipment and Denny-Brown roll reducer. Machinery: Parsons geared turbines. S.H.P.: 4,300 = 20 kts. Boilers: 2, of 3-drum type. Complement: 192.

Notes.—Owing to large amount of extra equipment added, these ships have not proved quite so satisfactory in service as original *Black Swan* type, and have required a certain amount of strengthening. *Starling* has discarded armament while employed as Navigation School tender, vide photo. War losses: *Kite* (Cammell Laird), *Lapwing*, *Lark* (both Scotts), *Chanticleer* (Denny). Cancelled ships: *Nonsuch*, *Nymphe*, *Partridge*, *Waterhen*, *Wryneck*.

STARLING 1946, *Wright & Logan.*

1 *Thornycroft:* **PELICAN** (Sept. 12, 1938).

Displacement: 1,250 tons. Complement: 188. Dimensions: 276 (*w.l.*) $\times 37\frac{1}{2} \times 8\frac{1}{4}$ feet (*mean*). Guns: **8**—4 inch d.p., **7** smaller. Machinery: Parsons single reduction geared turbines. 2 shafts. S.H.P.: 3,600 = 19·25 kts. Boilers: 2 Admiralty 3-drum type. Oil fuel.

Note.—Laid down in Sept., 1937, under Estimates for that year, and completed in April, 1939. Sister ships *Auckland* and *Egret* became war losses.

Added 1944, Official.

7 Black Swan Class.

WILD GOOSE. 1946, *London Studio.*

4 *Yarrow:* **BLACK SWAN** (July 7, 1939), **FLAMINGO** (April 18, 1939), **WHIMBREL** (Aug. 25, 1942), **WILD GOOSE** (Oct. 14, 1942).
1 *Furness S.B. Co.:* **ERNE** (Aug. 5, 1940).
1 *Denny:* **WREN** (Aug. 11, 1942). 1 *Fairfield:* **WOODCOCK** (Nov. 26, 1942).

Displacement: 1,470 tons (actual), 1,300 tons (designed). Dimensions: $299\frac{1}{2} \times 38 \times 8\frac{1}{2}$ feet. Guns: **6**—4 inch d.p., **10** smaller. Machinery: Geared turbines (by Richardson, Westgarth & Co. in *Erne*). S.H.P.: 3,600 = 19·25 kts. Boilers: 2, of 3-drum type. Complement: 180.

Note.—*Black Swan* laid down June 20, 1938; *Flamingo*, May 26, 1938, both under 1937 Estimates; *Erne* (to become R.N.V.R. drillship, Southampton) Sept. 21, 1939, under that year's Estimates. This design has proved most successful in service. *Whimbrel*, *Wild Goose*, *Woodcock*, and *Wren*, though officially counted as units of *Black Swan* class, are practically indistinguishable from modified *Black Swan* type as completed. War losses: *Ibis*, *Woodpecker*.

STORK. 1946, *Wright & Logan.*

1 *Denny:* **STORK** (April 21, 1936).

Displacement: 1,190 tons. Complement: 125. Dimensions: 266 (*w.l.*) $\times 37 \times 8\frac{1}{4}$ feet (*mean*). Guns: 4—4 inch d.p., 2—20 mm. AA. Machinery: Parsons geared turbines. S.H.P. 3,300 = 18·75 kts. Boilers: 2 Admiralty 3-drum type. Oil fuel: 270 tons.

Note.—*Stork* was built under 1934 Estimates as a Surveying Vessel at a cost of £160,392, but was refitted as a Sloop in 1939. Armament modified 1946 by removal of "A" mounting on selection for duty as S.O. ship, Fishery Protection and Minesweeping Flotillas. Sister ship *Bittern* is a war loss.

2 Aberdeen Class

ABERDEEN. (Mainmast now struck and after superstructure reduced.) 1936.

2 *Devonport Dockyard:* **ABERDEEN** (Jan. 22, 1936), **FLEETWOOD** (March 24, 1936).

Displacement: 990 tons. Dimensions: 250 (*pp.*), 262 (*w.l.*), 266 (*o.a.*) $\times 36 \times 7\frac{1}{2}$ feet (*mean*). Guns: **4**—4 inch AA., **2**—20 mm. AA., **1** hedgehog. Machinery: 2 sets Parsons geared turbines. S.H.P.: 2,000 = 16·5 kts. Boilers: 2 Admiralty 3-drum type. Oil fuel: 280 tons. Complement, 100.

Notes.—Built under 1934 Estimates. Are improvements on the *Leith* design, closely resembling Australian sloops *Yarra* and *Swan*. *Aberdeen* carried only two 4-inch guns before war. *Fleetwood* has had armament removed and bridge structure extended to provide extra accommodation while employed as Radar Experimental Ship, attached to Signal School.

Sloops

1943, *Official.*

1 *Devonport Dockyard :* **LEITH** (Sept. 9, 1933).

Displacement : 990 tons. Dimensions : 250 (*pp.*), 262 (*w.l.*), 266 (*o.a.*) × 34 × $7\frac{1}{4}$ (*mean*), $8\frac{3}{4}$ feet (*max*). Guns : 2—4·7 inch, 1—3 inch AA., etc. Machinery : 2 sets Parsons geared turbines by J. S. White & Co., Ltd. S.H.P. : 2,000 = 16·5 kts. Boilers : 2 Admiralty 3-drum type. Oil fuel : 275 tons. Complement : 100.

Notes.—Built under 1931 Estimates. War loss : *Grimsby.*

5 Older Types.

2 *Devonport :* **FALMOUTH** (April 19, 1932), **MILFORD** (June 11, 1932).
Displacement : 1,060 tons. Dimensions : 250 (*pp.*), 266 (*o.a.*) × 34 × $8\frac{3}{4}$ feet.

1 *Chatham :* **ROCHESTER** (July 16, 1931).
Displacement : 1,105 tons. Dimensions : 250 (*pp.*), 266 (*o.a.*) × 34 × 9 feet.

1 *Swan Hunter :* **SCARBOROUGH** (March 14, 1930).

1 *Hawthorn Leslie :* **SANDWICH** (Sept. 28, 1928).
Displacement : 1,045 tons. Dimensions : 250 (*pp.*), 266 (*o.a.*) × 34 × $8\frac{1}{4}$ feet (*mean*).

Following particulars apply to all : Guns : Originally, **2**—4 inch AA., **9** to **13** smaller. Various modifications made since. Machinery : Parsons impulse reaction turbines (single reduction gearing). 2 shafts. 2 Admiralty 3-drum type boilers, pressure 250 lbs. Designed S.H.P. : 2,000 = 16 kts. Oil : 275 tons. Complement : 100. All are fitted for minesweeping. *Sandwich* built under 1927 Estimates and completed March, 1929. Under 1928 Estimates : *Scarborough*, completed 1930–31. Under 1929 Estimates : *Rochester*, now attached to Navigation School. Under 1930 Estimates : *Falmouth*, *Milford*, both R.N.V.R. drillships. War losses : *Dundee*, *Penzance.*

2 Ex-German Escort Vessels.

F2, F4 (1935). Displacement : 600 tons. Dimensions : 241 (*pp.*), $249\frac{1}{3}$ (*o.a.*) × $28\frac{2}{3}$ × $8\frac{1}{4}$ feet (*mean*). Guns : 2—4·1 inch, **4**—37 mm. AA., **2** M.G. Machinery : Geared turbines. 2 shafts. S.H.P. : 9,000 = 26 kts. Boilers : 4 Wagner. Oil fuel : 245 tons. Complement : 124.

Frigates

22 "Bay" Class.

St. Bride's Bay. 1944, *Official.*

7 *Harland & Wolff :* **ST. AUSTELL BAY** (ex-*Loch Lydoch*, Nov. 18, 1944), **ST. BRIDE'S BAY** (ex-*Loch Achillty*, Jan. 16, 1945), **START BAY** (ex-*Loch Arklet*, Feb. 15, 1945), **TREMADOC BAY** (ex-*Loch Arnish*, March 29, 1945), **WHITSAND BAY** (ex-*Loch Lubnaig*, Dec. 16, 1944), **WIDEMOUTH BAY** (ex-*Loch Frisa*, Oct. 19, 1944), **WIGTOWN BAY** (ex-*Loch Garasdale*, April 26, 1945).

3 *Charles Hill & Sons :* **BURGHEAD BAY** (ex-*Loch Harport*, March 3, 1945), **PORLOCK BAY** (ex-*Loch Seaforth*, ex-*Loch Muick*, June 14, 1945), **VERYAN BAY** (ex-*Loch Swannay*, Nov. 11, 1944).

4 *Pickersgill :* **LARGO BAY** (ex-*Loch Fionn*, Oct. 3, 1944), **LUCE BAY** (ex-*Loch Glass*, Oct. 3, 1944), **MOUNTS BAY** (ex-*Loch Kilbirnie*, June 8, 1945), **PEGWELL BAY** (ex-*Loch Mochrum*, Sept. 1, 1945).

3 *Robb :* **CARDIGAN BAY** (ex-*Loch Laxford*, Dec. 28, 1944), **CARNARVON BAY** (ex-*Loch Maddy*, March 15, 1945), **PADSTOW BAY** (ex-*Loch Coulside*, Aug. 23, 1945).

2 *Smith's Dock :* **ENARD BAY** (ex-*Loch Bracadale*, Oct. 31, 1944), **SURPRISE** (ex-*Gerrans Bay*, ex-*Loch Carron*, March 14, 1944).

2 *Blyth S.B. Co. :* **ALERT** (ex-*Dundrum Bay*, ex-*Loch Scamadale*, July 10, 1945), **CAWSAND BAY** (ex-*Loch Roan*, Feb. 26, 1945).

1 *Hall Russell :* **BIGBURY BAY** (ex-*Loch Carloway*, Nov. 16, 1944).

Displacement : 1,600 tons. Dimensions : $307\frac{1}{3}$ × $38\frac{1}{2}$ × $12\frac{3}{4}$ feet. Guns : **4**—4 inch d.p., **8**—40 mm. AA., **2**—20 mm. AA., **1** or **2** hedgehogs (see Notes below). Machinery : Triple expansion. 2 shafts. I.H.P. : 5,500 = 19·5 kts. Boilers : 2 Admiralty 3-drum type. Oil fuel : 720 tons. Complement : 157.

Note.—Designed primarily for AA. escort duties. Have shown excellent sea-keeping qualities in spite of considerable top weight carried, having ridden out China Sea typhoons without mishap. *Alert* and *Surprise*, refitted for service as Commanders-in-Chief's yachts on China and Mediterranean Stations, respectively, have large deckhouses aft, extending from mainmast to stern, and mount a single 4-inch forward. Cancelled ships : *Hollesley Bay* (ex-*Loch Fannich*), *Morecambe Bay* (ex-*Loch Heilen*), *Runswick Bay*, *Thurso Bay* (ex-*Loch Muick*).

25 "Loch" Class.

Loch Dunvegan. 1944, *courtesy Messrs. Charles Hill & Sons.*

2 *Ailsa S.B. Co. :* **LOCH TARBERT** (Oct. 19, 1944), **LOCH VEYATIE** (Oct. 8, 1945).
1 *Barclay Curle :* **LOCH ALVIE** (April 14, 1944).

1 *Blyth S.B. Co. :* **LOCH QUOICH** (Sept. 2, 1944).
3 *Burntisland S.B. Co. :* **LOCH FYNE** (May 24, 1944), **LOCH GLENDHU** (Oct. 18, 1944), **LOCH KILLIN** (Nov. 29, 1943).
4 *Caledon S.B. Co. :* **LOCH ARKAIG** (June 7, 1945), **LOCH LOMOND** (June 19, 1944), **LOCH MORE** (Oct. 3, 1944), **LOCH TRALAIG** (Feb. 12, 1945).
1 *Clydebank :* **LOCH FADA** (Dec. 14, 1943).
3 *Harland & Wolff :* **LOCH CRAGGIE** (May 23, 1944), **LOCH GORM** (June 8, 1944) (both completed at Clydebank), **LOCH KILLISPORT** (July 6, 1944).
3 *Charles Hill & Sons :* **LOCH DUNVEGAN** (March 25, 1944), **LOCH RUTHVEN** (June 3, 1944), **LOCH SCAVAIG** (Sept. 9, 1944).
3 *Robb :* **LOCH ACHANALT** (ex-*Naver*, March 23, 1944), **LOCH INSH** (May 10, 1944), **LOCH KATRINE** (Aug. 21, 1944).
2 *Smith's Dock :* **LOCH ACHRAY** (July 7, 1944), **LOCH ECK** (April 25, 1944).
2 *Swan Hunter :* **LOCH MORLICH** (Jan. 25, 1944), **LOCH SHIN** (Feb. 23, 1944).

Displacement : 1,435 tons. Dimensions : 307 × $38\frac{1}{2}$ × 12 feet. Guns : **1**—4 inch d.p., **4**—2 pdr. pompoms, **10**—20 mm. AA. (some have **2**—40 mm., **6**—20 mm.), **2** squids. Machinery : Triple expansion (but *Loch Arkaig* and *Loch Tralaig* have double reduction geared turbines). 2 shafts. I.H.P. : 5,500 = 19·5 kts. (2 turbine ships are reported to have reached 21 kts.). Boilers : 2 Admiralty 3-drum type. Complement : 103.

Notes.—Two ships of this class, the former *Loch Assynt* and *Loch Torridon*, were converted into depot and repair ships and renamed *Derby Haven* and *Woodbridge Haven* respectively. Three are in S. African N.F. Cancelled names were *Loch Affric, Loch Awe, Loch Badcall, Loch Caroy, Loch Clunie, Loch Creran, Loch Doine, Loch Earn, Loch Enoch, Loch Ericht, Loch Erisort, Loch Eye, Loch Eynort, Loch Garve, Loch Glashan, Loch Goil, Loch Griam, Loch Harray, Loch Hourn, Loch Inchard, Loch Ken, Loch Kirbister, Loch Kirkaig, Loch Kishorn, Loch Knockie, Loch Lano, Loch Linfern, Loch Linnhe, Loch Lurgan, Loch Lyon, Loch Maberry, Loch Minnick, Loch Nell, Lock Odairn, Loch Ossain, Loch Ronald, Loch Ryan, Loch Scrivain, Loch Sheallag, Loch Shell, Loch Skaig, Loch Skerrow, Loch Stemster, Loch Stenness, Loch Striven, Loch Sunart, Loch Swin, Loch Tanna, Loch Tilt, Loch Tummell, Loch Urigill, Loch Vanavie, Loch Vennacher, Loch Watten.*

Frigates

36 "River" Class.

Note.—Fal is being transferred to Burmese Government.

3 *Blyth S.B. Co.:* **BALLINDERRY** (Dec. 7, 1942), **DART** (Oct. 10, 1942), **RIBBLE** (ex-*Duddon*, Nov. 10, 1943).

1 *Geo. Brown & Co.:* **CHELMER** (March 27, 1943).

1 *John Crown & Sons:* **ETTRICK** (Feb. 5, 1943).

3 *Fleming & Ferguson:* **AWE** (Dec. 28, 1943), **DOVEY** (ex-*Lambourn*, Oct. 14, 1943), **EXE** (March 19, 1942).

4 *Hall, Russell & Co.:* **HELFORD** (Feb. 6, 1943), **LOCHY** (Oct. 30, 1943), **TEES** (May 20, 1943), **TEVIOT** (Oct. 12, 1942).

4 *Charles Hill & Sons:* **AVON** (June 19, 1943), **JED** (July 30, 1942), **TAFF** (Sept. 11, 1943), **TAVY** (April 3, 1943).

4 *A. & J. Inglis, Ltd.:* **HALLADALE** (Jan. 28, 1944), **HELMSDALE** (June 5, 1943), **KALE** (June 24, 1942), **MEON** (Aug. 4, 1943).

4 *Henry Robb, Ltd.:* **DERG** (Jan. 7, 1943), **NESS** (July 30, 1942), **NITH** (Sept. 25, 1942), **WYE** (Aug. 16, 1943).

12 *Smith's Dock Co., Ltd.:* **FAL** (Nov. 9, 1942), **NENE** (Dec. 9, 1942), **ODZANI** (May 19, 1943), **PLYM** (Feb. 4, 1943), **ROTHER** (Nov. 20, 1941), **SPEY** (Dec. 18, 1941), **SWALE** (Jan. 16, 1942), **TAY** (March 18, 1942), **TOWY** (March 4, 1943), **USK** (April 3, 1943), **WAVENEY** (April 30, 1942), **WEAR** (June 1, 1942).

Displacement: 1,460 tons (actual), 1,370 tons (designed). Dimensions: $301\frac{1}{3} \times 36\frac{2}{3} \times 12$ feet. Guns: 2—4 inch d.p., 10—20 mm. AA., 1 hedgehog. Machinery: Geared turbine in *Chelmer, Ettrick, Halladale, Helmsdale*, triple expansion in others. 2 shafts. H.P.: 5,500 = 20 kts. Boilers: 2 Admiralty 3-drum type. Complement: 140.

Notes.—These ships have shown very good endurance and sea-keeping qualities. Some of earlier units tended to develop structural weakness and had to be strengthened. In several, 20 mm. have been replaced by 40 mm. *Ribble* transferred to R. Netherland Navy; *Annan* and *Monnow* to R. Danish Navy; *Braid, Frome, Moyola, Strule, Torridge, Windrush* to French Navy; *Bann, Test, Trent, Deveron* and *Nadder* to R. Indian Navy. War losses: *Itchen* (Fleming & Ferguson), *Mourne, Tweed* (Inglis). Scrapped as result of heavy damage: *Cam* (Geo. Brown), *Lagan, Teme* (Smith's Dock).

HELMSDALE. (Several have cinder screen as in this ship.) 1944, *courtesy Messrs. A. & J. Inglis, Ltd.*

NESS. 1942, *Official.*

NENE. 1943, *Official.*

PARRET. 1944, *Lieut. D. Trimingham, R.N.V.R.*

Corvettes

24 "Castle" Class.

1 *Ailsa S.B. Co.:* **TINTAGEL CASTLE** (Dec. 13, 1943).

1 *S. P. Austin & Son, Ltd.:* **AMBERLEY CASTLE** (Nov. 27, 1943).

1 *Barclay Curle:* **BERKELEY CASTLE** (Aug. 19, 1943).

2 *Blyth S.B. Co.:* **KNARESBOROUGH CASTLE** (Sept. 29, 1943), **LAUNCESTON CASTLE** (Nov. 27, 1943).

1 *Geo. Brown & Co.:* **ALNWICK CASTLE** (May 23, 1944).

2 *Caledon S.B. Co.:* **CARISBROOKE CASTLE** (July 31, 1943), **DUMBARTON CASTLE** (Sept. 28, 1943).

2 *John Crown & Sons:* **FARNHAM CASTLE** (April 25, 1944), **HEDINGHAM CASTLE** (ex-*Gorey Castle*, Oct. 30, 1944).

2 *Fleming & Ferguson:* **ALLINGTON CASTLE** (ex-*Amaryllis*, Feb. 29, 1944), **LANCASTER CASTLE** (April 14, 1944).

2 *Harland & Wolff:* **OXFORD CASTLE** (Dec. 11, 1943), **PEVENSEY CASTLE** (Jan. 11, 1944).

1 *A. & J. Inglis, Ltd.:* **OAKHAM CASTLE** (July 20, 1944).

2 *John Lewis & Sons:* **BAMBOROUGH CASTLE** (Jan. 11, 1944), **CAISTOR CASTLE** (May 22, 1944).

2 *Wm. Pickersgill & Sons:* **LEEDS CASTLE** (Oct. 12, 1943), **MORPETH CASTLE** (Nov. 26, 1943).

1 *Henry Robb, Ltd.:* **FLINT CASTLE** (Sept. 1, 1943).

2 *Smith's Dock Co., Ltd.:* **HADLEIGH CASTLE** (June 21, 1943), **KENILWORTH CASTLE** (Aug. 17, 1943).

2 *Swan Hunter:* **PORTCHESTER CASTLE** (June 21, 1943), **RUSHEN CASTLE** (July 15, 1943).

HADLEIGH CASTLE. 1946, *Wright & Logan.*

Displacement: 1,060 to 1,100 tons. Dimensions: 252 (*o.a.*) $\times 36\frac{2}{3} \times 13\frac{1}{2}$ feet (*mean*), $15\frac{3}{4}$ feet (*max*). Guns: 1—4 inch d.p., 6 to 10—20 mm. AA., 1 squid. Machinery: Triple expansion. I.H.P.: 2,880 = 16·5 kts. Boilers: 2 Admiralty 3-drum type.

Corvettes

LANCASTER CASTLE. 1944, *Official.*

Notes.—Smith's Dock Co., Ltd., were largely responsible for design of these ships, which represented a very definite improvement on the "Flower" type. *Shrewsbury Castle* transferred to R. Norwegian Navy and lost. Twelve more turned over to R. Canadian Navy. War losses: *Denbigh Castle, Hurst Castle* (Caledon). *Maiden Castle, Scarborough Castle, Rayleigh Castle, York Castle* were completed as Rescue ships *Empire Lifeguard, Empire Peacemaker, Empire Rest* and *Empire Comfort*, respectively. Others either cancelled, or not completed as warships, were *Alton Castle, Appleby Castle, Aydon Castle, Barnard Castle, Barnwell Castle, Beeston Castle, Bere Castle, Bodiam Castle, Bolton Castle, Bowes Castle, Bramber Castle, Bridgnorth Castle, Brough Castle, Caldecot Castle, Calshot Castle, Canterbury Castle, Carew Castle, Chepstow Castle, Chester Castle* (Collingwood Shipyards), *Christchurch Castle, Clare Castle, Clavering Castle, Clitheroe Castle, Clun Castle, Colchester Castle, Corfe Castle, Cornet Castle, Cowes Castle, Cowling Castle, Criccieth Castle, Cromer Castle, Devizes Castle, Dover Castle, Dudley Castle, Dunster Castle, Egremont Castle, Fotheringay Castle, Helmsley Castle, Malling Castle, Malmesbury Castle, Monmouth Castle, Norwich Castle, Oswestry Castle, Pendennis Castle, Raby Castle, Rhuddlan Castle, Thornbury Castle* (ordered from Ferguson Bros.), *Tonbridge Castle, Trematon Castle, Tutbury Castle, Warkworth Castle, Wigmore Castle.* One of these, built by George Brown & Co., became Rescue ship *Empire Shelter.*

---

22 "Flower" Class.

Note.—Majority of these ships are expected to be sold; others, deleted from here, have already been discarded, placed on disposal list, or utilised for non-naval purposes.

1943, *Official.*

1 *John Crown & Sons:* **HELIOTROPE** (ex-U.S.S. *Surprise*, ex-*Heliotrope*, June 5, 1940).

1 *Ferguson Bros.:* **JASMINE** (Jan. 14, 1941).

1 *Fleming & Ferguson:* **MONKSHOOD** (April 17, 1941).

1 *Grangemouth Dockyard Co.:* **CELANDINE** (Dec. 28, 1940).

1 *Alexander Hall & Co.:* **HYDERABAD** (ex-*Nettle*, Sept. 23, 1941).

2 *Hall, Russell & Co.:* **MARGUERITE** (July 8, 1940), **MIGNONETTE** (Jan. 28, 1941).

4 *Harland & Wolff:* **CAMELLIA** (May 4, 1940), **COWSLIP** (May 28, 1941), **HIBISCUS** (ex-U.S.S. *Spry*, ex-*Hibiscus*, April 6, 1940), **MALLOW** (ex-*Nada*, ex-*Mallow*, May 22, 1940).

3 *Charles Hill & Sons:* **COLUMBINE** (Aug. 13, 1940), **MEADOWSWEET** (March 28, 1942), **ROCKROSE** (July 26, 1941).

1 *A. & J. Inglis:* **SPIRAEA** (Oct. 31, 1940).

1 *John Lewis & Sons:* **DAHLIA** (Oct. 31, 1940).

1 *Philip & Son:* **NIGELLA** (Sept. 21, 1940).

1 *Wm. Simons & Co.:* **VIOLET** (Dec. 30, 1940).

2 *Smith's Dock Co.:* **NASTURTIUM** (ex-*La Paimpolaise*, July 4, 1940), **TULIP** (Sept. 4, 1940).

2 *Canadian built:* **BITTERSWEET** (Sept. 12, 1940), **FENNEL** (Aug. 20, 1940).

Displacement: 925 tons. Complement: 85. Dimensions: 190 (*pp.*), 205 (*o.a.*) × 33 × 14½ feet. Guns: **1**—3 or 4 inch d.p., **1** pompom, **2** to **6**—20 mm., **1** hedgehog. Machinery: Triple expansion. I.H.P.: 2,750 = 16 kts. Boilers: In majority, 2 S.E.; but one or two may have 2 Admiralty 3-drum type. Oil fuel: 232 tons.

2 Modified "Flower" Class.

1 *Ferguson Bros.:* **BURNET** (ex-H.M.I.S. *Gondwana*, ex-H.M.S. *Burnet*, May 31, 1943).

1 *A. Hall & Co.:* **BETONY** (ex-H.M.I.S. *Sind*, ex-H.M.S. *Betony*, April 22, 1943).

Displacement: 980 tons. Complement: 85. Dimensions: 193 (*pp.*), 208¼ (*o.a.*) × 33 × 13¾ feet (*mean*). Guns: **1**—4 inch d.p., **2**—20 mm. AA., **1** hedgehog. Machinery: Triple expansion. I.H.P.: 2,880 = 16 kts. Boilers: 2 of 3-drum type. Fuel: 282 tons.

Notes.—Two corvettes of this type have been transferred to R. Indian Navy, and two to R. New Zealand Navy. Differences between these ships and original "Flower" class are largely internal.

Notes.—Smith's Dock Co., Ltd., were responsible for the original design of "Flower" type, which could be quickly and easily built and is inexpensive to operate. Under 1939 Supplementary Estimates 56 of them were built; later programmes nearly trebled this figure. Various units have been transferred to the R. Danish, French, R. Hellenic, and R. Norwegian Navies, in which they will be found. Cancelled ships: *Gloriosa, Harebell, Hemlock, Ivy, Ling, Marjoram.* War losses: *Arbutus* (Blyth), *Asphodel, Auricula* (both Geo. Brown & Co.), *Bluebell* (Fleming & Ferguson), *Erica* (Harland & Wolff), *Fleur de Lys, Gardenia* (Simons), *Gladiolus, Godetia* (first of name), *Hollyhock* (Crown), *Marigold* (Hall, Russell), *Orchis, Picotee* (both Harland & Wolff), *Polyanthus* (Robb), *Salvia, Samphire* (Smith's Dock), *Snapdragon* (Simons), *Vervain* (Harland & Wolff), *Zinnia.* In addition, *Pink* (Robb) had to be scrapped owing to heavy damage.

---

1 Kingfisher Class.

KINGFISHER (Feb. 14, 1935). Built by Fairfield.

Displacement: 510 tons. Complement: 60. Dimensions: 234 (*pp.*), 240 (*w.l.*), 243⅙ (*o.a.*) × 26½ × 6 feet (*mean*). Guns: **1**—4 inch AA., **8** smaller. Machinery: Parsons geared turbines. S.H.P.: 3,600 = 20 kts. Boilers: 2 Admiralty 3-drum type. Fuel: 160 tons.

Notes.—Survivor of a group of nine. *Pintail* became a war loss; others have been discarded.

KINGFISHER (Bridge now covered in.) 1935, *R. Perkins, Esq.*

81 Algerine Class.

2 *Blyth S.B. & D.D. Co.:* **BRAVE** (April 3, 1943), **FANCY** (April 5, 1943).

1 *Fleming & Ferguson:* **COCKATRICE** (Oct. 27, 1942).

22 *Harland & Wolff:* **ACUTE** (ex-*Alert*, April 14, 1942), **ALBACORE** (April 2, 1942), **CADMUS** (May 27, 1942), **CHAMELEON** (May 6, 1944), **CHEERFUL** (May 22, 1944), **CIRCE** (June 27, 1942), **ESPIEGLE** (Aug. 12, 1942), **FANTOME** (Sept. 22, 1942), **HARE** (June 20, 1944), **JEWEL** (July 20, 1944), **LIBERTY** (Aug. 22, 1944), **MUTINE** (Oct. 10, 1942), **ONYX** (Oct. 27, 1942), **PICKLE** (Aug. 3, 1943), **PINCHER** (Aug. 19, 1943), **PLUCKY** (Sept. 29, 1943), **READY** (Jan. 11, 1943), **RECRUIT** (Oct. 26, 1943), **RIFLEMAN** (Nov. 25, 1943), **RINALDO** (March 20, 1943), **ROSARIO** (April 3, 1943), **SPANKER** (April 20, 1943).

RINALDO. 1946, *Wright & Logan.*

17 *Lobnitz:* **BRAMBLE** (Jan. 26, 1945), **FIERCE** (Sept. 11, 1945), **FLY** (June 1, 1942), **HOUND** (July 29, 1942), **HYDRA** (Sept. 29, 1942), **LENNOX** (Oct. 15, 1943), **NIGER** (ex-*Disdain*, May 1, 1945), **ORESTES** (Nov. 25, 1942), **PELORUS** (June 18, 1943), **RATTLESNAKE** (Feb. 23, 1943), **ROWENA** (June 5, 1944), **STORMCLOUD** (Dec. 28, 1943), **SYLVIA** (Feb. 28, 1944), **TANGANYIKA** (April 12, 1944), **WATERWITCH** (April 22, 1943), **WAVE** (Aug. 18, 1944), **WELCOME** (Nov. 14, 1944).

10 *Port Arthur Shipyards:* **LYSANDER** (ex-*Hespeler*, Nov. 11, 1943), **MARINER** (ex-*Kincardine*, May 9, 1944), **MARMION** (ex-*Orangeville*, June 15, 1944), **ORCADIA** (Aug. 8, 1944), **OSSORY** (Oct. 3, 1944), **PLUTO** (Oct. 21, 1944), **POLARIS** (Dec. 13, 1944), **PYRRHUS** (May 19, 1945), **ROMOLA** (May 19, 1945), **ROSAMUND** (Dec. 20, 1944).

29 *Redfern Construction Co.:* **COQUETTE** (ex-*Bowmanville*, Nov. 24, 1943), **COURIER** (ex-*Arnprior*, Dec. 22, 1943), **FLYINGFISH** (ex-*Tillsonburg*, Feb. 16, 1944), **GOLDEN FLEECE** (ex-*Humberstone*, Feb. 29, 1944), **JASEUR** (April 19, 1944), **LAERTES** (March 25, 1944), **LIONESS** (ex-*Petrolia*, March 15, 1944), **MÆNAD** (June 8, 1944), **MAGICIENNE** (June 24, 1944), **MAMELUKE** (July 19, 1944), **MANDATE** (Aug. 9, 1944), **MARVEL** (Aug. 30, 1944), **MARY ROSE** (ex-*Toronto*, Aug. 5, 1943), **MELITA** (Dec. 8, 1942), **MICHAEL** (Sept. 20, 1944), **MINSTREL** (Oct. 5, 1944), **MOON** (ex-*Mimico*, Sept. 2, 1943), **MYRMIDON** (Oct. 21, 1944), **MYSTIC** (Nov. 11, 1944), **NERISSA** (Nov. 25, 1944), **OCTAVIA** (Dec. 31, 1942), **PROMPT** (ex-*Huntsville*, March 30, 1944), **PROVIDENCE** (ex-*Forest Hill*, Oct. 27, 1943), **SEABEAR** (ex-*St. Thomas*, Nov. 6, 1943), **SERENE** (ex-*Leaside*, Oct. 18, 1943), **SKIPJACK** (ex-*Solebay*, April 7, 1943), **THISBE** (April 12, 1943), **TRUELOVE** (July 8, 1943), **WELFARE** (July 15, 1943).

MARMION. 1946, *Wright & Logan.*

Displacement: 950 to 1,040 tons (actual), 850 tons (designed). Dimensions: 225 (*pp.*), 235 (*o.a.*) × 35½ × 10½ to 11½ feet max. Guns: **1**—4 inch d.p., **4**—40 or 20 mm. AA., **2** D.C.T. Machinery: Geared turbines in some, triple expansion in others. 2 shafts. H.P.: 2,000 = 16·5 kts. Boilers: 2 of 3-drum type. Complement: peace, 85; war, 104 to 138.

MUTINE. 1943, *Official.*

Notes.—Have been described as the fastest and most efficient minesweepers in the Royal Navy. Frequently used as escort vessels. *Lennox*, *Mariner*, *Marmion*, *Ossory*, *Romola*, *Wave* and *Welcome* are now doing duty as Fishery Protection Vessels. *Fierce*, employed as S.O. ship of M/S flotillas, has extra deckhouse aft. Cancelled ships: *Happy Return*, *Nicator*, *Nox*, *Styx*. War losses: *Alarm*, *Algerine*, *Loyalty* (all Harland & Wolff), *Regulus* (Redfern), *Squirrel*, *Vestal* (both Harland & Wolff). Probably owing to heavy damage, *Larne* and *Felicity* have been scrapped.

36 Bangor Class.

(Triple Expansion Type.)

2 *Blyth S.B. Co.:* **BLYTH** (Sept. 2, 1940), **PETERHEAD** (Oct. 31, 1940).

6 *Lobnitz:* **BUDE** (Sept. 4, 1940), **EASTBOURNE** (Nov. 5, 1940), **FRASERBURGH** (May 12, 1941), **RHYL** (June 21, 1940), **ROMNEY** (Aug. 3, 1940), **SEAHAM** (June 16, 1941).

2 *Robb:* **SIDMOUTH** (March 15, 1941), **STORNOWAY** (June 10, 1941).

9 *Canadian Yards:* **BAYFIELD** (May 26, 1941), **CANSO** (June 9, 1941), **FORT YORK** (ex-*Mingan*, Aug. 24, 1941), **INGONISH** (July 30, 1941), **PARRSBOROUGH** (June 26, 1941), **QUALICUM** (Sept. 3, 1941), **SHIPPIGAN** (Aug. 12, 1941), **TADOUSSAC** (Aug. 2, 1941), **WEDGEPORT** (Aug. 2, 1941).

EASTBOURNE. 1943, *Official.*

Displacement: 656 to 672 tons (*Peterhead*, 700 tons). Dimensions: 171½ (*pp.*), 180 (*o.a.*) × 28½ × 9½ feet (*max.*). Guns: **1**—3 inch AA., **2**—20 mm. AA., **4** M.G. Machinery: Triple expansion (with governor gear in *Blyth* and *Peterhead*). 2 shafts. I.H.P.: 2,400 = 16 kts. Boilers: 2 Admiralty 3-drum small tube type. Complement: 60. War losses: *Cromer*, *Felixstowe* (both Lobnitz), *Guysborough* (lent R.C.N.).

Fleet Minesweepers

ROTHESAY. (Turbine Type.) 1946, *Wright & Logan*

6 *Ailsa* : **BEAUMARIS** (Oct. 31, 1940), **BOOTLE** (Oct. 23, 1941), **BOSTON** (Dec. 30, 1940), **DORNOCH** (Feb. 4, 1942), **POLRUAN** (July 18, 1940), **RYE** (Aug. 19, 1940).
3 *Blyth* : **ARDROSSAN** (July 22, 1941), **BRIXHAM** (Oct. 21, 1941), **DUNBAR** (June 5, 1941).
3 *Hamilton* : **ILFRACOMBE** (Jan. 29, 1941), **ROTHESAY** (March 18, 1941), **TENBY** (Sept. 10, 1941).
1 *Philip* : **WHITEHAVEN** (May 29, 1941).
2 *Stephen* : **LYME REGIS** (ex-*Sunderland*, March 19, 1942), **POOLE** (June 25, 1941).
Displacement: 605 to 656 tons. Dimensions: 174 (*o.a.*) × 28½ × 9¼ feet (*max.*). Guns: **1**—3 inch AA., **1**—2 pdr., **2**—20 mm. AA., **4**—M.G. Machinery: Geared turbines. 2 shafts. S.H.P.: 2,400 = 16 kts. Boilers: 2 Admiralty, small tube type. Complement: 60. War losses: *Clacton, Cromarty* (Blyth), *Hythe*.

2 *Denny* : **BRIDLINGTON, BRIDPORT** (both Feb. 29, 1940). (Diesel Type.)
Displacement: 590 tons. Dimensions: 162 × 28 × 8⅓ feet. Guns: **1**—3 inch AA., **2**—20 mm. AA., 4 M.G. Machinery: 2 sets H. & W. Diesels. 2 shafts. B.H.P.: 2,000 = 16 kts. Complement: 60.

Notes.—An exceedingly useful type, especially for Oropesa sweeping; capable also of being used for anti-submarine escort purposes. Machinery suppliers: *Bridlington, Bridport*, Harland & Wolff, Govan; *Blyth*, White's Marine Engineering Co., Hebburn; *Dunbar*, Metropolitan Vickers; *Beaumaris, Boston*, English Electric Co.; *Polruan, Rye*, Thornycroft; *Ilfracombe, Llandudno*, British Thomson-Houston Co.; *Rothesay, Tenby*, J. Samuel White & Co.; *Rhyl*, Lobnitz; *Stornoway*, Plenty & Son. First 20 built under 1939 Estimates. *Bangor, Blackpool* have been transferred to R. Norwegian Navy. *Blyth* has had armament removed and additional superstructure built aft, for duty as S.O. ship, Minesweeping Flotillas. Cancelled units included *Beaulieu, Looe, Portland, Seaford.*

BRIDPORT. 1941.

Ex-German Types.

M 201, 261, 272, 302, 306, 321-323, 326, 327, 361, 362, 364, 366, 424, 436, 442, 452, 454, 475, 601-605, 612, 806 (1943–45). Displacement: 550 tons. Dimensions: 205 × 28 × 9 feet. Guns: **1**—4·1 inch, **1**—37 mm. AA., **6**—20 mm. AA., **2** M.G. Machinery: Triple expansion with exhaust turbine. 2 shafts. H.P.: 2,200 = 16 kts. Boilers: 2 Schulz. Coal: 142 tons.

M 23, 33, 82, 102, 104, 132 (1940–42). Displacement: 600 tons. Dimensions: 228⅔ × 28¼ × 9 feet. Guns: **2**—4·1 inch, **2**—37 mm. AA., **8**—20 mm. AA. Machinery: Triple expansion. 2 shafts. I.H.P.: 3,200 = 18 kts. Boilers: 2 Wagner. Oil fuel: 125 tons.

Note.—These were amongst the ships allotted to the British Government in the division of German naval material. It is unlikely that they will be retained when the need for their services is at an end.

4 Halcyon Class.

SPEEDWELL. 1946, *Wright & Logan.*

1 *Ailsa* : **JASON** (October 6, 1937).

1 *Gray* : **HAZARD** (Feb. 26, 1937).

1 *Hamilton* : **SPEEDY** (Nov. 23, 1938).

1 *Thornycroft* : **HARRIER** (April 17, 1934).

Displacement: 815 tons (*Hazard, Jason*, 835 tons; *Speedy*, 875 tons). Complement: 80.

Dimensions: 230 × 33½ × 7⅚ feet (*max.*), 6⅚ feet (*mean*), except *Speedy*, 7¼ feet (*mean*).

Guns: **2**—4 inch d.p., **5** smaller.

Machinery: 2 sets 3-cylinder compound engines, fitted with poppet valves operated by rotary cam gear under totally enclosed forced lubrication system, in *Harrier* only; geared turbines in others (by J. S. White & Co. in *Speedy*, and by Thornycroft in *Jason*). 2 shafts. I.H.P.: 1,770 = 16·5 kts. in *Harrier* only; S.H.P.: 1,750 = 17 kts. in others. Boilers: 2 Admiralty 3-drum type. Oil fuel: 220 tons.

Notes.—Most of this class are named after minesweepers of 1914. Outstanding feature of earlier units is the novel machinery design. *Harrier* built under 1932 Estimates; *Hazard*, 1935 estimates; *Jason*, 1936; *Speedy*, 1937. Cost averaged over £100,000 each. War losses: *Bramble, Britomart, Gossamer, Hebe, Hussar, Leda, Niger, Skipjack, Sphinx*. In addition, *Salamander* was scrapped owing to heavy damage.

Monitors

ROBERTS. 1946, *London Studio.*

ABERCROMBIE (March 31, 1942), **ROBERTS** (Feb. 1, 1941). Built by Vickers-Armstrongs Ltd. (Tyne) and Clydebank, respectively. Displacement: 7,850 and 7,970 tons, respectively. Dimensions: 373⅓ (*o.a.*) × 89¾ × 11 feet (*mean*). Guns: **2**—15 inch, 42 cal., **8**—4 inch d.p., **12**—2 pdr., **20**—20 mm. AA. Machinery: Parsons geared turbines. 2 shafts. Boilers: 2 Admiralty 3-drum type. *Abercrombie* was laid down 29/5/41 and completed 5/5/43. *Roberts* completed 27/10/41.

Note.—These ships were armed with guns formerly mounted in *Marshal Soult* and other discarded monitors. *Abercrombie* now serves as Gunnery Training Ship, Nore Command.

Radar Training Ship

BOXER (Dec. 12, 1942). Built by Harland & Wolff. Displacement: 5,970 tons. Complement: 500. Dimensions: 390 (*pp.*), 400 (*o.a.*) × 49 × — feet. Guns: Small AA. only. Machinery: Parsons geared turbines. 2 shafts. Speed: 16 kts. Boilers: Foster-Wheeler "D" type. Originally laid down as a large Landing Ship, she was completed as a Fighter Direction Ship. Her equipment includes 6 high-power radar sets and an unprecedented quantity of radio apparatus for various purposes. She is the only vessel in the Royal Navy with four masts, and is now a seagoing Radar Training Ship attached to the Navigation School.

BOXER. 1946, *Wright & Logan.*

Aircraft Maintenance Ships

PERSEUS. 1945, *J. W. Kennedy, Esq.*

PERSEUS (ex-*Edgar*, March 26, 1944), **PIONEER** (ex-*Mars*, May 20, 1944).

Displacement: 12,265 and 12,000 tons, respectively.

Length: 694½ feet. Beam: 80⅓ feet. Draught: 23 feet.

Guns:
24–2 pdr. pompoms
19—40 mm. AA.

Aircraft:
(None carried in peacetime.)

Armour:
None over flight deck.

Machinery: Parsons geared turbines, 2 shafts. S.H.P.: 40,000=25 kts. Boilers: 4 of 3-drum type.

Name	*Builders*	*Machinery*	*Begun*	*Completed*
Perseus	Vickers-Armstrong, Tyne	V.-A., Barrow	1/6/42	8/45
Pioneer	Do. Barrow	Do.	2/12/42	8/2/45

Note.—These ships when laid down were intended to be additional units of *Colossus* class, but were completed as "aircraft maintenance ships," and are apparently modified versions of *Unicorn*.

UNICORN (November 20, 1941)

Displacement: 14,750 tons (20,300 tons *full load*).

UNICORN 1945, *Flight Lieut. P. A. Vicary.*

Length: (*o.a.*) 640 feet. Beam: 90 feet. Draught: 19 feet.

Guns:
8—4 inch d.p.
2 multiple pompoms.
Numerous 20 mm. AA.

Aircraft:
35

Machinery: Parsons geared turbines. 2 shafts. S.H.P. 40,000=22 kts. Boilers: 4 Admiralty 3-drum type.

Note.—Built by Harland & Wolff, Ltd. under 1938 estimates; laid down 29/6/39 and completed 12/3/43. Is equipped for duty as Aircraft Repair Ship, fulfilling for aircraft squadrons much the same duties as undertaken by *Adamant* for submarine flotillas.

UNICORN. 1945, *Francis H. A. Baker, Esq.*

Gunboats

PAMELA. 1945, *courtesy Rear-Admiral Viscount Mountbatten of Burma.*

UNA. 1945, *courtesy Rear-Admiral Viscount Mountbatten of Burma.*

PAMELA, UNA (both April 9, 1945). Displacement: 25 tons. Dimensions: 52 × 13 × 2¼ feet. Guns: **1**—40 mm. AA., **1**—20 mm. AA., **4** M.G. Machinery: 3 Ford engines. Speed: 10 kts. Endurance equal to 200 miles without refuelling. Complement: 10.

Notes.—These vessels were built of teak and launched at Kalewa, on the Chindwin River, in Burma, by the R. Engineers of the 14th Army. Commissioned and manned by the Royal Navy, they operated with success against the Japanese on the Chindwin and Irrawaddy during the closing stages of the war in the Far East. Both received hits in action with the enemy, on whom they inflicted a considerable number of casualties.

Gunboats

GREY GOOSE. 1946.

1 *Denny*: **GREY WOLF** (ex-*SGB* 8).

2 *Hawthorn Leslie*: **GREY OWL** (ex-*SGB* 5), **GREY SHARK** (ex-*SGB* 6, Feb. 14, 1942).

1 *White*: **GREY GOOSE** (ex-*SGB* 9).

2 *Yarrow*: **GREY FOX** (ex-*SGB* 4, Sept. 25, 1941), **GREY SEAL** (ex-*SGB* 3, Aug. 29, 1941).

Displacement: 198 tons. Dimensions: 137¾ (*pp.*), 145⅓ (*o.a.*) × 20 × 10 feet. Guns: **1**—3 inch, **2**—20 mm. AA. or **2**—2 pdr., **4** to **8** M.G. Tubes: **2**—18 inch. Machinery: Single reduction geared turbines. 2 shafts. S.H.P.: 8,000 = 30 kts. Boiler: 1 Foster-Wheeler or Lamont. Oil fuel: 50 tons. Complement: 34.

Note.—This was an experimental Coastal Forces design which was not pursued further. Towards close of war these vessels were used as fast minesweepers. War loss: *SGB* 7. Two others, *SGB* 1 and 2, were ordered but not completed.

MOSQUITO (since lost). 1939, *courtesy of Messrs. Thornycroft (Builders).*

LOCUST (1940). Displacement: 585 tons. Dimensions: 197 × 33 × 5 feet. Complement, 74. Guns: **2**—4 inch, **1**—3·7 inch howitzer, **4**—2 pdr., **8** M.G. Machinery: Parsons geared turbines. S.H.P.: 3,800 = 17 kts. Fuel: 90 tons. Built under 1938 Estimates by Yarrow & Co., Ltd. War losses of this type: *Dragonfly, Grasshopper, Mosquito.*

Added 1937, courtesy Arthur Sye, late R.N.

SEAMEW (1927), designed and built by Messrs. Yarrow & Co., Ltd. Displacement: 262 tons. Dimensions: 160 (*w.l.*), 167½ (*o.a.*) × 27 × 5⅙ feet *max.* draught. Guns: **2**—3 inch AA., **8** M.G. Armoured bridge and shields to guns. Machinery: Geared turbines. Boilers: Yarrow. Designed H.P.: 1,370 = 14 kts. Fuel: 50 tons oil. Complement: 55. War loss: *Tern.*

APHIS. 1943, *Official.*

APHIS (1915), by Ailsa Co., **COCKCHAFER** (1915), by Barclay Curle, **SCARAB** (1915), by Wood, Skinner and Co. Displacement: 625 tons. Complement: 54–65. Dimensions: 237½ (*o.a.*) × 36 × 4 feet. Guns: **2**—6 inch, **1**—3 inch AA., **10** smaller. Machinery: Triple expansion. Twin screws in tunnels fitted with Yarrow's patent balanced flap. Boilers: Yarrow. Designed H.P.: 2,000 = 14 kts. Fuel: 35 tons coal, 54 tons oil. *Scarab* is lent to Burma.

Note.—Messrs. Yarrow & Co., Ltd., were solely responsible for the design of these vessels, which were built under their supervision. *Tarantula* has been discarded. War losses: *Cicala, Cricket, Gnat, Ladybird, Moth.*

Coastal Craft

Motor Torpedo Boats.

MTB 523. 1944, *courtesy Messrs. Vosper.*

Vosper Type: **MTB 523-539.** Displacement: 47 tons. Dimensions: 73 × 19½ × 5½ feet (*max.*). Armament: **4**—18 inch tubes, **2**—20 mm. AA. (forward), **4** M.G. Machinery: 3 Packard engines. B.H.P.: 3,960 = 39·5 kts. Sea speed: 34 kts. Complement: 13.

MTB 488. 1944 *courtesy British Power Boat Co.*

British Power Boat Type: **MTB 457, 468, 470, 480, 488, 493, 496, 498, 502-510, 519-522.** Displacement: 52 tons. Dimensions: 71⅓ × 20½ × 5¾ feet (*max.*). Armament: **2**—18 inch tubes, **1**—6 pdr. (forward), **2**—20 mm. AA., **4** M.G. Machinery: 3 Packard engines. B.H.P.: 4,050 = 39 kts. Sea speed: 31 knots. Complement: 17.

Motor Torpedo Boats

MTB 5007. 1946, *Wright & Logan.*

MTB 701. 1944, *Lieut. D. Monro, R.N.V.R.*

Modified Fairmile "D" Type: **MTB 5002, 5003, 5005, 5007-5010, 5013, 5015, 5020.** Displacement: 120 tons. Dimensions: 115 (*o.a.*) × 21¼ × 5¼ feet. Armament: **2**—21 inch tubes, **2**—6 pdr., **2**—20 mm. AA., **8** M.G., **1** or **2** rocket projectors (5008 reported to have mounted experimentally a larger gun than any of these). Machinery: 4 Packard engines. B.H.P.: 5,000 = 30 kts. Sea speed: 27 kts.

Fairmile "D" Type: **MTB 616-621, 704, 711, 713, 716, 717, 719, 720-723, 729-731, 750-758, 767, 773, 774, 779, 780, 784-787, 790, 792-795, 797.** Displacement: 91 tons (trials), later much increased. Dimensions: 115 (*o.a.*) × 21¼ × 5 feet. Armament: **4**—18 inch tubes, **2**—6 pdr. (forward and aft), **2**—20 mm. AA., **8** M.G. Machinery: 4 Packard engines. B.H.P.: 5,000 = 31 kts. Sea speed: 27·5 kts. Complement: 30.

MTB 306 *Added*, 1946

Thornycroft and other Types: **MTB 275-306.** Displacement: 52 tons. Dimensions: 75½ (*o.a.*) × 16½ × 5½ feet (*max.*). Armament: **2**—21 inch tubes, **4** M.G. Machinery: 4 RY12 Thornycroft engines. B.H.P.: 2,600 = 29 kts. Sea speed: 26 kts.

Ex-German M.T.B. 1946, *Wright & Logan.*

MTB 2015. 1946, *Wright & Logan.*

Camper and Nicholsons Type: **MTB 2009, 2011-2018.** Displacement: 115 tons. Dimensions: 117 × 22¼ × 4⅓ feet (*max.*). Armament: **4**—18 inch tubes, **2**—6 pdr., **6**—20 mm. AA., **1** rocket projector. Machinery: 3 V12 Packard engines, supercharged. B.H.P.: 4,050 = 31 kts. Sea speed: 26 kts. Complement: 30.

Note.—Following ex-German MTB were taken over after surrender: S 7, 13, 19, 20, 25, 48, 62, 67, 69, 83, 89, 92, 95, 105, 115, 120, 130, 168, 195, 196, 205, 208, 212, 215, 217, 221, 228, 303, 705.

Motor Launches.

ML 134. (Observe 40 mm. Bofors forward.) 1944, *Official.*

ML 188. *Added* 1944, *Official.*

Fairmile "B" Type: **ML 100-919** *type.* Displacement: 65 tons. Dimensions: 112 × 18¼ × 4¾ feet (*max.*). Guns: **1**—3 pdr., or 40 mm. AA., **3**—20 mm. AA., **4** M.G. At least 12 D.C. carried. Machinery: 2 Hall-Scott Defender engines. B.H.P.: 1,200 = 20 kts. Sea speed: 16·5 kts. Complement: 16 to 18.

(Former Fairmile "C" type MGB have been sold or converted to other purposes.)

Note.—A few HDML also remain in service, mostly armed with 1—40 mm. and 1—20 mm. AA.

Netlayers and Target Towing Vessels.

1937, *P. A. Vicary, Cromer.*

PROTECTOR (Aug. 20, 1936). Laid down by Messrs. Yarrow & Co., Ltd., August 15, 1935, under 1934 Estimates. Completed end 1936. Displacement: 2,900 tons. Complement: 190. Dimensions: 310 (*pp.*), 338 (*o.a.*) × 50 × 11½ feet (*mean*). Guns: 1—4 inch, some smaller. Machinery: Parsons geared turbines. (Re-engined 1945.) S.H.P.: 9,000 = 20 kts. Boilers: 2 Admiralty 3-drum type. Oil fuel: 690 tons. Cost: £326,230.

Note.—*Protector* is a handier and faster ship than *Guardian*, her design embodying experience gained with that vessel. She has greater lifting power for dealing with nets.

1939, *P. A. Vicary, Cromer.*

GUARDIAN (Chatham Dockyard, Sept. 1, 1932). Laid down October 15, 1931; completed June 13, 1933. Displacement: 2,860 tons. Complement: 181. Dimensions: 310 × 53 × 12¼ feet (*max.*), 11⅙ feet (*mean*). Guns: 2—4 inch AA., 10—20 mm. AA., 6 Lewis. Machinery: Parsons geared turbines by Wallsend Co. H.P.: 6,500 = 18 kts., (now about 16 kts.). Boilers: 2 Admiralty 3-drum type. Oil fuel: 720 tons. Cost: £333,595.

Notes.- Designed for Net-laying and Fleet Photography work. The nets, sinkers and buoys are stowed to port and starboard, on the upper deck from just forward of the main-mast under the forecastle deck to the stern. The structure aft, placed on the deck spanning the nets, is the photographic cabin. This ship is very beamy in relation to her length, the proportion being 1:6 only.

Depot and Repair Ships

WOODBRIDGE HAVEN. 1946, *Wright & Logan.*

DERBY HAVEN (ex-*Loch Assynt*, 1944), **WOODBRIDGE HAVEN** (ex-*Loch Torridon*, 1944). Both built by Swan Hunter. Displacement: 1,652 tons. Dimensions: 307¼ × 38½ × 12¾ feet. Machinery: Triple expansion. 2 shafts. I.H.P.: 5,500 = 19·5 kts. Boilers: 2 Admiralty 3-drum type. (Depot and Repair Ships for Coastal Craft.)

1946, *Lieut. (E) Graeme Maclennan, R.N.*

BEACHY HEAD, BERRY HEAD, CAPE WRATH, DODMAN POINT, DUNCANSBY HEAD, GIRDLE NESS, HOLM SOUND, MULL OF GALLOWAY (ex-*Kinnaird Head*), **MULL OF KINTYRE, PORTLAND BILL, RAME HEAD** (all 1944–45). Built in Canada. Displacement: 8,580 tons (*Cape Wrath*, 8,755 tons). Dimensions: 439 × 62 × 29 feet. Guns: 32—20 mm. AA. Machinery: Geared turbines. S.H.P.: 6,000 = 17 kts. Boilers: 2 Foster-Wheeler. (Maintenance Ships, except *Holm Sound*, classed as Aircraft Component Repair Ship.)

BEACHY HEAD lent to R. Netherland Navy, 1947.

Note.—Ships discarded include *Beauly Firth, Buchan Ness, Cuillin Sound, Dullisk Cove, Dungeness, Fife Ness, Flamborough Head, Hartland Point, Moray Firth, Mullion Cove, Mull of Oa, Orfordness, Rattray Head, Selsey Bill, Solway Firth, Spurn Point, Tarbat Ness.*

TYNE. Added 1943.

TYNE (1940). Built by Scotts' S.B. & E. Co., Ltd., under 1937 Estimates. Displacement: 11,000 tons. Length: (*o.a.*) 623 feet. Guns: 8—4·5 inch, 2 multiple pompoms. Machinery: Parsons geared turbines. 2 shafts. S.H.P.: 7,500 = 17 kts. 4 boilers of 3-drum type. (Destroyer Depot Ship).

Notes.—Equipment includes two furnaces, each capable of melting 500 lb. of metal at any temperature up to 1,500° centigrade; a foundry; machine shops with milling and grinding machines; and a bakery with a daily output of 25,000 lb. of bread. Sister ship *Hecla* (Clydebank) became a war loss.

FORTH. 1943, *Official.*

MAIDSTONE (Oct. 21, 1937), **FORTH** (Aug. 11, 1938). Both built at Clydebank. Displacement: 8,900 tons. Complement: 502 (including 64 repair staff and 43 as spare submarine crew). Dimensions: 497 (*pp.*), 531 (*w.l.*), 574 feet (*o.a.*) × 75 × 20 feet (*mean*). Guns: 8—4·5 inch, 2 multiple pompoms, 4—3 pdr., 4 smaller. Machinery: Brown-Curtis geared turbines. S.H.P.: 7,000 = 17 kts. (Depot Ships for Submarines.)

Notes.—*Maidstone* ordered Aug. 17, 1936, under 1935 estimates and completed May 5, 1938; *Forth* laid down June 30, 1937 under estimates for that year, and completed May 14, 1939. Armament is notable, being the heaviest yet mounted in a British depot ship. Guns are in pairs, two forward, two aft and two sponsoned on either beam. Equipment includes a foundry; coppersmiths', plumbers' and carpenters' shops; heavy and light machine shops; electrical and torpedo repair shops; and plant for charging submarine batteries.

Depot and Repair Ships

ADAMANT (Nov. 30, 1940). Built by Harland & Wolff, Ltd., at Belfast. Displacement: 12,500 tons. Length: (*o.a.*) 646 feet. Guns: **8**—4·5 inch, 2 multiple pompoms. Machinery: Parsons geared turbines. S.H.P.: 8,000 = 17 kts. (Submarine Depot Ship).

Note.—Laid down 18/5/39, under 1938 Estimates. Completed 28/2/42. Resembles *Tyne* in appearance.

Ex-**TSINGTAU** (June 6, 1934). Displacement: 1,970 tons. Complement: 143. Dimensions: $278\frac{3}{4} \times 44\frac{1}{4} \times 12\frac{2}{3}$ feet. Guns: **2**—3·5 inch AA., **4** M.G. Machinery: Diesel. 2 shafts. B.H.P.: 4,100 = 17 kts. Fuel: 182 tons. (Doubtful if this ex-German ship will be retained.)

1935, *Wright & Logan.*

WOOLWICH (Fairfield, Sept. 20, 1934). Displacement: 8,750 tons. Complement: 406. Dimensions: $575 \times 64 \times 14\frac{2}{3}$ feet (*mean* draught). Guns: **4**—4 inch AA., **10** smaller. Machinery: 2 sets single reduction geared turbines. 2 shafts. S.H.P.: 6,500 = 15 kts. Boilers: 4 Admiralty 3-drum type. Oil fuel: 1,170 tons. Authorised under 1932 Estimates. Laid down May 24, 1933, and completed June, 1935. Carries a full equipment of machine tools of the latest type, with a total motor H.P. exceeding 2,000. (Depot ship for Destroyers.)

1934 *Photo, Wright & Logan.*

RESOURCE (Vickers, Nov. 27, 1928). (Fleet Repair Ship). Displacement: 12,300 tons. Complement: 450. Dimensions: 500 (*pp.*) $\times 83 \times 22\frac{1}{4}$ feet (*max.*). Guns: **4**—4 inch AA., 4 smaller. Machinery: 2 sets Parsons single reduction geared turbines. S.H.P.: 7,500 = 15 kts. Boilers: 4 Admiralty type 3-drum type, 235 lbs. pressure. Oil: 1,100 + 350 tons for other vessels.

1944, *Official.*

BONAVENTURE (1942). Displacement: 9,166 tons. Dimensions: $487 \times 63 \times$ — feet. Guns: **2**—4 inch d.p., **12**—20 mm. AA. Machinery: Triple expansion with l.p. exhaust turbine. 2 shafts. I.H.P.: 8,300 = 10 kts.

Note.—During the war this ship served as depot ship for midget submarines.

1943, *Official.*

ALAUNIA (1925), **ARTIFEX** (ex-*Aurania*, 1924), **AUSONIA** (1921). 13,867 to 14,030 tons *gross*. Dimensions: $519\frac{3}{4} \times 65\frac{1}{4} \times 31\frac{1}{2}$ feet. Machinery: Geared turbines. 2 shafts. S.H.P.: 8,500 = 15 kts. Oil fuel: 2,287 tons. (Repair ships.)

1946, *Wright & Logan.*

RANPURA (Hawthorn Leslie, 1925). Displacement: 16,120 tons. Dimensions: $548\frac{1}{4} \times 71\frac{1}{4} \times 28\frac{1}{4}$ feet. Machinery: Quadruple expansion. I.H.P.: 15,000 = 17 kts. Fuel: 2,370 tons. (Destroyer Depot and Repair Ship.)

MONTCLARE. 1946, *Wright & Logan.*

MONTCLARE (1922), **WOLFE** (ex-*Montcalm*, 1921). 16,314 and 16,418 tons *gross*, respectively. Dimensions: $550 \times 70 \times 28$ feet. Machinery: Geared turbines. 2 shafts. S.H.P.: 12,500 = 17 kts. Oil fuel: 2,250 tons. Complement: 480, including repair staff. (Submarine depot ships.)

WOLFE. 1946, *Wright & Logan.*

Surveying Vessels

DAMPIER (ex-*Herne Bay*, ex-*Loch Eil*, May 15, 1945). Displacement: 1,600 tons. Dimensions: 307⅓ × 38½ × 12¾ feet. Machinery: Triple expansion. 2 shafts. I.H.P.: 5,500 = 19·5 kts. Boilers: 2 Admiralty 3-drum type. Oil fuel: 720 tons.

FRANKLIN. 1946, *Group Captain K. G. Winicki.*

FRANKLIN (Ailsa S.B. Co., Dec. 22, 1937), **SCOTT** (Caledon S.B. Co., Aug. 23, 1938), **SEAGULL** (Devonport, Oct. 28, 1937), **SHARPSHOOTER** (Devonport, Dec. 10, 1936). Displacement: 830 tons. Complement: 80. Dimensions: 230 × 33½ × 7 feet (*mean*). Machinery: Parsons geared turbines. 2 shafts. S.H.P.: 1,750 = 17 kts. Boilers: 2 Admiralty 3-drum type. Oil fuel: 220 tons. Built under 1935, 1936 and 1937 Estimates.

1946, *Wright & Logan.*

CHALLENGER (Chatham, June 1, 1931). Displacement: 1,140 tons. Complement: 84. Dimensions: 200 (*pp.*), 220 (*o.a.*) × 36 × 12½ feet (*mean*). Machinery: Triple expansion. I.H.P.: 1,200 = 12·5 kts. Oil fuel: 340 tons. Radius of operation: 9,000 miles.

1946, *Wright & Logan.*

WHITE BEAR. Ex-yacht with exceptional equipment, including printing presses for the production of charts. Further particulars wanted.

Coastal Minelayers

(Certain trawlers are also fitted for minelaying.)

MINER VII. 1946, *Wright & Logan.*

MINER I–VIII (1939–44). Built by Philip & Son, Ltd. Displacement: 275 tons. Dimensions: 110¼ × 26½ × — feet. Machinery: Ruston & Hornby Diesel. 2 shafts. B.H.P.: 360.

Coastal Minelayers—*continued.*

LINNET. 1938, *Wright & Logan.*

LINNET (May 3, 1938), **RINGDOVE** (June 15, 1938). Former built by Ardrossan Dockyard Co., Ltd. under 1936 Estimates, latter by Henry Robb, Ltd., under 1937 Estimates. Displacement: 498 tons. Complement: 24. Dimensions: 145 (*pp.*), 163¾ (*o.a.*) × 27⅛ × 8 feet. Machinery: Triple expansion, by Ferguson Bros., Ltd., in *Linnet*; by White's Marine Engineering Co. Ltd. in *Ringdove*. I.H.P. 400 = 10·5 kts. Both are minelaying tenders to *Vernon*. War loss: *Redstart*.

PLOVER. 1943, *Official.*

PLOVER (Denny, June 8, 1937). Displacement: 805 tons. Complement: 69. Dimensions: 180 (*pp.*), 195¼ (*o.a.*) × 37½ × 8⅙ feet. Guns: 2 M.G. Machinery: Triple expansion. I.H.P.: 1,400 = 14·75 kts. Laid down Oct. 7, 1936, and completed in Sept., 1937. Minelaying tender to *Vernon*.

Controlled Minelayers (ex-Trawlers).

BLACKBIRD. 1943, *Official.*

1 *Cochrane*: **REDSHANK** (ex-*Turbot*, Aug. 28, 1942). Displacement: 680 tons. Dimensions: 162 × 25⅛ × 12½ feet.

3 *Cook, Welton & Gemmell*: **BLACKBIRD** (ex-*Sheppey*) (Feb. 20, 1943), **DABCHICK** (ex-*Thorney*) (March 9, 1943), **STONECHAT** (Aug. 28, 1944). Displacement: 560 tons. Dimensions: 150 × 27½ × — feet. Specially equipped for controlled minelaying. Guns: 1—4 inch AA., etc. Machinery: Triple expansion. Another of this type in R.C.N. War loss: *Corncrake* (Cochrane).

Motor Minesweepers

MMS 272. 1944, *J. W. Kennedy, Esq.*

MMS 1 series (about 40 still in service). Wood. Displacement: 240 to 255 tons. Length: 105 (*pp.*), 119 (*o.a.*) × 13 × 9½ feet. Guns: 2—20 mm. AA., 2 M.G. Machinery: Diesel. B.H.P.: 500 = 10 kts. Complement: 20.

Note.—*MMS* 233 and 261 are being refitted as tenders to R.N.V.R. Divisions.

Motor Minesweepers—*continued*.

MMS 1001. 1946, *J. W. Kennedy, Esq.*

MMS 1001 series. Wood. Displacement: 360 tons. Dimensions: 126 (*pp.*), 139¾ (*o.a.*) × 26 × 10½ (*mean*), 12½ feet (*max.*). Guns: 2—20 mm. AA., 2 M.G. Machinery: Diesel. B.H.P.: 500 = 10 kts.

Note.—*MMS* 1017, 1030, 1034, 1048, 1075, 1089, 1090 are being refitted for duty as tenders to R.N.V.R. Divisions.

BYMS 2027 (2001-2030 all like this). 1946.

BYMS 2244. 1944, *Official.*

BYMS 2001-2284 series. (All previously bore numbers from 1 upwards.) Wood. Displacement: 207 to 215 tons. Dimensions: 136 (*o.a.*) × 24½ × 6 feet. Guns: 1—3 inch, 2—20 mm. AA. Machinery: Diesel. B.H.P.: 1,000 = 13 kts.

23 ex-German vessels: **R 21, 31, 47-49, 83, 115, 143, 167, 168, 170, 174-176, 181, 220, 240, 244, 246, 251, 252, 255, 268.**

Displacement: 100 tons (except first pair, 90 tons). Dimensions: 125¾ × 21 × 6¼ feet (first pair, 115¾ × 16½ × 5¼ feet). Guns: 1 or 2—20 mm. AA. Machinery: Diesel. 2 shafts. B.H.P.: 1,800 = 18 kts. (first pair, B.H.P. 1,200 = 18 kts.).

Trawlers

1944, *courtesy Messrs. Hall, Russell & Co.*

(Round Table Class)

1 *John Lewis & Sons*: **SIR TRISTRAM** (Jan. 17, 1942). Displacement: 440 tons. Dimensions: 137 (*o.a.*) × 23¾ × 11½ feet. Guns: 1—4 inch, etc. Machinery: Triple expansion.

1945, *J. W. Kennedy, Esq.*

(Shakespearian Class)

1 *Cook, Welton & Gemmell*: **HAMLET** (July 24, 1940).

1 *Goole S.B. & R. Co.*: **MACBETH** (Oct. 3, 1940).

Displacement: 545 tons. Dimensions: 164 × 27⅔ × 13½ feet. Otherwise resemble "Tree" class. War losses: *Coriolanus* (Cochrane); *Horatio, Laertes* (both C.W.G.); *Othello* (Hall Russell).

1944, *Official.*

Shillay as Danlayer. 1946, *London Studio.*

Steepholm as Wreck Dispersal Vessel. 1946, *Wright & Logan.*

(Isles Class)

3 *Ardrossan Dockyard Co.*: **COLL** (April 7, 1942), **GORREGAN** (Dec. 30, 1943), **GRAEMSAY** (Aug. 3, 1942).

1 *George Brown & Co.*: **DAMSAY** (June 27, 1942).

HERMETRAY has been sold.

6 *Cochrane*: **FETLAR** (July, 1941), **HERMETRAY** (April, 1944), **IMERSAY** (Aug., 1944), **ORONSAY** (Oct. 30, 1943), **ORSAY** (Jan., 1945), **RONA** (Feb., 1945).

17 *Cook, Welton & Gemmell*: **ANNET** (March 25, 1943), **BERN** (May 2, 1942), **BRYHER** (April 8, 1943), **FLATHOLM** (May 8, 1943), **LINDISFARNE** (June 17, 1943), **LUNDY** (Aug. 29, 1942), **NEAVE** (July 16, 1942), **SANDRAY** (Oct. 5, 1944), **SCALPAY** (June 2, 1942), **SHILLAY** (Nov. 18, 1944), **SURSAY** (Dec. 16, 1944), **TAHAY** (Dec. 31, 1944), **TOCOGAY** (Feb. 7, 1945), **TRODDAY** (March 3, 1945), **VACEASAY** (March 17, 1945), **VALLAY** (April 10, 1945), **WIAY** (April 26, 1944).

Trawlers

(Isles Class—*continued*.)

1 *John Crown & Sons*: **EARRAID** (ex-*Gruna*) (Dec. 18, 1941).

1 *Fleming & Ferguson*: **BARDSEY** (July 17, 1943).

1 *Goole S.B. & R. Co.*: **TIREE** (Sept. 6, 1941).

1 *A. & J. Inglis*: **SWITHA** (April 3, 1942).

5 *John Lewis & Sons*: **CALDY, FOULNESS** (March 23, 1942), **SKOMER** (June 17, 1943), **STEEPHOLM** (July 15, 1943), **TRONDRA** (Oct. 4, 1941).

1 *Henry Robb*: **SKYE** (March 17, 1942).

1 *Canadian built*: **GATESHEAD.**

Displacement: 560 tons. Dimensions: 150 (*pp.*) × 27½ × — feet. Guns: 1—4 inch AA., 4 smaller. (Removed from those used for wreck dispersal). Machinery: Triple expansion. Boiler: 1 cylindrical. Four transferred to R.N.Z.N., and three to Portuguese Navy. War losses: *Campobello, Canna, Flotta, Gairsay, Ganilly, Orfasy, Rysa, Stronsay, Wallasea.*

1946, *Wright & Logan.*

(Tree Class)

1 *Hall, Russell & Co.*: **OLIVE** (Feb. 26, 1940).
1 *Smith's Dock Co.*: **WALNUT** (1939).

Both ordered in July, 1939, under Estimates for that year. Displacement: 530 tons. Dimensions: 150 (*pp.*), 164 (*o.a.*) × 27½ × 10½ feet. Guns: 1—4 inch AA., etc. Machinery: Triple expansion. I.H.P. 850 = 11·5 kts. War losses: *Almond, Ash, Chestnut, Hickory, Juniper, Pine.*

Basset (Now has foretopmast). 1937, *R. Perkins.*

BASSET. (Henry Robb, Ltd., Leith, Sept. 28, 1935). Displacement: 461 tons (full load, 696 tons). Complement, 15. Dimensions: 150 (*pp.*), 160½ (*o.a.*) × 27½ × 10½ feet. Guns: 1—4 inch. Reciprocating engines and cylindrical boiler. I.H.P. 850 = 12 kts. Fuel: 180 tons coal. Designed for Anti-Submarine duty. Sister ship *Mastiff* mined.

Syringa. 1945, *J. W. Kennedy, Esq.*

(Holly Class)

2 *Cochrane & Sons*: **LILAC** (ex-*Beachflower*, 1930). 593 tons. 150½ × 25½ × 12 feet. **SYRINGA** (ex-*Cape Kanin*, 1930). 574 tons. 140 × 24½ × 12 feet.

2 *Cook, Welton & Gemmell*: **HOLLY** (ex-*Kingston Coral*, 1930). **LAUREL** (ex-*Kingston Cyanite*, 1930). Both 590 tons. 140¼ × 24½ × 11½ feet.

In all: Guns: 1—4 inch AA. D.C. carried. I.H.P.: 600 = 11 kts. All purchased 1935 and 1939, and used for minesweeping. War losses: *Alder, Beech, Myrtle.*

1936, *Wright & Logan.*

VULCAN (ex-*Mascot*, ex-*Aston Villa*), (Smith's Dock Co. Ltd., 1933). Purchased and converted, 1936. Displacement: 623 tons. Dimensions: 155 (*o.a.*) × 26½ × 12 feet. Reciprocating engines. I.H.P.: 678 = 11·5 kts. 1 cylindrical boiler. Depot Ship for Coastal Craft.

Excellent. 1935, *R. Perkins.*

EXCELLENT (ex-*Nith*, ex-*Andrew Jewer*, 1916). Built by Messrs. Cochrane. Displacement: 551 tons. Dimensions: 138⅓ (*pp.*) × 22¾ × 13½ feet. Triple expansion engines. 1 boiler. I.H.P.: 600 = 11 kts. Coal: 204 tons. War loss: *Ouse.*

Boom Defence Vessels

(Bar Class—63 Ships.)

Barndale. 1945, *J. W. Kennedy, Esq.*

4 *Ardrossan Dockyard*: **BARBECUE** (Dec. 19, 1944), **BARCAROLE** (March 14, 1945), **BARHOLM** (Dec. 31, 1942), **BARTIZAN** (May 20, 1943).

15 *Blyth D.D. & S.B. Co.*: **BARBAIN** (Jan. 8, 1940), **BARBETTE** (Dec. 15, 1937), **BARBICAN** (March 14, 1938), **BARBOUR** (April 9, 1941), **BARBROOK** (May 28, 1938), **BARCASTLE** (July 23, 1938), **BARCLOSE** (July 9, 1941), **BARCOCK** (Sept. 3, 1941), **BARCOTE** (Feb. 8, 1940), **BARDELL** (Jan. 12, 1942), **BARDOLF** (April 14, 1942), **BARLAKE** (Sept. 16, 1940), **BARMILL** (Oct. 16, 1940), **BARNEHURST** (Oct. 21, 1939), **BARNSTONE** (Nov. 25, 1939).

4 *Ferguson Bros.*: **BARBERRY** (1943), **BARHILL** (1942), **BARKIS** (1945), **BARSPEAR** (1943).

2 *Hall, Russell:* **BARRAGE** (Dec. 2, 1937), **BARRANCA** (Jan. 18, 1938).

4 *Charles Hill:* **BARONIA** (April 23, 1941), **BAROVA** (July 5, 1941), **BARRICADE** (ex-*Ebgate*, Feb. 7, 1938), **BARRIER** (ex-*Bargate*, May 17, 1938).

2 *Goole S.B. & R. Co.:* **BARCOMBE** (July 28, 1938), **BARCROFT.**

7 *John Lewis:* **BARFIELD** (July 28, 1938), **BARFOOT** (Sept. 25, 1942), **BARGLOW** (Nov. 9, 1942), **BARILLA, BARLEYCORN, BARNARD, BARNEATH.**

7 *Lobnitz:* **BARBRIDGE, BARCLIFF** (ex-*Barwick*, May 10, 1940), **BARKING, BARLANE** (June 27, 1938), **BARNDALE** (Nov. 30, 1939), **BARNWELL** (Feb. 13, 1940), **BARTHORPE** (March 22, 1940).

4 *Philip:* **BARBASTEL** (1945), **BARFOIL** (1943), **BARITONE** (1945), **BARON** (1944).

14 *Simons:* **BARBOURNE, BARFOAM, BARFORD, BARFOSS** (Feb. 17, 1942), **BARFOUNT, BARLOW** (Aug. 26, 1938), **BARMOND** (Dec. 24, 1942), **BARMOUTH** (Oct. 11, 1938), **BARNABY, BARRHEAD, BARRINGTON, BARSING, BARSOUND, BARSTOKE.**

Built under 1935, 1936, 1937, 1939 and War Estimates. Displacement: 730 tons. Dimensions: 150 (*pp.*), 173¾ (*o.a.*) × 32¼ × 9½ feet. Guns: 1—3 inch AA. Machinery: Triple expansion. I.H.P. 850 = 11·75 kts. 2 S.E. boilers. Complement: 32. Two transferred to S.A.N.F., two to Burma, and two to Turkey. *Barcock* is on charter to Belgium, *Barlow* and *Barnehurst* to Netherlands. War losses: *Barflake, Barlight.*

PLANTAGENET. 1939, *courtesy Messrs. Lobnitz & Co., Ltd.* (*Builders*).

(BAYONET CLASS—10 SHIPS)

6 *Blyth DD. & S.B. Co.:* **FALCONET** (ex-*Barnham*), (Dec. 5, 1938), **BOWNET** (Jan. 19, 1939), **BURGONET** (March 14, 1939), **DRAGONET** (June 2, 1939), **SIGNET** (May 3, 1939), **SONNET** (1939).

2 *Smith's Dock Co.:* **MAGNET** (ex-*Barnsley*), (Nov. 22, 1938), **MARTINET** (ex-*Barnstone*), (Dec. 8, 1938).

2 *Lobnitz:* **PLANET** (ex-*Barnwell*), (Dec. 26, 1938), **PLANTAGENET** (ex-*Barwood*), (Feb. 23, 1939).

Displacement: 530 tons. Dimensions: 135 × 30½ × 9 feet. Guns: 1—3 inch AA. Machinery: Triple expansion (By North-Eastern Marine Engineering Co., Ltd. in *Bownet, Burgonet, Dragonet;* by White's Marine Engineering Co., Ltd. in *Signet, Sonnet*). I.H.P.: 850 = 11·5 kts. Cylindrical boilers. Authorised under 1937 and 1938 Estimates. War loss: *Bayonet.*

BARNET. 1934, *Grand Studio, Malta.*

BARNET (ex-*Earl Haig*). (Cochrane & Sons, Selby, 1919.) Purchased and converted, 1934. Displacement: 423 tons. Complement: 15. Dimensions: 138⅓ (*o.a.*) × 23¾ × 11¼ feet. Guns: 1—3 inch. Reciprocating engines and cylindrical boiler. I.H.P.: 600 = 11 kts. Fuel: 175 tons coal. Boom working vessel.

Drifters and Motor Fishing Craft.

MFV 1080. 1946, *Wright & Logan.*

Over 500 motor fishing vessels of above type are employed in Naval service, and have largely replaced drifters for various subsidiary duties.

SEABREEZE. 1937, *R. Perkins.*

Brine, *Fumarole, Halo, Harmattan, Indian Summer, Leeward, Noontide, Raleigh (ex-*Glitter*), ***Whirlpool.*** * = Wood.

Displacement: 199 tons. Dimensions: 87 × 19¾ × 9½ feet. I.H.P.: 270 = 9 kts. Guns: 1—6 pdr. or 3 pdr. Coal: 31–39 tons. War losses: *Eddy, Sunset.*

Cable Vessels.

BULLHEAD. (Others very similar.) 1946, *courtesy Builders.*

(BULLFINCH CLASS)

BULLFINCH (Aug. 19, 1940), **BULLFROG** (Jan. 1944), **BULLHEAD** (Oct. 3, 1944), **ST. MARGARETS** (Oct. 1943).

All built by Swan, Hunter & Wigham Richardson, Ltd. 1,524 tons *gross.* Dimensions: 252 (*o.a.*) × 36½ × 16⅓ feet (*mean*). Guns: 1—4 inch d.p., 4—20 mm. AA.

1938, *Wright & Logan.*

LASSO (March 17, 1938). Built by Messrs. Thornycroft under 1936 Estimates. Displacement: 903 tons. Dimensions: 180 (*pp.*), 205 (*o.a.*) × 35½ × 9⅞ feet. No guns. Machinery: Triple expansion. I.H.P.: 1,100 = 13 kts. Tender to Anti-Submarine School, Portland.

Miscellaneous

Royal Yacht.

VICTORIA AND ALBERT (1899). Displacement: 4,700 tons. Dimensions: 380 (*pp.*) × 40 × 18 feet (*mean* draught). Guns: 2—6 pdr. (bronze). Machinery: 2 sets triple expansion. I.H.P. 11,800 = 20 kts. Belleville boilers. Coal: *normal*, 350 tons; *maximum*, 2,000 tons. Complement: 363.

Note.—*V. and A.* was used for gunnery training duties during War. She is considered no longer seaworthy.

Tenders

1946, *Wright & Logan.*

DEEPWATER. Ex-German vessel, now employed as Diving Tender, attached to *Vernon*. Particulars wanted.

1939, *courtesy Messrs. Vosper, Ltd.*

BLOODHOUND (Vosper, 1937). Displacement: 35 tons. Complement: 5. Dimensions: 68 × 19 × 3 feet. 1—21 inch torpedo tube (3 torpedoes carried). Lorraine-Orion engines. H.P.: 1,600 = 25 kts. Tender to *Vernon*, used for torpedo practice. Built under 1937 Estimates.

1937, *Wright & Logan.*

DWARF. (1936). Built by Philip & Son, Ltd., Dartmouth. Displacement: 172 tons. Dimensions: 83¾ (*pp.*), 91 (*o.a.*) × 19 × 6½ feet (*mean*), 7 feet (*max.*). No guns. 2 sets reciprocating engines and 1 cylindrical boiler. I.H.P.: 350 = 9·25 kts. Fuel: 16 tons coal. Tender to Submarine Headquarters, Portsmouth.

REDWING. 1934 *Photo, R. Perkins.*

REDWING (Oct. 19, 1933). Built by J. Samuel White & Co., Ltd., Cowes. Displacement: 225 tons. Complement: 12. Dimensions: 112 (*o.a.*) × 25 × 6⅝ feet. Machinery: 2 sets reciprocating. I.H.P. 250 = 9·5 kts. 1 cylindrical boiler. Tender to *Defiance*, Torpedo School, Devonport.

ELFIN. 1935, *R. Perkins.*

ELFIN (Nov. 20, 1933). Built by J. Samuel White & Co., Ltd., Cowes. Displacement: 222 tons. Complement: 12. Dimensions: 108 (*o.a.*) × 25 × 6½ feet. 2 sets reciprocating engines and 1 cylindrical boiler. I.H.P.: 250 = 9·5 kts. Tender to Submarine Depot, Portland.

NIGHTINGALE. 1931 *Photo, Cribb.*

NIGHTINGALE (Sept. 30, 1931), **VERNON** (ex-*Skylark*), (Nov. 15, 1932). Both built at Portsmouth. Displacement: 298 and 302 tons, respectively. Complement: 15. Dimensions: *Nightingale*, 110 (*o.a.*) × 24½ × 7½ feet.; *Vernon*, 106⅓ (*o.a.*) × 24½ × 7½ feet. No guns. 2 sets reciprocating engines and 1 cylindrical boiler. I.H.P.: 400 = 10 kts. Fuel: 15 tons coal. Mining tenders to *Vernon* Establishment.

Note.—Ex-German tender *Paul Beneke* (1936) was also in possession of Royal Navy, but may have been sold.

Oilers

OAKOL. 1946, *Official.*

BIRCHOL (Feb. 19, 1946), **CEDAROL** (ex-*Ebonol*, May 15, 1946), **OAKOL** (Aug. 28, 1946), **TEAKOL** (Nov., 1946). All built by Lobnitz. Displacement: 2,670 tons. Dimensions: 218 (*pp.*), 232 (*o.a.*) × 39 × 15¾ feet. Machinery: Triple expansion. I.H.P.: 1,140 = 11 kts. Deadweight capacity: 1,050 tons. Complement: 26.

WAVE KING. 1944 *Official.*

(WAVE CLASS.)

10 *Furness S.B. Co.:* **WAVE BARON** (ex-*Empire Flodden*, Feb. 19, 1946), **WAVE EMPEROR** (Oct. 16, 1944), **WAVE GOVERNOR** (Nov. 30, 1944), **WAVE LIBERATOR** (ex-*Empire Milner*, Feb. 9, 1944), **WAVE PREMIER** (June 27, 1946), **WAVE PROTECTOR** (ex-*Empire Protector*, July 20, 1944), **WAVE REGENT** (March 29, 1945), **WAVE RULER** (ex-*Empire Evesham*, Jan. 17, 1946), **WAVE SOVEREIGN** (Nov. 20, 1945), **WAVE VICTOR** (ex-*Empire Bounty*, Sept. 30, 1943).

2 *Harland & Wolff (Govan):* **WAVE KING** (April 6, 1944), **WAVE MONARCH** (July 6, 1944).

5 *Laing:* **WAVE CHIEF** (ex-*Empire Edgehill*, April 4, 1946), **WAVE DUKE** (ex-*Empire Mars*, Nov. 16, 1944), **WAVE KNIGHT** (ex-*Empire Naseby*, Oct. 22, 1945), **WAVE LAIRD** (ex-*Empire Dunbar*, April 3, 1946), **WAVE PRINCE** (ex-*Empire Herald*, July 27, 1945).

Displacement: 16,476 to 16,483 tons. Dimensions: 465 (*pp.*), 492 (*o.a.*) × 64¼ × 28½ feet. Machinery: Parsons double reduction geared turbines. S.H.P.: 6,800 = 15 kts. Boilers of 3-drum type. D.W. capacity: 11,900 tons.

OLNA (1944). Displacement: 25,096 tons (*full load?*). Dimensions: 550 (*pp.*) × 70 × 31¾ feet. Guns: 1—4 inch AA., 4—40 mm. AA., 8—20 mm. AA. Machinery: Turbo-electric. S.H.P. 13,000 = 17 kts. Boilers: 3 Babcock & Wilcox. Fuel: 2,130 tons. Deadweight capacity: 17,500 tons. Complement: 77.

BLACK RANGER. Added 1944, *Official.*

(RANGER CLASS.)

2 *Caledon S.B. Co.:* **GOLD RANGER** (March 12, 1941), **GREEN RANGER** (Aug. 21, 1941).

3 *Harland & Wolff (Govan):* **BLACK RANGER** (Aug. 22, 1940), **BLUE RANGER** (Jan. 29, 1941), **BROWN RANGER** (Dec. 12, 1940).

3,313 to 3,417 tons *gross.* Dimensions: first two, 339½ (*pp.*), 355¼ (*o.a.*) × 47 × 20 feet; other three, 349⅓ (*pp.*), 365⅔ (*o.a.*) × 47 × 20 feet. Machinery: Diesel. B.H.P. 2,750. War loss: *Gray Ranger* (Caledon).

1939, *courtesy Messrs. Harland & Wolff.*

1 *Blythswood S.B. Co.:* **CEDARDALE** (March 25, 1939).

1 *Cammell Laird:* **DEWDALE** (1941).

2 *Furness S.B. Co.:* **EAGLESDALE, EASEDALE** (1942).

2 *Harland & Wolff (Govan):* **DERWENTDALE, DINGLEDALE** (1941).

1 *Hawthorn Leslie:* **ECHODALE** (1941).

1 *Swan Hunter:* **ENNERDALE** (1941).

Displacement: 17,000 tons. Complement: 40. Dimensions: 460 (*pp.*), 483 (*o.a.*) × 59 × 27½ feet (*mean*). Machinery: Burmeister & Wain 4-cycle Diesels. B.H.P.: 3,500 = 11·5 kts. Deadweight capacity: 12,000 tons. War losses: *Cairndale, Darkdale.* In addition, *Denbydale* was so badly damaged that she has ceased to be seagoing.

ABBEYDALE. Added 1943, *Lieut. D. Trimingham, R.N.V.R.*

2 *Swan Hunter:* **ABBEYDALE** (Dec. 28, 1936), **ARNDALE** (Aug. 5, 1937). Displacement: 17,210 tons.

1 *Lithgows:* **BISHOPDALE** (March 31, 1937). 17,357 tons.

1 *Harland & Wolff* (Govan): **BROOMDALE** (Sept. 2, 1937). 17,338 tons.

Following applies to all 4: Complement: 40. Dimensions: 464¼ (*pp.*), 481½ (*o.a.*) × 62 × 27½ feet (*mean*). Machinery: Doxford Diesels in first 2, Burmeister & Wain in others. B.H.P.: 4,000 = 11·5 kts. Deadweight capacity: 11,650 tons. Own fuel: 850 tons. War losses: *Aldersdale, Boardale.*

Photo, Abrahams, Devonport (added 1927).

1 *Hamilton:* **WAR HINDOO** (1919).

2 *Lithgows:* **WAR BRAHMIN, WAR PINDARI** (both 1920).

2 *Palmers:* **WAR BHARATA** (1920), **WAR NIZAM** (1918).

Displacement: from 11,660 to 11,681 tons. Dimensions: 400 × 52¼ × 25⅔ feet. Deadweight capacities vary from 6,300 tons to 8,000 tons. Triple expansion engines and cylindrical boilers. I.H.P.: 3,000 = 10 kts. War losses: *War Bahadur, War Diwan, War Mehtar, War Sepoy, War Sirdar.* Others have been omitted as no longer seagoing.

LEAF Type. *Photo added* 1927.

APPLELEAF (ex-*Texol*) (Workman Clark), **BRAMBLELEAF** (Lithgows), **CHERRYLEAF** (Sir R. Dixon & Co.), **ORANGELEAF** (J. L. Thompson & Sons), **PEARLEAF** (W. Gray & Co.). All launched 1917. Displacements: from 12,270 to 12,370 tons. Dimensions: 405 × 54½ × 27½ feet. Triple expansion engines and cylindrical boilers. I.H.P.: 6,750 = 14 kts. Deadweight capacity: *Appleleaf* and *Cherryleaf*, 5,400 tons; others, 5,000 tons. War loss: *Plumleaf.*

ELMOL. 1935, *R. Perkins.*

BOXOL (Barclay, Curle), **EBONOL** (Clyde S.B. Co.), **ELDEROL, ELMOL** (Swan Hunter), **HICKOROL** (McMillan), **LARCHOL, LIMOL** (Lobnitz). (All 1917.) **PHILOL** (Tyne Iron S.B. Co.), **KIMMEROL** (Craig, Taylor). (Both 1916.) Displacements: from 2,365 to 2,410 tons. Dimensions: 220 × 34⅝ × 13½ feet. Triple expansion engines and cylindrical boilers. I.H.P. 700 = 9 kts. Own oil: 40 tons. Complement: 19. Deadweight capacity: 1,000 tons. War loss: *Birchol.*

Oilers—*continued.*

CELEROL. 1938, *R. Perkins.*

BELGOL (Irvine's S.B. & D.D. Co.), **CELEROL** (Short Bros.), **FORTOL** (McMillan), **PRESTOL** (Napier & Miller), **RAPIDOL** (W. Gray), **SERBOL** (Caledon S.B. Co.). All launched 1917. Displacements: from 5,049 to 5,620 tons. Dimensions: 335 × 41½ × 20½ feet. I.H.P. 3,375 = 14 kts. Own Oil: 300 tons. Cylindrical boilers. Complement: 39. Deadweight capacity: 2,000 tons. War losses: *Francol, Montenol, Slavol.*

1920 *Photo, Coates, Harwich.*

MIXOL (Caledon S.B. & Eng. Co., 1916). Displacement: 4,326 tons. Dimensions: 270 × 38½ × 20¼ feet. I.H.P.: 1,200 = 11 kts. Oil: 150 tons. Deadweight capacity: 2,000 tons. To be discarded shortly.

Petrol Carriers.

AIRSPRITE (Dec. 22, 1942), **NASPRITE** (Nov. 28, 1940). Both built by Blythswood S.B. Co. 965 tons *gross.* Dimensions: 204½ × 33¼ × 12¾ feet. Machinery: Triple expansion. I.H.P. 900 = 11 kts.

PETRONEL. (See Water Carriers) 1934 *Photo, R. Perkins.*

PETROBUS (Dunlop, Bremner, 1918). Displacement: 1,024 tons. Dimensions: 164 × 28 × 11½ feet. I.H.P.: 500 = 9 kts. Own oil: 50 tons. Cylindrical boilers. Deadweight capacity: 300 tons. Complement: 16.

SPA. 1944, *courtesy Messrs. Philip & Son, Builders.*

SPA (1942), **SPABECK** (1943), **SPABROOK** (1944), **SPABURN** (1946), **SPALAKE** (Aug. 10, 1946), **SPAPOOL** (1946). Displacement: 1,219 tons. Dimensions: 160 (*pp.*), 163 (*o.a.*) × 30 × — feet. Machinery: Triple expansion. I.H.P.: 675. 1 boiler. D.W. capacity: 500 tons. Coal: 90 tons.

FRESHBROOK, FRESHBURN, FRESHENER, FRESHET, FRESHFORD, FRESHLAKE, FRESHMERE, FRESHPOOL, FRESHSPRAY, FRESHTARN, FRESHWATER, FRESHWELL.

PETRONEL (1918). Sister ship to Petrol Carrier *Petrobus.*

Hospital Ships.

AMARAPOORA. 1943, *Official.*

AMARAPOORA (1920). Displacement: 10,000 tons. Dimensions: 465¾ × 59¼ × 26½ feet. Machinery: Triple expansion. I.H.P.: 3,000 = 13 kts.

Added 1946, courtesy Surgeon Captain H. M. Willoughby, R.N.V.R.

OXFORDSHIRE (1912). Displacement: 10,500 tons. Dimensions: 474½ × 55¼ × 28 feet. Machinery: Quadruple expansion. Speed: 15 kts.

MAINE. 1935, *R. Perkins.*

MAINE (ex-Pacific Steam Navigation Company's s.s. *Panama*) (Fairfield Co., 1902). Purchased in 1920 and equipped for present duties. Displacement: 10,100 tons. Dimensions: 401¼ × 58¼ × 23½ feet. Machinery: Triple expansion. I.H.P. 4,000 = 13 kts. 2 D.E. and 2 S.E. boilers. Coal: 1,300 tons.

Fleet Tugs.

ENFORCER. 1946, *Wright & Logan.*

(5 ENVOY CLASS.)

ENCHANTER (Nov. 1944), **ENCORE** (Dec. 1944), **ENFORCER** (July, 1944), **ENIGMA** (June, 1944), **ENVOY** (Feb. 1944). All built by Cochrane & Sons, Ltd. Displacement: 1,332 tons; 762 tons *gross.* Dimensions: 174½ × 36 × 17 feet (*max.*). Guns: 1—3 inch AA., 2—20 mm. AA., 2 M.G. Machinery: Triple expansion. I.H.P. 1,700 = 13 kts. Boilers: 2 cylindrical. Oil fuel: 398 tons. Complement: 33.

Note.—Enticer lost in heavy weather in S. China Sea, Dec. 21, 1946.

GROWLER. 1943, *Official.*

(7 BUSTLER CLASS.)

BUSTLER (Dec. 4, 1941), **GROWLER** (Sept. 10, 1942), **MEDIATOR** (June 21, 1944), **REWARD** (Oct, 31, 1944), **SAMSONIA** (April 1, 1942), **TURMOIL** (July 14, 1944), **WARDEN** (Aug. 16, 1944). All built by Henry Robb, Ltd. Displacement: 1,800 tons; 1,100 tons *gross*. Dimensions: 190 (*pp.*), 205 (*o.a.*) × 38½ × 17 feet (*mean*), 18½ feet (*max.*). Guns: **1**—3 inch AA., **1**—2 pdr. pompom, **2**—20 mm. AA., 4 Lewis. Machinery: 2 sets Polar Diesels. B.H.P.: 4,000=15 kts. Oil fuel: 405 tons. Complement: 42. War loss: *Hesperia.*

Note.—Samsonia is temporarily renamed *Foundation Josephine* while on long-term charter in Canadian waters.

EARNER. 1944, *Official.*

(16 ASSURANCE CLASS.)

ALLEGIANCE (Feb. 1943), **ANTIC** (March, 1943), **ASSIDUOUS** (June, 1943), **CHARON** (Nov. 1941), **DEXTEROUS** (April 1942), **EARNER** (ex-*Earnest*) (July, 1943), **FRISKY** (May, 1941), **GRIPER** (May, 1942), **HENGIST** (Dec. 1941), **JAUNTY** (June, 1941,) **PROSPEROUS** (June, 1942), **PRUDENT** (Aug. 1940), **RESTIVE** (Sept. 1940), **SAUCY** (Oct. 1942), **STORMKING** (Nov. 1942), **TENACITY** (June, 1940). All built by Cochrane & Sons, Ltd. Displacement: 1,045 tons; 597 tons *gross*. Dimensions: 157 × 35 × — feet. Guns: **1**—3 inch AA., 1—20 mm. AA., 2 M.G. Machinery: Triple expansion. I.H.P. 1,350=13 kts. 1 cylindrical boiler. Oil fuel: 262 tons. Complement: 31. War losses: *Adept, Adherent, Assurance, Horsa, Sesame.*

CAPABLE. 1946, *Wright & Logan.*

(4 NIMBLE CLASS.)

CAPABLE (Hall, Russell, Nov. 22, 1945), **CAREFUL** (A. Hall & Co., Oct. 23, 1945), **EXPERT** (1944), **NIMBLE** (Dec. 4, 1941), both by Fleming & Ferguson. Displacement: 890 tons. Dimensions: 165 (*pp.*), 175 (*o.a.*) × 35¾ × 13¾ feet. Machinery: Triple expansion. 2 shafts. I.H.P. 3,500 = 16 kts. Boilers: 2 of 3-drum type. Fuel: 300 tons.

BRITON. 1946, *Wright & Logan.*

(4 BRIGAND CLASS.)

BRIGAND (July 8, 1937), **BRITON** (ex-*Bandit*, Feb. 15,1938), **MARAUDER** (Nov. 9, 1938), **FREEBOOTER** (Nov. 29, 1940). Built by Fleming & Ferguson, Paisley, under 1936, 1937, 1938 Estimates. Displacement: 840 tons. Complement: 43. Dimensions: 165 (*pp.*), 174 (*o.a.*) × 32 × 10⅔ feet. Guns: 1—3 inch AA., 1—20 mm. AA., 2 Lewis. Triple expansion engines. 2 shafts. Designed H.P.: 3,000=15·5 kts. Boilers: 2 of 3-drum type. Oil fuel: 390 tons.

Notes.—Fitted for salvage work, and have towing winches for work with battle practice targets. *Buccaneer* sunk by accident during gunnery practice, Aug. 25, 1946.

ROYSTERER (*Resolve, Retort,* no Fx. deck). 1929, *N. T. Tangye, Esq.*

(5 ROLLICKER TYPE).

RESOLVE, RESPOND (both by Ayrshire D.Y. Co.), **RETORT** (Day, Summers & Co.), **ROLLICKER** (Ferguson Bros.). **ROYSTERER** (Thornycroft). (1918–19.) Displacement: 1,400 tons. Dimensions: 175 × 34 × 17 (*maximum* draught). 2 shafts. I.H.P.: 2,400 = 14 kts. Complement: 24.

Notes.—All on Harbour Service List. *Rollicker* was transferred to Nigerian Government, but was reacquired by Admiralty in March, 1934.

ST. MELLONS. 1944, *J. W. Kennedy, Esq.*

(7 SAINT CLASS.)

ST. CLEARS, ST. DAY, ST. DOGMAEL, ST. MARTIN, ST. MELLONS, ST. MONANCE, ST. OMAR. Built by various yards, 1918–19. Displacement: 570 tons. Dimensions: 135½ × 29 × 14½ feet (*maximum* draught). 1 screw. I.H.P.: 1,250=12 kts. Coal: 240 tons. Complement: 21.

Note.—Two more tugs of this type, *Toia* (ex-*St. Boniface*) and *Ocean Eagle* (ex-*St. Arvans*), transferred to New Zealand Harbour Dept. and Canadian Government respectively. Others will be found in Brazilian, Iraqi and Spanish Navies, and in commercial harbours such as Shanghai, Sydney, Fremantle, etc.

Miscellaneous

Salvage Vessels.

SALVESTOR 1946, *J. W. Kennedy, Esq.*

(KING SALVOR CLASS.)

KING SALVOR, OCEAN SALVOR, PRINCE SALVOR (March 1943), **SALVAGE DUKE, SALVALOUR, SALVENTURE, SALVESTOR, SALVICTOR, SALVIGIL, SALVIOLA, SEA SALVOR.** 1,100 tons *gross*. Dimensions: 200 × 57 × 13 feet (*max.*). Machinery: Triple expansion. 2 shafts. I.H.P. 1,500. Complement: 52 to 72.

SALVEDA. 782 tons *gross*. Dimensions: 184 × 34½ × 11¼ feet (*mean*). H.P. 1,200=12 kts. Complement: 62.

DISPENSER, HELP, KINBRACE, KINGARTH, KINLOSS, LIFELINE, SUCCOUR, SWIN, UPLIFTER. 775 tons *gross*. Dimensions: 150×35×11 feet (*max.*) I.H.P. 600. Complement: 34.

MOORPOUT, MOORSMAN (both 1944). Salvage and mooring vessels. Fitted with salvage pumps, air compressors and diving equipment.

Fleet Supply Ship.

1934 *Official.*

RELIANT (ex-*London Importer*). (Purchased, March, 1933.) Built by Furness Shipbuilding Co., 1923. Displacement: 17,000 tons. Gross tonnage: 7,938. Dimensions: 450½ (*pp.*), 471½ (*o.a.*) × 58 × 30 feet (*max.*). 2 Brown-Curtis geared turbines. S.H.P.: 5,000 = 14 kts. 4 cylindrical boilers, 190 lbs. working pressure. Oil fuel: 2,170 tons.

Munition Carriers.

THROSK. 1944, *courtesy Messrs. Philip & Son, Ltd.*

KINTERBURY (1943), **THROSK** (1944). Both built by Philip & Son, Ltd. Displacement: 1,488 tons. Dimensions: 185 × 33 × 14½ feet. Machinery: Triple expansion. I.H.P. 900. Coal: 153 tons. Deadweight capacity: 769 tons.

Store Carriers.

BACCHUS. 1936, *courtesy Builders.*

BACCHUS. (Caledon Shipbuilding & Engineering Co., Ltd., July 15, 1936). Displacement: 5,150 tons *standard*, 5,790 tons *full load*. Complement, 44. Dimensions: 320 (*pp.*), 337½ (*o.a.*) × 49 × 18 feet (*max.* draught). No guns. Machinery: Triple expansion. I.H.P.: 2,000 = 12 kts. 3 cylindrical boilers. Oil fuel: 643 tons. Equipped with distilling plant. Deadweight capacity: 3,300 tons.

ROBERT MIDDLETON. 1946, *Wright & Logan.*

ROBERT DUNDAS (July 28, 1938), **ROBERT MIDDLETON** (June 29, 1938). Both built by Grangemouth Dockyard Co., Ltd. Displacement: 900 tons. Complement: 17. Dimensions: 210 × 35 × 13½ feet (*mean*). Machinery: Atlas Polar Diesel by British Auxiliaries Ltd., Govan. 1 shaft. B.H.P.: 960 = 10·5 kts. Fuel: 60 tons. Deadweight capacity: 1,100 tons.

Naval Aviation Store Carriers.

RIPON. 1946, *Wright & Logan.*

3 *Blyth S.B. Co.:* **BLACKBURN, ROC, WALRUS.**

4 *Pollock:* **RIPON, SEAFOX, SEA GLADIATOR, SEA HURRICANE.**

Displacement: 990 tons. Dimensions: 210 (*o.a.*) × 35 × 13¾ feet. Machinery: Crossley 2-stroke Diesels. B.H.P.: 960 = 10·5 kts. Fuel: 60 tons. Fitted with 6-ton and 12-ton derricks for handling aircraft.

Controlled Target Vessels.

CT 41 1946, *London Studio.*

Most of these appear to be redundant craft adapted for target service.

ROYAL AUSTRALIAN NAVY

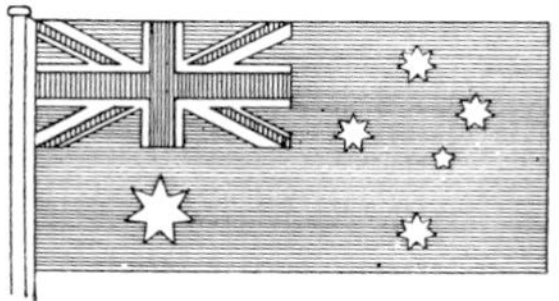

ENSIGN.

Australian Naval Board.

President: Minister of State for the Navy, Hon. W. J. F. Riordan, M.P.

1st Naval Member: Admiral Sir Louis Hamilton, K.C.B., D.S.O.

2nd Naval Member: Commodore J. M. Armstrong, D.S.O., AdC., R.A.N.

3rd Naval Member: Eng. Rear-Admiral A. B. Doyle, C.B.E., R.A.N.

Finance Member: Raymond Anthony, Esq.

Business Member: H. G. Brain, Esq.

Secretary, Dept. of the Navy: A. R. Nankervis, Esq.

Secretary to Naval Board: T. J. Hawkins, Esq.

Liaison Officer, London: Capt. (S) J. B. Foley, C.B.E., R.A.N.

Commonwealth Navy Personnel.

1946: A total strength of 13,500 officers and men has been approved *ad interim*.

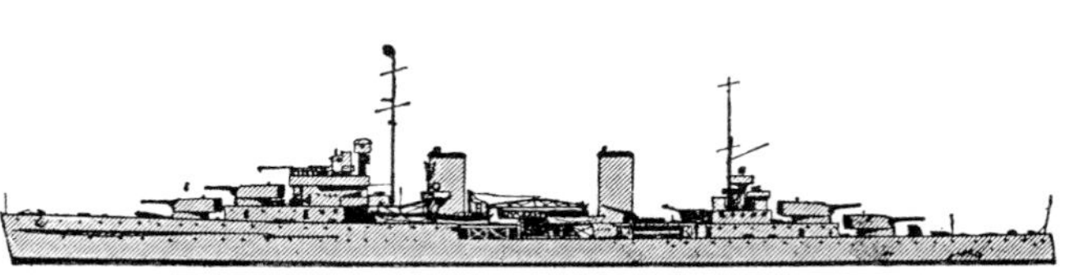

HOBART.

ADELAIDE.

BATHURST *class*.

AUSTRALIA.

QUEENBOROUGH *class*.

SWAN. (WARREGO similar.)

SHROPSHIRE.

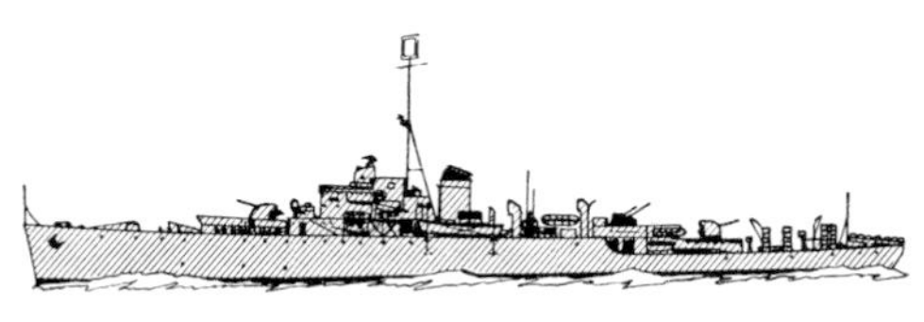

MURCHISON *class*.

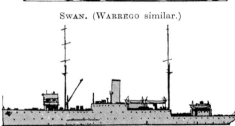

PLATYPUS.

Cruisers

HOBART. 1946, *Roy E. Scrivener, Esq.*

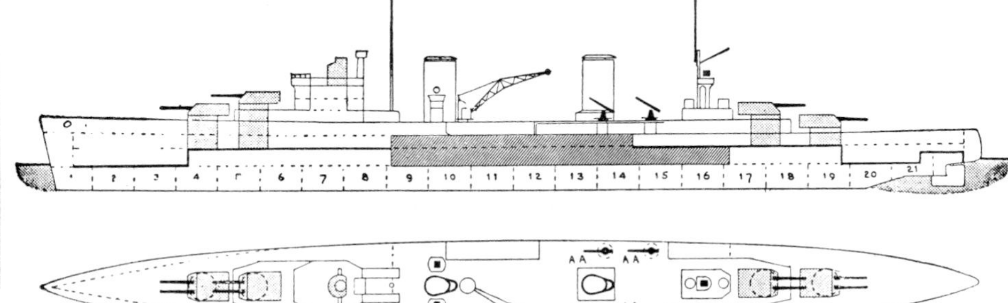

HOBART (ex-*Apollo*), (Oct. 9, 1934).

Displacement: 7,105 tons. Complement: 550.

Dimensions: 530 (*pp.*), 555 (*w.l.*) × $56\frac{2}{3}$ × $15\frac{2}{3}$ feet (*mean* draught).

Guns: 8—6 inch.
8—4 inch d.p.
8—2 pdrs.
11 smaller.
8 M.G.

Armour:
1″ turrets.
1″ bridges.
2—3″ side.
2″ deck.

Tubes: 8—21 inch (quadrupled).

Note to Plan.—Torpedo tubes are above water, in position shown in photo, and AA. guns are in pairs.

Machinery: 4 Parsons geared turbines. 4 shafts. S.H.P.: 72,000 = 32·5 kts. Boilers: 4 Admiralty 3-drum type. Oil: 1,725 tons.

Note.—Acquired from Royal Navy in 1938. Though officially described as of "modified *Leander* type", she differs entirely from that class in appearance. She cost nearly £1,450,000 to build, and was badly damaged aft by a torpedo off the New Hebrides in 1943. War losses of this type: *Perth*, *Sydney*.

Est.	*Name*	*Builder*	*Machinery*	*Ordered*	*Begun*	*Completed*
1932	*Hobart*	Devonport	Beardmore	1/3/33	15/8/33	1/36

Cruisers

SHROPSHIRE. 1946, *London Studio.*

SHROPSHIRE (July 5, 1928).

Displacement: 9,830 tons. Complement: 650.

Length (*pp.*), 595 feet; (*o.a.*), 633 feet. Beam, 66 feet. Draught, 17 feet (*mean*).

Guns: 8—8 inch, 50 cal.
8—4 inch d.p.
16—2 pdr.
15 smaller.
10 M.G.

Armour: 4″ Deck.
2″—1½″ Gun houses.
3″ C.T.

Torpedo tubes: 8—21 inch (quadrupled).

(Plan as H.M.S. *Sussex*, etc., on an earlier page.)

Machinery: Parsons geared turbines. 4 shafts. S.H.P. 80,000 = 32·25 kts. Boilers: 8 Admiralty 3-drum type. Oil fuel: 3,200 tons.

Notes.—Laid down by Beardmore, Feb. 1926, and completed Sept. 1929. She was officially presented to R.A.N. June 25, 1943, to replace *Canberra*, lost in action, and arrived in Australian waters the following October.

AUSTRALIA. 1945, *Francis H. A. Baker, Esq.*

AUSTRALIA (17th March, 1927).

"Standard" displacement, 10,000 tons (as reconstructed) (13,630 *deep load*). Complement, 679 (710 as flagship).

Length (*pp.*) 590 feet, (*o.a.*) 630 feet. Beam, 68¼ feet. Draught, 16¼ feet (*mean*).

Guns:
6—8 inch, 50 cal.
8—4 inch d.p.
16—2 pdr.
12 smaller.
19 M.G.

Armour:
3″—5″ Side at w.l.
4″ Deck
2″—1½″ Gun Houses
3″ C.T.
Bulges

Machinery: Brown-Curtis geared turbines. 4 screws. Designed S.H.P. 80,000 = 31·5 kts. Boilers: 8 Admiralty 3-drum type. Oil fuel: 3,400 tons. Radius at full speed, 2,300 miles; at economical speed (11—14 kts.), 10,400 miles.

General Notes.—Sister to *Kent* class, in British Navy Section. Designed by Sir E. H. Tennyson d'Eyncourt. Laid down by John Brown & Co., Ltd., Clydebank, in 1925, and completed in April, 1928. (See also detailed notes under *Kent* class, of Royal Navy, on an earlier page.) Under refit at Devonport Dockyard, 1945. Sister ship *Canberra* was lost in action.

Special Note.

In April, 1944, it was stated officially that an Australian cruiser was to be built in a Commonwealth shipyard at an estimated cost of £4,500,000. It was expected that construction would take at least five years, as it was proposed to manufacture guns and armour in Australia. There is no news of this ship having been ordered.

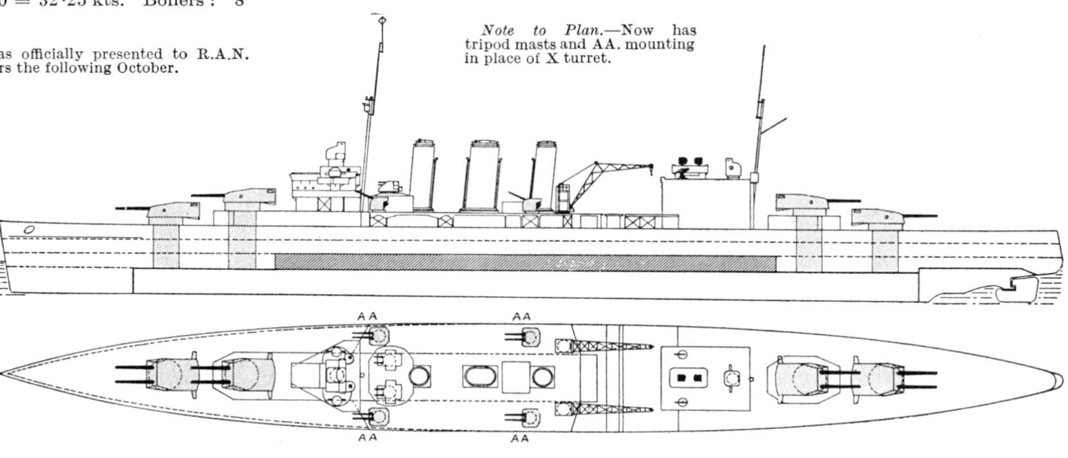

Note to Plan.—Now has tripod masts and AA. mounting in place of X turret.

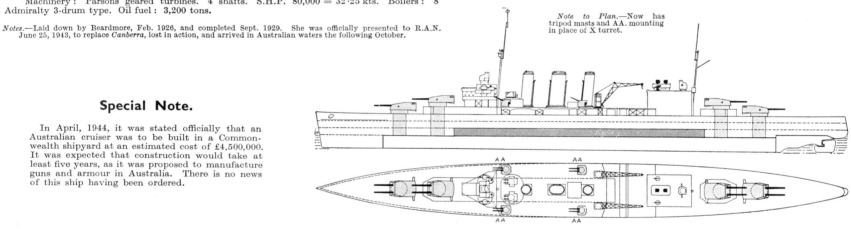

ADELAIDE (July, 1918).

Displacement, 5100 tons. Complement, 470.

Length (*o.a.*), 462⅔ feet. Beam, 49⅝ feet. Draught, 15⅝ feet (*mean*), 17¾—19 (*max.*).

Guns:
8—6 inch, 50 cal.
3—4 inch d.p.
4—3 pdr.
12—smaller.

Note to Plan.—Only 1—6 inch gun is now mounted on forecastle.

Armour:
2″ Deck (on slopes).
3″ (on sides) amidships.
1½″ (on sides) fore and aft.

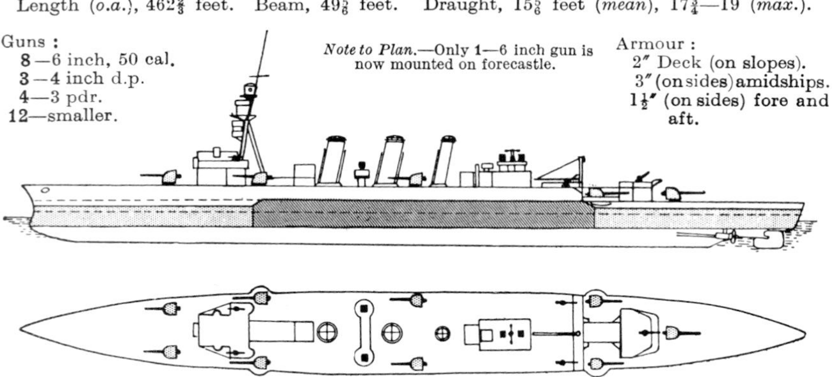

ADELAIDE. *Added 1946, Real Photographs Co.*

Machinery: Parsons turbines. Boilers: Yarrow. Designed S.H.P.: 25,000 = 25·5 kts. Oil fuel: 1,412 tons. 2 shafts.

Notes.—Laid down at Cockatoo Dockyard in Jan. 1915 and completed Aug. 1922. Cost £1,271,782 to build. Completely refitted 1938–39, when number of funnels was reduced from 4 to 3 and armament modified. Placed in reserve, and may be used for squadron gunnery practice.

Destroyers.

Two, of "Battle" type, ordered from Cockatoo Docks & Engineering Co., Pty., Ltd., and from Williamstown Naval Dockyard.

Displacement: 2,315 tons. Dimensions: 379 (*o.a.*) × 40¼ × 12¾ feet. Guns: **5**—4·5 inch d.p., **8**—40 mm. AA. Tubes: **10**—21 inch. Machinery: Parsons geared turbines. 2 shafts. S.H.P.: 50,000 = 34 kts. Boilers: 3 Admiralty 3-drum type.

5 Queenborough Class.

QUIBERON. 1946, *I. K. S. Paterson, Esq.*

1 *Hawthorn*: ***Quadrant.*** 2 *Swan Hunter*: ***Quality, Queenborough.***

2 *White*: ***Quiberon, Quickmatch.***

Displacement: 1,705 tons. Dimensions: 358¾ × 35¾ × 9½ feet. Guns: **4**—4·7 inch, **4**—2 pdr., **2**—40 mm., sundry 20 mm. AA. Tubes: **8**—21 inch. Machinery: Parsons geared turbines. 2 shafts. Boilers: 2 Admiralty 3-drum type. Complement: 220 (war). Lent to R. Australian Navy in 1943 (*Quiberon, Quickmatch*) and 1945 (others). *Quality, Queenborough* placed in reserve, 1946. *Quilliam* (Hawthorn) transferred to R. Netherland Navy. War losses: *Quail* (Hawthorn), *Quentin* (White).

Name	*Begun*	*Launch*	*Completed*
Quadrant	24/9/40	28/2/42	26/11/42
Quality	10/10/40	6/10/41	7/9/42
Queenborough	6/11/40	16/1/42	10/12/42
Quiberon	4/10/40	31/1/42	22/7/42
Quickmatch	6/2/41	11/4/42	30/9/42

3 "Tribal" Class.

BATAAN. 1946, *I. K. S. Paterson, Esq.*

Arunta (Nov. 30, 1940), ***Warramunga*** (Feb. 7, 1942), ***Bataan*** (ex-*Kurnai*) (Jan. 15, 1944). All built by Cockatoo Docks & Engineering Co. Proprietary, Ltd.

Displacement: 1,927 tons. Complement: 250. Dimensions: 355½ × 36½ × 9 feet. Guns: **8**—4 inch d.p., **10** smaller, **4** M.G. Tubes: **4**—21 inch. Machinery: Parsons geared turbines. S.H.P.: 44,000 = 36·5 kts. Boilers: 3 Admiralty 3-drum type. *Bataan* was completed in July, 1945.

Frigates.

MURCHISON. 1946, *courtesy Messrs. Evans, Deakin & Co. (Builders).*

CONDAMINE (Oct. 20, 1943), **MURCHISON** (1944), **SHOALHAVEN** (Dec. 14, 1944). Displacement: 1,544 tons (2,106 tons *full load*). Dimensions: 283 (*pp.*), 301½ (*o.a.*) × 36½ × 12 feet (*mean* draught). Guns: **4**—4 inch d.p., **3**—40 mm. AA., **8**—20 mm. AA., **1** hedgehog, **4** D.C.T. Machinery: Triple expansion. 2 shafts. I.H.P.: 5,500 = 20 kts. Boilers: 2 Admiralty 3-drum type. Complement: 177.

Note.—Respective builders of these 3 ships, which are an Australian variation of the "Bay" class, were N.S.W. Govt. Engineering & Shipbuilding Undertaking, Newcastle; Evans, Deakin & Co., Ltd., Brisbane; and Walkers, Ltd., Maryborough.

BURDEKIN. 1946, *courtesy Messrs. Evans, Deakin & Co.*

BARCOO (Aug. 26, 1943), **BARWON** (Aug. 3, 1944), **BURDEKIN** (June 30, 1943), **CULGOA** (ex-*Macquarie*, Sept. 22, 1945), **DIAMANTINA** (April 6, 1944), **GASCOYNE** (March 20, 1943), **HAWKESBURY** (July 24, 1943), **LACHLAN** (March 25, 1944), **MACQUARIE** (ex-*Culgoa*, March 3, 1945).

Displacement: 1,420 tons. Dimensions: 301⅓ × 36⅝ × 12 feet. Guns: **2**—4 inch d.p., **2**—40 mm. AA. (in *Lachlan* only), **6** to **20** M.G., **4** D.C.T. Machinery: Triple expansion. 2 shafts. I.H.P.: 5,500 = 20 kts. Boilers: 2 Admiralty 3-drum type. Complement: 140. Cancelled ships: *Bogam, Murrumbidgee, Namoi, Warburton.*

Sloops.

SWAN (1936), **WARREGO** (Feb. 10, 1940). Built by Cockatoo Docks & Engineering Co. Pty. Ltd. Displacement: 1,060 tons. Complement: 100. Dimensions: (250 *pp.*), 262 (*w.l.*) 266 (*o.a.*) × 36 × 7½ feet (*mean*). Guns: **3**—4 inch d.p., **4**—3 pdr., **6** M.G. Machinery: 2 sets Parsons geared turbines. S.H.P.: 2,000 = 16·5 kts. Boilers: 2 Admiralty 3-drum type. Oil fuel: 275 tons. War losses of this type: *Parramatta, Yarra.*

SWAN. *Added 1942, Ted Stone.*

Fleet Minesweepers.

Gympie. 1946, *courtesy Messrs. Evans, Deakin & Co.*

Bunbury. 1946, *courtesy Messrs. Evans, Deakin & Co.*

(Bathurst Class—38 Ships.)

ARARAT (1943), ***BALLARAT** (Dec. 10, 1940), ***BATHURST** (1940), ***BENDIGO** (March 1, 1941), **BOWEN, BUNBURY** (1943), **BUNDABERG, CASTLEMAINE, *CESSNOCK, COLAC, COOTAMUNDRA, COWRA, DELORAINE, DUBBO, ECHUCA, FREMANTLE, GLADSTONE, GLENELG, *GOULBURN, GYMPIE, HORSHAM, INVERELL, JUNEE, KAPUNDA, KATOOMBA, KIAMA, LATROBE** (1942), **LITHGOW** (Dec. 21, 1940), ***MARYBOROUGH** (Oct. 1940), **MILDURA, PARKES, ROCKHAMPTON, STAWELL, STRAHAN, TOWNSVILLE, WAGGA, WARRNAMBOOL, *WHYALLA** (ex-*Glenelg*). All built in Australia; those marked * were originally ordered for the Royal Navy, but have been manned by R.A.N. Design is generally similar to *Bangor* type. Displacement: 650 tons, except *Ballarat, Bathurst, Bendigo, Goulburn, Maryborough, Whyalla*, 733 tons; and *Cootamundra, Cowra, Junee*, 790 tons. Complement: 60. Dimensions: $162 \times 28 \times 8\frac{1}{3}$ feet (*mean* draught). Guns: **1**—4 inch, **1**—40 mm. AA., **5** or **6** M.G., except *Bathurst, Cessnock, Stawell*, which have **1**—3 inch instead of **1**—4 inch. Machinery: Triple expansion. 2 shafts. I.H.P.: 1,800 = 15 kts. Commonly referred to in Australia as corvettes, and were mainly employed on escort duties in 1941–45. War losses: *Armidale, Geelong, Wallaroo.*

Note.—4 more ships of this type were built in Australia for R. Indian Navy, 8 sold to R. Netherland Navy and 5 to Turkish Navy. *Bathurst* and *Lismore* differ in appearance from others in having a flying bridge.

Depot and Repair Ship.

R.A.N. Official Photo, 1922.

PLATYPUS (ex-*Penguin*, ex-*Platypus*) (Clydebank, Oct. 28th, 1916). Displacement: 3,455 tons. Dimensions: 310 (*w.l.*), 325 (*o.a.*) $\times 44 \times 15\frac{2}{3}$ feet. (*max.* draught). Guns: Not reported. Machinery: 2 sets triple expansion. 2 shafts. I.H.P. 3,500 = 15·5 kts. 4 cylindrical return-tube boilers. Coal: 450 tons. Complement: 357. (Now in reserve.)

Surveying Vessels.

BENALLA, SHEPPARTON. Laid down as units of *Bathurst* class, but completed for present duty. Displacement: 560 tons. Dimensions: $162 \times 28 \times 8\frac{1}{4}$ feet (*mean* draught). Machinery: Triple expansion. 2 shafts. I.H.P.: 1,800 = 15 kts.

Note.—Frigate *Lachlan* and "corvette" *Whyalla* were also employed on surveying duties during the war.

Fleet Tugs.

1944, *Official.*

RESERVE, SPRIGHTLY. Built in U.S.A. Displacement: 763 tons. Dimensions: $143 \times 33 \times 13\frac{1}{2}$ feet. Guns: **1**—40 mm. AA., **4** M.G. and **1**—3 inch AA., **2** M.G. respectively. Machinery: Diesel-electric. B.H.P. 1,875 = 14 kts. Fuel: 186 tons. Complement: 34.

Boom Working Vessels.

KARANGI (Aug. 16, 1941), **KOALA, KANGAROO** (1939). Displacement: 730 tons. Dimensions: 150 (*pp.*), $173\frac{3}{4}$ (*o.a.*) $\times 32\frac{1}{6} \times 9\frac{1}{2}$ feet. Guns: **1**—3 inch AA. Machinery: Triple expansion. I.H.P.: 850 = 11·5 kts. 2 boilers. Oil fuel: 140 tons. Complement: 32. Appearance as "Bar" type, Royal Navy.

1942, *Wide World Photos.*

KOOKABURRA (Oct. 29, 1938). Built at Cockatoo Dockyard. Displacement: 533 tons. Dimensions: 120 (*pp.*), 135 (*o.a.*) $\times 26\frac{1}{2} \times 10\frac{1}{4}$ feet. Guns: **1**—3 inch AA. Machinery: Triple expansion. I.H.P.: 450 = 9·5 kts. Cylindrical boiler. Oil fuel: 82 tons.

Fleet Auxiliaries.

BINGERA (Naval Store Carrier). 922 tons *gross*. Dimensions: $200 \times 34 \times 9$ feet. Guns: **1**—4 inch, **1**—40 mm. AA., **4** M.G.

WILCANNIA (Victualling Store Issuing Ship). 1,050 tons *gross*. Dimensions: $226 \times 36\frac{1}{2} \times 12\frac{3}{4}$ feet. Guns: **1**—4 inch, **1**—40 mm. AA., **6** M.G. Speed: 11 kts.

URALBA (Armament Store Carrier). 603 tons *gross*. Dimensions: $154 \times 37 \times 10$ feet. Guns: **2** M.G. Speed: 8 kts.

WOOMERA (Armament Store Carrier). 300 tons *gross*. Speed: 8 kts.

LST 3008, 3014, 3017, 3026, 3035, 3501 (on loan from R.N.). Displacement: 2,300 tons. Dimensions: $347\frac{1}{2} \times 55\frac{1}{4} \times 12\frac{1}{2}$ feet. Guns: **4**—40 mm. AA., **16**—20 mm. AA. Speed: 13·5 kts.

Coastal Craft.

ML 424—429, 431, 801—827. All of Fairmile "B" type. Also **HDML 1074, 1129, 1161, 1321—1327, 1329, 1338—1343, 1352, 1353, 1358, 1359.**

ROYAL CANADIAN NAVY

Governor-General: Field-Marshal the Rt. Hon. Viscount Alexander of Tunis, G.C.B., C.S.I., D.S.O., M.C.

Minister of National Defence: The Hon. Douglas C. Abbott.

Naval Board.

Chief of the Naval Staff: Vice-Admiral H. E. Reid, C.B., R.C.N.

Chief of Naval Personnel: Captain G. R. Miles, O.B.E., R.C.N.

Chief of Naval Equipment and Supply: Rear-Admiral H. T. W. Grant, C.B.E., D.S.O., R.C.N.

Chief of Naval Engineering and Construction: Commander (E) J. G. Knowlton, C.B.E., R.C.N.

Assistant Chief of Naval Staff: Commodore F. L. Houghton, R.C.N.

Financial and Civil Member and Deputy Minister for Naval Service: Mr. W. Gordon Mills.

Secretary to the Naval Board: Captain (S) H. R. Northrup, O.B.E., R.C.N.

Navy Estimates, 1944–45: $410,000,000.

Personnel (1946): 10,000.

Ships of the R.C.N. fly White Ensign.

Head of Naval Mission, London: Commodore A. M. Hope, O.B.E., R.C.N.

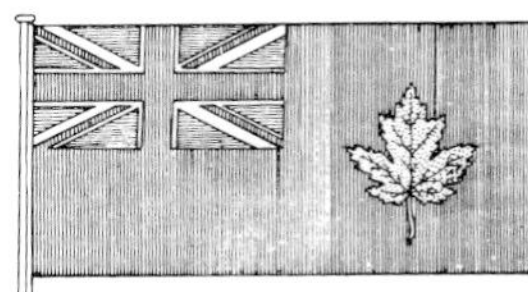

Ensign.

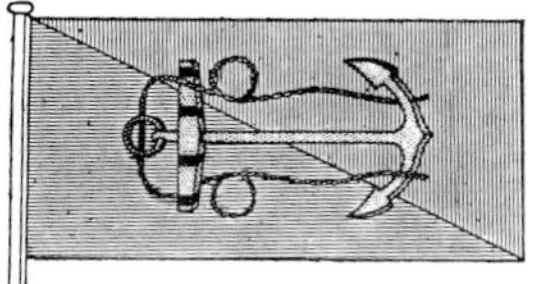

Canadian Admiralty Flag.

WARRIOR.

"TRIBAL" *class.*

GATINEAU, QU'APPELLE.

UGANDA.

CRESCENT, CRUSADER

FRIGATES.

ONTARIO.

ALGONQUIN, SIOUX.

WINNIPEG *class.*

Light Fleet Aircraft Carriers.

WARRIOR. 1946, *Associated Press.*

MAGNIFICENT (Nov. 16, 1944), **WARRIOR** (May 20, 1944).

Displacement: 14,000 and 13,350 tons, respectively. Complement: 1,350.
Length: (*w.l.*) 650 feet; (*o.a.*) 693¼ feet. Beam: (*w.l.*) 80⅓ feet; (*o.a.*) 112½ feet. Draught: 23 feet.

Guns:
24—2-pdr.
19—40 mm. AA. (Bofors).

Aircraft:
40.

Machinery: Parsons geared turbines. 2 shafts. S.H.P.: 40,000 = 25 kts. Boilers: 4 Admiralty 3-drum type.

Notes.—Both built by Harland & Wolff, Ltd., Belfast, and lent from Royal Navy. *Warrior* laid down 12/12/42 and completed 24/1/46. Completion of *Magnificent* likely to be delayed.

Cruisers.

ONTARIO (ex-*Minotaur*, July 29, 1943).

Displacement: 8,000 tons. Dimensions: 555½ (*o.a.*) × 63 × 20 feet

Guns:
9—6 inch
10—4 inch d.p.
19—2 pdr.
13—40 mm. AA.

Torpedo tubes:
6—21 inch.

Armour:
Similar to *Uganda*.

Machinery: Parsons geared turbines. 4 shafts. S.H.P. 72,500=31·5 kts. Boilers: 4 Admiralty 3-drum type. Fuel: 1,850 tons.

Notes.—Laid down 20/11/41 by Harland & Wolff, Ltd., for Royal Navy, and presented to Royal Canadian Navy on completion, 25/5/45.

ONTARIO. 1944, *R.C.N. Official.*

ONTARIO. 1944 *R.C.N. Official.*

UGANDA (August 7, 1941).

Displacement: 8,000 tons. Complement: 900. Length: (*pp.*) 549 feet, (*o.a.*) 555½ feet. Beam: 62 feet. Draught: 16½ feet (*mean*).

Guns:
9—6 inch
10—4 inch d.p.
Numerous 40 mm. and 20 mm. AA.

Torpedo tubes:
6—21 inch.

Armour:
3″—4½″ Side

Machinery: Parsons geared turbines. 4 shafts. S.H.P. 72,500=31·5 kts. Boilers: 4 Admiralty 3-drum type.

Notes.—Laid down by Vickers-Armstrongs, Ltd., on the Tyne 20/7/39, and completed 3/1/43. Was presented to the R.C.N. on October 21, 1944, and claims the distinction of having been the first ship in that Service to sail round Cape Horn.

(Plan as in R.N. section.)

UGANDA. 1944, *R.C.N. Official.*

UGANDA. 1944, *R.C.N. Official.*

UGANDA. 1944, *R.C.N. Official.*

2 Crescent Class.

(Photo wanted.)

2 *Clydebank:* **Crescent** (July 20, 1944), **Crusader** (Oct. 5, 1944). Displacement: 1,710 tons. Dimensions: $362\frac{3}{4} \times 35\frac{3}{4} \times 10$ feet. Guns: **4**—4·5 inch d.p., **4**—40 mm. AA., **4**—20 mm. AA. Tubes: **4**—21 inch (quadrupled). Machinery: Parsons geared turbines. 2 shafts. S.H.P.: 40,000 = 34 kts. Boilers: 2 Admiralty 3-drum type. Complement: Peace, 165; War, 250. (Presented to R.C.N., 1945.)

2 "V" type.

ALGONQUIN. 1943, *R.C.N. Official.*

1 *Clydebank:* **Algonquin** (ex-*Valentine*, ex-*Kempenfelt*, Sept. 2, 1943).
1 *White:* **Sioux** (ex-*Vixen*, Sept. 14, 1943).

Transferred from Royal Navy early in 1944. Displacement: 1,710 tons. Dimensions: $362\frac{3}{4} \times 35\frac{3}{4} \times 10$ feet. Guns: **4**—4·7 inch (Mark XII), **4**—40 mm. AA., **4**—20 mm. AA. Tubes: **8**—21 inch (quadrupled). Machinery: Parsons geared turbines. 2 shafts. S.H.P.: 40,000 = 34 kts. Boilers: 2 Admiralty 3-drum type. Complement: 230.

7 "Tribal" Class.

MICMAC. 1944, *R.C.N. Official*

3 *Vickers-Armstrongs (Tyne):* **Haida** (Aug. 25, 1942), **Huron** (June 25, 1942), **Iroquois** (Sept. 23, 1941).
4 *Halifax Shipyards:* **Athabaskan** (building), **Cayuga** (July 28, 1945), **Micmac** (Sept. 18, 1943), **Nootka** (April 26, 1944).

Displacement: 1,927 tons (2,745 tons *full load*). Complement: 240. Dimensions: $355\frac{1}{2} \times 37\frac{1}{2} \times 9\frac{1}{2}$ feet. Guns: **8**—4 inch d.p., **10**—20 mm. Oerlikon. Tubes: **4**—21 inch. Machinery: Parsons geared turbines. 2 shafts. S.H.P.: 44,000 = 36·5 kts. Boilers: 3 Admiralty 3-drum type. War loss: *Athabaskan*.

2 Gatineau Class.

GATINEAU. 1942, *Official.*

QU'APPELLE. 1943, *Official.*

1 *Clydebank:* **Qu'appelle** (ex-*Foxhound*, Oct. 12, 1934).
1 *Swan Hunter:* **Gatineau** (ex-*Express*, May 29, 1934).

Both transferred from Royal Navy in 1943. Displacement: 1,375 and 1,350 tons, respectively. Dimensions: 326 (*w.l.*) × $33\frac{1}{4} \times 8\frac{1}{2}$ feet. Guns: **2**—4·7 inch, **1**—3 inch AA., several smaller. Tubes: **4**—21 inch. Machinery: Parsons geared turbines. S.H.P.: 36,000 = 36 kts. Boilers: 3 Admiralty 3-drum type. Oil fuel: 480 tons. (Both lent from Royal Navy.)

18 Frigates.

WASKESIU. (Since discarded.) 1943, *R.C.N. Official.*

ANTIGONISH (Feb. 10, 1944), **BEACON HILL** (Nov. 6, 1943), **CAPILANO** (April 8, 1944), **CHARLOTTETOWN** (Sept. 16, 1943), **GROU** (Aug. 7, 1943), **KIRKLAND LAKE** (ex-*St. Jerome*, April 27, 1944), **LA HULLOISE** (Oct. 29, 1943), **LEVIS** (Nov. 26, 1943), **MONTREAL** (June 12, 1943), **NEW WATERFORD** (July 3, 1943), **ORKNEY** (Sept. 18, 1943), **PORT COLBORNE** (April 21, 1943), **ROYALMOUNT** (ex-*Alvington*, April 15, 1944), **ST. JOHN** (Aug. 25, 1943), **ST. STEPHEN** (Feb. 6, 1944), **SPRINGHILL** (Sept. 7, 1943), **SWANSEA** (Dec. 19, 1942), **WENTWORTH** (March 6, 1943).

Of similar design to British "River" class. Displacement: 1,445 tons. Dimensions: $301\frac{1}{2} \times 36\frac{1}{2} \times 12$ feet. Guns: **2**—4 inch d.p., **10**—20 mm. AA. Machinery: Triple expansion. 2 shafts. I.H.P.: 5,500 = 20 kts. Boilers: 2 Admiralty 3-drum type. Complement: 140. War losses: *Chebogue*, *Valleyfield*.

Note.—Charlottetown was the only one of above frigates in commission in Dec. 1946.

11 Minesweepers.

SAULT STE. MARIE. 1943, *R.C.N. Official.*

BORDER CITIES (May 3, 1943), **FORT FRANCIS** (Oct. 30, 1943), **KAPUSKASING** (July 22, 1943), **NEW LISKEARD** (Jan. 14, 1944), **OSHAWA** (Oct. 6, 1943), **PORTAGE** (Nov. 21, 1942), **ROCKCLIFFE** (Aug. 19, 1943), **ST. BONIFACE** (Nov. 5, 1942), **SAULT STE. MARIE** (ex-*Soo*, Aug. 5, 1942), **WALLACEBURG** (Dec. 17, 1942), **WINNIPEG** (Sept. 19, 1942).

Steel. Of same type as British *Algerine* class. Displacement: 950 tons. Length: 230 feet. Guns: **1**—4 inch d.p., **4**—20 mm. Oerlikon, **1** hedgehog, **2** D.C.T. Machinery: Geared turbines. 2 shafts. Speed: 15 kts. Boilers: 2, of 3-drum type. Complement: 104.

Note.—New Liskeard is employed as seagoing training ship. *Middlesex* was wrecked on coast of Nova Scotia, Dec. 3, 1946.

Controlled Minelayers.

1946, *R.C.N. Official.*

SACKVILLE (May 15, 1941). Displacement: 925 tons. Dimensions: 190 (*pp.*), 205 (*o.a.*) × 33 × 14½ feet. Guns: 1—4 inch d.p., some smaller. Machinery: Triple expansion. I.H.P. 2,750 = 16 kts. Boilers: 2 S.E.

WHITETHROAT (Sept. 6, 1944). Built by Cook, Welton & Gemmell, Ltd. Displacement: 580 tons. Dimensions: 150 × 27½ × 10½ feet. Guns: 1—4 inch AA., etc. Machinery: Triple expansion.

Surveying and Meteorological Vessel.

1946, *R.C.N. Official.*

WOODSTOCK (Dec. 10, 1941). Displacement: 925 tons. Dimensions: 190 (*pp.*), 205 (*o.a.*) × 33 × 14½ feet. Guns: Not reported. Machinery: Triple expansion. I.H.P. 2,750 = 16 kts. Boilers: 2 S.E.

Motor Minesweepers.

1943, *R.C.N. Official.*

LLEWELLYN, LLOYD GEORGE (both Aug. 12, 1942), **REVELSTOKE.** Wood. Displacement: 360 tons. Dimensions: 126 (*pp.*), 140 (*o.a.*) × 26 × 10½ (*mean*), 12½ feet (*max*). Machinery: Diesel. B.H.P. 500 = 10 kts. Complement: 20.

Coastal Craft.

1942, *Official.*

ML 106, 116, 121, 124. Of the "Fairmile B" type. Dimensions: 112 × 18¼ × 4⅚ feet. Armament: 1—20 mm., 2 M.G. and D.C. Machinery: 2 Hall-Scott internal combustion engines. H.P.: 1,260 = 20 kts. Complement: 18.

Training Ship.

SANS PEUR (ex-*Trenora*, 1933). 856 tons *gross*. Dimensions: 210 × 30½ × 13 feet. Machinery: Diesel. 2 shafts. Speed: 15 kts.

Miscellaneous Auxiliaries.

CLIFTON. Tug. Diesel engines.

MOONBEAM, SUNBEAM. Oilers.

PROVIDER. Store Carrier. Speed: 9 kts.

MOONBEAM and **SUNBEAM** have been sold, and **PROVIDER** is likely to be disposed of shortly.

ROYAL INDIAN NAVY

Flag Officer Commanding R.I.N. Vice-Admiral Sir Geoffrey Miles, K.C.B.
Flags.—Vessels of R.I.N. fly White Ensign and pendant as H.M. Ships. The Indian flag is flown as a Jack. Flag Officers when afloat fly the flag appropriate to their naval rank.
Personnel (Dec. 1946): 1,000 officers, 10,000 ratings.

Official Photos have mostly been furnished by courtesy of the Flag Officer Commanding R.I.N.

Cruisers.

It is proposed to purchase H.M.S. *Achilles*, *Ajax* and *Leander* in 1947–48.

Sloops.

KISTNA. 1946, *Official.*

2 *Yarrow:* **CAUVERY** (June 15, 1943), **KISTNA** (April 22, 1943).
Displacement: 1,470 tons (1,735 tons *full load*). Dimensions: $292\frac{1}{2}$ (*pp.*), $299\frac{1}{2}$ (*o.a.*) × $38\frac{1}{2}$ × $11\frac{1}{4}$ feet. Guns: **6**—4 inch d.p., **2**—40 mm. AA., **2**—20 mm. AA. Machinery: Parsons geared turbines. 2 shafts. S.H.P. 4,300 = 19 kts. Boilers: 2 of 3-drum type. Complement, 214.

NARBADA 1943, *Official.*

2 *Thornycroft:* **GODAVARI** (Jan. 21, 1943), **NARBADA** (Nov. 21, 1942).

Displacement: 1,340 tons (1,760 tons *full load*). Dimensions: 266 (*w.l.*), $292\frac{1}{2}$ (*o.a.*) × $37\frac{1}{2}$ × $10\frac{5}{6}$ feet (*mean*). Guns: **6**—4 inch d.p., **2**—2 pdr., **4**—20 mm. AA. Machinery: Parsons geared turbines. 2 shafts. S.H.P. 3,600 = 18 kts. Boilers: 2 of 3-drum type. Complement, 195.

SUTLEJ. 1946, *Official.*

2 *Denny:* **JUMNA** (Nov. 16, 1940), **SUTLEJ** (Oct. 1, 1940). Displacement: 1,300 tons (1,715 and 1,750 tons *full load*). Dimensions: 266 (*w.l.*), $292\frac{1}{2}$ (*o.a.*) × $37\frac{1}{2}$ × $10\frac{5}{6}$ feet (*mean*). Guns: **6**—4 inch d.p., **6**—20 mm. AA. Machinery: Parsons geared turbines. 2 shafts. S.H.P.: 3,600 = 18 kts. Boilers: 2 Admiralty 3-drum type. Complement, 160 to 197.

HINDUSTAN. 1930 *Photo, favour of Messrs. Swan Hunter.*

HINDUSTAN. (Swan Hunter & Wigham Richardson). Laid down 1929, launched May 12, 1930 and completed October, 1930. Standard Displacement: 1190 tons. Dimensions: $296\frac{1}{2}$ (*o.a.*) × 35 × $8\frac{3}{4}$ feet (*mean*). Complement: 119. Guns: **2**—4 inch, **4**—3 pdr., 10 smaller. Machinery: Parsons impulse reaction Turbines with single reduction gearing; 2 shafts. 2 Admiralty 3-drum type boilers, 250 lbs. pressure. S.H.P.: 2000 = 16·5 kts. Oil: 275 tons. Recently employed on surveying duties.

5 Frigates.

1 *Hall Russell:* **NEZA** (ex-*Test*, May 30, 1942).

2 *Hill:* **KUKRI** (ex-*Trent*, Oct. 10, 1942), **TIR** (ex-*Bann*, Dec. 29, 1942).

2 *Smith's Dock:* **DHANUSH** (ex-*Deveron*, Oct. 12, 1942), **SHAMSHER** (ex-*Nadder*, Sept. 15, 1943).

Displacement: 1,460 tons, except last pair, 1,370 tons. Dimensions: $301\frac{1}{3}$ (*o.a.*) × $36\frac{2}{3}$ × 12 feet. Guns: **2**—4 inch d.p., **8**—20 mm. AA. Machinery: Triple expansion. I.H.P.: 5,500 = 20 kts. Boilers: 2 Admiralty 3-drum type. Complement, 118.

2 Corvettes.

1 *John Crown:* **ASSAM** (ex-*Bugloss*, June 21, 1943).

1 *Ferguson Bros.:* **MAHRATTA** (ex-*Charlock*, Nov. 16, 1943).

Displacement: 980 tons. Dimensions: 193 (*pp.*), $208\frac{1}{3}$ (*o.a.*) × $33\frac{1}{4}$ × 13 feet. Guns: **1**—4 inch, **1**—40 mm. AA., **6**—20 mm. AA., **1** hedgehog. Machinery: Triple expansion. I.H.P.: 2,880 = 16 kts. Boilers: 2 of 3-drum type. Complement, 109.

16 Fleet Minesweepers.

KONKAN. 1946, *Official.*

3 *Lobnitz.* **KONKAN** (ex-*Tilbury*, Feb. 18, 1942), **ORISSA** (ex-*Clydebank*, Nov. 12, 1941), **RAJPUTANA** (ex-*Lyme Regis*, Dec. 31, 1941). Displacement: 656 tons. Dimensions: $171\frac{1}{2}$ (*pp.*), 180 (*o.a.*) × $28\frac{1}{2}$ × $9\frac{1}{2}$ feet. Machinery: Triple expansion. 2 shafts. I.H.P.: 2,000 = 15 kts.

Miscellaneous

2 *Blyth* : **BALUCHISTAN** (ex-*Greenock*, May 11, 1942), **KATHIAWAR** (ex-*Hartlepool*, July 14, 1942).

4 *Hamilton* : **CARNATIC** (ex-*Newhaven*, July 9, 1942), **KHYBER** (ex-*Harwich*, Feb. 17, 1942), **KUMAON** (ex-*Middlesbrough*, May 2, 1942), **ROHILKHAND** (ex-*Padstow*, Oct. 29, 1942). Displacement: 660 tons. Dimensions: 171½ (*o.a.*) × 28½ × 10½ feet. Machinery: Geared turbines. 2 shafts. I.H.P.: 2,000 = 15 kts.

3 *Australian built* : **BENGAL** (1942), **BOMBAY, MADRAS.** Displacement: 650 tons. Dimensions: 186½ × 31 × 8⅓ feet. Machinery: Triple expansion. 2 shafts. I.H.P. 2,000 = 15 kts.

4 *Calcutta built* : **BIHAR** (July 7, 1942), **DECCAN** (April 24, 1944), **MALWA** (June 21, 1944), **OUDH** (March 3, 1942). Displacement: 650 tons. Dimensions: 182 × 28 × 8¼ feet. Machinery: Triple expansion by Lobnitz. I.H.P.: 2,000 = 15 kts.

Following particulars are common to all: Guns: **1**—3 inch AA., **1**—40 mm. AA., **2**—20 mm. AA., **4** M.G. Boilers: 2 Admiralty 3-drum, small tube type. Complement: 87.

BIHAR 1946, *Official.*

Surveying Vessel.

1946, *Official.*

INVESTIGATOR. Ex-cable ship *Patrick Stewart* (Simons, 1924). Displacement : 1,572 tons. Complement: 109. Dimensions : 226 (*pp.*), 248 (*o.a.*) × 37½ × 13¼ feet (*mean* draught). No guns. Triple expansion engines. 2 shafts. H.P. : 1,137 = 12·5 kts. 2 cylindrical boilers. Oil fuel : 292 tons. Complement, 118.

6 Trawlers.

1946, *Official.*

AMRITSAR (Dec. 19, 1941), **CALCUTTA** (March 8, 1943), **COCHIN** (Dec. 29, 1943), **LUCKNOW** (April 3, 1942), **NASIK** (May 24, 1944), **RAMPUR** (July 19, 1941). Displacement: 545 tons. Dimensions: 164 (*o.a.*) × 27½ × 13½ feet. Guns: **1**—3 inch, **3**—20 mm. AA. Machinery: Triple expansion. I.H.P.: 850 = 11·5 kts. Boiler: 1 cylindrical. Coal: 181 tons. Complement: 48.

6 Motor Minesweepers.

BARQ (ex-*MMS* 132), **MMS 129, 130, 131, 151, 154.** Wood. Displacement: 255 tons. Dimensions: 105 (*pp.*), 119 (*o.a.*) × 13 × 9½ feet. Guns: **2**—20 mm. AA., **2** M.G. Machinery: Diesel. B.H.P.: 500 = 10 kts. Complement: 20.

8 Motor Launches.

1946, *Official.*

HDML 1110, 1112, 1117, 1118, 1261, 1262, 1263, 1266. Displacement: 54 tons. Dimensions: 72 (*o.a.*) × 15⅚ × 5¼ feet. Guns: **1**—3 pdr., **1**—20 mm. AA. Machinery: Diesel. 2 shafts. B.H.P.: 320 = 12 kts. Complement: 14.

KENYA AND ZANZIBAR

ROSALIND (May 3, 1941). Built by A. & J. Inglis. Displacement: 545 tons. Dimensions: 164 × 27⅔ × 11 feet. Guns: **1**—4 inch AA., **2** smaller. Machinery: Triple expansion. Boiler: 1 cylindrical.

NDOVU, ALHATHARI. Ex-tugs. Built by Bow, McLachlan & Co., Paisley (1928). *Standard* displacement: 380 tons. Dimensions: 125 × 25 × 8 feet. Guns: **1**—3 inch, **2** Lewis, **1** D.C.T. Fitted for minesweeping. I.H.P.: 500 = 10 kts. Complement: 25.

MALAYA

It is proposed to establish the Royal Malay Navy in 1947.

BURMA

Frigate **FAL** is to be acquired in 1947.

Motor Launches.

1942, *Official.*

ML 1104. Built by Messrs. Thornycroft, and manned by Burmese R.N.V.R. Dimensions: 76½ (*o.a.*) × 13½ × 4¾ feet. Armed with **1**—3 pdr., **1**—20 mm. AA. Fitted for minesweeping. Machinery: Three RL/6 Thornycroft Diesels. Total B.H.P.: 650 = 14 kts.

ML 1102, 1103. Of similar design, but propelled by two RL/6 Thornycroft Diesels and one RY/12 petrol engine. B.H.P.: 780 = 16 kts.

HDML 1272, 1299, 1304, 1306, 1369, 1456, 1462, 1463, 1467, 1477, 1478, 1486, 1488.

Motor Minesweepers.

Two (numbers not reported). Particulars as given under R.I.N. in adjoining column.

Boom Defence Vessels.

BARRYMORE, BARWIND. Built by Simons and Ferguson Bros., respectively. Of same type as "Bar" class, in Royal Navy section.

ROYAL NEW ZEALAND NAVY

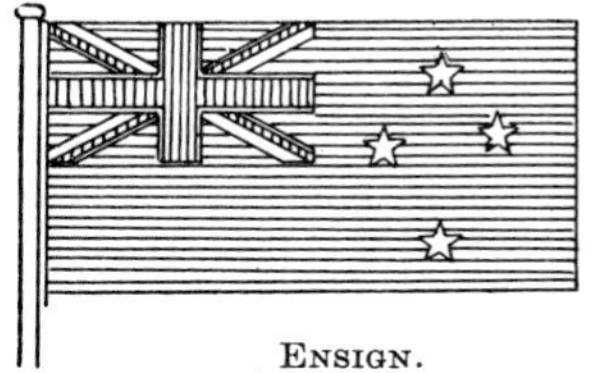

Ensign.

Commander-in-Chief: H.E. Lieut.-General Sir Bernard Freyberg, V.C., G.C.M.G., K.C.B., K.B.E., D.S.O.

Naval Board.

President: The Minister of Defence, the Hon. Frederick Jones, M.P.
First Naval Member and Chief of Naval Staff: Commodore G. H. Faulkner, D.S.C., R.N.
Second Naval Member: Captain J. G. Hewitt, D.S.O., Ad.C., R.N.
Naval Secretary: Captain (S) W. J. G. Prophit, O.B.E., R.N.
Personnel, May 1946: 2,200.

Cruisers.

BELLONA, BLACK PRINCE (both 1942). Displacement: 5,700, 5,770 tons, respectively. Other particulars as recorded on an earlier page, in Royal Navy section. Both are lent by the Admiralty to the New Zealand Government, who pay for their annual maintenance.

Corvettes.

ARABIS (Oct. 28, 1943), **ARBUTUS** (Jan. 26, 1944). Displacement: 980 tons. Dimensions: 193 (*pp.*), 208¼ (*o.a.*) × 33⅛ × 13 feet (*mean*). Guns: **1**—4 inch d.p., **8**—20 mm. AA. Machinery: Triple expansion. I.H.P.: 2,880 = 16 kts. Boilers: 2 of 3-drum type. Built by George Brown & Co., and presented to R.N.Z.N. in 1944.

Trawlers.

Tui. 1946, *Lieut. (L) J. P. Shelley, R.N.Z.N.V.R.*

KIWI (July 7, 1941), **TUI** (Aug. 26, 1941). Both by Henry Robb, Ltd. Displacement: 600 tons. Dimensions: 156 × 30 × 13 feet. Guns: **1**—4 inch, several smaller. Machinery: Triple expansion. Boiler: One cylindrical. War loss: *Moa.*

Trawlers—*continued*

Hautapu. 1946, *Lieut. (L) J. P. Shelley, R.N.Z.N.V.R.*

HAUTAPU (Aug. 1943), **HINAU** (Aug. 28, 1941), **MANUKA, RIMU** (both June, 1942). Built in New Zealand. Displacement: 625 tons (*full load*). Dimensions: 126 (*o.a.*) × 23½ × 14 feet. War loss: *Puriri.*

INCHKEITH (July 10, 1941), **KILLEGRAY** (May 25, 1941), **SANDA** (July 12, 1941), **SCARBA** (June 26, 1941). All of "Isles" class, as illustrated in Royal Navy section. Displacement: 560 tons. Dimensions: 150 × 27½ × 10½ feet. Guns: **1**—3 inch, etc. *Inchkeith* built by Lewis; *Sanda* by Goole S.B. Co.; and other two by Cook, Welton & Gemmell.

Coastal Craft.

HDML 1183, 1184, 1191–1194. All of "Fairmile" type, built in New Zealand. Length: 72 feet.

SOUTH AFRICA

Director, S. African Naval Forces: Commodore J. Dalgleish, C.B.E., S.A.N.F.

Personnel (1946): 863 officers and ratings.

Frigates.

1 *Blyth D.D. Co.:* **GOOD HOPE** (ex-*Loch Boisdale*, July 5, 1944).

1 *Harland & Wolff (Govan):* **TRANSVAAL** (ex-*Loch Ard*, Aug. 2, 1944).

1 *Swan Hunter:* **NATAL** (ex-*Loch Cree*, June 19, 1944).

Displacement: 1,400 tons. Dimensions: 307 × 38½ × 17 feet. Guns: **1**—4 inch d.p., **1** quadruple 2 pdr. pompom, **2**—40 mm. AA., **2**—20 mm. AA. Machinery: Triple expansion. 2 shafts. I.H.P.: 5,500 = 19·5 kts. Boilers: 2 Admiralty 3-drum type. Complement: 140. *Transvaal* was completed by Messrs. Lobnitz. All 3 ships presented to S. Africa in 1944-45.

Transvaal. 1944, *Official.*

Surveying Vessel.

A Surveying Vessel is to be acquired in 1947.

Coastal Craft.

1944, *Official.*

Six of **HDML 1100–1300** series. All built in South Africa. Length: 72 feet. Machinery: 2 Gardner 8-cylinder Diesels. B.H.P.: 130 = 11 kts.

Controlled Minelayer.

SPINDRIFT (ex-German Trawler *Polaris*). Displacement: 926 tons. Dimensions: 160 × 26 × 16 feet. Machinery: Compound Uniflow Lentz valve engines.

Boom Defence Vessels.

BARCROSS. 1942, *Official.*

BARCROSS (Oct. 21, 1944), **BARBRAKE.** Built by Blyth S.B. Co. and Simons, respectively. Of same type as "Bar" class described in Royal Navy section.

NEWFOUNDLAND

Transports, etc.

(All photos, courtesy H. A. Le Messurier, Esq.)

CABOT STRAIT (Fleming & Ferguson, Feb. 27, 1947). 2,000 tons *gross.* Accommodation for 142 persons. (Two more new ships are to be built in British yards).

BACCALIEU, BURGEO (Fleming & Ferguson, 1940). 1,421 tons *gross.* Dimensions: 233½ (*pp.*), 242 (*o.a.*) × 37 × 18¾ feet. Machinery: Triple expansion. I.H.P.: 1,600. Strengthened for ice navigation.

Added 1938.

NORTHERN RANGER (Fleming & Ferguson, Paisley, 1936). 1,365 tons *gross.* Complement, 32. Dimensions: 220 × 36 × 16⅔ feet draught. I.H.P.: 1,000 = 11·5 kts. Coal: 270 tons. Strengthened for ice navigation.

MOYRA (Swan Hunter, 1931). 1,396 tons *gross.* Dimensions: 248 × 39½ × 17 feet. Machinery: Triple expansion. I.H.P.: 700.

NORTHTON (Swan Hunter, 1924). 2,227 tons *gross.* Dimensions: 248 × 43 × — feet. Machinery: Triple expansion. I.H.P.: 1,150.

RANDOM (ex-*Hondu*, ex-*Carl*, ex-*Siggy*, ex-*Artensis*, ex-*Gustav Fischer*) (Stettin, 1921). 1,792 tons *gross.* Dimensions: 267½ × 42¼ × — feet. Machinery: Triple expansion.

Added 1938.

KYLE (Swan Hunter, 1913). 1,055 tons *gross.* Complement, 34. Dimensions: 220 × 32 × 16⅔ feet draught. Speed: 13·5 kts. Strengthened for ice navigation.

Added 1938.

CLYDE, HOME (A. & J. Inglis, Glasgow, 1900). 439 tons *gross.* Complement: 20. Dimensions: 154½ × 25 × 12 feet draught. Speed: 10 kts.

Added 1938.

GLENCOE (A. & J. Inglis, Glasgow, 1899). 767 tons *gross.* Complement, 24. Dimensions: 208 × 30 × 16 feet draught. Speed: 11 kts.

Note.—Argyle, Portia, Prospero and *Sagona* have been sold. War loss: Carsbon.

EIRE

Director of Naval Service: Captain H. J. A. S. Jerome, D.S.O. (Commander, R.N., retired).

Corvettes.

CLIONA (ex-*Oxlip*, Aug. 28, 1941), **MACHA** (ex-*Bellwort*, Aug. 11, 1941), **MAEV** (ex-*Borage*, Nov. 22, 1941). Displacement: 925 tons. Dimensions: 190 (*pp.*), 205 (*o.a.*) × 33 × 14½ feet. Guns: 1—4 inch d.p., 1—2 pdr., 2—20 mm. AA. Machinery: Triple expansion. I.H.P.: 2,750 = 16 kts. Boilers: 2 S.E. Purchased in 1946; three more to be acquired in 1947.

Motor Torpedo Boats.

1940, *courtesy "The Motor Boat"*

5 *Thornycroft type:* **M1, M2, M3, M4, M5** (1939). Displacement: 32 tons. Dimensions: 72 × 16½ × 3¾ feet. Armament: 2—21 inch torpedoes, 2 M.G. AA., also D.C. Machinery: 4 Thornycroft petrol motors. B.H.P.: 2,600 = 40 kts.

Fishery Protection Vessel.

FORT RANNOCH. (1936). 258 tons *gross.* Machinery: Triple expansion.

BELGIUM

Minister of Defence:—Colonel de Fraiteur.

Naval personnel, 1946: 1,000 officers and men. Mercantile Marine (Sept. 30, 1945), 200,000 tons.

Flags.

Ships belonging to the State

Directeur Général de la Marine.

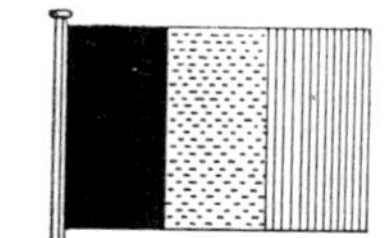

Mercantile Marine

Sloops.

1946, *Official.*

ARTEVELDE (ex-*K4*, ex-*Lorelei*, ex-*Artevelde*). Laid down at the Cockerill Yard at Antwerp in 1939 to replace the *Zinnia.* Displacement: 1,640 tons (2,270 tons *full load*). Dimensions: 292 (*pp.*), 323 (*o.a.*) × 34½ × 12 feet. Guns: **3**—4·1 inch, **2**—40 mm. AA., **2**—37 mm. AA., **16**—20 mm. AA. **30** D.C. carried. Machinery: Parsons-Rateau geared turbines. 2 shafts. S.H.P. 30,000 = 30 kts. Boilers: 2 Babcock & Wilcox. Complement: 180.

Note.—This ship was seized by the Germans in 1940, and completed by Wilton-Fijenoord, but was recovered intact at Cuxhaven after the war.

1946, *Official.*

ZINNIA (ex-*Barbara*, ex-*Zinnia*, August 1915). Built by Swan Hunter and acquired in June, 1920. Displacement: 1,200 tons. Dimensions: 250 (*pp.*), 262½ (*o.a.*) × 33 × 11 feet (*mean*). Guns: **1**—4·1 inch, **14**—20 mm. AA. Machinery: Triple expansion. I.H.P. 1,400 = 14 kts. Boilers: 2 cylindrical. Coal: 250 tons (*max.*). Complement: 120.

Note.—H.M.S. *Loch Eck* will be acquired to replace this ship.

Sail Training Ship.

Mercator. *Added* 1941, *courtesy D. R. Bolt, Esq., M.B.E.*

MERCATOR (Ramage & Ferguson, Leith, Dec. 9, 1931). Barquentine. Displacement: 1,200 tons (770 tons *gross*). Complement: 80. Dimensions: 190¼ × 34¾ × 14 feet. Auxiliary Diesel. B.H.P.: 500 = 11 kts. Sail area: 13,584 sq. feet.

Motor Minesweepers.

Eight are on loan from Royal Navy, including **MMS 187, 188, 1020.** Last mentioned is to be converted into a Surveying Vessel.

Boom Defence Vessel.

BARCAROLE (Ardrossan Dockyard, March 14, 1945). Displacement: 730 tons. Dimensions: 150 (*pp.*), 173¾ (*o.a.*) × 32¼ × 9½ feet. Guns: **1**—3 inch AA. Machinery: Triple expansion. I.H.P. 850 = 11·5 kts. Boilers: 2 S.E. Complement: 32. (On loan from R.N.)

BULGARIA

Flags. = Red. = White. = Green. = Yellow.

Note that the red of the flag is crimson.

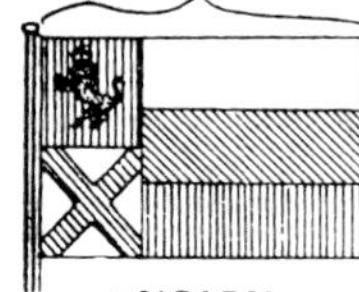

ENSIGN

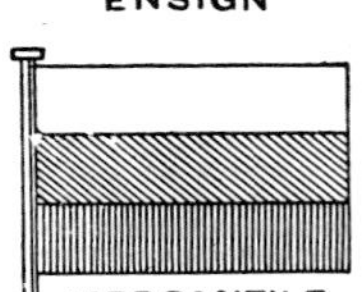

MERCANTILE

Jack: A white flag with a green saltire and superimposed over all the Cross of St. George.

Strength of fleet is restricted by Peace Treaty to 7,500 tons.

Mercantile Marine: 14 steamers of 17,476 tons.

Torpedo Boats.

2 *Motor Type:* ***Nos. 1, 2*** (Lürssen, Vegesack, 1938–39). Displacement: 60 tons. Complement, 18. Dimensions: 92 × 14¾ × 5½ feet. Armament: 1 M.G. AA., 2—21 inch T.T. Machinery: 3 Mercedes-Benz engines. B.H.P. 3,150 = 36 kts.

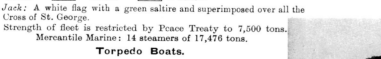

3 *Creusot* boats: ***Khrabri, Derzki, Strogi*** (built in sections in France; reassembled at Varna. 1907-8). 100 tons. Dimensions: 126½ × 13¼ × 8¾ feet. Armament: 2—47 mm., 1 M.G., 2—18-inch torpedo tubes. Designed H.P.: 2,000 = 26 kts. 1 screw. Du Temple boilers. Coal: 27 tons. Complement: 23. Reported to be fitted for minesweeping.

Patrol Boats.

Maritza, Vardar (1944). Built at Kavalla. Particulars wanted.

Belomoretz (ex-French C 27), ***Chernomoretz*** (ex-C 80). Both purchased 1922. 77 tons. 3 sets of 220 B.H.P. standard petrol motors, totalling 660 B.H.P. = 17 kts. Petrol: 9 tons. Endurance: 700 miles at 10 kts. Guns: 1—47 mm., 2 M.G. Complement: 26.

Auxiliary Sail Training Vessels.

Assen (1912). 240 tons. Guns: 2—65 mm., 1 M.G. H.P.: 120 = 7 kts. (Refitted 1933–34.)

Kamcia (1898). Speed 10 kts. (Refitted 1925.)

BRAZIL

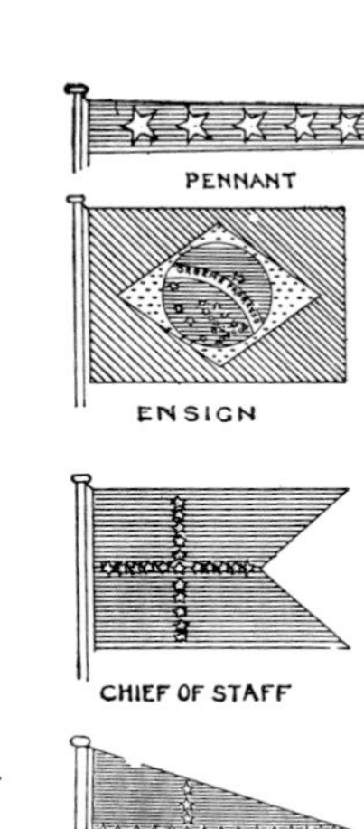

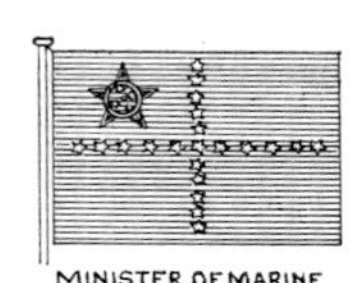

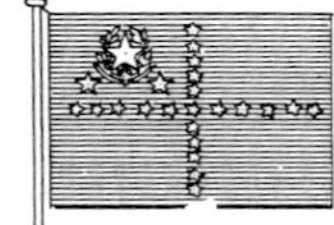

Uniforms.

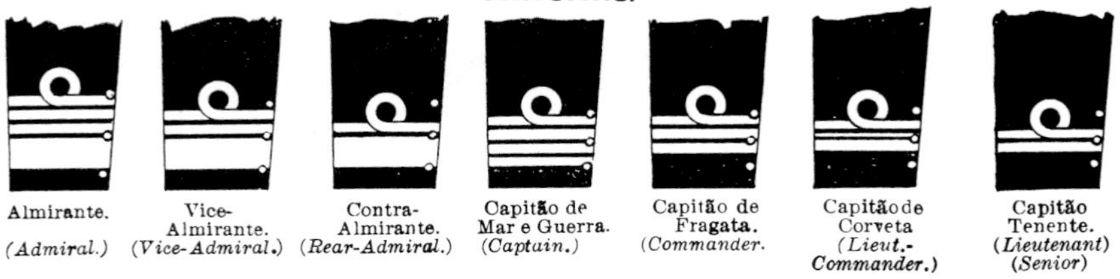

Almirante. *(Admiral.)* — Vice-Almirante. *(Vice-Admiral.)* — Contra-Almirante. *(Rear-Admiral.)* — Capitão de Mar e Guerra. *(Captain.)* — Capitão de Fragata. *(Commander.)* — Capitão de Corveta *(Lieut.-Commander.)* — Capitão Tenente. *(Lieutenant) (Senior)*

Primeiro Tenente. *(Lieut.) (Junior.)* — Segundo Tenente. *(Sub-Lieut.)* — Guarda Marinha. *(Midshipman.)* — Reserve Officer.

Caps :—Similar to British Navy.

Non-executive officers wear no curl, but have badges of rank above top stripe as at foot.

Marine Corps wear distinctive uniforms, but ranks and stripes correspond with those of Navy.

Naval Constructors and Marine Corps officers wear both curl and badge of branch.

Minister of Marine : Almirante de Esquadra Sylvio de Noronha.
Chief of Naval Staff : Vice-Almirante Adalberto Lara de Almeida.
Naval Attaché, London : Captain Paulo Nogueira Penido.
Naval Agent, London : Captain Natal Arnaud.

Mercantile Marine.

(From "Lloyd's Register," 1939.)
305 vessels of 487,820 gross tonnage.

Guns in Service.

Notation.	Calibre.		Length in calibres	Weight of A.P. shell.	Muzzle Velocity.	*Max.* penetration A.P. capped at K.C. at 5000 yards.	3000 yards.	Danger Space against average ships at 10,000 yards.	5000 yards.	3000 yards.	*Service* rounds per minute
	inch.	c/m.	cals.	lbs.	ft. secs.	inch.	inch.	yds.	yds.	yds.	
HEAVY	12	*30·5*	45	850	2800	...	...	...	...	...	2
LIGHT	4·7 4·7 4·7 4 3.9 3	*12* *12* *12* *10* *10* *7·6*	45 50 45 50 47 50	48 45 48 .. 30 14	2780 2630 2286 .. 1968 2560	$1\frac{3}{4}$	3	153	55	11	8

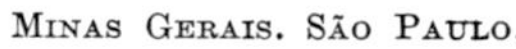

MINAS GERAIS. SÃO PAULO.

BAURU *class.*

ALMIRANTE SALDANHA

RIO GRANDE DO SUL

CARIOCA *class*

BARRETO MENEZES *class.*

JAVARI *class.*

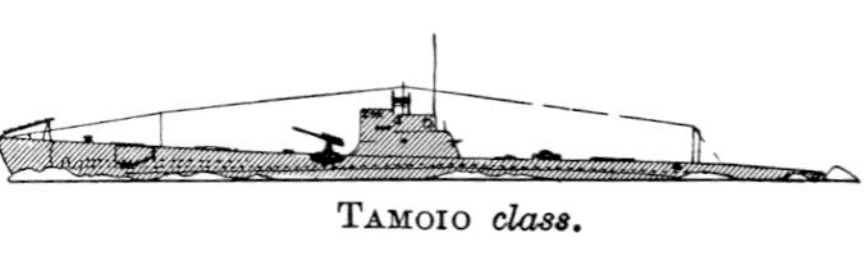

TAMOIO *class.*

M. DIAS *class.*

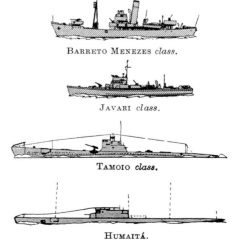

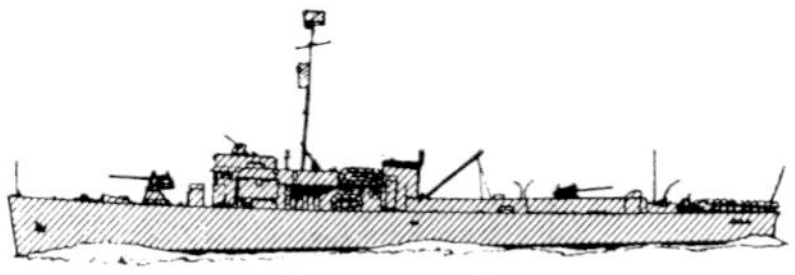

GUAPORE *class.*

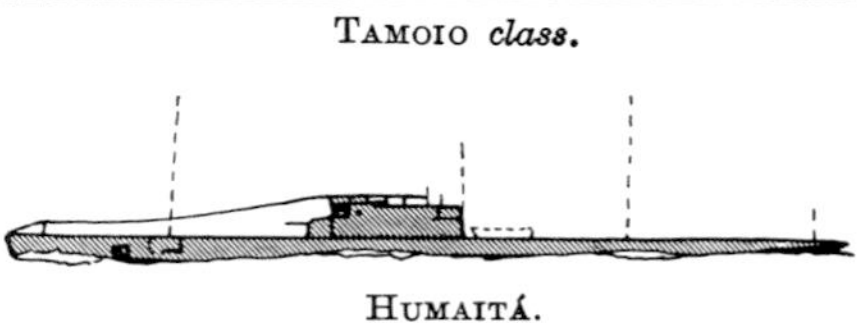

HUMAITÁ.

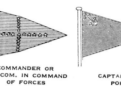

Battleships (*Encouraçados*)

MINAS GERAIS (Sept. 10, 1908).
SÃO PAULO (April 19, 1909).

Normal Displacement: 19,200 tons.
Complement: 1,087 and 1,113, respectively.
Dimensions: 533 (*w.l.*), 500 (*p.p.*) × 83 × 25 feet (*max.*).

Guns (Armstrong):
12—12 inch, 45 cal.
14—4·7 inch, 50 cal.
4—3 inch AA.
4—40 mm. AA.
8 M.G.

Armour (Krupp):
9″ Belt
6″—4″ Belt (bow) N.C.
6″—4″ Belt (aft) N.C.
9″—6″ Upper belt
9″ & 3″ Bulkheads
9″ Battery (main deck)
9″—8″ Turrets (K.C.)
12″ Conning tower (fore)
9″ Conning tower (aft)
8″—3″ Com. Tubes
1½″ Torp. Pro. Bulkh'd.

MINAS GERAIS. 1940, *Official.*

Note to Plan.—Disregard apparent main deck battery in elevation. Number of 4·7 inch will be as given above, though exact arrangement has still to be reported.

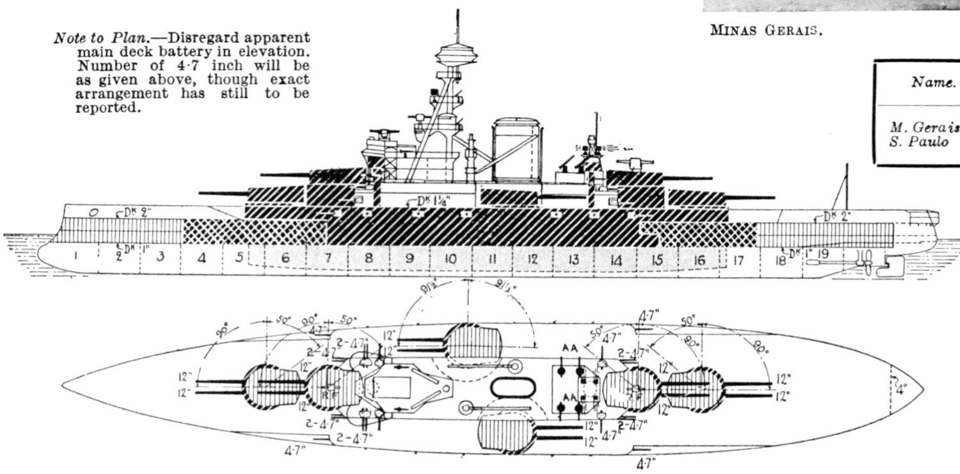

Name.	*Builder.*	*Machinery.*	*Laid down.*	*Completed.*	*Trials. 30 hour at ⅘.*	*Full power*	*Boilers.*	*Refit.*
M. Gerais	Armstrong	Vickers	1907	Jan.'10			Thornycroft	1934-39
S. Paulo	Vickers	Vickers	1907	July '10	16,067 = 19·85	25,517 = 21·2	Babcock	1937-40

Machinery: 2 sets triple expansion. 2 shafts. S.H.P.: 30,000 = 21 kts.
Boilers: 6 Thornycroft. Oil fuel only.

General Notes.—*M. Gerais* reconstructed and modernised, improved fire control arrangements being fitted, in 1934–39; *S. Paulo* to be transformed similarly in due course.

Engineering Notes.—The former No. 1 stokehold was converted into four oil-fuel deep-tanks,—the space available between top of tanks and main deck being used as distilling plant, with all necessary auxiliaries. 12 side coal bunkers converted into wing oil-fuel tanks, there being 2 service oil tanks for each stokehold. All upper coal bunkers removed. Internal arrangements entirely changed, in accordance with the requirements of new uptakes with single funnel. The whole Thornycroft supply includes:—main and auxiliary feed water pumps, oil fuel pumps, oil heaters and filters, teledep-installation, ventilating-plant, pipes, etc., etc.

MINAS GERAIS. 1942, *Official, courtesy H.E. the Brazilian Ambassador.*

Cruiser (*Cruzadore*)

1942, *Pictorial Press*

RIO GRANDE DO SUL (April, 1909).

Normal displacement 3150 tons. Complement 368.

Length, (*p.p.*), 380 feet. (*o.a.*), 401½ „ Beam, 39 feet. *Mean* draught, 13 feet 7½ ins.

Guns:
10—4·7 inch, 50 cal. (Armstrong)
4—3 inch A.A.
4—3 pdr. saluting.
8—M.G.
Torpedo tubes (21 in. Bliss):
4 *above water*, in twin mountings.

Armour:
1½″ Deck
3″ Conning tower

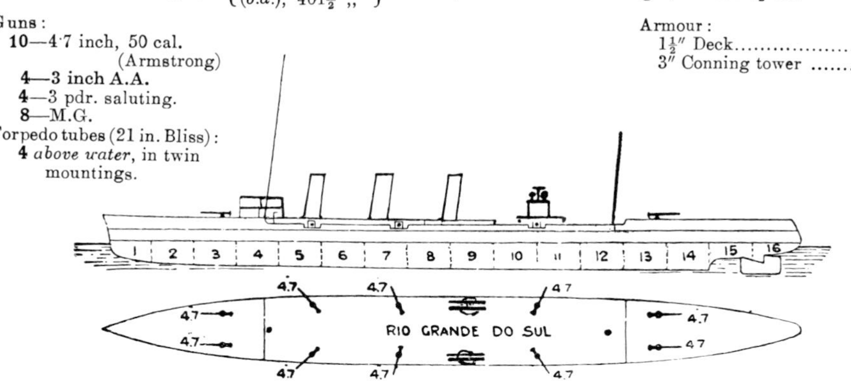

Machinery: 3 Brown-Curtis geared turbines. 3 shafts. Boilers: 6 Thornycroft oil-burning. S.H.P. 22,000 = 27 kts. 1926 *Trials*: H.P., 23,000 = 28·6. Oil fuel: 640 tons. Endurance: *about* 2400 miles at 24 kts., 3092 miles at 18 kts., 6600 miles at 10 kts.

Gunnery Notes.—Fire control Director system is now installed.

General Notes.—Built by Armstrong; engined by Vickers; was begun 1908 (under 1907 Naval Programme) and completed 1910. Completely refitted 1925-26, by Companhia Nacional de Navegação Costeira, Rio, new engines and boilers (to burn oil fuel) being installed by Messrs. Thornycroft. Heating Surface 26,027 sq. ft.

Destroyers (*Contratorpedeiros*)

1944, *U.S. Navy Official.*

8 *Ex-American Destroyer-Escorts:* **Babitonga** (ex-*Alger*, 1943), **Baependi** (ex-*Cannon*, May 25, 1943), **Baurú** (ex-*Reybold*, Aug. 22, 1943), **Beberibe** (ex-*Herzog*, Sept. 5, 1943), **Benevente** (ex-*Christopher*, June, 1943), **Bertioga** (ex-*Pennewill*, Aug. 8, 1943), **Bocaina** (ex-*Marts*, Aug. 8, 1943), **Bracui** (ex-*McAnn*, Sept. 5, 1943).

These were transferred from the United States Navy in 1944.

Displacement: 1,240 tons (1,520 tons *full load*). Dimensions: 306 (*o.a.*) × 36 × — feet. Guns: 3—3 inch (dual purpose), 2—40 mm., 4—20 mm., also D.C.T. Tubes: 3—21 inch. Machinery: Diesel-electric. 2 shafts. B.H.P.: 6,000 = 20 kts.

6 *British design:* **Amazonas, Araguaia** (both Nov. 29, 1943), **Acre,** (May 30, 1945), **Ajuricaba, Apa,** (May 30, 1945), **Araguarí.** First pair laid down at Rio in July, 1940, others on Dec. 28, 1940. Displacement: 1,376 tons. Dimensions: 323 (*o.a.*) × 35 × 8½ feet (*mean*). Guns: 4—4·7 inch. 7 smaller. Tubes: 8—21 inch (quadrupled). Machinery: Parsons geared turbines. S.H.P. 34,000 = 35.5 kts. Boilers: 3 of 3-drum type. Oil fuel: 150 tons. Complement: 150.

1946, *Official*

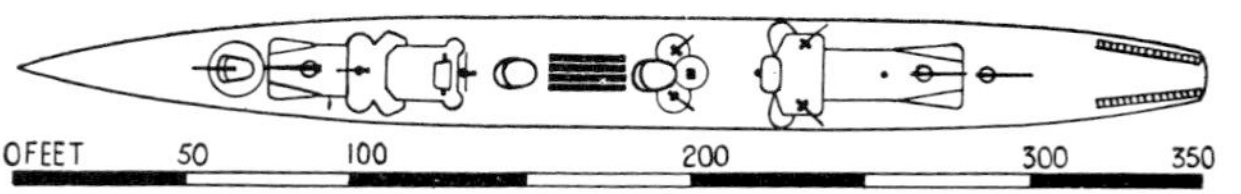

3 *U.S.A. design:* **Greenhalgh** (July 8, 1941), **Marcilio Dias** (July 20, 1940), **Maris e Barros** (Dec. 28, 1940). Built at Ilha das Cobras, Rio de Janeiro, with material from U.S.A. Displacement: 1,500 tons. Dimensions: 341 (*pp.*), 357 (*o.a.*) × 34⅜ × 9⅜ feet (*mean*). Guns: 5—5 inch, 38 cal. (dual purpose), 4—40 mm. AA., 4—20 mm. AA. Tubes: 12—21 inch (quadrupled). Machinery: Geared turbines by General Electric Co. S.H.P.: 42,800 = 36·5 kts. 4 high pressure water tube boilers of Express type by Babcock & Wilcox. Oil fuel: 550 tons. Radius: 6,000 miles. Complement: 190.

Note.—
These ships are generally similar to ***Mahan*** class, of U.S. Navy, and are armed with guns of American manufacture. Pendant Nos. are M1, *M. Dias*; M2, *Maris e Barros*; M3, *Greenhalgh*. All 3 commissioned Nov. 29, 1943.

Submarines

TUPÍ. 1937, *courtesy Engineer Captain Natal Arnaud.*

3 *Odero-Terni-Orlando* type. **Tamoio** (ex-*Ascianghi*, Feb. 14, 1937), **Tupí** (ex-*Neghelli*, Nov. 28, 1936), **Timbira** (ex-*Gondar*, Dec. 30, 1936). Built at Spezia. Displacement: 615 tons on *surface*, 853 tons *submerged*. Dimensions: 197½ × 21 × 13 feet. Armament: 1—3·9 inch, 47 cal., 2—13 mm. M.G., 6—21 inch torpedo tubes. Fiat Diesels. H.P.: 1,350/800 = 14/7·5 kts. Complement: 37. All three delivered in September, 1937. Are generally similar to Italian *Perla* type.

HUMAITÁ *Added* 1939, *courtesy W. H. Davis, Esq.*

1 *Ansaldo* type: **Humaitá.** (Ansãldo San Giorgio Co., Spezia, April, 1927.) Displacement: 1450 tons *surface*, 1884 tons *submerged*. Dimensions: 284¼ × 25½ × 14 feet. Fiat type Diesel engines. Designed H.P. $\frac{4900}{2200} = \frac{18 \cdot 5}{10}$ kts. Armament: 1—4·7 inch, 45 cal., 4—13 mm. AA., 6—21 inch tubes (4 bow, 2 stern). Similar in general design to Italian *Balilla* type (*vide* notes in Italian Section for further details). Ordered in 1926 and completed in 1927, but not delivered in Brazilian waters until two years later. Complement: 74.

Repair Ship.

1938, *D.G. Lambert, Esq.*

BELMONTE (ex-German S.S. *Valesia*, Rostock, 1912). 5,227 tons *gross*. Dimensions: 364¾ × 51 × 15 feet. Guns: 4—4·7 in., 2—6 pdr. H.P.: 2,700 = 12 kts. Can take about 6,500 tons as cargo. Complement: 338.

Trawlers. (rated as *Corvetas.*)

1946, *Official.*

BARRETO DE MENEZES (ex-*Paru*, Feb., 1945), **FELIPE CAMARÃO** (ex-*Papaterra*, July, 1942), **FERNANDES VIEIRA** (ex-*Parati*, 1942), **HENRIQUE DIAS** (ex-*Pargo*, Aug., 26, 1942), **MATIAS DE ALBUQUERQUE** (ex-*Pampano*, June 11, 1942), **VIDAL DE NEGREIROS** (ex-*Pelegrime*, 1942). All laid down in 1941 at Ilha Vianna, Rio de Janeiro, for the Royal Navy, but transferred to the Brazilian flag in the following year. Displacement: 920 tons (*full load*). Dimensions: 160 (*pp.*), 176½ (*o.a.*) × 28 × 16 feet (*max.* draught). Guns: 1—3 inch, 4—20 mm., 4 D.C.T. Machinery: Triple expansion. I.H.P., 1,000 = 12·5 kts. Coal-fired boilers. *B. Menezes* is to be fitted as Surveying Vessel.

Submarine Chasers (Motor Launches).

(Caças-Submarinos.)

GOIANA. 1946, *Official.*

GUAIBA (ex-*PC 604*), **GUAPORÉ** (ex-*PC 544*), **GURUPÍ** (ex-*PC 547*), **GOIANA** (ex-*PC 554*, May 1, 1942), **GRAJAU** (ex-*PC 1236*, April 24, 1943), **GRAUNA** (ex-*PC 561*), **GUAJARÁ** (ex-*PC 607*), **GURUPA** (ex-*PC 605*). Built by Defoe Boat & Motor Works, and acquired from U.S. Navy in 1942–43. Steel. Displacement: 280 tons. Dimensions: 170 (*w.l.*), 173½ (*o.a.*) × 23 × 7½ feet. Guns: **1**—3 inch dual purpose, **1**—40 mm. AA., **5**—20 mm. AA., **4** D.C.T. Machinery: Diesel. 2 shafts. B.H.P.: 2,880 = 20 kts. Fuel: 60 tons. Complement: 65. Pendant Nos. of *Guaporé* and *Gurupi* are *CS* 1 and 2.

JUTAI. 1946, *Official.*

JAVARÍ (ex-*SC 763*), **JUTAÍ** (ex-*SC 762*), **JURUÁ** (ex-*SC 764*), **JURUENA** (ex-*SC 766*), **JAGUARÃO** (ex-*SC 765*), **JAGUARIBE** (ex-*SC 767*), **JACUÍ** (ex-*SC 1288*), **JUNDIAÍ** (ex-*SC 1289*) (1942–43). Acquired from U.S. Navy in 1942–43. Wood. Displacement: 95 tons. Dimensions: 107½ × 17 × 6½ feet. Armament: **1**—40 mm. AA, **2**—20 mm. AA., many D.C. Machinery: 2 sets G.M. Diesels. 2 shafts. B.H.P.: 800 = 15 kts. Complement: 28. Pendant Nos. are *CS 51* to *58*, respectively.

RIO NEGRO, RIO PARDO (both Nov. 29, 1943), **BELLO HORIZONTE, DISTRITO FEDERAL, JOÃO PESSÃO, NITHEROI, PORTO ALEGRE, SÃO VICENTE.** All built at Rio to Canadian design. Wood. Displacement: 132 tons. Dimensions: 120 (*pp.*), 128 (*o.a.*) × 21 × 5¾ feet (*mean*). 3 motors. B.H.P.: 1,890 = 20 kts.

Minelayers (*Mineioros*)

CARIOCA. 1939, *Official.*

CANANEIA (Oct., 1938), **CARIOCA** (1938), **CAMOCIM, CABEDELO, CARAVELA** (all 3 Sept.–Oct., 1939). Built at Rio. (First pair laid down on Nov. 6, 1937.) Displacement: 552 tons. Dimensions: 188⅔ × 25½ × 8 feet (*mean*). Guns: 2—4 inch, 4—20 mm. AA. 50 Mines. Machinery: 2 sets vertical triple expansion by Thornycroft. I.H.P.: 2,200 = 14 kts. (exceeded on trials). Oil fuel: 70 tons. Complement: 97.

Note.—Pendant Nos. are *Carioca*, C 1; *Cananeia*, C 2; *Camocim*, C 3; *Caravela*, C 4; *Cabedelo*, C 5.

1937, *Courtesy Eng. Capt. Natal Arnaud.*

ITAPIMIRIM (ex-*Maria do Couto*). Displacement: 340 tons. Dimensions: 116 × 21 × 12 feet. Guns: 2—3 pdr. Mines: 30. Complement: 45.

ITACURUSSÁ (Ramage & Ferguson, Leith, 1901). Displacement: 210 tons. Dimensions: 95¼ (*pp.*), 102⅓ (*o.a.*) × 19½ × 10⅓ feet (*max.* draught). Guns: 1—37 mm. Machinery: Reciprocating. I.H.P.: 110 = 10 kts. Coal: 35 tons. Complement: 45.

Surveying Vessels (*Navios Hidrograficos*).

1937, *Courtesy Eng. Capt. Natal Arnaud.*

JACEGUAI (ex-*Flecha*, ex-*H.M.S. Fairfield*), (Clyde Shipbuilding Co., 1919). Ex-minesweeper, purchased for use as a surveying vessel in 1937. Displacement: 710 tons. Dimensions: 231 (*o.a.*) × 28½ × 7½ feet. Guns: None reported. I.H.P.: 2,200 = 16 kts. Coal: 185 tons. Complement: 79.

1935, *Official.*

RIO BRANCO (ex-Canadian Government vessel *Margaret*). (Thornycroft, 1914). Displacement: 896 tons. Dimensions: 200 × 32 × 10 feet. Guns: 2—6 pdr. I.H.P.: 2,000 = 15 kts. Coal: 200 tons. Complement: 91.

1935, *Official.*

JOSÉ BONIFACIO (ex-*Itapema*, 1909). Built by Ailsa S.B. Co., Troon. Displacement: 1,300 tons. Dimensions: 270 × 42 × 14 feet. Guns: 2—4 inch, 2—6 pdr. H.P.: 540 = 9 kts. Complement: 152.

CHINA

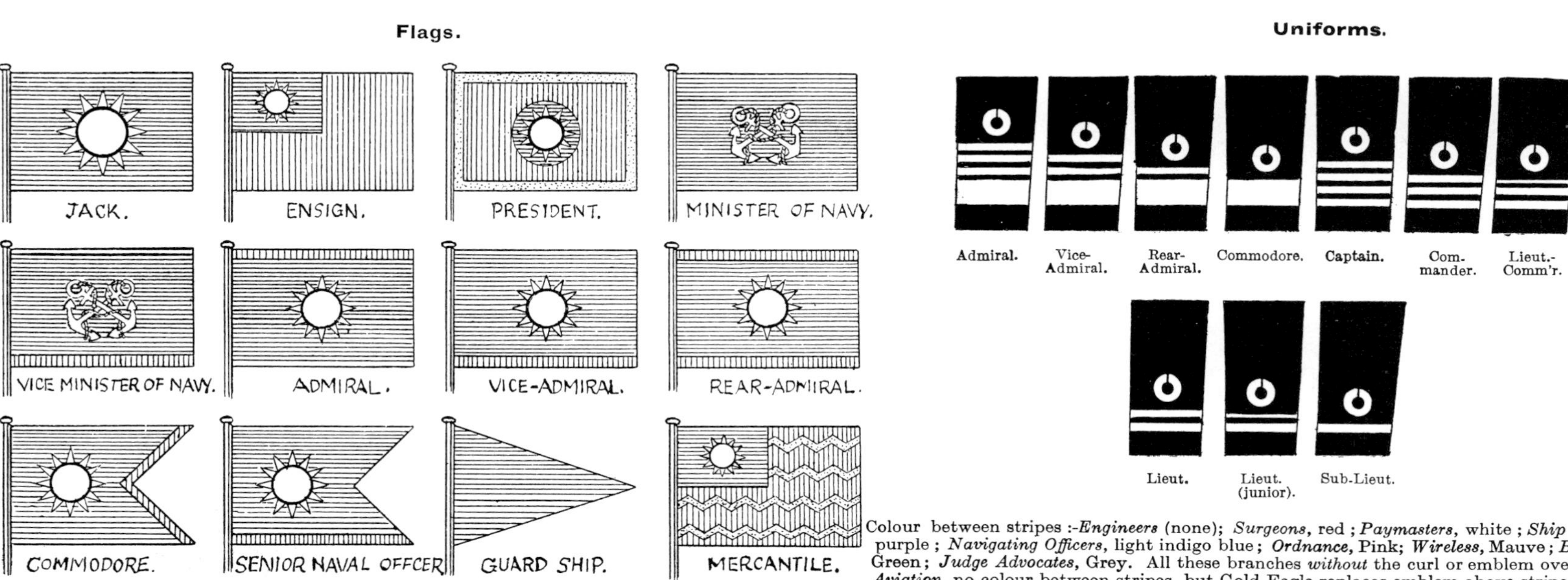

Colour between stripes :-*Engineers* (none); *Surgeons*, red ; *Paymasters*, white ; *Ship Constructor*, purple ; *Navigating Officers*, light indigo blue ; *Ordnance*, Pink; *Wireless*, Mauve ; *Bandmasters*, Green ; *Judge Advocates*, Grey. All these branches *without* the curl or emblem over top stripe. *Aviation*, no colour between stripes, but Gold Eagle replaces emblem above stripe.

Commander in Chief, Naval Forces : Admiral S. K. Chen.
Chief of Naval Staff : Vice-Admiral C. L. Chen.
Naval Attaché, London : Captain N. Soong.

Cruisers

Special Note.—It has been reported that these ships have been recovered from Japanese hands, but official confirmation is so far lacking.

NING HAI (Harima S.B. Co., Japan. 1931).
PING HAI (Kiangnan Dock Co., Shanghai. 1932).

Displacement : 2,500 tons. Complement : 340

Dimensions : 350 (*pp.*) 360 (*o.a.*) × 39 × 13 feet.

Guns :
6—5·5 inch.
6—3·5 inch, Krupp.
8—M.G.

Tubes :
4—21 inch.

Protection :
Thin plating on gunhouses and side amidships.
1″ deck.

Machinery : Geared turbines. H.P. 9500 = 22¼ kts. (Trials, 10,500 = 24 kts.). Coal fired.

PING HAI. 1937, *Courtesy Admiral S. K. Chen.*

General Notes.—This design is an exceedingly interesting production, displaying considerable originality. *Ping Hai*, though laid down on July 9, 1931, was not completed till late in 1936, construction having been suspended in 1933. Machinery and main armament of these ships were supplied from Japan.

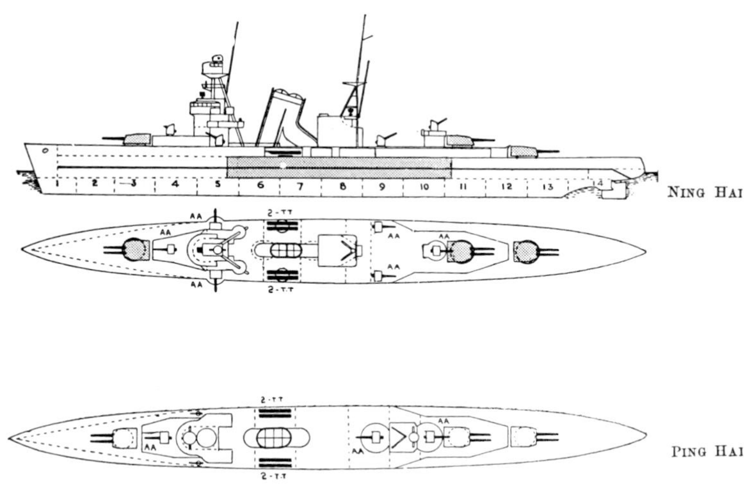

PING HAI. 1937, *Courtesy Admiral S. K. Chen.*

Cruisers

NING HAI. 1934 *Photo.*

Special Note.

It is understood that the cruiser **AURORA**, of 5,270 tons, is to be acquired from the Royal Navy in the course of 1947.

Destroyers

1944, *U.S. Navy Official.*

TAI KANG (ex-U.S.S. *Decker*, 1943), **TAI PING** (ex-U.S.S. *Wyffels*, 1943), and 4 others (to be acquired in 1947).

Displacement: 1,150 tons (1,360 tons, *full load*). Complement: 200. Dimensions: 283½ (*w.l.*), 289 (*o.a.*) × 35 × 10⅔ feet. Guns: **3**—3 inch, 50 cal. dual purpose, **2**—40 mm. AA., **9**—20 mm. AA., **8** D.C.T. Machinery: Diesel with electric drive. 2 shafts. H.P. 5,500 = 19 kts.

Note.—First two vessels built at Philadelphia and Boston Navy Yards, respectively, and delivered in 1946.

It is proposed to acquire a Destroyer of the "Hunt" Class from the Royal Navy in the course of 1947.

Sloop

Sloop (officially rated as Cruiser).

1931 *Photo, Official.*

YAT SEN (1930). Displacement: 1,650 tons. Dimensions: 275 (*o.a.*), 252 (*pp.*) × 34 × 11 feet. Guns: **1**—6 inch, **1**—5·5 inch, **4**—3 inch AA., **2**—3 pdr., **4** M.G. H.P.: 4,000 = 20 kts. Coal: 280 tons. Complement: 173.

Corvette.

FU PO (ex-H.M.S. *Petunia*, Sept. 19, 1940). Displacement: 925 tons. Dimensions: 190 (*pp.*), 205 (*o.a.*) × 33 × 14½ feet (*max.* draught). Guns: **1**—4 inch AA., **1**—2 pdr. pompom, several 20 mm. AA. Machinery: Triple expansion. I.H.P.: 2,750 = 16 kts. Boilers: 2 S.E., 225 lb. pressure. Oil fuel: 230 tons.

Notes.—Built by Henry Robb, Ltd., of Leith; engined by John G. Kincaid & Co.; and purchased by Chinese Navy in 1945. Present name means "Calming of the Waves". A number of Canadian corvettes which were transferred to the Chinese flag in 1946 are understood to be for mercantile service.

Minesweepers.

YUNG HSING (ex-U.S.S. *Mainstay*, July 31, 1943), **YUNG NING** (ex-U.S.S. *Lucid*, June 5, 1943), **YUNG TAI** (ex-U.S.S. *Magnet*, June 5, 1943), **YUNG TING** (ex-U.S.S. *Logic*, April 10, 1943). Displacement: 625 tons (945 tons *full load*). Complement: 104. Dimensions: 180 (*w.l.*), 184½ (*o.a.*) × 33 × 9¾ feet (*max.* draught). Guns: **1**—3 inch d.p., **2**—40 mm. AA., **6**—20 mm. AA. Machinery: Diesel. 2 shafts. B.H.P. 1,710 = 14·5 kts.

Note.—20 more minesweepers are to be acquired from the U.S. Navy.

Patrol Vessels.

YUNG SHENG (ex-U.S.S. *PCE* 867, Dec. 3, 1942), **YUNG SHUN** (ex-*PCE* 869, Feb. 6, 1943). Displacement: 795 tons (903 tons *full load*). Dimensions: 180 (*w.l.*), 184½ (*o.a.*) × 33 × 9½ feet (*max.* draught). Guns: **1**—3 inch d.p., **2**—40 mm. A.A., **6**—20 mm. AA., **4** D.C.T. Machinery: Diesel. 2 shafts. B.H.P. 1,800 = 17 kts.

Note.—28 wooden submarine chasers of *SC* type are also to be acquired from the U.S. Navy, together with 6 motor gunboats and 8 m.t.b.

Transfer from U.S. Navy of 271 surface ships, below destroyer status, has been authorised.

Corvette **FU PO** was sunk by collision with s.s. *Hai Ming*, while on passage from Amoy to Formosa, March 19, 1947.

Eight Harbour Defence motor launches are on loan from the Royal Navy, 1947.

Gunboats

1929, *Official Photo.*

YUNG SUI (1929). Built by Kiangnan Dock Co., Shanghai. Displacement: 650 tons. Complement: 100. Dimensions: 225 × 30 × 6 feet. H.P.: 4000 = 18·5 kts. Guns: **1**—6 inch, **1**—4·7 inch, **3**—3 inch AA., **4**—6 pdr., **1**—1 pdr. pom-pom, **4** MG.

1930.

MING CHUEN (1929). Built by Kiangnan Dock Co., Shanghai. Displacement: 550 tons. Dimensions: 196¾ × 26 × 6 feet (*mean*). Guns: **1**—4·7 inch, **1**—4 inch, **1**—3 inch AA., **2**—6 pdr., **1**—1 pdr. pompom, **4** M.G. I.H.P.: 2,200 = 17 kts. (Coal fired.) Complement: 115.

1929, *Official Photo.*

HSIEN NING (Kiangnan Dock Co., Shanghai, Aug. 16, 1928). Displacement: 418 tons. Complement: 115. Dimensions: 170 (*p.p.*), 180 (*o.a.*) × 24 × 6½ feet. H.P.: 2500 = 17 kts. Guns: **1**—4·7 inch, **1**—4 inch, **3**—6 pdr., **5** MG. Cost $300,000.

River Gunboats

(Now has mainmast.) 1933 *Photo, courtesy of builders.*

YING HAO (ex-H.M.S. *Sandpiper*). (June 9, 1933). Built by Thornycroft. Displacement: 185 tons. Dimensions: 160 × 30⅔ × 2 feet (*mean*). Guns: **1**—3·7 inch howitzer, **9** smaller. Machinery: 2 sets Reciprocating. 2 shafts. 1 Admiralty 3-drum type boiler. H.P.: 600 = 11¼ kts. Complement: 40. Presented to China by the British Government in Feb., 1942. Name means "British Hero".

1931 *Photo, favour of Messrs. Yarrow.*

YING TEH (ex-H.M.S. *Falcon*) (1931). Built by Messrs. Yarrow & Co., Ltd. Displacement: 372 tons. Dimensions: 150 × 28⅔ × 5 feet (*mean*). Guns: **1**—3·7 inch howitzer, **2**—6 pdr., **10** M.G. Machinery: Parsons geared turbines. Boilers: 2 Admiralty 3-drum type. S.H.P.: 2,250 = 15 kts. Fuel: 84 tons oil. Complement: 55. Presented to China by the British Government, in Feb., 1942. Name means "British Virtue".

1932.

YING SHAN (ex-H.M.S. *Gannet*) (1927). Designed and built by Messrs. Yarrow & Co., Ltd. Displacement: 310 tons. Dimensions: 177 (*w.l.*), 184⅔ (*o.a.*) × 29 × 3 ft. 2½ ins. draught. Guns: **2**—3 inch AA., **8** M.G. Machinery: Geared turbines. Boilers: Yarrow. Designed H.P.: 2250 = 16 kts. Fuel: 60 tons oil. Complement: 55. Presented to China by the British Government in Feb., 1942. Name means "British Mountain".

1928 *Official Photo.*

MEI YUAN (ex-U.S.S. *Tutuila*) (June 14, 1927), and another (ex-*Tatara*, ex-U.S.S. *Wake*, ex-U.S.S. *Guam*) (May 28, 1927). Displacement: 370 tons *standard*, 150 (*w.l.*), 159½ (*o.a.*) × 27 × 5¼ feet *mean* draught (fresh water), 6 feet (*max.*). Guns: **2**—3 inch, 23 cal., **10** M.G. Triple expansion engines. I.H.P.: 1,950 = 14·5 kts. Oil fuel: 75 tons. Complement: 58. *Mei Yuan* was presented to China by the U.S. Government in March, 1942. Sister ship was recovered from Japanese hands and presented to China in 1946. *Mei Yuan* means "American Origin".

River Gunboats

SAN MIN (ex-French *Balny*, 1920). Displacement: 201 tons. Dimensions: $167\frac{1}{4} \times 23 \times 4\frac{1}{2}$ feet. Guns: 2—3 inch, 2—37 mm., 4 M.G. Machinery: Triple expansion. 2 shafts. I.H.P. 920 = 14 kts. Boilers: 2 Fouché. Coal: 45 tons. Complement: 59.

1929 *Photo.*

YUNG HSIANG (Kawasaki Co., Kobé, Japan, 1912–13). 830 tons. Dimensions: 205 (*pp.*) $\times 29\frac{1}{2} \times 8$ feet. Guns: 1—4·1 inch, 1—3 inch, 4—3 pdr., 2—1 pdr. H.P.: 1,350 = 13·5 kts. Coal: 190 tons. 2 screws. Complement: 105. 1 inch steel protective deck.

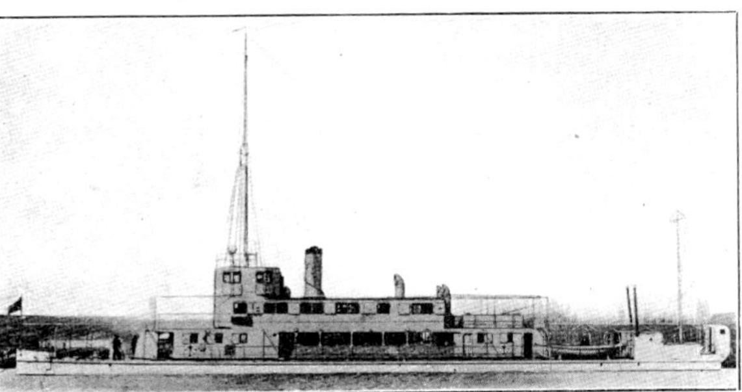

1929 *Official Photo.*

KIANG HSI (Krupp, 1911). Displacement: 150 tons. Dimensions: 144 × 25 × 3 feet. H.P.: 450 = 9 kts. Boilers: 2 Schulz. Coal: 35 tons. Guns: 1—3·4 inch howitzer, 1—1 pdr., 4 M.G. Complement: 58.

1929 *Official Photo.*

Chu Kwan. (Chu Tung has no superstructure aft.) 1929 *Photo.*

CHU KWAN (1907), **CHU TUNG** (1906). Built by Kawasaki Co., Kobe. Displacement: 740 tons. Dimensions: 200 × 30 × 8 feet. Guns: 2—4·7 inch, 2—3 inch, 3—6 pdr., 1—2 pdr. AA., 2 M.G. Machinery: Triple expansion. 2 shafts. I.H.P.: 1,350 = 11 kts. Watertube boilers. Coal: 150 tons. Complement: 135.

1929 *Official Photo.*

KIANG YUAN (1905). Built by Kawasaki Co., Kobe. Displacement: 550 tons. Dimensions: 170 (*pp.*), 180 (*o.a.*) × 28 × 7 feet. Guns: 1—4·7 inch, 1—4 inch, 4—3 pdr., 4 M.G. Machinery: Triple expansion. 2 shafts. I.H.P.: 950 = 9 kts. Watertube boilers. Coal: 113 tons. Complement: 123.

YUNG CHIEN (Kiangnan Dock Co., Shanghai, 1915). Displacement: 860 tons. Dimensions: 205 (*pp.*), $215\frac{1}{2}$ (*o.a.*) $\times 29\frac{1}{2} \times 11\frac{1}{2}$ feet. Guns: 1—4 inch, 1—3 inch, 4—3 pdr., 1—2 pdr. AA. Designed H.P.: 1,350 = 13 kts. Coal: 150 tons. Complement: 105.

CHANG CHIH (ex-Japanese *Uji*, Sept. 26, 1940). Displacement: 1,350 tons. Length: 225 feet. Guns: 3—4·7 inch, 9—25 mm., 3 M.G. Speed: 20 kts.

AN TUNG (ex-Japanese *Ataka*, ex-*Nakoso*, April, 1922). Displacement: 725 tons. Dimensions: $222 \times 32 \times 7\frac{1}{2}$ feet. Guns: 2—3 inch, 5—25 mm., 6 M.G. Machinery: Triple expansion. I.H.P. 1,700 = 16 kts. Boilers: 2 Kanpon.

CHANG TEH. Displacement: 486 tons. Guns: 3—3 inch, 3—25 mm., 3 M.G.

TAI YUAN. Displacement: 390 tons. Armed as *Chang Teh.*

YUNG AN, YUNG CHI, YUNG PING. Displacement: 370 tons. All armed as *Chang Teh.*

Landing Craft.

(174 of these are being acquired.)

7 *LST*: **CHUNG CHIEN, CHUNG CHUAN, CHUNG HAI, CHUNG HSING, CHUNG HSUN, CHUNG TING, CHUNG YEH.** Guns: 6—40 mm. AA., 12—20 mm. AA.

5 *LSM*: **MEI CHEN, MEI LEH, MEI PENG, MEI SUNG, MEI YI.** Guns: 1 or 2—40 mm. AA., 4—20 mm. AA.

4 *LCI*: **LIENG CHEN, LIENG HWA, LIENG KUANG, LIENG SHEN.** Guns: 3 to 5—20 mm. AA.

3 *LCT*. **HO CHIEN, HO CHUN, HO CHUNG.**

Miscellaneous.

OMEI (ex-U.S.S. *Maumee*, 1915). Displacement: 4,990 tons. Dimensions: $475\frac{2}{3}$ (*o.a.*) × 56 × 10 feet (*mean*). Guns: 5—3 inch, 2—40 mm. AA., 8—20 mm. AA. Machinery: Diesel. 2 shafts. B.H.P. 5,000 = 14 kts. Cargo capacity: 7,850 tons. Fuel: 820 tons. (Oiler.)

(2 more Oilers, 2 Repair Ships, 1 Surveying Vessel, and 6 Lighthouse Tenders are to be acquired from the U.S. Navy in 1947.)

Ex-**ATR 26** (April 23, 1944). Displacement: 852 tons. Dimensions: $165\frac{1}{2} \times 33\frac{1}{3} \times 15\frac{1}{2}$ feet. Machinery: Triple expansion. I.H.P. 1,600 = 12 kts. (Tug.)

DENMARK

Flags.

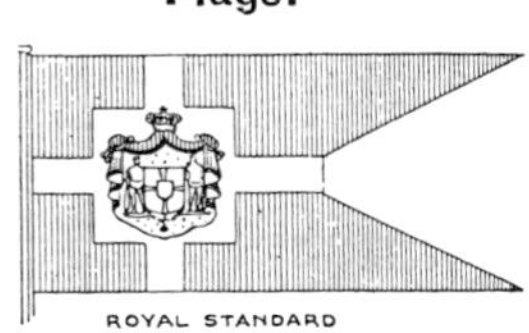

ENSIGN AND JACK. ROYAL STANDARD. MINISTER of MARINE.

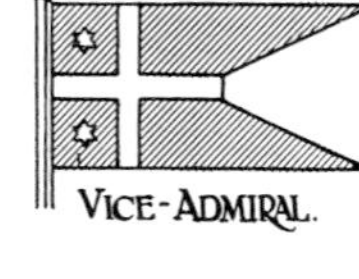
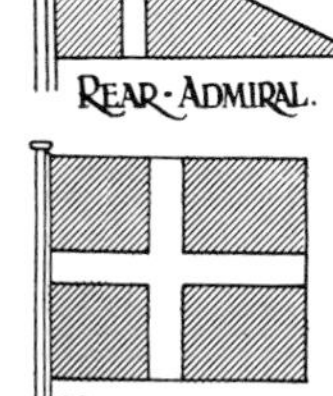
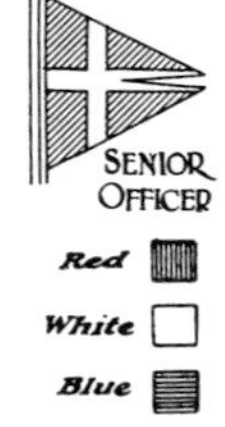

ADMIRAL. VICE-ADMIRAL. REAR-ADMIRAL. SENIOR OFFICER

COMMODORE. FLOTILLA C.O. MERCANTILE FLAG.

Red. White. Blue. Green. Yellow.

Insignia of Rank on Sleeves.

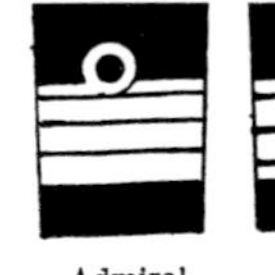

	Admiral.	Vice-Admiral.	Kontre-Admiral.	Kommandör.	Kommandör kaptajn.	Orlogs-kaptajn.	Kaptajn-löjtnant.	Sölöjtnant 1' Grad.
British or U.S.A.	*Admiral.*	*Vice-Admiral.*	*Rear-Admiral.*	*Commodore.*	*Captain.*	*Commander*	*Lieutenant-Commander.*	*Lieutenant.*

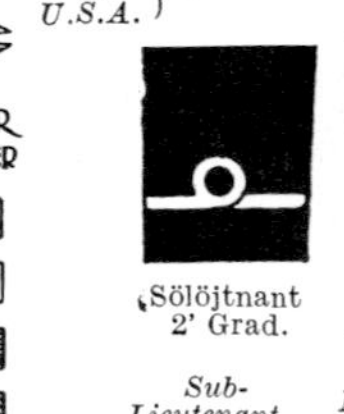

Sölöjtnant 2' Grad. — *Sub-Lieutenant.*
Sökadet Ældste Klasse — *Midshipman.*

Personnel: About 4000, all ranks.
Oversea Possessions: Greenland, Faröe Islands.
Minister of Defence: Mr. Harald Petersen.
C. in C. and Director-General, Ministry of Marine: Vice-Admiral A. H. Vedel, K.C.B.
Naval Attaché, London: Captain E. J. C. Qvistgaard.

Mercantile Marine.

(Sept. 30, 1945), 500,000 tons gross.

Note.—Division flag is pendant, otherwise as commodore.

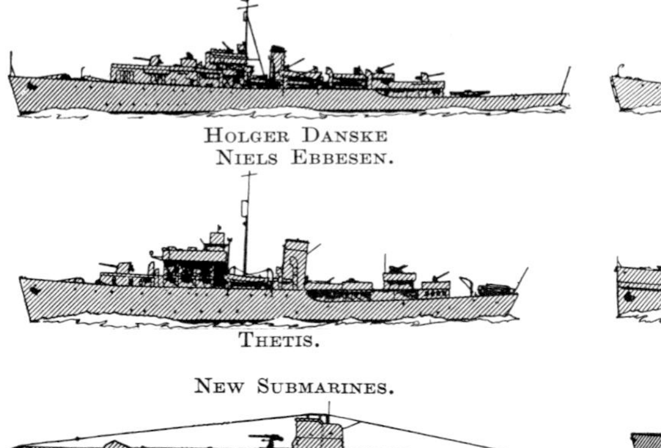

HOLGER DANSKE
NIELS EBBESEN.

THETIS.

NEW SUBMARINES.

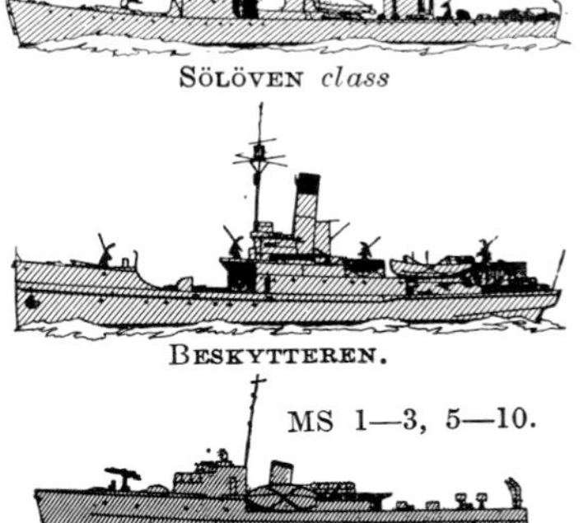

SÖLÖVEN *class*

BESKYTTEREN.

MS 1—3, 5—10.

LINDORMEN.

FREJA.

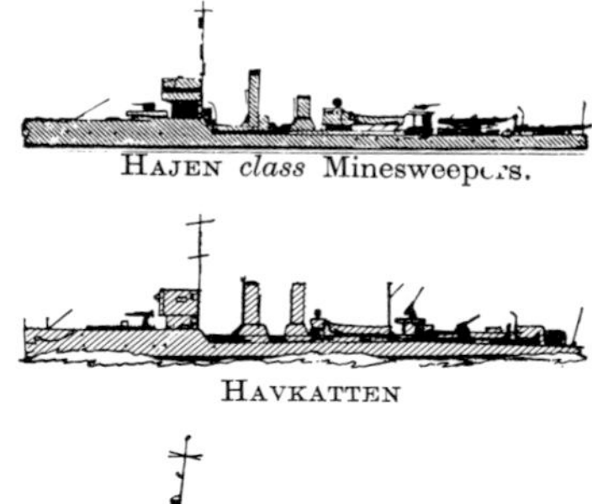

HAJEN *class* Minesweepers.

HAVKATTEN

HEJMDAL.

All displacements are "Standard". Where measurement of length is not stated, it can be taken as between perpendiculars (*pp.*). All draughts *max. load aft.* unless otherwise stated.

Danish warships are referred to officially with the prefix H.D.M.S.

Destroyers.

1939, *Official Sketch*

HVITFELDT (ex-*Nymfen*, 1943), **WILLEMOES** (ex-*Najaden*, 1942). Both laid down at Royal Dockyard, Copenhagen, 1939. Displacement: 710 tons. Dimensions: 279 (*pp.*) × 27⅓ × 8 feet. Guns: **2**—3·5 inch, **2**—40 mm. AA., **4**—20 mm. Madsen. Tubes: **6**—21 inch. 60 mines carried. Machinery: Geared turbines. 2 shafts. S.H.P.: 21,000 = 35 kts. Oil fuel: 100 tons. Complement: 100.

(These ships will be completed early in 1947.)

Minelayer (*Mineskib*).

1944, *courtesy Commander R. Steen Steensen, R.D.N.*

LINDORMEN (Royal Dockyard, Copenhagen, March 30, 1940). 614 tons. Complement: 58. Dimensions: $167\frac{1}{4}$ (*pp.*) × 29 × 8 feet. Guns: **2**—3 inch, **3**—20 mm. AA. Mines: 150. Machinery: Triple expansion. 2 shafts. I.H.P.: 1,200 = 14 kts. Boilers: 2 Thornycroft 3-drum type. Oil fuel: 35 tons. Scuttled in Copenhagen Harbour, August 29, 1943, but was salved and will be refitted. Now used for training.

Torpedo Boats. (*Torpedobaade*)

BILLE (Sept. 21, 1946), **BUHL, HAMMER, HOLM, KRABBE** (June 27, 1946), **KRIEGER** (May 4, 1946). All built in Royal Dockyard at Copenhagen. Displacement: 329 tons (400 tons *full load*). Dimensions: 210 × 21 × 14 feet. Armament: **2**—3·5 inch, **2**—20 mm. AA. Madsen, **2** D.C.T., **6**—18 inch tubes. Machinery: Danish Atlas geared turbines. 2 shafts. S.H.P. 6,900 = 29 kts. Will resemble *Willemoes* type in silhouette.

(*Under reconstruction after scuttling.*)

HÖGEN (1933), **HVALEN** (1930), **ÖRNEN** (Oct. 19, 1934). All by Royal Dockyard, Copenhagen. Displacement: 290 tons. Dimensions: $198\frac{3}{4}$ (*o.a.*) × $19\frac{1}{2}$ × $7\frac{3}{4}$ feet. Armament: **2**—3·5 inch, **2**—20 mm. AA., **2** M.G., **2** D.C.T., **6**—18 inch tubes. Machinery: Danish Atlas geared turbines. S.H.P. 6,000 = 27·5 kts. Oil fuel: 40 tons. Complement: 55.

Submarines.

1945, *courtesy M. Henri Le Masson.*

(Names not yet reported). (ex-H.M.S. *Vulpine*, Dec. 28, 1943), (ex-*Morse*, ex-H.M.S. *Vortex*, Aug. 19, 1944.) Displacement: 545/735 tons. Complement: 36. Dimensions: 203 × 16 × $14\frac{3}{4}$ feet. Guns: **1**—3 inch, **3** M.G. Tubes: **4**—21 inch. Machinery: 2 Davey Paxman Diesels, 2 electric motors. B.H.P. 800/760 = 13/9 kts. Fuel: 56 tons.

(Name not yet reported). (ex-*Dzik*, ex-*P* 52, Oct. 11, 1942). Displacement: 540/730 tons. Complement: 36. Dimensions: 200 × 16 × $14\frac{3}{4}$ feet. Guns: **1**—3 inch, **3** M.G. Tubes: **4**—21 inch. Machinery: 2 Davey Paxman Diesels, 2 electric motors. B.H.P. 615/825 = 11/9 kts. Fuel: 50 tons.

Havfruen, Havkalen, Havmanden, Havörnen (1937-39). Displacement: 320/402 tons. Dimensions: $154\frac{1}{3}$ × $15\frac{1}{2}$ × $8\frac{1}{3}$ feet. (These 4 submarines were scuttled in August 1943, and have been salved with a view to being refitted if their condition warrants it.)

Frigates.

HOLGER DANSKE 1946, *courtesy Com. R. S. Steensen, R.D.N.*

HOLGER DANSKE (ex-H.M.S. *Monnow*, Dec. 4, 1943), **NIELS EBBESEN** (ex-H.M.S. *Annan*, Dec. 12, 1943). Displacement: 1,445 tons. Dimensions: $301\frac{1}{2}$ × $36\frac{1}{2}$ × 12 feet. Guns: **2**—4 inch AA., **10**—20 mm. AA. Madsen. Tubes: **2**—18 inch (for instructional use). Machinery: Triple expansion. 2 shafts. I.H.P.: 6,500 = 20 kts. Boilers: 2, of 3-drum type. Complement: 140. Purchased from R.N.

Note.—Employed as sea-going Training Ships for midshipmen and for boys, respectively.

Surveying Vessels.

1939, *Com. R. Steen Steensen, R.D.N.*

AFREJ (Dec. 22, 1938). Built at Royal Dockyard, Copenhagen. Displacement: 322 tons. Complement: 40. Dimensions: $124\frac{3}{4}$ (*pp.*), 134 (*o.a.*) × $25\frac{1}{4}$ × $7\frac{1}{4}$ feet. Guns: **2**—3 inch, **2**—20 mm. AA. (Not mounted when on Surveying Service.) Machinery: Triple expansion. 1 shaft. I.H.P.: 300 = 10·5 kts. Boilers: 1 cylindrical. Oil fuel: 15 tons. Classed as *Opmaalingsskib* (Surveying Vessel).

1946, *Official.*

HEJMDAL (Royal Dockyard, Copenhagen, Feb. 1 1935). Displacement: 705 tons. Complement: 40. Dimensions: 175 (*o.a.*) × 30 × 12 feet. Guns: **2**—3 inch, **4**—20 mm. AA., **2**—8 mm. AA. Machinery: Triple expansion. 1 shaft. I.H.P.: 800 = 13 kts. Boilers: 2 cylindrical. Oil: 100 tons. Radius: 4,000 miles at 12 kts. Completed April, 1935. Classed as a Surveying Vessel, but also employed on Fishery Protection duties.

Minesweepers (ex-Torpedo Boats).

HAVKATTEN. 1946, *Com. R. S. Steensen, R.D.N.*

Hajen (ex-*Söridderen*, ex-*Sölöven*, 1916), ***Havkatten*** (1919), ***Narhvalen*** (1917). All built at Royal Dockyard, Copenhagen. Displacement: 110 tons. Complement: 26. Dimensions: 126½ (*o.a.*) × 14 × 8¾ feet (*max. draught*). Guns: 2—20 mm. AA., 2 D.C.T. (in *Havkatten* only). Machinery: Triple expansion. I.H.P. 2,000 = 24 kts. Coal: 15 tons.

Note.—*Havkatten* is at present employed as a Tender to Training establishments.

MS 7. 1946, *Com. R. Steen Steensen, R.D.N.*

MS 1–3, 5–10 (1941). Wood. Displacement: 74 tons. Dimensions: 78¾ × 21 × 5 feet. Guns: 1—20 mm., 2 M.G. Speed: 11 kts.

Note.—*MS* 4 was scuttled in August, 1943, and became a complete loss.

SÖRIDDEREN. 1946, *Com. R. Steen Steenson, R.D.N.*

SÖHUNDEN (1943), **SÖLÖVEN** (Dec. 3, 1938), **SÖRIDDEREN** (1942), all built at Royal Dockyard, Copenhagen. Displacement: 270 tons. Complement: 47. Dimensions: 176½ (*o.a.*), 170 (*pp.*) × 20¾ × 6½ feet. Guns: 2—3 inch, 4—20 mm. AA., 4—8 mm. AA., 2 D.C.T. Equipped for minelaying. Machinery: Geared turbine, 1 shaft. S.H.P.: 2,200 = 19 kts. Boiler: 1 Thornycroft 3-drum type. Oil fuel: 30 tons.

Note.—*Sölöven* means Sealion; *Söhunden*, Seadog; *Soridderen*, Sea Knight. These 3 vessels wear pendant numbers M 1, M 6, and M 4, respectively.

SÖHUNDEN. 1946, *R.S.S.*

Motor Minesweepers.

MR 225. 1946, *R.S.S.*

MR 18, 26, 32, 36, 152—157, 160, 173, 214, 225, 226, 229, 230, 233, 236, 242, 259, 263. Ex-German craft. Displacement: 90 tons. Guns: 2—20 mm. AA. Machinery: Diesel. B.H.P. 1,800 = 18 kts. Complement: 17.

ME 83, 84, 86, 263, 307. On loan from Royal Navy. Wood. Displacement: 240 tons. Dimensions: 105 (*pp.*), 119 (*o.a.*) × 13 × — feet. Guns: 2—20 mm. AA., etc. Machinery: Diesel. B.H.P. 500 = 10 kts. Complement: 20.

ME 1038, 1042, 1044. On loan from Royal Navy. Wood. Displacement: 360 tons. Dimensions: 126 (*pp.*), 139⅝ (*o.a.*) × 26 × 10½ feet (*mean*). Machinery: Diesel. B.H.P. 500 = 10·5 kts.

MSK 1—3 (1945). Displacement: 70 tons (*full load*). Dimensions: 70½ × 17⅓ × 9 feet. Machinery: Diesel. B.H.P. 210 = 10 kts.

MSK 4—6 (1944–45). Displacement: 50 tons (*full load*). Dimensions not reported. Machinery: Diesel. B.H.P. 120.

ML 1—3 (1944). Displacement: 21 tons. Dimensions: 50 × 13 × 3¼ feet.

Note.—A number of motor fishing craft are also employed in minesweeping.

Fishery Patrol Vessels

1944, *courtesy Commander R. Steen Steensen R.D.N.*

THETIS (ex-H.M.S. *Geranium*, April 23, 1940). Displacement: 925 tons. Dimensions: 190 (*pp.*), 205 (*o.a.*) × 33 × 14½ feet (*max.* draught). Guns: 1—4 inch AA., 1—40 mm. AA., 4—20 mm. AA. Machinery: Triple expansion. I.H.P.: 2,750 = 16 kts. Boilers: 2 S.E. Oil fuel: 230 tons. Complement: 85. Operates in North Sea and off Faroes.

1932 *Photo, Commdr. R. S. Steensen, R.D.N.*

MAAGEN (Frederikssund, 1930). Wood. Displacement: 90 tons. Dimensions: 71½ (*o.a.*) × 16½ × 9½ feet. Guns: 1—37 mm. 1 Tuxham motor. B.H.P.: 108 = 8 kts. Complement: 11.
For service in Greenland waters. Classed as Fishery Patrol Cutter (*Fiskeriinspektionsfartöj*).

Miscellaneous

Fishery Patrol Vessels—*continued.*

TERNEN. 1938, *Official.*

TERNEN (Faaborg, 1937.) Wood. Displacement: 82 tons. Complement: 11. Dimensions: 68½ (*o.a.*) × 16⅞ × 9¾ feet. Guns: 1—37 mm. 1 Möller & Jochumsen Diesel engine. B.H.P.: 110 = 8 kts. Employed on fishery research and coastal surveying duties, Greenland. Classed as Surveying Tender (*Opmaalingsfartöj*).

1946, *Photo Commdr. R. S. Steensen, R.D.N.*

BESKYTTEREN (1900). 415 tons. Comp. 47. 134 (*pp.*), 142·5 (*o.a.*) × 24·8 × 12·5 feet. Guns: **1**—6 pdr. **2**—8 mm. AA. I.H.P. 620 = 11 kts. (*f.d.*). Cruising speed is 9 kts. Re-boilered 1920. Employed in North Sea and inside Shaw. May be discarded shortly.

Royal Yacht (*Kongeskib*).

1936, *Commdr. R. S. Steensen, R.D.N.*

DANNEBROG (Royal Dockyard, Copenhagen, 1931). 1,130 tons. Complement: 57. Dimensions: 246 (*o.a.*) × 34 × 11⅕ feet. Guns: 2—37 mm. Two Burmeister & Wain 8-cylinder, 2-cycle Diesels. B.H.P.: 1,800 = 14 kts.

Tenders (used for transport purposes).

DEN LILLE HAVFRUE, KIRSTEN PIIL (1935). Displacement: 88 tons. Dimensions: 150 × 19 × 7¼ feet. Machinery: Diesel. (Manned by Coast Artillery personnel.)

Mining Tenders (*Minefartöier.*)

LAALAND, LOUGEN (1941). Displacement: 260 tons. Dimensions: 101½ × 19⅔ × — feet. **2** M.G. Speed: 11 kts. Both scuttled in August, 1943, but salved and rebuilt, 1945—46.

EGYPT

A :—Royal Egyptian Navy.

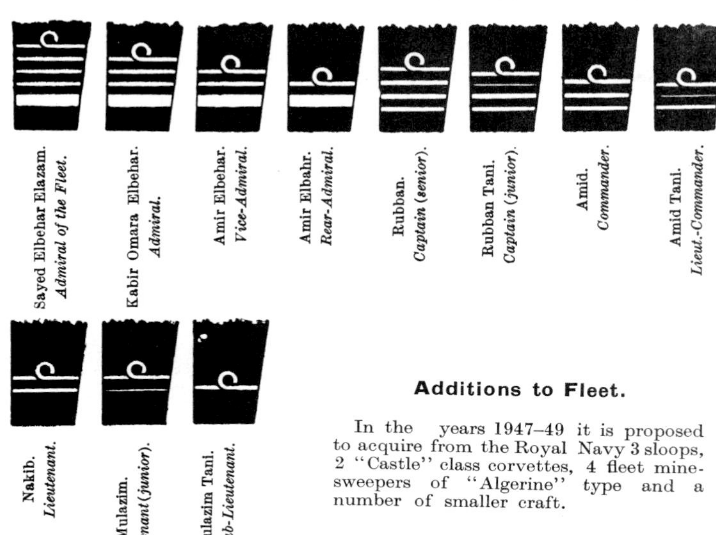

Additions to Fleet.

In the years 1947–49 it is proposed to acquire from the Royal Navy 3 sloops, 2 "Castle" class corvettes, 4 fleet mine-sweepers of "Algerine" type and a number of smaller craft.

Mercantile Marine: ("Lloyd's Register" 1939 figures) 56 vessels of 109,825 tons gross.

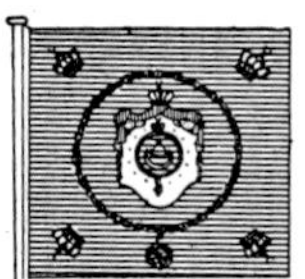

Royal Standard.

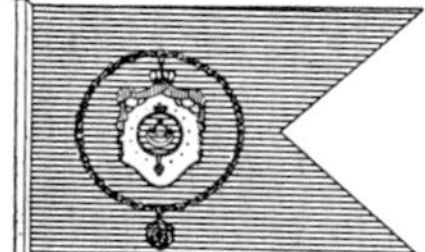

Crown Prince's Standard.

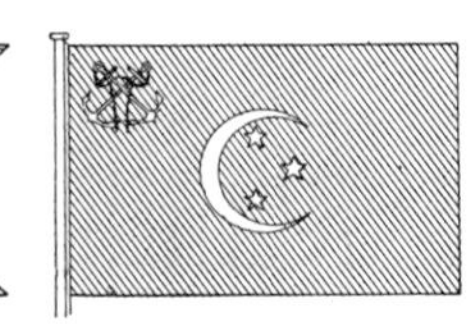

Ensign.

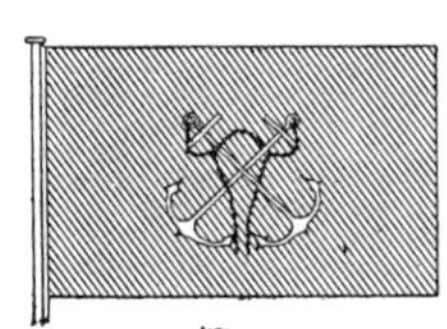

Jack.

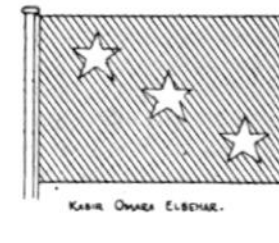

Minister of Defence.

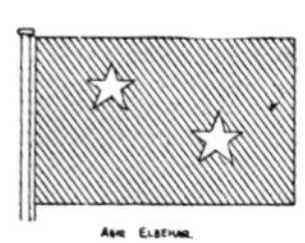

Kabir Omara Elbehar.

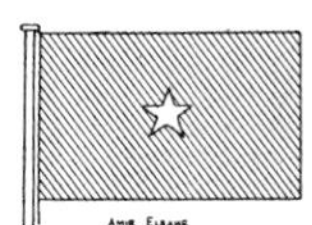

Amir Elbehar.

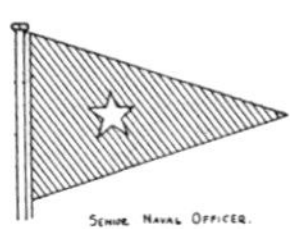

Amir Elbahr.

Senior Naval Officer.

Royal Yacht.

MAHROUSSA. Iron. Built by Samuda Bros., Poplar, 1865. Reconstructed by A. & J. Inglis, Glasgow, 1905, and re-fitted in 1946–47 at Malta Dockyard. Displacement: 4561 tons. Dimensions: 400 (*p.p.*), 420 (*w.l.*), $477\frac{5}{8}$ (*o.a.*) × $42\frac{3}{4}$ × $17\frac{1}{4}$ feet draught. Machinery: 3 Parsons turbines. 3 shafts. S.H.P. 5500 = 16 kts. Boilers (new 1905): 5 main and 1 auxiliary Inglis multitubular. Oil: 346 tons. Complement, 164.

1946, *London Studio.*

B :—Coastguard and Fisheries Administration.

Transport.

1930 *Photo, Swan, Hunter.*

EL AMIRA FAWZIA (Swan, Hunter, July 8th, 1929). 2,640 tons. Dimensions: 275 × 36 × 14 feet. Guns: 2—3 pdr. Machinery: Triple expansion. 2 shafts. I.H.P.: 2,130 = 14 kts. 2 S.E. boilers (working pressure, 180 lbs.). Oil fuel. Fitted as transport for 400 men and 40 horses. Normally employed on coasting service carrying passengers. Complement, 79.

Sloop.

EL AMIR FAROUQ (Hawthorn, Leslie, 1926). 1441 tons. Dimensions: 247 × 34 × $13\frac{1}{4}$ feet. Guns: 1—6 pdr. 4 M.G. Machinery: Triple expansion. 2 shafts. I.H.P.: 2,800 = 17 kts. 2 s.e. boilers, working pressure, 180 lbs. Oil fuel. Complement: 70.

Motor Patrol Vessels.

(All lent to Royal Navy during War, and rated as HDML.)

1939, *Official.*

RAQIB (Alexandria, 1938). Dimensions: 66 × $12\frac{1}{2}$ × 4 feet. Guns: 1—37 mm. Machinery: 2 Otto Deutz 8-cyl. Diesel engines. 2 shafts. B.H.P.: 540 = 15 kts. Fuel: 520 gallons. Complement: 9.

AL SAREA (J. S. White & Co., Ltd., 1936). Displacement: 20 tons. Dimensions: 55 × $11\frac{1}{2}$ × $3\frac{1}{4}$ feet. Guns: 1—37 mm. Machinery: 2 Kermath 12-cyl. petrol engines. H.P.: 900 = 35 kts. Fuel: 340 gallons. Complement: 9.

DARFEEL. 1939, *Official.*

DARFEEL, NOOR-EL-BAHR (Thornycroft, 1925). Displacement: 20 tons. Dimensions: 56 × 11 × $3\frac{1}{2}$ feet. Guns: 1—37 mm. Machinery: 3 Thornycroft 6-cyl. petrol engines. 3 shafts. B.H.P.: 330 = 17 kts. Fuel: 600 gallons. Complement: 9.

Research Vessel.

1930 *Photo, Swan, Hunter.*

MABAHISS—Built by Swan, Hunter, and completed 1930. Displacement: 618 tons. Dimensions: 138 × $23\frac{1}{2}$ × $13\frac{1}{2}$ feet. Machinery: Triple expansion. 1 shaft. I.H.P.: 650 = 11 kts. 1 s.e. boiler. Fuel: Coal. Complement: 39.

Coastal Motor Launches.

QAMAR	23 tons.	71 feet.	11 kts.
EL HOOT	24 tons.	46 feet.	7 kts.

C :—Ports and Lighthouses Administration.

Transports

1942, *Official.*

(Name not reported.) (Ex-H.M.S. *Fowey*, Nov. 4, 1930.) Displacement: 1,105 tons. Dimensions: 250 (*pp.*), 266 (*o.a.*) × 34 × 9 feet. Machinery: Parsons geared turbines. 2 shafts. S.H.P.: 2,000 = 16 kts. Boilers: 2, of 3-drum type. Oil fuel: 275 tons.

Miscellaneous

1939, *Official.*

NAPHTYS (Howaldt, Kiel, 1905). Displacement: 620 tons. Dimensions: 187¾ (*pp.*) × 35 × 8½ feet. Machinery: Triple expansion. 1 shaft. I.H.P.: 360 = 7 kts. Complement: 47.

Lighthouse Tender.

Foretopmast since struck.

AÏDA (A. & Ch. de la Loire, Nantes, 1911). 1428 tons *gross*. Dimensions: 246⅓ × 31¾ × 13½ feet draught. I.H.P. 1200 = 10 kts. 1 shaft. Serves in Red Sea. Complement, 63.

FINLAND

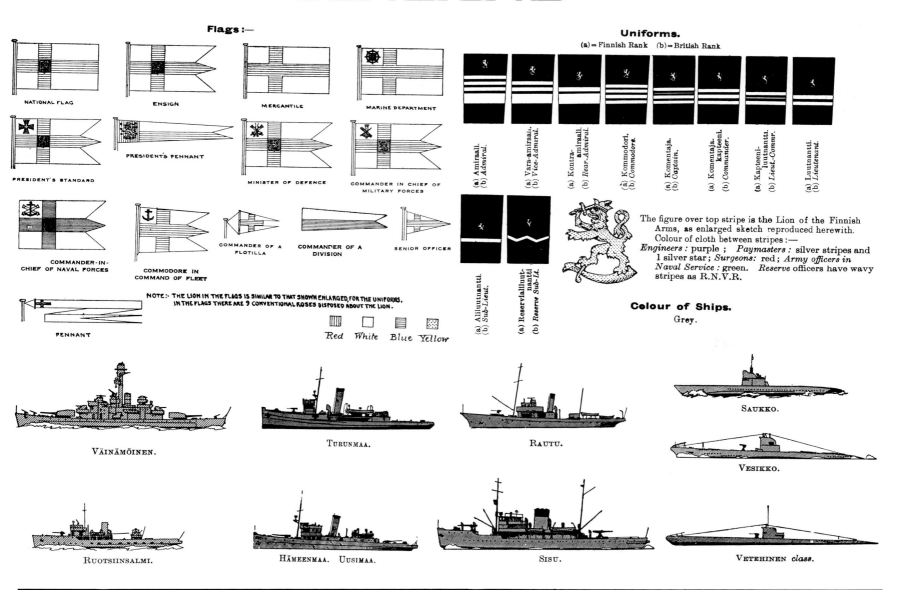

Flags :—

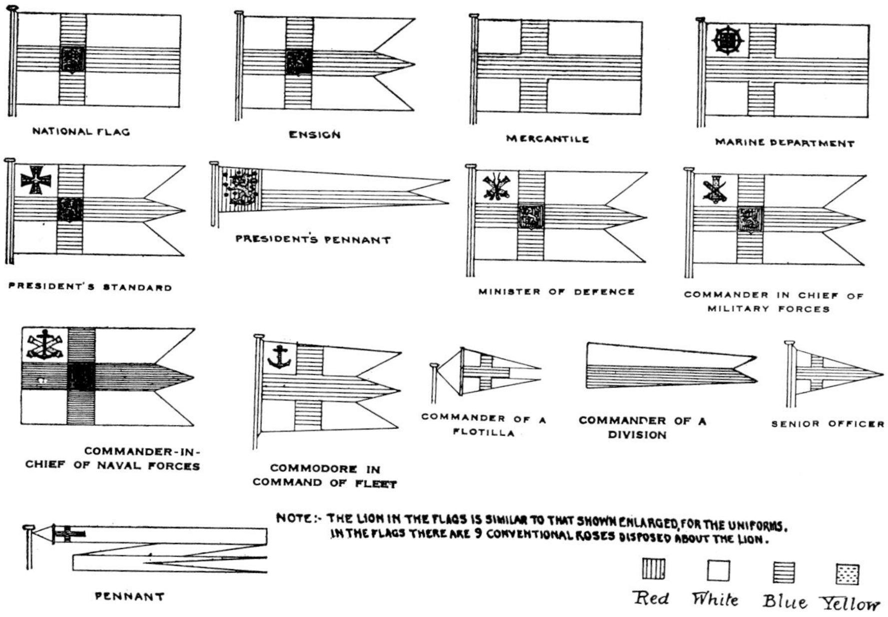

NATIONAL FLAG. ENSIGN. MERCANTILE. MARINE DEPARTMENT.

PRESIDENT'S STANDARD. PRESIDENT'S PENNANT. MINISTER OF DEFENCE. COMMANDER IN CHIEF OF MILITARY FORCES.

COMMANDER-IN-CHIEF OF NAVAL FORCES. COMMODORE IN COMMAND OF FLEET. COMMANDER OF A FLOTILLA. COMMANDER OF A DIVISION. SENIOR OFFICER.

PENNANT.

NOTE:- THE LION IN THE FLAGS IS SIMILAR TO THAT SHOWN ENLARGED FOR THE UNIFORMS. IN THE FLAGS THERE ARE 9 CONVENTIONAL ROSES DISPOSED ABOUT THE LION.

Red White Blue Yellow

Uniforms.

(a) = Finnish Rank (b) = British Rank

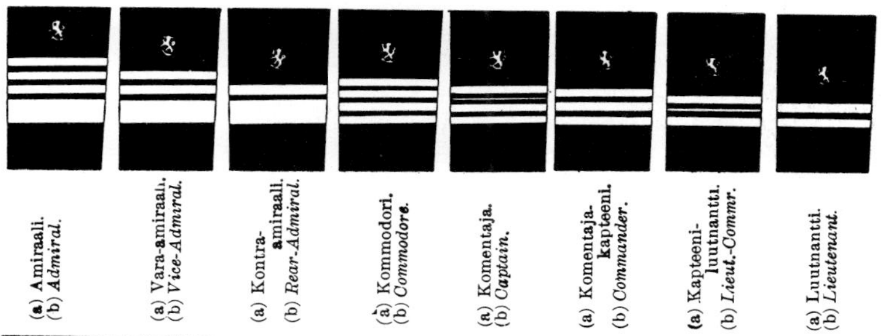

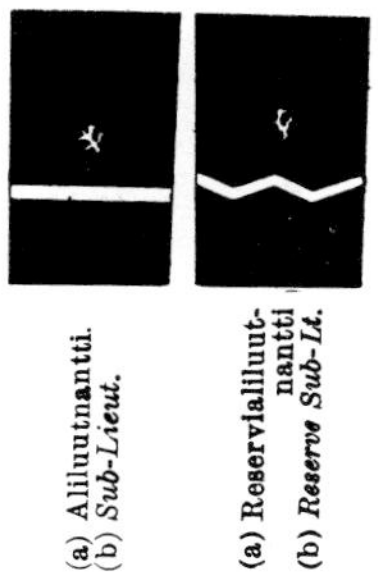

(a) Amiraali. (b) *Admiral.*
(a) Vara-amiraali. (b) *Vice-Admiral.*
(a) Kontra-amiraali. (b) *Rear-Admiral.*
(a) Kommodori. (b) *Commodore.*
(a) Komentaja. (b) *Captain.*
(a) Komentaja-kapteeni. (b) *Commander.*
(a) Kapteeni-luutnantti. (b) *Lieut.-Commr.*
(a) Luutnantti. (b) *Lieutenant.*
(a) Aliluutnantti. (b) *Sub-Lieut.*
(a) Reservialiluutnantti. (b) *Reserve Sub-Lt.*

The figure over top stripe is the Lion of the Finnish Arms, as enlarged sketch reproduced herewith. Colour of cloth between stripes :—*Engineers :* purple ; *Paymasters :* silver stripes and 1 silver star; *Surgeons:* red; *Army officers in Naval Service :* green. *Reserve* officers have wavy stripes as R.N.V.R.

Colour of Ships.

Grey.

VÄINÄMÖINEN.  TURUNMAA.  RAUTU.  SAUKKO.  VESIKKO.

RUOTSIINSALMI.  HÄMEENMAA. UUSIMAA.  SISU. 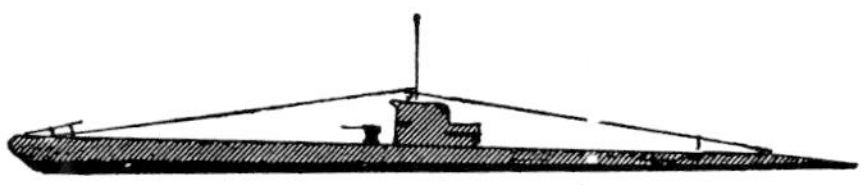 VETEHINEN *class.*

Coast Defence Ship and Gunboats

Coast Defence Ship.

1944, *courtesy Mr. T. Hallonblad.*

VÄINÄMÖINEN (Dec. 20, 1930).

Built by A. B. Crichton-Vulcan, Turku. (Abo).
Displacement: 3,900 tons. Complement: 343.
Dimensions: $305 \times 55\frac{1}{2} \times 14\frac{3}{4}$ feet.

Guns (Bofors):
4—10 inch, 46 cal.
8—4·1 inch AA.
4—40 mm. AA.
6—20 mm. AA. (Madsen)

Armour:
4″—$4\frac{1}{2}$″ Turrets.
$\frac{1}{2}$″-$\frac{3}{4}$″ Deck.
$2\frac{1}{4}$″ Side.
5″ C.T.

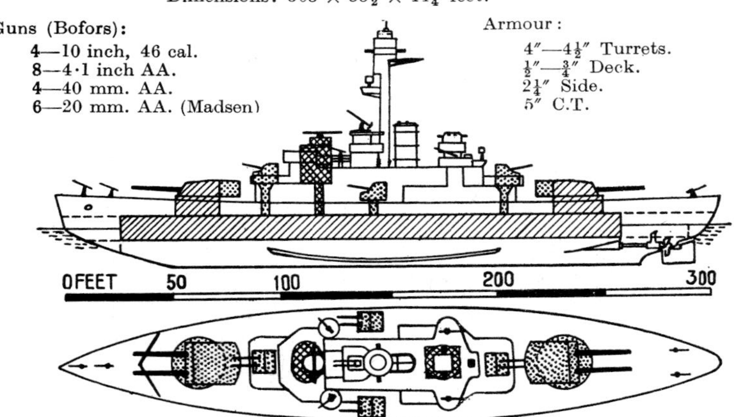

Machinery: Germania Diesels with electric drive, Leonard system, by Brown, Boveri & Co. 2 shafts. B.H.P.: 5,000=15·5 kts. Fuel: 93 tons.

Notes.—Laid down Aug., 1929. Completed 1932. Guns: Max. elevation of 10 inch is 50°.

Gunboats (*Tykkiveneet*)

UUSIMAA. (Mainmast since struck and foremast shortened.) 1934 *Photo.*

UUSIMAA (ex-German *Beo*, ex-*Golub*, 1917), **HÄMEENMAA** (ex-German *Wulf*, ex-*Pingvin*, 1917). Built at Helsinki to order of late Imperial Russian Government. Displacement: 400 tons. Complement, 54. Dimensions: 160 (*p.p.*), $170\frac{1}{2}$ (*o.a.*) $\times 24\frac{1}{2} \times 11$ feet. Guns: 2—3·9 inch, 1—40 mm. AA., 3 M.G. Machinery: 2 sets triple expansion. Designed H.P.: 1,400 = 15 kts. Cylindrical boilers. Coal: 70 tons.

Note.—Sisters to Russian *Pioner* and *Kopchik*.

Gunboats and Submarines

Gunboats—*continued.*

(Mainmast since struck and foremast shortened.) 1934, *Official.*

KARJALA (ex-Russian *Filin*, 1918). Built by Crichton A/B., Turku. Displacement: 342 tons. Complement: 52. Dimensions: 154 (*pp.*), 164 (*o.a.*) $\times 22\frac{1}{2} \times 9\frac{1}{2}$ feet. Guns: 2—3 inch, 3 M.G. Machinery: 2 sets triple expansion. I.H.P.: 1,000=15 kts. Boilers: Normand. Coal: 60 tons.

5 Submarines (*Sukellusveneet*).

Vesikko (1933), built by A/B Crichton-Vulcan as a private speculation and taken over by Finnish Navy Jan. 1936. Displacement: 250/300 tons. Complement, 16. Dimensions: $134\frac{1}{3} \times 13 \times 13\frac{1}{2}$ feet. 1 M.G. Torpedo tubes: 3—21 inch. Machinery: Mannheim B.M.V. H.P. 700/360 = 13/7 kts. Fuel: 9 tons. Radius of action, 1,500/50 miles. Diving limit reported to be 50 fathoms. Is actually a German design.

VETEHINEN. 1932 *Official Photo.*

Vetehinen (June 1, 1930), ***Vesihiisi*** (Aug. 2, 1930), ***Iku-Turso*** (May 5, 1931). Built by A/B Crichton-Vulcan, Turku, Abo, the first keel being laid in Sept., 1926, other two early in 1927. Displacement: 490/715 tons. Complement, 27. Dimensions: $208\frac{1}{3}$ (*o.a.*) $\times 20\frac{1}{3} \times 10\frac{1}{5}$ feet. Torpedo Tubes: 4—21 inch. Guns: 1—3 inch, 1—M.G. Reported to carry 20 mines. Machinery: Atlas Diesels and Brown-Boveri electric motors. H.P.: 1,060/600 = 14/8 kts. Fuel: 20 tons. Radius of action: 1,500/75 miles. Diving limit: 40 fathoms.

1932 *Official Photo.*

Saukko (July 2, 1930). Laid down 1929 by Hietalahden Laivatelakka of Helsinki. Displacement: 100/136 tons. Complement, 13. Dimensions: $106\frac{1}{2} \times 13\frac{1}{2} \times 10\frac{1}{2}$ feet. 1 M.G. 2—18 inch torpedo tubes. 9 mines. Machinery: Germania Diesels. H.P. 200/150 = 9/6 kts. Radius of action, 375/45 miles.

Patrol Vessel.

TURSAS (Crichton-Vulcan, 1941). Machinery: Diesel. Further particulars wanted.

Minelayers. (*Miinanlaskijat*)

RUOTSIINSALMI (May, 1940). Displacement: 300 tons. Dimensions: $206\frac{1}{2} \times 29 \times 6\frac{1}{2}$ feet. Guns: 1—3 inch AA., 2—20 mm. AA. Mines: 100. Machinery: 2 Rateau Diesels. B.H.P.: 1,120 = 15 kts.

1924 *Photo, Commdr. Raninen.*

RAUTU (ex-Russian *Murman*, 1917). Displacement: 268 tons. Complement, 35. Dimensions: $147\frac{2}{3}$ (*o.a.*) $\times 20\frac{1}{3} \times 6\frac{1}{2}$ feet. Guns: 1—3 inch, 2 M.G. Machinery: 2 sets triple expansion. Designed H.P. 450 = 12 kts. Boilers: Yarrow and Schulz respectively. Oil: 19 tons. Can carry 30 mines.

Mining Tenders.

POMMI (MIINA similar). 1933 *Photo.*

POMMI (ex-*M.* 7, 1916), **MIINA** (ex-*T.* 17, 1917). Built by Porin Konepaja O.Y., Pori. Displacement: 80 tons. Complement, 6. Dimensions: $65\frac{3}{4} \times 17 \times 4$ feet. Machinery: 2 sets of B.M.V. petrol motors. Designed I.H.P. 90 = 9 kts. Fuel: $1\frac{1}{4}$ ton.

LOIMU. 1934 *Photo.*

LOIMU (ex-*T.* 21, 1915), **LIESKA** (ex-*T.* 16, 1916), **PAUKKU** (ex-*T.* 15, 1916). Built by Porin Konepaja O.Y., Pori. Displacement: 60 tons. Complement, 6. Dimensions: $62\frac{1}{3} \times 17 \times 3\frac{2}{3}$ feet. Machinery: 2 sets of B.M.V. petrol motors. Designed I.H.P. 60 = 7·5 kts. Fuel: $1\frac{1}{4}$ ton.

Motor Minesweepers. (*Raivaajat*).

KUHA and others, of similar but slightly larger design to *Ahven* type, below. (Several of these vessels have been lost.)

AHVEN, KIISKI, MUIKKU, SARKI, KUORE, LAHNA (Turun Veneveistämö Yard, 1936–37). Displacement: 17 tons. Complement: 8. Dimensions: $56\frac{1}{3} \times 12 \times 4\frac{1}{2}$ feet. H.P.: 60 = 10·5 kts.

AF. 2 1934 *Photo.*

11 *boats*: **BVA., BVD., A.37, A.38, A.40, A.42, A.43, A.45, B.3, AF.2, HAUKKA.** Displacement: *BVA.*—*A.*45, 9 tons; *B.*3, 18 tons; *AF.*2, 15 tons; *Haukka*, 12 tons. Complement, 6. Dimensions: $53 \times 11\frac{1}{4} \times 4$ feet (first 8). Engines: Petrol motor. Designed I.H.P.: 45–60 = 8–9·5 kts.

A.37. 1934.

HAUKKA. *Photo* 1934.

Motor Patrol Boats.
(*Vartiomoottoriveneet.*)

VMV. 9 1935.

VMV. 1, 5, 6 (1930–31). **VMV. 8, 9, 11, 13, 15, 16** (1935). Built in Germany. Displacement: 30 tons. Dimensions: $82 \times 13\frac{3}{4} \times 3\frac{1}{2}$ feet. Guns: 1—20 mm. Machinery: Benzol motors in first 3, semi-Diesel in others. H.P.: 1,220 = 25 kts. Complement 8.

Motor Torpedo Boats.
(*Moottoritorpedoveneet.*)

5 ordered in March 1940 from Higgins Ind., Inc., U.S.A., have probably not been delivered. Some of those below have been sunk.

SYÖKSY. 1937.

4 boats: ***Syöksy*** (ex-*M.T.V.* 4), ***Nuoli*** (ex-*M.T.V.* 5), ***Vinha*** (ex-*M.T.V.* 6), and ***Raju*** (ex-*M.T.V.* 7). *Syöksy* and *Nuoli* built 1928 by Thornycroft. *Vinha* 1929 by Turun Veneveistämö, and *Raju* 1929 by Porvoon Veneveistämö. Displacement: 12 tons. Complement, 7. Dimensions: $55 \times 11 \times 3\frac{1}{4}$ feet. Guns: 2 Lewis. Torpedoes 2—17·7 inch. 2 D.C. I.H.P. 750 = 40 kts.

Miscellaneous

Torpedo Boats—*continued*

1 boat: ***Isku*** (ex-*M.T.V.* 3). Built by Porvoon Veneveistämö in 1926. Displacement: 11 tons. Dimensions: $54 \times 11 \times 3\frac{2}{3}$ feet. 2 M.G. Torpedoes: 2—17·7 inch, carried in dropping gears. Machinery: 2 sets Fiat motors. I.H.P. 650 = 31 kts.

1924 *Photo, Commdr. Raninen.*

2 boats ***Sisu II.*** (ex-*M.T.V.*1) ***Hurja*** ex-*M.T.V.* 2, (ex-*M.A.S.* 220, 221). Built for Royal Italian Navy by Flli. Orlando 1916 and purchased, 1920. Displacement: 13 tons. Complement, 7. Dimensions: $53 \times 9\frac{4}{5} \times 4$ feet. Guns: 2 M.G. on high angle mounts. Torpedoes: 2—17·7 inch (450 mm.). Machinery: 2 sets Isotta Fraschini motors. I.H.P. 500 = 26 kts.

Cadets' Training Ship.

1932 *Official Photo.*

TURUNMAA (ex-Russian *Orlan*, 1916). Built by Crichton A/B Turku. Ordered by late Imperial Russian Government, 1914. Displacement: 342 tons. Complement, 52. Length (*p.p.*) 154 feet, (*o.a.*) 164 feet. Beam, $22\frac{1}{2}$ feet. Designed load draught, $9\frac{1}{2}$ feet. Guns: 2—3 inch, 3 M.G. Machinery: 2 sets triple expansion. Boilers: Normand. Designed I.H.P.: 1,000 = 15 kts. Coal capacity: 60 tons.

Sail Training Ship.

(*Koululaiva.*)

1932 *Official Photo.*

SUOMEN JOUTSEN (ex-*Oldenburg*) (St. Nazaire, 1902). Purchased by Finnish Navy in 1931. Displacement: 3,200 tons. Complement, 27 + 60 cadets. Dimensions: $316\frac{3}{4} \times 40\frac{2}{3} \times 16\frac{1}{2}$ feet. Machinery: 2 auxiliary Diesels. H.P. 400 = 6 kts. Fuel: 40 tons.

Submarine Depot Ship and Icebreaker.

1940, *Official.*

SISU (Sandvikens, Sept. 24, 1938), Displacement: 2,000 tons. Dimensions: $194\frac{3}{4}$ (*w.l.*), $210\frac{1}{2}$ (*o.a.*) $\times 46\frac{1}{2} \times 16\frac{3}{4}$ feet. Guns: 2—3·9 inch, AA. Machinery: 3 sets Atlas Polar Diesels with electric drive. 2 shafts and a bow propeller. H.P.: 4,000 = 16 kts. Complement, 100.

Icebreakers.

(*Jäänsärkijät*)

1940, *Official.*

OTSO (1936). Displacement: 800 tons. Dimensions: $134\frac{1}{2} \times 35\frac{1}{2} \times 15\frac{3}{4}$ feet. H.P.: 1,800 = 13 kts. Oil fuel: 60 tons.

Added 1938, *courtesy Messrs. Armstrong.*

TARMO (ex-*Sampo II*), (Armstrong, 1907). Displacement: 2,300 tons. Dimensions: $210\frac{1}{2} \times 47 \times 18\frac{1}{2}$ feet. Machinery: Triple expansion. I.H.P.: 3,850 = 12 kts.

Added 1938, *courtesy Messrs. Armstrong.*

SAMPO (Armstrong, 1898). Displacement: 1,850 tons. Dimensions: $202 \times 43 \times 18\frac{1}{4}$ feet. Machinery Triple expansion. 2 shafts. I.H.P.: 3,000 = 12 kts. Complement, 43.

Illustrated in "Fighting Ships," 1919, p. 375.

AFU (ex-*Avance*), (Howaldt, Kiel, 1899). Displacement: 800 tons. Dimensions: 136 (*pp.*), 144 (*o.a.*) $\times 35\frac{1}{2} \times 18$ feet. I.H.P.: 1,385 = 10 kts.

Illustrated in "Fighting Ships," 1919, p. 375.

MURTAJA (Stockholm, 1890). Displacement: 815 tons. Dimensions: $137\frac{1}{2} \times 36 \times 15\frac{1}{2}$ feet. H.P.: 1,130 = 11 kts.

Coastal Craft Depot Ship

Ex-*Von Döbeln* (1876, rebuilt 1929). Iron. Displacement: 250 tons. Dimensions: $175\frac{1}{4}$ (*pp.*), 182 (*o.a.*) $\times 26 \times 9$ feet. Machinery: Compound. I.H.P. 750=11 kts. (Acquired 1941).

It is reported that, under terms of Peace Treaty with Russia, the coast defence ship **VAINAMOINEN,** five submarines, and all the motor torpedo boats in the Finnish fleet are being handed over to Soviet Navy.

FRANCE

Flags.

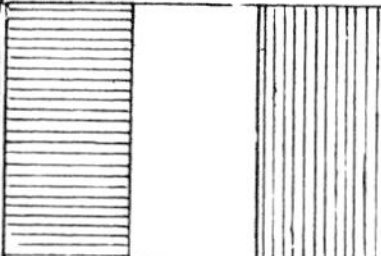

Ensign & Jack

Amiral de la Flotte

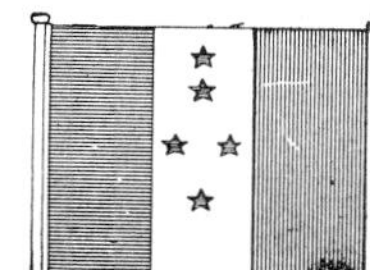

Amiral

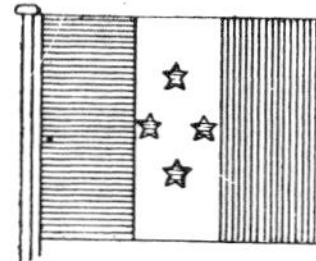

Vice-Amiral d'Escadre (commanding Fleet).

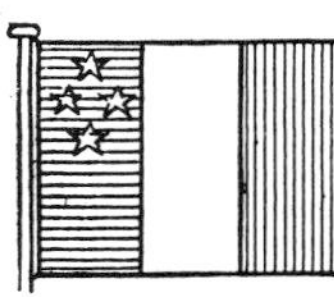

Vice-Amiral d'Escadre.

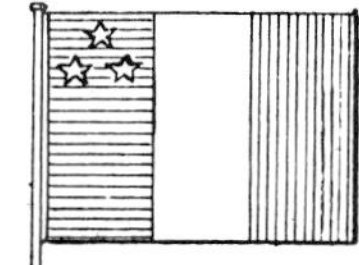

Autres Vice-Amiraux

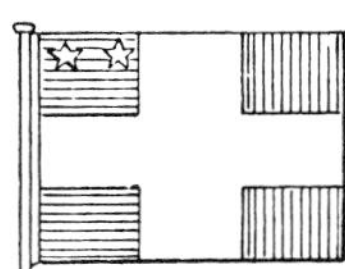

Contre-Amiral

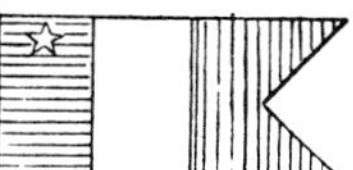

Capitaine de Vaisseau Chef de Division (independante ou en sous ordre).

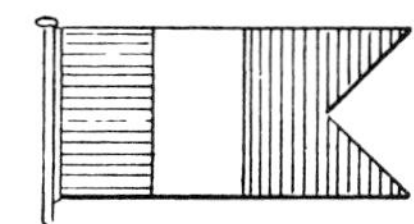

Capitaine de Vaisseau Comm't un groupe de bâtiments, ou Major-Général commandant la Marine.

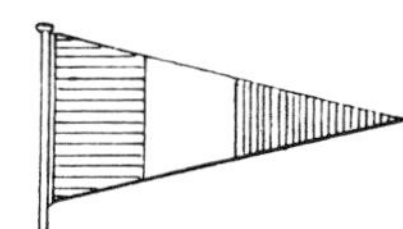

Capitaine de Frégate ou de Corvette, Comm't un groupe de bâtiments ou commandant la Marine.

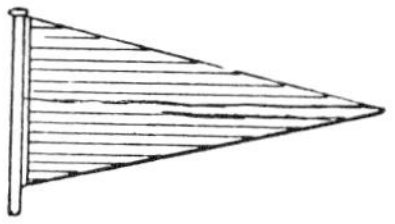

Comm't supérieur temporaire de tout grade.

Rouge *Blanc* *Bleu*

Uniforms.

Amiral de la Flotte ou Amiral.

Vice-Amiral d'Escadre.

Vice-Amiral.

Contre-Amiral.

Capitaine de vaisseau.

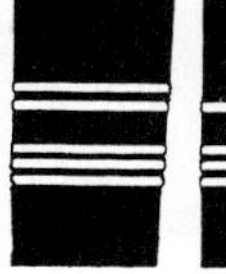

Capitaine de frégate †

Capitaine de corvette.

Lieutenant de vaisseau.

(*Gold stripe and 2 light blue patches*)

Enseigne.

Enseigne 2e classe.

Aspirant

Corresponding to British } *Vice-Ad.* *Rear-Ad.* *Captain.* *Commander.* *Lieut.-Comm'der.* *Lieut.* *Lieut.* (junior.) *Sub-Lieut.* *Midshipman*

†Only three of the Capitaine de frégate's stripes are gold: the second and fourth are silver.
Epaulettes with parade uniform are of the usual sort, *except* that—
A Vice-Admiral's epaulettes have the usual anchor and 3 stars
A Rear-Admiral's ,, ,, ,, ,, 2 ,,
Caps are similar to British Navy in shape but badge differs, being more like Italian, and there are stripes right round corresponding to rank. The cocked hat carries the tri-colour.

Minister of Marine.—M. Louis Jacquinot.
Chief of the Naval Staff.—Vice-Amiral A. G. Lemonnier.
Vice-Chief of Naval Staff.—Vice-Amiral Jaugard.
Deputy Chief of Naval Staff.—Contre-Amiral Deramond.
Naval Attaché, London.—Contre-Amiral A. Sala, C.B.E., D.S.O.

Personnel (1946), 55,000.

Torpedoes. (Details official.)

(Made at St. Tropez Torpedo Factory.)

Date	French Designation.	Diameter.	Length.	Charge.	Pressure	*Maximum* range.	Speed Kts.
1923	1923 D	550 mm.	8 m. 58	310 kg.	200 or 220 kg. by cm. 2	18,000 m.	30
1923	1923 DT	,,	,,	,,	,,	13,000 m.	37
1924	1924 V	,,	6 m. 63	,,	170 kg. by cm. 2	3,000/7,000 m.	45

Mines.

Moored mines only —
(a) Breguet B.4, charge 80 kg., contact pistols, length mooring rope 400 m. Weight : 525 kg.
(b) Sautter Harlé H4, H5, HS4, charge 220 kg., contact pistols, length mooring rope 200 m. up to 500 & 1,000 m., for some patterns. Weight : 1,150 kg.

General Notes.

COLOUR OF SHIPS: *Surface ships.*—Dark grey hull. Light grey upperworks. Black funnel tops.
Submarines.—Light or dark grey.

EFFECTIVE LIFE OF SHIPS: Fixed in **1936** as—Battleships, **26 years**; Aircraft Carriers, 20 years; Cruisers, **20 years**; Torpedo Craft, **16** years; Submarines, **13** years. All reckoned from date of first commissioning for trials.

Washington Treaty standard has been adopted for regulation of displacements.

Mercantile Marine.

(1946) *Ca.*, 1,000,000 tons.

NAVAL ORDNANCE.

(There are also a 15 inch (*Richelieu* class), 1932–33 models of 5·5, 5·1 and 3·9 inch, and a 3 inch AA. of 35 cal.)

Calibres (inches)	15	13·4	8	6·1	6	5·5			5·1		3·9	3·5	3	..
Calibres (mm.)	380	340	203	155	152	138			130		100	90	75	..
Modèle	1935	1912	1924	1920	1930	1929	1924	1910	1924	1919	1925	1926	1924	..
Longueur (en calibres)	45	45	50	50	55	50	40	55	40	40	45	50	50	..
Poids du canon (Kgs.)	100,000	66,280	20,716	8530	8128	4114	4113	5300	3875	4392	1500	1600	1095	..
Poids du projectile (Kgs.)	880	554	123	56	54	40	40	39	32	32	15	9·5	6	..
Poids de la charge (Kgs.)	270	151	47	19·6	17	..	9	11	8	8	4	3	2	..
Pression Kg./cm.	2800	2800	2750	3050	3200	..	2500	2500	2420	2420	2200	3200	2560	..
Vitesse initiale m/sec.	830	794	850	850	870	860	700	830	734	734	765	850	850	..

Battleships

Richelieu, Jean Bart.

Lorraine

Aircraft Carriers

Colossus.

Dixmude.

Béarn. (Funnel on starboard side).

Cruisers

Emile Bertin.

Jeanne d'Arc.

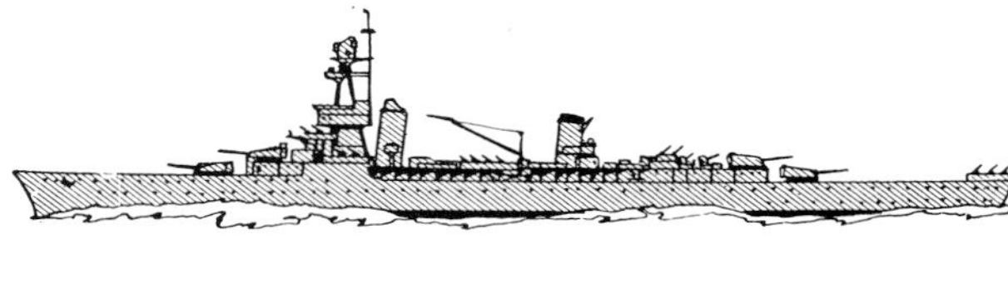

Suffren.

Duguay-Trouin.

Duquesne, Tourville.

Gloire, Montcalm, G. Leygues.

Destroyers

Hoche.

La Melpomène *class.*

Le Fantasque *class.*

Marceau.

Baccarat, Bir Hakeim.

Tigre.

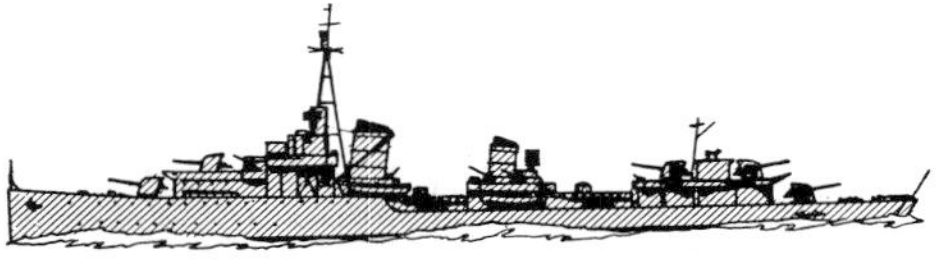

Desaix, Kléber.

Alsacien, Lorrain.

Simoun *and* Alcyon *classes.*

Destroyer

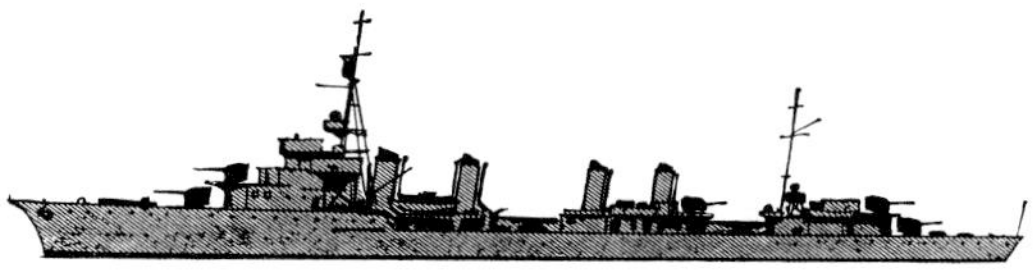

ALBATROS.

Submarines

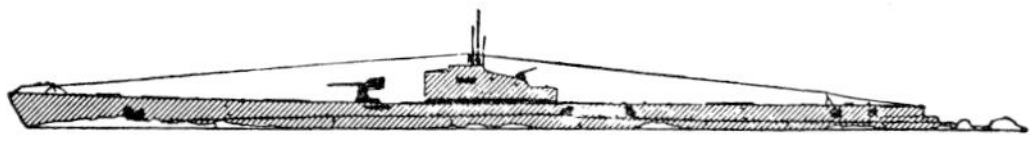

ARCHIMÈDE *class*.

DIANE *class*.

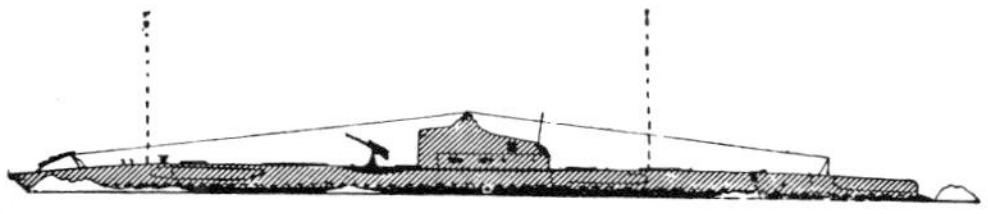

CURIE *class*.

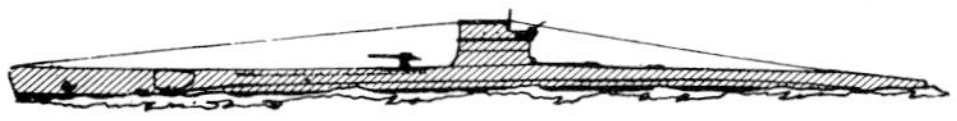

NARVAL.

RUBIS.

Auxiliaries

LOBELIA *class*.
(Individual ships vary.)

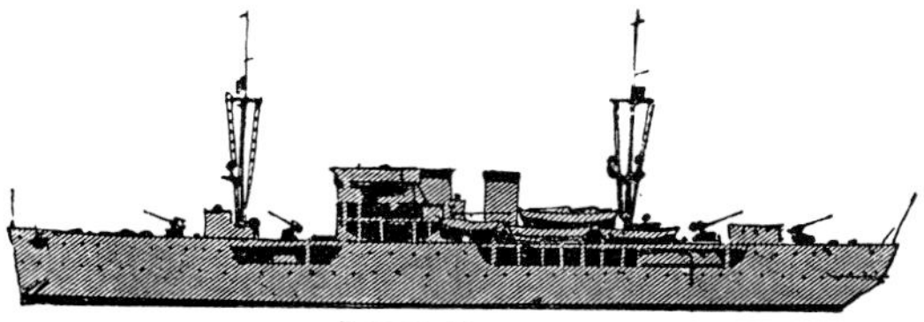

JULES VERNE.

DUMONT D'URVILLE *class*.

AMIRAL MOUCHEZ.

ELAN *class*

L'AVENTURE *class*.

CHEVREUIL *class*.

BEAUTEMPS-BEAUPRÉ, LAPÉROUSE.

CH 10—43.

SENEGALAIS *class*.

CARABINIER *class*.

Battleships

(RICHELIEU CLASS—2 SHIPS.)

RICHELIEU (Jan. 17, 1939), **JEAN BART** (March 6, 1940).

Displacement : 35,000 tons (48,500 tons *full load*). (Actual standard displacement probably approaches 40,000 tons). Complement : 1,946.

Length : 794 feet. Beam, 108 feet 7 inches. Draught, 26½ feet (*mean*)

Guns (as rearmed) :
- **8**—15 inch.
- **9**—6 inch.
- **12**—3·9 inch AA.
- **69**—40 mm. AA. (Bofors).
- **37**—20 mm. AA. (Oerlikon).

Armour :
- 9″—16″ Belt.
- 8″ Deck (upper and lower combined).
- 13″–17″ Main Turrets.
- 5″ Secondary Turrets.
- 13″ Conning Tower.

(Total weight of armour, 14,000 tons ; of machinery, over 3,000 tons.)

RICHELIEU. 1946, *courtesy M. Henri Le Masson.*

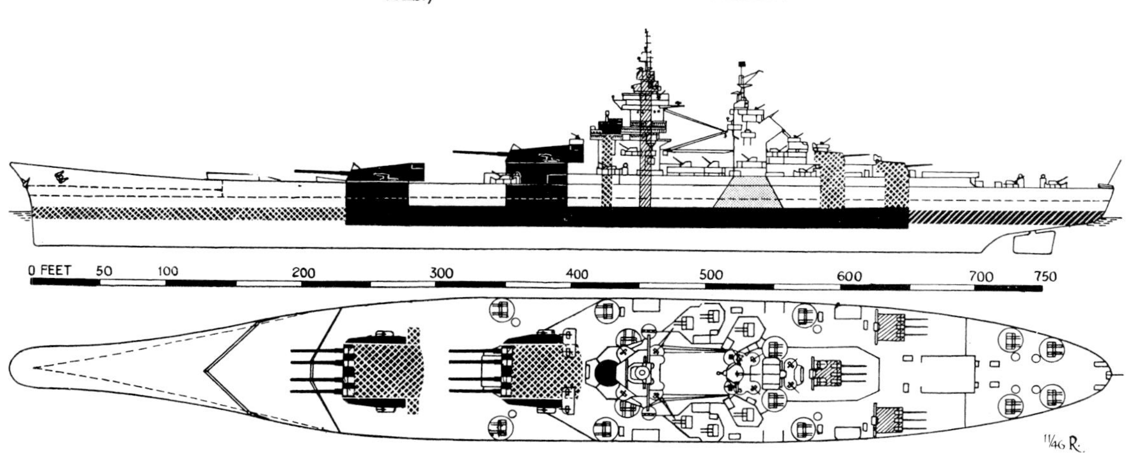

RICHELIEU. 1946, *French Navy Official.*

Battleships

Machinery: Parsons geared turbines. 4 shafts. S.H.P.: 150,000 = 30 kts. (In service she has reached 32 kts. with 180,000 S.H.P.) Boilers: 6 Indret. Oil fuel: 6,000 tons. Radius of action: 6,000 miles at 15 kts.

General Notes.—Percentage of displacement devoted to armour is higher than in any previous ships. *Jean Bart* built in Loire yard, but construction shared by Penhoët concern. Both ships were built in dry docks, their cost exceeding 2,000,000,000 francs each. Uncompleted hull of a third ship, *Clemenceau*, was sunk by Allied heavy bombers during siege of Brest. A fourth ship, the *Gascogne*, was projected, but never begun. *Jean Bart*, now being completed, will be given a new type of bridge and improved AA. armament. Her missing 15 inch guns will be replaced by pieces originally intended for *Clemenceau* and *Gascogne*.

Programme	*Name*	*Builder*	*Machinery*	*Laid down*	*Completed*
1935	*Richelieu*	Brest	Loire	22/10/35	July 1940
	Jean Bart	Penhoët, Loire	Penhoët	1/1/37	1948

JEAN BART. 1946, *courtesy M. Henri Le Masson.*

RICHELIEU. 1946, *Wright & Logan.*

RICHELIEU. 1946, *Wright & Logan.*

RICHELIEU (p. 176). 1946, *courtesy M. Henri Le Masson.*

RICHELIEU. 1946, *Wright & Logan.*

RICHELIEU 1945, *French Navy Official.*

DUNKERQUE (Oct. 2, 1935). **STRASBOURG** (Dec. 12, 1936).

Standard Displacement, 26,500 tons. Complement: 1,431.

Dimensions: Length (*w.l.*) 686; (*o.a.*) 702 feet. Beam: 101¾ feet. Draught: 28 feet (*mean*)

Guns:
8—13 inch.
16—5·1 inch (dual purpose).
4—47 mm.
8—37 mm. AA.
32—13 mm. AA.

Aircraft: 4, with 1 catapult (on q.d.).

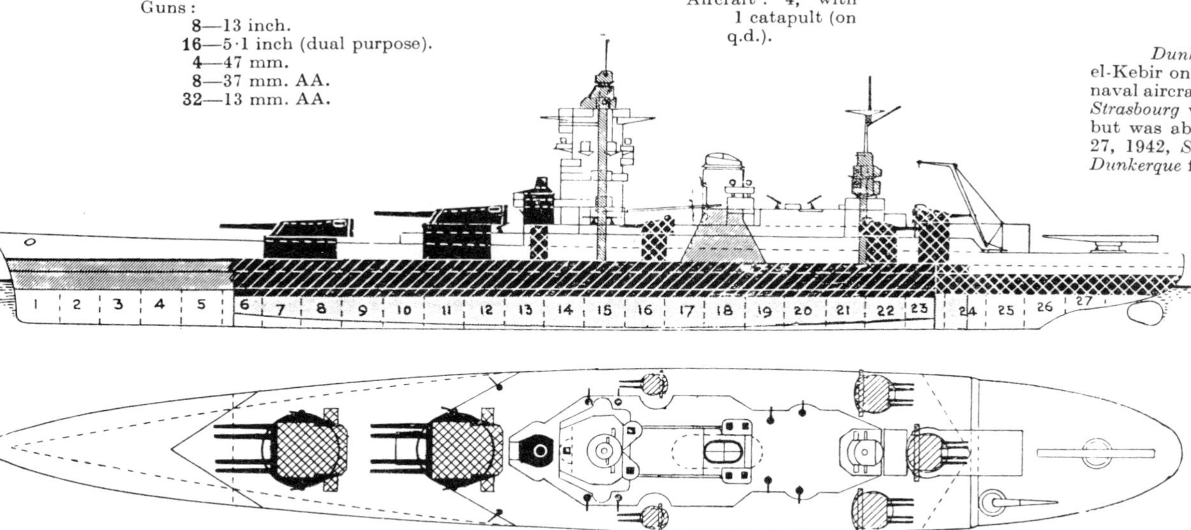

Special Notes.

Dunkerque was heavily shelled, set on fire and beached at Mers-el-Kebir on July 3, 1940; and on July 6 she was torpedoed by British naval aircraft. Early in 1942 she was taken to Toulon to be refitted. *Strasbourg* was torpedoed by a British naval aircraft on July 3, 1940, but was able to proceed to Toulon under her own power. On Nov. 27, 1942, *Strasbourg* was scuttled in shallow water at that port, and *Dunkerque* flooded and otherwise damaged in dry dock.

Armour:
14″ C.T.
14″ Turrets.
9″—11″ Side (at w.l.).
7″ do. (at main deck).
1½″ Longitudinal Torpedo Bulkhead.
Protective Decks:
5″ Upper.
2″ Lower.
(Total weight of armour, *over* 10,000 tons.)

(*Other illustrations on preceding page.*)

Machinery: Parsons Geared Turbines. S.H.P.: 100,000 = 29·5 kts. (trials, 136,900 = 31·5). Radius: 7500 miles at 15 kts. 6 Indret boilers.

General Notes.—These two ships are to replace the *France* (lost in 1922) and the *Océan*. Cost approximately Frcs. 700,000,000 each. Modelled on the *Nelson*, the quadruple turrets were finally adopted after a variety of other gun dispositions had been considered, this grouping having been selected for the pre-War ships of the *Normandie* and *Tourville* classes. The turrets are widely separated to localise the effects of shell fire and reduce blast on the tower when trained abaft the beam. Bridge structure is also modelled on that of *Nelson*. It includes a lift in its interior. The percentage of displacement devoted to protection is higher than in any previous capital ship. A feature which does not show in illustrations is the extraordinary height between decks.

Dunkerque was built in dry dock. Being too long for the dock, the stem piece was constructed separately and attached to hull after floating out.

The construction of *Strasbourg*, although nominally by Penhoët, was shared by Ch. Loire.

Gunnery Notes.—13 inch guns fire projectiles of 1,200 lbs. weight. Rate of fire 3 rounds a minute. All-round loading position. Elevation 35°. 5·1 inch guns can fire with extreme elevation and are said to have an average rate of fire of 10 rounds per minute and a range of 11,000 yards when so discharged.

Name	*Builder*	*Machinery*	*Laid down*	*Completed*
Dunkerque	Brest	Loire	26/12/32	*April* 1937
Strasbourg	Penhoët	Penhoët	25/11/34	*Dec.* 1938

Distinctive features.—*Dunkerque* has 2 white bands around funnel, *Strasbourg* only 1 band.

DUNKERQUE. 1937, *R. Perkins.*

STRASBOURG. 1938, *courtesy M. Henri Le Masson.*

DUNKERQUE. 1937, *R. Perkins.*

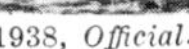

STRASBOURG. 1938, *Official.*

DUNKERQUE 1937, *R. Perkins.*

Battleships

PROVENCE. *Added 1941, E. P. Saraf, Alexandria.*

PROVENCE (April 20, 1913).

Standard displacement, 22,189 tons. Complement, 1,133 (+ 57 as Flagship).
Length (*waterline*), 541⅓ feet, *over all*, 544½ feet. Beam, 88½ feet. *Maximum* draught, 32 feet.

Guns:
10—13·4 inch, 45 cal.
14—5·5 inch, 55 cal. (M.'10).
8—3 inch AA, 60 cal.
7—47 mm.
16—13 mm.
Torpedo tubes (Removed)

Armour (chromo-nickel):
10¾" Belt (amidships) ...
7" Belt (ends) ....
Deck (*see Notes*) ....
10"—6" Lower deck side
17"—10" Turrets........
11" Turret bases (N.C.)
7" Secondary battery ...
12½" Conning tower .....

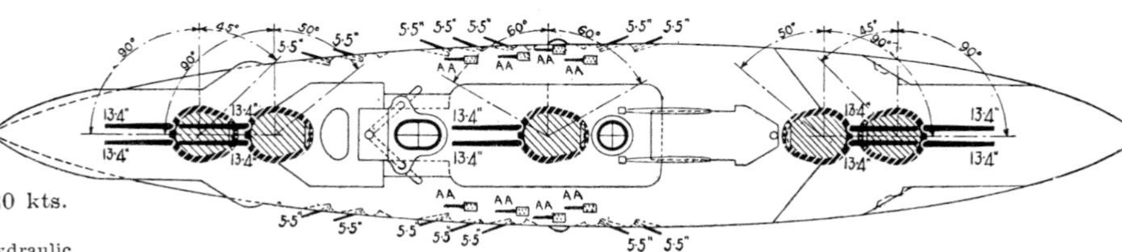

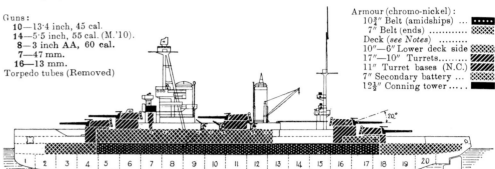

Machinery: Parsons turbine. 4 shafts. Boilers: Indret. Designed H.P.: 29,000 = 20 kts. (since increased). Oil fuel: 2,600 tons. Radius at 10 kts., over 7,000 miles.

**Gunnery Notes.*—Carry 100 rounds per gun for 13·4 inch and 275 per gun for the 5·5 inch. Janney electro-hydraulic mountings to big guns. Special cooling for magazines—temperature 77° Fahr. Magazines can be completely flooded inside ten minutes. Height of guns above l.w.l.: 1st turret, 30½ feet; 2nd, 37¾ feet; 3rd, 33½ feet; 4th, 28½ feet; 5th, 21⅓ feet. Arcs of training: Nos. 1 and 5, 270°; Nos. 2 & 4, 280°; No. 3, 120° either beam. Arcs of secondary guns: 120°. Big gun elevation increased from 18° to 23°: *max.* range is 23,000 metres. *Lorraine* has had turret removed amidships to make room for catapult.

**Armour Notes.*—Turrets of maximum thickness at ports, instead of uniform thickness as in *Courbet* type. According to the 1917 Edition of "Flottes de Combat," the barbette shields are not of uniform design. Those for the end barbettes are 13·4" thick, for the super-firing barbettes 9¾" thick and for the central barbette 15¾" thick. The double bottom is carried to the under side of protective deck. Main belt is 13⅓ feet wide, $5\frac{7}{12}$ feet below and 7¾ above l.w.l. Battery 197 feet long with 7 in. bulkheads. Protective decks: lower 2" slopes, 1¾" flat. Upper, 1¾" flat on top of belt.

**Engineering Notes.*—Is now converted to oil fuel. 6 new Indret small tube type now supply turbines with steam, giving a large reserve of power beyond the designed figure.

Name	*Builder*	*Machinery*	*Laid down*	*Com-pleted*	*Trials*	*Turbines*	*Boilers*	*Best recent speed*
Lorraine	Penhoët	Penhoët	Nov. '12	July '16	21·4 kts.	Parsons	Indret	22
Provence	Lorient	La Seyne	June '12	June '15		Parsons		20·5

*Unofficial.

Notes.— *Provence* and *Lorraine* belong to 1912 programme, one being a replace ship for the *Liberté*, blown up September, 1911. Estimated cost, £2,908,000 per ship = £126 per ton. In 1919–20 tripod foremasts and directors were installed. Both converted to partial oil burning, 1927–30. In 1932–35 they were extensively refitted, being given new 13·4 inch guns (originally ordered for *Normandie* class), additional AA. and machine guns, enhanced protection, and small-tube boilers, burning oil, and subsequently made 20 kts. continuously at sea.

Special Notes.

Provence was heavily shelled at Mers-el-Kebir on July 3, 1940, and severely damaged, though she was afterwards taken to Toulon for refit. On Nov. 27, 1942, she received further heavy damage from her own ship's company at Toulon, her stern compartments being submerged.

***COURBET** (Sept. 23, 1911), ***PARIS** (Sept. 28, 1912).

Standard displacement, 22,189 tons. *Full load*, 25,850 tons. Complement, 1108.
Length (*pp.*) 541 feet, (*o. a.*) 551 feet. Beam, 92½ feet. *Maximum* draught, 32½ feet.

Guns (M. '06—10):
12—12 inch, 45 cal.
22—5·5 inch, 55 cal. (M. '10).
7—3 inch AA. (M. 1922).
2—47 mm. AA.
Torpedo tubes (18 inch):
4 *submerged*.

Armour: (Chromo-nickel):
10¾" Belt (amidships)......
7" Belt (bow) (N.C.) ...
7" Belt (aft) (N.C.) ......
2¾" Deck ....
10"—6" Lower deck side
12½" Turrets (N.C.) .....
11" Turret bases (N.C.)...
7" Secondary battery ...
11¾" Conning tower (N.C.)

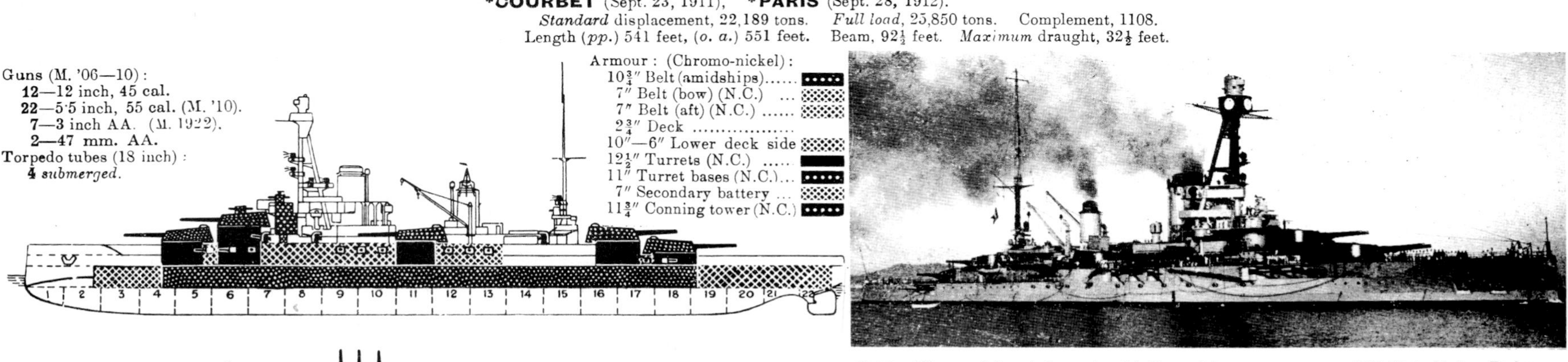

PARIS. (Observe 2 funnels forward and bridgework.) 1929 *Photo, M. Bar, Toulon.*

Name	*Builder*	*Machinery*	*Laid down*	*Com-pleted*	*Trials Full power*	*Boilers*	*Best recent speed*
Courbet	Lorient	St. N'z're (Ch. de l'Atlantique)	Sept., '10	Sept. '13	=20·81	Belleville & small tube in each	16
Paris	La Seyne	F.&C. de la Méd	Nov., '11	Aug. '14	35,610=21·6		

General Notes.—Designed by M. Lyasse. Average cost about £2,475,000. All this class were reconstructed 1928–1929. *Courbet* was completely re-boilered at La Seyne (1929) with small tube boilers (originally ordered for *Normandie* class). *Océan*, of this type, has been demilitarised for training purposes. Since June, 1940, *Courbet* and *Paris* have been lying in British ports.

Machinery: Parsons turbine. **4 shafts.** 24 Boilers: see Notes. H.P. **43,000 = 20** kts after refit. Coal: *normal*, 906 tons; *maximum*, 2700 tons; also **310** tons oil (two boiler rooms are fitted for oil burning). ***Endurance, 2700 at 18¾ kts.**

Armour Notes.—Belt, 13¼ feet wide; 7¾ feet of it above water, 5½ feet of it below. For about 325 feet it is 10¾". Upper belt, 7" thick forms redoubt for secondary battery. The 4—5·5 inch aft. are in casemates. Prot. decks: 2¾" curved from lower edge of belt to l.w.l. level. Above that a flat 1¾" deck from end to end on top of main belt. Above again is a 1½" splinter deck against aerial attack. Conning tower is in three stories. 10¾" communication tube. Two armoured fire control stations on top.

**Gunnery Notes.*—Amidship 12 inch 180°, the centre line turrets 270° each. The 5·5 inch 120°. Elevation of guns reported increased to give range of 24,000 metres. Height of guns above water: Turrets (1) 30½ feet, (2) 37¾ (amidships) 25 feet, (5) 28½ feet, (6) 21⅓ feet; upper deck battery, 5·5 inch, 21⅓ feet; main deck, 5·5 inch aft, 11⅔ feet. Ammunition carried: 100 for each 12 in., 275 for each 5·5 inch, 300 for each 3 pdr. Westinghouse refrigerators in magazines. 77°F.

**Torpedo Notes.*—8 searchlights (36 inch), also 2—30 inch. Carries 12 torpedoes and 30 blockade mines.

**Engineering Notes.*—Outer shafts: H.P. turbines; inner, L.P. Condensers (2): 32,076 sq. feet cooling surface. Turbines: 300 r.p.m. Belleville oil fuel system.

* Unofficial.

Battleship

LORRAINE (September 30, 1913).
Standard displacement : 22,189 tons. Complement, 977.
Length (*w.l.*) $541\frac{1}{3}$ feet, (*o.a.*) $544\frac{1}{2}$ feet. Beam, $88\frac{1}{2}$ feet. *Max.* draught, 32 feet.

Machinery : Parsons turbines. 4 shafts. Boilers : 6 Indret. S.H.P. : 43,000 = 21 kts. (exceeded on trials with new boilers). Oil fuel : 2,600 tons.

General Notes.—Lorraine was extensively reconstructed in 1934–35, "Q" turret amidships being removed to make room for aircraft and catapult, which were discarded in 1943. Now serves as Gunnery Training Ship.

Guns :
8—13·4 inch
14—5·5 inch, 55 cal.
8—3 inch, AA.
14—40 mm. AA.
25—20 mm. AA.

Armour (Chromo-nickel)
$10\frac{3}{4}$" Belt (amidships)
7" Belt (ends)
$3\frac{1}{2}$" Deck
10"—6" Lower deck side
17"—10" Turrets
11" Turret bases (N.C.)
7" Secondary Battery
$12\frac{1}{2}$" Conning tower

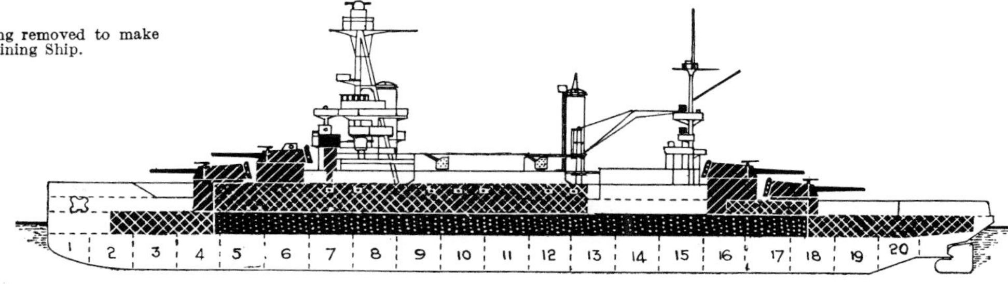

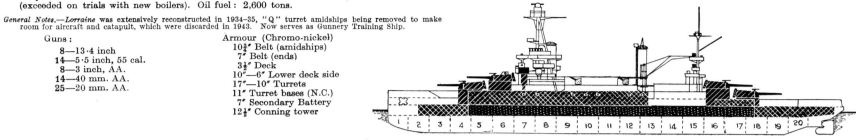

1944, *French Navy Official.*

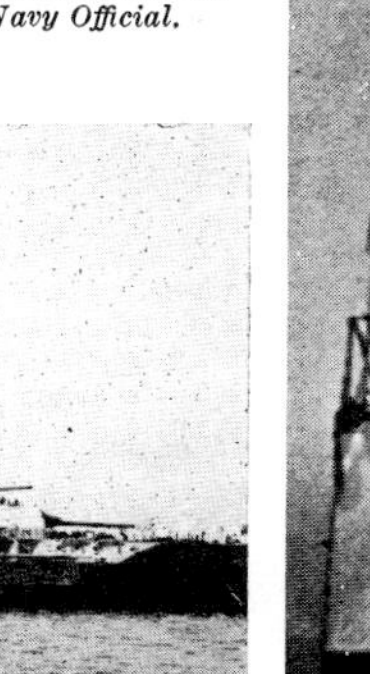
1946, *French Navy Official.*

1944, *Official.*

Aircraft Carrier

COLOSSUS (Sept. 30, 1943).

Displacement : 13,190 tons (18,040 tons *full load*).

Complement : 1,350.

Length : 694 ft. 6 in. Beam : 80 ft. 3 in. Draught : 23 ft.

Guns :
24—2 pdr. pompoms.
19—40 mm. AA.

Aircraft :
39 to **44**, according to type.

Machinery : Parsons geared turbines. 2 shafts. S.H.P. : 40,000=25 kts. Boilers : 4, of 3-drum type (400 lb. working pressure, 700° maximum superheat), arranged *en echelon*.

Note.—This ship has been lent to the French Navy for five years, from August, 1946, in order that training in naval flying may be conducted on up-to-date lines. She was laid down by Vickers-Armstrongs, Ltd., on the Tyne, 1/6/42, and completed 16/12/44 for the Royal Navy.

COLOSSUS. 1946, *Francis H. A. Baker, Esq.*

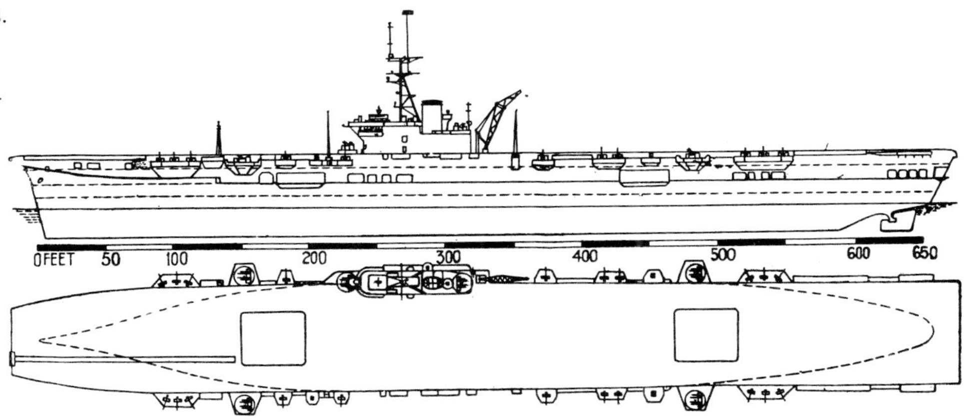

Aircraft Carrier

COLOSSUS. 1946, *Planet News.*

COLOSSUS. 1946, *Planet News.*

Escort Aircraft Carrier.

DIXMUDE. 1943, *Official.*

DIXMUDE (ex-H.M.S. *Biter*, ex-*Rio Parana*, 1941).

Displacement : 8,200 tons (14,500 tons *full load*). Complement : 800.

Length : 496 feet (*o.a.*). Beam : 69½ feet. Draught : 25½ feet. (*max.*)

Guns :
3—4 inch AA.
8—20 mm. AA.
4 M.G.
(This armament is believed to have been modified.)

Aircraft :
20 to **30**,
according to type.

Machinery : 2 sets Diesels. B.H.P. : 8,500 = 16·5 kts.

Notes.—Built by Seattle-Tacoma S.B. Corpn. Taken over by French Navy, April 9, 1945. Generally similar to U.S.S. *Charger* and *Long Island.*

Cruiser

DE GRASSE.

Displacement : 8,000 tons.

Length : 592 feet. Beam : 60 feet 4½ ins.

Guns:
9—6 inch.
12—3·9 inch AA.
28—40 mm. AA.
12—20 mm. AA.

Tubes:
6—21·7 inch.

Complement : 1,074.

Draught : 18 feet 2 ins. (*mean*).

Armour :
Generally similar to *La Galissonnière.*

Machinery : Rateau-Chantiers de Bretagne geared turbines. 2 shafts. S.H.P. : 110,000 = 33·5 kts.
Boilers : 4.

Estimates	*Name*	*Builder*	*Machinery*	*Laid down*	*Completed*
1937	*De Grasse*	Lorient	A. & C. de Bretagne	Nov. 1938	

Notes.—Construction of *De Grasse* was suspended during enemy occupation of Lorient, but has since been resumed. Design will follow that of *Algérie* in its main features. Two more ships, *Chateaurenault* and *Guichen*, were to have been begun in 1940, but owing to German invasion this proved impossible, and there seems no immediate prospect of their materialising.

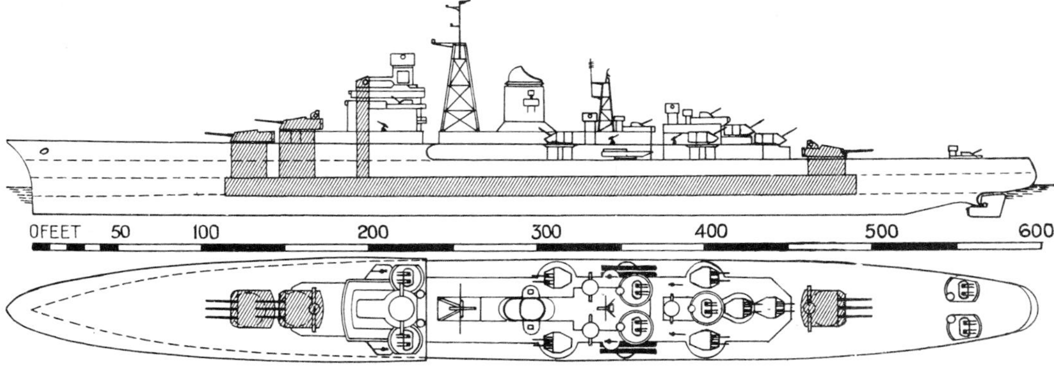

Cruisers

(Gloire Class—3 Ships)

GLOIRE (Sept. 28, 1935). **MONTCALM** (Oct. 26, 1935). **GEORGES LEYGUES** (*ex-Chateaurenault*) (March 24th 1936).

Displacement: 7,600 tons (10,850 tons *full load*). Complement: 674 peace, 764 war.

Length: (*pp.*) 548 feet, (*o.a.*) 580¾ feet. Beam: 57⅓ feet. Draught: 17⅓ feet (*max.*).

Guns:
- 9—6 inch
- 8—3·5 inch AA.
- 24—40 mm. AA.
- 16—20 mm. AA.

Tubes:
- 4—21·7 inch.

Armour (unofficial):
- 4¾"—3" Vert. Side.
- 2⅓" Deck
- 5½" Turret faces.
- 2" Turret sides.
- 3¾" C.T.

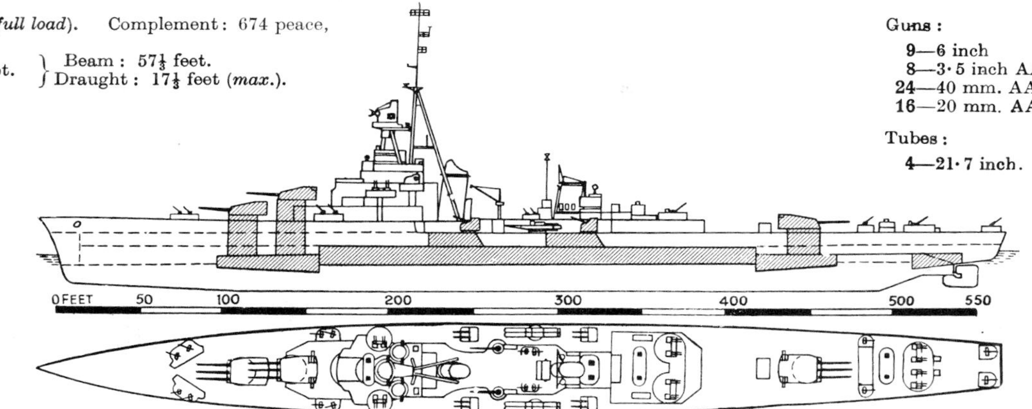

Machinery: 2 Rateau-Chantiers de Bretagne (*Gloire* only) or Parsons geared turbines. S.H.P.: 84,000 = 31 kts. Boilers: 4 Indret small tube. Fuel: 1,870 tons oil. Radius: 5,500 miles at 18 kts.

Programme	*Name*	*Builder*	*Machinery*	*Laid down*	*Completed*
1932	*Gloire* *Montcalm* *G. Leygues*	F. C. Gironde F. C. Med. C. A. St. Nazaire (Penhoët)	Ch. de Bretagne Builders in each case	1933	4.12.37

General Notes.—These ships resemble the *Emile Bertin* with additional protection which is said to be capable of resisting 6-inch shell. A feature of the design is the long quarter-deck. The bow flare is angled and not curved. Altogether the design of these cruisers is a remarkably successful one, embodying the maximum advantage to be obtained from their relatively low displacement. Trials: *Montcalm*, 35·7 kts. Sea speed about 30 kts. Fuel consumption reported to be exceptionally low in this class. Three sister ships, *La Galissonnière*, *J. de Vienne*, and *Marseillaise*, were scuttled at Toulon.

G. Leygues.

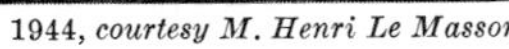

1944, *courtesy M. Henri Le Masson.*

Montcalm. 1946, *French Navy Official.*

Gloire. 1946, *French Navy Official.*

Cruiser (Minelayer)

EMILE BERTIN (Penhoët, St. Nazaire.) (May 9, 1933).

Displacement: 5,886 tons (8,480 tons *full load*). Complement: 567 peace, 705 war. Length: (*pp.*) 548 feet, (*o.a.*) 580¾ feet. Beam: 51¾ feet. Draught: 17¾ feet (*max.*).

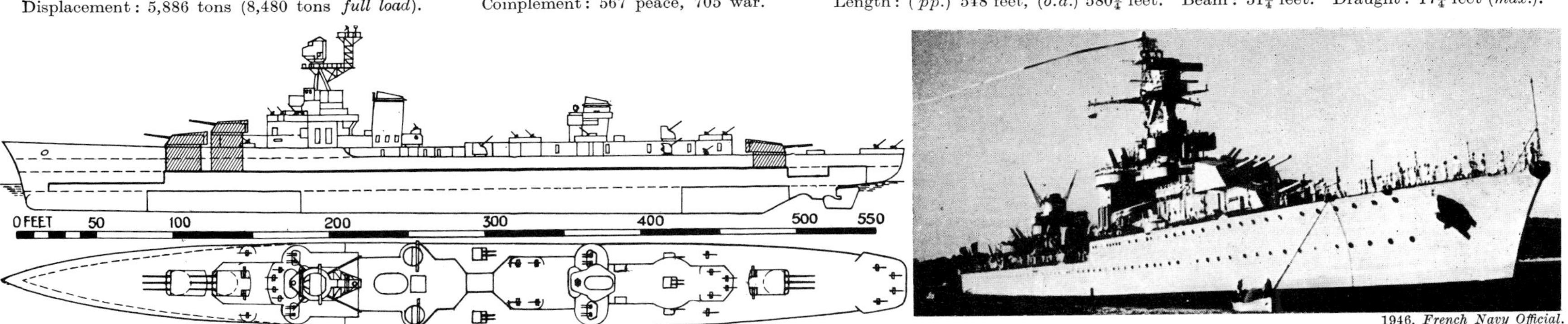

1946, *French Navy Official.*

Cruisers

1946, *French Navy Official.*

1946, *French Navy Official.*

Guns:
- 9—6 inch.
- 8—3·5 inch AA.
- 1υ—40 mm. AA.
- 20—20 mm. AA.

Tubes:
- 6—21·7 inch (tripled).

Mines: 200 (unofficial).

Armour: 1″—2″ Deck.

Machinery: Parsons geared turbines. 4 shafts. S.H.P.: 102,000 = 34 kts. Boilers: 6 Penhoët. Oil fuel: 1,360 tons.

Notes.—Authorised under the 1930 Programme. Laid down 1931. Completed in 1934. The triple mounting made its first appearance in the French Navy in *E. Bertin*, which is named after the famous naval architect. On trials, the ship exceeded expectations, maintaining 37 kts. for an hour in a 13 ft. swell. Maximum power and speed on trials, 123,000 = 39·8 kts. Hull strengthened beneath turrets to permit salvo firing, 1935.

SUFFREN (May 3rd, 1927).

Standard displacement, 10,000 tons (14,400 tons *full load*).
Complement, 637 peace, 773 war.

Length (*pp.*) 607 feet, (*o.a.*) 643 feet. Beam, 65⅝ feet.
Draught, 24½ feet (*max.*).

Guns:
- 8—8 inch
- 8—3 inch AA.
- 8—40 mm. AA.
- 20—20 mm. AA.
- 12—13 mm. AA.

Torpedo tubes:
- 6—21·7 inch (tripled).

Armour:
Has a patch of thin armour over engine and boiler spaces, with 17 W.T. bulkheads carried right up to upper deck. Fitted with internal bulges.

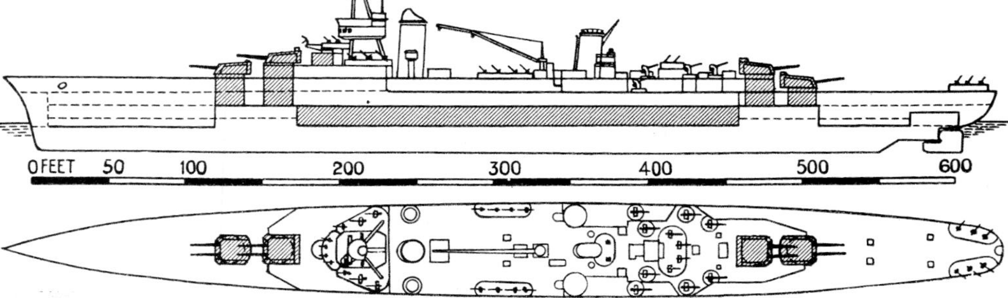

General Notes.—Laid down at Brest in May, 1926, as a modified edition of *Tourville* class but with about two knots speed sacrificed in order to gain better protection. Completed in 1930 at a cost of 144,000,000 francs. Three sister ships, *Colbert*, *Dupleix* and *Foch*, were scuttled at Toulon in November, 1942.

Machinery: 3 Rateau-Chantiers de Bretagne geared turbines. 3 shafts. Boilers: 9 Guyot (8 main and 1 auxiliary). Designed S.H.P.: 90,000 = 31·3 kts. Is able to steam at 29 kts. with half-power. Fuel: 2,700 tons *max.* Auxiliary equipment driven through 3 Diesels (Renault type) with dynamos. Radius: 4,600 miles at 15 kts., 3,000 at 25 kts.

SUFFREN. 1945, *courtesy M. Henri Le Masson.*

SUFFREN. 1946, *Marius Bar, Toulon.*

Cruiser

ALGÉRIE, (Brest, May 21st, 1932).

Standard Displacement, 10,000 tons. Complement, 616. (629 as flagship.)
Length (*w.l.*) 610¼ feet; (*o.a.*) 617 feet. Beam, 65⅝ feet. Draught, 24 feet. (*max.*)

Special Note.

his ship was scuttled in shallow water at Toulon, on Nov. 27, 1942.

Guns:
8—8 inch (new model).
12—3·9 inch AA.
8—37 mm. AA.
16—13 mm. AA.

Torpedo tubes:
6—21·7 inch (tripled).

Aircraft: 3.

Catapults: 2, of 3-ton type.

Armour:
4½" Vert. Side.
3" Deck.
Internal bulges, with hull thickness of 1½".
(Total weight of Armour 2,000 tons.)

Machinery: 4 Rateau-Chantiers de Bretagne geared Turbines.

S.H.P.: 84,000 = 31 kts. Radius: 5,000 miles at 15 kts.

Boilers: 8 Indret. Fuel: 1,900 tons

Trials: Average of 86,000 = over 32 kts. Max. speed, over 33 kts.

Note to Plan.—There are actually 3 S.L. mounted on tower amidships.

1934 *Photo, Capt. M. Adam.*

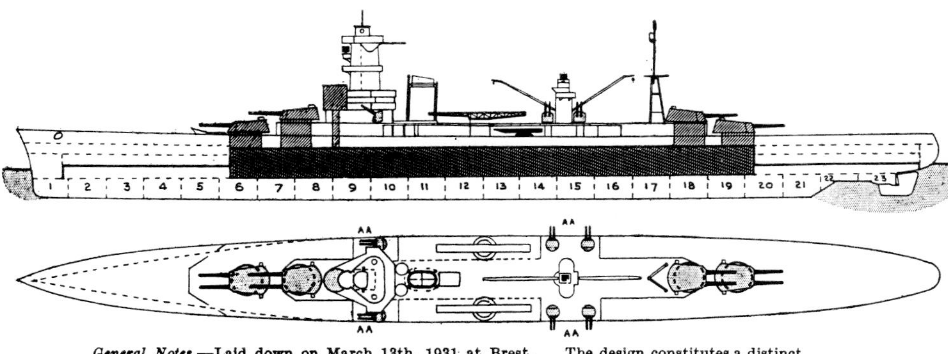

General Notes.—Laid down on March 13th, 1931 at Brest. The design constitutes a distinct departure from the "Tin-clad" vogue, and is more along the lines of a modern edition of the armoured cruiser of thirty years ago, being a reply to the Italian *Zara* type. A novel distribution of internal armour has been introduced giving special anti-aerial and torpedo protection, while the big guns and hoists are adequately armoured instead of being mounted in gunhouses made up of thin plating with unarmoured hoists. Speed has not been reduced as a result of these modifications and equals that of the *Foch* group but with less designed h.p. The 8 inch gun introduced in this ship, firing improved shells, has a greater range than the previous model. She was completed in 1934.

Aircraft Notes.—Unlike those of earlier cruisers, *Algérie's* catapults are of explosive type. Previously compressed air had been the motive power.

1938, *D. W. Hargreaves, Esq.*

Minelaying Cruiser

PLUTON (April 10th, 1929).

Standard Displacement, 4,850 tons. Complement, 406. Length, 472½ feet. Beam, 51 feet. Draught, 17 feet.

Guns:
4—5.5 inch.
10—37 m/m. AA.
12 M.G.

Armour: Nil.

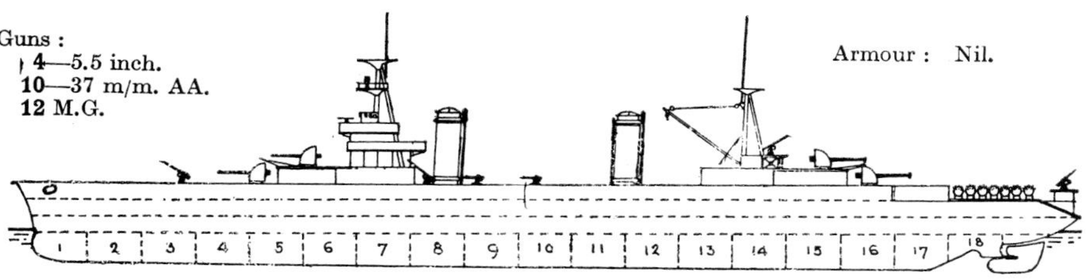

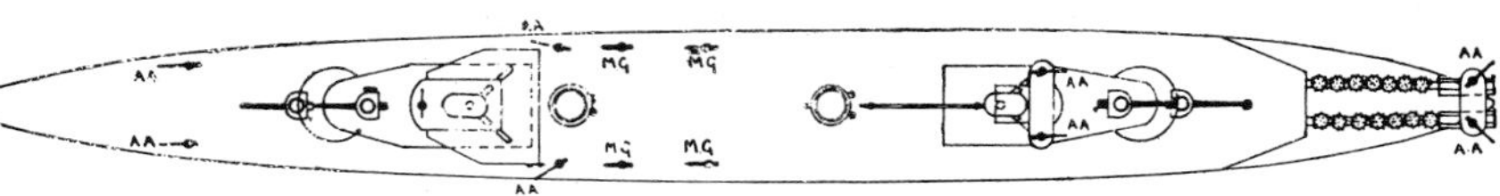

Machinery: 2 Breguet geared turbines. S.H.P. 57,000=30 kts. Oil=1,200 tons. Boilers: 4 small tube.

Note.—Authorised under 1925 Programme, and laid down at Lorient Dockyard in April, 1928, completed April, 1931. Trials: H.P., 56,000=30·6 kts.

PLUTON. 1931, *Official Photo.*

(TOURVILLE CLASS—2 SHIPS.)

DUQUESNE (Dec. 17th, 1925), **TOURVILLE** (Aug. 24th, 1926). *Standard* displacement, 10,000 tons (11,900 tons *deep load*). Complement, 605.
Length (*pp.*), 607 feet; (*o.a.*), 626⅔ feet. Beam, 62⅓ feet. Draught, 23 feet (*max.*)

DUQUESNE. 1946, *London Studio.*

TOURVILLE. 1946, *French Navy Official.*

Machinery: 4 Rateau-Chantiers de Bretagne geared turbines. Boilers: 9 Guyot (8 main and 1 auxiliary). Designed S.H.P.: 120,000 = 33 kts. 4 shafts. Oil: 2,070 ons. Radius: 3,000 miles at 13 kts.; 1,600 at 29 kts.

Name	Builder	Machinery	Laid down	Completed	Trials
Tourville	Lorient	A. & C. de Bretagne	14 April, 1925	1928	130,000 = 36·15
Duquesne	Brest		30 Oct., 1924	1928	135,000 = 35·3

General Note.—Above ships are practically enlarged copies of *Duguay-Trouin* design with an improved form of hull and heavier armament. Torpedo tubes, aircraft and catapult removed in 1945.

Engineering Notes.—Boiler and engine rooms are arranged alternately, and not in two separate groups, as suggested in plans appearing elsewhere. *Tourville's* trial speed of over 36 kts. was obtained while running on normal displacement. Auxiliaries driven through 3 Diesels (Renault Type) with dynamo.

Guns
8—8 inch
8—3 inch AA.
8—40 mm. AA.
16—20 mm. AA.

Armour:
Practically nil except for thin gun-shields and a splinter-proof C.T.

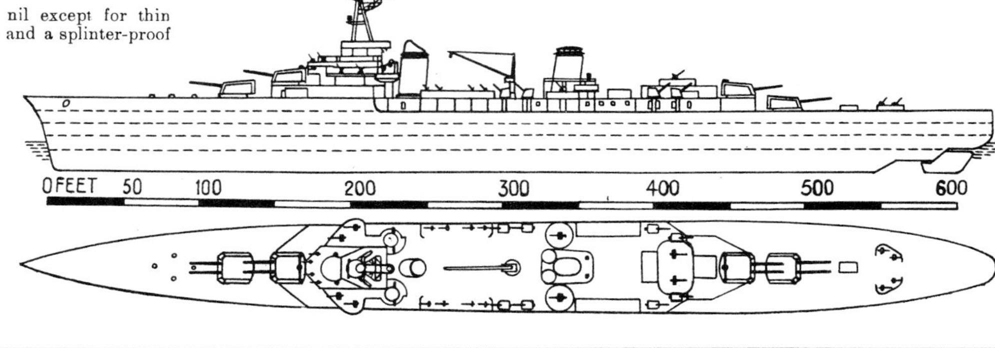

1945, *H. Emery, Toulon.*

JEANNE D'ARC (Feb. 14th, 1930.)

Standard displacement: 6,496 tons (9,200 tons *full load*). Complement: 506 peace, 643 war.
Length (*pp.*), 525 feet; (*o.a.*), 557¾ feet. Beam, 57½ feet. Draught, 17¾ feet (*mean*); 20⅔ feet (*max.*).

Guns:
8—6·1 inch.
4—3 inch AA.
6—40 mm. AA.
20—20 mm. AA.

Armour:
Protective deck and light plating to gun-houses and conning tower.

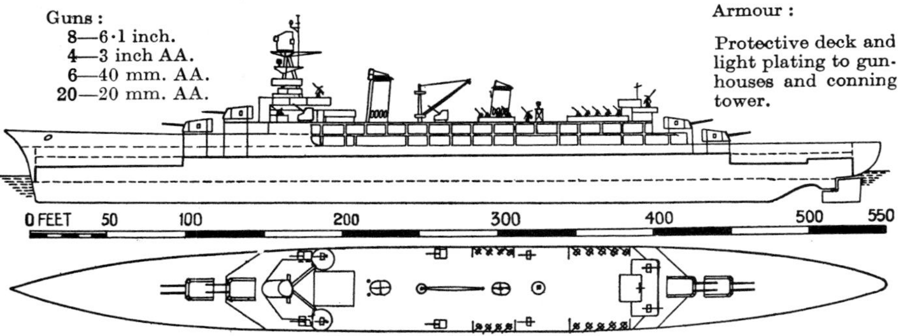

Machinery: Parsons geared turbines. 2 shafts. Designed H.P.: 32,500 = 25 kts. Boilers: 4 Penhoët. Oil: 1,400 tons. Radius: 5,200 miles at 11 kts., 3,200 at 21 kts.

General Notes.—This ship was specially designed for duty as a training cruiser and can accommodate 156 midshipmen and cadets and 20 instructional officers, in addition to ordinary complement. Authorised under 1927 Programme and laid down at Penhoët Yard, St. Nazaire in 1928. Completed in 1931.
Trials:—3 hours' full power: 39,200 H.P. = 27·03 kts. (*mean*), 27·84 kts. (*max.*).

1945, *French Navy Official.*

DUGUAY-TROUIN (14th Aug., 1923).

Standard displacement, 7,249 tons. (*Full load*, 10,100 tons.) Complement, 647.
Length (*pp.*) 575 feet, (*o.a.*) 594⅔ feet. Beam, 57½ feet. Draught, 17¼ feet *mean*; 20⅔ feet *maximum* at load.

Guns:
8—6·1 inch, 50 cal.
4—3 inch AA.
6—40 mm. AA.
20—20 mm. AA.

Armour:
Practically nil, except for thin gunshields, splinter-proof C.T., and double armoured deck.

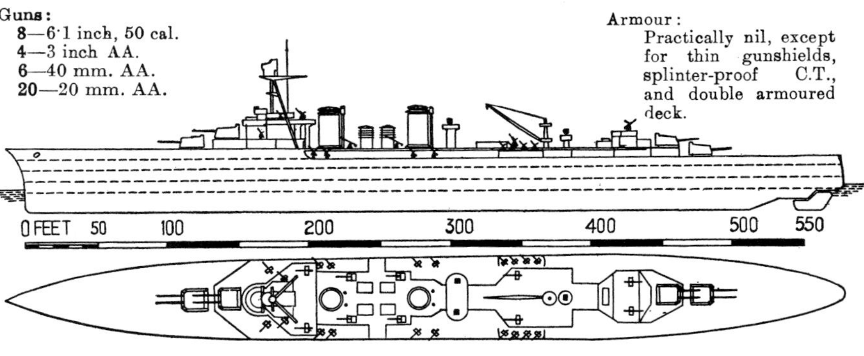

Machinery: Parsons geared turbines. 4 shafts. Designed S.H.P.: 102,000 = 33 kts. Boilers: 8 Guyot. Oil: 500 tons *normal*, 1,500 tons *maximum*. Radius: 4,300 miles at 14 kts.; 1,900 at 25 kts.

General Notes.—Laid down at Brest 4/8/22 and completed 10/9/26, *Duguay-Trouin* has shown excellent sea-keeping qualities.

Gunnery Notes.—6·1 inch guns are 1920 model. Range reported to be 28,000 yards, elevation 35°. Gunhouses are reported to be gas-tight, and to have a special method of ventilation by forced draught. New AA. armament installed 1943.

Engineering Notes.—On trials averaged 116,235 = 33·6 kts. over 6 hours with full complement of fuel and stores. *Maximum* speed for 1 hour, 34·5 kts. At half power 30 kts. was maintained for 24 hours' continuous steaming. Heating surface, 13,209 sq. feet. Machinery supplied by F. & C. de la Méditerranée.

Destroyers

2 ex-German Type (Classed as *Contretorpilleurs*)

HOCHE 1946, *French Navy Official.*

MARCEAU 1946, *French Navy Official.*

Hoche (ex-*Z* 25, 1940), ***Marceau*** (ex-*Z* 31, 1941).

Displacement: 1,870 tons (German official figure—actually 2,400 tons). Dimensions: $388\frac{3}{4}$ (*pp.*), $403\frac{1}{2}$ (*o.a.*) × $38\frac{1}{3}$ × $9\frac{1}{2}$ feet (*light* draught). Guns: In *Hoche*, **4**—5·9 inch, **8**—37 mm. AA., **12**—20 mm. AA., **4** D.C.T.; in *Marceau*, **3**—5·9 inch, **1**—4·1 inch, **14**—37 mm. AA., **8**—20 mm. AA., **4** D.C.T. Tubes: **8**—21 inch. Mines: 60. Machinery: Geared turbines. 2 shafts. S.H.P.: 70,000 = 36·5 kts. Boilers: **6** Wagner, 176 lb. working pressure. Oil fuel: 620 tons. Radius of action, 3,200 miles at 16·5 kts. 2,800 miles at 20 kts. Complement: 320.

Gunnery Notes.—5·9 inch guns are not AA., having only 45° maximum elevation. Substitution of one 4·1 inch for a pair of 5·9 inch in *Marceau* was presumably dictated by desire to reduce weight forward.

General Notes.—Laid down 1940 and completed 1943. Acquired by French Navy in 1946.

4 ex-German Type (Classed as *Torpilleurs*)

(Fitted for Minelaying)

ALSACIEN 1946, *French Navy Official.*

Alsacien (ex-*T* 23, Nov. 1941), ***Lorrain*** (ex-*T* 28, Nov. 1942).

Displacement: 1,100 tons. Dimensions: 310 (*pp.*), 319 (*o.a.*) × 30 × $8\frac{1}{4}$ feet. Guns: **4**—4·1 inch, **4**—37 mm. AA., **12**—20 mm. AA., **2** M.G., **6** D.C.T. Tubes: **6**—21 inch. Mines: Stowage for 70. Machinery: Geared turbines. 2 shafts. S.H.P.: 35,000 = 32 kts. Boilers: 4 Wagner, 155 lb. working pressure. Oil fuel: 290 tons. Complement: 186.

Baccarat (ex-*T* 11, March 1939), ***Bir Hakeim*** (ex-*T* 20, Oct. 1941).

Displacement: 600 tons. Dimensions: $265\frac{3}{4}$ × $28\frac{1}{4}$ × $6\frac{1}{4}$ feet (*light* draught). Guns: **1**—4·1 inch, **1**—40 mm. AA., **2**—37 mm. AA., **12**—20 mm. AA., **21** rockets. Tubes: **6**—21 inch. Stowage for 60 mines. Machinery: Geared turbines. 2 shafts. S.H.P.: 22,000 = 33 kts. Boilers: 4 Schichau. Oil fuel: 200 tons.

2 ex-German Type.

(Classed as *Contretorpilleurs*)

Desaix (ex-*Paul Jacobi*, March 1936), ***Kléber*** (ex-*Theodor Rieder*, 1936).

Displacement: 1,625 tons (3,000 tons *full load*). Dimensions: 374 (*pp.*), 381 *o.a*) × $37\frac{3}{4}$ × $9\frac{1}{3}$ feet (*light* draught). Guns: **5**—5 inch, **8**—37 mm. AA. **12**—20 m.m. AA. Tubes; **8**—21 inch. Machinery: Geared turbines. 2 shafts. S.H.P.: 50,000 = 36 kts. Boilers: 6 Wagner. Oil fuel: 700 tons. Complement: 340.

KLÉBER (Now has clipper bow). 1937, *Renard.*

4 Fantasque Class. *1930 Programme.*

(Classed as *Croiseurs Légers*)

LE FANTASQUE. 1945, *French Navy Official.*

Le Fantasque	(March 15, 1934).	***Le Terrible***	(Nov. 29, 1933).
Le Malin	(Aug. 17, 1933).	***Le Triomphant***	(April 16, 1934).

Displacement: 2,569 tons (3,230 tons *full load*). Complement: 220.
Dimensions: $411\frac{1}{2}$ (*pp.*), $434\frac{1}{3}$ (*o.a.*) × $39\frac{1}{3}$ × 14 feet (*mean*).
Guns: **5**—5·5 inch, **8**—40 mm. AA., **10**—20 mm. AA., **4** D.C. throwers. Tubes: **6**—21·7 inch (tripled).
Machinery: 2 sets geared turbines. Parsons in *Le Malin* and *Le Triomphant*; Rateau-Chantiers de Bretagne in others. S.H.P.: 74,000 = 37 kts. Boilers: 4 small tube, of Penhoët, Guyot, Yarrow and Babcock types, respectively. Oil fuel: 650 tons.

Builders: Le Fantasque, Lorient; *Le Malin*, F. Ch. de la Mediterranée, La Séyne; *Le Terrible*, Ch. Nav. Français, Blainville; *Le Triomphant*, Ch. de France, Dunkerque.

Notes.—On trials, *Le Terrible* reached record speed of 45·25 kts. with about 100,000 H.P., average for one hour being 44·9 with 94,200 H.P. On her 8 hours' trial she averaged 43 kts. All the ships of this class are excellent sea boats, able to maintain 37 kts. continuously. They were completely refitted in U.S.A., 1942–44.

Appearance Notes.—No mainmast in these ships, w.t. aerials being slung from brackets on second funnel.

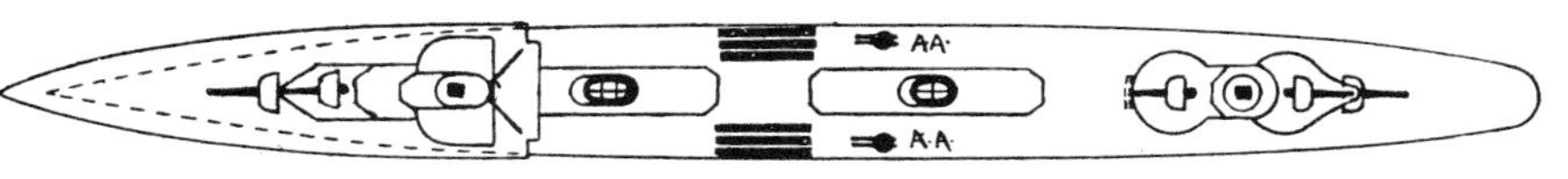

LE TERRIBLE 1946, *French Navy Official.*

LE TERRIBLE. 1946, *French Navy Official.*

Destroyers

1922 Programme

		Begun.	Launched.	Compl.	Trials.
Jaguar	Lorient Dockyard		7/11/23	1926	52,000=36·1
Panthère			28/10/24	1926	=35·5
Léopard ..	Ch. de Loire St. Nazaire		20/9/24	1927	
Lynx ..			24/2/25	1927	=35·5
Chacal ..	Penhoët		13/7/24	1926	52,000=36 1
Tigre ..	Ch. de Bretagne Nantes.		2/8/24	1926	58,000=36·7

Displacement: 2,126 tons; 2,700 tons full load.

Dimensions: 392¾ (*p.p.*), 416 (*o.a.*)×36×11·1 feet. Complement: 204.

Guns: **5**—5·1 inch.
2—2·9 inch A.A.
4—D.C. Throwers.

Oil: 250/540 tons.
Radius: 3,500 miles at 15 kts.
2,500 ,, ,, 18 ,,
900 ,, ,, full speed.

Tubes: **6**—21·7 inch.

S.H.P. 50,000=35·5 kts. Breguet turbines (*Leopard* and *Lynx*.) Rateau in other four. 5 small tube boilers.

TIGRE. 1926 *Photo, M. Bar, Toulon.*

Note.—Classified on a tonnage basis these ships would rank as cruisers being above 2,000 tons standard displacement. They are employed in divisions and not as flotilla leaders.

2 + *4* (Authorised) Volta class.
(Classed as *Contre-Torpilleurs*)

MOGADOR. 1939, *Wright & Logan.*

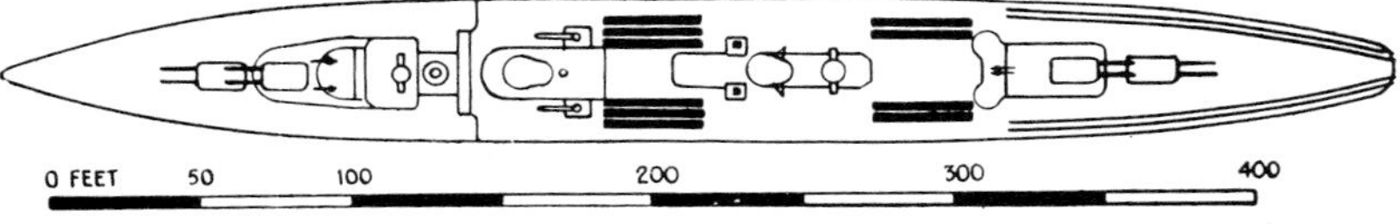

2 *Lorient:* ***Desaix, Mogador.***
3 *Ch. de Bretagne:* ***Volta, Hoche, Marceau.***
1 *At. et Ch. de France:* ***Kléber.***
Displacement: 2,884 tons. (About 3,500 tons full load.) Complement: 238.
Dimensions: 451 × 41 × 14¾ feet (*mean*).
Guns: **8**—5·5 inch, **4**—37 mm. AA., **4**—13 mm. AA., **4** D.C.T.
Tubes: **10**—21·7 inch (2 triple mounts and 2 pairs).
Machinery: Rateau-Chantiers de Bretagne geared turbines by A. & C. de Bretagne in *Volta* and *Marceau*; Parsons in others. S.H.P.: 90,000 = 38 kts. Boilers: 6 Indret small tube. Oil fuel: 630 tons.

Gunnery Notes.—5·5 inch are of a new model, semi-automatic, and have a range of 25,000 yards. A rate of fire of 16 rounds a minute can be maintained.

General Notes.—*Mogador* was badly damaged at Oran on July 3rd, 1940, but was afterwards repaired. Both this vessel and *Volta* were scuttled at Toulon in Nov., 1942. Last 4 ships of this class will probably never be built.

Programme	*Name*	*Laid down*	*Launch*	*Completed*
1932	*Mogador*	Dec. 1934	9/6/37	1/6/38
1934	*Volta*	Jan. 1935	26/11/36	15/9/38
1938	*Desaix*, *Hoche*, *Marceau*, *Kléber*	1940 (?)		

5 Guépard Class.

1 *At. et Ch. de France:* ***Lion.***
1 *Lorient:* ***Guépard.***
Dimensions of both: 427 × 38¾ × 15¾ feet
1 *At. et Ch. de la Loire:* ***Verdun.***
1 *At. et Ch. de France:* ***Vauban.***
1 *At. et Ch. de St. Nazaire (Penhoët):* ***Valmy.***
Dimensions of these 3: 427 × 39 × 16¾ feet.

All scuttled at Toulon, Nov. 27, 1942.

All 5 ships: Displacement: 2,436 tons (about 3,080 tons *full load*). Complement: 209. Guns: **5**—5·5 inch, **4**—37 mm., **4** D.C.T. Tubes: **6**—21·7 inch. Machinery: 2 sets geared turbines—Parsons in *Guépard*, *Valmy*, *Verdun*; Zoelly-Fives-Lille in *Lion* and *Vauban*. S.H.P.: 64,000=36 kts. Boilers: Small tube, varying types. Oil fuel: 550 tons. Radius of action: 3,000 miles at 18 kts.

VAUBAN 1938, *Grand Studio.*

8 Aigle Class.

1 *At. et Ch. de France:* ***Aigle.***
1 *Ch. de Bretagne:* ***Gerfaut.***
1 *F. et Ch. de la Med. (Havre):* ***Vautour.***
1 *Lorient:* ***Milan.***
Dimensions of these 4: 423¼ × 40 × 16 feet.
1 *Ch. de Bretagne:* ***Cassard.***
1 *At. et Ch. de France:* ***Vauquelin.***
2 *At. et Ch. de la Loire:* ***Kersaint, Tartu.***
Dimensions of these 4: 424¼ × 39 × 15¾ feet.

All 8 ships: Displacement: 2,441 tons (3,090 tons full load). Complement: 220. Guns: **5**—5·5 inch, **4**—37 mm., **4** D.C.T. Tubes: **7**—21·7 inch, except *Aigle, Gerfaut, Vautour* with 6. Machinery: 2 sets geared turbines—of Parsons type in *Milan, Vautour, Kersaint, Tartu*; Zoelly-Fives-Lille in *Aigle* and *Vauquelin*; Rateau-Ch. de Bretagne in *Cassard, Gerfaut*. Boilers: 4 small tube, Yarrow or Penhoët. S.H.P.: 64,000 = 36 kts. except *Milan*, 68,000 = 36·5 kts. Oil fuel: 650 tons. Radius: 3,000 miles at 18 kts.

Note.—*Milan* totally disabled at Casablanca, Nov. 9, 1942. Others were scuttled at Toulon, Nov. 27, 1942.

Programme	*Name*	*Begun*	*Launch*	*Completed*	*Trials*
1927	*Aigle*	1929	19/2/31	1932	39·67
	Gerfaut	1929	14/6/30	1932	93,000 = 42·78
	Vautour	1929	26/8/30	1932	80,000 = 40·2
	Milan	6/30	13/10/31	1933	83,000 = 43·4
1928–29	*Cassard*	11/30	8/11/31	1932	80,600 = 43·4
	Vauquelin	3/30	29/9/32	1934	39·4
	Kersaint	9/30	14/11/31	1933	39·1
	Tartu	1930	7/12/31	1932	41·02
1925	*Lion*	4/27	5/8/29	1931	66,298 = 40·4
	Guépard	2/27	19/4/28	1929	69,100 = 38·4
1926	*Verdun*	1927	4/7/28	1930	72,400 = 40·1
	Vauban	1927	1/2/29	1931	40·2
	Valmy	1927	19/5/29	1930	69,300 = 39·8

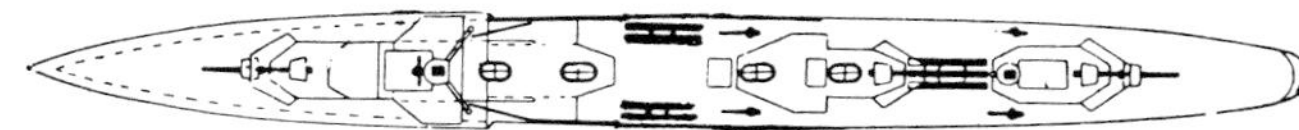
MILAN, and 4 of CASSARD group.

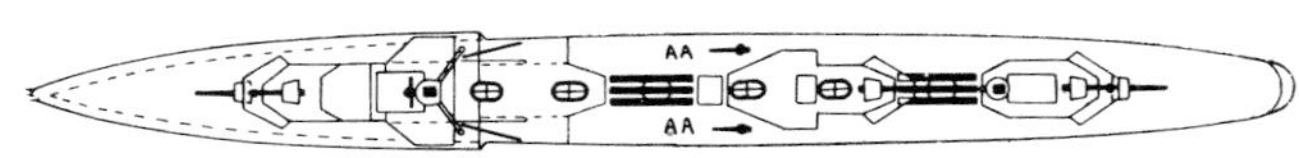
GUÉPARD CLASS.
Also AIGLE, GERFAUT, VAUTOUR.

(Classed as *Contretorpilleurs.*)

1938, *Grand Studio.*

1 *At. et Ch. de la Loire:* **Albatros** (June 28, 1930).

Displacement: 2,441 tons (3,090 tons *full load*). Dimensions: 423¼ × 40 × 16 feet. Complement: 220. Guns: 5—5·5 inch, 4—37 mm., 4 D.C.T. Tubes: 6—21·7 inch. Machinery: 2 sets Parsons geared turbines. Boilers: 4 small tube, Yarrow or Penhoët. S.H.P.: 64,000 = 36 kts. Oil fuel: 650 tons. Radius: 3,000 miles at 18 kts.

Note.—Built under 1927 Programme. Under reconstruction at present.

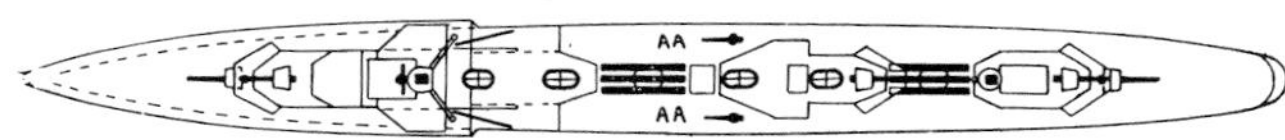

TIGRE. 1945, *French Navy Official.*

1 *Ch. de Bretagne:* **Tigre** (August 2, 1924).

Displacement: 2,126 tons (3,550 tons *full load*). Dimensions: 392⅔ (*pp.*), 416 (*o.a.*) × 37½ × 17¼ feet (*max.*). Guns: 4—5·1 inch, 2—40 mm. AA., 10—20 mm. AA. 4 D.C.T. Tubes: 3—21·7 inch. Machinery: Rateau-Ch. de Bretagne turbines. S.H.P.: 44,000 = 30 kts. Boilers: 4 small tube Du Temple. Oil: 250/550 tons. Radius: 2,600 at 12 kts., 1,200 at 25 kts., 1,000 at 30 kts. Complement: 235.

Note.—Built under 1922 Programme. *Tigre* was temporarily in Italian hands during part of 1943, but has since had complete refit, 1944–45, in which a fifth boiler was removed to provide additional fuel space.

Note to Plan:—Additional AA. gun positions not indicated.

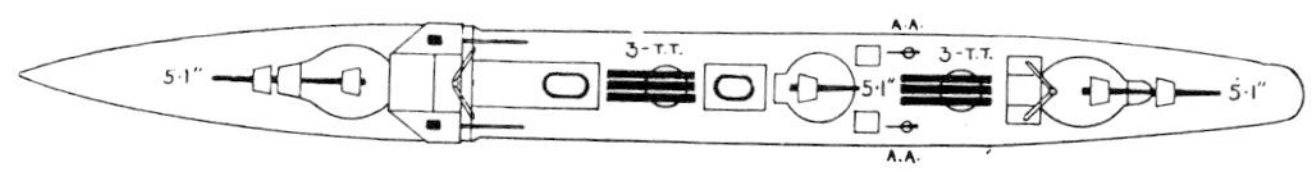

4 Alcyon class.

(Classed as *Torpilleurs*)

L'ALCYON. 1946, *Wright & Logan.*

L'Alcyon (June 26th, 1926). (Launched at Harfleur and towed to Bordeaux for completion.)

Forbin (July 17th, 1928). **Basque** (May 25th, 1929). **Le Fortuné** (Nov. 15, 1926).

Displacement: 1,378 tons *standard* (2,100 tons *full load*). Dimensions: 330·9 × 32½ × 9½ feet. Complement: 167. Guns: 3—5·1 inch, 1—40 mm. AA., 8—20 mm. AA. 6 D.C.T. Torpedo tubes: 3—21·7 inch, in triple mounting. Machinery: 2 sets geared turbines of Zoelly type in *Alcyon*, Rateau-Ch. de Bretagne in *Basque*, Parsons in other two. 2 shafts. S.H.P.: 3,2000=28 kts. Boilers: 3 small tube. Oil fuel: 340 tons.

Notes.—Ordered under Programmes of 1925 (*Basque* and *Forbin*) and 1924 (other two). As compared with *Simoun* type, these vessels possess improved stability, higher rate of salvo firing, better aerial defence and lower fuel consumption. 5·1 inch guns said to possess a range of 19,000 yards, and can fire eight rounds a minute. *L'Alcyon* has been rearmed experimentally with a pair of 4·1 inch German guns, in place of after 5·1 inch.

Name	*Builder*	*Engines*	*Begun*	*Completed*
L'Alcyon	F. & Ch. de la Gironde	Ch. de la Gironde	} 1925	1929
Le Fortuné	Ch. Navals Français, Blainville	A. & Ch. de la Loire		1928
Basque	Ch. de la Seine Maritime (Worms)	A. & Ch. de Bretagne	Sept. 1926	1930
Forbin	F. & Ch. de la Med., Havre	F. & Ch. de la Med.	1927	1930

BASQUE. 1945, *courtesy M. Henri Le Masson.*

5 Simoun Class.

1 *F. & Ch. de la Méditerranée (Havre):* **Mistral** (June 6th, 1925).
1 *Ch. Navals Français (Blainville):* **Ouragan** (Dec. 6th, 1924).
1 *A. & Ch de St. Nazaire (Penhoët):* **Simoun** (June 2rd, 1924).
1 *Ch. Dubigeon:* **Tempête** (Feb. 21st, 1925).
1 *F & Ch. de la Gironde:* **Trombe** (Dec. 29th, 1925).

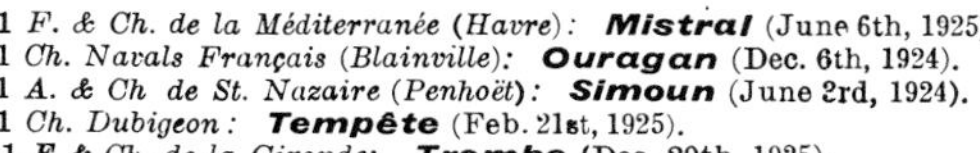

SIMOUN. 1946, *French Navy Official.*

Displacement: 1,319 tons *standard* (2,000 tons *full load*). Dimensions: 326 (*pp.*), 347 (*o.a.*) × 33 × 13¾ feet. Complement: 167. Guns: 3—5·1 inch, 1—40 mm. AA., 8—20 mm. AA. (*Mistral* has 3—4 inch in place of 5·1). Torpedo tubes: 3—21·7 inch (none in *Simoun*). Geared turbines of Zoelly type in *Trombe*; Parsons in other ships. H.P.: 33,000=28 kts. Boilers: 3 small tube. 2 shafts. Oil fuel: 345 tons *max.* Radius: 2,350 miles at 10 kts.

Notes.—Authorised by Law of 18th August, 1922. All completed 1926-27. These vessels lose their speed rapidly in a seaway. *Trombe* was temporarily in Italian hands between Nov., 1942, and Oct., 1943.

Destroyers (Classed as *Torpilleurs*)

5 Melpomene Class.

LA MELPOMÈNE. 1942, *P.D.*

LA FLORE. 1937, *Capt. M. Adam.*

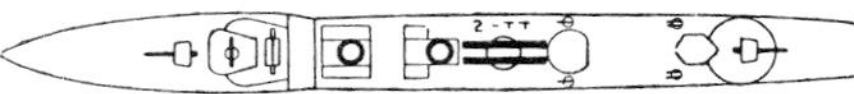

2 *Ch. de Bretagne, Nantes:* **La Flore** (May 4, 1935), **La Melpomène** (Jan. 24, 1935).

2 *Ch. Worms, Rouen:* **Bouclier** (Aug. 9, 1937), **L'Incomprise** (April 14, 1937).

1 *Ch. Augustin Normand:* **La Cordelière** (Sept. 9, 1936).

Displacement: 610 tons (970 tons *full load*). Complement: 92. Dimensions: $245\frac{1}{3}$ (*pp.*), $264\frac{3}{4}$ (*o.a.*) × 26 × $9\frac{1}{4}$ feet (*mean* draught). Guns: **2**—3·9 inch, **4** M.G. Tubes: **2**—21·7 inch. Machinery: Parsons geared turbines in all except *La Cordelière, L'Incomprise, Bouclier*, which have Rateau-Bretagne type. H.P.: 22,000 = 34·5 kts. (exceeded on trials). Oil fuel: 90 tons. Radius: 1,700 at 14 kts.

Notes.—Provided for under 1931 and 1932 Programmes. All completed during 1936–38. They have not proved very satisfactory in service, and are now laid up in reserve.

Submarines

FRENCH SUBMARINE CRUISER "SURCOUF" 1931 *Photo, Official*

1 Cruiser Type.

Surcouf (Nov. 18th, 1929) laid down at Cherbourg Dec. 1927, under 1926 Programme. Dimensions: 393·7 × 29·5 × 23 feet = 2880/4300 tons. Machinery: Diesels 7,600 B.H.P. = 18 kts. *surface.* Motors 3,400 H.P. = 10 kts. *submerged.* Guns: **2**—8″, tubes: **10**—21″ adapted for salvo firing. Carries 22 torpedoes. Complement, 150. Radius of action: 10,000 miles at 10 kts.

25 Redoubtable Class.

VENGEUR. 1930 *Photo, favour of M. of Marine.*

31 *Fuzier-Roquebert type.*

1924 Programme.

Redoubtable (Feb. 24th, 1928) } Cherbourg.
Vengeur (Sept., 1928) }

1925 Programme.

Pascal } (July 19th, 1928), Brest.
Pasteur }
Henri Poincare } (April 10th, 1929), Lorient.
Poncelet }
Fresnel (June 8th, 1929), St. Nazaire (Penhoët).

1926 Programme.

Archimede (   ), Ch. Nav. Fr. Blainville.
Monge (June 25th, 1929), La Seyne.
Acteon (April 10th, 1929) } A. C. Loire.
Acheron (Aug. 6th, 1929) }
Argo (April 11th, 1929), Ch. Dubigeon, Nantes.
Achille } (May 28th, 1930) Brest.
Ajax }

1927 Programme.

Prométhée (   ), Cherbourg.
Persée (   ), C. N. F. Blainville.
Protée (Aug., 1930), F. C. Havre.

Pégase (   ), A. C. Loire.
Phénix (   ), Dubigeon.

1928 Programme.

Glorieux } Cherbourg.
Centaure }
Heros } Brest.
Conquerant }
Tonnant A. C. Loire.
Espoir La Seyne.

1930 Programme.

Agosta
Beveziers Cherbourg.
Ouessant
Sidi-Ferruch
Sfax
Casablanca

Displacement: 1,384 tons *surface*; 2,080 tons *submerged* for first two; remainder 1,379 tons *surface*; 2,060 tons *submerged.* Dimensions: $302\frac{1}{2} \times 30\frac{1}{2} \times 15\frac{1}{2}$ feet. Machinery: 2 sets Sulzer Diesels, combined H.P. 6,000 = 18 kts. (Trials, 19.5 kts.) Electric motors of H.P. 2,000 = 10 kts. *submerged.* 1 auxiliary Diesel, H.P. 750. 2 screws. Armament: **1**—3·9″ AA., **1**—37 m/m AA., **1**—M.G., **11**—21·7″ tubes, including 2 sets of revolving tubes, 1 bow, 1 stern. (Reported that in later boats **1**—5·5″ will replace the 3·9″. Radius of action = 30 days cruising.

Notes.—Have proved very successful on trials. *Vengeur* and *Redoubtable* performed a cruise to the West Indies in 1930 without mishap, and were able to make 19 kts. easily without being pressed. *H. Poincairé* maintained an average of 17·60 kts. for 48 hours on trials

4 Lagrange Class.

ROMAZZOTTI. 1924 *Photo, M. Bar, Toulon.*

4 *Hutter* type: **Lagrange** (1917), **Regnault** (25th June, 1924), and **Romazzotti** (1917). All built at Toulon D.Y. **Laplace** (Rochefort D.Y., 1919). Displacements: 836 tons *on surface*, 1317 tons *submerged.* Dimensions: $246\frac{3}{4} \times 20.9 \times 13.2$ feet. Machinery: *on surface*, 2 sets 1300 B.H.P. Sulzer-Diesel engines, totalling 2600 B.H.P for $16\frac{1}{2}$ kts. *Submerged* speed: 11 kts. Endurance: *on surface*, 2500 miles at 14 kts., 4200 miles at 10 kts., 6000 miles at 8 kts. When *submerged*, 115 miles at 5 kts. Armament: **2**—14 pdr. guns. **8**—17.7 inch torpedo discharges, arranged as in *Dupuy de Lôme*, below. Stowage for 10 torpedoes and 440 rounds of ammunition for guns. Complement, 47.

Notes.—Begun as *Q* 111—114 of 1914 Programme. General design as *D. de Lôme* class.

2 Dupuy de Lôme Class.

SANÉ. 1930 *Photo, Lt. T. D. Manning, R.N.V.R.*

2 *Hutter* type: **Dupuy de Lôme** (1915) and **Sané** (1916). Both built at Toulon D.Y. Displacements: 748 tons *on surface*, 1291 tons *submerged.* Dimensions: 246 × 20.9 × 13.7 feet. Machinery: *on surface*, Diesel engines (recently renewed) of 2900 H.P. = 16 kts. *Submerged* speed: 10 kts. Armament: **2**—14 pdr. guns and discharge positions for **8**—18 inch torpedoes as follows: 2 *submerged* tubes, W.T. parallel, built into bows; 2 *above water*, fixed, divergent, built into superstructure forward; 2 revolving, in twin mount, under superstructure abaft C.T.; 2 fixed, divergent, built into superstructure aft. Oil: 100 tons. Complement, 43.

Notes.—Begun as *Q* 105 and *Q* 106 of 1913 Programme. Both completed 1916. Are enlargements of M. Hutter's design for the *Bellone* class. *Dupuy de Lôme's* 2 Diesels are by Krupp *Sané* has two Koerting motors.

Curie (built in England, 1942). No particulars published.

Aurore Class.

Note.—Most of the vessels building in territory occupied in 1940 are believed to have been effectually demolished. Only one known to have been completed is *Aurore*, reported to have been scuttled at Toulon on Nov. 27, 1942. *Cornélie* and *Phénix* may never have been begun.

2 *Toulon*: ***Aurore, Phénix.***
1 *Schneider*: ***Antigone***
5 *Normand*: ***La Bayadère La Creole, Artemis, Gorgone, Hermione***
4 *Ch. Worms*: ***L'Africaine, La Favorite, Andromaque, Armide***
4 *Ch. Dubigeon*: ***Andromède, Astrée, Clorinde, Cornélie***
Displacement: 393/1,170 tons.
Dimensions: 241 × 21⅓ × 11½ feet.
Guns: **1**—3·9 inch, **2**—13 mm. AA. Tubes: **9**—21·7 inch.
Machinery: Schneider Diesels in *Aurore, Antigone, L'Africaine, La Favorite*; Sulzer type in others.
H.P.: 3,000/1,400 = 17/9 kts.

Programme	*Name*	*Laid down*	*Launch*	*Completed*
1934	*Aurore*	9/36	26/7/39	6/40
1937	*L'Africaine*	9/38		
	La Favorite	7/38		
	La Bayadere	8/38		
	La Creole	8/38	1940	

Programme	*Name*	*Laid down*	*Launch*	*Completed*
1938	*Antigone*	1939		
	Artemis			
	Gorgone			
	Hermione			
	Andromaque			
	Armide			
	Andromede			
	Astrée			
	Clorinde			
	Cornélie			
1939	*Phénix*	2/40		

Saphir Class (Minelayers).

TURQUOISE. 1930 *Photo, A. Ganda.*

10 *Normand-Fenaux* type: ***Saphir*** (Dec. 20th, 1928); ****Turquoise*** (May 16th, 1929); ****Nautilus*** (Mar. 21st, 1930); ****Rubis*** (Sept. 30th, 1931); ***Diamant*** (May 18th, 1933); ****Perle*** (July 30th, 1935); ***Emeraude*** (laid down Sept., 1938) ***Agate, Corail, Escarboucle,*** (all 3 laid down 1940). All built at Toulon. Displacement: 669 tons *on surface*; 925 *submerged*. Dimensions: 216½ × 23¾ × 16 feet. Machinery: 2 sets Vickers-Normand 4-cycle Diesels. B.H.P.: 1,300 = 12 kts. *Submerged* H.P.: 1,000 = 9 kts. Armament: **1**—3 inch AA., **5**—21·7 inch tubes, **32** minelaying chutes, arranged on Normand-Fenaux system. Carry **6** torpedoes and **32** mines of 460 lbs. weight. *Saphir* and *Turquoise* 1925 Programme, *Nautilus* 1926, *Rubis* 1927, *Diamant* 1928–29, *Perle* 1930, *Emeraude* 1937, remaining three 1938. Complement: 40. Radius of action: 2,500 miles *surface*; 850 miles *submerged*.

Notes.—Mines are stowed in wells in outer ballast tanks, with direct release arrangement. Last four do not appear to have been completed. *Saphir* and *Diamant* were both scuttled at Toulon, Nov. 27, 1942. *Rubis* is the vessel referred to in Press by the unofficial name of *Jour de Gloire*.

14 Redoutable Class.

CASABIANCA. 1943, *Official.*

14 *Roquebert design.*

1924 Programme.
Redoutable (Feb. 24th, 1928) } Cherbourg.
Vengeur (Sept. 1st, 1928) }

1925 Programme.
Pascal (July 19th, 1928), Brest.
Henri Poincare (April 10th, 1929), Lorient.
Fresnel (June 8th, 1929), St. Nazaire (Penhoët).
****Archimede*** (Sept. 6th, 1930), Ch. Nav. Fr. Blainville.

1926 Programme.
Achéron (Aug. 6th, 1929), A. C. Loire.
****Argo*** (April 11th, 1929), Ch. Dubigeon, Nantes.

1927 Programme.
****Protée*** (July 31st, 1930), F. C. Havre.
****Pégase*** (July 28th, 1930), A. C. Loire.

1928 Programme.
****L'Espoir*** (July 18th, 1931) } Cherbourg.
****Le Glorieux*** (Nov. 29th, 1932) }
****Le Centaure*** (Oct. 14th, 1932), Brest.

1930 Programme.
****Casabianca*** (Feb. 2nd, 1935) (ex *Casablanca*), A. C. Loire.

Displacement: 1,379/2,060 tons, except *Redoutable* and *Vengeur*, 1,384/2,080 tons. Dimensions: 302½ × 27 × 16 feet. Diesels: 2 sets Sulzer or Schneider-Carel type. 2 shafts. H.P. 6,000 = 17 kts. Vessel of 1930 Programme, H.P. 8,400 = 18 kts. Electric motors of H.P. 2,000 = 10 kts. *submerged*. 1927 and 1928 boats all reached 19 kts. with 6,500 H.P., and *Casabianca* with 8,600 H.P. was able to do 20·5 kts. Armament: **1**—3·9 inch AA, **2** M.G. (first two have **1**—37 mm. AA. and **1** M.G. as secondary armament), **11**—21·7 inch tubes, including 2 sets of revolving tubes in triple and quadruple mountings, the latter at the stern. Complement: 67.

Radius of action = 30 days' cruising.

Notes.—Have proved very successful Vessels. *Redoutable, Vengeur, Pascal, H. Poincaré, Fresnel, Achéron*, reported scuttled at Toulon, Nov. 27, 1942; and *Le Tonnant* at Cadiz in same month.

6 Requin Class.

6 *Fuzier-Roquebert* type: ***Requin*** (19th July, 1924), ***Caïman*** (3rd March, 1927), (both Cherbourg), ***Dauphin*** (1925), ***Espadon*** (28th May, 1926), (both Toulon), ****Marsouin*** (Dec. 27th, 1924). ***Phoque*** (16th March, 1926), (both Brest). 974 tons (*on surface*), 1441 tons (*submerged*). Dimensions: 257½ (*p.p.*) × 23 × 17¾ feet. Complement: 51. Machinery: 2 Diesel motors, of Sulzer or Schneider-Carel type, each 1450 H.P. Total 2900 H.P. = 16 kts. Electric drive: 248 "D" type batteries, 1800 H.P. = 10 kts. Radius: 7000 miles at 9 kts. (*on surface*), 105 miles at 5 kts. (*submerged*). Endurance: equal to 30 days' cruising. Guns: **1**—3·9 inch, **2** M.G. AA. Torpedo tubes: **10**—21·7 inch (4 bow and 2 stern submerged; 4 above water, revolving in pairs before and abaft C.T.). 32 torpedoes (24 of 1922 model, 8 of 1919 model) carried by *Caïman, Espadon, Phoque*; 16 by others.

Notes.—All completed 1926-27. Freeboard about 7 feet. Can dive with safety to 100 metres (say, 55 fathoms). *Requin, Caïman, Dauphin, Espadon, Phoque*, all scuttled at Toulon, Nov. 27, 1942.

(All this class modernised, with complete refit of hull and machinery, 1935–37.)

9 Sirene Class.

SIRÈNE. 1927 *Official Photo.*

3 *Simonot* type, built by A. & C. de la Loire, St. Nazaire: ***Naïade*** (Oct. 20, 1925), ***Sirène*** (August 6, 1925), ***Galatée*** (Dec. 18, 1925). Displacement: 548 tons surface, 764 tons submerged. Dimensions: 210 (*p.p.*) × 21 × 14¾ feet. Machinery: 2 sets 2-cycle Sulzer Diesels, B.H.P. 1,300 on *surface*, = 14 kts. 1,000 submerged = 7·5 kts. Complement, 40. (All three reported scuttled at Toulon, Nov. 27, 1942.)

Following particulars apply to all **9**. Complement: 40. 140 to 144 "D" type electric batteries. Speed: 14 kts. on *surface*, 7·5 kts. *submerged*. Radius: *surface*, 2,000 miles at 10 kts.; *submerged*, 90 miles at 5 kts. Endurance equal to 20 days' cruising. Can dive to 45 fathoms. Guns: **1—3** inch AA., **2** M.G. Torpedo tubes (21·7 inch): 7-13 torpedoes carried. Cost stated to be Frs. 8,500,000 each.

ARIANE. 1927 *Official Photo.*

3 *Normand-Fenaux* type, built by C. & A. Augustin Normand, Le Hâvre: ***Ariane*** (August 6, 1925), ***Danae*** (Sept. 11, 1927), ***Eurydice*** (May 31, 1927). Displacement: 576 tons *surface*, 765 tons *submerged*. Dimensions: 216½ (*p.p.*) × 20⅓ × 13½ feet. Machinery: 2 sets 4cycle Diesels, Vickers-Normand type. Electric motors by Schneider et Cie. 1,200 B.H.P. on *surface* = 14 kts. 1,000 *submerged*—7.5 kts. Complement, 40.

Note.—This type is reported to have given great satisfaction in service. *Eurydice* believed scuttled at Toulon, Nov. 27, 1942.

3 *Schneider-Laubeuf* type, built by Schneider et Cie, Chalon-sur-Saône: ***Circé*** (Oct. 29, 1925), ***Calypso*** (Jan. 1926) ****Thétis*** (June 30, 1927). Displacement: 552 tons *surface*, 785 tons *submerged*. Dimensions: 204½ (*pp.*) × 21⅓ × 12¾ feet. Machinery: 2 sets 2-cycle Schneider-Carels Diesels. B.H.P.: 1,250 = 14 kts. H.P.: 1,000 = 7·5 kts. *submerged*. (Two former reported to have been scuttled at Toulon, Nov. 27, 1942.)

Notes.—*Ariane, Calypso, Circé, Naïade, Sirène,* were laid down under 1922-23 Programme; others under Coast Defence Vote of Sept. 30, 1923.

16 Diane Class.

1926 PROGRAMME
****Aréthuse*** (Aug. 8th, 1929) Schneider
Diane (May 13th, 1930) Normand

1927 PROGRAMME
Antiope (Aug. 19th, 1930) } Worms
Amazone (Dec. 28th, 1931) }
Atalante (Aug. 5th, 1930) Schneider

1928 PROGRAMME
****Orphée*** (Nov. 10th, 1931) Normand
Orion (April 21st, 1931).. Loire
Ondine (May 4th, 1931).. Dubigeon

1929 PROGRAMME
La Vestale (May 25th, 1932) } Schneider
La Sultane (Aug. 9th, 1932) }

1930 PROGRAMME
****Minerve*** (Oct. 23, '34) Cherbourg
****Junon*** (Sept. 15th, 1935) Normand
Vénus (April 6th, 1935) Worms
Iris (Sept. 23rd, 1934) Dubigeon

1936 PROGRAMME
Cérès (Dec. 9th, 1938) Worms
Pallas (Aug. 25th, 1938) Normand

JUNON. 1942, *Official.*

1943, *Official.*

Displacements: *Aréthuse, Atalante, La Vestale, La Sultane,* 565/800 tons; *Diane, Antiope, Amazone, Orphée,* 571/809 tons; *Orion, Ondine,* 558/787 tons; *Minerve, Junon, Vénus, Iris,* 597/825 tons; *Cérès, Pallas,* 662/858 tons. Complement: 48. Dimensions: *Aréthuse, Atalante,* 208 × 21 × 13¾ feet; *Orion, Ondine,* 219 × 22 × 15 feet; *Cérès, Pallas,* 221 × 18½ × 15 feet; remainder, 211 × 20 × 13¾ feet. Armament: **1**—3 inch AA. **1** M.G., **8**—21·7 inch tubes in first 8 boats; but **7**—21·7 inch and **2**—15·7 inch in remaining 8 which have latter tubes mounted on either side of a larger tube in after triple group. Machinery: 2 sets Diesels, of Schneider-Carel type in *Aréthuse, Atalante, La Vestale, La Sultane, Cérès, Pallas;* Vickers-Normand in *Diane, Amazone, Antiope, Orphée, Minerve, Junon;* Sulzer in *Orion, Ondine.* B.H.P.: 1,300 to 1,800 = 14 kts. *surface.* Electric motors. H.P.: 1,000 = 9 kts. *submerged.* Radius: 3,000 miles at 10 kts. *surface;* 78 miles at 5 kts. *submerged.*

Notes.—Designs of these submarines are by Normand, Loire-Simonot (*Orion* and *Ondine*) and 1930-36 batch by Ministry of Marine. All are of same general type with minor differences, reflected in appearance, according to builders. *Méduse* sunk at Casablanca, Nov., 1942. *Iris* interned at Barcelona, Nov. 29, 1942.

4 Sloops.

(Classed as *Avisos Coloniaux.*)

La Grandière. 1944, *Marius Bar, Toulon.*

1 *F. et Ch. Gironde:* **DUMONT D'URVILLE** (March 21, 1931).

2 *Ch. Sud-Ouest:* **SAVORGNAN DE BRAZZA** (June 18, 1931), **D'ENTRECASTEAUX** (June 22, 1931).

1 *Ch. Provence:* **LA GRANDIÈRE** (ex-*Ville d'Ys*) (June, 1939).

Displacement: 1,969 tons *standard* (2,600 tons *full load*). Complement: 135 peace, 194 war. Dimensions: 340 × 41⅔ × 14¾ feet. Guns: **3**—5·5 inch, **4**—40 mm. AA., **11**—20 mm. AA.; but *S. de Brazza* has **8**—37 mm. AA., **3**—25 mm. AA., **2**—20 mm. AA., and *D'Entrecasteaux* **4**—37 mm. AA., **6** M.G., as anti-aircraft armament. Stowage for 40 mines. Machinery: 2 sets Sulzer Diesels. 2 shafts. B.H.P.: 3,200 = 15·5 kts. Fuel: 220 tons + 60 tons for use in auxiliary boilers. Radius: 13,000 miles at 8·5 kts., 7,600 at 15 kts.

Notes.—Authorised under 1927, 1928 and 1937 Programmes, respectively. Designed for tropical service, with a special arrangement for circulation of cool air, and auxiliary plant is electrically driven through 3 Diesel groups 125 kws. each and 2 auxiliary petrol groups 22 kws. each. All are fitted as flagships. Hulls, roofs and bridges are protected against bullets and splinters. They have proved most efficient and reliable in service. On trials, *Dumont d'Urville* averaged 17·2 kts. *Sav. de Brazza,* 18·1 kts. Consumption at 10 kts. averages 26·55 lbs. per mile.

6 Aventure Class.

Tonkinois. (Observe new mast.) 1946, *French Navy Official.*

1 *Simons:* **L'AVENTURE** (ex-H.M.S. *Braid,* Nov. 30, 1943).

2 *Robb:* **CROIX DE LORRAINE** (ex-H.M.S. *Strule,* ex-*Glenarm,* March 8, 1943), **LA DÉCOUVERTE** (ex-H.M.S. *Windrush,* June 18, 1943).

2 *Blyth S.B. & D.D. Co.:* **L'ESCARMOUCHE** (ex-H.M.S. *Frome,* June 1, 1943), **LA SURPRISE** (ex-H.M.S. *Torridge,* Aug. 16, 1943).

1 *Smith's Dock Co.:* **TONKINOIS** (ex-H.M.S. *Moyola,* Aug. 27, 1942).

Displacement: *averages* 1,400 tons (2,130 tons *full load*). Dimensions: 301⅓ (*pp.*), 305⅓ (*o.a.*) × 36⅝ × 12 feet. Guns: **2**—4 inch AA., **11**—20 mm. AA., **6** D.C.T. Machinery: Triple expansion. 2 shafts. I.H.P.: 5,500 = 19 kts. Boilers: 2, of 3-drum type. Complement: 140.

Note.—These are all ex-British frigates of "River" type, taken over in 1943-44.

La Surprise. 1946, *French Navy Official.*

Frigates

6 Senegalais Class. (Classed as *Torpilleurs d'Escorte*)

ALGÉRIEN (Nov. 27, 1943), **HOVA** (Jan. 22, 1944), **MAROCAIN** (Jan. 1, 1944), **SENEGALAIS** (Nov. 11, 1943), **SOMALI** (Feb. 12, 1944), **TUNISIEN** (Dec. 17, 1943). Ex-U.S. DE 106–111, built by Dravo Corporation at Wilmington, Del. Acquired in 1944.

SOMALI. 1944, *courtesy M. Henri Le Masson.*

HOVA. 1946, *London Studio, Malta.*

Displacement: 1,300 tons (1,750 tons *full load*). Dimensions: 306 (*o.a.*) × $36\frac{5}{6}$ × $10\frac{2}{3}$ feet. Guns: **3**—3 inch dual purpose, **2**—40 mm. Bofors, **12**—20 mm. Oerlikon. **8** D.C.T. Machinery: Diesel-electric. 2 shafts. B.H.P.: 6,000 = 19 kts. Complement: 185. Radius of action: 11,500 miles at 11 kts., 5,500 at 19 kts.

Corvettes

7 Lobelia Class.

COMMANDANT D'ESTIENNE D'ORVES. 1942, *Official.*

1 *Ailsa S.B. Co.:* **ACONIT** (ex-H.M.S. *Aconite*, March 31, 1941).
1 *Alex. Hall & Co.:* **LOBÉLIA** (ex-H.M.S. *Lobelia*, Feb. 15, 1941).
1 *Hall, Russell & Co.:* **COMMANDANT DETROYAT** (ex-H.M.S. *Coriander*, ex-*Iris*, June 9, 1941).
1 *Harland & Wolff:* **COMMANDANT DROGOU** (ex-H.M.S. *Chrysanthemum*, April 11, 1941).
1 *Charles Hill & Sons:* **COMMANDANT D'ESTIENNE D'ORVES** (ex-H.M.S. *Lotus*, Jan. 17, 1942).
1 *John Lewis & Sons:* **ROSELYS** (ex-H.M.S. *Sundew*, May 28, 1941).
1 *Simons:* **RENONCULE** (ex-H.M.S. *Ranunculus*, June 25, 1941).

Displacement: 925 tons. Dimensions: 190 (*pp.*), 205 (*o.a.*) × 33 × $14\frac{1}{2}$ feet (*max.*). Guns: **1**—4 inch AA., **2**—57 mm. AA., **1**—40 mm. AA., **2**—20 mm. AA., **6** D.C.T. Machinery: Triple expansion. I.H.P.: 2,750 = 15·5 kts. Boilers: 2 cylindrical. Oil fuel: 232 tons. Complement: 85.

Note.—*Lobelia* is employed on fishery protection duties, Newfoundland area, and at present mounts only 1—4 inch, 1—40 mm. AA., 4—20 mm. AA.

Aviation Transport (*Transport d'Hydravions.*)

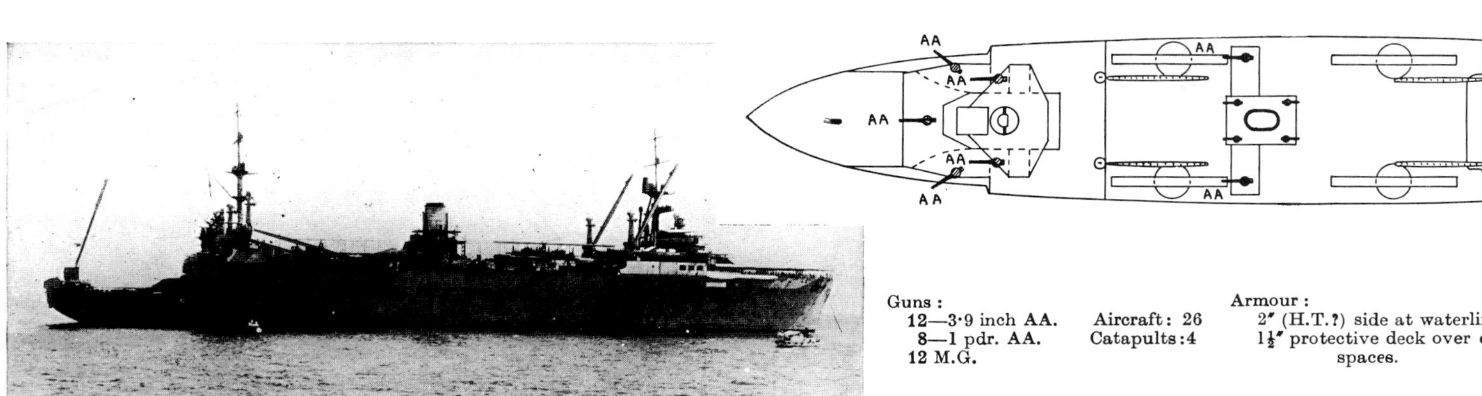

(Undergoing reconstruction, which may alter appearance) 1934, *Nautical Photo Agency* (*added* 1935).

Guns:
12—3·9 inch AA.
8—1 pdr. AA.
12 M.G.

Aircraft: 26
Catapults: 4

Armour:
2" (H.T.?) side at waterline.
$1\frac{1}{2}$" protective deck over engine and boiler spaces.

COMMANDANT TESTE. (F. et C. de la Gironde, Bordeaux, April 12th, 1929.)

Standard displacement: 10,000 tons (about 11,500 tons *deep load*). Length: $512\frac{3}{4}$ feet (*pp.*), 558 feet (*o.a.*). Beam: $71\frac{1}{2}$ feet ($88\frac{1}{2}$ feet, extreme). Draught: $22\frac{1}{4}$ feet. Complement: 686.

Machinery: 2 Schneider-Zoelly geared turbines. 2 shafts. S.H.P. 21,000 = 20·5 kts. 4 Yarrow-Loire boilers (mixed firing). Fuel:—Oil 290, coal 720 tons. Radius of action: 6,000 miles at 10 kts. Trials: Average speed of 21·77 kts. maintained for 3 hours.

Notes.—Authorised under 1926 Programme, ordered in May, 1927, and completed in 1931. Catapults are of Penhoët 3-ton type. There is accommodation for 26 seaplanes in a hangar measuring 275 × $88\frac{1}{2}$ × 23 feet high. Though scuttled in shallow water at Toulon on Nov. 27, 1942, damage was less extensive than in other cases, and ship has been salved and will be refitted, possibly as an escort carrier.

Aircraft Maintenance Ship

BÉARN (April, 1920)

Standard displacement: 22,146 tons; 28,400 tons *full load.*

Dimensions: 576 (*w.l.*), 560 (*pp.*) 599 (*o.a.*) feet × 89 feet × 30½ feet (*max.* draught). (Extreme beam is 115½ feet.) Complement: 651

Guns:

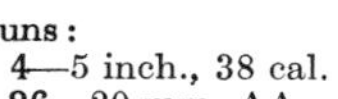

4—5 inch., 38 cal.
26—20 mm. AA.

Armour:

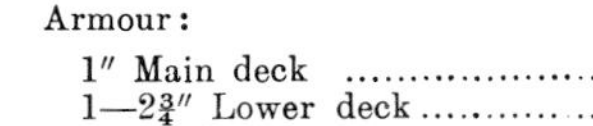

1″ Main deck ....
1—2¾″ Lower deck ....
1″ Flight deck ....

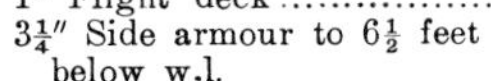

3¼″ Side armour to 6½ feet below w.l.

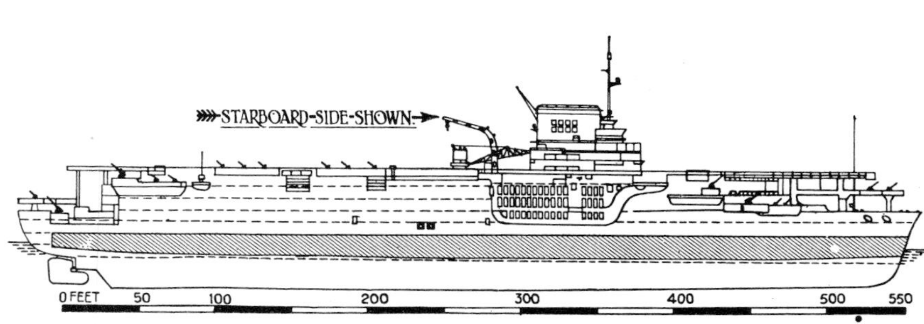

BÉARN. 1945, *French Navy Official.*

Machinery: 2 turbines on inner shafts (for main propulsion) = 22,200 S.H.P. and 2 sets reciprocating engines on outer shafts (for cruising and manœuvring purposes only) = 15,000 I.H.P. Total H.P. with 4 shafts, 37,200 = 21·5 kts. (reached on trials with 40,000 H.P.). 12 Du Temple-Normand small tube boilers. Oil fuel: 4,500 tons. Radius: 6,000 miles at 10 kts.

Notes.—Laid down in Jan. 1914, by F. et Ch. de la Mediterranée, as a battleship. Redesigned as an aircraft carrier, and conversion begun at La Seyne in August, 1923. Completed in May, 1927. Refitted by builders, 1935. Rebuilt in U.S.A., 1944–45, and reclassified as an aircraft transport.

BÉARN. 1945, *courtesy M Henri Le Masson.*

Minesweepers (*Aviso-Dragueurs*)

7 Chevreuil Class (*Series Coloniale*).

ANNAMITE. 1944, *courtesy M. Henri Le Masson.*

4 *Lorient Dockyard:* **ANNAMITE, CHEVREUIL, GAZELLE** (all three June 17, 1939), **BISSON** (March 6, 1946).

2 *Ch. Dubigeon:* **COMMANDANT AMIOT D'INVILLE, COMMANDANT DE PIMODAN** (both 1941).

1 *F. et Ch. de la Gironde:* **COMMANDANT DUCUING** (building).

Standard displacement: 647 tons (900 tons *full load*). Dimensions: 256 × 27¾ × 7¾ feet. Guns: *Annamite* and *Gazelle*: **2**—3·5 inch, **1**—40 mm. AA., **6**—20 mm. AA., **6** D.C.T.; *Chevreuil*, **2**—3·9 inch AA., **8**—20 mm. AA., **6** D.C.T.; others, **2**—4·1 inch, **2**—40 mm. AA., **4**—20 mm. AA., **6** D.C.T. Machinery: 2 sets Sulzer Diesels. 2 shafts. B.H.P.: 4,000 = 20 kts. Radius: 10,000 miles at 9 kts. Complement: 100. Fuel 100 tons.

Notes.—*Chevreuil* and *Gazelle* built under 1935 Programme, *Annamite* under that for 1937.

CHEVREUIL. 1946, *French Navy Official.*

Minesweepers

9 Elan Class.

La Gracieuse. 1946, *French Navy Official.*

2 *Lorient Dockyard:* **ÉLAN** (July 27, 1938), **LA MOQUEUSE** (Jan. 21, 1940).

3 *At. et Ch. de France:* **LA BOUDEUSE** (Sept. 1939), **COMMANDANT BORY** (Jan. 26, 1939), **COMMANDANT DELAGE** (Feb. 25, 1939).

3 *Ch. Dubigeon:* **LA CAPRICIEUSE** (April 19, 1939), **COMMANDANT DOMINÉ** (ex-*La Rieuse*, May 2, 1939), **COMMANDANT DUBOC** (Jan. 16, 1938).

1 *Ch. et At. de Provence:* **LA GRACIEUSE** (Nov. 30, 1939).

Standard displacement: 630 tons (890 tons *full load*). Dimensions: $256 \times 27\frac{3}{4} \times 7\frac{3}{4}$ feet. Guns: **2**—3·5 inch AA., **1**—40 mm. AA., **6**—20 mm. AA., 6 D.C.T. (*Cdt. Dominé, Cdt. Duboc* and *La Moqueuse* each have **2**—3·9 inch AA., **8**—20 mm. AA., 6 D.C.T.). Machinery: 2 sets Sulzer Diesels. 2 shafts. B.H.P.: 4,000=20 kts. Fuel: 100 tons.

Notes.—*Elan* built under 1934 Programme, *Bory, Delage* and *Duboc* under that for 1936; others, 1937.

La Capricieuse. 1946, *London Studio.*

30 ex-American type.

D 301 (ex-*YMS* 169)
311 („ „ 34)
312 („ „ 63)
313 („ „ 58)
314 („ „ 226)
315 („ „ 28)
316 („ „ 37)
317 („ „ 13, June 13, 1942)
318 („ „ 78)
321 („ „ 36)
322 („ „ 16)
323 („ „ 62)
324 („ „ 43)
325 („ „ 82)
326 („ „ 83)

D 327 (ex-*YMS* 20, Nov. 1, 1941)
331 („ „ 55)
332 („ „ 18)
333 („ „ 27)
334 („ „ 3)
335 („ „ 29, April 10, 1942)
336 („ „ 64)
337 („ „ 69)
338 („ „ 15)
351 (ex-*D* 201, ex-*YMS* 23)
352 („ 211, „ „ 26)
353 („ 212, „ „ 31)
354 („ 271, „ „ 207)
355 („ 272, „ „ 208)
356 („ 273, „ „ 227)

Built of wood. Displacement: 280 tons. Dimensions: $134\frac{1}{2} \times 24\frac{1}{4} \times 12$ feet. Guns: **1**—3 inch, d.p., **2**—20 mm. AA., 2 M.G. Machinery: 2 sets Diesels. B.H.P.: 1,000=15 kts. All acquired in 1944.

1946, *French Navy Official.*

22 ex-British type.

1943, *Official*

D 341 (ex-*MMS* 1069)
342 („ „ 1054)
D 343 (ex-*MMS* 1065)
344 („ „ 1055)
D 345 (ex-*MMS* 1070)
346 („ „ 1056)

Built of wood. Displacement: 360 tons. Dimensions: 126 (*pp.*), $139\frac{5}{6}$ (*o.a.*) $\times 26 \times 10\frac{1}{2}$ feet (*mean*), $12\frac{1}{2}$ feet (*max.*). Guns: **2**—20 mm. AA., etc. Machinery: Diesel. B.H.P. 500 = 10·5 kts.

Minesweepers.

D 361 (ex-*D* 241, ex-*MMS* 21)
362 („ 242, „ „ 184)
363 („ 251, „ „ 47)
364 („ 252, „ „ 9)

D 365 (ex-*D* 261, ex-*MMS* 116)
366 („ 262, „ „ 118)
367 („ 291, „ „ 133)
368 („ 292, „ „ 134)

D 371 (ex-*MMS* 221)
372 („ „ 202)
373 („ „ 220)

D 374 (ex-*MMS* 91)
375 („ „ 75)
376 („ „ 204)

D 377 (ex-*MMS* 49)
378 („ „ 13)

Built of wood. Displacement: 240 tons. Dimensions: 105 (*pp.*), 119 (*o.a.*) × 13 × — feet. Guns: 2—20 mm. AA., etc. Machinery: Diesel. B.H.P.: 500 = 10 kts. Complement: 20.

1943, *Central Press*

15 ex-German type.

M 9, 24, 28, 38, 85. Displacement: 600 tons. Dimensions: 228¾ × 28¼ × 9 feet. Guns: 2—4·1 inch, 2—37 mm. AA., 8—20 mm. AA. Machinery: Triple expansion. 2 shafts. I.H.P. 3,200 = 18·5 kts. Boilers: 2 Wagner. Complement: 100.

M 275, 277, 404, 408, 432, 434, 442, 452, 454, 476. Displacement: 550 tons. Dimensions: 205 × 28 × 9 feet. Guns: 1—4·1 inch, 1—37 mm. AA., 6—20 mm. AA., 2 M.G. Machinery: Triple expansion, with exhaust turbine. 2 shafts. I.H.P. 1,600 to 2,200 = 17 kts. Boilers: 2 Schulz. Coal: 142 tons.

Coastal Craft

Motor Torpedo Boats.
(*Vedettes Torpilleurs à Moteurs*)

V 121 1946, *courtesy M. Henri Le Masson.*

2 *German type:* **V 120, 121** (ex-*S* 300, 301). Built at Meulan. Displacement: 65 tons. Dimensions: 99¾ × 19 × 5½ feet. Guns: 12 M.G. B.H.P.: 3,600=35 kts.

2 *German type:* **V 130, 131** (ex-*S* 21, 22). Displacement: 30 tons. Length: 93 feet (*o.a.*). Armament: 7 M.G. Machinery: Diesel. B.H.P.: 2,600=39 kts. Complement: 11.

1 *French type:* **VTB 13** (1939). Displacement: 28 tons. 2 tubes. B.H.P.; 2,200=45 kts. (Photo in Addenda.)

4 *German type:* **VR 41–44.** Displacement: 24 tons. Dimensions: 67 × 15 × 6¼ feet. Guns: 2—20 mm. AA. Speed: 22 kts. (Rhine flotilla.)

VR 41 1946, *courtesy M. Henri Le Masson.*

1945, *French Navy Official.*

Motor Launches.
4 "Fairmile" B Type.

1946, *courtesy John Bartlett, Esq.*

Ved. 101 (ex-*ML* 244), **Ved. 102** (ex-*ML* 271), **Ved. 103** (ex-*ML* 266), **Ved. 104** (ex-*ML* 302). Displacement: 82 tons. Dimensions: 112 × 18 × 9 feet. Guns: 1—47 mm., 1—20 mm. AA., 4 M.G., D.C. Machinery: 2 Hall Scott motors. B.H.P.: 1,290=19 kts. Complement: 19.

Coastal Craft

Submarine Chasers

30 Carabinier Class.

L'EFFRONTÉ. 1946, *courtesy M. Henri Le Masson.*

L'Attentif (ex-*PC* 551)
Carabinier (ex-*PC* 556, April 24, 1943)
Cavalier (ex-*PC* 627)
Cimeterre (ex-*PC* 1250)
Coutelas (ex-*PC* 1560, Feb. 4, 1944)
Dague (ex-*PC* 1561)
Dragon (ex-*PC* 557)
L'Effronté (ex-*PC* 481)
L'Emporté (ex-*PC* 480, Oct. 25, 1941)
L'Eveillé (ex-*PC* 471)
Fantassin (ex-*PC* 621)
Franc Tireur (ex-*PC* 546)
Goumier (ex-*PC* 545)
Grenadier (ex-*PC* 625)
Hussard (ex-*PC* 1235, April 3, 1943)
L'Indiscret (ex-*PC* 474)
Javelot (ex-*PC* 1562, March 4, 1944)
Lancier (ex-*PC* 1227)
Lansquenet (ex-*PC* 626)
Legionnaire (ex-*PC* 1226)
Mameluck (ex-*PC* 562)
Le Resolu (ex-*PC* 475)
Pique (ex-*PC* 1249)
Le Rusé (ex-*PC* 472)
Sabre (ex-*PC* 1248)
Spahi (ex-*PC* 591)
Tirailleur (ex-*PC* 542)
Le Vigilant (ex-*PC* 550)
Le Volontaire (ex-*PC* 543)
Voltigeur (ex-*PC* 559)

Steel. Acquired in 1944. Displacement: 280 tons (430 tons *full load*). Dimensions: 170 (*w.l.*), $173\frac{2}{3}$ (*o.a.*) × 23 × $6\frac{1}{2}$ feet. Guns: **1**—3 inch d.p., **1**—40 mm. AA., **5**—20 mm. AA., **6** D.C.T. Machinery: Diesel. 2 shafts. B.H.P.: 2,880=20 kts. Fuel: 60 tons. Complement: 59.

49 Wooden Type.

CH 93. 1946, *London Studio.*

CH 5 (ex-*SC* 1359)
CH 6 (ex-*SC* 1331)
CH 51 (ex-*SC* 1336)
CH 52 (ex-*SC* 1335)
CH 61 (ex-*SC* 1345)
CH 62 (ex-*SC* 1344)
CH 71 (ex-*SC* 1337)
CH 72 (ex-*SC* 1346)
CH 81 (ex-*SC* 516, Oct. 11, 1941)
CH 82 (ex-*SC* 517, Oct. 11, 1941)
CH 83 (ex-*SC* 519)
CH 84 (ex-*SC* 529)
CH 85 (ex-*SC* 507)
CH 91 (ex-*SC* 649, April 18, 1942)
CH 92 (ex-*SC* 697)
CH 93 (ex-*SC* 639)
CH 94 (ex-*SC* 977)
CH 95 (ex-*SC* 508)
CH 96 (ex-*SC* 497)
CH 101 (ex-*SC* 524)
CH 102 (ex-*SC* 525)
CH 103 (ex-*SC* 532)
CH 104 (ex-*SC* 533)
CH 105 (ex-*SC* 676)
CH 106 (ex-*SC* 690)
CH 107 (ex-*SC* 693)
CH 111 (ex-*SC* 522)
CH 112 (ex-*SC* 503, March 14, 1942)
CH 113 (ex-*SC* 506)
CH 114 (ex-*SC* 526)
CH 115 (ex-*SC* 530)
CH 121 (ex-*SC* 515, Sept. 20, 1942)
CH 122 (ex-*SC* 534)
CH 123 (ex-*SC* 1029, Aug. 26, 1942)
CH 124 (ex-*SC* 771)
CH 125 (ex-*SC* 1043)
CH 126 (ex-*SC* 1044)
CH 131 (ex-*SC* 692)
CH 132 (ex-*SC* 691)
CH 133 (ex-*SC* 695)
CH 134 (ex-*SC* 666)
CH 135 (ex-*SC* 651)
CH 136 (ex-*SC* 1030, Aug. 26, 1942)
CH 141 (ex-*SC* 770)
CH 142 (ex-*SC* 498)
CH 143 (ex-*SC* 535)
CH 144 (ex-*SC* 655)
CH 145 (ex-*SC* 978)
CH 146 (ex-*SC* 979)

Wood. Acquired 1944. Displacement: 95 tons (138 tons *full load*). Dimensions: $107\frac{1}{2}$ (*w.l.*), $110\frac{5}{6}$ (*o.a.*) × 17 × $6\frac{1}{2}$ feet. Guns: **1**—40 mm. AA., **3**—20 mm. AA. Numerous D.C. Machinery: 2 G.M. Diesels. 2 shafts. B.H.P.: 800 = 15 kts. Complement: 25.

Coastal Craft

CH 42. (CH 21 differs from others, having no funnel.) 1941, *Official.*

3 *Ch. de Normandie* (*Fécamp*): **CH 41** (**AUDIERNE**) (May 1, 1939), **CH 42** (**LARMOR**), **CH 43** (**LAVANDOU**) (all 1939). Built under 1937 Programme. Wood. Displacement: 126 tons. Dimensions: 136 × 17 × $8\frac{1}{4}$ feet. Guns: 1—3 inch. M.A.N. Diesel engines. 2 shafts. B.H.P.: 1,100 = 16 kts.

4 *Ch. Worms:* **CH 13** (**CALAIS**), **CH 14** (**DIELETTE**), **CH 15** (**PAIMPOL**) (1939), **CH 16.**

4 *F. et C. de la Mediterranée:* **CH 10** (**BAYONNE**), **CH 11** (**BOULOGNE**), **CH 12** (**BENODET**) (1939), **CH 21** (1940). All ordered under 1937 Programme. Steel. Displacement: 107 tons. Dimensions: $121\frac{1}{3}$ × $16\frac{1}{2}$ × $6\frac{1}{2}$ feet. Guns: **1**—3 inch, etc. (*CH* 21 has **1**—3 inch, **4**—20 mm. AA.) M.A.N. Diesels. 2 shafts. B.H.P.: 1,100 = 16 kts.

Note.—Above craft were specially designed for employment as seaplane tenders when required. During war some were further distinguished by names, as given in parentheses. Names borne by certain other French-manned motor launches, since returned to Royal Navy, were *St. Alain* (ML 247), *St. Guenole* (245), *St. Ronan* (123), and *St. Yves* (246).

1944, *French Navy Official.*

VP 1-16, 21-23, 31, 32 (ex-*HDML* 1249, 1138, 1223, 1240, 1166, 1228, 1133, 1132, 1127, 1250, 1152, 1225, 1142, 1136, 1144, 1139, 1072, 1141, 1231, 1164, 1143), **41, 42, 51, 52, 61-63** (former numbers not reported). Displacement: 46 tons. Dimensions: 72 (*o.a.*) × $15\frac{1}{6}$ × $4\frac{1}{3}$ feet (*mean*). Guns: **1**—2 pdr., **1**—20 mm. AA. Machinery: Diesel. B.H.P.: 260 = 11 kts.

Note.—*VP* 31, 32 were known during war as *Baalbeck* and *Palmyre.*

River Gunboat

1934, *Courtesy of Mons. H. Le Masson.*

TOURANE (Saigon, 1933). Displacement: 95 tons (*Standard*). Complement: 16. Dimensions: $114\frac{3}{4}$ × $17\frac{1}{2}$ × 3 feet. Guns: **1**—3 inch Howitzer (Army pattern), **1**—37 mm., 2 M.G. Machinery: 2 Diesels. H.P.: 250 = 10 kts. Radius: 560 miles at 10 kts.

Note.—River gunboats *Francis-Garnier* and *Balny* have been turned over to Chinese Navy.

Fleet Repair Ship.

Photo 1932, *Official.*

JULES VERNE (Lorient, Feb. 3, 1931). Displacement: 4,347 tons. Complement: 259. Dimensions: 377½ (*pp.*), 400¼ (*o.a.*) × 56½ × 19 feet. Guns: 4—3·5 inch AA., 4—37 mm. AA., 9 M.G. 2 sets Sulzer-Diesels. 2 shafts. B.H.P.: 7,000 = 16 kts. Previously served as submarine depot ship.

Trawlers (*Chalutiers-Patrouilleurs*).

1944, *Marius Bar.*

L'AJACCIENNE (ex-*Mildenhall*, 1936), **LA SÉTOISE** (ex-*Oriental Star*, 1934), **LA TOULONNAISE** (ex-*Hampshire*, 1934). Displacement: 590 to 640 tons. Dimensions: 178¾ × 27½ × 16½ feet. Guns: 1—4 inch, 5—20 mm. AA., 2 M.G. I.H.P.: 800 = 10 kts. Coal: 205 tons. Complement: 35. All acquired from Royal Navy early in 1940.

Seaplane Tender.

COMMANDANT GIRAUD (ex-German *Immelmann*). Particulars wanted.

Note.—Named after a brilliant naval officer who lost his life when destroyer *Bison* was sunk, May 3, 1940.

Surveying Vessels.

Usually commissioned for the six months April—November, and reduced to Reserve during other six months of the year.

BEAUTEMPS-BEAUPRÉ (ex-*Sans Souci*, 1940), **LAPÉROUSE** (ex-*Sans Peur*, 1940). Built by Penhoët and At. et Ch. de la Loire, respectively. Displacement: 1,372 tons. Dimensions: 311⅔ × 38½ × 10½ feet. Guns: 2—4·1 inch, 4—40 mm. AA., 4—20 mm. AA. Machinery: Sulzer Diesels. Speed: 16 kts.

Six ex-German vessels of trawler type have been fitted for surveying, and named: **ALIDADE, ASTROLABE, BOUSSOLE, ESTAFETTE, SENTINELLE, SEXTANT.**

1944, *French Navy Official.*

AMIRAL MOUCHEZ (Aug. 3, 1936). Laid down at Cherbourg, Jan., 1935. Displacement: 719 tons. Dimensions: 203½ × 33¾ × 11 feet. Guns: 2—3.9 inch, 4—20 mm. Machinery: Sulzer Diesel. B.H.P.: 800 = 12 kts. Complement: 81.

INGENIEUR-HYDROGRAPHE NICOLAS (ex-German *VP* 206). Particulars wanted.

Target Ship

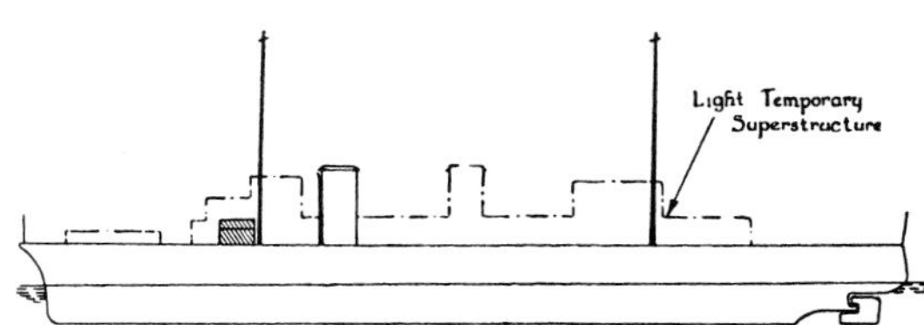

IMPASSIBLE (Lorient, June 17, 1939). Displacement: 2,450 tons. Dimensions: 328 × 39⅓ × 13 feet. S.H.P.: 10,000 = 20 kts. Ordered, Feb., 1937, under 1936 Programme, laid down, May 23, 1938, and completed May, 1940. Designed to be controlled by wireless. Complement, 46.

Submarine Depot Ship.

1930, *Photo, courtesy of Ministry of Marine.*

POLLUX (ex-*Ilya Murometz*, 1915). Built by Swan Hunter as an icebreaker; converted into a minelayer in 1928-29, and now used as a depot ship. Displacement: 2,461 tons. Dimensions: 260 (*pp.*), 211 (*o.a*) × 50½ × 20 feet. Guns: 4—3·9 inch, 2—37 mm. AA. Machinery: Triple expansion. 2 shafts. I.H.P. 4,000 = 14 kts. Boilers: 6 cylindrical. Coal: 367 tons. Complement: 162.

Oilers (*Transports Pétroliers*).

DURANCE (ex-Japanese *Hoei Maru*). Displacement: 1,500 tons. Particulars wanted.

CHARENTE. (Sister ships differ slightly.) 1946, *French Navy Official.*

CHARENTE (1940), **BAISE, MAYENNE.** All ordered from Ch. Worms, Le Trait, under 1938 Programme. Displacement: 4,220 tons; deadweight, 7,400 tons. Dimensions: 433 × 52½ × 20¾ feet. Guns: 2—3·9 inch. Machinery: Parsons geared turbines. S.H.P. 5,200 = 15 kts. Radius: 10,000 miles at 13 kts. Rated as *Ravitailleurs d'Escadre.*

LAC NOIR (ex-U.S.S. *Guyandot*, ex-*Veedol No.* 2, 1930), **LAC PAVIN** (ex-U.S.S. *Aroostook*, ex-*Esso Delivery No.* 11, 1938). Displacement: 3,570 tons (*full load*). Dimensions: 251⅔ × 43½ × — feet. Guns: 1—3 inch AA., 4—20 mm. AA. Machinery: Diesel-electric. H.P.: 1,360 = 9·5 kts. Formerly rated as Petrol Carriers. Acquired Jan. 1945.

ELORN (VAR similar). *Added* 1944, *Marius Bar.*

VAR (1931), **ELORN** (1930). Both built by Deutsche Werft A.G., Hamburg, on War Reparations account.

LE MÉKONG. *Added* 1944, *Marius Bar.*

LE MÉKONG, by Ch. & At. de St. Nazaire (Penhoët) (Aug. 31, 1928). Displacement: 5,482 tons *standard*; 15,150 tons *full load.* Dimensions: 436¼ (*pp.*), 456 (*o.a.*) × 61¾ × 26 feet *mean* draught. Guns: 2—3·9 inch, 2—1 pdr. 2 sets Burmeister & Wain Diesel engines. B.H.P.: 4,850 = 13·5 kts. (6,000 on trials). Capacity of tanks: 33,900 cubic metres. Deadweight: 9,600 tons, of which oil fuel absorbs 9,000; distilled water, 500; lubricating oil, 100. Complement: 76.

Oilers—*continued.*

DROME. 1921 *Photo, H. Freund.*

DROME (ex-*Aube*), (July, 1920), built by Lorient D.Y. 1,055 tons. Complement, 70. Dimensions: 242¾ × 38 × 15¾ feet. Guns: 2—3 inch AA. Machinery: Breguet turbines. S.H.P.: 1,000 = 10 kts. Radius: 1,580 miles at 10 kts. Capacity for 1,500 tons of oil.

Coastal Oilers.

LAC CHAMBON (ex-*Anticline*), **LAC TCHAD** (ex-*Syncline*), **LAC TONLE-SAP** (ex-*Pumper*). Ex-American fuel oil barges. Displacement: 2,670 tons (*full load*). Guns: 3—20 mm. AA. Machinery: Diesel. B.H.P.: 1,150 = 11 kts. Acquired Dec. 1944–March 1945.

Admiralty Yacht.

1945, *courtesy M. Henri Le Masson.*

GIRUNDIA II (ex-*Eileen*, ex-*Doris*, 1910). Built at Clydebank. Displacement: 1,200 tons. Dimensions: 231 × 31 × — feet. Guns: 1—3 inch, 2—20 mm. AA. Machinery: Triple expansion. 2 shafts. I.H.P. 1,600 = 14 kts. Oil fuel.

(This ship is listed for disposal.)

Transports.

1946, *French Navy Official.*

ILE D'OLERON (ex-*München*, ex-*Mur*, 1939). Displacement: 3,300 tons. Dimensions: 350 × 50 × — feet. Machinery: Diesel. B.H.P.: 4,500. (Used as hospital ship.)

ALPHÉE (ex-yacht). 900 tons.

ETEL (ex-*Sperber*, ex-*Bonn*, 1922). Displacement: 2,000 tons. Dimensions: 216 × 32½ × — feet. Machinery: Triple expansion.

Boom Defence Vessels.

ARAIGNÉE (ex-*Hackberry*, ex-*Maple*, March 6, 1941), **SCORPION** (ex-*Yew*, Sept. 1941), **TARENTULE** (ex-*Pepperwood*, ex-*Walnut*, Aug. 25, 1941). Displacement: 500 tons (700 tons *full load*). Dimensions: 146 (*w.l.*), 163 (*o.a.*) × 30½ × 11⅝ feet. Guns: 1—3 inch AA., some M.G. Machinery: Diesel-electric. H.P.: 800 = 12 kts. Complement: 39.

TARANTULE — 1946, *J. W. Kennedy, Esq.*

Fleet Tugs.

Most of the following have reciprocating engines:

Ex-**YT 458, 459** (1943). Transferred from U.S. Navy, 1944. Particulars wanted.

BUFFLE (May 4, 1939). Laid down 1936 by A. & C. de Bretagne. Displacement: 1,115 tons. Complement: 32. Dimensions: 167⅓ × 33 × — feet. Machinery: 2 sets Triple expansion. I.H.P.: 2,000 = 12 kts.

LOCMINE. — 1943, *Official.*

ACTIF, APPLIQUÉ, CÉPET, COTENTIN, LOCMINE (ex-*Attentif*), **TÉBESSA.** All laid down 1937-38, *Actif* by Ch. de la Loire, Nantes, *Tébessa* by F. & C. de la Méditerranée, La Seyne, *Cépet* and *Cotentin* by Ch. Dubigeon, Nantes, others by F. & C. de la Gironde, Bordeaux. Displacement: 672 tons. Dimensions: 114¾ × 27¾ × — feet. Machinery: Triple expansion. I.H.P.: 1,000 = 11 kts.

FORT (1933). Displacement: 600 tons. H.P.: 1,000 = 13 kts.

INFATIGABLE (ex-*Polangen*), **IMPLACABLE** (ex-*Fohn II*). I.H.P. 1,200.

ACHARNÉ (ex-*Gigant*), **IMBATTABLE** (ex-*Nesserland*), **INTRAITABLE** (ex-*Nordergrunde*). I.H.P. 1,000.

HIPPOPOTAME (1918), **MAMMOUTH** (1918), **MASTODONTE** (1919). Displacement: 954 tons. I.H.P.: 1,800 = 12 kts.

PINGOUIN (1917). Displacement: 700 tons. I.H.P.: 700 = 10 kts.

Fleet Tugs—*continued.*

RAMIER (1917). Displacement: 685 tons. I.H.P.: 750 = 10 kts.

NESSUS (1913). Displacement: 590 tons. I.H.P.: 1,500 = 12 kts.

TAUREAU (ex-*Albatros*, ex-*Zwarte Zee*, 1903). 615 tons *gross*. Dimensions: 164½ × 30 × — feet. I.H.P. 1,600.

ELEPHANT (ex-*Bär*). Displacement: 1,182 tons. I.H.P. 2,000 = 12 kts.

HUELGOAT (ex-*Tegeler Platte*). Displacement: 600 tons. I.H.P. 1,000.

SAMSON. Displacement: 660 tons. I.H.P. 1,000.

TOURTERELLE. Displacement: 650 tons. I.H.P. 1,000.

Others:

HALEUR 1,000 H.P.

PADARAN, **TULEAR**, **VARELLA** } 600 H.P.

Sailing Vessels.

(Used for training purposes)

BELLE POULE — 1942, *Official.*

LA BELLE-POULE, L'ÉTOILE. Built by Chantiers de Normandie (Fécamp), 1932. Displacement: 227 tons. Dimensions: 128 (*o.a.*) × 23⅜ × 11¾ feet. Accommodation for 3 officers, 30 cadets, 5 petty officers, 12 seamen. Machinery: Sulzer-Diesels. B.H.P.: 120 = 6 kts.

Two small transports, **FORFAIT** and **HAMELIN**, are being brought back into Navy, though former has lately been serving with mercantile marine.

Two additional sail training vessels for boys are named **NOTRE DAME D'ETEL** and **PREMIER MAITRE LE GOFF.**

GERMANY

Uniforms.

INSIGNIA OF RANK ON SLEEVES

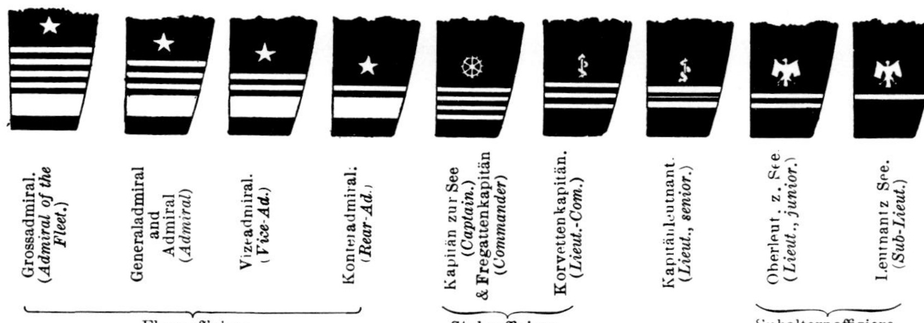

Flaggoffiziere. Stabsoffiziere. Subalternoffiziere.

NOTE.—In above sketch, a *star* should replace devices which appear in the 5 junior ranks.

Uniforms and distinguishing marks of rank are the same for officers of all branches of the service; but in place of the star on the sleeve, which distinguishes the military branch, there is worn by:

Engineer Officers, a pinion wheel
Medical Officers, the rod of Æsculapius
Accountant Officers, the winged staff of Hermes
} As in sketches above.

The difference between a *Kapitän zur See* and a *Fregattenkapitän* is indicated by stars on the shoulder straps.

Kommodores wear the same sleeve stripes as a *Kapitän zur See*, but with the cords and shoulder bands of a Flag Officer.

Flags.

ENSIGN

NATIONAL FLAG AND JACK

STATE SERVICE FLAG (Fleet Auxiliaries)

NATIONAL FLAG FOR MERCHANT SHIPS COMMANDED BY NAVAL RESERVE OFFICERS

ADMIRAL

VICE ADMIRAL

REAR ADMIRAL

FÜHRER'S STANDARD

C-IN-C. OF NAVY

Black *White* *Yellow* *Red*

(a) COMMODORE WHEN FLOWN FROM MAIN MAST
(b) SENIOR OFFICER WHEN FLOWN FROM UPP' SIGNAL YARD

S. O. CDG. MINESWEEPING DESTROYER OR SUBMARINE FLOTILLAS

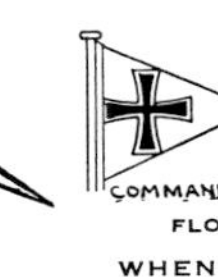

COMMANDER OF A FLOTILLA WHEN FLOWN FROM MAIN MAST, BUT LEADER'S PENNANT WHEN FLOWN FROM UPPER SIGNAL YARD

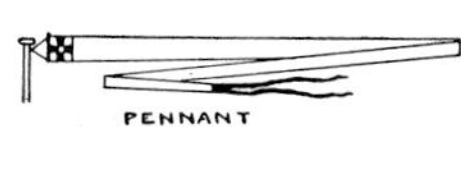

PENNANT

Personnel.

Total personnel, 1938, 75,000 officers and men. (Since increased)

Colour of Ships.

Light Grey, *except* Sail Training Ships, which are white with yellow superstructures.

Mercantile Marine.

(From "Lloyd's Register," 1939 figures.)
2,466 vessels of 4,492,708 gross tonnage.

Naval Guns.

Calibre.	Usual Naval Designation.	Length in cals.	Date of Model.	Weight of Gun.	Weight of A.P. shot.	Initial Velocity.	*Maximum* penetration, direct impact against K.C. at 9000 yds.	6000 yds.	3000 yds.	Danger space against average ships at 10,000 yds.	5000 yds.	3000 yds.	*Approximate* Muzzle Energy.
inch.	c/m.			tons.	lbs.	foot-secs.	in.	in.	in.	yards	yards.	yards.	foot tons.
15	*38·1*	...	'36	...		...	...	...	...	...	...	...	...
11	*28*		'28		670								
11	*28*	40	'01	32·2	661·4	2756	6	10	14	150	450	740	31,600
8	*20.3*												
5·9	*15*	50	...	5·5		3084	...	...	...	...	...	...	6,690
5.9	*15*	45	'09	5	101·4	2920	...	...	5	...	200	420	5,990
5	*12.7*												
4·1	*10·5*	45	'16	...	38·2	...	...	...	...	...	...	...	...
4·1	*10·5*	50	'28										
4·1	*10·5*	60	A.A.										
3·5	*90*	50	A.A.										

Brass cartridge cases to all guns.

11 inch, 40 cal., M. '01 in *Schlesien* and *Schleswig-Holstein*.

Lesser guns: 3·4 inch (88 m/m) firing 22 lb. projectiles in modern and 15 lb. in old models.

A.A. guns: 4·1 inch, 3·5 inch on H.A. mounts ("Flak").

Projectiles: Guns of 11 inch and over fire A.P., Ersatz A.P., H.E., and common shell.

All models have the recoil utilized to return the gun to firing position for pieces over 5.9 inch. In 5.9 in. springs are employed. German guns have a lower muzzle pressure than normally obtains.

Torpedoes.

21 inch (reported to be of electric "trackless" type) is in general use except for aircraft, which carry 18 inch.

TIRPITZ.

GNEISENAU
SCHARNHORST.

LÜTZOW.
(Now has cinder screen to funnel.)

ADMIRAL SCHEER.

Silhouettes

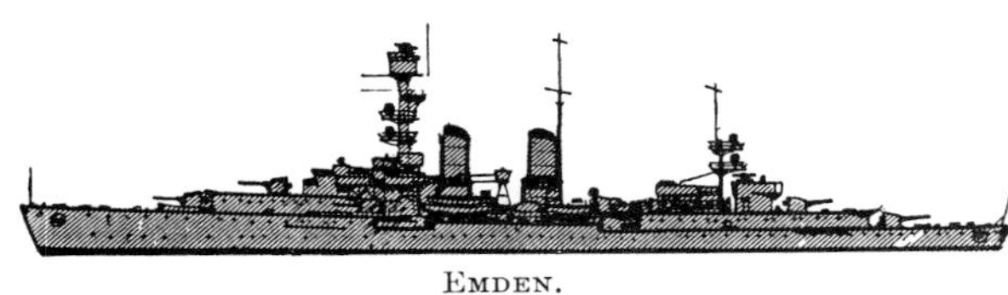
Emden.

Admiral Hipper.

Schlesien.
Schleswig-Holstein.

Nürnberg.
(Mizzenmast since added and funnel modified.)

Prinz Eugen

Leipzig
(Mainmast now taller and a different type of crane fitted.)

T 1—30.

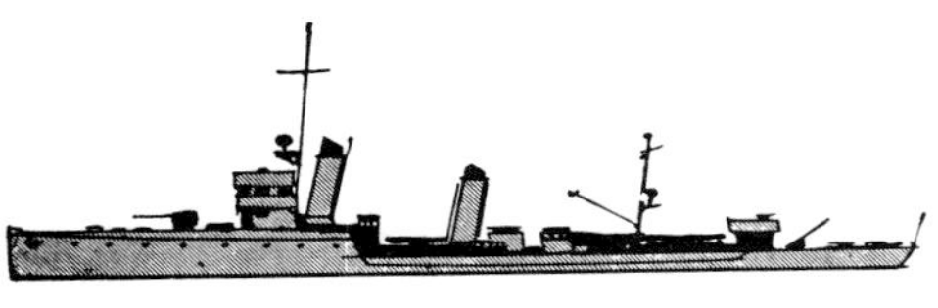
T 107, 108, 110, 111.
(T 123 similar but no Torpedo Tubes.)

C. van Bevern.

T 196.

E. Jungmann *class*.

Wolf *Class.*
(Möwe *Class* as part sketch.)

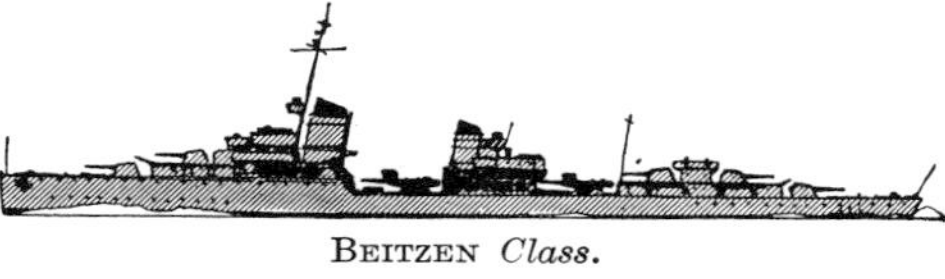
Beitzen *Class.*

K. Galster.

Z 23—39.

Hai, F 1, F 2, F 4, F 5, F 7—10

Erwin Wassner.

Tanga.

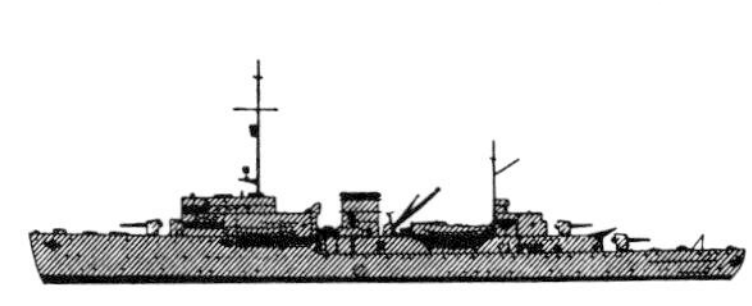
Saar.

Tsingtau.

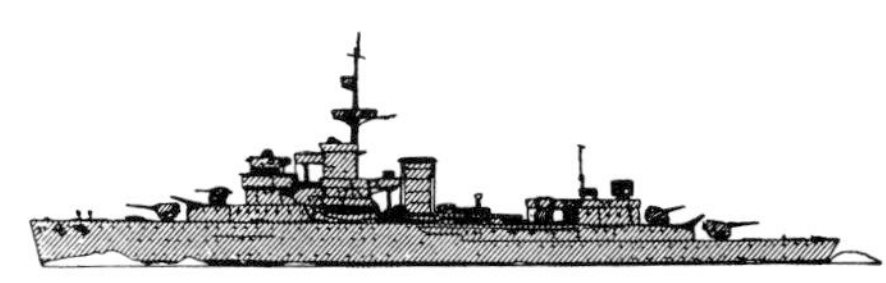
Brummer.

Grille.

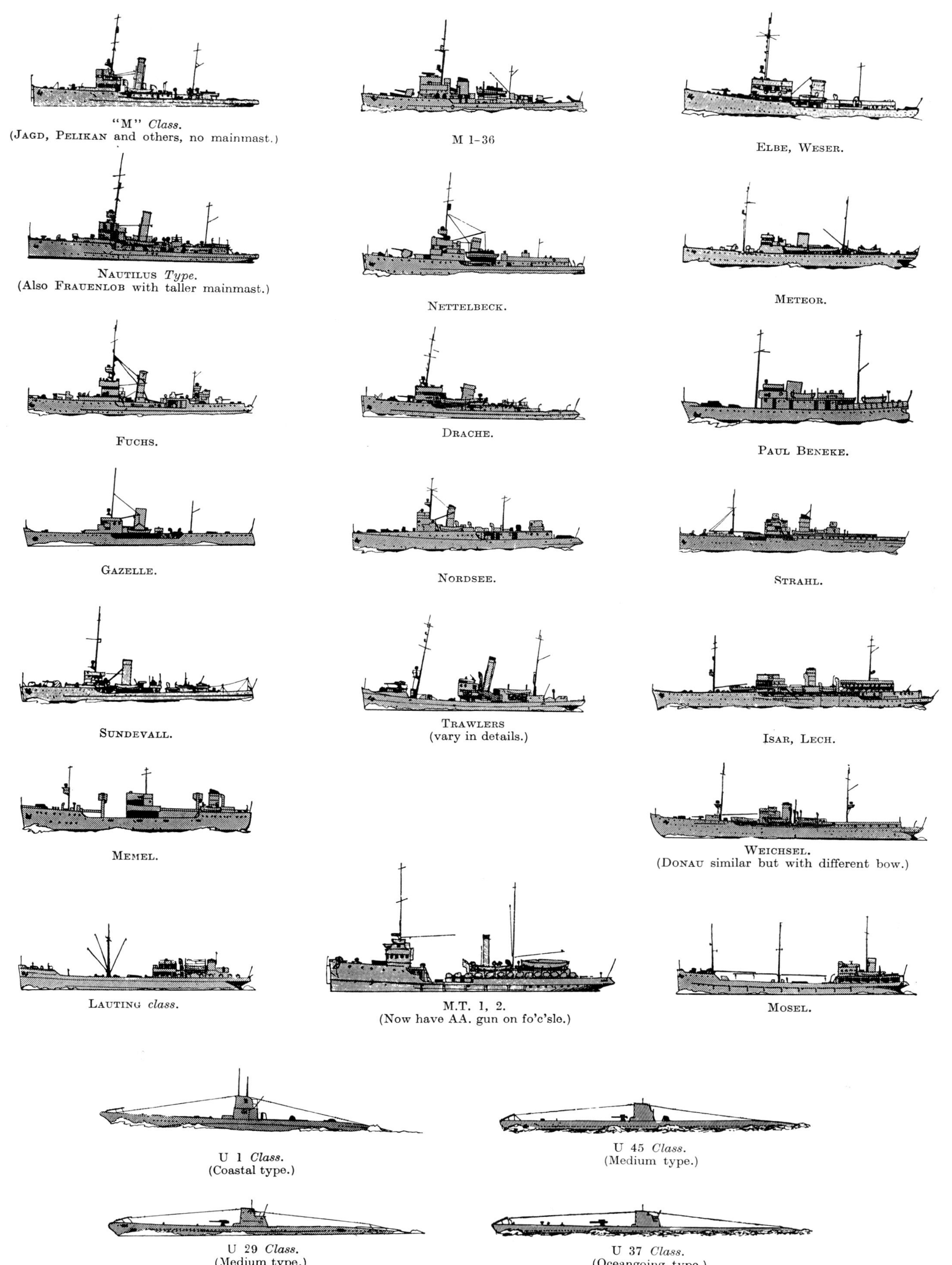

"M" *Class.*
(Jagd, Pelikan and others, no mainmast.)

M 1-36

Elbe, Weser.

Nautilus *Type.*
(Also Frauenlob with taller mainmast.)

Nettelbeck.

Meteor.

Fuchs.

Drache.

Paul Beneke.

Gazelle.

Nordsee.

Strahl.

Sundevall.

Trawlers
(vary in details.)

Isar, Lech.

Memel.

Weichsel.
(Donau similar but with different bow.)

Lauting *class.*

M.T. 1, 2.
(Now have AA. gun on fo'c'sle.)

Mosel.

U 1 *Class.*
(Coastal type.)

U 45 *Class.*
(Medium type.)

U 29 *Class.*
(Medium type.)

U 37 *Class.*
(Oceangoing type.)

Battleships

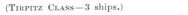

(Tirpitz Class—3 ships.)

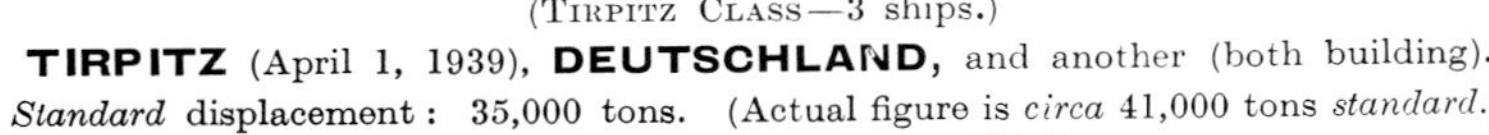

TIRPITZ (April 1, 1939), **DEUTSCHLAND**, and another (both building).

Standard displacement: 35,000 tons. (Actual figure is *circa* 41,000 tons *standard*.)

Complement: 1,500. Length (*w.l.*), 791 feet. Beam, 118 feet. Draught, 28 feet (*mean*).

Guns:
8—15 inch
12—5·9 inch
16—4.1 inch

Aircraft:
4, with 2 catapults.

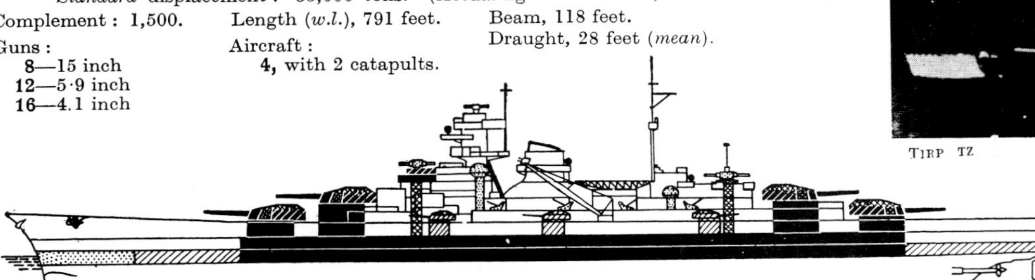

TIRP TZ 1942, *Associated Pr ess*

Name.	*Builder.*	*Laid down.*	*Completed.*
Tirpitz	Wilhelmshaven	1936	1941
Deutschland	Blohm & Voss	1938	
I	Wilhelmshaven	1939	

Armour:
Not reported, but is certainly equal to that of contemporary battleships of other navies, and probably amounts to close on 16,000 tons in weight.

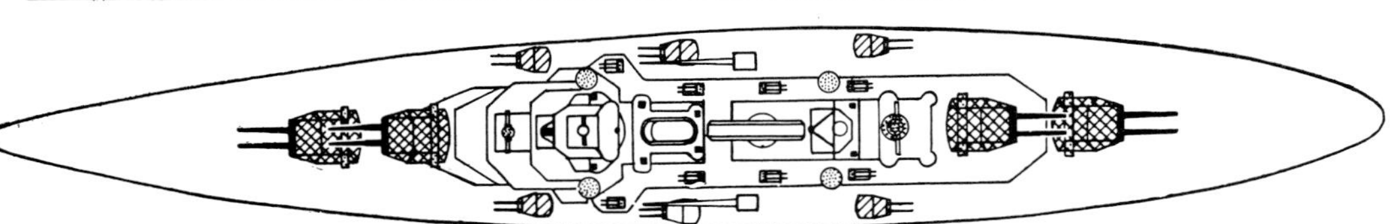

Machinery: Geared turbines. 2 shafts. High pressure water-tube boilers. S.H.P. 150,000
Oil fuel: 8,000 tons (*max.*).

BISMARCK (1939). 45,000 tons. Torpedoed by H.M.S. *Dorsetshire* after being reduced to a sinking condition by gunfire of H.M.S. *King George V* and *Rodney*, May 27, 1941. (She had previously been damaged by torpedoes discharged by Naval aircraft from H.M.S. *Victorious* and *Ark Royal*.)

Notes.—Bismarck, the first unit of this class to be completed, was sunk in action on May 27, 1941. Unofficial suggest that the second of the two still under construction may be named either *Friedrich der Grosse* or *Hinde* Very little progress appears to have been made with them since war began, and it is questionable whether th ever be completed.

TIRPITZ. 1941, *Associated Press.*

SCHARNHORST (October 3, 1936).
GNEISENAU (December 8, 1936).

Standard displacement: 26,000 tons. Complement: 1,461.

Length (*w.l.*) 741½ feet. Beam, 98½ feet. Draught, 24¾ feet (*mean*).

Guns:
9—11 inch.
12—5·9 inch.
14—4·1 inch A.A.
16—37 mm. AA.

Aircraft: 4

Catapults: 2
(No torpedo tubes.)

Armour: (Unofficial)
12"—13" Belt amidships,
3"—4" ends.
12" Turrets.
6" Decks.

Note to plan.—See remarks under *Gneisenau* photo, which apply to both ships. Hangar is between funnel and after superstructure.

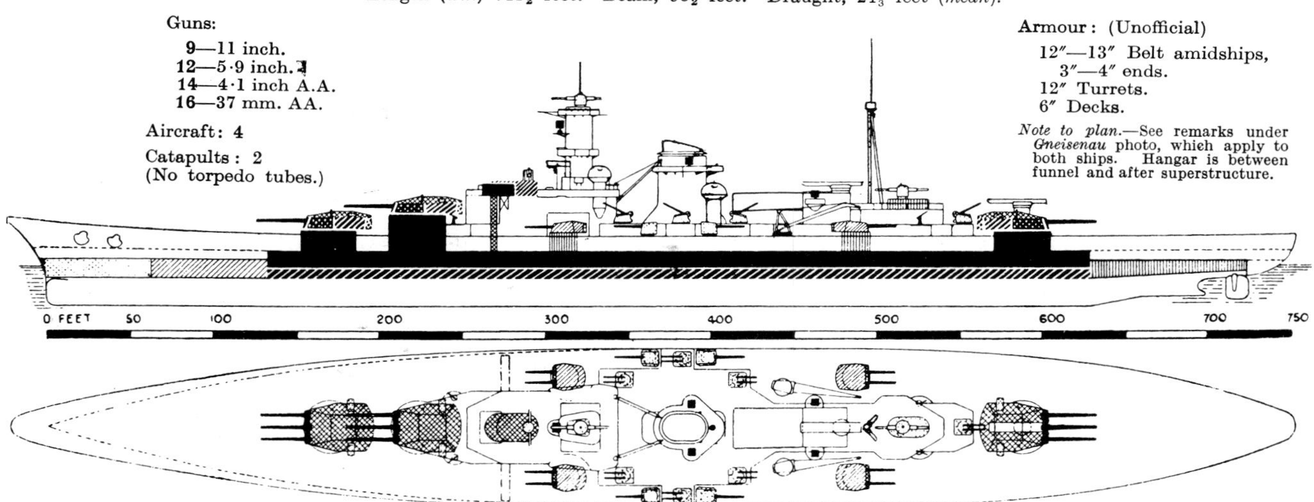

Machinery: Geared turbines, combined with Diesels for cruising speeds. 3 shafts. High pressure water tube boilers. Designed speed: 27 kts., considerably exceeded on trials. Actual full speed believed to be about 29 knots.

Name.	*Builder.*	*Laid down.*	*Completed*
Scharnhorst	Wilhelmshaven	1934	7 Jan., 1939
Gneisenau	Deutsche Werke	1934	21 May, 1938

General Notes.—Names of these battleships commemorate those of 2 cruisers sunk at the Battle of the Falklands, Dec. 8, 1914. In 1941 both received extensive damage from heavy bombing attacks, and both were under refit for the greater part of 1942.

Gunnery Notes.—11 inch calibre was accepted for these ships in order to allow a greater proportion of weight to be devoted to protection.

GNEISENAU. Funnel cap since reduced in size, and mainmast moved to a position just abaft first catapult, where it is stepped as a tripod. 1939, *W. Schäfer*.

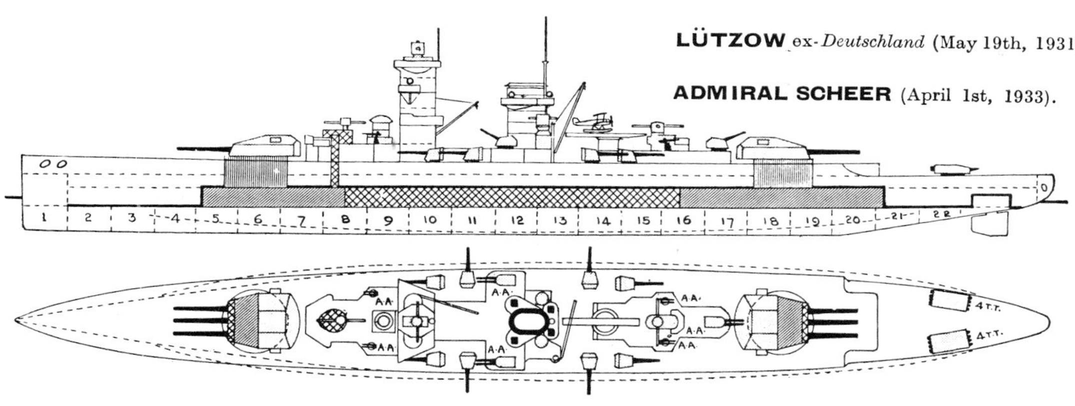

LÜTZOW ex-*Deutschland* (May 19th, 1931).

ADMIRAL SCHEER (April 1st, 1933).

Plan of ADMIRAL SCHEER.

Standard displacement, 10,000 tons. (Probably over 12,000 tons is nearer true figure.) Complement, 926.

Length, 593 (*w.l.*). 609¼ (*o.a.*) feet. Beam, 67½ feet (*Deutschland*), 69½ (*Scheer*). Draught, 21⅔.

Guns :
- 6—11 inch.
- 8—5·9 inch.
- 6—4·1 inch AA.
- 8—3 pdr. AA.
- 10—M.G.

Torpedo tubes :
- 8—21 inch (*above water*).

Aircraft :
- 2, with catapult.

Armour :
- Belt—4″ with 1½″ internally.
- Turrets : 4″ bases.
- 5½″ faces.
- 2—3″ sides.
- C.T. 5″
- 2″ roof.
- Deck 1½″—2¼″
- 3″ over magazine.
- External bulges.

Note—Following alterations in appearance were effected in 1937. 2 new cranes have replaced the former one; a small deckhouse has been added at base of catapult; derrick posts have been cut down and S.L. rearranged on a platform around upper part of funnel. There is a pole mast on after director.

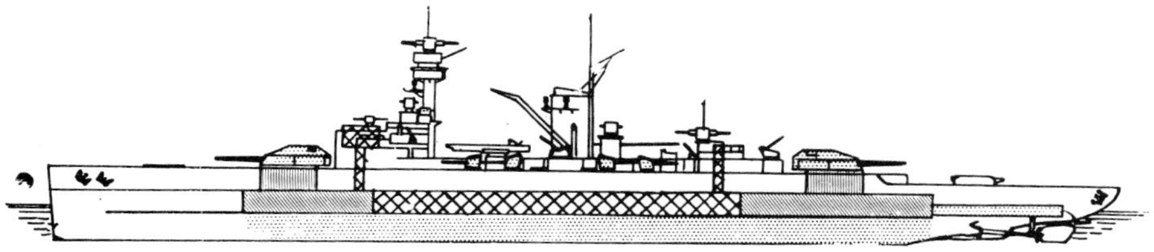

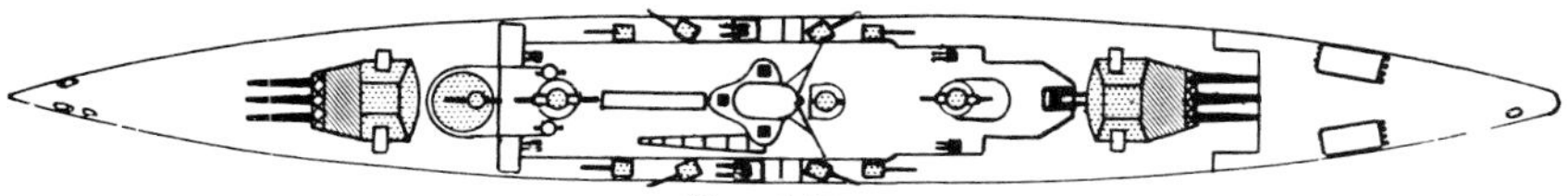

Plan of LÜTZOW

ADMIRAL GRAF SPEE (1934). 10,000 tons. Scuttled off Montevideo after being defeated in action four days earlier by H.M.S. *Ajax*, *Achilles* and *Exeter*, December 17, 1939.

AD. SCHEER.

Name.	*Builder.*	*Laid down*	1935. *Completed.*
Lützow	Deutsche Werke	5/ 2/29	1/4/33
Ad. Scheer	Wilhelmshaven	25/ 6/31	12/11/34

(A third ship, the *Admiral Graf Spee*, scuttled herself to avoid action in the River Plate on Dec. 17, 1939.)

LÜTZOW 1938, *Schäfer.*

Machinery : 8 sets M.A.N. Diesels, of 6,750 H.P. each. 2 shafts. Total H.P. : 54,000 = 26 kts. Fuel : 3,500 tons. Radius : 20,000 miles at 15 kts.

General Notes.—These are the first ships of such size to have electrically welded hulls and to be propelled by Diesel engines. By these means a saving in weight of 550 tons is said to be effected. Are officially rated as "Armoured Ships" (*Panzerschiffe*), and popularly referred to as "Pocket Battleships." Actually, they are equivalent to armoured cruisers of an exceptionally powerful type. Cost £3,750,000 = £375 per ton.

Gunnery Notes.—The 11 inch guns are a new Krupp model, firing a 670 lb. projectile, with a range of 30,000 yards and an elevation of 60°.

Machinery Note.—8 sets compressorless double-acting two-stroke M.A.N. Diesels each of 6,750 B.H.P. at 450 r.p.m. Each group of four drives a single propeller shaft through Vulcan gear, which reduces speed to 250 r.p.m. Net weight of engines about 17·6 lb. per b.h.p. excluding Vulcan drive, shafting, propeller and air reservoirs. Total weight of whole plant, about 48·5 lb. per b.h.p. Electrically welded plate framing employed for the first time. It is stated that Diesels have operated satisfactorily in service, without undue vibration or noise from exhaust; but unofficial reports suggest that they have not entirely answered expectations in these respects.

Special Note.—*Lützow* was torpedoed by a British aircraft off the Norwegian coast on June 13, 1941, receiving extensive damage.

ADMIRAL SCHEER. *Added* 1940, *W. Schäfer.*

Aircraft Carriers

GRAF ZEPPELIN (Deutsche Werke, Kiel, Dec. 8, 1938), **PETER STRASSER** (Germania, Kiel, building.) Both laid down in 1936, under the Programme for that year. *Standard* displacement: 19,250 tons.

Length: 820¼ feet. Beam: 88½ feet. Draught: 18⅓ feet (*mean*).

Guns:
16—5·9 inch
10—4·1 inch AA.
22—37 mm. AA.

Aircraft: 40.

Armour:
Casemates for 5·9 inch guns. No bulges. Also *see* notes.

Machinery: Geared turbines. Speed: 32 kts.

Notes.—Flight deck reported to measure 790 × 88½ feet. Sides appear to be armoured for two-thirds of length amidships, and to a lesser extent as far as bow, which is of bulbous form. Will have island superstructure on starboard side. One of these aircraft carriers was photographed from the air, fitting out alongside a quay in the Naval Dockyard at Kiel, in July, 1940, whence she is believed to have proceeded to Gdynia. *P. Strasser* does not appear to have been completed.

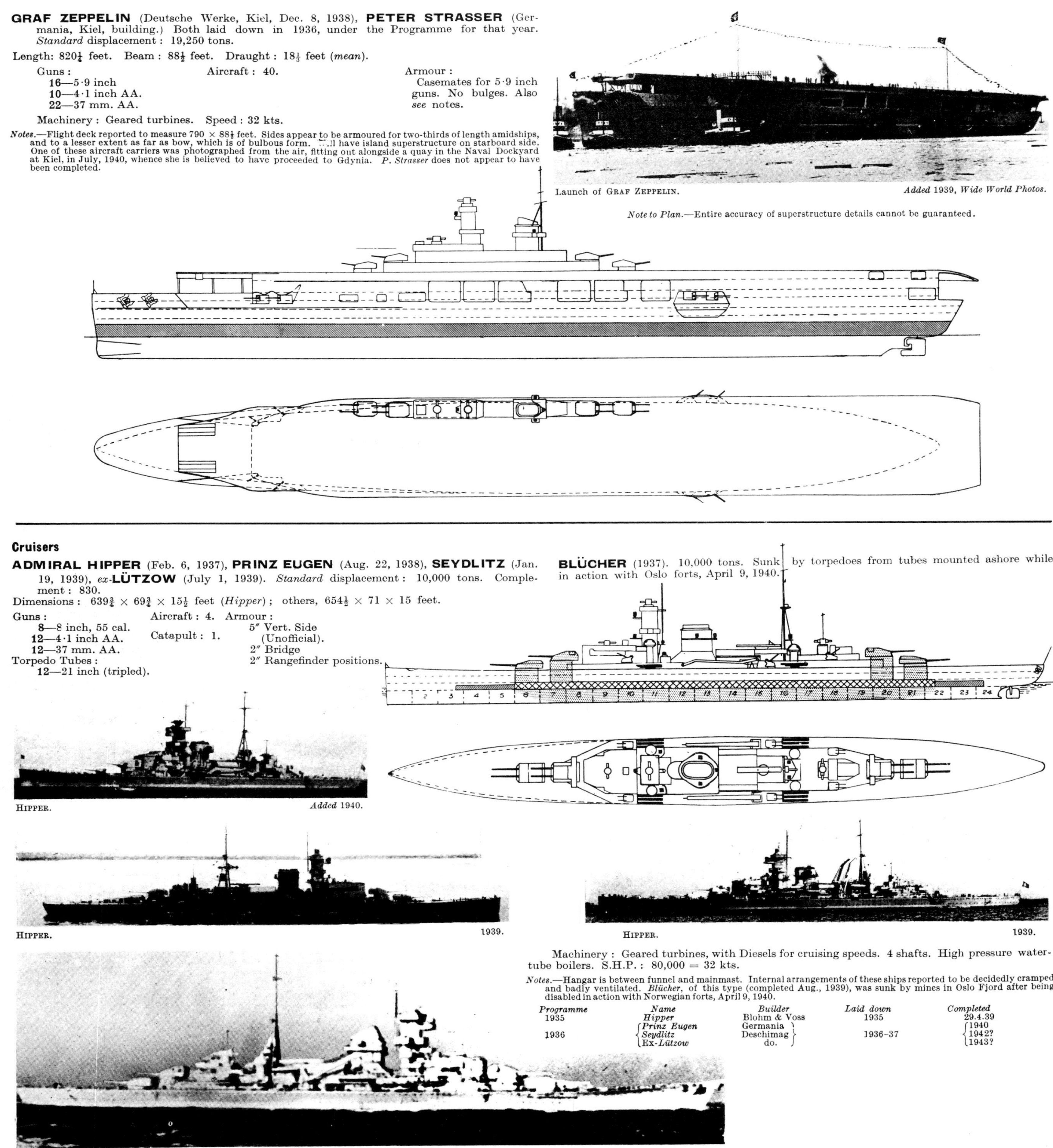

Launch of GRAF ZEPPELIN. *Added* 1939, *Wide World Photos.*

Note to Plan.—Entire accuracy of superstructure details cannot be guaranteed.

Cruisers

ADMIRAL HIPPER (Feb. 6, 1937), **PRINZ EUGEN** (Aug. 22, 1938), **SEYDLITZ** (Jan. 19, 1939), *ex*-**LÜTZOW** (July 1, 1939). *Standard* displacement: 10,000 tons. Complement: 830.

Dimensions: 639¾ × 69¾ × 15½ feet (*Hipper*); others, 654½ × 71 × 15 feet.

Guns:
8—8 inch, 55 cal.
12—4·1 inch AA.
12—37 mm. AA.

Torpedo Tubes:
12—21 inch (tripled).

Aircraft: 4.

Catapult: 1.

Armour:
5″ Vert. Side (Unofficial).
2″ Bridge
2″ Rangefinder positions.

BLÜCHER (1937). 10,000 tons. Sunk by torpedoes from tubes mounted ashore while in action with Oslo forts, April 9, 1940.

HIPPER. *Added* 1940.

HIPPER. 1939.

HIPPER. 1939.

Machinery: Geared turbines, with Diesels for cruising speeds. 4 shafts. High pressure water-tube boilers. S.H.P.: 80,000 = 32 kts.

Notes.—Hangar is between funnel and mainmast. Internal arrangements of these ships reported to be decidedly cramped and badly ventilated. *Blücher*, of this type (completed Aug., 1939), was sunk by mines in Oslo Fjord after being disabled in action with Norwegian forts, April 9, 1940.

Programme	*Name*	*Builder*	*Laid down*	*Completed*
1935	*Hipper*	Blohm & Voss	1935	29.4.39
1936	*Prinz Eugen*	Germania	1936–37	1940
	Seydlitz	Deschimag		1942?
	Ex-*Lützow*	do.		1943?

PRINZ EUGEN 1941.

Cruiser

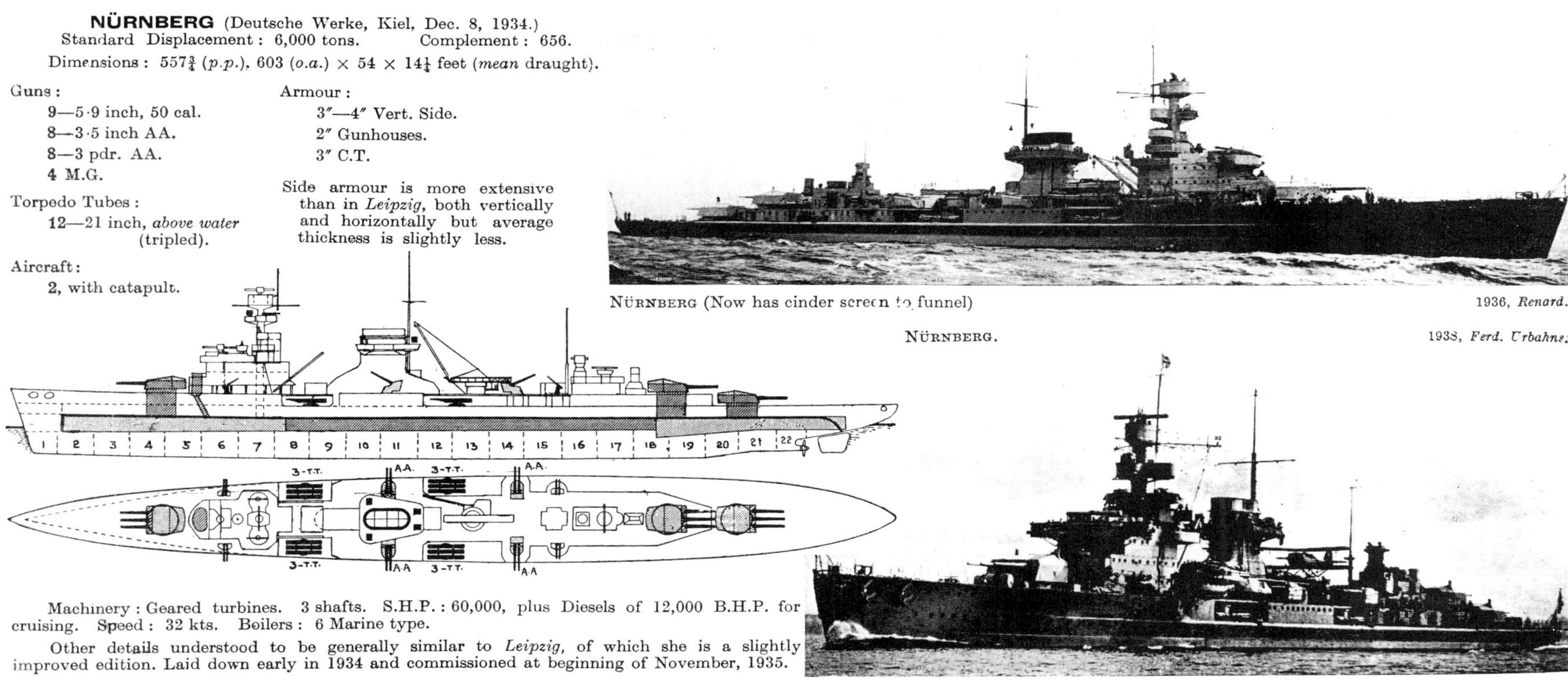

NÜRNBERG (Deutsche Werke, Kiel, Dec. 8, 1934.)
Standard Displacement: 6,000 tons. Complement: 656.
Dimensions: 557¾ (*p.p.*), 603 (*o.a.*) × 54 × 14¼ feet (*mean* draught).

Guns:
- 9—5·9 inch, 50 cal.
- 8—3·5 inch AA.
- 8—3 pdr. AA.
- 4 M.G.

Torpedo Tubes:
- 12—21 inch, *above water* (tripled).

Aircraft:
- 2, with catapult.

Armour:
- 3″—4″ Vert. Side.
- 2″ Gunhouses.
- 3″ C.T.

Side armour is more extensive than in *Leipzig*, both vertically and horizontally but average thickness is slightly less.

NÜRNBERG (Now has cinder screen to funnel) 1936, *Renard.*

NÜRNBERG. 1938, *Ferd. Urbahns.*

Machinery: Geared turbines. 3 shafts. S.H.P.: 60,000, plus Diesels of 12,000 B.H.P. for cruising. Speed: 32 kts. Boilers: 6 Marine type.

Other details understood to be generally similar to *Leipzig*, of which she is a slightly improved edition. Laid down early in 1934 and commissioned at beginning of November, 1935.

LEIPZIG (Wilhelmshaven, Oct. 18, 1929).

Standard Displacement: 6,000 tons.
Dimensions: 544 (*p.p.*) 580 (*o.a.*) × 53½ × 15¾ ft.
Complement: 615.

Guns:
- 9—5·9 inch, 50 cal.
- 8—3·5 inch, AA.
- 8—3 pdr. AA.
- 4 M.G.

Torpedo tubes:
- 12—21 inch, *above water* (tripled).

Aircraft:
- 2, with catapult.

Armour:
- 3″—4″ Vert. Side.
- 2″ Gun houses.
- 2″ C.T.

LEIPZIG *Added* 1940, *Associated Press.*

Note to Plan.—2 extra 3·5 inch A.A. guns have since been mounted.

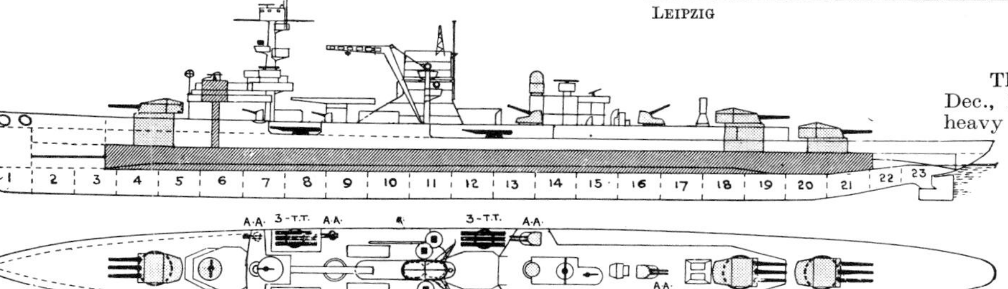

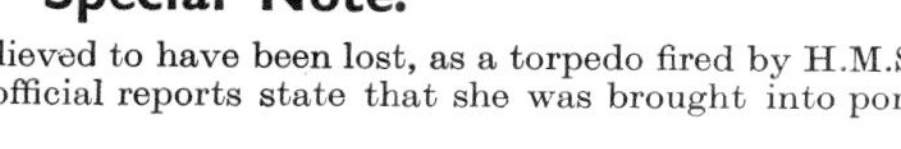

Special Note.

This cruiser was at one time believed to have been lost, as a torpedo fired by H.M.S. *Salmon* in Dec., 1939, certainly hit her. Unofficial reports state that she was brought into port with very heavy damage.

Machinery: Geared turbines, 3 shafts. S.H.P. 60,000 plus Diesel engines of 12,000 B.H.P. Speed: 32 kts. Boilers: 6 "Marine" type (modified Schulz-Thornycroft), double-ended. Centre shaft Diesel driven: can be used for cruising or combined with turbines to give full speed. Radius of action with Diesel engines at 14·5 kts: 3,800 miles; with turbines at 14·5 kts.: 3,200 miles = 7,000 miles. Radius could be greatly augmented if all bunkers were filled with Diesel fuel only, but this would reduce speed at full power. Oil fuel: 1,200 tons + 378 tons Diesel fuel.

Machinery Notes.—Variable pitch propeller on inner shaft, which "feathers" when Turbines only are used. Under Diesels alone, wing shafts are spun by 500 b.h.p. motors through spur gearing from centre shaft, thus obviating loss of 3,000 b.h.p. if they were allowed to turn idly. Plant is four 7-cyl. M.A.N. two-stroke double-acting compressorless Diesels. Engine speed = 600 r.p.m. Four engines to each shaft, through Vulcan hyd. clutches and reducing gear, giving shaft speed of 400 r.p.m. Weight of machinery, including scavenging blower and its driving engine, and auxiliaries to propelling plant = 12·1 lb. per b.h.p. (5·5 kg.). Turbines are Germania type.

General Notes.—Laid down at Wilhelmshaven April 18th, 1928. Completed in 1931. Modification of *Köln* design with after turrets in centre-line and uptakes trunked into one funnel: fitted below water-line with bulges which are to be filled with oil fuel and are designed to improve speed lines rather than to act as a means of protection.

(A different type of crane has since been fitted, as shown in upper photo.) 1935, *courtesy "Taschenbuch der Kriegsflotten"*

Cruisers

KÖLN (May 23rd, 1928).

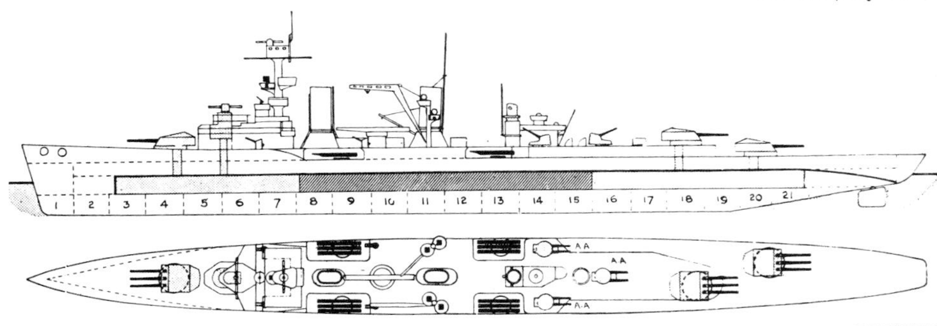

Displacement, 6000 tons. Complement, 571.

Length, 554 feet $5\frac{1}{2}$ inches (*w.l.*), 570 feet (*o.a.*),

Beam, 49 feet $10\frac{1}{2}$ inches.

Designed draught, 17 feet 9 inches.

Guns:
9—5·9 inch, 50 cal.
6—3·5 inch AA.
8—3 pdr. AA.
4 M.G.

Armour:
3″—4″ Vert. Side
2″ Gun Houses
3″ C.T.

Torpedo tubes:
12—21 inch, *above water*, tripled.

Aircraft: 2, with catapult.

Machinery: Geared turbines, with 10 cyl. 4-stroke Diesel engines or cruising purposes. Designed H.P.: 65,000 = 32 kts. Boilers: 6 Schulz-Thornycroft. Fuel: 1,200 tons oil + 300 tons Diesel fuel. Radius: at 14 kts., 5,500 miles; at 10 kts., 10,000.

KÖLN. *Added* 1940. *Central Press.*

General Notes.—Every possible expedient for saving weight was employed in this ship. A very high grade of steel was selected, and electric welding took the place of riveting. Laid down at Wilhelmshaven, Aug. 7, 1926, and completed in Jan., 1930. Two sister ships, *Karlsruhe* and *Königsberg*, have been lost, but this ship was photographed from the air while lying alongside the Germania shipyard at Kiel, in July, 1940.

KARLSRUHE (1927). 6,000 tons. Torpedoed by H.M.S. *Truant* off Kristiansand, April 9, 1940.

Gunnery Notes.—3—5·9 inch can fire simultaneously at rate of 6 salvoes a minute, and range to 2[illegible]000 yards. Disposition of after turrets is governed by arrangement of ammunition handling rooms.

Engineering Notes.—Designed horse-power of turbines is 63,000, and of Diesels, 2.000.

KÖNIGSBERG (1927). 6,000 tons. Sunk in dive-bombing attack by Skua aircraft from H.M.S. *Sparrowhawk*, at Bergen, April 9, 1940.

EMDEN (Wilhelmshaven, 7th January, 1925).

EMDEN. 1937, *Renard.*

Engineering Notes.—Designed to maintain a speed of 27·5 kts. in fair weather. Revs. per minute: 2435 H.P. turbines. 1568 L.P. turbines, geared down to 295 R.P.M. on propellers. On trials designed speed was slightly exceeded with 46,500 H.P.

General Notes.—The tubular foremast is about 5 feet in diameter. Masting modified and second funnel heightened, 1926–27. *Emden* was designed for foreign service, particular attention being paid to accommodation. Laid down in December, 1921, commissioned 15th October, 1925. Since used as sea-going training ship for cadets.

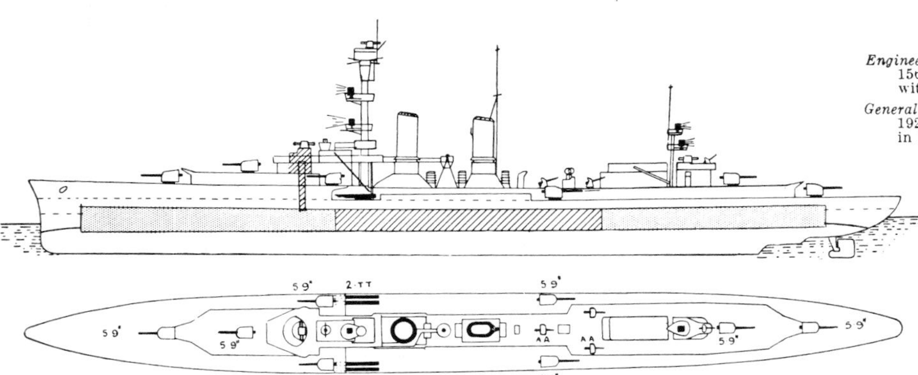

Standard displacement, 5,400 tons. Complement, 534.

Dimensions: $493\frac{3}{4}$ (*w.l.*), $508\frac{1}{4}$ (*o.a.*) × 47 × $17\frac{1}{2}$ feet (*mean* draught), 21 feet (*max.*)

Guns:
8—5·9 inch 45 cal.
3—3·5 inch AA.
4—M.G.

Torpedo tubes:
4—19·7 inch (*above wate* .

Armour:
3″—4″ Vert. Side ....
2″ Gun Houses ....
3″ C.T.

Machinery: Geared turbines. Boilers: 10 Schulz-Thornycroft "Marine" type (Converted to oil-burning 1934). Designed H.P. 46,500 = 29 kts. Oil fuel: 1,260 tons.

Added 1942.

Z 23—Z 39. Displacement: 1,870 tons (first four), 1,811 tons (others). Dimensions not reported, but believed to be the same as in *Karl Galster*, in adjoining column. Guns: **4**—5 inch, **6**—37 mm. AA., **4**—20 mm. AA. Tubes: **8**—21 inch. Otherwise resemble *K. Galster*. No information as to dates of launching or completion. Builders Deschimag, Deutsche Werke, Germania and Blohm & Voss. ***Z 23—26*** (apparently fitted as Leaders) built under 1938 Programme, ***Z 27—39*** under that for 1939. This group of destroyers is known in Germany as the "Narvik Flotilla."

K. GALSTER — 1939, *Schäfer.*

Karl Galster (1938). Built by Deschimag, Bremen, under 1936 Programme. Displacement: 1,811 tons. Dimensions: 384 × 38 × 9½ feet. Guns: **5**—5 inch, **4**—37 mm. AA., **4**—20 mm. AA. Tubes: **8**—21 inch (quadrupled). Machinery: Geared turbines. S.H.P.: 55,000 = 36 kts. Completed March 21, 1939, and is the only survivor of a class of six, the other five having been sunk at Narvik in April, 1940. Pendant No. is painted on sides as shown in photo.

8 *(or less)* Beitzen Class.

T. RIEDEL. — 1937, *Renard.*

F. IHN. — *Added* 1940, *Renard.*

1 *Deutsche Werke:* ***Richard Beitzen,*** (1935).
3 *Germania:* ***Paul Jacobi, Theodor Riedel, Hermann Schoemann,*** (All 1936).
1 *Deschimag:* ***Hans Lody*** (1936).
3 *Blohm & Voss:* ***Friedrich Ihn*** (1935), ***Erich Steinbrinck*** (1936), ***Friedrich Eckoldt*** (1937).

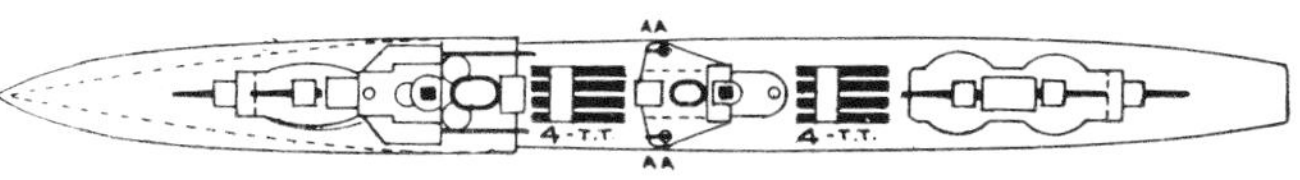

Standard Displacement: 1,625 tons. Complement: 283. Dimensions: 374 × 37 × 9⅓ feet.
Guns: **5**—5 inch, **4**—37 mm. AA., **4**—20 mm. AA. Tubes: **8**—21 inch, quadrupled.
Machinery: Geared turbines. S.H.P: 50,000 = 36 kts. High pressure watertube boilers.

Note.—Notable feature of these torpedo craft is the first appearance in German flotillas of quadruple torpedo tubes. First of class were laid down in autumn of 1934, latest in autumn of 1935. All authorised under 1934 Programme, and completed by end of 1938 or early 1939. Pendant Numbers, *R. Beitzen*, 11; *P. Jacobi*, 21; *T. Riedel*, 22; *H. Schoemann*, 23: *E. Steinbrinck*, 31: *F. Eckoldt*, 32; *F. Ihn*, 33; *H. Lody*, 82. The first figure in each case refers to the flotilla, the second to position of ship therein. Several of above ships have been sunk.

Torpedo Boats.

(Several of these have been lost.)

Added 1942.

Though this purports to represent one of ***T 1*** type, it will be observed that it bears a distinct resemblance to Norwegian *Sleipner* type

Added 1942.

30 boats: ***T1—T18*** (1938–39), ***T19—30*** (1940). (Seven launched during 1938, *T*11 in March, 1939, and *T*13 on June 15, 1939). *Standard* displacement: 600 tons. Dimensions: 267 × 28¼ × 6¼ feet. Guns: **1** *or* **2**—4·1 inch, 2—37 mm. Tubes: **6**—21 inch (tripled). Speed: 36 kts. First 12 laid down 1936. Some built by F. Schichau, Elbing, others by Deschimag, Bremen, under 1935–1939 programmes.

4 Wolf Class.

4 *Wilhelmshaven Yard:* ***Iltis, Wolf*** (both Oct. 12th, 1927), ***Jaguar, Tiger*** (both March, 1928). Laid down 1927. Standard Displacement: 800 tons (1,000 tons deep load). Dimensions: 292 (*p.p.*), 304 (*o.a.*) × 28 × 9 feet. Guns: 3—4·1 inch, 2—1 pdr. AA. T.T.: **6**—21 inch (tripled parallel). Designed S.H.P.: 25,000 = 34 kts. Geared turbines and Schulz-Thornycroft boilers. Oil fuel: 330 tons. Complement: 123. Are of same general type as *Möwe* class, with minor improvements. *Jaguar* formerly employed as Gunnery School Tender.

3 Möwe Class.

FALKE. — 1939, *Dr. Erich Gröner.*

3 *Wilhelmshaven Yard:* ***Möwe*** (March 24th, 1926), ***Falke, Kondor*** (both Sept. 22nd, 1926). Standard Displacement: 800 tons (960 tons deep load). Dimensions: 277¾ × 27½ × 9⅛ feet draught. Guns: **3**—4·1 inch, 50 cal., **2**—1 pdr. AA. T.T.: **6**—21 inch (tripled parallel). Geared turbines. 3 Schulz-Thornycroft boilers. Designed S.H.P. 24,000 = 33 kts. (exceeded on trials). Oil fuel: 320 tons. Complement, 121.

Notes.—Laid down under 1924 and 1925 Programmes. *Möwe* commissioned October 1st, 1926, others passed into service during 1927, replacing old and worn-out torpedo boats. Have longitudinal framing and double bottom to hull. Guns said to elevate to 80°. The cost of these vessels was extraordinarily high, working out at about £215 per ton.

Identification letters formerly painted on bows: FK, *Falke;* IT, *Iltis;* JR, *Jaguar;* KO, *Kondor;* MÖ, *Möwe;* TG, *Tiger;* WL, *Wolf.* These are believed to have been replaced by numerals.

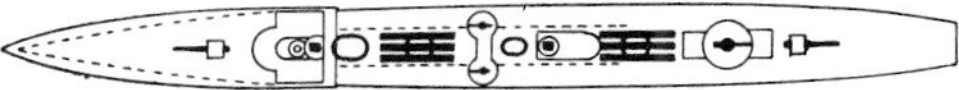

WOLF and MÖWE types.
Möwe has pointed stern.

Submarines

Oceangoing types.

Special Note.

A large number of the Submarines listed here have been destroyed since September, 1939. A great many more have, of course, been built or laid down during the same period, but details of these are not yet obtainable. *U* 574 is the highest number of which any record has been published. A notable feature of recent German submarine design is that the double-hull form used in the larger U-boats of 1914–18 has been discarded in favour of a single-hull type with saddle-tanks. This simplifies and accelerates construction, though it increases vulnerability to depth charge attack. Spare torpedoes are carried on deck as well as in torpedo compartment forward. There is no basis for reports of engines of a novel type having been adopted.

H.M.S. *Seal* (of the *Porpoise* type), reported missing in May, 1940, is believed to have been repaired and put into commission under the German flag in December, 1940.

Note.—Turkish minelaying submarine *Batiray* is understood to have been taken over by Germany; for particulars see Turkish section. Possibly she may be *U* 77 or *U* 78.

U77, U78 (1939). Displacement: 1,060 tons. Dimensions: $275\frac{1}{2} \times 27\frac{3}{4} \times 12\frac{3}{4}$ feet. Armament: **1**—4·1 inch, 45 cal., **2**—1 pdr. AA., **2**—21 inch tubes (bow). Fitted for minelaying. H.P.: 3,600/1,100 = 18·5/8 kts.

U 37 — 1938, *Schäfer.*

U37 (Deschimag, 1938), **U65—68** (1939), **U79—82** (1940), **U88—92** (1940). Displacement: 740 tons. Complement: 40. Dimensions: $244\frac{1}{2} \times 20\frac{1}{2} \times 13\frac{1}{2}$ feet. Armament: **1**—4·1 inch 45 cal., **2**—1 pdr. AA., **6**—21 inch tubes (4 bow, 2 stern). H.P.: 3,200/1,000 = 18·5/8 kts.

Notes.—*U* 37 completed Aug. 4, 1938. Some of these vessels may be minelayers. In later modifications of above type, tubes No. 5 (4 bow, 1 stern), and surface speed is 17·5 kts. with 2,800 H.P. Dimensions also differ slightly.

Seagoing types.

1938, *Schäfer.*

U 45—55 (Germania, 1938), **U 69—72, U 74—76** (1939), **U83, U 84, U 86, U 87** (1939), **U93, U 94, U 96—98** (1940). Displacement: 517 tons. Complement: 35. Dimensions: $213\frac{1}{4} \times 19\frac{3}{8} \times 13$ feet. Armament: **1**—3·5 inch, **1**—1 pdr. AA., **5**—21 inch tubes (4 bow, 1 stern). H.P.: 2,100/750 = 16·5/8 kts. First 7 laid down early in 1937, others begun by end of year. *U* 45 commissioned June 25, 1938; *U* 46, Nov. 2, 1938; *U* 47, Dec. 7, 1938; *U* 51, Aug. 6, 1938; *U* 52, Feb. 4, 1939; *U* 53, June 24, 1939. *U* 99 and *U* 100 are known to have been lost in Atlantic operations, and *U* 73 was captured by Russian naval forces in Barentsz Sea.

Seagoing Type—*continued.*

1937, *Schäfer.*

U 29, U 30, U 34 (1936). Standard displacement: 500 tons. Complement, 35. Dimensions: $206\frac{3}{4} \times 19\frac{1}{3} \times 13$ feet. Armament: **1**—3·5 inch, **1**—1 pdr. AA.; **5**—21 inch tubes (4 bow, 1 stern). H.P.: 2,000/750 = 16·5/8 kts.

Notes.—Laid down under 1935 and 1936 Programmes and completed during 1936–37. *U* 34 built by Germania, *U* 29, *U* 30 by Deschimag.

No.	*Launch*	*No.*	*Launch*
U 29	29/8/36	*U* 34	17/7/36
U 30	8/4/36		

Coastal types.

U 59. — 1939 *Schäfer.*

U 1 to **U 11, U 17, U 20** to **U 24** (1935–36), **U 56** to **U 63** (1938). *Standard* displacement: 250/330 tons. Complement: 23. Dimensions: $136\frac{1}{2} \times 13 \times 12\frac{2}{3}$ feet. Armament: **1**—1 pdr. AA., **3**—21 inch torpedo tubes. H.P.: 700/360 = 13/7 kts. Diving limit reported to be 50 fathoms.

Appearance Note.—Of those so far reported, identification numbers are painted in *black* on C.T. of U 1—6, and in *white* on C.T. of later boats

No.	*Builder*	*Begun*	*Launch*	*Comp.*
U 1	*Deutsche Werke, Kiel*	1935	15/6/35	1935
2			1/7/35	
3			19/7/35	
4			31/7/35	
5			14/8/35	
6			21/8/35	
7	*Germania, Kiel.*		29/6/35	
8			16/7/35	
9			30/7/35	
10			13/8/35	
11			27/8/35	

No.	*Builder*	*Begun*	*Launch*	*Comp.*
17	*Germania*	1935	14/11/35	1936
20			14/ 1/36	
21	*Deschimag, Bremen*	1936	13/ 7/36	
22			29/ 7/36	
23			28/ 8/36	
24			24/ 9/36	
56	*Deutsche Werke*	1938	26/11/38	
57			29/12/38	
58			4/2/39	
59			39	
60			39	
61			15/6/39	
62			39	
63			39	

Sloop, rated as Gunnery Training Ship.

BRUMMER (Deschimag, Bremen, May 29, 1935.)

Standard Displacement: 2,410 tons. Complement, 214.

Dimensions: $354\frac{1}{3} \times 44\frac{1}{3} \times 11\frac{1}{2}$ feet.

(Fitted for Minelaying).

(This ship may have been sunk). — 1936 *Renard.*

1936 *Schäfer.*

Guns: **4**—3·5 inch AA. (new model), **2**—3·5 inch AA. (of older pattern), **4**—3 pdr. AA. (Number and calibre of guns has varied from time to time.)

Machinery: Geared turbines. High pressure w.t. boilers. S.H.P.: 7,500 = 20 kts. (in service), but believed capable of considerably more.

Notes.—Laid down 1934 under current programme: commissioned Feb. 8, 1936. Used as AA. gunnery training ship. In emergency she would become a combatant unit of fleet. Unofficial reports suggest that she is not an unqualified success. She spent several months of 1936 in dockyard hands, undergoing repairs and alterations. A new gunnery training ship was projected under 1939 programme.

1939, *Schäfer.*

ERWIN WASSNER (ex-*Gran Canaria*), (Hamburg, 1938). Displacement: 5,000 tons. Dimensions: 379¾ × 54¾ × — feet. Machinery: Geared turbines. 1 shaft. I.H.P.: 5,000. Submarine Depot Ship.

Note.—A sister ship, the *Santa Cruz*, is also reported to have been acquired.

1939, *Schäfer.*

MEMEL (1937). Displacement: 998 tons. Speed: 13 knots. Parent Ship of "Weddigen" Submarine Flotilla.

1939, *Schäfer.*

TANGA (Neptun Werft, Rostock, 1938). Classed as *Schnellbootsbegleitschiff.*

MARS (ex-*Samoa*, ex-*Altair*), (Emden, 1937). 2,414 tons *gross.* Dimensions: 324¼ × 46¾ × — feet. Machinery: Quadruple expansion. Speed: 11 kts. Tender to Gunnery School.

LECH. 1939, *Dr. Erich Gröner*

ISAR (ex-*Puma*), **LECH** (ex-*Panther*), (Bremer Vulkan, Vegesack, 1930). Displacement: 3,850 tons. Dimensions: 319 × 45½ × 13 feet. Machinery: Triple expansion. H.P.: 2,000 = 12 kts. Both purchased 1938 for use as Submarine Depot Ships.

1937, *Schäfer.*

WEICHSEL (ex-*Syra*), (Howaldt, Kiel, 1923). Displacement: 3,974 tons. Dimensions: 309¼ × 44 × 13½ feet. Guns: 4—20 mm. AA. Machinery: Triple expansion. H.P.: 1,400 = 10·5 kts. Coal: 425 tons. 2 watertube boilers. Complement, 135. (Depot Ship for Submarines.)

Note.—Purchased in summer of 1936 and rebuilt at Stettin.

1938, *Schäfer.*

DONAU (ex-*Nicea*), (Lübeck, 1922). Displacement: 3,886 tons. Dimensions: 287½ × 41½ × 14 feet. Guns: 4—20 mm. AA. Machinery: Triple expansion. H.P.: 1,150 = 10 kts. Coal: 335 tons. 2 watertube boilers. Complement, 135. (Depot Ship for Submarines.)

1937, *Schäfer.*

MOSEL (ex-*Frieda*). (Hamburg, 1921). Displacement: 796 tons. Guns: 2—20 mm. AA. Speed: 9 kts. Complement, 34. Further particulars wanted. (Depot Ship for Submarines.)

WARNOW (ex-*Vorwärts*), (Vegesack, 1906). 726 tons *gross.* Dimensions: 206 × 41¼ × — feet. I.H.P.: 600 = 13 kts. (Depot Ship for Submarines.)

Minesweepers.

(*Minensuchboote*)

M 7 1939, *Ferd. Urbahns.*

M1—4, M6—36 (1937–1940). Displacement: 600 tons. Complement: 82. Guns: 2—4·1 inch, 2—37 mm. Machinery: Triple expansion. Speed: 17 kts. Coal: 150 tons. All laid down during 1936 and 1937 under 1935–37 Programmes.

Builders of these vessels are: H. C. Stülcken Sohn, Hamburg; Schichau, Elbing; Stettiner Oderwerke, Stettin; and Lübecker Flenderwerke, Lübeck.

Notes.—*M* 1 commissioned Sept. 1938; *M* 2—8 all completed by end Jan. 1939. *M* 20 was launched June 16, 1939. First 20 believed all to have been completed in 1939. *M* 5 (as well as others unidentified) believed to have been lost.

Minesweepers and Tenders

M. 117. 1934 Photo, *Schäfer*.

M 157	**M 117**	**M102**	**M 72**
M 145	**M 111**	**M 98**	**TAKU** (*ex*-**M146**)
M 126	**M 110**	**M 84**	
M 122	**M 104**	**M 75**	

Built 1916–1920. Displacement: 360 tons. Dimensions: 184 (*w.l.*), 192 (*o.a.*) × 24¼ × 7¼ feet. Guns: 1—4·1 inch, 1 M.G. Engines: 2 sets triple expansion. Boilers: 2 watertube "Schulz." I.H.P.: 1,850 = 16 kts. 2 screws. Coal: 145-160 tons. Complement: 51.

Note.—Sundry other units of this class have been given names on appropriation for various special services, vide later pages. *M* 132 was lost off the West coast of Jutland in January, 1940, and various others since.

Tenders.

Note.—Ex-*Geleitboot Hai* (on an earlier page) is rated as a Fleet Tender.

HELA (1939). Particulars wanted. Rated as *Flottentender*.

Nettelbeck. 1939, *Schäfer*.

NETTELBECK (ex-*Zieten*, ex-*M* 138, Tecklenborg, Feb. 17, 1919). Displacement: 550 tons. Dimensions: 184 × 24 × 7½ feet. Guns: 1—4·1 inch, 2—1 pdr. AA. 2 sets Diesel engines. B.H.P.: 840 = 12 kts. Complement: 40. Fuel: 90 tons.

Fuchs. *Added* 1939, *Schäfer*.

FUCHS (ex-*M* 130, 1919). Displacement: 525 tons. Dimensions: 184 × 24 × 7¼ feet. Guns: 3—3·5 inch AA. Machinery: 2 sets triple expansion. Boilers: 2 Schulz w.t. 2 screws. I.H.P.: 1,850 = 16 kts. Coal: 160 tons. Complement: 54.

Note.—On occasions mounts 2—4·1 inch instead of 3—3·5 inch guns, being Gunnery School Tender.

Pelikan (ex-*M*. 28). 1934 *Photo, Schäfer*.

PELIKAN (ex-*M*.28, 1916). Displacement: 500 tons. Complement: 49. Dimensions: 180½ × 24 × 7½ feet. Guns: 1—4·1 inch, 1—1 pdr. AA. Machinery: 2 sets triple expansion. 2 shafts. I.H.P.: 1,800 = 16·5 kts. Boilers: 2 Schulz w.t. Coal: 145 tons. Classed as *Versuchsboot*.

1936, *Schäfer*.

DRACHE (Germania, 1908). 790 tons. Dimensions: 176 × 31¾ × 10½ feet. Complement: 69. Guns: 6—4·1 inch. 1—20 mm. AA. Machinery: Geared turbines. High pressure watertube boilers. Oil fuel. Speed nominally 15 kts., but believed to exceed 18 kts. since 1936 refit.

Note.—Rated as Gunnery School Tender (*Artillerieschulboot.*)

Brommy. 1938, *Schäfer*.

BROMMY (ex-*M* 50, 1916). Displacement: 480 tons. Dimensions: 180½ × 24 × 7½ feet. Guns: 1—4·1 inch, 2—1 pdr. AA. Machinery: 2 sets triple expansion. 2 shafts. I.H.P.: 1,800 = 16·5 kts. Boilers: 2 Schulz w.t. Coal: 145 tons.

Note.—Rated as *Räumbootsbegleitschiff*.

Gazelle. 1938, *Schäfer*.

HECHT (ex-*M* 60, 1917), **JAGD** (ex-*M* 82, 1917), **DELPHIN** (ex-*M* 108, 1919), **ACHERON** (ex-*M* 113, 1918), **FRAUENLOB** (ex-*M* 134, 1919), **GAZELLE** (ex-*Hela*, ex-*M* 135, March 15, 1919), Ex-Minesweepers of 525 tons. Complement: 49. Dimensions: 184 × 24¼ × 7¼ feet. Guns: 1—4·1 inch in some, none in others. Machinery: 2 sets triple expansion. 2 shafts. I.H.P.: 1,850 = 16 kts. Boilers: 2 Schulz w.t. Coal: 160 tons. *Acheron* classed as Submarine Tender (*Unterseebootstender*). *Frauenlob*, Station Tender. *Delphin*, Gunnery School Tender. *Gazelle, Hecht, Jagd* classed as Fleet Tenders.

Störtebeker. 1938, *Schäfer*.

STÖRTEBEKER (ex-*M* 66, 1918), **NAUTILUS** (ex-*M* 81, 1919), **ARKONA** (ex-*M* 115, 1918), **OTTO BRAUN** (ex-*M* 129, 1919), **RAULE** (ex-*Wacht*, ex-*M* 133). Displacement: 525 tons. Complement: 49. Dimensions: 184 × 24¼ × 7¼ feet. Guns: 1—4·1 inch, 1 M.G. Machinery: 2 sets triple expansion. 2 shafts. I.H.P.: 1,850 = 16 kts. Boilers: 2 Schulz w.t. Coal: 160 tons. All classed as *Versuchsboote*.

1939, *Schäfer.*

STRAHL (ex-*Latona*, ex-*Soneck*, 1902). Displacement: 1,643 tons. Complement: 35. Dimensions: 235 × 33½ × 11¼ feet. Machinery: Triple expansion. I.H.P.: 800 = 10 kts. 1 cyl. boiler. First commissioned Oct. 20, 1936. Classed as *Versuchsschiff.*

1939, *Schäfer.*

NORDSEE (Atlas Werke, Bremen, 1914). 830 tons. Complement, 46. Dimensions: 175¾ × 30¾ × 12 feet. Armament: Nil. Machinery: Triple expansion. H.P.: 1,680 = 12 kts. 2 screws. Coal: 105 tons. Well deck built up 1923. Tender to Navigation School.

1939, *Schäfer.*

PAUL BENEKE (ex-*Admiral*), (Memel, 1936). Displacement: 460 tons. Dimensions: 165 (*o.a.*), 156 (*w.l*) × 25 × 10½ feet. No guns. Diesel engine. 1 shaft. B.H.P.: 800 = 12·5 kts. Complement: 30. Navigation School Tender. (Acquired in 1937 and refitted.)

1939, *Dr. E. Gröner.*

DAHME (ex-trawler *Carsten Rehder*) (1936). 475 tons *gross.* Dimensions: 186 × 26½ × 13 feet. Machinery: Triple expansion. Submarine School Tender.

NIXE. 1935 *Photo.*

NIXE (ex-*Fiora*, Harburg, 1914). Displacement: 108 tons. Dimensions: 96¾ × 16⅓ × 5½ feet. Machinery: 2 Daimler 4-cylinder 4-stroke benzol engines. 2 screws. H.P.: 200 = 13 kts. Fuel: 10 tons. Complement: 13. (Purchased 1916.) Used as Commander-in-Chief's yacht, Kiel.

MT 1 1930 *Photo.*

MT1 (ex-*Heppens*), **MT**2 (ex-*Mariensiel*). Both launched 1917 at Neptun Yard, Rostock. Displacement: 550 tons. Dimensions: 164 × 30½ × 7½ feet. Armament: 1 M.G. Machinery: 2 screws triple expansion. Boilers: 2 single-ended coal-burning Schulz-Thornycroft. 2 screws. Designed H.P.: 375 = 10 kts. Radius: 1,200 miles at 7 kts. Coal: 37 tons. Complement: 47. Classed as *Sperrübungsfahrzeuge.* (Minelaying tenders.)

C 21 1938, *Schäfer.*

C 21—C 24 (1935–37). Displacement: 120 tons. Speed: 9 kts. Minelaying Tenders.

A, B (1939), **C, D** (1940).

1939, *Dr. Erich Gröner.*

ORKAN (ex-*Welle*, ex-*Grille*, ex-*Star of Eve*, ex-*Von der Goltz*). (Hamburg, 1916.) Purchased 1927. Displacement: 470 tons. Complement: 22. Dimensions: 120 × 24 × 12½ feet. H.P.: 400 = 10 kts. Coal: 65 tons.

Note.—Sank in heavy weather, 1937, but salved and refitted. Used for recovery of practice Torpedoes. Classed as *Torpedobergungsdampfer*, and flies State Service Flag.

SPREE (ex-*Vorwärts*). Tender to Submarine School.

CARL ZEISS (ex-*H.L.M. Russ*). Tender to Gunnery School.

TAUCHER 1935, *Renard.*

TAUCHER (Stulcken & Sohn, Hamburg, 1934). Displacement: 195 tons. Complement: 17. Dimensions: 88½ × 22⅓ × 6¼ feet. Diesel engine. H.P.: 60 = 6·5 kts. No armament. Diving School Tender (*Taucherfahrzeug*).

Tenders (ex-Torpedo Boats)

T 123. *Added* 1940, *W. Schäfer.*

T 123 (ex-*S* 23), (Schichau, March 29, 1913). Displacement: 640 tons. Dimensions: 233 × $24\frac{1}{3}$ × $9\frac{3}{4}$ feet. Armament: 2 M.G. Machinery: Schichau turbines. Designed S.H.P.: 15,700 = 31 kts. (now only 22 kts.). Fuel: 71 tons oil. Complement: 80. Used as Submarine Tender.

T 107 1938, *courtesy Dr. Erich Gröner.*

4 *Krupp-Germania*: ***T 107, 108*** (ex-*G* 7, *G* 8) (both 1911), ***T 110, 111*** (ex-*G* 10, *G* 11) (both 1912).

Displacement: 760 tons. Dimensions: $247\frac{3}{4}$ × 25 × $10\frac{1}{2}$ feet. Armament: 1—4·1 inch, 45 cal., 2 M.G. AA. Torpedo tubes: 3—19·7 inch in *G* 8, *G* 10; 3—21 inch and 1—19·7 inch in others. Machinery: 2 sets Satz-Germania turbines. Designed H.P.: 16,000 = 31 kts. (now about 25 kts.) 3 Schulz-Thornycroft boilers (oil burning). Oil fuel: 173 tons. Complement: 85.

All four were lengthened $14\frac{3}{4}$ feet during alterations 1928–31. Triple tubes abaft mast. Single tube between funnels in *T* 110, 111. Used as training tenders (*Torpedoschulboote*) and will be discarded in near future.

T 196 (Observe AA. guns added aft). 1938, *Schäfer.*

C. van Bevern, *Added* 1940, *Dr. E. Gröner.*

1 *Krupp Germania*, ***T196*** (ex- *G196*). 1 *Vulkan.* **CLAUS VAN BEVERN** (ex-*T* 190 ex-*V* 190). (1911.)
Displacement: 800 tons. Dimensions: *T* 196, $242\frac{3}{4}$ × $26\frac{1}{4}$ × $10\frac{3}{4}$ feet; *T* 190, $241\frac{1}{2}$ × 26 × $10\frac{1}{2}$ feet. Armament: 2—4·1 inch, 45 cal., 2 M.G. AA. Machinery: Germania turbines in *T* 196; A.E.G. Vulcan type in *T* 190. Designed H.P.: *T* 196, 18,200 = 32·5 kts.; *T* 190, 18,000 = 30·5 kts. Present best speed, 25 kts. Fuel: *T* 196, 204 tons; *T* 190, 198 tons. 3 Schulz-Thornycroft boilers (oil burning). Complement: 80.

Notes.—*T* 196 classed as *flottentender*. *C. van Bevern* is experimental tender (*Versuchboot*), and has 2—19·7 inch torpedo tubes, mounted singly in centre line.

T 156. 1938, *courtesy Dr. Erich Gröner.*

EDUARD JUNGMANN (ex-T 153), T 155, 156, 157, 158 (Vulcan, 1907–8).
Displacement: 675 tons. Dimensions: 237 × $25\frac{1}{2}$ × $10\frac{1}{2}$ feet (*max.* draught).
Guns: 1 or 2 M.G. AA. in all but *T* 158, which has 1—3·5 inch in addition, and *E. Jungmann*, which is not armed.
Machinery: Triple expansion. Designed H.P.: 10,900 = 30 kts. how only 22 kts.). Oil: 181 tons. Complement: 74 in *E. Jungmann*, 83 in others. All originally bore numbers with V prefixed.
Note.—E. Jungmann used as Gunnery School Tender, others as tenders to submarines.

Miscellaneous

Patrol Trawlers. (*Vorpostenboote*)

Note.—Some of these have been lost. Many more trawlers have been taken into service.

Frithjof. 1937, *Schäfer.*
(All similar except *Hagen*, in which deckhouse extends further aft.)

BEOWULF (ex-*Joh. Vester*, ex-*Beowulf*), **FREYR** (ex-*Glücksburg*) **FRITHJOF** (ex-*N. Ebeling*, ex-*Frithjof*), **HEIMDALL** (ex-*Lauenburg*), **SIGFRID** (ex-*Esteburg*, ex-*Sigfrid*), **WOTAN** (ex-*Augustenburg*), **HAGEN** (ex-*Anton Palm*, ex-*Gustav Harms*), **HILDEBRAND** (ex-*Seelöwe*, ex-*Wilhelm Grünhage*), **HUGIN** (ex-*Gorch Fock*, ex-*Hugin*), **MUNIN** (ex-*Ditmar Koel*, ex-*Munin*), **ODIN** (ex-*Österreich*), **VOLKER** (ex-*Niedersachsen*), (1912–21). Ex-Trawlers, acquired 1937. Displacement: 496 tons. Dimensions vary from 117 × 22 × 11 to 136 × 24 × $11\frac{1}{2}$ feet. Guns: 1—3·5 inch, 3—1 pdr. AA. Machinery: Triple expansion. I.H.P.: 400 = 10 kts. Complement: 38.

Target Service Ships (*Zielschiffe*).

1937, *Schäfer.*

HESSEN (ex-Battleship). (1903). Reconstructed 1936–37 as a wireless-controlled target ship. Displacement: 13,040 tons. Dimensions: $400\frac{1}{4}$ × 73 × $23\frac{1}{2}$ feet. H.P.: 16,000 = 20 kts. Oil fuel and automatically fired boilers. Equipment includes special smoke screen apparatus.

1934 *Photo.*

ZÄHRINGEN (ex-Battleship), (1901), reconstructed 1927–28 for use as a wireless controlled target ship on similar lines to British *Centurion*. Displacement: 11,800 tons. Dimensions: $393\frac{1}{2}$ × $68\frac{1}{4}$ × 25 feet. H.P. 5,000 = 13 kts. 2 screws. Oil fuel and automatically fired boilers. Complement: 104.

GREECE

Royal Hellenic Navy:

Flags.

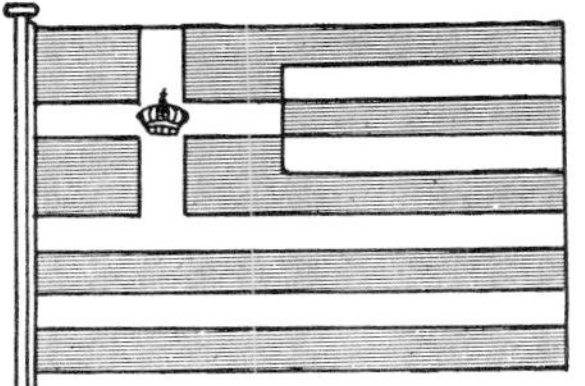
Ensign

H.M. the King
(Crown Prince's similar, but crown in upper left canton only.)

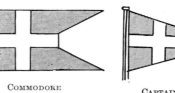

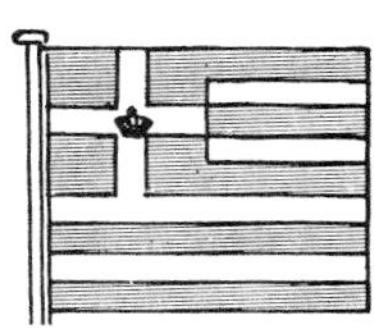
Minister of Marine

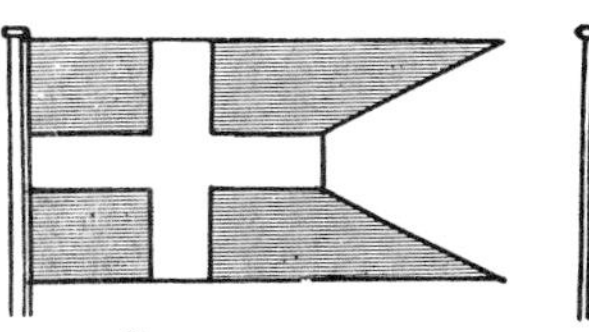
Commodore

Captain (D)

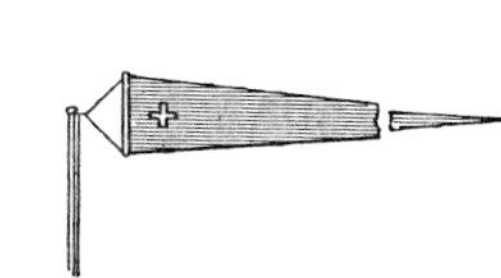
Pendant

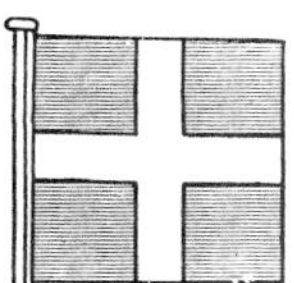
Admiral

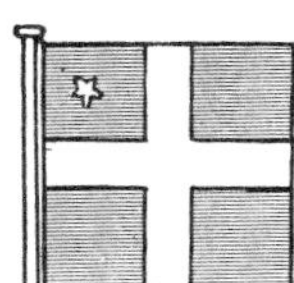
Vice-Admiral

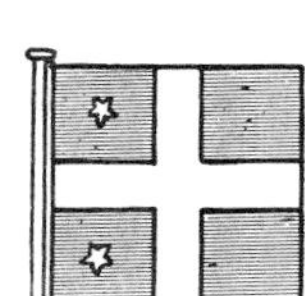
Rear-Admiral

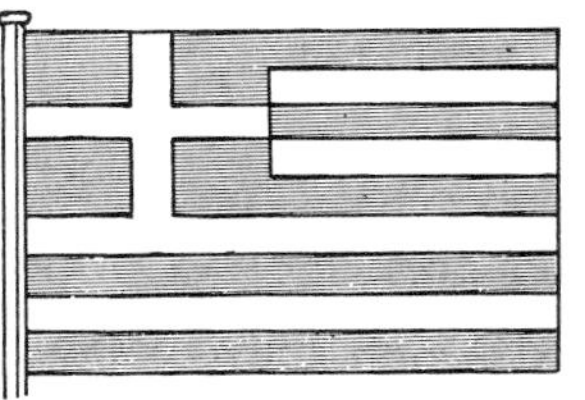
Mercantile

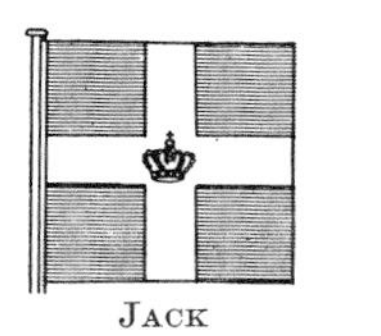
Jack

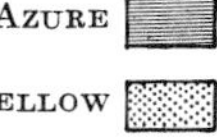

Minister for Navy:—Mr. Demetrios Londos.
Under Secretary Navy:—Captain Coundouriotis.
Commander-in-Chief:—Rear-Admiral G. Mezekais.
Naval Attaché, London:—Captain E. Georgacopoulos.
Personnel:—About 10,000 (conscript, 18 months or enlistment).

Uniforms.

(Rank of Admiral of the Fleet, with 4 stripes, is held only by the King.)

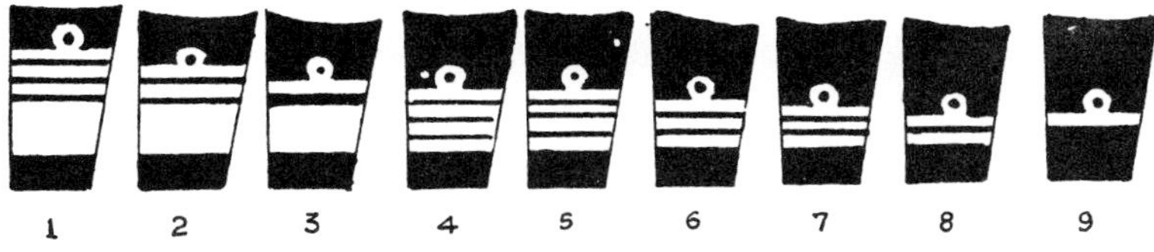

(1) Navarkhos *Admiral.* (2) Andinavarkhos. *Vice-Admiral.* (3) Yponavarkhos. *Rear-Admiral.* (4 Ploiarkhos. *Captain.* (5) Andiploiarkhos. *Commander.* (6) Plotarkhis. *Lieutenant-Commander* (with brass hat). (7) Ypoploiarkhos. *Lieutenant.* (8) Anthipoploiarkhos. *Sub-Lieut.* (9) Simæophoros. *Act. Sub-Lieut.*

Other branches (all with curl):
Engineers: *Dark violet velvet.*
Constructors: *Black velvet.*
Electricians: *Light violet velvet.*
Surgeons: *Scarlet cloth.*
Judicals: *Violet cloth.*
Supply Officers: *White cloth.*
Pharmacists: *Dark green velvet.*
Research Chemists: *Light green velvet.*

Tonnage.

At Standard Displacement.

Mercantile Marine.

(Sept. 30, 1945), 500,000 tons gross.

Naval Ordnance

Nominal Calibre In.	mm.	Maker and Date		Length in Calibres	Weight of Gun	Weight of Projectile	Muzzle Velocity Foot-sec.	Muzzle Energy Foot-tons
					Tons	lb.		
4·7	120	T.	1929	50	3	48	3,117	2,200
4	102	B.	1910	50	2·6	33	2,998	1,937
3·5	88	K.	1907	30	1	18	2,500	1,000
3 H.A.	76·2	V.	1924	50	1·1	12·8	2,789	675
2·6	66	S.	1905	30	12 cwt.	9	2,000	400
1·58 H.A.	40	T.	1917	39	5 cwt.	2	2,000	55

V = Vickers; T = Terni; B = Bethlehem; K = Krupp; S = Skoda; H.A. = High Angle.

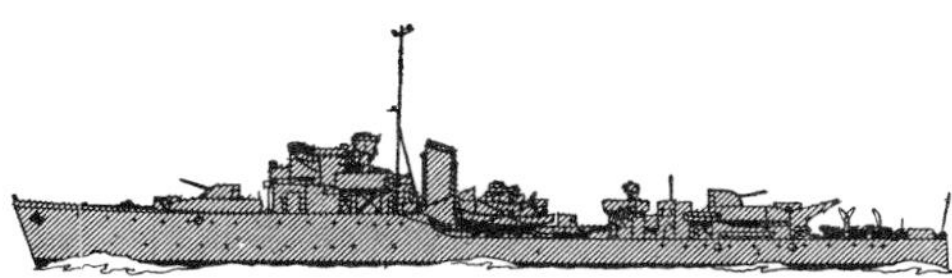
Adrias *class.*

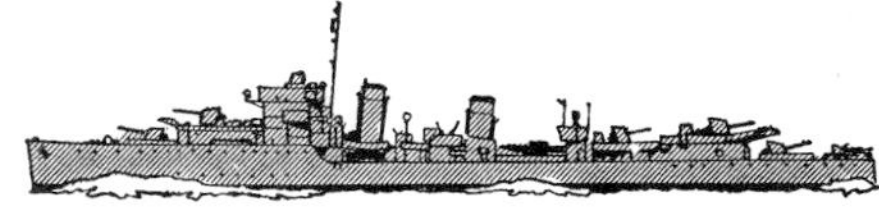
Salamis.

Apostolis *class.*

Themistocles *class.*

Navarinon.

Vasilevs Georgios II.

Silhouettes

AFROESSA *class.*

AMPHITRITI, XIFIAS.

PIPINOS *class.*

Destroyers

5 Adrias Class.

2 *Swan Hunter:* **Miaoulis** (ex-H.M.S. *Modbury*, April 13, 1942), **Pindos** (ex-*Bolebroke*, Nov. 5, 1941).
1 *Vickers-Armstrongs (Tyne):* **Kanaris** (ex-*Hatherleigh*, Dec. 18, 1941).
1 *Vickers-Armstrongs (Barrow):* **Hastings** (ex-*Catterick*, Nov. 22, 1941).
1 *Yarrow:* **Adrias** (ex-*Tanatside*, April 30, 1942).

All belong to modified "Hunt" type. Displacement: 1,050 tons (1,490 tons *full load*). Dimensions: 280 × 31½ × 7⅝ feet (*mean*). Guns: **4**—4 inch, **1**—4-barrelled 2 pdr. pompom, **2** or **3**—20 mm. AA. Tubes: **2**—21 inch. Machinery: Parsons geared turbines. S.H.P. 19,000 = 27 kts. Boilers: 2, of 3-drum type. Oil fuel: 280 tons. Complement: 168. All transferred from Royal Navy, 1942–44.

PINDOS. 1946, *London Studio.*

HASTINGS. 1946, *London Studio.*

Note.—Another destroyer of this type, *Adrias* (ex-*Border*), was scrapped owing to heavy damage received when a mine blew away her forecastle on October 22, 1943. *Hastings* is named after a retired British naval officer in Greek service who during the War of Independence destroyed a much superior Turkish squadron at Salona, Sept. 30, 1827. *Miaoulis* is fitted as Leader.

3 Themistoklis Class

1 *Stephen:* **Themistoklis** (ex-H.M.S. *Bramham*, Jan. 29, 1942).
1 *Swan Hunter:* **Kriti** (ex-*Hursley*, July 25, 1941).
1 *Thornycroft:* **Aigaion** (ex-*Lauderdale*, May 8, 1941).

Displacement: 1,050 tons (1,490 tons *full load*). Dimensions: 280 × 31½ × 7⅝ feet (*mean*). Guns: **6**—4 inch, **1**—4-barrelled multiple pompom, **3**—20 mm. AA. No tubes. Machinery: Parsons geared turbines. S.H.P.: 19,000 = 27 kts. Boilers: 2, of 3-drum type. Oil fuel: 280 tons. Complement: 168.

THEMISTOKLIS. 1942, *Lieut.-Com. W. A. Fuller, R.N.V.R.*

Old Destroyers.

(*Relegated to training duties.*)

NAVARINON. 1942, *Official.*

1 *Denny:* **Navarinon** (ex-H.M.S. *Echo*) (Feb. 16, 1934). Displacement: 1,375 tons. Dimensions: 318¼ (*pp.*), 329 (*o.a.*) × 33¼ × 8½ feet (*mean*). Guns: 4—4·7 inch, 1—3 inch AA., 4—20 mm. AA. Tubes: 4—21 inch (in quadruple mounting). Machinery: Parsons geared turbines. 2 shafts. S.H.P. 36,000 = 36 kts. Boilers: 3, of 3-drum type, 300 lb. working pressure. Oil fuel: 480 tons. Complement: 145.

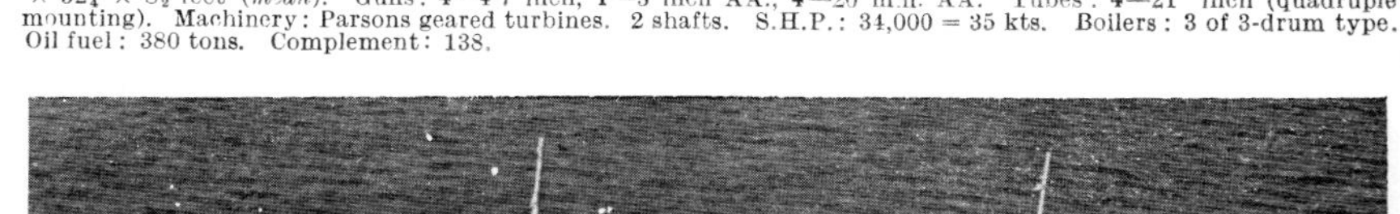

1 *Palmer:* **Salamis** (ex-H.M.S. *Boreas*) (July 18, 1930). Displacement: 1,360 tons. Dimensions: 312 (*pp.*) 323 (*o.a.*) × 32¼ × 8½ feet (*mean*). Guns: **4**—4·7 inch, **1**—3 inch AA., **4**—20 mm. AA. Tubes: **4**—21 inch (quadruple mounting). Machinery: Parsons geared turbines. 2 shafts. S.H.P.: 34,000 = 35 kts. Boilers: 3 of 3-drum type. Oil fuel: 380 tons. Complement: 138.

Added 1946, Charles E. Brown.

Submarines.

PIPINOS. 1945, *London Studio.*

4 *Vickers-Armstrongs (Barrow)*: ***Argonaftis*** (ex-*Virulent*, May 23, 1944), ***Delfin*** (ex-*Vengeful*, July 20, 1944), ***Pipinos*** (ex-*Veldt*, July 19, 1943), ***Triaina*** (ex-*Volatile*, June 20, 1944). Displacement: 545/735 tons. Dimensions: 206 × 16 × 14¾ feet. Guns: **1**—3 inch, **3**—20 mm. AA. Tubes: **4**—21 inch. B.H.P.: 800/760 = 13/9 kts. Fuel: 56 tons.

XIFIAS. 1946, *London Studio.*

1 *Vickers-Armstrongs (Tyne)*: ***Amfitriti*** (ex-*Untiring*, Jan. 20, 1943).
1 *Vickers-Armstrongs (Barrow)*: ***Xifias*** (ex-*Upstart*, Nov. 24, 1942).

Displacement: 540/721 tons. Dimensions: 200 × 16 × 14¾ feet.

Other particulars as in four preceding vessels. All 6 transferred from Royal Navy, 1943-46.

Note.—Older Submarines *Matrozors, Nereus* and *Papanikolis* have been discarded.

Submarines.

4 Glavkos Class.

GLAVKOS. 1929 *Photo, by favour of M. Henri Le Masson.*

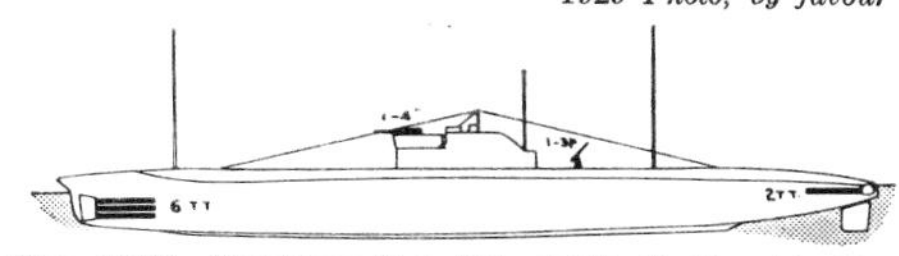

4 *Simonot* type. ***Nereus*** (Dec., 1927), ***Proteus*** (Oct. 24th, 1927), ***Triton*** (April 4th, 1928), all built by At. & Ch. de la Loire, at Nantes, ***Glavkos*** (1928), by Chantiers Navals Francais, at Blainville. Displacement: 700/930 tons (metric). Dimensions: 225 (*p.p.*) × 18.8 × 13.7 feet. Machinery (supplied by At. & Ch. de la Loire): On *surface*, 2 sets 2-cycle Sulzer-Diesels, totalling 1420 B.H.P. for 14 kts.: *submerged* 1200 B.H.P. for 9½ kts. Endurance on *surface*: *normal* 1500 miles, *maximum* 4000 miles; both at 10 kts. When *submerged*, 100 miles at 5 kts. Armament: **1**—4 inch, **1**—3 pdr. AA., **6**—21 inch internal bow tubes, **2**—21 inch internal stern tubes. Stowage for 8 torpedoes, 150 rounds of 4 inch ammunition. Complement, 41. *Maximum* depth of submergence: 40 fathoms. Approximate cost £119,000 each.

2 Katsonis Class.

KATSONIS. 1929 *Photo, M. Bar, Toulon.*

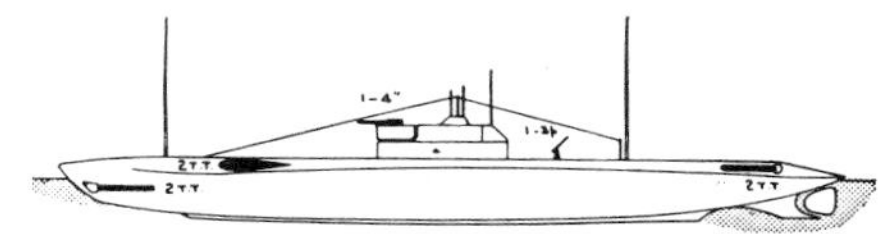

2 *Schneider-Laubeuf* type. ***Katsonis*** (20 March, 1926), by Ch. de la Gironde, at Bordeaux; ***Papamicolis*** (Nov. 1926), by At. & Ch. de la Loire, at Nantes. Displacement: 576/775 tons. Dimensions: 204½ × (*p.p.*) 17½ × 11 feet. On *surface*, 2 sets of 2-cycle Machinery: Schneider-Carels Diesels, totalling 1300 B.H.P. for 14 kts. *Submerged*, 1000 B.H.P. for 9½ kts. Endurance, on *surface*: *normal* 1500 miles, *maximum* 3500 miles, both at 10 kts; when *submerged*, 100 miles at 5 kts. Armament: **1**—4 inch, **1**—3 pdr. AA., **2**—21 inch internal bow tubes, **2**—21 inch external bow tubes, **2**—21 inch external stern tubes. Stowage for 7 torpedoes, 100 rounds of 4 inch ammunition. Complement, 39. *Maximum* depth of submergence: 40 fathoms. First boat delivered at Piraeus, Dec. 29th, 1927.

(1907) Armoured Cruiser.

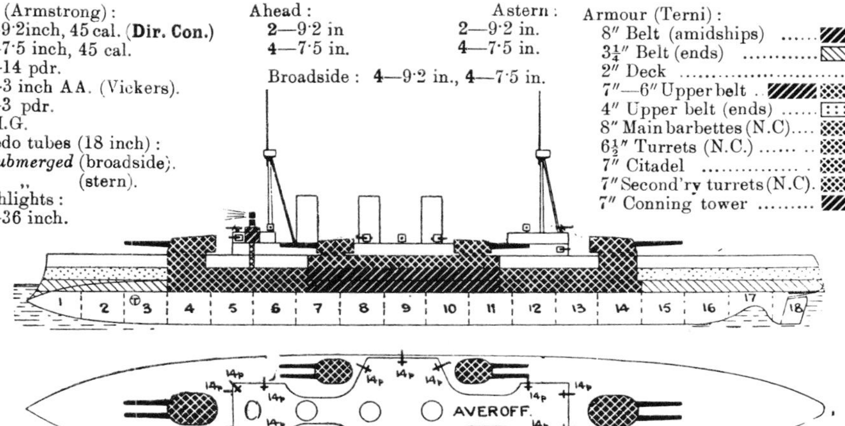

AVEROFF 1931 *Photo, Official.*

AVEROFF (March, 1910).

Displacement, 9,450 tons. Complement, 670.

Length (*over all*), 462 feet. Beam, 69 feet. *Maximum* draught, 24⅔ feet.

Guns (Armstrong):
4—9·2inch, 45 cal. (**Dir. Con.**)
8—7·5 inch, 45 cal.
16—14 pdr.
2—3 inch AA. (Vickers).
4—3 pdr.
2 M.G.

Torpedo tubes (18 inch):
2 *submerged* (broadside).
1 ,, (stern).

Searchlights:
2—36 inch.

Ahead:
2—9·2 in
4—7·5 in.

Astern:
2—9·2 in.
4—7·5 in.

Broadside: **4**—9·2 in., **4**—7·5 in.

Armour (Terni):
8″ Belt (amidships) ......
3¼″ Belt (ends) ....
2″ Deck ....
7″—6″ Upper belt ..
4″ Upper belt (ends) ......
8″ Main barbettes (N.C)....
6½″ Turrets (N.C.) ....
7″ Citadel ....
7″ Second'ry turrets (N.C).
7″ Conning tower ....

Machinery: 2 sets 4 cylinder triple expansion. 2 screws. Boilers: 22 Belleville. Designed H.P. 19,000 = 22·5 kts. Trials: 21,500 = 23·9. Coal: *normal* 660 tons; *maximum* 1500 tons = 7125 miles at 10 kts.; 2489 miles at 17¾ kts. Built by Orlando.

Cruiser Minelayer.

HELLE. 1931 *Photo, Official.*

HELLE (ex-Chinese *Fei Hung*, May, 1912).

Displacement, 2115 tons. Complement, 232.

Length (*over all*), 322 feet. Beam, 39 feet. Draught, 14 feet.

Guns (Armstrong):
3—6 inch.
2—3 inch. AA. (Vickers).
4—6 pdr.

Torpedo tubes (18 inch):
2 *above water.*

110 *Mines carried.*

Armour (steel):
2″ Deck on slopes ...
2″ Deck on flat.........

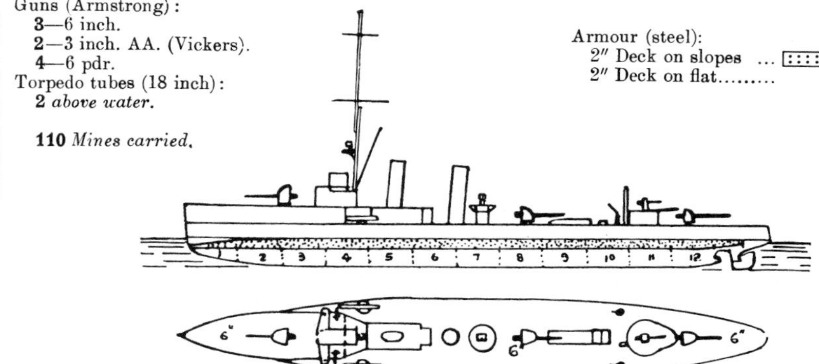

Machinery: 3 Parsons geared turbines. 3 screws. Boilers: 3 Yarrow. Designed H.P. 7500 = 20.5 kts. Oil: *normal* 600 tons = 7000 miles at 10 kts.

Name	Builder	Machinery	Laid down	Completed	Trials: 4 hours.	Trials: Full Power.	Boilers	Best recent speed
Helle	N.Y. Shipblg.	N.Y. Shipblg.	1910	Nov.,'13	7500=20·3	8650=21	Yarrow	

Repair Ships.

1938, Grand Studio.

HIFAISTOS (ex-*Khios*) (ex-German cargo ship *Marie Reppel*, Rostock, 1920). *Gross* tonnage: 4,549. Dimensions: 360½ × 50 × 23 feet. I.H.P.: 2,500 = 11·5 kts. Guns: 4—4 inch AA. Converted into a Repair Ship by Messrs. Palmers, Jarrow-on-Tyne, 1925. Fitted with up-to-date workshops and plant.

1946, London Studio.

HERMES (ex-*Product*, ex-*Port Jackson*, 1941). Displacement: 400 tons. Dimensions: 133 × 27¾ × 11 feet. Machinery: Triple expansion.

Motor Launches

(*Photos in Addenda.*)

9 *Fairmile B type:* **DOLIANA, DOMOKOS, DOXATON, DRAMA, KALAMPAKA, KALINI, KARPENISI, KHALKI, TSATALTZA** (ex-*ML* 295, 232, 307, 341, 483, 478, 867, 578, 861, respectively). Displacement: 75 tons.

8 *Harbour Defence type:* **BIZANI, DAVLIA, DISTRATON, FARSALA, KARYA, KASTRAKI, KLISOURA, PORTARIA** (ex-*HDML* 1221, 1032, 1292, 1252, 1007, 1375, 1149, 1051, respectively). Displacement: 40 tons.

Coastal Transports.

(*Photo in Addenda.*)

ANKHIALOS, DISTOMON, ELASSON, KALAVRYTA, LEKHOVON, VELESTINON (ex-*FT* 11, 12, 13, 65, 66, 71; ex-*APC* 65, 66, 67, 71, 73, 75). All built 1943. Displacement: 229 tons. Guns: 2—20 mm. AA.

Though it is understood that five fleet minesweepers, late H.M.S. **COMBATANT, FLORIZEL, GORGON, JASPER** (ex-*Garnet*), and **STEADFAST,** have been transferred to the Greek flag, it is believed that it is not intended to use them for naval purposes.

FARSALA 1946, *R. H. N. Official.*

KALINI 1946, *R. H. N. Official.*

LEKHOVON *type* 1946, *R. H. N. Official.*

ARGYROKASTRON 1946, *R. H. N. Official.*

HUNGARY

(Danube Flotilla.)

Ensign

Flag Officer

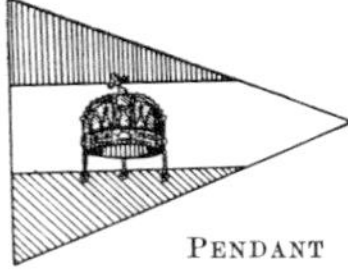

Pendant

Principal Base.—Budapest.

Under Law XIV of 1922 the Royal Hungarian Honvéd River Force (Magyar Királyi Honvéd Folyamerök) was established for police purposes on the Danube, under the control of the Ministry of the Interior.

Colour of Ships: Khaki, and Green below waterline.

River Patrol Vessels.

1938, *courtesy Dr. E. Gröner.*

GODOLLO (ex-Czechoslovak *Birago*, ex-Hungarian *Siofok*, ex-Austro-Hungarian *Czuka*). Laid down Jan. 1915 as patrol vessel "K" at the Ganz-Danubius Shipyard, Budapest. Completed and commissioned March 1, 1916. Purchased by Austria in Aug. 1929. Displacement: 60 tons. Complement: 18. Dimensions: 118 × 15 × 2¾ feet. Protected by bullet-proof belt of chrome steel. Guns: 1—70 mm., 30 cal., 1—1 pdr. AA., 3 M.G. Machinery: Reciprocating. I.H.P.: 800 = 11 kts.

Debrecen. (Masts now of equal height.) 1925 *Official Photo.*

BAJA (ex-*Barsch*), **GYOR** (ex-*Compo*), **DEBRECEN** (ex-*Komaron*, ex-Austro-Hungarian *Lachs*), (Ganz-Danubius Yard, Budapest, 1918). Displacement: 140 tons. Dimensions: 149¼ × 19½ × 3¼ feet *mean* draught. Guns: 2—70mm., 2 M.G. 1 S.L. Machinery: A.E.G. turbines. Tunnel screws. S.H.P. 1,200 = 15 kts. 2 Yarrow boilers. Oil fuel: 18 tons. Complement, 44. Refitted 1924–26.

River Patrol Vessels—*continued.*

Györ 1933 *Photo, Official.*

SOPRON (ex-Austro-Hungarian *Stöhr*). (Ganz-Danubius Yard, Budapest, 1918). Refitted 1928 and re-engined with M.A.N. Diesels. B.H.P. 1600 = 18 kts. Fuel: 20 tons.

Details otherwise as *Debrecen* class above.

Szeged. 1925 *Official Photo.*

SZEGED (ex-*Bregainica*, ex-Austro-Hungarian *Wels*, 1915), **KECSKEMÉT** (ex-Austro-Hungarian *Viza*, 1916). Both built at Ganz-Danubius Yard, Budapest. Displacement: 133 tons. Dimensions: 144½ × 16½ × 3¼ feet *mean* draught. Guns: 2—70 mm., 2 M.G. 1 S.L. Machinery: A.E.G. turbines. Tunnel screws. S.H.P. 1100 = 15 kts. 2 Yarrow boilers. Oil fuel: 18 tons. Complement, 44. *Szeged* refitted 1921, *Kecskemét*, 1923.

Depôt Ship.

1934 *Photo, Official.*

CSOBÁNC (Ganz-Danubius Yard, Budapest, 1928). 305 tons. Dimensions: 132 × 18 × 4½ feet. 2 Diesels. Tunnel screws. B.H.P. 180 = 8 kts. Oil: 8 tons. Complement, 18.

In addition to the above, there are 3 Motor Launches of 17 tons, **HONVED, HUSZAR, TÜZER,** and a training vessel of 225 tons, **BADACSONY,** H.P.: 400 = 10·5 kts.

ITALY

Flags.

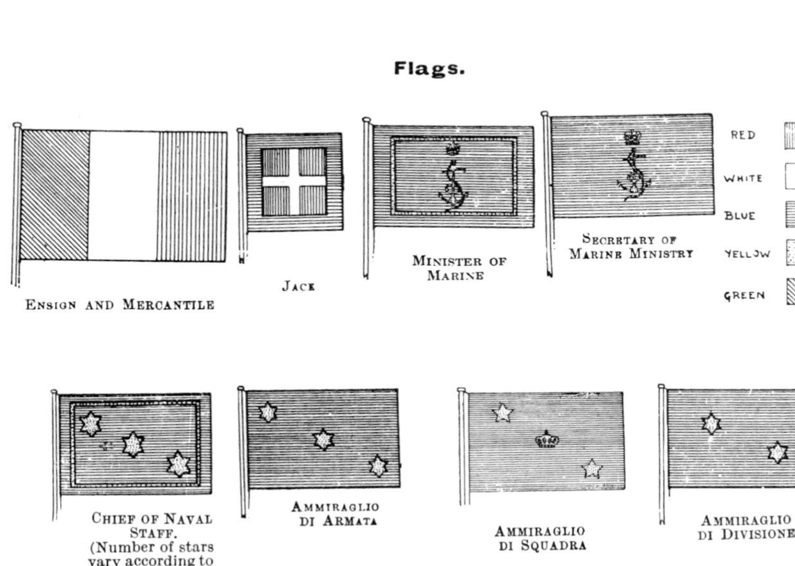

Ensign and Mercantile. Jack. Minister of Marine. Secretary of Marine Ministry.

Chief of Naval Staff. (Number of stars vary according to rank.) Ammiraglio di Armata. Ammiraglio di Squadra. Ammiraglio di Divisione.

Contrammiraglio. Capitano di Vascello (commanding division.) Senior Naval Officer. Flotilla Leader.

Uniforms.

Note.—A five pointed silver star (or gold in the case of flag officers) is worn on lapel of coat.

INSIGNIA OF RANK ON SLEEVES.

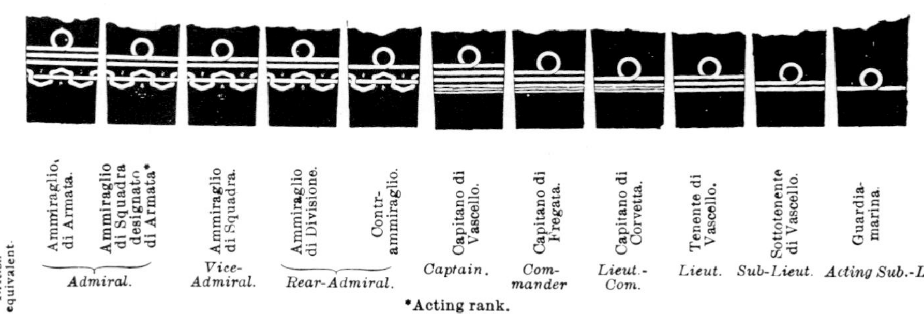

Ammiraglio di Armata. Ammiraglio di Squadra designato di Armata*. Ammiraglio di Squadra. Ammiraglio di Divisione. Contr-ammiraglio. Capitano di Vascello. Capitano di Fregata. Capitano di Corvetta. Tenente di Vascello. Sottotenente di Vascello. Guardia-marina.

British equivalent: *Admiral. Vice-Admiral. Rear-Admiral. Captain. Commander. Lieut.-Com. Lieut. Sub-Lieut. Acting Sub.-Lt.*

*Acting rank.

Second and third sketches embody varying devices on lower cuff, only shown faintly above.

The rank of Grande Ammiraglio (four stripes) equivalent to Admiral of the Fleet can only be conferred for special merit on flag officers who have commanded fleets in time of war.

Lesser ranks are: Aspirante (*Midshipman*); Allievo dell' Accademia Navale (*Naval Cadet*).

Other branches distinguished by following Colours: Armi Navali (*Ordnance Constructors*), yellow-brown; Genio Navale (*Naval Constructors* and *Engineers*), dark purple; Sanitario (*Doctors*), blue; Commissariato (*Paymasters*), red; Chemists, green; Harbour Masters, grey-green.

Note.—All officers under arms on duty wear a blue sash over right shoulder, ending in a blue knot at left hip; worn with belt. Officers on staff duty wear it on opposite shoulder, with or without belt. Tropical white tunic has insignia of rank on shoulder straps, with stars to correspond with number of stripes. Senior lieutenants wear a piece of gold under the stars of shoulder strap.

Minister of Defence: Signor Luigi Gasparotto.

Chief of Naval Staff: Ammiraglio di Divisione Francesco Maugeri.

Mercantile Marine.

From "Lloyd's Register" 1939 figures.
1.235 vessels of 3,448,453 gross tonnage.

Conditions of Peace Treaty, 1946.

Material of Navy (excluding *Doria* and *Duilio* and auxiliaries) not to exceed 67,500 tons (*standard*). Personnel not to exceed 22,500 officers and men.

No battleship, aircraft carrier, submarine, M.T.B., or specialised assault craft shall be constructed, acquired, employed or experimented with by Italy.

No warship to be constructed or acquired before Jan. 1, 1950, except in replacement of accidental losses.

Silhouettes Battleships, Cruisers

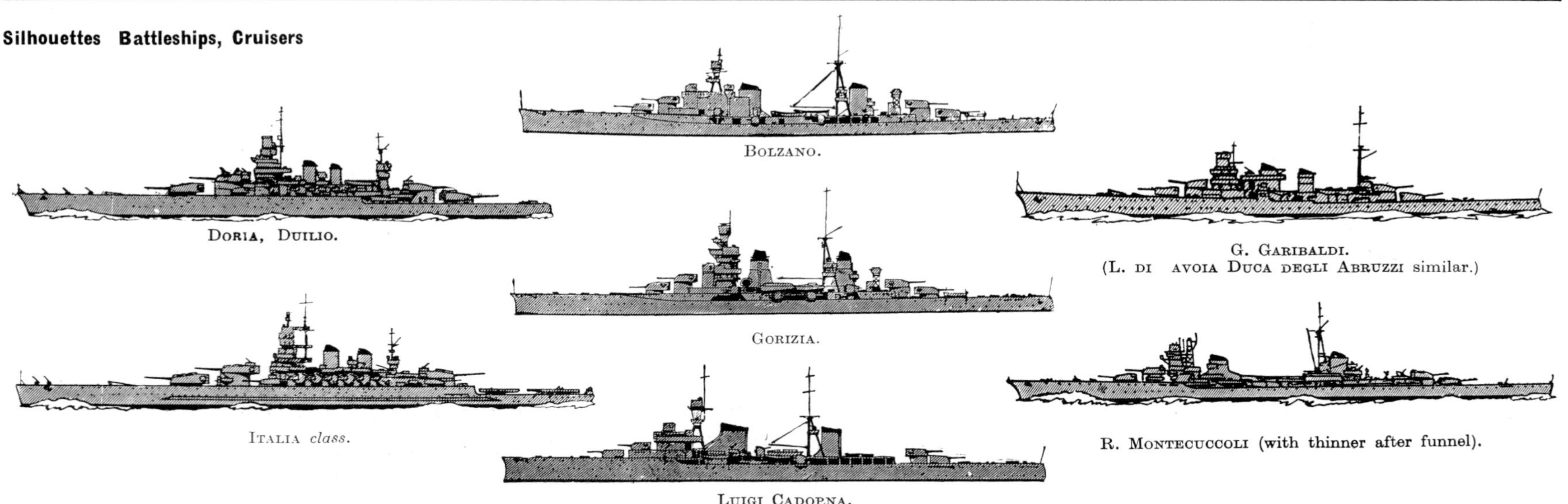

Bolzano.

Doria, Duilio.

G. Garibaldi. (L. di Savoia Duca degli Abruzzi similar.)

Gorizia.

Italia *class.*

R. Montecuccoli (with thinner after funnel).

Luigi Cadorna.

CARABINIERE, GRANATIERE.

ORIONE, ORSA.

G. CARINI, N. FABRIZI.

GRECALE.

MONZAMBANO

G. MIRAGLIA.

E. GIOVANNINI.

N. DA RECCO.

A. PACINOTTI.

ARIETE

GABBIANO *class.*

LIBRA and SIRIO *classes.*

ABBA *class.*

AZIO.

OFFICIAL TABLE OF NAVAL ORDNANCE.

Official Designation.— Calibre mm length cal. Mark A=Armstrong, V=Vickers An=Ansaldo, S=Schneider. O.T.O.=Odero-Terni-Orlando. Date of introduction.	203/54 An. 1929	152/53 An. O.T.O. 1927-29	120/50 An. 1926. O.T.O. 1931	120/45 A. 1918 O.T.O. 1928–31	102/45 S.-A. 1917	100/47 O.T.O. 1929	76/50 A., V. 1909	76/40 A. 1916
Designation by Calibre, c/m.	20.3	15.24	12	12	10.2	10.0	7.62	7.62
Calibre, in inches	8	6	4.75	4.75	4	3.9	3	3
Lengths: Total, in feet	36.545	27.83	19.57	18.38	15.715	15.721	13.271	10.292
Lengths: Rifled Bore, in inches	358·66	—	—	174.64	150.74	12.365	126	101.57
Lengths: Powder Chamber, in inches	64.66	—	—	35.03	27.16	3.112	22	—
Lengths: Bore, in calibres	—	—	—	36.96	37.53	15.371	42	28.42
No. of Grooves	52	44	36	36	40	26	28	16
Twist of Rifling, in calibres	—	30	30	30	—	30	30	33
Total Weight, in tons	19.170	7.700	3.00	4.035	2.327	2.020	1.122	0.660
Firing Charge: Armour-piercing projectile lb.	112	43	19	—	—	—	—	—
Firing Charge: Common Shell H.E., lb.	—	—	—	9.589	9.479	10.319	3.02	2.281
Weight: Armour-piercing projectile, lb.	275.573	103.5	50.5	—	—	—	—	—
Weight: Shell H.E., lb.	—	—	—	48.74	30.31	30.318	14.05	13.954
Weight: Shrapnel, lb.	—	—	—	—	—	—	—	—
Bursting Charge: Armour-piercing projectile, lb.	—	—	—	—	—	—	—	—
Bursting Charge: Shell H.E., lb.	—	—	—	2.711	2.866	—	1.102	—
Bursting Charge: Shrapnel, lb.	—	—	—	—	—	—	—	—
Muzzle Velocity, in ft. secs.	3031.180	2785	2786	2460	2788	2438.40	2460	2214
Muzzle Energy — Total tons per sq. inch	—	—	—	15.75	18.37	—	18.37	—

Note.—There is also an O.T.O. model 12·6 inch.

12·6 inch in *Doria* and *Duilio*.
6 „ 53 cal. in *Cadorna* and later cruisers.
4.7 „ 50 „ „ *N. da Recco* and later destroyers.
3.9 „ 47 „ „ *Cadorna* and later cruisers.

Displacement.

Now given in English Tons, "Standard" calculation.

Directors, Rangefinders, &c.

Supplied by the Galileo and S. Giorgio Companies, of Florence and Genoa, respectively. Rangefinders are of a new model both co-incident and stereoscopic, of 5 and 7.20 metres base for main armament and 3 metres for secondary guns.

Torpedoes.

Supplied by Silurificio Italiano di Fiume.
Cal. 533·4 mm. *Length,* 7·2 m. *Charge* 250 kg. *Speed,* 4,000 m. = 50 kts. 6,000 = 43 kts., 8,000 = 39 kts., 10,000 = 34 kts., 12,000 = 30 kts.

Battleships

CAIO DUILIO (April 24, 1913), ANDREA DORIA (March 30, 1913).

Standard displacement (as reconstructed): 23,622 tons (over 25,000 full load). Complement: 1,198. Dimensions: 597 (*w.l.*), 611½ (*o.a.*) × 92 × 30 feet (*mean* draught).

Guns:
- 10—12·6 inch, 44 cal.
- 12—5·3 inch, 45 cal.
- 10—3·5 inch AA., 48 cal.
- 39—M.G., AA.

Armour (originally, now improved over magazines, machinery and boiler spaces):
- 9¾″–8″ Belt (amidships)
- 5″ Belt (ends)
- 9½″ Barbettes
- 11″ Turrets to these
- 11″ Conning tower (fore)

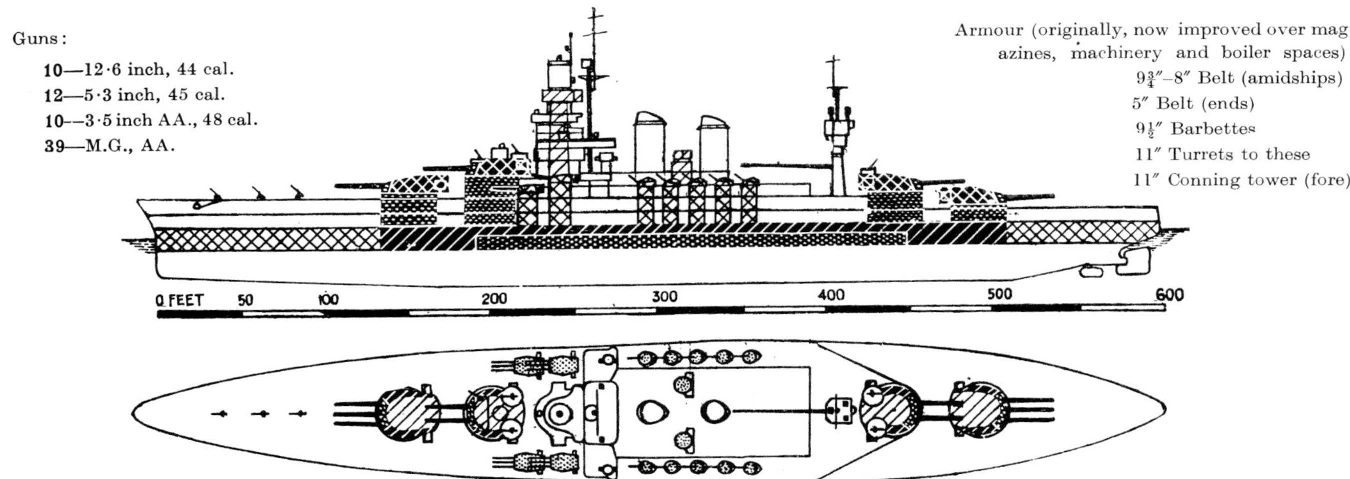

DORIA. *Added* 1946, *E. Mioni.*

Machinery: Belluzzo geared turbines. 2 shafts. S.H.P.: 75,000 = 27 kts. (actual speed does not exceed 22 kts). 8 boilers of 3-drum type (working pressure reported to be 500 lb. to sq. inch). Oil fuel: 2,000 tons.

Note.—These ships were originally of entirely different appearance, with a main armament of 13—12 inch guns, in 3 triple and 2 double turrets and a secondary battery of 6-inch guns.

Gunnery Note.—12·6 inch guns are a Terni model, reported to have given remarkably successful results in proof tests. They are 43·8 calibres in length.

Name	*Builder*	*Machinery*	*Laid down*	*Completed*	*Rebuilt by*
Doria	Spezia	Ansaldo	24/3/12	Mar. 16	Cant. Riuniti dell' Adriatico } 1937–40.
Duilio	Castellammare	„	25/4/12	May 15	Cant. Nav. del Tirreno } 1937–40.

DORIA.

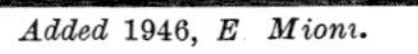

Added 1946, *E Mioni.*

CESARE. 1938, *Grand Studio*

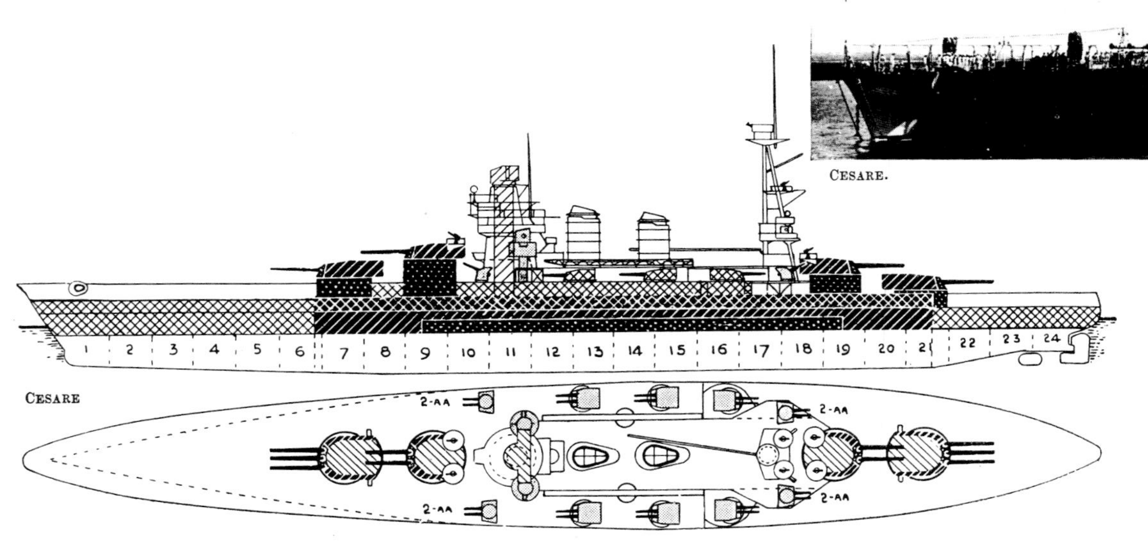

CESARE

*GIULIO CESARE (Oct. 15, 1911), CONTE DI CAVOUR (Aug. 10, 1911).

- 10—12·6 inch, 44 cal.
- 12—5·3 inch, 45 cal.
- 10—3·5 inch AA., 48 cal.
- 39—M.G., AA.

ITALY

Battleships

(Italia Class—3 Ships.)

***ITALIA** (ex-*Littorio*) (Aug. 27, 1937), ***VITTORIO VENETO** (July 25, 1937), **IMPERO** (Nov. 15, 1939). *Standard* displacement: 35,000 tons. Complement: 1,600. Length: 754¼ (*pp.*), 762½ (*w.l.*), 775 feet (*o.a.*). Beam: 106⅓ feet. Draught: 28 feet (*mean*), 30½ feet (*max.*).

Guns:
- **9**—15 inch, 50 cal.
- **12**—6 inch, 55 cal.
- **12**—3·5 inch AA., 48 cal.
- **40** M.G. AA.

Aircraft: **3**
Catapults: **2**

Armour:
9″—12″ Belt.

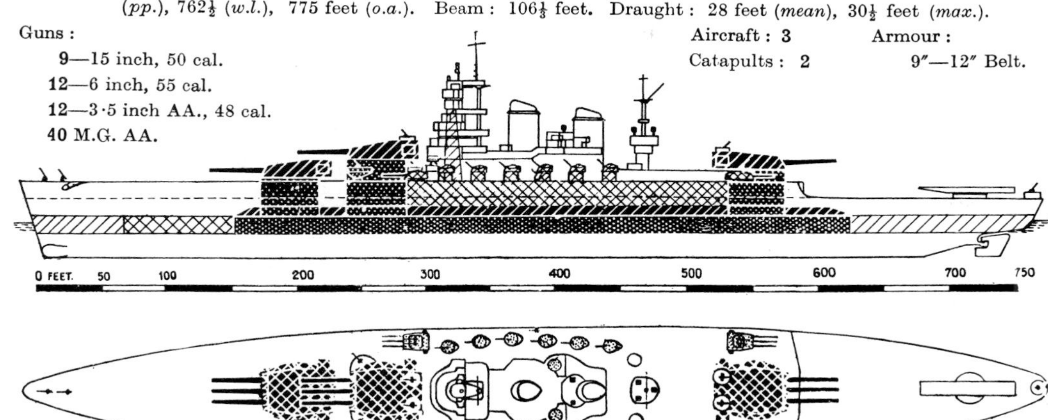

Machinery: Parsons geared turbines. 4 shafts. S.H.P.: 130,000=30 kts. (exceeded on trials.) High pressure water-tube boilers of 3-drum type. Oil fuel.

Name.	*Builder and Machinery*	*Laid down.*	*Completed.*
Italia	Ansaldo	28 Oct., 1934	1 May, 1940.
Vittorio Veneto	C.R.D.A., San Marco, Trieste	28 Oct., 1934	30 April, 1940.
Impero	Ansaldo	14 May, 1938	1943?

Notes.—Designed by Engineer Inspector-General Umberto Pugliese. Though trials of first two ships started in Dec. 1939, it was not until four or five months later that delivery was accepted from builders. Completion of *Impero*, though planned for 1941, has been delayed considerably for reasons still to be explained. Though shortage of steel has been alleged as an excuse, it seems more likely that the ship suffered damage of some kind subsequent to her launch. *Italia's* name was changed in August, 1943. A fourth ship of this class, *Roma*, was torpedoed and sunk by German aircraft on Sept. 9, 1943. *Italia* was also torpedoed on this occasion (for the third time in her career), and when she reached Malta is reported to have been drawing 37 feet.

Vittorio Veneto. 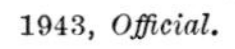 1943, *Official.*

Italia. 1943, *Official.*

Italia. 1943, *Official.*

Cruisers

(Garibaldi Class—2 Ships.)

GIUSEPPE GARIBALDI
LUIGI DI SAVOIA DUCA DEGLI ABRUZZI

(Both April 21, 1936.)

Standard displacement: 7,874 tons as designed, but actual figures are 8,134 and 8,605 tons, respectively (11,776 tons full load).

Complement, 600

Length: 593 (*w.l.*), 613¾ feet (*o.a.*). Beam, 61 feet. Draught, 17 feet (*mean*).

Guns:
- **10**—6 inch, 53 cal.
- **8**—3·9 inch, 47 cal. (**10** in *Abruzzi*).
- **8**—37 mm. AA.
- **10**—20 mm. AA.
- **2** to **6** M.G.
- **2** D.C.T.

Torpedo tubes:
6—21 inch (tripled).
(Removed from *Abruzzi*).

Mines:
Equipped for minelaying.

Aircraft:
2, with **1** catapult.

Armour:
1½″—4½″ Vert. Side.
2¼″ Deck.
4″ Turrets
5″ C.T.

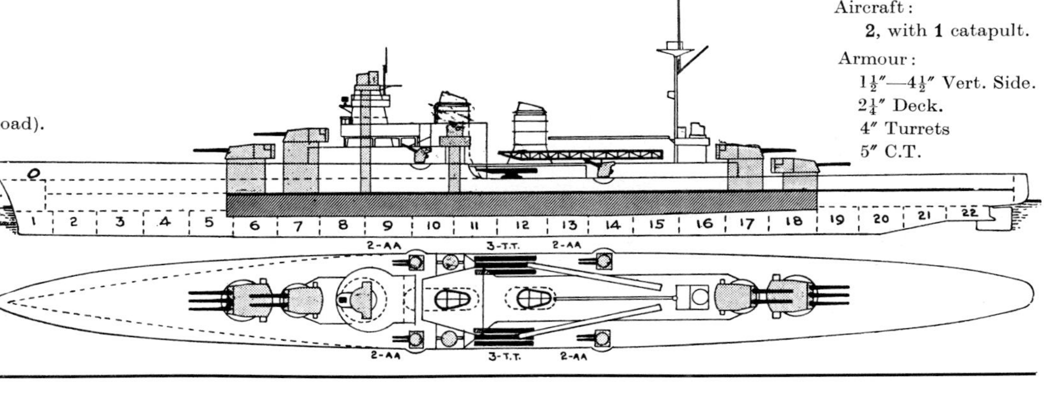

L. di Savoia Duca degli Abruzzi. 1946, *Raymond E. Smith, Esq.*

G. Garibaldi. 1946, *London Studio.*

Machinery: Parsons geared turbines. 2 shafts. Designed S.H.P.: 100,000 = 32 kts. Boilers: 8, of 3-drum type. Oil fuel: 1,680 tons.

Name	*Builder*	*Laid down*	*Completed*
G. Garibaldi	C.R. dell' Adriatico	Dec. 1933	1937
L. di Sav. Duca degli Abruzzi	Odero-Terni-Orlando	Dec. 1933	1937

Notes.—These ships represent the ultimate expansion of the original "Condottieri" design. The 6-inch guns are a new model, more powerful than the 53 cal. weapons with which previous cruisers have been armed. On trials, *Garibaldi* exceeded 33·6 kts. with 104,030 S.H.P.

RAIMONDO MONTECUCCOLI (Ansaldo, Sestri Ponente, August 2, 1934).
Standard displacement: 6,941 tons (about 8,000 tons full load). Complement, 522.
Dimensions: 575¼ (*pp.*), 577 (*w.l.*), 597¾ (*o.a.*) × 54½ × 14¾ feet (*mean* draught).

R. Montecuccoli. 1944.

Guns: 8—6 inch, 53 cal.
6—3·9 inch, 47 cal. AA.
8—37 mm. AA.
8—13 mm. AA.
2 D.C.T.

Torpedo Tubes: 4—21 inch.
Mines: Equipped for laying.

Armour:
Similar to "A" and "B" types of this class, but side armour decidedly thicker at w.l.

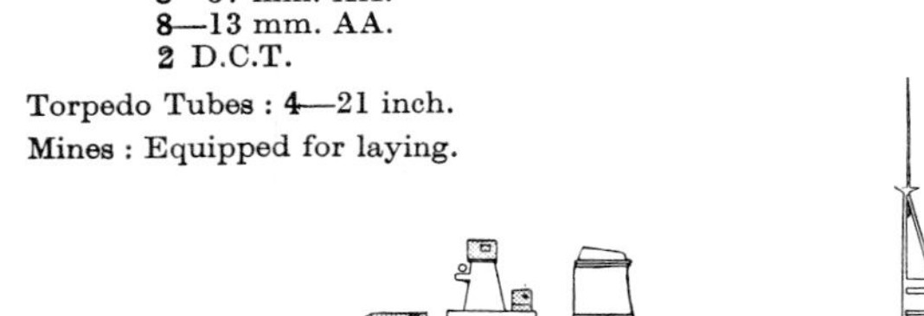

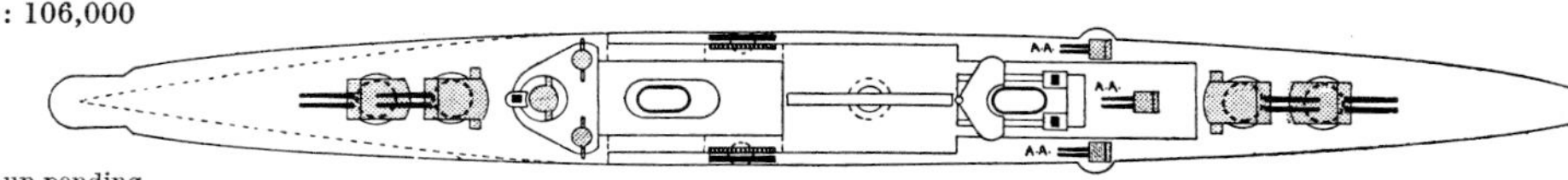

Machinery: Belluzzo geared turbines. 2 shafts. 6 boilers of 3-drum type. S.H.P.: 106,000 = 37 kts. Oil fuel: 500/1,200 tons.

Note.—*R. Montecuccoli* was laid down in October, 1931, under 1930 Programme, but construction was held up pending alterations to plans. Completed in July, 1935, she made 39·4 kts. on trials, without stores or ammunition on board. Sister ship, *Muzio Attendolo*, was sunk by bombing at Naples in Dec. 1942.

LUIGI CADORNA (Cant. Riuniti dell' Adriatico, San Marco, Trieste, Sept. 30, 1931).
Displacement: 5,008 tons. Complement: 500. Dimensions: 547 (*w.l.*), 554½ (*o.a.*) × 50⅕ × 14 feet (*mean*) draught.

Guns: 8—6 inch 53 cal.
6—3·9 inch AA.
8—37 mm. AA.
8—13 mm. AA.
2 D.C.T.

Armour:
Thin plating only on Side, Turrets and Decks.

Torpedo Tubes: 4—21 inch.
Mines: Equipped for laying.

Luigi Cadorna. *Added* 1946, *Official.*

Machinery: 2 Parsons geared turbines. 2 shafts. S.H.P. 95,000 = 37 kts. 6 boilers of 3-drum type. Oil: 500/1,000 tons. Radius: 2,500 miles at 25 kts.

BOLZANO. Ansaldo, Sestri-Ponente. (Aug. 31, 1932).

Standard displacement, 10,000 tons. Complement, 723.
Length 627 (*p.p.*), 637½ (*w.l.*), 646¼ (*o.a.*). Beam 68 feet.
Draught 18⅜ feet (*mean*).

Guns:
8—8 inch. 54 cal.
12—3·9 inch. 47 cal. AA.
10—37 mm. AA.
8—13 mm. AA.
Torpedo tubes:
8—21 inch.

Aircraft:
2, with 1 catapult (amidships)
Armour (unofficial)
2¾" side amidships.
3" Turrets.
3" C.T.
2" Deck.

Note to Plan.—Aftermost pair of AA. on either side replaced by 4—13 mm. T.T. are mounted on either side, amidships. Catapult is amidships.

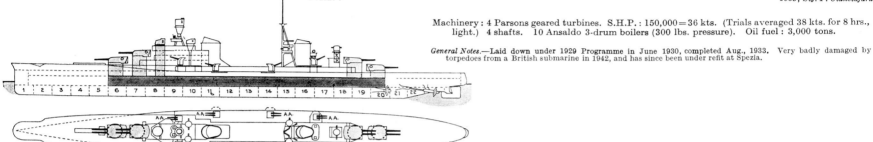

BOLZANO. 1935, *Sig. F. Cianciafara.*

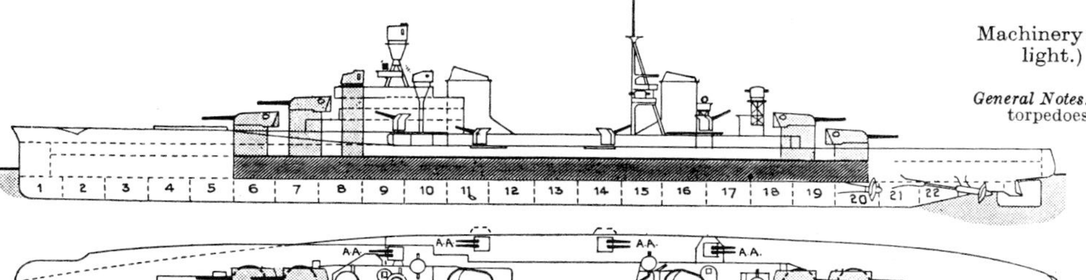

Machinery: 4 Parsons geared turbines. S.H.P.: 150,000=36 kts. (Trials averaged 38 kts. for 8 hrs., light.) 4 shafts. 10 Ansaldo 3-drum boilers (300 lbs. pressure). Oil fuel: 3,000 tons.

General Notes.—Laid down under 1929 Programme in June 1930, completed Aug., 1933. Very badly damaged by torpedoes from a British submarine in 1942, and has since been under refit at Spezia.

(TRENTO CLASS.—2 SHIPS.)

TRENTO (Orlando, Leghorn, Oct. 4th, 1927).

TRIESTE (Stab. Tecnico, Trieste, Oct. 24th, 1926).

Standard displacement, 10,000 tons. Complement, 723.

Length (*p.p.*), 624, (*w.l.*) 636⅓. (*o.a.*), 645 feet.

Beam, 67½ feet. *Mean* draught, 19 feet.

TRENTO. 1933 *Photo, Official.*

Guns:
8—8 inch, 50 cal.
12—3·9 inch, 47 cal.
18 smaller AA.
Torpedo tubes (21 inch):
8, *above water*, on main deck.

Aircraft: 2, with catapult.

Note to Plan:—Aftermost pair of 3·9 inch on either side removed, and 4—13 mm. AA. substituted.

Armour:
3" Side amidships
3" Turrets
3" C.T.
2" Deck

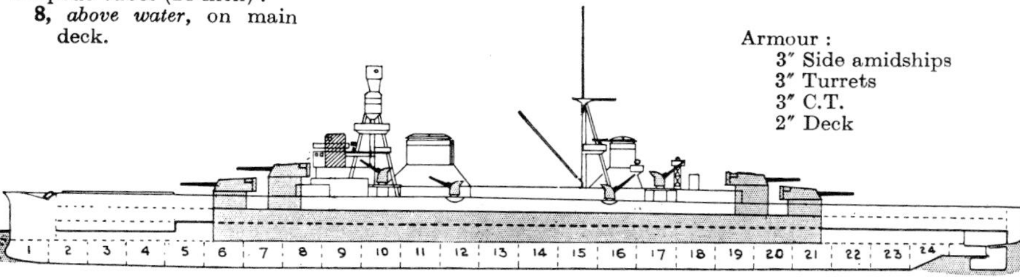

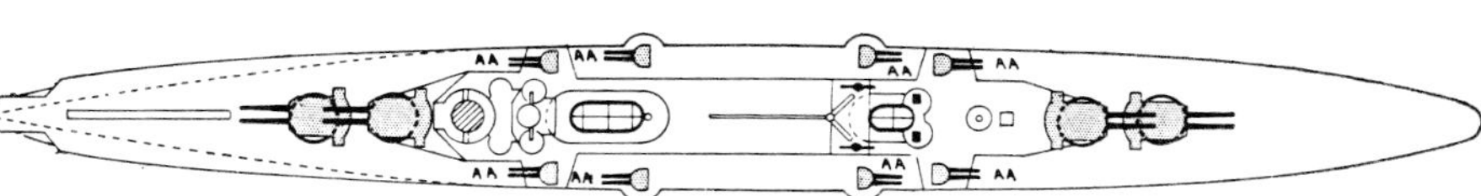

Plan revised 1934.

Machinery: 4 Parsons geared turbines. 4 shafts. S.H.P.: 150,000 = 35 kts. 12 3-drum boilers (300 lbs. pressure). Oil fuel: 3,000 tons.

General Notes.—Laid down under 1923-24 Programme. *Trento*, 8/2/25; *Trieste*, in June, 1925. Carry three scouting seaplanes, equipped for bombing. Design modified during construction. They were originally to have had hangar amidships, but this idea has been abandoned and a catapult installed on forecastle. In the revised design, after C.T. is dispensed with, AA. armament redistributed, and additional mast control tops added. These ships are believed to be much more lightly constructed than British *Kent* class, in order to attain a high speed. Completion dates: *Trento*, April, 1929; *Trieste*, March, 1930.

Gunnery Notes.—8 inch reported to be remarkably powerful weapons with exceptional range. *Maximum* elevation is 45°.

Engineering Notes.—Trials in August, 1928, are said to have given consumption of 68 tons of oil per hour. *Maximum* figure, *Trento*, 38·7 kts. Displacement was 11,000 tons (*normal*) at the time. Average trial figures: *Trento*, 146,640 = 36·6 kts. *Trieste*, 124,761 = 35·6 kts. Weight of engines is about 33 lbs. per S.H.P.

Special Note.

One of these 2 ships was torpedoed by British naval aircraft and sunk by a submarine in the Central Mediterranean, June 15, 1942. Either her sister ship or *Bolzano* was torpedoed and sunk by H.M. submarine *Urge* (announced April 9, 1942).

TRIESTE. 1932 *Lt. A. E. T. Christie, R.N.*

Cruisers

GORIZIA (Dec. 28, 1930).

Standard displacement, 10,000 tons. Complement, 705.

Length (*p.p.*) 589¼; (*o.a.*) 599½ feet. Beam, 67⅔ feet. Draught, 19½ feet.

Guns:
- **8**—8 inch, 54 cal.
- **12**—3·9 inch, 47 cal.
- **10**—37 mm. AA.
- **8**—13 mm. AA.

Torpedo tubes:
Nil.

Aircraft:
2, with catapult.

Armour:
- 5½″ Side ....
- 5″ Turrets.............
- 4½″ Transverse Bulkheads
- 3″ C.T. ....
- 2″ Deck................

Added 1942.

Note to Plan:—Aftermost pair of 3·9 inch on either side removed, and **4**—13 mm. A.A. substituted.

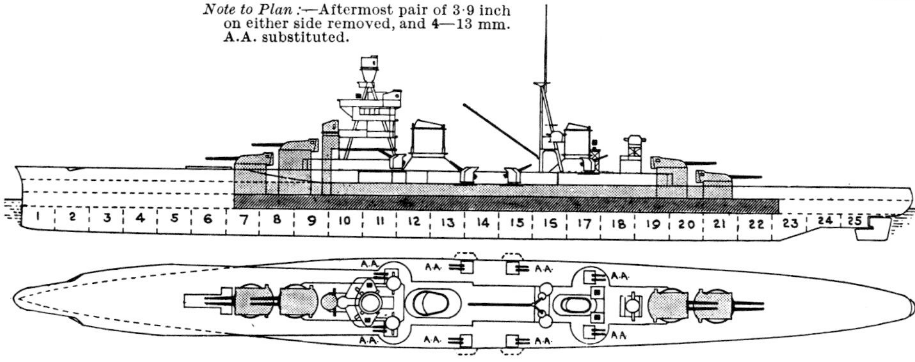

Added 1942.

Machinery: 2 Parsons geared turbines. S.H.P.: 95,000 = 32 kts. 2 shafts. Oil fuel: 1,450 tons *normal*, 2,200 tons *maximum*. Radius: 3,200 miles at 25 kts. 8 boilers, 3-drum type, 300 lbs. pressure.

General Notes.—Though torpedoed by a British submarine on June 29, 1941, this ship appears to have been beached and salved in a badly damaged condition. She is the survivor of a class of 4 cruisers. Laid down by Odero-Terni-Orlando in March, 1930, she was completed about the end of 1931.

(Condottieri Class.—" D " Type.)
(Emanuele Filiberto Class—2 Ships.)

EUGENIO DI SAVOIA (March 16, 1935).
EMANUELE FILIBERTO DUCA D'AOSTA (April 22, 1934).

Standard displacement: 7,283 tons. (About 8,500 tons full load.)
Complement: 551
Dimensions: 592 (*w.l.*) 610½ (*o.a.*) × 57⅓ × 16⅓ feet (*mean* draught).

Guns:
- **8**—6 inch, 53 cal.
- **6**—3·9 inch, 47 cal. AA.
- **8**—37 mm. AA.
- **8**—13 mm. AA.
- 2 D.C.T.

Torpedo Tubes: **6**—21 inch (tripled).

Aircraft: 3 with 1 catapult.

Armour: (*Unofficial*)
- 1½″–3″ Vert. side.
- 1½″ Deck.
- 1″ Turrets.
- 1″ C.T.

Mines: Equipped for Minelaying.

Note to Plan.—Torpedo tubes are tripled, not paired, as shown.

Emanuele Filiberto Duca d'Aosta 1935

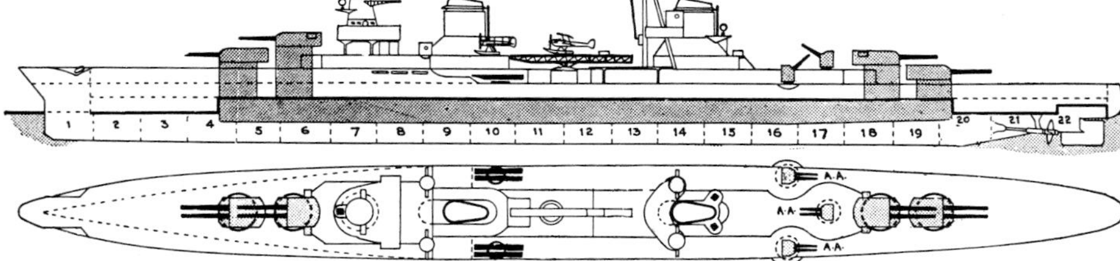

Emanuele Filiberto Duca d'Aosta. 1936

Machinery: Geared turbines (Belluzzo in *Eugenio di Savoia*, Parsons in *E. Filiberto*). 2 shafts. 6 boilers, 3-drum type. Designed S.H.P.: 110,000 = 36·5 kts. Oil fuel: 1,200 tons.

Name	*Builders*	*Laid down*	*Completed*
E. di Savoia	Ansaldo	Jan., 1932	Jan., 1936
E. F. Duca d'Aosta	Odero-Terni-Orlando	Jan., 1932	July, 1935

Notes.—These two ships are enlarged editions of the *Montecuccoli* class. Reported to be very lightly constructed.

Eugenio di Savoia 1937

("Condottieri" Class—"A" Type.)

GIOVANNI DELLE BANDE NERE (Castellammare, April 27, 1930).

("Condottieri" Class—"B" Type.)

LUIGI CADORNA (Cant. Riuniti dell' Adriatico, San Marco, Trieste, Sept. 30, 1931).

Displacement: 5,069 and 5,008 tons respectively. Complement: 500.

Dimensions: 547 (*w.l.*), 554½ (*o.a.*) × 50⅕ × 14 feet (*mean*) draught.

Guns:
- 8—6 inch 53 cal.
- 6—3·9 inch AA.
- 8—37 mm. AA.
- 8—13 mm. AA.
- 2 D.C.T.

Aircraft:
2, with Catapult.

Torpedo Tubes: 4—21 inch.

Mines: Equipped for laying.

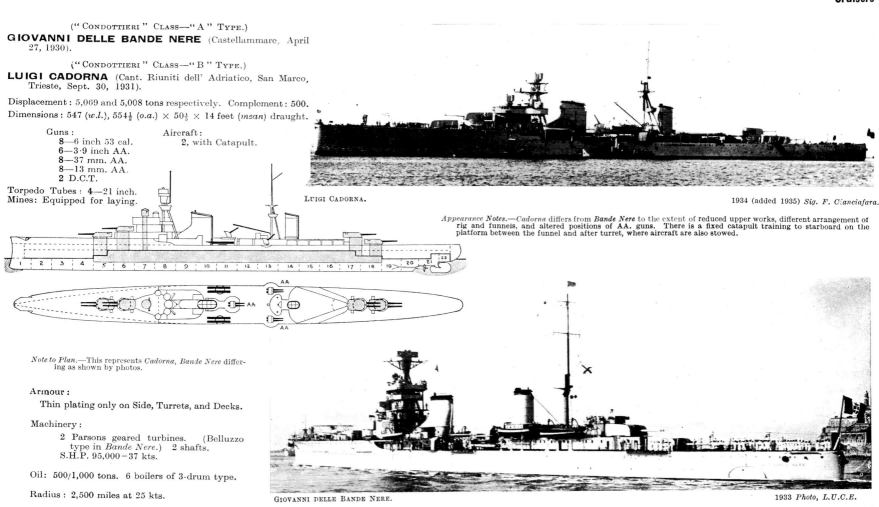

Luigi Cadorna. 1934 (added 1935) *Sig. F. Cianciafara.*

Appearance Notes.—*Cadorna* differs from **Bande Nere** to the extent of reduced upper works, different arrangement of rig and funnels, and altered positions of AA. guns. There is a fixed catapult training to starboard on the platform between the funnel and after turret, where aircraft are also stowed.

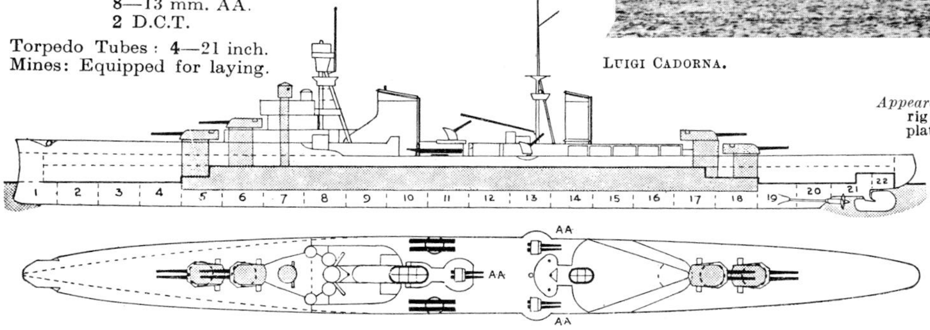

Note to Plan.—This represents *Cadorna, Bande Nere* differing as shown by photos.

Armour:
Thin plating only on Side, Turrets, and Decks.

Machinery:
2 Parsons geared turbines. (Belluzzo type in *Bande Nere.*) 2 shafts. S.H.P. 95,000=37 kts.

Oil: 500/1,000 tons. 6 boilers of 3-drum type.

Radius: 2,500 miles at 25 kts.

Giovanni delle Bande Nere. 1933 *Photo, L.U.C.E.*

Obsolete Cruisers

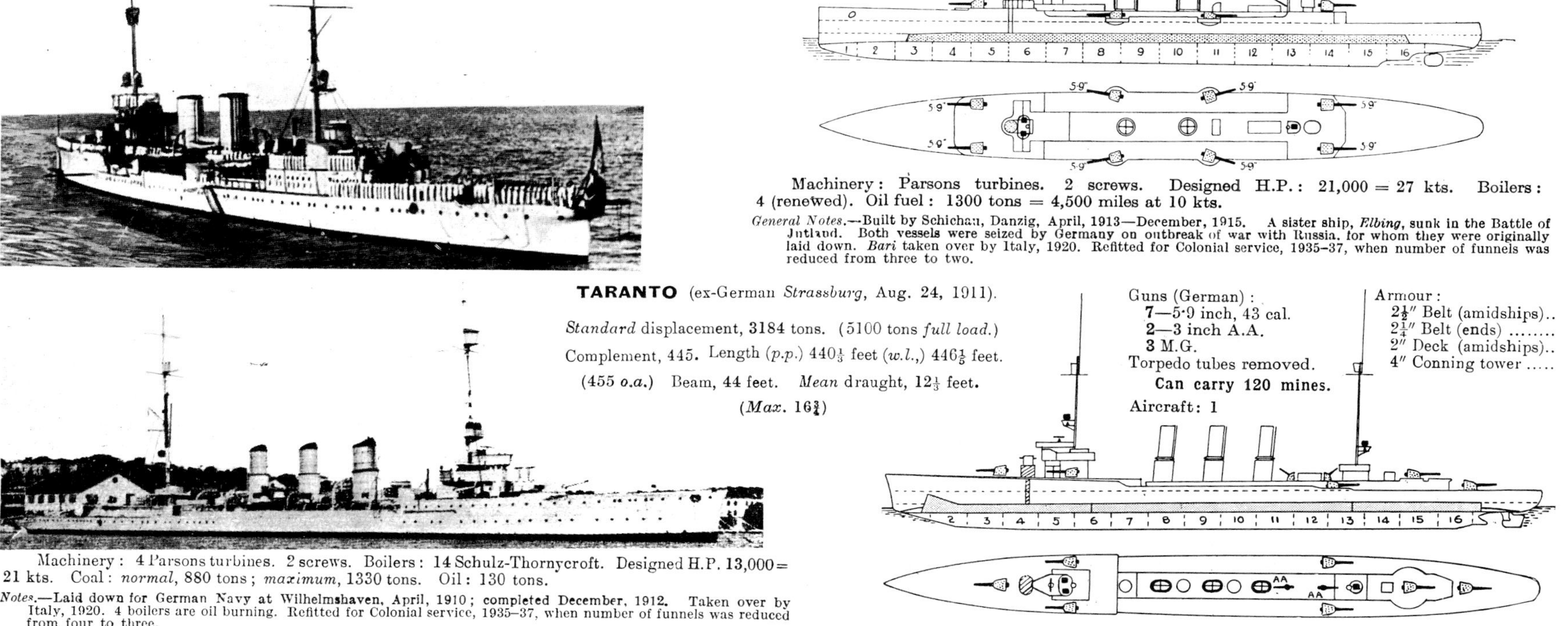

BARI (ex-German *Pillau*, ex-Russian *Muraviev Amurski*, April, 1914).

Standard displacement, 3,248 tons. Complement, 398.

Length { 435½ feet *w.l.* / 444 feet *o.a.* } Beam, 44½ feet. { *Mean* draught, 13½ feet. / *Max.* „ 19 feet. }

Armour:
- 3¼″ side..................
- 1½″ Deck (on slopes)...
- ¾″ Deck (bow) ....
- 3″ Deck (over rudder)
- 4″ Conning tower ......

Guns (German):
- 8—5·9 inch, 42 cal., S.A.
- 3—3 inch AA.
- 3 M.G.

Torpedo tubes removed.

Can carry 120 mines.

Machinery: Parsons turbines. 2 screws. Designed H.P.: 21,000 = 27 kts. Boilers: 4 (renewed). Oil fuel: 1300 tons = 4,500 miles at 10 kts.

General Notes.—Built by Schichau, Danzig, April, 1913—December, 1915. A sister ship, *Elbing*, sunk in the Battle of Jutland. Both vessels were seized by Germany on outbreak of war with Russia, for whom they were originally laid down. *Bari* taken over by Italy, 1920. Refitted for Colonial service, 1935–37, when number of funnels was reduced from three to two.

TARANTO (ex-German *Strassburg*, Aug. 24, 1911).

Standard displacement, 3184 tons. (5100 tons *full load.*)

Complement, 445. Length (*p.p.*) 440⅓ feet (*w.l.*,) 446⅕ feet. (455 *o.a.*) Beam, 44 feet. *Mean* draught, 12⅓ feet. (*Max.* 16¾)

Guns (German):
- 7—5·9 inch, 43 cal.
- 2—3 inch A.A.
- 3 M.G.

Torpedo tubes removed.

Can carry 120 mines.

Aircraft: 1

Armour:
- 2½″ Belt (amidships)..
- 2¼″ Belt (ends) ....
- 2″ Deck (amidships)..
- 4″ Conning tower .....

Machinery: 4 Parsons turbines. 2 screws. Boilers: 14 Schulz-Thornycroft. Designed H.P. 13,000=21 kts. Coal: *normal*, 880 tons; *maximum*, 1330 tons. Oil: 130 tons.

Notes.—Laid down for German Navy at Wilhelmshaven, April, 1910; completed December, 1912. Taken over by Italy, 1920. 4 boilers are oil burning. Refitted for Colonial service, 1935–37, when number of funnels was reduced from four to three.

Cruisers

(Ciano Class—2 Ships)

AMMIRAGLIO COSTANZO CIANO, VENEZIA.

Displacement : 8,000 tons. Complement : 600.
Length : Beam : Draught :

Guns :
10—6 inch, 53 cal.
Torpedo Tubes :
8—21 inch.

Aircraft :
4, with 2 catapults.

Armour :
Believed to be somewhat more extensive than in *Garibaldi* type.

Machinery : Geared turbines. Speed : 35 kts.

Note.—Authorised under Programme for 1939. Very little progress has been made with construction of these ships.

(Regolo Class—12 Ships)

ATTILIO REGOLO, SCIPIONE AFRICANO, CAIO MARIO, CLAUDIO TIBERIO, PAOLO EMILIO, CORNELIO SILLA, OTTAVIANO AUGUSTO, POMPEO MAGNO, ULPIO TRAIANO, VIPSANIO AGRIPPA, CLAUDIO DRUSO, GIULIO GERMANICO.

Displacement : 3,362 tons. Complement :
Length : (*w.l.*) 444½ feet. Beam : 44¾ feet. Draught : 13 feet (*mean*).

Guns :
8—5·3 inch, 45 cal.
6—65 mm. AA.
14 M.G. AA.
Torpedo Tubes :
8—21 inch.
Mines : Equipped for laying.

Armour :
Practically *nil*.

Machinery : 2 sets geared turbines. 2 shafts. S.H.P. : 120,000 = 41 kts. Boilers : 4 of 3-drum type. Oil fuel.

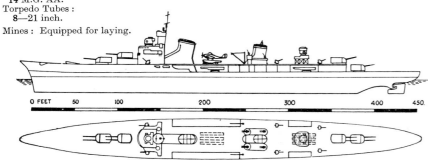

O FEET 50 100 200 300 400 450.

Name.	*Builder.*	*Laid down.*	*Completed.*
A. Regolo	O.T.O., Leghorn	Sept. 1939	1942
Scip. Africano	O.T.O., Leghorn	Sept. 1939	1942
Caio Mario	O.T.O., Leghorn	Sept. 1939	1942–43
C. Tiberio	O.T.O., Spezia	1939	1942–43
P. Emilio	Ansaldo	Oct. 1939	1942–43
C. Silla	Ansaldo	Oct. 1939	1942–43
O. Augusto	Riuniti, Ancona	23 Sept. 1939	1942–43
Pompeo Magno	Riuniti, Ancona	23 Sept. 1939	1942–43
U. Traiano	Riuniti, Palermo	Sept. 1939	1942–43
V. Agrippa	Tirreno	Oct. 1939	1942–43
C. Druso	Tirreno	Sept. 1939	1942–43
G. Germanico	Navalmeccanica, Castellammare	April 1939	1942–43

Scouts

3 Leone Class.

Leone. (*Pantera* has S.L. on platform, low on foremast.) 1925 *Photo, by favour of Messrs. Ansaldo.*

Tigre. 1925 *Photo, by favour of Messrs. Ansaldo.*

3* *Ansaldo type* : **Leone, Pantera, Tigre** (1923). 1550 tons (*standard*), 2283 tons (*full load*). Dimensions : 372 (*o.a.*), 359½ (*p.p.*) × 34 × 11·5 feet (*mean*). Guns : **8**—4.7 inch (45 cal.), **2**—14 pdr. (40 cal.) AA., **2**—2 pdr. AA. Tubes : **6**—18 inch, in two triple deck mountings. Designed S.H.P. 42,000 = 34 kts. (Trials, 50,000 = 35 kts.). Best recent speeds, 33 kts. or less. 4 Parsons turbines (geared). 4 Yarrow oil-burning boilers. 2 screws. Oil fuel : 200 tons *normal*, 400 tons *max*. Carry 60 mines (*normal* stowage), or 100 (*maximum*).
**Leopardo* and *Lince* cancelled.

Notes.—Internally these ships are most elaborately fitted. Each is equipped with a different system of fire-control—British, Italian and German respectively. 4.7 inch guns are paired very closely—only 1 foot apart. *Max.* elevation : 30°. Special apparatus for smoke screen production is fitted on starboard quarter of each. The distinctive appearance conferred by the upright funnels, of unequal height, and straight stem is a noteworthy feature of these vessels.

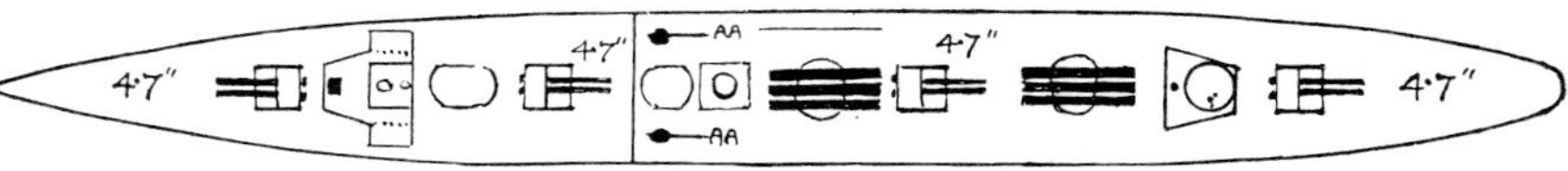

Funnel bands : *Pantera*, none ; *Leone*, 1 white on fore funnel ; *Tigre*, 1 white on after funnel.

Tigre. *Photo added* 1931, *W. A. Fuller, Esq.*

Destroyers

2 Folgore Class

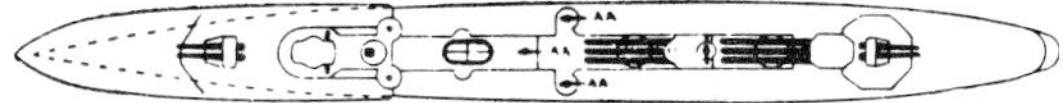

LAMPO. *Added* 1942.

2 *Partenopei* : **Folgore** (Apl. 26th, 1931), **Lampo** (July 26th, 1931).

Displacement : 1,220 tons (*standard*). Dimensions : 309 (*pp.*), $315\frac{1}{4}$ (*o.a.*) × $30\frac{1}{2}$ × $10\frac{1}{4}$ feet.
Guns : **4**—4·7 inch, 50 cal., **4**—37 m/m. AA., **4**—13 m/m. AA. Tubes : **6**—21 inch, tripled.
Machinery : 2 sets Belluzzo geared turbines. 2 shafts.
S.H.P. 44,000 = 38 kts. 3 boilers of 3-drum type.
Oil : 225 tons. Complement, 150.
All ordered 1929, laid down 1930 and completed 1932.

Note.—Lampo was beached after action with British warships on April 15, 1941, but has since been salved.

4 Dardo Class

STRALE. Now has cinder screen to funnel. 1932 *Photo, Official.*

2 *Odero*: **Dardo** (Sept. 6th, 1930), **Strale** (Mar. 26th, 1931).
2 *Tirreno*: **Freccia** (Aug. 3rd, 1930), **Saetta** (Jan. 17, 1932).

Displacement : 1,206 tons *standard*, 1,450 tons *normal*. Dimensions : $302\frac{1}{2}$ (*pp.*), 315 (*o.a.*) × 32 × $9\frac{1}{2}$ feet (*mean*).
Guns : **4**—4·7 inch, 50 cal., **4**—37 m/m. AA., **4**—13 m/m. AA. Tubes : **6**—21 inch, tripled.
Machinery : 2 sets Parsons geared turbines. S.H.P. 44,000 = 38 kts. 3 boilers of 3-drum type. Oil fuel : 225 tons. Complement, 150. All ordered 1928. *Freccia* completed 1931, others 1932.

Dardo class —As first designed these boats had two funnels and a straight bow, resembling *Turbine* in profile. During construction the design was changed, the uptakes being trunked into one stack, and the bridge and upperworks modified, while the bows were given an overhang. After launching further modifications were made, the tripod foremast was abolished, control platforms and a searchlight tower were added to the bridgework and the funnel raised.

8* "Navigatori" class

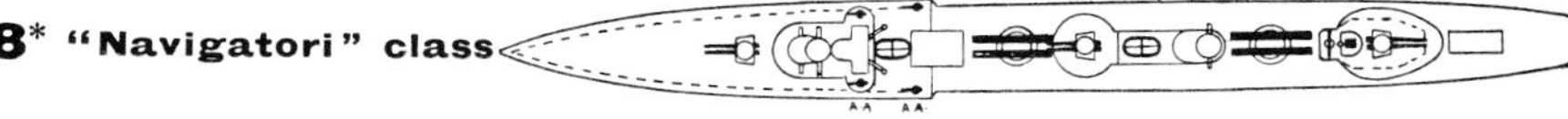

* One sunk by H.M.S. *Turbulent* has not been identified. *L. Pancaldo* has also been reported lost.

A. USODIMARE. 1939.

1 *Ansaldo* : **Lanzerotto Malocello** (March 14th, 1929).
2 *Odero* : **Ugolino Vivaldi** (Jan. 9th, 1929), **Antoniotto Usodimare** (May 12th, 1929).
2 *Tirreno* : **Leone Pancaldo** (Feb. 6th, 1929), **Antonio da Noli** (May 21st, 1929).
2 *Riuniti* (Ancona) : **Emanuele Pessagno** (August 12th, 1930), **Nicoloso da Recco** (Jan. 5, 1930).
2 *Quarnaro* : **Nicolo Zeno** (Aug. 11, 1928). **Antonio Pigafetta.** (Nov. 10th, 1929.)

Displacement : 1,628 tons, *standard ;* 2,010 tons *deep load.* Dimensions : 352 (*o.a.*), 351 (*p.p.*) × $33\frac{1}{2}$ × $16\frac{3}{4}$ feet. Guns : **6**—4·7 inch, 50 cal., **4**—37 m/m. AA., **6**—13 m/m. AA. Tubes : **4**—21 inch, paired. Some carry 50 mines.

Machinery and boilers : 2 Parsons turbines and 4 Odero boilers in *L. Malocello, U. Vivaldi, A. Usodimare, L. Pancaldo, A. da Noli, E. Pessagno.* 2 Belluzzo turbines and 4 modified Yarrow boilers in *N. Zeno, A. Pigafetta ;* 2 Tosi turbines and 3 boilers of 3-drum type in *N. da Recco.* S.H.P. 50,000 = 38 kts. Complement, 185.

Notes.—All ordered 1926, and laid down in 1927, except last-named ship, which was begun in 1928. *U. Vivaldi* and *L. Malocello* were still afloat up to June, 1942, according to Italian communiqués.

3 "Turbine" Class.

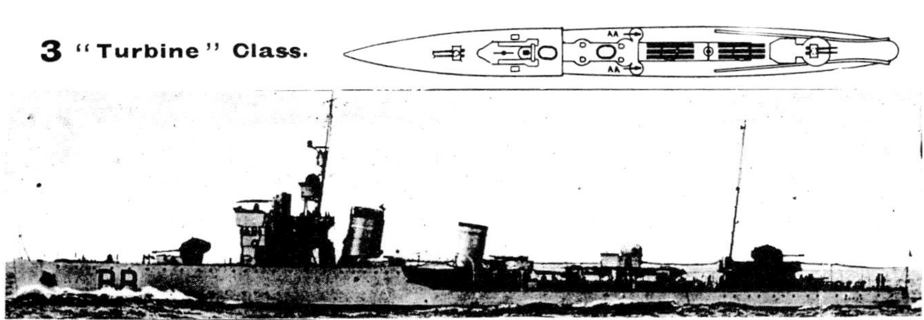

BOREA. *Added* 1942.

1 *Ansaldo*: **Borea** (Jan. 1927).
1 *Odero* : **Turbine** (21st April, 1927).
1 *Cant. del Tirreno, Riva Trigoso* : **Euro** (July 7th, 1927).

All ordered or laid down 1924-25. Displacement: *Borea* 1,073 tons. Others 1,092 tons. Dimensions : $299\frac{1}{2}$ (*p.p.*), $307\frac{1}{2}$ (*o.a*) × $30\frac{1}{2}$ × $10\frac{3}{4}$ feet. Guns : **4**—4·7 inch, 45 cal., **4**—37 mm. AA., **2**—13 mm. AA. Tubes : **6**—21 inch, in triple deck mountings. Machinery : Parsons geared turbines. S.H.P. 40,000 = 36 kts. 3 Express boilers, with superheaters. Oil : 270 tons. Complement, 142.

Mean speed on trials : *Euro* 38·9 ; *Borea* 36·5 ; *Turbine* 39·6.

Note.—Euro reported to have been lost, but particulars are lacking.

2 *Odero* boats: **Cesare Battisti** (11th Dec., 1926), **Nazario Sauro** (12th May, 1926).
2 *Quarnaro* boats : **Daniele Manin** (24th June 1925), **Francesco Nullo** (Oct., 1925). All designed by Odero and laid down 1924. Displacement : 1075 tons *standard*. Dimensions: $295\frac{1}{2}$ × $30\frac{1}{2}$ × $10\frac{1}{2}$ feet. Parsons geared turbines. 3 Thornycroft oil-fired boilers, with superheaters. S.H.P. 32,000 = 35 kts. (On trials. *N. Sauro* 37,000 = 36.5, *D. Manin* 36.8). Guns : **4**—4.7 inch, **3**—40 m/m. AA., **2** M.G. Tubes : **6**—21 inch, in triple deck mountings. 30 mines carried. Oil : 230 tons.

Deck plan, *Sauro* and *Turbine* classes.

SAURO. 1927 *Official Photo.*

4 Sella class ("Improved Palestro design").

G. NICOTERA 1928 *Photo, Pucci.*

Q. SELLA. 1926 *Photo, by courtesy of Ministry of Marine.*

4 *Pattison* type : **Francesco Crispi** (Oct., 1925), **Giovanni Nicotera** (24th June, 1926), **Bettino Ricasoli** (29th Jan., 1926), **Quintino Sella** (25th April, 1925). All laid down 1922-23. 950 tons *standard*. Dimensions : $270\frac{3}{4}$ × 27 × $9\frac{3}{4}$ feet. Guns : **3**—4.7 inch (45 cal.), **2**—40 m/m. AA., 4 M.G. Torpedo tubes : **4**—21 inch in two pairs. Machinery : Turbines (Belluzzo in *Crispi*, Parsons in others). 28,000 S.H.P. = 35 kts. (Trial speeds have been from 35.9 to 38 kts.) 3 Thornycroft boilers. Oil fuel : 200 tons *normal*, 255 tons *max.* Radius : 2750 miles at 15 kts. Complement, 120.

Note.—On *trials B. Ricasoli* is reported to have exceeded 38 kts. with H.P. 40,000; *F. Crispi* 38.7; *Q. Sella* 37.6. Average figures : *B. Ricasoli*, 35 kts. ($8\frac{1}{2}$ tons consumption) ; *F. Crispi*, 34 kts. ($9\frac{1}{2}$ tons) ; *Q. Sella*, 35 kts. (8 tons); *G. Nicotera*, 34.5 kts. (9 tons).

Destroyers and Torpedo Boats

2 "Sella" class.

F. CRISPI. 1935, *Bassan.*

2 *Pattison:* **Francesco Crispi** (Oct., 1925,) **Quintino Sella** (25th April. 1925), Both laid down 1922–23. Displacement: 935 tons *standard*. Dimensions: $275\frac{1}{2} \times 27 \times 9\frac{3}{4}$ feet. Guns: 4—4·7 inch (45 cal.), 2—40 m/m AA., 2 M.G. Torpedo tubes: 4—21 inch in two pairs. Machinery: Turbines (Belluzzzo in *Crispi*, Parsons in *Sella*). S.H.P.: 36,000 = 35 kts. 3 Thornycroft boilers. Oil fuel: 200 tons *normal*, 255 tons *maximum*. Radius: 2,750 miles at 15 kts. Complement: 120.

Note.—2 more vessels of this type, *Nicotera* and *Ricasoli*, were sold to Sweden in 1940. *Crispi* re-engined, 1937.

2 Mirabello class.

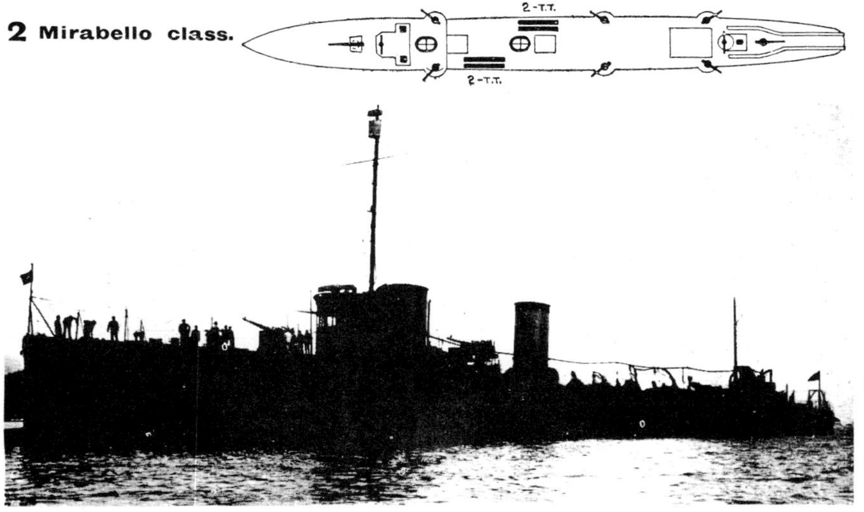

1926 *Photo, Capitan M. Mille.*

Height of Fore-funnel reported to have been increased as in *Sella* class.

2 *Ansaldo* type: **Carlo Mirabello** (1914), **Augusto Riboty** (1915). Displacement: 1383 tons. Dimensions: 331·4 (*pp.*) × 32 × $10\frac{1}{2}$ feet (*mean*). Guns: 8—4 inch, 2—40 mm. AA., 2 M.G. Tubes: 4—18 inch. Carry 100 mines. Machinery: 2 Parsons geared turbines. 2 shafts. Designed S.H.P. 35,000 = 35 kts. 4 Yarrow oil-burning boilers. Oil fuel; *normal* 200 tons, *maximum* 350 tons. Endurance: 2840 miles (15 kts.), 500 miles (full speed). Complement, 145.

18 "Partenope" Class.

LUPO. 1939, *Sig. Aldo Fraccaroli.*

4 Torpedo Boats (probably of this type) were built under the 1939 Programme. (Guns — 3·9 inch.)

4 *Napoletani* boats: **Partenope** (Feb. 27, 1938), **Polluce** (Oct, 24, 1937), **Pallade** (Dec. 19, 1937), **Pleiadi** (Sept. 5, 1937.)

4 *Quarnaro* boats: **Libra** (Oct. 3, 1937), **Lince** (Jan. 15, 1938), **Lira** (Sept. 12, 1937), **Lupo** (Nov. 7, 1937).

6 *Ansaldo* boats: **Airone** (Jan. 23, 1938), **Aretusa** (Feb. 6, 1938), **Calipso** (June 12, 1938), **Calliope** (April 15, 1938), **Circe** (June 29, 1938), **Clio** (April 3, 1938).

Standard displacement: 679 tons. Complement: 94. Dimensions: $254\frac{2}{3}$ (*w.l.*), 267 (*o.a.*) × 26 × $7\frac{3}{4}$ feet (*mean*). Guns: 3—3·9 inch, 6—37 mm. AA., 2—13 mm. AA., 2 D.C.T. Tubes: 4—18 inch, paired in all *except* Quarnaro boats, which have tubes arranged as in later units of *Climene* type. Machinery: 2 sets Tosi geared turbines. 2 shafts. S.H.P.: 19,000 = 34 kts. 2 boilers of 3-drum type. All laid down Oct., 1936—March, 1937.

11 Aviere Class.

CAMICIA NERA. 1938, *Courtesy Dott. Ing. L. Accorsi.*

5 *Odero-Terni-Orlando:* **Aviere** (Sept. 20, 1937), **Ascari** (July 31, 1938), **Camicia Nera** (Aug. 8, 1937), **Corazziere** (May 22, 1938), **Geniere** (ex-*Pontiere*), (Feb. 27, 1938).
2 *Riuniti, Ancona:* **Alpino** (Sept. 18, 1938), **Fuciliere** (July 31, 1938).
2 *Riuniti, Palmero:* **Bersagliere** (July 3, 1938), **Granatiere** (April 24, 1938).
2 *Tirreno:* **Carabiniere** (July 24, 1938), **Lanciere** (Dec. 18, 1938)

Displacement: 1,620 tons (*standard*), about 1,900 tons full load. Complement: 165. Dimensions: 339 (*w.l.*), 350 (*o.a.*) × $38\frac{1}{2}$ × $10\frac{3}{4}$ feet (mean). Guns: 4—4·7 inch, 50 cal., 6—37 mm. AA., 2—13 mm. AA., 2 D.C.T. Torpedo tubes: 6—21 inch (tripled). Machinery: 2 sets geared turbines (Parsons in O.T.O. boats, Belluzzo in others). 2 shafts. S.H.P.: 48,000 = 39 kts. 3 boilers of 3-drum type. Oil fuel: 250 tons. All laid down Jan.—May, 1937.

According to Italian official statements *Ascari* was still afloat in June, 1942.

2 Oriani Class.

A. ORIANI. *Added* 1942.

2 *Odero-Terni-Orlando*: **Alfredo Oriani** (July 30, 1936). **Vittorio Alfieri** (Dec. 20, 1936). Ordered 1935, and laid down Oct. 1935 and 1936, respectively. *Standard* displacement: 1,729 tons (about 1,950 tons full load). Dimensions: 341 (*w.l.*), $350\frac{1}{3}$ (*o.a.*) × $33\frac{1}{3}$ × $11\frac{1}{4}$ feet (*mean*), 12 ft. (*max.*). Guns: 4—4·7 inch, 50 cal., 8—37 mm. AA., 4—13 mm. AA. 2 D.C.T. Torpedo tubes: 6—21 inch (tripled). Machinery: 2 sets Parsons geared turbines. 2 shafts. S.H.P.: 48,000 = 39 kts. 3 boilers of 3-drum type. Oil fuel: 250 tons. Complement: 157.

Note.—*V. Alfieri* may possibly have been sunk at Battle of Cape Matapan, March 28, 1941.

ORIANI TYPE.

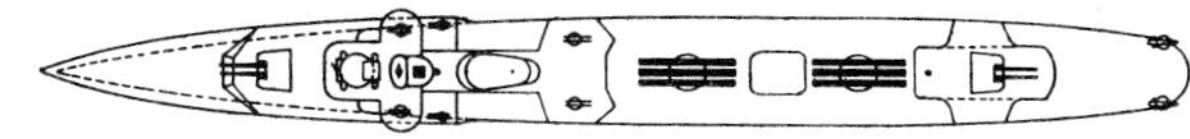

2 Grecale Class.

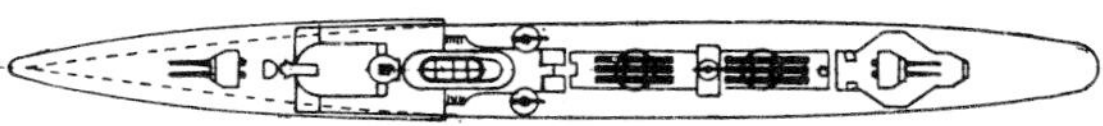

1 *Riuniti, Ancona:* **Grecale** (June 17th, 1934).

1 *Tirreno:* **Scirocco** (April 22nd, 1934).

Displacement: 1,449 tons. Complement, 153. Dimensions: $333\frac{1}{3}$ (*w.l.*), 350 (*o.a.*) × $33\frac{1}{3}$ × 10 feet. Guns: 4—4·7 inch, 50 cal., 8—37 mm. AA., 4—13 mm. AA. Tubes: 6—21 inch. Machinery: 2 sets Parsons geared turbines. 2 shafts. S.H.P. 44,000 = 38 kts. 3 boilers of 3-drum type. Oil fuel: 250 tons.

Built under 1930 Programme. Laid down end 1931 and completed 1934. Are enlarged editions of the *Dardo* class with the same general design.

GRECALE. 1936.

Destroyers

General Note.—Only these 4 Destroyers will be retained by Italy under Peace Treaty.
(*All fitted for Minelaying.*)

The following list of distinctive letters, painted on bows of destroyers and torpedo boats, has been furnished officially to "Fighting Ships".

A B *Abba*
A E *Ariete*
A U *Aretusa*

C A *Carini*
C B *Carabiniere*
C L *Clio*
C P *Calliope*
C S *Cassiopea*

D R *Da Recco*
F B *Fabrizi*

G N *Granatiere*
G R *Grecale*
G V *Giovannini*

L B *Libra*

M B *Monzambano*
M T *Mosto*

ON *Orione*
O S *Orsa*

P L *Pilo*

S G *Sagittario*
S I *Sirio*

GRECALE. (Mainmast since struck.) *Added* 1946.

1 *Riuniti, Ancona*: ***Grecale*** (June 17th, 1934).

Displacement: 1,449 tons. Complement, 153. Dimensions: 333⅓ (*w.l.*), 350 (*o.a.*) × 33⅓ × 10 feet. Guns: **4**—4·7 inch, 50 cal., **8**—20 mm. AA., 2 M.G. (Torpedo tubes removed.) Machinery: 2 sets Parsons geared turbines. 2 shafts. S.H.P. 44,000 = 38 kts. 3 boilers of 3-drum type. Oil fuel: 250 tons.

Built under 1930 Programme. Laid down end 1931 and completed 1934.

2 Granatiere Class.

GRANATIERE. 1943, *Official.*

1 *Riuniti, Palermo*: ***Granatiere*** (April 24, 1938).
1 *Tirreno*: ***Carabiniere*** (July 24, 1938).

Displacement: 1,620 tons (*standard*), about 1,900 tons full load. Complement: 165. Dimensions: 339 (*w.l.*), 350 (*o.a.*) × 33½ × 10¾ feet (*mean*). Guns: **5**—4·7 inch, 50 cal., **6**—37 mm. AA., **2**—13 mm. AA., 2 D.C.T. Torpedo tubes: **6**—21 inch (tripled) in *Carabiniere*, 3 in *Granatiere*, which has 16—20 mm. as secondary armament. Machinery: 2 sets Belluzzo geared turbines. 2 shafts. S.H.P.: 48,000 = 39 kts. 3 boilers of 3-drum type. Oil fuel: 250 tons. Both laid down early in 1937.

1 *Riuniti, Ancona*: ***Nicoloso da Recco*** (Jan. 5, 1930). Ordered 1926 and laid down 1927.

Displacement: 1,628 tons, *standard*; 2,010 tons *deep load*. Dimensions: 352 (*o.a.*), 351 (*pp.*) × 33½ × 16⅔ feet. Guns: **6**—4·7 inch, 50 cal., **2**—37 mm. AA., **9**—20 mm. AA. (Tubes removed.)
Machinery: 2 Tosi turbines. 2 shafts. S.H.P.: 50,000 = 38 kts. Boilers: 3 of 3-drum type. Complement, 185.

Note.—Survivor of a once numerous class, named after navigators.

Torpedo Boats (*All fitted for Minelaying.*)

4 Libra Class.

LIBRA. 1943, *Official.*

2 Orsa Class.

Added 1940.

2 *Riuniti* (*Palermo*) boats: ***Orione*** (April 22, 1937), ***Orsa*** (March 21, 1937).

Standard displacement: 855 tons. Dimensions: 274¼ (*pp.*), 279 (*w.l.*), 292¾ (*o.a.*) × 31 × 11½ (*max.*), 8 feet (*mean* draught). Guns: **2**—3·9 inch, 47 cal., **8** M.G., **6** D.C.T. Tubes: **4**—18 inch, paired. Machinery: Tosi geared turbines. 2 shafts. S.H.P.: 16,000 = 28 kts. 2 boilers of 3-drum type.

Notes.—Ordered 1935, and laid down early in 1936. Were rated as Escort Vessels (*Avvisi Scorta*) when first completed.

1 *Quarnaro*: ***Libra*** (Oct. 3, 1937).
3 *Ansaldo*: ***Aretusa*** (Feb. 6, 1938), ***Calliope*** (April 15, 1938), ***Clio*** (April 3, 1938).

Standard displacement: 679 tons. Complement: 94. Dimensions: 254⅔ (*w.l.*), 267 (*o.a.*) × 26 × 7¾ feet (*mean*). Guns: **3**—3·9 inch, **6**—37 mm. AA., **2**—13 mm. AA., 2 D.C.T. Tubes: **4**—18 inch, paired in all except *Libra*, which has tubes arranged as in later units of *Sirio* type. Machinery: 2 sets Tosi geared turbines. 2 shafts. S.H.P.: 19,000 = 34 kts 2 boilers of 3-drum type. All laid down Oct., 1936—March, 1937.

3 Sirio Class.

PERSEO. (Since lost.) 1938, *Cav. Angelo Priore.*

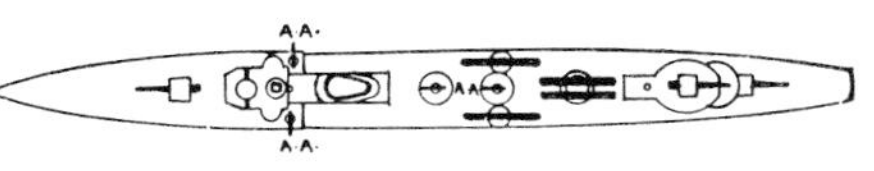

CASSIOPEA.

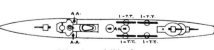

Other two of this class, *also* LIBRA.

1 *Riuniti* (*Ancona*): ***Cassiopea.***
2 *Quarnaro*: ***Sirio*** (Nov. 14, 1935), ***Sagittario*** (June 21, 1936).

Standard displacement: *Cassiopea*, 652 tons; other two vessels, 642 tons. Respective lengths (*o.a.*) 267 and 269 feet. Beam: 27 feet. Respective draughts: 7½ and 7 feet (*mean*). Complement: 94. Guns: **3**—3·9 inch, 47 cal., 6—37 mm. AA., 2—13 mm. AA., 2 D.C.T. Tubes: **4**—18 inch, arranged as shown in plans below. Machinery: 2 Tosi geared turbines. 2 shafts. S.H.P.: 19,000 = 34 kts. (exceeded on trials). 2 boilers of 3-drum type. Oil fuel. 2 more ships of this type, *Remus* and *Romulus*, will be found in Swedish Navy section.

Name	*Laid down*	*Compl.*	*Name*	*Laid down*	*Compl.*
Sirio	Nov. 1934	Feb. 1936	*Sagittario*	Nov. 1935	1937
			Cassiopea	Dec. 1935	1936

Torpedo Boats *(All fitted for Minelaying.)*

MONZAMBANO. 1946, *Lieut. Aldo Fraccaroli.*

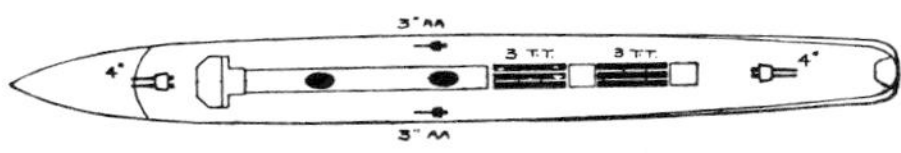

1 *Orlando* type: ***Monzambano*** (6th August, 1923).

Displacement: 966 tons (1,190 *full load*). Dimensions: 262½ × 24⅔ × 8½ feet. Guns: **4**—4 inch, **2**—3 inch AA. Tubes: **6**—18 inch. **10** mines. 2 Zoelly turbines. 2 shafts. S.H.P.: 22,000 = 32 kts. 4 Thornycroft boilers. Oil fuel: 200 tons. Complement: 105.

1 *Pattison* type: ***Ernesto Giovannini*** (1921).

Standard displacement: 182 tons. Dimensions: 170½ × 19 × 5⅔ feet (*mean*). Guns: **2**—4 inch, 35 cal., **2** M.G. Tubes: **2**—18 inch, paired. Fitted for minelaying. Machinery: Triple expansion. 2 shafts. Designed H.P.: 2,400 = 23 kts. (Trials: 3,262 = 23·7 kts.) 2 boilers. Oil fuel: 40 tons. Radius: 900 miles at 20 kts.

Notes.—Originally classed as an Escort Vessel. Survivor of a class of six.

1946, *Official.*

2 Carini Class.

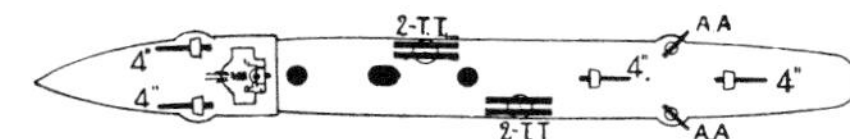

1925 *Photo, Pucci.*

2 *Odero:* ***Nicola Fabrizi*** (1917), ***Giacinto Carini*** (1916).

Displacement: 635 tons (810 *full load*). Dimensions: 238 (*pp.*) × 24 × 9·2 feet (*mean*). Guns: **4**—4 inch, **2**—3 inch AA., **4** M.G. Tubes (in both): **4**—18 inch, in two twin-deck mountings. 2 Tosi turbines. 2 shafts. S.H.P.: 15,500 = 32 kts. (On trials made 34·1 kts. Now cannot make 30 kts.) 4 Thornycroft oil-burning boilers. Fuel: 150 tons. Complement, 100. Endurance: 1,700 miles (15 kts.), 470 miles (full speed).

3 Abba Class.

1 *Pattison:* ***Antonio Mosto*** (1914).

2 *Odero:* ***Rosolino Pilo, Giuseppe Abba*** (both 1914).

Displacement: 615 tons. Dimensions: 236¼ (*pp.*) × 24 × 8¾ feet (*mean*). Guns: **5**—4 inch, **2**—40 mm. AA., **4**—20 mm. AA. Tubes: **4**—18 inch. Machinery: 2 Tosi turbines. 2 shafts. S.H.P.: 15,500 = 32 to 33·8 kts., except *Mosto*, S.H.P.: 14,500 = 30·8 kts. Boilers: 4 Thornycroft. Fuel: 150 tons. Endurance: 1,700 miles (15 kts.), 440 miles (full speed). Complement: 94.

(Motor Torpedo Boats will be found on a later page.)

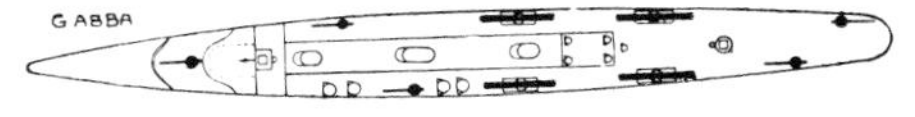

R. PILO. *Added* 1946, *Lieut. Aldo Fraccaroli.*

Corvettes

20 Gabbiano Class. *(Fitted for Minesweeping)*

APE, BAIONETTA, CHIMERA, CORMORANO, DANAIDE, DRIADE, FENICE, FLORA, FOLAGA, GABBIANO, GRU, IBIS, MINERVA, PELLICANO, POMONA, SCIMITARRA, SFINGE, SIBILLA, URANIA, and another (to be completed or salved).

Displacement: 642 tons (some may be less). Dimensions: 192¾ (*w.l.*), 203 (*o.a.*) × 28½ × 8⅓ feet. Guns: **1** or **2**—3·9 inch, 47 cal., **5** or **6**—20 mm. AA. (Some mount instead **2**—37 mm. AA., **8**—20 mm. AA.) 10 D.C.T. Machinery: Fiat Diesels. 2 shafts. B.H.P.: 3,500 = 18·5 kts. Also 2 electric motors for cruising, H.P.: 150 = 6 kts.

Notes.—There are believed to be more than one type. Differences uncertain, except that some were designed to carry two 18 inch torpedo tubes, mounted singly. Altogether 60 of these vessels were ordered, but how many were completed has not been made clear. Some were destroyed on slips, or construction abandoned. They are distinguished by pendant numbers painted on bows, as given below.

C 11 *Gabbiano*	C 25 *Ape*	C 46 *Flora*
13 *Cormorano*	33 *Scimitarra*	47 *Sfinge*
14 *Pellicano*	34 *Baionetta*	48 *Chimera*
16 *Folaga*	42 *Minerva*	49 *Sibilla*
17 *Ibis*	43 *Driade*	50 *Fenice*
18 *Gru*	44 *Danaide*	65 *Urania*
	45 *Pomona*	

SFINGE. *Added* 1946, *E. Mioni.*

Torpedo Boats

1944, *courtesy M. Henri Le Masson.*

Added 1946, *E. Mioni.*

SFINGE. *Added* 1946, *E. Mioni.*

Seaplane Carrier and Minelayer

Seaplane Carrier. (*Nave Appoggio Aerei.*)

(To be refitted as Supply Ship.)

G. MIRAGLIA. 1939, *courtesy Dott. Ing. L. Accorsi.*

GIUSEPPE MIRAGLIA (ex-*Città di Messina*, 20th December, 1923). Displacement: 4,880 tons. Dimensions: 377 × 49 × 17 feet. Guns: 4—4 inch AA., 4—M.G. Parsons geared turbines. 8 Yarrow boilers. I.H.P.: 12,000 = 21 kts. Oil fuel: 440 tons. Complement: 180. Reconstructed at Spezia D.Y., 1924–27.

Minelayer. (*Nave Posamine.*)

(To be converted into a Surveying Vessel.)

AZIO. *Added* 1946, *Official.*

1 *Riuniti* (*Ancona*): **AZIO** (May 4th, 1927). Displacement: 615 tons (*full load,* 850 tons). Dimensions: 204 × 28½ × 8½ feet. Guns: 2—4 inch, 35 cal., 1—3 inch AA., 2 M.G. Machinery: Triple expansion. 2 shafts. H.P.: 1,500 = 15 kts. Oil fuel. 2 watertube boilers.

Motor Minesweepers (*Motodragamine Veloci.*)

RDV 149 (in foreground) 1946, *Lieut. Aldo Fraccaroli.*

RDV 102-105, 111, 113, 117-122, 129, 131-134, 147-149 (1944-46). Displacement: 100 tons. Dimensions: 111½ × 19 × 4½ feet. Guns: 1—20 mm. AA. Machinery: Petrol motors. 2 shafts except in *RDV* 113, 149, which have 4. B.H.P. 2,300 = 17·5 kts.

RD 20, 32, 34, 38, 40, 41 (1919-20). Displacement: 156 tons. Dimensions: 116 × 19 × 6 feet. Guns: 1—3 inch. Machinery: Triple expansion. I.H.P. 750 = 10 kts. Boiler: 1 Thornycroft (coal-fired).

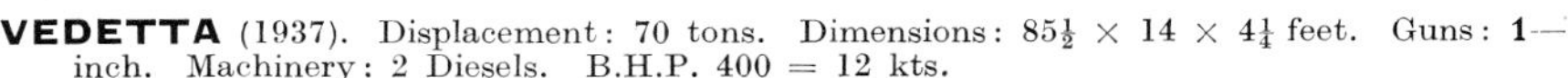

VEDETTA (1937). Displacement: 70 tons. Dimensions: 85½ × 14 × 4¼ feet. Guns: 1—3 inch. Machinery: 2 Diesels. B.H.P. 400 = 12 kts.

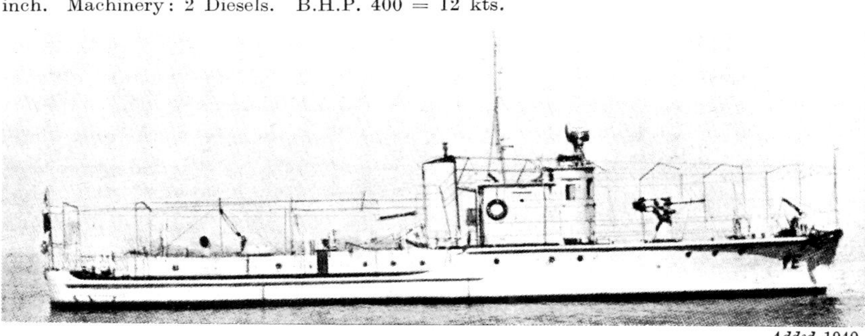

Added 1940.

Note.—A considerable number of Italian submarines have been lost since June 10, 1940, in addition to those already deleted from this section.

8 St. Bon Class.

6 authorised under 1939 Programme.

2 *Adriatico*: ***Ammiraglio Saint Bon, Ammiraglio Cagni*** (1940). Displacement: 1,461/— tons. Dimensions: $288\frac{1}{3} \times 25\frac{1}{2} \times 17$ feet. Guns: 2—3·9 inch, 4 M.G. Tubes: 14—18 inch. Machinery: Fiat Diesels. B.H.P.: 4,600 = 18 kts.

Note.—Last two, 1938 Programme. A remarkable feature of this type is the reversion to a smaller pattern of torpedo tube.

2 Bagnolini Class.

2 *Tosi*: ***Alpino Attilio Bagnolini*** (Oct. 28, 1939). ***Reginaldo Giuliani*** (Dec. 3, 1939). Displacement: 1,031/—— tons. Dimensions: $252\frac{1}{2} \times 23 \times 13\frac{3}{4}$ feet. Guns: 2—3·9 inch, 4 M.G. Tubes: 8—21 inch. Machinery: Tosi Diesels. B.H.P.: 3,500 = 18 kts.

Note.—Both belong to 1938 Programme and were laid down in 1938. On diving trials in Dec., 1939, *Bagnolini* reached a depth of 62 fathoms.

5 Marconi Class.

L. DA VINCI. 1942, *courtesy David Woodward, Esq.*

2 *Adriatico*: ***Guglielmo Marconi*** (July 27, 1939), ***Leonardo da Vinci*** (1940).
3 *Odero-Terni-Orlando*: ***Luigi Torelli*** (Jan. 6, 1940), ***Alessandro Malaspina*** (Feb. 18, 1940), ***Maggiore Francesco Baracca*** (April 21, 1940). Displacement: 1,036/—— tons. Dimensions: $251 \times 22\frac{1}{3} \times 15\frac{1}{2}$ feet. Guns: 2—3·9 inch, 4 M.G. Tubes: 8—21 inch. Machinery: Adriatico Diesels. B.H.P.: 3,600 = 18 kts.

Notes.—Built under 1938 Programme. *Bianchi* (since lost) reached a depth of 63 fathoms during diving trials.

2 Cappellini Class.

2 *Odero-Terni-Orlando*: ***Comandante Cappellini*** (May 14, 1939), ***Comandante Faa di Bruno*** (June 18, 1939). Displacement: 951/1,270 tons. Dimensions: $239\frac{1}{2} \times 23\frac{2}{3} \times 15$ feet. Guns: 2—3·9 inch, 4 M.G. Tubes: 8—21 inch. Machinery: Fiat Diesels. B.H.P.: 3,000/800 = 17/9 kts.

Notes.—Built under 1938 Programme. Appear to be a modified version of *Dandolo* design.

6 "Dandolo" Class.

Added 1940.

6 *Adriatico*: ***Dandolo, Mocenigo*** (both Nov. 20, 1937), ***Barbarigo*** (June 12, 1938), ***Morosini*** (July 28, 1938), ***Provana*** (March 16, 1938), ***Veniero*** (Feb. 14, 1938).

Displacement: 941/1,260 tons. Dimensions: 235 (*w.l.*), $239\frac{1}{2}$ (*o.a.*) $\times 23\frac{2}{3} \times 15\frac{1}{2}$ feet (*mean*). Guns: 2—3·9 inch, 2—13 mm. AA. Tubes: 8—21 inch. 2 Sulzer Diesels by builders (except *Mocenigo* and *Veniero*, which have Fiat Diesels) and 2 electric motors. H.P.: 3,000/800 = 17/9 kts. Diving Limit, 58 fathoms.

2 "Brin" Class.

GUGLIELMOTTI. *Added* 1940.

2 *Tosi* boats: ***Brin*** (April 3, 1938), ***Guglielmotti.*** (Sept. 11, 1938).

Displacement: 896/1,247 tons. Dimensions: $228\frac{3}{4}$ (*w.l.*), $231\frac{1}{3}$ (*o.a.*) $\times 22\frac{1}{2} \times 13\frac{1}{2}$ feet (*mean*). Guns: 1—3·9 inch 2 13 mm. AA. Tubes: 8—21 inch. 2 Tosi Diesels and 2 electric motors. H.P.: 3,000/840 = 17/9 kts. Diving limit, 60 fathoms.

3 Foca Class (Minelayers).

FOCA. 1938, *courtesy Dott. Ing. L. Accorsi.*

3 *Tosi* boats: ***Foca*** (June 26, 1937), ***Zoea*** (Dec. 5, 1937), ***Atropo*** (Nov. 20, 1938). First two laid down at Taranto in January and February, 1936, respectively, *Atropo* in 1937. Displacement: 1,109/1,533 tons (*Atropo*, 1,121 tons). Dimensions: $253\frac{1}{2}$ (*w.l.*), $266\frac{3}{4}$ (*o.a.*) $\times 23\frac{1}{2} \times 12\frac{1}{3}$ feet (*Atropo*, $255\frac{1}{4} \times 23\frac{1}{2} \times 15\frac{1}{4}$ feet). Guns: 1—3·9 inch, 47 cal., 2—13 mm. AA. Tubes: 6—21 inch (bow). 2 mine-discharging chutes. Fiat Diesels (except *Atropo*, which has Tosi) and 2 electric motors. H.P.: 2,880/1,250 = 16/8 kts. *Atropo* reached 58 fathoms in diving trials.

2 "Finzi" Class.

(Improved "BALILLA" design.)

G. FINZI. 1937.

G. FINZI. 1937.

2 *Odero-Terni-Orlando* type: ***Enrico Tazzoli*** (Oct. 14, 1935). ***Giuseppe Finzi*** (June 29, 1935).

Standard displacement: 1,332/1,965 tons. Complement, 66.
Dimensions: 272 (*w.l.*), $276\frac{1}{2}$ (*o.a.*) $\times 25\frac{1}{3} \times 13$ feet (*mean*).
Guns: 2—4·7 inch, 45 cal., 4—13 mm. AA. Tubes: 8—21 inch (6 bow, 2 stern).
2 Fiat Diesels. H.P.: 4,400/1,800 = $17/8\frac{3}{4}$ kts.
Radius: *Surface*: 13,500 miles at 9 kts; *submerged*: 80 miles at 4 kts.

Notes.—Laid down 1932, under 1930 Programme. Normal diving limit, 55 fathoms (reached on trials at Spezia).

Added 1940.

1 *Bernardis* type: ***Otaria*** (March 20, 1935), (Cant. Riuniti dell' Adriatico, Trieste). Displacement: 863/1,167 tons. Complement, 48. Dimensions: $239\frac{1}{2} \times 23\frac{1}{2} \times 14\frac{1}{2}$ feet. Guns: 2—3·9 inch, 47 cal., 2—13 mm. AA. Tubes: 8—21 inch. Machinery: 2 sets Fiat Diesels. H.P. 3,000 = 17 kts. 2 motors H.P. 1,400 = 8·5 kts. *submerged.*

1 Minelaying Type

1936.

1 *Cavallini* type: ***Pietro Micca*** (Cant. Nav. Franco Tosi, Taranto, March 31, 1935). Displacement: 1,371/1,883 tons. Complement, 66. Dimensions: $296\frac{1}{4}$ (*o.a.*) $\times 25\frac{1}{4} \times 17\frac{1}{2}$ feet. Guns: 2—4·7 inch, 45 cal., 4—13 mm. AA. Mines: 40. Tubes: 6—21 inch (in bow.) Machinery: Tosi Diesels. H.P. 3,000/1,600 = 15·5 kts. *surface*, 8·5 kts. *submerged.*

1 *Cavallini* type: ***Archimede*** (Dec. 10, 1933). Built by Cantiere Navale Franco Tosi, Taranto. Displacement: 880/1,231 tons. Complement, 50. Dimensions: $231\frac{1}{2} \times 22\frac{1}{2} \times 13$ feet. Guns 2—3·9 inch, 47 cal., 2—13 mm. AA. Tubes: 8—21 inch. Machinery 2 Tosi Diesels and 2 Ansaldo electric motors. H.P. 3,000/1,300 = 17/8·5 knots.

E. FIERAMOSCA. *Added* 1940, *Official.*

1 *Bernardis* type: ***Ettore Fieramosca*** (April 15th, 1929). Laid down August, 1926, by Cantiere Navale Franco Tosi, Taranto. 1,340 tons *surface* displacement, 1,788 tons *submerged.* Complement, 64. Dimensions; $270\frac{1}{4}$ (*o.a.*) $\times 27\frac{1}{2} \times 14\frac{3}{4}$ feet (*mean*). Guns: 1—4·7 inch, 45 cal., 4—13 mm. AA. 8—21 inch tubes. Can carry a small seaplane. Machinery: 2 sets Tosi Diesels. B.H.P. 5,500 = 19 kts. *surface.* Electric motors, H.P. 2,000 = 10 kts. *submerged.* Fuel: 150 tons.

4 "Balilla" Class.

D. MILLELIRE. *Added* 1940.

4 *Odero* type: ***Balilla*** (20th Feb., 1927), ***Antonio Sciesa,*** (Aug 12th 1928), ***Enrico Toti,*** (14th April, 1928), ***Domenico Millelire*** (Sept. 19th, 1927). Built at Spezia by Odero-Terni Co. *Surface* displacement, 1368 tons; *submerged*, 1,874 tons. Dimensions: 282 (*o.a.*) $\times 24\frac{1}{2} \times 14$ feet *mean* draught. Guns: 1—4·7 inch, 45 cal., 4—13 mm. AA. Tubes: 6—21 inch (4 bow, 2 stern). Complement: 64. Machinery: 2 sets Fiat Diesels, of H.P: 4,400 = 17·5 kts. *on surface*; electric motors of H.P.: 2,200 = 9·5 kts. *submerged.* Fuel: 140 tons.

Submarines

5 "Cobalto" Class.

1939 Programme:

5, names and builders no reported. Completed during 1941-42. Main particulars believed to be similar to *Perla* type. *Cobalto*, of this class, has been sunk.

18 "Perla" Class.

DESSIE — 1938, *courtesy Dott. Ing. L. Accorsi.*

7 *Odero-Terni-Orlando:* ***Beilul*** (May 22, 1938). ***Scire*** (Jan. 6, 1938). ***Tembien*** (Feb. 6, 1938). ***Ascianghi*** (Dec. 5, 1937). ***Ambra*** (May 28, 1936), ***Malachite*** (July 15, 1936), ***Onice*** (June 15, 1936.)

3 *Tosi:* ***Uarsciek*** (Sept. 19, 1937). ***Dagabur, Dessie*** (both Nov. 22, 1936).

8 *Adriatico:* ***Adua*** (Sept. 13, 1936), ***Alagi*** (Nov. 11, 1936), ***Aradam*** (Oct. 18, 1936), ***Axum*** (Sept. 27, 1936). ***Corallo*** (Aug. 2, 1936), ***Diaspro*** (July 5, 1936), ***Turchese*** (July 19, 1936), ***Perla*** (May 1, 1936).

Displacement: 620/853 tons, *except* O.T.O. vessels. 615, and Tosi, 613 tons. Dimensions: 195 (*w.l.*), 197½ (*o.a.*) × 21 × 13 feet (*mean*). *Corallo, Turchese,* and 4 of *Adua* group, Adriatico-Sulzer Diesels; *Ambra, Malachite,* and Tosi boats, Tosi Diesels; all the remainder have Fiat type. Armament, horsepower, and speed same as *Sirena* class (following). Diving limit: 50 fathoms. Built under 1935, 1936 and 1937 Programmes.

Note.—Brazilian submarines *Tamoyo, Timbyra* and *Tupy* were originally units of this class, and first bore the respective names *Ascianghi, Gondar* and *Neghelli.*

2 "Argo" Class.

VELELLA — 1937, *W. H. Davis, Esq.*

2 *Adriatico* boats: ***Argo,*** (Nov. 24, 1936), ***Velella*** (Dec. 18, 1936). Laid down at Monfalcone, Sept., 1935. Displacement: 689/857 tons. Dimensions: 195¾ (*w.l.*), 206¾ (*o.a.*) × 22½ × 10½ feet (*mean*). Guns: 1—3·9 inch, 47 cal., 2 M.G. AA. Tubes: 6—21 inch (bow). Fiat Diesels and 2 electric motors. H.P.: 1,350/800 = 14/8 kts.

Note.—These two submarines were originally put in hand for the Portuguese Navy, but after cancellation of the contracts they were taken over by the Italian Government.

8 "Sirena" Class.

ZAFFIRO. — *Added* 1942.

4 *Adriatico:* ***Sirena*** (Jan. 26, 1933), ***Nereide*** (May 25, 1933), ***Galatea*** (Oct. 5, 1933), ***Ondina*** (Dec. 2, 1933).

1 *Tosi:* ***Smeraldo*** (July 23, 1933).

2 *Odero-Terni-Orlando:* ***Ametista*** (April 26, 1933), ***Zaffiro*** (July 28, 1933).

1 *Quarnaro:* ***Topazio*** (May 15, 1933).

Displacement: 590/787 tons. Dimensions: 194¼ (*w.l.*), 197½ (*o.a.*) × 21 × 12 (*mean*). 13¾ feet (*max.*). Guns: 1—3·9 inch 47 cal., 2—13 mm. AA. Tubes: 6—21 inch. Machinery: 2 sets Fiat Diesels in all except Tosi and Quarnaro vessels, which have 2 sets Tosi Diesels. H.P. 1,350/800 = 14/8·5 kts. Complement 41.

5* "Fisalia" Class. (*Bernardis type*).

* One of this class was sunk by British destroyers in the Central Mediterranean on Jan. 14, 1943.

MEDUSA. — *Added* 1942.

2 *Adriatico:* ***Fisalia*** (May 2, 1931), ***Medusa*** (Dec. 12, 1931).

2 *Tosi:* ***Serpente*** (Feb. 28, 1932), ***Salpa*** (May 8, 1932).

2 *Odero-Terni-Orlando:* ***Jalea*** (June 15, 1932), ***Jantina*** (May 16, 1932).

Displacement: 599/778 tons. Dimensions: 200½ (*w.l.*), 201¾ (*o.a.*) (except Tosi boats 218 *o.a.*) × 18½ × 14½ feet. Guns: 1—4 inch, 35 cal., 2—13 mm. AA. Tubes: 6—21 inch. Machinery: 2 sets. Fiat Diesels in *Fisalia, Jalea, Jantina;* 2 sets Tosi Diesels in *Serpente, Salpa;* 2 sets Adriatico type in *Medusa.* H.P.: 1,200/800 = 14/8·5 kts. Complement: 41.

2 "Settembrini" Class.

LUIGI SETTEMBRINI. — 1935, *Sig. F. Cianciafara.*

2 *Cavallini* type: ***Luigi Settembrini,*** (Sept. 28, 1930), ***Ruggiero Settimo*** (March 29, 1931), (Cant. Nav. F. Tosi, Taranto). 798 tons *surface* and 1,134 tons *submerged.* Complement, 48. Dimensions: 225¼ (*w.l.*), 226¾ (*o.a.*) × 25¼ × 11½ feet (*mean*). 2 Tosi Diesels. H.P. 3,000 = 17·5 kts. Electric motors, H.P. 1,400 = 9 kts. *submerged.* Guns: 1—4 inch 2—13 mm. AA. Tubes: 8—21 inch. Radius: 9,000 miles at 8 kts. *surface,* 80 miles *submerged.*

4 "Squalo" Class.

TRICHECO. — 1934 *Photo, Pucci.*

4 *Bernardis* type: ordered 1928 from Cant. Nav. Triestino, Monfalcone: ***Delfino*** (April 27, 1930), ***Narvalo*** (March 15, 1930), ***Squalo*** (Jan. 15, 1930), ***Tricheco*** (Sept. 11, 1930).
Names translated are respectively *Dolphin, Swordfish, Shark, Walrus.*

Displacement: 810/1,077 tons. Complement, 48. Dimensions: 229 × 18¾ × 16¼ feet. Machinery: 2 sets Fiat Diesels. H.P. 3,000 = 16·5 kts. 2 electric motors. H.P. 1,400 = 9 kts. Guns: 1—4 inch. 2—13 mm. AA. Tubes: 8—21 inch. *Delfino* has dived to 58 fathoms.

2 "Corridoni" Class (*Minelayers*).

F. CORRIDONI. — *Added* 1935, *Official.*

2 *Bernardis* type: ***Marcantonio Bragadino*** (July 3rd, 1929), ***Filippo Corridoni.*** (March 30th, 1930). Both by Cant. Nav. F. Tosi, Taranto. Displacement: 803 tons *surface,* 1,051 tons *submerged.* Complement, 47. Dimensions: 232¾ (*w.l.*), 234¼ (*o.a.*) × 20 × 13¼ feet (*mean*). 2 Tosi Diesels of H.P. 1,500 = 14 kts. *surface* speed. Electric motors of 1,000 H.P. = 8 kts. *submerged.* Guns: 1—4 inch, 2 M.G. Tubes: 4—21 inch. 2 mine-launching chutes. 24 mines.

4 "Santarosa" Class.

4 *Bernardis* type: ***Santorre Santarosa*** (Oct. 22nd, 1929), ***Ciro Menotti*** (Dec. 29th, 1929), (both Odero-Terni Co., Spezia); ***Fratelli Bandiera*** (Aug. 7th, 1929), ***Luciano Manara*** (Oct. 5th, 1929), (both Cant. Nav. Triestino, Monfalcone).

Displacement: 815 tons on *surface,* 1,078 tons *submerged.* Complement, 48. Dimensions: 227½ (*w.l.*), 229 (*o.a.*) × 23¾ × 13½ feet (*mean*). 2 Fiat Diesels. H.P. 3,000 = 17·5 kts. *surface;* electric motors, B.H.P. 1,300 = 9 kts. *submerged.* Guns: 1—4 inch, 3—13 mm. AA. Tubes: 8—21 inch. Are an improvement of *Pisani* design. Ordered 1928, and completed 1930.

SANTAROSA. — 1934 *Photo, Pucci.*

Submarines

5 "H" Class

(Used for Training purposes)

H. 2. 1931 *Photo.*

5 *Electric Boat Co.* design: ***H1, H2*** (1916), ***H4, H6, H8*** (1917), by Canadian Vickers Co., Montreal. Displacement: 336 tons *on surface* 434 tons *when submerged.* Dimensions: $150\frac{1}{4} \times 15\frac{3}{4} \times 12\frac{1}{3}$ feet. 4—18 inch bow tubes. Machinery: 2 Nelseco Diesel engines *on surface*; 2 Electric Dynamic Co. motors *when submerged.* H.P. 480 = 13 kts. *on surface*, H.P. 620 = 11 kts. *when submerged.* Radius: 3,000 miles at 9 kts. *on surface.* 130 miles at 2 kts. *when submerged.* Complement, 22. Oil: 18 tons. *H*5 War loss. *H*3, *H*7 scrapped.

2 "X" Class (*Minelayers*).

X 3. (Gun since removed). 1928 *Photo, Pucci.*

2 *Bernardis* type: ***X2, X3*** (Ansaldo, Sestri Ponente, 1916). Displacement: 389 tons *on surface*; 453 tons *submerged.* Dimensions: 140 × 18 × 13 feet. 1 M.G. Torpedo tubes: 2—18 inch. Carry 18 mines in 9 discharge chutes. Machinery: 2 Sulzer Diesels *on surface*; 2 Ansaldo electric *submerged.* 660 H.P. = 10 kts. *on surface*; 320 H.P. = 6 kts. *when submerged.* Carry 18 tons of fuel. Radius: 1,360 miles at 6·5 kts. *on surface*; 96 miles at 4 kts. *when submerged.*

Note.—The existence of a number of very small submarines, each manned by a crew of four, has been doubtfully reported.

4 "Pisani" class.

Vittor Pisani. 1930 *Official Photo.*

M. Colonna. 1930 *Official Photo.*

4 *Bernardis* type: ***Vittor Pisani*** (Nov. 24, 1927), ***Giovanni Bausan*** (March 24, 1928), ***Marcantonio Colonna*** (Dec. 26, 1927), ***Ammiraglio des Geneys*** (Nov. 14, 1928). Ordered from Cantiere Navale Triestino, Monfalcone, 1924–25. Displacement: 791 tons *on surface*, 1,040 tons *submerged.* Dimensions: 223 × 19 × 14 feet. Machinery: 2 Tosi Diesels, H.P.: 2,700 = 17·5 kts. *on surface.* Electric motors of 1,200 H.P. = 9 kts. *submerged.* Guns: 1—4 inch, 2—13 mm. A.A. Tubes: 6—21 inch. Complement, 46.

3 "Mameli" class.

G. Mameli. 1928 *Official Photo.*

4 *Cavallini* type: ***Goffredo Mameli*** (ex-*Masaniello*, 9th Dec., 1926), ***Tito Speri*** (May 25, 1928), ***Giovanni da Procida*** (April 1, 1928). Ordered from Cantiere Navale F. Tosi, Taranto, 1924–25. Displacement: 770 tons *on surface.* 994 tons *submerged.* Dimensions: $213\frac{1}{4} \times 21\frac{1}{4} \times 13$ feet. 2 Tosi Diesel 8-cyl. 4-cycle engines. H.P.: 3,000 = 17 kts. *on surface.* Electric motors of 1,100 H.P. = 9 kts. *submerged.* Guns: 1—4 inch, 2—13 mm. AA. Torpedo tubes: 6—21 inch. Complement. 46.

Note.—In March, 1929, *G. Mameli* dived to a depth of 64 fathoms during trials, remaining submerged for 20 minutes, and in March, 1930, to 58 fathoms for 1 hour.

Miscellaneous

Transports (*Navi Trasporto.*)

AMALIA MESSINA.
MONTEGRAPPA.
TARANTOLA.
} No particulars received.

Hospital Ship (*Nave Ambulanza.*)

MARECHIARO (1928). Displacement: 127 tons. Dimensions: $108\frac{1}{4} \times 29 \times 12\frac{1}{2}$ feet. Machinery: 2 sets Kört Diesels. 2 shafts. B.H.P. 490 = 12 kts.

Oilers (*Navi Cisterna per Nafta.*)

Nettuno. 1928 *Photo, by courtesy of Ministry of Marine.*

NETTUNO (Cant. Nav. Riuniti, Palermo, 1916). 9,540 tons. Dimensions: $416\frac{1}{2} \times 51\frac{1}{2} \times 24$ feet. Guns: 3—4·7 inch, 2—3 inch AA. Machinery; Triple expansion. 2 shafts. 4 Yarrow oil-fired boilers. H.P.: 4,200 = 14 kts. Cargo: 6,000 tons oil fuel.

1939, *courtesy Dott. Ing. L. Accorsi.*

LETE (Riva Trigoso, 1915). Displacement: 1,163 tons. Dimensions: $168\frac{1}{4} \times 30\frac{1}{2} \times 11$ feet. Guns: 3—3 inch AA. Machinery: Tosi Diesels. 1 shaft. H.P. 750 = 10 kts. (*light*), 8·5 kts. (*loaded*). Cargo: 760 tons.

Water Carriers (*Navi Cisterna per Acqua*).

1938, *courtesy Sig. F. Cianciafara.*

PO (1936), built by C. N. Riuniti, Ancona. Displacement: 3,336 tons. Dimensions: $265\frac{3}{4} \times 38\frac{3}{4} \times 16\frac{3}{4}$ feet. Guns: 2—4·7 inch. 4 M.G. AA. Machinery: Triple expansion. 1 shaft. I.H.P.: 1,700 = 11·5 kts. Oil-fired watertube boilers. Capacity: 2,000 tons.

1937.

SESIA (Adriatico, 1933). 1,050 tons. Dimensions: 213¼ × 33 × 11¼ feet. **4** M.G. (Fitted for minelaying.) Fiat Diesels. 2 shafts. B.H.P.: 600 = 9·5 kts.

ARNO *Added* 1941

ARNO (Odero-Terni, 1929). 635 tons. Dimensions: 138¾ × 26 × 10 feet. Fiat Diesels. H.P.: 350 = 9 kts.

Added 1946, *Lieut. Aldo Fraccaroli.*

MINCIO (Venice, 1929). 645 tons. Dimensions: 138⅓ × 26¼ × 10 feet. Tosi Diesels. H.P.: 350 = 9 kts.

FRIGIDO (ex-*Fukuju Maru*). (Osaka, 1912.) (Purchased 1916.) 398 tons. Dimensions: 116½ × 21½ × 10 feet. **2** M.G. Triple expansion engines. 1 cylindrical boiler. H.P. 221 = 9 kts.

Lighthouse Tender

(*Nave addette al Servizio Fari.*)

BUFFOLUTO. 1928 *Photo, Pucci.*

BUFFOLUTO (1924). Displacement: 915 tons. Dimensions: 172¼ (*pp.*), 184½ (*o.a.*) × 29½ × 11 feet. Machinery: Triple expansion, I.H.P.: 1,400 = 11 kts. Boilers: 2 Thornycroft.

Note.—This vessel, reported to have been sunk at Leghorn in Sept. 1943, has since been salved.

Tugs (*Rimorchiatori*)

GAGLIARDO (1939). Displacement: 389 tons. I.H.P.: 1,000 = 12 kts.

1936

PORTO FOSSONE, PORTO PISANI, PORTO RECANATI (1936–37). Displacement: 226 tons. Dimensions: 88¾ × 22 × 10 feet. Guns: **1—3** inch. I.H.P.: 600 = 11 kts.

1936

ATLANTE (1928). Displacement: 355 tons. Guns: **1—3** inch. I.H.P. 900 = 11 kts.

PORTO EMPODOCLE (1914). Displacement: 330 tons. Guns: **1—3** inch. I.H.P. 500 = 11 kts.

Cable Ship.

1946, *Lieut. Aldo Fraccaroli.*

RAMPINO. Particulars wanted.

Minesweepers

RD 201-216. Ex-British units of MMS type, on loan to Italy. Displacement: 240 to 255 tons. Dimensions: 105 (*pp.*), 119 (*o.a.*) × 13 × 9 feet. Guns: 2—20 mm. AA. Machinery: Diesel. B.H.P. 500 = 10 kts. Complement: 20.

Note.—Above include ex-*MMS* 34 and 185, but other former numbers have not been communicated.

(*Motodragamine Magnetici.*)

ex-MMS 34.

Coastal Craft.

(*Vedette Antisommergibile.*)

VAS 201, 204, 211, 218, 222, 224 (1942). Displacement: 69 tons. Dimensions: 92 × 14 × 4½ feet. Guns: 2—20 mm. AA., 4 M.G. 1 D.C.T. 2—18 inch torpedoes. Machinery: 2 Fiat motors and 1 Carraro. 3 shafts. B.H.P. 1,110 = 19 kts. Complement: 26.

VAS 233, 235 (1942). Displacement: 68 tons. Dimensions: 92 × 15½ × 4½ feet. Guns: 2—20 mm. AA. 1 D.C.T. Machinery: 1 Isotta-Fraschini and 2 Carraro motors. 3 shafts. B.H.P. 1,450 = 19 kts. Complement: 26.

Note.—Above craft have been used for minesweeping.

Trawlers.

(Classed as *Dragamine.*)

RD 301. 1946, *London Studio.*

RD 301–316, all ex-British trawlers of Admiralty design. Displacement: 523 tons. Dimensions: 150 (*pp.*), 164 (*o.a.*) × 27⅔ × 11 feet. Guns: 1—4 inch, 4 M.G. Machinery: Triple expansion. I.H.P. 950 = 12 kts.

Former respective identities of above have not all been ascertained, but following of "Isles" class are known:

RD 301, ex-*Burra*.
,, 302, ex-*Cumbrae*.
,, 303, ex-*Unst*.
,, 304, ex-*Staffa*.
,, 305, ex-*Filla*.
,, 311, ex-*Mousa*.
,, 314, ex-*Ensay*.

Others include ex-*Egilsay*, *Foula*, *Grain*, and *Stroma*.

RD 311. 1946, *Lieut. Aldo Fraccaroli.*

Trawlers—*continued.*

ex-*Twostep*. 1946, *London Studio.*

Following belong to "Dance" class:
RD 307, ex-*Minuet*; also ex-*Gavotte, Hornpipe,* and *Twostep.*
Remaining unit is ex-*Othello*, of "Shakespearian" class.

Training Ship (*Nave Scuola*).

1932, *Rear-Admiral G. R. Ferretti.*

AMERIGO VESPUCCI (March 22, 1930). Built at Castellammare. Displacement: 3,543 tons. Dimensions: 229·6 × 51 × 22 feet. Machinery: Two Fiat Diesels, with electric drive to 2 Marelli motors. 1 shaft. H.P.: 1,900 = 10·5 kts. Sail area: 22,600 sq. feet. Complement: 400 + 150 midshipmen.

Note.—Hull, masts and yards are of steel. Loud-speakers and echo sounding gear are included in equipment.

Surveying Vessel (*Nave Idrografiche*).

CHERSO. *Added 1946, Lieut. Aldo Fraccaroli.*

CHERSO (ex-*Amalfi*). (A. G. Neptun, Rostock, 1912). Displacement: 3,988 tons. Dimensions: 300 × 41 × 17½ feet. Guns: 4—4·7 inch, 2—3 inch AA. Machinery: Triple expansion. I.H.P. 1,100 = 10·5 kts.

Repair Ship (*Nave Officina.*)

ANTONIO PACINOTTI. *Added 1946, Lieut. Aldo Fraccaroli.*

ANTONIO PACINOTTI. Reconstructed at Castellammare D.Y., 1924-25. Displacement: 2,720 tons Dimensions: 288¾ × 36 × 15 feet. Guns: 4—3 inch AA. Machinery: Orlando-Zoelly geared turbines. 2 shafts. S.H.P.: 7,500 = 19 kts. 4 cylindrical oil-fired boilers.

JAPAN

Minister of the Navy: Admiral Shigetaro Shimada.
Vice-Minister of the Navy: Vice-Admiral Sawamoto.
Chief of Naval Staff: Admiral Osami Nagano.

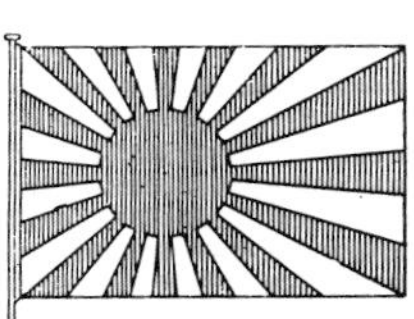

JACK & MERCANTILE ENSIGN

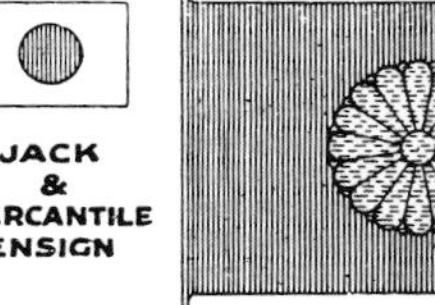

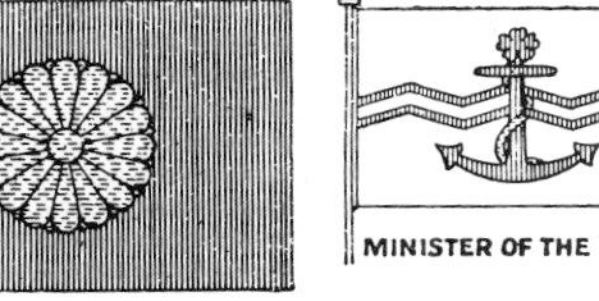

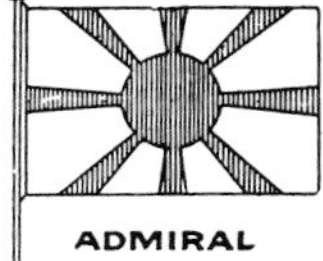

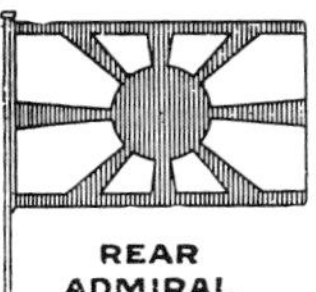

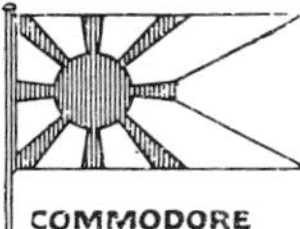

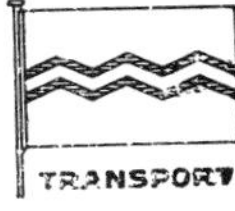

Flags.

1 *Standard of H.I.M. the Empress.*—A forked flag with a gold chrysanthemum on a red ground (as sketch for Imperial Standard).

2 *Standard of H.I.H. the Crown Prince.*—As Imperial Standard, but the chrysanthemum is enclosed in a square white border set a little distance within edges of flag.

3 *Imperial Princes and Princesses.*—A square white flag, with red border run round edges of flag and gold chrysanthemum in centre.

4 *Duty Flag.*—As transport flag, but *white* stripes over *red* ground.

5 *Repair Ship Flag.*—As transport flag, but with red stripes along upper and lower edges of flag, instead of across centre.

6 *Pendant for Men of War.*—Usual narrow triangulated shape, with Rising Sun next to hoist, as in Commodore's broad pendant.

Navy Estimates.

(excluding Supplementary Credits and China Expense Fund).

1939-40, Yen 826,752,432 1940-41, Yen 1,029,075,517 1941-42, Yen 1,241,034,064*

Personnel: *About* 325,000, all ranks

* With extra items as above, Yen 2,549,986,726.

Mercantile Marine.

(From "Lloyd's Register," 1939 figures).
2,337 vessels of 5,629,845 gross tonnage.

INSIGNIA OF RANK—EXECUTIVE OFFICERS—SLEEVES.

CAP.

The cap is the same as the British (but without gold embroidery in the senior ranks).

CAP BADGE.

Small anchor, surrounded by cherry leaves and blossom

Executive Branch:	Tai-sho.	Chu-sho.	Sho-sho.	Tai-sa.	Chu-sa.	Sho-sa.	Tai-i.	Chu-i.	Sho-i	Sho-i Ko-hosei.
Corresponding British:	*Admiral.*	*Vice-Ad.*	*Rear-Ad.*	*Captain.*	*Commander.*	*Lieut. Com.*	*Lieutenant.*	*Sub-Lieut.*	*Acting Sub-Lieut.*	*Midshipman.*

BAND between stripes. (BRANCHES, with but after Executive).

Violet	Kikwan (*Engineer*) (with executive rank and curl. Titles as above with the prefix Kikwan).
Red	Gun-i (*Surgeon*).
White	Shukei (*Paymaster*). } with curl, as Executive.
Brown	Zosen (*Constructor*). }
,,	Zoki (*Engineer-Constructor*). }
Purple-Brown	Zohei (*Ordnance Constructor*). }
Blue	Suiro (*Surveyor*). }

The senior officer of any branch on board one of H.I.J.M. ships always carries the affix "*cho*." Thus: Ho-jitsu-cho (*Gunnery*), Sui-rai-cho (*Torpedo*), Ko-kai-cho (*Navigator*), Gun-i-cho (*Principal Medical Officer*), Shukei-cho (*Senior Paymaster*).

Undress is a military tunic (dark blue) with the sleeve insignia of rank in black braid only, with curl, and with collar insignia of rank and branch.

NOMENCLATURE OF JAPANESE WARSHIPS.

The system of nomenclature recently in use (with occasional exceptions) is thus:—

Battleships: Named after ancient Provinces.
Aircraft Carriers: Named after Dragons and Birds.
Heavy Cruisers: Named after Mountains.
Light Cruisers: Named after Rivers.
Destroyers (First Class). Meteorological Names in poetic style.
Destroyers (Second Class) Named after Trees, Flowers and Fruits.
Torpedo Boats: Named after Birds.
Minelayers: Named after Islands, Straits, Channels and (formerly) Birds.

Colour of Ships: Dark grey usually.

Spelling of Japanese Ship Names

As confusion has occasionally arisen owing to the revised official spellings of certain ship names approved by the Navy Department, Tokyo, in 1936, a list is given below of such names together with the spellings formerly current and still sometimes used outside Japan.

BATTLESHIPS

Official Spelling	*Formerly*
SATUMA	SATSUMA
MUTU	MUTSU
HUSO	FUSO
YAMASIRO	YAMASHIRO
HIEI	HIYEI
KIRISIMA	KIRISHIMA
TAKAMATU	TAKAMATSU
TITIBU	CHICHIBU

AIRCRAFT CARRIERS

SYOKAKU	SHOKAKU
RYUZYO	RYUJO
HOSYO	HOSHO

CRUISERS

TYOKAI	CHOKAI
NATI	NACHI
ASIGARA	ASHIGARA
HURUTAKA	FURUTAKA
TIKUMA	CHIKUMA
ZINTU	JINTSU
OI	OHI
TATUTA	TATSUTA

DESTROYERS

Official Spelling	*Formerly*
SIRANUI	SHIRANUI
KUROSIO	KUROSHIO
OYASIO	OYASHIO
HATUKAZE	HATSUKAZE
HAYASIO	HAYASHIO
NATUSIO	NATSUSHIO
TOKITUKAZE	TOKITSUKAZE
AMATUKAZE	AMATSUKAZE
ARASI	ARASHI
ASASIO	ASASHIO
ARASIO	ARASHIO
OSIO	OSHIO
MITISIO	MITSUSHIO
NATUGUMO	NATSUGUMO
SUZUKAZE	SUDZUKAZE
SIRATUYU	SHIRATSUYU
SIGURE	SHIGURE
YUDATI	YUDACHI
HATUHARU	HATSUHARU
HATUSIMO	HATSUSHIMO
HUBUKI	FUBUKI
SIRAYUKI	SHIRAYUKI
HATUYUKI	HATSUYUKI
SINONOME	SHINONOME
SIRAKUMO	SHIRAKUMO
SIKINAMI	SHIKINAMI
USIO	USHIO
AKATUKI	AKATSUKI
IKADUTI	IKADSUCHI
INADUMA	INADSUMA
MUTUKI	MUTSUKI
UDUKI	UDZUKI
SATUKI	SATSUKI
MINADUKI	MINADSUKI
HUMIDUKI	FUMIDSUKI
NAGATUKI	NAGATSUKI
KIKUDUKI	KIKUDSUKI
MIKADUKI	MIKADSUKI
MOTIDUKI	MOCHIDSUKI
YUDUKI	YUDSUKI
MATUKAZE	MATSUKAZE
SIOKAZE	SHIOKAZE
TATIKAZE	TACHIKAZE
SANAE	SANAYE
HUYO	FUYO
TUGA	TSUGA
TIDORI	CHIDORI
MANADURU	MANADZURU
TOMODURU	TOMODZURU
HATUKARI	HATSUKARI

OTHER VESSELS

Official Spelling	Formerly	Official Spelling	Formerly	Official Spelling	Formerly	Official Spelling	Formerly	Official Spelling	Formerly	Official Spelling	Formerly
Kasima	Kashima	Sirakami	Shirakami	Idumo	Idzumo	Hutami	Futami	Komahasi	Komahashi		
Hatutaka	Hatsutaka	Hasidate	Hashidate	Titose	Chitose	Hodu	Hodzu	Siriya	Shiriya		
Okinosima	Okinoshima	Hatijo	Hachijo	Tiyoda	Chiyoda	Akasi	Akashi	Turumi	Tsurumi		
Siratakа	Shirataka	Natusima	Natsushima	Miduho	Mitsuho	Kasino	Kashino	Siretoko	Shiretoko		
Katuriki	Katsuriki	Sarusima	Sarushima	Nissin	Nisshin	Turugizaki	Tsurugizaki	Nozima	Nojima		
Itukusima	Itsukushima	Tubame	Tsubame	Karatu	Karatsu	Zingei	Jingei	Sikisima	Shikishima		
		Aduma	Adzuma	Husimi	Fusimi	Tyogei	Chogei	Huzi	Fuji		

Shipbuilding Establishments and Dockyards of which the spelling has also been revised are:

Official Spelling	Formerly	Official Spelling	Formerly	Official Spelling	Formerly
Maiduru	Maidzuru	Mitubisi	Mitsubishi	Saseho	Sasebo

Naval Ordnance

Principal Naval Guns.

Notation.	Calibre.	Length in calibres.	Model.	Weight of Gun.	Weight of A.P. shot.	*Maximum* Initial Velocity.	*Maximum* penetration firing AP. capped at K.O. 5000 yards.	*Maximum* penetration firing AP. capped at K.O. 3000 yards.	Danger space against average ship, at 10,000 yards.	Danger space against average ship, at 5000 yards.	Danger space against average ship, at 3000 yards.	*Service* rate of Fire. Rounds per minute.
	inches.			tons.	lbs.	F. S.	inches.	inches.	yards.	yards.	yards.	
HEAVY	16	45	K.M.	105	...	2600	...	...	...	...	...	...
	14	45	V	82	1400	...	...	...	...	...	...	...
MEDIUM.	8	50										
	8	45	A	17⅓	250	2740	7	10	110	425	600	1·2
	8	40	A	15½	250	2580	5½	7½	100	400	580	1·2
	6	45	('04)	8½	100	3000	4½	6½	75	250	475	...
	6	50	V	8	100	3000	4½	6½	75	250	475	6
	6	40	A	6½	100	2500	3	4½	65	210	435	7
	6	40	A	6	100	2220	2½	4	35	150	360	8
	5·5	50	...	6¼	82	2725	...	...	...	...	...	12
	4·7	45	...	...	...	...	...	...	...	...	...	...
	4·7	40	A	2	45	2150	...	2½	...		...	8
	4·7	32	A	1⅔	36	1938	...	...	...	...	...	8·6
LIGHT	3	...	...	...	14	...	...	...	...	...	...	...
	3	40	...	2	12	2200	...	...	...	...	...	...
AA	3	40	...	...	13	...	...	...	...	...	...	...

In the Model column A = Armstrong; V = Vickers; K.M. = Kure Arsenal and Muroran Steel Works.

There are also mounted in recent ships, 6·1 inch (*Mogami* and *Tone* types); 6 inch, 50 cal. K.M. 5 inch, 50 cal. high and low angle, 1927 K.M.; 4·7 inch, 50 cal. AA.; and various marks of 4 inch and 3 inch.

(**All details tabulated above are unofficial.**)

Torpedoes: 21 inch heater type (also carried by shore-based naval aircraft).

Third Fleet Replenishment Law, 1937.

4 battleships, 4 armoured ships, 4 aircraft carriers, and a number of cruisers, destroyers and submarines. To be completed at end of 1942.

Fourth Replenishment Law, 1940.

To involve the expenditure of Yen 5,401,000,000 (of which Yen 3,458,000,000 will be spent on new construction and 436,000,000 for warship rearmament) up to end of 1944.

Japanese Alphabet. Read name from right to left in syllables made by consonants (down) and vowels (across), in names painted on sides of smaller ships.

	A	E	I	O	U	YA	YO	YU	WA
	ア	エ	イ	オ	ウ	/	/	/	/
B	バ	ベ	ビ	ボ	ブ	ビャ	ビョ	ビュ	/
D	ダ	デ	ヂ	ド	ツ	ヂャ	ヂョ	ヂュ	/
G	ガ	ゲ	ギ	ゴ	グ	ギャ	ギョ	ギュ	グヮ
H	ハ	ヘ	ヒ	ホ	フ	ヒャ	ヒョ	ヒュ	/
K	カ	ケ	キ	コ	ク	キャ	キョ	キュ	クヮ
M	マ	メ	ミ	モ	ム	ミャ	ミョ	ミュ	/
N	ナ	ネ	ニ	ノ	ヌ	ニャ	ニョ	ニュ	/
P	パ	ペ	ピ	ポ	プ	ピャ	ピョ	ピュ	/
R	ラ	レ	リ	ロ	ル	リャ	リョ	リュ	/
S	サ	セ	シ	ソ	ス	シャ	ショ	シュ	/
T	タ	テ	チ	ト	ツ	チャ	チョ	チュ	/
W	ワ	ヱ	ヰ	ヲ	/	/	/	/	/
Y	ヤ	/	/	ヨ	ユ	/	/	/	/
Z	ザ	ゼ	ジ	ゾ	ズ	ジャ	ジョ	ジュ	/

N = ン

Silhouettes

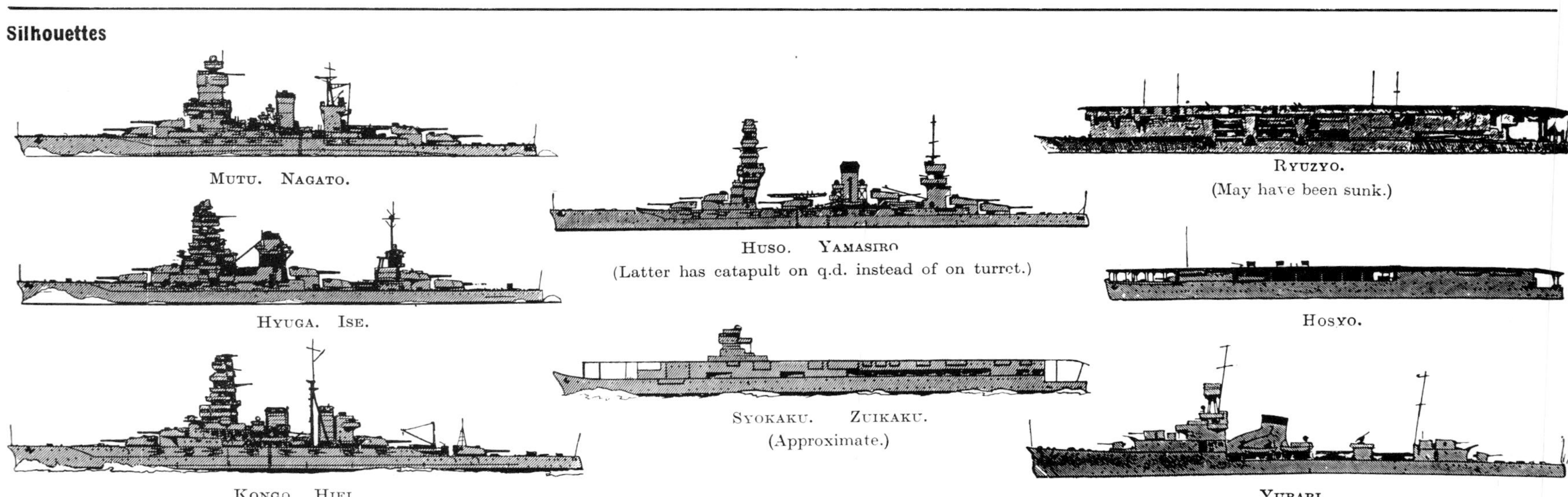

Mutu. Nagato.

Huso. Yamasiro (Latter has catapult on q.d. instead of on turret.)

Ryuzyo. (May have been sunk.)

Hyuga. Ise.

Hosyo.

Syokaku. Zuikaku. (Approximate.)

Kongo. Hiei. (Also Haruna and Kirisima, with funnels of unequal height).

Yubari.

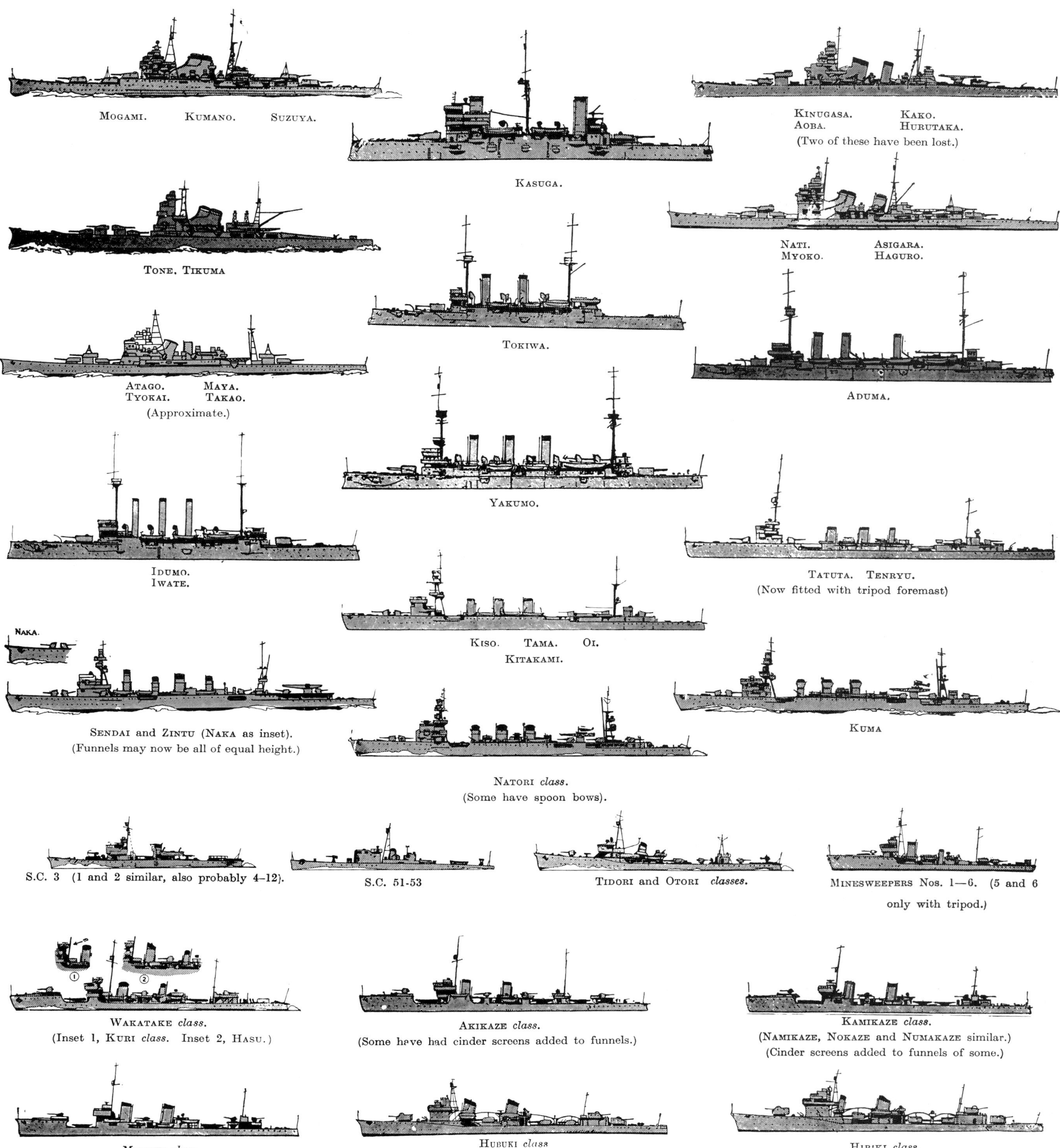

MOGAMI. KUMANO. SUZUYA.

KASUGA.

KINUGASA. KAKO.
AOBA. HURUTAKA.
(Two of these have been lost.)

TONE, TIKUMA

NATI. ASIGARA.
MYOKO. HAGURO.

TOKIWA.

ATAGO. MAYA.
TYOKAI. TAKAO.
(Approximate.)

ADUMA.

YAKUMO.

IDUMO.
IWATE.

TATUTA. TENRYU.
(Now fitted with tripod foremast)

NAKA.

KISO. TAMA. OI.
KITAKAMI.

SENDAI and ZINTU (NAKA as inset).
(Funnels may now be all of equal height.)

KUMA

NATORI *class*.
(Some have spoon bows).

S.C. 3 (1 and 2 similar, also probably 4–12).

S.C. 51-53

TIDORI and OTORI *classes*.

MINESWEEPERS Nos. 1—6. (5 and 6 only with tripod.)

WAKATAKE *class*.
(Inset 1, KURI *class*. Inset 2, HASU.)

AKIKAZE *class*.
(Some have had cinder screens added to funnels.)

KAMIKAZE *class*.
(NAMIKAZE, NOKAZE and NUMAKAZE similar.)
(Cinder screens added to funnels of some.)

MUTUKI *class*.
(Note bow and amidships t.t.)

HUBUKI *class*
(Some have no shields to tubes, others a more slender fore funnel.)

HIBIKI *class*.

Silhouettes

Battleships

YAMATO (August 8th, 1940) **MUSASHI** (November 1st, 1940)

Standard displacement, 62,315 tons (about 69,990 tons full load)

Complement, 2,500

Length (*p.p*) 800½ feet, (*o.a.*) 840 feet. Beam, 121 feet.

Daught, 34 feet.

Armour:
16″ Belt
9″ – 8″ Deck
21½″ – 2″ Barbettes
25½″ – 7½″ Turrets
19¾ – 11¾ Conning tower

Guns:
9 – 18 inch, 45 cal
12 – 6 inch, 60 cal
12 – 5 inch, 40 cal DP
24 – 25mm AA
4 – 13.2mm AA
7 aircraft

Machinery: 4-shaft geared turbines, 12 boilers, 150,000shp = 27 knots. Oil, 6,300 tons.

YAMATO sunk by US Navy aircraft April 7th, 1945
MUSASHI sunk by US Navy aircraft in the Battle of the Sibuyan Sea, October 24th, 1944.

NAGATO (Nov. 9th, 1919), **MUTU** (May 31st, 1920).

Standard displacement, **32,720** tons.

Complement, { 74 officers / 1,258 men } = **1,332.**

Length, { *p.p.*, 660⅔ feet. / *o.a.*, 700 feet approximate } Beam, 95 feet. Draught, 30 feet *max.*

Aircraft: 3 with catapult.

Guns (Japanese):
8—16 inch, 45 cal.
20—5.5 inch, 50 cal.
8—5 inch AA.
7 M.G.
Torpedo tubes (21 inch):
4 *submerged.*
Searchlights: **8.**

Armour: (*unofficial*)
13″ *or* 12″ Belt ....
8″—4″ Ends ....
3½″ Deck ....
7″ deck above magazines, boilers and engine rooms.

14″ Turrets ....
″ Battery ....
12″ Conning tower ...
(Bulges and other special anti-torpedo protection.)

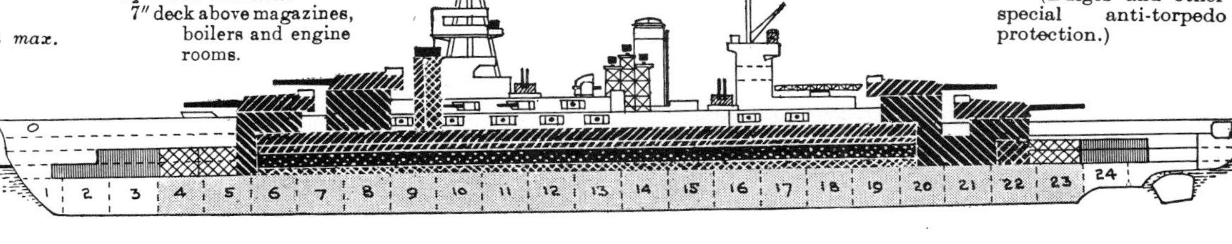

NAGATO. 1937

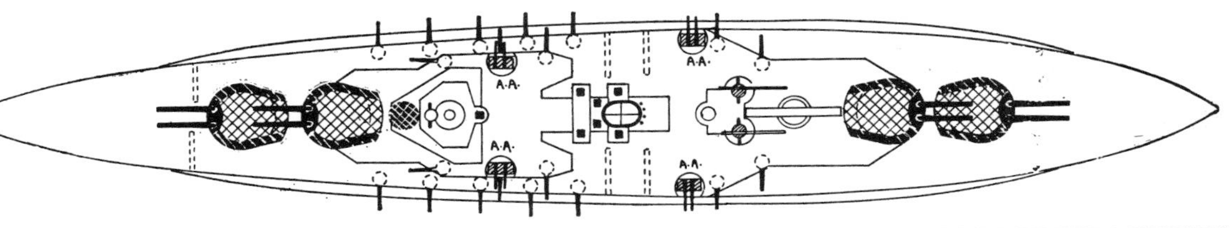

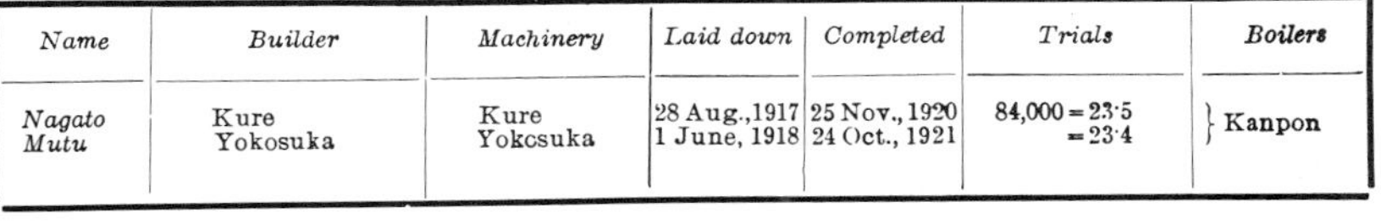

Name	*Builder*	*Machinery*	*Laid down*	*Completed*	*Trials*	*Boilers*
Nagato	Kure	Kure	28 Aug., 1917	25 Nov., 1920	84,000 = 23·5	} Kanpon
Mutu	Yokosuka	Yokosuka	1 June, 1918	24 Oct., 1921	= 23·4	

Machinery: Geared turbines. 4 shafts. Boilers: 21 Kanpon. Designed H.P.: 80,000 = 23 kts. (Reported increased, see notes.) Oil fuel: about 4,500 tons.

Notes.—Both built at Naval Yards as shown in table. Extensively reconstructed at same yards in 1934–36, being given bulges and triple bottoms for protection against torpedo attack, new machinery, aircraft, increased deck protection and increased elevation of 16-inch guns. Trial speed after reconstruction and reboilering reported as 26 kts.

MUTU. 1938 *added* 1939.

ISE (Nov. 12, 1916), **HYUGA** (Jan. 27, 1917).
Standard Displacement, 29,990 tons. Complement, 1,360.

Length (*p.p*). 640 feet. Beam, 94 feet. *Max.* draught, 28⅝ feet. Length (*o.a.*), 683 feet.

Machinery: Brown-Curtis turbines in *Ise*; Parsons turbines in *Hyuga*. 4 shafts. Boilers: 24 Kanpon.* Designed H.P. 45,000 = 23 kts. Oil fuel: 4,500 tons.

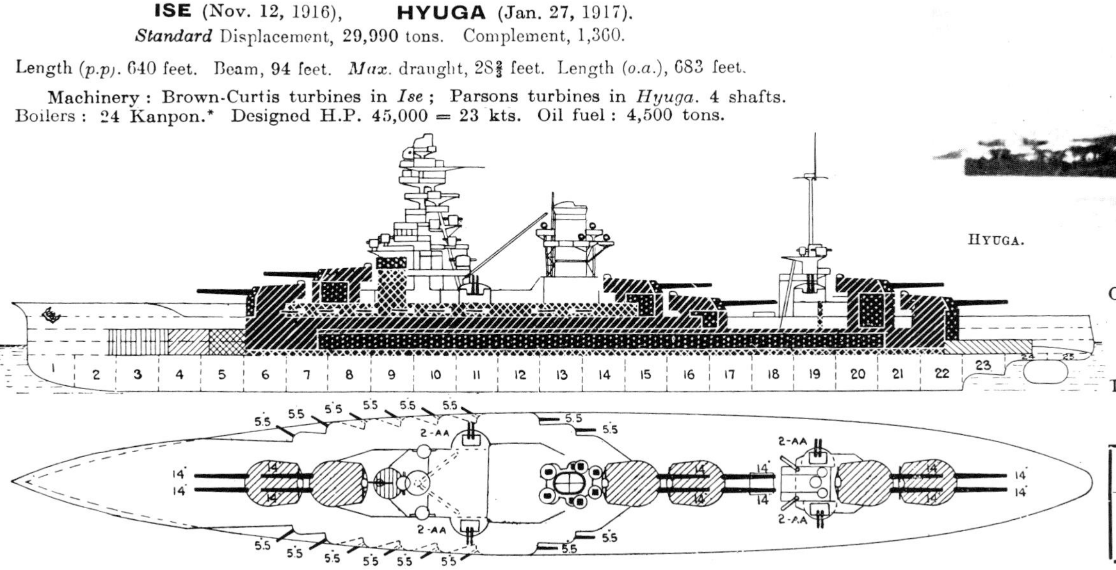

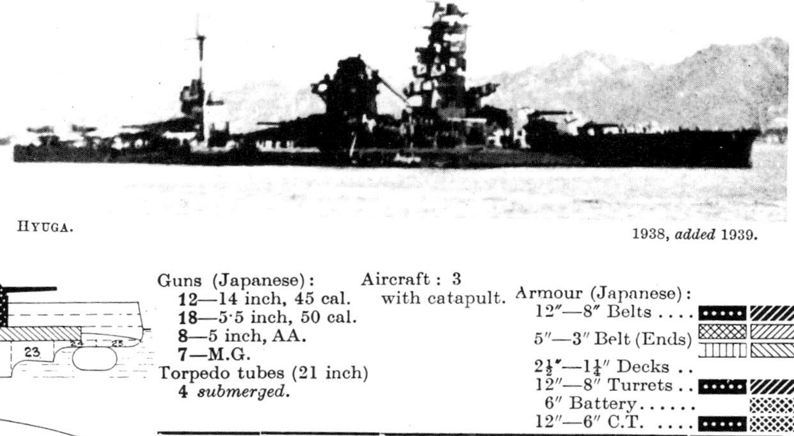

HYUGA. 1938, *added* 1939.

Guns (Japanese):
12—14 inch, 45 cal.
18—5·5 inch, 50 cal.
8—5 inch, AA.
7—M.G.
Torpedo tubes (21 inch)
4 *submerged.*

Aircraft: 3 with catapult.

Armour (Japanese):
12″—8″ Belts ....
5″—3″ Belt (Ends)
2½″—1¼″ Decks ..
12″—8″ Turrets ..
6″ Battery......
12″—6″ C.T. ....

Name	*Built by*	*Machinery*	*Laid down*	*Completed*	*Trials. H.P. = kts*
Ise	Kawasaki Co.	Kawasaki Co.	10.5.15	15.12.17	= 23·3.
Hyuga	Mitubisi Co.	Mitubisi Co.	6.5.15	30.4.18	

Battleships

HUSO (March 28th, 1914), YAMASIRO (Nov. 3rd, 1915).

Standard Displacement, 29,330 tons.

Complement, 1243 and 1272, respectively.

Length { (*p.p.*) 630 feet. (*o.a.*) 673 feet. } Beam, 94 feet. *Max.* draught, 28½ feet.

Guns (Japanese):
12—14 inch, 45 cal.
16—6 inch, 50 cal.
8—5 inch AA.
26 machine.
4 landing.
Torpedo tubes (21 inch):
2 *submerged*.

Aircraft:
3, with catapult—on turret amidships in *Huso* and on q.d. in *Yamasiro*.

YAMASIRO — 1936 *Official.*

Machinery: Brown-Curtis turbines. 4 **shafts.** Boilers: Kanpon. Designed H.P. 40,000 = 22·5 kts. Fuel: 4,500 tons oil.

General Notes.—Both ships were thoroughly reconstructed 1932-33 and altered in profile. The replacing of the 24 Miyabara boilers by (?) 8 Kanpon has enabled the forward boiler room to be converted to other uses, and there is now only one funnel fitted with an anti-flare top. The base of the foremast has been enlarged and fitted with wings, and the tripod mainmast is replaced by a tower base on which AA guns are mounted. No. 3 turret in *Huso* only now bears forward, and has a catapult on the crown, while additional searchlights have been grouped around the funnel. A large amount of additional armour and anti-torpedo structure has been worked into the ships, but details are lacking. Formerly 14 inch guns were reported as having an elevation of 25°, but this has probably now been increased. Anti-aircraft armament augmented during 1936–37 refit.

Name.	*Builder.*	*Machinery.*	*Laid down*	*Com-pleted*	*Trials.* H.P. = kts.	*Turbine*	*Boilers*	*Best recent speed*
Huso	Kure	Kawasaki	11 3.12	8.11.15	46,500 = 23.	Curtis	Kanpon	
Yamasiro	Yokosuka	Kawasaki	20.11.13	31. 3.17	... ...	Curtis	Kanpon	

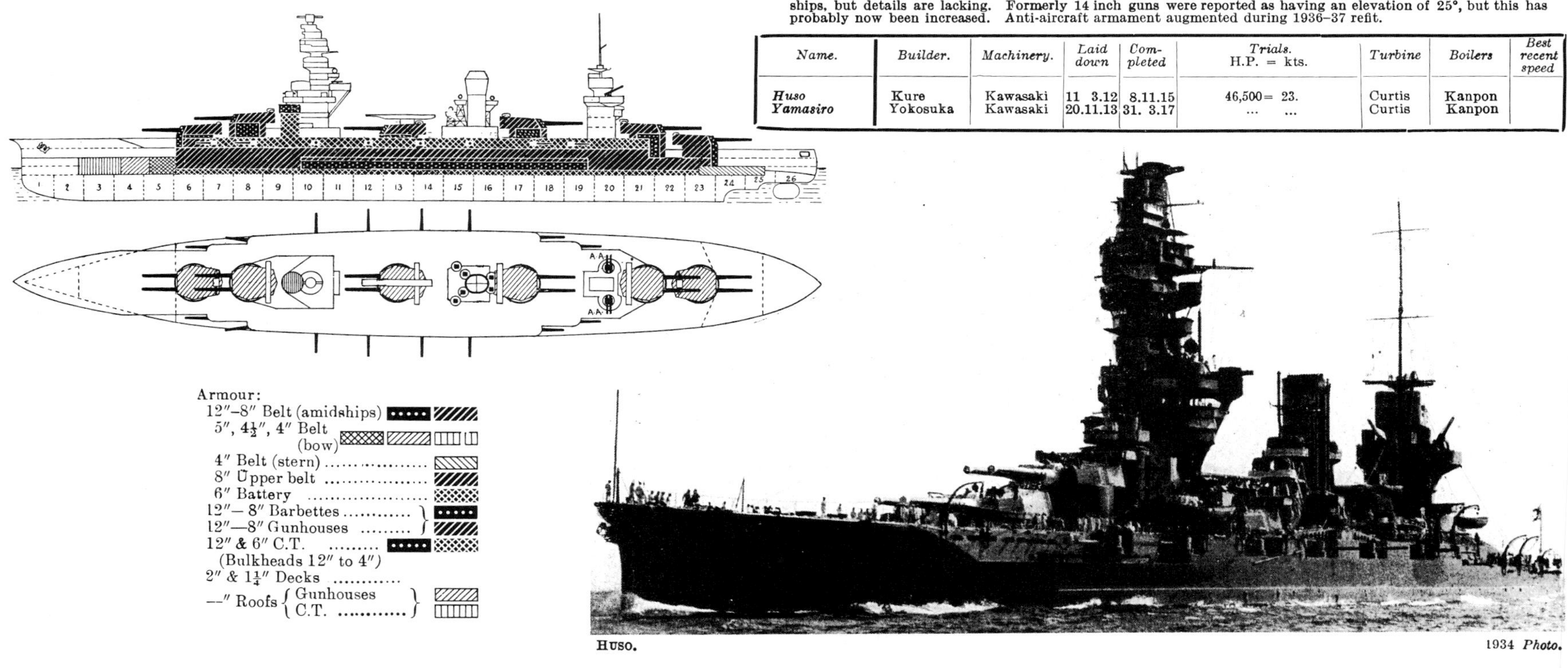

HUSO. — 1934 *Photo.*

KONGO (May 18th, 1912). HIEI (Nov. 21, 1912). HARUNA (Dec. 14th, 1913), KIRISIMA (Dec. 1st, 1913).

Standard displacement, 29,330 tons. Complement, 980.

Length { (*p.p.*) 653½ feet. (*o.a.*) 704 " } *Kirisima* Beam, 95 feet. *Kongo* " 92 ". *Hiei* " 92 ". *Haruna* " 95 ". *Max.* draught, 27½ feet. *Mean, 20¾ feet.*

Machinery: Parsons 4-shaft (in *Haruna* only, Curtis 4-shaft) turbines. Designed H.P.: 64,000 = 26 kts. **Boilers: 16 Kanpon. Fuel: About 4,500 tons oil.**

Name	*Builder*	*Machinery*	*Laid down*	*Com-pleted*	*Trials* F.P.	*Turbine*	*Re-fit*
Hiei	Yokosuka	Mitubisi	4.11 11	4.8.'14		Parsons	
Kongo	Vickers	Vickers	17.1.11	16.8.'13		Parsons	1936
Haruna	Kawasaki	Kawasaki	16.3.12	} 19.4.'15		Curtis	1926
Kirisima	Mitubisi	Mitubisi	17.3.12			Parsons	1925

Guns (*see Notes*):
8—14 inch, 45 cal.
16—6 inch, 50 cal.
8—5 inch AA.
4 machine.
4 landing.
Torpedo tubes (21 inch):
4 *submerged*.

Aircraft: 3

HARUNA (Funnels now of unequal height.) — 1934 (*added* 1935).

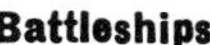

Battleships

General Notes.—*Kongo* 1910–11 Programme, others 1911–12 Programme. Designed by Sir George Thurston. For *Haruna* 30% of material was imported and erected in Japan. 3 planes added to equipment, 1927. All 4 refitted 1926–30, and bulges added, reducing speed by over a knot. Funnels altered on conversion to oil fuel only. *Kongo* completely rebuilt, 1935–37, being given additional protection against torpedo and aircraft attack. *Hiei*, de-militarised for Training purposes under London Naval Treaty of 1930, has been rearmed as a first line battleship. Originally these ships were rated as battle cruisers, hence their being named after mountains, and not after provinces as in case of other battleships.

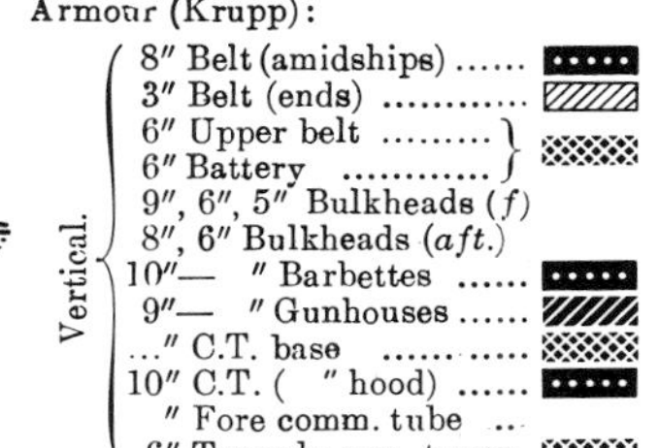

Armour (Krupp):

Vertical.
- 8″ Belt (amidships) ......
- 3″ Belt (ends) ....
- 6″ Upper belt ....
- 6″ Battery ....
- 9″, 6″, 5″ Bulkheads (*f*)
- 8″, 6″ Bulkheads (*aft.*)
- 10″— ″ Barbettes ......
- 9″— ″ Gunhouses ......
- ...″ C.T. base ....
- 10″ C.T. (″ hood) ......
- ″ Fore comm. tube ...
- 6″ Torpedo con. tower
- 8″ Tube (C.T. tower) ...

Armour (H.T.?):

Decks.
- ″ Forecastle ....
- 2¾″ Main......................
- ″ Middle ....
- ″ Lower ....

Special Protection H.T.
Torpedo Protection Bulkheads.

During reconstruction 4″ was added to deck protection, raising displacement by 3,000 tons.

These Notes are not from any official data.

Gunnery Notes.—In *Kongo* guns are Vickers models; but in other three ships all calibres are of Japanese manufacture. *Kongo* has combined Vickers (hydraulic) and Janney-Williams (electric) manœuvring systems for her barbettes; there is also a small auxiliary hydraulic installation, generally used for cleaning purposes, which can be used in emergency for working the 14-inch guns.

Armour Notes.—Main belt is 12′ 5″ deep, 8″ thick, and extends between Barbettes Nos. 1 and 4. Upper belt between Barbettes Nos. 1 and 3, 6″ thick, and carried up to forecastle deck. Bulkheads: Main belt is closed by diagonal bulkheads of 8″—6″ aft and by a 6″—5″ bulkhead forward. Upper belt closed by 6″ bulkhead aft and 9″—6″ bulkhead forward. There is also a narrow 3 inch strip of armour, 2 feet 6 inch deep under whole length of main belt; this is not shown on plans.

Anti-Torpedo Protection Notes.—Internal sub-division by longitudinal and cross bulkheads. Extra protection given by armour to all magazine spaces. Port and starboard engine rooms are divided by an unpierced longitudinal bulkhead along keel-line.

Torpedo Notes.—Tubes are twin submerged type, at varying levels, some being only 6 feet below waterline. Except in the case of the tubes in wake of No. 3 Barbette, Starboard Tube is before Port Tube. *Kongo* has combined hydraulic and electrically-operated tubes. In *Haruna*, tubes are Armstrong 21-inch side-loading, hydraulically operated.

Engineering Notes.—In *Kongo*, and *Kirisima* Parsons turbines have H.P. rotors on outboard shafts and L.P. on inner shafts with astern turbines aft and in same casing. Reconstruction included new Kanpon boilers.

KONGO (funnels of equal height). (HIEI probably similar). 1938, *added* 1939.

KIRISIMA. 1935.

Aircraft Carriers

RYUJO (Yokohama D.Y., April 2, 1931).

Displacement, 7,600 tons.

Length 548 feet. Beam 60½ feet. Draught 15⅓ feet.

Complement 600.

Guns: **12**—5·1 inch (12·7 cm.) AA.

Machinery: Geared turbines. Kampon boilers. D.H.P. 40,000 =25 kts. Laid down in Jan., 1930. To be completed in 1932.

RYUJO. *Photo*, April, 1931.

KAGA. 1929 *Photo.*

KAGA

がか

Displacement, 28,100 tons.

Length (*p.p.*) 715 feet. Beam 102¾ feet. Draught 21⅓ feet.

(Kawasaki Co., Kobe, 17th Nov., 1921).

Aircraft Carriers

KAGA

Guns:
10—8 inch.
4—4.7 inch.
12—4.7 inch AA.

Armour:
" Belt.
" Gunhouses.

Machinery: Geared turbines. Designed S.H.P. 91,000 = 25 kts. (23 kts. was to have been speed originally). Fuel:

KAGA. 1931 Photo

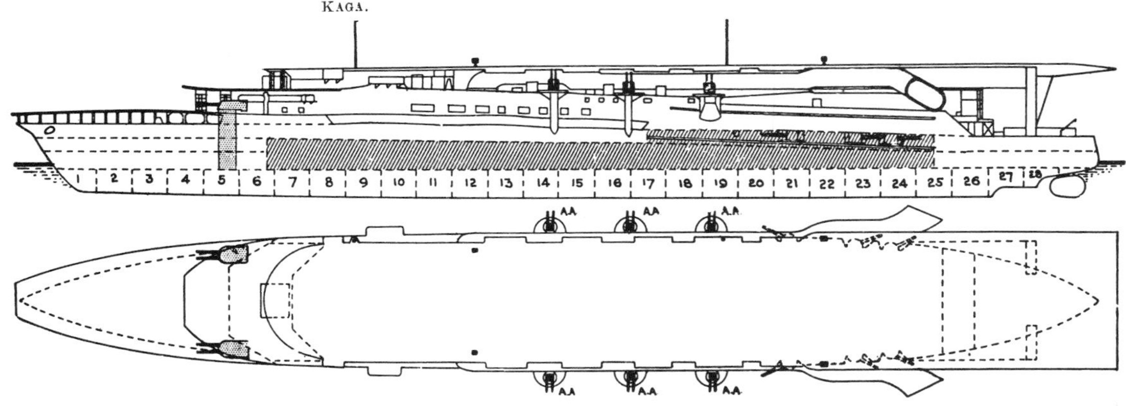

Notes.—Originally laid down July 20th, 1920, as a battleship of 39,900 tons, but has been converted into an aircraft carrier as the result of the Washington Treaty: Smoke is discharged through huge trunks on both sides, extending for nearly half the length of the ship and turning outboard towards the stern: There is accommodation for 60 planes.

ぎかあ AKAGI (Kure Dockyard, April 22nd, 1925).

Displacement: 28,100 tons. Length (*p.p.*), 763 feet. Beam, 92 feet. Draught, 21¼ feet.

3—8" Guns AA. Guns. AA. Guns. AA. Guns. Funnels. 8" Turret. 1930 *Photo.*

Machinery: Geared turbines. Original designed S.H.P. 131,200 = 28.5 kts. (likely to be exceeded). Fuel: Coal + oil in original design.

Notes.—Originally laid down on 6th Dec., 1920, as battle cruiser of 42,000 tons, but converted into aircraft carrier as result of Washington Treaty. Funnels are arranged on starboard side so that the foremost (which is internally divided into four) is trunked outward and downward amidships, while the second projects slightly above flight deck abaft of the first. Though she has accommodation for 50 planes, only about 30 are carried normally. There are 2 aircraft lifts on starboard side, one abaft funnels and a smaller one right astern.

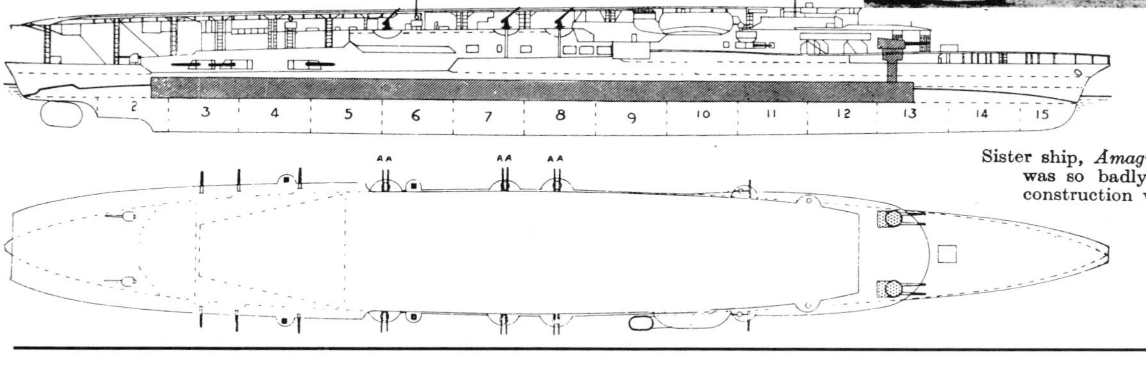

Guns:
10—8 inch
4—4.7 inch
12—4.7 inch AA.

Armour:
" Belt.
" Gunhouses.

Sister ship, *Amagi,* laid down at Yokosuka Dockyard, and launched late in 1922, was so badly damaged by earthquake and fire, September, 1923, that her construction was abandoned, and *Kaga's* hull was appropriated to replace her.

SYOKAKU (June 2, 1939), **ZUIKAKU** (Nov. 27, 1939).

Displacement: 20,000 tons.
Dimensions: 800 (*o.a.*) × — × — feet.
Guns: 12—5 inch A.A. Aircraft: 60.
Machinery: Geared turbines. Speed: over 30 kts.

Name	*Builder*	*Laid down*	*Completed*
Syokaku	Yokosuka	11 Dec. 1937	1941
Zuikaku	Kawasaki	1938	1941

Note.—These names mean *Crane* and *Lucky Stork* respectively. A third ship of this class, *Ryukaku*, has been lost. A fourth may exist.

SYOKAKU. 1942, *U.S. Navy, Official.*

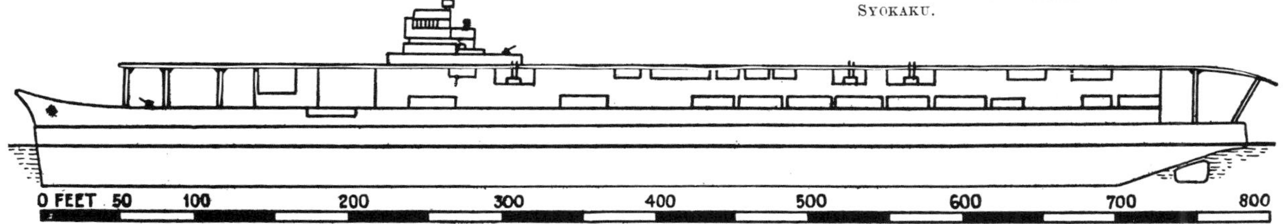

RYUZYO (April 2, 1931).

RYUZYO 1933 *Photo, Official.*

Note.—Smoke discharge is arranged through 2 funnels projecting from starboard side. This ship, though completed at Yokosuka Naval Yard, was actually laid down and launched at the Yokohama Dock Company's establishment.
In Sept., 1942, she was severely damaged in action with Allied naval forces off the Solomon Islands, and her survival is doubtful.

Displacement: 7,100 tons. Complement: 600.
Length: 548 feet. Beam: $60\frac{1}{2}$ feet. Draught: $15\frac{1}{3}$ feet.
Guns: 12—5 inch AA. 24 M.G. 24 aircraft carried (unofficial).
Machinery: Geared turbines. Kanpon Boilers. S.H.P. 40,000 = 25 kts.
Laid down Nov. 26, 1929. Completed May 9, 1933.

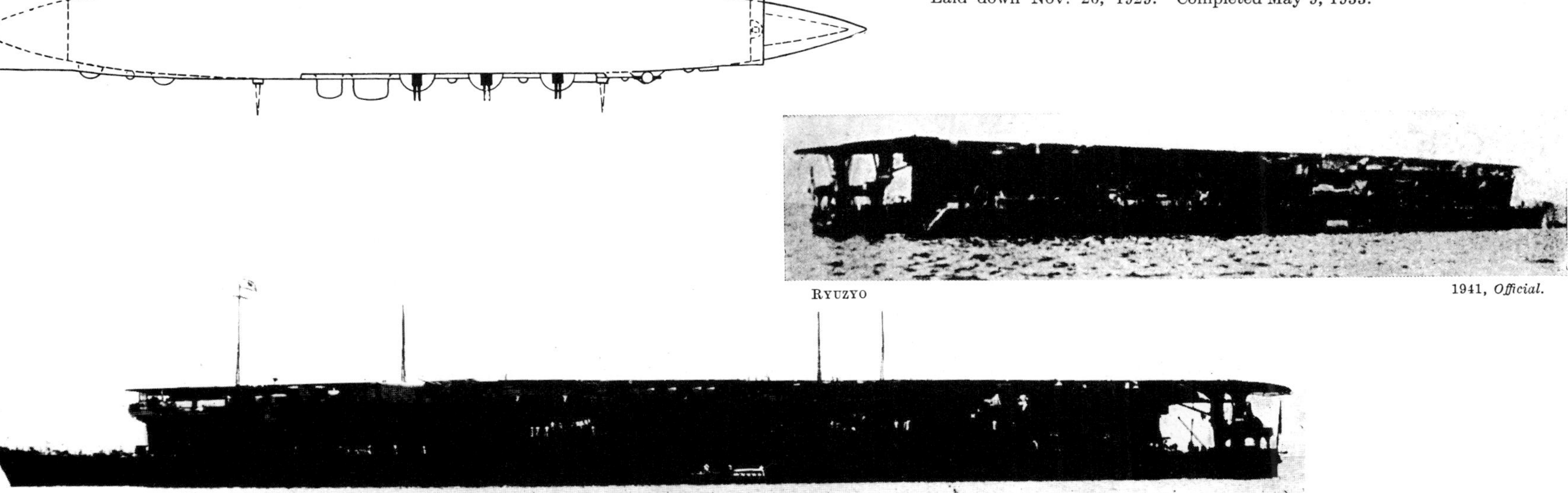

RYUZYO 1941, *Official.*

RYUZYO. 1934 *Photo, Official.*

Aircraft Carrier

HOSYO (Asano Co., Turumi, November 13, 1921). Displacement: 7,470 tons. Dimensions: 510 (*p.p.*) × 62 × 20¼ feet. Guns: 4—5·5 inch. 2—3 inch AA. 2 M.G.

Machinery: 2 sets geared turbines. S.H.P.: 30,000 = 25 kts. 8 Kanpon boilers. Fuel: Oil only, 550 tons. Can carry 26 aircraft with all accessories, etc., though normal complement seldom exceeds 20. (Unofficial). Sperry gyro-stabiliser fitted. 2 searchlights.

Note.—Laid down December 16, 1919; completed December 27, 1922. The building of a second ship of this type (to have been named *Syokaku*) was cancelled owing to Washington Treaty, but this name was ultimately appropriated for an aircraft carrier launched in 1939. Big refit 1939-40.

(Plan reversed to illustrate funnel arrangement.)

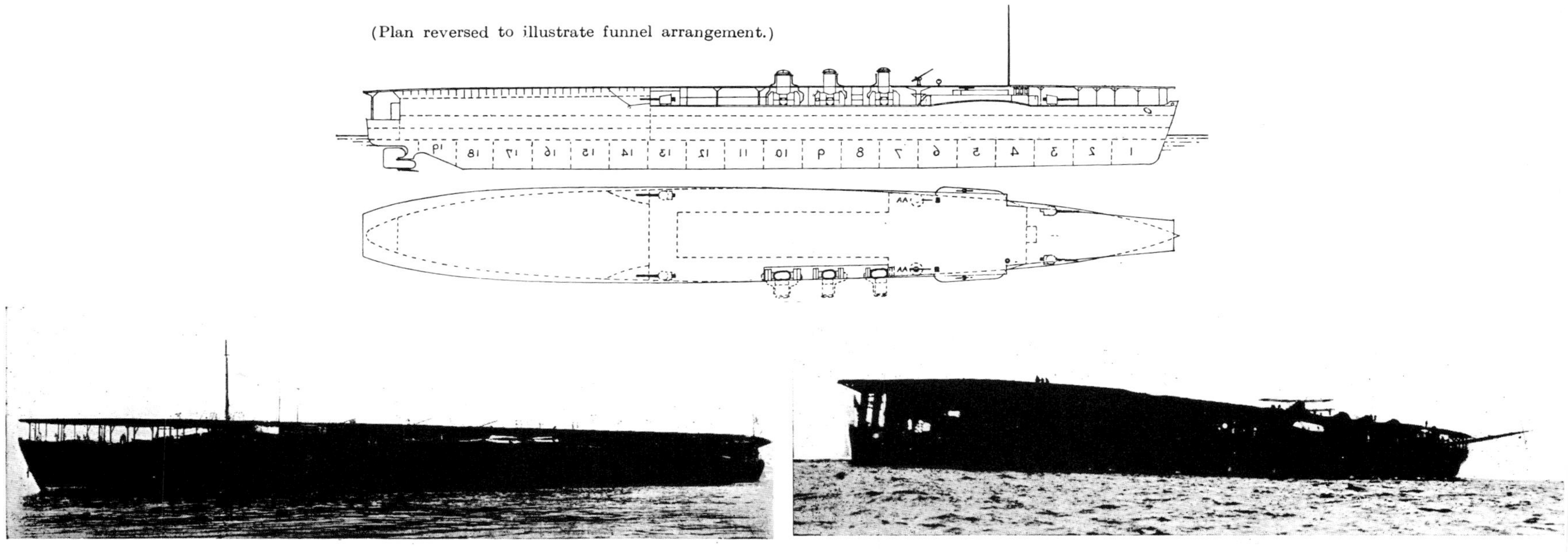

HOSYO. *Added* 1935.

HOSYO with funnels lowered to horizontal position. 1932 *Photo.*

First Class Cruisers

MAYA. 1932 *Photo.*

ATAGO (June 16th, 1930), **TAKAO** (May 12th, 1930), **TYOKAI** (April 5, 1931), **MAYA** (Nov. 8, 1930).

Standard displacement, 9,850 tons.
Complement, 692.

Length: 630 (*p.p.*), 650 (*o.a.*) feet. Beam: 62¼ feet. Draught: 16⅓ feet (*mean*).

Notes.—Provided for under 1925 and later Programmes. Triple hull, designed to give greatest possible protection against submarines. Vertical and deck protection over boiler and machinery spaces is 410 feet long. Guns are a new model with very high muzzle velocity. Cost £2,200,000 each.

Guns:
10—8 inch, 50 cal.
4—4·7 inch AA.
8—47 mm. AA.
8 M.G.
Torpedo tubes (21 inch):
8 *above water.*

Armour (unofficial):
3-4″ Side....................
3″ Deck ....
3″ Turrets ....
Aircraft:
4, with 2 catapults.

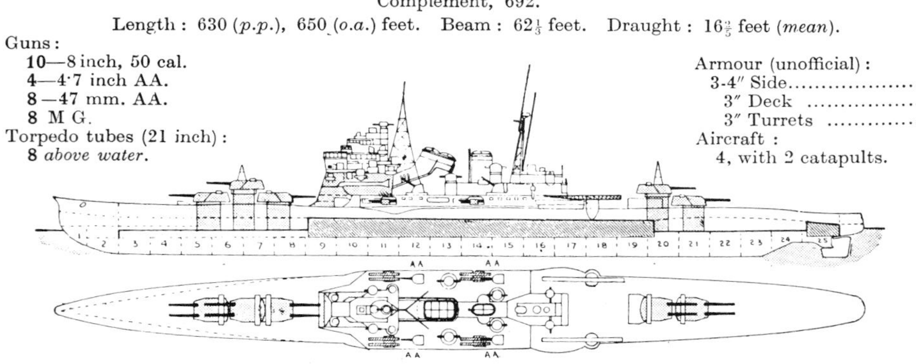

Machinery: Geared turbines. Boilers: 12 Kanpon. S.H.P. 100,000 = 33 kts. *max.* (32 kts. at deep load). Oil: 2,000 tons. Radius at 14–15 kts.: 14,000 miles.

ATAGO. 1932 *Photo.*

First Class Cruisers

ATAGO. 1933 *Official Photo.*

MAYA. 1933 *Photo.*

Name	Builder	Machinery	Laid down	Completed
Atago	Kure	Kure	28/4/27	30 March 1932
Takao	Yokosuka	Yokosuka	28/4/27	31 May 1932
Tyokai	Mitubisi	Mitubisi	26/3/28	30 June 1932
Maya	Kawasaki, Kobe	Kawasaki	4/12/28	30 „ 1932

NATI (June 15th, 1927), **MYOKO** (April 16th, 1927), **ASIGARA** (April 22nd, 1928), **HAGURO** (March 24th, 1928).

Standard displacement, 10,000 tons.

Complement, 692.

Length (*p.p.*), 630 feet, (*o.a.*), 640 feet. Beam, 62⅓ feet. Draught, 16½ feet (*mean*).

Guns:
10—8 inch, 50 cal.
6—4·7 inch AA. (8 in *Asigara*)
8—47 mm. AA.
8—M.G.
Torpedo tubes (21 inch):
8 *above water.* (quadrupled).

Note to plan: T.T. actually are slightly further aft than shown, above section 18.

Armour (unofficial):
3″ Side ....
2-3″ Deck ....
3″ Turrets ....

Aircraft: 4 with 2 Catapults.

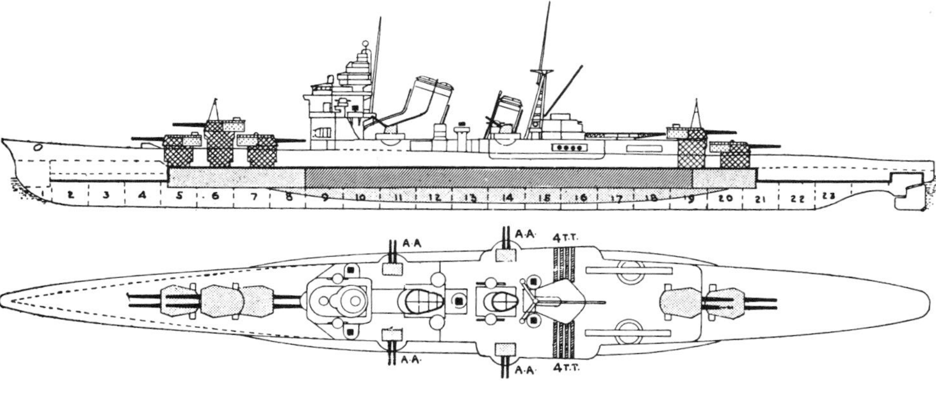

MYOKO. 1941.

ASIGARA.

Machinery: Geared turbines. Boilers: 12 Kanpon. S.H.P. 100,000 = 33 kts. *max.* (32 kts. at deep load). Oil: 2,000 tons. Radius at 14-15 kts.: 14,000 miles.

Notes.—Provided for under 1923 and later Programmes. Triple hull, designed to give greatest possible protection against submarines. Vertical and deck protection over boiler and machinery spaces is 410 feet long. Guns are a new model with very high muzzle velocity. Cost £2,200,000 each.
All 4 ships extensively refitted 1934-36, fore funnel being heightened, after control structure extended, anti-aircraft armament augmented and torpedo tubes rearranged in quadruple mountings. Further refits undertaken, 1939-41.

Name	Builder	Machinery	Laid down	Completed	Trials
Nati	Kure	Kure	26/11/24	26 Nov. 1928	
Myoko	Yokosuka	Yokosuka	25/10/24	31 July, 1929	
Asigara	Kawasaki Kobe	Kure	11/4/25	20 Aug. 1929	
Haguro	Mitubisi	Yokosuka	16/3/25	25 April, 1929	

ASIGARA.

First Class Cruisers

Asigara.

Asigara.

KAKO (April 10, 1925), **HURUTAKA** (Feb. 25, 1925), **KINUGASA** (Oct. 24th, 1926), **AOBA** (Sept. 25th, 1926).

Standard Displacement, 7,100 tons. Complement, 604.

Length (*w.l.*) 580 feet. (*o.a.*) 595 feet. Beam: 50¾ feet. Draught: 14¾ feet (*mean*).

Aircraft: 2, with catapult

Guns:
- 6—8 inch.
- 4—4·7 inch AA.
- 10—M.G

Torpedo tubes (21 inch):
- 12, *above water*.
- (May be quadrupled now in all.)

Armour: (Unofficial)
- 2" Side amidships ....
- 2" Deck ....
- 1½" Turrets ....
- (Bulges added, 1938–39)

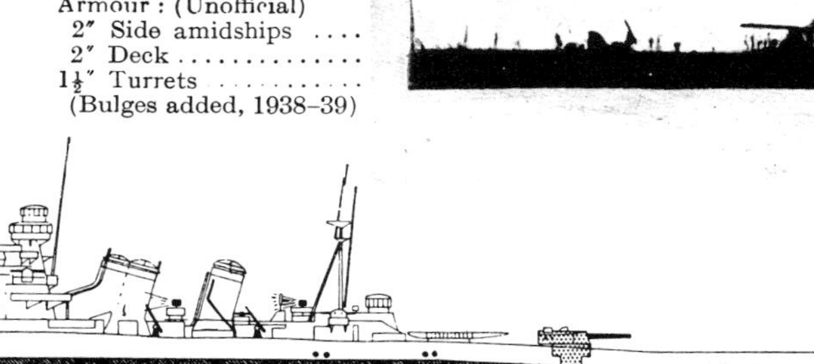

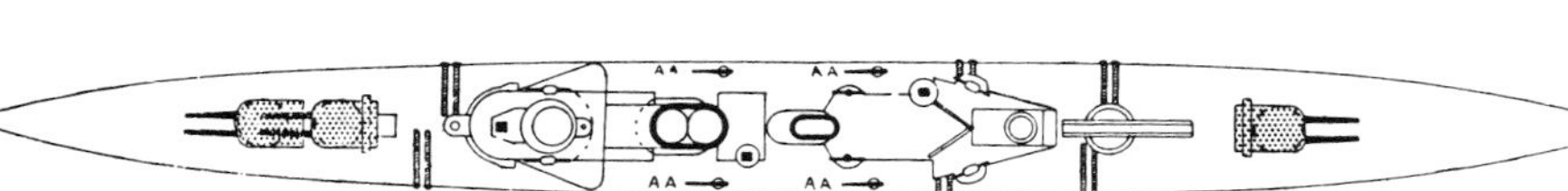

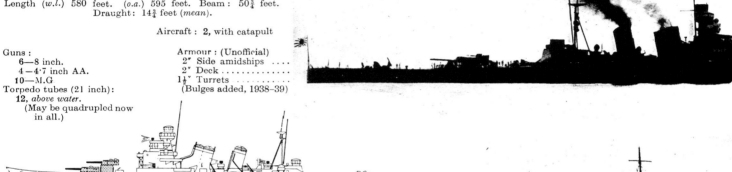

Machinery: Geared turbines. Boilers: 12 Kanpon (10 oil, 2 mixed). S.H.P.: 95,000 = 33 kts. (said to have been considerably reduced by addition of bulges). Fuel: 1,800 tons oil.

Name	*Builder*	*Machinery*	*Laid down*	*Completed*	*Trials*
Kako	Kawasaki, Kobe	Kawasaki	17 Nov., 1922	20 July, 1926	
Hurutaka	Mitubisi, Nagasaki	Mitubisi	5 Dec., 1922	31 Mar., 1926	
Kinugasa	Kawasaki, Kobe	Kawasaki	23 Jan., 1924	30 Sept., 1927	
Aoba	Mitubisi, Nagasaki	Mitubisi	4 Feb., 1924	20 Sept., 1927	

1927 *Photo* (*added* 1928).

Notes.—Provided for under 1922 and 1923 Programmes. Noteworthy features introduced in these ships are the undulating deck line, unusual bridgework and masts, trunked and heavily raked funnels and angled hull form. As originally completed with six single turrets, *Kako* and *Hurutaka* proved deficient in seakeeping qualities. They were therefore rebuilt at Kure on similar lines to two later ships in 1938–39. In *Kako* and *Hurutaka* superstructure extends as far as turret and carries a catapult forward of mainmast. After funnel in these two ships is noticeably thinner than in other pair.

TONE (Nov. 21, 1937), **TIKUMA** (March 19, 1938).

Displacement: 8,500 tons. Complement: 850.

Length: 614¼ feet (*pp.*). Beam: 63 feet. Draught: 14¾ feet (*mean*).

Guns:
- 8—8 inch.
- 8—5 inch AA.
- 12 M.G.

Torpedo Tubes: 12—21 inch.

Aircraft: 6

Armour:
- 2" Deck.
- 2" Side.

Machinery: 4 sets geared turbines. 4 shafts. S.H.P.: 90,000 = 33 kts. Boilers: 8 Kanpon.

Name.	*Builder and Machinery.*	*Laid down.*	*Completed.*
Tone	Mitubisi	1 Dec., 1934	20 Nov., 1938
Tikuma	Mitubisi	1 Oct., 1935	1939

Note.—Design incorporates various improvements resulting from experience with *Mogami* type, armament being reduced to save weight. Both laid down under 1933 Fleet Replenishment Law.

MOGAMI (March 13, 1934), SUZUYA (Nov. 20, 1934), KUMANO (Oct. 15, 1936).

Standard displacement: 8,500 tons. Complement: 850.

Length (*pp.*) 625 feet, (*o.a.*) 639¾ feet; Beam, 59¾ feet; Draught, 14¾ feet (*mean*).

Guns:
15—6·1 inch.
8—5 inch AA.
12 M.G.

Aircraft:
4, with 2 catapults.

Torpedo Tubes:
12—21 inch, *above water*
(in triple mounts)

Armour: (Unofficial)
2″ Deck.
2″ Side.

Searchlights:
3

Machinery: 4 sets geared turbines. 4 shafts.
Designed S.H.P.: 90,000 = 33 kts. Boilers: 10 Kanpon.

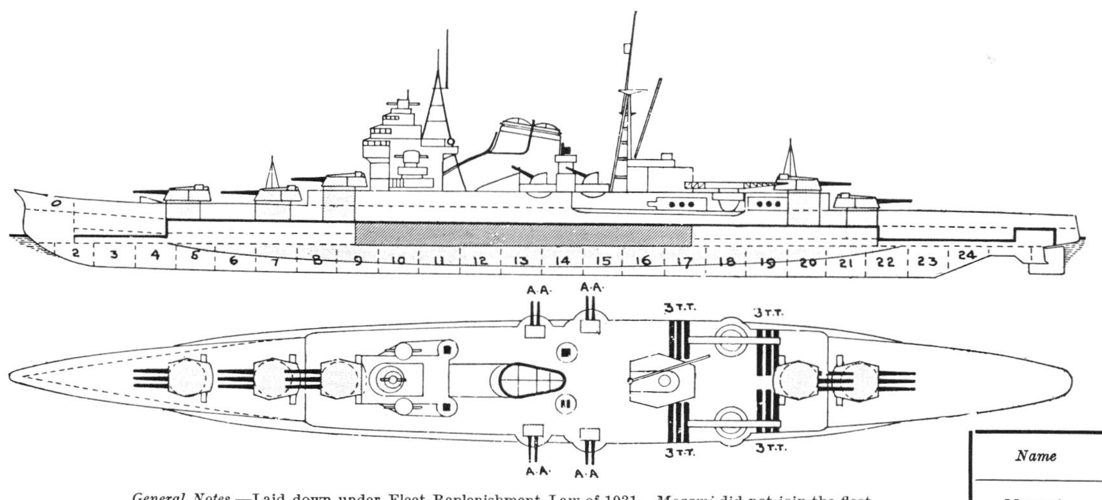

Name	*Builder*	*Machinery*	*Begun*	*Completed*
Mogami	Kure		27 Oct., 1931	28 July, 1935
Suzuya	Yokosuka		11 Dec., 1933	31 Oct., 1937
Kumano	Kawasaki	Kawasaki	5 April, 1934	31 Oct., 1937

General Notes.—Laid down under Fleet Replenishment Law of 1931. *Mogami* did not join the fleet until more than a year after date given above for completion, various modifications having to be made before she was considered satisfactory. Actual completion dates of 2 latter ships uncertain. Trials began in July, 1937.

Appearance Notes.—There are sundry small differences in appearance as completed.

KUMANO 1938.

ZINTU (8th Dec., 1923), NAKA (24th March, 1925), SENDAI (30th Oct., 1923).

Standard displacement, 5195 tons. Complement, 450.

Length (*p.p.*), 500 feet; (*o.a.*) 535 feet. Beam, 46¾ feet
Draught, 15 feet 10½ in.

Guns:
7—5·5 inch, 50 cal.
2—3 inch, 13 pdr., 40 cal. AA.
6 M.G.

Armour: (Unofficial)
2″ Side (amidships)
2″ C.T.

Torpedo tubes:
8—21 inch, *above water.*

Aircraft:
1, with catapult.

Note to Plan.—Now carry catapult in position shown in photos. Some, if not all, have funnels of equal height.

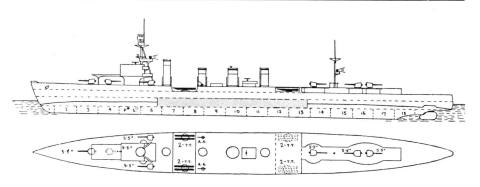

Machinery: 4 geared turbines. 4 shafts. Boilers: 12 Kanpon. Designed S.H.P. 70,000 = 33 kts. Fuel: 300 tons *coal.* 1200 tons *oil.*

General Notes.—Slightly enlarged and improved editions of *Natori* class on following page. The launch of *Naka* was delayed by earthquake of Sept., 1923. Catapult fitted 1929. Foremost boiler is fitted for mixed firing.

All this class underwent extensive refits, 1939–40.

Name	*Builder*	*Machinery*	*Begun*	*Completed*	*Trials*
Zintu	Kawasaki, Kobe	Kawasaki	4 Aug., '22	31 July, '25	
Sendai	Mitubisi, Nagasaki	Mitubisi	16 Feb., '22	29 Apr., '24	
Naka	Yokohama Dock Co.	Mitubisi	10 June, '22	30 Nov., '25	

ZINTU. 1938, *Official courtesy of Navy Dept., Tokyo.*

SENDAI. Funnels of this ship are now all of equal height.

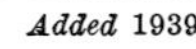

Added 1939.

Second Class Cruisers

"Natori" Class (6 Ships)

ISUZU (29th Oct., 1921). **NAGARA** (25th April, 1921).

NATORI (16th Feb., 1922). **YURA** (15th Feb., 1922)

KINU (29th May, 1922). **ABUKUMA** (16th March, 1923)

Standard displacement, 5170 tons. Comp., 438.
Length (*p.p.*) 500 feet, (*o.a.*) 535 feet. Beam, 46¾ feet.
Draught, 15 feet 10½ in.

Guns :—
7—5·5 inch, 50 cal.
2—3 inch, 13 pdr. 40 cal. AA.
2 M.G.
Torpedo tubes : (21 inch)
8 (*above water*).
Aircraft :
1, with catapult.

Armour : (Unofficial).
2" Side (amidships).
2" C.T.

Isuzu. (*Yura* similar). 1934 (*added* 1935).

Machinery : 4 geared turbines. 4 shafts. Boilers : 12 Kanpon, 8 oil and 4 coal burning. Designed S.H.P. : 70,000 = 33 kts. Fuel : 350 tons coal, 1,150 tons oil.

Plan: Details generally as *Kuma*. Formerly had aircraft hangar forward but this has been removed from most if not all of class.

Kinu. Aug. 1937.

Name	Builder	Machinery	Begun	Completed	Trials (unofficial)
Isuzu	Uraga Dock Co.	Mitubisi	10 Aug., '20	15/8/23	
Nagara	Saseho	Kawasaki	9 Sept., '20	21/4/22	65,000 = 33.4
Natori	Mitubisi, Nagasaki	Mitubisi	14 Dec., '20	15/9/22	
Kinu	Kawasaki Co., Kobe	Kawasaki	17 Jan., '21	10/11/22	
Yura	Saseho	Kawasaki	21 May, '21	20/3/23	
Abukuma	Uraga Dock Co.	Mitubisi	8 Dec., '21	26/5/25	

Natori and Abukuma (showing catapult mounted between guns Nos. 5 and 6). 1934 *Photo.*

Notes.—Commencement authorised by 1919 Naval Programme. Cost of each ship is said to be £1,250,000. Completion of *Abukuma* was delayed owing to earthquake damage at Uraga Yard in Sept., 1923. *Abukuma* taken in hand for modernisation, 1939.

Kuma Class—5 Ships.

KUMA (July 14th, 1919), **TAMA** (Feb. 10th, 1920),

OI (July 15th, 1920),

KITAKAMI (July 3rd, 1920), **KISO** (Dec.14th, 1920).

Standard displacement, 5100 tons. Complement, 439
Length (*p.p.*) 500 feet, (*o.a.*) 535 feet. Beam, 46¾ feet. *Mean* draught, 15¾ feet.

Guns :
7—5·5 inch, 50 cal.
2—3 inch (13 pdr.), 40 cal.
2 M.G.
Torpedo tubes (21 inch):
8 *above water*.
Searchlights :
3—30 inch.
Mines:
80 can be carried
Aircraft : 1.

Armour (*unofficial*) :
2" (H.T.) Side (amidships) ....
2" C.T. ....

Note to Plan.—Apparent rake shown in plan does not exist. Foremast control tops now as in photos.

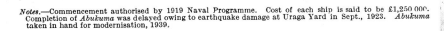

Ahead : 3—5·5 inch. Broadside : 6—5·5 inch, 4—21 inch T.T. Astern : 1—5·5 inch.

Machinery: Geared Parsons or Curtis Turbines. 4 shafts. Boilers: 12 Kanpon, 10 oil fuel, 2 mixed firing. Designed H.P. 70,000 = 33 kts. Fuel: *normal*, 350 tons ; *maximum*, about 1500 tons = 8500 miles at 10 kts.

General Notes.—*Kuma* and *Tama* begun under the 1917 Naval Programme ; *Oi*, *Kitakami*, *Kiso* under 1918 Programme. Completion of *Oi* delayed by failure of one of her engines when she was running trials at end of Dec., 1920. Said to be very efficiently sub-divided. Fuel supply is somewhere above the average = 6,000 miles at 15 kts., and between 1,000 and 1,100 miles at full speed. No official data published concerning trials, but are reported to have averaged about 64,500 H.P. and about 33 kts. Cost about £1,000,000 each. An aeroplane was added to the equipment of these ships in 1927.

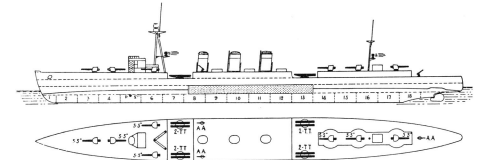

Kiso. 1938, *B. R. Goodfellow, Esq.*

Name	Builder	Machinery	Laid down	Com-pleted	First Trials.	Boilers
Oi	Kawasaki	Kawasaki	24/11/19	3/10/21		
Kitakami	Saseho	Kawasaki	1/9/19	15/4/21		
Kiso	Mitubisi Nagasaki	Mitubisi	10/6/19	4/5/21	—34	All 12 Kanpon.
Kuma	Saseho	Kawasaki	29/8/18	31/8/20		
Tama	Mitubisi Nagasaki	Mitubisi	10/8/18	29/1/21		

KUMA 1937

KUMA (fitted with anti-flare tops to funnels). 1935 *Official.*

YUBARI (5th March, 1923).

Standard displacement, 2890 tons. Complement, 328.
Length (*p.p.*), 435 feet. Beam, 39½ feet. Draught, 11 feet 9 ins.

Guns:
6—5·5 inch, 50 cal.
1—3 inch AA.
2—M.G.
Torpedo tubes (21 inch):
4 (*above water*).
Mines:
Storage for 34.
Searchlights: 2.

Armour (unofficial):
2″ side (H.T.)

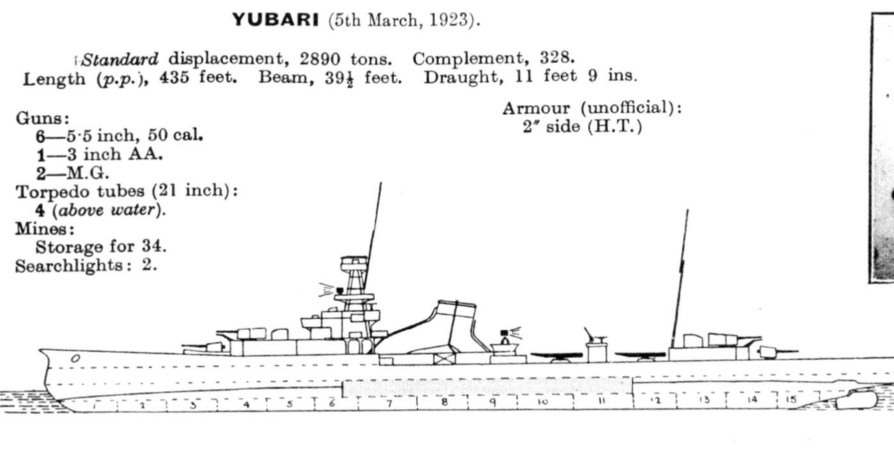

1928 *Photo.*

Machinery: Geared Turbines. 3 shafts. Boilers: 8 Kanpon (coal and oil-burning). Designed S.H.P.: 57,000 = 33 kts. Fuel: 820 tons.

Note.—Laid down on 5th June, 1922, at Saseho Dockyard. Completed July 31, 1923. Under refit, 1940.

Torpedo Notes.—Tubes are arranged so that they can be trained on either broadside.

Engineering Notes.—Machinery was built by Saseho Dockyard.

(TENRYU CLASS—2 SHIPS.)

TATUTA (29th May, 1918) **TENRYU** (11th Mar., 1918)

Standard displacement, 3230 tons. Complement, 332.
Length (*o.a.*) 468 feet (*p.p.*), 440 feet. Beam: 40¾ feet. *Mean* draught: 13 feet.

Guns:
4—5·5 inch, 50 cal.
1—3 inch (13 pdr.) 40 cal. AA.
2 M.G.
Torpedo tubes: (21 in.)
6 *above water* in two triple U.D. mountings.
Searchlights:
2—30 inch.
Mines:
May be carried.

Note to Plan.—Both ships now have tripod foremast.

Armour (unofficial):
2″ or 1½″ (H.T.) Side amidships ......
—″ Deck (H.T.) at ends ....
—″ C.T. ....

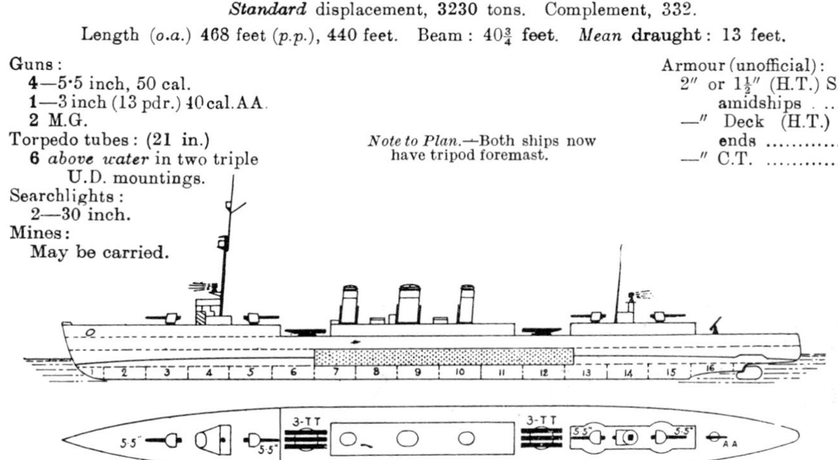

TENRYU. 1939.

Machinery: Curtis and Parsons turbines, respectively. 3 shafts. Boilers: 10 Kanpon. Designed H.P.: 51,000 = 31 kts. Fuel: Coal and oil, 900 tons = 6,000 miles at 10 kts. (unofficial).

Name	Builder	Machinery	Laid down	Com-pleted	Trials
Tatuta	Saseho	Kawasaki	24/7/17	31 Mar., '19	51,000 = 33 kts.
Tenryu	Yokosuka	Mitubisi	17/5/17	20 Nov., '19	

Destroyers and Torpedo Boats

Meanings of names of Destroyers and Torpedo Boats. (Supplied officially to "Fighting Ships.")

Many of these names are poetical in conception; and where adequate translation is not possible the English version should be taken merely as an approximate indication of the meaning of the names.

KAGERO *class.* 1ST CLASS.
- *Siranui* .. .. Phosphorescent foam (literally, "Unknown fires")
- *Kagero* .. .. Gossamer.
- *Kurosio* .. .. Black tide.
- *Oyasio* .. .. Parent tide.
- *Hatukaze* .. .. Early breeze.
- *Hayasio* .. .. Fast running tide.
- *Yukikaze* .. Snowstorm.
- *Natusio* .. .. Summer tide.
- *Kurukaze* .. .. Head wind.
- *Isokaze* .. .. Shore breeze.
- *Urakaze* .. .. Wind in the bay.
- *Tokitukaze* .. Fair wind.
- *Amatukaze* .. Divine wind.
- *Arasi* .. .. Gale.
- *Nowake* .. .. Strong autumn wind (literally, "Separator of fields".)
- *Tanikaze* .. .. Wind in the valley.

ASASIO *class.*
- *Asasio* .. .. Morning tide.
- *Arasio* .. .. Rough tide.
- *Osio* .. .. High tide.
- *Mitisio* .. .. Tide running full.
- *Asagumo* .. .. White clouds of the morning.
- *Yamagumo* .. White clouds on the hillsides.
- *Minegumo* .. White clouds on the mountain peak.
- *Natugumo* .. White clouds of summer.
- *Kasumi* .. .. Haze (literally, "Mist of flowers").
- *Arare* .. .. Hail.

SIGURE *class.*
- *Yamakaze* .. Wind from the hills.
- *Suzukaze* .. .. Cool breeze of summer.
- *Kawakaze* .. Wind on the river.
- *Umikaze* .. .. Sea breeze.
- *Siratuyu* .. White dew.
- *Sigure* .. .. Autumn shower.
- *Murasame* .. Scattered showers.
- *Yudati* .. .. Evening thunder shower in summer.
- *Harusame* .. Spring shower.
- *Samidare* .. Early summer rain.

HATUHARU *class.*
- *Hatuharu* .. First days of spring.
- *Nenohi* .. .. A day of New Year celebrations in old Japan.
- *Wakaba* .. .. Fresh verdure (young leaves shooting).
- *Hatusimo* .. First frost of the season.
- *Ariake* .. .. Dawn (still the moon remains in the sky).
- *Yugure* .. .. Evening.

HUBUKI *class.*
- *Hubuki* .. .. Blizzard (snowstorm).
- *Sirayuki* .. White snow.
- *Hatuyuki* First snow of the season.
- *Murakumo* .. Cloud clusters.
- *Sinonome* .. .. Dawn.
- *Usugumo* .. Fleecy clouds.
- *Sirakumo* .. White clouds.
- *Isonami* .. .. Waves on the beach.
- *Uranami* .. .. Waves in the bay.
- *Ayanami* .. .. Waves whose beauty suggests figures woven in silk.
- *Sikinami* .. .. Waves chasing one another.
- *Asagiri* .. .. Morning mist.
- *Yugiri* .. .. Evening mist.
- *Amagiri* .. .. Mist in the sky.
- *Sagiri* .. .. Mist.
- *Oboro* .. .. Haziness diffusing moonlight.
- *Akebono* .. .. Daybreak.
- *Sazanami* .. .. Ripples.
- *Usio* .. .. Tide.
- *Akatuki* .. .. Dawn.
- *Hibiki* .. .. Echo.
- *Ikaduti* .. .. Thunder.
- *Inaduma* .. Lightning.

MUTUKI *class*

Mutuki, Kisaragi, Yayoi, Uduki, Satuki, Minaduki, Humiduki, Nagatuki, Kikuduki. These are poetical names for January, February, March, April, May, June, July, and September (two examples), respectively.
- *Mikaduki* .. New moon.
- *Motiduki* .. .. Full moon.
- *Yuduki* .. .. Evening moon.

KAMIKAZE *and* MINEKAZE *classes.*
- *Kamikaze* .. Divine wind.
- *Asakaze* .. .. Morning breeze.
- *Harukaze* .. .. Spring breeze.
- *Matukaze* .. .. Wind among the pine trees.
- *Hatakaze* .. .. Wind which causes the flapping of a flag.
- *Oite* .. .. Fair wind (i.e., favourable wind).
- *Hayate* .. .. Squall.
- *Asanagi* .. .. Morning calm.
- *Yunagi* .. .. Evening calm.
- *Akikaze* .. .. Autumn wind.
- *Yukaze* .. .. Evening breeze.
- *Hokaze* .. .. Wind on the sail.
- *Siokaze* .. .. Wind springing up at the turn of the tide.
- *Tatikaze* .. .. Wind caused by the stroke of a sword.
- *Namikaze* .. .. Wind on the waves.
- *Numakaze* .. Wind over the marsh.
- *Nokaze* .. .. Wind over the field.
- *Sawakaze* .. Wind from the swamp.
- *Hakaze* .. .. Wind of a bird's flight.
- *Yakaze* .. .. Wind of an arrow's flight.
- *Minekaze* .. Wind from the mountain peak.
- *Okikaze* .. .. Wind in the offing.

WAKATAKE *class.* 2ND CLASS.
- *Wakatake* .. .. Young bamboo.
- *Kuretake* .. .. Certain variety of bamboo.
- *Sanae* .. .. Rice seedling.
- *Asagao* .. .. Morning glory.
- *Huyo* .. .. A species of rose.
- *Karukaya* .. Sage.

KURI *class.*
- *Kuri* .. .. Chestnut.
- *Tuga* .. .. Japanese hemlock-spruce.
- *Hasu* .. .. Lotus.

TIDORI *class.* TORPEDO BOATS
- *Tidori* .. .. Dotterel plover.
- *Manaduru* .. White-naped crane.
- *Tomoduru* .. Flight of cranes.
- *Hatukari* .. .. First wild goose of the season.
- *Otori* .. .. Japanese stork.
- *Hiyodori* .. .. Brown-eared bulbul.
- *Hayabusa* .. Peregrine falcon.
- *Kasasagi* .. .. Magpie
- *Kizi* .. .. Pheasant
- *Kari* .. .. Wild goose.
- *Sagi* .. .. Snowy heron.
- *Hato* .. .. Dove.

Over 17 Kagero class.

Photo wanted.
Reported to resemble ASASIO *type.*

Kagero, Siranui, Kurosio, Oyasio, Hatukaze, Natusio, Yukikaze, Kurukaze, Isokaze, Hayasio, Amatukaze, Tokitukaze, Urakaze, Arasi, Nowake, Tanikaze, Hagikaze and others (number uncertain, but may be 8 to 12).
Displacement: 2,000 tons. Dimensions: 364 × 35 × 11 feet.
Guns: **6**—5 inch, **2** M.G. Torpedo tubes: **8**—21 inch.
Machinery: Geared turbines. 2 shafts. S.H.P.: 45,000 = 36 kts. Boilers: 3 Kanpon.
Note.—*Hamakaze* (meaning "Wind from the beach"), of this type, was sunk in Sept. 1942. *Arasi* may also have been lost.

Name.	*Builder.*	*Laid down.*	*Launch.*	*Completed.*
Kagero	Maiduru	Sept. 3, 1937	Sept. 27, 1938	Nov. 6, 1939
Siranui	Uraga	Aug. 30, 1937	June 28, 1938	Dec. 20, 1939
Kurosio	Hudinagata	Aug, 31, 1937	Oct. 25, 1938	Jan. 27, 1940
Oyasio	Maiduru	1938	Nov. 29, 1938	1940
Hatukaze	Kawasaki	Dec. 3, 1937	Jan. 24, 1939	Feb. 15, 1940
Natusio	Hudinagata	1938	Feb. 23, 1939	1940
Hayasio	Uraga	1938	April 19, 1939	1940
Yukikaze	Saseho	Aug. 2, 1938	March 24, 1939	Jan. 20, 1940
Kurukaze	Uraga	1938	June 1, 1939	1940
Isokaze	Saseho	1938	June 19, 1939	194C
Tokitukaze	Uraga	1938	Nov. 10, 1939	1940
Amatukaze	Maiduru	1938	Oct. 19, 1939	1940
Urakaze	Hudinagata	1939	April 10, 1940	1941
Arasi	Maiduru	1939	April 22, 1940	1941
Hagikaze	Uraga	1939	Sept. 17, 1940	1941
Nowake	Maiduru	1939	Sept. 17, 1940	1941
Tanikaze	Hudinagata	1939	Nov. 1, 1940	1941

10 Asasio class.

ASAGUMO. 1938.

Asasio, Arasio, Osio, Mitisio, Asagumo, Yamagumo, Minegumo, Natugumo, Kasumi, Arare.
Displacement: 1,500 tons. Complement: 190.
Dimensions: 356 × 33½ × 9 feet.
Guns: **6**—5 inch, **2** M.G. Torpedo Tubes: **8**—21 inch.
Machinery: Geared turbines. 2 shafts.
S.H.P.: 38,000 = 34 kts.
Boilers: 3 Kanpon. Oil fuel: About 400 tons. (*Osio* is suspected to have been lost.)

10 Sigure class.

KAWAKAZE. 1937.

SAMIDARE. 1937.

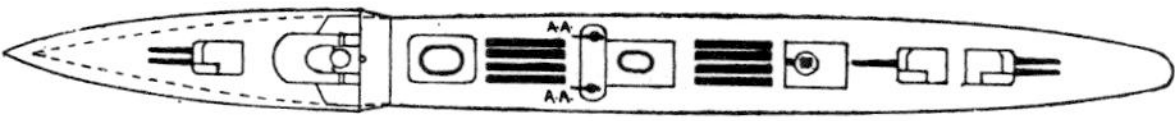

Sigure, Siratuyu, Murasame, Yudati, Harusame, Samidare, Yamakaze, Suzukaze, Kawakaze, Umikaze.

Displacement: 1,368 tons. Complement: 180.
Dimensions: 335½ × 31¾ × 9¼ feet (*mean*).
Guns: 5—5 inch, 2 M.G. Torpedo tubes: 8—21 inch (quadrupled).
Machinery: Geared turbines. S.H.P.: 37,000 = 34 kts.
Boilers: 3 Kanpon. Oil fuel: About 400 tons.
Notes.—It is reported that the guns of these and later destroyers have nearly 90° elevation, so they may be regarded as "dual purpose" guns.

6 Hatuharu class.

HATUSIMO. (Plan as *Sigure* class, but 6 T.T. in triple mounts). 1937.

Ariake, Nenohi, Hatuharu, Hatusimo, Wakaba, Yugure.

Displacement: 1,368 tons *standard*. Complement, 180.
Dimensions: 337¾ × 32½ × 8¾ feet (*mean* draught).
Guns: 5—5 inch, 2 M.G. Torpedo tubes: 6—21 inch.
Machinery: Geared turbines. S.H.P. 37,000 = 34 kts.
Boilers: 3 Kanpon. Oil fuel: About 400 tons.

Name	*Builder*	*Laid down*	*Launch*	*Completed*
Hatuharu	Saseho	May 14, 1931	Feb. 27, 1933	Sept. 30, 1933
Nenohi	Uraga	Dec. 15, 1931	Dec. 22, 1932	Sept. 30, 1933
Wakaba	Saseho	Dec. 12, 1931	Mar. 18, 1934	Oct. 31, 1934
Hatusimo	Uraga	Jan. 31, 1933	Nov. 4, 1933	Sept. 27, 1934
Ariake	Kawasaki	Jan. 14, 1933	Sept. 23, 1934	Mar. 25, 1935
Yugure	Maiduru	April 9, 1933	May 6, 1934	Mar. 30, 1935
Siratuyu	Saseho	Nov. 14, 1933	April 5, 1935	Aug. 20, 1936
Sigure	Uraga	Dec. 9, 1933	May 18, 1935	Sept. 7, 1936
Murasame	Hudinagata	Feb. 1, 1934	June 20, 1935	Jan. 7, 1937
Yudati	Saseho	Oct. 16, 1934	June 21, 1936	Jan. 7, 1937
Harusame	Maiduru	Feb. 3, 1935	Sept. 21, 1935	Aug. 26,1937
Samidare	Uraga	Dec. 19, 1934	July 6, 1935	Jan. 29, 1937
Yamakaze	Uraga	May 25, 1935	Feb. 21, 1936	July 30, 1937
Suzukaze	Uraga	July 9, 1935	Mar. 11, 1937	Aug. 31, 1937
Kawakaze	Hudinagata	April 25, 1935	Nov. 1, 1936	April 30, 1937
Umikaze	Maiduru	May 4, 1935	Nov. 27, 1936	May 31, 1937
Asasio	Saseho	Sept. 7, 1935	Dec. 16, 1936	Aug. 31, 1937
Arasio	Kawasaki	Oct. 1, 1935	May 26, 1937	Dec. 20, 1937
Osio	Maiduru	Aug. 5, 1936	April 19, 1937	Oct. 31, 1937
Mitisio	Hudinagata	Nov. 5, 1935	Mar. 15, 1937	Oct. 31, 1937
Asagumo	Kawasaki	Dec. 23, 1936	Nov. 5, 1937	Mar. 31, 1938
Yamagumo	Hudinagata	Nov. 4, 1936	July 24, 1937	Jan, 15, 1938
Minegumo	Hudinagata	Mar. 22, 1936	Nov. 4, 1937	April 30, 1938
Natugumo	Saseho	July 1, 1936	May 26, 1937	Feb. 10, 1938
Kasumi	Uraga	Dec. 1, 1936	Nov. 18, 1937	June 28, 1938
Arare	Maiduru	Mar. 5, 1937	Nov. 16, 1937	April 15, 1938

Notes.—As the result of the capsizing of the torpedo boat *Tomoduru*, the design of these destroyers was modified, the number of torpedo tubes being reduced and forward guns paired. A high percentage of electric welding was used.

23 Hubuki Class.

(A) "Amagiri" type. 11 Vessels.

URANAMI. 1933 *Photo*.

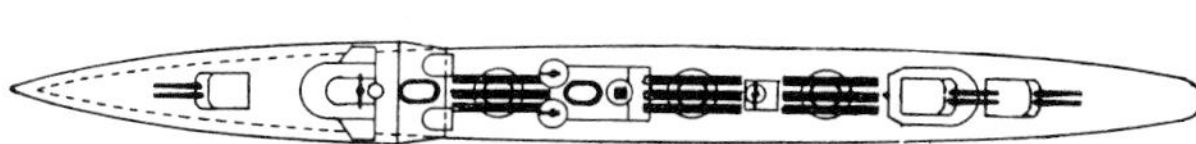

Notes:—*Hibiki* was the first rivetless ship in the Japanese Navy. *Miyuki* (built by Uraga Co.) lost by collision in 1934. *Uranami* has probably been lost in action.

ASAGIRI. 1933 *Photo*.

(AMAGIRI, AKEBONO, AYANAMI, OBORO, SAGIRI, SAZANAMI, SIKINAMI, USIO, YUGIRI similar, with collar ventilators around funnels, and bridge control tower level with funnel caps which in all this class (23) are anti-flare fittings.)

Hubuki, Sirayuki, Hatuyuki, Murakumo, Uranami, Sinonome, Usugumo, Sirakumo, Isonami, Ayanami, Asagiri, Amagiri, Sagiri, Sikinami, Yugiri, Usio, Oboro, Akebono, Sazanami, Akatuki, Hibiki, Ikaduti, Inaduma

Authorised under 1926 and subsequent sections of the Fleet Replenishment Law 1700 tons (2125 tons full load).
Dimensions: 371½ × 33¾ × 9¾ feet (*mean*). Armament: 6—5 inch, 50 cal., 4 AA. M.G. and 9—21 inch tubes.
Machinery: Parsons geared turbines. Boilers: 4 Kanpon. H.P. 40,000 = 34 kts. Oil: 420 tons. Complement, 197.

Destroyers

(B) "Hibiki" type. 4 Vessels.

IKADUTI. 1937 (*added* 1938).
(AKATUKI, HIBIKI, INADUMA, similar with small fore funnel, high bridge, and big flat-sided shields to Torpedo Tubes.)

Name	Builder	Laid dn.	Launch.	Compl.	Name	Builder	Laid dn.	Launch.	Compl.
Hubuki	Maiduru	19/6/26	15/11/27	10/8/28	*Yugiri*	Maiduru	1/4/29	12/5/30	3/12/30
Sirayuki	Yokohama	19/3/27	20/3/28	18/12/28	*Amagiri*	Isikawazima	28/11/28	27/2/30	10/11/30
Hatuyuki	Maiduru	12/4/27	29/9/27	30/3/28	*Sagiri*	Uraga	28/3/29	23/12/29	31/1/31
Murakumo	Hudinagata	25/4/27	27/9/27	10/5/28	*Oboro*	Saseho	29/11/29	8/11/30	31/10/31
Sinonome	Saseho	12/8/26	26/11/27	25/7/28	*Akebono*	Hudinagata	25/10/29	7/11/30	31/7/31
Usugumo	Isikawazima	21/10/26	26/12/27	26/7/28	*Sazanami*	Maiduru	21/2/30	6/6/31	19/5/32
Sirakumo	Hudinagata	27/10/26	27/12/27	28/7/28	*Usio*	Uraga	24/12/29	17/11/30	14/11/31
Isonami	Uraga	18/10/26	24/11/27	30/6/28	*Akatuki*	Saseho	17/2/30	7/5/32	30/11/32
Uranami	Saseho	28/4/27	29/11/28	30/6/29	*Hibiki*	Maiduru	21/2/30	16/6/32	31/3/33
Ayanami	Hudinagata	20/1/28	5/10/29	30/4/30	*Ikaduti*	Uraga	7/3/30	22/10/31	15/8/32
Sikinami	Maiduru	6/7/28	22/6/29	24/12/29	*Inaduma*	Hudinagata	7/3/30	25/2/32	15/11/32
Asagiri	Saseho	12/12/28	18/11/29	30/6/30					

(C) "Sinonome" type. 8 Vessels.

SIRAKUMO (note shields to Tubes). 1932 *Photo.*

HUBUKI. 1933 *Photo.*
(HATUYUKI, ISONAMI, MURAKUMO, SINONOME, SIRAKUMO, SIRAYUKI, USUGUMO, similar with smaller bridge and cowls abreast funnels.)

12 Mutuki Class.

UDUKI. *Photo* 1933.

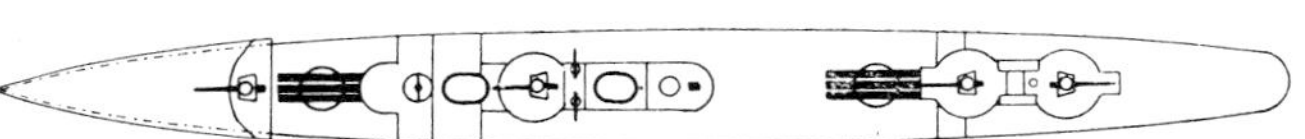

12 boats; ***Mutuki*** (ex-No. 19), (by Saseho), ***Kisaragi*** (ex-No. 21), (by Maiduru), ***Yayoi*** (ex-No. 23), (by Uraga Dock Co.), ***Uduki*** (ex-No. 25), (by Isikawazima Co.), ***Satuki*** (ex-No. 27), (by Hudinagata Co.), ***Minatuki*** (Uraga Dock Co.), ***Humituki*** (Hudinagata Co.), ***Nagatuki*** (Isikawazima Co.), ***Kikutuki*** (Maiduru), ***Mikaduki*** (Saseho), ***Motiduki*** (Uraga Dock Co.), ***Yuduki*** (Hudinagata Co.), (ex-Nos. 28–34). Enlarged editions of *Kamikaze*. Built under 1923, 1924 and 1925 sections of Navy Law. 1,315 tons. Dimensions: 320 (*p.p.*) × 30 × $9\frac{5}{6}$ feet (*max.* draught). Armament: **4**—4·7 inch, 50 cal., **2** AA. M.G. and **6**—21 inch tubes (in triple deck mountings). 3 S.L. Machinery: Parsons 2-shaft turbines, 4 Kanpon boilers. Designed H.P.: 38,500 = 34 kts. Oil: 350 tons. Endurance: 4,000 miles at 15 kts. Complement, 150.

Name.	Begun.	Launch.	Comp.	Name.	Begun.	Launch.	Comp.
Minatuki	24/3/25	25/5/26	22/3/27	*Mutuki*	21/5/24	23/7/25	25/3/26
Humituki	20/10/24	16/2/26	3/7/26	*Kisaragi*	3/6/24	5/6/25	21/12/25
Nagatuki	16/4/25	6/10/26	30/4/27	*Yayoi*	11/1/24	11/7/25	28/8/26
Kikutuki	15/6/25	15/5/26	20/11/26	*Uduki*	11/1/24	15/10/25	14/9/26
Mikaduki	21/8/25	12/7/26	7/5/27	*Satuki*	1/12/24	25/3/25	15/11/25
Motiduki	23/3/26	28/4/27	31/10/27				
Yuduki	27/11/26	4/3/27	25/7/27				
Kamikaze	15/12/21	25/9/22	28/12/22	*Hayate*	11/11/22	23/3/25	21/12/25
Asakaze	16/2/22	8/12/22	16/6/23	*Asanagi*	5/3/23	21/4/24	29/12/24
Harukaze	16/5/22	18/12/22	31/5/23	*Yunagi*	17/9/23	23/4/24	24/4/25
Matukaze	2/12/22	30/10/23	5/4/24				
Hatakaze	3/7/23	15/3/24	30/8/24	*Hokaze*	30/11/20	12/7/21	22/12/21
Oite	16/3/23	27/11/24	30/10/25	*Siokaze*	15/5/20	22/10/20	29/7/21
Akikaze	7/6/20	14/12/20	1/4/21	*Tatikaze*	18/8/20	31/3/21	5/12/21
Yukaze	14/12/20	28/ 5/21	24/8/21	*Nokaze*	16/4/21	1/10/21	31/3/22
Namikaze	7/11/21	24/6/22	11/11/22	*Sawakaze*	7/1/18	7/1/19	16/3/20
Numakaze	10/8/21	25/2/22	24/7/22	*Hakaze*	11/11/18	21/6/20	16/9/20
Minekaze	20/4/18	8/2/19	29/3/20	*Yakaze*	15/8/18	10/4/20	19/7/20
Okikaze	22/2/19	3/10/19	17/8/20				

9 Kamikaze Class.

ASAKAZE. 1934 *Photo.*

4·7" 2-T.T. 4·7" 2-T.T 2-T.T. 4·7" 4·7"

9 *boats:* ***Kamikaze*** (ex-No. 1) and ***Asakaze*** (ex-No. 3) (both by Mitubisi Z.K.), ***Harukaze*** (ex-No. 5), ***Matukaze*** (ex-No. 7), ***Hatakaze*** (ex-No. 9), (all three by Maiduru D.Y.), ***Oite*** (ex-No. 11), (by Uraga Dock Co.), ***Hayate*** (ex-No. 13), (by Isikawazima Co.), ***Asanagi*** (ex-No. 15), (by Hudinagata Co.), ***Yunagi*** (ex-No. 17), (by Saseho).

Built under 1922 and 1923 Sections of Navy Law. 1270 tons. Dimensions: 320 (*p.p.*) × 30 × $9\frac{7}{12}$ feet (*max. draught*). Armament: **4**—4·7 inch, 50 cal., **2** AA. M.G. and **6**—21 inch torpedo tubes. 2 S.L. Machinery: Parsons 4-shaft turbines. 4 Kanpon boilers. Designed H.P. 38,500 = 34 kts. Oil: 350 tons. Endurance: 4000 miles at 15 kts. Complement, 148.

13 Akikaze class.

13 *Akikaze* class: ***Akikaze*** and ***Yukaze*** (both by Mitubisi Z.K., Nagasaki); ***Minekaze, Okikaze, Hokaze, Siokaze, Tatikaze, Namikaze, Numakaze, Nokaze.*** All by Maiduru. ***Sawakaze, Hakaze*** and ***Yakaze*** all built by Mitubisi Co., at Nagasaki. Displacement: 1215 tons. Dimensions: 320 (*p.p.*), $336\frac{1}{2}$ (*o.a.*) × $29\frac{1}{4}$ × $9\frac{1}{2}$ feet (*mean* draught). Armament: **4**—4·7 inch, 45 cal., **2** M.G. (AA.), and **6**—21 inch torpedo tubes. **2**—30 inch searchlights in Maiduru built vessels: only **1** in others. Designed S.H.P.: 38,500 = 34 kts. Machinery: Parsons 4 shaft turbines and 4 Kanpon boilers. Oil: 315 tons. Complement: *Sawakaze*, 145, others 148. *Sawakaze* belongs to the 1917 Programme; *Hakaze* and *Yakaze* to the 1918 Programme. Remainder authorised under 1919 and 1920 sections of the 1918–24 Navy Law.

MINEKAZE
4·7" 2-TT 4·7" 4·7" 2-TT 2-TT RF 4·7"

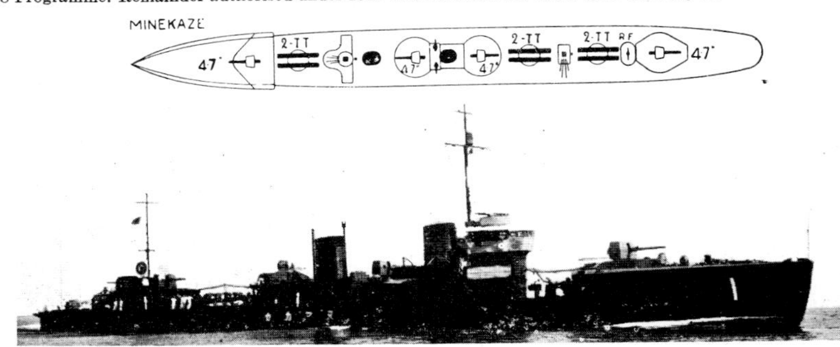

NUMAKAZE (NAMIKAZE and NOKAZE similar). 1937.

6 Wakatake Class.

Built under 1921 Naval Programme. Displacement: 820 tons. Complement: 110. Dimensions: 275 × 26½ × 8¼ feet. Guns: **3**—4·7 inch, 45 cal., **2** M.G. Tubes: **4**—21 inch (paired). Machinery: Parsons geared turbines. 2 shafts. S.H.P. 21,500 = 31·5 kts. 3 Kanpon boilers. Oil: 275 tons.

All originally bore numbers only. Names were conferred on August 1st, 1928. *Sawarabi* lost off Formosa, Dec. 5, 1932, and *Yugao* removed from list in 1940.

Name.	*Begun.*	*Launch.*	*Comp.*
Wakatake	13/12/21	24/7/22	30/ 9/22
Kuretake	15/3/22	21/10/22	21/12/22
Sanae	5/4/22	15/2/23	5/11/23
Asagao	14/3/22	4/11/22	10/5/23

Name.	*Begun.*	*Launch.*	*Comp.*
Huyo	16/2/22	23/9/22	16/3/23
Karukaya	16/5/22	19/3/23	20/8/23

KARUKAYA. 1937.

6 *Wakatake class:* **Wakatake** (ex-No. 2) and **Kuretake** (ex-No. 4), (both by Kawasaki Co., Kobe); **Sanae** (ex-No. 6 by Uraga Dock Co.); **Asagao** (ex-No. 10) (by Isikawazima Co.); **Huyo** (ex-No. 16) and **Karukaya** (ex-No. 18), (both by Hudinagata Co.).

KURETAKE. 1936 (*added* 1938). *B. R. Goodfellow, Esq.*

3 Kuri Class

TUGA (painted white). 1936, *Official, added* 1937.

3 *Kuri* class: **Kuri** (Kure), **Hasu** (Uraga Dock Co.), **Tuga** (Isikawazima Co.). Displacement: 770 tons. Dimensions: 275 (*pp.*) × 26 × 8 feet. Armament: **3**—4·7 inch, 45 cal., **2** M.G. (AA.). **4**—21 inch torpedo tubes in two twin-deck mountings. **1**—30 inch searchlight (*Hasu* has 2). Designed S.H.P.: 17,500 = 31·5 kts., *except Hasu*, 21,500 = 31·5 kts. Machinery: Parsons direct drive turbines. 3 Kanpon boilers. 2 shafts. Oil: 275 tons. Endurance: 3,000 miles at 15 kts. Complement: 110. Built under 1918–19 and 1920 Programmes.

Notes.—*Warabi*, of this class, lost by collision, Aug. 24, 1927. *Momi* scrapped, 1932, and 16 others during 1939–40.

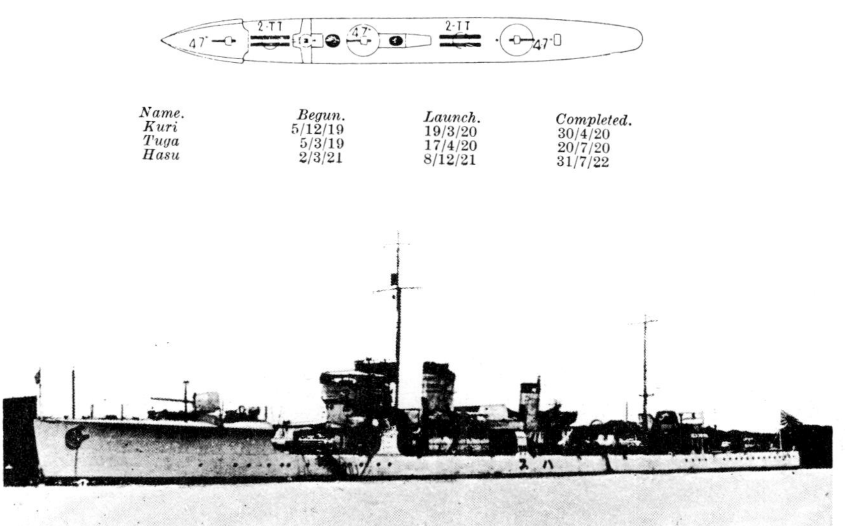

Name.	*Begun.*	*Launch.*	*Completed.*
Kuri	5/12/19	19/3/20	30/4/20
Tuga	5/3/19	17/4/20	20/7/20
Hasu	2/3/21	8/12/21	31/7/22

HASU (Observe forefunnel). 1936, *Official, added* 1937.

12 Torpedo Boats.

Note.—A number of motor torpedo boats have been built. There are also two old torpedo boats taken from China, **Yamasemi** (ex-*Chien Kang*), 390 tons, and **Kawasemi** (ex-*Hu Oah*), 96 tons, but neither possesses any fighting value.

SAGI 1938.

3-TT.

OTORI class (*Tidori* class similar, but only 2 tubes).

8 *Otori* class: **Otori, Hiyodori, Hayabusa, Kasasagi, Kizi, Kari, Sagi, Hato.** Displacement: 595 tons *standard*. Dimensions: 263 × 26 × 6¾ feet. Guns: **3**—4·7 inch, **1** M.G. Torpedo tubes; **3**—21 inch. 1 S.L. Machinery: Parsons geared turbines. 2 shafts. S.H.P.: 9,000 = 28 kts. Boilers: Kanpon. Oil fuel.

Notes.—Authorised by 2nd Fleet Replenishment Law, 1933. Design modified in consequence of capsizing of *Tomoduru*. *Hato* is believed to have been lost.

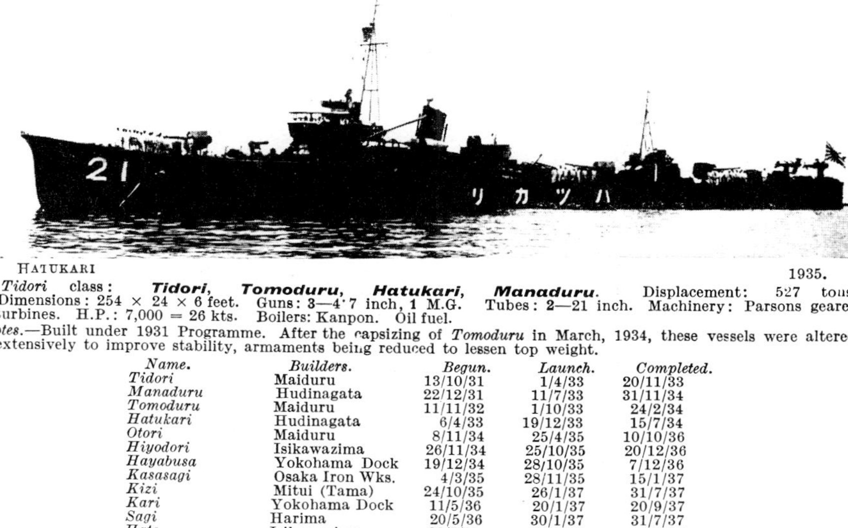

HATUKARI 1935.

4 *Tidori* class: **Tidori, Tomoduru, Hatukari, Manaduru.** Displacement: 527 tons. Dimensions: 254 × 24 × 6 feet. Guns: **3**—4·7 inch, **1** M.G. Tubes: **2**—21 inch. Machinery: Parsons geared turbines. H.P.: 7,000 = 26 kts. Boilers: Kanpon. Oil fuel.

Notes.—Built under 1931 Programme. After the capsizing of *Tomoduru* in March, 1934, these vessels were altered extensively to improve stability, armaments being reduced to lessen top weight.

Name.	*Builders.*	*Begun.*	*Launch.*	*Completed.*
Tidori	Maiduru	13/10/31	1/4/33	20/11/33
Manaduru	Hudinagata	22/12/31	11/7/33	31/11/34
Tomoduru	Maiduru	11/11/32	1/10/33	24/2/34
Hatukari	Hudinagata	6/4/33	19/12/33	15/7/34
Otori	Maiduru	8/11/34	25/4/35	10/10/36
Hiyodori	Isikawazima	26/11/34	25/10/35	20/12/36
Hayabusa	Yokohama Dock	19/12/34	28/10/35	7/12/36
Kasasagi	Osaka Iron Wks.	4/3/35	28/11/35	15/1/37
Kizi	Mitui (Tama)	24/10/35	26/1/37	31/7/37
Kari	Yokohama Dock	11/5/36	20/1/37	20/9/37
Sagi	Harima	20/5/36	30/1/37	31/7/37
Hato	Isikawazima	28/5/36	25/1/37	7/8/37

Submarines

(a) Oceangoing

10 "I 15" Class.

1942.

I 15—24. Displacement: 2,180 tons. Dimensions: 348 × 30 × 16 feet. Guns: **1**—5·5 inch, **2** M.G. AA. Tubes: **8**—21 inch. 2 sets Diesels. B.H.P.: 9,000 = 20 kts. *I* 16 was laid down at Kure on Sept. 15, 1937, launched July, 28, 1938, and completed March 30, 1940. *I* 18 was launched at Saseho on Nov. 12, 1938, and *I* 15 and *I* 17 at Yokosuka in March 1939 and on July 19, 1939 respectively. *I* 19—21 launched by Mitubisi, *I* 22 by Kawasaki, *I* 23 at Yokosuka and *I* 24 at Saseho, all during 1939. These are the biggest submarines ever built in Japan. Several, if not all, are believed to include a seaplane in their equipment.

10 "I 6" Type.

I 6. *Added* 1941.

1 *boat*: ***I 6*** (Kawasaki, March 31, 1934). Displacement: 1,900/2,500 tons. Dimensions: 309⅓ (*pp.*), 343½ (*o.a.*) × 29¾ × 15½ feet. Guns: **1**—5 inch, **2** M.G. A.A. Tubes: **6**—21 inch. 2 sets Diesels. H.P.: 6,000 = 17 kts. *surface. Submerged*, 9 kts. Completed 1935.

I 8. *Added* 1940.

9 *boats*: ***I 7*** (Kure, July 3, 1935), ***I 8*** (Kawasaki, July 20, 1936). Displacement: 1,950/2,600 tons. Dimensions; 343½ (*pp.*), 356¾ (*o.a.*) × 29¾ × 14½ feet (*mean* draught). Guns: **2**—5·5 inch, **2** M.G. AA. Tubes: **6**—21 inch, **1** S.L. 2 sets Kanpon Diesels. H.P.: 6,000 = 17 kts., *surface. Submerged*, 9 kts.

I 9—14. No official particulars of these vessels are available, but it is thought probable that they are generally similar to *I* 7 and *I* 8, described above. Built at Kure and Kawasaki yards.

Note.—*I* 7, *I* 8, were laid down Sept. 12 and Oct. 1, 1934 respectively. *I* 7 completed March 31, 1937, *I* 8 on Dec. 5, 1938.

4 Kawasaki Boats.

I 1. 1926 *Photo, by courtesy of Navy Department.*

4 *boats*: ***I 1*** (*ex*-No. 74, Oct., 1924), ***I 2*** (*ex*-No. 75, Feb. 23., 1925), ***I 3*** (*ex*-No. 76, June 8, 1925), ***I 4*** (May 22, 1928). All by Kawasaki, Kobe. Displacement: 1,955/2,480 tons. Dimensions: 320 × 30¼ × 15¾ feet. Guns: 2—5·5 inch, 2 M.G. A.A. Tubes: **6**—21 inch. Machinery: Diesels, H.P. 6,000 = 17 kts. *surface*. Motors H.P. 1,800 = 9 kts. Design is based in its main features on the ex-German Submarine *O* 1 (*ex-U* 125). First three authorised by 1922 Programme, and completed 1926. *I* 1 carried out a test cruise of 2,500 miles with complete success. *I* 4, laid down at Kawasaki in April, 1926 built under direct superintendence of Naval Construction Department and completed in Dec., 1929.

(b) Seagoing.

9 Kaigun Type.

I 25—33. Believed to be slightly enlarged versions of *I* 71 type, below. Displacement: *circa* 1,500 tons. No other particulars reported. *I* 29 was launched at Saseho on June 6, 1940. *I* 25 (Nov. 1939) and 26 built at Mitubisi; *I* 27 and 28 at Kure.

Seagoing—continued.

8 Kaigun Type.

I 71. 1936, *Official.*

5 *boats*: ***I 71*** (Kawasaki, Aug. 25, 1934), ***I 72*** (Mitubisi, April 6, 1935), ***I 73*** (Kawasaki, June 20, 1935), ***I 74*** (Saseho, March 28, 1937), ***I 75*** (Mitubisi, Sept. 16, 1936). Displacement, dimensions, etc., as preceding group below, but armed with **1**—4·7 inch gun, **6**—21 inch tubes.

3 boats: ***I 68*** (Kure, June 26, 1933), ***I 69*** (Mitubisi, Kobe, Feb. 15, 1934), ***I 70*** (Saseho, June 14, 1934). *Surface* displacement: 1,400 tons. Dimensions: 331⅓ × 27 × 13 feet. Guns: **1**—4 inch, **1** M.G. Tubes: **6**—21 inch. 2 sets Diesels. H.P.: 6,000 = 20 kts., *surface. Submerged* 9 kts.

I 71 completed Dec. 24, 1935. *I* 72, *I* 73 both completed Jan. 7 1937. *I* 74 in 1938, *I* 69, *I* 70 in 1935, and *I* 68 in 1934. All reported to have a radius of action of 16,000 miles.

2 Kaigun Type.

I 66. 1941 *Official.*

I 65 1941 *Official.*

2 *boats*: I ***65*** (Kure, June 2, 1931), I***66*** (Saseho, June 2, 1931). Displacement: 1,638/2,100 tons. Dimensions: 321½ × 27 × 16 feet, Guns: **1**—**4** inch, **1** M.G. Tubes: **6**—21 inch. 2 sets Diesels. H.P. 6,000 = 19 kts. *surface*. Electric motors, H.P. 1800 = 9 kts.

Note.—I ***67*** foundered during exercises on August 29, 1940.

11 or 12 *(See Notes)* Kaigun Type.

I 55. 1928 *Photo.*

I 58 (?). 1941 *Official.*

12 boats: I ***53*** (ex-*No.* 64, Kure, Aug. 5, 1925), I ***54*** (ex-*No.* 77, Saseho, March 15, 1926), I ***55*** (ex-*No.* 78, Kure, Sept. 2, 1925), I ***56***(Kure, March 23, 1928), I ***57*** (Kure, Oct. 1, 1928), I***58*** (Yokosuka, Oct. 3, 1925), I ***59*** (Yokosuka, March 25, 1929). I ***60*** (Saseho, April 24, 1929), I ***61*** (Mitubisi, Nov. 12, 1927), I ***62*** (Mitubisi. Nov. 29, 1928), I ***63*** (Saseho, Sept. 28, 1927), I ***64*** (Kure, Oct. 5, 1929). Displacement: 1,635/2,100. Dimensions: 331 × 26 × 16 feet (except *I* 62, 63, 64, which are 321½ × 25½.) Armament: **1**—4·7 inch, **1** M.G., **8**—21 inch tubes (except *I* 62, 63, 64, which have only **6** tubes). Machinery: 2 sets Diesels. B.H.P.: 6,000 = 19 kts. Electric motors, H.P.: 1,800 = 9 kts. Believed begun under 1923–25 Programmes. Cruising radius is undoubtedly very large, 16,000 miles being reported. They are supposed to be capable of crossing the Pacific and returning without refuelling. This design is the fruit of experience gained with *I* 51 and *I* 52.

Note.—*I* 63 sunk by collision in Bungo Channel, Feb. 2, 1939, but salved a year later, and has presumably been refitted. *I* 61 sunk by collision during exercises in Oct., 1941; her salvage is reported to have been effected in Feb. 1942.

Seagoing—(continued)

1 Kaigun Experimental Type.

1926 *Photo.*

I 52 (ex-*No.* 51, Kure, June 12, 1922). Built under 1920 Programme. Displacement: 1,390/2,000 tons. Dimensions: 331 × 25 × 17 feet. Armament: 1—4·7 inch, 1 M.G., 8—21 inch tubes. H.P.: 6,000/1,800. Speed: 19/9 kts. Completed in May, 1925.

(c) *Coastal* from 500 to 1000 tons.

2 Kaigun type.

Ro. 33. 1937.

2 *boats*: ***Ro. 33*** (Kure, Oct. 10, 1934), ***Ro. 34*** (Mitubisi, Dec. 12, 1935). Displacement, 700/—tons. Dimensions 239½ × 22 × 12 feet. Armament: 1—3 inch AA., 4—21 inch tubes (believed all in bow). H.P.: 2,600/— = 16/9 kts. Complement: 42.

9 Mitubisi Type.

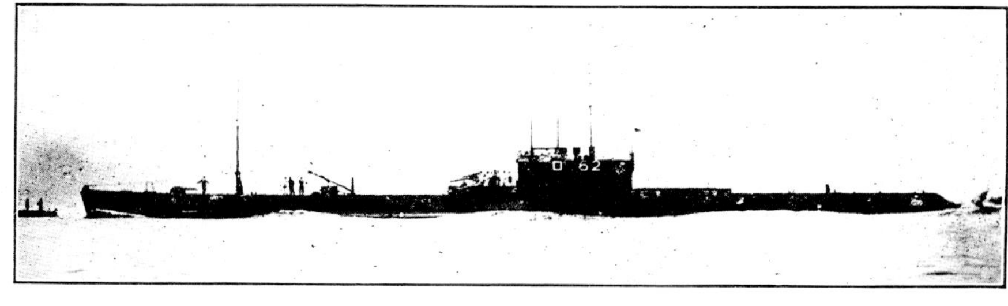

Ro. 64. *Photo added* 1926.

9 boats: ***Ro. 60*** (ex-*No.* 59), ***Ro. 61*** (ex-*No.* 72), ***Ro. 62*** (ex-*No.* 73), ***Ro. 63*** (ex-*No.* 84), ***Ro. 64—68***. All built by Mitubisi, Kobe, 1923–25. Displacement: 988/1,300 tons. Dimensions: 250 (*p.p.*) × 24 × 13 feet. Guns: 1—3 inch, 1 M.G. Torpedo tubes: 6—21 inch. Vickers Diesels H.P. 2,400 = 16 kts. Motors: 1,800 H.P. = 10 kts. Fuel: 75 tons. Complement: 48.

Notes.—Built under 1920–22 Programmes. Apparently an enlargement of the *Ro.* 51—59 type. Completed—*Ro.* 60, 1923; *Ro.* 61—63, 1924 *Ro.* 64 and 68, 1925; *Ro.* 65 and 67, 1926 *Ro.* 66, 1927.

3 Kawasaki Boats

1926 *Photo, by courtesy of Navy Department.*

3 boats: ***Ro. 30—32*** (ex-*Nos.* 69—71). (Kawasaki Co., Kobe, 1923–26). Dimensions: 243½ (*p.p.*) × 20 × 12 feet. Displacement: 655/1,000 tons. Guns: 1—4·7 inch, 1—3 pdr. Torpedo tubes: originally carried 5—21 inch, now 4—21 inch. Fiat Diesels. H.P.: 1,200/1,200 = 13/10 kts.

Notes.—Built under 1919 Programme, and completed 1923–24 *Ro.* 31. (ex-*No* 70) sank during trials at Kobe, August, 1923, but was salved and rebuilt. She was finally completed at Kure, 1927, owing to financial crisis at Kawasaki Yard. *Ro.* 30 and *Ro.* 32 both completed during 1924.

4 Kawasaki Boats

I 122. 1930 *Photo.*

I 121. 1927 *Photo, by courtesy of Navy Dept.*

4 boats: ***I 121*** (ex-*I* 21, ex-48) (March 30, 1926), ***I 122*** (ex-*I* 22, ex-49) (Nov. 8, 1926), ***I 123*** (*ex-I* 23, ex-50) (March 19, 1927), ***I 124*** (ex-*I* 24) (Dec. 12, 1927), all by Kawasaki Co., Kobe, the first probably laid down under 1919 Programme. Displacement: 1,142/1,470 tons. Dimensions: 279½ × 24¾ × 14¼ feet. Armament: 1—5·5 inch, 4—21 inch tubes, 42 mines. Machinery: Diesels, H.P.: 2,400 = 14 kts. Electric motors, H.P.: 1,200 = 9·5 kts. *I* 122, *I* 123 completed at Kure, owing to temporary suspension of business by Kawasaki Co. Construction of *I* 124 completed at Kawasaki by Nava Construction Dept. Design believed to be based on German *U B* types.

Special Note.

Old submarines *Ro.* 57–59, though withdrawn from effective list, are believed still to exist. They are probably being used for training purposes.

"Midget" submarines appear to be tenders, carried by special depot ships, so are not listed here. It is reported that some of them are of 87 tons submerged displacement, others being rather smaller.

Seagoing Training Ships.

(Katori Class—3 ships)

KASIMA (October 2, 1939), **KATORI** (June 17, 1939), **KASII** (October 15, 1940).

Displacement: 5,800 tons. Length: 425 feet. Beam: 52 feet. Draught: 18 feet (*mean*).

Guns:
4—5·5 inch.
2—5 inch AA.
— M.G.
Torpedo Tubes:
8—21 inch.

Armour:
2″ Deck.
(*unofficial*).

Machinery: Geared turbines. 2 shafts. S.H.P.: 8,000 = 18 kts. Boilers: 3 Kanpon.

Katori. 1940, *Official.*

Notes.—All three built at Mitubisi yard in Yokohama and rated officially as "Training Cruisers". Are probably fitted for minelaying. *Katori* laid down Aug. 24, 1938, and completed April 20, 1940. *Kasima* has also been reported as launched Sept. 25, 1940, but this is more likely to be date of completion. *Kasii* was launched in a very advanced stage of construction, and was completed early in 1941. Speed is too low for these ships to be reckoned as effective cruisers. Cruiser *Oi* and coast defence ships *Kasuga*, *Iwate* and *Yakumo* have been used as seagoing training ships.

Minelayers, First Class

1937.

OKINOSIMA (Harima S.B. Co., Nov. 15, 1935.) *Standard* displacement : 4,400 tons. Dimensions : $386\frac{1}{2} \times 51\frac{1}{3} \times 16\frac{1}{2}$ feet (*mean*). Guns : 4—5·5 inch, 4 M.G. Geared turbines. S.H.P : 9,000 = 20 kts. 4 Kanpon boilers.

Note.—Laid down Sept. 27, 1934, and completed Sept. 30, 1936. Name is that of an island off which the Battle of the Japan Sea was fought in May, 1905.

YAEYAMA (Now painted white). 1933 *Photo, Official.*

YAEYAMA (Kure, October 15, 1931). *Standard* displacement : 1,135 tons. Complement : 150. Dimensions : $280\frac{1}{2} \times 34\frac{1}{2} \times 8$ feet. Guns : 2—4·7 inch AA., 2 M.G. Machinery : 2 sets triple expansion. H.P. : 4,800 = 20 kts. 2 Kanpon boilers. Fuel: Mixed firing.

Note.—Is also fitted for laying anti-submarine nets. Laid down Aug. 2, 1930 and completed Aug. 31, 1932.

SIRATAKA. 1939

SIRATAKA (Isikawazima Co., Tokyo, 25th January, 1929). Displacement : 1,345 tons *standard*. Dimensions : 260×38×9 feet. Guns : 3—4·7 inch AA., 1 M.G. Machinery : 2 sets triple expansion. H.P. 2,200=16 kts. Boilers : 2 Kanpon.

Notes.—Also fitted for anti-submarine netlaying. Was laid down on Nov. 24, 1927, and completed April 9, 1929. *Sirataka* means White Hawk.

1920 *Photo, Navy Dept., Tokyo.*

KATURIKI (Kure, Oct., 1916). 1,540 tons. Dimensions : 240'× 39 × 14 feet. Guns : 3—3 inch. Machinery : 2 sets triple expansion. H.P. : 1,800 = 13 kts. Built under 1915–16 Programme. Fitted with 4 gallows for sweeps. Reported to carry 150 mines.

1930 *Photo.*

TOKIWA (Armstrong, July 6, 1898) 9,240 tons. Dimensions : 408 (*pp.*), 442 (*o.a.*) × $67\frac{1}{4} \times 24\frac{1}{4}$ feet. Guns : 2—8 inch, 40 cal., 8—6 inch, 40 cal., 2—3 inch, 1—3 inch AA. Armour : 7" belt, tapering to $3\frac{1}{2}$", 2" deck, 6" turret, 6" casemates. Machinery : 2 sets triple expansion. Boilers : 16 Miyabara. H.P. : 18,000 = $21\frac{1}{4}$ kts. Coal : 1,400 tons. Originally a cruiser.

Note.—*Tokiwa* means Evergreen. After turret removed 1929, when she was adapted for minelaying.

ITUKUSIMA (May 22nd, 1929).

Standard displacement, 1,970 tons.

Dimensions, 328×42×10 feet. Complement, 235.

Guns :
3—5·5 inch, 50 cal.
2—3 inch AA.

Armour: Nil.

Mines :
250 large or 500 small.

Depth charge throwers :
1—each side amidships.

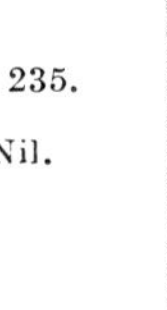

1930 *Photo.*

General Notes.—Laid down by Uraga Co., in Feb. 1928, and completed Dec. 1929. Is the first experimental Diesel-driven ship in the Japanese Navy. Design suggested by H.M.S. *Adventure* of which she is a small edition. First searchlight shown in plan has been replaced by a 6 ft. anti-aircraft range-finder. Officers' cabins in superstructure deck under fore gun and bridge. Upper deck is for mine stowage, 4 lines of minelaying rails extending from forecastle to stern. Two outer lines start abaft of bridge and extend to the wing-ports at stern. There is a single line on the forecastle from starboard bow to gun for transport back to store of picked-up practice mines. Two sizes of mines can be carried and number stowed varies as the type—roughly twice as many of the smaller size.

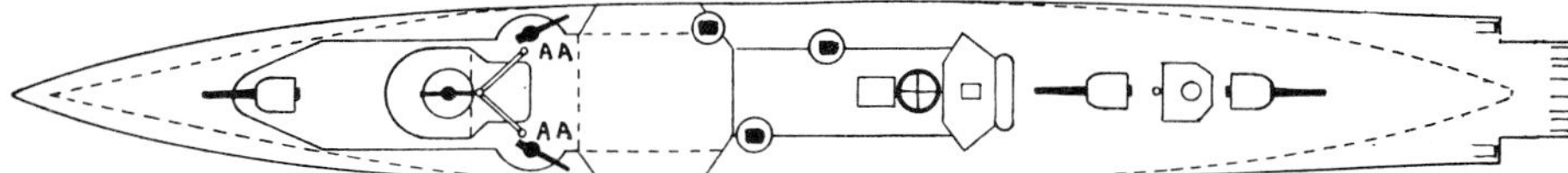

Machinery : 3 sets Diesel engines. B.H.P. 3,000 = 16 kts. 3 shafts. Radius of action is 5,000 miles at 16 kts.

1930 *Photo.*

1930 *Photo.*

Minelayers

SOKUTEN (Mitubisi, Yokohama, April 27, 1938), **SIRAKAMI** (Isikawazima, June 25, 1938), **NARIU** (Mitubisi, Yokohama, Aug. 28, 1939), **KYOSAI** (Isikawazima, June 29, 1939), **KUNAZIRI** (Turumi Steel Works, May 6, 1940), **HASIDATE** (Hudinagata, Dec. 23, 1939), **SUMISU** (Tama Works, Dec. 30, 1939), **HATIJO** (Saseho, April 10, 1940), **ISIGAKI** (Tama Works, Sept. 1940), **TANZURU** (Kawasaki, Kobe, August 1940), and about 12 others. Displacement: 720 tons. Dimensions: $239 \times 25\frac{3}{4} \times 8\frac{1}{3}$ feet. Guns: **2** or **3**—4·7 inch. Machinery: 2 sets Diesels. H.P.: 3,600 = 20 kts. **1** S.L.

NASAMI 1936, *official*

NATUSIMA (*Sarusima* has shorter funnel, with plain top). 1934, *Official.*

NATUSIMA (Isikawazima S.B. Co., March 24, 1934).
SARUSIMA (Yokohama Dock Co., Dec. 16, 1933).
NASAMI (Harima Co., March 26, 1934).

Displacement: 443 tons. Dimensions: $225 \times 24\frac{1}{2} \times 5\frac{1}{2}$ feet. Guns: **2**—3 inch AA., **1** M.G. Machinery: 2 sets Diesels. H.P.: 2,300 = 19 kts, except *Sarusima*, H.P.: 2,100 = 19 kts.

TUBAME. 1931 *Photo.*
Kamome similar but 2 white bands on funnel).

TUBAME (now has 1 white band on funnel as in upper photo). 1930 *Photo, Navy Dept., Tokyo.*

KAMOME (Osaka Ironworks, 27th April, 1929), **TUBAME** (Yokohama Dock Co., 24th April, 1929). Displacement: 450 tons *standard.* Dimensions: $206\frac{2}{3} \times 23\frac{1}{2} \times 6\frac{1}{3}$ feet. Guns: **1**—3 inch A.A., **1** M.G. Machinery: Triple expansion. H.P. 2,500 = 19 kts. Also equipped for netlaying.

Notes.—Both laid down in 1928. Meanings of names are as follows: *Kamome*—Seagull. *Tubame*—Swallow.

Coast Defence Ships

IDUMO. 1938, *Official, courtesy of Navy Dept., Tokyo.*

ADUMA (St. Nazaire, June 24, 1899). Displacement: 8,640 tons. Complement: 644. Length: (*w.l.*) 430; (*o.a.*) $452\frac{1}{2}$ feet. Beam: $59\frac{1}{2}$ feet. *Max.* draught: 25 feet. Guns (Armstrong): **4**—8 inch, 40 cal., **8**—6 inch, 40 cal., **4**—3 inch, **1**—3 inch AA. Torpedo tubes: **4** *submerged.* Armour (Krupp mostly): 7″ Belt (amidships), $3\frac{1}{2}$″ Belt (ends), $2\frac{1}{2}$″ Deck (on slopes), 6″ Turrets and bases (H.N.), 6″ Casemates (H.N.), 5″ Side above belt. (Total weight, 2,000 tons.) Machinery: 2 sets vertical triple expansion. 2 screws. Boilers: 24 Belleville. Designed H.P.: 17,000 = 21 kts. **Coal: *normal*, 600 tons; *maximum*, 1,200 tons. Good for about 16 kts. now.**

1931 *Photo, Official.*

IDUMO (Sept. 19, 1899), and **IWATE** (March 29, 1900). Built by Armstrong. Displacement: 9,180 tons. Complement: 658. Length (*p.p.*), 400 feet; (*o.a.*) 434 feet. Beam: $68\frac{1}{2}$ feet. *Max.* draught: $24\frac{1}{4}$ feet. Guns (Armstrong): **4**—8 inch, 40 cal., **8**—6 inch, 40 cal., **1**—3 inch AA., **4**—3 inch, **3** M.G., 4 S.L. Torpedo tubes: **4** *submerged.* Armour (Krupp): 7″ Belt (amidship), $3\frac{1}{2}$″ Belt (ends), $2\frac{1}{2}$″ Deck (slopes), 5″ Lower deck (redoubt), 6″ Turrets and bases, 6″ Casemates, 14″ Conning tower. (Total 2,100 tons.) Machinery by Humphrys & Tennant: 2 sets 4-cylinder triple expansion. 2 screws. Boilers: Belleville in *Idumo*; 6 Yarrow in *Iwate*. *Idumo*, I.H.P.: 14,700 = 20·75 kts. *Iwate*, I.H.P.: 7,000 = 16 kts. Coal: *normal* 550 tons; *maximum*, 1,400 tons. Begun at Elswick 1898–99, and completed 1900–01. *Iwate* used as seagoing Training Ship. Full armament (not mounted in peace time) includes **14**—6 inch guns.

Coast Defence Ships

YAKUMO. (Deckhouse since added abaft foremast). 1929 *Photo.*

YAKUMO (Vulcan Co., July 8, 1899). Displacement : 9,010 tons. Complement : 698. Length : (*pp.*) 409 feet ; *over all*, 434 feet. Beam : 64¼ feet. *Mean* draught : 23¾ feet. Guns : **4**—8 inch, 40 cal., **8**—6 inch, 40 cal., **4**—3 inch, 4 S.L. Torpedo tubes (18 inch) : 2 *submerged*. Armour (Krupp) : 7″ Belt (amidships), 3½″ Belt (ends), 2½″ Deck (slopes), 6″ Turrets (N.C.), 6″ Turret bases (N.C.), 5″ Lower deck side, 6″ Casemates (8), 10″ Conning tower. (Total weight, 2,040 tons.). Machinery : 2 sets vertical triple expansion. 2 screws. Boilers : 6 Yarrow. I.H.P. : 7,000 = 16 kts. Coal : *normal*, 550 tons ; *max.*, 1,200 tons. Employed as Midshipmen's Training Ship, and speed reduced. Full armament (not mounted at present) includes **12**—6 inch.

KASUGA *Photo* 1931.

KASUGA (October 22, 1902). Displacement : 7,080 tons. Complement : 595. Length (*waterline*) : 357 feet. Beam : 61 feet 11 ins. *Maximum* draught : 25¼ feet. Guns (Armstrong) : **1**—10 inch, **2**—8 inch, 45 cal., **4**—6 inch, 45 cal., **4**—3 inch, **1**—3 inch AA., **2** M.G. Torpedo tubes (18 inches) : 4 *above water* (in casemates). Armour (Terni) : 6″ Belt (amidships), 4½″ (ends), 1½″ Deck (on slopes), 5½″ Turrets and bases, 6″ Lower deck side and battery, 4½″ Lower deck bulkheads and Battery bulkheads, 4¾ Conning tower. 4 Searchlights. Machinery : 2 sets 3-cylinder vertical triple expansion. 2 screws. Boilers : 12 Kanpon. Designed H.P. : 13,500 = 20 kts. (Now much less) Coal : *normal*, 650 tons ; *maximum*, 1,200 tons.

Note.—*Kasuga* (ex-*Rivadavia*, ex-*Mitra* built by Ansaldo purchased from Argentina, 1904. Full armament includes 14—6 inch guns.

Seaplane Carriers

MIDUHO. 1939.

MIDUHO. 1939.

TITOSE (Nov. 29, 1936), **TIYODA** (Nov. 19, 1937), **MIDUHO** (May 16, 1938). **NISSIN** (Nov. 30, 1939). *Standard* displacement : 9,000 tons. Dimensions : 577½ × 61⅔ × 19 feet (*mean*). Guns : **6**—5 inch AA. (paired), **20** M.G. AA. **20** aircraft, **4** catapults. Machinery : Geared turbines. H.P. : 15,000 = 20 kts. (*Miduho*, 9,000 = 17 kts.). Built under Second Fleet Replenishment Law, *Titose* having been laid down on Nov. 26, 1934, *Tiyoda* on December 14, 1936, *Miduho* on May 1, 1937, and *Nissin* in Sept., 1937, three of them at Kure and the *Miduho* at Kawasaki, Kobe.

1941.

NOTORO (Kawasaki Co., Kobe, May 3, 1920). *Standard* displacement : 14,050 tons (8,000 tons *gross*). Complement : 155. Dimensions : 455 (*pp.*), 470¾ (*o.a.*) × 58 × 26½ feet. Guns : **2**—4·7 inch, **2**—3 inch AA. Reciprocating engines. H.P. : 5,850 = 12 kts. Oil Fuel : 1,000 tons. Converted from a tanker of the *Erimo* class (*vide* a later page). Laid down Nov. 24, 1919 and completed Aug. 10, 1920. Reported to carry from 8 to 16 aircraft, latter figure presumably representing maximum stowage.

KAMIKAWA (Maru). 1939.

KAGU (MARU) (Harima, 1936). 6,807 tons *gross*. Dimensions : 453¾ × 61 × 27½ feet. **KAMIKAWA (MARU)** (Kawasaki, 1937). 6,853 tons *gross*. Dimensions : 479⅓ × 62¼ × 27½ feet. **KINUGASA (MARU)** (Kawasaki, 1936). 6,808 tons *gross*. Dimensions : 453½ × 60¾ × 27¼ feet. **KINAGAWA (MARU)**. (Mitubisi, Nagasaki, 1938). 6,937 tons *gross*. Dimensions : 436⅓ × 58½ × — feet. In all : Guns : **2**—3 inch. Aircraft : **12.** Machinery : Diesel. B.H.P. : 14,500 = 17 kts.

Note.—All 4 of the foregoing are ex-mercantile vessels, converted into temporary Seaplane Carriers. In addition, certain large liners are believed to have been fitted out as Seaplane Carriers. Some of them have been lost. Those still in service are reported to include *Fujikawa Maru*, *Kasuga Maru*, *Kiyokawa Maru*, *Kenyo Maru*, *Awata Maru*, *Kamakura Maru*, *Tatuta Maru*. It is possible that some of these have merely been used to transport aircraft from one port to another. *Maru* means merchant ship.

KAMOI. (Now has crane aft.) 1924 *Photo, Official.*

KAMOI (New York S.B. Co., June 8, 1922). *Standard* displacement : 17,000 tons (10,222 tons *gross*). Dimensions : 496 (*w.l.*), 478½ (*p.p.*) × 67 × 27⅔ feet. Guns : 2—5·5 inch, 2—3 inch AA. Machinery : G.E. (Curtis) turbines and electric drive. Boilers : 4 Yarrow. S.H.P. : 8,000 = 15 kts. Fuel : 2,500 tons coal. Laid down Sept. 14, 1921 and completed Sept. 12, 1922. Converted from a tanker 1932–33. The first Japanese warship to have electric drive installed. Reported to carry from 10 to 16 aircraft, former being normal complement.

Submarine Chasers.

Note.—More of these have been built.

No. 53. 1938.

No. 51 (June 9, 1937), **No. 52** (Aug. 25, 1937), both by Turumi Steel Works; **No. 53** (July 15, 1937), by Osaka Iron Works.

Displacement: 170 tons. Dimensions: $146 \times 15\frac{1}{3} \times 5\frac{1}{2}$ feet. Armed with D.C. and **1** AA. gun. Machinery: Diesel (except No. 53, reported to be steam turbine). H.P.: 3,000 = 23 kts.

No. 2. 1935.

This represents No. 3, no longer in service. Nos. 4–12 are understood to be of similar appearance.

Nos. 4 (Osaka Iron Works, Sept. 13, 1938), **5** (Mitubisi, Yokohama, July 28, 1938), **6** (Turumi Steel Works, Feb. 6, 1939), **7** (Turumi, 1939), **8** (Tama Works, Aug. 9, 1938), **9** (Mitubisi, Yokohama, 1938), **10** (Osaka Iron Works, Jan. 31, 1939), **11** (Turumi Steel Works, 1939), **12** (Tama Works, Feb. 8, 1939. Displacement: 290 tons. Dimensions: $180 \times 18 \times 6\frac{1}{2}$ feet. Armed with **4** M.G. and D.C. H.P.: 2,600 = 20 kts.

No. 1 (Uraga Dock Co., Dec., 1933), **No. 2** (Isikawazima, Dec., 1933). Displacement: 300 tons. Dimensions: $210\frac{1}{2} \times 19\frac{3}{4} \times 5$ feet. Armed with Depth Charges and **4** M.G. Machinery: Diesel. H.P.: 3,400 = 24 kts.

Minesweepers

No. 7 (Tama Works, June 16, 1938)
No. 8 (Uraga Dock Co., May 28, 1938).
No. 11 (Uraga Dock Co., Dec. 28, 1938).
No. 9 (Maiduru, Sept. 10, 1938)
No. 10 (Isikawazima Co., Sept. 22, 1938).
No. 12 (Isikawazima Co., Feb. 18, 1939).

Displacement: 630 tons. Complement: 88. Dimensions: $226 \times 25\frac{3}{4} \times 7\frac{3}{8}$ feet. Guns 3—4·7 inch, 2 M.G. Machinery: Triple expansion. 2 shafts. I.H.P.: 3,850 = 20 kts. Boilers 3 Kanpon, coal-fired.

No. 13. 1935.

No. 13 (Hudinagata S.B. Co., March 30, 1933).
No. 14 (Osaka Iron Works, May 20, 1933).
No. 15 (Hudinagata S.B. Co., Feb. 14, 1934).
No. 16 (Tama Works, March 30, 1934).
No. 17 (Osaka Iron Works, Aug. 3, 1935).
No. 18 (Tama Works, Sept. 19, 1935).

Nos. 13—16: Displacement: 492 tons. Dimensions: $232\frac{1}{4} \times 25 \times 6$ feet.
Nos. 17, 18: Displacement: 511 tons. Dimensions: $218 \times 25\frac{1}{3} \times 6\frac{1}{2}$ feet.
In all: Guns: 2—4·7 inch, 2 M.G. Machinery: Triple expansion. I.H.P.: 3,200 = 20 kts., except *Nos.* 17, 18, only 19 kts. Coal-fired.

Notes.—All built under First Fleet Replenishment Law of 1931.

MINESWEEPER No. 6 (Tripod foremast in this one and No. 5). 1930, *Photo.*

MINESWEEPER No. 1. 1938, *Official, courtesy of Navy Dept., Tokyo.*

Nos. 1 (Harima S.B. Co., March 6, 1923), **2** (Tama Works, March 17, 1923), **3** (Osaka Iron Works, March 29, 1923), **4** (Saseho, April 24, 1924), **5** (Tama Works, Oct. 30, 1928), **6** (Osaka I.W., Oct. 29, 1928). All provided by 1920–28 Fleet Replenishment Law. 615 tons. $235 \times 26\frac{1}{4} \times 7\frac{1}{2}$ feet. Guns: 2—4·7 inch, 1—3 inch AA., 2 D.C. throwers. Complement: 87. Triple expansion engines. I.H.P.: 4,000 = 20 kts. 3 Kanpon boilers, coal-fired.

Repair Ship.

AKASI (Saseho, June 29, 1938). Displacement: 9,000 tons. Dimensions: $500 \times 67\frac{1}{4} \times 18\frac{2}{3}$ feet. Guns: 4—5 inch AA., 12 M.G. Machinery: 2 sets geared turbines. S.H.P.: 10,000 = 19 kts. First big repair ship built for the Imperial Japanese Navy, and the largest vessel ever launched at Saseho up to that date. Laid down Jan. 18, 1937, under Second Fleet Replenishment Law.

Submarine Depot Ships

KASINO (Mitubisi, Jan. 26, 1940), **SOYA** (1940), **TUGARU** (Yokosuka, June 5, 1940). All these 3 are believed to be Submarine Depot Ships or Fleet Auxiliaries of some kind. (*Tugaru* has been reported as a large minelayer.)

TURUGIZAKI (Yokosuka June 1, 1935), **TAKASAKI** (Yokosuka, June 19th, 1936). Standard displacement: 12,000 tons. Dimensions: 660¼ × 59½ × 21 feet. Guns: 4—5 inch AA., 12 M.G. H.P.: 13,000 = 19 kts. Both built under Second Replenishment Law of 1933, and completed Jan. 15, 1939, and 1940, respectively. (*For appearance, vide silhouette.*)

Note.—May both be parent ships for midget submarines.

1936.

TYOGEI (2 steam pipes to first funnel). 1934 *Photo.*

TAIGEI (Yokosuka, Nov. 16, 1933). Displacement: 10,000 tons. Dimensions: 647 (*w.l.*), 689 (*o.a.*) × 59 × 17 feet. Guns: 4—5 inch AA., 12 M.G. 4 sets Diesels. H.P.: 13,000 = 20 kts. Complement: 413. 3 Aircraft included in equipment, with 2 catapults.

Notes.—Laid down April 12, 1933; completed March 31, 1934. *Taigei* means Great Whale. Reported to roll badly owing to light draught. Possibly employed as parent ship for midget submarines.

ZINGEI. (Now has white band round first funnel.) *Photo added* 1926.

ZINGEI (May 4, 1923), **TYOGEI** (March 24, 1924). Both by Mitubisi Co., Nagasaki. 5,160 tons. Dimensions: 380 × 53 × 19½ feet (*mean*), 22⅔ (*max.*). Geared turbines. 2 shafts. *Zingei*, 6 Kanpon boilers; *Tyogei*, 5. H.P.: 7,000 = 16 kts. Guns: 4—5·5 inch, 2—3 inch AA., 2 M.G. 2 searchlights. Each equipped to carry 1 seaplane. Both laid down in 1922, completed in August 1923 and August 1924, respectively.

Zingei—Swift swimming Whale. *Tyogei*—Long Whale.

Gunboats.

UJI (Hudinagata, Sept. 26, 1940). Particulars almost entirely lacking, though believed to be a good-sized vessel of sloop type with a heavy bridge and a single funnel. Guns: 3—4·7 inch, two of them super-imposed forward, and the third mounted aft. Has relieved *Ataka*, below, as flagship on the Yangtse.

ATAKA (Now has tripod foremast, as in silhouette). 1936, *Official.*

ATAKA (ex-*Nakoso*). (Yokohama Dock Co., April, 1922). 725 tons. Complement: 118. Dimensions: 222 × 32 × 7½ feet. Guns: 2—4·7 inch, 2—3 inch AA. Machinery: Triple expansion. Designed H.P.: 1,700 = 16 kts. Boilers: 2 Kanpon. Authorised under 1920–28 Fleet Law, laid down 1921, and completed 1922. Equipped for submarine salvage work.

1936 *Official.*

SAGA (Saseho, 1912). 685 tons. Complement, 99. 210×29½×7¼ feet. Guns: 1—4·7 inch, 3—3 inch AA., 6 M.G. Machinery: Triple expansion, 3 screws. Boilers: 2 Kanpon. Designed H.P. 1600=15 kts. Coal: *maximum* 140 tons. Completed Nov., 1912.

ATAMI. 1937.

ATAMI (Tama Works, March 30, 1929), **HUTAMI** (Hudinagata Co., Nov. 20, 1929). Displacement: 170 tons. Dimensions: 148⅜ × 20⅔ × 3 feet. Guns: 1—3 inch AA., 6 M.G. Machinery: 2 sets triple expansion. H.P.: 1,200 = 16 kts. Boilers: 2 Kanpon. Completed 1929 and 1930 respectively.

SETA. 1937.

HIRA (March 24, 1923, Mitubisi, Kobe).
HODU (April 19, 1923, Mitubisi, Kobe).
KATADA (July 16, 1923, Harima S.B. Co.).
SETA (June 30, 1922, Harima S.B. Co.).

Displacement: 305 tons. Dimensions: 180 × 27 × 3⅓ feet. Guns: 2—3 inch AA., 6 M.G. Machinery: 2 sets triple expansion. Boilers: 2 Kanpon (mixed firing). Designed H.P.: 2,100 = 16 kts. Authorised under 1920–28 Fleet Law. Laid down 1922 and completed 1923.

1937.

TOBA (1911). 215 tons. Complement: 59. Dimensions: 180 × 27 × 2⅜ feet. Guns: 2—3 inch AA., 6 M.G. H.P.: 1,400 = 15 kts. Coal: 80 tons. Built at Saseho.

NETHERLANDS

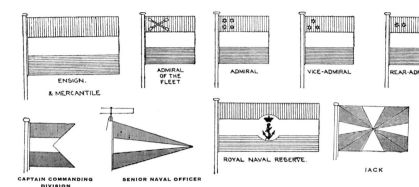

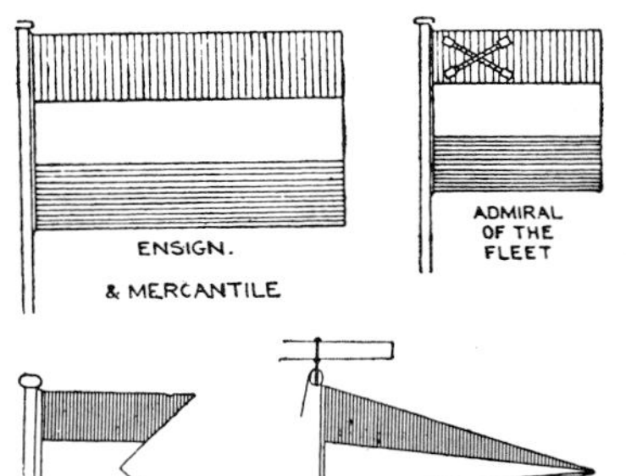
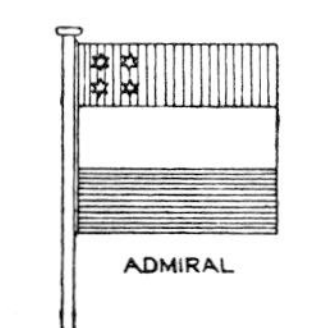
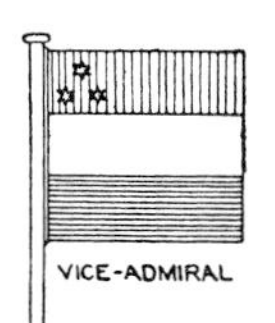
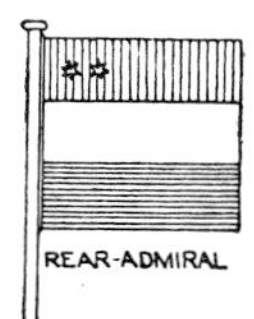
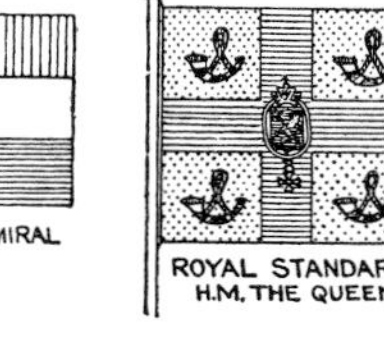
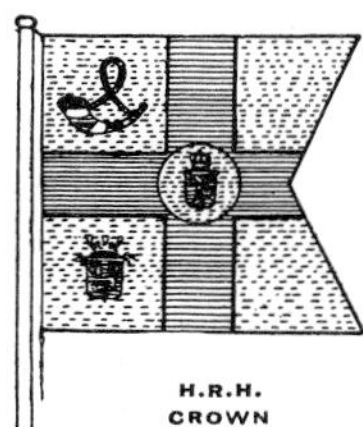
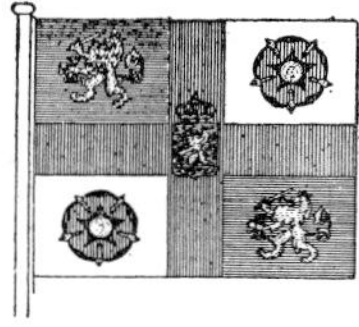

Officers commanding Divisions fly a yellow pendant with black letter D in centre, from signal yard.

Officers commanding Flotillas fly a black pendant with yellow letter F in centre, from signal yard.

Notes to Flags.

Royal Standard / *H.R.H. The Crown Princess* } Colours of these are *Nassau* blue (*dark* blue) and *deep* orange.

Governor-General of Netherland Indies : A broad pendant (Red, White, Blue) above Ensign.

Governors of Surinam and of Curaçao: Three white balls replace stars, in flag of Vice-Admiral's type.

Naval Guns (Officially revised, 1946)

	Cal. inch	Cal. cm.	Official Mark No.	Length cals.	Weight of Shell	Initial Vel. ft. secs.	K. = Krupp, B. = Bofors F. = Wilton-Fijenoord V. = Vickers, B. = British. U.S. = United States	
MEDIUM	5·9	15	11	50	101½	2953	Twin mounting, *Tromp*, A.A.	F.
	5·9	15	7	50	101½	2953	*Flores* class	B.
	4·7	12	8	46	46	2444	Twin mounting, *v. Speyk.*	F.
	4·7	12	7	50	53	2444	*W. v. d. Zaan*	F.
	4·7	12	6	50	53	2950	*v. Kinsbergen*, A.A.	F.
	4·7	12	Mk. XII**	45	50	2600	Twin mounting, *v. Galen* class.	Br.
	4·7	12	Mk. IX**	45	50	2600	*Evertsen* class.	Br.
LIGHT	4·1	10·5	1	50	39⅔	2897	*Gruno.*	K.
	4	10·2	Mk. XVI	45	35	2600	Twin mounting, A.A. *J. v. Heemskerck, Karel Doorman*	Br.
	4	10·2	Mk. XII	45	35	2600	Submarines *Zwaardvisch, Tijgerhaai*	Br.
	4	10·2	Mk. V	45	35	2600	*v. Galen* class.	Br.
	3·5	8·8	3	45	22	2625	Submarines *O21* class, A.A.	B.
	3	7·5	Mk. 22	50	13	2700	*Queen Wilhelmina.*	U.S.
	1·5	4	4	60	2	2953	Twin mounting, A.A.	B.
	1·5	4	Mk. IV * and IV	40	2	2400	Twin mounting, A.A.	Br.
	1·5	4	Mk. VIII	40	2	2400	Twin mounting, A.A.	Br.
	1·5	4	Mk. VII *P	40	2	2400	Quad. mounting, A.A.	Br.

Minister of the Navy : Mr. J. J. A. Schagen van Leeuwen (Commander, R.N.V.R.)
Commander-in-Chief : Admiral C. E. L. Helfrich.
Chief of Naval Staff : Vice-Admiral J. W. Termytelen.
British Naval Adviser : Rear-Admiral J. W. A. Waller.
Naval Attaché, London : Captain J. B. de Meester.
Colour of Ships : Greyish Blue, *except* Submarines, painted Dark Green in home waters and Black in E. Indies.

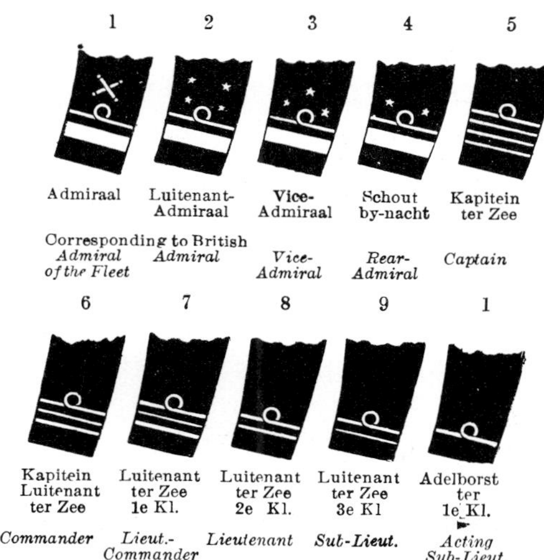

Uniforms.

In relative ranks (all with "curl"):

Doctors have insignia 4 to 9 in gold, with staff of Æsculapius on lapel.
Paymasters ,, 4 to 9 in gold, with silver anchor and crown on lapel, and silver cap badge.
Engineers ,, 4 to 9 in gold, and are to be distinguished by the badge of a torch, crossed by two arrows, on the lapel, instead of the usual anchor.

Flying Officers are of ranks 5, 6, 7, 8, 9, 10, and are to be distinguished by the badge of an aeroplane propeller on lapel instead of the usual anchor. R.N. Reserve Officers are of ranks 5, 6, 7, 8, 9, 10 and wear no special distinguishing mark. R.N.V.R. Officers (for special services) have a semi-triangular curl. Chaplains wear one silver stripe above two gold ones on each cuff, and are otherwise to be distinguished by the badge of a cross on the collar.

Navy Estimates.

1946, Fl. 448,000,000. 1947, Fl. 375,007,220.

New Construction Programme.

One light fleet carrier to be acquired or laid down in 1947 and one in 1948.
One cruiser to be laid down in 1947, and a second to be acquired, probably from Royal Navy.
Two destroyers to be laid down in 1947, and four more to be acquired, probably from Royal Navy.
One submarine to be laid down in 1947.
Eight minesweepers to be acquired in 1947.
One fast repair ship to be laid down in 1947, and a second to be acquired ; one anti-submarine training ship and one tender for torpedo school to be laid down in 1947.

Mercantile Marine.

(Sept. 30, 1945). 1,400,000 tons.

1946, *Wright & Logan.*

Silhouettes

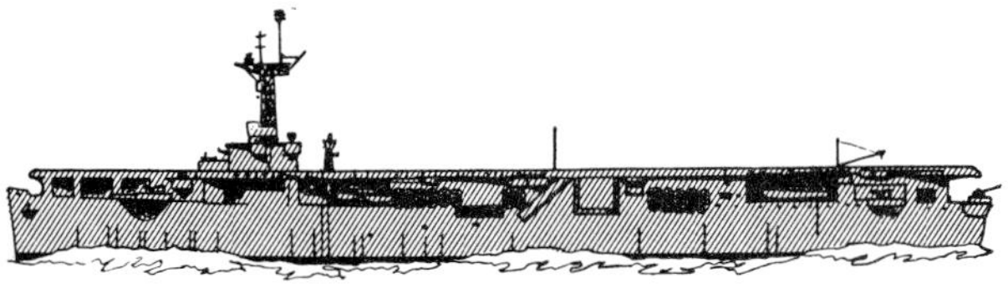

KAREL DOORMAN.

JAN VAN BRAKEL.

VAN SPEIJK.

HEEMSKERCK.

VAN KINSBERGEN.

HYDROGRAAF.

W. VAN DER ZAAN.

GRUNO.

TROMP

QUEEN WILHELMINA.

AMELAND *class.*

EVERTSEN *class.*

DOUWE AUKES.

VOORNE *class.*

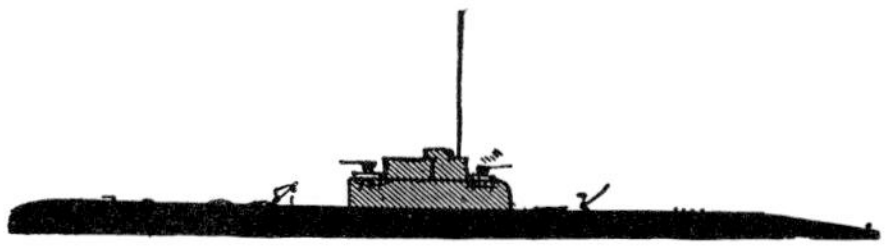

O 15.

VAN GALEN.
TJERK HIDDES.

FLORES.

DOLFIJN.

O 21, 23, 24.

BANCKERT.

A. CRIJNSSEN.

O 27.

JOHAN MAURITS.

SOEMBA.

TIJGERHAAI, ZWAARDVISCH.

Aircraft Carrier

KAREL DOORMAN (ex-H.M.S. *Nairana*, May 20, 1943).

Standard displacement: 14,046 tons (17,485 tons *full load*). Complement: 558.
Dimensions: $528\frac{1}{2} \times 68\frac{1}{4} \times 21$ feet.

Guns: **2**—4 inch D.P., **16**—40 mm. AA., **16**—20 mm. AA.

Aircraft: 20 to 24 Fireflies.

Machinery: 2 sets 5-cyl. Doxford Diesels. 2 shafts. B.H.P. 11,000 = 17 kts.
Fuel: 1,932 tons.

Notes.—Built at Clydebank, and taken over from Royal Navy 20 March, 1946

1946, *Wright & Logan.*

Cruisers

DE ZEVEN PROVINCIEN (Dec. 24, 1944), EENDRACHT (ex-*Kijkduin*).

Displacement: 8,350 tons. Complement: 900. Dimensions: 598 (*pp.*), $609\frac{5}{6} \times 56\frac{3}{4} \times$ 18 feet 7 in. Original plans, as given in earlier issues of "Fighting Ships," are understood to have been altered radically to embody war lessons.

Guns:
8—5·9 inch.
14—40 mm. AA.
8—M.G.

Torpedo tubes:
6—21 inch.

Armour:
3″—4″ side.

Machinery: Parsons geared turbines. S.H.P.: 78,000 = 33 kts. Boilers: 6 of 3-drum type.

Notes.—Laid down at Rotterdam by Wilton-Fijenoord (5.9.39) and Rotterdam Dry Dock Co. (19.5.39), respectively. Machinery by K. M de Schelde. Construction resumed in 1946.

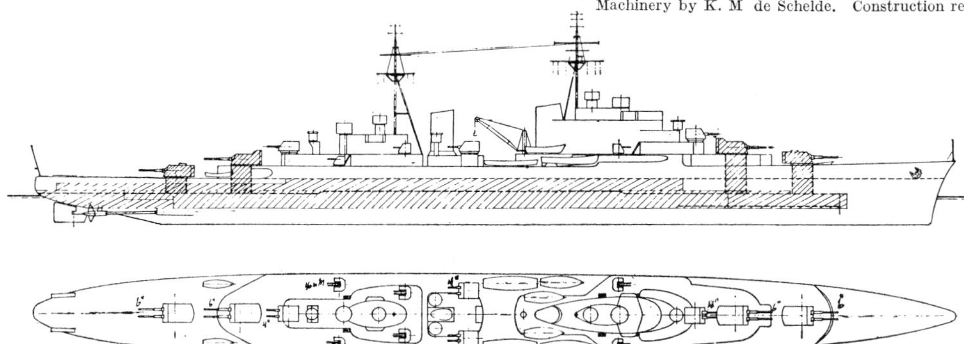

Zeven Provincien

TROMP (May 24, 1937), JACOB VAN HEEMSKERCK (Sept. 16, 1939.)

Displacement: 4,150 tons *standard*; 4,860 tons *full load*.
Complement: 380 and 420, respectively.

Length, (*pp.*) 426½ feet; (*o.a.*) 433 feet. Beam, 40¾ feet. *Maximum* draught, 15 feet.

Guns in *Tromp:*
6—5·9 inch, 50 cal. (Bofors).
8—40 mm. AA. (2 pdr.) (Bofors).
2—20 mm. AA. (Oerlikon).
4—D.C.T.

In *Heemskerck:*
10—4 inch AA.
8—40 mm. AA. (Bofors).
8—20 mm. AA. (Oerlikon).

Armour:
2″—2½″ Vert. Side.
1½″ Deck.

Torpedo Tubes:
6—21 inch (tripled).

Note to Plan.—This represents *Tromp*; *Heemskerck* differs as photo and silhouette.

Machinery: Parsons geared turbines. 2 shafts. Designed H.P.: 56,000 = 32·5 kts. (34·5 on trials). Boilers: 4 Yarrow. Oil: 860 tons.

Notes.—Tromp **authorised in 1931,** laid down 17/1/36, and completed 18/8/38 **by Nederlandsche Scheepsbouw Mij., Amsterdam.** Machinery by Werkspoor. *Heemskerck* laid down Oct. 31, 1938, by same builders as replacement **of former ship** of that name, and completed in a British yard in 10/2/40. *Tromp* taken in hand July, 1946, for a complete refit, to occupy 14 months.

Gunnery Notes—**The 5·9 inch guns have 60° elevation and can be used as AA. weapons.**

Tromp. (Mainmast since struck.) *Added* 1939, *Wright & Logan.*

Heemskerck. 1946, *Official.*

Heemskerck. 1946, *Official.*

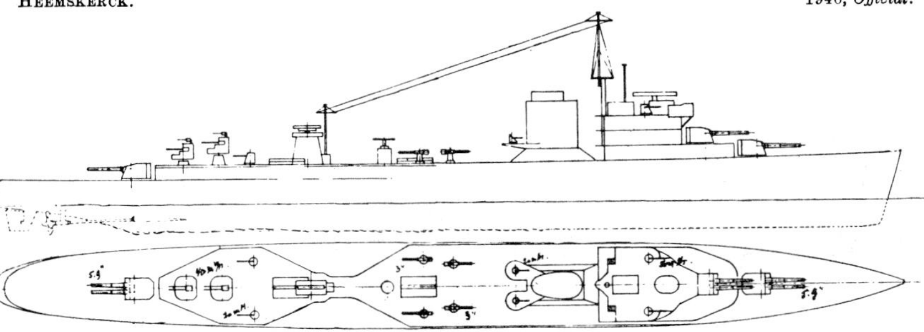

Tromp

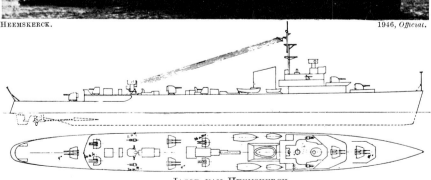

Jacob van Heemskerck

Cruisers

DE RUYTER. 1936, *courtesy Wilton-Fijenoord (Builders).*

DE RUYTER (1935). 6,450 tons. Torpedoed in Battle of Java Sea, February 27, 1942.

DE RUYTER (March 11th, 1935)

Normal displacement, 6,450 tons (about 7,548 tons full load)

Complement, 435

Length (*o.a*) 560⅓ feet. Beam, 51½ feet. Draught, 16¾ feet.

Armour:
2" – 1¼" Belt
1¼" Barbettes
1¼" Turrets
1¼" Bulkheads
1¼" Decks
1¼" Conning Tower

Guns:
7 – 5.9 inch (50cal)
10 – 40mm AA
8 – .5 inch machine guns

Machinery: 2-shaft Parsons geared turbines, 6 Yarrow boilers, 66,000shp = 32 knots. Oil, 1300 tons.

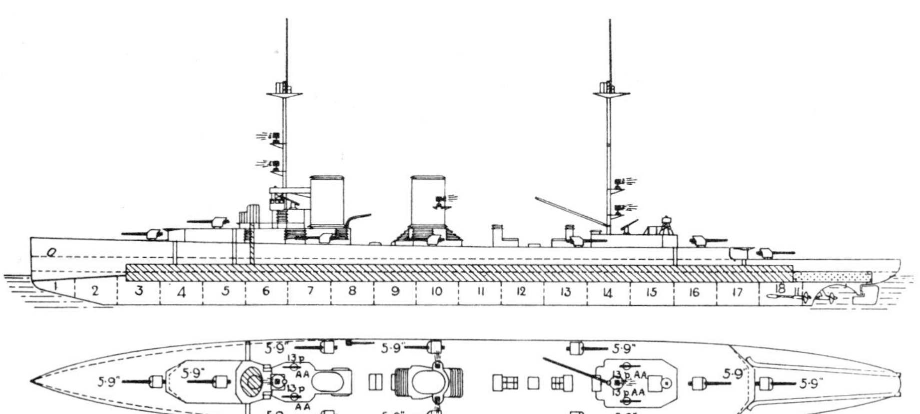

JAVA (Aug. 6th, 1921) & **SUMATRA** (Dec. 29th, 1920).

Normal displacement, 6670 tons.
Complement, 480 (504 with E.I. personnel added).
Length (*o.a.*), 509·5 feet. Beam, 52½ feet. *Max.* draught, 18 feet.

Guns (Bofors):
10—5·9 inch (50 cal.) "No. 6"
4—13 pdr. S.A., 55 cal. (anti-aircraft) "No. 4"
4 machine.
Torpedo tubes:
None.
Mines: 12.
Searchlights: 6—47".
Paravanes: 4.
Range Finders: 4

Armour (Coventry):
3" Belt ....
Deck { 1" flat / 2" slopes
4" Gun shield faces (much thinner at sides and roof)
2" Funnel bases ...
5" Conning tower

Ahead: **4**—5·9in. Broadside: **7**—5·9 in. Astern: **4**—5·9 in.

Machinery: 3 sets Krupp-Germania turbines. 3 screws. Boilers: 8 Schulz-Thornycroft. Designed H.P., 65,000=30 kts. Fuel, oil only: *normal*, 1070 tons; *maximum*, 1200 tons. Radius of action: 4800 miles at 12 kts, 3600 miles at 15 kts.

Armour Notes.—C.T. divided into gunnery control and navigation compartments. 3" belt is 392½ feet long. Towards stern and over steering gear, belt is narrower for a length of 42½ feet, and is only 2" thick.

Name	*Builder*	*Machinery*	*Laid down*	*Completed*	*Trials*	*Boilers*	*Best recent speed*
Sumatra	Nederlandsche Scheepsbouw Maatschappij, Amsterdam	Krupp, Germania	July,'16	Nov. 1925	82.000=31·8	Schulz	30.3
Java	K. M. de Schelde, Flushing	Krupp, Germania	May,'16*	1924	73,000=31.5 (St. Abbs, 7/7/25)	Schulz	

* Contracted for, June, 1917.

Aircraft Notes.—Each ship carries 2 Fairey III D type seaplanes, with 450 h.p. Napier "Lion" engines, crew 3 men. To handle these, 2 small cranes are now mounted abeam, to port and starboard, just abaft first funnel.

General Notes.—The German design of these ships is evident in their appearance. A third ship of this type (*Celebes*) was authorised, but cancelled. *Java*, though completed in 1924, did not enter into service until May, 1925.

Gunnery Notes.—5.9 inch guns elevate to 25-30°. Electric hoists.

JAVA. 1937 *R. Perkins.*

JAVA (1921). 6,670 tons. Torpedoed in Battle of Java Sea, February 27, 1942.

JAVA. 1924 *Photo, by courtesy of the Ministry of Marine.*

8 Destroyers (*Torpedobootjagers*).

PIET HEIN. 1928 *Photo.*

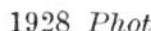

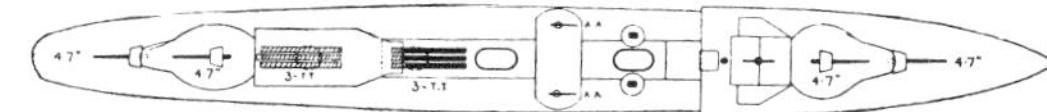

8 *Yarrow* type: ***De Ruijter*** (K. M. de Schelde, Flushing, Oct. 23, 1926), ***Evertsen*** (29 Dec., 1926), ***Kortenaer*** (June 30, 1927), ***Piet Hein*** (April 2, 1927), all by Burgerhouts, Rotterdam; ***Van Galen*** (June 28th, 1928), ***Witte de With*** (Sept. 11th, 1928), both by M. Fijenoord. ***Banckert, Van Nes,*** both by Burgerhouts. Displacement: 1316 tons. Dimensions: 307 (*p.p.*), 322 (*o.a.*) × 31¼ × 9¾ feet *max.* draught. Armament: **4**—4.7 inch (50 cal.), **2**—3 inch AA., **6**—20.8 inch tubes in triple deck mountings in first four. Other four carry AA., armament of **1**—3 inch and **4**—2 pdr. pom poms. Parsons geared turbines and Yarrow super heated boilers (250 lbs. pressure in first four, 400 lbs. in others). Designed H.P. 31,000=34 kts. in loaded condition, 36 kts. light. Oil: 330 tons. Complement, 126.

Notes.—These destroyers have been designed throughout by Messrs. Yarrow & Co., Ltd., and constructed under their supervision. The design was selected by the Dutch Government from several submitted by firms in England, France, Germany and the U.S.A. Included in the equipment of the vessels are a seaplane, bomb throwers and 24 mines. There is also a complete fire control system. *De Ruijter* and *Evertsen* both completed late in 1927, former said to have made 36 kts. with 90% full load. All are intended for East Indies Station. ***Piet Hein*** and ***Kortenaer*** completed 1928, ***Van Galen*** 1929, ***Witte de With*** 1930, ***Banckert*** 1930, ***Van Nes*** 1931.

PIET HEIN. 1929 *Photo, by courtesy of Messrs. Burgerhouts (builders).*

EVERTSEN. 1935, *Grand Studio, Malta.*

S/M.

(East Indies Marine.) 1925 *Official Photo, by courtesy of Chief of Naval Staff, The Hague.*

3 *Navy* type: ***K XIII*** (Dec., 1924), ***K XII*** (Nov., 1924), ***K XI*** (April, 1924), all by M. Fijenoord, Rotterdam. Displacement: 670 tons *on surface*, 820 tons *submerged*. Dimensions: 231 × 20½ × 12¼ feet. Engines: 2 sets M.A.N. Diesels, each 1200 B.H.P. = 15 kts. *surface* speed (17 kts. reached on trials). *Submerged* speed: 8 kts. Armament: **1**—3.5 inch AA. and **2**—21 and **4**—17.7 inch tubes (of which 4 are in bow and 2 at stern). **12** torpedoes carried. Complement, 31. Provided for under 1918 Naval Programme.

Note.—*K XIII* completed the voyage from Amsterdam to Surabaya, via the Panama Canal, unescorted, without mishap. Period occupied was from May 27 to Dec. 12, 1926.

K X. 1926 *Photo, R. F. Scheltema, Esq.*

O 9. 1926 *Photo, R. F. Scheltema, Esq*

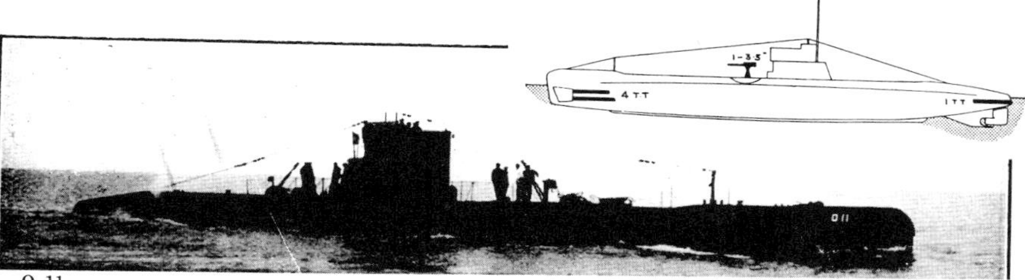

O 11. 1926 *Photo, by courtesy of Chief of Staff, The Hague.*

3 *Navy* (Home Service) type: ***O 11*** (M. Fijenoord, 19th March, 1925), ***O 10*** (Nederlandsche Scheepsbouw, 30th July, 1925), ***O 9*** (K. M. de Schelde. 1925). Displacement: 515 tons *on surface*, 645 tons *submerged*. Dimensions: 180 × 19 × 11½ feet. Engines: 2 sets Sulzer Diesels, each 450 B.H.P. = 13 kts. *on surface*. *Submerged* speed: 8·5 kts. Armament: **1**—3.5 inch AA. and **5** torpedo tubes (of which **2**—21 inch are in bow, **2**—17.7 inch bow, and **1**—17.7 inch stern). **10** torpedoes carried. Provided for under 1917 Programme.

K VIII, IX, X. **(East Indies Marine.)** 1925 *Photo, by favour of R. F. Scheltema, Esq.*

Holland type: ***K X*** (May, 1923), ***K IX*** (1923), and ***K VIII*** (1922), all by K. M. de Schelde. Displacements: 570 tons *on surface*, about 715 tons *submerged*. Dimensions: 211 × 18½ × 12 feet. Armament: **1**—3·5 inch AA. and **4**—17·7 inch tubes. Machinery: *K VIII* has two sets of 900 B.H.P. Diesel engines, M.A.N. type while *K IX*, and *K X* have 2 Schelde-Sulzer Type of 800 h.p. each for a *surface* speed of 15 kts. (16 reached *on trials*). Electric motors B.H.P. 630 = 8 kts. *Submerged* speed. Endurance about 3500 miles at 11 kts. *on surface* Complement, 29. Provided for by the 1916 Naval Programme. Note arrangement of hydroplanes and anchor recesses

Destroyers

Note.—2 more destroyers are to be built in Netherlands.

EVERTSEN. 1946, *Wright & Logan.*

PIET HEIN. 1945, *Official.*

2 *Cammell Laird :* **Evertsen** (ex-*Scourge*, Dec. 8, 1942), **Kortenaer** (ex-*Scorpion*, Aug. 26, 1942).
1 *Scotts :* **Piet Hein** (ex-*Serapis*, March 25, 1943).
Displacement: 1,796 tons (over 2,500 tons *full load*). Dimensions: $362\frac{3}{4} \times 35\frac{2}{3} \times 10$ feet. Guns: **4**—4·7 inch, **4**—40 mm. AA., **8**—20 mm. AA. (*Evertsen*, only **2**—40 mm.). Torpedo tubes: **8**—21 inch (quadrupled). Machinery: Parsons geared turbines. 2 shafts. S.H.P.: 40,000 = 36·5 kts. Boilers: 2 of 3-drum type. Complement: 232. Pendant Nos. are J 2, J 6, J 4, respectively.

1 *Hawthorn Leslie :* **Banckert** (ex-*Quilliam*, Nov. 29, 1941). Displacement: 1,750 tons. Dimensions: $358\frac{3}{4} \times 35\frac{3}{4} \times 9\frac{1}{2}$ feet. Guns: **4**—4·7 inch, **4**—40 mm. AA., **6**—20 mm. AA. Torpedo tubes: **8**—21 inch (quadrupled). Machinery: Parsons geared turbines. 2 shafts. S.H.P.: 40,000 = 36·5 kts. Boilers: 2 of 3-drum type. Complement: 232. Pendant number is J 1.

Notes.—Above 4 ships were acquired from the Royal Navy in 1945. Names were previously borne by destroyers lost in action in the E. Indies, 1942.

Note.—Both these ships were transferred to the R. Netherland Navy by the Royal Navy in 1942.

2 *Denny :* **Van Galen** (ex-*Noble*), **Tjerk Hiddes** (ex-*Nonpareil*) (both June 5, 1941). Displacement: 1,760 tons Complement: 246. Dimensions: 348 × 35 × 9 feet. Guns: **6**—4·7 inch, **4**—40 mm. AA., **6**—20 mm. AA. (only **4**—20 mm. in *Tjerk Hiddes*). Tubes: **10**—21 inch (quintupled). Machinery: Parsons geared turbines. 2 shafts. S.H.P.: 40,000 = 36 kts. Boilers: 2 of 3-drum type. Pendant numbers are J 3 and J 5 respectively.

VAN GALEN. 1942, *Official.*

Submarines

Note.—All are double-hull design.

TIJGERHAAI. 1946, *Official.*

2 *Vickers-Armstrongs (Barrow) :* **Tijgerhaai** (ex-*Tarn*, Nov. 29, 1944), **Zwaardvisch** (ex-*Talent*, July 17, 1943). Completed April 6, 1945, and Dec. 6, 1943, respectively. Displacement: 1,295/1,557 and 1,354/1,621 tons, respectively. Complement: 65. Dimensions: $273\frac{1}{2} \times 26\frac{1}{2} \times 14\frac{3}{4}$ feet. Guns: **1**—4 inch, **1**—20 mm. AA., **3** M.G. Tubes: **11**—21 inch (8 bow, 3 stern) (3 stern and 2 bow tubes are external). Machinery: 2 Vickers Diesels. B.H.P.: 2,500/1,800 = 15/8 kts. Pendant Nos. are O 2 and O 3 respectively.

DOLFIJN. 1943, *Official.*

1 *Vickers-Armstrongs (Barrow) :* **Dolfijn** (ex-*P* 47, July 27, 1942). Completed October 8 and delivered November, 1942. Displacement: 632/735 tons. Complement: 50. Dimensions: $197 \times 16 \times 14\frac{1}{2}$ feet. Guns: **1**—3 inch AA., **3** M.G. Tubes: **4**—21 inch (bow). Machinery: 2 Paxman-Ricardo Diesels. B.H.P.: 800/760 = 13/9 kts. Fuel: 56 tons. Pendant No. is O 1.

O 24. 1946, *Official.*

O 21. 1946, *Official.*

1 *K. M. de Schelde :* **O 21.**
3 *Rotterdam Dry Dock Co. :* **O 23, O 24, O 27.**
Displacement: 962/1,175 tons. Complement: 55. Dimensions: $255 \times 21\frac{1}{2} \times 13$ feet. Armament: **1**—3·5 inch, **1**—20 mm. AA., **8**—21 inch tubes (4 bow, 2 stern, 2 deck). 2 Sulzer Diesels, by K. M. de Schelde. B.H.P.: 5,200 = 19·5 kts. *Submerged* B.H.P.: 1,000 = 9 kts.

Notes.—*O* 27 differs slightly in appearance from others, c.t. being of German style. She was completed by the Germans (who renumbered her *UD* 5), and surrendered in 1945. Stern tubes had been suppressed by enemy, but will be restored during next refit. Others of this type were destroyed on slips, except *O* 25 (*UD* 3), which was launched May 1, 1940, and scuttled later.

No.	*Begun*	*Launched*	*Completed*	*No.*	*Begun*	*Launched*	*Completed*
O 21	20/11/37	21/10/39	10/5/40	O 24	3/5/38	18/3/40	..../40
O 23	6/4/38	5/12/39	..../40	O 27	3/8/39	26/9/41	1/11/41

Miscellaneous

Frigate.

1946, *Official.*

JOHAN MAURITS (ex-*Ribble*) (April 23, 1943). Built by Simons, at Renfrew, and acquired June 25, 1943. Displacement: 1,463 tons (1,994 tons *full load*). Dimensions: 301¼ × 36½ × 14¼ feet. Guns: **2**—4 inch, **4**—20 mm. Oerlikon. Machinery: 2 sets 4-cyl. triple expansion. 2 shafts. I.H.P.: 5,500 = 20 kts. Boilers: 2 of 3-drum type. Complement: 120. Pendant No. PF 1.

Sloop, rated as Gunnery Training Ship.

VAN KINSBERGEN. 1943, *Official.*

VAN KINSBERGEN (January 5, 1939). *Standard* displacement: 2,095 tons (2,703 tons *full load*). Complement: 205. Dimensions: 338 (*o.a.*) × 38 × 11 feet. Guns: **4**—4·7 inch, **6**—20 mm. AA. Armour: Possesses some slight protection, probably confined to armoured deck and C.T. Machinery: Geared turbines by Gebr. Stork. S.H.P.: 16,000 = 25 kts. Boilers: 2 Yarrow. Oil fuel: 128 tons. Complement: 220. Pendant No. is N 3.

Note.—Ordered Nov. 1936 from Rotterdam Dry Dock Co., laid down 11/9/37 and completed 21/8/39.

Sloops (Classed as *Kanonneerbooten*)

SOEMBA as radar training ship (FLORES illustrated in Addenda.) 1946, *Wright & Logan.*

FLORES (Aug. 15, 1925), **SOEMBA** (Aug. 24, 1925). Built at Rotterdam by Fijenoord and Wilton yards, respectively. Displacement: 1,734 and 1,683 tons, respectively. Dimensions: 248 × 37½ × 11¾ feet. Guns (removed from *Soemba*): **3**—5·9 inch, **3**—40 mm. AA., **4**—20 mm. AA. Machinery: 2 sets triple expansion. I.H.P.: 2,000 = 15 kts. Boilers: 4 Yarrow. Oil fuel: 285 tons. Complement: 135. Respective pendant numbers are N 1 and HX I.

FLORES 1946.

Note.—*Flores* recently served as accommodation ship; *Soemba* has been refitted and disarmed for duty as radar training ship.

Gunboat (*Kanonneerboot*)

1946, *Official.*

VAN SPEIJK (ex-*K* 3, March 22, 1941). Built by Smit, Rotterdam. Displacement: 1,365 tons. Dimensions: 246¾ (*pp.*), 255½ (*o.a.*) × 33½ × 10½ feet. Guns: **4**—4·7 inch, **4**—37 mm. AA., **4**—20 mm. AA., **2** D.C.T. Machinery: 2 sets Löckner-Humboldt-Deutz 4-stroke Diesels. B.H.P.: 1,400 = 15·5 kts. Fuel: 157 tons. Complement: 106.

Note.—A second ship of this type (ex-*K* 2), built by Werf Gusto, Schiedam, has been salved and is being rebuilt. She has Burmeister & Wain single-acting 2-stroke Diesels, B.H.P.: 3,500 = 18 kts.

Submarine Chaser (Rated as Patrol Vessel)

1944, *Lieut. D. Trimingham, R.N.V.R.*

QUEEN WILHELMINA (ex-U.S.S. *PC* 468) (April 29, 1942). Displacement: 280 tons. Dimensions: 165 (*w.l.*), 173⅔ (*o.a.*) × 23 × 6½ feet. Guns: **1**—3 inch D.P., **5**—20 mm. AA. Machinery: Fairbanks Diesel. 2 shafts. B.H.P.: 2,880 = 20 kts. Fuel: 60 tons. Complement: 52. Pendant No. is PO 1.

Note.—Built by Geo. Lawley & Sons, Neponset, Mass., and transferred to Netherlands flag in Aug., 1942, under provisions of Lease-Lend Act, name *Queen Wilhelmina* being selected by President Roosevelt.

Minelayer (*Mijnenlegger*).

1946, *Official.*

WILLEM VAN DER ZAAN (Dec. 15, 1938). Laid down 1937 by Netherland Dry Dock Co. *Standard* displacement: 1,267 tons. Complement: 144. Dimensions: 229⅔ (*pp.*), 247 (*o.a.*) × 36¾ × 11 feet. Guns: **2**—4·7 inch, 50 cal., **4**—40 mm. AA., **4**—20 mm. AA., **2** M.G. (92 mines). Machinery: 2 sets triple expansion. H.P.: 3,540 = 15 kts. Boilers: 2 Yarrow. Completed, Aug., 1939.

Minesweepers (*Mijnenvegers*)

Banda. (All similar except *Batjan*, with flying bridge. 1942, *Official.*

AMBON (ex-*Cairns*), **BANDA** (ex-*Wollongong*), **BATJAN** (ex-*Lismore*), **BOEROE** (ex-*Toowoomba*), **CERAM** (ex-*Burnie*), **MOROTAI** (ex-*Ipswich*), **TERNATE** (ex-*Tamworth*), **TIDORE** (ex-*Kalgoorlie*). All built 1940–41, and acquired in 1946. Displacement: 560 tons. Dimensions: 162 × 28 × 8⅓ feet. Guns: **1**—3 inch, **1**—40 mm. AA., **2**—20 mm. AA. Machinery: Triple expansion. 2 shafts. I.H.P.: 1,800 = 15 kts. Complement: 56. Pendant Nos. MV 21–28. All serving in E. Indies.

Minesweepers—*continued.*

A. Crijnssen. 1946, *Official.*

Jan van Gelder.

ABRAHAM CRIJNSSEN (Sept. 22, 1936), **ABRAHAM VAN DER HULST** (May 27, 1937), **JAN VAN GELDER** (April 17, 1937), all by Werf Gusto; **PIETER FLORISZ** (May 11, 1937), by Smit. Displacement: 460 tons. Complement: 47. Dimensions: 183 × 25½ × 7 feet. Guns: **1**—40 mm. AA., **2**—20 mm. AA. (but *A. Crijnssen* has **1**—4 inch in place of 40 mm.). Machinery: Triple expansion. I.H.P.: 1,690 = 15 kts. Boilers: 2 Yarrow. Oil fuel: 110 tons. Pendant Nos. MV 1–4.

Voorne. 1946, *Official.*

DUIVELAND (ex-*MMS* 1044), **IJSELMONDE** (ex-*MMS* 1026), **OVERFLAKKEE** (ex-*MMS* 1046), **SCHOKLAND** (ex-*MMS* 1082), **THOLEN** (ex-*MMS* 1014), **VOORNE** (ex-*MMS* 1043), **WIERINGEN** (ex-*MMS* 1025) (all 1943–44). Wood. Displacement: 350 tons. Dimensions: 126 × 26 × 10½ feet. Guns: **2**—20 mm. AA., **4** M.G. Machinery: Diesel. B.H.P.: 500 = 9·5 kts. Complement: 22. Pendant Nos. MV 13, 20, 14, 15, 16, 17, 19, respectively.

BORNDIEP (ex-*BYMS* 2210), **HOLLANDSCH DIEP** (ex-*BYMS* 2050), **MARSDIEP** (ex-*BYMS* 2030), **TEXELSTROOM** (ex-*BYMS* 2156), **VLIESTROOM** (ex-*BYMS* 2155), **WESTERSCHELDE** (ex-*BYMS* 2046) (all 1942–43). Wood. Displacement: 223 tons. Dimensions: 136 × 24½ × 6 feet. Guns: **1**—3 inch, **2**—20 mm. AA. Machinery: Diesel. B.H.P.: 1,000 = 12 kts. Complement: 26. Pendant Nos. MV 34–39.

Ameland. 1946, *Official.*

AMELAND (ex-*MMS* 231), **BEVELAND** (ex-*MMS* 237), **MARKEN** (ex-*MMS* 34), **PUTTEN** (ex-*MMS* 138), **ROZENBORG** (ex-*MMS* 292), **TERSCHELLING** (ex-*MMS* 234), **TEXEL** (ex-*MMS* 73), **VLIELAND** (ex-*MMS* 226) (all 1942). Wood. Displacement: 219 tons. Dimensions: 105 × 13 × — feet. Guns: **2** M.G. Machinery: Diesel. B.H.P.: 500 = 10 kts. Complement: 18. Pendant Nos. MV 5–12.

Patrol Vessel.

1944, *Lieut. D. Trimingham, R.N.V.R.*

JAN VAN BRAKEL (Feb. 8, 1936). Built by K. M. de Schelde. Displacement: 970 tons. Dimensions: 181½ × 30 × 10 feet *mean*, 13 feet *max.* Guns: **2**—3 inch, **6**—20 mm. AA., **8** M.G., **2** rocket projectors. Machinery: Triple expansion. 2 shafts. H.P.: 1,600 = 15 kts. 2 Yarrow boilers. Oil fuel: 72 tons. Complement: 55.

Miscellaneous

Old Gunboat (*Kanonneerboot*)

GRUNO (May 26, 1913). Built by Amsterdam D.Y. Displacement: 533 tons (545 tons *full load*). Complement: 52. Dimensions: 172¼ (*o.a.*) × 28 × 9¼ feet *max.* draught. Armament: 4—4·1 inch, 2—40 mm. AA., 2 M.G. Armour: 2″ belt, ⅜″ deck, 2″ conning tower. Machinery: 2 sets Sulzer Diesels (new in 1934). B.H.P.: 1,500 = 14 kts. Oil: 34 tons. Complement: 50.

Coastal Minelayers

DOUWE AUKES. (Now rigged as silhouette.) 1933 *Photo.*

DOUWE AUKES (Feb. 23, 1922). Built under 1918 Programme by Werf Gusto, Schiedam. Displacement: 687 tons. Dimensions: 180½ × 28½ × 10½ feet. Guns: 3—3 inch AA., 2 M.G. Engines: 2 sets triple expansion. 2 shafts. I.H.P.: 1,000 = 13 kts. Coal 115 tons. Complement: 50.

MEDUSA (1911). Built at Amsterdam Dockyard. Displacement: 593 tons. Complement: 53. Dimensions: 163 × 29½ × 9 feet. Guns: 3—3 inch AA., 2 M.G. I.H.P.: 800 = 11 kts. Coal: 72 tons. Used as accommodation ship.

Depot Ship.

Note.—2 new Fleet Auxiliaries are authorised.

1939, *courtesy F. W. Endert, Esq.*

ZUIDERKRUIS (1923). Displacement: 2,660 tons. Dimensions: 256 × 36¾ × 14¼ feet. Machinery: Triple expansion. 2 shafts. I.H.P.: 1,600 = 12·5 kts. Complement: 97.

Motor Launches.

ML 1408 1946, *Official.*

MV 42 (ex-*ML* 138), **ML 1407** (ex-161), **1408** (ex-260). Displacement: 82 tons. Dimensions: 112 × 17¾ × 4 feet. Guns: 2—20 mm. AA., 2 M.G. B.H.P. 1,100 = 20 kts. Complement: 13. (Latter two employed in Surveying Service.)

RP 101-104 (ex-*HDML* 1479, ——, 1470, 1337), **105-112.** Displacement: 46 tons. Dimensions: 72 × 15 × 4⅓ feet (*mean*). Guns: 1—20 mm. AA., 1 M.G. B.H.P.: 260 = 11 kts. (Stationed in E. Indies.)

Surveying Vessels.

(A new Surveying Vessel is to be built.)

BANGKALAN (ex-*Hydrograaf*, ex-*W. van Braam*, 1926). 397 tons *gross*.

ZEEFAKKEL (ex-*Miene*, 1919). Displacement: 78 tons. Dimensions: 73⅔ × 16½ × — feet. Machinery: 1 Kromhout Diesel. B.H.P.: 60 = 7 kts.

HYDROGRAAF (1911). Displacement: 297 tons. Dimensions: 132¾ × 22 × 9½ feet. Machinery: Triple expansion. I.H.P. 360 = 9 kts. Coal: 30 tons. Complement: 18.

Landing Craft.

LT 5. 1946, *Official.*

LT 1-10 (ex-*LCT* 562, 781, 1128, 1136, 7031, 7033, 7118, 7121, 7122, 7125). In European waters.

LT 101-106 (ex-*LCT* 1102, 1237, 1153, 1055, 1154, 1175). Stationed in E. Indies.

LV 1-14 (ex-*LCM* type) In European waters.

LV 101-126 (ex-*LCM* type. Stationed in E. Indies.

Tenders.

1939, *Ir. R F. Scheltema.*

(*Rated as Torpedo Transport.*)

MERCUUR (Feb. 26, 1936). Displacement: 265 tons *standard*, 284 tons *full load*. Dimensions: 137½ (*pp.*), 140 (*o.a.*) × 23 × 9 feet. No guns. H.P. 325 = 12 kts.

MOK I (Den Helder, 1939). Displacement: 177 tons. Dimensions: 114 × 20½ × — feet. Machinery: 2 Kromhout Diesels. B.H.P.: 400 = 12 kts. (Communication tender for Air Arm.)

GERBERDINA JOHANNA (1912). Displacement: 353 tons. Speed: 12 kts.

POELOE WEH (ex-Trawler.) In E. Indies.

GOEREE (ex-*Dolfijn*, 1920). 168 tons *gross*. Speed: 12 kts.

SMEROE 1946, *R. Neth. N. Official.*

NORWAY

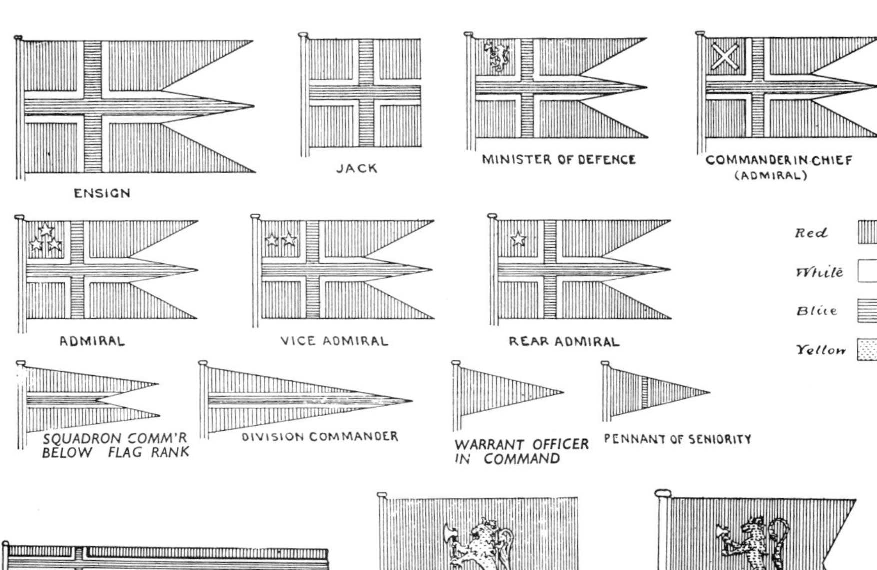

PENDANT

ROYAL STANDARD

CROWN PRINCE'S STANDARD

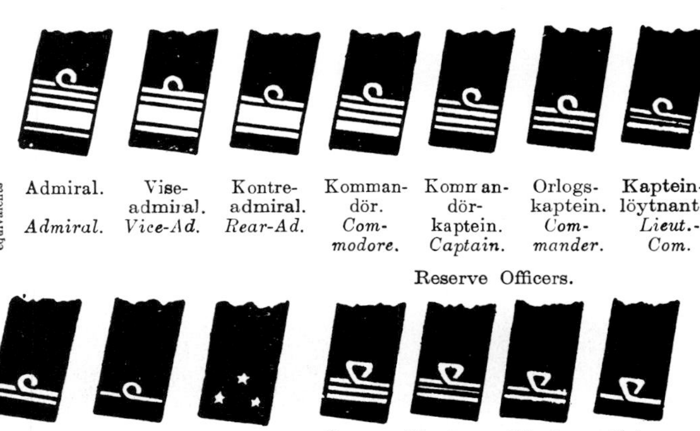

Admiral.	Vise-admiral.	Kontre-admiral.	Komman-dör.	Komman-dör-kaptein.	Orlogs-kaptein.	**Kaptein-löytnant.**
Admiral.	*Vice-Ad.*	*Rear-Ad.*	*Com-modore.*	*Captain.*	*Com-mander.*	*Lieut.-Com.*

British equivalents (italic).

Reserve Officers.

Löytnant.	Fenrik.	Kadett, klasse 3*	Com-mander	Lieut.-Com.	Lieut.	Sub-Lieut.
Lieut.	*Sub-Lieut.*	*Acting Sub-Lieut.*				

Other branches have same insignia, but with colours between stripes as follows: Engineers, purple; Surgeons, red; Paymasters, white; Constructors, grey; Instructors, blue; Technical and Special branches, green.

* 2 stars, klasse 2, Midshipman; 1 star, klasse 1, Cadet.

Note.—Peaks of caps of Commanders and higher ranks, formerly plain, are now decorated with gold lace as in British Navy.

Modern Guns

Notation.	Designation		Length in calibres	Model.*	Weight of Gun.	Weight of A.P. shot.	Initial velocity	*Max.* penetration firing A P. capped at K.C.		Danger Space against average warship, at			*Nom.* Rounds per minute.
								5000 yards.	3000 yards.	10,000 yards.	5000 yards.	3000 yards.	
	c/m.	inches.			tons.	lbs.	ft. secs.	ins.	ins.	yds.	yds.	yds.	
MEDIUM.	..	..	..	..	..	..	..	..	..	..	..	..	..
	12	4·7	44	B	2½	46	2625	...	...	...	...	...	10
	..	..	..	..	..	..	..	...	...	...	...	...	..
LIGHT.	*10·16*	4	40	B	2	32	2545	...	...	...	...	...	20
	7·6	3	50	B	1	12	2820	...	...	...	...	...	...
	7·6	3†	28	B	·4	12	1640	...	...	...	...	...	...
	7·6	3†	21	B	·33	12	1500	...	...	...	...	...	...
	4	1·57	60	B	·2	2	2790	..	..	..	..	..	..
	2	·8	70	O	·12	·31	2725	..	..	..	..	..	..
	2	·8	60	O	·12	·31	2460	..	..	..	..	..	..

* B = Bofors. O = Oerlikon. † Anti-Aircraft.

Minister of Defence.—Hr. J. Chr. Haug.
Commander in Chief.—Rear-Admiral Thore Horve.
Chief of Naval Staff.—Commodore S. V. Storheill.
Naval Attaché, London.—Commodore J. E. Jacobsen, O.B.E.
General Notes.—Personnel: About 7,500 officers and men in 1945.
Mercantile Marine.—(July 1, 1946). About 3,000,000 tons gross.

NORDKYN *class.*

SLEIPNER *class.*

BERGEN *class.*

ARENDAL.

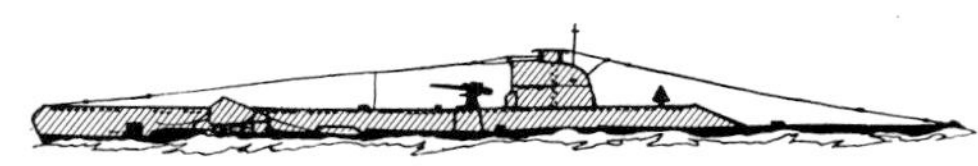

ULA, UTSIRA.

STORD.

NARVIK.

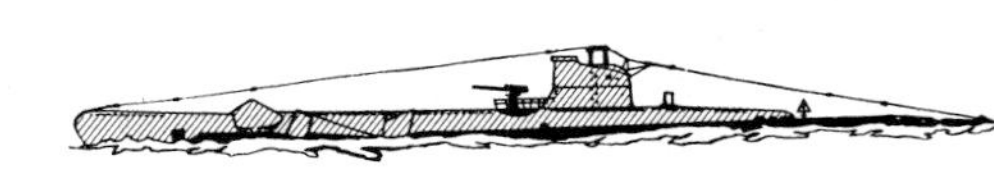

UTHAUG, UTSTEIN, UTVAER.

NORWAY

Silhouettes—*continued.*

H.M.S. *Arethusa* is being acquired on loan.

KONG HAAKON VII.

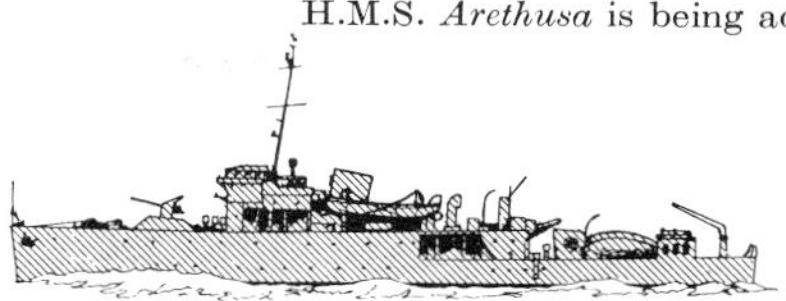

GLOMMA, TANA.

NORDKAPP.

HEIMDAL.

Destroyers (*Jagere*)

BERGEN. 1946, *courtesy Builders.*

2 *Scotts:* **Bergen** (ex-H.M.S. *Cromwell*, ex-*Cretan*, Aug. 6, 1945), **Oslo** (ex-H.M.S. *Crown*, Dec. 19, 1945).
2 *Yarrow:* **Stavanger** (ex-H.M.S. *Crystal*, Feb. 12, 1945), **Trondheim** (ex-H.M.S. *Croziers*, Sept. 19, 1944).

All purchased from Royal Navy in 1946. Displacement: 1,710 tons, except *Oslo*, 1,730 tons. (Respective deep load figures are 2,510 and 2,530 tons.) Dimensions: 362¾ × 35¾ × 10 feet. Guns: **4**—4·5 inch D.P., **4**—40 mm. AA., **2**—20 mm. AA. Tubes: **4**—21 inch, in quadruple mount. Machinery: Parsons geared turbines. 2 shafts. S.H.P.: 40,000 = 36 kts. Boilers: 2, of 3-drum type. Complement: 235.

Notes.—Construction of these destroyers is entirely welded. *Oslo* is fitted as Leader.

STORD. 1943, *Official.*

1 *White:* **Stord** (ex-H.M.S. *Success*, April 3, 1943). Displacement: 1,796 tons. Dimensions: 362¾ × 35¾ × 10 feet. Guns: **4**—4·7 inch, **10**—20 mm. AA. Tubes: **8**—21 inch (quadrupled). Machinery: Parsons geared turbines. 2 shafts. S.H.P.: 40,000 = 36 kts. (Sea speed 32 kts.) Boilers: 2 of 3-drum type. Complement: 220.

NARVIK. 1943, *Official.*

2 *Cammell Laird:* **Arendal** (ex-H.M.S. *Badsworth*, March 17, 1941), **Narvik** (ex-H.M.S. *Glaisdale*, Jan. 5, 1942). Displacement: 1,050 tons (1,430 tons *full load*). Dimensions: 264¼ (*pp.*), 280 (*o.a.*) × 31½ × 7⅝ feet. Guns: (*Arendal*) **6**—4 inch AA., **4**—20 mm. Oerlikon; *Narvik* has **4**—4 inch AA., **1**—2 pdr. pompom, **3**—20 mm. AA. Tubes: **2**—21 inch in *Narvik*. Machinery: Parsons geared turbines. 2 shafts. S.H.P.: 19,000 = 27 kts. Boilers: 2, of 3-drum type. Fuel: 280 tons. Complement: 208 and 185, respectively.

ARENDAL. 1944, *Official.*

Miscellaneous

Destroyers

No. 130, laid down at Horten, in April, 1939, was launched in 1941. Displacement: 1,220 tons (1,770 tons *full load*). Complement: 130. Dimensions: 300 (*pp.*), 319 (*o.a.*) × 32¾ × 9 feet. Guns: **4**—4·7 inch, **2**—40 mm. AA., **2**—12·7 mm. Tubes: **4**—21 inch (paired). Machinery: De Laval geared turbines. S.H.P.: 30,000 = 34 kts. Oil fuel: 300 tons. A sister ship was completely wrecked by sabotage; and the surviving unit, which was considerably damaged, is being re-designed before completion. Superstructure and armament as shown above are likely to be modified, and completion will therefore be delayed till 1948.

Torpedo Boats (*Torpedobaater*).

SLEIPNER. 1946, *Official.*

Sleipner (May 7, 1936), **Gyller** (July 2, 1938), **Odin** (Jan. 17, 1939), **Balder** (Oct. 11, 1939), **Tor** (1939). *Standard* displacement: 597 tons. Complement: 96. Dimensions: 236¼ (*pp.*), 243¾ (*o.a.*) × 25½ × 7 feet (*mean*), 9 feet (*max.*). Guns: **3**—4 inch (*Sleipner*, only 2), **1**—40 mm. AA., **2** M.G., **4** D.C.T. Fitted for minelaying. Torpedo tubes: **2**—21 inch, paired (except *Gyller*, **4**). Machinery: 2 De Laval geared turbines. 2 shafts. Designed H.P.: 12,500 = 32 kts. 3 water-tube boilers, working pressure: 450 lbs. Oil fuel: 100 tons. All built at Horten except *Tor*, by Frederikstad Mek. Verksted. While in German hands the latter four were known as *Löwe*, *Leopard*, *Panter* and *Tiger*. All now used for training.

SLEIPNER *class* (GYLLER has 4 tubes.)

SLEIPNER

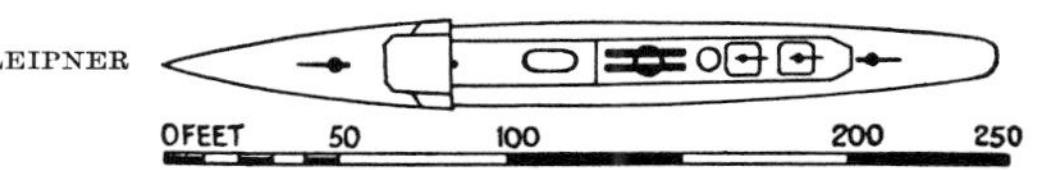

Sleipner class. To be refitted as patrol vessels, with reduced armament and boiler power.

Corvettes.

ANDENES. 1942, *Lieut.-Com. W. A. Fuller, R.N.V.R.*

1 *Ailsa:* **Andenes** (ex-*Acanthus*, May 26, 1941).
2 *Harland & Wolff:* **Nordkyn** (ex-*Buttercup*, April 10, 1941), **Söröy** (ex-*Eglantine*, June 11, 1941).

Displacement: 925 tons. Dimensions: 190 (*pp.*), 205 (*o.a.*) × 33 × 14½ feet (*max.*). Guns: **1**—4 inch AA., **1** pompom, M.G. and D.C.T. Machinery: Triple expansion. I.H.P.: 2,750 = 16 kts. Boilers: 2 S.E. Complement: 85. All acquired from Royal Navy.

Battleships

Note.—**3** pdr. AA. gun now mounted on each turret and masts owered. 1918 *Photo, Wilse, Oslo.*

NORGE (March, 1900), EIDSVOLD (June, 1900).

Displacement, 4166 tons. Complement, 270.

Length (*p.p.*), 290 feet. Length (*over all*), $301\frac{1}{4}$ feet. Beam, $50\frac{1}{2}$ feet. *Max.* draught, $17\frac{2}{3}$ feet.

Guns:
- **2**—8·2 inch, 44 cal.
- **6**—5·9 inch, 46 cal.
- **8**—12 pdr.
- **2**—3 pdr. AA.

Torpedo tubes (18 inch):
- **2** *submerged.*

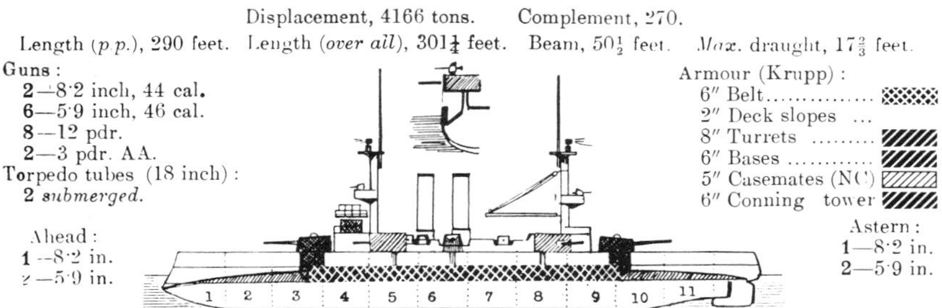

Armour (Krupp):
- 6″ Belt
- 2″ Deck slopes
- 8″ Turrets
- 6″ Bases
- 5″ Casemates (NC)
- 6″ Conning tower

Ahead:
- **1**—8·2 in.
- **2**—5·9 in.

Astern:
- **1**—8·2 in.
- **2**—5·9 in.

Machinery: 2 screws. Boilers: 6 Yarrow. Designed H.P. 4500=16·5 kts. Coal: *normal* 440 tons; *maximum* 550 tons.

TORDENSKJOLD. *June, 1927, Photo, H. C. Bywater, Esq.*

HARALD HAARFAGRE (Jan., 1897), TORDENSKJOLD (March, 1897).

Displacement, 3858 tons. Complement, 249.

Length (*p.p.*), 279 feet. Length (*over all*), 304 feet. Beam, $48\frac{1}{2}$ feet. *Maximum* draught, $17\frac{2}{3}$ feet. *Mean* draught, $16\frac{1}{2}$ feet.

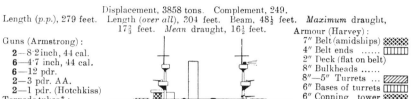

Guns (Armstrong):
- **2**—8·2 inch, 44 cal.
- **6**—4·7 inch, 44 cal.
- **6**—12 pdr.
- **2**—3 pdr. AA.
- **2**—1 pdr. (Hotchkiss)

Torpedo tubes*:
- **2** *submerged.*

Armour (Harvey):
- 7″ Belt (amidships)
- 4″ Belt ends
- 2″ Deck (flat on belt)
- 8″ Bulkheads
- 8″—5″ Turrets
- 6″ Bases of turrets
- 6″ Conning tower

Ahead:
- **1**—8·2 in.
- **2**—4·7 in.

Astern:
- **1**—8·2 in.
- **2**—4·7 in.

Machinery: Boilers: 3 cylindrical. 2 screws. Designed H.P. 4500=16·9 kts. (made 17·2 on *trial*, 1897-8). Coal: *normal* 400 tons; *maximum* 540 tons.

Notes.—Built by Armstrong, and completed 1897–8. Engines by Hawthorn, Leslie & Co. Belt is 174 feet long by $6\frac{1}{2}$ feet deep. Excellent seaboats, good for **14** kts. still.

* Tubes are 18 inch in *H. Haarfagre* and 17·7 inch in *Tordenskjold.*

Destroyers

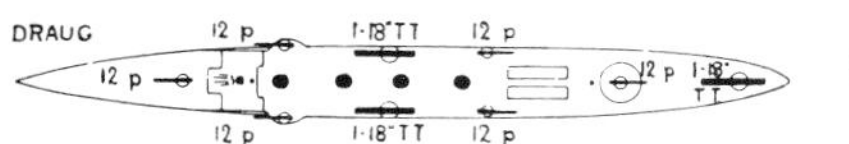

3 Destroyers (*Torpedobaatsjagare*).

Garm (1913), ***Draug*** (1908), and ***Troll*** (1910). All built at Horten. 540 tons. Dimensions: 227 × $23\frac{1}{2}$ × $8\frac{3}{4}$ feet. Armament: **6**—12 pdr., **3**—18 in. tubes. H.P. 7500 (8000 in *Garm*)=27 kts. Reciprocating engines in last two, turbines in *Garm*. Coal: 95 tons. Complement, 76.

GARM. 1930 *Photo, by courtesy of the Ministry of Defence.*

(Funnels raised and graded.)

TROLL. *Photo added 1930, by favour of "Flottes de Combat."*

Submarines

9 Submarines (*Undervandsbaater*).

B 2. 1925 *Photo, by favour of the Ministry of Defence.*

6 *Holland* type: ***B 1*** (1923), ***B 2*** (1 Oct.), 1924), ***B 3*** (1926), ***B 4*** (1 May, 1927) ***B 5*** (17 June, 1929), ***B 6*** (August, 1929) (all built at Horten). 420 tons *on surface* 545 tons *submerged.* H.P. 900 = $14\frac{3}{4}$ kts. *on surface*, 700 = $9\frac{3}{4}$ kts. *when submerged.* Dimensions: $167\frac{1}{3}$ × $17\frac{1}{2}$ × $11\frac{1}{2}$ feet. Sulzer type Diesel engines, built at Horten. Electric motors built in Norway. Armament: **1**—12 pdr., **4**—18 inch torpedo tubes (2 bow, 2 stern). Complement, 23. Laid down 1915. *B 1* completed 1923, and reported to have been very successful, maintaining a speed of 14·5 kts on trial. *B 2* completed in 1924, *B 3* in 1926, *B 4* in 1927. *B 5*, *B 6* both laid down in Dec. 1925, and will be completed in 1929 and 1930 respectively.

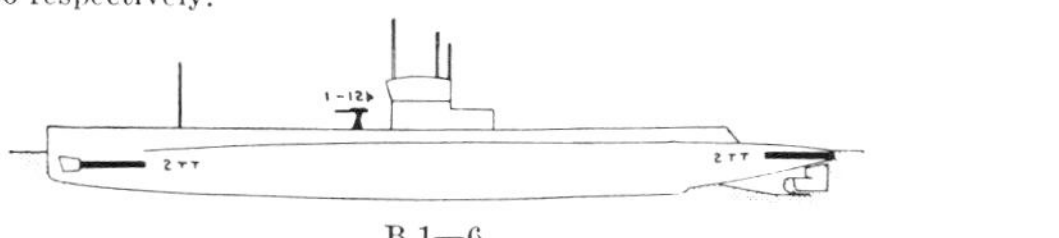

B 1—6.

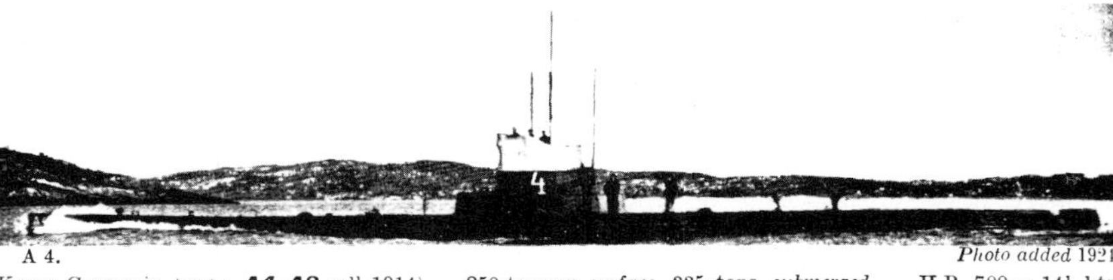

A 4. *Photo added 1921.*

3 *Krupp-Germania* type: ***A4-A2*** (all 1914). 250 tons *on surface*, 335 tons *submerged.* H.P. 700 = $14\frac{1}{4}$ kts. *on surface*, 380 = 9 kts. *submerged.* Complement, 15. Dimensions: $152\frac{1}{4}$ × $16\frac{1}{2}$ × $9\frac{1}{4}$ feet. Surface engines: Krupp-Diesel. **3**—18 inch tubes, 1 bow, 2 stern. **4** torpedoes carried.

Note.—*A5* completing at Kiel, was appropriated by Germany on outbreak of war and became the German *UA*. Was surrendered at Harwich with other German Submarines; ceded to France for experiments, and demolished at Toulon, 1920-1.

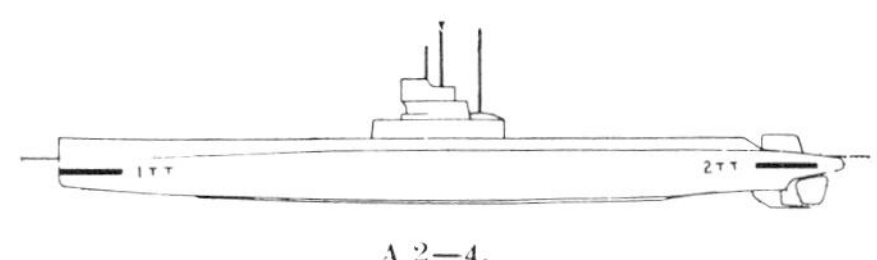

A 2—4.

Minesweepers.

GLOMMA. *Added* 1946, *Official.*

GLOMMA (ex-H.M.S. *Bangor*, May 23, 1940), **TANA** (ex-H.M.S. *Blackpool*, July 4, 1940). Displacement: 590 tons. Dimensions: 162 × 28 × 8¼ feet. Guns: **1**—3 inch AA., **2**—20 mm. AA., **4** M.G. Machinery: 2 sets Diesels. 2 shafts. B.H.P.: 2,000 = 16 kts. Complement: 60.

ORKLA (ex-*MMS* 1085), **VEFSNA** (ex-*MMS* 1086). Wood. Displacement: 350 tons. Dimensions: 126 × 26 × 10½ feet. Guns: **2**—20 mm. AA., **4** M.G. Machinery: Diesel. B.H.P.: 500 = 9·5 kts. Complement: 19.

HESSA (ex-*NYMS* 379, ex-*YMS* 379), **HITRA** (ex-*NYMS* 380, ex-*YMS* 380), **VIGRA** (ex-*NYMS* 381, ex-*YMS* 381). Wood. Displacement: 223 tons. Dimensions: 136 × 24½ × 6 feet. Guns: **1**—3 inch, **2**—20 mm. AA. Machinery: Diesel. B.H.P. 1,000 = 12 kts. Complement: 26.

Note.—*YMS* 247, 305, 377, 406 have also been serving in R. Norwegian Navy under Lend-Lease scheme, but will be returned to U.S.N.

PENANG, POLARNACHT, ROTGES, SÖLÖVEN. Whalers fitted as auxiliary minesweepers. May be acquired permanently in due course.

Submarine Chaser.

1946, *Official.*

KONG HAAKON VII (ex-*U.S.S. PC 467*) (April 29, 1942). Displacement: 280 tons. Dimensions: 165 (*w.l.*), 173⅜ (*o.a.*) × 23 × 6½ feet. Guns: **1**—3 inch d.p., **1**—40 mm. AA., **5**—20 mm. AA., **4** D.C.T. Machinery: Diesel. 2 shafts. B.H.P. 2,880 = 20 kts. Fuel: 60 tons. Complement: 59.

Minelayer

1921 *Photo, by courtesy of the Ministry of Defence.*

LAUGEN (Akers, Oslo, 1917). Displacement: 335 tons. Complement: 39. Dimensions: 137¾ × 28 × 6¼ feet. Guns: **2**—3 inch. Machinery: Triple expansion. I.H.P.: 170 = 9·5 kts. Coal: 21 tons. Stowage for about 50 mines.

Submarines (*Undervandsbaater*).

ULA. 1944, *Official.*

1 *Vickers-Armstrongs (Tyne)*: ***Uthaug*** (ex-H.M.S. *Votary*, Aug. 21, 1944).
4 *Vickers-Armstrongs (Barrow)*: ***Ula*** (ex-H.M.S. *Varne*, Jan. 22, 1943), ***Utsira*** (ex-H.M.S. *Variance*, May 22, 1944), ***Utstein*** (ex-H.M.S. *Venturer*, May 4, 1943), ***Utvaer*** (ex-H.M.S. *Viking*, May 5, 1943).
Displacement: 632/735 tons. Dimensions: 206 × 16 × 14⅔ feet. Guns: **1**—3 inch, **3** M.G. Tubes: **4**—21 inch (bow). Machinery: 2 Davey Paxman Diesels, 2 electric motors. B.H.P.: 800/760 = 13/9 kts. Fuel: 56 tons. Complement, 37. *Ula* is name of the birthplace of Ulabrand, the navigator.

Draught of submarines is 12¾ feet.

Motor Torpedo Boats.

1946, *Official.*

MTB 704, 711, 713, 716, 717, 719-723 (1944). Displacement: 128 tons. Dimensions: 115 × 20 feet. Guns: **2**—6 pdr., **2**—20 mm. AA., **8** M.G. Tubes: **4**—18 inch. Machinery: Packard engines. Sea speed: 30 kts.

Ten motor torpedo boats have been purchased from Royal Navy.

Motor Launches.

ML 125, 213, 573. Dimensions: 112 × 17¾ × 4 feet. Guns: **1**—40 mm. AA., **4**—20 mm. AA., **4** M.G. Machinery: 2 Hall-Scott engines. B.H.P.: 1,120 = 21 kts. Complement: 18.

Fishery Protection Vessel.

NORDKAPP. 1937 *Official.*

NORDKAPP (Aug. 18, 1937), (Horten). *Standard* displacement: 243 tons (275 tons *full load*). Complement: 22. Dimensions: 130½ × 21½ × 7½ feet. Guns: **1**—47 mm., **2**—20 mm. 2 Sulzer Diesels, with electric drive. 1 shaft. H.P.: 830= 13·75 kts. Fuel: 30 tons.

POLAND

Note.—The Emblem in the centre of the Jack is a flesh-coloured arm holding a steel-blue scimitar with gold hilt. The covering over shoulder of the arm is pale blue and has a gold-tasselled fringe. Eagle in all flags should be of same design as in Presidential standard.

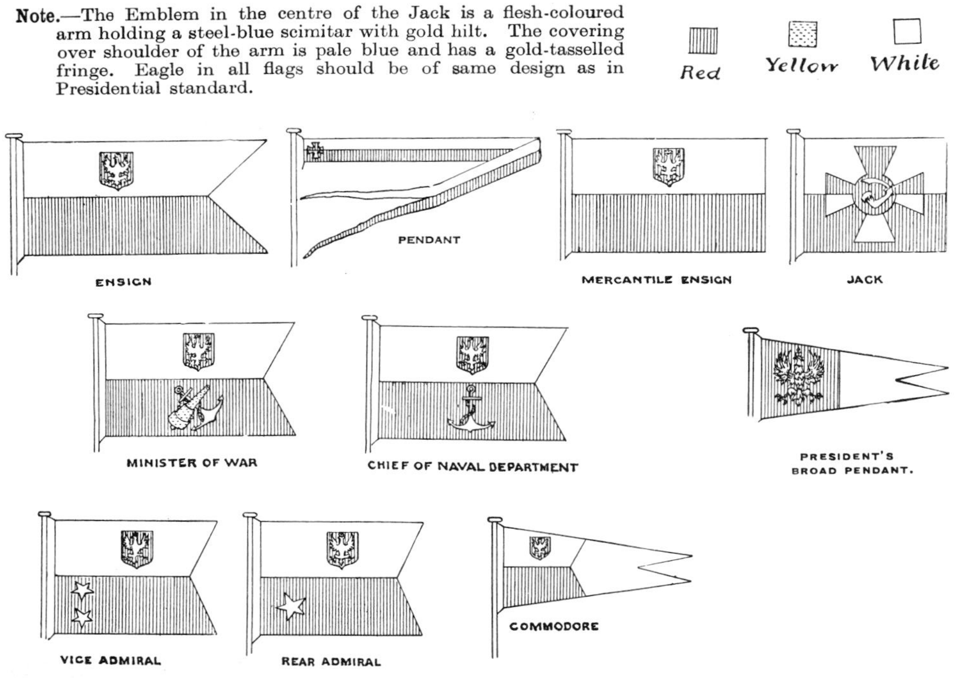

Red   Yellow   White

Minister of Defence : Marshal Michal Zymierski.

Naval Attaché, London : Captain Jerzy Klossowski.

ENSIGN   PENDANT   MERCANTILE ENSIGN   JACK

MINISTER OF WAR   CHIEF OF NAVAL DEPARTMENT   PRESIDENT'S BROAD PENDANT.

VICE ADMIRAL   REAR ADMIRAL   COMMODORE

Uniforms.

(*a*) = Polish Rank. (*b*) = Equivalent British Rank.

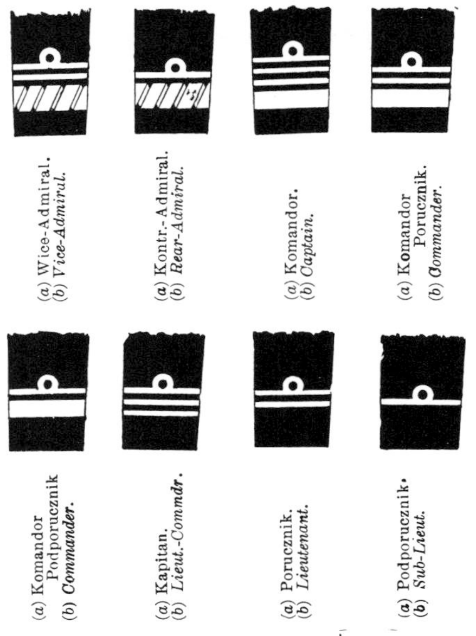

(*a*) Wice-Admiral. (*b*) *Vice-Admiral.*

(*a*) Kontr.-Admiral. (*b*) *Rear-Admiral.*

(*a*) Komandor. (*b*) *Captain.*

(*a*) Komandor Porucznik. (*b*) *Commander.*

(*a*) Komandor Podporucznik (*b*) *Commander.*

(*a*) Kapitan. (*b*) *Lieut.-Commdr.*

(*a*) Porucznik. (*b*) *Lieutenant.*

(*a*) Podporucznik. (*b*) *Sub-Lieut.*

BLYSKAWICA.   BURZA.   CZAJKA *class*

SEP.   WILK *class.*

2 Destroyers (*Kontrtorpedowce*). (Both in British ports at end of 1946.)

BLYSKAWICA. 1943, *Official.*

BURZA. 1942, *Official.*

Blyskawica (Oct. 1, 1936). Built by J. Samuel White & Co., Ltd., Cowes. *Standard* displacement: 2,144 tons. Complement: 180. Dimensions: 357 (*pp.*), 374 (*o.a.*) × 37 × 10¼ feet. Guns: **8**—4 inch AA., **1**—3 inch AA., **4**—47 mm. AA., **4** M.G. Tubes: **6**—21 inch (tripled), **2** D.C.T. Fitted for minelaying. Machinery: Parsons geared turbines. 2 shafts. H.P.: 54,000 = 39 kts. Boilers: 4 of 3-drum type. Name means Lightning.

Burza (April 16, 1929). Laid down by Chantiers Navals Français, Blainville, Nov. 1. 1926. Displacement: 1,540 tons. Dimensions: 344 (*w.l.*), 351 (*o.a.*) × 29 × 9¾ feet draught. Guns: **2**—4·7 inch, **1**—4 inch AA., **2**—47 mm. AA., several smaller AA. Torpedo tubes: **3**—21 inch, in triple deck mounting. Machinery: Geared turbines (supplied by At. & Ch. de la Loire). H.P.: 35,000 = 33 kts.

Notes.—Design of this vessel follows closely that of French *Simoun* class. Meaning of name is: Squall. Completed 1930. Sister ship *Wicher* (Hurricane) sunk at Gdynia, Sept. 1939.

Submarines (*Okrety Podwodne*).

Sep (Oct. 17, 1938). Laid down, 1936, by Rotterdam Dry Dock Co. Displacement: 1,110/1,473 tons. Complement: 56. Dimensions: 273½ (*pp.*), 275½ (*o.a.*) × 22 × 13 feet. Guns: **1**—3·5 inch, **2**—40 mm. AA. Torpedo tubes: **8**—21 inch. Fitted for minelaying. Machinery: 2 Sulzer Diesels. B.H.P.: 4,740/1,000 = 19/9 kts.

Note.—This name means Vulture. A sister ship, the *Orzel* (Eagle), paid for by funds subscribed by the Polish Navy League, was lost in June, 1940.

Miscellaneous

Submarines—*continued*.

WILK. 1930 *Photo, by courtesy of Messrs. Augustin Normand.*

3 *Normand-Fenaux* type: ***Rys*** (At. & Ch. de la Loire, Nantes), April 22, 1929, ***Zbik*** (Ch. Navals Français, Blainville, June 14, 1930), ***Wilk*** (Ch. & At. Augustin Normand, Le Havre, April 12, 1929). Displacement: $\frac{980}{1250}$ tons. Dimensions: 246 × 18 × 13 feet. Guns: **1**—3·9 inch, **1**—1·5 inch AA. Torpedo tubes: **6**—21·7 inch. Mines carried: **38.** 2 sets Vickers-Normand Diesels, H.P. 1800 = 14 kts. on *surface*. Electric motors, B.H.P. 1200 = 9 kts. *submerged*. Radius of action: 3500 miles on *surface* at 10 kts., 100 miles *submerged*. Diving limit: 44 fathoms. Carry **10** torpedoes and **38** mines.

Notes.—Meanings of names are as follows: *Rys*, Lynx; *Wilk*, Wolf; *Zbik*, Wild Cat. *Wilk* is prototype of the class, and all were built to Normand plans. Are distinguished by initials of names, painted on C.T. *Wilk* was still in a British port at end of 1946.

Coastal Craft.

MTB 76, 116 (1944–45). Ex-Russian, possibly of American PT type. Wood. No. 76 carries 2 torpedoes and **1**—20 mm. AA. No. 116, **2** torpedoes and **4** M.G. Speed: 38 kts.

Bezwzgledny (BW), ***Blyskawiczny*** (BL), ***Bystry*** (BS), ***Dziarski*** (DR), ***Dzielny*** (DL), ***Karny*** (KR), ***Niedoscigly*** (ND), ***Nieuchwytny*** (NW), ***Odwazny*** (OW), ***Smialy*** (SM), ***Sprawny*** (SP), ***Szybki*** (SZ). (Ex-Russian Nos. 325–329, 368, 369–372, 546, 552.) Wood. Displacement: 40 tons. Dimensions: 65 × 11 × — feet. Guns: **1**—20 mm. AA., **2** M.G., except *Blyskawiczny* with **2**—20 mm. AA., **4** M.G. Machinery: Diesel. Speed: 28 kts. Complement: 22.

Note.—Are differentiated by letters painted on bows as noted against each name above. *Blyskawiczny* differs slightly from others in appearance. Meanings of these names are respectively: Absolute, Lightning-swift, Acute, Brisk, Brave, Disciplined, Inaccessible, Intractable, Courageous, Bold, Efficient, and Rapid.

13 Minesweepers (*Wylawiaczemin*).

Albatros (AL), ***Czapla*** (CP), ***Jaskolka*** (ex-*T* 465) (JK), ***Jastrzab*** (JS), ***Kania*** (KN), ***Kondor*** (KD), ***Kormoran*** (KR), ***Krogulec*** (KG), ***Orlik*** (OK). All built in Russia, 1944–45. Displacement: 130 tons. Complement: 32. Dimensions: 100 × 16 × 4½ feet. Guns: **2**—20 mm. AA., **4** M.G. Machinery: Diesel. 3 shafts. B.H.P.: 480 = 10 kts.

Note.—Reported to be similar in appearance to Russian motor launches 201–212. Engines are American. Respective meanings of above names (which are abbreviated to letters painted on bows for identification, as shown against each) are: Albatross, Heron, Swallow, Hawk, Kite, Condor, Cormorant, Sparrowhawk, Eaglet.

Czajka (April 10, 1935), ***Mewa*** (1935), ***Rybitwa*** (April 26, 1935), ***Zuraw*** (Aug. 22, 1938). All built in Poland. Displacement: 183 tons. Dimensions: 139½ × 21⅓ × 5½ feet. Guns: **1**—3 inch. Machinery: Diesel. B.H.P.: 1,040 = 15 kts. Complement: 30.

Note.—These four vessels were recovered from German hands in 1945. *Czajka* (meaning Lapwing) had been renamed *Westerplatte*, and *Zuraw* (meaning Crane), *Oxhoft*. *Mewa* means Seagull, and *Rybitwa*, Tern; these two were numbered *MT* 6 and 7, respectively, by the Germans.

Arrangements are in progress for return of **BLYSKAWICA, BURZA, WILK** and sail training vessel **ISKRA** to Poland. It is also reported that Russia proposes to allot 19 vessels of the former German Navy to Poland.

PORTUGAL

ENSIGN
BANDEIRA NACIONAL

JACK
JAQUE

MINISTRO DA MARINHA

MAIOR GENERAL DA ARMADA

CHEFE DO ESTADO MAIOR NAVAL

KEY: RED GREEN

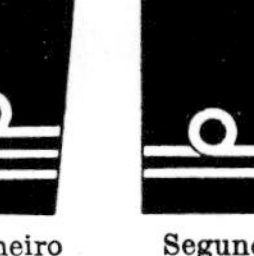

	Almirante.*	Vice-almirante.†	Contra-almirante.‡	Capitão de mar e guerra.	Capitão de fragata.	Capitão-tenente.	Primeiro tenente.	Segundo Tenente.	Guarda marinha.
British rank.	*Admiral.*	*Vice-Admiral.*	*Rear-Admiral.*	*Captain.*	*Commander. (Senior.)*	*Commander. (Junior.)*	*Lieut.-Commander.*	*Lieut.*	*Midshipman*

Naval Uniforms.

There is also the rank of Sub-Tenente (*Sub-Lieutenant*), but only in non-executive branches.

* Admiral has four *gold* stars. † Vice-Admiral has three *gold* stars. ‡ Rear-Admiral has three *silver* stars.

Staff officers same but *without* executive curl. Colour between stripes—*Surgeons*: red; *Engineers*: violet; *Paymasters*: blue; *Constructors*: black. On visor of cap, *Admirals*: 2 oak leaves; *Captains*: 1 oak leaf; *Commanders*: 1 narrow stripe. Uniforms like British Navy. Chin strap of gold cord, but officers of lieutenant's rank and below have black chin straps.

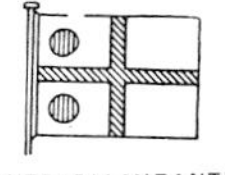

CONTRA-ALMIRANTE COMANDANTE EM CHEFE

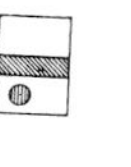

OFICIAL GENERAL DA ARMADA, QUANDO EMBARCADO SEM FUNCÕES DETERMINADOS

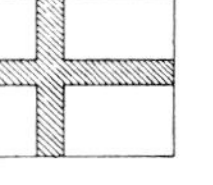

INSPECTOR DA MARINHA OU QUALQUER OFICIAL GENERAL EM SERVIÇO DE INSPECCÃO

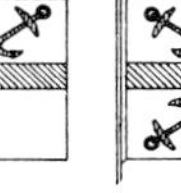

DIRECTOR GERAL DA MARINHA

INTENDENTE DA MARINHA NO ALFEITE

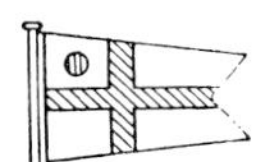

COMODORO

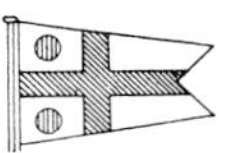

CAPITÃO DE MAR E GUERRA DE FORCA NAVAL DEBAIXO DE ORDENS, OU COMANDANTE SUPERIOR DE NAVIOS NO PORTO DE LISBOA

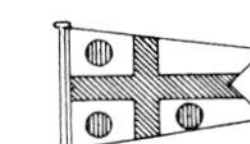

CAPITÃO DE FRAGATA OU CAPITÃO TENENTE COMANDANTE DE FLOTILHA OU ESQUADRILHA

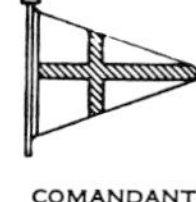

COMANDANTE MAIS ANTIGO NUMA REUNIÃO ACIDENTAL DE NAVIOS

Minister of Marine: Captain Americo Deus Rodrigues Tomaz.
Commander-in-Chief (*Maior-General da Armada*)*:* Vice-Admiral A. G. Souza Ventura.
Chief of the Naval Staff: Rear-Admiral Correia Pereira.
Naval Attaché, London: Commander José Conceição da Rocha.
Personnel: 719 officers and 5,550 men. *Colour of ships:* Light grey.
Mercantile Marine: (From "Lloyd's Register," 1939 figures) 266 vessels, *gross* tonnage, 269,118
Navy Estimates, 1946: Escudos 350,478,045.

Mode of address: N.R.P. "——". (Navio da Republica Portuguesa). *Displacements:* Standard

VOUGA *class.*

GONÇALVES ZARCO. GONÇALO VELHO.

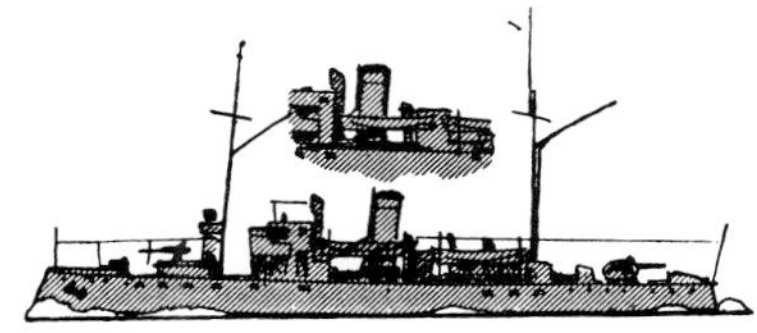

DIU
(*Inset:* IBO).

AFONSO DE ALBUQUERQUE.
BARTOLOMEU DIAS.

JOÃO DE LISBOA, P. NUNES.

ZAIRE

Silhouettes

Almirante Lacerda.

Dom João de Castro.

C. Araujo.

Faro. Lagos.

S. Miguel *class*.

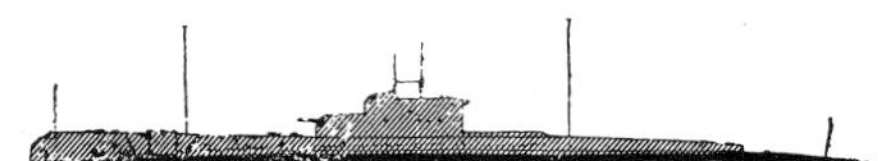

Delfim. Espadarte. Golfinho.

Destroyers

Destroyers (*Contra-Torpedeiros*).

3 authorised for construction, but none yet begun. Displacement: 1,400 tons.

5 Vouga Class.

Douro. 1946, *courtesy Eng. Lieut.-Com. Aluino Martins da Silva.*

5 *Yarrow* type: **Dão** (July 27, 1934), **Vouga** (Jan. 25, 1933), **Lima** (May 29, 1933), **Tejo** (May 4, 1935), **Douro** (Aug. 16, 1935). Displacement: 1,219 tons *standard*, 1,563 tons *full load.* Complement: 163 *normal*, 184 *full*. Dimensions: 319 (*pp.*), 322 (*o.a.*) × 31 × 11 feet (*mean draught*). Guns: 4—4·7 inch, 50 cal., 5—20 mm. AA., 4 D.C.T. Torpedo tubes: 4—21 inch, quadrupled. Mine rails fitted and 20 mines carried.

Machinery: Parsons geared turbines. S.H.P. 33,000 = 36 kts. 3 Yarrow boilers (400 lb. pressure). Oil: 296 tons *normal*, 345 tons *maximum*. Radius: 5,400 miles at 15 kts. Trials gave speeds of from 36·65 to 37 kts. with ample margin of power and boiler capacity.

Note.—Two earlier ships of this class, originally named *Douro* and *Tejo*, were sold to Colombia, fresh ships with these names being built to replace them. All built at Lisbon except *Vouga* and *Lima*, constructed on the Clyde by Messrs. Yarrow, as were machinery and boilers of all five. In 1946 a contract was entered into with Yarrow & Co. Ltd., and Vickers-Armstrongs, Ltd., for the reconstruction and modernisation of these destroyers at a cost of £1,400,000, the work to occupy three years.

Distinguishing letters on bows: D—*Dão*, D R—*Douro*, L—*Lima*, T—*Tejo*, V—*Vouga*

Tejo. 1946, *courtesy Eng. Lieut.-Com. Aluino Martins da Silva.*

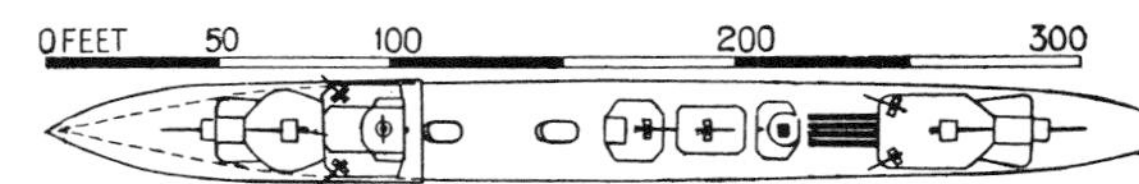

Submarines

3 Submarines (*Submersiveis*).

3 authorised for construction, but not yet laid down. Displacement: 900 tons.

Delfim. 1946, *Eng. Lieut.-Com. Aluino Martins da Silva.*

3 *Vickers-Armstrongs* type: **Delfim** (May 1, 1934), **Espadarte, Golfinho** (both May 30, 1934).

Displacement: 800/1,092 tons. Dimensions: 227·2 × 21·3 × 12·7 feet. Complement, 36.
Armament: **1**—4 inch, 2 M.G. Tubes: **6**—21 inch (4 bow, 2 stern). 12 torpedoes carried.

Machinery: Vickers Diesels, B.H.P. 2,300 = 16·5 kts. Motors H.P. 1,000 = 9·25 kts. Radius: 2,080 miles full speed, 5,000 miles at 10 kts.; *submerged* = 8 miles at full speed and 110 miles at 4 kts.

Notes.—All three laid down at Barrow, 9th March 1933, and completed 1935. Distinguished by initial letters of names painted on C.T.

Delfim. 1934, *courtesy Messrs. Vickers-Armstrongs.*

Sloops

1st class. (*Avisos de Primeira Classe.*)

B. Dias. (Observe funnel band.) 1944, *courtesy Eng. Lieut.-Com. Aluino Martins da Silva.*

AFONSO DE ALBUQUERQUE (May 28, 1934), **BARTOLOMEU DIAS** (Oct. 10, 1934). Built by R. & W. Hawthorn, Leslie & Co. Displacement: (*standard*), 1,783 and 1,788 tons, respectively; (*full load*), 2,434 and 2,439 tons, respectively. Complement: 189 (peace), 229 (war). Dimensions: $326\frac{3}{4} \times 44\frac{1}{4} \times 12\frac{1}{2}$ feet (*mean*). Guns: **4**—4·7 inch, 50 cal. **2**—3 inch AA., **8**—20 mm. AA., **4** D.C.T. Fitted to carry 40 mines. Machinery: Parsons geared turbines. S.H.P.: 8,000 = 21 kts. Oil fuel: 660 tons. Radius: 8,000 miles at 10 kts. 2 Yarrow boilers.

Notes.—Original contract placed with Odero-Terni-Orlando, 1931, cancelled 1932, and design modified by new builders when fresh contract was made. Both ships made 22 kts. on trials without being pressed. They are differentiated by the white band around funnel of *B. Dias*.

AFONSO DE ALBUQUERQUE. 1944, *courtesy Eng. Lieut.-Com. Aluino Martins da Silva.*

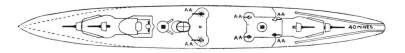

2nd Class (*Avisos de 2a Classe*).

G. VELHO. (Mainmast now reduced to a staff.) 1933 *Photo, courtesy of builders.*

GONÇALVES ZARCO (Nov. 28, 1932), **GONCALO VELHO** (Aug. 3, 1932). Built by R. & W. Hawthorn, Leslie & Co. Both vessels laid down October 9, 1931. Displacement: (*Standard*) 950 tons; (*full load*) 1,414 tons. Complement: 128. Dimensions: 250 (*pp.*), 268 (*o.a.*) × 35½ × 11¼ feet (*mean*). Guns: 3—4·7 inch, 50 cal., 5—20 mm. AA., 4 D.C.T. Machinery: Parsons geared turbines. S.H.P.: 2,000 = 16·5 kts. 2 shafts. Boilers: 2 Yarrow. Radius: 9,831 miles at 11 kts. Oil: 335 tons *normal*, 470 tons *maximum*. Trials: 4 hours full speed = 17·4 kts.

G. ZARCO. 1943, *Lieut.-Com. P. Zilhão, P.N.*

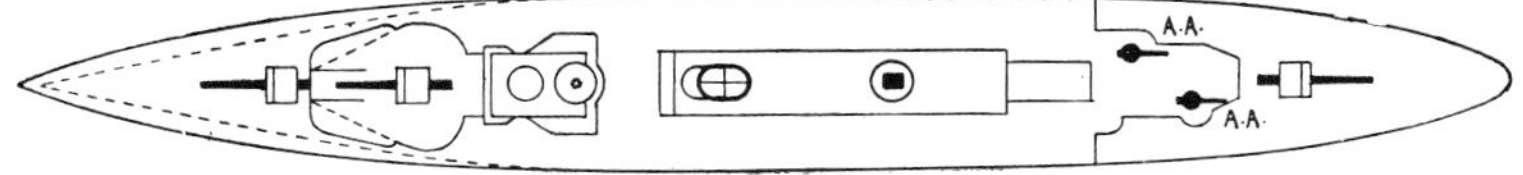

2nd Class (*Avisos de 2a Classe*)—*continued.*

JOÃO DE LISBOA. 1943, *Eng. Lt.-Com. Aluino Martins da Silva.*

PEDRO NUNES (1933), **JOAO DE LISBOA** (ex-*Infante D. Henrique*). (May 21, 1936).
Displacement: (*Standard*), 1,090 and 1,091 tons, respectively; (*full load*), 1,197 and 1,218 tons, respectively. Complement: 112/138.
Dimensions: *J. de Lisboa*, 234⅓ (*pp.*), *P. Nunes*, 223 (*pp.*) × 32¾ × 9⅓ feet (*mean*). 10½ feet (*max.*)
Guns:
2—4·7 inch, 50 cal.
4—20 mm. AA.
4—D.C.T.

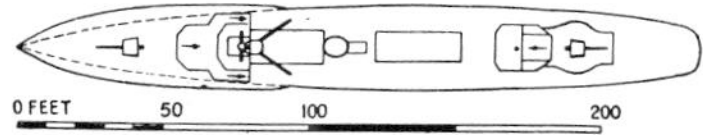

Machinery: 2 sets M.A.N. 8 cycle Diesels. B.H.P.: 2,400 = 16·5 kts. Radius: 8,850 miles at 12 kts., 4,800 at 16 kts. Oil: 110 tons *normal*, 126 tons *max.*

Notes.—Both built at the Naval Arsenal, Lisbon. *P. Nunes* laid down early in 1930. Unlike her sister ship, she is not part of ten-year programme introduced that year.

P. NUNES 1946, *Lieut. Malheiro do Vale.*

JOÃO DE LISBOA (Observe funnel band.) 1945, *Eng. Lt.-Com. Aluino Martins da Silva.*

PEDRO NUNES. 1946, *Official.*

ROUMANIA

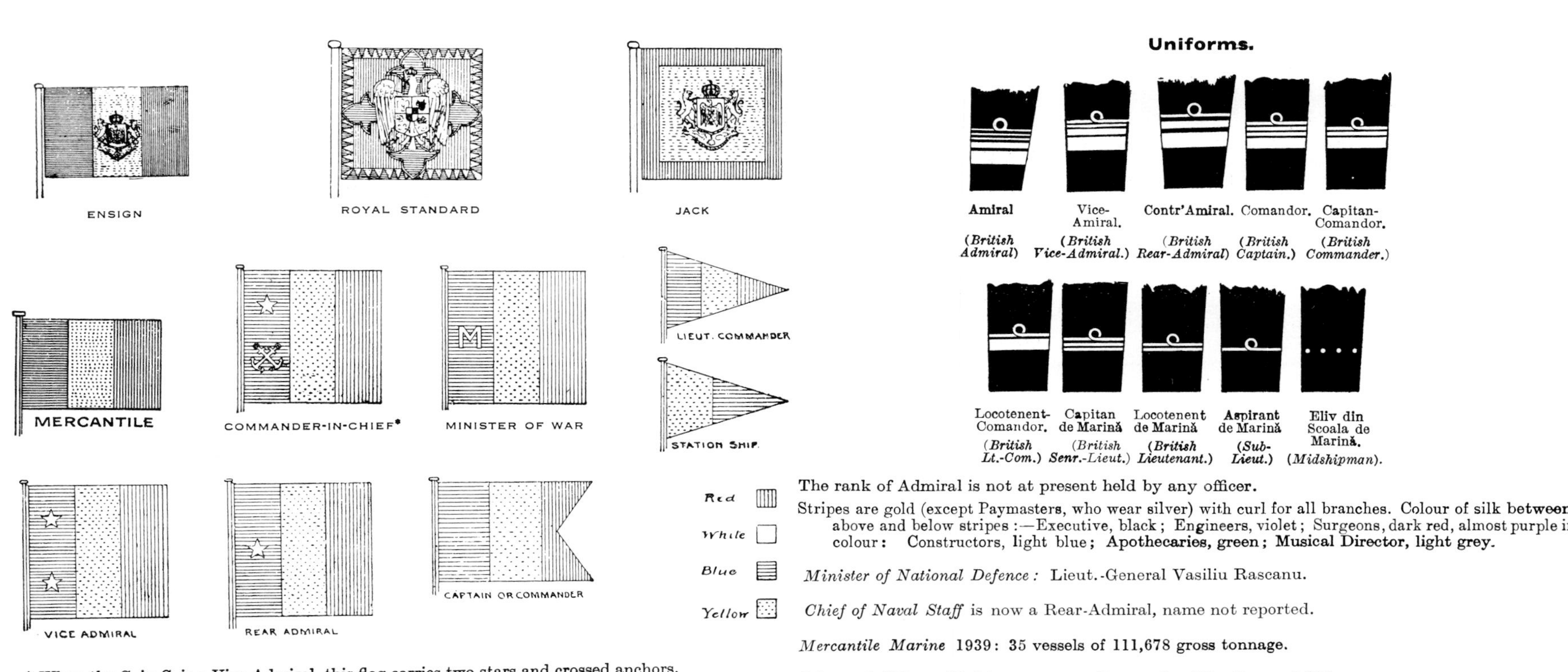

* When the C. in C. is a Vice-Admiral, this flag carries two stars and crossed anchors.

The rank of Admiral is not at present held by any officer.

Stripes are gold (except Paymasters, who wear silver) with curl for all branches. Colour of silk between, above and below stripes :—Executive, black ; Engineers, violet ; Surgeons, dark red, almost purple in colour : Constructors, light blue ; Apothecaries, green ; Musical Director, light grey.

Minister of National Defence : Lieut.-General Vasiliu Rascanu.

Chief of Naval Staff is now a Rear-Admiral, name not reported.

Mercantile Marine 1939 : 35 vessels of 111,678 gross tonnage.

Colour of Ships : Light grey. *Personnel :* 480 officers, 4,500 men.

Form of Address : "N.M.S." ("Nava Majestații Sale").

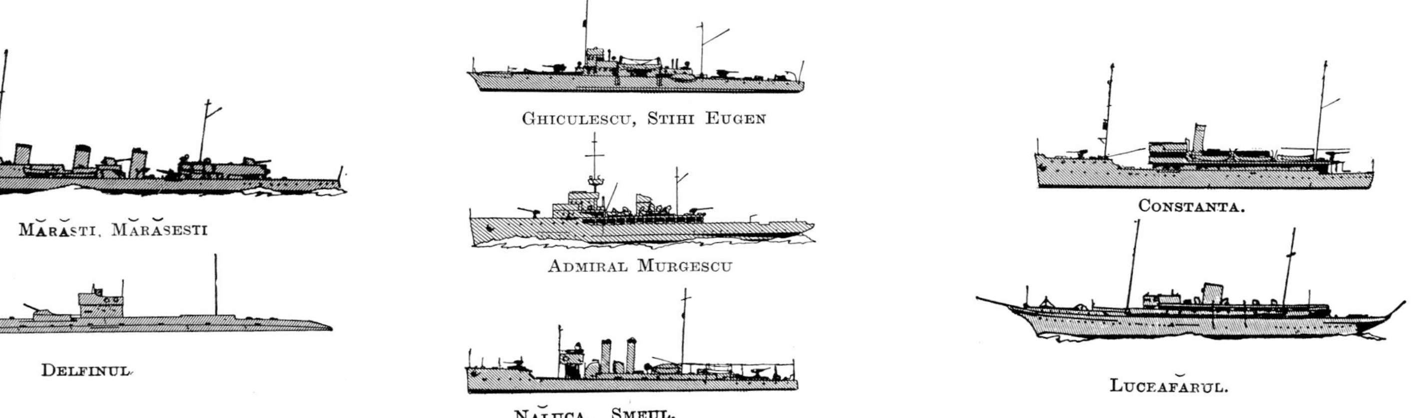

MĂRĂSTI, MĂRĂSESTI — GHICULESCU, STIHI EUGEN — CONSTANTA. — ADMIRAL MURGESCU — DELFINUL — LUCEAFĂRUL. — NĂLUCA. SMEUL.

Destroyers (*Distrugatoáre*)

Black Sea Division (*Divizia de Mare*).

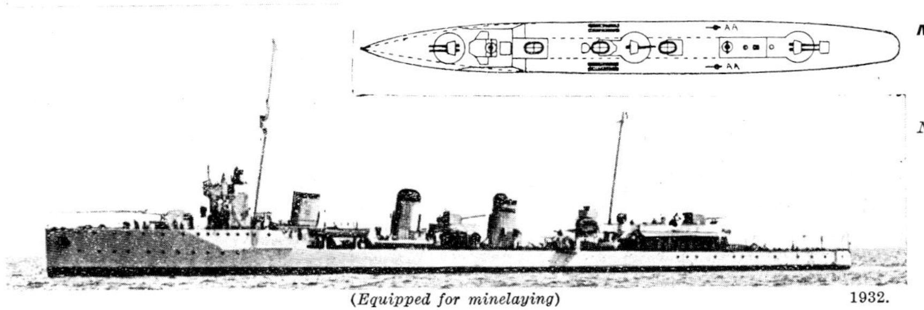

(*Equipped for minelaying*) 1932.

Mărăsti (ex-Italian *Sparviero*, 1919), ***Mărăsesti*** (ex-Italian *Nibbio*, 1918). Standard displacement : 1,410 tons (1,723 tons *full load*). Dimensions : 309½ (*pp.*) × 31 × 11½ feet. Guns : **4**—4·7 inch, **2**—37 mm. AA., **2** M.G. Tubes : **4**—17·7 inch in twin deck mountings. Machinery : 2 Tosi turbines. 2 shafts. Designed S.H.P. : 45,000 = 34 kts. 5 Thornycroft oil-burning boilers. Oil : 260 tons = 1,700 miles (15 kts.), 380 miles (full speed). Complement : 139.

Notes.—Built by Pattison, Naples; ordered for Roumanian Navy about 1913, and requisitioned by Italy in 1915. They were repurchased by Roumania, 1920, and renamed after actions fought in 1917. Refitted and rearmed at Galatz and Naples, 1925–26.

Motor Torpedo Boats.

Six, of British Power Boat type, are reported to exist. Particulars wanted.

Submarine.

1 *Quarnaro* boat: ***Delfinul*** (June 22, 1930). Displacement: $\frac{640}{886}$ tons. Dimensions: 225 × 19½ × 12 feet. **Guns: 1—4 inch, 35 cal. Tubes: 8—21 inch.** Machinery: Sulzer Diesels and electric motors. Speed $\frac{14}{9}$ **kts. Completed 1931, but not taken over by Roumania until April, 1936.** Received considerable damage during the war, and is now of doubtful efficiency.

Minelayers (*Puitoare de Mine*).

1944, *courtesy M. Henri Le Masson.*

AMIRAL MURGESCU (Galatz, June 14, 1939), **CETETEA ALBA** (1940). *Standard:* displacement: 812 tons. Complement: 78. Dimensions: 252⅓ (*o.a.*) × 29½ × 8¼ feet (*mean* draught). Guns: 2—4 inch (dual purpose), 2—37 mm. AA., 2 D.C.T. Mines: 135. Machinery 2 Krupp Diesels. B.H.P.: 2,100 = 16 kts. Radius of action: 3,400 miles at 12 kts. (Existence of second ship has been questioned.)

Submarine Depot Ship (*Navă Bază*).

CONSTANTA (November 8, 1928). Laid down at the Quarnaro Yard, Fiume, August 15, 1927, completed in 1931. Displacement: 1,329 tons. Dimensions: 255¾ × 37 × 13¼ feet. Guns: 2—4 inch, 2—40 mm. Machinery: 2 sets Diesels. B.H.P.: 1,000 = 13 kts. Radius: 12,000 miles. Fitted with engineering and torpedo shops; bakery; torpedo loading room; salvage, diving and submarine signalling apparatus.

(Black Sea) Gunboats (*Canoniere*).

STIHI EUGEN. 1944, *courtesy M. Henri Le Masson.*

LOCOTENENT-COMANDOR STIHI EUGEN (ex-French *Friponne*, Lorient D.Y., 1916). **SUBLOCOTENENT GHICULESCU** (ex-French *Mignonne*, Brest D.Y., 1917)

Displacement: 443 and 344 tons respectively. Dimensions: 199¾ × 22½ × 9¼ and 7¾ feet, respectively. Guns: 2—3·9 inch, 2 M.G. Machinery: 2 sets of Sulzer Diesel motors. B.H.P. 900 = 15 kts. Fuel carried: 30 tons oil = 3000 miles (10 kts.), 1600 miles (15 kts.) Complement: 50.

Notes.—Purchased from French Navy, Jan. 9, 1920. Entered service Jan. 15, 1920. Are differentiated by coloured rings around crowsnest and initials on bow. Names are those of naval officers killed in action, 1916–18.

Royal Yachts (*Jachturi Regele*).

LUCEAFARUL. *Added* 1937, *courtesy Messrs. G. L. Watson & Co. (Designers).*

LUCEAFARUL (ex-*Nahlin*). (Clydebank, 1930). Purchased 1937. Displacement, 2,050 tons. Dimensions: 250 (*w.l.*), 296 (*o.a.*) × 36 × — feet. Machinery: 4 Brown-Curtis geared turbines. 2 shafts. S.H.P.: 4,000 = 17·5 kts. Boilers: 2 Yarrow. Oil fuel.

TAIFUN (J. Samuel White & Co. Ltd., Cowes, 1938). Wood. 34 tons Thames measurement. Dimensions: 54 × 12½ × 3 feet. Machinery: 2 petrol motors. 2 shafts.

(Black Sea) Sail Training Ship (*Navă Şcoală*).

1940, *Official.*

MIRCEA (Blohm & Voss, Hamburg, Sept. 22, 1938). Displacement: 1,604 tons. Dimensions: 239½ (*o.a.*), 267⅓ (*with bowsprit*) × 39⅓ × 16½ feet. Auxiliary M.A.N. 6-cylinder Diesel. B.H.P.: 500 = 9·5 kts. Sail area: 18,830 sq. ft. Complement: 83 + 140 midshipmen for training. Laid down April 30, 1938, and delivered March 29, 1939.

Miscellaneous

Monitors (*Monitoare*)

Note.—With exception of *Bratianu* class, all ships on this page are named after Roumanian provinces acquired after the War of 1914–18. Two are reported to have been sunk, but this lacks confirmation.

(Now has 2 white bands around funnel. Has flush deck forward.)

BUCOVINA (ex-Austro-Hungarian *Sava*, launched 1915). Displacement, 541 tons. Dimensions: 190¼ × 33·8 × 4¼ feet. Guns: 2—4.7 inch, 45 cal. Skoda (paired in single turret forward) + 2—4.7 inch, 10 cal. howitzers (fortress type, singly mounted in pits with cupola protection), 2—66 m/m. (AA., twin-mounted in turret), 2—47 m/m., and 6 M.G. 1—24 inch searchlight. Armour: 1½" Belt and Bulkheads, 1" Deck, 2" C.T., 2" Turret and Cupolas. 3 magazines with water-jackets and electric-controlled refrigerators. Designed H.P. 1600 = 12 kts. Boilers: Yarrow. Fuel: 75 tons, oil *only*. Complement, 90 to 100. Built under 1914-15 Austro-Hungarian Naval Programme, completed 1915. Interned at Novi Sad 1919-20 and handed over by Yugo-Slavs at Orsova early in 1921. Sister ship, *Drava*, now unit of Yugo-Slav Danube Flotilla.

L CATARGIU. 1934.

ION C. BRĂTIANU (1907), **MIHAIL KOGĂLNICEANU** (1907), **ALEXANDRU LAHOVARI** (1908), and **LASCĂR CATARGIU** (1907). Displacement: 670 tons. Complement, 110. Dimensions: 208¼ × 33¾ × 5¼ feet. Guns (Skoda): 3—4.7 inch, 35 cal. (2—4.7 inch howitzers removed during the War), 1—3 inch. AA., 2—47 m/m., 2 M.G. 1—30.7 inch searchlight. Armour: 1½" Belt, 1" Deck, 3"—2" Turrets. H.P. 1800 = 13 kts. Coal: 60 tons. Built by Stabilimento Tecnico Triestino, at Trieste, in sections, re-erected at Galatz. Deck cabins, military masts and howitzers removed during the War, and funnel modified. All named after nineteenth century Roumanian statesmen. Are the heaviest armoured ships on the Danube.

BASARABIA (ex-Austro-Hungarian *Inn*, launched 1915). Displacement, 541 tons. Dimensions: 203½ (*o.a.*) × 34¼ × 4¼ feet. Guns: 2—4.7 inch, 45 cal. + 3—4.7 inch, 10 cal. howitzers, 2—47 m/m., 9 M.G. Armour: 1½" Belt and Bulkheads, 1" Deck, 2" Turret and Cupolas, 2" C.T. Designed I.H.P. 1500 = 12 kts. Boilers: Yarrow. Fuel: 70 tons, oil *only*. Complement, 100. Built under Austro-Hungarian 1912 Naval Programme; interned at Novi Sad 1919-20, handed over by Yugo-Slavs at Orşova early in 1921. Sister ship, *Vardar*, now unit of Yugo-Slav Danube Flotilla is shown above.

1922 *Photo.*

ARDEAL (ex-Austro-Hungarian *Temes*, 1904). Displacement: 443 tons. Complement, 80 to 90. Dimensions: 183½ × 31¼ × 3¾ feet. Guns: 2—4.7 inch, 35 cal., 1—3.5 inch AA., 2—47 m/m., 4 M.G. Armour: 1½" Belt, 3" and 1½" Turrets, 1½" Bulkheads, 1" Deck. H.P. 1400 = 10 kts. Fuel capacity: 60 tons. Was originally built as a sister-ship to *Sava*, of Yugo-Slav Navy. While serving on Danube as Austro-Hungarian *Temes*, she was sunk in October, 1914, but was raised in June, 1916, and entirely rebuilt 1916-17; she is thus, compared with others of the same original design, a practically new Monitor. Re-entered service April, 1917. Interned at Novi Sad, 1919-20; handed over at Orşova by Yugo-Slavs early in 1921. Easily identified by her tall, thin funnel and raised gun aft, mounted during reconstruction, 1916-17. No other Monitor exists with this arrangement, except Yugo-Slav *Morava*, and her guns are not all in turrets.

Note.—*Ardeal* is the Roumanian name for the province of Transylvania.

Old Torpedo Boats (*Torpiloare*).

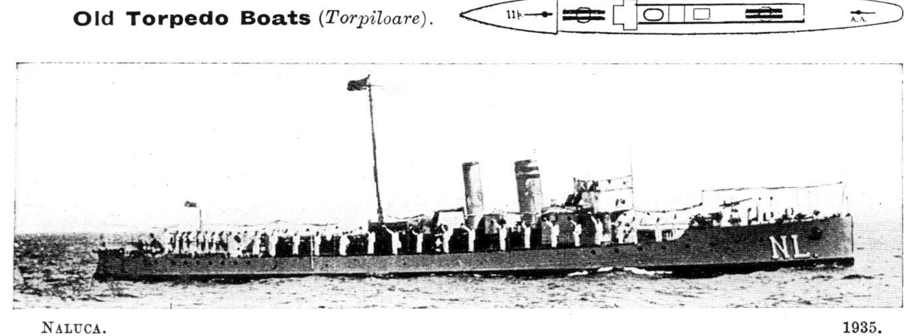

NALUCA. 1935.

2 Ex-Austrian boats: ***Năluca*** (ex-*82F*), ***Smeul*** (ex-*83F*), (Ganz-Danubius Co., Porto Ré, Fiume, 1913-14.) Displacement: 256 tons. Dimensions: 189¾ × 19 × 5 feet. Guns: 2—11 pdr., 2 M.G. No tubes. 1—16·5 inch S.L. Machinery: Turbines. S.H.P.: 5,000 = 24 kts. Boilers: Yarrow. Fuel: 20 tons coal + 34 tons oil. *Smeul* = Dragon. *Năluca* = Phantom.

RUSSIA (SOVIET UNION)

It is extremely difficult to secure accurate information regarding the Russian Navy, but the particulars given in these pages have been revised and compared with data from reliable sources.

Displacements of more important ships are standard.

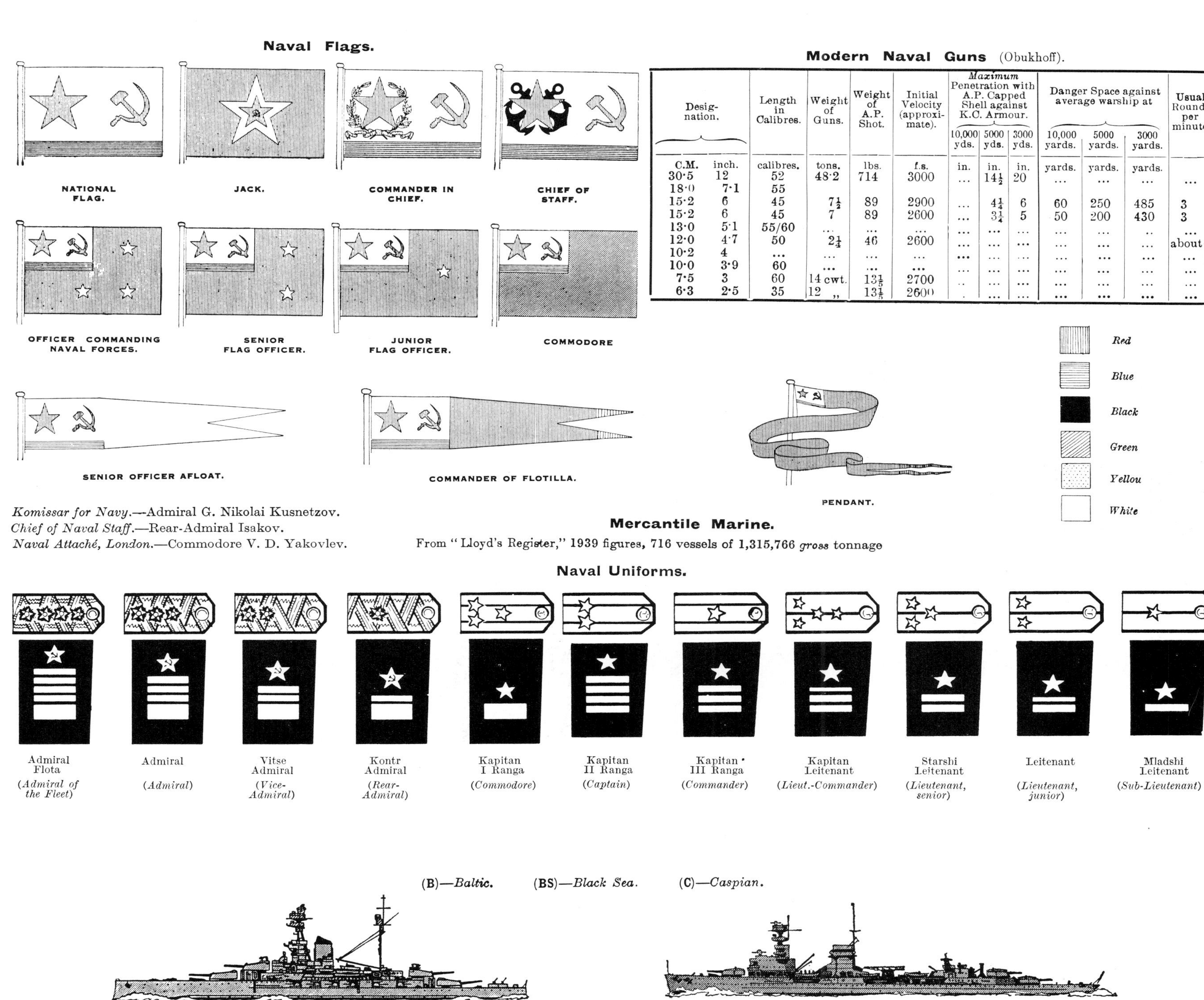

Modern Naval Guns (Obukhoff).

Designation.		Length in Calibres.	Weight of Guns.	Weight of A.P. Shot.	Initial Velocity (approximate).	*Maximum* Penetration with A.P. Capped Shell against K.C. Armour.			Danger Space against average warship at			Usual Rounds per minute.
						10,000 yds.	5000 yds.	3000 yds.	10,000 yards.	5000 yards.	3000 yards.	
C.M.	inch.	calibres.	tons.	lbs.	f.s.	in.	in.	in.	yards.	yards.	yards.	
30·5	12	52	48·2	714	3000	...	14½	20	...	...	...	...
18·0	7·1	55										
15·2	6	45	7½	89	2900	...	4¼	6	60	250	485	3
15·2	6	45	7	89	2600	...	3¼	5	50	200	430	3
13·0	5·1	55/60	...	...	...	...	...	...	...	...	..	...
12·0	4·7	50	2¼	46	2600	...	...	...	...	...	...	about 4
10·2	4	...	...	...	...	...	...	...	...	...	...	...
10·0	3·9	60	...	...	...	...	...	...	...	...	...	...
7·5	3	60	14 cwt.	13⅕	2700	..	...	...	...	...	...	...
6·3	2·5	35	12 „	13⅕	2600	.	...	...	...	...	...	...

Komissar for Navy.—Admiral G. Nikolai Kusnetzov.
Chief of Naval Staff.—Rear-Admiral Isakov.
Naval Attaché, London.—Commodore V. D. Yakovlev.

Mercantile Marine.

From "Lloyd's Register," 1939 figures, 716 vessels of 1,315,766 *gross* tonnage

(B)—*Baltic.* (BS)—*Black Sea.* (C)—*Caspian.*

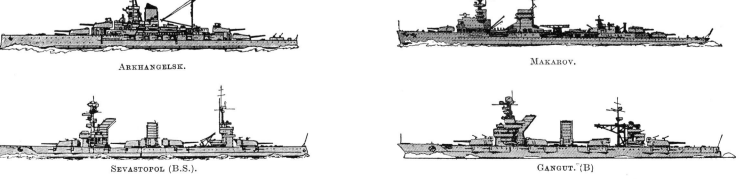

ARKHANGELSK.

MAKAROV.

SEVASTOPOL (B.S.).

GANGUT. (B)

RUSSIA (SOVIET UNION)

Silhouettes

(B)—*Baltic*. (BS)—*Black Sea*. (C)—*Caspian*.

Cruisers

KIROV *class*. (B) and (B.S.)
(Individual ships may vary.)

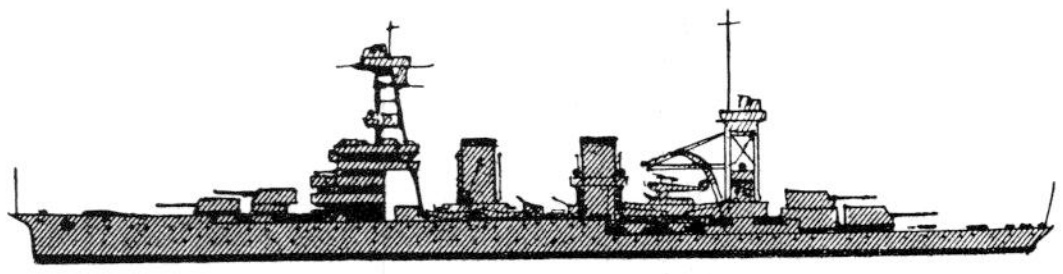

KRASNI-KAVKAZ. (B.S.)

KRASNI KRIM.

MURMANSK. (B.)

Destroyers

GROMKI *class*. (B)

LENINGRAD *class*. (B)

SILNI *class*. (B and B.S.)

BEZPOSHTADNI *type*. (B.S.)

Ex-REGELE FERDINAND.
Ex-REGINA MARIA.

Torpedo Craft and Sloops

NEZAMOSHNIK, ZHELESNIAKOV. (B.S.)

URITSKI *class*. (B)

DERZKI *class*.

MARKIN *class*. (C)

Ex-Z 33.

Ex-KARL GALSTER.

Ex-E. STEINBRINCK, *ex*-F. IHN.

KONSTRUKTOR. (B)

Ex-F 7.

AMETIST. (B)

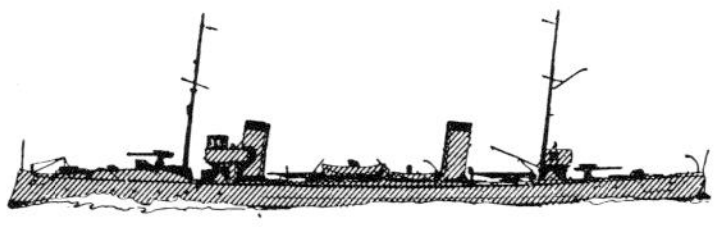

MARTINOV *class*. (B)

Ex-T 12, *ex*-T 17.

SASOVIETZ *class*. (B. and Far East.)

SHTORM *class*. (B., B.S. and Far East.)

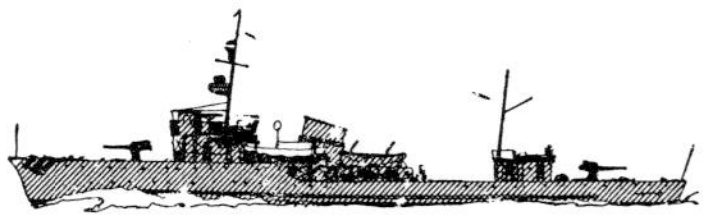

DZERZHINSKI *type* (Far East).

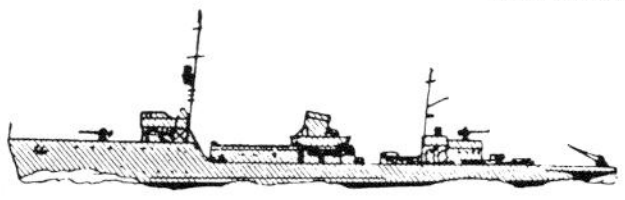

FUGAS *class* and later minelayers.
(B. and Far East).

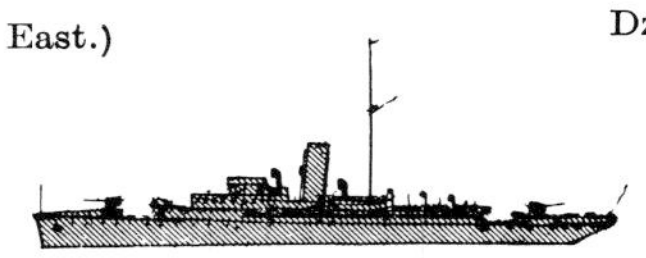

VOROVSKY (B.S.)

RUSSIA (SOVIET UNION)

(B)—*Baltic.* (BS)—*Black Sea.* (C)—*Caspian.*

Silhouettes

Auxiliaries

SVIR. (B)

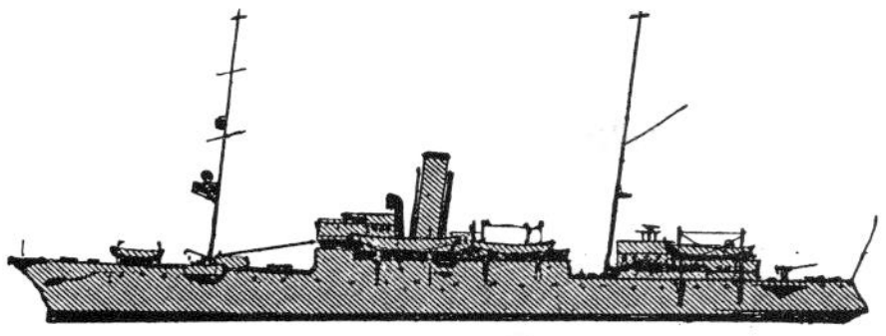

DEVIATOYE-YANVARYA. (B) PERVOYE-MAYA. (B.S.)
(Latter is without after superstructure.)

Ex-SMETONA (B)

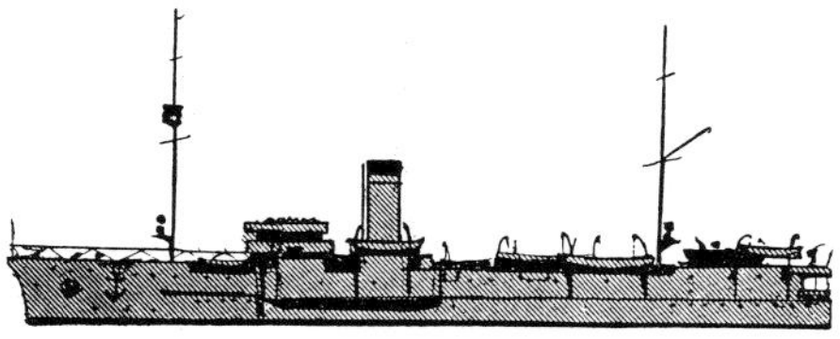

25 OKTIABRYA. (B)

UDARNIK (B)

VIRSAITIS (B)

KRASNI GCRN (B)

PIONER *class* (B)

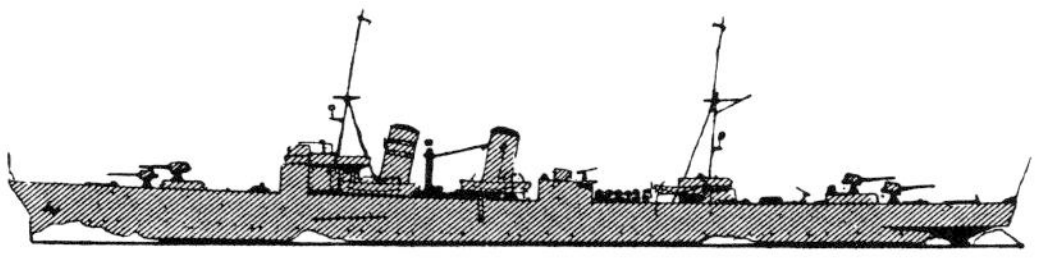

MARTY (B)

SEKSTANT (B)

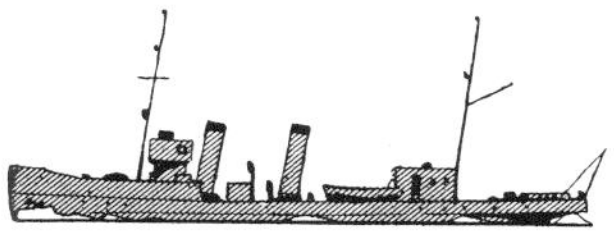

DOZORNI, RAZVYEDCHIK (B)

POLARNAYA SVIEZDA. (B)

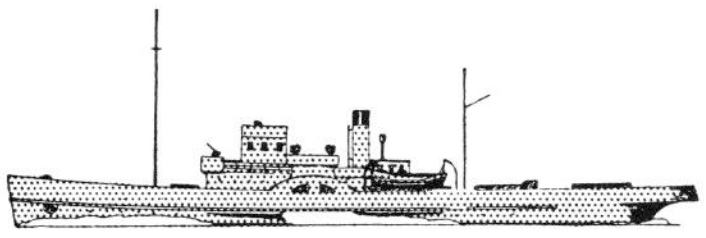

BERESINA *class.* (B)

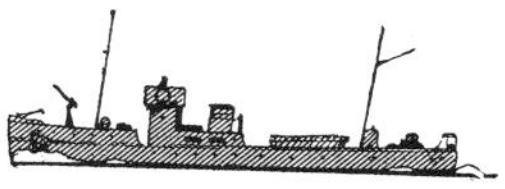

MU. 40–54. (B)

Submarines

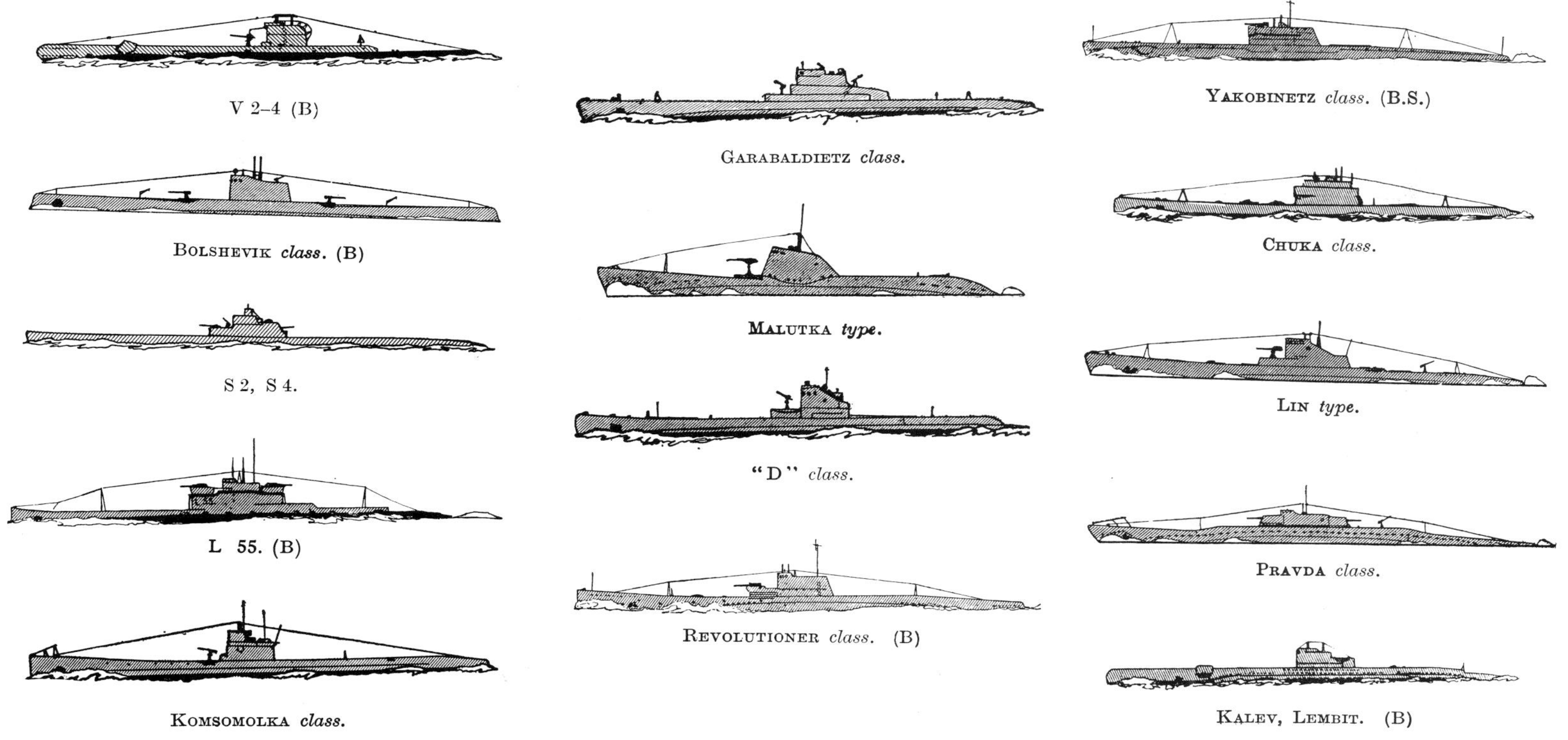

V 2–4 (B)

GARABALDIETZ *class.*

YAKOBINETZ *class.* (B.S.)

BOLSHEVIK *class.* (B)

CHUKA *class.*

MALUTKA *type.*

S 2, S 4.

LIN *type.*

"D" *class.*

L 55. (B)

PRAVDA *class.*

REVOLUTIONER *class.* (B)

KOMSOMOLKA *class.*

KALEV, LEMBIT. (B)

Battleships

ARKHANGELSK (ex-H.M.S. *Royal Sovereign*, April 29, 1915). Displacement, 29,150 tons, *about* 33,500 tons *full load*. Complement, 1009-1146.
Length (*pp.*) 580 feet, (*w.l.*) 614½ feet, (*o.a.*) 620½ feet. Beam, about 102½ feet. *Mean* draught, 28½ feet.

Guns:
- **8**—15 inch, 42 cal.
- **12**—6 inch, 50 cal.
- **8**—4 inch AA.
- Numerous 40 mm. and 20 mm. AA.
- (besides multi-M.G.)

Armour (H.T.):

Deck.
- 1″ Fo'xle over Battery
- 1¼″—1½″ Upper ......
- 2″, 1½″, 1″ Main ......
- 2½″, 1″ (forw'd), 4″, 3″, 2½″ (aft) Lower

Special Protection:
- 1½″—1″ Torp. Prot. b.h. between end barbettes.

(Also bulges, of varying types.)

Armour (Krupp):

Vertical
- 13″ Belt ....
- 6″—4″ Belt (ends) ....
- 1″ Belt (bow) ....
- 6″, 4″ Bulkheads (f. & a.)
- 6″ Battery ....
- 10″—7″ Barbettes .....
- 13″—5″ Gunhouses.....
- 6″—3″ C.T. Base .....
- 11″ C.T. (6″—3″ hood) .
- 6″ Fore com. tube ....
- 6″ Torp. con. tower ...
- 4″ Tube (T.C. tower) ..

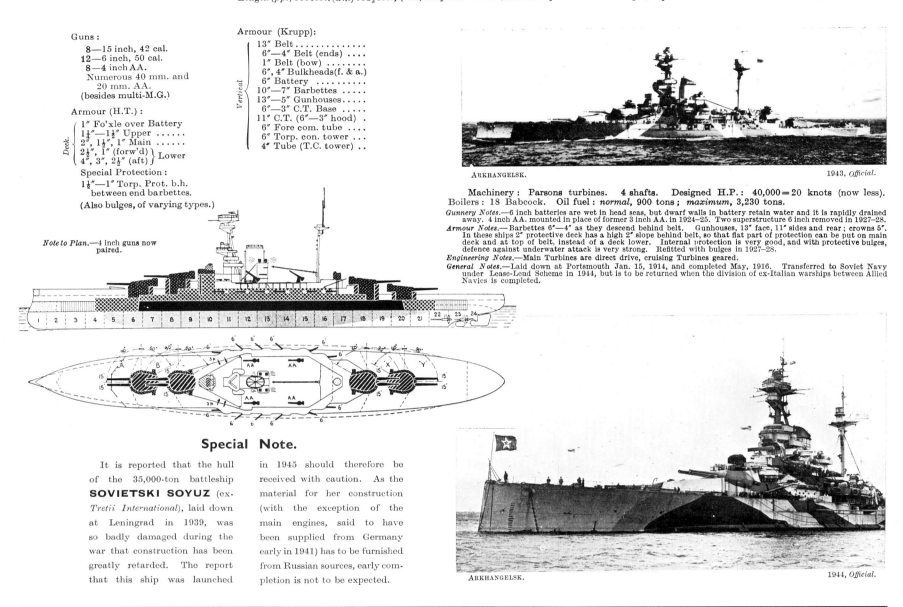

ARKHANGELSK. 1943, *Official*.

Note to Plan.—4 inch guns now paired.

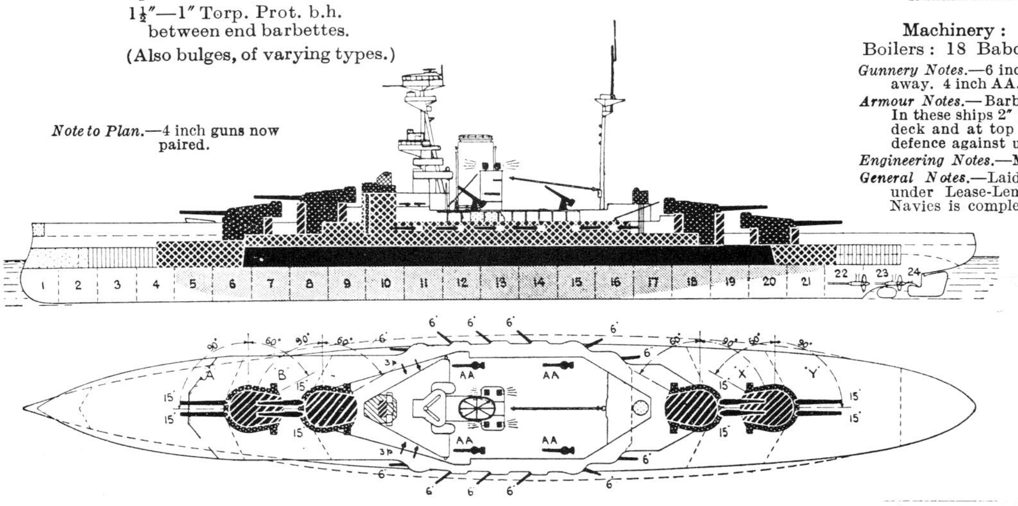

Machinery: Parsons turbines. 4 shafts. Designed H.P.: 40,000 = 20 knots (now less). Boilers: 18 Babcock. Oil fuel: *normal*, 900 tons; *maximum*, 3,230 tons.

Gunnery Notes.—6 inch batteries are wet in head seas, but dwarf walls in battery retain water and it is rapidly drained away. 4 inch AA. mounted in place of former 3 inch AA. in 1924–25. Two superstructure 6 inch removed in 1927–28.

Armour Notes.—Barbettes 6″—4″ as they descend behind belt. Gunhouses, 13″ face, 11″ sides and rear; crowns 5″. In these ships 2″ protective deck has a high 2″ slope behind belt, so that flat part of protection can be put on main deck and at top of belt, instead of a deck lower. Internal protection is very good, and with protective bulges, defence against underwater attack is very strong. Refitted with bulges in 1927–28.

Engineering Notes.—Main Turbines are direct drive, cruising Turbines geared.

General Notes.—Laid down at Portsmouth Jan. 15, 1914, and completed May, 1916. Transferred to Soviet Navy under Lease-Lend Scheme in 1944, but is to be returned when the division of ex-Italian warships between Allied Navies is completed.

Special Note.

It is reported that the hull of the 35,000-ton battleship **SOVIETSKI SOYUZ** (ex-*Tretii International*), laid down at Leningrad in 1939, was so badly damaged during the war that construction has been greatly retarded. The report that this ship was launched in 1945 should therefore be received with caution. As the material for her construction (with the exception of the main engines, said to have been supplied from Germany early in 1941) has to be furnished from Russian sources, early completion is not to be expected.

ARKHANGELSK. 1944, *Official*.

GANGUT (ex-*Oktiabrskaya Revolutia*, ex-*Gangut*, October 7, 1911).
SEVASTOPOL (ex-*Pariskaya Kommuna*, ex-*Sevastopol*, June 20, 1911).

Standard displacement, 23,606 and 23,256 tons, respectively; *full load*, over 26,000 tons. Complement, 1125 (1230 as flagship).

Length (*w.l.*) 590½; (*o.a.*) 619 feet. Beam, 87 feet. *Mean* draught, 27½ feet.

Guns (*Gangut*):
- **12**—12 inch, 52 cal.
- **10**—4·7 inch, 50 cal.
- **8**—3 inch AA.
- **12**—37 mm. AA.

Guns (*Sevastopol*):
- **12**—12 inch, 52 cal.
- **16**—4·7 inch, 50 cal.
- **6**—3 inch AA.
- **16**—37 mm. AA.

Torpedo tubes (18 inch):
4 *submerged.*

Armour (Krupp):
- 8¾″ Belt (amidships) ...
- 5″-2″ Belt (ends)
- 3″-4″ Internal belt (*see notes*)
- 3″ Deck ....
- 12″-10″ Turrets.........
- 8″ Turret bases.........
- 6″ Battery...............
- 10″ Conning tower.... ..

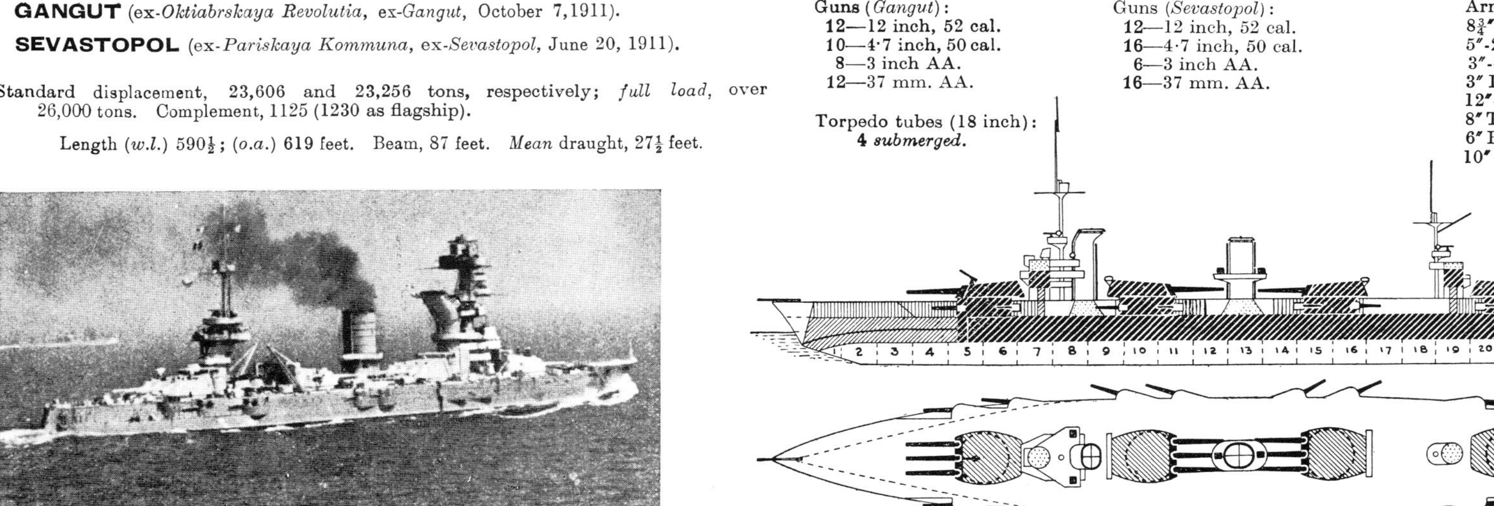

SEVASTOPOL 1944, *Pictorial Press*.

Battleships

Machinery: Parsons turbine. 4 shafts. Designed H.P. 42,000=23 kts. Boilers: 25 Yarrow in *Gangut*, 22 of 3-drum type in *Sevastopol* (installed 1938). Coal ***normal***, 1,000 tons; ***maximum***, 2000 tons. Also 1,170 tons oil. Radius of action: 900 miles at 23 kts., 4,000 miles at 16 kts.

Gunnery Notes.—The port plate above each gun is in the form of a hinged flap, allowing each 12-inch gun to elevate to 30—40° *maximum*. Arcs of fire: End triple 12-inch barbettes, 310°; central barbettes, 130° *each beam*; aft group of 4—4·7 inch, 90°; other 4·7 inch, 85°. Anti-aircraft armament extended in recent years.

Armour Notes.—Belt is about 15 feet wide, 5 feet of it below water, uniform thickness. There is a *secondary* 3"-4" internal belt 11 feet inboard above protective deck, extending between the end barbettes. The space between main belt and internal belts is divided up into w.t. compartments.

Name	*Builder*	*Machinery*	*Laid down*	*Completed*	*Trials: Full power*	*Boilers*	*Best recent speed*
Sevastopol	Baltic Works	Baltic Works	June,'09	Jan. '15	About 50,000=23·4	Yarrow	16
Gangut	Galernii	Franco-Rus. Works	June,'09	Jan. '14			

General Notes.—The late Gen. Vittorio Cuniberti prepared the original designs for this type. The Ministry of Marine afterwards altered the plans to include Russian ideas of armouring, ice-breaking bows and other special features. Further, to obtain a higher speed, hull design is relatively lighter than in contemporary battleships of other fleets. Said to be most unhealthy, insanitary and badly ventilated. Early in 1930 *Sevastopol* proceeded to Black Sea where she was refitted. *Gangut* refitted 1926–28. A third ship, *Petropavlovsk* (ex-*Marat*), was so badly damaged forward by enemy air attack at Kronstadt in 1941 that she is reported to have been scrapped.

GANGUT. 1935, *Nautical Photo Agency.*

Special Note.

Finnish Coast Defence Ship **VAINAMOINEN**, described and illustrated, has recently been acquired by Soviet Navy.

Aircraft Carrier

KRASNAYA ZNAMYA *Completing?*

Displacement: 22,000 tons. Complement: .

Dimensions: 722 × 92 × — feet.

Guns:
12—4 inch AA.

Aircraft: 60. Machinery: Geared turbines. Speed: 30 kts.

Note.—*Krasnaya Znamya* is said to have been laid down at Leningrad in 1939, and may have been launched in 1945. Existence of a second ship named *Voroshilov* is decidedly doubtful. An aircraft carrier named *Stalin*, reported to exist in Black Sea, is now believed to be only a small seaplane carrier (vide a later page).

Cruisers

(KIROV CLASS—4 Ships).

KIROV (Dec. 1, 1936), **MAKSIM GORKI** (Dec. 1937), **MOLOTOV** (Feb. 23, 1939), **VOROSHILOV** (1940). Displacement: 8,800 tons. Complement: 624.

Length: 613½ (*pp.*), 627¼ feet (*o.a.*). Beam: 64 feet. Draught: 17 feet (*mean*), 21 feet (*max.*)

Guns:
9—7·1 inch.
8—4 inch AA.
10—37 mm. AA.
6 M.G.
Torpedo tubes: 6—21 inch (in triple deck mountings).
Mines: Stowage for **60.**

Armour:
2"—3" Side.
2" Deck.
3"—4" Gunhouses.
4" C.T.

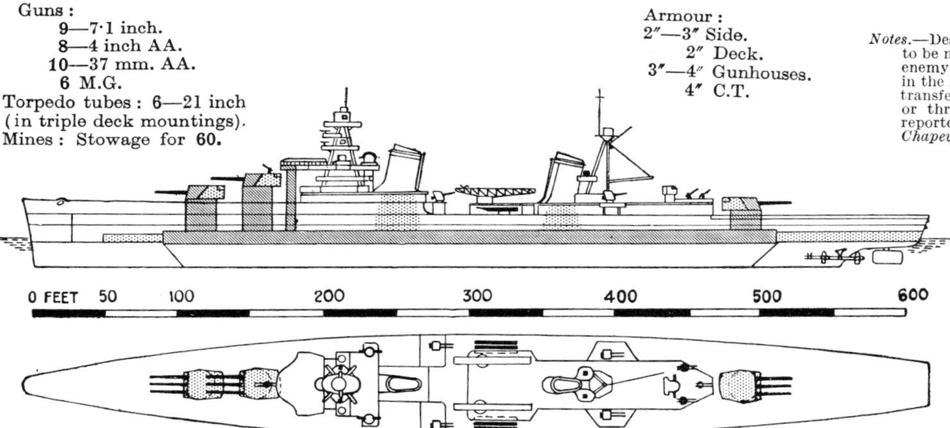

Machinery: Geared turbines with Diesels for cruising speeds. 4 shafts. S.H.P.: 100,000 = 35 kts. (actually less). Boilers: 6 Yarrow or Normand. Fuel: 1,280 tons.

Name.	*Builder.*	*Machinery.*	*Laid down.*	*Completed.*
Kirov	Putilov D.Y.	Tosi, Taranto	1934	Aug., 1937
M. Gorki	Putilov D.Y.	Tosi, Taranto	1934	1939
Molotov	Marti Yard, Nikolaiev		1935	1940–41?
Voroshilov	Marti Yard, Nikolaiev		1936	1940–41?

Notes.—Design and technical direction of construction said to have been furnished by Ansaldo. Two more ships, said to be named *Frunze* and *Kaganovich*, under construction at Nikolaiev, were wrecked by high explosives before the enemy occupied that port in August, 1941. At least one cruiser of this type (probably *M. Gorki*) was badly damaged in the Baltic in August 1941. Germans claimed to have destroyed the incomplete cruiser (ex-*Lützow*) which they transferred to Soviet Navy early in 1940, but it is possible she still exists and may yet go into service. Two or three more ships of *Kirov* type are said to be under construction, but names *Kubyshev* and *Orjonikidze*, reported as assigned to them, are now known to be borne by destroyers. Latest information suggests their names as *Chapev* and *Chekalov*.

MOLOTOV. 1944, *Pictorial Press*

MAKAROV (ex-*Nürnberg*) (Deutsche Werke, Kiel, Dec. 8, 1934.)
Standard Displacement: 6,000 tons. Complement: 656.
Dimensions: 557¾ (*pp.*), 603 (*o.a.*) × 54 × 14¼ feet (*mean* draught).

Guns:
9—5·9 inch, 50 cal.
8—3·5 inch AA.
8—37 mm. AA.
4 M.G.

Torpedo Tubes:
12—21 inch, *above water* (tripled).

Armour:
3"—4" Vert. Side.
2" Gunhouses.
3" C.T.

MAKAROV. 1936, *Renard.*

Cruisers

Note to Plan.—Aircraft formerly carried is believed to have been removed.

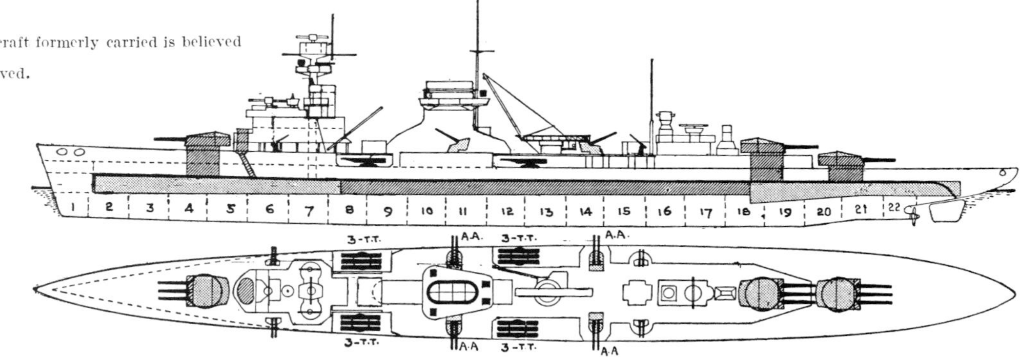

Machinery : Geared turbines. 3 shafts. S.H.P. : 60,000, plus Diesels of 12,000 B.H.P. for cruising. Speed : 32 kts. Boilers : 6 Marine type.

Notes.—Laid down early in 1934 and commissioned at beginning of November, 1935. Taken over by Soviet Navy in 1946. Named after the admiral commanding the Russian Far Eastern Fleet who lost his life when his flagship was mined outside Port Arthur in 1904.

MAKAROV. 1938, *Ferd. Urbahns.*

MAKAROV. 1944.

MURMANSK (ex-U.S.S. *Milwaukee*, March 24, 1921).

Displacement : 7,050 tons. Complement : 458.

Length : (*w.l.*) 550, (*o.a.*) 555½ feet.

Beam : 55⅓ feet. Draught : 13½ (*mean*), 20 feet *max.*

Guns :
10—6 inch, 53 cal.
6—3 inch AA.
8—40 mm. AA.
14—20 mm. AA.

Torpedo tubes :
6—21 inch (tripled) *above water.*

Armour :
3″ Side.
1½″ Upper deck.

Aircraft : 2.
Catapult : 1.

Machinery : Westinghouse geared turbines. 4 shafts. S.H.P. 90,000 = 35 kts. (now less). Boilers : 12 Yarrow. Oil fuel : 2,000 tons.

Notes.—Laid down Dec. 13, 1918, by Todd, Tacoma, and completed for the U.S. Navy in June, 1923. Transferred to Soviet Navy under Lend-Lease scheme, April 20, 1944.

KRASNI KAVKAZ (ex-*Admiral Lazarev*, June, 1916. Nikolaiev).

KRASNI KAVKAZ. 1934 *Photo, favour of Lieut. R. T. T. Falkner, R.N.*

Displacement : 8,030 tons. **Complement** : 850. **Length**, 530 feet. **Beam**, 50½ feet. **Draught**, 20½ feet.

Guns : **4**—7·1 inch, **12**—4 inch AA., **2**—3 inch AA., **4**—45 mm. AA., **8**—37 mm. AA., **14** M.G.

Tubes : **12**—21 inch (tripled).

Mines : 100.

Aircraft. 1, with catapult.

Correction to Plan.—Torpedo Tubes are tripled and AA. guns paired.

Armour :
2″—3″ Side.
1″ Deck.
3″ Gunhouses.
3″ C.T.

Machinery : Brown-Boveri Turbines. 2 shafts. H.P. : 55,000 = 30 kts. (actual best speed, 25 kts.). **Boilers** : 13 Yarrow. **Coal** : 540 tons. **Oil** : 690 tons = 3,700 miles at 14 kts.

Note.—Laid down in 1914, the construction of this ship was held up for many years. As completed, *Krasni Kavkaz* mounts an entirely different armament from *Chervonaya Ukraïna*, to which she was originally to have been a sister. She is said to be fitted for minelaying. Germans claimed to have sunk either this ship or *Krasni Krim*, but confirmation of the report is lacking.

KRASNI KRIM (ex-*Profintern*, ex-*Sovnarkom*, ex-*Klara Zetkin*, ex-*Svietlana*, June 1915.)

Displacement, 6,934 tons. **Complement**, 684. **Length**, 507¾ feet. **Beam**, 50⅓ feet. **Draught**, 18⅓ feet.

Guns :
15—5·1 inch, 55 cal.
8—4 in. AA.
4—45 mm. AA.
10—37 mm. AA.
Torpedo Tubes (21 inch) :
6 in Triple Mounts.
Mines : 100.

Note to Plan—Now carries T.T. above sections 9 and 13.

Armour :
2″ Side at w.f. amidships ....
1″ Deck ....
3″ Gun shields ....
3″ Conning tower .....

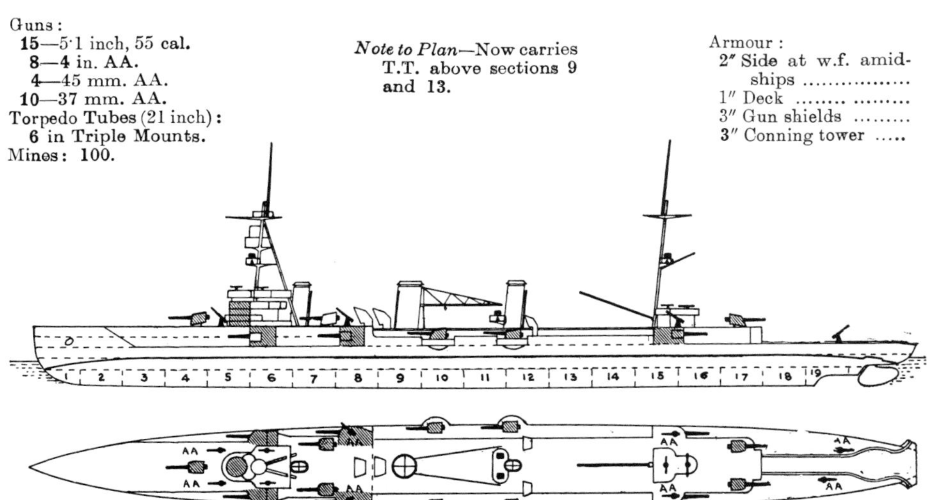

Krasni Krim.

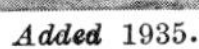

Added 1935.

Krasni Krim (smoke conceals after funnel). 1944, *Pictorial Press*

Machinery : A.E.G. turbines. 2 shafts. **Boilers** : 13 Yarrow. **S.H.P.** 50,000 = 29·5 kts., (actual best speed is under 25 kts.). **Coal** : 540 tons. **Oil** : 690 tons. **Radius of action** : 470 miles at full speed, 3,700 at 14 kts.

General Notes.—Built under the 1912 Naval Programme and laid down in 1913 at Reval. Construction was held up for many years, being completed in December, 1924. Germans claimed to have sunk either this ship or *Krasni Kavkaz*, but confirmation of the report is lacking.

Destroyers (*Eskadrenyi Minonosetz*)

1944, *courtesy M. Henri Le Masson.*

Ex-Z 30**, ex-**Z 33 (1942). Displacement : 2,600 tons. Dimensions : 393½ × 39⅓ × 9½ feet. Guns : **4**—5·9 inch, **8**—37 mm. AA., **4**—20 mm. AA. (*Z* 33 reported to have had this armament reduced). Tubes : **8**—21 inch. Machinery : Geared turbines. S.H.P.: 72,000 = 36 kts. 2 shafts. High pressure watertube boilers.

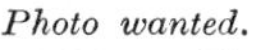

Photo wanted.

Ex-T 33 (1942). (Ex-German.) Displacement : 1,100 tons. Dimensions : 295 (*pp.*) 313 (*o.a.*) × 31 × 9 feet. Guns : **4**—4·1 inch, **4**—37 mm. AA., **8**—20 mm. AA., **2** D.C.T. Tubes : **6**—21 inch. Stowage for 70 mines. Machinery : Geared turbines. 2 shafts. S.H.P. : 35,000 = 31 kts. Boilers : 3 Schulz. Oil fuel : 290 tons.

Destroyers

Opitni Class

VNUSHITELNI. 1941, *Official.*

Drozd (ex-*Stoiki*), ***Letuchi, Likhoi, Opitni*** (ex-*Serge Orjonikidze*), ***Silni, Slavni, Storoshevoi, Strashni, Strogi, Stroini, Sviryepi*** (1939–45). All reported in Baltic, but only six effective.
Raziastchi, Volochevka (1938–45). Both in Far East.
Vnimatelni, Vnushitelni (1939). In Black Sea.

Displacement: *ca.* 2,050 tons. Dimensions: 387 × $38\frac{1}{2}$ × $15\frac{1}{2}$ feet. Guns: **4**—5·1 inch, **3**—3 inch 50 cal. AA., **2**—45 mm. AA., **4**—37 mm. AA., **4** M.G. Tubes: **6**—21 inch. Stowage for 70 mines reported. Machinery: Geared turbines. 2 shafts. S.H.P.: 55,000 = 36 kts. Boilers of 3-drum type. Oil fuel.

Note.—Other names reported but not confirmed are *Skori, Sposobni, Statni, Surovi.* Above figure is probably full load displacement.

K. GALSTER 1939 *Schäfer.*

Ex-***Karl Galster*** (1938). (Ex-German.) Displacement: 2,500 tons. Dimensions: 384 × 38 × $9\frac{1}{2}$ feet. Guns: **5**—5 inch, **4**—37 mm. AA., **4**—20 mm. AA. Tubes: **8**—21 inch. Machinery: Geared turbines. 2 shafts. S.H.P.: 67,000 = 36 kts. High pressure watertube boilers.

F. IHN. *Added* 1940, *Renard.*

Ex-***Erich Steinbrinck*** (1936), *ex*-***Friedrich Ihn*** (1935). (Both ex-German.) Displacement: 2,300 tons. Dimensions: 374 × 37 × $9\frac{1}{3}$ feet. Guns: **5**—5 inch, **4**—37 mm. AA., **4**—20 mm. AA. Tubes: **8**—21 inch. Machinery: Geared turbines. 2 shafts. S.H.P.: 65,000 = 36 kts. High pressure watertube boilers.

Leningrad Class. (Only 5 of these are believed to be in effective existence.)

LENINGRAD (Baltic). 1937, *courtesy H. C. Bywater, Esq.*

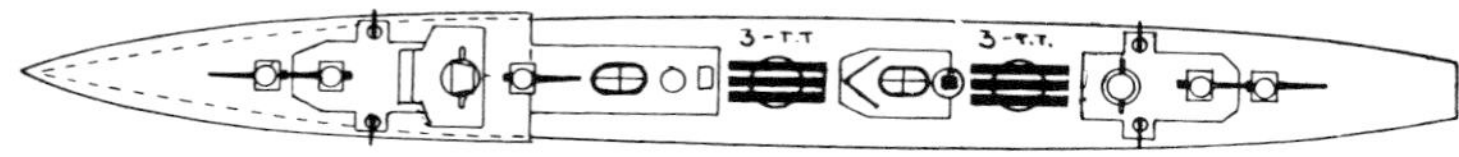

17 *French type:* ***Leningrad*** (1935), ***Baku*** (ex-*Arkhangelsk* ?), ***Kharbinsk, Tomsk, Tula, Tver, Petrosavodsk.*** All built at Leningrad. ***Ochakov, Kazan, Rostov, Tiflis, Sivash, Perekop, Stalinsk, Krasnoyarsk, Vernoleninsk, Tibilissi.*** All built in Black Sea yards. *Standard* displacement: 2,900 tons (3,500 *full load*). Dimensions: 430 (*pp.*) $459\frac{1}{3}$ (*o.a.*) × 45 × 14 feet. Guns: **5**—5·1 inch 55 cal., **2**—3 inch 50 cal. AA., **2**—37 mm. AA., **4** D.C.T. Tubes: **6**—21 inch (tripled). Fitted for minelaying. Machinery: Geared turbines. S.H.P.: 90,000 = 36 kts. (Trials of *Leningrad*, light, said to have given 39·3 kts.) Watertube boilers of 3-drum type. Oil fuel.

Note.—These ships resemble French *contretorpilleurs* of recent design, and construction of earlier units is understood to have been supervised by French technical experts. Reported to be poor sea boats, very wet forward. Majority of names given above must be regarded as doubtful, and it seems probable that the ships which were to have borne them were never built. It is possible one of Black Sea units listed may have been renamed *Kiev.*

Gromki Class.

GROMKI (Baltic). *Added* 1940.

BEZPOSHTADNI (Black Sea). 1942, *Official.*

Gremiastchi, Gromki, Grosni, Liepni, Opasni, (1936–41). All in Baltic or White Sea.
Ryani. In Far East.
Bezpokoini, Bezposhtadni, Bezupreshtni, Biedovi, Bodri, Bravi, Buini, Graveni, Metki, Molodetski, Ryeshitelni, Zadorni, Zavietni, Zhivoi, Zorki. All reported to be in Black Sea, but existence of so many must be regarded as somewhat doubtful pending further evidence.

Displacement: 1,860 tons. Dimensions: $380\frac{1}{2}$ × 36 × 13 feet. Guns: **4**—5·1 inch, **2**—3 inch 50 cal. AA., **4**—37 mm. AA., **1**—20 mm. AA., **8** D.C.T. Tubes: **6**—21 inch (tripled). Fitted for minelaying. Machinery: Geared turbines of Tosi design. 2 shafts. S.H.P.: 50,000 = 37 kts. Boilers of 3-drum type. Oil fuel.

Notes.—These destroyers are said to be better sea boats than *Leningrad* class, having less top weight. They are understood to be of Odero-Terni-Orlando design. Other names reported: *Razyarenni, Razumni, Subrazatelni.* Figure given above is suspected to be full load displacement.

Ex-REGINA MARIA (Note band around after funnel.) 1937, *R. Perkins.*

2 *Thornycroft type:* *Ex*-***Regele Ferdinand*** (Dec. 2, 1928), *ex*-***Regina Maria*** (March 2, 1929). Built at Naples to design of Messrs. Thornycroft, and captured from Roumanian Navy in 1944. Displacement: 1,821 tons. Dimensions: $334\frac{1}{2}$ × $31\frac{1}{2}$ × $11\frac{1}{2}$ feet. Guns (Bofors): **5**—4·7 inch, 50 cal., **1**—3 inch AA., **2**—40 mm. AA., **2** M.G. Tubes: **6**—21 inch (tripled). 50 mines carried. Machinery: Parsons geared turbines by Stab. Tecnico Triestino. 2 shafts. S.H.P.: 48,000 = 35 kts. Complement: 212.

7 Derzki Class.

ZHARKI. 1942, *Official.*

Derzki (ex-*Chelsea*, ex-*Crowninshield*, July 24, 1919), ***Doblestni*** (ex-*Georgetown*, ex-*Maddox*, Oct. 27, 1918), ***Dostoini*** (ex-*St. Albans*, ex-*Thomas*, July 4, 1918), ***Zharki*** (ex-*Brighton*, ex-*Cowell*, Nov. 23, 1918), ***Zhguchi*** (ex-*Leamington*, ex-*Twiggs*, Sept. 28, 1918), ***Zhivuchi*** (ex-*Richmond*, ex-*Fairfax*, Dec. 15, 1917), ***Zhostki*** (ex-*Roxborough*, ex-*Foote*, Dec. 14, 1918). Transferred from R.N., 1944.

Displacement: 1,060 to 1,090 tons. Dimensions: 309 (*w.l.*), $314\frac{1}{3}$ (*o.a.*) × $30\frac{1}{2}$ × $8\frac{1}{2}$ feet (*mean*). Guns: **2**—4 inch. several smaller. Machinery: Geared turbines. 2 shafts. S.H.P.: 24,200 = 35 kts. (now less). Boilers: 4. Oil fuel: 300–375 tons.

Note.—Two other destroyers of this type transferred at same date no longer exist, *Churchill* having been lost and *Lincoln* expended for spare fittings and machinery parts. Names are those of qualities, *e.g.*, *Derzki* = Audacious; *Doblestni* = Valiant; *Dostoini* = Worthy; *Zharki* = Ardent; *Zhguchi* = Fiery; *Zhivuchi* = Enduring; *Zhostki* = Enterprising.

Destroyers

2 Nezamoshnik Class.

1935, *J. Weinberg.*

Nezamoshnik (ex-*Zante*, 1917), **Zhelesniakov** (ex-*Petrovski*, ex-*Korfu*, 1917). Both built at Nikolaieff. Displacement: 1,323 tons and 1,308 tons respectively. Dimensions: $303\frac{1}{2} \times 29\frac{1}{2} \times 9$ feet. Armament: **4**—3·9 inch, **1**—3 inch AA., **1**—37 mm. AA., **12**—18 inch tubes, in triple mountings. Originally designed to carry 80 mines of pre-war pattern, but now have 45 of heavier type. Turbine engines. Oil fuel only: 390 tons. S.H.P.: 29,000 = 33 kts. (Actual speed considerably less.) Complement: 161. *Nezamoshnik* not completed till 1923, *Zhelesniakov* till 1925.

5 Uritski Class (*All fitted for minelaying.*)

KUBYSHEV. 1932.

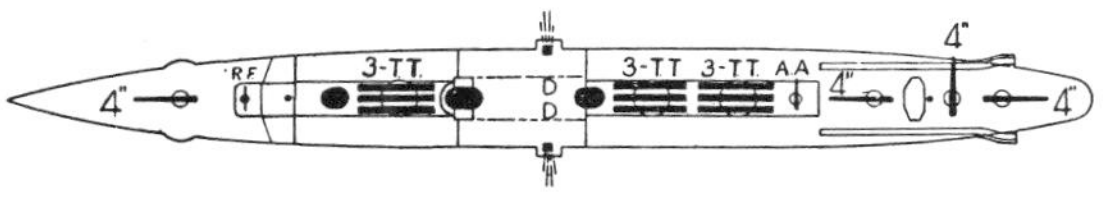

3 *Leningrad Metal Works:* **Uritski** (ex-*Zabiaka*, 1914), **Stalin** (ex-*Samson*), **Kubyshev** (ex-*Shadnov*, ex-*Rykov*, ex-*Kap. Kern*). All 1914–15.
2 *Putilov Works, Leningrad:* **Karl Liebknecht** (ex-*Kap.-Lt. Belli*), **Voikov** (ex-*Trotski*, ex-*Leit. Ilyin*). All 1914–15.

Displacement: 1,150 to 1,417 tons. Dimensions: $314\frac{3}{4}$ to $321\frac{1}{2} \times 30\frac{1}{2} \times 9\frac{3}{4}$ feet. Complement: 157. Guns: **4**—3·9 inch, **1**—3 inch AA., **1** M.G. Torpedo tubes: **9**—18 inch (tripled). All carry mines. Machinery: Turbines. S.H.P.: 30,000 = 28 to 30 kts. Thornycroft boilers. Oil fuel: 400 tons. All laid down under 1912 Programme, and mostly completed after War. *Kubyshev* and *K. Liebknecht* were not commissioned till 1927 and 1928, respectively.

Appearance Notes.—These destroyers vary in appearance according to builders. Some reported to have raking funnel tops. *Stalin* has been reconstructed and differs from rest of class in appearance. *Uritski* was reconstructed in 1937. *Stalin* and *Voikov* were last reported in Far East.

Rated as Patrol Vessels.

ALBATROSS (1940). Displacement: 920 tons. Dimensions: $279 \times 27\frac{1}{2} \times 10$ feet. Speed: 34 kts.

YASTREB (1939). Displacement: 842 tons. Dimensions: $275 \times 27\frac{1}{4} \times 9\frac{1}{2}$ feet. Guns: **3**—4 inch, **4**—37 mm. AA., **8** M.G. Speed: 36 kts.

MOLNYA, SERP, ZARNITZA (1937–39). Displacement: 670 tons. Dimensions: $236\frac{1}{3} \times 24\frac{2}{3} \times 9\frac{1}{2}$ feet. Guns: **2**—3·9 inch, **4**—37 mm. AA., **2** M.G. Tubes: **3**—18 inch. Stowage for 50 mines. Speed: 31·5 kts. Reported to be a great improvement on design of *Shtorm* class. (*Tucha* may have been lost.)

Added 1942.

1944, *courtesy M. Henri Le Masson.*

Ex-**T 17**, *ex*-**T 12** (1938–39). (Both ex-German.) Displacement: 600 tons. Dimensions: $267 \times 28\frac{1}{4} \times 6\frac{1}{4}$ feet. Guns: **2**—4·1 inch, **2**—37 mm. AA. Tubes: **6**—21 inch (tripled). Machinery: Geared turbines. 2 shafts. S.H.P.: 33,000 = 36 kts. Boilers: 2 Schulz.

Ex-**F 7** (1935). (Ex-German.) Displacement: 600 tons. Dimensions: 241 (*pp.*), $249\frac{1}{3}$ (*o.a.*) $\times 28\frac{3}{4} \times 8\frac{1}{4}$ feet (*mean* draught). Guns: **2**—4·1 inch, 50 cal., **4**—37 mm. AA., **2** M.G. and D.C.T. Machinery: Geared turbines. 2 shafts. S.H.P.: 9,000 = 28 kts. Boilers: 4 Schulz. Oil fuel: 245 tons. (Fitted for minelaying.)

Photo wanted.

KONSTRUKTOR 1932 *Photo.*

1 *Kondratenko* type: **Konstruktor** (ex-*Sibirski-Strelok*, Helsinki, 1906). 625 tons. Dimensions: $246 \times 27\frac{1}{2} \times 8\frac{1}{4}$ feet. Guns: **3**—3·9 inch, **2**—4 pdr. AA. Tubes: **1**—18 inch. 50 mines. H.P.: 7,300 = 25 kts. Coal: 215 tons. Complement: 101. (Serving as Leader of Minesweepers, Baltic.)

Torpedo Boats, etc.

1934 *Photo.*

Grom, Groza, Metel, Shkval, Shtorm, Siklon, Smertch, Snieg, Uragan, Vikhr, Viyuga (1932–6). Displacement: 635 tons. Complement: 72. Dimensions: 233 (*pp.*) $\times 24 \times 8\frac{1}{4}$ feet. Guns: **2**—3·9 inch, **2**—37 mm. AA., **4** M.G., **2** D.C.T. Tubes: **3**—18 inch (tripled). 50 Mines carried. Machinery: Geared turbines. 2 shafts. H.P.: 13,200 = 25 kts.

Notes.—Reported to be poorly constructed and to roll heavily, owing to excessive tophamper. *Shtorm* and *Shkval* stationed in Black Sea, *Vikhr* and 2 more in Far East, others in Baltic. *Purga*, of this type, wrecked in White Sea during autumn of 1938.

1934

Ametist (ex-*Sulev*, ex-*A* 32). Built at Elbing, 1916. (Sunk off Estonian coast, October, 1917, salved and refitted 1923.) Displacement, 228 tons. Dimensions: $165\frac{1}{2} \times 17\frac{1}{2} \times 6$ feet. Guns: **2**—3 inch, 50 cal. Torpedo tubes: **2**—18 inch, in double deck mounting. Can carry 10 mines. Designed S.H.P. 3500 = 26 kts. Oil: 50 tons = 975 miles at 20 kts. Complement, 35. Mainmast shortened 1932. Refitted, 1935.

Note.—This vessel was formerly a unit of the Estonian Navy, and previously German.

Submarines (*Podrodniya Lodki*)

Note.—About 100 submarines of seagoing types are believed to exist. Most of these are now known by numerals. These appear to change as vessels are transferred from one flotilla to another, increasing the confusion. Submarines allotted from the German Navy for experimental use include the former U 1057, 1058, 1064 (all 517-ton type), 1231 (type IXc, 740 tons), 2353 (233 tons), 2529, 3035, 3041, 3515 (all 1,600 tons).

"K" Class

1944, *Pictorial Press.*

K 1 and upwards (1939). (Total number uncertain.) Displacement: 1,390 tons. Dimensions: 308 × 23 × 13 feet. Guns: **2**—4 inch, **2**—45 mm. AA. Tubes: **10**—21 inch. Speed: 18 kts. Apparently developed from "P" type. May include 2 submarines built by public subscription in 1943 and said to be named *Chelyabinski Komsomoletz* and *Yaroslavski Komsomoletz.*

"D" Class.

1942, *Official.*

D 2, 4, 5 (1939). Displacement: 989 tons. Dimensions: 282 × 21⅓ × 12½ feet. Guns: **1**—4 inch, **1**—45 mm. AA., 1 M.G. Tubes: **8**—21 inch. Speed: 15 kts.

"V" Class.

V 4. *Added* 1940, *courtesy Messrs. Vickers-Armstrongs, Ltd.*

3 *Vickers-Armstrongs:* **V2** (ex-*Unbroken*, Nov. 4, 1941), **V3** (ex-*Unison*, Nov. 5, 1941), **V4** (ex-*Ursula*, Feb. 16, 1938). All built at Barrow, and transferred from Royal Navy in 1944. Displacement: 540/730 tons. Dimensions: 180 × 16 × 12¾ feet. Armament: **6**—21 inch tubes, **1**—3 inch gun. B.H.P.: 615/825 = 11·25/10 kts.

"S" Class

1937.

1944, *Pictorial Press.*

S 4, 9, 12—15, 31, 35, 51, 54—56, 101—104 (1937). Displacement: 780 tons. Dimensions: 256 × 21 × 13 feet. Guns: 1—4 inch, 1—45 mm. AA. Tubes: 6—21 inch. Speed: 21 kts. Appear to be enlarged editions of *Chuka* class.

"P" Class.

Added 1940.

Sviezda (*P* 2), **Iskra** (*P* 3), (1936). Displacement: 1,200/1,800 tons. Dimensions: 295½ × 26¼ × 10 feet. Guns: 2—4 inch, 45 cal., 2—45 mm. AA. Torpedo tubes: **10**—21 inch. Speed: 18 kts. Said to be quite a successful type, capable of rapid diving.

Italian type.

1942, *Pictorial Press.*

6 *Adriatico design:* **Blücher, Budenni, Chartist, Galler, Garibaldietz, Karbonari.** Completed 1933-35. Displacement: 1,039/1,335 tons. Guns: **1**—4 inch, 45 cal., **1**—37 mm. AA. Tubes: **6**—21 inch. Speed: 14/8·5 kts. In Black Sea.

"Chicha" Class.

No. 260. *Added* 1940.

1937.

Originally named **Sig** (313), **Lin** (305), **Delfin** (309), **Kassatka** (311), **Nalim, Osetr, Bitshok, Kesal, Paltus, Plotva, Skat, Som, Losos, Sterliad, Forel, Kumsa, Piksha, Semga, Treska, Bieluga, Peskar,** and others. Built 1935-38. Displacement: 650/748 tons. Dimensions: 190½ × 19½ × 13 feet. Guns: 2—45 mm. AA., 2 M.G. Tubes: **6**—21 inch. Reported to be minelayers. Speed 13/9 kts. Numbers reported include various figures from 101 to 428, the higher numbers being of a slightly improved design. Apparently those in Baltic and White Sea are numbered 301 and upwards; in Black Sea, 201 and upwards; and in Far East, 101 and upwards.

1942, *Pictorial Press.*

3 special boats: **Komsomolka, Komsomoletz, Dvigatel** (1933). Displacement: 889/1,212 tons. Dimensions: 265¾ × 21¾ × 14½ feet. Guns: **1**—4 inch, 45 cal., 1—1 pdr. AA., **2** M.G. Tubes: **8**—21 inch (6 bow, 2 stern). Other particulars believed to be similar to "*L*" class. First two built by subscription from Communist Youth movement. *Komsomolka* used for training.

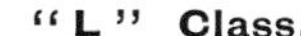

"L" Class.

YAKOBINETZ 1935, *J. Weinberg.*

1935.

Bezbojnik (*L* 4), ***Bezvirnik, Dekabrist*** (*L* 12), ***Gamarnik, Krasni Spania, Profilski Ukraina, Spartakovetz*** (*L* 13), ***Sviezdoshka, Yakobinetz*** (*L* 11). All in Black Sea. ***Frunzovetz, Krasnogvardietz*** (*L* 3), ***Leninetz, Mudrovetz, Narodovoletz*** (*L* 2), ***Revolutioner*** (*L* 1), ***Stalinetz, Sverdlovetz.*** All in Baltic (1929–35). Displacement: 896/1,318 tons. Complement: 44. Dimensions: 279 × 23 × 16½ feet. Guns: **1**—4 inch AA., **1**—37 mm. AA., **2** M.G. Torpedo tubes: **8**—21 inch (6 bow, 2 stern). Fitted for minelaying. H.P.: 2,500/1,200 = 15/8 kts. *Surface* radius: 7,000 at 9 kts. One of this class sank during exercises in Gulf of Finland, July, 1935; reported to have been salved. Another vessel of this type reported lost on trials. Highest number mentioned recently is *L* 25.

LEMBIT. 1937, *Wright & Logan.*

1 *Vickers-Armstrongs* (*Barrow*): **Lembit** (July 7, 1936). Displacement: 600/820 tons. Complement: 30. Dimensions: 190 (*o.a.*) × 24½ × 11½ feet. Armament: **1**—40 mm. AA., **1**—20 mm. AA., **4**—21 inch tubes (bow), **20** mines. Machinery: 2 Vickers Diesels. B.H.P.: 1,200 = 13·5 kts. on *surface*. Electric motors. H.P.: 450 = 8·5 kts. *submerged*. Radius of action, 2,000 miles at 10 kts.

Note—This submarine was originally built for the Estonian Navy, and may have been given an identification number in lieu of her name.

"Malutka" Type.

1942, *Pictorial Press.*

M 72. *Added* 1940.

46 boats. Of a small design. Built 1935–40. Displacement: 205 tons *surface*. Dimensions: 147⅔ × 11½ × 9¾ feet. Guns: **1**—45 mm. AA., **1** M.G. Tubes: **2**—21 inch. Speed: 13/8 kts. "Malutka" means "baby" or "little one." Are built on a mass production basis, notably at Gorki, and sent to their assembly ports in sections. Can be easily transported by rail, but have a very limited radius of action. Numbers reported range from *M* 26 to *M* 98. One of this type lost in Gulf of Finland, Nov., 1937, and others since.

Unidentified type. 1944, *Pictorial Press.*

MOSKVA and 2 others (1940). Displacement: 1,500 tons. Dimensions not reported. Guns: **6**—4 inch, **4**—37 mm. AA., **4**—20 mm. AA. Further particulars wanted.

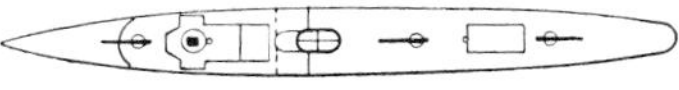

2 *Ansaldo* type: **DZERZHINSKI** (ex-*P.S.* 8), (Aug. 19, 1934), **KIROV** (ex-*P.S.* 26), (Sept. 18, 1934). Built by Ansaldo. *Standard* displacement: 810 tons. Complement: 120. Dimensions: 249⅓ (*pp.*), 262½ (*o.a.*) × 27¼ × 16¾ feet. Guns: **3**—4 inch, **4**—40 mm. AA. Fitted for minelaying. Machinery: 3 Fiat and Tosi Diesels respectively. 3 shafts. B.H.P.: 4,800 = 20 kts. (Trials: H.P.: 5,400 = 21 kts.) Fuel: 44 tons. (In Far East.)

KIROV. *Added* 1935.

Fleet Minesweepers

1946, *London Studio.*

T 901—943 (ex-German M type). Displacement: 550 tons. Ex-**M 3, 7, 17, 29, 30, 34, 151, 155, 203, 204, 254—256, 265, 267, 279, 291, 324, 330, 341, 342, 348, 369, 377, 386, 401, 405—407, 411, 415, 423, 425, 431, 437, 443, 446, 456, 461, 467, 470, 484, 496.**

GAK (*T* 210). **RYM** (*T* 211), **SYPIL** (*T* 207), *T* **205,** *T* **212,** *T* **215,** *T* **217—219** (1942–44). Displacement: 441 tons. Dimensions: 187 × $23\frac{1}{2}$ × $7\frac{3}{4}$ feet. Guns: **1**—4 inch, **1**—45 mm. AA., **1**—37 mm. AA. Speed: 18 kts. (*T* 219 is reported to have been named *Khoroskin.*)

1946, *S. C. Heal, Esq.*

10 *American type*: Ex-*Advocate, Agent, Alarm, Alchemy, Apex, Arcade, Arch, Armada, Aspire, Assail* (1942). Acquired during 1943. Displacement: 625 tons. Dimensions: 180 (*w.l.*), $184\frac{1}{2}$ (*o.a.*) × 33 × $9\frac{3}{4}$ feet. Guns: **1**—3 inch D.P., **4**—40 mm. AA. Machinery: Diesel. B.H.P.: 1,700 = 14 kts. Complement: 104.

1942 *Official.*

VLADIMIR POLUKHIN, VASSILI GROMOV and 4 others (1938–40). Displacement: 600 tons. Dimensions: 259 (*o.a.*) × 26 × $8\frac{1}{4}$ feet. Guns: **2**—4 inch, **3**—37 mm. AA., **2**—20 mm. AA., **4** M.G. Speed: 24 kts. These vessels appear to be an enlargement of *Fugas* type, in following column.

Minelayers

MATROS. 1939, *Associated Press.*

PROVODNIK 1939, *Associated Press.*

BUI, CHEKA, CHISIT, FUGAS, GAFEL, GRUZ, HARPUN, ISKATEL, KAPSIUL, KORSHUN, MATROS, MINA, MINREP, PAROVAN, PATRON, PLAMYA, PODJIGATEL, PROVODNIK, RUBIN, STRELA, TRAL, TROS, VELTA, VERP, VZRYF, YAKOR, ZAPAL (1935–36).
Displacement: 441 tons. Dimensions: 203 (*o.a.*) × $23\frac{1}{4}$ × $7\frac{1}{4}$ feet. Guns: **1**—4 inch, **1**—45 mm. AA., **1**—37 mm. AA. Fitted for minelaying and minesweeping (stowage for 40 mines). Machinery: Diesel. 2 shafts. B.H.P.: 2,000 = 16 kts.

Note.—Six of these vessels were previously known as *P.S.* 1 to 6. Initials *P.S.* stand for *Pogranitchni Storoshevoi*, meaning Frontier Patrol. They now bear numbers, *T* 401 and upwards.

ARGUN (1939). Displacement: 5,000 tons. Dimensions not reported. Guns: **4**—5·1 inch, **3**—3 inch, **4**—37 mm. AA. Mines: 800. Speed: 14 kts.

OKHOTSK (1938). Displacement: 3,200 tons. Dimensions: $265\frac{3}{4}$ × $42\frac{1}{2}$ × $18\frac{1}{4}$ feet. Guns: **3**—5·1 inch, **2**—3 inch, **2** M.G. Speed: 15 kts.

MURMAN (1937). Displacement: 3,500 tons. Dimensions: 266 × $42\frac{2}{3}$ × $15\frac{3}{4}$ feet. Guns: **3**—5·1 inch, **4**—3 inch. Mines: 150. Speed: 14 kts.

VOROSHILOVSK. Displacement: 2,300 tons. Dimensions: 236 × $39\frac{1}{3}$ × $16\frac{1}{2}$ feet. Guns: **4**—3 inch. Mines: 400.

GIZHIGA (1932). Displacement: 1,500 tons. Dimensions: $229\frac{1}{2}$ (*pp.*), $242\frac{3}{4}$ (*o.a.*) × 34 × $10\frac{1}{2}$ feet. Guns: **1**—3 inch, **2**—45 mm. AA. Machinery: Diesel. 2 shafts.

ZIUID. Displacement: 700 tons. Dimensions: 187 × $30\frac{1}{2}$ × 12 feet. Guns: **2**—3 inch, **4**—45 mm. AA. Mines: 100. Machinery: 2 sets Diesels.

Photo wanted.
For appearance, see silhouette.

KRASNAYA ABKHASIA, KRASNI AJARISTAN, KRASNAYA GRUSIA, KRASNI ARMENIA (ex-*Krasni Krim*) (1916). Displacement: 1,100 tons. Guns: **2**—5·1 inch, **2**—3 inch AA., **2** M.G. (Some reported to mount **3**—5·1 inch.) 248 mines carried. Machinery: Triple expansion. I.H.P.: 640 = 9 kts. Oil fuel: 150 tons. (In Black Sea.)

1932 *Photo.*

DEVIATOYE YANVARYA (ex-*Volga*, 1905). 1711 tons. Dimensions: 229 × 45 × 13 feet. Complement, 266. Armament: **4**—3 inch. Carries 236 mines. H.P. 1600 = 13 kts. Babcock boilers. Coal: 160 tons. Present best speed. 10 kts.

Added 1940

MARTY (ex-*Shtandart,* 1895). Displacement: 5,980 tons. Dimensions: 370 (*w.l.*) × 52½ × 20 feet (*mean*). Guns: **4**—5·1 inch, 55 cal., **7**—3 inch, **3**—45 mm. AA., **3** M.G. Mines: 500. Armour: 2″ Deck. Machinery: Geared turbines. 2 shafts. Speed: 18 kts. Oil fuel.

Note.—This ship is the former Imperial yacht, laid down at Copenhagen in 1893, and re-engined and rebuilt as a minelayer at Leningrad in 1935–7.

DVADSATPYATAVO OKTIABRYA (ex-*Narova*, ex-*General Admiral,* 1873). Displacement: 4,250 tons. Dimensions: 284½ × 48 × 22 feet. Guns: **4**—3 inch, **4** M.G. 600 mines. H.P.: 4,500 = 9 kts. (Minelaying Training Ship.)

Motor Torpedo Boats.

29 *German type:* Ex-*S* 11, 16, 24, 50, 65, 81, 82, 86, 99, 101, 109, 110, 113, 118, 123, 132, 135, 175, 204, 209, 211, 214, 219, 222, 227, 704, 707–709. First 3 of 62-ton type; others all 95 tons.

Added 1940.

A1–150 (1943–45) (Ex-*PT* 85–87, 89, 197, 265–276, 289–294, 400–504, 506–508, 510–521, 552–556, 560–563, 661–687, 731–760; ex-*RPT* 1–5, 11; and ex-*BPT* 53–60). Some of Vosper 70 ft. design, and others built by Elas or Higgins. Armed with **2** torpedo tubes, **2**—20 mm. AA., and **2** M.G.

Note.—There are still some units of Italian M.A.S. type. Usual armament, 2 torpedoes. Machinery of Italian design. Distributed between Baltic, Black Sea and Far East. Those built at Marti Yard, Leningrad, in 1937, are of 11 tons with a speed of 42 kts. Distinctive numbers are painted on C.T.'s.

VIRSAITIS. 1926.

SMETONA (ex-*M* 59), **VIRSAITIS** (ex-*M* 68). (Both 1917.) Ex-German minesweepers reconstructed. Displacement: 380 tons. Complement: 48. Dimensions: 184 (*w.l.*), 193 (*o.a.*) × 24¼ × 8½ feet (*max.* draught). Guns: **2**—3 inch, **3** M.G. Machinery: 2 sets triple expansion. 2 shafts. I.H.P.: 1,800 = 16 kts. Boilers: 2 Schulz. Coal: 160 tons.

T 107 1938, *courtesy Dr. Erich Gröner.*

Ex-**T 107** (ex-*G* 107, 1911). Old ex-German torpedo boat, acquired 1946. Displacement: 760 tons. Dimensions: 247¾ × 25 × 10½ feet. Guns: **1**—4·1 inch, **2** M.G. Machinery: 2 sets turbines. 2 shafts. S.H.P.: 16,000 = 25 kts. Boilers: 3 Schulz. Oil fuel: 173 tons.

Ex-**T 196** (ex-*G* 196, 1911). Old ex-German torpedo boat, acquired 1946. Displacement: 800 tons. Dimensions: 242¾ × 26¼ × 10¾ feet. Guns: **2**—4·1 inch, **2** M.G. Machinery: 2 sets turbines. 2 shafts. S.H.P.: 18,200 = 25 kts. Boilers: 3 Schulz. Oil fuel: 204 tons.

Ex-**T 158** (1908). Old ex-German torpedo boat, acquired 1946. Displacement: 675 tons. Dimensions: 237 × 25½ × 10½ feet. Guns: **1**—3·5 inch, **1** M.G. Machinery: Triple expansion. 2 shafts. I.H.P.: 10,900 = 22 kts.

Patrol Vessels and Tenders

Photo added 1933.

MARTYNOV (ex-*Vnushitelni*), **ARTEMIEV** (ex-*Vinoslivi*), **OSSOAVIAKHIM** (ex-*Vnimatelni*). All built by Schichau, 1905. Displacement: 375 tons. Dimensions: 210 × 24 × 8¼ feet. Guns: **2**—3 inch, **4** M.G. May also carry mines. H.P.: 6,200 = 28 kts. (15—20 kts. present speed). Coal: 125 tons. Complement: 69.

BAKINSKI RABOTCHI. *Photo, Dmitri Novik (added* 1929).

ALFATER (ex-*Turkmenetz-Stavropolski*), **MARKIN** (ex-*Ukraina*), **BAKINSKI-RABOTCHI** (ex-*Voiskovoi*) (all 1904). Built by Lange's Yard, Riga. Displacement: 580 tons. Dimensions: 240 × 23¾ × 7½ feet. Guns: **3**—3·9 inch, **2**—45 mm. AA., **2**—37 mm. AA., **4** M.G. H.P.: 6,200 = 25 kts. (now less). Boilers: 4 Normand. Coal: 50 tons *normal*, 135 tons *full load.* Complement: 88—85. Carry 16 mines. All three are in Caspian.

Coastal Craft

Motor Launches

Nos. 201–212 (1937–38). Motor vessels, similar to Finnish V.M.V. type. Displacement: 30 tons. Guns: 2—47mm. Speed: 25 kts. or more.

Many others exist, of which the photo below is an example, including vessels of 18, 20, 25, 26 and 42 tons, usually armed with 1 or 2—3 inch guns and varying numbers of M.G.

No. 38. 1942, *Official.*

No. 201. 1941 *Official.*

1946, *S.C. Heal, Esq.*

BO 1–46 (Ex-*SC* 719–721, 1073–1076, 1283–1287, 1475–1493, 1496–1499, 1502–1508, 1510–1512, 1517). Displacement: 95 tons. Dimensions: 107½ (*w.l.*), 111 (*o.a.*) × 17 × 6½ feet. Guns: **1**—40 mm. AA., etc. Machinery: 2 sets Diesels. 2 shafts. B.H.P.: 800 = 15 kts. Complement: 28.

M 1–75 (Ex-*PTC* 37–49, 54–66; ex-*RPC* 1–49). Displacement: 23 tons (*full load*). Dimensions: 59 (*w.l.*), 63 (*o.a.*) × 15¼ × 3½ feet (*max.* draught). Guns: **1**—20 mm. AA., **2** M.G. Machinery: Hall-Scott motors. 2 shafts. S.H.P.: 650 = 30 kts. *max.* Complement: 10.

50 *German types:* Ex-*R* 23, 28. 90-ton type. Ex-*R* 53, 58, 63, 65, 87, 90, 103, 105, 107, 113, 122, 124, 149, 234, 238, 245, 254, 257, 258, 262, 265, 269, 270, 288, 289, 302, 303, 305, 307, 308, 310–312, 409–423. 100-ton type.

Fishery Protection Vessel.

1924 *Photo, Abrahams, Devonport.*

VOROVSKY (ex-*Yaroslavna*, ex-yacht *Lysistrata*, Denny, Dumbarton, 1900). 2,089 tons T.M. Dimensions: 285 (*pp.*), 319 (*o.a.*) × 40 × 18 feet. Machinery: Triple expansion. 2 shafts. H.P.: 3,500 = 18 kts. Guns: **2**—4·7 inch, **2**—3 pdr., **2** M.G. Complement: 127. (In Far East.)

River Monitors.

KHASAN. Displacement: 1,900 tons. Dimensions: 298½ × 39 × 10 feet. Guns: **4**—5·1 inch, **4**—3 inch, **6**—47 mm. Machinery: 4 sets Diesels. B.H.P.: 3,200.

Added 1940.

LENIN (ex *Shtorm*), **SUN-YAT-SEN** (ex-*Shkval*), **KRASNI-VOSTOK** (ex-*Viyuga*), **SVERDLOV** (ex-*Uragan*), **CHICHERIN** (ex-*Vikhr*) (1910). Displacement: 965 tons. Complement: 104. Dimensions: 242¾ × 39⅓ × 6½ feet. Guns: **8**—4·7 inch, **2**—37 mm. AA., **9** M.G. Armour: 4½″ turrets. Machinery: 4 sets Diesels. B.H.P.: 3,000 = 15 kts. Fuel: 100 tons. (Amur Flotilla.)

Krasni Azarbaijan. 1931 *Photo.*

KRASNI AZARBAIJAN (ex-*Trotsky*, ex-*Ardagan*), **LENIN** (ex-*Kars*). (Both 1909.) Displacement: 700 tons. Dimensions: 203 × 28¼ × 9½ feet. Guns: **3**—4 inch, **2**—45 mm. AA., **2**—37 mm. AA., **4** M.G. Machinery: Diesel. B.H.P.: 2,200 = 11 kts. Complement: 126. (Both in Caspian Sea.)

River Gunboats.

AKTIVNI. Displacement: 300 tons. Dimensions: 167 × 27 × 5¼ feet. Guns: **2**—4 inch, **4**—45 mm. AA., **6** M.G. Machinery: 2 sets Diesels. B.H.P.: 1,600.

ZHELESNIAKOV. Displacement: 240 tons. Dimensions: 157½ × 25 × 4¼ feet. Guns: **2**—4 inch, **3**—45 mm. AA., **2**—37 mm. AA. Machinery: 2 sets Diesels. B.H.P.: 300.

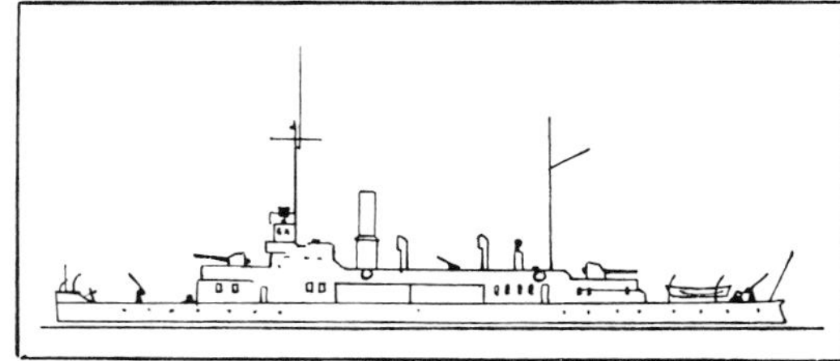

KRASNOYE ZNAMYA (ex-*Sibiriak*), **BIEDNOTA** (ex-*Vogul*), **PROLETARI** (ex-*Buriat*), **RABOTCHI** (ex-*Kalmuk*) (1907). 190 tons. Dimensions: 164 × 27 × 2 feet. Guns: **2**—4·7 inch, **2** M.G. H.P. 500 = 11 kts. Fuel: 145 tons. (Amur Flotilla.)

Coastal Minesweepers.

(*Appearance as YMS* 449, *in U.S. section.*)

12 *American type*: Ex-*YMS* 447, 448, 453, 455–457, 460, 462, 464–466, 469 (1943). All acquired in 1945. Displacement: 215 tons. Dimensions: 136 × 24½ × 6 feet. Guns: **1**—3 inch D.P., **2**—20 mm. AA., **2** D.C.T. Machinery: Diesel. B.H.P.: 1,000 = 12 kts. Complement: 50.

1945, *J. C. R. Ayias, Esq.*

12 *British type*: Ex-*Alder Lake, Beech Lake, Cedar Lake, Elm Lake, Hickory Lake, Larch Lake, Pine Lake, Poplar Lake, Spruce Lake, Willow Lake* (1944–45). Built in Canadian shipyards on "Mutual Aid" account, and delivered 1945–46. Ex-*MMS* 1005, 1023, acquired from Royal Navy. Displacement: 360 tons. Dimensions: 126 (*pp.*), 140 (*o.a.*) × 26 × 10½ feet. Guns: 2—40 mm. AA., 2—20 mm. AA. Machinery: Diesel. B.H.P.: 500 = 10 kts.

4 *British type*: Ex-*MMS* 90, 202, 203, 212. Acquired from Royal Navy. Displacement: 250 tons. Dimensions: 105 (*pp.*), 119 (*o.a.*) × 13 × 9½ feet. Guns: 2—20 mm. AA., etc. Machinery: Diesel. B.H.P.: 500 = 10 kts. Complement: 20.

N. 1—5 (1934–35). 200 tons. Guns: 1—3 pdr., 1 M.G. Diesel engines. Speed: 16 kts.

HAV, SHIKA, SHUSA, SILSA, STEFA, SUMBA, SVEGA (1929–31). 249–253 tons *gross*. Ex-whalers fitted for minesweeping, and transferred from Royal Navy in 1942.

JALITA (1926). 359 tons. **DOROTEA** (1924). 443 tons. Guns: 1—45 mm. AA. Speed: 8 kts.

NIEVOD, YAKOR (Norway, 1916). Ex-whalers of 400 tons. Guns: 2—3 inch, 1—37 mm. AA. Speed: 11 kts.

KRAMBOL, ZMEYA (1916). Displacement: 185 tons. Guns: 1—3 inch. Speed: 11 kts.

1932 *Photo.*

KLIUZ, UDARNIK (1916). Displacement: 268 tons. Complement: 35. Dimensions: 147⅞ (*o.a.*) × 20¼ × 6½ feet. Guns: 1—3 inch, 2 M.G. Machinery: Triple expansion. I.H.P.: 450 = 12 kts.

IJORA (ex-*Patron*), **PLAMYA** (Middlesbrough, 1913–14). 500 tons. Dimensions: 146 × 24½ × 10 feet. Guns: 2—3 inch, 1—37 mm. AA. H.P.: 650 = 11 kts.

Note.—A number of German motor minesweepers (*Räumboote*) have been acquired. There are also a number of small sweepers of from 9 to 16 tons.

Mining Tenders.

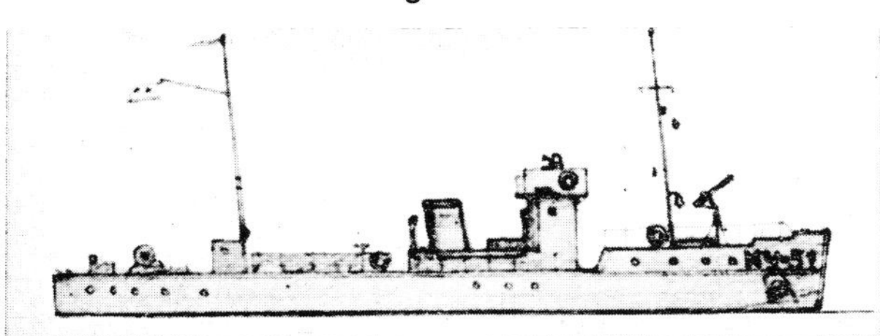

M.U. 50—54 (1936–37). 180 tons. 1 M.G. Diesel-driven. Speed: 12 kts. Are attached to Mining School as Tenders.

Seaplane Carrier.

STALIN (ex-*Krasnaya Bessarabia*) (Oct. 4, 1937). Displacement: 9,000 tons (?). Dimensions: Not reported. Guns: 12—4 inch AA., etc. Aircraft: From 12 to 22 seaplanes are reported to have been carried. Machinery: Geared turbines. Speed: 30 kts. (probably an exaggeration).

Note.—Considerable mystery surrounds this ship, whose importance appears to have been exaggerated. At one time she was believed to have been laid down at Nikolaiev in 1914 as the cruiser *Admiral Kornilov*, but it now seems fairly certain that she is a converted mercantile hull. She is said to have been completed in 1939.

Surveying Vessels.

CHUKCHA. Displacement: 2,700 tons. Dimensions: 246 × 43½ × 14 feet. Machinery: Triple expansion. I.H.P.: 900 = 10 kts. Coal: 900 tons.

PARTIZAN, POLARNI (1937). Displacement: 1,300 tons. Dimensions: 210 × 32¾ × 11 feet. Machinery: Triple expansion. I.H.P.: 700 = 9·5 kts. Coal: 400 tons.

LEBED. Displacement: 1,100 tons. Dimensions: 180½ × 29½ × 16 feet. Machinery: Triple expansion. I.H.P.: 680 = 12 kts.

AZIMUT, OST, PRIEMNYL, RULEVOI, SAMOYED, SUID, ZAGRADITEL. Displacement: 1,000 tons. Dimensions: 170 × 30½ × 10 feet. Machinery: 2 sets Diesels. B.H.P.: 600 = 10 kts.

GALS. Displacement: 540 tons. Dimensions: 121¼ × 25 × 11 feet. Machinery: Triple expansion. I.H.P.: 240 = 8 kts. Coal: 45 tons.

BAROGRAF. Displacement: 260 tons. Dimensions: 92 × 19 × 12½ feet. Machinery: Triple expansion. I.H.P.: 425 = 7·5 kts.

SEKSTANT (1918). Displacement: 415 tons. Dimensions: 143 × 21 × 12 feet. Machinery: Triple expansion. I.H.P.: 260 = 6 kts. Complement: 20.

1944, *courtesy M. Henri Le Masson.*

METEOR (Jan. 18, 1915). Displacement: 1,200 tons. Dimensions: 219⅘ × 33½ × 12½ feet. Guns: 1—3·5 inch, 1 M.G. Machinery: 2 sets 8-cyl. 4-stroke Diesels. 2 shafts. B.H.P.: 2,200 = 14·5 kts.

Training Ships.

Added 1938.

SVIR (ex-Rotterdam Lloyd liner *Patria*), (K. M. de Schelde, Flushing, 1919). 9,686 tons *gross*. Dimensions: 480½ × 57¼ × 29 feet. Guns: 4—37 mm. Machinery: Single reduction geared turbines. Speed: 15 kts. Seamen's Training Ship.

AMUR (1907). Displacement: 3,600 tons. Dimensions: 320 (*o.a.*) × 46 × 14½ feet (*max.*). Guns: 1—4·7 inch, 1—3 inch. Machinery: 2 sets triple expansion. I.H.P.: 4,700 = 17 kts. Boilers: Belleville. Coal: 500 tons.

KRASNOYE ZNAMYA (ex-*Khrabri*, Nov. 21, 1895). Displacement: — tons. Dimensions: 223 × 41⅜ × 13 feet. Guns: 5—5·1 inch, etc. Machinery: Triple expansion. I.H.P.: 2,640 = 12 kts.

Added 1938.

POLARNAYA SVIEZDA (1890). Displacement: 3,640 tons. Dimensions: 315½ × 46 × 17½ feet. Guns: 3—3 inch, 3—45 mm. AA. Machinery: M.A.N. Diesels. B.H.P.: 5,000 = 15 kts. Re-engined 1936. Used as Training Ship for artificers and stokers. (Ex-Imperial Yacht, rebuilt 1936–7.)

Note.—Old Training Ships *Trevolev, Komsomoletz*, etc., are no longer seagoing.

Miscellaneous

Depôt Ships.

VOLGA. Displacement: 11,300 tons. Dimensions: 459 × 56 × 21½ feet. Guns: **2**—3 inch, **3**—45 mm. AA., **5** M.G. Machinery: Parsons turbines. 2 shafts. S.H.P.: 5,500 = 14 kts. Oil fuel: 1,090 tons.

KRONSTADT (1940). Displacement: 5,800 tons. Dimensions: 328 × 46 × 19½ feet. Guns: **4**—3 inch, **3**—45 mm. AA., **2** M.G. I.H.P.: 1,500 = 12 kts.

1946, *London Studio.*

TEREK (ex-*Hela*, 1939). Displacement: 2,300 tons. Dimensions: 328 × 42½ × 11 feet. Guns: **2**—4·1 inch, **1**—37 mm. AA., **2**—20 mm. AA. Speed: 18 kts.

SMOLENSK (1931). Displacement: 6,000 tons. Dimensions: 314½ (*pp.*), 331 (*o.a.*) × 46 × 19½ feet. Guns: Not reported. Machinery: Triple expansion. I.H.P.: 1,500 = 11 kts.

1939, *Dr. Erich Gröner.*

ISAR (ex-*Puma*, 1930). Displacement: 3,850 tons. Dimensions: 319 × 45½ × 13 feet. Machinery: Triple expansion. I.H.P.: 2,000 = 12 kts. (Depot Ship for Submarines.)

WEICHSEL (ex-*Syra*), (Howaldt, Kiel, 1923). Displacement: 3,974 tons. Dimensions: 309¼ × 44 × 13½ feet. Guns: **4**—20 mm. AA. Machinery: Triple expansion. H.P.: 1,400 = 10·5 kts. Coal: 425 tons. 2 watertube boilers. Complement, 135. (Depot Ship for Submarines.)

NEVA (ex-*Essequibo*, 1914). Displacement: 13,300 tons. Dimensions: 450¼ (*pp.*), 466 (*o.a.*) × 57⅔ × 24¼ feet. Guns: **3**—3 inch, **6**—45 mm. AA., **8** M.G. Machinery: Quadruple expansion. I.H.P.: 5,800 = 15 kts. Oil fuel: 960 tons.

SIBIR (ex-*Empire Tarne*, ex-*Oceana*, ex-*Neptunia*, ex-*Peer Gynt*, ex-*Avare*, ex-*Sierra Salvada*, 1912). 3,767 tons *gross*. Dimensions: 439½ × 56 × — feet. Guns: **6**—45 mm. AA., **4** M.G. Machinery: Triple expansion. 2 shafts. I.H.P.: 3,300 = 12 kts.

ALDAN (ex-*Brunswijk*, 1912). Displacement: 4,700 tons. Dimensions: 287½ (*pp.*), 288¾ (*o.a.*) × 42 × 16 feet. Machinery: Triple expansion. I.H.P.: 1,200 = 9 kts. Coal: 500 tons.

UMBA (ex-*Keret*, 1910). Displacement: 1,400 tons. Dimensions: 195½ (*pp.*), 200 (*o.a.*) × 30 × 12 feet. Guns: **5**—45 mm. AA., **2** M.G. Machinery: Triple expansion. I.H.P.: 825 = 10 kts.

PRIMORIE (ex-*Hai Yen*, ex-*Bulga*, ex-*Signal*, 1903). Displacement: 4,000 tons. Dimensions: 262½ × 36 × 14½ feet. Machinery: Triple expansion. I.H.P.: 940 = 9 kts. Coal: 400 tons.

ELBORUS. Displacement: 2,600 tons. Dimensions: 302 × 39 × 13½ feet. Guns: **2**—3 inch, **1**—45 mm. AA. Machinery: Diesel-electric. H.P.: 2,800 = 13 kts. Oil fuel: 180 tons.

Water Carriers.

VODOLEI II (1905). Built at Sandvikens. 660 tons. 9·5 kts.
VODOLEI I (1907). 730 tons. 9·5 kts.

Note.—In 1945, 15 miscellaneous auxiliaries (AG 51-65) were acquired from the U.S. Navy on Lend-Lease terms.

Netlayer.

ONEGA. Displacement: 530 tons. Dimensions: 185⅓ × 30½ × 4¼ feet. Guns: **3**—45 mm. AA. Speed: 8 kts.

Fleet Tugs.

CHF 18. 1946, *London Studio.*

CHF 1-19. Particulars wanted.

Target Service Ships.

1937, *Schäfer.*

Ex-**HESSEN** (ex-Battleship). (1903). Reconstructed 1936–37 as a wireless-controlled target ship. Displacement: 13,040 tons. Dimensions: 400¼ × 73 × 23½ feet. H.P.: 16,000 = 18 kts. Oil fuel and automatically fired boilers. Equipment includes special smoke-screen apparatus.

BLITZ 1939, *Schäfer.*

Ex-**BLITZ** (ex-*T.* 185, Vulcan, 1910). Ex-Torpedo boat, used for wireless target control. Displacement: 800 tons. Speed: 20 kts.

Icebreakers.

Note.—Majority of following are immensely strong in framing and scantlings, with exceptionally thick plating, and decks strengthened to permit of guns being mounted in war time.

SERGEI KIROV, VALERIAN KUBYSHEV, KASAK KHABAROV (1938-40). Built at Leningrad. Displacement: 12,000 tons. Dimensions: 357½ × 69¼ × 23½ feet. Machinery: Diesel-electric. B.H.P.: 12,000. 3 shafts (2 stern, 1 bow). Radius: 12,000 miles.

L. KAGANOVICH 1939, *Midshipman T. B. Healey, R.N.R.*

LAZAR KAGANOVICH (April 30, 1937), **YOSIF STALIN** (Aug. 14, 1937), **MIKOYAN** (ex-*Otto Schmidt*, March 8, 1939). First ship built at Nikolaiev, others at Baltic Works, Leningrad. Displacement: 11,000 tons; 4,866 tons *gross*. Dimensions: 335¾ (*pp.*), 351 (*o.a.*) × 75½ × 22 feet. Machinery: 3 sets triple expansion, with Diesel-electric propulsion for cruising speeds. 3 shafts. H.P.: 10,050 = 15·5 kts. 9 boilers. Coal: 4,000 tons. 3 aircraft, 1 catapult included in design, though not apparent in above photo. *L. Kaganovich* is in Far East.

Icebreakers *continued.*

1939 *Official.*

KRISJANIS VALDEMARS (Beardmore, 1925). Displacement: 2,800 tons; 1,932 tons *gross*. Dimensions: 196½ × 55¾ × 22 feet. Machinery: Triple expansion. I.H.P.: 5,200 = 15 kts. Coal: 350 tons. Complement: 55. (Baltic.)

Added 1938, courtesy Messrs. Smit.

JAAKARHU (Smit, Rotterdam, 1926). Displacement: 4,825 tons. Dimensions: 246 × 63 × 21 feet. Machinery: Triple expansion. 3 shafts. I.H.P.: 9,200 = 15 kts. 8 boilers. Oil fuel.

Added 1938, courtesy Messrs. Armstrongs.

KRASSIN (ex-*Sviatogor*, Armstrong, 1917). Displacement: 9,300 tons; 4,902 tons *gross*. Dimensions: 297 (*w.l.*), 323¼ (*o.a.*) × 71 × 26 feet. Machinery: 3 sets triple expansion. 3 shafts. I.H.P.: 10,000 = 15 kts. 10 single-ended boilers. Coal: 3,200 tons. Complement: 190. (Stationed in Arctic.)

1946, *Keith P. Lewis.*

LENIN (ex-*Aleksandr Nevski*). (Armstrong, 1917). Displacement: 6,260 tons; 3,828 tons *gross*. Complement: 122. Dimensions: 273 (*w.l.*), 281 (*o.a.*) × 64 × 19 feet. Machinery: 3 sets triple expansion. 3 shafts. H.P.: 8,000 = 19 kts. 8 boilers. Coal: 1,200 tons. (Arctic.)

(This ship was refitted on the Mersey, 1946–47.)

1940, *Official.*

VOIMA (Sandvikens, 1917). Displacement: 2,070 tons. Dimensions: 210¾ × 46½ × 16¾ feet. Machinery: Triple expansion. 1 shaft. I.H.P.: 4,100 = 13·5 kts.

Added 1938, courtesy Messrs. Swan, Hunter.

STEFAN MAKAROFF (ex-*Kniaz Pojarski*), (Swan, Hunter, 1916). *Standard* displacement: 3,150 tons; 2,156 tons *gross*. Dimensions: 236 (*pp.*), 248 (*o.a.*) × 57 × 22 feet. Machinery: 3 sets triple expansion. 3 shafts. I.H.P.: 6,400 = 14·5 kts. 6 boilers. Coal: 700 tons. (Black Sea.)

Added 1938, courtesy Messrs. Swan, Hunter.

DOBRINA NIKITICH (Swan, Hunter, 1916). *Standard* displacement: 2,460 tons. 1,664 tons *gross*. Dimensions: 200 (*pp.*), 211 (*o.a.*) × 50½ × 20 feet. Machinery: Triple expansion. 2 shafts. I.H.P.: 4,000 = 14 kts. 6 boilers. Coal: 370 tons. (Far East.)

1939, *Official.*

VOLHYNETZ (ex-*Suur Töll*, ex-*Vainamoinen*, ex-*Volhynetz*, ex-*Tsar Mikhail Feodorovitch*, 1914). Displacement: 4,000 tons. Dimensions: 236½ × 57 × 18¾ feet. Machinery: 3 sets triple expansion. 3 shafts. I.H.P.: 5,800 = 13·5 kts. Coal: 800 tons. (Baltic.)

MALYGIN (ex-*Solovei Budimirovitch*, ex-*Bruce*). (Napier & Miller, 1912). Displacement: 2,200 tons; 1,571 tons *gross*. Dimensions: 250½ × 36 × 17½ feet. Machinery: Triple expansion. 1 shaft. I.H.P.: 3,000 = 15 kts. (Arctic.)

Icebreakers *continued.*

Added 1938, courtesy Messrs. Swan, Hunter

SADKO (ex-*Lintrose*), (Swan, Hunter, 1913). Displacement: 2,000 tons; 1,613 tons *gross*. Dimensions: 255 × 37½ × 21 feet. Machinery: Triple expansion. 1 shaft. I.H.P.: 3,500 = 14 kts. 4 boilers. (Arctic.)

Note.—This ship was sunk during First World War off the Arctic coast of Russia, where she lay for many years until raised and refitted.

TAIMYR. *Added* 1938.

TAIMYR (1909). Displacement: 1,290 tons. Speed: 10·5 kts.

(May no longer be in service.)

GEORGEI SEDOFF (ex-*Beothic*), **VLADIMIR RUSSANOFF** (ex-*Bonaventure*). Built 1909, by D. & W. Henderson & Co. and by Napier & Miller, respectively. Displacement: 3,217 tons; 1,383–1,588 tons *gross*. Dimensions: 240½ × 36 × 16½ feet. Machinery: Triple expansion. 1 shaft. I.H.P.: 3,000 = 13·5 kts. Coal: 500 tons. (Arctic.)

Note.—In 1939 *G. Sedoff* achieved a record latitude in her ice-bound drift northward.

Added 1938, courtesy Vickers-Armstrongs, Ltd.

FEODOR LITKE (ex-*Kanada*, ex-*Earl Grey*). (Vickers, 1909). Displacement: 3,400 tons; 2,216 tons *gross*. Dimensions: 250 (*pp.*), 265 (*o.a.*) × 47½ × 17¾ feet. Machinery: Triple expansion. 2 shafts. I.H.P.: 6,000 = 17 kts. Transferred from Canadian Govt. Service, 1915. (Baltic.)

Photograph in "Fighting Ships," 1921, p. 134.

MONTCALM (Napier & Miller, 1904). Displacement: 3,270 tons; 1,432 tons *gross*. Dimensions: 245 × 40½ × 15¾ feet. Machinery: 2 sets triple expansion. 2 shafts. I.H.P.: 3,600 = 14 kts. Boilers: 4 Babcock & Wilcox. Coal: 600 tons. Transferred from Canadian Govt. Service, 1942. (Far East.)

Photograph in "Fighting Ships," 1921, p. 607.

ERMAK (Armstrong, 1898). Displacement: 8,800 tons; 4,955 tons *gross*. Dimensions: 305 × 71 × 25 feet. Machinery: 3 sets triple expansion. 3 shafts. I.H.P.: 9,500 = 15 kts. Boilers: 10 S.E. Coal: 2,100 tons. Complement: 112. (Baltic.)

Added 1938, courtesy Messrs. Burmeister & Wain.

DAVIDOFF (ex-*Krasni Oktiabr*, ex-*Nadiejni*). (Burmeister & Wain, 1897). Displacement: 1,525 tons; 1,212 tons *gross*. Dimensions: 184 × 43 × — feet. Machinery: Compound. I.H.P.: 2,200 = 13 kts. (Far East.)

(There are a large number of smaller icebreakers of insufficient importance to warrant their inclusion here.)

SIAM

ADMIRAL OF THE FLEET'S FLAG.—A blue flag with a white elephant, and in the upper canton next the staff two yellow anchors crossed surmounted by the Siamese crown.

ADMIRAL'S FLAG.—A blue flag with a white elephant in the centre.

VICE-ADMIRAL'S FLAG.—The same as the Admiral's flag but with a white "Chakra" in the upper canton next the staff.

REAR-ADMIRAL'S FLAG.—The same as the Admiral's flag but with two white "Chakras" near the staff.

Personnel: 4726. Officers: 352.

Minister of Defence: Lieut.-General Luang Promyothi.

Chief of Naval Staff: Rear-Admiral Luang Sindhu.

Commander-in-Chief of Navy: Eng. Captain Phya Vicharn Chakrakich.

Mercantile Marine.

14 steamers of 9,186 tons gross (Bureau Veritas figures).

Flags.

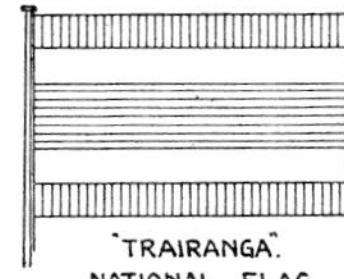

"TRAIRANGA." NATIONAL FLAG.

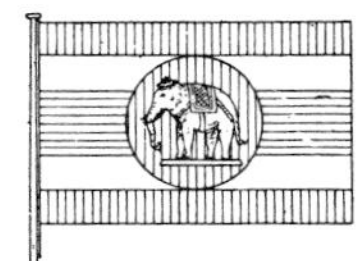

NAVAL ENSIGN.

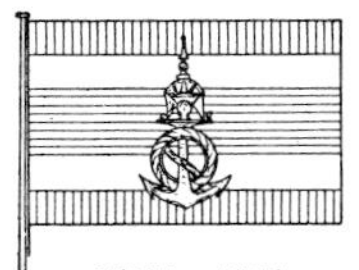

NAVAL JACK.

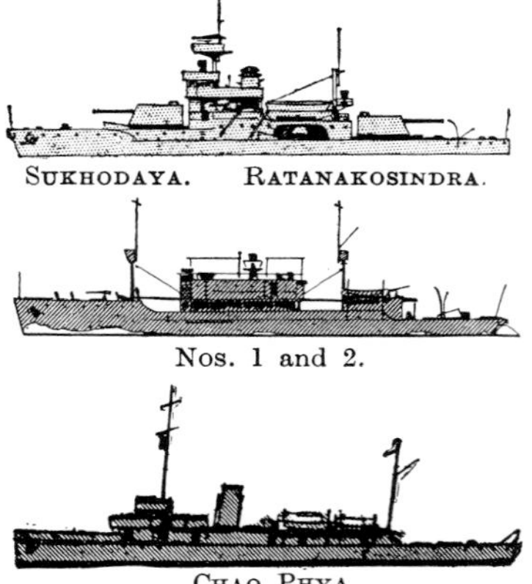

SUKHODAYA. RATANAKOSINDRA.

Nos. 1 and 2.

CHAO PHYA.

Silhouettes

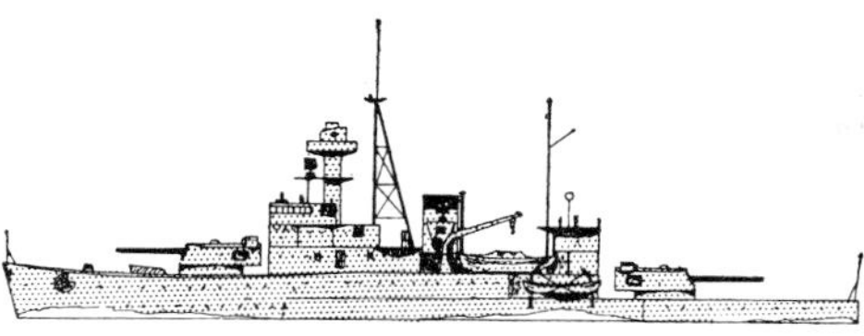

Dhonburi.

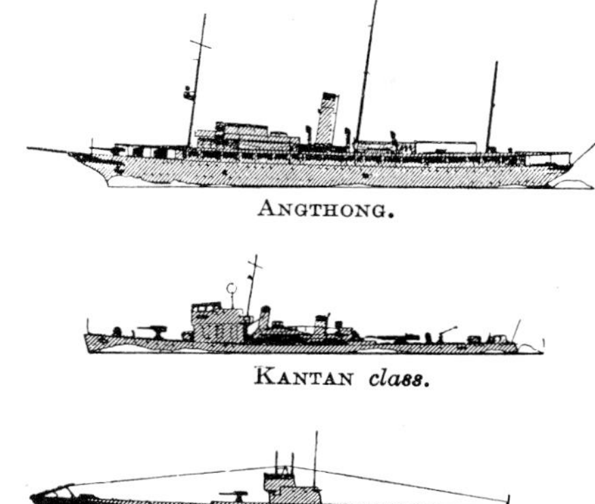

Angthong.

Kantan *class.*

Machanu *class.*

Phra Ruang.

Meklong, Tachin.

Trad *class.*

Cruisers.

(*For plan, see Appendix.*)

NARESUAN, TAKSIN, laid down by Cantieri Riuniti dell' Adriatico, Trieste, Aug. 26 and Sept. 25, 1939, respectively. One was launched in October, 1940, and the other in September, 1941; but both were last reported as sunk in shallow water. Displacement: 4,268 tons. Dimensions: $482\frac{1}{4} \times 47 \times 13\frac{3}{4}$ feet. Guns: **6**—6 inch, **6**—3 inch AA., **4**—40 mm. AA. Torpedo tubes: **6**—18 inch. Geared turbines. S.H.P.: 45,000 = 30 kts. These ships were both requisitioned by Italy, renamed *Etna* and *Vesuvio*, and ordered to be armed with **6**—5·3 inch d.p., **10**—3·9 inch AA. and 1[illegible] smaller AA., but no tubes. It is improbable that they will ever be completed.

Coast Defence Ships

Dhonburi 1938.

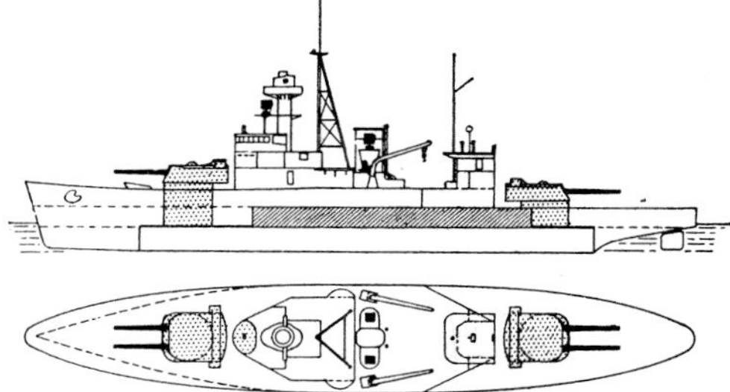

DHONBURI (Jan. 31, 1938). (Laid down by Kawasaki Co., Kobe, in 1936.) Displacement: 2,265 tons. Dimensions: $252\frac{2}{3} \times 47\frac{1}{4} \times 13\frac{3}{4}$ feet. Guns: **4**—8 inch, **4**—3 inch AA., **4**—20 mm. AA. Machinery: 2 sets M.A.N. Diesels. 2 shafts. B.H.P.: 5,200 = 15·5 kts. Fuel: 150 tons. Complement: 155.

Note.—Apparently an expansion of *Ratanakosindra* design. This ship and a sister, the *Ayuthia*, were in action in January, 1941, with a French squadron including the cruiser *Lamotte-Picquet* and 4 smaller ships. *Dhonburi* was reduced to a wreck, and *Ayuthia* driven ashore. *Dhonburi* was refitted in Japan, but it is doubtful whether she has returned to Siam.

Sukhodaya. 1930 *Photo, by courtesy of Messrs. Vickers-Armstrongs.*

SUKHODAYA (Vickers Armstrongs, Nov. 19, 1929), **RATANAKOSINDRA** (Armstrong, April 21, 1925). Displacement: 1000 tons. Dimensions: 160 (*pp.*), 173 (*o.a.*) × 37 × $10\frac{3}{4}$ feet. Guns: **2**—6 inch, **4**—3 inch AA. Protection: Side $2\frac{1}{2}''$ (amidships), $1\frac{1}{4}''$ ends, nickel steel. Barbette rings, $2\frac{1}{2}''$ nickel steel. C.T. $4\frac{3}{4}''$ cast steel armour. Upper deck, $\frac{3}{4}''$ to $1\frac{1}{2}''$ high tensile steel. Machinery: Triple expansion. 2 shafts. I.H.P. 850 = 12 kts. 2 oil-burning water-tube boilers, working pressure 225 lb. Oil: 102 and 96 tons respectively. Complement: 103.

Ratanakosindra laid down 29th Sept., 1924, and completed August, 1925. *Sukhodaya* completed 1930.

Ratanakosindra. 1926 *Photo, by courtesy of Messrs. Armstrongs.*

Miscellaneous

Destroyer.

PHRA RUANG. 1921 *Photo, by courtesy of J. Bailey, Esq.*

PHRA RUANG

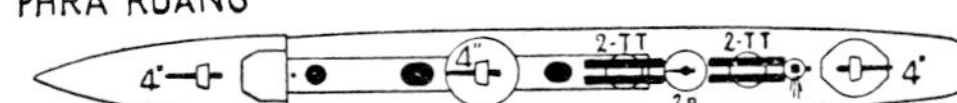

Phra Ruang (ex-H.M.S. *Radiant*, launched by Thornycroft, Nov. 5, 1916. Purchased during July, 1920). 1,035 tons. Dimensions: 274 (*o.a.*), 265 (*p.p.*), × 27⅓ × 11 feet (*max.* draught) and 8½ feet (*mean*). Guns: **3**—4 inch, **1**—3 inch AA., **2**—20 mm., **1** M.G. Tubes: **4**—21 inch, in two twin deck mountings. Machinery: Brown-Curtis (all geared) turbines. Designed S.H.P.: 29,000 = 35 kts. (39·67 trials). 3 Yarrow boilers. Oil fuel: *about* 285 tons (*max.*). Complement, 100.

Submarines.

BLAJUNBOL, SINSAMUDAR. 1938.

4 *Mitubisi* type: ***Machanu, Vilun*** (both Dec. 24, 1936), ***Blajunbol, Sinsamudar*** (both May 14, 1937). *Standard* displacement: 370 tons. Dimensions: 167⅓ × 13½ × 12 feet. Armament: **5**—21 inch tubes, **1** M.G. H.P.: 1,000/540 = 14·5/8 kts. Fuel: 27 tons. Complement: 24.

Notes.—First pair laid down on April 6, 1936, second pair Oct. 1, 1936. Reported to be in poor condition.

Motor Torpedo Boats.

Added 1938, *courtesy Messrs. Thornycroft.*

4 *Thornycroft* type: Nos. **6** to **9** (1935). 16 tons. B.H.P. 950 = 40 kts. 2 M.G., 2 torpedoes, 2 D.C.

4 *Thornycroft* type: Nos. **2** to **5** (1922). 11 tons. 55 × 11 feet. B.H.P.: 750 = 37 kts. (40 kts. *extreme*). Petrol carried: 300 gallons *normal*, 500 *max.* 4 Lewis guns, 2 torpedoes, 2 D.C. Complement, 5.

Torpedo Boats.

PUKET. 1936.

TRAD. 1936, *courtesy Commander R. Steen Steensen.*

7 *Adriatico* type: ***Trad*** (No. 11) (Oct. 26, 1935), ***Puket*** (No. 12) (Sept. 28, 1935), ***Patani*** (No. 13) (Oct. 16, 1936), ***Surasdra*** (No. 21) (Nov. 28, 1936), ***Chandraburi*** (No 22) (Dec. 16, 1936), ***Rayong*** (No. 23) (Jan. 11, 1937), ***Chunphorn*** (No. 31) (Jan. 18, 1937). *Standard* displacement: 318 tons (470 tons *full load*). Dimensions: 219 (*pp.*), 223 (*o.a.*) × 21 × 7 feet *max.* draught. Armament: **3**—3 inch AA., **2**—20 mm. AA., **4**—8 mm., **6**—18 inch tubes (2 single, 4 paired). Parsons geared turbines. 2 shafts. H.P.: 9,000 = 31 kts. Boilers: Yarrow. Fuel: 102 tons. Radius: 1,700 miles at 15 kts. Complement: 70.

Notes.—First 2 laid down Feb. 8, 1935 by Cantieri Navali Riuniti dell'Adriatico, Monfalcone, for delivery by end of 1935. Armament supplied by Vickers-Armstrongs, Ltd. First boat reached 32·54 kts. on trials with 10,000 H.P. All delivered by summer of 1937. Three were reported to have been sunk in action with a French squadron early in 1941, but local information mentions only *Cholburi* and *Songkla* as having become total losses. *Trad*, though claimed by the French as sunk, appears to have been beached and subsequently salved, but her fighting efficiency is questionable.

Coastal Torpedo Boats.

TAKBAI. 1937.

KANTAN (No. 7), **KLONGYAI** (No. 5), **TAKBAI** (No. 6) (Isikawazima Co., March 26, 1937). Displacement: 110 tons *standard*, 135 tons *full load*. Complement: 31. Dimensions: 131½ × 15½ × 4 feet. Guns: 1—3 inch, 2—20 mm. Tubes: **2**—18 inch. Machinery: Geared turbines. 2 shafts. S.H.P.: 1,000 = 19 kts. 2 water tube boilers. Oil fuel: 18 tons.

Notes.—Above 3 completed June 21, 1937.

Sloops (Training Ships).

MEKLONG. 1937.

TACHIN (July 24, 1936), **MEKLONG** (Nov. 27, 1936), both by Uraga Dock Co. Displacement: 1,400 tons. Dimensions: 269 × 34½ × 10½ feet (*mean*). Guns: **4**—4.7 inch, **2**—20 mm. AA. Tubes: **4**—21 inch (paired). Machinery: Triple expansion. 2 shafts. I.H.P.: 2,500 = 17 kts. Boilers: 2 water-tube. Oil fuel: 487 tons. Fitted for minesweeping. Complement (as training ships), 155.

Note.—Both delivered in June, 1937.

SPAIN

Flags.

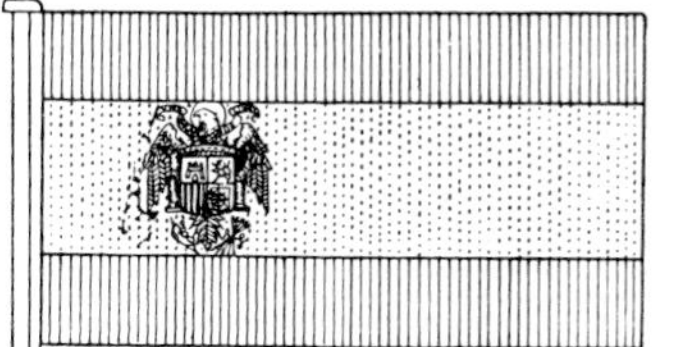

ENSIGN.

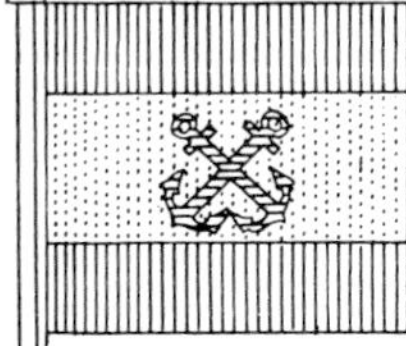

MINISTER OF MARINE.

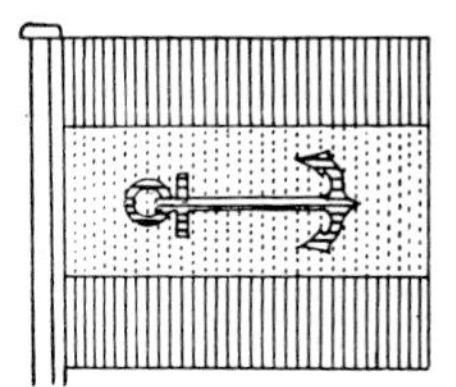

ADMIRAL OF THE FLEET. (Chief of Staff's flag similar, but anchor vertical.)

ADMIRAL.

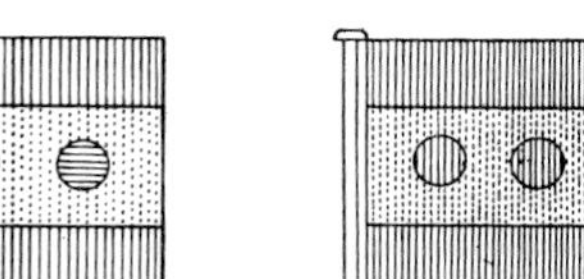

VICE-ADMIRAL IN COMMAND.

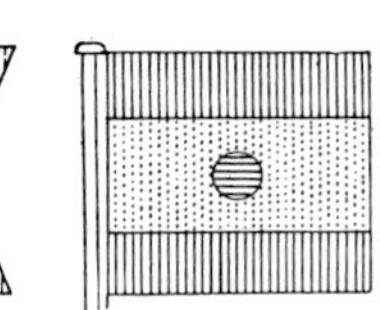

VICE-ADMIRAL SUBORDINATE.

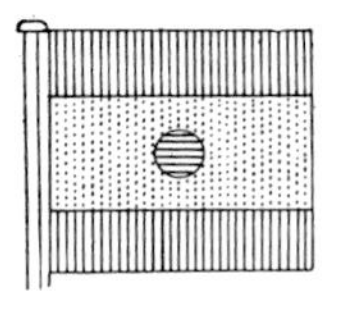

REAR-ADMIRAL IN COMMAND.

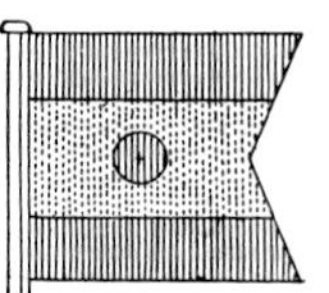

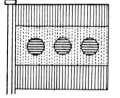

REAR-ADMIRAL SUBORDINATE.

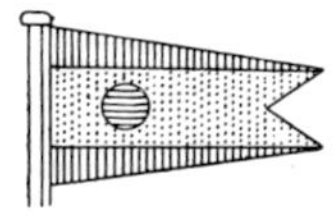

CAPTAIN IN COMMAND OF A DIVISION.

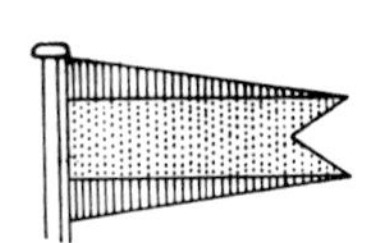

COMMANDER OR LIEUT.-COMMANDER IN COMMAND OF A DIVISION.

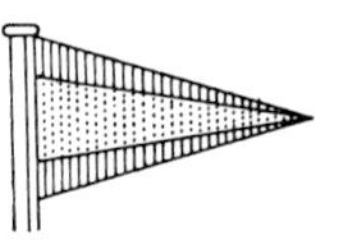

SENIOR OFFICER.

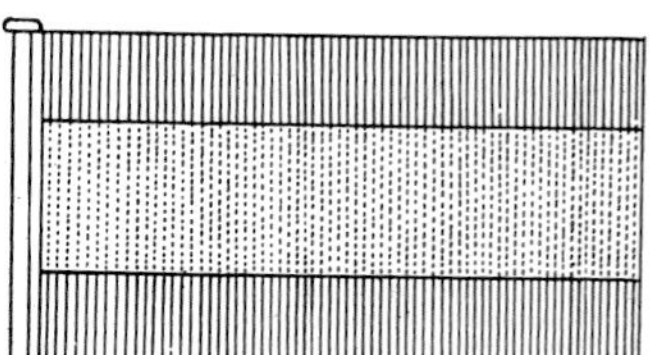

MERCANTILE FLAG.

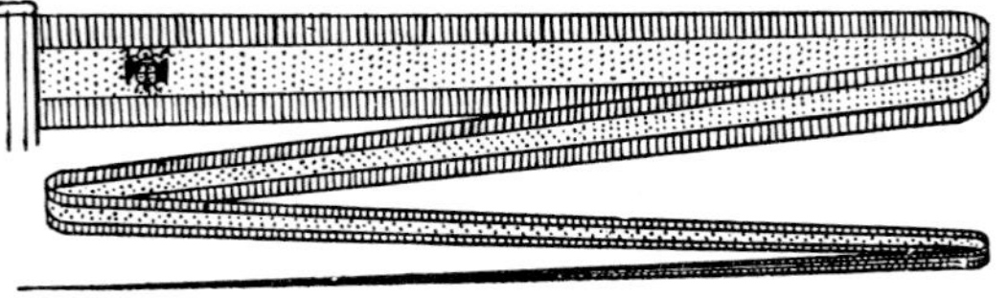

PENDANT.

RED.

YELLOW.

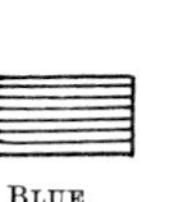

BLUE.

Naval Ordnance.

Notation.	Nominal Calibre.		Model.	Length in calibres	Weight of Gun.	Weight of A.P. shell.	Initial velocity	Max. penetration A.P. capped direct impact at K.C. at		Danger Space against average ship, at			Rounds per minute.
								5000 yards.	3000 yards.	10,000 yards.	5000 yards.	3000 yards.	
	c/m.	inches.			tons.	lbs.	ft. secs.	inches.	inches.				
HEAVY	*20 3*	8	V.	50	15	256	3000	...	...	...	...	...	6
MEDIUM	*15·2*	6	*V.	50	7¾	100	3100	...	8¾	...	...	...	10
LIGHT	12	4·7	V.	45	3·1	48·5	2788	...	...	...	...	...	12
	10·2	4	V.	50	2·1	31	3030	...	...	...	...	...	15
	7·6	3	V.										
	7·6	3	A.										

V = Vickers. A = Armstrong. * = Arsenal de Carraca.
There are also a 10·5 cm. (4·1 inch), and a 8·8 cm. (3·4 inch) AA.

Capitan-General de la Armada. *Admiral of the Fleet.*

Almirante *Admiral.*

Vice-Almirante. *Vice-Admiral*

Contra Almirante. *Rear-Admiral.*

Capitan de Navio *Captain.*

Capitán de Fragata. *Commander.*

Capitán de Corbeta. *Lieutenant-Commander.*

Teniente de Navio. *Lieutenant.*

Alferez de Navio. *Sub-Lieut*

Alferez de Fragata. *Midshipman*

Minister of Marine: Vice-Admiral Don Francisco Regalado.
Chief of Naval Staff: Vice-Admiral Don A. Arriaga Adam.
Naval Attaché, London: Commander The Duke of Luna.
Navy Estimates, 1946: 672,564,247 pesetas.

(The rank of Admiral of the Fleet is held only by the Caudillo, General Franco.)

Other branches, *without a curl*, have distinguishing colours as follows:—

Engineers ...	*green.*	Accountant and Supply Officers ...	*white.*
Constructors ...	*blue.*	Astronomical	*sage.*
Surgeons. ...	*red.*	Pharmacists.	*yellow.*
Ordnance ...	*black*	Juridical	*purple*

Personnel.

Officers: 950. P.O.'s: 1,350. Sailors and Marines: 20,000.

Training Establishments.

For Executive Officers, Naval School (*Escuela Naval Militar*), Marin, Galicia. For Engineering Branch and Cadets, Ferrol. For Petty Officers, San Fernando.

Colour of Ships.

Light grey.

Mercantile Marine.

Official figures, 1 Jan. 1,946: 1,064 vessels of 1,068,902 gross tonnage.

CANARIAS.

GALICIA *class.*

MENDEZ NUÑEZ.

NAVARRA.

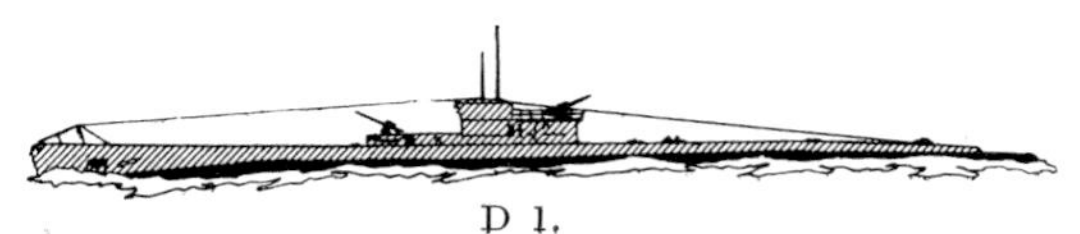

D 1.

"C" *Class.*

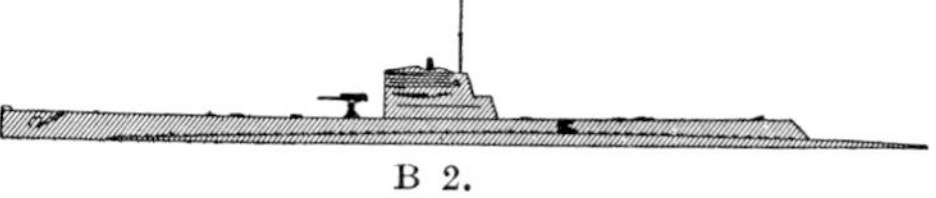

B 2.

Silhouettes

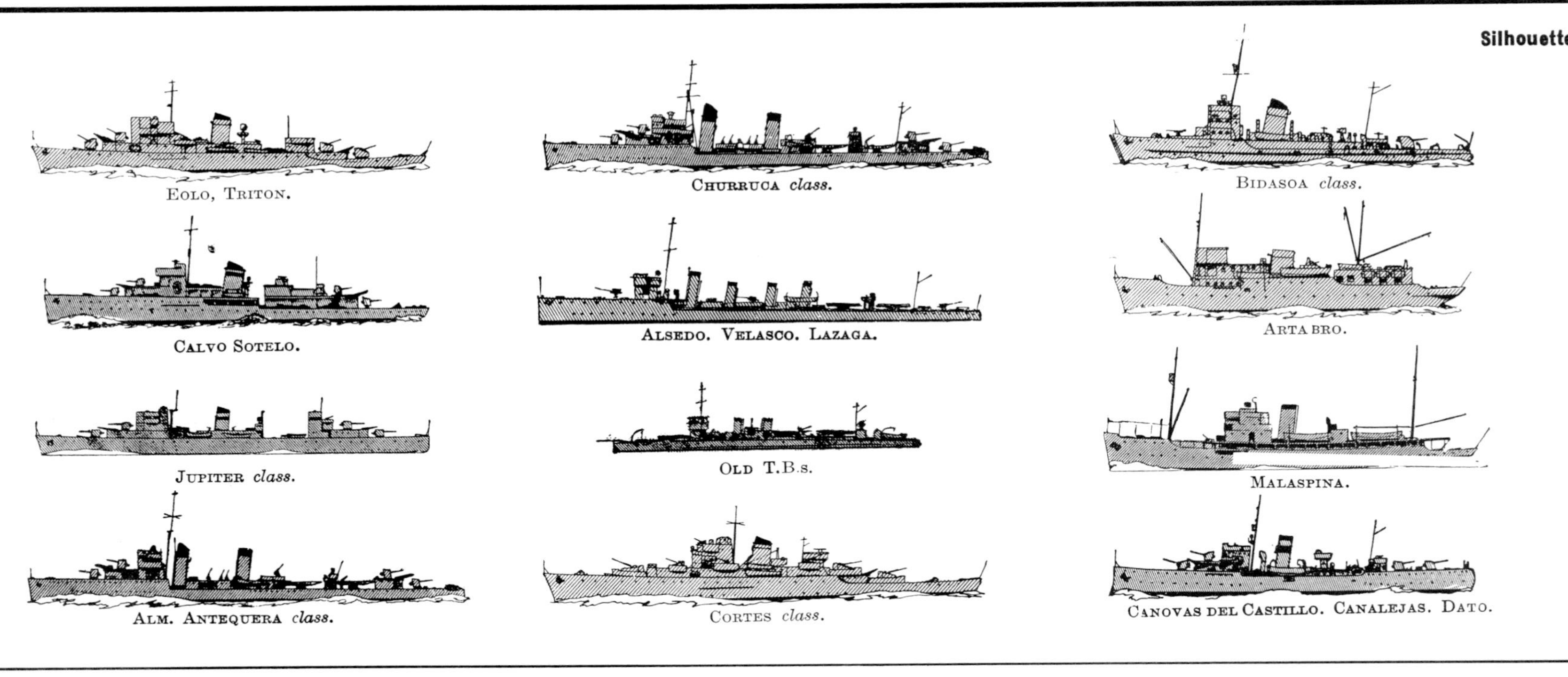

1st Class Cruiser (*Cruçero de Primera Clase*)

CANARIAS (May 28th, 1931).

Guns:
- 8—8 inch., 50 cal.
- 8—4·7 inch AA., 45 cal.
- 12—40 mm. AA.

Torpedo tubes (21 inch):
- 12 (*above water*, tripled).

Note to Plan.—Aircraft and catapult are not carried.

Armour:
- 1½"—2" Side
- 1" Turrets
- 4" Magazines

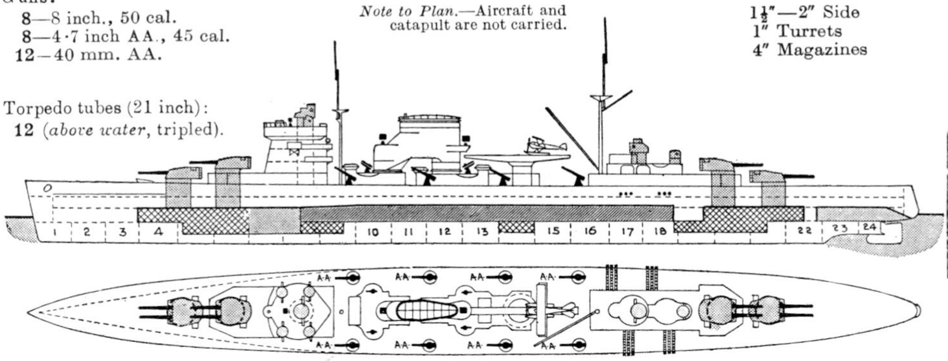

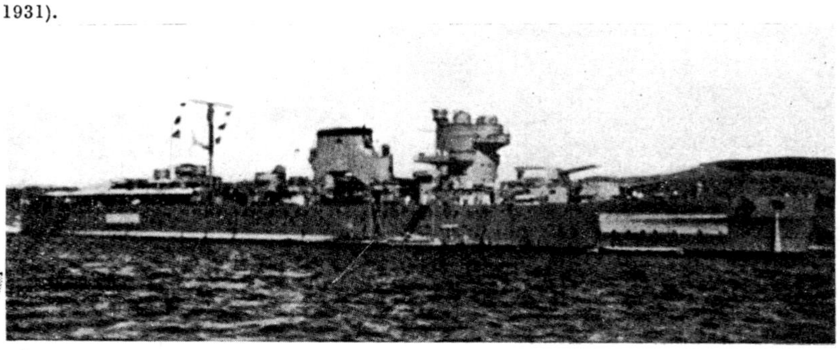

CANARIAS. 1944, *Official.*

Displacement: 10,670 tons *standard* (12,230 tons *full load*). Complement, 765.
Length, 636 feet.
Beam, 64 feet.
Draught, 17½ feet (*mean*).

Machinery: Parsons geared turbines. 2 shafts. Designed S.H.P. 90,000 = 33 kts. Boilers: 8 Yarrow. Oil: 2,794 tons. Radius: 8000 miles at 15 kts.

General Notes.—Laid down at Ferrol, August 15, 1928, and completed in Sept. 1936. Sister ship *Baleares* torpedoed and sunk, March 6, 1938.

Gunnery Note.—Maximum elevation of 8-inch guns is 70°.

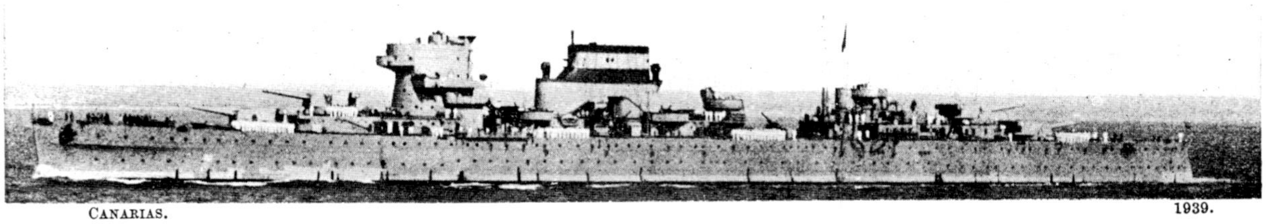

CANARIAS. 1939.

Cruisers

GALICIA (ex-*Libertad*, ex-*Principe Alfonso*) (Jan. 3rd, 1925), ALMIRANTE CERVERA (Oct. 16th, 1925), MIGUEL DE CERVANTES (May 19th, 1928).

Standard Displacement, 7,976 tons (*Cervera*), 8,250 tons (others). *Full load*, 9,240 and 9,900 tons, respectively.
Length, 575 feet (*pp.*), 579½ feet (*o.a.*) Beam, 54 feet.
Draught, *mean* 16½ feet, *deep load* 20½ feet
Complement, 564.

Guns:
- 8—6 inch, 50 cal.
- 8—3·5 inch AA.
- 8—37 mm. AA.
- 20—20 mm. A.A.

Tubes:
- 6—21 inch (tripled) in revolving mounts on upper deck.

But *Cervera* has
- 8—6 inch.
- 4—4·1 inch AA.
- 8—37 mm. AA.
- 4—20 mm. AA.

Tubes:
- 12—21 inch.

Armour:
- 3" Side (amidships.) ....
- 2" Side (forward.) ....
- 1½" Side (aft.) ....
- 1" Deck. ....
- 2" (H.T. ?) over rudder. ?.........

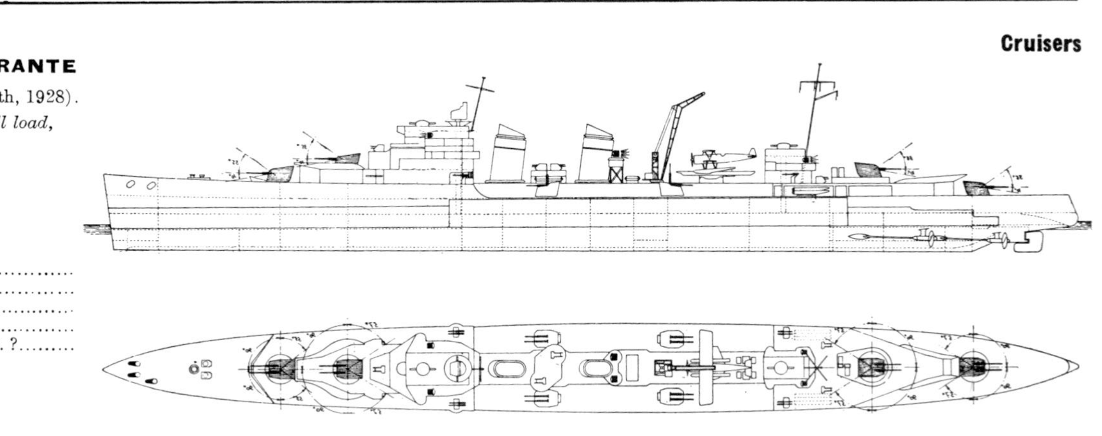

Cruisers

Machinery: Parsons Geared Turbines. 4 shafts. Designed S.H.P. 80,000 = 33 kts. Boilers: 8 Yarrow (large tube). Fuel capacity: 500 tons oil, *normal*; 1,700 tons oil, *maximum*. Endurance: 5000 at 15 kts., 1200 at *full power*.

Name	*Builder*	*Machinery*	*Laid down*	*Completed*	*Trials*	*Boilers*
Galicia *Alm. Cervera* *M. de Cervantes*	Ferrol D.Y.	S. E. C. N.	Aug. '22 25 Nov. '22 Apr. '26	Dec. '25 May '27 1931	83000 = 34·7.	Yarrow

Notes.—Laid down by S.E.C.N. at Ferrol D.Y., under Navy Law of 17th Feb., 1915. Cost estimated at about 8122 pesetas a ton.

Designed under direction of late Sir Philip Watts, K.C.B., Director of Sir W. G. Armstrong, Whitworth & Co., Ltd., for Spanish Government. Were originally modifications of British "E" class design, with second, third and fourth gun positions paired and beam guns omitted. Reconstructed and modernised during 1940–44.

ALMIRANTE CERVERA. 1944, *Official.*

ALM. CERVERA. 1944, *Official.*

GALICIA. 1946, *Official.*

1946, *Official.*

MENDEZ NUÑEZ (3rd March, 1923).

Standard Displacement: 4,680 tons (*full load,* 6,045 tons). Complement, 370.
Length, (*pp.*) 440 feet, (*o.a.*) 462 feet. Beam, 46 feet. Draught, 14⅓ feet *mean* 19 feet *max.*

Guns:
8—6 inch, 50 cal.
10—37 mm. AA.
8—20 mm. AA.

Torpedo Tubes (21 inch):
6 *above water* (triple mountings).

Armour:
¾—1″ Side amidships ....
½—1″ Side (ends)...............
1″ Deck ....

Machinery: Parsons geared turbines. 4 shafts. Designed H.P.: 45,000 = 29 kts. Boilers: 12 Yarrow (6 oil burning, 6 mixed firing). Coal: 806 tons + 727 tons oil. Radius: 5,000 miles at 13 kts. *Blas de Lezo*, wrecked July 11, 1932, was a sister ship.

Name	*Builder*	*Machinery*	*Laid down*	*Completed*	*Trials*	*Boilers*
M. Nuñez	Ferrol D.Y.	S. E. C. N.	28 Sept.'17	1924	43,776 = 29·28	Yarrow

Historical Note.—Named after the Admiral who was Commander-in-Chief of the Spanish Fleet in the Pacific in 1866. He bombarded Valparaiso on March 31 of that year, but was repulsed with a wound at Callao on May 2.

1944, *Official.*

NAVARRA (ex-*Republica*, ex-*Reina Victoria Eugenia*) (21st April, 1920).

Standard Displacement, 4,857 tons (6,500 tons *full load.*) Complement, 404.
Length (*pp.*) 440 feet, (*o.a.*) 462 feet. Beam, 50 feet. *Mean* draught, 15¾ feet; **max., 21¾ feet.**

Guns (Vickers):
6—6 inch, 50 cal.
4—3.5 inch AA.
4—20 mm. AA.

Armour (Nickel and H.T.):
3″ Side ....
2½-1¼″ Ends ......
3″ Deck ....
6″ Conning tower

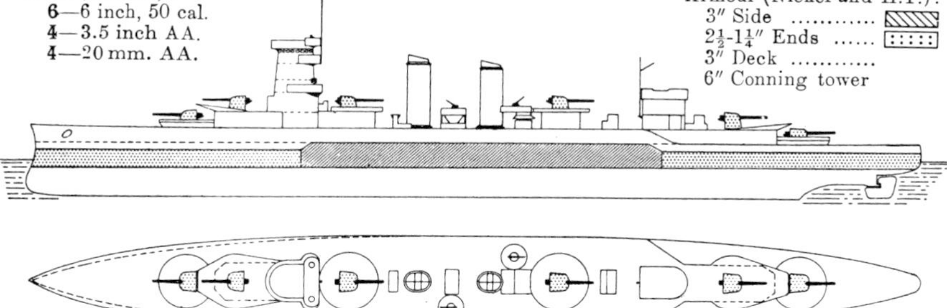

Machinery: Parsons turbines. 2 shafts. Designed H.P.: 25,500 = 25·5 kts. Boilers: 8 Yarrow. Oil fuel: 1,200 tons. Radius: 4,500 miles at 15 kts.

Name	*Builder*	*Machinery*	*Ordered*	*Laid down*	*Completed*	*Trials*	*Boilers*	*Best recent speed*
Navarra	Ferrol D.Y.	S. E. C. N.	Aug. '14	Mar. '15	15 Jan., '23	8 hours: 26,049 = 25·77 4 hours: 28,387 = 26·9	Yarrow	

General Notes.—Built under Navy Law of July 30, 1914. Refitted and reboilered at Cadiz, 1937–38, changes involved being reduction of funnels from 3 to 2, removal of 3 guns of main armament, new bridgework and masts.

Gunnery Notes.—6 inch are Vickers models, built at La Carraca.

Destroyers (*Destructores*).

9 Oquendo Class. *Building.*

Blasco de Garay, Blas de Lezo, Bonifaz, Gelmirez, Langara, Marques de la Enseñada, Oquendo, Recalde, Roger de Lauria. All building or about to be laid down at Ferrol. Displacement: 2,050 tons. Dimensions: 382 × 36 × 12 feet (*mean*). Guns: **8**—4·1 inch AA., **12**—37 mm. AA., **4**—20 mm. AA. Tubes: **7**—21 inch. Machinery: Geared turbines of Rateau-Bretagne type. 2 shafts. S.H.P.: 60,000 = 39 kts. Boilers: 3 of 3-drum type. Fuel: 659 tons. Radius of action: 5,000 miles at 20 kts. Complement: 267.

Historical Notes.—Don Blas de Lezo (1687–1741) lost a leg at the Battle of Malaga, an eye in the siege of Toulon, and an arm during the second siege of Barcelona. He died after repulsing Admiral Vernon's attack on Cartagena. Bonifaz, Marques de Montferrat, was a prominent figure in the Fourth Crusade. Don Juan de Langara commanded the Spanish fleet at Toulon in 1793, and at the Battle of Cape St. Vincent in 1780. Enseñada (1690–1772), one of the chief ministers of Ferdinand VI, fostered the Spanish Navy and maritime commerce. Admiral don Antonio de Oquendo (1577–1640) defeated the Dutch off Pernambuco in 1633, but lost his life in action against Tromp in the Downs seven years afterwards. Don Juan Martinez de Recalde was second-in-command of the Armada in 1588. Lauria (1250–1305) expelled the French from Sicily and defeated the Turks at sea.

2 Alava Class. *Building.*

Alava, Liniers. Displacement: 1,650 tons. Dimensions: 332 × 31½ × 15 feet (*mean*). Guns: **4**—4·7 inch, **2**—37 mm. AA., **3**—20 mm. AA. Tubes: **6**—21 inch (tripled). Machinery: Parsons geared turbines. 2 shafts. S.H.P.: 44,000 = 36 kts. Boilers: 4 of 3-drum type.

Note.—These two destroyers, a development of the *Churruca* design, were originally ordered in 1936, but construction was held up by the Civil War. After being resumed, it was again suspended in 1940, only to be started once more at Cartagena, 1944.

Historical Notes.—Don Miguel Ricardo de Alava (1771–1843), originally a naval officer, fought against the French at the Battle of Vitoria, and rose to the rank of General. Don Santiago de Liniers (1756–1810) defended Buenos Aires against British attack in 1807, and subsequently became Governor of that province. He supported the cause of Ferdinand VII against the usurpation of Joseph Buonaparte, and was executed in consequence.

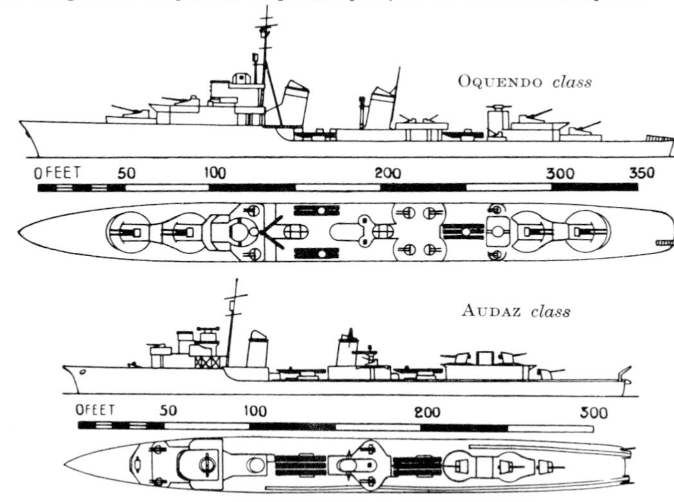

13 Churruca Class.

ALMIRANTE VALDES. 1944, *Official.*

First Group (6). Appearance as first photo.

Sanchez Barcaiztegui (July 24, 1926), ***José Luis Diez*** (Aug. 25, 1928), ***Lepanto*** (Nov. 7 1929), ***Alcalá Galiano*** (April 12, 1930), ***Almirante Valdés*** (Sept. 8, 1930), ***Churruca*** (1929).

Second Group (7). Appearance as second photo.

Almirante Antequera (Dec. 29, 1930), ***Almirante Miranda*** (June 20, 1931), ***Gravina*** (Dec. 24, 1931), ***Escaño*** (June 28, 1932), ***Ulloa*** (July 24, 1933), ***Jorge Juan*** (March 28, 1933), ***Ciscar*** (Oct. 26, 1933).

All built at Cartagena by S.E. de C.N. Displacement: 1,676 tons *standard*, 2,087 tons *full load*. Dimensions: 320 (*pp.*), 333 (*o.a.*) × 31¾ × 17 feet *max.* draught. Complement: 175. Guns: **4**—4·7 inch, **4**—37 mm. AA., **4**—20 mm. AA. **4** D.C. Throwers. Armament of all these ships has recently been modified to permit of increased anti-aircroft fire. Torpedo tubes: **6**—21 inch (tripled). Machinery: 2 sets Parsons geared turbines. 2 shafts. S.H.P.: 42,000 = 36 kts. Boilers: 4 of 3-drum type. Oil fuel: 540 tons. Radius: 4,500 miles at 14 kts.

Notes.—Design generally follows that of British flotilla leaders of *Scott* class. Two earliest ships of this class, originally named *Alcalá Galiano* and *Churruca*, were sold to Argentina, 1927, new units bearing same names being built to replace them. *Alm. Juan Ferrandiz* and *Ciscar* sunk in Civil War, Sept., 1936 and Oct., 1937, respectively, but latter ship was salved and refitted in 1938–39. *Churruca* torpedoed by submarine, but repaired.

Following initials are painted on bows: *Sanchez Barcaiztegui, SB; José Luis Diez, DZ; Lepanto, LO; A. Galiano, AG; Ciscar, CR.; Alm. Valdés, VS; Alm. Antequera, AA; Alm. Miranda, MA; Gravina, GA; Escaño, EO; Ulloa, UA; J. Juan, JJ.; Churruca, CH.*

Historical Notes.—Admiral don Federico Gravina died of wounds received at Trafalgar, where he commanded the Spanish fleet. Rear-Admiral don Antonio Escaño was his chief of staff. Commodore Galiano commanded the *Bahama*, don Cosme Churruca the *San Juan Nepomuceno*, and don Cayetano Valdès the *Neptuno*, in the same battle. Don Antonio de Ulloa (1716–1795) was a flag officer who served with distinction in S. America, and became Governor of Louisiana in 1764. Don Jorge Juan (1713–1773) was a celebrated naval architect and scientist. Lepanto was the victory gained over the Turks in 1571.

GRAVINA. 1944, *Official.*

Torpedo Boats (*Torpederos*).

9 Audaz Class. (*Building.*)

Ariete, Atrevido, Audaz, Furor, Intrepido, Osado, Rayo, Relampago, Temerario. All laid down at Ferrol in 1944–45. Displacement: 1,010 tons. Dimensions: 305 × 30¾ × 10 feet *mean*). Guns: **3**—4·1 inch, **4**—37 mm. AA., **8**—20 mm. AA. 2 D.C.T. Torpedo tubes: **6**—21 inch (tripled). Machinery: Geared turbines. S.H.P.: 28,000 = 33 kts. Boilers: 3 of 3-drum type. Oil fuel: 290 tons. Radius: 3,800 miles at 14 kts. Complement, 145.

Note.—Respective meanings of these names are: Battering ram, bold, audacious, fury, fearless, daring, thunderbolt, lightning flash, venturesome.

3 Alsedo Class.

Alsedo class: ***Alsedo*** (Oct. 26, 1922), ***Velasco*** (1923), ***Lazaga*** (March, 1924). All built at Cartagena. Displacement: 1,145 tons (*normal*), 1,315 tons (*full load*). Dimensions: 275 (*p.p.*), 283 (*o.a.*) × 27 × 15 feet. (*max.*) Parsons geared turbines. 4 Yarrow boilers. H.P. 33,000 = 34 kts. (36 kts. reached on trials). Fuel: 272 tons oil only. Radius: 2,500 miles at 15 kts. Guns: **2**—4 inch, 45 cal., **1**—3·5 inch AA., **4**—20 mm. AA., 2 D.C.T. Torpedo tubes: **4**—21 inch in 2 twin deck mountings. Complement, 86.

Notes.—Provided under Law of 1915. First of class laid down about June, 1920. *Lazaga* was originally known as *Juan Lazaga*. Are distinguished by initial letters painted on bows, viz., *Alsedo, A; Lazaga, L; Velasco, V.*

Historical Notes.—Don Francisco Alsedo y Bustamente was killed while commanding the *Montañes* at Trafalgar. Don Luis Vicente de Velasco lost his life in the defence of the Morro Castle against the British at Havana, 1762. Captain Lazaga was killed in command of the cruiser *Oquendo* at the Battle of Santiago, 1898.

ALSEDO. 1928 *Photo, Abrahams & Sons, Devonport.*

Old Torpedo Boats (*Classed as Minelayers*).

2 *Vickers-Normand* type: Nos. ***14*** (1915), ***17*** (1918). Displacement: 177 tons. Dimensions: 164 × 16½ × 6⅓ feet (*max.* draught). Armament: **3**—3 pdr., **3**—18 inch tubes, twin amidships and single aft. Parsons turbines and Normand boilers. 2 shafts. H.P.: 3,750 = 26 kts. Coal: 33 tons. Complement: 31. 24 boats sanctioned under Law of the 7th January, 1908, but Nos. 23 and 24 were abandoned 1919. No. 2 lost in Sept., 1937. Others have been scrapped.

1931 *Photo, Capitán M. Mille*

Submarines (*Submarinos*).

C 2 — 1933 *Photo, Capitán Mateo Mille.*

2 *Electric Boat Co.* design: ***C 1*** (March 28, 1927), ***C 2*** (May 4, 1928). Built at Cartagena. Displacement: 842 tons *on surface*, 1,290 tons *submerged*. Dimensions: 247 (*o.a.*) × $20\frac{3}{4}$ × $13\frac{1}{2}$ feet. Machinery: 2 sets 6-cylinder Vickers Diesel engines. H.P.: 2,000 = 16 kts. (*surface*), $8\frac{1}{2}$ kts. (*submerged*). Guns: **1**—3 inch AA., **1** M.G. AA. Torpedo tubes: **6**—21 inch (4 bow, 2 stern). Diving limit, 45 fathoms (reached by *C* 1 on trials in 1928). Complement: 46.

Notes.—About Sept. 1930 *C* 1 was named ***Isaac Peral.*** Peral, a naval officer, was the first Spaniard to design a submarine. *C* 3 was sunk at Malaga in Dec., 1936, but was salved some months later and towed to Cadiz for refit. She has since been discarded, together with *C* 5. *C* 6 sunk at Gijon. *C* 4 was sunk by collision with *Lepanto*, during exercises off the Balearic Islands in June, 1946.

D 1. — 1946, *Official.*

3 *Admiralty* type: ***D1*** (May 11, 1944), ***D2*** (Dec. 21, 1944), ***D3.*** All built at Cartagena. Displacement: 1,050/1,375 tons. Dimensions: $275\frac{1}{2}$ × $21\frac{3}{4}$ × $13\frac{1}{2}$ feet (*mean*). H.P.: 5,000/1,350 = 20·5/9·5 kts. Tubes: **6**—21 inch (4 bow, 2 stern). Guns: **1**—4·7 inch, **4**—37 mm.AA. Diving limit, 50 fathoms. Radius *on surface*: 9,000 miles.

Minelayers

TRITON — Added 1946, *Official.*

Eolo (August 30, 1939), ***Tritón*** (Feb. 1940). Both built by S.E. de C.N. at Ferrol. Displacement: 1,500 tons. Dimensions: 278 × $38\frac{1}{2}$ × 10 feet. Guns: **4**—4 inch, **4**—40 mm. AA., **4** M.G. Stowage for 70 mines. Machinery: Parsons geared turbines. 2 shafts. S.H.P. 5,000 = 19·5 kts. Boilers: 2 Yarrow. Fuel: 300 tons. Design resembles Mexican *Queretaro* type.

VULCANO. — 1944, *Official.*

JUPITER (Sept. 14, 1935), **VULCANO** (Oct. 18, 1935), **MARTE** (June 19, 1936), **NEPTUNO** (Dec. 19, 1937). All built at Ferrol. Displacement: 2,100 tons. Dimensions: $302\frac{3}{4}$ (*pp.*), 315 (*o.a.*) × $41\frac{1}{2}$ × $11\frac{1}{2}$ feet. Guns: **4**—4·7 inch, **2**—3 inch AA. (except *Vulcano*, **2**—3·5 inch AA.), **4**—20 mm. AA. (twin mounts), **2** D.C. Throwers. Machinery: 2 sets Parsons geared turbines. 2 shafts. S.H.P.: 5,000 = 18·5 kts. Yarrow boilers. Fuel: 280 tons. Stowage for 264 mines. Complement: 123.

Sloops, rated as Gunboats (*Cañoneros*).

8 Cortes Class.

PIZARRO. — 1946, *Official.*

HERNAN CORTES, MARTIN ALONSO PINZON, PIZARRO, VASCO NUÑEZ DE BALBOA (all Aug. 3, 1944). **LEGAZPI, MAGALLANES, SARMIENTO DE GAMBOA, VICENTE YAÑEZ PINZON** (all Aug. 8, 1945). Built at Ferrol. Displacement: 1,710 tons. Dimensions: 279 (*pp.*), $312\frac{1}{3}$ (*o.a.*) × $39\frac{1}{2}$ × 11 feet. Guns: **6**—4·1 inch, **8**—37 mm. AA., **6**—20 mm. AA., **2** D.C.T. Machinery: 2 sets Diesels. B.H.P.: 5,000 = 18·5 kts. Fuel: 373 tons. Radius: 3,000 miles at 14 kts.

Historical Notes.—Francisco Pizarro (1475–1541) and his kinsman Cortes (1485–1547) were the conquerors of Peru and Mexico, respectively. M. A. Pinzon and V. Y. Pinzon accompanied Columbus on his first voyage. Balboa (1475–1517) discovered Yucatan in company with V. Y. Pinzon, and was the first European to sight the Pacific. Magallanes was the first to navigate that ocean. Legazpi colonised the Philippines, 1566–71. Sarmiento (1530–1587) first charted the Strait of Magellan.

Added 1940.

CALVO SOTELO (ex-*Zacatecas*) (Echavarrieta y Larrinaga, Cadiz, August 27, 1934). Displacement: 1,600 tons. Dimensions: 282 × 40 × 10 feet. Guns: **4**—4 inch, **2**—3 inch AA., **3**—20 mm. AA. Machinery: Parsons geared turbines. 2 shafts. S.H.P.: 6,500 = 20 kts. 2 Yarrow boilers.

Note.—This ship was completing for the Mexican Navy in 1936, when she was acquired by the Spanish Government.

DATO. — 1939, *Official.*

CANOVAS DEL CASTILLO (Jan. 21, 1922), **CANALEJAS** (Dec. 1, 1922), **DATO** (1923). Built by S.E.C.N., at Cartagena. Displacement: 1,314 tons. Complement: 220. Dimensions: $236\frac{1}{2}$ (*pp.*), $251\frac{1}{3}$ (*o.a.*) × $33\frac{3}{4}$ × $11\frac{3}{4}$ feet. Guns: **4**—4 inch (except *Canalejas*, **4**—4·1 inch), **2**—3 inch AA., **2** pom-poms (for landing). No torpedo tubes. Machinery: 2 sets triple expansion. Boilers: 2 Yarrow. Designed I.H.P.: 1,700. Speed: 15 kts. Fuel: 324 tons coal *or* oil = 6,500 miles at 10·5 kts. Provided for by Law of Feb. 17, 1915, and ordered Jan., 1920. *C. del Castillo* and *Canalejas* completed 1923, *Dato* completed 1924. These ships were originally named *Antonio Canovas del Castillo, Jose Canalejas,* and *Eduardo Dato,* but names have since been shortened.

Miscellaneous

GALATEA. 1944, *Official.*

GALATEA (ex-Barque *Clarastella*, 1896). Purchased in Italy, 1922. 2,713 tons. Dimensions: 243 × 38¾ × 17¾ feet. Guns: 4—6 pdr. 2 auxiliary Diesel motors, combined H.P.: 900 = 8·5 kts. Fuel: 46 tons. T.S. for boys.

Oilers.

1935 *Photo, Capitan M. Mille.*

PLUTÓN (ex-*Campilo*) (Valencia, 1931). Purchased in Dec., 1934. Displacement: 4,550 tons (in light condition). Dimensions: 342½ × 53¾ × 19½ feet. Machinery: 2 sets B. & W. Diesels, built in Barcelona. B.H.P.: 2,530 = 13·5 kts.

Transports

CONTRAMAESTRE CASADO. 1929 *Photo, Capitán M. Mille.*

CONTRAMAESTRE CASADO (Oct. 26, 1920). Built by Armstrong. Displacement: 7,275 tons. Complement, 107. Dimensions: 320 (*pp.*), 332¼ (*o.a.*) × 45 × 23½ feet. Guns: 4—42 mm. Machinery: 1 set triple expansion. I.H.P. 2,000=10.5 kts. Boilers: 3 cylindrical, with Howden's forced draught. Coal: 826 tons.

PP 1, PP 2 (Santander, 1939). Displacement: 470 tons. Dimensions: 138 (*pp.*), 147½ (*o.a.*) × 25 × 9½ feet. Diesel engines. B.H.P.: 220 = 10 kts.

TARIFA. Displacement: 1,325 tons. Dimensions: 270 × 35 × — feet. I.H.P.: 840 = 10 kts.

TURKEY

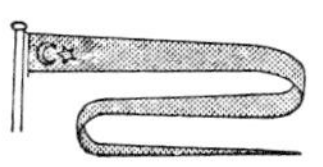

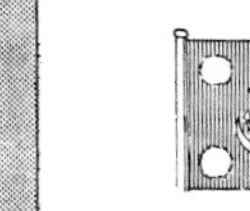

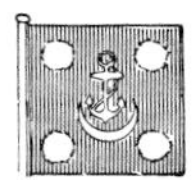

ENSIGN AND JACK. PENDANT. PRESIDENT'S STANDARD. COMMANDER-IN-CHIEF. COMMANDER OF NAVAL BASE.

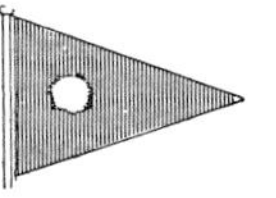

OR AMIRAL.* TÜM AMIRAL. TUĞ AMIRAL. COMMODORE. † SENIOR OFFICER (AT YARDARM) SENR. OFFICER (SUBORDINATE)

*(Kor Amiral has three balls.) † Commodore 1st class has 3 balls, if Albay 2, and if Yarbay 1.

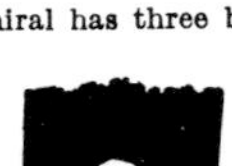

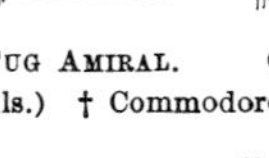

Büyük Amiral. Or Amiral. Kor Amiral. Tüm Amiral. Tuğ Amiral. Albay.

Yarbay. Binbaşi. Yüzbaşi and On Yüzbasi. Üstegmen. Tegmen. Astegmen.

DISTINGUISHING BADGES WORN BY TURKISH NAVAL OFFICERS.

1. All Turkish Naval Officers wear coloured tabs, similar to the patches worn by Midshipmen in the Royal Navy, to indicate the branch of the service to which they belong. These are:—

Flag Officers.	Scarlet.
Qualified Staff Officers.	Red.
Executive Officers.	Dark Blue.
Engineer Officers.	Light Blue, with Dark Blue diamond in centre.
All Dockyard Engineer Officers.	Light Blue (if holding a University degree, with a compass and protractor in centre).
Hydrographic Officers.	Green.
Accountant Officers.	Mauve.
Medical Officers.	Maroon velvet, with Yellow snake and staff in centre.
Dental Officers.	Maroon velvet, with Yellow snake and dental mirror in centre.
Chemical Officers.	Maroon velvet, with Yellow "U" tube and test tubes in centre.
Instructor Officers.	Brown, with White book in centre.
Legal Officers.	Brown velvet, with White scales in centre.
Band Officers.	Brown velvet, with White lyre in centre.
Clerical Officers.	Brown velvet, with White crossed quills in centre.

2. All Officers in the Submarine Service wear on the left side of their waist a badge consisting of a submarine in white metal with yellow metal oak leaves superimposed upon it.

Admiral of the Fleet (*Non-existent in peacetime*)	Büyük Amiral
Admiral (Senior)	Or Amiral
Admiral (Junior)	Kor Amiral
Vice-Admiral	Tüm Amiral
Rear-Admiral	Tuğ Amiral
Commodore	Tuğbay
Captain (Senior)	Albay

Minister of National Defence: Or General C. C. Toydemir.
Under-Secretary for Navy: Rear-Admiral Ridvan Koral.
Commander-in-Chief: Admiral Ali Ülgen.
Commanding Seagoing Fleet: Rear-Admiral Sadik Altincan.
Naval Attaché, London: Captain Asim Sinik.

Captain (Junior)	Yarbay
Commander	Binbaşi
Lieutenant-Commander	Ön Yüzbaşi
Lieutenant	Yüzbaşi
Sub-Lieutenant	Üstegmen
Acting Sub-Lieutenant	Teğmen
Midshipman	Asteğmen

Mercantile Marine.

(From "Lloyd's Register," 1939 figures). 185 Vessels of 224,461 gross tonnage.

Silhouettes

3. On white uniform and great-coats Turkish Naval Officers wear shoulder straps fitted with yellow metal badges similar to those worn by Turkish Military Officers of similar rank. These are:—

Admiral (Kor Amiral)	Three stars and three bars.
Vice-Admiral (Tum Amiral)	Two stars and three bars.
Rear Admiral (Tug Amiral)	One star and three bars.
Commodore (Tugbay)	Three stars and two bars.
Captain (Albay)	Three stars and two bars.
Captain, junior (Yarbay)	Two stars and two bars.
Commander (Binbasi)	One star and two bars.
Lieut.-Cmdr. (On Yuzbasi)	Three stars and one bar.
Lieutenant (Yuzbasi)	Three stars and one bar.
Sub-Lieut. (Ustegmen)	Two stars and one bar.
Acting Sub-Lieut. (Tegmen)	One star and one bar.
Midshipman (Astegmen)	One bar.

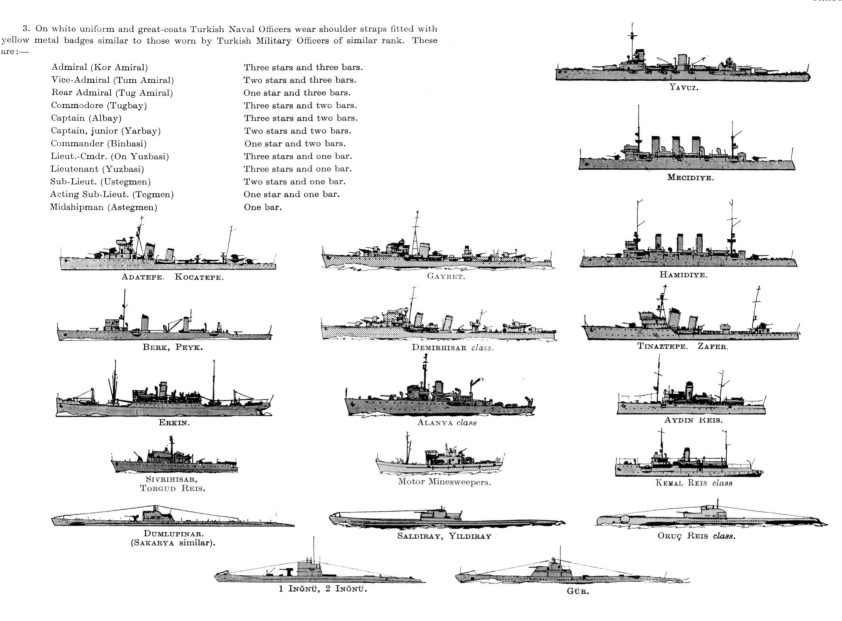

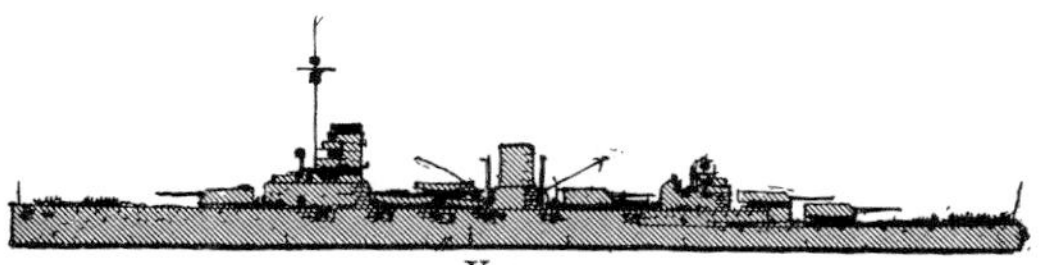

YAVUZ.

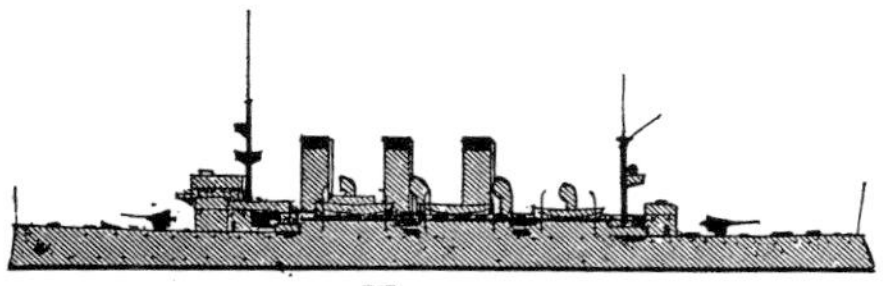

MECIDIYE.

ADATEPE. KOCATEPE.

GAYRET.

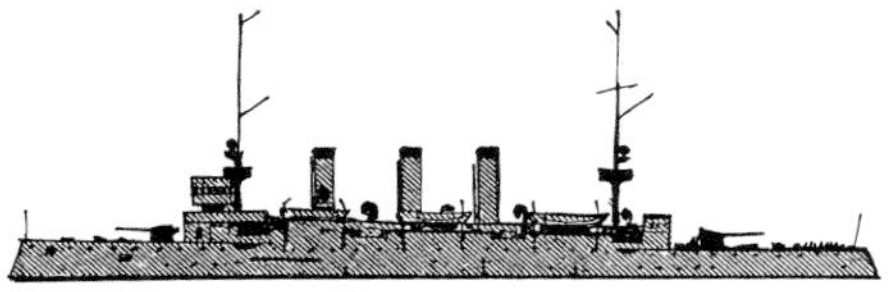

HAMIDIYE.

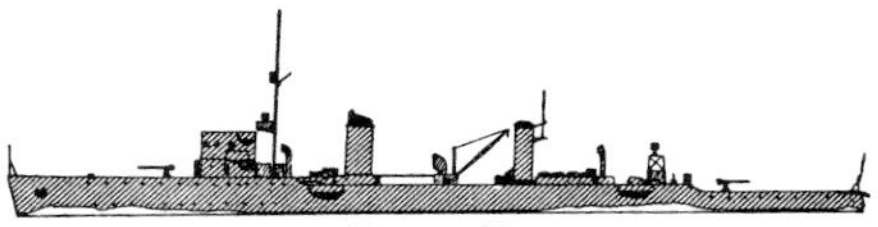

BERK, PEYK.

DEMIRHISAR *class.*

TINAZTEPE. ZAFER.

ERKIN.

ALANYA *class*

AYDIN REIS.

SIVRIHISAR, TORGUD REIS.

Motor Minesweepers.

KEMAL REIS *class*

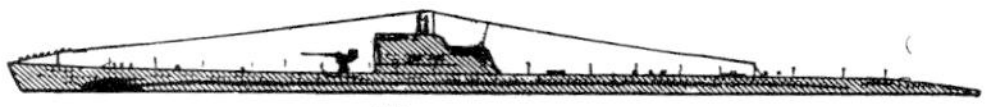

DUMLUPINAR. (SAKARYA similar).

SALDIRAY, YILDIRAY

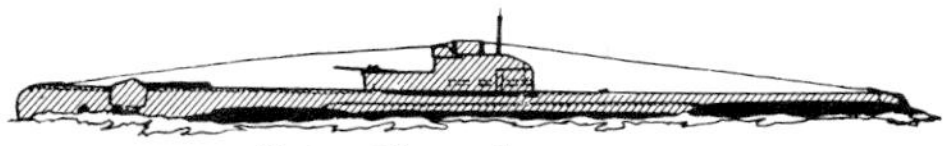

ORUÇ REIS *class.*

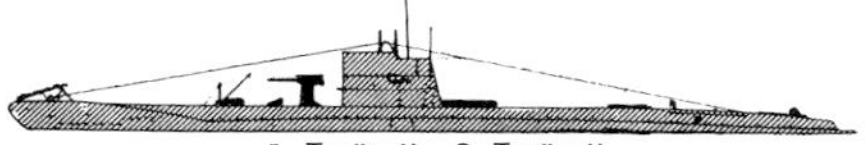

1 INÖNÜ, 2 INÖNÜ.

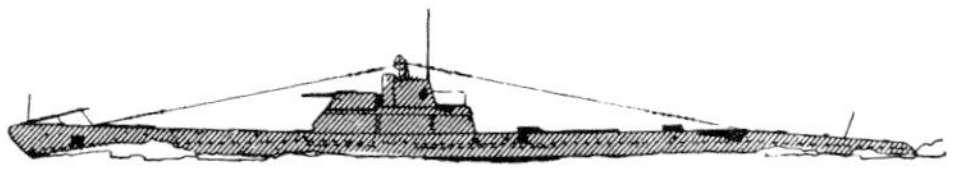

GÜR.

YAVUZ (ex-German *Goeben,*) (Blohm & Voss, March 28, 1911).

Standard Displacement, 23,100 tons. Complement, 1,300 (as Flagship).
Length (*w.l.*), 610¼ feet. Beam, 96 ft. 10 in. Draught (*max. load*), 26 ft. 11 in.

Machinery: Parsons turbine, 4 shaft, direct drive. Boilers: 24 Schulz-Thornycroft (German "Marine Type.") Designed H.P.: nominally 52,000 = 25·5 kts. (21 kts. now best speed). Coal: *normal* about 1,000 tons; *maximum* 3,050 tons + 200 tons oil.

Guns:
10—11 in. 50 cal.
10—5·9 in. 45 cal.
8—3.5 inch A.A.
12—40 mm. AA.
4 M.G.
Torpedo tubes (19·7 in.)
2 *submerged.*

Anti-Torp. Pro.:—
2″—1″ deep H.T. Steel B.H., between extreme barbettes: Minute internal subdivision.

Armour (Krupp):
10½″ Belt (amidships) tapers to 6″ at top and 5″ below
3¾″ Belt (bow and stern)
9″—8″ Barbettes
8″ Gunhouses
5″ Battery
10″ Fore C.T. 3″ Roof
8″—3″ Double com. tube
8″ After C.T.
6″—3″ Com. tube
3″—1″ Decks

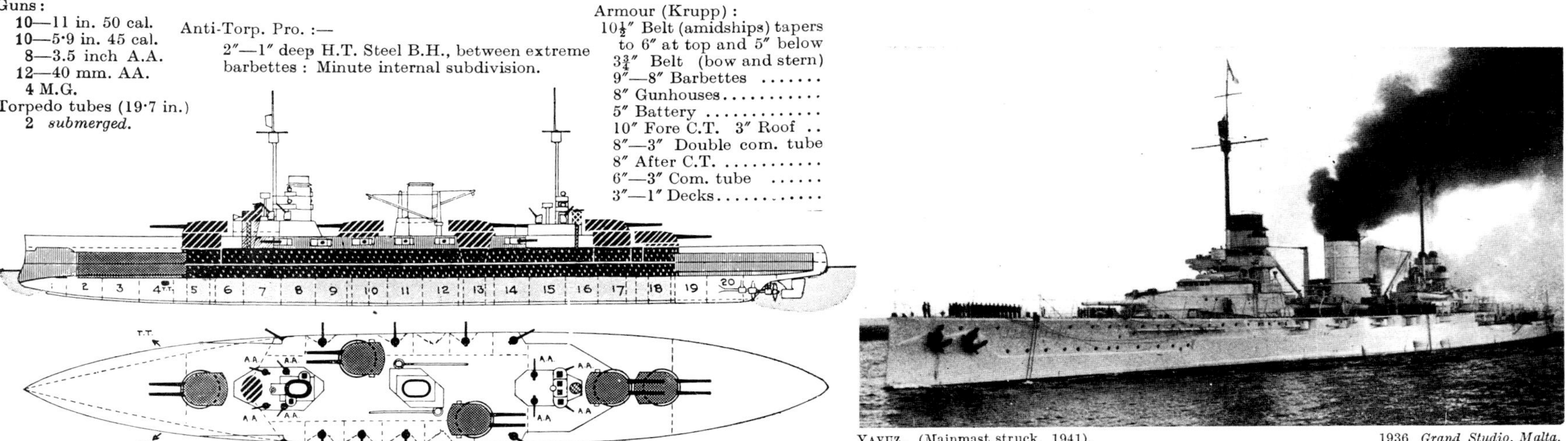

YAVUZ. (Mainmast struck, 1941). 1936 *Grand Studio, Malta.*

Battle-Cruiser

1934 *Photo, Official.*

Engineering Notes.—Endurance is *(a)* 5,350 miles at 10 kts., *(b)* 2,370 miles at a continuous *max.* sea-going speed of 23 kts. **She made 26·8 knots on Trials for 6 hours, and 27·1 kts. for 4 hours, on Mar. 17, 1930.**

General Notes.—Laid down, August, 1909, by Blohm & Voss, Hamburg, under 1909 German Navy Programme, as a sister to German *Moltke*. Completed, July, 1912. Transferred to the Turkish Navy in 1914, and during the war was twice mined, striking 5 mines in all. A contract was signed in December, 1926, with the Chantiers de St. Nazaire (Penhoët), for the repair and refit of this battle-cruiser at Ismid; the work was considerably delayed owing to a floating dock proving unequal to her weight, and completion was not reached till 1930. She was again refitted in 1938. Mainmast was removed in 1941 to provide space for AA. fire control.

1931, *Official.*

Destroyers

1946, *Wright & Logan.*

1 *Fairfield:* **Gayret** (ex-H.M.S. *Oribi*, ex-*Observer*, Jan. 14, 1941). Displacement: 1,540 tons. Dimensions: $338\frac{1}{2}$ (*pp.*), 345 (*o.a.*) × 35 × 9 feet. Guns: **4**—4·7 inch, **4**—2 pdr. pompoms, **8**—20 mm. AA. Tubes: **8**—21 inch. Machinery: Parsons geared turbines. 2 shafts. S.H.P.: 40,000=36 kts. Boilers: 2, of 3-drum type.

3 Demirhisar Class.

SULTANHISAR. 1946, *London Studio.*

2 *Denny:* **Demirhisar, Sultanhisar.**
1 *Vickers-Armstrongs (Barrow):* **Muavenet** (ex-H.M.S. *Inconstant*, ex-*Muavenet*).

Displacement: 1,360 tons. Dimensions: 312 (*pp.*), 323 (*o.a.*) × 33 × $8\frac{1}{2}$ feet (*mean*). Guns: **4**—4·7 inch, **6** smaller. Tubes: **8**—21 inch. Machinery: Parsons geared turbines, 2 shafts. S.H.P.: 34,000 = 35·5 kts. Boilers: 3, of 3-drum type, 300 lb. working pressure. Oil fuel: 450 tons. Complement: 150.

Name	*Begun.*	*Launched.*	*Completed.*	*Name*	*Begun.*	*Launched.*	*Completed*
Demirhisar } *Sultanhisar* }	1939	1941	1942	*Muavenet*	24/5/39	15/12/40	24/1/42

ZAFER. 1933 *Photo, Official.*

2 *C.N. del Tirreno* boats: **Tinaztepe** (July 27, 1931), **Zafer** (Sept. 20, 1931). Built at Riva Trigoso.
Displacement: 1,206 tons (*standard*), 1,610 tons (*full load*). Dimensions: 307 (*pp.*), 315 (*o.a.*) × $30\frac{1}{2}$ × $10\frac{3}{4}$ feet. Guns: **4**—4·7 inch, 50 cal., 2—40 mm. AA., 2—20 mm. AA. Tubes: **6**—21 inch in triple mountings. Machinery: Parsons geared turbines. S.H.P.: 35,000=36 kts. Boilers: 3 Thornycroft with superheaters. Oil: 350 tons. Complement: 149.

1935.

KOCATEPE.

2 *Ansaldo* boats: **Kocatepe** (Feb. 7, 1931), **Adatepe** (March 19, 1931). Built at Sestri Ponente.
Displacement: 1,250 tons (*standard*), 1,650 tons (*full load*). Dimensions: $321\frac{1}{2}$ (*pp.*) $328\frac{3}{8}$ (*o.a.*) × $30\frac{3}{4}$ × $9\frac{1}{2}$ feet (*mean*). Guns: **4**—4·7 inch, 50 cal., 2—40 mm. AA. and 2—20 mm. AA. Tubes: **6**—21 inch in triple mountings. Machinery: Parsons geared turbines. S.H.P.: 40,000=36 kts. Boilers: 3 Thornycroft with superheaters. Oil: 360 tons. Complement: 149.
Note.—These ships are named after mountains near Smyrna associated with Turkish military glories.

Submarines

BURAK REIS. 1946, *London Studio.*

3 *Vickers-Armstrongs (Barrow):* **Burak Reis** (Oct. 19, 1940), **Murat Reis** (July 20, 1940), **Oruç Reis** (July 19, 1940). Ordered March, 1939. Displacement: 683/856 tons. Dimensions: 193 (*pp.*), $201\frac{1}{2}$ (*o.a.*) × $22\frac{1}{3}$ × $10\frac{1}{2}$ feet (*mean*), $11\frac{2}{3}$ feet (*max.*). Guns: **1**—3 inch, **1** M.G. Tubes: **5**—21 inch (4 bow, 1 stern). H.P.: 1,550/1,300 = 13·75/9 kts. Fuel: 40 tons. All completed 1942.

Note.—These submarines served in Royal Navy as *P* 611, 612, 614 during the *Second World War*.

SALDIRAY 1939

2 "Ay" Class.

2 *Germania* type: **Yildiray** (Aug. 26, 1939), (built at Istambul), **Saldiray** (Germania, Kiel, July 23, 1938). Both laid down 1937. Displacement: 934/1,210 tons. Dimensions: $262\frac{1}{2}$ × 21 × 14 feet. Guns: **1**—4 inch, **1**—20 mm. AA. Tubes: **6** (4 bow and 2 stern). 2 sets Burmeister & Wain Diesels. H.P.: 3,500 = 20/9 kts. Diving limit: 55 fathoms. Complement: 44.

Note.—*Atilay*, of this type, lost during submerged trials off Canakkale, July 14, 1942. The minelaying submarine *Batiray*, launched at Kiel for the Turkish Navy in 1939, was never delivered by the Germans, and was scuttled by them in May, 1945.

Submarines

1935, *courtesy of Capitán M. Mille.*

1 *German* design: **Gür** (Echavarrieta y Larrinaga, Cadiz, 1932). Purchased 1934 and delivered in Jan. 1935. Displacement: 750/960 tons. Dimensions: $237\frac{1}{2} \times 20\frac{1}{3} \times 13\frac{1}{2}$ feet. Armament: **1**—4 inch, **1**—20 mm. AA. guns, **6**—21 inch tubes (**4** bow, **2** stern). 14 torpedoes carried. 2 sets M.A.N. Diesels. H.P. 2,800/1,000, speed, 20/9 kts. Radius: 6,400 miles at $9\frac{1}{2}$ kts. on *surface*; 1,880 miles at $18\frac{1}{2}$ kts. on *surface*; 101 miles at 4 kts. *submerged*. Diving limit, 44 fathoms. Complement: 42.

Note.—Many of the parts for this submarine were made in the Netherlands.

1 *Bernardis* type: **Sakarya** (Cant. Nav. Triestino, Monfalcone, Feb. 2, 1931). Displacement: 710/940 tons. Dimensions: 196 (*p.p.*) $\times 22\frac{1}{3} \times 13$ feet. Guns: **1**—4 inch, **1**—20 mm. AA. Tubes: 6—21 inch. M.A.N Diesels. H.P.: 1,600 = 16 kts. *surface*. Electric motors. H.P.: 1,100 = 9·5 kts. *submerged*. Radius: 4,000 miles at 10 kts. Complement: 41.

DUMLUPINAR. 1936, *Grand Studio.*

1 *Bernardis* minelaying type: **Dumlupinar** (4 March, 1931). Built by Cantiere Navale Triestino, Monfalcone. Displacement: 920/1,150 tons. Dimensions: $223 \times 19 \times 14$ feet. Armament: **1**—4 inch gun, **1** M.G., **6**—21 inch tubes (4 bow, 2 stern). 48 mines carried. Machinery: M.A.N. Diesels H.P.: 3,000 = 17·5 kts. *on surface*. Electric motors of 1,400 H.P. = 9 kts. *submerged*. Complement: 47.

BIRINCI INÖNÜ 1936, *Grand Studio.*

2 *Fijenoord* type: **Birinci Inönü** (February 1, 1927), **Ikinci Inönü** (March 12, 1927). Built by Fijenoord Co., Rotterdam. Displacement: 505/620 tons. Dimensions: $192\frac{1}{2} \times 19 \times 11\frac{1}{2}$ feet. 2 sets M.A.N. Diesels. H.P.: 1,100 = 13·5/8·5 kts. Guns: **1**—3 inch, **1**—20 mm. Tubes: **6**—17·7 inch (4 bow, 2 stern). Complement: 29.

Note.—These two names refer to the first and second Turkish victories gained at Inönü, in Asia Minor.

Old Cruisers (*Muhafazali Kruvazör*)

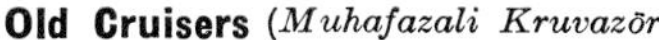

(These two ships, with gunboats *Berk* and *Peyk* on following page, together constitute the Reserve Fleet.)

1932 *Photo, Official.*

HAMIDIYE (ex-*Abdul Hamid*, Armstrong, Sept., 1903). Displacement: 3830 tons. Complement, 302. Dimensions: $368 \times 47\frac{1}{2} \times 16$ feet (*mean* draught). Guns: **2**—5·9 inch, 45 cal. Krupp, **8**—3 inch 50 cal. (Schneider). Armour: 4″ Deck. Machinery: 2 sets 4-cylinder triple expansion. 2 shafts. Designed H.P.: 12,000 = 22 kts. (*forced* draught). Present best speed about 16–18 kts. Boilers: 6 cylindrical. Coal: 750 tons. Endurance: 5,000 miles at 10 kts. At present serves as Training Ship for Naval Cadets.

1932 *Photo, Official.*

MECIDIYE (ex-Russian *Prut*, ex-Turkish *Medjidieh*, July 25, 1903). Displacement: 3,500 tons. Complement: 330. Dimensions: $330 \times 42 \times 17\frac{1}{2}$ feet (*max.* draught). Guns (as re-armed): **6**—5·1 inch (Vickers), **4**—3 inch, 50 cal. (Schneider), **2** M.G. Armour: 1″ Deck. Machinery: Triple expansion. I.H.P.: 12,000 = about 18 kts. now. Babcock and Wilcox boilers. Coal: 600 tons. Endurance: 4,700 miles at 10 kts. Built by Cramps, Philadelphia. (Refitted and reboilered 1930.)

Notes.—Mined and sunk in Black Sea, April, 1915. Salved and taken to Nikolaieff, 1915–16. Seized by Austro-German Armies at Sevastopol, 1918, and returned to Turkish Navy, to be refitted in 1919.

Yachts

1938.

SAVARONA (Blohm & Voss, Feb. 28, 1931). Displacement: 5,710 tons. Dimensions: $349\frac{1}{2}$ (*w.l.*), $408\frac{1}{2}$ (*o.a.*) $\times 53 \times 20\frac{1}{2}$ feet (*mean*). Guns: **2**—3 pdr. Machinery: 6 geared turbines. 2 shafts. S.H.P.: 10,750 = 21 kts. (about 18 kts. now). 4 watertube boilers, 400 lb. working pressure. Oilfuel. Radius: 9,000 miles at 15 kts. Equipment includes Sperry gyro-stabilisers. Is probably the most sumptuously fitted yacht afloat. Complement: 79.

1937 "*Yavuz.*"

ERTUĞRUL (Armstrong, 1903). Displacement: 964 tons. Dimensions: 260 (*pp.*) $\times 27\frac{1}{3} \times 11\frac{1}{2}$ feet. Guns: **8**—3 pdr. Machinery: Triple expansion by Hawthorn Leslie. H.P.: 2,500 = 21 kts. Boilers: Cylindrical.

Note.—Above yachts are not part of Turkish Navy in peace time, but come under Ministry of Communications.

Minelayers

SIVRIHISAR (April 10, 1940), **TORGUD REIS** (ex-*Yüzbasi Hakki*, 1940). Built by John I. Thornycroft & Co., Ltd., Southampton. Displacement: 350 tons (375 tons *full load*). Dimensions: $172 \times 26 \times 5\frac{3}{4}$ feet. Guns: 1—3 inch. Mines: **40**. Machinery 2 sets Atlas Polar Diesels. 2 shafts. B.H.P.: 1,200 = 15 kts.

1942, *courtesy Messrs. Thornycroft.*

USA

FLAGS.

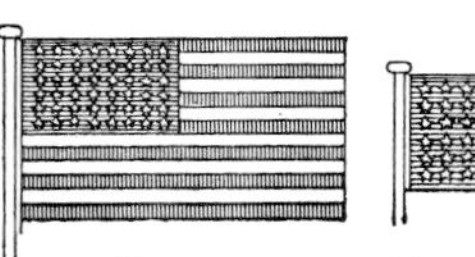
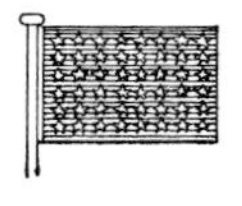

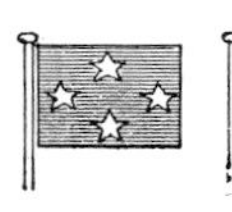
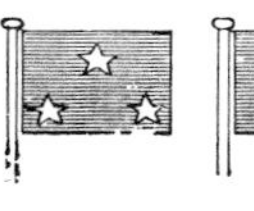
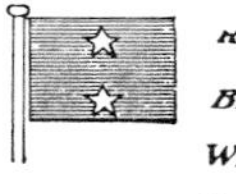

ENSIGN. UNION-JACK. PRESIDENT. ADMIRAL. VICE-ADMIRAL. REAR-ADMIRAL.

Red *Blue* *White* *Yellow*

COMMODORE. S.N.O. SQUADRON COMMANDER. DIVISION COMMANDER. NAVAL RESERVE. NAVAL MILITIA.

Note.—Fleet Admiral wears a 5-star flag, pentagonally arranged.

UNIFORMS.

The rank of Fleet Admiral (4 stripes) was established in Dec. 1944.

ADMIRAL. VICE-ADMIRAL. REAR-ADMIRAL. CAPTAIN. COMMANDER. LIEUT-COMMR. LIEUTENANT. LIEUTENANT. JUNIOR GRADE. ENSIGN. CHIEF WARRANT OFFICER. WARRANT OFFICER.

Note.—Chief Warrant Officers one stripe broken with blue. Line Warrant Officers have one half stripe broken with blue. Staff Warrant Officers under Chiefs have no sleeve mark. Engineers same as Line Officers (interchangeable). Other branches than executive wear no sleeve star, but have following badges of branch above top stripe.

Carpenter. Machinist. Pharmacist. Aerographer. Photographer. Boatswain.

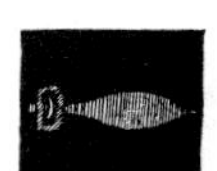

Torpedoman. Gunner. Pay Clerk. Ship's Clerk. Electrician. Radio-Electrician.

Commander in Chief: President Harry S. Truman.
Chief of Staff to C.-in-C.: Fleet Admiral William D. Leahy.
Secretary of the Navy: Mr. James V. Forrestal.
Under Secretary of the Navy: Mr. John L. Sullivan.
Assistant Secretary of the Navy: Mr. W. John Kenney.
Chief of Naval Operations and C.-in-C. U.S. Fleet: Fleet Admiral Chester W. Nimitz.
Vice Chief of Naval Operations: Vice-Admiral D. C. Ramsey.
Deputy Chief of Naval Operations (Air): Vice-Admiral A. W. Radford.
Naval Attaché, London: Commodore T. Shelley.

Future Strength of Fleet.

In 1946 strength of U.S. Navy was established at 18 battleships; 3 battle cruisers; 27 fleet aircraft carriers; 70 escort aircraft carriers; 31 heavy and 48 light cruisers; 367 destroyers; 296 destroyer-escorts; and 200 submarines. There was provision for 6,000 aircraft in operation and 2,400 in reserve. Future strength of personnel, including Marine Corps, 550,000.

Principal Guns in the U.S. Fleet.

Built at Washington Gun Factory, proved at Indian Head, Dahlgren, Va., and Potomac Range.

Notation.	Nominal Calibre.	Mark or Model.	Length in Calibres.	Weight of Gun.	Weight of A.P. Shot.	*Service* Initial Velocity.	*Maximum* penetration firing *capped* A.P. direct impact against K.C. armour. 9000 yards	600 yards	3000 yards	Muzzle Energy.
	inch.			tons.	lbs.	ft. secs.	in.	in.	in.	ft-tons.
HEAVY	16	II	50	128	2100	2800	...	...	...	...
	16	I	45	105	2100	2600	...	...	...	98,531
	14	IV	50	81	1400	2800	...	...	...	76,087
	14	I	45	63⅓	1400	2600	18	...	...	...
MEDIUM	8	IX	55	19·7	250	3000	...	...	...	16,240
	6	XII	53	10	105	3000	...	...	...	6,551
	5	VII	51	5·0	50	3150	1·4	1·8	3·4	3,439
LIGHT and AA.	4*	IX	50	3·0	33	2900	...	...	..	1,926
	4*	VIII	50	2·9	33	2800	1·2	1·5	2·6	1,794
	4*	VII	50	2·6	33	2500	1·2	1·4	2·2	1,430
	4*	III,IV,V,VI	40	1·5	33	2000	...	1·2	1·7	915
	3§	X	50	1·15	13	2700	...	...	...	657
	3	V, VI, *S-A*	50	1·0	13	2700	...	0·8	1·2	658
	3*	II, III	50	0·9	13	2700	...	0·8	1·2	658

(There are besides a new model 12 inch; a 6 inch, 47 cal.,* a 5 inch, 25 cal. AA.; a 5 inch 54 cal. and a 5 inch 38 cal. dual purpose, and a 3 inch dual purpose.) Latest models up to and including 8 inch are entirely automatic.

* = Brass cartridge case. § Anti-aircraft gun.

Naval Appropriations.

1944-45, $28,533,839,301. 1945-46, $24,116,411,064. 1946-47, $4,119,659,300.

Personnel: Total on duty (Aug. 1946) including U.S. Marine Corps, 644,857.

Colour of U.S. Warships: Apart from certain experimental colour schemes, majority have hulls painted "battle grey" (almost black), with light grey upperworks in Atlantic Fleet; and medium grey with light grey upperworks in Pacific Fleet.

Mercantile Marine.

Total *gross* tonnage, Sept. 30, 1945, was 40,100,000, since considerably reduced.

CLASSIFICATION OF U.S. WARSHIPS

Every vessel on the Navy List is given a distinctive serial number, prefaced by initials denoting the category to which she belongs. A list of most of these initials, with their significance, appears below, though many of the minor categories are not of sufficient importance to be described in *Fighting Ships*.

(a) Seagoing Fighting Ships

BB Battleships
CB Large Cruisers (i.e., Battle Cruisers)
CVB Large Fleet Aircraft Carriers
CV Fleet Aircraft Carriers
CVL Light Fleet Aircraft Carriers
CVE Escort Aircraft Carriers
CA Heavy Cruisers
CL Light Cruisers
DD Destroyers
DE Escort Vessel
SS Submarines
SM Submarines, Minelaying type
CM Minelayers
CMc Minelayers, Coastal type
DM Light Minelayers (ex-Destroyers)
DMS Minesweepers, Fast type (ex-Destroyers)
AM Fleet Minesweepers (Steel)
AMc Minesweepers, Coastal type (Wooden)
AMc (U) Minesweeper (Coastal), Underwater Locator
AMb Minesweepers, Harbour (Base) type
PG Gunboats (Sloops and Corvettes)
PGM Gunboats (Motor)
PF Escort Vessels (Frigates)
PY Patrol Vessels (Converted Yachts)
PYc Patrol Vessels, Coastal type (Converted Yachts)
PT Motor Torpedo Boats
PC Submarine Chasers (Steel)
PCE Submarine Chasers (Steel), Escort type
PCE (R) Submarine Chasers (Steel), fitted for Rescue work
PCS Submarine Chasers (Wooden), fitted for Minesweeping
SC Submarine Chasers (Wooden)

(b) Auxiliaries

AB Crane Ship
AC Collier
AD Destroyer Tender
AE Ammunition Ship
AF Provision Storeship
AG Miscellaneous Auxiliary
AGC Amphibious Force Flagship
AGL Lighthouse Tender (Coast Guard)
AGP Motor Torpedo Boat Tender
AGS Surveying Ship
AH Hospital Ship
AK Cargo Ship
AKA Cargo Ship—Attack
AKD Deep-hold Cargo Ship
AKN Net Cargo Ship
AKS General-stores-issue Ship
AKV Cargo Ship and Aircraft Ferry
AL Lightship (Coast Guard)
AN Net-laying Ship
AO Oiler (Fuel Oil Tanker)
AOG Gasoline Tanker (Petrol Carrier)
AP Transport
APA Transport—Attack
APB Barrack Ship—Self-propelled
APc Coastal Transport (Small)
APD High Speed Transport
APF Administration Flagship
APG Supporting Gunnery Ship
APH Transport fitted for Evacuation of Wounded
APL Labour Transport or Barrack Ship
APM Mechanized-artillery Transport
APN Non-mechanized-artillery Transport
APR Rescue Transport
APV Transport and Aircraft Ferry
AR Repair Ship
ARB Repair Ship—Battle Damage
ARC Cable Repairing or Laying Ship
ARD Floating Dry Dock
ARDC Repair Dock—Concrete
ABD Advance Base Dock
ABSD Advance Base Sectional Dock
AFD Mobile Floating Dry Dock
ARG Repair Ship—Internal combustion Engine
ARH Heavy-hull Repair Ship
ARL Repair Ship—Landing Craft
ARM Heavy-machinery Repair Ship
ARS Salvage Vessel
ARS (D) Salvage Lifting Vessel
ARS (T) Salvage Craft Tender
ARV (A) Aircraft Repair Ship (Airframe)
ARV (E) Aircraft Repair Ship (Engine)
AS Submarine Tender
ASR Submarine Rescue Vessel
ATA Ocean Tug—Auxiliary
ATF Ocean Tug—Fleet
ATO Ocean Tug—Old
ATR Ocean Tug—Rescue
AV Seaplane Tender
AVC Catapult Lighter
AVD Seaplane Tender (Destroyer)
AVP Seaplane Tender (Small)
AVR Aircraft Rescue Vessel

Classification of U.S. Warships, Nomenclature, Silhouettes etc.

AVS	Aviation Supply Ship
AW	Distilling Ship
AWK	Water Tanker
AZ	Airship Tender (Lighter-than-Air)
IX	Unclassified Vessel

(c) Yard and District Craft

YA	Ash Lighter
YAG	District Auxiliary, Miscellaneous
YC	Open Lighter
YCF	Car Float (Railroad)
YCK	Open Cargo Lighter
YCV	Aircraft transportation Lighter
YD	Floating Derrick
YDG	Degaussing Vessel
YDT	Diving Tender
YE	Ammunition Lighter
YF	Covered Lighter
YFB	Ferry Boat or Launch
YFD	Floating Dry Dock
YFT	Torpedo transportation Lighter
YG	Garbage Lighter
YH	Ambulance Boat
YHB	House Boat
YHT	Heating Scow
YLA	Open Landing Lighter
YM	Dredge
YMS	Motor Mine Sweeper
YN	Net Tender
YNg	Gate Vessel
YNT	Net Tender (Tug Class)
YO	Fuel Oil Barge
YOG	Gasoline Barge
YOS	Oil Storage Barge
YP	District Patrol Vessel
YPD	Pile Driver (Floating)
YPK	Pontoon Stowage Barge
YR	Floating Workshop
YRD (H)	Floating Workshop, Drydock (Hull)
YRD (M)	Floating Workshop, Drydock (Machinery)
YS	Stevedoring Barge
YSD	Seaplane Wrecking Derrick
YSP	Salvage Pontoon
YSR	Sludge Removal Barge
YTB	Harbour Tug, Big
YTL	Harbour Tug, Little
YTM	Harbour Tug, Medium
YTT	Torpedo Testing Barge
YW	Water Barge

SHIP NOMENCLATURE.

Battleships are named after States; heavy and light cruisers after large cities; aircraft carriers after historical naval vessels or battles; destroyers after officers and enlisted men of the Navy and Marine Corps, Secretaries of the Navy, Members of Congress and inventors.

Submarines are named after fish and marine creatures; minesweepers and submarine rescue vessels after birds; gunboats and escort vessels after small cities; submarine tenders after pioneers in submarine development and mythological characters; repair ships after mythological characters; oilers after rivers; store and cargo ships after stars; destroyer tenders after natural areas of the United States, e.g., mountain ranges, valleys, etc.; large seaplane tenders and aircraft escort vessels after sounds; ammunition ships after volcanoes and ingredients of explosives; transports after flag officers, general officers, and officers of the Marine Corps; attack transports and attack cargo ships after counties; coastal minesweepers after abstract qualities, etc.; small seaplane tenders after bays, straits and inlets; ocean-going tugs after Indian tribes; and harbour tugs after Indian chiefs and words of the Indian dialect.

Owing to war exigencies, occasional exceptions to this system will be found.

CONSTRUCTIONAL NOTES.

All modern battleships, aircraft carriers, cruisers, depot ships, etc., have bows of bulbous form. This has been found advantageous when ships are being pressed to their utmost speeds. In the *Washington* class the effect is only felt at 28 knots and over, and in large cruisers at about 29 knots and over.

Aircraft carriers are identified from the air by their official identification numbers, e.g. CV 32 painted prominently on flight deck towards stern. These are also painted on funnels.

Accommodation in all U.S. warships is so arranged that men mess forward and sleep aft, in three-tier bunks.

Recent alterations include the removal of boats and derricks from battleships and cruisers, and the plating over of lower deck scuttles in destroyers.

COMPLEMENTS.

These are mostly war-time figures. In some instances both peace and war figures are given.

Battleships and Battle Cruisers

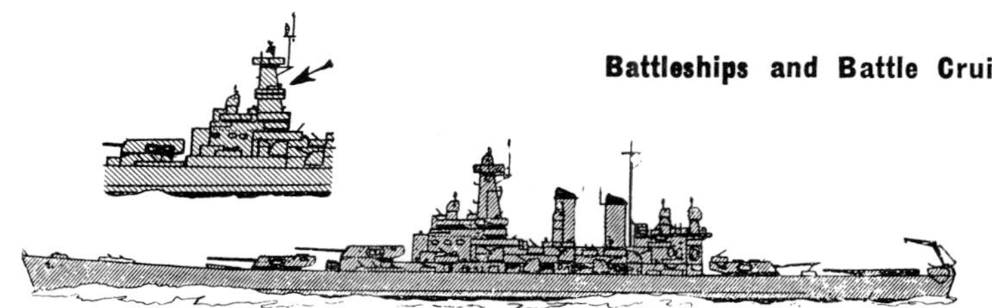

WASHINGTON, N. CAROLINA.

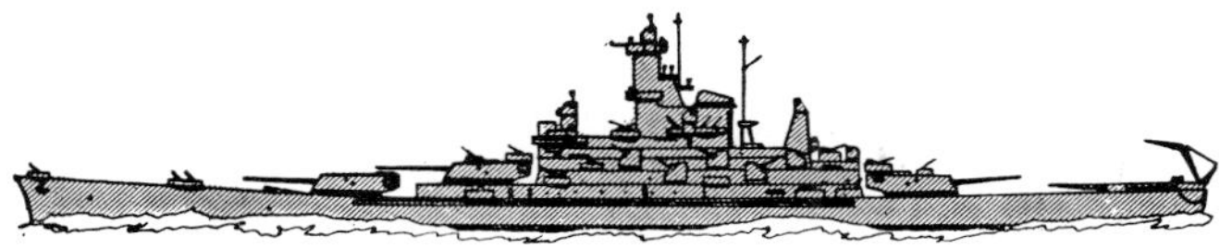

S. DAKOTA *class.*

IOWA *class.*

WEST VIRGINIA, CALIFORNIA, TENNESSEE.

COLORADO, MARYLAND.

ALASKA *class.*

NEW MEXICO *class.*

Aircraft Carriers

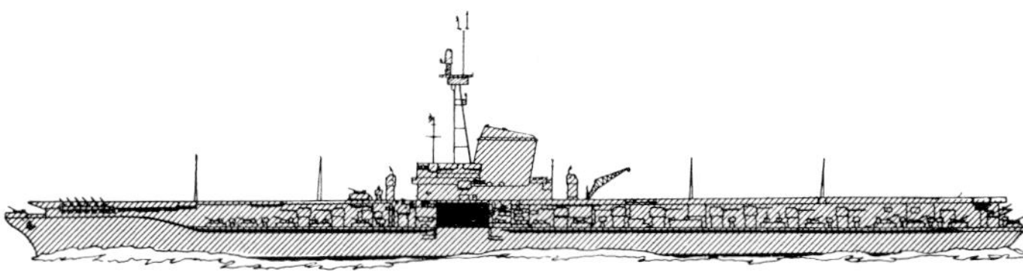

MIDWAY *class.*

ESSEX *class.*

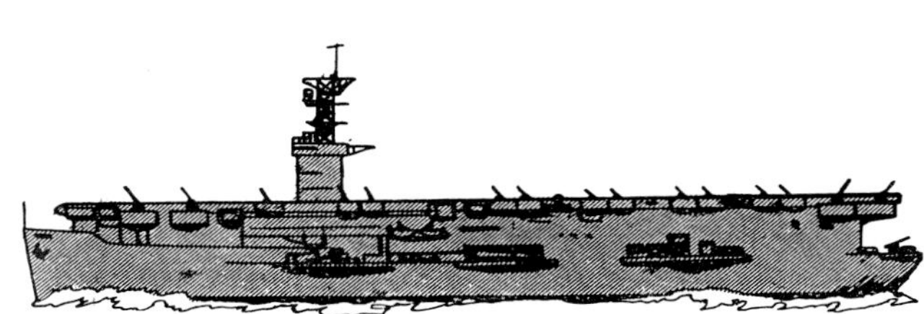

CASABLANCA *class.*

CHENANGO *class.*

Silhouettes

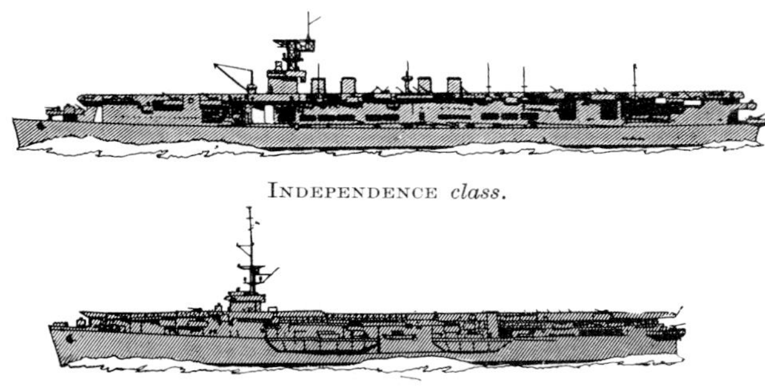

INDEPENDENCE *class*.

COMMENCEMENT BAY *class*.

SAIPAN, WRIGHT.

ALTAMAHA *type*.

Cruisers

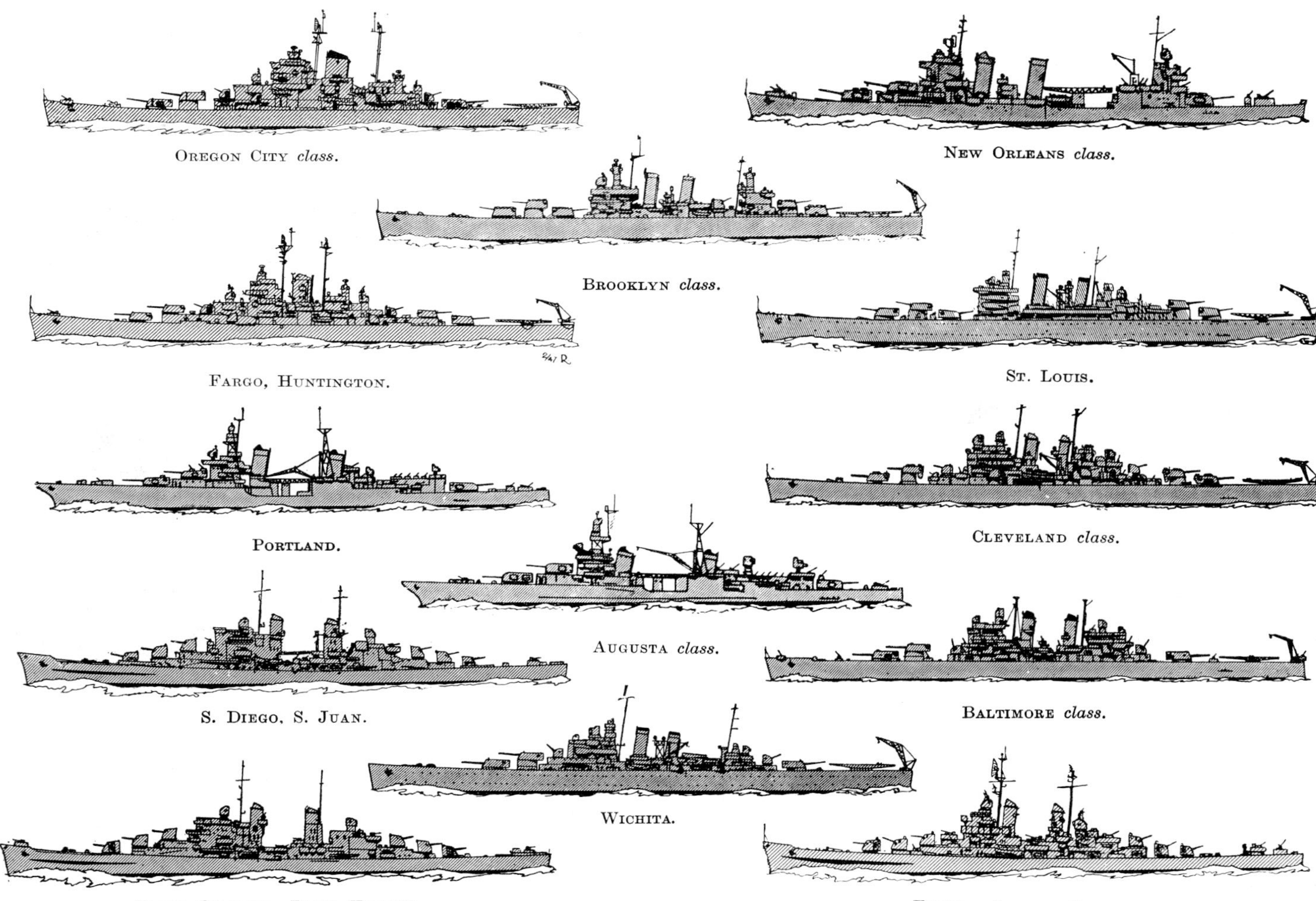

OREGON CITY *class*.

NEW ORLEANS *class*.

BROOKLYN *class*.

FARGO, HUNTINGTON.

ST. LOUIS.

PORTLAND.

CLEVELAND *class*.

AUGUSTA *class*.

S. DIEGO, S. JUAN.

BALTIMORE *class*.

WICHITA.

FLINT, OAKLAND, RENO, TUCSON.

FRESNO, JUNEAU, SPOKANE.

Destroyers, etc.

BUCHANAN *class*.
(BENSON *class* similar.)

FLETCHER *class*.

GEARING *class*.
(Some have light AA. in place of after T.T.)

TURNER, H. W. TUCKER.

A. M. SUMNER *class*.

BUCKLEY *type*.

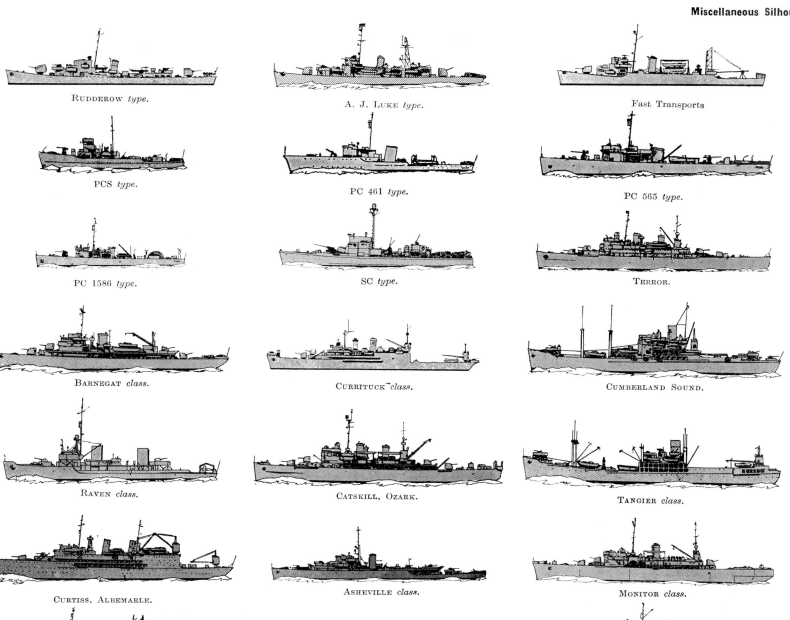

Miscellaneous Silhouettes

RUDDEROW *type.*

A. J. LUKE *type.*

Fast Transports

PCS *type.*

PC 461 *type.*

PC 565 *type.*

PC 1586 *type.*

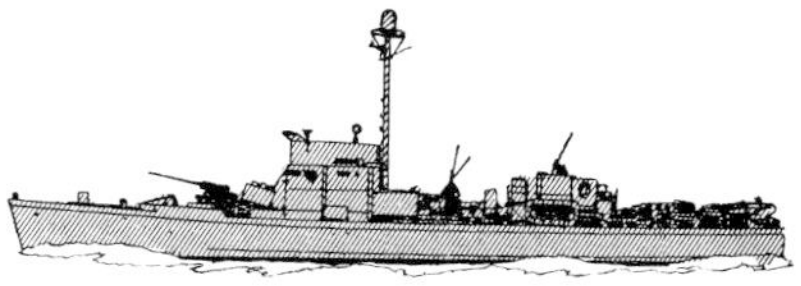

SC *type.*

TERROR.

BARNEGAT *class.*

CURRITUCK *class.*

CUMBERLAND SOUND.

RAVEN *class.*

CATSKILL, OZARK.

TANGIER *class.*

CURTISS, ALBEMARLE.

ASHEVILLE *class.*

MONITOR *class.*

CHANTICLEER *class.*

ADMIRABLE *class.*
(Some have no funnel.)

YMS *type.*
(Later vessels, only 1 funnel or none.)

Auxiliaries

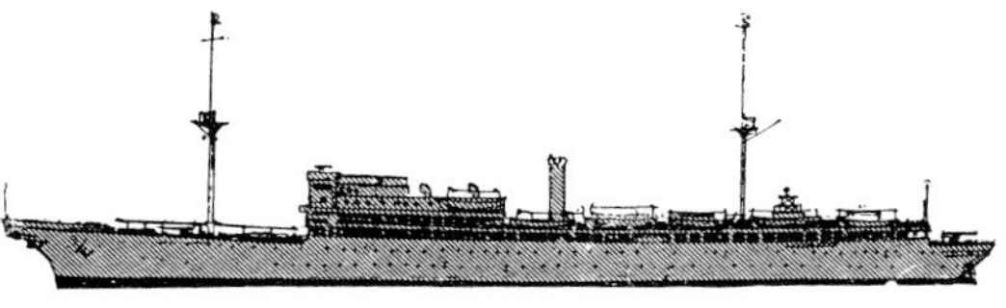

HOLLAND.
(Topmasts now shortened).

DIXIE, PRAIRIE.

GRIFFIN, PELIAS.

BOWDITCH.

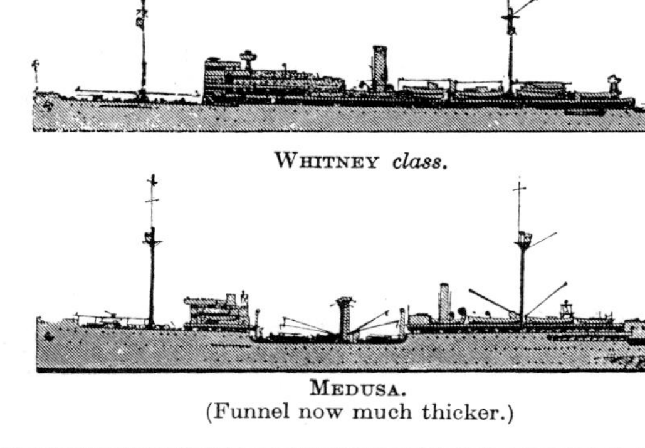

WHITNEY *class.*

FULTON *class.*

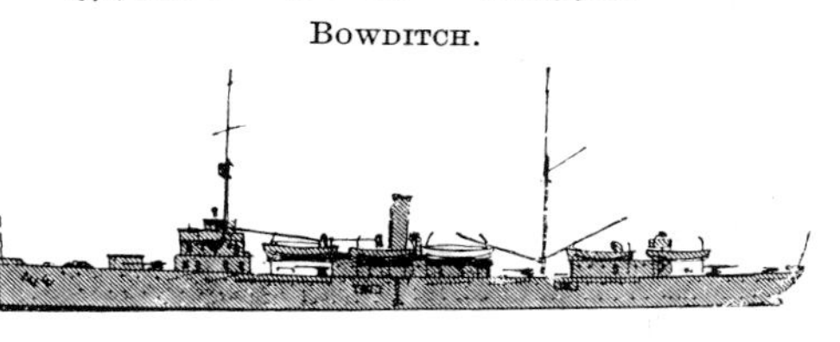

MELVILLE.

MEDUSA.
(Funnel now much thicker.)

VULCAN *class.*

Silhouettes — Coast Guard Cutters

CHAMPLAIN *class.*

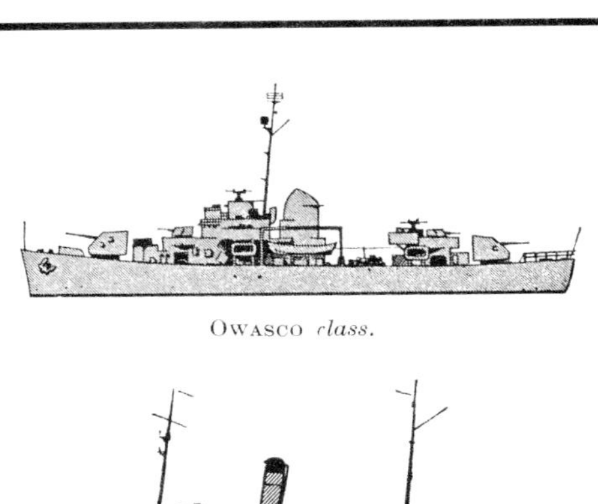

OWASCO *class.*

TALLAPOOSA.
(OSSIPEE similar).

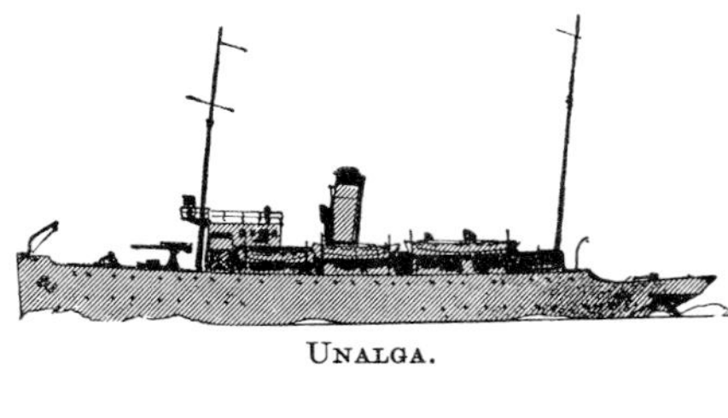

UNALGA.

ALGONQUIN *class.*

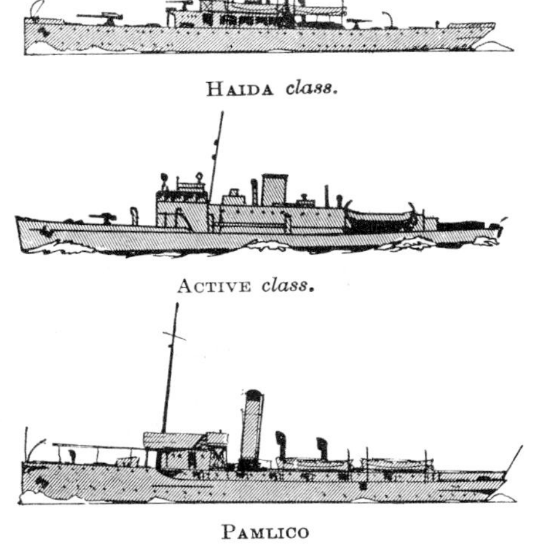

HAIDA *class.*

ACTIVE *class.*

PAMLICO

ARGO *class except* AURORA, DAPHNE, PERSEUS, only 1 funnel.
(Some have thinner 2nd funnel)

SHAWNEE.

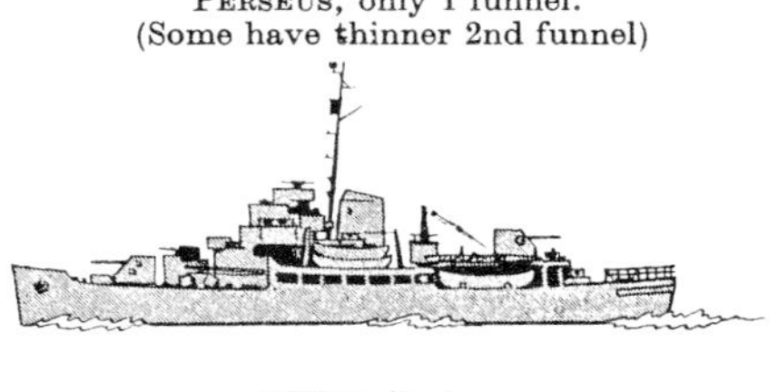

"WIND" *class.*

CAMPBELL *class.*

Submarines

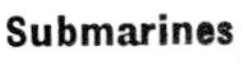

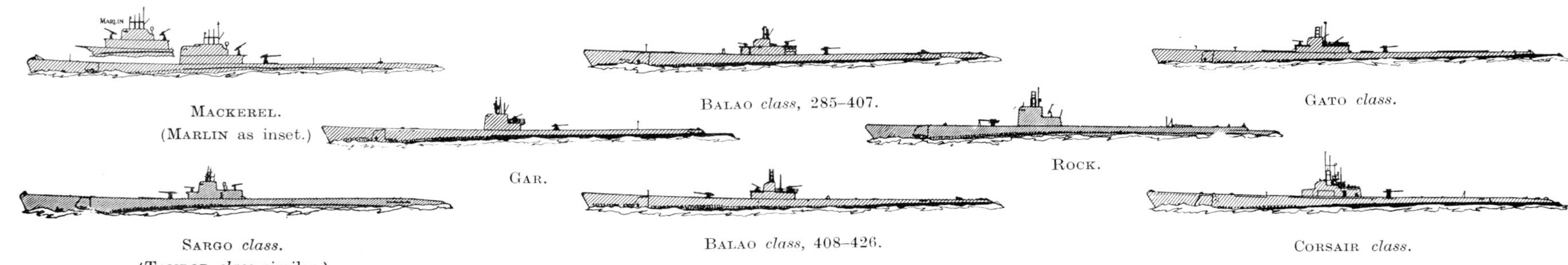

MACKEREL.
(MARLIN as inset.)

BALAO *class*, 285–407.

GATO *class.*

GAR.

ROCK.

SARGO *class.*
(TAMBOR *class* similar.)

BALAO *class*, 408–426.

CORSAIR *class.*

Following is latest official report on Lend-Lease warships:

A total of 2,216 were returned from all countries; 643 became war losses, and 1,943 are still retained. The Royal Navy returned 2,207, lost 635, and still had 814 in March 1947. Soviet Navy still has 580, having lost 3 m.t.b. France lost 4 ships and retains 243. China has 92, Brazil 66, Greece 33, Netherlands 23, Norway 10, Yugoslavia 8, Venezuela 4, Peru 10, Paraguay 6, Haiti 1, Colombia 13, Uruguay 4, Ecuador 9, Chile 9, the Dominican Republic 4 and Cuba 12.

Following ships have been stricken from effective list: Battleship **NEW MEXICO;** destroyer escorts **DUFFY, EMERY, STADTFELD;** frigates **GROTON** and **WOONSOCKET;** oiler **PECOS** (sold to Chile); petrol carrier **MAQUOKETA;** general stores issue ship **HESPERIA;** attack cargo ships **OTTAWA, ARTEMIS** and **SARITA;** submarine rescue vessel **MALLARD;** and net tenders **CHINABERRY** and **LARCH.**

Battleships

(IOWA CLASS—5 Ships).

IOWA (Aug. 27, 1942)
NEW JERSEY (Dec. 7, 1942)
MISSOURI (Jan. 29, 1944)
WISCONSIN (Dec. 7, 1943)
KENTUCKY

WISCONSIN

Iowa. 1944, *Associated Press.*

Iowa. 1944, *U.S. Navy Official.*

Missouri. 1944, *U.S. Navy Official.*

Missouri. 1946, *Mr. Wm. H. Davis.*

Standard displacement: 45,000 tons (52,000 tons *full load*). Complement: 2,700.
Length: (*pp.*) 861¼ feet; (*o.a.*) 890 feet. Beam: 108 feet. Draught: 36 feet (*max.*).

Guns:
9—16 inch, 50 cal.
20—5 inch, 38 cal.
80—40 mm. AA.
50—20 mm.

Aircraft:
3

Catapults:
2

Armour:
16″ Side.
Otherwise not reported, but will be more extensive than in *Alabama* class.

Programme.	Name and No.	Builder	Machinery	Laid down	Completed.
1940	*Iowa* (61)	New York Navy Yard.	Gen. Electric Co.	27/6/40	22/2/43
	New Jersey (62)	Philadelphia Navy Yard.	Westinghouse Co.	16/9/40	23/5/43
	Missouri (63)	New York Navy Yard.	Gen. Electric Co.	6/1/41	11/6/44
	Wisconsin (64)	Philadelphia Navy Yard.	Westinghouse Co.	25/1/41	16/4/44
	Kentucky (66)	Norfolk Navy Yard.	do.	6/12/44	

Special Note.—*Kentucky's* construction was suspended for a year from August, 1946. Her armament will be modified to include a number of rocket projectors, in addition to 16 inch and some other guns.

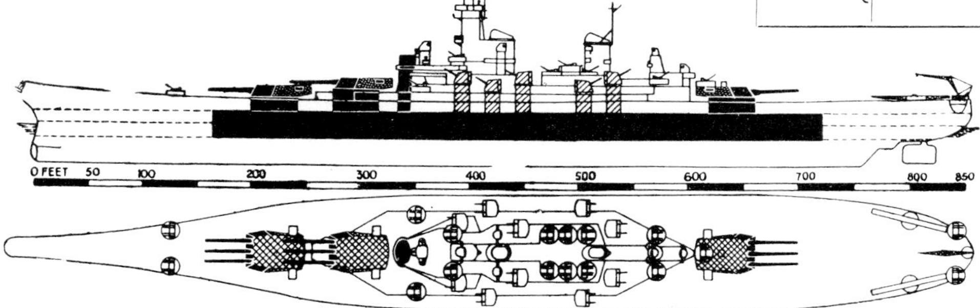

Machinery: Geared turbines. 4 shafts. S.H.P.: 200,000 = 33 kts. (35 kts. reached in service). Boilers: 12 Babcock & Wilcox. Oil fuel.

Notes.—Inclusive cost officially stated to exceed $100,000,000 each. *Iowa* and *New Jersey* were each built in 2¾ years, same period as occupied by the *Alabama*, a smaller ship. Construction of *Kentucky*, after being suspended for a time, was resumed in Dec., 1944; but the *Illinois* (65), authorised in 1940 and ordered from Philadelphia Navy Yard in Dec., 1942, was cancelled when 22 per cent. complete, on Aug. 11, 1945.

Appearance Note.—While serving as Third Fleet flagship, *New Jersey* had a lattice mainmast stepped against her after-funnel to accommodate flag-hoists.

Missouri 1945, courtesy "*Ships & Aircraft*".

Iowa. 1944, *U.S. Navy Official.*

Battleships

WISCONSIN. 1944, *U.S. Navy Official.*

NEW JERSEY. 1944, *U.S. Navy Official.*

IOWA. 1944, *Associated Press*

ALABAMA. 1943, *Keystone.*

(SOUTH DAKOTA CLASS—4 SHIPS)

ALABAMA (Feb. 16, 1942), **INDIANA** (Nov. 21, 1941), **MASSACHUSETTS** 23, 1941), **SOUTH DAKOTA** (June 7, 1941).

Standard displacement: 35,000 tons (42,000 tons *full load*). Complement: 2,500.

Length: 680 feet (*o.a.*). Beam: 108 feet 2 inches. Draught: 26 feet 9 inches.

Guns:
- **9**—16 inch, 50 cal.
- **20**—5 inch, 38 cal., dual purpose. (*S. Dakota* has only 16.)
- **68**—40 mm. AA.
- **40**—20 mm. AA.

Aircraft: 3

Catapults: 2

Armour:
- 16″ Side.
- 18″ Turrets.
- 6″ Upper Deck.
- 4″ Main Deck.

Understood that these ships have enhanced protection as compared with *Washington* type.

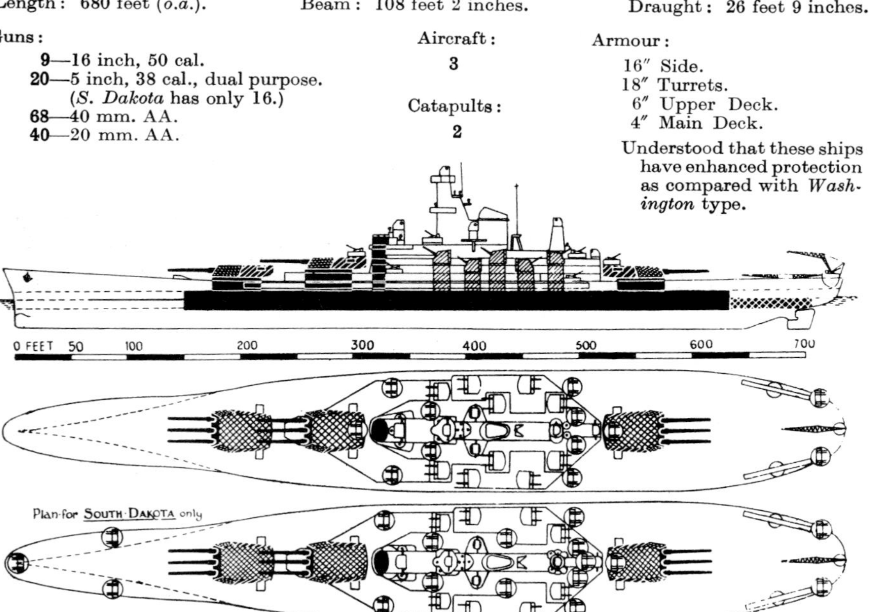

Machinery: Geared turbines. 4 shafts. S.H.P.: 130,000 = 30 kts. Boilers: Babcock & Wilcox in *S. Dakota* and *Massachusetts*; Foster Wheeler in *Indiana* and *Alabama*. Working pressure reported as 600 lb. per sq. inch with 400° of superheat. Oil fuel.

General Notes.—These ships are a modification of *Washington* design with increased freeboard and reduced length, embodying sundry improvements. *Alabama* was built in $2\frac{3}{4}$ years from date of laying keel. *S. Dakota* played a prominent part in naval victory over Japanese squadron in Battle of Guadalcanal, Nov. 13–15, 1942.

Gunnery Notes.—Outstanding feature of these ships is the very large number of 40 mm. Bofors and 20 mm. Oerlikon guns included in AA. armament. 5 inch are mounted at a higher level than in *N. Carolina* and *Washington*.

MASSACHUSETTS. 1942, *U.S. Navy, Official.*

Programme	*Name and No.*	*Builder*	*Machinery*	*Laid down*	*Completed*	*Cost*
1938	*S. Dakota* (57)	New York S.B. Corpn.	Gen. Electric Co.	July 5, 1939	Aug. 16, 1942	$77,000,000 each
	Indiana (58)	Newport News Co.	Westinghouse Co.	Nov. 20, 1939	Oct., 1942	
	Massachusetts (59)	Bethlehem Steel Co. (Quincy)	Gen. Electric Co.	July 20, 1939	Sept., 1942	
	Alabama (60)	Norfolk Navy Yard	Westinghouse Co.	Feb. 1, 1940	Nov., 1942	

Battleships

(WASHINGTON CLASS—2 Ships)

NORTH CAROLINA (June 13, 1940)
WASHINGTON (June 1, 1940)

Standard displacement: 35,000 tons. (*About* 41,000 tons, *full load*.)
Complement: 2,500

Length: 704 ft. (*w.l.*); 729 ft. (*o.a.*). Beam: 108 ft.
Draught: 26 ft. 8 in. (*mean*).

Aircraft: 3 Catapults: 2

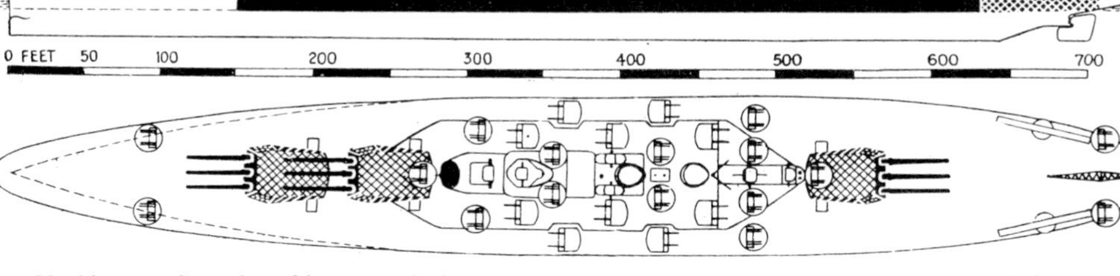

Guns:
9—16 inch, 50 cal.
20—5 inch, 38 cal. (dual purpose).
Over **100**—40 mm. and 20 mm.

Armour: (Unofficial)
16″ Side amidships.
18″ Turrets.
6″ Upper Deck.
4″ Main Deck.
Triple hull below *w.l.* and internal bulges.

Machinery: Geared turbines. 4 shafts. S.H.P.: 115,000 = over 27 kts. Babcock and Wilcox boilers of a new pattern (working pressure reported to be 600 lb. per sq. inch, with 400° of superheat). Oil fuel.

General Notes.—Delays in laying down these ships were due to changes in design, late delivery of materials and necessity for extending and strengthening building slips. Ships are fully 35 per cent. welded. Engine room is arranged on a novel plan to save weight.
Gunnery Notes.—16 inch are a new model, reported to weigh 125 tons. Each turret weighs 650 tons complete.
Engineering Notes.—Weight of machinery has been reduced in comparison with earlier battleships. Steam pressures and temperatures are reported to be greater than in any other battleship afloat.

Programme	*Name and No.*	*Builder*	*Machinery*	*Laid down*	*Completed*	*Cost*
1936	*N. Carolina* (55)	New York Navy Yard	Gen. Electric Co.	Oct. 27, 1937	Aug., 1941	$76,885,750 each
	Washington (56)	Philadelphia Navy Yard	Gen. Electric Co.	June 14, 1938	March, 1942	

NORTH CAROLINA. 1946, *Mr. Wm. H. Davis.*

WASHINGTON 1941, *U.S. Navy Official.*

WASHINGTON. 1945, *courtesy Commander P. A. Morgan, R.N.R.*

(COLORADO CLASS—3 SHIPS.)

COLORADO (March 22nd, 1921), **MARYLAND** (March 20th, 1920), **WEST VIRGINIA** (Nov. 19th, 1921).

Standard displacement, *Colorado*, 32,500 tons. ***Maryland*, 31,500.** ***W. Virginia*, 31,800 tons.** *Full load*, 33,590 tons.

Complement, 2100 (of *W. Virginia* as fleet flagship, 2350)

Length (*w.l.*), 600 feet. (*o.a.*), 624 feet.
Beam, 97½ feet. (*W. Virginia*, 110 feet.)

Mean draught, 30½ feet, 29⅔ feet and 30 feet respectively.
Max. draught of all, 35 feet.

Note to Plan.—This represents *Colorado* and *Maryland* only. *W. Virginia* is reconstructed as in photo.

Machinery: In *Colorado* Westinghouse turbines and electric drive; in *Maryland* and *W. Virginia*, G.E. turbines and electric drive. 4 shafts. Designed S.H.P. 27,300 = 21 kts. Boilers: 8 Babcock & Wilcox. Fuel (oil only): *normal* 2500 tons; *maximum* 4000 tons (unofficial figures).

General Notes.—Authorised 1916. ***W. Virginia*** and ***Maryland*** both fitted as Flagships. ***W. Virginia*** was reduced to a wreck by Japanese attack at Pearl Harbour on Dec. 7, 1941, being hit by four torpedoes and two heavy bombs. She settled down on an even keel, and has since been reconstructed to a silhouette identical in nearly all respects with *California*, including anti-torpedo bulge. *Maryland* received a considerable amount of bomb damage on same occasion. At that date *Colorado* is understood to have been under refit.

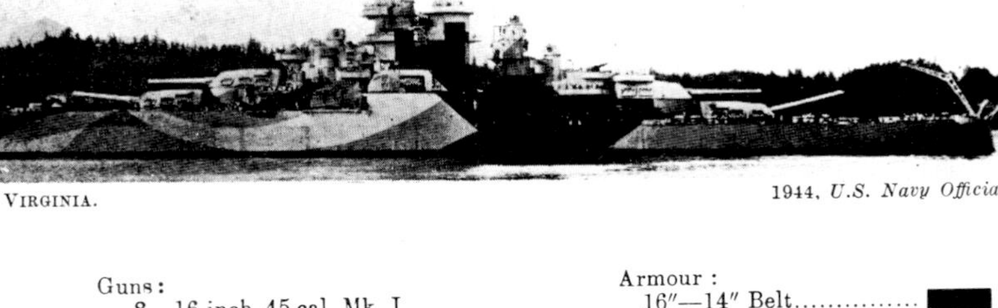
W. VIRGINIA. 1944, *U.S. Navy Official.*

Guns:
8—16 inch, 45 cal. Mk. I.
8—5 inch, 38 cal.
10—5 inch, 51 cal.
W. Virginia **16**—5 inch, 38 cal.
Many 40 mm. and 20 mm. AA.

Aircraft: **3**

Catapults:
1 on Quarter Deck.

Armour:
16″—14″ Belt
8″ Belt (aft)
3″ Deck (ends)
16″—9″ Funnel bases
18″—9″ Turrets
16″ Conning tower and tube
3½″ upper and 2½″ lower armour decks.

Battleships

COLORADO. (MARYLAND similar.) 1944, *U.S. Navy, Official.*

Gunnery Notes.—Maximum elevation of 16 inch 30°; Maximum range at this elevation unofficially stated to be 33,300 yards. Turrets electrically manœuvred and with electric hoists. Excepting increase of calibre to 16 inch, otherwise as Notes for *Tennessee* Class.

Armour Notes. As for *California* and *Tennessee.*

Engineering Notes.—"Electric Drive" is identical with that for the *Tennessee* Class, but in these ships electric installation has been extended. Part of steam generated in boilers is diverted for running six auxiliary turbo-generators, supplying current to anchor gear, workshop lathes, refrigerating plant, bakeries, &c. Guns are also electrically manœuvred, ammunition hoists are electric. In fact, every possible item of equipment, even down to potato peelers and ice-cream freezers, is run by electric power. Estimated weight of machinery, 2002 tons. Heating surfaces as *Tennessee* on a later page.

Anti-Torpedo Protection.—Ferrati type triple hull and minute internal subdivision by longitudinal and transverse unpierced bulkheads.

Name and No.	*Builder*	*Machinery*	*Laid down*	*Completed*	*Trials*	*Boilers*
Colorado (45)	New York S.B. Cpn.	Westinghouse Co.	May '19	Aug.,'23	37,480 = 20·67	Babcock
Maryland (46)	Newport News	Gen. Elec. Co.	Apl.,'17	July '21	36,167 = 21·07	Babcock
W. Virginia (47)	Newport News	Gen. Elec. Co.	Apl.,'20	Dec. '23	= 21·1	Babcock

(TENNESSEE *class*—2 ships.)

CALIFORNIA (Nov. 20th, 1919), **TENNESSEE** (April 30th, 1919).

Displacement: *Standard* 32,600 and 32,300 tons, respectively. *Full load,* 35,190 tons. Complement: 2,200.

Length (*w.l.*) 600 feet. (*o.a.*) 624 feet. Beam 110 feet, outside bulges. *Mean* draught, 30½ and 30⅓ ft. respectively. *Max.* „ 35½ and 35 ft. respectively.

Guns:
12—14 inch, 50 cal., Mk. IV.
16—5 inch, 38 cal.
Many 40 mm. and 20 mm. AA.

Aircraft: 4 and 3 respectively.

Catapults: 1 on Q.D.

Armour:
14″ Belt
8″ Belt (aft)
3″ Deck (ends)
15″—9″ Funnel bases
18″—9″ Turrets
16″ Conning tower and tube
3½″ upper 2½″ lower armour decks

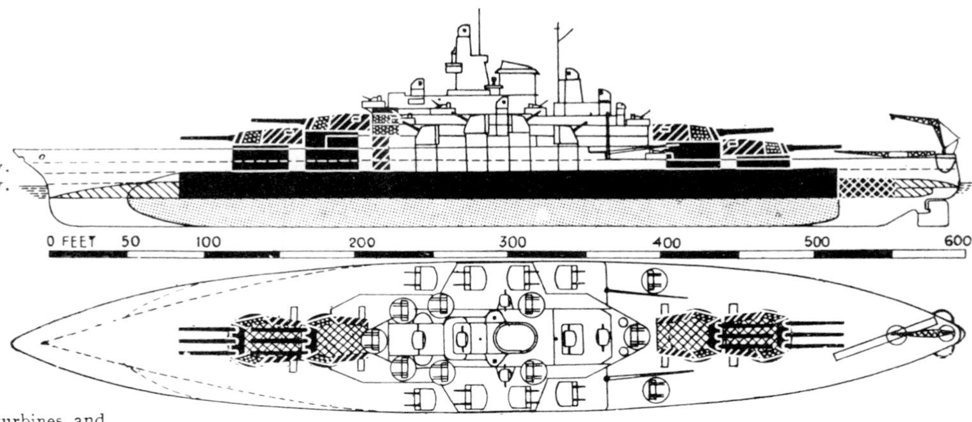

Machinery: *California*, G. E. turbines and electric drive. *Tennessee*, Westinghouse turbines and electric drive. 4 shafts in both ships. Designed H.P.: 26,800 = 21 kts. Boilers: 8 Bureau Express type in *California*. 8 Babcock and Wilcox in *Tennessee*. Fuel (oil only): *normal* 2,200, *maximum* 3,328 tons.

Name and No.	*Builder*	*Machinery*	*Laid down*	*Com-pleted*	*Refit*	*Trials*	*Boilers*
California (44)	Mare Island Yard	G. E. Co.	Oct.,'16	15/9/21	1942	21·46	Express
Tennessee (43)	New York Yard	Westinghouse Co.	May,'17	16/9/20	1942	30,908 = 21·01	Babcock

***General Notes.*—Authorised 1915 as *No.* 43 (*Tennessee*) and 44 (*California*). The above design is practically identical with *New Mexico* class as originally completed. *California* fitted as Flagship.** She was heavily damaged at Pearl Harbour on Dec. 7, 1941. Having been torpedoed and set on fire, she had to be flooded to save the magazines exploding, and settled down with a pronounced list. She has since been completely reconstructed, with the addition of bulges. *Tennessee* received extensive damage of a less serious nature from bombs on same occasion, and has undergone similar transformation.

TENNESSEE. 1944, *U.S. Navy Official.*

CALIFORNIA. 1944, *U.S. Navy Official.*

Gunnery Notes.—The 14 inch mounted in separate sleeves; elevation, up to 30°. Maximum range stated to be over 35,000 yards. *Tennessee* had new main fire control system installed and splinter screens added during 1940–41.

Armour Notes.—Internal subdivision by unpierced bulkheads developed to the utmost degree below waterline.

Engineering Notes.—Estimated weight of machinery: *California*, 1,805 tons; *Tennessee*, 2,045 tons. Heating surface: 50,984 sq. ft. for Bureau Express boilers in *California*; 41,768 sq. ft. + 4,168 sq. ft. (superheated) for Babcock boilers in *Tennessee*. Each boiler is in a separate w.t. compartment. Boiler rooms are abeam of engine rooms (4 to port, 4 to starboard), and boilers are under central control. Turbines are in tandem on centre line. On *trials*, *Tennessee* brought to rest from full speed within 3 minutes; tactical diameter: 700 yards (full helm, both screws turning forward).

(New Mexico Class—2 ships.)

IDAHO (June 30th, 1917).

NEW MEXICO (April 23rd, 1917).

Standard displacement: 33,400 tons. Complement, 1,930.

Special Note.

These 2 ships are to be discarded on completion of *Kentucky* and *Hawaii*, if not earlier.

Armour:
14″ Belt (amidships)
8″ Belt (aft)
*″ Deck ends
15″—9″ Funnel base
18″—9″ Turrets
16″ Conning tower & tube
*(Reported as 6″ upper and 4″ lower over vital areas)

(Bulges fitted, 1934–36.)

Note to Plan.—Sundry minor modifications since effected as shown in photos.

New Mexico.

Added 1944, *U.S. Navy Official.*

Notes.—These two ships were not at Pearl Harbour when the Japanese made their surprise attack on December 7, 1941, but have been modernised to a certain extent. *New Mexico* may differ slightly from *Idaho*, as she underwent further alterations after a severe bomb hit on the bridge, Jan. 6, 1945. A third unit of this class, *Mississippi*, is being refitted as a gunnery training ship, and will be found on a later page.

Guns:
12—14 inch, 50 cal., Mk. IV.
8—5 inch, 38 cal.
6—5 inch, 51 cal.
Many 40 mm. and 20 mm. AA.

Catapults:
1 on quarterdeck.

Aircraft: **3**

Length { *waterline*, 600 feet. *over all*, 624 feet. } Beam, **106¼** feet { *Mean* draught, **29½** feet. *Max.* „ **34** feet

Machinery: Westinghouse geared turbines. 4 shafts. Designed H.P.: 40,000 = 21·5 kts. Boilers: *Idaho*, 6 Bureau Express; *New Mexico*, 4 White-Forster. Fuel: Oil only, 2,200 tons (pre-alterations figures). Since modernisation speed has been raised to 22–23 kts.

No.	*Name*	*Builder*	*Machinery*	*Laid down*	*Completed*
BB 42	*Idaho*	N.Y.S.B. Corpn.	Builders	20/1/15	24/3/19
40	*New Mexico*	N.Y. Navy Yard		14/10/15	15/8/18

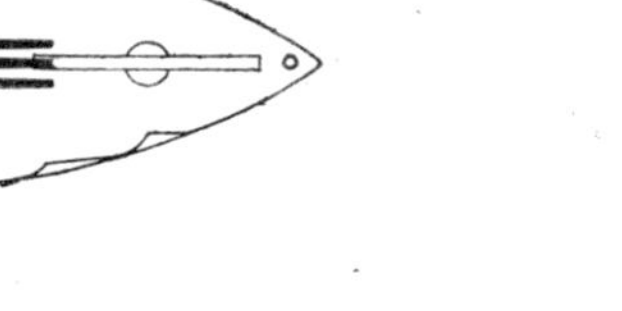

Idaho. 1944, *U.S. Navy Official.*

Battle Cruisers

(Alaska Class—3 Ships.)

ALASKA (August 15, 1943), **GUAM** (Nov. 21, 1943), **HAWAII** (Nov. 3, 1945).

Displacement: 27,500 tons (32,000 tons *full load*). Complement: 1,979.

Length: 808½ feet (*o.a.*). Beam: 89½ feet. Draught: 31 feet 6 inches.

Guns (*Alaska* and *Guam*):
9—12 inch, 50 cal.
12—5 inch, 38 cal.
56—40 mm. AA.
34—20 mm. AA.

Aircraft: **4**.
Catapults: **2**.

Armour:
6—9″ Side.
3¼″ Upper deck.
2″ Main deck.
Protection generally is on the lines of a cruiser rather than of a battleship.

Note to Plan.—Stern is actually squarer in form than shown here.

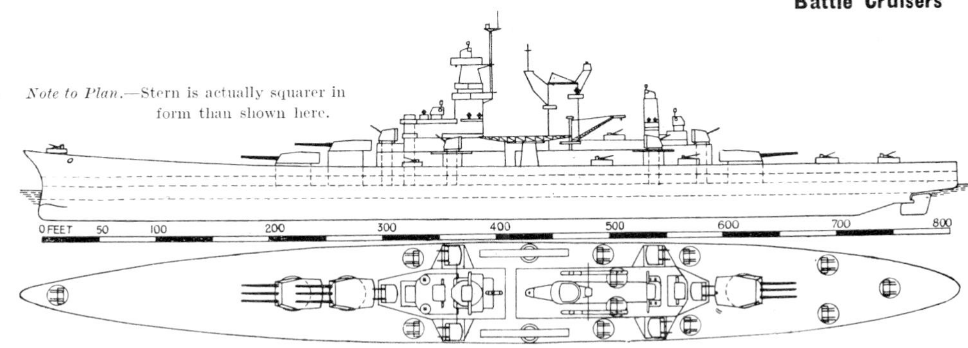

Machinery: General Electric geared turbines. **4** shafts. S.H.P.: 150,000 = 33 kts. (exceeded in service). Boilers: 8 Babcock & Wilcox.

Guam. 1944, *U.S. Navy Official.*

No.	*Name*	*Builders*	*Machinery*	*Laid down*	*Completed*
CB 1	*Alaska*	New York Shipbuilding Corporation	General Electric Co.	16/12/41	17/6/44
2	*Guam*			2/2/42	17/9/44
3	*Hawaii*			20/12/43	

Notes.—All ordered in Sept. 1940 and officially described as "Large Cruisers". In fact, they are the first battle cruisers to be ordered by any Navy since the Washington Conference met in 1921. The 12-inch guns are of a new and powerful model. Inclusive cost is officially estimated at $74,066,000 per ship. Three more ships of this type *Philippines*, *Puerto Rico* and *Samoa*, authorised in 1940, were cancelled on June 24, 1943. *Hawaii*, still incomplete, has been laid up awaiting final decision concerning armament, which may be modified to include rocket projectors.

Alaska. 1944, *U.S. Navy Official.*

Battleships

PENNSYLVANIA. (Height of funnel since increased and a sky lookout platform added at mainmasthead as in NEVADA.) 1933 *O. W. Waterman.*

PENNSYLVANIA (16th March, 1915). *Standard* Displacement, 33,100 tons.

Length {*w.l.* 600 feet / *o.a.* 608 feet} Beam, 106 feet, 3 in. {*Mean* draught, 28 feet. / *Maximum* draught, 33½ feet.

Complement, 1358.

Guns:
- **12**—14 inch, 45 cal. Mark I.
- **12**—5 in., 51 cal.
- **12**—5 in. (AA.), 25 cal.
- **4**—3 pdr. (saluting).
- (Torpedo tubes removed).

Aircraft: **3**

Catapults:
- **1** on "X" Turret
- **1** on quarter deck.

Armour:
- 14" Belt (amidships) ....
- 8" Belt (aft) ....
- 3" Deck (ends) ....
- 15"—9" Funnel base ....
- 18"—9" Turrets
- 16" Conning tower & tube ...
- (Total, 8072 tons.)
- 6" deck amidships (4" upper, 2" lower).

Machinery: Curtis turbines, L.P. ahead and astern, H.P. astern. Westinghouse geared turbines, H.P. ahead and cruising. 4 shafts. Designed H.P. 32,000 = 21 kts. (unaffected by modernisation). Boilers: 1 Bureau Express, 5 White-Forster. Fuel: Oil only, *normal* 2,322 tons (694,830 gallons).

Name	*Builder*	*Machinery*	*Laid down*	*Completed*	*Trials Full Power: 12 hrs.*
Pennsylvania	Newport News	Newport News	Oct.'13	June,'16	29,366 = 21·05

Tons Fuel per day		
10—	15—	19—kts.
65/—	90/—	—/—

General Notes.—*Pennsylvania* authorised 1912, as *No. 38.* She is an enlarged and improved *Nevada*, and is reported to be an excellent sea boat, very steady gun platform, and very economical. She has been extensively reconstructed, alterations including: Battery raised a deck and AA. armament increased; tripods fitted, funnel moved further aft; bulges and increased internal protection; additional bridges, and catapults fitted. In appearance she differs from *Nevada* in having higher conning tower and bridge which reaches funnel level. Sister ship *Arizona* was destroyed by enemy action at Pearl Harbour, Dec. 7, 1941.

Armour Notes.—Generally as for *Nevada* class. Increase of armour weight due to increased internal protection against submarine explosions and greater length of belt. Armour for each triple barbette, 226½ tons.

Gunnery and Fire Control Notes.—14 inch guns mounted in single sleeve, and can be fired as one piece. *Max.* range at 15° elevation reported to be 21,000 yards. Triple positions weigh about 650 tons each (guns, mountings and armour). Turrets are capable of putting 2—3 salvoes a minute through a target at short range practice. Breech blocks worked by hand power. Interior of the shields to 14 inch guns very roomy and well arranged.

NEVADA (July 11th, 1914). OKLAHOMA

Standard Displacement 29,000 tons. Complement, 1301.

Length {*waterline*, 575 feet. / *over all*, 583 feet.} Beam, 107 ft. 11 in. *Mean* draught 27½ feet. *Maximum* draught 32½ feet.

Guns:
- **10**—14 inch, 45 cal.
- **12**—5 inch, 51 cal.
- **12**—5 inch, 25 cal. AA.
- **4**—6 pdr.
- **8**—M.G.
- (Torpedo tubes removed.)

Aircraft: **3.**

Catapults:
- **1** on "X" Turret.
- **1** on quarter deck.

Armour:
- 13½" Belt (amidships) ....
- 8" Belt (aft)...........................
- 13½" Bulkheads ....
- 13½" Funnel base ....
- 5" Deck (amidships). (3" upper and 2" main).
- 3" Deck (ends) ....
- 18"—9" Triple turrets ..
- 16"—9" Double turrets...
- 16" Conning tower and tube ......
- (Total weight, 7664 tons.)
- (Bulges fitted).

Machinery: Parsons turbines with reduction gear. 2 shafts. Designed H.P.: 25,000 = 20·5 kts. Boilers: 6 Bureau Express. Fuel: Oil, 598,400 gallons (2,000 tons), *maximum capacity.* Radius of action: 4,000 miles at full speed, 10,000 miles at 10 kts.

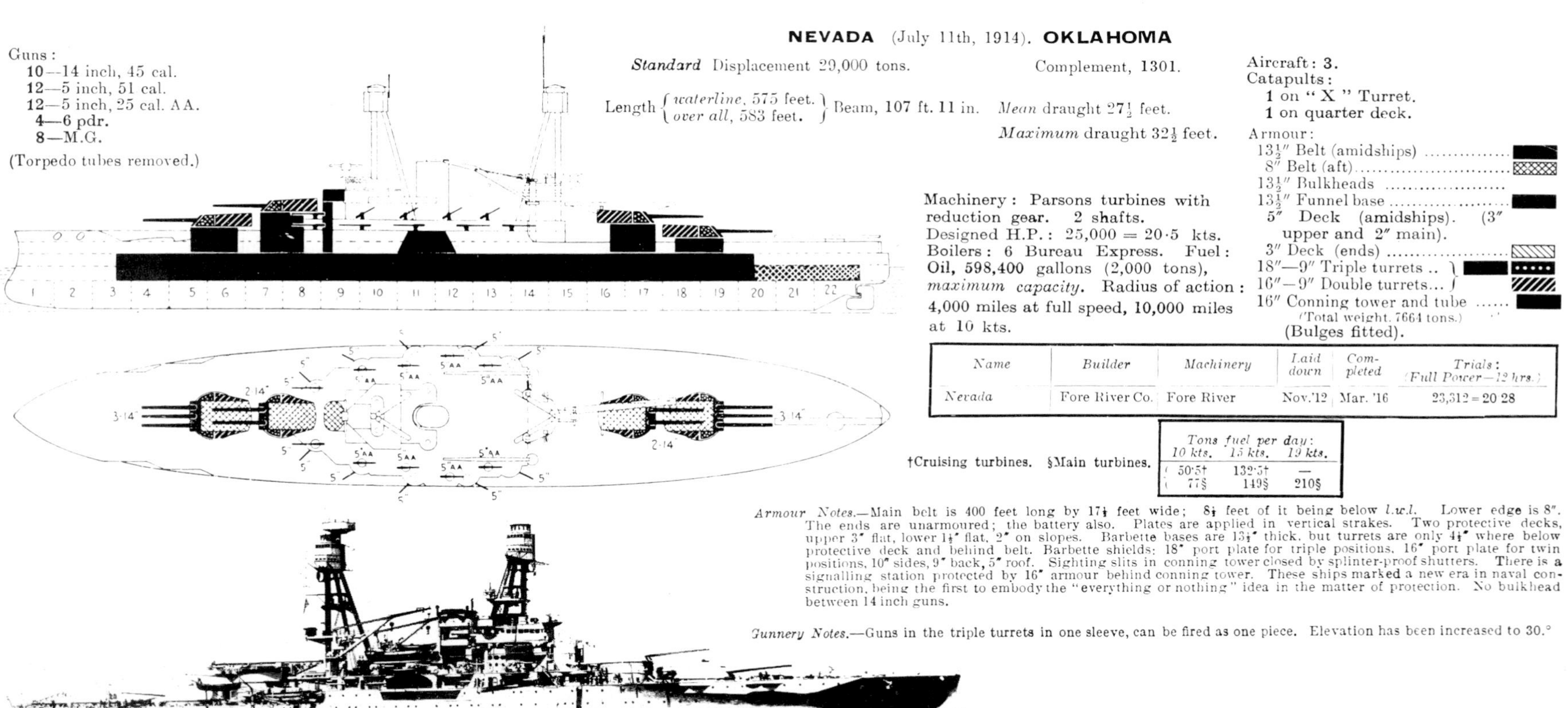

Name	*Builder*	*Machinery*	*Laid down*	*Completed*	*Trials: Full Power—12 hrs.*
Nevada	Fore River Co.	Fore River	Nov.'12	Mar. '16	23,312 = 20·28

†Cruising turbines. §Main turbines.

Tons fuel per day:		
10 kts.	*15 kts.*	*19 kts.*
50·5†	132·5†	—
77§	149§	210§

Armour Notes.—Main belt is 400 feet long by 17½ feet wide; 8½ feet of it being below *l.w.l.* Lower edge is 8". The ends are unarmoured; the battery also. Plates are applied in vertical strakes. Two protective decks, upper 3" flat, lower 1½" flat, 2" on slopes. Barbette bases are 13½" thick, but turrets are only 4½" where below protective deck and behind belt. Barbette shields: 18" port plate for triple positions, 16" port plate for twin positions, 10" sides, 9" back, 5" roof. Sighting slits in conning tower closed by splinter-proof shutters. There is a signalling station protected by 16" armour behind conning tower. These ships marked a new era in naval construction, being the first to embody the "everything or nothing" idea in the matter of protection. No bulkhead between 14 inch guns.

Gunnery Notes.—Guns in the triple turrets in one sleeve, can be fired as one piece. Elevation has been increased to 30.°

NEVADA. (Appearance since altered by reconstruction.) 1935, *O. W. Waterman.*

(Texas Class—

NEW YORK (Oct. 30th, 1912), **TEXAS** (May 18th, 1912).

Displacement, { *Standard*, 27,000 tons. / *Full load*, 32,000 tons. } Complement, 1314.

Length (*waterline*), 566 feet. / Length (*over all*), 573 feet. } Beam, 106 feet.

Mean draught, 26ft.
Max. „ 31½ ft.

Guns:
10—14 inch, 45 cal.
16—5 inch, 51 cal.
8—3 inch AA., Mk. III.
4—3 pdr. (saluting).
2—1 pdr.
8 M.G.
2 landing.
(Torpedo tubes removed).

Aircraft: 3.
Catapults:
1 on turret amidships.

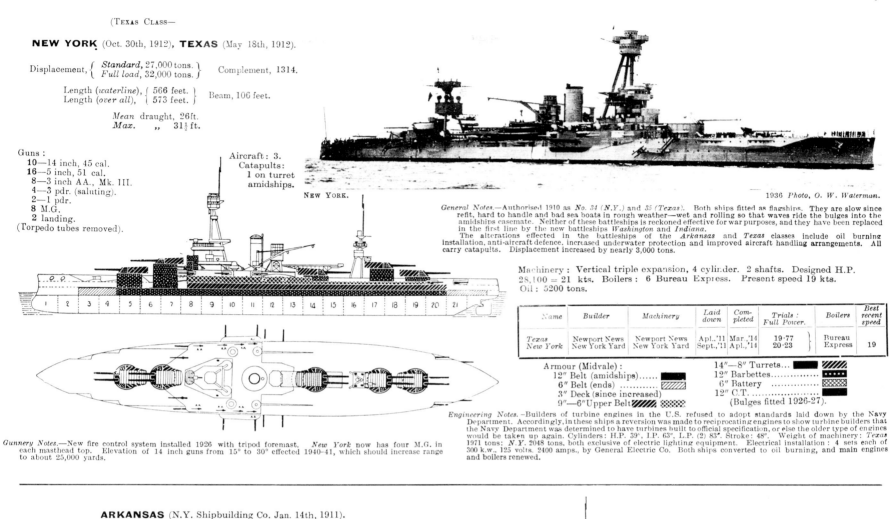

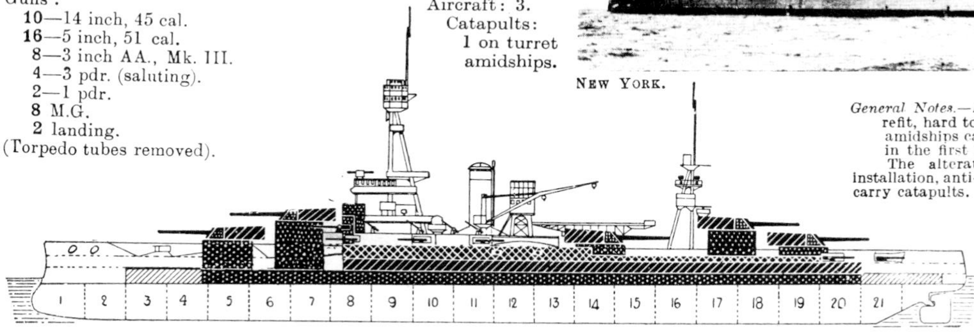

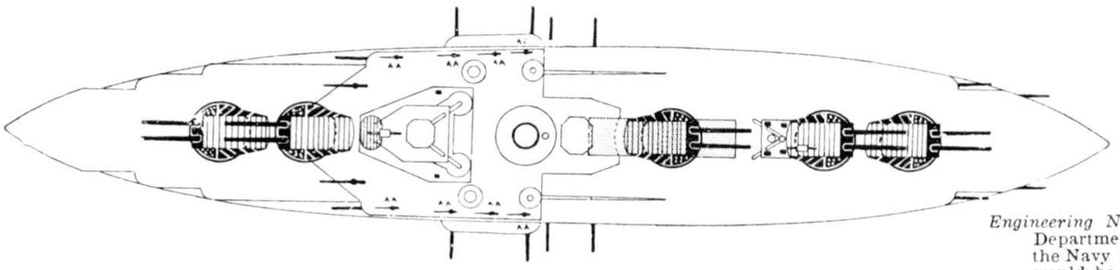

New York.

1936 *Photo, O. W. Waterman.*

General Notes.—Authorised 1910 as *No. 34 (N.Y.)* and *35 (Texas)*. Both ships fitted as flagships. They are slow since refit, hard to handle and bad sea boats in rough weather—wet and rolling so that waves ride the bulges into the amidships casemate. Neither of these battleships is reckoned effective for war purposes, and they have been replaced in the first line by the new battleships *Washington* and *Indiana*.

The alterations effected in the battleships of the *Arkansas* and *Texas* classes include oil burning installation, anti-aircraft defence, increased underwater protection and improved aircraft handling arrangements. All carry catapults. Displacement increased by nearly 3,000 tons.

Machinery: Vertical triple expansion, 4 cylinder. 2 shafts. Designed H.P. 28,100 = 21 kts. Boilers: 6 Bureau Express. Present speed 19 kts. Oil: 5200 tons.

Name	*Builder*	*Machinery*	*Laid down*	*Com-pleted*	*Trials: Full Power.*	*Boilers*	*Best recent speed*
Texas	Newport News	Newport News	Apl.,'11	Mar.,'14	19·77	Bureau Express	19
New York	New York Yard	New York Yard	Sept.,'11	Apl.,'14	20·23		

Armour (Midvale):
12″ Belt (amidships)......
6″ Belt (ends) ....
3″ Deck (since increased)
9″—6″ Upper Belt
14″—8″ Turrets...
12″ Barbettes..............
6″ Battery ....
12″ C.T. ....
(Bulges fitted 1926-27).

Engineering Notes.—Builders of turbine engines in the U.S. refused to adopt standards laid down by the Navy Department. Accordingly, in these ships a reversion was made to reciprocating engines to show turbine builders that the Navy Department was determined to have turbines built to official specification, or else the older type of engines would be taken up again. Cylinders: H.P. 39″, I.P. 63″, L.P. (2) 83″. Stroke: 48″. Weight of machinery: *Texas* 1971 tons: *N.Y.* 2048 tons, both exclusive of electric lighting equipment. Electrical installation: 4 sets each of 300 k.w., 125 volts. 2400 amps., by General Electric Co. Both ships converted to oil burning, and main engines and boilers renewed.

Gunnery Notes.—New fire control system installed 1926 with tripod foremast. *New York* now has four M.G. in each masthead top. Elevation of 14 inch guns from 15° to 30° effected 1940–41, which should increase range to about 25,000 yards.

ARKANSAS (N.Y. Shipbuilding Co. Jan. 14th, 1911).

Displacement, { *Standard*, 26,100 tons. / *Full load*, 31,000 tons. } Complement, 1330.

Length { (*w.l.*), 555½ feet. / (*o.a.*), 562 feet. } Beam, 106 feet.

Mean draught, 26 feet.
Max. „ 32 „

Guns:
12—12 inch, 50 cal.
16—5 inch, 51 cal.
8—3 inch AA., Mk III.
4—3 pdr. (saluting).
(Torpedo tubes removed).

Aircraft: 3
Catapults:
1 on 3rd turret.

Armour (Midvale):
11″—9″ Belt amidships
5″ Belt (ends) ....
12″—9″ Turrets.........
11″ Turret bases ....
6½″ Battery ....
12″ Conning tower.........
(Bulges fitted 1926-27)

Machinery: Parsons turbines. 4 shafts. S.H.P. 28,000 = 20·5 kts. Boilers: 4 White-Forster. Oil: 5,100 tons. Present speed 19·2 kts.

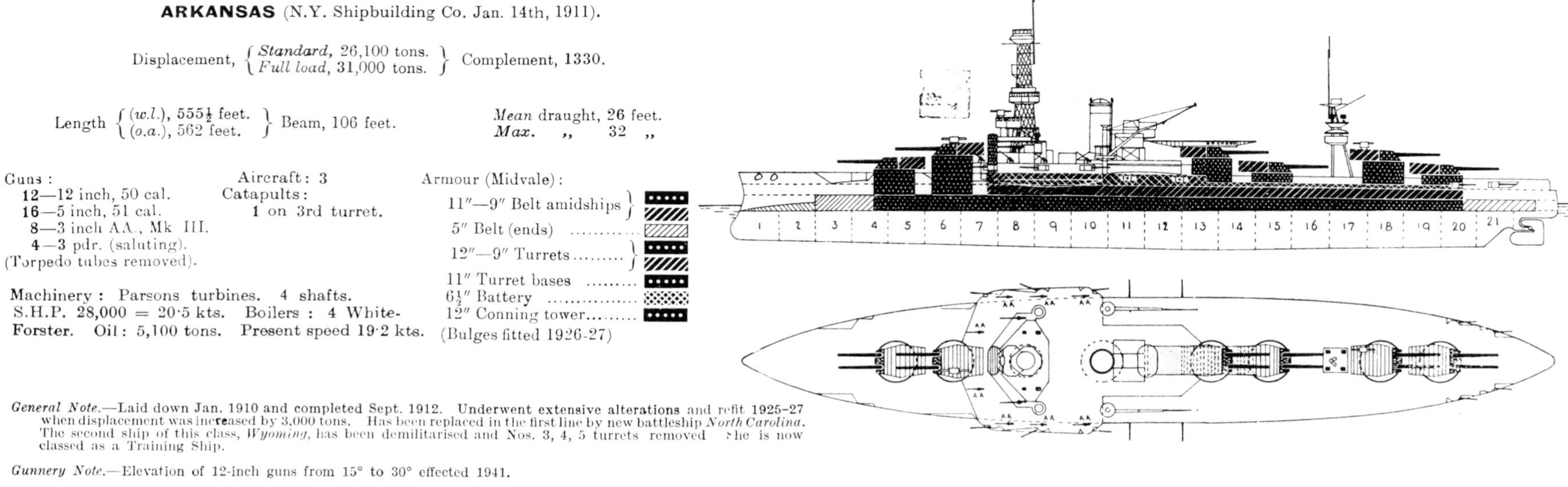

General Note.—Laid down Jan. 1910 and completed Sept. 1912. Underwent extensive alterations and refit 1925–27 when displacement was increased by 3,000 tons. Has been replaced in the first line by new battleship *North Carolina*. The second ship of this class, *Wyoming*, has been demilitarised and Nos. 3, 4, 5 turrets removed She is now classed as a Training Ship.

Gunnery Note.—Elevation of 12-inch guns from 15° to 30° effected 1941.

1934 *Photo, R. Perkins*

1927 *Official*

Large Fleet Aircraft Carriers

General Note.—All fleet carriers are differentiated by pendant numbers on funnels.

(Midway Class—3 Ships.)

CORAL SEA (April 2, 1946), **FRANKLIN D. ROOSEVELT** (ex-*Coral Sea*, April 29, 1945), **MIDWAY** (March 20, 1945).

Displacement: 45,000 tons (55,000 tons *full load*). Complement: 4,085.
Length: 968 feet (*o.a.*). Beam: 113 feet; 136 feet (*max.*). Draught: 32 feet 9 inches.

Guns:
18—5 inch, 54 cal.
84—40 mm. AA. (quadrupled).
82—20 mm. AA.

Aircraft:
137 (including large bombers of latest type).

Armour:
—" Side.
—" Deck.

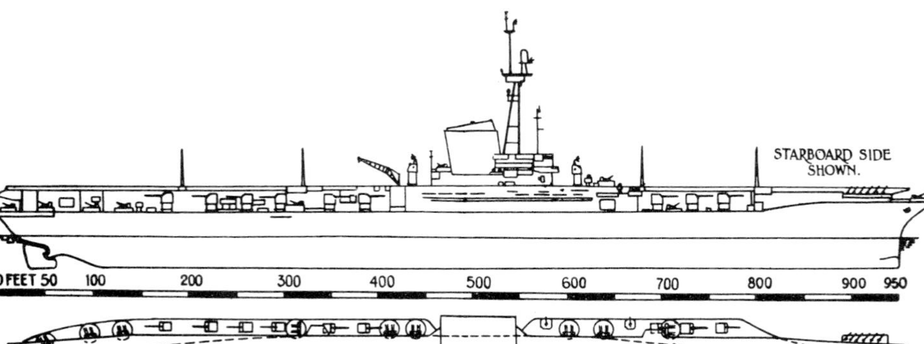

Machinery: Geared turbines. 4 shafts. S.H.P.: 200,000=33 kts. Boilers: 12.

Midway. 1946, *Mr. Wm. H. Davis.*

Name and No.	*Builders*	*Machinery*	*Laid down*	*Completed*
Coral Sea (CVB 43)	Newport News Co.	Builders	1944	
F. D. Roosevelt (CVB 42)	New York Navy Yd.		1/12/43	27/10/45
Midway (CVB 41)	Newport News Co.	Builders	10/43	11/9/45

Notes.—Three more ships of this class (CVB 44, 56, 57) were projected, but cancelled in 1945. Are the most extensively welded ships in U.S. Navy. Officially stated that they are protected by heavy armour, intricate watertight compartments and an improved system of damage control. Armoured flight deck is 932 × 113 feet, covered with non-skid surface material. Cost $90,000,000 each.

F. D. Roosevelt. 1946. *U.S. Navy Official.*

Princeton. 1946, *Ted Stone.*

Leyte. 1946, *U.S. Navy Official.*

Wasp. 1945, *U.S. Navy Official.*

Randolph. 1946, *Mr. Wm. H. Davis.*

Fleet Aircraft Carriers

ANTIETAM. 1945, *U.S. Navy Official.*

LEXINGTON. 1945, *U.S. Navy Official.*

MIDWAY. 1946, *Mr. Wm. H. Davis.*

(ESSEX CLASS—24 ships.)

ANTIETAM (Aug. 20, 1944), **BENNINGTON** (Feb. 26, 1944), **BON HOMME RICHARD** (April 29, 1944), **BOXER** (Dec. 14, 1944), **BUNKER HILL** (Dec. 7, 1942), **ESSEX** (July 31, 1942), **FRANKLIN** (Oct. 14, 1943), **HANCOCK** (ex-*Ticonderoga*, Jan. 24, 1944), **HORNET** (ex-*Kearsarge*, Aug. 29, 1943), **INTREPID** (April 26, 1943), **KEARSARGE,** (May 5, 1945), **LAKE CHAMPLAIN,** (Nov. 1944), **LEXINGTON** (ex-*Cabot*, Sept. 26, 1942), **LEYTE** (ex-*Crown Point* Aug. 23, 1943), **ORISKANY** (Oct. 13, 1945), **PHILIPPINE SEA** (ex-*Wright*, Sept. 5, 1945), **PRINCETON** (ex-*Valley Forge*, July 8, 1945), **RANDOLPH** (June 28, 1944), **SHANGRI-LA** (Feb. 24, 1944), **TARAWA** (May 12, 1945), **TICONDEROGA** (ex-*Hancock*, Feb. 7, 1944), **VALLEY FORGE** (Nov. 18, 1945), **WASP** (ex-*Oriskany*, Aug. 17, 1942), **YORKTOWN** (ex-*Bon Homme Richard*, Jan. 21, 1943).

Displacement: 27,100 tons (33,000 tons *full load*). Complement: 2,900.

Length: 874 feet (*pp.*), 888 feet (*o.a.*). Beam: 93 feet. Draught: 29 feet (*max.*).
(First 8 ships built are only 885 feet 10 in. *o.a.*)

Guns:
12—5 inch, 38 cal.
72—40 mm. AA.
52—20 mm.
(quadruple mounts).
(Later ships have only **10**—5 inch.)

Aircraft:
82 (**103** have been carried).

Armour:
2″—3″ Side amidships.
1½″ Flight deck.
1½″ Upper deck.
3″ Hangar deck.

BOXER. 1945, *U.S. Navy Official.*

Note to Plan.—Amidships lift should be shown as at flight deck level.

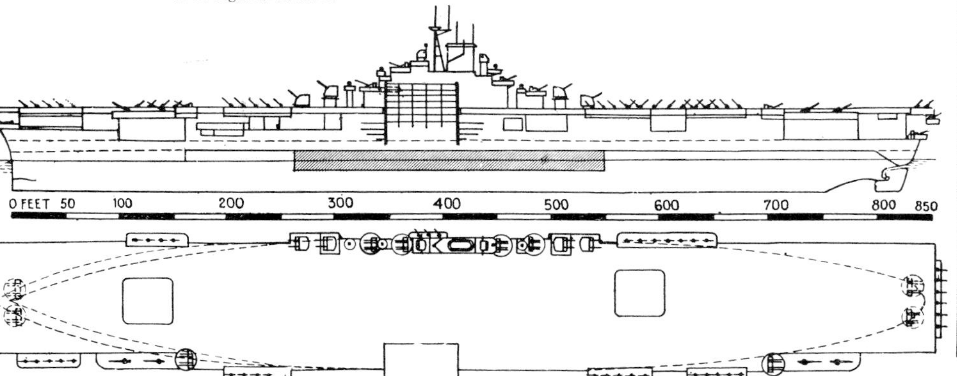

No.	Name	Builders	Machinery	Laid down	Completed
CV 9	*Essex*			28/4/41	31/12/42
10	*Yorktown*			1/12/41	16/5/43
11	*Intrepid*	Newport News S.B. & D.D. Co.	Builders.	1/12/41	16/8/43
12	*Hornet*			1942	29/11/43
13	*Franklin*			7/12/42	31/1/44
14	*Ticonderoga*			1942	8/5/44
15	*Randolph*			15/7/41	9/10/44
16	*Lexington*			15/9/41	17/3/43
17	*Bunker Hill*	Bethlehem Steel Co., Quincy	do.	1941	24/5/43
18	*Wasp*			1942	24/11/43
19	*Hancock*			1942	15/4/44
20	*Bennington*	New York Navy Yard	Not reported.	15/12/42	6/8/44
21	*Boxer*	Newport News Co.	Builders.	1943	16/4/45
31	*B. H. Richard*	New York Navy Yard	Not reported.	2/1/43	26/11/44
32	*Leyte*	Newport News Co.	Builders.	1944	11/4/46
33	*Kearsarge*	New York Navy Yard	Not reported.	1/3/44	2/3/46
34	*Oriskany*	do.	do.	1944	
36	*Antietam*	Philadelphia Navy Yard	do.	1943	28/1/45
37	*Princeton*	do.	do.	1944	18/11/45
38	*Shangri-La.*	Norfolk Navy Yard.	do.	1942	15/4/44
39	*Lake Champlain*	do.	do.	1944	3/6/45
40	*Tarawa*	do.	do.	1944	8/12/45
45	*Valley Forge*	Philadelphia Navy Yard	do.	1944	3/11/46
47	*Philippine Sea*	Bethlehem Co., Quincy	Builders.	1944	11/5/46

Machinery: Geared turbines. 4 shafts. S.H.P.: 150,000 = 33 kts.
Boilers: 8 Babcock & Wilcox.

Notes.—First 11 of class ordered 1940. Inclusive cost officially estimated to average $68,932,000, but *Princeton* is said to have cost $76,000,000 and *Kearsarge* $90,000,000. *Essex* was built in 20 months, *Yorktown* in 17½ months. Contracts were changed from original assignments in some instances. Later ships of this class are of improved design, with stronger flight decks, and are more thoroughly sub-divided. Two ships under construction at New York Navy Yard (*Reprisal*) and Newport News (*Iwojima*, ex-*Crown Point*) were cancelled in August, 1945, and six others in March, 1945. Construction of *Oriskany* has been held up for a year from August, 1946, presumably with a view to modification of design.

Engineering Note.—In November 1945, *Lake Champlain* made Atlantic crossing from Gibraltar to Newport News in 4 days, 8 hours, 51 minutes, equal to an average speed of 32·048 kts.

Appearance Note.—All ships of this class now reported to have bow and stern of same form as *Antietam*

BOXER. 1945, *U.S. Navy Official.*

Aircraft Carriers

SARATOGA. 1928 *Photo, by favour of H. C. Bywater, Esq.*

LEXINGTON (3rd Oct., 1925.)

SARATOGA (7th April, 1925.)

Standard Displacement, 33,000 tons.

Complement (including flying personnel) 169 Officers, 1730 men.

Length (*p.p.*), 850 feet ; (*o.a.*) 888 feet. Beam, 106 feet (*extreme*). Draught, 24 feet $1\frac{1}{2}$ inches (*mean*).

Guns :
- **8**—8 inch, 55 cal.
- **12**—5 inch AA., 25 cal.
- **4**—6 pdr. saluting.

Armour :
Unofficially reported to have 6" Belt, 600 feet in length, and 3" deck. Triple hull and bulge protection.

Notes on Lexington and Saratoga.

These two ships were originally authorised in 1916 for construction as Battle Cruisers of 35,300 tons, with *seven* funnels and boilers disposed on two deck levels. After the War, and as a result of the lessons thereof, plans were to a large extent re-cast, v. F.S. 1919—1921 Editions.

As Aircraft Carriers, these ships show a reduction (from the second Battle Cruiser design) in displacement of about 8,500 tons, achieved mainly by the elimination of eight 16-inch guns in four twin turrets, with mounts, armour, &c. It is believed the main belt protection is retained and that deck protection has been heavily reinforced. The general lines of the hull remain unaltered, and the special system of underwater protection is also adhered to. Flight deck is 880 feet long, from 85 to 90 feet in width, and 60 feet above waterline.

Handling of Aircraft.—The Landing Net is placed just before the recessed stern portion of the Flight Deck ; it is about 100 ft. long. Before it is a large T-shaped lift for moving aircraft from Flight to Hangar Deck. There is another and similar T-shaped lift abeam of the mast and C.T. At the bow is a catapult, 155 feet in length, capable of launching the heaviest aircraft into the air at flying speed with a travel of 60 feet. Before the C.T. and abaft the Navigating Officers' Deck House, and right over to starboard beam, are powerful derricks for lifting seaplanes and flying boats from the water. As a result of experiments with *Langley*, certain modifications have been made which should enable planes to land safely on deck in any weather.

Reported that 120 planes can be carried. Photos show them with from 70 to 80 planes on deck ready for flight, but number varies as the type of plane employed.

Total cost of these ships, with aircraft, was over $45,000,000 each.

Engineering Notes.—Each boiler 11,250 H.P. Steam pressure, 295 lbs. to sq. inch. Fuel consumption estimated at 2000 tons daily under full power. Machinery is the most powerful ever installed in a warship ; it is all controlled, so far as main engines are concerned, from one central position. There are over 1000 auxiliary motors, ranging from 425 H.P. ventilating plant down to the small electric motors connected with the self-synchronising electric fire-control arrangements, which develop 1-200th of one H.P. For general distribution through the ship, current is supplied by six turbo-generators of 750 K.W. each. There are eight propelling motors of 22,500 H.P. (two to each of the four shafts), speed 317 R.P.M. The combined illuminating power of the S.L. is equal to 3,260,000 c.p. Altogether, these ships represent the climax of American practice in applying electric power to warship construction. On trials, it is stated that 97% of designed speed was obtained with 85% of designed power. *Lexington* did the voyage from San Diego to Honolulu (2228 miles) at an average speed of 30·7 kts. A speed of 34·5 kts. was maintained for one hour by the latter ship with S.H.P. 210,000.

Machinery: G.E. Turbines, electric drive. Designed S.H.P. 180,000 = 33·25 kts. Boilers : *Lexington*, 16 Yarrow ; *Saratoga*, 16 White-Forster. 4 screws.

Name	*Builder*	*Machinery*	*Laid down*	*Completed*	*Trials*	*Boilers*
Lexington	Fore River S B. Co.	Gen. Elec. Co.	8/1/21	Dec.'27	153,600 = 33·04	Yarrow
Saratoga	New York S.B. Co.	Gen. Elec. Co.	25/9/20	Nov.'28	158,375 = 33·42	White-Forster

---

RANGER (Newport News S.B. Co., Feb. 25, 1933).

Displacement : 14,500 tons.

Complement (including flying personnel) : 1,788, of whom 162 are commissioned officers.

Dimensions : 728 (*w.l.*), 769 (*o.a.*) × $80\frac{1}{12}$ × $19\frac{2}{3}$ ft. (*mean*).

Guns :
- **8**—5 inch 38 cal. dual purpose.
- **40** smaller

Aircraft :
- 72 (peace-time complement).
- 86 can be carried.

Armour :
- 1" Flight Deck
- Double Hull and internal subdivision, but no side armour beyond small patch shown.

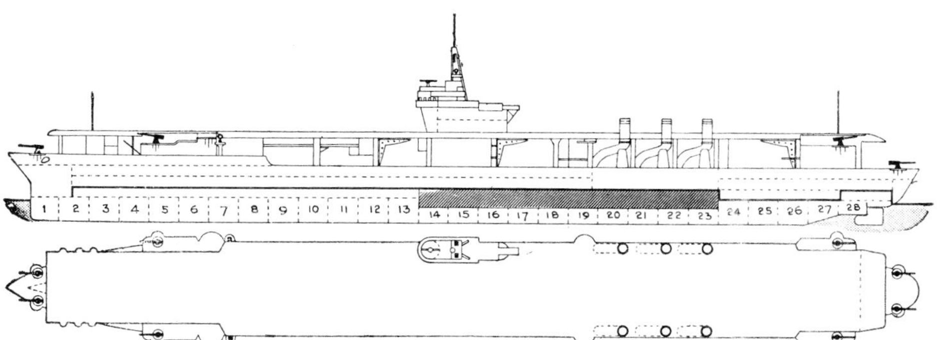

Machinery : Geared Turbines (high pressure Curtis ; low pressure Parsons). 2 shafts. S.H.P.: 53,500 = $29\frac{1}{4}$ kts. Boilers : 6 Babcock & Wilcox sectional Express.

General Notes.—Laid down Sept. 26 1931. Completed June 4, 1934. Trials : 58,700 = 30·35 kts. (*max.*). The six funnels can be lowered to horizontal position, as shown in photo. Cost approached $20,000,000. *Ranger* was first U.S. aircraft carrier designed as such.

Added 1935, *courtesy U.S. Naval Institute.*

RANGER. *Added* 1937, *O. W. Waterman.*

With funnels lowered. 1936, *O. W. Waterman.*

ENTERPRISE (Oct. 3, 1936).
Displacement : 19,900 tons.
Complement, 2,072 (including flying personnel).
Length : 761 feet (*w.l.*), 809½ feet (*o.a.*). Beam, 83¼ feet.
Draught, 21⅓ feet (*mean*).

Guns :
8—5 inch 38 cal. (dual purpose).
16—1·1 inch M.G. A.A.
16 smaller M.G.

Aircraft :
81-85 (space for over 100).

Armour : A patch of side armour at water line over machinery and boiler spaces (unofficially reported to be 4″) and a heavy protective deck.

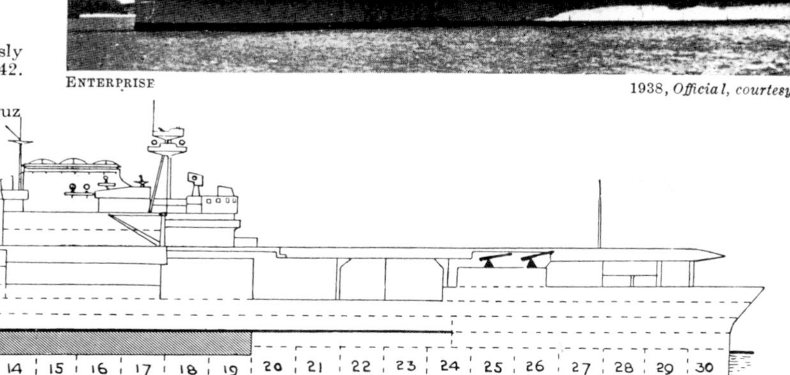

ENTERPRISE 1938, *Official, courtesy "Our Navy."*

YORKTOWN (1936). 19,900 tons.
Foundered after being torpedoed by a Japanese submarine, having previously been damaged by aircraft torpedoes and bombs in Battle of Midway, June 7, 1942.

HORNET (1940). 20,000 tons.
Sunk by U.S. Naval forces after being irreparably damaged in Battle of Santa Cruz Islands, October 26, 1942.

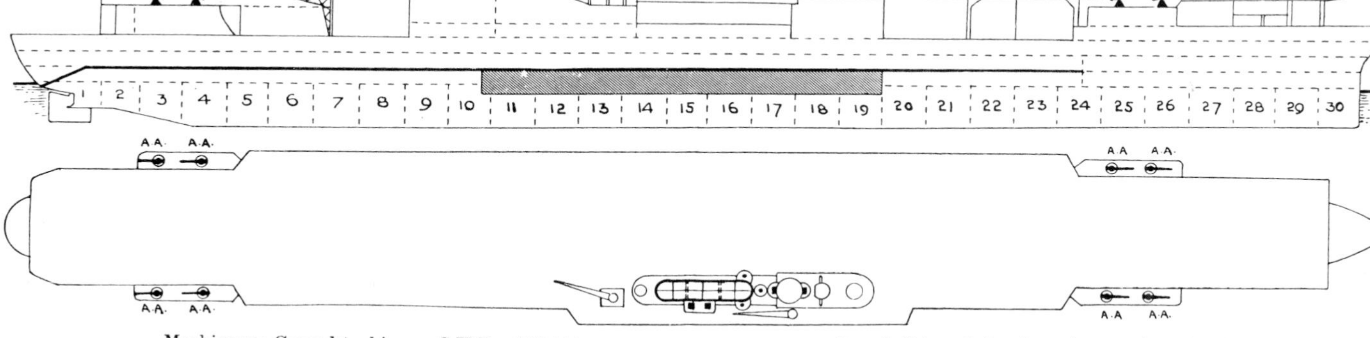

Machinery : Geared turbines. S.H.P. : 120,000 = 34 kts. (exceeded on trials). Boilers : 9 Babcock & Wilcox Express type

Name	*Builder*	*Laid down*	*Completed*
Enterprise	Newport News Co.	16 July, 1934	18 July, 1938

General Notes.—Owing to serious mechanical defects, involving replacement of the reduction gearing and over 1,200 boiler tubes, completion of *Enterprise* was postponed until late in 1938. Said to have cost about $25,000,000.

Aircraft Notes.—Aircraft can be catapulted from hangar deck as well as from flight deck, thus increasing the number that can be put into the air at short notice. There are 3 lifts from hangars to flight deck.

WASP (April 4th, 1939)

Standard displacement, 14,700 tons (about 18,450 tons full load)

Complement, 2,167

Length (*o.a.*) 720 feet. Beam, 100 feet. Draught, 23 feet.

Armour:
2/3″ Belt
1 1/4″ Deck

Guns:
8 – 5 inch, 38cal
16 – 1.1 inch AA
24 – 0.5 inch machine guns

Aircraft:
76

Machinery: 2-shaft Parsons turbines, 6 Yarrow boilers, 70,000 shp= 29.5 knots. Oil, 1602 tons

WASP. 1940, *U.S. Navy Official*

WASP (1939). 14,700 tons.
Torpedoed by a Japanese submarine in the Pacific, September 15, 1942.

Light Fleet Aircraft Carriers

SAIPAN (July 8, 1945), **WRIGHT** (Sept. 1, 1945).

Displacement: 14,500 tons (20,000 tons *full load*).

Complement: 1,500.

Length: 683 feet 7 in. Beam: 76 feet 9 in. Draught not reported.

Machinery: Geared turbines. 4 shafts. S.H.P.: 120,000 = 33 kts. Boilers: Babcock & Wilcox. Fuel: 2,400 tons.

No.	*Name.*	*Builders and Machinery.*	*Laid down.*	*Completed.*
CVL 48	*Saipan*	New York S.B. Corpn.	10/7/44	14/7/46
49	*Wright*		21/8/44	9/2/47

Guns:
4—5 inch, 38 cal.
40—40 mm. AA.
25—20 mm. AA.

Aircraft:
48

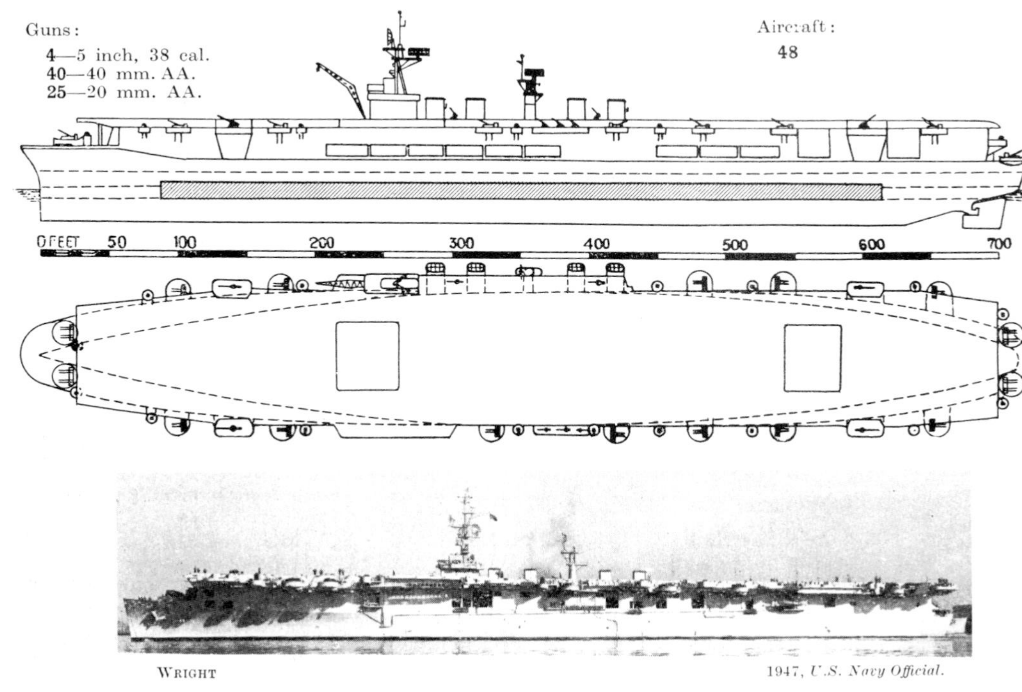

WRIGHT. 1947, *U.S. Navy Official.*

SAIPAN. 1947, *U.S. Navy Official.*

(INDEPENDENCE CLASS—7 SHIPS.)

BATAAN (ex-*Buffalo*), (Aug. 1, 1943), **BELLEAU WOOD** (ex-*New Haven*, Dec. 6, 1942), **CABOT** (ex-*Wilmington*, April 4, 1943), **COWPENS** (ex-*Huntington*, Jan. 17, 1943), **LANGLEY** (ex-*Crown Point*, ex-*Fargo*, May 22, 1943), **MONTEREY** (ex-*Dayton*, Feb. 28, 1943), **SAN JACINTO** (ex-*Reprisal*, ex-*Newark*, Sept. 26, 1943).

Displacement: 11,000 tons (13,000 tons *full load*). Complement: 1,400.

Length: 600 feet (*w.l.*), 618 feet (*o.a.*). Beam: 71½ feet. Draught: 20 feet.

Guns:
16—40 mm. AA.
40—20 mm. AA.

Aircraft:
45.

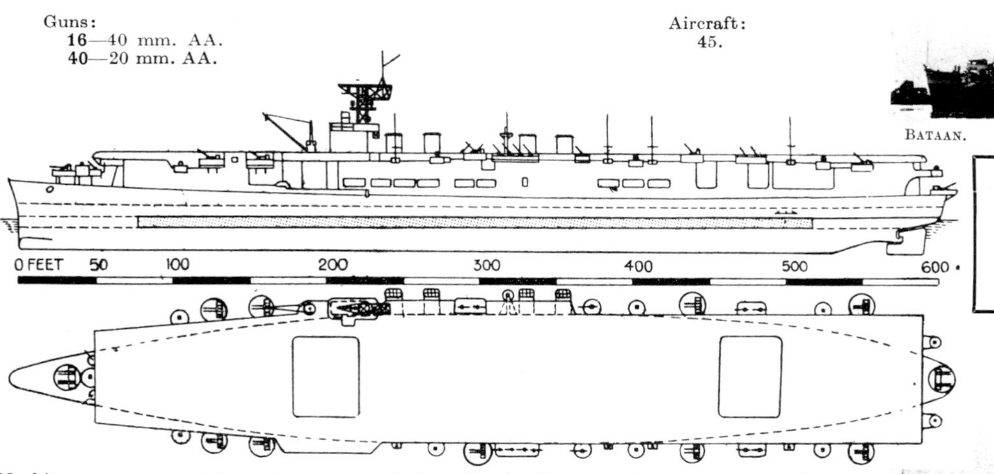

Machinery: Geared turbines. 4 shafts. S.H.P.: 100,000=33 kts. Boilers: Babcock & Wilcox.

S. JACINTO. 1944, *U.S. Navy Official.*

COWPENS. 1944, *U.S. Navy Official.*

BATAAN. 1944, *U.S. Navy Official.*

No.	*Name.*	*Builders and Machinery.*	*Laid down.*	*Completed.*
CVL 24	*Belleau Wood*	New York S.B. Corpn.	11/8/41	31/3/43
25	*Cowpens*		17/11/41	28/5/43
26	*Monterey*		29/12/41	17/6/43
27	*Cabot*		11/4/42	31/8/43
28	*Langley*		16/8/42	24/7/43
29	*Bataan*		31/8/42	17/11/43
30	*S. Jacinto*		26/10/42	15/12/43

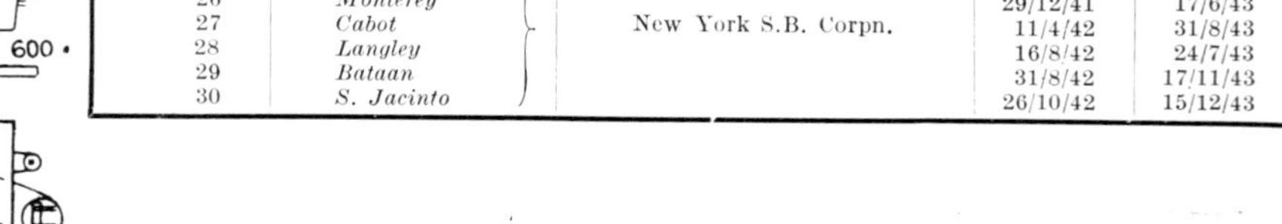

BATAAN. 1944, *U.S. Navy Official.*

Note.—These vessels were all laid down as cruisers of the *Cleveland* class, described on a later page, but were ordered to be completed as aircraft carriers. *Princeton* (CVL 23), ex-*Tallahassee*, lost in action; and *Independence* (CVL 22) utilised for Bikini atom-bomb experiments, 1946.

Gunnery Note.—Were originally designed to include 4—5 inch in armament.

(Commencement Bay Class—19 Ships, CVE 105–123.)

Commencement Bay. 1944, *U.S. Navy Official.*

BADOENG STRAIT (ex-*San Alberto Bay*, Feb. 15, 1945), **BAIROKO** (ex-*Portage Bay*, Jan. 25, 1945), **BLOCK ISLAND** (ex-*Sunset Bay*, June 10, 1944), **CAPE GLOUCESTER** (ex-*Willapa Bay*, Sept. 12, 1944), **COMMENCEMENT BAY** (ex-*St. Joseph's Bay*, May 9, 1944), **GILBERT ISLANDS** (ex-*St. Andrew's Bay*, July 20, 1944), **KULA GULF** (ex-*Vermilion Bay*, Aug. 15, 1944), **MINDORO** (June 27, 1945), **PALAU** (Aug. 6, 1945), **POINT CRUZ** (ex-*Trocadero Bay*, May 18, 1945), **PUGET SOUND** (ex-*Hobart Bay*, Nov. 30, 1944), **RABAUL** (July 14, 1945), **RENDOVA** (ex-*Mosser Bay*, Dec. 28, 1944), **SAIDOR** (ex-*Saltery Bay*, March 17, 1945), **SALERNO BAY** (ex-*Winjah Bay*, Sept. 26, 1944), **SIBONEY** (ex-*Frosty Bay*, Nov. 9, 1944), **SICILY** (ex-*Sandy Bay*, April 14, 1945), **TINIAN** (Sept. 5, 1945), **VELLA GULF** (ex-*Totem Bay*, Oct. 19, 1944).

Displacement: 12,000 tons. Dimensions: 553 (*o.a.*) × 75 × 30½ (*max.* draught). Guns: **2**—5 inch 38 cal. when first completed; but now reported to carry **26**—40 mm. AA., **30**—20 mm. AA. Aircraft: 34. Machinery: Geared turbines. 2 shafts. S.H.P.: 16,000=20 kts. Complement: 1,000.

Notes.—All built by Todd Pacific Shipyards, Tacoma; cost reported to be $11,000,000 each. Design modelled on that of *Sangamon* type. Sixteen more ships of this class, *Bastogne*, *Eniwetok*, *Lingayen*, *Okinawa*, and 128–139, were cancelled in August, 1945.

(Chenango Class—3 Ships, CVE 27–29.)

Added 1944, *U.S. Navy Official.*

CHENANGO (ex-*Esso New Orleans*, Jan. 4, 1939), **SANTEE** (ex-*Seakay*, March 4, 1939), **SUWANEE** (ex-*Markay*, March 4, 1939). Ex-oilers converted into Aircraft Carriers.

Displacement: 12,000 tons. Complement: Over 1,000.

Dimensions (prior to conversion): 525 (*w.l.*), 556 (*o.a.*). × 75 × 30 feet. Guns: **1** or **2**—5 inch, 51 cal., **8**—40 mm. AA., **15**—20 mm. AA. Aircraft: 34. Machinery: Geared turbines. 2 shafts. S.H.P.: 13,500 = 18 kts.

(Casablanca Class—37 Ships, CVE 55–104.)

1946, *Ted Stone.*

ADMIRALTY ISLANDS (ex-*Chapin Bay*, May 10, 1944), **ANZIO** (ex-*Alikula Bay*, ex-*Coral Sea*, May 1, 1943), **BOUGAINVILLE** (ex-*Didrickson Bay*, May 16, 1944), **CAPE ESPERANCE** (ex-*Tananek Bay*, March 3, 1944), **CORREGIDOR** (ex-*Atheling*, ex-*Anguilla Bay*, May 12, 1943), **FANSHAW BAY** (Nov. 1, 1943), **GUADALCANAL** (ex-*Astrolabe Bay*, June 5, 1943), **HOGGATT BAY** (Dec. 4, 1943), **HOLLANDIA** (ex-*Astrolabe Bay*, April 28, 1944), **KADASHAN BAY** (Dec 11, 1943), **KASAAN BAY** (Oct. 24, 1943), **KITKUN BAY** (Nov. 8, 1943), **KWAJALEIN** (ex-*Bucareli Bay*, May 4, 1944), **LUNGA POINT** (ex-*Alazon Bay*, April 11, 1944), **MAKASSAR STRAIT** (ex-*Ulitaka Bay*, March 23, 1944), **MANILA BAY** (ex-*Bucareli Bay*, July 10, 1943), **MARCUS ISLAND** (ex-*Kanalku Bay*, Dec. 16, 1943), **MATANIKAU** (ex-*Dolomi Bay*, May 22, 1944), **MISSION BAY** (May 26, 1943), **MUNDA** (ex-*Tonowek Bay*, June 8, 1944), **NATOMA BAY** (ex-*Begum*, July 20, 1943), **NEHENTA BAY** (ex-*Khedive*, Nov. 28, 1943), **PETROF BAY** (Jan. 5, 1944), **RUDYERD BAY** (Jan. 12, 1944), **SAGINAW BAY** (Jan. 19, 1944), **SARGENT BAY** (Jan. 31, 1944), **SAVO ISLAND** (ex-*Kaita Bay*, Dec. 22, 1943), **SHAMROCK BAY** (Feb. 3, 1944), **SHIPLEY BAY** (Feb. 12, 1944), **SITKOH BAY** (Feb. 19, 1944), **STEAMER BAY** (Feb. 26, 1944), **TAKANIS BAY** (March 10, 1944), **THETIS BAY** (March 16, 1944), **TRIPOLI** (ex-*Didrickson Bay*, Sept. 2, 1943), **TULAGI** (ex-*Fortaleza Bay*, Nov. 15, 1943), **WHITE PLAINS** (ex-*Elbour Bay*, Sept. 27, 1943), **WINDHAM BAY** (March 29, 1944).

Displacement: 6,730 tons *standard*, 10,200 tons *full load*. Complement: 800. Dimensions: 487 (*w.l.*), 498⅚ (*o.a.*) × 80 × 19¾ feet *max.* draught. Guns: **1**—5 inch, 38 cal., **24**—20 mm. AA. (Later ships have **8**—40 mm. AA., **24**—20 mm. AA.) Machinery: Skinner Unaflow (reciprocating) engines. 2 shafts. I.H.P.: 11,200=18 kts.

Notes.—All these ships were built by the Henry J. Kaiser Co., Inc., at Vancouver, Wash., or by the Oregon S.B. Corpn. at Portland, Oregon. They are of an improved design, differing from converted ships of *Bogue* class, which were found difficult to land upon in light airs. Beam given above is width of flight deck. *Admiralty Islands* and *Bougainville* each took 76 days to build. War losses: *Bismarck Sea* (CVE 95), *Gambier Bay* (73), *Liscome Bay* (56), *Ommaney Bay* (79), *St. Lo* (63). Sold or scrapped since: *Attu*, *Casablanca*, *Kalinin Bay*, *Makin Island*, *Roi*, *Salamaua*, *Solomons*, *Wake Island*.

(Bogue Class—10 ships.)

Altamaha. (Observe funnel.) 1944, *U.S. Navy Official.*

Copahee. 1942, *U.S. Navy Official.*

Card. 1943, *Associated Press.*

ALTAMAHA (May 22, 1942), **BARNES** (May 22, 1942), **BOGUE** (Jan. 15, 1942), **BRETON** (June 27, 1942), **CARD** (Feb. 21, 1942), **COPAHEE** (ex-*Steel Architect*, Oct. 21, 1941), **CORE** (May 15, 1942), **CROATAN** (Aug. 3, 1942), **NASSAU** (April 4, 1942), **PRINCE WILLIAM** (Aug. 23, 1942).

All converted from mercantile hulls by Seattle-Tacoma S.B. Corpn., and vary slightly in appearance. Displacement: 7,800 tons (except *Prince William*, 8,300 tons). Dimensions: 465 (*pp.*), 494 (*o.a.*) × 69½ × 23¼ feet (except *Prince William*, 492 × 70 × 25½ feet). Guns: **1** or **2**—5 inch, 51 cal., **16**—40 mm. Bofors, **20**—20 mm. Oerlikon. Aircraft: Normal complement is 12 fighters and 9 torpedo-bombers. Machinery: Westinghouse geared turbines. B.H.P.: 8,500 = 16 to 16·5 kts. Boilers of Foster Wheeler type. Complement: 650.

Notes.—All are named after sounds. These vessels are equipped with derricks for retrieving seaplanes. Flight deck is 450 feet long. They are numbered as follows: *Bogue*, CVE 9; *Card*, 11; *Copahee*, 12; *Core*, 13; *Nassau*, 16; *Altamaha*, 18; *Barnes*, 20; *Breton*, 23; *Croatan*, 25; *Prince William*, 31. Most of them are expected to be listed for disposal shortly.

Heavy Cruisers

(Des Moines Class—4 Ships)

DALLAS, DES MOINES (Sept. 27, 1946), **NEWPORT NEWS** (March 6, 1947), **SALEM**

Displacement: 17,000 tons (21,000 tons *full load*)

Complement not reported.

Length: 716 feet 6 in. (*o.a.*). Beam: 75 feet 4 in. Draught not reported.

Guns:
9—8 inch, 55 cal.
16—5 inch, 38 cal.
60—40 mm. AA.

Aircraft: 4.
Catapults: 2.

Armour:
6″—8″ Side.
3″+2″ Decks.

Machinery: Geared turbines. 4 shafts. S.H.P.: 120,000 = 32 kts. Boilers: Babcock & Wilcox. Fuel: 2,600 tons.

No.	Name.	Builders & Machinery.	Laid down.	Completed.
CA 134	*Des Moines*	Bethlehem Steel Co., Quincy.	28/3/45	
139	*Salem*		45	
140	*Dallas*		45	
148	*Newport News*	Newport News Co.	45	

Notes.—These ships represent an expansion of *Oregon City* design, with same engine power, but all guns are to be of fully automatic type. Cartridge cases have replaced wrapped charges, and shells have an automatic fuze setting. Much of extra tonnage is likely to be absorbed by rapid loading gear and extra magazine space, though part of this will be made up by saving in complement. Four others of class cancelled (CA 141–143 and 149).

NEWPORT NEWS and **SALEM** launched respectively on March 6 and 25, 1947.

(Insufficient information available for a plan; but main features of design are expected to resemble *Oregon City*.)

(Oregon City Class—3 Ships)

ALBANY (June 30, 1945), **OREGON CITY** (April 9, 1945), **ROCHESTER** (August 28, 1945).

Displacement: 13,700 tons (17,000 tons *full load*).
Complement: 1,715.

Length: 673 feet 6 in. (*o.a.*). Beam: 69 feet 9 in. Draught not reported.

Guns:
9—8 inch, 55 cal.
12—5 inch, 38 cal.
48—40 mm. AA.
40—20 mm. AA.

Aircraft: 4
Catapults: 2.

Armour:
6″—8″ Side.
3″ + 2″ Decks.

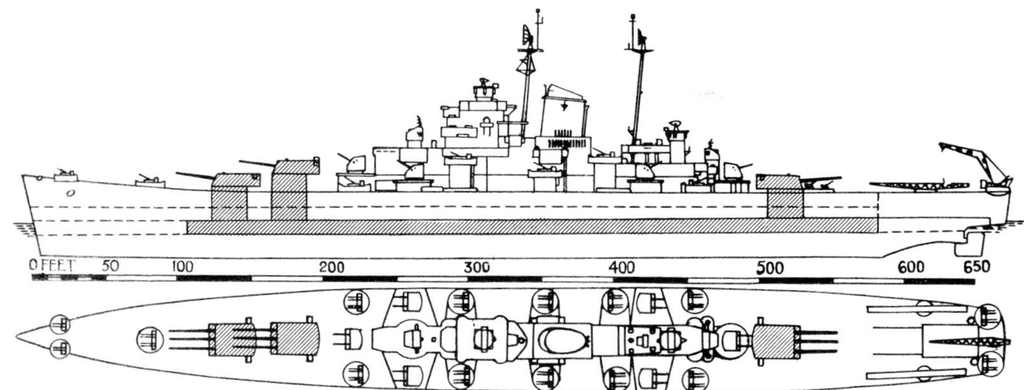

Machinery: General Electric geared turbines. 4 shafts. S.H.P.: 120,000 = 33 kts. Boilers: Babcock & Wilcox. Fuel: 2,500 tons.

No.	Name.	Builders and Machinery.	Laid down.	Completed.
CA 122	*Oregon City*	Bethlehem Steel Co., Quincy.	8/4/44	16/2/46
123	*Albany*		6/3/44	15/6/46
124	*Rochester*		29/5/44	46

Rochester (p. 355).

Oregon City. 1946, *U.S. Navy Official.*

Notes.—These ships are modified *Baltimores*, with a single funnel and simplified superstructure. Seven more units of this class were cancelled, CA 125–129 (*Northampton, Bridgeport, Cambridge, Kansas City, Tulsa*), 137 and 138 (*Norfolk, Scranton*).

Engineering Notes.—Cruising turbines are not included in engine design. In event of port or starboard fuel tanks being ruptured, change-over of suction to other side could be accomplished in a minute, oil burner lines being divided at boiler face.

(Baltimore Class—14 ships.)

BALTIMORE (July 28, 1942), **BOSTON** (Aug. 26, 1942), **BREMERTON** (July 2, 1944), **CANBERRA** (ex-*Pittsburgh*, April 19, 1943), **CHICAGO** (Aug. 20, 1944), **COLUMBUS** (Nov. 30, 1944), **FALL RIVER** (Aug 13, 1944), **HELENA** (ex-*Des Moines*, April 28, 1945), **LOS ANGELES** (Aug. 20, 1944), **MACON** (Oct. 15, 1944), **PITTSBURGH** (ex-*Albany*, Feb. 22, 1944), **QUINCY** (ex-*St. Paul*, June 23, 1943), **ST. PAUL** (ex-*Rochester*, Sept. 16, 1944), **TOLEDO** (May 6, 1945).

Displacement: 13,600 tons (over 16,000 tons *full load*). Complement: 1,700.
Length: 673½ feet (*o.a.*). Beam: 69¾ feet. Draught not reported.
Baltimore class: Maximum thickness of side armour reported to be 6″.

Guns:
9—8 inch, 55 cal.
12—5 inch, 38 cal.
44—40 mm. AA.
22 to 28—20 mm. AA.

Aircraft: 4
Catapults: 2

Armour:
6″—8″ Side.
3+2″ Decks.

Note to Plan.—Only one crane now at stern.

HANGAR.

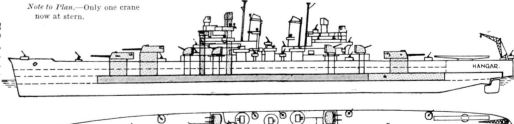

HATCH

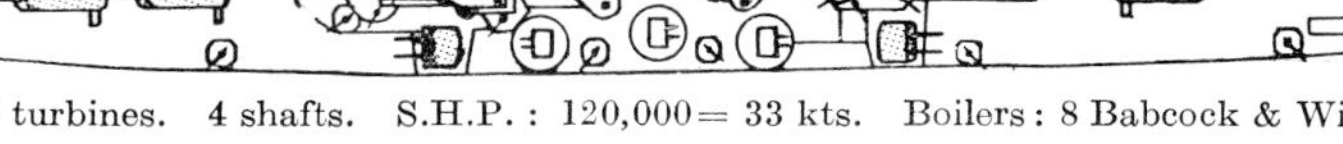

Machinery: Geared turbines. 4 shafts. S.H.P.: 120,000 = 33 kts. Boilers: 8 Babcock & Wilcox. Fuel: 2,500 tons.

Toledo

Los Angeles. 1946, *S. C. Heal, Esq.*

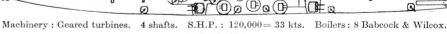

No.	Name	Builders and Machinery	Laid down	Completed
CA 68	*Baltimore*	Bethlehem Steel Co., Quincy	26/5/41	15/4/43
69	*Boston*		30/6/41	30/6/43
70	*Canberra*		3/9/41	14/10/43
71	*Quincy*		9/10/41	15/12/43
72	*Pittsburgh*		3/2/43	10/10/44
73	*St. Paul*		3/2/43	17/2/45
74	*Columbus*		28/6/43	8/6/45
75	*Helena*		9/9/43	4/9/45
130	*Bremerton*	New York S.B. Corpn.	1/2/43	29/4/45
131	*Fall River*		12/4/43	1/7/45
132	*Macon*		14/6/43	25/8/45
133	*Toledo*		13/9/43	27/10/46
135	*Los Angeles*	Philadelphia Navy Yard	28/7/43	22/7/45
136	*Chicago*		28/7/43	10/1/45

Notes.—*Boston* was built in two years. Average inclusive cost of earlier units officially estimated at $39,342,000 each. Are much enlarged and improved editions of *Wichita*. Last 6 ships belong to War Programme.

Gunnery Note.—8-inch guns are a new model, firing a heavier shell than those mounted in earlier cruisers.

Aircraft Notes.—An aircraft can if necessary be stowed on each catapult, leaving space for another pair in the hangar.

HELENA. 1946, *Wright & Logan.*

CHICAGO. 1944, *U.S. Navy Official.*

WICHITA (Nov. 16, 1937).

Displacement: 9,324 tons (*standard*). (13,400 tons *full load.*) Complement: 882/1,200.

Length, 600 feet (*w.l.*), 614 feet (*o.a.*). Beam, $61\frac{3}{4}$ feet. Draught, $19\frac{5}{6}$ feet (*mean*).

Guns:
- **9**—8 inch, 55 cal.
- **8**—5 inch 38 cal. (dual purpose).
- **16**—40 mm. AA.
- **14**—20 mm. AA.

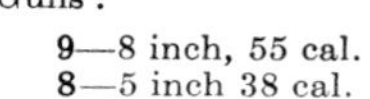

Aircraft: **4**

Catapults: **2**

Armour:
- $1\frac{1}{2}$″ Side (fore and aft)
- 5″ Side (amidships)
- 3″ + 2″ Decks
- 5″—6″ Turret faces
- 3″ Turret sides and backs
- 8″ C.T.

WICHITA. 1944, *U.S. Navy Official.*

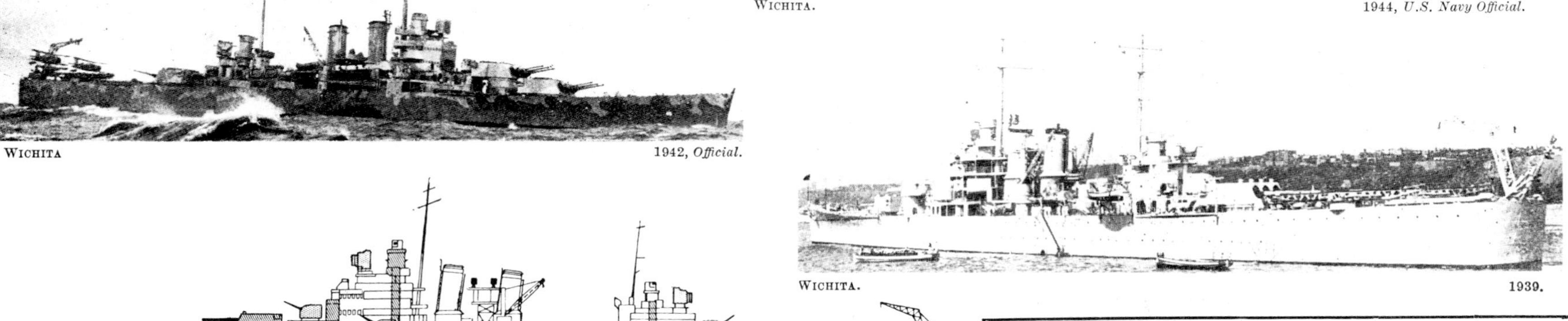

WICHITA 1942, *Official.*

WICHITA. 1939.

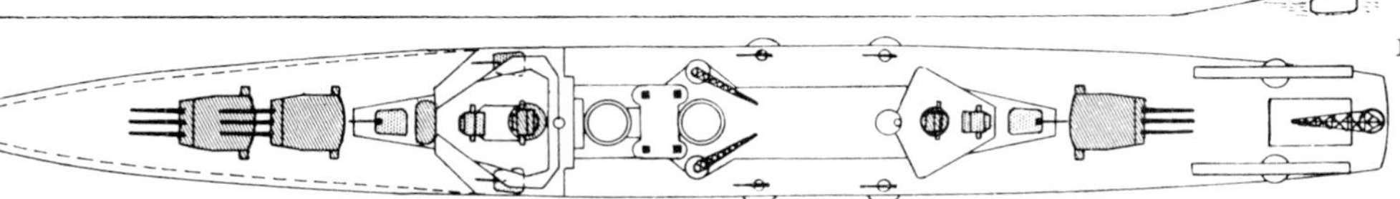

Name	Builder	Machinery	Laid down	Completed
Wichita (CA 45)	Philadelphia Navy Yard	Westinghouse Co.	Oct. 28, 1935	March, 1939

Machinery: Westinghouse geared turbines. 4 shafts. S.H.P.: 100,000 = 32·5 kts. Boilers: 8 Babcock & Wilcox. Fuel: 1,650 tons.

Notes.—Though originally to have been a unit of *New Orleans* class, this ship was completed as a modified *Brooklyn* with 8 inch guns.

Heavy Cruiser

(New Orleans Class—4 Ships)

NEW ORLEANS (April 12, 1933).
MINNEAPOLIS (Sept. 6, 1933).
TUSCALOOSA (Nov. 15, 1933).
SAN FRANCISCC (March 9, 1933).

Displacement: 9,950 tons, except *Tuscaloosa*, 9,975 tons.

Complement: 876/1,200.

Dimensions: 574 (*w.l.*), 588 (*o.a.*) × 61$\frac{3}{4}$ × 19$\frac{5}{12}$ feet (*mean*), 23$\frac{1}{2}$ (*max.*).

Guns:
- **9**—8 inch, 55 cal.
- **8**—5 inch AA., 25 cal.
- **16**—40 mm. AA.
- **19**—20 mm. AA.

Armour:
- 1$\frac{1}{2}$" Side (fore and aft).
- 5" Side (amidships between sections 10—17).
- 3"+2" Decks.
- 5"—6" Turret faces.
- 3" Turret sides and backs.
- 8" Conning Tower.

Aircraft: 4.
Catapults: 2.

Tuscaloosa. Observe petrol pipe line extended outboard to reduce fire risk. 1944, *U.S. Navy Official.*

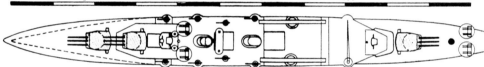

No.	*Name*	*Builders*	*Machinery*	*Laid down*	*Completed*
CA 36	*Minneapolis*	Philadelphia Navy Yard	Westinghouse Co.	27/6/31	20/6/34
32	*New Orleans*	New York Navy Yard	Do.	14/3/31	18/4/34
37	*Tuscaloosa*	New York S.B. Corp.	N.Y.S.B. Corp.	3/9/31	17/8/34
38	*San Francisco*	Mare Isld. Navy Yard	Westinghouse Co.	9/9/31	23/4/34

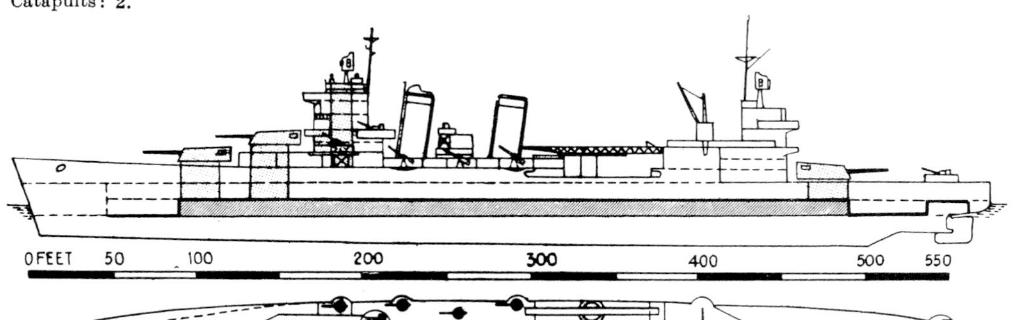

Machinery: Parsons geared turbines in *Tuscaloosa;* Westinghouse in others. 4 shafts. S.H.P.: 107,000 = 32·7 kts. 8 Babcock & Wilcox boilers. Fuel: 1,650 tons.

San Francisco. 1944, *U.S. Navy Official.*

General Notes.—In this class, the forecastle deck has been extended to the second funnel with a slight lowering of the freeboard; the bow form altered and overhang dispensed with; height of bridges increased and form altered; AA. guns re-distributed; hangars moved aft and extended to shelter deck, all the boats excepting the lifeboats being stowed on top to avoid interference with the AA. guns. These ships possess better protection than the *Portland*, as the armour has been distributed to better advantage in the new design. The utmost economy has been effected in construction, electric welding having been employed extensively and weight saved in every direction even to the extent of using aluminium paint internally. 8 inch guns and mountings are of a lighter model and the weight so saved has been put into armour. There is a certain amount of plating on the bridgework, not shown in the plan. Cost, $11,000,000 to $12,000,000 each.

Gunnery Notes.—8 inch guns elevate to 45°. Anti-aircraft armament augmented in 1940–41.

PORTLAND (May 21, 1932).

Standard displacement: 9,800 tons. Complement: 876/1,200.
Dimensions: 582 (*w.l.*), 610$\frac{1}{4}$ (*o.a.*) × 66 × 17$\frac{1}{12}$ feet (*mean*).

Guns:
- **9**—8 inch, 55 cal.
- **8**—5 inch AA., 25 cal.
- **24**—40 mm. AA.
- **16**—20 mm. AA.

Aircraft: 4
Catapults: 2.

Armour:
- 3"—4" Vert.Side
- 2"+2" Decks.
- 1$\frac{1}{2}$"—3" Turrets.

} Not Official.

Portland. 1944, *U.S. Navy Official.*

Machinery: Parsons geared turbines. 4 shafts. S.H.P. 107,000 = 32·7 kts. Boilers: 8 Yarrow Fuel: 1,600 tons.

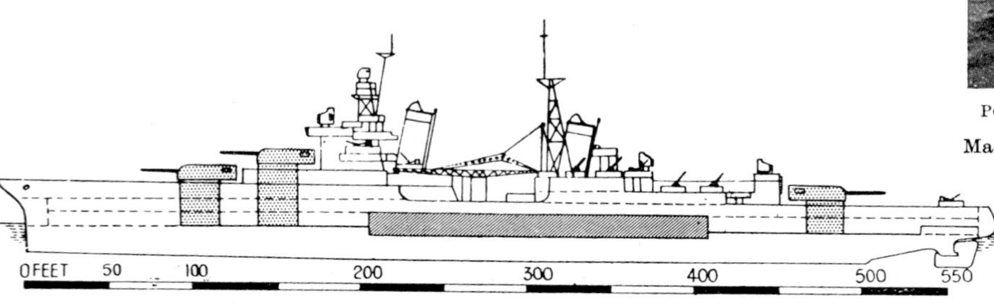

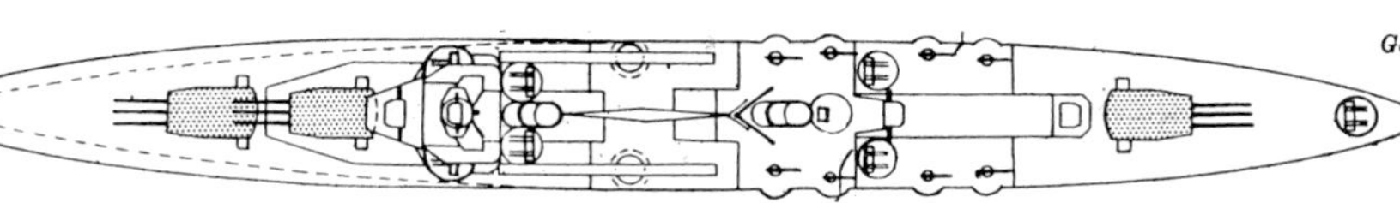

General Notes.—This ship follows the general design of the *Chester* class, with alterations in weight distribution to improve stability. Some 40 tons of plating were spread over the bridge work, which is higher than in *Chester*, with a 30 feet reduction in the height of the masthead control top. *Portland* laid down Feb. 17, 1930, completed Feb. 23, 1933, by Bethlehem Steel Co., Quincy. *Portland* used to be a bad roller until fitted with bilge keels. Machinery supplied by builders. Distinctive number is CA 33. War loss: *Indianapolis*.

Gunnery Notes.—Anti-aircraft armament augmented, 1941.

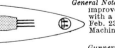

(Chester Class—3 ships).

AUGUSTA (Feb. 1st, 1930). **CHESTER** (July 3rd, 1929). **LOUISVILLE** (Sept. 1st, 1930).

Standard displacement, 9,050 tons (except *Chester*, 9,200 tons). Complement, 872/1,200.

Dimensions : 569 (*w.l.*), 600¼ (*o.a.*) × 66 × 16½ feet (*mean*), 23 feet (*maximum*), except *Chester*, 570 (*w.l.*), 16½ feet (*mean*).

Guns :
9—8 inch, 55 cal.
8—5 inch AA., 25 cal.
32—40 mm. AA.
27—20 mm. AA.

Aircraft : 4
Catapults : 2.

(*Plan very like* Portland.)

Armour :
3" Vert. Side.
2" + 1" Deck.
1½" Gunhouses.

Augusta. 1944, *New York Times.*

Machinery : Parsons geared turbines. 4 shafts. Designed S.H.P. 107,000 = 32·7 kts. 8 White-Forster boilers. Radius : 13,000 miles at 15 kts. Fuel : 1,500 tons.

General Notes.—Authorised 1926-27 under Act of December, 1924. Centre of gravity being placed too low, they were inclined to roll at low speed until fitted with bigger bilge keels. War losses: *Chicago, Houston, Northampton.*

Gunnery Notes.—Elevation of 8 inch guns, 45°. Control very accurate. AA. armament increased, 1940-41.

Engineering Notes.—Heating surface, 95,040 sq. feet. Machinery weighs 2,161 tons. 4 Turbo generator sets ; 250 kilowatts each ; 120—240 volts ; built by General Electric Co. There are 4 boiler rooms.

No.	*Name*	*Builders*	*Machinery*	*Laid down*	*Completed*	*Trials*
CA 31	*Augusta*	Newport News Co.	Builders	2/7/28	Jan., 1931	33·11
27	*Chester*	New York S.B. Cpn.	Builders	6/3/28	June, 1930	33·04
28	*Louisville*	Puget Sound Navy Yard	Builders	4/7/28	March, 1931	32·74

ROANOKE, WORCESTER (Feb. 5, 1947).

Ordered from New York S.B. Corporation, June 15, 1943.

Displacement : 14,700 tons.

Machinery: Geared turbines. 4 shafts. No other particulars published.

Guns :
12—6 inch, 47 cal. d.p.
12—3 inch d.p.
68—40 mm. AA.

Notes.—Distinctive numbers are CL 144 (*Worcester*) and 145 (*Roanoke*). Two more ships, *Vallejo* (146) and *Gary* (147), were cancelled on Aug. 11, 1945. These ships will have two funnels, with 6 inch guns of a new automatic model, arranged similarly to 5 inch in *Spokane*.

WORCESTER launched February 4, 1947.

(Fargo Class—2 Ships)

FARGO (Feb. 25, 1945), **HUNTINGTON** (April 8, 1945).

Displacement: 10,000 tons.

Complement: 900/1,200.

Length (*w.l.*) 600 feet; *o.a.*, 611 feet. Beam: 66 feet.

Mean draught (at *normal* displacement): 20 feet.

Guns:
12—6 inch, 55 cal.
12—5 inch, 38 cal. d.p.
24—40 mm. AA.
20—20 mm. AA.

Aircraft: 3.
Catapults: 2.

Armour:
Similar to *Cleveland* class.

Fargo. 1946, *courtesy the Hon. D. H. Erskine.*

Machinery: Geared turbines. 4 shafts. S.H.P.: 100,000 = 33 kts. Boilers: 8 Babcock & Wilcox.

No. and Name	*Builders and Machinery.*	*Laid down*	*Completed*
106 *Fargo*	New York S.B. Corpn.	23/8/43	9/12/45
107 *Huntington*	New York S.B. Corpn.	4/10/43	23/2/46

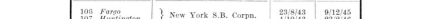

Huntington. 1946, *U.S. Navy Official.*

Notes.—These two ships are modified *Clevelands*, with single funnels and simplified superstructures, intended to enlarge the arc of fire of AA. armament. Cancelled units: *Newark* (108), *New Haven* (109), *Buffalo* (110), *Wilmington* (111), *Tallahassee* (116), *Cheyenne* (117), *Chattanooga* (118).

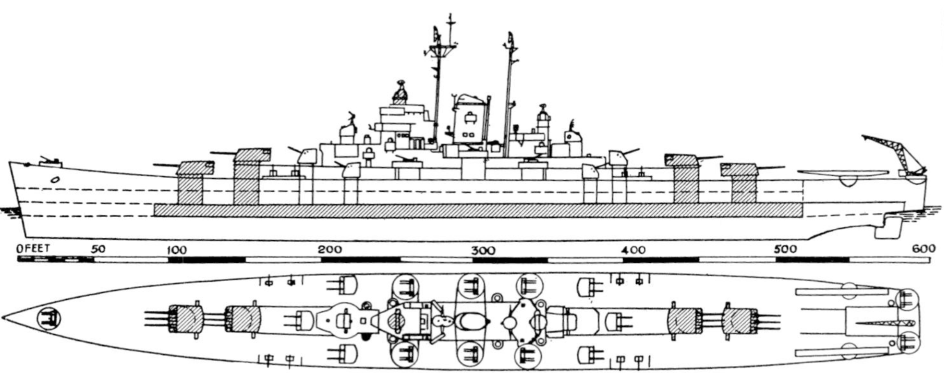

Fargo. 1946, *London Studio.*

Light Cruisers

Fargo — 1946, *Monsieur P. Banet-Rivet.*

Fargo — 1946, *Monsieur P. Banet-Rivet.*

Huntington — 1946, *Associated Press.*

Fargo — 1946, *Monsieur P. Banet-Rivet*

(Cleveland Class—27 Ships.)

Guns:
12—6 inch, 47 cal.
12—5 inch 38 cal. (dual purpose), paired.
24—40 mm. AA.
19—20 mm. AA.

Aircraft: 3

Catapults: 2

Armour:
$1\frac{1}{2}''$—5″ Side.
3″+2″ Decks.
3″—5″ Gunhouses.

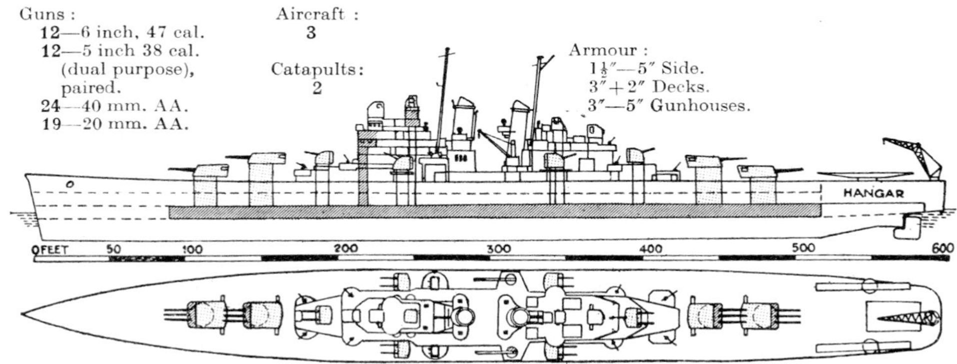

Machinery: Geared turbines. 4 shafts. S.H.P.: 100,000=33 kts. Boilers: 8 Babcock & Wilcox.

AMSTERDAM (April 25, 1944), **ASTORIA** (ex-*Wilkes-Barre*, March 6, 1943), **ATLANTA** (Feb. 6, 1944), **BILOXI** (Feb. 23, 1943), **BIRMINGHAM** (March 20, 1942), **CLEVELAND** (Nov. 1, 1941), **COLUMBIA** (Dec. 17, 1941), **DAYTON** (March 19, 1944), **DENVER** (April 4, 1942), **DULUTH** (Jan. 13, 1944), **GALVESTON** (April 22, 1945), **HOUSTON** (ex-*Vicksburg*, June 19, 1943), **LITTLE ROCK** (Aug. 27, 1944), **MANCHESTER** (March 1946), **MIAMI** (Dec. 8, 1942), **MOBILE** (May 15, 1942), **MONTPELIER** (Feb. 12, 1942), **OKLAHOMA CITY** (Feb. 20, 1944), **PASADENA** (Dec. 28, 1943), **PORTSMOUTH** (Sept. 20, 1944), **PROVIDENCE** (Dec. 28, 1944), **SANTA FE** (June 10, 1942), **SPRINGFIELD** (March 9, 1944), **TOPEKA** (Aug. 19, 1944), **VICKSBURG** (ex-*Cheyenne*, Dec. 14, 1943), **VINCENNES** (ex-*Flint*, July 17, 1943), **WILKES-BARRE** (Dec. 24, 1943).

Displacement: 10,000 tons (12,000 tons *full load*). Complement: 900/1,200. Length: 600 feet (*w.l.*); $608\frac{1}{3}$ feet *o.a.* Beam: 63 feet. Draught: 20 feet (*mean*).

Notes.—This is the largest group of cruisers of a single design ever put in hand. Several originally ordered from New York S.B. Corpn. were converted into aircraft carriers of the *Independence* class. Official estimate of average cost of earlier ships is $31,090,000, and it has also been stated officially that *Houston* cost $42,000,000. *Duluth* and *Vicksburg* were originally to have been built by Federal S.B. & D.D. Co., but contracts were transferred. *Birmingham* was torpedoed 8/11/43; again severely damaged when *Princeton* blew up alongside her in Oct. 1944; and nearly sunk by a Japanese suicide aircraft whose bomb penetrated three of her decks off Okinawa on 4/5/45. *Houston* was heavily damaged by a torpedo from a Japanese aircraft off Formosa in Oct. 1944.

Note.—Cancelled on 11/8/45: *Youngstown* (94).

Houston. — 1944, *U.S. Navy Official.*

Light Cruisers

No. and Name	Builders & Machinery	Laid down	Completed
55 *Cleveland*	New York S.B. Corp.	1/7/40	15/6/42
56 *Columbia*		19/8/40	29/6/42
57 *Montpelier*		2/12/40	9/9/42
58 *Denver*		26/12/40	15/10/42
60 *Santa Fe*		7/6/41	24/11/42
103 *Wilkes-Barre*		14/12/42	1/7/44
104 *Atlanta*		25/1/43	3/12/44
105 *Dayton*		8/3/43	7/1/45
62 *Birmingham*	Newport News Co.	17/2/41	29/1/43
63 *Mobile*		14/4/41	24/3/43
80 *Biloxi*		9/7/41	31/8/43
81 *Houston*		4/8/41	20/12/43
86 *Vicksburg*		26/10/42	12/6/44
87 *Duluth*		9/11/42	18/9/44
101 *Amsterdam*		3/3/43	8/1/45
102 *Portsmouth*		28/6/43	25/6/45
89 *Miami*	Cramp S.B. Co.	2/8/41	28/12/43
90 *Astoria*		6/9/41	17/5/44
91 *Oklahoma City*		8/12/42	22/12/44
92 *Little Rock*		6/3/43	17/6/45
93 *Galveston*		20/2/44	-- --46
64 *Vincennes*	Bethlehem Co., Quincy	7/3/42	21/1/44
65 *Pasadena*		6/2/43	8/6/44
66 *Springfield*		13/2/43	9/8/44
67 *Topeka*		21/4/43	23/12/44
82 *Providence*		27/7/43	15/5/45
83 *Manchester*		25/9/44	29/10/46

LITTLE ROCK. 1946, *Mr. Wm. H. Davis.*

(SAN DIEGO CLASS—9 SHIPS).

FLINT (ex-*Spokane*, Jan. 25, 1944), **FRESNO** (March 5, 1946), **JUNEAU** (July 15, 1945), **OAKLAND** (Oct. 25, 1942), **RENO** (Dec. 23, 1942), **SAN DIEGO** (July 26, 1941), **SAN JUAN** (Sept. 6, 1941), **SPOKANE** (Sept. 22, 1945), **TUCSON** (Sept. 3, 1944).

Displacement: 6,000 tons (7,500 tons *full load*.)

Complement: 597/700.

Length: 541 feet. Beam: 52 feet 10 in. Draught: $14\frac{3}{4}$ feet (*mean*), 20 feet (*max*).

Guns:
12—5 inch, 38 cal. (dual purpose).
28 to 32—40 mm. AA.
12 to 16—20 mm. AA.

(*S. Diego, S. Juan,*
16—5 inch
24—40 mm. AA.
8—20 mm. AA.)

Armour:
$3\frac{1}{2}''$ Side.
$2''$ Deck.

Torpedo Tubes:
8—21 inch, in quadruple deck mountings.
(None in *Juneau, Fresno, Spokane.*)

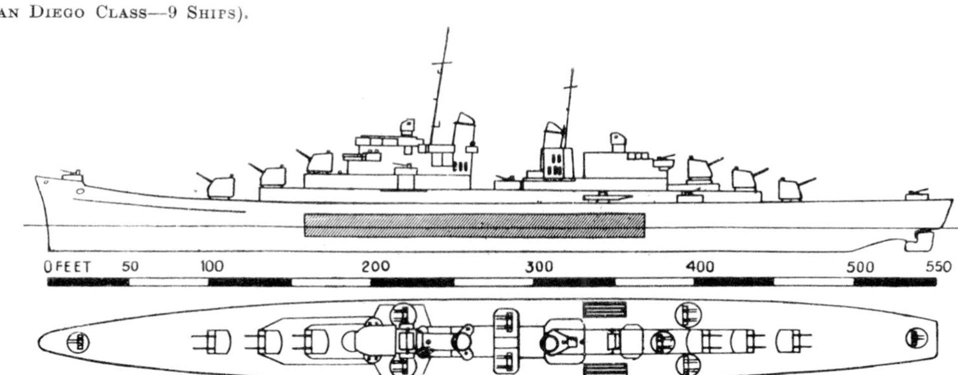

Machinery: Geared turbines. 2 shafts. S.H.P.: 75,000=35 kts. (exceeded on trials).

Note to Plan.—*S. Diego* and *S. Juan* have two wing turrets, as shown in photo of former. In *Juneau, Spokane* and *Fresno*, "B" and "X" turrets are placed a deck lower than in earlier ships, and T.T. have been omitted, to improve stability.

Notes.—Cost averages $23,261,500 each, inclusive. Arrangement of main armament forward and aft is reminiscent of British *Dido* class. Bridges are reported to be armoured. War losses: *Atlanta, Juneau.* Two new ships of these names have been built, of which the former belongs to 10,000 ton *Cleveland* class.

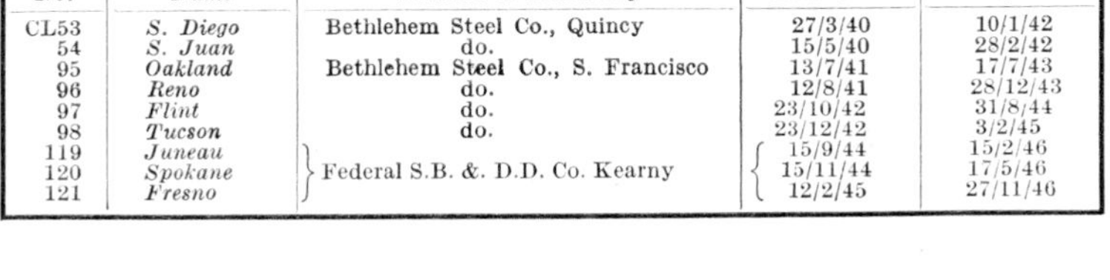

No.	Name	Builders & Machinery	Laid down	Completed
CL53	*S. Diego*	Bethlehem Steel Co., Quincy	27/3/40	10/1/42
54	*S. Juan*	do.	15/5/40	28/2/42
95	*Oakland*	Bethlehem Steel Co., S. Francisco	13/7/41	17/7/43
96	*Reno*	do.	12/8/41	28/12/43
97	*Flint*	do.	23/10/42	31/8/44
98	*Tucson*	do.	23/12/42	3/2/45
119	*Juneau*	Federal S.B. & D.D. Co. Kearny	15/9/44	15/2/46
120	*Spokane*		15/11/44	17/5/46
121	*Fresno*		12/2/45	27/11/46

SAN DIEGO. 1944, *U.S. Navy Official.*

SPOKANE. 1946, *U.S. Navy Official.*

Light Cruisers

ST. LOUIS (April 15, 1938).

Displacement: 9,700 tons. Complement: 888/1,200.

Length: 600 feet (*w.l.*), $608\frac{1}{4}$ (*o.a.*). Beam: $61\frac{1}{2}$ feet. Draught: $19\frac{3}{4}$ feet (*mean*).

General Notes.—Laid down by Newport News S.B. Co. under 1934 Programme on Dec. 10, 1936, and completed in December 1939. Differs from *Brooklyn* class in having 5 inch guns mounted in pairs behind shields on high bases; a different scheme of boat stowage; a small tripod mast immediately abaft second funnel and after gunnery control arrangements redistributed. Boiler pressure is higher than in *Brooklyn* class. Distinctive number is CL 49. War loss: *Helena*.

Note.—This ship is expected to be discarded in 1947.

ST. LOUIS.

1940, *Official.*

HANGAR.

0 FEET 50 100 200 300 400 500 600

Guns:
15—6 inch, 47 cal.
8—5 inch, 38 cal. (dual purpose).
16—40 mm. AA.
24—20 mm. AA.

Aircraft:
4

Catapults:
2

Armour:
$1\frac{1}{2}''$—5″ Side.
3″+2″ Decks.
3″—5″ Gunhouses.
8″ C.T.

Machinery: Westinghouse geared turbines. 4 shafts. S.H.P.: 100,000 = 32·5 kts. Boilers: 8 Babcock & Wilcox Express type. Oil fuel: 2,100 tons. Radius: 14,500 miles at 15 kts.

ST. LOUIS. 1944, *U.S. Navy Official.*

BROOKLYN CLASS (7 SHIPS)

BROOKLYN (Nov. 30, 1936), PHILADELPHIA (Nov. 17, 1936), SAVANNAH (May 8, 1937), NASHVILLE (Oct. 2, 1937), PHOENIX (March 12, 1938), BOISE (Dec. 3, 1936), HONOLULU (Aug. 26, 1937).

Displacement: 9,700 tons (*Brooklyn* and *Philadelphia*), 9,475 tons (*Savannah*), 9,650 tons (*Honolulu*), others estimated as 10,000 tons.
Complement: 975/1,200. Dimensions: 600 (*w.l.*) × $61\frac{1}{2}$ × $19\frac{3}{4}$ feet (*mean*) ($69\frac{1}{2}$ feet beam with sponsons).

BROOKLYN. 1944, *U.S. Navy Official.*

Machinery: Westinghouse geared turbines. 4 shafts. S.H.P.: 100,000 = 32·5 kts. Boilers: 8 Babcock & Wilcox Express type. Oil fuel: 2,100 tons. Radius: 14,500 miles at 15 kts.

Note.—The first four of this class were ordered under the Emergency Programme of 1933: the other three under the provisions of the "Vinson Bill." Cost ranges from \$18,000,000 to \$19,000,000 each. *Honolulu* was severely damaged by a bomb at Pearl Harbour on Dec. 7, 1941; and on Oct. 20, 1944, off Leyte, she was again badly damaged by a torpedo from a Japanese aircraft. *Brooklyn*, *Honolulu* and *Savannah*, when refitted, had anti-torpedo bulges added increasing beam by 8 feet. *Boise* and *Phoenix* will both be discarded in 1947, and *Nashville* may follow.

Aircraft Note.—The hangar included in hull right aft can, if necessary, accommodate 6 aircraft, with duplicate parts and spare engines, though 4 is normal complement. Presence of this hangar accounts for very wide flat counter and high freeboard aft, which is also utilised to give after guns higher command. The two catapults are mounted as far outboard as possible and the revolving crane is placed at the extreme stern, overhanging the hatch.

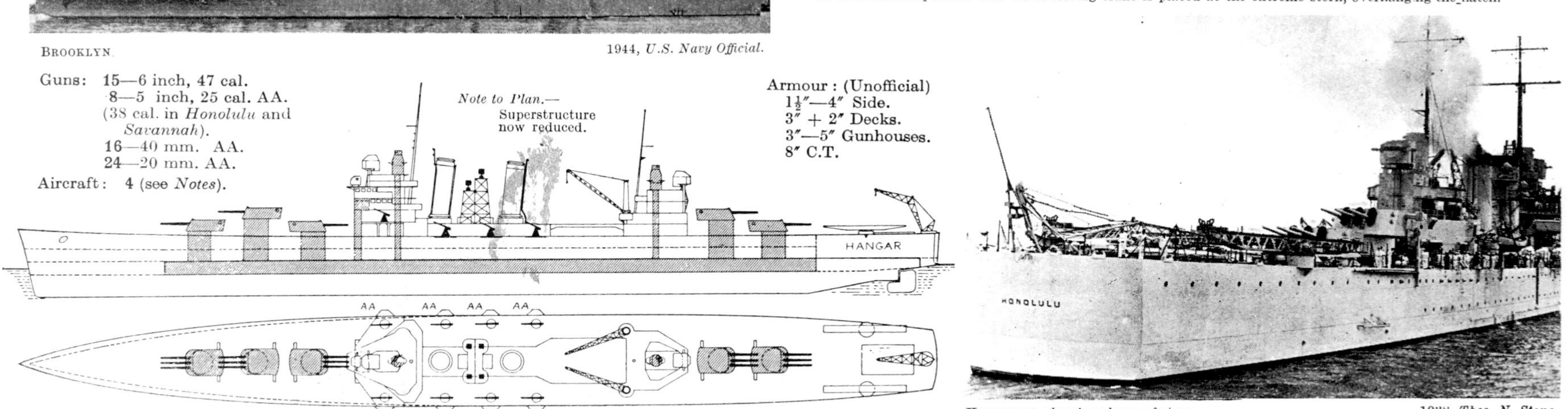

Guns: 15—6 inch, 47 cal.
8—5 inch, 25 cal. AA. (38 cal. in *Honolulu* and *Savannah*).
16—40 mm. AA.
24—20 mm. AA.
Aircraft: 4 (see *Notes*).

Note to Plan.—Superstructure now reduced.

Armour: (Unofficial)
$1\frac{1}{2}''$—4″ Side.
3″ + 2″ Decks.
3″—5″ Gunhouses.
8″ C.T.

HONOLULU, showing shape of stern. 1938, *Theo. N. Stone.*

Heavy Cruisers

(Pensacola Class).

PENSACOLA (April 25th, 1929),
SALT LAKE CITY (Jan. 23rd, 1929).

Displacement, 9,100 tons.
Complement, 700.
Length (*w.l.*) 558 feet; *o.a.*, 585½ feet. Beam, 65¼ ft.
Mean draught (at *normal* displacement), 16 ft. 2 in.
Max. draught, 22 ft.

Guns:
10—8 inch, 55 cal.
8—5 inch, 25 cal. AA.
2—3 pdr.
Torpedo tubes: Removed.
Aircraft: 4.
Catapults 2.

Armour:
3″ side.
2″+1″ deck.
1½″ gunhouses.

PENSACOLA. (Now has pole mainmast.) 1935 *Photo, O. W. Waterman.*

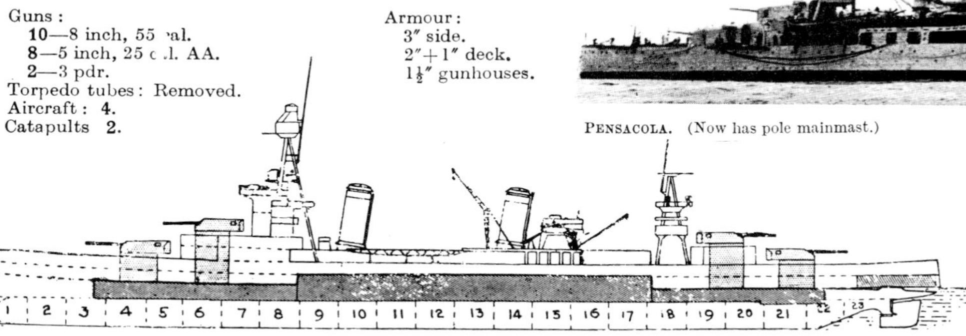

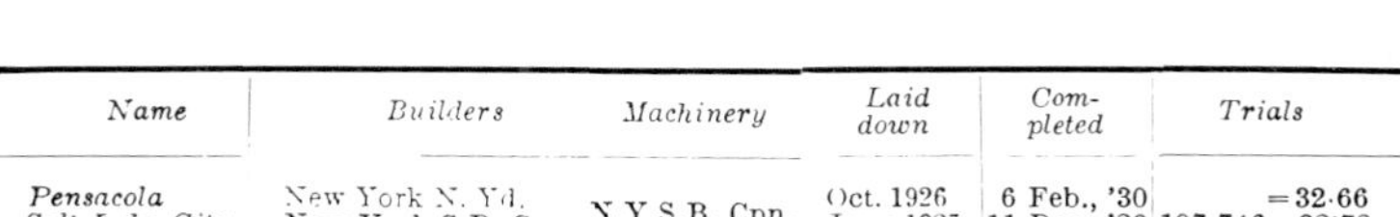

Name	*Builders*	*Machinery*	*Laid down*	*Completed*	*Trials*
Pensacola	New York N. Yd.	N.Y.S.B. Cpn.	Oct. 1926	6 Feb., '30	=32·66
Salt Lake City	New York S.B. Cpn.		June 1927	11 Dec., '29	107,746=32·78

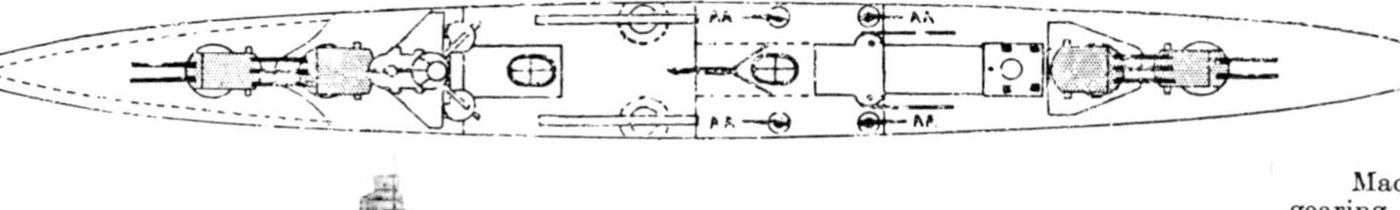

SALT LAKE CITY. (Now has pole mainmast.) 1935, *Official.*

Machinery: 4 sets of Parsons geared Turbines. Cramp type, with de Laval single reduction gearing. 4 shafts. Designed S.H.P. 107,000 = 32·7 kts. 8 White-Forster boilers, working pressure reported as 300 lbs. per square inch. Radius of action: 13,000 miles at 15 kts. Fuel: 1500 tons.

General Notes.—Laid down under Act of December 18, 1924. Tons per inch immersion, 60·7. Utmost economy in weights practised in design and construction. Aluminium alloy fittings replacing steel and aluminium paint is used internally. Welding has been employed wherever possible instead of riveting. They suffer from lack of freeboard, but no longer vibrate, although they roll at low speeds. Above 20 kts. they are extremely steady even in bad weather. Mainmast reduced to a pole to save weight, 1941.

Gunnery Notes.—The 8 in. 55 cal. guns. have an elevation of 45°: fore control station at the mast head is about 120 feet above w.l.: the after control is abaft second funnel, and AA. control on fore bridge. Additional AA. guns mounted, 1941.

Engineering Notes.—Heating surface, 95,000 square feet. Machinery weighs 2,161 tons. Can steam at 30 kts. with 60 per cent H.P. There are 2 engine and 2 boiler rooms, the outboard shafts coming from the foremost engine rooms.

Light Cruisers

(Omaha Class—10 Ships.)

OMAHA (Dec. 14th, 1920),
RALEIGH (Oct. 25th, 1922),
CONCORD (Dec. 15th, 1921),
MEMPHIS (April 17th, 1924),
MARBLEHEAD (Oct. 9th, 1923),
MILWAUKEE (Mar. 24th, 1921),
DETROIT (June 29th, 1922),
TRENTON (April 16th, 1923),
RICHMOND (Sept. 29th, 1921),
CINCINNATI (May 23rd, 1921).

Name.	*Built and Engined by*	*Laid down*	*Completed*	*Trials*	*Turbines.*	*Boilers*	*Heating Surface (sq. ft.)*
Omaha	Todd Co., Tacoma	6 Dec. '18	Feb. '23	94,290=34·87	Westghs.	12 Yarrow	90600
Milwaukee	" "	13 Dec. '18	June '23	90,060=34·64	"	12 Yarrow	
Cincinnati	" "	15 May '20	Dec. '23	94,290=34·44	"	12 Yarrow	
Raleigh	Bethlehem Co., Quincy	16 Aug. '20	Feb. '24	97,722=34·63	Curtis	12 Yarrow	90084
Detroit	" " "	10 Nov. '20	July '23	97,375=34·63	"	12 Yarrow	
Richmond	Wm. Cramp & Sons	16 Feb. '20	June '23	95,000=34·2	Parsons	12 White-F	90840
Concord	" " "	29 Mar. '20	Nov. '23	92,772=33·48	"	12 White-F	
Trenton	" " "	18 Aug. '20	April, '24	33·91	"	12 White-F	
Marblehead	" " "	4 Aug. '20	Sept. '24	95,950=34·42	"	12 White-F	
Memphis	" " "	14 Oct. '20	Jan. '25	34·43	"	12 White-F	

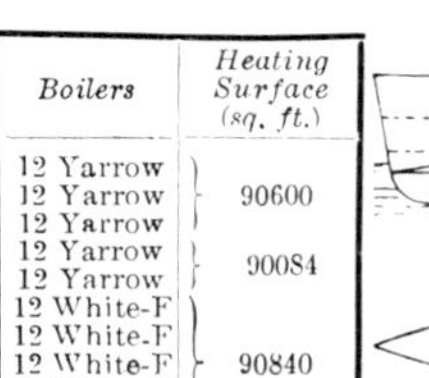

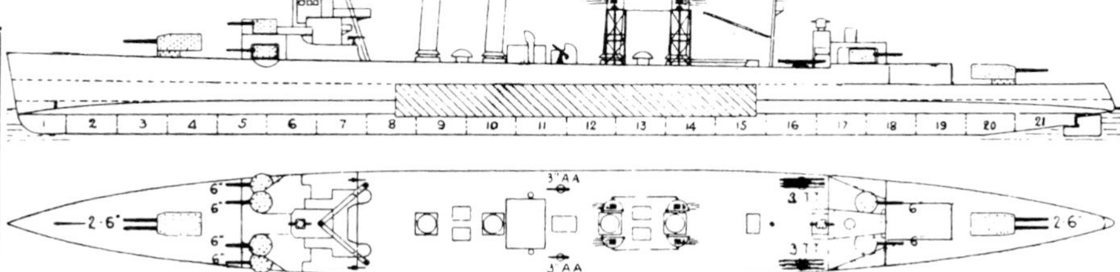

Displacement: 7,050 tons. Complement: 458

Dimensions: 550 (*w.l.*), 555½ (*o.a.*) × 55⅓ × 13½ feet (*mean*), 20 feet (*max*).

Guns:
10—6 inch, 53 cal. Mk. XII.
(12—6 inch in *Concord, Memphis, Milwaukee, Omaha, Trenton*).
8—3 inch, 50 cal. AA.
2—3 pdr. (saluting).
8—M.G. AA.
(AA. armament since increased.)
Torpedo tubes (21 inch):
6 (tripled) *above water*.
Aircraft: 2.
Catapults: 2.

Armour:
3″ Side ....
1½″ Upper Deck .....

Machinery: Turbines (see Table for types), with reduction gears. Designed S.H.P. 90,000 = 35 kts. 4 screws. Boilers: see Table. Fuel: oil only; *about* 2,000 tons (300,000 gallons). Radius of action: 10,000 miles at 15 knots, 7,200 at 20 kts.

CINCINNATI. 1937, *O. W. Waterman.*

Light Cruisers

No.	Name	Builders	Machinery	Laid down	Completed
CL 40	*Brooklyn*	New York Navy Yd.	Builders in each case	12/3/35	18/7/38
41	*Philadelphia*	Philadelphia Navy Yd		28/5/35	28/7/38
42	*Savannah*	New York S.B. Corp.		31/5/34	30/8/38
43	*Nashville*	Do.		24/1/35	25/11/38
46	*Phœnix*	Do.		15/4/35	18/3/39
47	*Boise*	Newport News Co.		1/4/35	1/2/39
48	*Honolulu*	New York Navy Yd.		10/9/35	7/9/38

HONOLULU, with jury bow. 1944, *U.S. Navy Official.*

Destroyers

105 Gearing Class.

(Construction of 11 units marked * was suspended in June, 1946.)

FRANK KNOX. (Some have heavier mast, of tripod type.) 1944, *U.S. Navy Official.*

30 *Bath Iron Works:*

Agerholm
Baussell
Benner (Nov. 20, 1944)
Charles P. Cecil (April 22, 1945)
Chevalier (Oct. 29, 1944)
Dennis J. Buckley (Dec. 20, 1944)
Ernest G. Small (June 9, 1945)
Everett F. Larson (Jan. 28, 1945)
Fiske (Sept. 8, 1945)
Frank Knox (Sept. 17, 1944)
George K. Mackenzie (May 13, 1945)
Glennon (July 14, 1945)
Goodrich (Feb. 25, 1945)
Hanson (March 11, 1945)
Herbert J. Thomas (March 25, 1945)
Higbee (Nov. 12, 1944)
Myles C. Fox (Jan. 13, 1945)
Noa (July 30, 1945)
Ozbourn
Perry (Nov. 25, 1945)
Power (June 30, 1945)
Richard E. Kraus (March 2, 1946)
***Robert A. Owen**
Robert L. Wilson (Jan. 5, 1946)
Sarsfield (May 27, 1945)
Southerland (Oct. 5, 1944)
Timmerman
Turner (April 8, 1945)
Warrington (Sept. 27, 1945)
Witek (Feb. 2, 1946)

4 *Bethlehem, Quincy:*

Charles H. Roan (March 15, 1946)
Joseph P. Kennedy Jr. (July 26, 1945)
Leonard F. Mason
Rupertus (Sept. 21, 1945)

7 *Bethlehem, S. Francisco:*

***Abner Read**
***Hoel**
Keppler
***Lansdale**
Lloyd Thomas (Oct. 5, 1945)
***Seymour D. Owens**
William C. Lawe (Feb. 25, 1945)

4 *Bethlehem, S. Pedro:*

Fred T. Berry (Jan. 28, 1945)
Harwood (May 24, 1945)
McCaffery (April 12, 1945)
Norris (Feb. 25, 1945)

11 *Bethlehem, Staten Island:*

Arnold J. Isbell (Aug. 6. 1945)
Brownson (July 7, 1945)
Charles R. Ware (April 12, 1945)
Cone (May 10, 1945)
Damato (Nov. 21, 1945)
Fechteler (Sept. 19, 1945)
Forrest Royal (Jan. 17, 1946)
Harold J. Ellison (March 14, 1945)
Steinaker (Feb. 13, 1945)
Stribling (June 8, 1945)
Vogelgesang (Jan. 15, 1945)

27 *Consolidated Steel Corpn.*

***Basilone** (Dec. 21, 1945)
Bordelon (March 3, 1945)
Brinkley Bass (May 26, 1945)
***Carpenter**
Corry (July 28, 1945)
Duncan (Oct. 27, 1944)
Dyess (Jan. 26, 1945)
Floyd B. Parks (March 31, 1945)
Furse (March 9, 1945)
Hawkins (ex-*Beatty*, Oct. 7, 1944)
Henry W. Tucker (Nov. 8, 1944)
Holder (Aug. 25, 1945)
John R. Craig (April 14, 1945)
Johnston (Oct. 19, 1945)
Leary (Jan. 20, 1945)
Meredith (June 28, 1945)
New (Aug. 18, 1945)
Newman K. Perry (March 17, 1945)
O'Hare (June 22, 1945)
Orleck (May 12, 1945)
Perkins (Dec. 7, 1944)
Rich (Oct. 5, 1945)
Robert H. McCard (Nov. 9, 1945)
Rogers (Nov. 20, 1944)
Samuel B. Roberts
Stickell (June 16, 1945)
Vesole (Dec. 29, 1944)

12 *Federal S.B. & D.D. Co.:*

***Castle**
***Epperson** (Dec. 22, 1945)
Eugene A. Greene (March 18, 1945)
Gearing (Feb. 18, 1945)
Gyatt (April 15, 1945)
Hamner (Nov. 24, 1945)
Kenneth D. Bailey (June 17, 1945)
Theodore E. Chandler (Oct. 20, 1945)
William M. Wood (July 29, 1945)
William R. Rush (July 8, 1945)
Wiltsie (Aug 31, 1945)
***Woodrow R. Thompson**

10 *Todd Pacific Shipyards:*

Eversole (Dec. 7, 1945)
Gurke (ex-*John A. Bole*, Feb. 15, 1945)
Henderson (May 28. 1945)
Hollister (Oct. 9, 1945)
James E. Kyes (Aug. 4, 1945)
McKean (March 31, 1945)
Richard B. Anderson (July 7, 1945)
Rowan (Dec. 29, 1944)
***Seaman**
Shelton

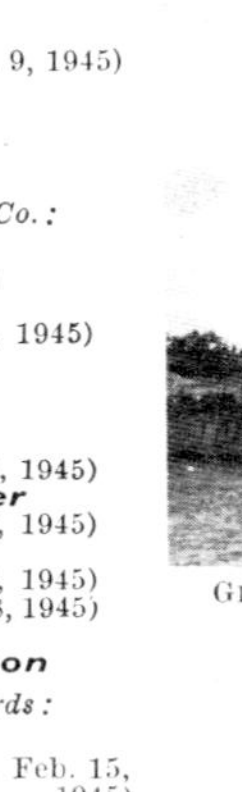

Displacement: 2,400 tons. Dimensions: $390\frac{1}{2}$ (*o.a.*) × $40\frac{5}{8}$ × $12\frac{1}{2}$ feet. Guns: **6**—5 inch, 38 cal., **12** to **16**—40 mm. AA., **11**—20 mm. AA. Tubes: **10**—21 inch (quintupled); but some have only 5, and others (including *Dyess*) none. Machinery: Geared turbines. 2 shafts. S.H.P.: 60,000 = 35 kts. Boilers: 4. Complement: 350.

Note.—These ships are merely enlarged editions of *Allen M. Sumner* type, with extra 14 feet length, necessitated by additional installations of various kinds. Pendant Nos. are DD. 710/721, 742, 743, 763/769, 782/791, 805/808, 817/853, 858/890. Cancellations: 809/816, 854/856, 891/926.

Constructional Notes.—It is reported that heavy weights carried on forecastle have resulted in cracks developing in hulls in way of forward turrets. There are also reports of "A" turret face being stove in by heavy seas and having to be reinforced. Full load displacement exceeds 3,000 tons.

CONE. 1946, *Wright & Logan.*

GLENNON. 1946, *Wright & Logan.*

TURNER. (*H. W. Tucker* is similarly rigged.) 1945, *U.S. Navy Official.*

Note.—Five ex-German destroyers, *Z* 39; *T* 4, 14, 19 and 35, were taken over in 1945–46. Of these *Z* 39 and *T* 35 have been renumbered DD 939 and 935, respectively.

63 Allen M. Sumner Class.

17 *Bath Iron Works Corpn.:*

Adams (M) (July 23, 1944)
Barton (Oct. 10, 1943)
Collett (March 5, 1944)
De Haven (Jan. 9, 1944)
Harry F. Bauer (M) (July 9, 1944)
Hyman (April 8, 1944)
Laffey (Nov. 21, 1943)
Lyman K. Swenson (Feb. 12, 1944)
Maddox (March 19, 1944)
Mansfield (Jan. 29, 1944)
O'Brien (Dec. 8, 1943)
Purdy (May 7, 1944)
Robert H. Smith (M) (May 25, 1944)
Shannon (M) (June 24, 1944)
Thomas E. Fraser (M) (June 10, 1944)
Tolman (M) (Aug. 13, 1944)
Walke (Oct. 27, 1943)

6 *Bethlehem Steel Co. (S. Francisco):*

Buck (March 11, 1945)
Henley (April 8, 1945)
John W. Thomason (Sept. 29, 1944)
Lofberg (Aug. 12, 1944)
Putnam (March 26, 1944)
Strong (April 22, 1944)

6 *Bethlehem Steel Co. (S. Pedro):*

Bristol (Oct. 29, 1944)
Gwin (M) (April 9, 1944)
James C. Owens (Oct 1, 1944)
Lindsey (M) (March 5, 1944)
Lowry (Feb. 6, 1944)
Willard Keith (Aug. 29, 1944)

12 *Bethlehem Steel Co. (Staten Island):*

Alfred A. Cunningham (Aug. 3, 1944)
Beatty (Nov. 30, 1944)
Blue (Nov. 28, 1943)
Brush (Dec. 28, 1943)
Frank E. Evans (Oct. 3, 1944)
Harry E. Hubbard (March 24, 1944)
Henry A. Wiley (April 21, 1944)
John A. Bole (Nov. 1, 1944)
John R. Pierce (Sept. 1, 1944)
Samuel L. Moore (Feb. 23, 1944)
Shea (M) (May 20, 1944)

Destroyers

ZELLARS 1946, *Ted Stone.*

Taussig (Jan. 25, 1944)

17 *Federal S.B. & D.D. Co.:*

Allen M Sumner (Dec. 15, 1943)
Ault (March 26, 1944)
Borie (July 4, 1944)
Charles S. Sperry (March 13, 1944)
Compton (Sept. 17, 1944)
English (Feb. 27, 1944)
Gainard (Sept. 17, 1944)
Hank (May 21, 1944)
Harlan R. Dickson (Dec. 17, 1944)
Haynsworth (April 15, 1944)
Hugh Purvis (Dec. 17, 1944)
Ingraham (Jan. 16, 1944)
John W. Weeks (May 21, 1944)
Moale (Jan. 16, 1944)
Soley (Sept. 8, 1944)
Waldron (March 26, 1944)
Wallace L. Lind (June 14, 1944)

5 *Todd Pacific Shipyards:*

Douglas H. Fox (Sept. 30, 1944)
Massey (Aug. 19, 1944)
Robert K. Huntington (Dec. 10, 1944)
Stormes (Nov. 4, 1944)
Zellars (July 19, 1944)

Displacement: 2,200 tons. Dimensions: 376½ × 40½ × 12½ feet. Guns: **6**—5 inch, 38 cal., **12**—40 mm. AA., **11**—20 mm. AA. Tubes: **10**—21 inch (quintupled). Machinery: Geared turbines. 2 shafts. S.H.P.: 60,000 = 36·5 kts. Boilers: 4. Complement: 350.

Note.—Distinctive numbers are 692/694, 696/709, 722/725, 727/732, 734/740, 744/762, 770/781, 857. Those marked (M) were fitted for minelaying and re-rated as DM 23–34 during war in Pacific. These ships, as well as those of *Gearing* class, are apt to roll badly when light. They are faster than any destroyers previously constructed, and have a larger radius of action. Type is an enlargement and modification of *Fletcher* design. Cost reported to be $8,000,000 each, exclusive of armament, etc. War losses: *Cooper, Drexler, Mannert L. Abele, Meredith.* Scrapped: *Hugh W. Hadley.*

53 Improved Fletcher Class (*1942 Programme.*)

Displacement: 2,050 tons (over 2,500 tons *full load*). Complement: 353. Dimensions: 376½ (*o.a.*) × 39½ × 12¼ feet. Guns: **5**—5 inch, 38 cal., **10**—40 mm. AA., **8**—20 mm. AA. Tubes: **10**—21 inch (quintupled). Machinery: General Electric geared turbines. 2 shafts. S.H.P.: 60,000 = 36 kts. Boilers: 4 Babcock & Wilcox.

Notes.—Except that they have lower fire controls and flat-faced bridges, these ships are in most respects like *Fletcher* class, described on the following page. *Dortch* was built in 158 days. Pendant Nos.: 649/691, 793/800, 802, 804. War losses: *Callaghan, Colhoun, Little.*

COLAHAN. 1944, *Lieut. D. Trimmingham, R.N.V.R.*

8 *Bath Iron Works Corpn:*

Caperton (July 24, 1943)
Cogswell (June 5, 1943)
Ingersoll (June 28, 1943)
Knapp (July 10, 1943)
Mertz (Sept. 11, 1943)
Norman Scott (Aug. 28, 1943)
Remey (July 24, 1943)
Wadleigh (Aug. 7, 1943)

2 *Bethlehem Steel Co. (S. Francisco):*

Stockham (July 25, 1943)
Wedderburn (Aug. 1, 1943)

5 *Bethlehem Steel Co. (S. Pedro):*

Cassin Young (Sept. 12, 1943)
Hopewell (May 2, 1943)
Irwin (Oct. 31, 1943)
Porterfield (June 13, 1943)
Preston (Dec. 12, 1943)

8 *Bethlehem Steel Co. (Staten Island):*

Benham (Aug. 29, 1943)
Charles J. Badger (April 3, 1943)
Colahan (May 2, 1943)
Cushing (Sept. 30, 1943)
Halsey Powell (June 30, 1943)
Monssen (Oct. 29, 1943)
Picking (May 31, 1943)
Uhlmann (July 30, 1943)

3 *Boston Navy Yard:*

Bennion (July 4, 1943)
Heywood L. Edwards (Oct. 6, 1943)
Richard P. Leary (Oct. 6, 1943)

2 *Charleston Navy Yard:*

Albert W. Grant (May 29, 1943)
Bryant (May 29, 1943)

18 *Federal S.B. & D.D. Co.:*

Black (March 28, 1943)
Chauncey (March 28, 1943)
Clarence K. Bronson (April 18, 1943)
Bullard (Feb. 28, 1943)
Cotten (June 12, 1943)
Dashiell (Feb. 6, 1943)
Dortch (June 20, 1943)
Gatling (June 20, 1943)
Healy (July 4, 1943)
Hickox (July 4, 1943)
Hunt (Aug. 1, 1943)
Kidd (Feb. 28, 1943)
Lewis Hancock (Aug. 1, 1943)
McDermut (Oct. 17, 1943)
McGowan (Nov. 14, 1943)
McNair (Nov. 14, 1943)
Marshall (Aug. 29, 1943)
Melvin (Oct. 17, 1943)

3 *Gulf S.B. Corpn.:*

Bearss (July 25, 1943)
John Hood (Oct. 23, 1943)
Van Valkenburgh (Dec. 19, 1943)

4 *Todd Pacific Shipyards (late Seattle-Tacoma Corpn.)*

Gregory (May 8, 1944)
Jarvis (Feb. 14, 1944)
Porter (March 13, 1944)
Rooks (June 6, 1944)

98 Fletcher Class (*1940–41 Programmes*).

Appearance Note.—All Bethlehem-built ships of this class reported to have flat-sided funnels.

NICHOLAS. 1943, *U.S. Navy Official.*

(*For launch dates, etc., see table 2 pp. beyond.*)

9 *Boston Navy Yard:*

Bennett
Charette
Conner
Fullam
Guest
Hall
Haraden
Hudson
Hutchins
Izard
Paul Hamilton
Stanly
Stevens

6 *Charleston Navy Yard:*

Bell
Burns

7 *Puget Sound Navy Yard:*

Halford
Hart (ex-*Mansfield*)
Howorth
Killen
Metcalfe
Shields
Wiley

18 *Bath Iron Works Corpn.:*

Abbot
Anthony
Braine
Converse
Conway
Cony
Eaton
Erben
Foote
Hale
Nicholas
O'Bannon
Sigourney
Stembel
Taylor
Terry
Wadsworth
Walker

11 *Federal S.B. & D.D. Co.:*

Fletcher
Jenkins
La Vallette
Philip
Radford
Renshaw
Ringgold
Saufley
Schroeder
Sigsbee
Waller

13 *Bethlehem (S. Francisco):*

Ammen
Hazelwood
Heerman
McCord
Miller
Mullany (ex-*Beatty*)
Owen
Stephen Potter
Sullivans (ex-*Putnam*)
Tingey
Trathen
Twining
Yarnall

5 *Bethlehem (Staten Island):*

Bache
Beale
Daly
Isherwood
Kimberly

4 *Bethlehem (S. Pedro):*

Boyd
Bradford
Brown
Cowell

11 *Seattle-Tacoma S.B. Corpn., Seattle:*

Franks
Hailey
Laws
Prichett
Robinson
Ross
Rowe
Smalley
Stoddard
Watts
Wren

11 *Consolidated Steel Corpn., Orange, Texas:*

Aulick
Charles Ausburn
Claxton
Dyson
Harrison
John Rodgers
McKee
Murray
Sproston
Wickes
Young

3 *Gulf S.B. Corpn., Chickasaw, Ala.:*

Capps
David W. Taylor
John D. Henley

Standard displacement: 2,050 tons (*ca.* 2,500 tons full load). Complement: 353. Dimensions: 376½ (*o.a.*) × 39⅓ × 12¼ feet. Guns: **5**—5 inch, 38 cal., **6**—40 mm. Bofors, **10**—20 mm. Oerlikon, etc. Tubes: **10**—21 inch. Machinery: General Electric geared turbines. 2 shafts. S.H.P.: 60,000 = 36·5 kts. Boilers: 4 Babcock & Wilcox. Six units (including *Halford*) were experimentally fitted with a seaplane and catapult, and did not have deckhouse between "Q" and "X" turrets (armament being temporarily reduced by **1**—5 inch and **5** T.T.); and some, including *Young*, had only one set of tubes. Cost averages $11,086,000 per ship, inclusive. War losses: *Abner Read, Brownson, Bush, Chevalier, De Haven, Halligan, Hoel, Johnston, Longshaw, Luce, Morrison, Pringle, Spence, Strong, Twiggs, Wm. D. Porter.* Heavily damaged and reported scrapped: *Evans, Haggard, Leutze, Newcomb, Thatcher.* Cancelled: *Percival, Watson.*

RADFORD. 1944, *U.S. Navy Official.*

AMMEN. 1944, *U.S. Navy Official.*

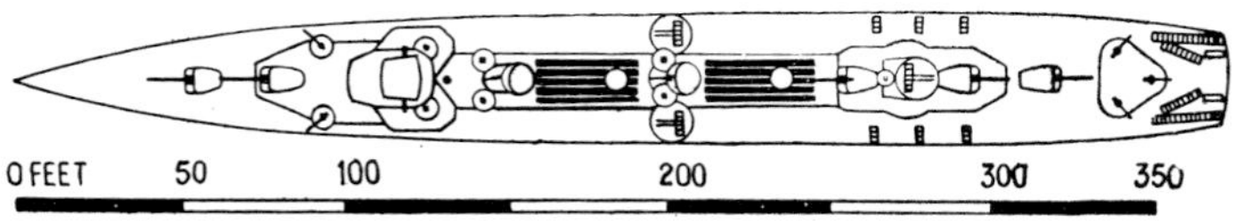

CONY. 1942, *U.S. Navy Official.*

79 Benson and Buchanan Class (*1940–41 and 1937–39 Programmes*).

HOBBY. 1944, *U.S. Navy Official.*

KENDRICK. 1944, *U.S. Navy Official.*

Appearance Note.—Seattle-built ships of this class have square-faced bridges, with director on bridge instead of mounted on a pedestal. Those built by Bethlehem Co. have flat-sided funnels.

(*For launch dates, etc., see table on following page.*)

9 *Boston Navy Yard:*
Cowie
Doran
Earle
Fitch
Forrest
Knight
Madison
Nicholson
Wilkes

2 *Charleston Navy Yard:*
Hobson
Tillman

5 *Philadelphia Navy Yard:*
Butler
Gherardi
Grayson
Hilary P. Jones
Swanson

1 *Norfolk Navy Yard:*
Herndon

1 *Puget Sound Navy Yard:*
Charles F. Hughes

7 *Bath Iron Works Corpn.:*
Eberle
Gleaves
Livermore (ex-*Grayson*)
Ludlow
Macomb
Niblack
Woolsey

20 *Federal S.B. & D.D. Co.:*
Buchanan
Davison
Edison
Edwards
Ellyson
Ericsson
Hambleton
Jeffers
Kearny
Lansdowne
Lardner
McCalla
Mervine
Nelson
Plunkett
Quick
Rodman
Stevenson
Stockton
Thorn

7 *Bethlehem (Quincy):*
Bancroft
Benson
Boyle
Champlin
Mayo
Nields
Ordronaux

8 *Bethlehem (S. Francisco):*
Caldwell
Coghlan
Frazier
Gansevoort
Gillespie
Hobby
Kalk
Woodworth

5 *Bethlehem (Staten Island):*
Bailey
Farenholt
Meade
Murphy
Parker

4 *Bethlehem (S. Pedro):*
Kendrick
Laub
Mackenzie
McLanahan

10 *Seattle-Tacoma S.B. Corpn. Seattle:*
Baldwin
Carmick
Doyle
Endicott
Frankford
Harding
McCook (ex-*Farley*)
Satterlee
Thompson
Welles

BANCROFT. 1942, *U.S. Navy Official.*

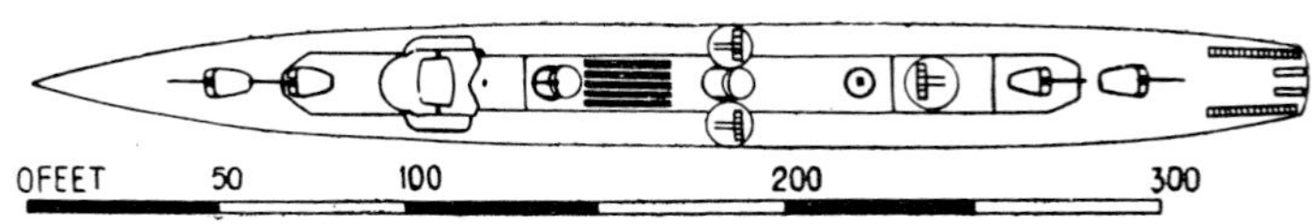

Standard displacement: 1,630 tons—actually now about 1,700 tons (2,000 tons full load). Dimensions: 341 (*w.l.*), 348⅓ (*o.a.*) × 36 × 10 feet. Complement: 250. Guns: **4**—5 inch, 38 cal., **4**—40 mm. Bofors, **7**—20 mm. Oerlikon. Tubes: **5**—21 inch. Machinery: Gen. Electric geared turbines. 2 shafts. S.H.P.: 50,000 = 36·5 kts. Boilers: 4 Babcock & Wilcox. Cost averages $8,814,000 per ship, inclusive. *Butler, Carmick, Cowie, Davison, Doran, Doyle, Ellyson, Endicott, Fitch, Forrest, Gherardi, Hale, Hambleton, Harding, Hobson, Jeffers, Knight, McCook, Macomb, Mervine, Quick, Rodman, Thompson,* were fitted out as Fast Minesweepers during war in Pacific. War losses: *Aaron Ward, Beatty, Bristol, Corry, Duncan, Emmons, Glennon, Gwin, Ingraham, Laffey, Lansdale, Maddox, Meredith, Monssen, Turner.* In addition, *Shubrick* was so badly damaged that she was scrapped.

19 Benson Class. (*1937–39 Programmes*)

(Another photo of this type will be found in Addenda.)

CHARLES F. HUGHES. (*Benson, Mayo, Madison*, all similar.) 1942, *Keystone.*

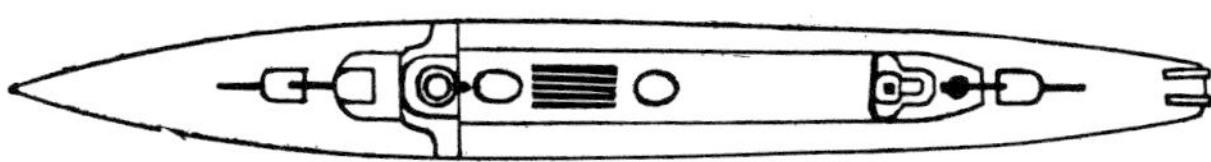

2 *Bethlehem (Quincy)*: **Benson, Mayo.**
6 *Bath Iron Works Corpn.*: **Gleaves, Niblack, Eberle, Livermore** (ex-*Grayson*), **Woolsey, Ludlow.**
3 *Boston Navy Yard*: **Madison, Wilkes, Nicholson.**
3 *Charleston Navy Yard*: **Hilary P. Jones, Grayson** (ex-*Livermore*), **Swanson.**
1 *Puget Sound Navy Yard*: **Charles F. Hughes.**
4 *Federal S.B. & D.D. Co.*: **Kearny, Plunkett, Edison, Ericsson.**

Standard displacement: 1,630 tons. Complement: 210. Dimensions: 341 (*w.l.*), 348 (*o.a.*) × 35$\frac{1}{3}$ × 10$\frac{1}{8}$ feet (*mean*). Guns: **4**—5 inch, 38 cal., 10 smaller. (A fifth 5 inch was removed to allow space for additional AA. guns.) Tubes: 5—21 inch (quintupled). Otherwise similar to *Anderson* class.

Name	*No.*	*Laid down*	*Launched*	*Completed*
Benson	421	16/5/38	15/11/39	25/7/40
Mayo	422	16/5/38	26/3/40	18/9/40
Gleaves	423	16/5/38	9/12/39	/5/40
Niblack	424	8/8/38	18/5/40	1/8/40
Madison	425	19/12/38	20/10/39	12/40
H. P. Jones	427	16/11/38	14/12/39 }	12/40
C. F. Hughes	428	3/1/39	16/5/40 }	
Livermore	429	6/3/39	3/8/40	7/10/40
Eberle	430	12/4/39	14/9/40	4/12/40
Plunkett	431	1/3/39 }	9/3/40	{ 16/7/40
Kearny	432	1/3/39 }		{ 13/9/40
Grayson	435	17/7/39	7/8/40	15/4/41
Woolsey	437	9/10/39	12/2/41	/41
Ludlow	438	18/12/39	11/11/40	5/3/41
Edison	439 }	18/3/40	23/11/40 {	30/1/41
Ericsson	440 }			11/3/41
Wilkes	441 }	1/11/39	31/5/40	
Nicholson	442 }			/41
Swanson	443	15/11/39	2/11/40	/41

Note.—There are probably variations in displacement as well as small differences in appearance in later units of this class. Most are reported to have square sterns. Reversion to 2 funnels is a noteworthy feature; shape of these appears to vary, some being circular and others oval. War losses: *Buck, Gwin, Ingraham, Lansdale, Meredith, Monssen.*

7 Anderson Class (*1936 Programme*)

MUSTIN. 1940, *Official.*

1 *Bath Iron Works Corpn.*: **Hughes.**
2 *Newport News Co.*: **Mustin, Russell.**
1 *Federal S.B. & D.D. Co.*: **Anderson.**
2 *Norfolk Navy Yard*: **Morris, Wainwright.**
1 *Charleston Navy Yard*: **Roe.**

Standard displacement: 1,570 tons. (See notes below.) Dimensions: 341 (*w.l.*) × 35 × 10 feet (*mean*). Guns: **4**—5 inch, 38 cal., several smaller. Tubes: **8**—21 inch (quadrupled). (Some may have only 4 tubes now.) Machinery: Parsons geared turbines. S.H.P.: 44,000 = 36·5 kts. (trials approached 40 kts.) Boilers: 4 Express, 600 lb. working pressure, with 850° *max.* superheat. Oil fuel: 600 tons. Cost about $7,000,000 apiece.

Notes.—This type combines the most successful features of *Gridley* and *Mahan* classes. General arrangement similar to *Dunlap* and *Fanning*, but with a single funnel. Defective stability has been remedied in earlier units of class by the addition of 60 tons of steel to the keel as ballast. Official designed displacement given above has therefore been exceeded in such cases, and ranges from 1,640 to 1,670 tons. In later units weight has been saved by use of lighter auxiliary plant, and reduction in thickness of plating for decks and superstructures. Sundry weights have been redistributed to improve stability. These were first destroyers fitted with central gunnery control station below deck. Decks are armoured over vital parts against M.G. bullets. Bridges and edges of forecastle deck are streamlined, which helps to keep forecastle dry in rough weather. War losses: *Hammann, O'Brien, Sims, Walke.*

Name	*No.*	*Laid down*	*Launched*	*Completed*
Hughes	410	15/9/37	17/6/39	21/9/39
Anderson	411	15/11/37	4/2/39	21/7/39
Mustin	413	20/12/37	8/12/38	15/9/39
Russell	414	20/12/37	8/12/38	40
Morris	417	7/6/38	1/6/39	30/4/40
Roe	418	23/4/38	21/6/39	15/3/40
Wainwright	419	7/6/38	1/6/39	31/5/40

17 Gridley Class (*1934–35 Programmes*)

STACK. 1940, *Official, courtesy "Our Navy".*

RHIND. 1940, *courtesy "Our Navy".*

2 *Bethlehem Steel Co., S. Francisco*: **Maury, McCall.**
2 *Bethlehem Steel Co., Quincy*: **Gridley, Craven.**
3 *Norfolk Navy Yard*: **Bagley, Helm, Stack.**
4 *Boston Navy Yard*: **Mugford, Ralph Talbot, Mayrant, Trippe.**
2 *Puget Sound Navy Yard*: **Patterson, Wilson.**
2 *Federal S.B. & D.D. Co.*: **Ellet, Lang.**
1 *Philadelphia Navy Yard*: **Rhind.**
1 *Charleston Navy Yard*: **Sterett.**

Standard displacement: 1,500 tons. Complement: 200. Dimensions: 334 (*w.l.*), 341$\frac{2}{3}$ (*o.a.*) × 34$\frac{2}{3}$ × 9$\frac{5}{8}$ feet (*mean*). Guns: **4**—5 inch, 38 cal. (dual purpose), some smaller. Tubes: **16**—21 inch (quadrupled) (probably reduced to 8). Machinery: Parsons geared turbines. S.H.P.: 42,800 = 36·5 kts. Boilers: 4 Express type (except *Gridley* and *Craven*, 4 Bethlehem Yarrow), 350 lb. working pressure. Oil fuel: 600 tons. Radius: 9,000 miles at 15 kts. Cost ranges from $4,500,000 to $5,000,000.

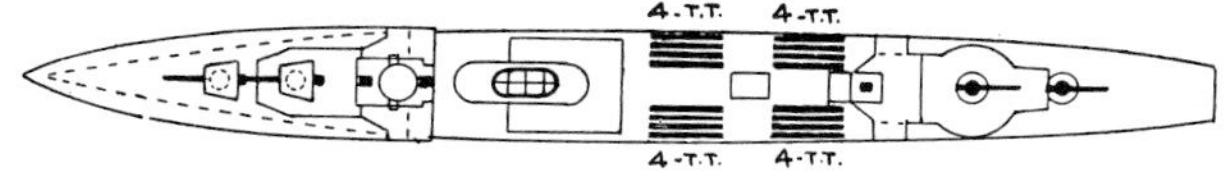

Notes.—Many of this class have exceeded designed speed on trials. *Ellet* and *Lang* said to have approached 40 kts. Several ships were delayed in delivery through difficulties with high pressure and superheated installations. War losses: *Benham, Blue, Henley, Jarvis, Rowan.*

Name	*No.*	*Laid down*	*Launched*	*Completed*
Gridley	380	3/6/35	1/12/36	30/6/38
Craven	382	3/6/35	25/2/37	29/7/38
Bagley	386	31/7/35	3/9/36	10/8/38
Helm	388	25/9/35	27/5/37	16/9/38
Mugford	389	28/10/35	31/10/36	23/9/38
Ralph Talbot	390	28/10/35	31/10/36	23/9/38
Patterson	392	22/7/35	6/5/37	11/10/38
Ellet	398	3/12/36	11/6/38	18/4/39
Lang	399	5/4/37	27/8/38	26/5/39
McCall	400	17/3/36	20/11/37	19/12/38
Maury	401	24/3/36	14/2/38	17/1/39
Mayrant	402	15/4/37	14/5/38	1/11/39
Trippe	403	15/4/37	14/5/38	15/12/39
Rhind	404	22/9/37	28/7/38	15/1/40
Stack	406	25/6/37	5/5/38	3/1/40
Sterett	407	2/12/36	27/10/38	15/9/39
Wilson	408	22/3/37	12/4/39	14/8/39

2 Dunlap Class (*1934 Programme*)

DUNLAP. 1937, *Mr. James Downey.*

Plan as MAHAN *class*

2 *United Dry Docks*: **Dunlap, Fanning.**

Standard displacement: 1,490 tons. Dimensions: 334 (*w.l.*), 341$\frac{2}{3}$ (*o.a.*) × 34$\frac{5}{8}$ × 9$\frac{5}{8}$ feet (*mean*). Guns: **5**—5 inch, 38 cal. (dual purpose), etc. Tubes: **12**—21 inch (quadrupled). Machinery: Parsons geared turbines. S.H.P.: 42,800 = 36·5 kts. Boilers: 4 Express type. Oil fuel: 500 tons. Radius: 6,000 miles. Complement: 200.

Name	*No.*	*Laid down*	*Launched*	*Completed*
Dunlap	384	10/4/35	18/4/36	7/7/38
Fanning	385	10/4/35	18/9/36	4/8/38

Destroyers

5 Somers Class. (*1934-35 Programmes*).

DAVIS. 1940.

2 *Federal S.B. & D.D. Co.:* **Somers, Warrington.**
3 *Bath Iron Works Corpn.:* **Sampson, Jouett, Davis.**

Displacement; 1,850 tons. Complement: 230. Dimensions: 371 (*w.l.*) × 36$\frac{1}{8}$ × 10$\frac{1}{4}$ feet (*mean* draught). Guns: **8**—5 inch, 38 cal., **8**—1 pdr., **2** M.G. Tubes: **12**—21 inch. Machinery: Geared turbines. S.H.P.: 52,000 = 37·5 kts. 4 Babcock & Wilcox high pressure boilers (officially stated to operate at 850° F.) Oil fuel: *circa* 600 tons. Radius estimated to be over 7,000 miles. Cost of 3 later ships averages $7,830,000 each. This includes a special air-conditioning plant. (This class may have had armament modified as in *Selfridge* class, following.)

Name	*No.*	*Laid down*	*Launched*	*Completed*
Somers	381	27/6/35	13/3/37	30/6/38
Warrington	383	10/10/35	15/5/37	12/8/38
Sampson	394	8/4/36	16/4/38	3/10/38
Davis	395	28/7/36	30/7/38	16/12/38
Jouett	396	26/3/36	24/9/38	7/3/39

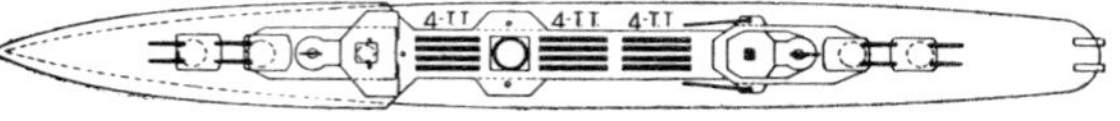

7 Selfridge Class (*1933 Programme*).

PHELPS. 1939, *O. W. Waterman.*

Appearance Note.—All of this class now rigged as silhouette, with pole foremast, but without mainmast, after fire control or "X" turret.

WINSLOW. 1938, *O. W. Waterman.*

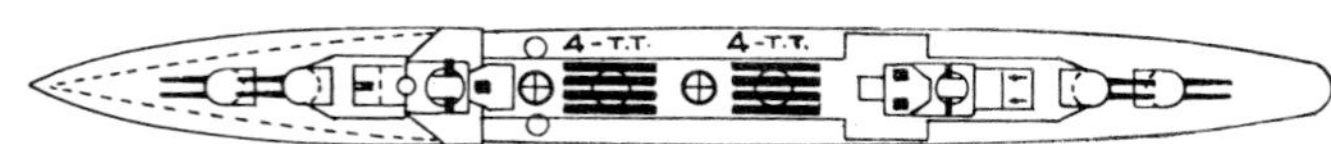

3 *New York S.B. Corpn.:* **Selfridge, McDougal, Winslow.**
4 *Bethlehem Steel Co., Quincy:* **Phelps, Clark, Moffett, Balch.**

Displacement: 1,850 tons (*Phelps* and *Clark* as completed, 1,805 tons; *Balch* and *Moffett*, 1,825 tons). Complement: 230. Dimensions: 371 (*w.l.*), 381 (*o.a.*) × 36$\frac{1}{8}$ × 10$\frac{1}{4}$ to 10$\frac{7}{12}$ feet (*mean* draught). Guns: **6**—5 inch, 38 cal., 6—40 mm. Bofors, etc. Tubes: **8**—21 inch. Machinery: Geared turbines. S.H.P.: 50,000 = 37 kts. (Trials, 39 kts.). 4 Babcock & Wilcox high pressure boilers. Oil fuel: *circa* 600 tons. Cost approaches $4,000,000 each.

Note.—In 1941 *Winslow* was painted light turquoise blue experimentally. War loss: *Porter.*

Name	*No.*	*Laid down*	*Launched*	*Completed*
Selfridge	357	18/12/33	18/4/36	26/10/37
McDougal	358	18/12/33	17/7/36	12/10/37
Winslow	359	18/12/33	21/9/36	19/10/37
Phelps	360	2/1/34	18/7/35	26/2/36
Clark	361	2/1/34	15/10/35	20/5/36
Moffett	362	2/1/34	11/12/35	28/9/37
Balch	363	16/5/34	24/3/36	5/10/37

11 Mahan Class (*1933 Programme*)

PERKINS. 1939, *O. W. Waterman.*

2 *Bath Iron Works Corpn.:* **Drayton, Lamson.**
2 *Boston Navy Yard:* **Case, Conyngham.**
1 *Philadelphia Navy Yard:* **Shaw.**
2 *United Dry Docks:* **Mahan, Cummings.**
2 *Federal S.B. and D.D. Co.:* **Flusser, Reid.**
1 *Norfolk Navy Yard:* **Tucker.**
1 *Mare Island Navy Yard:* **Smith.**

Standard displacement: 1,500 tons (except *Mahan*, 1,450 tons; *Cummings*, 1,465 tons. *Drayton, Lamson, Flusser, Reid, Smith*, 1,480 tons). Dimensions: 334 (*w.l.*), 341$\frac{1}{4}$ (*o.a.*) × 34$\frac{3}{8}$ × 9 ft. 8 in. (*Mahan*), 9 ft. 9 in. (1,465 and 1,480-ton ships), 9 ft. 10 in. others (*mean*): all about 17 feet *max.* Guns: 4—5 inch, 38 cal., several smaller. Tubes: 12—21 inch (quadrupled). Machinery: Double reduction geared turbines. S.H.P.: 42,800 = 36·5 kts. Boilers: 4 Express type. Oil fuel: 500 tons. Radius: 6,000 miles. Cost ranges from $3,400,000 to $3,750,000. *Shaw*, whose forward magazine blew up after she had been bombed in dry dock at Pearl Harbour, on Dec. 7, 1941, was repaired and refitted 1942. War losses: *Cassin, Cushing, Downes, Perkins, Preston.*

Name	*No.*	*Laid down*	*Launched*	*Completed*
Mahan	364	12/6/34	15/10/35	16/11/36
Cummings	365	26/6/34	11/12/35	26/1/37
Drayton	366	20/3/34	26/3/36	1/6/37
Lamson	367	20/3/34	17/6/36	4/1/37
Flusser	368	4/6/34	28/9/35	1/12/36
Reid	369	25/6/34	11/1/36	4/1/37
Case	370	19/9/34	14/9/35	19/3/37
Conyngham	371	19/9/34	14/9/35	10/4/37
Shaw	373	1/10/34	28/10/35	20/4/37
Tucker	374	15/8/34	26/2/36	30/3/37
Smith	378	27/10/34	20/2/36	31/12/36

8 Farragut Class (*1932 Programme.*)

AYLWIN. (Mainmast now reduced to a staff.) 1939, *Theo. N. Stone.*

DALE. (Mainmast now reduced to a staff.) 1937, *O. W. Waterman.*

1 *Bethlehem Steel Co., Quincy:* **Farragut** (ex-*Smith*, ex-*Farragut*).
2 *New York Navy Yard:* **Hull, Dale.**
1 *Bath Iron Works Corpn.:* **Dewey** (ex-*Phelps*, ex-*Dewey*).
2 *Boston Navy Yard:* **MacDonough, Monaghan.**
1 *Philadelphia Navy Yard:* **Aylwin.**
1 *Puget Sound Navy Yard:* **Worden.**

Standard displacement: 1,395 tons (except *Farragut*, 1,365 tons; *Dewey*, 1,345; *Aylwin*, 1,375; *Worden*, 1410 tons.) Length, (*o.a.*), 341$\frac{1}{4}$ feet; (*w.l.*), 331 feet (except *Farragut*, 330; *Dewey*, 329 feet). Beam, 34$\frac{1}{4}$ feet. *Mean* draught, 8$\frac{5}{6}$ feet (except *Farragut*, 8$\frac{2}{3}$ feet; *Dewey*, 8$\frac{7}{12}$ feet; *Aylwin*, 8$\frac{3}{4}$ feet). *Maximum* draught, 15$\frac{1}{2}$ feet. Complement, 162. Guns: **4**—5 inch, 38 cal., several smaller. Tubes: **8**—21 inch (quadrupled). Machinery: Geared turbines. 2 shafts. S.H.P. 42,800 = 36·5 kts. (exceeded on trials). Boilers: 4 Yarrow (by Bethlehem), high pressure. Oil fuel: 400 tons. Radius: 6,000 miles. Cost ranges from $3,400,000 to $3,750,000.

Name	*No.*	*Laid down*	*Launched*	*Compl.*
Farragut	348	20/9/32	15/3/34	18/6/34
Dewey	349	16/12/32	28/7/34	3/10/34
Hull	350	7/3/33	31/1/34	24/5/35
MacDonough	351	15/5/33	22/8/34	28/6/35
Worden	352	29/12/32	27/10/34	1/3/35
Dale	353	10/2/34	23/1/35	19/7/35
Monaghan	354	21/11/33	9/1/35	30/8/35
Aylwin	355	23/9/33	10/7/34	1/5/35

57 Flush Deck Type.

Vessels of this type which have been adapted for service as Light Minelayers, Seaplane Tenders, Fast Minesweepers and Transports will be found listed on later pages. According to latest reports, most of those listed below have been re-armed with 6—3 inch dual-purpose, 2 M.G. AA., and 6 torpedo tubes. Lower scuttles are being eliminated in all these destroyers as they come in for refit. War losses: *Borie, Edsall, Jacob Jones, Leary, Peary, Pillsbury, Pope, Reuben James, Stewart, Sturtevant, Truxtun.*

Note.—Numerals preceding name are the official Pendant Numbers, as painted on the bows of each ship. Numeral in parentheses after name refers to Builder (see list below).

TARBELL, with one funnel removed. (Other ships may have been altered similarly.) 1943.

Builders:—

1 Newport News S.B. & D.D. Co.
2 Wm. Cramp & Sons.
6 New York S.B. Corpn.
7 Fore River S.B. Co. (now Bethlehem Steel Co., Quincy).
8 Navy Yard, Mare Island.
9 Navy Yard, Norfolk.
10 Union Iron Works (now Bethlehem Steel Co., San Francisco).

FOX. 1940, *Theo. N. Stone.*

1st Group (5 Ships):

DD	Name	Laid down	Launched	Compl.
232	*Brooks* (6)	11/6/18	24/4/19	18/6/20
234	*Fox* (6)	25/6/18	12/6/19	17/5/20
233	*Gilmer* (6)	25/6/18	24/5/19	30/4/20
231	*Hatfield* (6)	10/6/18	17/3/19	16/4/20
235	*Kane* (6)	3/7/18	12/8/19	11/6/20

Displacement: 1,190 tons, *standard*. Complement, 122. Dimensions: 310 (*w.l.*), $314\frac{1}{3}$ (*o.a.*) × $30\frac{2}{3}$ × $9\frac{1}{4}$ feet (*mean* draught), $13\frac{1}{2}$ feet (*max.*). Armament: see notes at head of page. Machinery: Westinghouse geared turbines. 2 shafts. S.H.P. 26,000 = 35 kts. Boilers: 4 White-Forster. Total heating surface, 27,500 sq. ft. Oil fuel: 375 tons.

Observe AA. M.G. abaft fore-funnel. 1935, *O. W. Waterman.*

(All 2nd and 3rd groups were of above appearance except *Dahlgren* with only 3 funnels and others such as *Simpson* with taller fore-funnel.)

2nd Group (23 ships):

DD	Name	Laid down	Launched	Compl.
211	*Alden* (2)	24/10/18	7/6/19	24/11/19
246	*Bainbridge* (6)	27/5/19	12/6/20	9/2/21
213	*Barker* (2)	30/4/19	11/9/19	27/12/19
248	*Barry* (6)	26/7/19	28/10/20	28/12/20
210	*Broome* (2)	8/10/18	14/5/19	31/10/19
222	*Bulmer* (2)	11/8/19	22/1/20	16/8/20
341	*Decatur* (8)	15/9/20	29/10/21	9/8/22
216	*John D. Edwards* (2)	21/5/19	18/10/19	6/4/20
228	*John D. Ford* (2)	11/11/19	2/9/20	30/12/20
247	*Goff* (6)	16/6/19	2/6/20	19/1/21
236	*Humphreys* (6)	31/7/18	28/7/19	21/7/20
230	*Paul Jones* (2)	23/12/19	30/9/20	19/4/21
242	*King* (6)	28/4/19	14/10/20	16/12/20
250	*Lawrence* (6)	14/8/19	10/7/20	18/4/21
336	*Litchfield* (8)	15/1/19	12/8/19	12/5/20
220	*MacLeish* (2)	19/8/19	18/12/19	2/8/20
223	*McCormick* (2)	11/8/19	14/2/20	30/8/20
343	*Noa* (9) ‡	18/11/18	28/6/19	15/2/21
239	*Overton* (6)	30/10/18	10/7/19	30/6/20

2nd Group—*continued.*

DD	Name	Laid down	Launched	Compl.
218	*Parrott* (2)	23/7/19	25/11/19	11/5/20
243	*Sands* (6)	22/3/19	28/10/19	10/11/20
221	*Simpson* (2)*	9/10/19	28/4/20	3/11/20
217	*Whipple* (2)	12/6/19	6/11/19	23/4/20

Same as 1st Group. Parsons or Westinghouse geared turbines. Four White-Forster or Normand boilers. H.P. 24,200, 25,000 or 26,000 = 35 kts. T.H.S. 27,500 or 27,000 sq. ft.

3rd Group (1 ship):

DD	Name	Laid down	Launched	Compl.
187	*Dahlgren* (1)†	8/6/18	20/11/18	6/1/20

Same as 2nd Group, except 311 feet water-line length. Westinghouse geared turbines. Four White-Forster boilers. S.H.P. 27,000 = 35 kts. T.H.S. 27,500 sq. ft.

* *Simpson* and several others now have fore-funnel taller than remaining three.
† *Dahlgren* re-engined, 1938; speed being improved considerably. Third and fourth funnels have been combined in one large casing, and tubes removed.
‡ *Noa* has been fitted experimentally with a small seaplane and derrick, 1941. S.L. platform has been shifted farther forward to enable plane to be stowed.

Flush Deck Type, 4th Group (21 ships):

DD	Name	Laid down	Launched	Compl.
128	*Babbitt* (6)	19/2/18	30/9/18	24/10/19
126	*Badger* (6)	9/1/18	24/8/18	29/5/19
149	*Barney* (2)	26/3/18	5/9/18	14/3/19
151	*Biddle* (2)	22/4/18	3/10/18	22/4/19
150	*Blakeley* (2)	26/3/18	19/9/18	8/5/19
148	*Breckinridge* (2)	11/3/18	17/8/18	27/2/19
157	*Dickerson* (6)	25/5/18	12/3/19	3/9/19
152	*Du Pont* (2)	2/5/18	22/10/18	30/4/19
154	*Ellis* (2)	8/7/18	30/11/18	7/6/19
145	*Greer* (2)	24/2/18	1/8/18	31/12/18
141	*Hamilton* (8)*	8/6/18	15/1/19	7/11/19
160	*Herbert* (6)	9/4/18	8/5/19	21/11/19
118	*Lea* (2)	18/9/17	29/4/18	2/10/18
113	*Rathburne* (2)	12/7/17	27/12/17	24/6/18

Flush Deck Type, 4th Group—*continued.*

DD	Name	Laid down	Launched	Compl.
147	*Roper* (2)	19/3/18	17/8/18	15/2/19
159	*Schenck* (6)	26/3/18	23/4/19	30/10/19
114	*Talbot* (2)	12/7/17	20/2/18	20/7/18
156	*J. Fred Talbott* (2)	8/7/18	14/12/18	30/6/19
142	*Tarbell* (2)*	31/12/17	28/5/18	27/11/18
125	*Tattnall* (6)	1/12/17	5/9/18	26/6/19
144	*Upshur* (2)	19/2/18	4/7/18	23/12/18

Displacement: 1,090 tons *standard*. Dimensions: 309 (*w.l.*), $314\frac{1}{3}$ (*o.a.*) × $30\frac{1}{2}$ × $8\frac{3}{8}$ feet (*mean* draught), 12ft. (*max.*). Armament as Groups 1, 2, 3. Parsons geared turbines; Four White-Forster, Normand or Thornycroft boilers. H.P. 24,200, 26,000 or 27,000 = 35 kts. T.H.S.: 27,048, 27,000 or 27,500 sq. ft.

* *Hamilton*, *Tarbell*, and probably others have had a funnel removed.

J. FRED TALBOTT. 1938, *Theo. N. Stone.*

(All 4th and 5th groups were originally like this, though several, if not all, now have only 3 funnels.)

Flush Deck Type, 5th Group (7 ships):

	Name	Laid down	Launched	Compl.
106	*Chew* (10)	2/1/18	26/5/18	12/12/18
109	*Crane* (10)	7/1/18	4/7/18	18/4/19
164	*Crosby* (7)	23/6/18	28/9/18	24/1/19
138	*Kennison* (8)	14/2/18	8/6/18	2/4/19
137	*Kilty* (8)	15/12/17	25/4/18	17/12/18
103	*Schley* (10)	29/10/17	28/3/18	20/9/18
139	*Ward* (ex-*Cowell*)(8)	15/5/18	1/6/18	24/7/18

Displacement: 1,060 tons *standard*. Dimensions: 309 (*w.l.*) $314\frac{1}{3}$ (*o.a.*) × $30\frac{1}{2}$ × $8\frac{1}{2}$ feet (*mean* draught), 12 ft. (*max*). Armament as in other four Groups. Parsons turbines. Four Normand boilers. S.H.P. 25,000 = 35 kts. T.H.S.: 27,540 sq. ft. Oil fuel: 300 tons.

Photo wanted.

Allen (Bath Iron Works Corpn., 1916). Displacement: 920 tons *standard*. Complement: 136. Dimensions: 310 (*w.l.*), $315\frac{1}{4}$ (*o.a.*) × $29\frac{7}{12}$ × $8\frac{1}{8}$ feet (*mean*). Armament: 3—4 inch, 50 cal., 3—3 inch AA., 6—21 inch tubes. Machinery: Parsons geared turbines. S.H.P.: 17,500 = 30 kts. Boilers: 4 Normand. Oil fuel: 290 tons.

Note.—This old destroyer does not belong to the Flush Deck type, but is the survivor of an earlier class, numbered *DD* 66. Armament was modified on recommissioning for war service.

Destroyers

Particulars of Construction, Benson, Fletcher and Buchanan Classes.

No.	Name	Laid down	Launched	Completed
421	*Benson*	16/5/38	15/11/39	25/7/40
422	*Mayo*	16/5/38	26/3/40	18/9/40
423	*Gleaves*	16/5/38	9/12/39	5/40
424	*Niblack*	8/8/38	18/5/40	1/8/40
425	*Madison*	19/12/38	20/10/39	12/40
427	*H. P. Jones*	16/11/38	14/12/39	12/40
428	*C. F. Hughes*	3/1/39	16/5/40	
429	*Livermore*	6/3/39	3/8/40	7/10/40
430	*Eberle*	12/4/39	14/9/40	4/12/40
431	*Plunkett*	1/3/39	9/3/40	16/7/40
432	*Kearny*	1/3/39		13/9/40
435	*Grayson*	17/7/39	7/8/40	15/4/41
437	*Woolsey*	9/10/39	12/2/41	41
438	*Ludlow*	18/12/39	11/11/40	5/3/41
439	*Edison*	18/3/40	23/11/40	30/1/41
440	*Ericsson*			11/3/41
441	*Wilkes*	1/11/39	31/5/40	41
442	*Nicholson*			
443	*Swanson*	15/11/39	2/11/40	41
445	*Fletcher*	10/41	3/5/42	42
446	*Radford*			
447	*Jenkins*	11/41	21/6/42	42
448	*La Vallette*			
449	*Nicholas*	3/3/41	19/2/42	42
450	*O'Bannon*		14/3/42	6/42
*454	*Ellyson*	2/12/40	25/7/41	28/11/41
455	*Hambleton*	16/12/40	26/9/41	22/12/41
456	*Rodman*			27/1/42
*458	*Macomb*	3/9/40	22/9/41	42
*460	*Woodworth*	13/1/41	29/11/41	42
461	*Forrest*	6/1/41	14/6/41	42
462	*Fitch*			
*464	*Hobson*	14/11/40	8/9/41	42
465	*Saufley*	12/41	19/7/42	42
466	*Waller*	1/42	15/8/42	43
*468	*Taylor*	11/41	7/6/42	42
470	*Bache*	19/11/41	27/7/42	42
471	*Beale*	19/12/41	25/8/42	43
472	*Guest*	27/9/41	20/2/42	42
473	*Bennett*	10/12/41	16/4/42	42
474	*Fullam*			
475	*Hudson*	23/2/42	3/6/42	42
476	*Hutchins*	27/9/41	20/2/42	17/11/42
*478	*Stanly*	30/12/41	2/5/42	42
479	*Stevens*	30/12/41	24/6/42	42
480	*Halford*	6/41	30/1/43	43
*484	*Buchanan*	11/2/41	22/11/41	21/8/42
*486	*Lansdowne*	7/41	20/2/42	28/4/42
487	*Lardner*	7/41	20/3/42	12/5/42
488	*McCalla*	7/41		42
489	*Mervine*	9/41	3/5/42	42
490	*Quick*	9/41		
491	*Farenholt*	11/12/40	19/11/41	2/4/42
492	*Bailey*	29/1/41	19/12/41	42
493	*Carmick*	29/5/41	8/3/42	42
494	*Doyle*		17/3/42	42
495	*Endicott*	1/5/41	5/4/42	42
496	*McCook*		3/5/42	42
497	*Frankford*	6/41	16/5/42	42
498	*Philip*	42	13/10/42	43
499	*Renshaw*			
500	*Ringgold*	42	11/11/42	43
501	*Schroeder*	42		

No.	Name	Laid down	Launched	Completed
502	*Sigsbee*	42	7/12/42	43
*507	*Conway*	42	16/8/42	42
508	*Cony*			
509	*Converse*	42	30/8/42	20/11/42
510	*Eaton*	42	20/9/42	43
511	*Foote*	42	11/10/42	43
*513	*Terry*	42	22/11/42	43
*515	*Anthony*	42	20/12/42	43
516	*Wadsworth*	42	10/1/43	43
517	*Walker*	42	31/1/43	43
*519	*Daly*	42	24/10/42	43
520	*Isherwood*	42	24/11/42	43
521	*Kimberly*	42	4/2/43	43
*527	*Ammen*	11/41	17/9/42	43
528	*Mullany*	42	10/10/42	43
*530	*Trathen*	17/1/42	21/10/42	43
531	*Hazelwood*	12/4/42	20/11/42	43
532	*Heerman*	42	5/12/42	43
*534	*McCord*	42	1/43	43
535	*Miller*	18/8/42	7/3/43	43
536	*Owen*	42	21/3/43	43
537	*Sullivans*	42	4/4/43	43
538	*Stephen Potter*	42	28/4/43	43
539	*Tingey*	42	28/5/43	43
540	*Twining*	42	11/7/43	43
541	*Yarnall*	42	25/7/43	43
*544	*Boyd*	42	29/10/42	43
545	*Bradford*	42	12/12/42	43
546	*Brown*	27/6/42	22/2/43	43
547	*Cowell*	42	18/4/43	43
*550	*Capps*	7/41	31/5/42	43
551	*David W. Taylor*	7/41	15/6/42	42
*553	*John D. Henley*	7/41	15/11/42	43
554	*Franks*	42	7/12/42	43
*556	*Hailey*	42	9/3/43	43
*558	*Laws*	42	22/4/43	43
*561	*Prichett*	42	31/7/43	43
562	*Robinson*	42	28/8/43	43
563	*Ross*	42	11/9/43	43
564	*Rowe*	42	30/9/43	43
565	*Smalley*	42	27/10/43	44
566	*Stoddard*	42	19/11/43	44
567	*Watts*	42	31/12/43	44
568	*Wren*	43	29/1/44	44
569	*Aulick*	14/5/41	2/3/42	42
570	*Charles Ausburn*			
571	*Claxton*	7/41	2/4/42	42
572	*Dyson*	7/41	42	43
573	*Harrison*	7/41	42	43
574	*John Rodgers*	7/41	42	43
575	*McKee*		1/8/42	43
576	*Murray*	41	16/8/42	20/4/43
577	*Sproston*		42	42

No.	Name.	Laid down	Launched	Completed
578	*Wickes*	42	13/9/42	43
*580	*Young*	42	11/10/42	43
581	*Charette*	20/2/41	3/6/42	42
582	*Conner*	16/4/42	18/7/42	42
583	*Hall*			
*585	*Haraden*	3/6/42	19/3/43	43
*587	*Bell*	24/2/42	24/6/42	42
588	*Burns*	9/5/42	8/8/42	43
589	*Izard*			
590	*Paul Hamilton*	20/1/43	5/5/43	43
*592	*Howorth*	11/41	42	44
593	*Killen*			
594	*Hart*			44
595	*Metcalfe*			44
596	*Shields*		4/12/44	45
597	*Wiley*			45
598	*Bancroft*	20/5/41	31/12/41	42
*600	*Boyle*	41	14/6/42	42
601	*Champlin*	41	25/7/42	42
602	*Meade*	25/3/41	15/2/42	42
603	*Murphy*	5/41	29/4/42	42
604	*Parker*	6/41	12/5/42	42
605	*Caldwell*	24/3/41	15/1/42	42
606	*Coghlan*	28/3/41	16/2/42	42
607	*Frazier*	6/41	17/3/42	42
608	*Gansevoort*	6/41	11/4/42	42
609	*Gillespie*	6/41	8/5/42	42
610	*Hobby*	6/41	4/6/42	42
611	*Kalk*	6/41	15/6/42	42
612	*Kendrick*	1/5/41	2/4/42	42
613	*Laub*		1/6/42	42
614	*Mackenzie*	1/5/41	27/6/42	42
615	*McLanahan*	41	7/9/42	43
616	*Nields*	42	1/10/42	43
617	*Ordronaux*	42	9/11/42	43
618	*Davison*	41	19/7/42	42
619	*Edwards*			
*621	*Jeffers*	41	26/8/42	43
*623	*Nelson*	42	15/9/42	43
624	*Baldwin*	7/41	1/6/42	42
625	*Harding*	7/41	28/6/42	42
626	*Satterlee*	41	17/7/42	42
627	*Thompson*			
628	*Welles*	42	7/9/42	43
629	*Abbot*	42	17/2/43	43
630	*Braine*	42	7/3/43	43
631	*Erben*	42	21/3/43	43
632	*Cowie*	18/3/41	27/9/41	42
633	*Knight*			
634	*Doran*	14/6/41	10/12/41	42
635	*Earle*			
636	*Butler*	16/9/41	12/2/42	42
637	*Gherardi*			
638	*Herndon*	26/8/41	5/2/42	42
*641	*Tillman*	8/9/41	20/12/41	42
642	*Hale*	42	4/4/43	43
643	*Sigourney*	42	24/4/43	43
644	*Stembel*	42	8/5/43	43
645	*Stevenson*	42	11/11/42	11/1/43
646	*Stockton*	42		
*647	*Thorn*	42	28/2/43	43

* Nos. 451, 453, 457, 459, 463, 467, 469, 477, 481, 483, 485, 512, 514, 518, 522, 526, 529, 533, 552, 555, 557, 559, 560, 579, 584, 586, 591, 599, 620, 622, 639, 640, 648, lost or scrapped. Nos. 452, 482, 503/506, 523/525, 542, 543, 548, 549, cancelled.

Destroyers (Escort type)

General Notes on Destroyer-Escorts.—Many of those originally ordered were cancelled, i.e., DE 114–128, 284–300, 373–381, 425–437, 451–507, 511–515, 541–562, 607–632, 645–664, 723–738, 751–762, 772–788, 801–1005. These included *Creamer*, *Curtis W. Howard*, *Delbert W. Halsey*, *Ely*, *Gaynier*, *John J. van Buren*; also *Myles C. Fox* and *Vogelgesang*, names reallotted to destroyers. Ex-German vessels of somewhat similar type taken over were *F* 8 and *F* 10.

99 Rudderow Class.

RUDDEROW. 1944, *U.S. Navy Official.*

11 *Bethlehem-Hingham:*

DE
584 Charles J. Kimmel (Jan. 15, 1944)
585 Daniel A. Joy (Jan. 15, 1944)
583 George A. Johnson
580 Leslie L. B. Knox
586 Lough
581 McNulty
582 Metivier
588 Peiffer
579 Riley
587 Thomas F. Nickel
589 Tinsman

3 *Bethlehem, Quincy:*

685 Coates (Dec. 9, 1943)
684 De Long
686 Eugene E. Elmore (Dec. 23, 1943)

10 *Boston Navy Yard:*

536 Bivin
531 Edward H. Allen
533 Howard F. Clark (Nov. 8, 1943)
535 Lewis
538 Osberg
537 Rizzi
534 Silverstein (Nov. 8, 1943)
532 Tweedy
540 Vandivier
539 Wagner

20 *Brown S.B. Co., Houston:*

421 Chester T. O'Brien
405 Dennis (Dec. 4, 1943)
422 Douglas A. Munro
423 Dufilho
406 Edmonds
424 Haas
410 Jack Miller
409 La Prade
415 Lawrence C. Taylor
420 Leland E. Thomas
414 Le Ray Wilson
416 Melvin R. Nawman
417 Oliver Mitchell
403 Richard M. Rowell (Nov. 17, 1943)
402 Richard S. Bull
419 Robert F. Keller
411 Stafford
408 Straus
418 Tabberer
412 Walter C. Wann

1 *Charleston Navy Yard:*

231 Hodges

33 *Consolidated Steel Corpn., Orange:*

343 Abercrombie
366 Alvin C. Cockrell
368 Cecil J. Doyle
353 Doyle C. Barnes
346 Edwin A. Howard
367 French
349 Gentry
357 George E. Davis (April 8, 1944)
355 Jaccard
347 Jesse Rutherford
339 John C. Butler
370 John L. Williamson
360 Johnnie Hutchins (May 2, 1944)
354 Kenneth M. Willett
348 Key
356 Lloyd E. Acree
365 McGinty
358 Mack (April 11, 1944)
351 Maurice J. Manuel
352 Naifeh
340 O'Flaherty
363 Pratt (June 1, 1944)
371 Presley
341 Raymond
342 Richard W. Suesens
345 Robert Brazier (Jan. 22, 1944)
362 Rolf
364 Rombach
369 Thaddeus Parker
350 Traw
361 Walton
372 Williams
359 Woodson (April 29, 1944)

3 *Defoe Co.:*

706 Holt
707 Jobb
708 Parle

16 *Federal S.B. & D.D. Co., Port Newark:*

447 Albert T. Harris (April 16, 1944)
446 Charles E. Brannon (April 23, 1944)
439 Conklin (Feb. 13, 1944)
438 Corbesier (Feb. 13, 1944)
448 Cross (July 4, 1944)
509 Formoe (April 2, 1944)
508 Gilligan (Feb. 22, 1944)
444 Goss (March 19, 1944)
445 Grady (April 2, 1944)
449 Hanna (July 4, 1944)
510 Heyliger (Aug. 6, 1944)
443 Kendal C. Campbell (March 19, 1944)
450 Joseph E. Connolly (Aug. 6, 1944)
440 McCoy Reynolds (Feb. 22, 1944)
442 Ulvert M. Moore (March 7, 1944)
441 William Seiverling (March 7, 1944)

2 *Philadelphia Navy Yard:*

225 Day (October 14, 1943)
224 Rudderow (Oct. 14, 1943)

Displacement: 1,450 tons (1,780 tons *full load*). Complement: 220. Dimensions: 306 (*o.a.*) $\times 36\frac{5}{8} \times 10\frac{2}{3}$ feet. Guns: **2**—5 inch, 38 cal., **2**—40 mm. AA., **6**—20 mm. AA., and D.C.T. Tubes: **3**—21 inch in triple mount. Machinery: Geared turbines, except in 21 ships, built by Bethlehem and Defoe Companies and by Charleston and Philadelphia Navy Yards, which have turbo-electric propulsion. 2 shafts. S.H.P.: 12,000 = 28 kts. (26 kts. in service). War losses: *Eversole*, *Samuel B. Roberts*, *Shelton*.

Note.—Fifty-one ships of this class, with turbo-electric propulsion, were converted into fast Transports. *Oswald A. Powers* and *Sheehan* have been scrapped. Completion of *Vandivier* and *Wagner*, laid down at Boston 27/12/43, has been deferred for 12 months from August, 1946. Reported that some ships of *Rudderow* type have shown signs of structural weakness around forward turret.

52 Buckley Class.

WM. T. POWELL. 1946, *Mr. Wm. H. Davis.*

6 *Bethlehem-Hingham:*
- **575 Ahrens**
- **577 Alexander J. Luke** (Dec. 28, 1943)
- **51 Buckley** (Jan. 9, 1943)
- **57 Fogg** (March 20, 1943)
- **59 Foss** (April 10, 1943)
- **578 Robert I. Paine** (Dec. 30, 1943)

5 *Bethlehem, Quincy:*
- **681 Gillette**
- **679 Greenwood**
- **678 Harmon** (July 25, 1943)
- **683 Henry R. Kenyon** (Oct. 30, 1943)
- **680 Loeser** (Sept. 11, 1943)

9 *Bethlehem, S. Francisco:*
- **643 Damon M. Cummings** (April 18, 1944)
- **640 Fieberling**
- **633 Foreman** (Aug. 1, 1943)
- **639 Gendreau** (Dec. 12, 1943)
- **642 Paul G. Baker** (March 12, 1944)
- **644 Vammen** (May 21, 1944)
- **634 Whitehurst** (Sept. 5, 1943)
- **641 William C. Cole** (Dec. 28, 1943)
- **638 Willmarth** (Nov. 1943)

7 *Charleston Navy Yard:*
- **202 Eichenberger**
- **201 James E. Craig**
- **199 Manning** (Oct. 1, 1943)
- **200 Neuendorf** (Oct. 18, 1943)
- **210 Otter** (Oct. 23, 1943)
- **203 Thomason** (Aug. 24, 1943)
- **213 William T. Powell** (Nov. 27, 1943)

6 *Consolidated Steel Corpn., Orange*
- **795 Gunason** (Oct. 17, 1943)
- **800 Jack W. Wilke**
- **796 Major**
- **799 Scroggins**
- **798 Varian**
- **797 Weeden** (Oct. 27, 1943)

10 *Defoe Co.:*
- **704 Cronin**
- **700 Currier**
- **702 Earl V. Johnson** (Jan. 12, 1944)
- **705 Frybarger**
- **697 George**
- **703 Holton**
- **699 Marsh**
- **701 Osmus**
- **698 Raby**
- **696 Spangler**

1 *Dravo Corpn., Pittsburgh:*
- **667 Wiseman**

2 *Norfolk Navy Yard:*
- **198 Lovelace** (July 4, 1943)
- **153 Reuben James**

6 *Philadelphia Navy Yard:*
- **217 Coolbaugh** (May 29, 1943)
- **218 Darby** (May 29, 1943)
- **222 Fowler** (July 3, 1943)
- **220 Francis M. Robinson** (May 29, 1943)
- **219 J. Douglas Blackwood** (May 29, 1943)
- **223 Spangenburg** (July 3, 1943)

Displacement: 1,400 tons (1,720 tons *full load*). Complement: 220. Dimensions: 306 (*o.a.*) × 36⅞ × 10⅝ feet. Guns: 3—3 inch, 50 cal., d.p., 2—40 mm. AA., 6—20 mm. AA., and D.C.T. Tubes: 3—21 inch, in triple mount (removed from some, vide photo of *Robert I. Paine*). Machinery: Turbo-electric. 2 shafts. S.H.P.: 12,000 = 28 kts. (26 kts. in service). Fuel: 340 tons. War losses: *Fechteler, Underhill.* Destroyed by internal explosion, 30/4/46: *Solar.*

Notes.—46 ships of this class were transferred to Royal Navy under Lend-Lease scheme. Six of these were lost, and the remainder have been returned to U.S.A. for scrapping. Fifty more of *Buckley* class have been adapted for duty as fast Transports or for subsidiary purposes.

57 Bostwick Class.

6 *Dravo Corporation, Wilmington, Del.:*
- **103 Bostwick** (Aug. 30, 1943)
- **104 Breeman**
- **105 Burrows**
- **112 Carter** (Feb. 29, 1944)
- **113 Clarence L. Evans**
- **102 Thomas** (July 31, 1943)

30 *Federal S.B. & D.D. Co., Port Newark:*
- **167 Acree** (May 9, 1943)
- **168 Amick** (May 26, 1943)
- **169 Atherton** (May 26, 1943)
- **190 Baker** (Nov. 28, 1943)
- **166 Baron** (May 9, 1943)
- **170 Booth** (June, 1943)
- **189 Bronstein** (Nov. 14, 1943)
- **171 Carroll** (June, 1943)
- **191 Coffman** (Nov. 28, 1943)
- **172 Cooner** (August, 1943)
- **192 Eisner** (Dec. 12, 1943)
- **173 Eldridge** (1943)
- **193 Garfield Thomas** (Dec. 12, 1943)
- **182 Gustafson** (Oct. 3, 1943)
- **162 Levy** (March 28, 1943)
- **163 McConnell** (March 28, 1943)
- **176 Micka** (Aug. 22, 1943)
- **188 O'Neill** (Nov. 14, 1943)
- **164 Osterhaus** (April 18, 1943)
- **165 Parks** (April 18, 1943)
- **185 Riddle** (Oct. 17, 1943)
- **196 Rinehart** (Jan. 9, 1944)
- **183 Samuel S. Miles** (Oct. 3, 1943)
- **187 Stern** (Oct. 31, 1943)
- **181 Straub** (Sept. 18, 1943)
- **186 Swearer** (Oct. 31, 1943)
- **195 Thornhill** (Dec. 30, 1943)
- **180 Trumpeter** (Sept. 18, 1943)
- **184 Wesson** (Oct. 17, 1943)
- **194 Wingfield** (Dec. 30, 1943)

9 *Tampa S.B. Co:*
- **763 Cates** (Oct. 10, 1943)
- **765 Earl K. Olsen**
- **768 Ebert**
- **764 Gandy** (Dec. 12, 1943)
- **770 Muir** (June 4, 1944)
- **769 Neal A. Scott** (June 4, 1944)
- **767 Oswald**
- **766 Slater** (Feb. 13, 1944)
- **771 Sutton**

12 *Western Pipe & Steel Co.:*
- **739 Bangust** (June 6, 1943)
- **747 Bright** (Sept. 26, 1943)
- **746 Hemminger** (Sept. 12, 1943)
- **742 Hilbert** (July 18, 1943)
- **744 Kyne** (October, 1943)
- **743 Lamons** (Aug. 1, 1943)
- **750 McClelland** (Nov. 28, 1943)
- **749 Roberts** (Nov. 14, 1943)
- **745 Snyder** (Aug. 29, 1943)
- **748 Tills** (Oct. 3, 1943)
- **740 Waterman** (June 20, 1943)
- **741 Weaver** (July 4, 1943)

Displacement: 1,240 tons (1,520 tons *full load*). Complement: 220. Dimensions: 306 (*o.a.*) × 36⅞ × 10⅝ feet. Guns: 3—3 inch, 50 cal., d.p., 2—40 mm. AA., 4—20 mm. AA. and D.C.T. Tubes: 3—21 inch, in triple mount. Machinery: Diesel-electric. 2 shafts. B.H.P: 6,000 = 20 kts. (19 kts. in service).

Note.—Eight ships of this class were transferred to Brazilian Navy and six to French Navy.

81 Edsall Class.

KRETCHMER. 1946, *S. C. Heal, Esq.*

37 *Brown S.B. Co., Houston.*
- **390 Calcaterra** (Aug. 16, 1943)
- **251 Camp**
- **391 Chambers**
- **398 Cockrill**
- **389 Durant**
- **393 Haverfield** (Aug. 1943)
- **400 Hissem**
- **252 Howard D. Crow**
- **250 Hurst** (April, 1943)
- **396 Janssen**
- **243 J. Richard Ward** (Jan. 6, 1943)
- **241 Keith** (Dec. 21, 1942)
- **388 Lansing** (Aug. 3, 1943)
- **249 Marchand**
- **392 Merrill** (August, 1943)
- **383 Mills**
- **240 Moore** (Dec. 21, 1942)
- **244 Otterstetter** (Jan. 19, 1943)
- **253 Pettit**
- **382 Ramsden**
- **384 Rhodes** (June 29, 1943)
- **385 Richey** (June 20, 1943)
- **254 Ricketts**
- **386 Savage**
- **255 Sellstrom** (May 12, 1943)
- **245 Sloat**
- **246 Snowden**
- **247 Stanton**
- **238 Stewart** (Nov. 22, 1942)
- **399 Stockdale**
- **239 Sturtevant**
- **248 Swasey** (March 18, 1943)
- **394 Swenning**
- **242 Tomich**
- **387 Vance**
- **397 Wilhoite**
- **395 Willis**

44 *Consolidated Steel Corpn.:*
- **147 Blair** (April, 1943)
- **327 Brister** (Aug. 24, 1943)
- **148 Brough**
- **149 Chatelain**
- **337 Dale W. Peterson**
- **335 Daniel** (Nov. 16, 1943)
- **138 Douglas L. Howard** (Jan. 25, 1943)
- **129 Edsall** (Nov. 1, 1942)
- **324 Falgout**
- **139 Farquhar**
- **142 Fessenden**
- **328 Finch** (Nov. 1943)
- **135 Flaherty** (Jan. 17, 1943)
- **334 Forster** (Nov. 13, 1943)
- **144 Frost** (March 21, 1943)
- **131 Hammann** (ex-*Langley*)
- **316 Harveson**
- **137 Herbert C. Jones**
- **141 Hill** (Feb. 28, 1943)
- **145 Huse**
- **146 Inch** (April 4, 1943)
- **130 Jacob Jones**
- **317 Joyce**
- **140 J. R. Y. Blakeley** (March 7, 1943)
- **318 Kirkpatrick** (June 5, 1943)
- **331 Koiner**
- **329 Kretchmer** (Aug. 31, 1943)
- **325 Lowe**
- **338 Martin H. Ray** (Dec. 29, 1943)
- **320 Menges**
- **321 Mosley** (June 26, 1943)
- **150 Neunzer**
- **322 Newell**
- **330 O'Reilly**
- **152 Peterson**
- **133 Pillsbury**
- **151 Poole**
- **134 Pope**
- **332 Price** (Oct. 30, 1943)
- **323 Pride**
- **132 Robert E. Peary**
- **336 Roy O. Hale**
- **333 Strickland** (Nov. 2, 1943)
- **326 Thomas J. Gary**

Displacement: 1,200 tons (1,490 tons *full load*). Complement: 220. Dimensions: 306 (*o.a.*) × 36⅝ × 10⅝ feet. Guns: 3—3 inch, 50 cal., d.p., 2—40 mm. AA., 4—20 mm. AA. and D.C.T. Tubes: 3—21 inch. Machinery: Fairbanks-Morse Diesels. 2 shafts. B.H.P.: 6,000 = 20 kts. War losses: *Fiske, Frederick C. Davis, Holder, Leopold.*

43 Evarts Class.

LOVERING. 1944, *U.S. Navy Official.*

12 *Boston Navy Yard:*
- **10 Bebas**
- **265 Cloues**
- **11 Crouter**
- **5 Evarts**
- **7 Griswold**
- **528 John J. Powers** (1943)
- **530 John M. Bermingham** (Nov. 17, 1943)
- **529 Mason** (Nov. 17, 1943)
- **527 O'Toole** (1943)
- **257 Smartt**
- **8 Steele** (May 3, 1943)
- **258 Walter S. Brown** (Feb. 22, 1943)

24 *Mare Island Navy Yard:*
- **13 Brennan**
- **19 Burden R. Hastings**
- **306 Connolly** (April 6, 1944)
- **303 Crowley**
- **26 Dempsey** (April 22, 1943)
- **27 Duffy** (May, 1943)
- **16 Edgar G. Chase** (Sept. 1942)
- **34 Eisele**
- **28 Emery**
- **35 Fair**
- **307 Finnegan** (ex-H.M.S. *Calder*, Feb. 22, 1944)
- **32 Fleming**
- **305 Halloran**
- **21 Harold C. Thomas**
- **301 Lake**
- **20 Le Hardy**
- **302 Lyman**
- **36 Manlove**
- **30 Martin**
- **31 Sederstrom**
- **29 Stadtfeld** (Sept. 19, 1943)
- **33 Tisdale**
- **22 Wileman**
- **25 Wintle** (April 22, 1943)

2 *Philadelphia Navy Yard:*
- **45 Andres**
- **48 Dobler**

5 *Puget Sound Navy Yard:*
- **41 Brackett**
- **44 Donaldson**
- **37 Greiner**
- **39 Lovering** (May 4, 1943)
- **43 Mitchell** (Feb. 8, 1944)

Displacement: 1,150 tons (1,360 tons *full load*). Complement: 200. Dimensions: 283½ (*w.l.*), 289 (*o.a.*) × 35 × 10⅝ feet. Guns: 3—3 inch, 50 cal., dual purpose, 2—40 mm. AA., 4—20 mm. AA., 8 D.C.T. (No tubes.) Machinery: Diesel with electric drive. 2 shafts. H.P. 6,000 = 20 kts. (19 kts. in service).

Notes.—This type was built only in Navy Yards. In addition, 32 were delivered to Royal Navy under Lend-Lease scheme; five of these were lost and the remainder returned to U.S.N. for scrapping.

Fleet Submarines

Note.—All U.S. submarines are painted black.

Electric Boat Co.: **Perch** (Sept. 12, 1943), **Shark** (Oct. 17, 1943), **Sealion** (Oct. 31, 1943), **Barbel** (Nov. 14, 1943), **Barbero** (Dec. 12, 1943), **Baya** (Jan. 2, 1944), **Becuna** (Jan. 30, 1944), **Bergall** (Feb. 16, 1944), **Besugo** (Feb. 27, 1944), **Blackfin** (March 12, 1944).

Portsmouth Navy Yard: **Cabrilla** (Dec. 24, 1942), **Balao** (Nov. 1942), **Billfish** (Nov. 13, 1942), **Bowfin** (Dec. 7, 1942), **Crevalle** (Feb. 22, 1943), **Aspro** (April 7, 1943), **Batfish** (May 3, 1943), **Archerfish** (May 29, 1943), **Burrfish** (June 18, 1943), **Sandlance** (June 25, 1943), **Barche** (July 24, 1943), **Bang, Pilotfish** (both Aug. 30, 1943), **Pintado** (Sept. 15, 1943), **Pipefish** (Oct. 12, 1943), **Piranha, Pomfret, Sterlet** (all three Oct. 27, 1943), **Plaice** (Nov. 15, 1943), **Razorback, Redfish, Ronquil, Scabbardfish** (all four Jan. 27, 1944), **Seacat** (Feb. 21, 1944), **Seadevil** (Feb. 28, 1944), **Atule** (March 6, 1944).

Mare Island Navy Yard: **Seahorse** (Jan. 9, 1943), **Skate** (March 4, 1943), **Tilefish** (Oct. 25, 1943), **Spadefish** (Jan. 8, 1944).

Cramp S.B. Co.: **Dragonet, Escolar** (both April 18, 1943), **Devilfish, Hackleback** (both May 30, 1943), **Lancetfish, Ling** (both Aug. 18, 1943), **Lionfish, Manta** (both Nov. 7, 1943), **Trumpetfish** (Feb. 19, 1944).

Manitowoc S.B. Co.: **Hammerhead** (Nov. 1943), **Icefish** (Feb. 20, 1944).

No information concerning these submarines has been released officially, but it is believed that, to facilitate rapid building, all are of the same general type as *Gar* class, of all-welded construction, and with a high standard of accommodation, including separate messing and sleeping compartments. Average time of construction has been reduced to about nine months. Following particulars are believed to be accurate:

Displacement: 1,525 tons or over. Guns: **1**—4 inch, **2**—20 mm. Oerlikon. Tubes: **10**—21 inch (**6** bow, **4** stern). Machinery: G.M., Fairbanks-Morse or H.O.R. Diesels. B.H.P. 6,500 = 21 kts. Sundry minor improvements have doubtless been incorporated as results of experience with *Gar* class. All built under 1941–43 Programmes. War losses: *Capelin, Cisco* (both Portsmouth).

6 Salmon Class.

SNAPPER. *Added* 1940, *O. W. Waterman.*

3 *Electric Boat Co.:* **Salmon, Seal, Skipjack.**
2 *Portsmouth Navy Yard:* **Snapper, Stingray.**
1 *Mare Island Navy Yard:* **Sturgeon.**
Displacement: 1,450/2,198 tons (first 3), 1,445 tons (others). Dimensions: 298 (*w.l.*) × 26 × 14¼ feet (*mean*). Guns: **1**—4 inch, **2**—20 mm. Oerlikon. Tubes: **8**—21 inch (4 bow, 4 stern). H.O.R. Diesels in first 3, Fairbanks-Morse in others. Complement: 62.

Name and No.	*Laid down*	*Launched*	*Completed*	*Name and No.*	*Laid down*	*Launched*	*Completed*
Salmon (182)	15/4/36	12/6/37	/38	*Snapper* (185)	23/7/36	24/8/37	1/3/38
Seal (183)	25/5/36	25/8/37	/38	*Stingray* (186)	1/10/36	6/10/37	30/6/38
Skipjack (184)	22/7/36	23/10/37	/38	*Sturgeon* (187)	27/10/36	15/3/38	2/9/38

3 Plunger Class.

PLUNGER. (Now carries Pendant No. 179). 1938, *O. W. Waterman.*

1 *Electric Boat Co.:* **Permit** (ex-*Pinna*).
2 *Portsmouth Navy Yard:* **Plunger, Pollack.**
Displacement: 1,330/1,998 tons (except *Plunger* and *Pollack*, 1,335 tons). Complement: 57. Dimensions: 290 (*w.l.*), 300½ (*o.a.*) × 25 × 13¾ feet (*mean* draught). Guns: **1**—4 inch, **2**—20 mm. Oerlikon. Tubes: **6**—21 inch. Winton Diesels in *Permit*, with G.E. motors; Fairbanks-Morse Diesels and Elliott motors in *Plunger* and *Pollack*. War losses: *Perch, Pickerel, Pompano.* Cost averages $2,400,000 each unarmed.

Name and No.	*Laid down*	*Launched*	*Completed*	*Name and No.*	*Laid down*	*Launched*	*Completed*
Permit (178)	6/6/35	5/10/36	17/3/37	*Pollack* (180)	1/10/35	15/9/36	28/4/37
Plunger (179)	17/7/35	8/7/36	31/3/37				

3 Pike Class.

PORPOISE. (Now carries Pendant No. 172). 1937, *O. W. Waterman.*

2 *Portsmouth Navy Yard:* **Pike, Porpoise.** Displacement: 1,310/1,934 tons. Dimensions: 283 (*w.l.*), 301 (*o.a.*) × 25 × 13 feet (*mean*). Winton Diesels. Elliott motors.

1 *Electric Boat Co.:* **Tarpon.** Displacement: 1,315/1,968 tons. Dimensions: 287 (*w.l.*), 298 (*o.a.*) × 25 × 13¾ feet (*mean*). Winton Diesels, with electric drive. Elliott motors.

Both types: Complement: 57. Guns: **1**—4 inch, **2**—20 mm. Tubes: **6**—21 inch. Speed: 20/10 kts. First all-welded submarines in U.S. Navy. Radius of this and succeeding classes approaches 12,000 miles.

Name and No.	*Laid down*	*Launched*	*Completed*	*Name and No.*	*Laid down*	*Launched*	*Completed*
Porpoise (172)	27/10/33	20/6/35	15/1/36	*Tarpon* (175)	22/12/33	4/9/35	12/3/36
Pike (173)	20/12/33	12/9/35	17/4/36	War loss: *Shark* (174).			

2 Cachalot Class.

CUTTLEFISH. (Now carries Pendant No. 170). 1935, *O. W. Waterman.*

Cachalot (***170,*** ex-*V*.8) Portsmouth Navy Yard. Laid down Oct. 21, 1931. Launched Oct. 19, 1933. Completed March 1, 1934. **Cuttlefish** (***171,*** ex-*V*.9) Electric Boat Co. Laid down Oct. 7, 1931. Launched Nov. 21, 1933. Completed June, 1934.

Respective displacements: 1,110 and 1,120/1,650 tons. Complement, 52. Dimensions: 260 (*w.l.*), 271⅓ (*o.a.*) × 24¾ × 12⅚ feet (*Cachalot*): 25 × 12¾ (*Cuttlefish*). Machinery: 2 sets G.M. "V" type Diesels. H.P.: 3,400/800 = 17/9 kts. Armament: 1—3 inch AA. Tubes: **6**—21 inch. All-welded construction. Guns mounted abaft C.T. in this and subsequent classes. No external torpedo stowage.

Note.—Owing to design of original engines (with direct drive) having proved unsatisfactory, *Cachalot* and *Cuttlefish* were given new machinery under 1936 Programme.

DOLPHIN. (Now carries Pendant No. 169). 1935, *O. W. Waterman.*

Dolphin (***169,*** ex-*V*.7) Portsmouth Navy Yard. Laid down June 14, 1930. Launched March 8, 1932. Completed Oct. 14th, 1932.

Displacement: 1,540/2,215 tons. Complement, 64. Dimensions: 307 (*w.l.*), 319 (*o.a.*) × 27⅞ × 13 feet. M.A.N. Diesels, H.P.: 4,200 = 17 kts. *surface.* Electric motors, H.P.: 875 = 8 kts. *submerged.* Guns: **1**—4 inch, 50 cal., Tubes: **6**—21 inch + 3 Torpedoes stowed externally.

2 Narwhal Class.

NAUTILUS. (Now carries Pendant No. 168). *Added*, 1938, *Wide World Photos.*

Narwhal (***167,*** ex-*V*.5) (Dec. 17, 1929), **Nautilus** (***168,*** ex-*V*.6) (March 15, 1930). Laid down at Portsmouth and Mare Island Navy Yards, respectively, May 10 and August 2, 1927. Displacement: 2,730/3,960 tons. Dimensions: 371 (*o.a.*), 349 (*w.l.*) × 33¼ × 15¾ feet (*mean*). Armament: **2**—6 inch, **4**—20 mm Oerlikon, **10**—21 inch tubes. Fairbanks-Morse Diesels, H.P. 10,000 = 20 kts. *surface.* Westinghouse electric motors, H.P. 2,540 = 8·5 kts. *submerged.* Complement, 90. Estimated cost: Hull and machinery, $5,350,000; armament, $1,020,000. Authorised 1916 as Nos. 167–168. Completed July 21 and Oct. 18, 1930, respectively.

Note.—Also carry eight external Torpedo Stowage Tubes, two each side fore and aft under the half-deck amidships. Neither vessel could exceed 14 kts. with original engines, which were replaced in 1940–41 by Fairbanks, Morse & Co. for the sum of $2,850,000 for the 2 vessels. Number of tubes was increased at the same time. War loss: *Argonaut* (of similar displacement but differing in design).

3 Barracuda Class.

BONITA. (Now carries Pendant No. 165). 1935, *O. W. Waterman.*

3 *Bureau* design: **Barracuda** (ex-*V*.1), **Bass** (ex-*V*.2), **Bonita** (ex-*V*.3). Built at Portsmouth Navy Yard. Displacement: 2,000/2,506 tons. Complement: 80. Dimensions: 326 (*w.l.*), 341½ (*o.a.*) × 27 $\frac{1}{12}$ × 14½ feet. Guns: **1**—3 inch AA., 2 M.G. Tubes: **6**—21 inch. 16 torpedoes carried. Machinery: 2 sets Busch-Sulzer Diesels aft for main drive. H.P.: 6,700 = 18·75 kts. on *surface.* Also 2 sets M.A.N. auxiliary Diesels forward driving generators supplying current to electric motors, H.P.: 2,400 = 8 kts. *submerged.* Latter combination can be used for cruising on surface with electric drive. Radius of action: 12,000 miles. Designed speed never realised in service with original machinery, but have now been re-engined. Armament probably improved at the same time.

Name & No.	*Laid down*	*Launched*	*Compl.*	*Name & No.*	*Laid down*	*Launched*	*Compl.*
Barracuda (163)	20/10/21	17/7/24	1/11/24	*Bonita* (165)	16/11/21	9/6/25	17/6/26
Bass (164)	20/10/21	27/12/24	26/9/25				

36 "S" Classes.

Note on S Class.—An official report in 1925 stated that "experience in manœuvres indicates that these vessels cannot be considered as a satisfactory type of fleet submarines." All were taken in hand for refit and recommissioning in 1940–41.

S 47. 1943.

5 *Electric Boat Co.* design: ***S42, S43, S45, S46, S47*** (1923–24). All contracted for by Electric Boat Co.; hulls sub-contracted for by Bethlehem S.B. Co., Quincy. Authorised 1916–18. Displacement: 850/1,126 tons. Dimensions: $225\frac{1}{4} \times 20\frac{2}{3} \times 15$ feet. Guns: **1**—3 inch AA. Tubes: **4**—21 inch. **12** torpedoes carried. Machinery: Two sets 8-cylinder, 4-cycle Nelseco Diesels and 2 sets Elect. Dy. Co. motors. B.H.P.: 1,200/1,500 = 14·5/11 kts. Oil: 11,463—46,363 gallons. Complement: 45.

1 *Bureau* design: ***S 48*** (1921). By Lake T. B. Co. Displacement: 1000/1458 tons. Dimensions: 266 (*w.l.*), 267 (*o.a.*) $21\frac{5}{6} \times 13\frac{1}{4}$ feet. Guns: **1**—3 inch AA. Tubes: **5**—21 inch (4 bow, 1 stern). **14** torpedoes carried. Machinery: 2 sets M.A.N. (N.Y.) 4-cycle 6-cyl. Diesels and 2 sets electric motors. B.H.P.: 2,000/2,000 = 14·5/11 kts. (See note below.) Crash dive in 60 secs. *Max.* dive limit: 200 feet. Divided into 6 watertight compartments. Double hull amidships, single hull at ends. 3 periscopes. Oil: 23,411 gallons *normal*, 44,305 *max.* Radius: 8,000 at 10 kts. Authorised 1916. Complement: 45.

Note.—*S* 48 is stated to have been re-engined in 1929 with two new motors of 1000 H.P. each, oil storage being increased at same time. She underwent an extensive refit at Cristobal in 1938.

S 22. 1940, "*Ships and Aircraft.*"

22 *Electric Boat Co.* design: ***S 1, S 18, S 20—24, S 27—41*** (1918–22). All contracted for by Electric Boat Co., and sub-contracted for as follows: *S*1 by Fore River S.B. Co., *S* 18—*S* 29 by Bethlehem S.B. Co., Quincy, *S* 30—*S* 41 by Bethlehem S.B. Co., San Francisco. Displacement: 800/1,062 tons. Dimensions: $219\frac{1}{4} \times 20\frac{2}{3} \times 15$ feet. Machinery: 2 sets Nelseco Diesel engines. Motors: 2 sets Ridgeway or Electric Dynamic Co. (*S* 1). B.H.P.: 1,200/1,500 = 14·5/10·5 kts. Oil: 11,511/41,921 gallons. Have large radius of action *on surface*. Armament: **1**—3 inch AA. and **4**—21 inch bow tubes (**12** torpedoes carried). Authorised: *S* 1 (1916, as No. 105), *S* 18—21 (1916–17 as Nos. 123—126), *S* 22—41 (1916–17, as Nos. 127—146). *S*1 experimentally fitted, 1923, to carry a small seaplane in a cylindrical tank abaft C.T.

Note.—*S* 30 built at expense of Philippines Government. *S* 19 scrapped, 1937. *S* 20 used for experimental work. *S* 25 transferred to Polish Navy, Nov. 1941, and subsequently lost. *S* 26 lost in Jan. 1942.

3 *Bureau* design: ***S11—13*** (1919–21); all by Portsmouth Ny. Yd. Displacement: 790/1,092 tons. Dimensions: $231 \times 21\frac{5}{8} \times 13\frac{1}{12}$ feet. Guns: **1**—3 inch AA. Tubes: **5**—21 inch (**14** torpedoes carried). Machinery: 2 sets of 4-cycle "Bureau Design" M.A.N. (6-cyl.) Diesels and 2 sets 600 H.P. Westinghouse electric motors. B.H.P.: 2,000/1,200 = 15/10·5 kts. Oil: 19,271/36,950 gallons. Completed 1919–23, and numbered 116—118. *S* 4 sunk by collision on Dec. 17, 1927; salved March, 1928. After being used as a special vessel for experimental purposes, she was scuttled in 1936. Other numbers scrapped.

4 *Bureau* design: ***S 14—S 17*** (1919—20). All by Lake T.B. Co. Displacement: 790/1,092 tons. Dimensions: $231 \times 21\frac{5}{8} \times 13$ feet. Guns: **1**—3 inch AA. Tubes: **4**—21 inch (**12** torpedoes carried). Machinery: 2 sets M.A.N. (N.Y.) 4-cycle 6-cyl. Diesels. B.H.P.: 2,000 = 14 kts. *surface*. **2** sets Westinghouse electric motors. B.H.P.: 1200 = 12 kts. *submerged*. Complement, 38. Oil, 19,271/36,950 gallons. Official Nos. 119—122.

Coastal Submarines.

2 Mackerel Class.

MACKEREL. 1941, *U.S.N. official.*

1 *Electric Boat Co.*: ***Mackerel.*** (204). (Sept. 28, 1940).
1 *Portsmouth Navy Yard*: ***Marlin.*** (205). (Jan. 29, 1941).

Displacement: 800 tons. Dimensions: 231 (*pp.*), 253 (*o.a.*) $\times 21\frac{1}{2} \times 12$ feet. Guns: **1**—3 inch, **2** M.G. T.T., **6**—21 inch (4 bow, 2 stern). Machinery: Nelseco Diesels in *Mackerel*. American Locomotive Co. Diesels in *Marlin*. Electric Dynamic motors. B.H.P.: 1,600 = 14·5 kts. Provided for under 1939 Programme as Nos. 204, 205. *Mackerel* laid down Oct. 6, 1939, *Marlin*, May 28, 1940. Both completed in 1941. Trials gave a speed of 16 knots. Submerged speed reported to be 11 kts. (?)

17 "R" Class.

Official, added 1935.

17 *Electric Boat Co.* design: ***R1, 2, 4—7, 9—11, 13—20*** (1917–19). Contracted for by Electric Boat Co. Sub-contract assigned as follows: *R* 1 to *R* 14 by Fore River S.B. Co., *R* 15—20 by Union I.W. San Francisco. Displacement 530/680 tons. Dimensions: $186 \times 18 \times 13\frac{2}{3}$ feet. Armament: **1**—3 inch, 50 cal. gun, **4** torpedo tubes (8 torpedoes carried). Engines: 2 sets of 440 B.H.P. (400 r.p.m.) 6-cyl. 4-cycle Nelseco Diesel. Fuel: 7,691/18,880 gallons. Motors: 2—467 H.P. Electric Dynamic Co., with Cutler-Hammer Co. magnetic controllers. Batteries: Electric Storage Co. Type 31-WLL. Speed: 13·5/10 kts. *R* 1—20 were authorised 1916 as Nos. 78—97. Completed 1918-19 and mostly refitted 1940–41. *R* 3 transferred to Royal Navy in Nov. 1941. *R* 12 lost in 1943.

7 "O" Class.

O 6. 1920 *Photo.*

7 *Electric Boat Co.* design: ***O 2, 3, 4, 6, 7, 8, 10*** (1917–18), viz. *O* 2 by Puget Sound Navy Yard; others contracted for by Electric Boat Co. and sub-contracted for by Fore River Co. Dimensions: $172\frac{1}{3} \times 18 \times 14\frac{1}{2}$ feet. Displacement: 480/624 tons. **1**—3 inch, 23 cal. AA. gun. **4** torpedo tubes (8 torpedoes). Engines: 2 sets of 440 B.H.P. (400 r.p.m.) 6-cyl. 4-cycle Nelseco Diesel engines. Speed: 14/10 kts. Fuel: 10,089/21,897 gallons. Motors: 2—370 H.P. in *O* 2, by New York Navy Yard; in others, by Electric Dynamic Co., all with Cutler-Hammer Co. magnetic controller. Gould storage batteries, Type 29-WLL in *O* 2. Electric Storage Co., Type 49-WLL in others. Electric batteries weigh 65 tons. Radius of action: 3,500/3,000 miles, at 11 kts. *on surface*. Authorised 1915, as Nos. 63—71. Completed 1918. Complement: 32.

Note.—*O* 5 wrecked, Oct. 28, 1923, and not considered worth repair after salvage. *O* 1 converted into an experimental vessel, 1937, and discarded following year. *O* 9 foundered June 20, 1941.

Submarines

Notes.—Ex-German submarines *U* 234, 505, 530, 858, 873, 1105, 1406, 2513 and 3008 have been retained for experimental purposes, *U* 505 being temporarily renamed ***Nemo.*** In Nov. 1946, *U* 977 was expended in trials of a new type of torpedo. It is proposed to lay down two new submarines of 2,000 tons which will embody all improvements devised as result of study of German designs and war experience.

23 Corsair Class.

1946, *courtesy R. Lloyd Gwilt, Esq.*

CUTLASS 1944, *U.S. Navy Official.*

4 *Boston Navy Yard:*
Amberjack (Dec. 15, 1944)
Grampus (Dec. 15, 1944)
Grenadier (Dec. 15, 1944)
Pickerel (Dec. 15, 1944)

3 *Electric Boat Co.:*
Corsair (April 19, 1946)
Unicorn (Aug. 1, 1946)
Walrus (Sept. 20, 1946)

16 *Portsmouth Navy Yard:*
Argonaut (Oct. 1, 1944)
Conger (Oct. 17, 1944)
Cutlass (Nov. 5, 1944)
Diablo (Nov. 30, 1944)
Irex (Jan. 26, 1945)
Medregal (Dec. 15, 1944)
Odax (April 10, 1945)
Pomodon (Dec. 6, 1945)
Remora (Dec. 7, 1945)
Requin (Jan. 1, 1945)
Runner (Oct. 17, 1944)
Sarda (Aug. 24, 1945)
Sea Leopard (March 2, 1945)
Sirago (May 11, 1945)
Spinax (Nov. 20, 1945)
Volador (Jan. 17, 1946)

Displacement: 1,570 tons. No other particulars released, but appear to be an enlarged and improved version of *Balao* design. Guns: **1**—5 inch, 25 cal., **2**—40 mm. AA. Tubes: **10**—21 inch.

Note.—93 more of this class were cancelled during 1944–45, including *Chicolar, Comber, Dorado, Grayling, Needlefish* (493), *Pompano, Sculpin, Tiburon, Wahoo* (516). Completion of *Grampus, Grenadier, Pickerel, Unicorn, Volador* and *Walrus* temporarily suspended, 1946, with a view to incorporating novel features based on experiments with German prize submarines. *Irex* is being fitted with a "Schnorkel" breathing tube, the first of 80 submarines to be so equipped.

Pendant Nos. of "Corsair" Class.

4 *Boston Navy Yard:* 522–525.
3 *Electric Boat Co.:* 435–437.
16 *Portsmouth Navy Yard:* 475–490.

120 Balao Class.

HAWKBILL. (In later units, numbered 408 and above, gun is before C.T.) 1946, *Ted Stone.*

13 *Cramp S.B. Co.:*
Devilfish (May 30, 1943)
Dragonet (April 18, 1943)
Hackleback (May 30, 1943)
Lancetfish (Aug. 18, 1943)
Ling (Aug. 18, 1943)
Lionfish (Nov. 7, 1943)
Manta (Nov. 7, 1943)
Moray (May 14, 1944)
Roncador (May 14, 1944)
Sabalo (June 4, 1944)
Sablefish (June 4, 1944)
Trumpetfish (Feb. 19, 1944)
Tusk (July 8, 1945)

41 *Electric Boat Co.*
Archerfish (May 29, 1943)
Aspro (ex-*Acedia*, April 7, 1943)
Barbero (Dec. 12, 1943)
Batfish (ex-*Acoupa*, May 3, 1943)
Baya (Jan. 2, 1944)
Becuna (Jan. 30, 1944)
Bergall (Feb. 16, 1944)
Besugo (Feb. 27, 1944)
Blackfin (March 12, 1944)
Blenny (April 9, 1944)
Blower (April 23, 1944)
Blueback (May 7, 1944)
Boarfish (May 21, 1944)
Brill (June 25, 1944)
Bugara (July 2, 1944)
Bumper (Aug. 6, 1944)
Burrfish (ex-*Amillo*, June 18, 1943)
Cabezon (Aug. 27, 1944)
Caiman (ex-*Blanquillo*, March 30, 1944)
Capitaine (Oct. 1, 1944)
Carbonero (Oct. 15, 1944)
Carp (Nov. 12, 1944)
Catfish (Nov. 19, 1944)
Charr (ex-*Bocaccio*, May 28, 1944)
Chivo (Jan. 14, 1945)
Chopper (Feb. 14, 1945)
Chub (ex-*Bonaci*, June 18, 1944)
Clamagore (Feb. 23, 1945)
Cobbler (April 1, 1945)
Cochino (April 16, 1945)
Corporal (June 10, 1945)
Cubera (June 17, 1945)
Cusk (July 28, 1945)
Dentuda (Sept. 10, 1944)
Diodon (Sept. 10, 1945)
Dogfish (Oct. 27, 1945)
Entemedor (ex-*Chickwick*, Dec. 17, 1944)
Greenfish (ex-*Doncella*, Dec. 21, 1945)
Halfbeak (ex-*Dory*, Feb. 19, 1946)
Perch (Sept. 12, 1943)
Sealion (Oct. 31, 1943)

15 *Manitowoc S.B. Co.:*
Guavina (Aug. 29, 1943)
Guitarro (Sept. 26, 1943)
Hammerhead (Oct. 27, 1943)
Hardhead (Dec. 12, 1943)
Hawkbill (Jan. 9, 1944)
Icefish (Feb. 20, 1944)
Jallao (March 12, 1944)
Kraken (April 30, 1944)
Lamprey (June 18, 1944)
Lizardfish (July 16, 1944)
Loggerhead (Aug. 13, 1944)
Macabi (Sept. 19, 1944)
Mapiro (Nov. 9, 1944)
Menhaden (Dec. 20, 1944)
Mero (Jan. 17, 1945)

9 *Mare Island Navy Yard:*
Seahorse (Jan. 9, 1943)
Skate (March 4, 1943)
Spadefish (Jan. 8, 1944)
Spot (May 20, 1944)
Springer (Aug. 3, 1944)
Stickleback (Jan. 1, 1944)
Tilefish (Oct. 25, 1943)
Tiru
Trepang (March 23, 1944)

42 *Portsmouth Navy Yard:*
Atule (March 6, 1944)
Balao (Nov. 1942)
Bang (Aug. 30, 1943)
Billfish (Nov. 13, 1942)
Bowfin (Dec. 7, 1943)
Cabrilla (Dec. 4, 1942)
Crevalle (Feb. 22, 1943)
Pampanito (July 12, 1943)
Parche (July 24, 1943)
Picuda (ex-*Obispo*, July 12, 1943)
Pintado (Sept. 15, 1943)
Pipefish (Oct. 12, 1943)
Piper (ex-*Awa*, June 26, 1944)
Piranha (Oct. 27, 1943)
Plaice (Nov. 15, 1943)
Pomfret (Oct. 27, 1943)
Queenfish (Nov. 30, 1943)
Quillback (ex-*Trembler*, Oct. 1, 1944)
Razorback (Jan. 27, 1944)
Redfish (Jan. 27, 1944)
Ronquil (Jan. 27, 1944)
Sandlance (ex-*Orca*, ex-*Ojanco*, June 25, 1943)
Scabbardfish (Jan. 27, 1944)
Seacat (Feb. 21, 1944)
Seadevil (Feb. 28, 1944)
Seadog (March 28, 1944)
Seafox (March 28, 1944)
Sea Owl (May 7, 1944)
Sea Poacher (May 20, 1944)
Sea Robin (May 25, 1944)
Segundo (Feb. 5, 1944)
Sennet (June 6, 1944)
Spikefish (ex-*Shiner*, April 26, 1944)
Sterlet (Oct. 27, 1943)
Tench (July 7, 1944)
Thornback (July 7, 1944)
Threadfin (ex-*Sole*, June 26, 1944)
Tigrone (July 20, 1944)
Tirante (Aug. 9, 1944)
Toro (Aug. 19, 1944)
Torsk (Sept. 6, 1944)
Trutta (Aug. 18, 1944)

Displacement: 1,526 tons. Dimensions: $311\frac{3}{4} \times 27\frac{1}{8} \times 13\frac{3}{4}$ feet. Guns: **1**—3 inch, 50 cal., d.p., **2**—40 mm. AA. (Some have **1**—4 inch; others, **1**—5 inch 25 cal.) Tubes: **10**—21 inch (**6** bow, **4** stern). Machinery: G.M., Fairbanks-Morse or H.O.R. 2-stroke Diesels. B.H.P.: 6,500 = 21 kts. Complement, 75. War losses: *Barbel, Bullhead, Capelin, Cisco, Escolar, Golet, Kete, Lagarto, Shark, Tang.* 18 cancelled: *Dugong, Eel, Espada, Garloppa, Garuppa, Goldring, Jawfish, Needlefish* (379), *Nerka, Ono, Turbot, Ulua, Unicorn, Vandace, Walrus, Whitefish, Whiting, Wolffish.* Construction of *Tiru* was suspended, and *Apogon* and *Pilotfish* were scrapped, in 1946.

Notes.
—In order to facilitate rapid building, all are of the same general type as *Gato* class, of all-welded construction, and with a high standard of accommodation, including separate messing and sleeping compartments. Average time of construction during war was reduced to about nine months.

Pendant Nos. of "Balao" Class.

13 *Cramp S.B. Co.:* SS. 292, 293, 295–303, 425, 426.
42 *Electric Boat Co.:* 308–313, 315, 317–331, 333–352.
15 *Manitowoc S.B. Co.:* 362–368, 370, 372–378.
9 *Mare Island Navy Yard:* 304, 305, 307, 411–416.
43 *Portsmouth Navy Yard:* 285–288, 291, 381–410, 417–424.

54 Gato Class (*1939–41 Programmes*).

ROCK. (Most of class have principal gun abaft C.T.) 1944, *U.S. Navy, Official.*

31 *Electric Boat Co.:* ***Angler, Barb, Bashaw, Blackfish, Bluefish, Bluegill, Bream, Cavalla, Cero, Cobia, Cod, Croaker, Dace, Flasher, Flounder, Gabilan, Gato, Greenling, Grouper, Guardfish, Gunnel, Gurnard, Haddo, Hake, Hoe, Jack, Lapon, Mingo, Muskallonge, Paddle, Pargo.***

9 *Portsmouth Navy Yard:* ***Drum, Finback, Flying Fish, Haddock, Halibut, Kingfish, Sawfish, Shad, Steelhead.***

5 *Mare Island Navy Yard:* ***Silversides, Sunfish, Tinosa, Tunny, Whale.***

9 *Manitowoc S.B. Co.:* ***Peto, Pogy, Pompon, Puffer, Rasher, Raton, Ray, Redfin, Rock.***

Displacement: 1,525 tons. Dimensions: 307 × 27 × 14 feet. Guns: **1**—3 inch, 50 cal., d.p., **2**—20 mm. Oerlikon. Tubes: **10**—21 inch (6 bow, 4 stern). Machinery: G.M. Diesels and electric motors. Have 2 engine-rooms instead of 1 as in *Tambor* class, to reduce size of compartments. B.H.P.: 6,500 = 21 kts. Complement: 65 to 74. Are improved editions of *Tambor* class. Inclusive cost per ship officially estimated at $6,288,200. War losses: *Albacore, Amberjack, Bonefish, Corvina, Darter, Dorado, Flier, Growler, Grunion, Harder, Herring, Robalo, Runner, Scamp, Scorpion, Snook, Trigger, Tullibee, Wahoo.*

HAKE. 1944, *U.S. Navy Official.*

Fleet Submarines and Minelayers

GAR. 1944, *U.S. Navy Official.*

(Missing numbers have been lost.)

No.	*Name*	*Laid down*	*Launched*	*Completed*
212	*Gato*	5/10/40	21/8/41	42
213	*Greenling*	12/11/40	20/9/41	42
214	*Grouper*	28/12/40	27/10/41	42
217	*Guardfish*	1/4/41	20/1/42	42
220	*Barb*	7/6/41	2/4/42	42
221	*Blackfish*	7/41	18/4/42	42
222	*Bluefish*	8/41	21/2/43	43
224	*Cod*	42	21/3/43	43
225	*Cero*	42	4/4/43	43
228	*Drum*	11/9/40	12/5/41	11/41
229	*Flying Fish*	6/12/40	9/7/41	12/41
230	*Finback*	5/2/41	25/8/41	42
231	*Haddock*	31/3/41	20/10/41	42
232	*Halibut*	41	3/12/41	42
234	*Kingfish*	8/41	2/3/42	42
235	*Shad*	10/41	15/4/42	42
236	*Silversides*	4/11/40	26/8/41	42
239	*Whale*	28/6/41	14/3/42	42
240	*Angler*	42	4/7/43	43
241	*Bashaw*	42	25/7/43	43
242	*Bluegill*	42	8/8/43	43
243	*Bream*	43	17/10/43	44
244	*Cavalla*	43	14/11/43	44
245	*Cobia*	43	28/11/43	44
246	*Croaker*	43	19/12/43	44
247	*Dace*	22/7/42	25/4/43	43
249	*Flasher*		20/6/43	43
251	*Flounder*		22/8/43	43
252	*Gabilan*		19/9/43	43
253	*Gunnel*	21/7/41	17/5/42	42
254	*Gurnard*	9/41	1/6/42	42
255	*Haddo*	10/41	21/6/42	42
256	*Hake*	11/41	7/42	42
258	*Hoe*	42	17/9/42	42
259	*Jack*	42	16/10/42	43
260	*Lapon*	42	27/10/42	
261	*Muskallonge*	42	13/12/42	
262	*Paddie*	42	30/12/42	
263	*Mingo*	42	30/11/42	
264	*Pargo*	42	24/1/43	
265	*Peto*	18/6/41	30/4/42	21/11/42
266	*Pogy*	10/41	22/6/42	43
267	*Pompon*	11/41	8/42	43
268	*Puffer*	42	22/11/42	43
269	*Rasher*			
270	*Raton*			
271	*Ray*	42	43	43
272	*Redfin*			
274	*Rock*			
276	*Sawfish*	41	23/6/42	42
280	*Steelhead*	42	11/9/42	43
281	*Sunfish*	41	2/5/42	42
282	*Tunny*	10/11/41	1/7/42	42
283	*Tinosa*	42	8/10/42	43

5 Tambor Class (*1938 Programme*).

THRESHER. 1941, *U.S. Navy, Official.*

4 *Electric Boat Co.:* ***Gar, Tambor, Tautog, Thresher.***
1 *Mare Island Navy Yard:* ***Tuna.***

Displacement: 1,475 tons. Dimensions: 299 × 27 × $13\frac{3}{4}$ feet. Guns: **1**—4 inch, **2**—20 mm. Oerlikon. Tubes: **10**—21 inch (6 bow, 4 stern). Machinery: G.M. Diesels in first 3, Fairbanks-Morse in others, with all-electric drive. B.H.P.: 6,400 = 21 kts. (22 kts. reached on trials). Complement: 65. Differ from *Sargo* type in silhouette, hull form, and internal lay-out. Double-hull construction, with external control room as in German submarines. Bilge keels are fitted.

Name & No.	*Laid down*	*Launched*	*Completed*
Gar (206)	27/12/39	7/11/40	14/4/41
Tambor (198)	16/1/39	20/12/39	3/6/40
Tautog (199)	1/3/39	27/1/40	3/7/40
Thresher (200)	27/4/39	27/3/40	27/8/40
Tuna (203)	19/7/39	2/10/40	41

War losses: *Grampus, Grayback, Grayling, Grenadier, Gudgeon* (207–211), *Triton* (201), *Trout* (202). Remaining units of class will be discarded in near future.

3 Sargo Class (*1936–37 Programmes*).

SAILFISH. 1940, *courtesy "The Motor Boat".*

1 *Electric Boat Co.:* ***Seadragon,***
2 *Portsmouth Navy Yard:* ***Searaven, Sailfish*** (ex-*Squalus*).

Displacement: 1,475 tons. Complement: 62. Dimensions: 299 (*w.l.*), 310 (*o.a.*) × 27 × $13\frac{3}{4}$ feet (*mean*). Guns: **1**—4 inch, **2**—20 mm. Oerlikon. Tubes: **8**—21 inch (4 bow, 4 stern). Machinery: G.M. Diesels. B.H.P.: 6,140 = 20 kts.

Name and No.	*Laid down*	*Launched*	*Completed*
Sailfish (192)	18/10/37	14/9/38	12/5/40
Seadragon (194)	18/4/38	21/4/39	1940
Searaven (196)	9/8/38	21/6/39	1940

Notes.
—Cost about $5,000,000 each. *Squalus* foundered May 23, 1939, but was salved and renamed *Sailfish* in Feb. 1940. Repairs cost about $1,000,000. War losses: *Sculpin* (191), *Sealion* (195), *Seawolf* (197), *Swordfish* (193). All this class to be discarded shortly, as three of them already have been.

Minelayers.

LINDSEY. 1944, *U.S. Navy Official.*

SHEA. 1944, U.S. *Navy Official.*

Following 10 modern Destroyers have been fitted as Minelayers.

ADAMS, GWIN, HARRY F. BAUER, HENRY A. WILEY, LINDSEY, ROBERT H. SMITH, SHANNON, SHEA, THOMAS E. FRASER, TOLMAN. Displacement: 2,200 tons. All described on an earlier page, under *Allen M. Sumner* class of Destroyers. Numbered DM 23—30, 32, 33.

TERROR. 1943, *U.S. Navy Official.*

TERROR (June 6, 1941). Built at Philadelphia Navy Yard, under 1938 Programme. Displacement: 5,875 tons. Complement: 400. Dimensions: $453\frac{5}{6}$ (*o.a.*) × $60\frac{1}{6}$ × — feet. Guns: **4**—5 inch, 38 cal., numerous 40 mm. and 20 mm. Machinery: Geared turbines. 2 shafts. B.H.P.: 11,000=19 kts. Distinctive number is CM 5.

Training Ship

Gunnery Training Ship.

MISSISSIPPI before conversion. 1944, *U.S. Navy Official.*

MISSISSIPPI (Jan. 25, 1917). Displacement: 33,000 tons. Dimensions: 600 (*w.l.*), 624 (*o.a.*) × 106¼ × 29¼ feet (*mean* draught). Guns: Not yet reported. Machinery: Westinghouse geared turbines. 4 shafts. S.H.P.: 40,000 = 22 kts. Boilers: 6 Bureau Express. Oil fuel: 2,200 tons.

Note.—Built by Newport News S.B. Co. as a unit of *New Mexico* class, but converted into a Training Ship at Norfolk Navy Yard, 1947, to replace *Wyoming* (scrapped). Numbered AG 128.

Fast Minesweepers (Modified Destroyers.)

KNIGHT. 1946, *U.S. Navy Official.*

HAMBLETON 1946.

Following 23 modern Destroyers have been fitted for minesweeping, and were classed as Fast Minesweepers during war in Pacific:

BUTLER, CARMICK, COWIE, DAVISON, DORAN, DOYLE, ELLYSON, ENDICOTT, FITCH, FORREST, GHERARDI, HALE, HAMBLETON, HARDING, HOBSON, JEFFERS, KNIGHT, McCOOK, MACOMB, MERVINE, QUICK, RODMAN, THOMPSON. Displacement: 1,700 tons.

All will be found described on an earlier page, under *Buchanan* class of Destroyers. Numbered DMS 19—21, 23—30. War loss: *Emmons.*

Note.—Following 42 ex-German fleet minesweepers were taken over, but are unlikely to be retained permanently: *M* 4, 9, 12, 21, 32, 35, 81, 202, 205, 251-253, 278, 294, 328, 371, 373-375, 388, 389, 441, 453, 460, 495, 502, 509, 510, 528, 545, 572, 581, 582, 598, 606-611, 801, 803.

Fleet Minesweepers

63 Auk Class.

Added 1946, *U.S. Navy Official*

1 *Norfolk Navy Yard:* **AUK** (Aug. 26, 1941). (*AM* 57.)

14 *American S.B. Co.:* **SEER** (May 23, 1942), **SPEED** (April 18, 1942), **SPRIG** (Sept. 15, 1944), **STAFF** (June 17, 1942), **STEADY** (June 6, 1942), **STRIVE** (May 16, 1942), **SURFBIRD** (Aug. 31, 1944), **SUSTAIN** (June 23, 1942), **TANAGER** (Dec. 9, 1944), **TERCEL** (Dec. 16, 1944), **TOUCAN** (Sept. 15, 1944), **TOWHEE** (Jan. 9, 1945), **WAXWING** (March 10, 1945), **WHEATEAR** (April 21, 1945). (*AM* 112, 114, 116–119, 383–390.)

3 *Associated Shipbuilders:* **SPEAR, TRIUMPH** (both Feb. 25, 1943), **VIGILANCE** (April 5, 1943). (*AM* 322–324.)

4 *Defoe S.B. Co.:* **BROADBILL** (May 21, 1942), **CHICKADEE** (July 20, 1942), **NUTHATCH** (Sept. 16, 1942), **PHEASANT** (Oct. 24, 1942.) (*AM* 58–61.)

14 *General Engineering & D.D. Co.:* **ARDENT** (June 22, 1943), **CHAMPION** (Dec. 12, 1942), **CHIEF** (Jan. 5, 1943), **COMPETENT** (Jan. 9, 1943), **DEFENSE** (Feb. 18, 1943), **DEVASTATOR** (April 19, 1943), **GLADIATOR** (May 7, 1943), **HEED** (June 19, 1942), **HERALD** (July 4, 1942), **IMPECCABLE** (May 21, 1943), **MOTIVE** (Aug. 17, 1942), **ORACLE** (Sept. 30, 1942), **SHELDRAKE** (Feb. 12, 1942), **STARLING** (April 11, 1942). (*AM* 62, 64, 100–103, 314–320.)

9 *Gulf S.B. Corpn.:* **DEXTROUS** (Jan. 17, 1943), **ROSELLE** (Aug. 29, 1945), **RUDDY** (Oct. 29,1944), **SCOTER** (Sept. 26, 1945), **SHOVELER** (Dec. 10, 1945), **TOKEN** (March 28, 1942), **TUMULT, VELOCITY** (both April 19, 1942), **ZEAL** (Sept. 15, 1942). (*AM* 126–131, 341, 379–382.)

2 *John H. Mathis Co.:* **SWAY** (Sept. 29, 1942), **SWIFT** (Dec. 5, 1942). (*AM* 120, 122.)

3 *Pennsylvania Shipyard:* **PILOT** (July 5, 1942), **PIONEER** (July 26, 1942), **PREVAIL** (Sept. 13, 1942). (*AM* 104, 105, 107.)

9 *Savannah Machine & Foundry Co.:* **MURRELET** (Dec. 29, 1944), **PEREGRINE** (Feb. 17, 1945), **PIGEON** (March 28, 1945), **POCHARD** (June 11, 1944), **PTARMIGAN** (July 15, 1944), **QUAIL** (Aug. 20, 1944), **REDSTART** (Oct. 18, 1944), **SYMBOL** (July 2, 1942), **THREAT** (Aug. 15, 1942). (*AM* 123, 124, 372–378.)

4 *Winslow Marine Ry. & S.B. Co.:* **PURSUIT** (June 12, 1942), **REQUISITE** (July 25, 1942), **REVENGE** (ex-*Right*, Nov. 7, 1942), **SAGE** (Nov. 21, 1942). (*AM* 108–111.)

Displacement: 890 tons (1,250 tons *full load*). Dimensions: 215 (*w.l.*), 221⅙ (*o.a.*) × 32 × 10¾ feet (*max.*). Guns: 1—3 inch d.p., 2 or 4—40 mm. AA. Machinery: Diesel, with electric drive. 2 shafts. B.H.P.: 2,976–3,532 = 18 kts. Complement: 105. War losses: *Minivet, Portent, Sentinel, Skill, Skylark, Swallow, Swerve, Tide.*

Note.—Following 28 units of above type, transferred to Royal Navy in 1943-4 under Lend-Lease scheme, have been returned, or acquired by Allied navies: H.M.S. *Antares, Arcturus, Aries, Catherine, Chamois, Chance, Clinton, Combatant, Cynthia, Elfreda, Fairy, Florizel, Foam, Frolic, Friendship, Gazelle, Gorgon, Gozo, Grecian, Jasper, Lightfoot, Persian, Pique* (ex-*Celerity*), *Postillion, Steadfast, Strenuous* (ex-*Vital*), *Tattoo, Tourmaline* (ex-*Usage*).

RAVEN. 1941, *U.S. Navy Official.*

1 *Norfolk Navy Yard:* **RAVEN** (Aug. 24, 1940).

Displacement: 810 tons (1,040 tons *full load*). Dimensions: 215 (*w.l.*), 220½ (*o.a.*) × 32 × 9⅓ feet (*mean*). Guns: 1—3 inch d.p., 2—40 mm. AA. Machinery: Diesel. 2 shafts. B.H.P.: 1,800 = 17 kts. Complement: 105. Otherwise similar to *Auk* type.

Fleet Minesweepers

106 Admirable Class.

11 *American S.B. Co.:* **DISDAIN, DOUR** (both March 25, 1944), **EAGER** (June 10, 1944), **JUBILANT** (Feb. 20, 1943), **KNAVE** (March 13, 1943), **LANCE** (April 10, 1943), **MARVEL** (July 31, 1943), **MEASURE, METHOD** (both Oct. 23, 1943), **MIRTH, NIMBLE** (both Dec. 24, 1943). (*AM* 222–224, 255–266.)

9 *Associated Shipbuilders:* **SCURRY** (ex-*Skurry*, Oct. 11, 1943), **SIGNET, SKIRMISH** (both Aug. 16, 1943), **SPECTER, STAUNCH** (both Feb. 15, 1944), **STRATEGY, STRENGTH** (both March 28, 1944), **SUCCESS, SUPERIOR** (both May 11, 1944). (*AM* 302–303, 306–311.)

9 *General Engineering & D.D. Co.:* **RANSOM** (Sept. 18, 1943), **REBEL** (Oct. 28, 1943), **RECRUIT** (Dec. 11, 1943), **REFORM** (Jan. 29, 1944), **REFRESH** (April 12, 1944), **REIGN** (May 29, 1944), **REPORT, REPROOF** (both Aug. 8, 1944), **RISK** (Nov. 7, 1944). (*AM* 283–291).

Admirable. (Appearance varies according to builder; some have a funnel.) 1944, *U.S. Navy Official.*

14 *Gulf S.B. Corpn.:* **NUCLEUS** (June 26, 1943), **OPPONENT** (June 12, 1943), **PALISADE** (June 26, 1943), **PENETRATE** (Sept. 11, 1943), **PERIL, PHANTOM** (both July 25, 1943), **PINNACLE** (Sept. 11, 1943), **PIRATE** (Dec. 16, 1943), **PIVOT** (Nov. 11, 1943), **PLEDGE** (Dec. 23, 1943), **PROJECT** (Nov. 20, 1943), **PROWESS** (Feb. 17, 1944), **QUEST** (March 16, 1944), **RAMPART** (March 31, 1944). (*AM* 268–278, 280–282.)

4 *Puget Sound Bridge Co.:* **EXECUTE, FACILITY** (both June 22, 1944), **FANCY, FIXITY** (both Sept. 4, 1944). (*AM* 232–235.)

9 *Savannah Machine & Foundry Co.:* **IMPLICIT** (Sept. 6, 1943), **IMPROVE** (Sept. 26, 1943), **INCESSANT** (Oct. 22, 1943), **INCREDIBLE** (Nov. 21, 1943), **INDICATIVE** (Dec. 12, 1943), **INFLICT** (Jan. 16, 1944), **INSTILL** (March 5, 1944), **INTRIGUE** (April 8, 1944), **INVADE** (Feb. 6, 1944). (*AM* 246–254.)

13 *Tampa S.B. Co.:* **ADMIRABLE, ADOPT** (both Oct. 18, 1942), **ASTUTE, AUGURY, BARRIER, BOMBARD** (all four Feb. 23, 1943), **CRAG** (ex-*Craig*, March 21, 1943), **CRUISE** (March 21, 1943), **DEFT** (March 28, 1943), **DENSITY, DESIGN** (both Feb. 6, 1944), **DEVICE, DIPLOMA** (both May 21, 1944). (*AM* 136, 137, 148–151, 214–216, 218–221.)

26 *Willamette Iron & Steel Corpn.:* **ADJUTANT** (June 17, 1944), **BITTERN** (June 21, 1944), **BOND** (Oct. 21, 1942), **BREAKHORN** (July 4, 1944), **CANDID** (Oct. 14, 1942), **CAPABLE** (Nov. 16, 1942), **CAPTIVATE** (Dec. 1, 1942), **CARAVAN** (Oct. 14, 1942), **CARIAMA** (July 1, 1944), **CAUTION** (Dec. 7, 1942), **CHANGE** (Dec. 15, 1942), **CHUKOR** (July 15, 1944), **CLAMOUR** (Dec. 24, 1942), **CLIMAX** (Jan. 9, 1943), **COMPEL** (Jan. 16, 1943), **CONCISE** (Feb. 6, 1943), **CONTROL** (Jan. 28, 1943), **COUNSEL** (Feb. 17, 1943), **CREDDOCK** (July 22, 1944), **DIPPER** (July 26, 1944), **DOTTEREL** (Aug. 5, 1944), **DRIVER** (Aug. 19, 1944), **GADWALL** (July 15, 1943), **GRAYLAG** (Dec. 4, 1943), **HARLEQUIN** (June 3, 1944), **HARRIER** (June 7, 1944). (AM 152–165, 351–358, 360, 362, 364–366.)

11 *Winslow Marine Ry. & S.B. Co.:* **GARLAND** (Feb. 20, 1944), **GAYETY** (March 19, 1944), **HAZARD** (May 21, 1944), **HILARITY** (July 30, 1944), **INAUGURAL** (Oct. 1, 1944), **SCOUT** (May 2, 1943), **SCRIMMAGE** (May 16, 1943), **SCUFFLE** (Aug. 8, 1943), **SENTRY** (Aug. 15, 1943), **SERENE** (Oct. 31, 1943), **SHELTER** (Nov. 14, 1943). (*AM* 238–242, 296–301.)

Displacement: 625 tons (945 tons *full load*). Complement: 104. Dimensions: 180 (*w.l.*), $184\frac{1}{2}$ (*o.a.*) × 33 × $9\frac{3}{4}$ feet (*max.*). Guns: 1—3 inch d.p., 4—40 mm. AA. (but *Crag* and *Cruise*, completed by Charleston Navy Yard, are armed only with 2—40 mm. AA.). Machinery: Diesel. 2 shafts. B.H.P.: 1,710 = 14·5 kts. War loss: *Salute*. Scrapped or sold: *Buoyant, Delegate, Drake, Dunlin, Elusive, Embattle, Gavia, Notable, Prime, Saunter, Spectacle.* Transferred to Soviet Navy: *Advocate, Agent, Alarm, Alchemy, Apex, Arcade, Arch, Armada, Aspire, Assail*; and to Chinese Navy: *Logic, Lucid, Magnet, Mainstay.*

Minesweepers

209 Coastal Type.

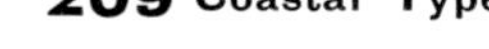

YMS 446–479 type (ex-PCS) 1944, *U.S. Navy Official.*

YMS 260, and others of YMS 135–445 type. 1944, *U.S. Navy Official.*

YMS 1–134 type. 1942, *U.S. Navy Official.*

10 *Associated Shipbuilders:* **287** (Oct. 27, 1942), **288** (Nov. 28, 1942), **289** (Jan. 26, 1943), **290** (Feb. 27, 1942), **291** (1943), **292** (June 8, 1943), **293** (July 7, 1943), **294–296** (1943).

9 *Astoria Marine Construction Co.:* **YMS 100** (April 12, 1942), **102, 135, 136, 139, 140, 422, 423, 425.**

6 *Ballard Marine Ry. Co.:* **YMS 326, 327** (Dec. 5, 1942), **328** (Dec. 19, 1942), **331, 332, 333** (Sept., 1943).

13 *Bellingham Marine Ry. Co.:* **YMS 269–274, 276, 342, 343, 410–413.**

3 *Burger Boat Co.:* **YMS 109, 159, 160.**

2 *Colberg Boat Works:* **YMS 94, 97.**

4 *Dachel-Carter S.B. Corpn.:* **YMS 163–165, 170.**

11 *Gibbs Gas Engine Co.:* **YMS 59, 60, 65, 348, 349, 354, 357, 467, 468, 470, 471.**

13 *Henry C. Grebe & Co.:* **YMS 85, 176–180, 405, 406, 408, 417–420.**

9 *Greenport Basin & Construction Co.:* **YMS 25** (Jan. 28, 1942), **183** (June 25, 1942), **184** (July 18, 1942), **192, 193** (Jan. 2, 1943), **375–377, 458.**

10 *Harbor Boat Building Co.:* **YMS 117** (Aug. 23, 1942), **119, 120** (April 4, 1942), **313, 314, 316, 393–396.**

7 *C. Hiltebrant D.D. Co.:* **YMS 33, 35, 442–445, 463.**

7 *Hubbards' South Coast Co.:* **YMS 88, 91** (March 7, 1942), **93, 259, 260, 317, 319.**

9 *Robert Jacob, Inc.:* **YMS 38** (1941), **215, 358, 359, 362** (May 22, 1943), **438, 440, 441, 446.**

4 *Kruse & Banks S.B. Co.:* **YMS 265–268.**

3 *Al. Larson Boat Shop:* **YMS 321, 324, 325.**

7 *J. M. Martinac S.B. Corpn.:* **YMS 216, 218, 219, 434–437.**

5 *Mojean & Erickson:* **YMS 426–429, 479.**

13 *Henry B. Nevins, Inc.:* **YMS 2** (Jan. 28, 1942), **7, 309, 311, 312, 397–404.**

2 *North Western S.B. Co.:* **YMS 285, 286.**

3 *Rice Bros. Corpn.:* **YMS 305–307.**

Coastal Minesweepers and Patrol Vessels (Frigates)

Minesweepers, Coastal Type—*continued*

3 *Frank L. Sample, Junr., Inc.:* **YMS 106, 228, 231.**

9 *San Diego Marine Construction Co.:* **YMS 113** (Feb. 13, 1942), **114, 116, 143-145, 281, 283, 475.**

4 *Seattle S.B. & Dry Dock Corpn.:* **YMS 335** (Nov. 21, 1942), **337** (Feb. 20, 1943), **339, 340,** etc.

15 *Stadium Yacht Basin:* **YMS 79-81, 235-239, 389-391, 414-416, 461.**

3 *Wm. F. Stone & Son:* **YMS 300-302.**

8 *Tacoma Boat Building Co.:* **YMS 129** (Dec. 18, 1941), **241, 297, 430-433, 477.**

8 *Weaver Shipyards:* **YMS 73, 75, 247, 250, 371-374.**

1 *Western Boat Building Co.:* **YMS 147** (Oct. 24, 1942).

8 *Wheeler S.B. Corpn.:* **YMS 42** (March 17, 1942), **45, 46, 51** (June 22, 1942), **364, 367-369.**

Wood. Displacement: *YMS* 1–134, 207 tons; 135–479, 215 tons. Dimensions: 136 × 24½ × 6 feet. Guns: **1**—3 inch, **2**—20 mm., **2** D.C.T. Machinery: 2 G.M. Diesels. B.H.P.: 1,000 = 13 kts. Complement: 50. War losses: *YMS* 14, 19, 21, 24, 30, 39, 48, 50, 70, 71, 84, 98, 103, 127, 133, 304, 341, 350, 365, 378, 383, 385, 409, 481. Other missing numbers have been discarded, or transferred to Royal Navy, R. Hellenic Navy, R. Norwegian Navy, French Navy, or Soviet Navy.

2 Ex-Patrol Craft.

(Similar to YMS 446 type in appearance)

MEDRICK (ex-*PCS* 1464), **MINAH** (ex-*PCS* 1465). (Both1944.) Displacement: *ca.* 220 tons. Dimensions: 130 (*w.l.*), 136 (*o.a.*) × 23⅓ × 8½ feet (*max.*). Guns: **1**—3 inch d.p., **1**—40 mm. AA. Machinery: G.M. Diesel. 2 shafts. B.H.P.: 1,000 = 14 kts. Complement: 47.

Note.—Following 48 ex-German coastal minesweepers were taken over, but are unlikely to be retained long: *R* 22, 24, 43, 52, 55, 67, 68, 71, 76, 91, 96, 98–102, 117, 118, 120, 127, 128, 130, 132–138, 140, 142, 144, 146, 147, 150, 241, 249, 253, 264, 266, 267, 401, 403–408.

10 Underwater Locator type.

AMc (U) 7-11 (ex-*LCI* 400, 409, 513, 515, 589). (1943–4.) Displacement: *ca.* 220 tons. Dimensions: 153 (*w.l.*), 159 (*o.a.*) × 23⅔ × 5⅝ feet (*max.*). Guns: **2**—20 mm. AA. Machinery: G.M. Diesel. 2 shafts. B.H.P.: 1,800 = 14 kts. Complement: 41.

AMc (U) 2-6 (ex-*LCT* 844, 887–890). (1944.) Displacement: 143 tons. Dimensions: 105 (*w.l.*), 119 × 32⅔ × 3¾ feet (*max.*). Guns: **2**—20 mm. AA. Machinery: Diesel. 3 shafts. B.H.P.: 675 = 10 kts. Complement: 21.

41 Frigates

Special Note.—Those marked * (28 in all) were on loan to Soviet Navy. So far there has been no news of their return.

1944, *U.S. Navy Official.*

2 *American S.B. Co., Cleveland:*

PF
- * **21 Bayonne** (Sept. 11, 1943)
- **101 Greensboro'** (1944)

3 *American S.B. Co., Lorain:*

- **16 Bangor** (1943)
- **93 Lorain** (ex-*Roanoke*) (March 18, 1944)
- **94 Milledgeville** (ex-*Sitka*) (1944)

8 *Walter Butler:*

- * **25 Charlottesville**
- **28 Emporia**
- * **22 Gloucester**
- **23 Groton**
- **24 Muskegon**
- * **27 Newport** (Aug. 15, 1943)
- * **26 Poughkeepsie** (Aug. 12, 1943)
- **32 Woonsocket**

13 *Consolidated Steel Corpn., Los Angeles:*

PF
- * **35 Belfast**
- * **46 Bisbee** (Sept. 8, 1943)
- * **51 Burlington** (Dec. 7, 1943)
- * **50 Carson City** (Nov. 19, 1943)
- * **38 Coronado** (June 17, 1943)
- * **47 Gallup** (Sept. 17, 1943)
- * **36 Glendale** (May 28, 1943)
- * **34 Long Beach** (May 5, 1943)
- * **49 Muskogee** (Oct. 18, 1943)
- * **39 Ogden** (June 23, 1943)
- **43 Orange** (Aug. 6, 1943)
- * **48 Rockford** (Sept. 27, 1943)
- * **37 San Pedro** (June 11, 1943)

4 *Froemming Bros.:*

- * **52 Allentown**
- * **55 Bath**
- * **53 Machias** (Aug. 22, 1943)
- * **54 Sandusky**

4 *Globe S.B. Co.:*

PF
- **58 Abilene** (ex-*Bridgeport*)
- **56 Covington**
- **61 Manitowoc**
- **63 Moberley** (ex-*Scranton*)

1 *Leathem D. Smith S.B. Co.:*

- * **70 Evansville**

6 *Permanente Metals Corpn.:*

- * **7 Albuquerque** (Sept. 14, 1943)
- * **8 Everett**
- * **5 Hoquiam** (July 31, 1943)
- * **6 Pasco**
- * **4 Sausalito**
- * **3 Tacoma**

Displacement: 1,430 tons. Complement: 194. Dimensions: 285½ (*w.l.*), 304 (*o.a.*) × 37½ × 13⅔ feet. Guns: **3**—3 inch, 50 cal., d.p., **4**—40 mm. AA., **4** D.C.T. Machinery: Triple expansion. 2 shafts. H.P.: 5,500 = 20 kts.

Notes.—These ships are of similar design to British frigates of the "River" class. PF 72–92 were transferred to Royal Navy under Lend-Lease scheme, and have since been returned for disposal. Contracts for PF 95–98 (*Macon, Roanoke, Sitka, Stamford*) were cancelled. *Alexandria, Annapolis, Asheville, Beaufort, Brownsville, Brunswick, Casper, Charlotte, Corpus Christi, Davenport, Dearborn, El Paso, Eugene, Forsyth, Gladwyne* (ex-*Worcester*), *Grand Forks, Grand Island, Grand Rapids, Gulfport, Hingham, Huron*, **Hutchinson, Key West, Knoxville, Natchez, New Bedford, Orlando, Peoria, Pocatello, Pueblo, Racine, Reading*, **Sheboygan, Shreveport, Uniontown* (ex-*Chattanooga*), *Van Buren*, have been sold.

Yachts and Coastal Craft

4 Yachts

WILLIAMSBURG. 1944, *U.S. Navy Official.*

WILLIAMSBURG (ex-*Aras*, 1931). Displacement: 1,730 tons. Dimensions: 224 (*w.l.*), 243¾ (*o.a.*) × 36 × 16 feet (*mean*). Guns: **2**—3 inch d.p. Machinery: Winton Diesel. 2 shafts. B.H.P.: 2,200 = 16 kts. (Presidential Yacht.)

MENTOR (ex-*Haida II*, May 26, 1942). Displacement; 182 tons (*full load*). Dimensions: 123¾ (*w.l.*), 127 (*o.a.*) × 21 × 6½ feet. Guns: **1**—40 mm. AA. Machinery: Diesel. 2 shafts. B.H.P.: 600 = 13 kts. (*PYc* 37.)

JASPER (ex-*Stranger*, 1938). Wood. Displacement: 395 tons (*full load*). Dimensions: 125 (*w.l.*), 134 (*o.a.*) × 23⅚ × 13½ feet. Guns: **2**—3 inch d.p. Machinery: Diesel. 2 shafts. B.H.P.: 800 = 12 kts. (*PYc* 13.)

AQUAMARINE (ex-*Seawolf*, ex-*Clader*, ex-*Vasanta*, 1925). Displacement: 215 tons (*full load*). Dimensions: 124 (*o.a.*) × 20½ × 15 feet. Guns: **2**—3 inch d.p. Machinery: Union Diesel. 2 shafts. B.H.P.: 1,200 = 12 kts.

Motor Torpedo Boats

1943, *U.S. Navy Official.*

PT 613, 616, 619, 620. All built by the Electric Boat Co., Bayonne, N.J. Displacement: 45 tons. Dimensions: 80 × 20⅔ × 5 feet. Machinery: Packard. 3 shafts. B.H.P.: 4,050 = 41 kts. (light). Armament: **1**—40 mm. AA., **4** torpedoes. Complement: 17. (Retained for instructional purposes, all other m.t.b. being discarded.)

Note.—30 ex-German m.t.b. taken over were: *S* 9, 10, 12, 15, 21, 64, 68, 76, 79, 85, 97, 98, 107, 117, 122, 127, 133, 174, 197, 206, 207, 210, 216, 218, 225, 302, 305, 306, 701, 706.

Motor Gunboats.

20 Steel Type.

Photo wanted. Appearance resembles PC 461 type.

PGM 10-16,19-26, 28-32 (ex-*PC* 805, 806, 1088–1091, 1148, 1550–1557, 1559, 1565–1568). Displacement: 280 tons. Dimensions: 170 (*w.l.*), 173⅔ (*o.a.*) × 23 × 7½ feet. Guns: **1**—3 inch d.p., **2**—40 mm. AA. and rockets. Machinery: 2 sets G.M. 2-stroke Diesels. B.H.P.: 2,880 = 20 kts. Complement: 65.

Notes.—Built by Consolidated S.B. Corpn. *PGM* 17 launched on 12/12/42, *PGM* 19 on 11/4/44, *PGM* 21 on 25/5/44, *PGM* 32 on 17/11/44.

1 Wooden Type.

Photo wanted. Appearance as SC 497 type.

PGM 8 (ex-*SC* 1366). Displacement: 95 tons. Dimensions: 107½ (*w.l.*), 110⅚ (*o.a.*) × 17 × 6 feet. Guns: **1**—3 inch d.p., **1**—40 mm. AA. and rockets. Machinery: 2 sets Diesels. 2 shafts. B.H.P.: 1,540 = 20 kts. Fuel: 15 tons. Complement: 28.

Submarine Chasers.

3 Steel Type (ex-Minesweepers).

PC 1591 (since scrapped). 1944 *U.S. Navy Official.*

3 *Commercial Iron Works:* **PC 1589** (ex-*Conflict*), **1590** (ex-*Constant*), **1592** (ex-*Dash*).
Displacement: 295 tons. Dimensions: 170 (*w.l.*), 173⅔ (*o.a.*) × 23 × 7½ feet. Guns: **1**—3 inch, 50 cal., d.p., **1**—40 mm. AA. Machinery: Diesel. 2 shafts. B.H.P.: 1,770 = 16·5 kts. Complement: 65. (Formerly numbered AM 85, 86, 88, but reclassified in 1944.) War lost: *PC* 1603.

42 Steel Type.

PCE 853. *Added* 1944

PCE 842–847, 868, 870–875, 877, 880–882, 884–886, 891–900, 902–904.
PCE (R) 849-853, 855-857, 859. Built by *Pullman Standard Mfg. Co., Albina Engine & Machinery Works* and *Willamette Iron & Steel Corpn.*

Displacement: 795 tons (903 tons, *full load*). Dimensions: 180 (*w.l.*), 184½ (*o.a.*) × 33 × 9½ feet. Guns: **1**—3 inch dual purpose, **6**—40 mm. AA., **4** D.C.T. (PCE (R) type have four fewer 40 mm.) Machinery: Diesel. 2 shafts. B.H.P.: 1,500 to 1,800 = 18 kts. Complement: 99.

Note.—*PCE (R)* type carry hospital equipment and personnel, complement being 107, with accommodation for 57 patients. *PCE* 827–841 were transferred to Royal Navy, and have since been placed on sale list. *PCE* 867, 869 were transferred to China.

40 Wooden Type

1944, *U.S. Navy Official.*

2 *Burger Boat Co.:* **PCS 1423, 1424** (June 1943).
1 *Colberg Boat Works:* **PCS 1403** (Sept. 28, 1943).
3 *Dachel-Carter S.B. Co.:* **PCS 1417, 1419, 1420.**
2 *Gibbs Gas Engine Co.:* **PCS 1430, 1431.**
1 *Greenport Basin & Construction Co.:* **PCS 1405** (Aug. 21, 1943).

Wooden Type—*continued*

3 *Harbor B.B. Co.:* **PCS 1441, 1442, 1444** (ex-*YMS* 474).
2 *C. Hiltebrant D.D. Co.:* **PCS 1425, 1426.**
4 *Hubbard's South Coast Co.:* **PCS 1397, 1399-1401** (ex-*YMS* 450–452).
1 *Mojean & Ericson:* **PCS 1455.**
2 *Robert Jacob, Inc.:* **PCS 1391, 1392.**
3 *San Diego Marine Constrn. Co.:* **PCS 1445, 1446, 1448** (ex-*YMS* 476).
2 *Stadium Yacht Basin:* **PCS 1413, 1414.**
1 *W. F. Stone & Son:* **PCS 1422.**
1 *Tacoma B.B. Co.:* **PCS 1451.**
1 *Western Boat Building Co.:* **PCS 1459** (July 2, 1943).
11 *Wheeler S.B. Corpn.:* **PCS 1376-1378, 1380-1387.**
Displacement: 267 tons. Dimensions: 136 × 24½ × 8½ feet (*max.*). Guns: **1**—3 inch dual purpose, **1**—40 mm. AA., **2**—20 mm. AA. Many D.C. Machinery: 2 G.M. Diesels. B.H.P.: 800 = 14 kts. Complement: 57.

Note.—A number of this class were reclassified as *YMS* 446—479.

194 Steel Type.

PC 461. 1943, *U.S. Navy Official.*

19 *Albina Engine & Machinery Works:* **PC 569–572, 579-582, 816-820, 1077-1082.**
12 *Brown S.B. Co.:* **PC 565-568, 608-611, 1251-1254.**
13 *Commercial Iron Works:* **PC 597, 776-804, 807, 808, 813.**
26 *Consolidated Shipbuilding Corpn.:* **PC 483** (Oct. 25, 1941), **484** (Dec. 6, 1941), **485** (Dec. 20, 1941), **486** (Jan. 25, 1942), **487** (Feb. 28, 1942), **563** (March 17, 1942), **564** (April 12, 1942), **600** (May 9, 1942), **601** (May 23, 1942), **602** (June 13, 1942), **603** (June 30, 1942), **1193** (Aug. 29, 1942), **1196, 1198, 1201, 1202, 1205, 1206 1207, 1208** (Sept. 15, 1943), **1237** (April 3, 1943), **1240, 1546, 1547** (Feb. 8, 1944), **1548, 1549** (March 12, 1944).
34 *Defoe Boat & Motor Works:* **PC 476, 477, 479, 549, 583, 585-587,1119-1123, 1125, 1127, 1130-1147, 1149.**
10 *Dravo Corporation:* **PC 490** (Oct. 18, 1941), **491-493, 495, 575, 576, 592-594.**
14 *George Lawley & Sons:* **PC 461** (Dec. 23, 1941), **463** (Feb. 27, 1942), **465** (March, 1942), **466** (April 29, 1942), **467-470, 616-618, 619** (Aug. 15, 1942), **1086, 1087.**
10 *Gibbs Gas Engine Co.:* **PC 614, 615, 1181-1187, 1190.**
1 *Jeffersonville Boat & Machine Co.:* **PC 560** (March 17, 1942).
30 *Leathem D. Smith S.B. Co.:* **PC 588, 589, 821-825, 1171-1180, 1225-1230, 1260-1263, 1563, 1564, 1569.**
7 *Luders Marine Construction Co.:* **PC 606, 1212-1214, 1216, 1218, 1220.**
8 *Nashville Bridge Co.:* **PC 620, 1241-1247.**
1 *Penn-Jersey S.B. Corpn.:* **PC 1224.**
9 *Sullivan Dry Dock & Repair Co.:* **PC 488** (Dec. 20, 1941), **553** (May 30, 1942), **1167, 1168** (both July 3, 1943), **1169, 1170** (both Oct. 16, 1943), **1231, 1232** (both Dec. 12, 1942), **1233** (Jan. 11, 1943).

All the above are of the same general design with minor differences. Displacement: 280 tons (450 tons *full load*). Dimensions: 170 (*w.l.*), 173⅔ (*o.a.*) × 23 × 7½ feet. Armament: **1**—3 inch dual purpose, **1**—40 mm. AA., **5**—20 mm. AA., **4** D.C.T. Machinery: 2 G.M. 2-stroke Diesels. 2 shafts. B.H.P.: 2,560 to 2,880 = 20 kts. Complement: 80.

Note.—Units of this class have been transferred to R. Norwegian, R. Netherland, R. Hellenic, Brazilian, French, Soviet and Uruguayan Navies. War losses: *PC* 496, 558, 815, 1129, 1261.

Miscellaneous

Submarine Chasers—*continued*

78 Wooden Type

SC 1497 (earlier units have funnel). 1944, *U.S. Navy Official.*

4 *American Cruiser Co.:* **SC 658, 683, 685, 687.**
1 *Annapolis Yacht Yard:* **SC 1314.**
2 *Burger Boat Co.:* **SC 660, 661.**
3 *Calderwood Yacht Yard:* **SC 1358, 1360, 1361.**
1 *Dachel Carter S.B. Co.:* **SC 665.**
2 *Daytona Beach Boat Works:* **SC 1305, 1308.**
1 *Delaware Bay S.B. Co.:* **SC 699.**
2 *Dingle Boat Works:* **SC 1000, 1001.**
3 *Elizabeth City Shipyard:* **SC 1277, 1278, 1280.**
2 *Fellows & Stewart:* **SC 1007, 1011.**
5 *Fisher Boat Works:* **SC 500, 663, 713, 716, 718.**
1 *Gulf Marine Ways:* **SC 1057.**
4 *Harris & Parsons:* **SC 1061, 1321, 1322, 1324.**
2 *C. Hiltebrant D.D. Co.:* **SC 674, 675.**
2 *Inland Waterways Inc.:* **SC 1059, 1060.**
1 *Island Docks:* **SC 997.**
1 *John E. Matton & Son:* **SC 986.**
1 *Julius Petersen:* **SC 1315.**
2 *Luders Marine Construction Co.:* **SC 1021, 1357.**
1 *Mathis Yacht Bldg. Co.:* **SC 634.**
1 *Perkins & Vaughan:* **SC 1300.**
7 *Peterson Boat Works:* **SC 537, 538, 643, 645 1031, 1034, 1036.**
4 *Peyton Co.:* **SC 773, 774, 1364, 1365.**
3 *Quincy Adams Yacht Yard:* **SC 750, 1267, 1272.**
1 *Rice Bros. Corporation:* **SC 1341.**
6 *Robinson Marine Construction Co.:* **SC 646, 647, 752, 754, 756, 759.**
5 *W. A. Robinson:* **SC 760, 1290, 1291, 1292, 1295.**
1 *Seabrook Yacht Corporation:* **SC 769.**
1 *Simms Bros.:* **SC 1330.**
4 *Vineyard S.B. Co.:* **SC 981, 982, 1352, 1354.**
4 *Walter E. Abrams Shipyard:* **SC 673, 678** (Aug. 17, 1942), **679, 1334** (1943).

All of same standardised design. Displacement: 95 tons (148 tons *full load*). Dimensions: 107½ (*w.l.*), 110⅚ (*o.a.*) × 17 × 6½ feet (*max.*). Armament: **1**—40 mm. AA., **2** or **3**—20 mm. AA., many D.C. Machinery: 2 sets Diesels. 2 shafts. B.H.P.: 800 = 15 kts. in some; 1,500 = 19 kts. in others. Fuel: 15 tons. Complement: 28.

Note.—Various units of this type have been transferred to Brazil, Mexico, Uruguay, France, and the Soviet Navy. War losses: *SC* 636, 694, 696, 744.

Seaplane Tenders

(a) Large Type.

4 Currituck Class.

CURRITUCK. 1944, *U.S. Navy Official.*

CURRITUCK (Sept. 11, 1943), **NORTON SOUND** (Nov. 28, 1943), **PINE ISLAND** (Feb. 26, 1944), **SALISBURY SOUND** (ex-*Puget Sound*) (June 18, 1944). First ship built by Philadelphia Navy Yard, others by Todd Shipyards, Los Angeles. Displacement: 9,090 tons. Dimensions: 520 (*w.l.*), 540½ (*o.a.*) × 69¼ × 22¼ feet (*max.*). Guns: **4**—5 inch, 38 cal., **20**—40 mm. AA. Machinery: Geared turbines (Parsons in *Currituck*, Allis-Chalmers in others). 2 shafts. S.H.P.: 12,000 = 18·5 kts. Boilers: 4 Babcock & Wilcox Express. Distinctive Nos. are AV 7, 11, 12, 13.

Seaplane Tenders (a) Large Type—*continued*

2 Curtiss Class.

CURTISS. 1942, *U.S. Navy Official.*

CURTISS (April 20, 1940), **ALBEMARLE** (July 13, 1940). Displacement: 8,625 tons. Dimensions: 508 (*w.l.*), 527⅓ (*o.a.*) × 69¼ × 22 feet (*max.*). Guns: **4**—5 inch, 38 cal., **14**—40 mm. AA. Aircraft: 25. Machinery: Parsons geared turbines. 2 shafts. S.H.P.: 12,000 = 19 kts. Boilers: 4 Babcock & Wilcox Express. Built by New York S.B. Corpn. under 1937 and 1938 Programmes, respectively. Distinctive Nos., AV 4, 5.

7 Tangier Class.

TANGIER. 1944, *U.S. Navy Official.*

CHANDELEUR (Nov. 29, 1941), **CUMBERLAND SOUND** (Feb. 23, 1944), **HAMLIN** (Jan. 11, 1944), **KENNETH WHITING** (Dec. 15, 1943), **POCOMOKE** (ex-*Exchequer*, June 8, 1940), **ST. GEORGE** (Feb. 14, 1944), **TANGIER** (ex-*Sea Arrow*, 1939). Displacement: 8,000 tons. Dimensions: 465 (*pp.*), 492 (*o.a.*) × 69½ × 23¾ feet (*max.*). Guns: **2**—5 inch, 38 cal., **12**—40 mm. AA., in *Cumberland Sound, Hamlin, St. George* and *Kenneth Whiting*; **1**—5 inch, 38 cal., **4**—3 inch, 50 cal., **8**—40 mm. AA., in other three. Machinery: 2 sets geared turbines (General Electric in *Chandeleur* and *Pocomoke*; De Laval in *Tangier*; Allis-Chalmers in others). S.H.P.: 8,500 = 17·5 kts. Boilers: 2 Foster-Wheeler. Oil fuel: 1,417 tons. All are modified C 3 type mercantile conversions. Distinctive Nos., AV 10, 17, 15, 14 9, 16, 8, respectively. (*Townsend*, AV 18, cancelled.)

(b) Small Type.

30 Barnegat Class.

MATAGORDA (as originally armed). 1944, *Lieut. D. Trimingham, R.N.V.R.*

3 *Puget Sound Navy Yard:* **BARNEGAT** (July, 1941), **CASCO, MACKINAC** (both 1942). (Nos. AVP 10–13.)
2 *Boston Navy Yard:* **HUMBOLDT** (March 17, 1941), **MATAGORDA** (March 18, 1941). (AVP 21, 22.)
5 *Lake Washington Shipyard:* **ABSECON** (March 8, 1942), **CHINCOTEAGUE** (April 15, 1942), **COOS BAY** (May 15, 1942), **HALF MOON** (1942), **BERING STRAIT** (March 30, 1944). (AVP 23–26, 34.)
4 *Associated Shipbuilders:* **ROCKAWAY** (Feb. 15, 1942), **SAN PABLO** (March 31, 1942), **UNIMAK** (1942), **YAKUTAT** (July 4, 1942). (AVP 29–32.)
Builders not reported: **BARATARIA, CASTLEROCK, COOK INLET, CORSON, DUXBURY BAY, FLOYD'S BAY, GARDINER'S BAY, GREENWICH BAY, ONSLOW, ORCA, REHOBOTH, SAN CARLOS, SHELIKOF, SUISUN, TIMBALIER, VALCOUR** (AVP 33, 35–41, 48–55).

Displacement: 1,695 tons (2,800 tons *full load*). Dimensions: 300 (*w.l.*), 310¾ to 311⅝ (*o.a.*) × 41 × 13½ feet (*max.*). Guns: **1**—5 inch, 38 cal., **5**—40 mm. AA. (except *Absecon*, **2**—5 inch). Machinery: 2 sets Diesels. 2 shafts. B.H.P.: 6,080 = 18 kts. (Other ships of this class have been adapted for various duties.)

Note.—Original main armament of 4—5 inch was severely reduced to save top weight.

Ammunition Ships.

WRANGELL. 1946, *courtesy Derek Mercer, Esq.*

DIAMOND HEAD (Feb. 3, 1945), **FIREDRAKE** (ex-*Winged Racer*), **GREAT SITKIN, MOUNT KATMAI, PARICUTIN, VESUVIUS** (ex-*Gamecock*), **WRANGELL.** Displacement: 13,910 tons. Dimensions: 435 (*w.l.*), 459⅙ (*o.a.*) × 63 × 28¼ feet. Guns: 1—5 inch, 4—3 inch, 4—40 mm. AA. Machinery: Geared turbines. S.H.P.: 6,000 = 15·5 kts. Complement: 267. (AE 19, 14, 17, 16, 15, 12.)

SHASTA. 1944, *U.S. Navy Official.*

MOUNT BAKER (ex-*Kilauea*, ex-*Surprise*, Aug. 6, 1940), **LASSEN** (ex-*Shooting Star*, Jan. 1, 1940), **RAINIER** (ex-*Rainbow*, March 1, 1941), **SHASTA** (ex-*Comet*, July 9, 1941), **MAUNA LOA** (April 14, 1943), **MAZAMA** (Aug. 15, 1943), **AKUTAN** (Sept. 17, 1944). Built by Tampa S.B. Co. Displacement: 9,950 tons. Dimensions: 435 (*w.l.*), 459 (*o.a.*) × 63 × 26½ feet. Guns: 1—5 inch, 4—3 inch, 4—40 mm. AA. Machinery: 2 Nordberg Diesels. B.H.P.: 6,000 = 15 kts. Complement: 281. (AE 4, 3, 5, 6, 8, 9, 13.) War loss: *Mount Hood.*

Photo wanted.

SANGAY (ex-*Cape Sable*, 1941). Displacement: 6,400 tons. Dimensions: 390 (*w.l.*), 412¼ (*o.a.*) × 60 × 23¼ feet. Guns: 1—5 inch, 4—3 inch, 4—40 mm. AA. Machinery: Diesel. B.H.P.: 4,000 = 14·5 kts. Complement: 308. (AE 10.)

Submarine Tenders.

Photo wanted.

AEGIR, ANTHEDON, APOLLO, CLYTIE, EURYALE. Displacement: 7,650 tons. Dimensions: 492 (*o.a.*) × 69½ × 23 feet. Machinery: Geared turbine. S.H.P.: 8,500 = 16·5 kts. (AS 22–26).

FULTON. 1942, *U.S. Navy Official.*

FULTON (Dec. 17, 1940), **SPERRY** (Dec. 17, 1941), **BUSHNELL** (Sept. 14, 1942), **HOWARD W. GILMORE** (ex-*Neptune*) (Sept. 16, 1943). All 4 by Mare Island Navy Yard. **NEREUS** (Puget Sound Navy Yard, Feb. 12, 1945), **ORION** (Oct. 14, 1942), **PROTEUS** (Nov. 12, 1942) (both by Moore Dry Dock Co., Oakland, Calif.). Displacement: 9,250 tons. Guns: 4—5 inch. Machinery: G.M. Diesels with electric drive. B.H.P.: 12,000 = 20 kts. *Fulton* authorised by 1938 Programme, others by 1940. (AS 11, 12, 15–19.)

Submarine Tenders—*continued.*

PELIAS. 1944, *U.S. Navy Official.*

GRIFFIN (ex-*Mormacpenn*, Nov. 10, 1939), **PELIAS** (ex-*Mormacyork*, Nov. 14, 1939). 7,886 tons *gross*. Dimensions: 492 × 69½ × 28½ feet. Guns: 4—5 inch. Machinery: 4 sets Busch-Sulzer Diesels. B.H.P.: 8,500 = 16·5 kts. (AS 13, 14.)

1937, *O. W. Waterman.*

HOLLAND (Puget Sound N. Yd., April 12, 1926). Begun April 11th, 1921. Displacement: 8,100 tons. Dimensions: 460 (*pp.*), 513 (*o.a.*) × 61 (*extreme*) × 22¾ feet (*mean* draught). Guns: 8—5 inch, 4—3 inch AA., 2—6 pdr. Torpedo tube: 1—21 inch, *submerged.* Machinery: Parsons geared turbines. 1 shaft. S.H.P. 7,000 = 16 kts. Boilers: 2 Bureau Modified Thornycroft. Oil: 1,050 tons. Complement: 398. Generally sister ship to *Whitney* and *Dobbin*, Destroyer Tenders. (AS 3.)

Note.—Following ex-German submarine tenders were taken over: *Tanga* (1938), *Saar* (1934), *Lech* (1930); but disposal has not been reported.

Destroyer Tenders

Photos wanted.

ARCADIA, BRYCE CANYON, EVERGLADES (Jan. 28, 1945), **FRONTIER, GRAND CANYON, ISLE ROYAL, KLONDIKE, SHENANDOAH, TIDEWATER** (June 30, 1945), **YELLOWSTONE.** By Todd Pacific Shipyards, S. Pedro, and other builders. Displacement: 11,755 tons. Dimensions: 465 (*w.l.*), 492 (*o.a.*) × 69½ × 27¼ feet. Guns: 1—5 inch, 4—3 inch, 4—40 mm. AA. Machinery: Geared turbines. S.H.P.: 8,500 = 18 kts. Boilers: 2 Foster-Wheeler or Babcock & Wilcox. Complement: 826. Three other ships (*Arrowhead*, *Canopus*, *New England*) were cancelled in 1945, and a fourth (*Great Lakes*) sold. Construction of *Bryce Canyon* suspended, 1946. (AD 22–29, 31, 36.)

HAMUL. 1943, *U.S. Navy Official.*

CASCADE (June 7, 1942), **HAMUL** (ex-*Dr. Lykes*, April 6, 1940), **MARKAB** (ex-*Mormacpenn*, Dec. 21, 1940). Displacement: 11,755 tons. Dimensions: 465 (*pp.*), 492 (*o.a.*) × 69½ × 28½ feet. Guns: 2—5 inch, 6—40 mm. AA. in *Cascade*; 1—5 inch, 4—3 inch, 4—40 mm. AA. in others. Machinery: Geared turbines. S.H.P.: 8,500 = 16·5 kts. Boilers: 2 Foster-Wheeler. Complement: 860. (AD 16, 20, 21.)

Fleet Auxiliaries

PRAIRIE. 1941, *U.S.N. Official.*

PIEDMONT. 1944, *U.S. Navy Official.*

DIXIE (May 27, 1939), **PRAIRIE** (Dec. 9, 1939). Both built by New York S.B. Corpn. under 1937 and 1938 Programmes respectively. **PIEDMONT** (Dec. 7, 1942), **SIERRA** (Feb. 23, 1943), **YOSEMITE** (May 16, 1943). All 3 by Tampa S.B. Co. Displacement: 14,037 tons. Dimensions: 520 (*w.l.*), 530½ (*o.a.*) × 73⅓ × 25½ feet. Guns: **4**—5 inch, 38 cal., **8**—40 mm. AA. Machinery: Geared turbines. 2 shafts. S.H.P. 11,000 = 19 kts. (AD 14, 15, 17, 18, 19.)

DOBBIN. 1925, *U.S. Navy Official.*

WHITNEY (Boston N.Yd., Oct. 12th, 1923), **DOBBIN** (Philadelphia N.Yd., May 5th, 1921). Displacement: 8,325 tons. Dimensions: 460 (*pp.*), 483⅝ (*o.a.*) × 61 × 24⅛ feet. Guns: **4**—5 inch, **4**—40 mm. AA. Machinery: Parsons geared turbines. S.H.P.: 7,000 = 16 kts. Boilers: 2 Bureau Modified Thornycroft. Oil: 1,107 tons. Complement: 589. Equipped to serve as Depot, Repair and Hospital Ships for 18 Destroyers. Possess special anti-torpedo protection. Generally sister ships to *Holland*, Tender to Submarines. Both fitted as flagships. (AD 4, 3.)

Official, added 1935.

MELVILLE (1915). Built by New York S.B. Corpn. Displacement: 5,250 tons. Complement: 574. Dimensions: 400 (*pp.*) × 54½ × 20 feet (*mean* draught). Guns: **2**—5 inch, **4**—3 inch, **4**—40 mm. AA. Machinery: Parsons geared turbines. S.H.P.: 4,000 = 15 kts. 2 Thornycroft boilers. Oil fuel: 930 tons. (AD 2.)

Repair Ships

K. ROOSEVELT. 1945, *S. C. Heal, Esq.*

CEBU (ex-*Francis P. Duffy*), **CHOURRE** (ex-*Dumaran*), **CULEBRA ISLAND** (ex-*John F. Goucher*), **DIONYSUS**, **HOOPER ISLAND** (ex-*Bert McDowell*), **KERMIT ROOSEVELT** (ex-*Deal Island*, Oct. 5, 1944), **LAERTES**, **LUZON** (ex-*Samuel Bowles*), **MAUI** (ex-*Leyte*), **MINDANAO** (ex-*Elbert Hubbard*), **MONA ISLAND**, **OAHU** (ex-*Caleb C. Wheeler*), **PALAWAN** (Aug. 12, 1944), **SAMAR**, **TUTUILA** (ex-*Arthur P. Gorman*), **WEBSTER** (ex-*Masbate*, Aug. 5, 1944), **XANTHUS.** Displacement: 11,500 tons. Dimensions: 416 (*w.l.*), 441½ (*o.a.*) × 57 × 23 feet (*mean* draught). Machinery: Triple expansion. I.H.P.: 2,500 = 11 kts. Boilers: 2 Babcock & Wilcox. *Dionysus*, *Laertes*, *Xanthus* numbered AR 19–21; *Chourre*, *Webster* (Aircraft Repair Ships), ARV 1, 2; others rated as Internal Combustion Engine Repair Ships, ARG 2–11 and 16, 17.

Photo wanted.

AMPHION (May, 1945), **CADMUS.** Displacement: 16,200 tons. Dimensions: 465 (*w.l.*), 492 (*o.a.*) × 69½ × 27½ feet. Guns: **2**—5 inch, **8**—40 mm. AA. Machinery: Westinghouse turbines. S.H.P.: 8,500 = 16·5 kts. Boilers: 2 Foster-Wheeler. (Two more of this type, *Deucalion* and *Mars*, cancelled.) (AR 13, 14.)

Photo wanted.

ACHELOUS, ADONIS, AEOLUS, AGENOR, AMPHITRITE, AMYCUS, ARISTAEUS, ASKARI, ATLAS, AVENTINUS, BELLEROPHON, CERBERUS, CHANDRA, CHIMAERA, CHLORIS, CONSUS, CORONIS, CREON, DAEDALUS, DEMETER, DIOMEDES, EGERIA, ENDYMION, FABIUS, FERONIA, GORDIUS, HELIOS, INDRA, KRISHNA, MEGARA, MENELAUS, MIDAS, MINERVA, MINOS, MINOTAUR, MYRMIDON, NUMITOR, OCEANUS, PANDEMUS, PATROCLUS, PENTHEUS, PHAON, POSEIDON, PROSERPINE, QUIRINUS, ROMULUS, SARPEDON, SATYR, SPHINX, STENTOR, TANTALUS, TELAMON, TYPHON, ULYSSES, ZEUS (ex-*LST* 10, 38, 310, 490, 1124, 489, 329, 1131, 231, 1092, 1132, 316, 350, 1137, 1094, 317, 1003, 1036, 1143, 1121, 1119, 136, 513, 332, 1145, 1127, 1147, 1149, 971, 514, 374, 644, 645, 948, 518, 954, 650, 955, 1115, 15, 1037, 1116, 1151, 962, 956, 852, 963, 858, 1117, 957, 1118, 967, and 132 respectively). Displacement: 3,960 tons. Dimensions: 316 (*w.l.*), 328 (*o.a.*) × 50 × 11 feet. Guns: **8**—40 mm. AA. Machinery: Diesel. 2 shafts. B.H.P.: 1,700 = 11 kts. Rated as Repair Ships for Battle Damage (ARB 1–12), for Landing Craft (ARD 1–4, 7–24, 26–33, 35–47), and for Aircraft (ARV 3, 6).

VULCAN. 1942, *U.S. Navy Official.*

VULCAN (Dec. 14, 1940). Built by New York S.B. Corpn. under 1939 Programme. **AJAX** (Aug. 22, 1942), **HECTOR** (Nov. 11, 1942), **JASON** (April 3, 1943). Built by Los Angeles S.B. & D.D. Corpn. under 1940 Programme. Displacement: 16,900 tons. Dimensions: 520 (*w.l.*), 529½ (*o.a.*) × 73⅓ × 23¼ feet. Guns: **4**—5 inch, **8**—40 mm. AA. Machinery: Geared turbines. 2 shafts. S.H.P.: 11,000 = 19 kts. Boilers: 4 Babcock & Wilcox 3-drum.

Note.—All these ships carry a most elaborate equipment of machine tools in order that they may undertake repairs of every possible description. *Jason* (ARH 1) is rated as a heavy hull repair ship. Others are numbered AR 5–7.

DELTA. 1944, *U.S. Navy Official.*

BRIAREUS (ex-*Hawaiian Planter*), **DELTA** (ex-*Hawaiian Packer*) (1941). Displacement: 14,000 tons. Dimensions: 465½ (*pp.*), 490½ (*o.a.*) × 69½ × 23½ feet. Guns: **1**—5 inch, **4**—3 inch, **4**—40 mm. AA. Machinery: Geared turbines. S.H.P.: 8,500 = 16·5 kts. Boilers: 2 Foster-Wheeler and 2 Babcock & Wilcox, respectively. (AR 12, 9.)

(Now has thicker funnel and foremast abaft bridge). 1925 *Photo, W. W. Stewart, Esq.*

MEDUSA (Puget Sound N.Yd., April 16, 1923). Displacement: 8,125 tons. Dimensions: 460 × 70 × 20 feet. Guns: **4**—5 inch, 51 cal., **2**—3 inch AA., etc. Machinery: Parsons geared turbines. Designed S.H.P. 7,000 = 16 kts. 2 Bureau Modified Thornycroft boilers. Oil: 1,834 tons. Complement: 466. (AR 1.)

M.T.B. Tenders.

ALECTO, ANTIGONE, CALLISTO, ORESTES, PORTUNUS (1943–45) (ex-*LST* 977, 773, 966, 135, 330, respectively). Displacement: 3,960 tons. Dimensions: 316 (*w.l.*), 328 (*o.a.*) × 50 × 11 feet. Machinery: Diesel. 2 shafts. B.H.P.: 1,700 = 11 kts. (AGP 14, 16, 15, 10, 4.)

1944, *U.S. Navy Official.*

MOBJACK (Aug. 2, 1942). Built by Lake Washington Shipyard. Displacement: 1,695 tons (2,800 tons *full load*). Dimensions: 300 (*w.l.*), 310¾ (*o.a.*) × 41 × 13½ feet. Guns: **2**—5 inch, 38 cal., **8**—40 mm. AA. Machinery: Diesel. 2 shafts. B.H.P.: 2,400 = 18 kts. (AGP 7.)

Oilers.

MATTAPONI (ex-*Kalkay*), **MONONGAHELA** (ex-*Ellkay*, 1942), **NECHES** (ex-*Aekay*), **TAPPAHANNOCK** (ex-*Jorkay*), (all 1941–42). Displacement: 22,325 tons. Dimensions: 500 (*w.l.*), 526 (*o.a.*) × 68 × 30 feet (*max.*). Machinery: Geared turbines. S.H.P.: 12,800 = 17·5 kts. Boilers: 2 Babcock & Wilcox. (AO 41–43, 47.)

SARANAC. 1944, *U.S. Navy Official.*

CHEPACHET (1943), **KENNEBAGO** (1943), **OCKLAWAHA** (June 9, 1943), **PECOS** (ex-*Corsicana*, 1942), **PONAGANSET** (1943), **SARANAC** (ex-*Cowpens*, Dec. 21, 1942). Displacement: 21,500 tons. Dimensions: 500 (*w.l.*), 520 (*o.a.*) × 68 × 30 feet. Guns: **1**—5 inch, **4**—3 inch, **8**—40 mm. AA. Machinery: Turbo-electric. S.H.P.: 6,000 = 14 kts. Boilers: 2 Babcock & Wilcox. (AO 78, 81, 84, 65, 86, 74.)

KANKAKEE (ex-*Colina*, 1941), **KENNEBEC** (ex-*Corsicana*, 1940), **MERRIMACK** (ex-*Caddo*, 1940). Displacement: 20,960 tons. Dimensions: 488½ (*w.l.*), 501½ (*o.a.*) × 68 × 30 feet (*max.*). Machinery: Geared turbines. S.H.P.: 12,000 = 16·5 kts. (AO 39, 36, 37.)

KASKASKIA. 1946, *S. C. Heal, Esq.*

ALLAGASH (1945), **ASHTABULA** (1943), **AUCILLA** (1943), **CACAPON** (June 6, 1943), **CALIENTE** (Aug. 26, 1943), **CALOOSAHATCHEE** (1945), **CANISTEO** (1945), **CHEMUNG** (ex-*Esso Annapolis*, Sept. 9, 1939), **CHIKASKIA** (Oct. 2, 1943), **CHIPOLA** (1944), **CHUKAWAN** (1945), **CIMARRON** (Jan. 7, 1939), **ELOKOMIN** (1943), **ENOREE** (ex-*Sachem*, 1942), **GUADALUPE** (ex-*Esso Raleigh*, Jan. 26, 1940), **KASKASKIA** (ex-*Esso Richmond*, 1939), **MANATEE** (Feb. 19, 1944), **MARIAS** (1943), **MISPILLION** (1945), **NANTAHALA** (1943), **NAVASOTA** (Aug. 30, 1945), **NIOBRARA** (ex-*Citadel*, Nov. 28, 1942), **PASSUMPSIC** (Oct. 31, 1945), **PAWCATUCK** (1945), **PLATTE** (July 8, 1939), **SABINE** (ex-*Esso Albany*, 1939), **SALAMONIE** (ex-*Esso Columbia*, 1939), **SEVERN** (May 31, 1944), **TALUGA** (1943), **TOLOVANA** (1944). Displacement: 23,235 tons. Complement: 64. Dimensions: 525 (*w.l.*), 553 (*o.a.*) × 75 × 32 feet. Guns: **1**—5 inch, **4**—3 inch, **8**—40 mm. AA. (except *Cimarron, Platte, Salamonie*, **4**—5 inch, **8**—40 mm. AA.). Machinery: Geared turbines. 2 shafts. S.H.P.: 13,500 = 18 kts. Boilers: 4 Foster-Wheeler, except *Cimarron*, 4 Babcock & Wilcox. Radius reported to be 18,000 miles. Cargo capacity exceeds 6,000,000 gallons. (AO 22, 24–27, 30, 32, 51–58, 60–64, 69–72, 97–100, 105–108.) War losses: *Mississinewa, Neosho.*

Note.—Ex-German oiler *Dithmarschen* has been taken over by U.S. Navy. Future disposal is uncertain.

Petrol Carriers.

PATAPSCO. 1944, *U.S. Navy Official.*

AGAWAM (May 6, 1943), **CHEHALIS** (April 15, 1943), **CHEWAUCAN** (July 22, 1944), **ELKHORN** (May 15, 1943), **GENESEE** (Sept. 23, 1943), **KERN** (ex-*Rappahannock*, Sept. 7, 1942), **KISHWAUKEE** (July 24, 1943), **MAQUOKETA** (Aug. 12, 1944), **MATTABESSET** (Nov. 11, 1944), **NAMAKAGON** (Nov. 4, 1944), **NATCHAUG** (Dec. 6, 1944), **NEMASKET** (Oct. 20, 1943), **NESPELEN** (April 10, 1945), **NOXUBEE** (April 3, 1945), **PATAPSCO** (Aug. 15, 1942), **RIO GRANDE** (Sept. 23, 1942), **SUSQUEHANNA** (Nov. 23, 1942), **TOMBIGBEE** (Nov. 18, 1943), **WABASH** (Oct. 28, 1942), **WACISSA.** Displacement: 2,020 tons. Dimensions: 292 (*w.l.*), 310¾ (*o.a.*) × 48½ × 15⅓ feet. Guns: **4**—3 inch, d.p. Machinery: Diesel-electric. 2 shafts. B.H.P.: 3,300 = 14 kts. (AOG 1–11, 48, 50–56, 59.)

AMMONUSUC, CHIWAUKUM, KALAMAZOO (Aug. 30, 1944), **TOWALIGA, WAUTAUGA** (ex-*Conroe*). Displacement: 700 tons. Dimensions: 212½ (*w.l.*), 220½ (*o.a.*) × 37 × 12¾ feet. Machinery: Diesel. B.H.P.: 800 = 10 kts. (AOG 23, 26, 30, 42, 22.)

Distilling Ships.

ABATAN (ex-*Mission San Lorenzo*, 1944), **PASIG** (ex-*Mission San Xavier*, 1944). Displacement: 22,350 tons. Dimensions: 504 (*pp.*), 523½ (*o.a.*) × 68 × 30 feet. Guns: **1**—5 inch, **4**—3 inch, **8**—40 mm. AA. Machinery: Turbo-electric. S.H.P.: 6,000 = 14 kts. Boilers: 2 Babcock & Wilcox. (AW 3, 4.)

WILDCAT (ex-*Léon Godchaux*, 1944). Displacement: 14,600 tons. Dimensions: 422¾ (*pp.*), 441½ (*o.a.*) × 57 × 28½ feet. Guns: **1**—5 inch, **2**—3 inch. Machinery: Triple expansion. I.H.P.: 2,500 = 11 kts. Boilers: 2 Babcock & Wilcox. (AW 2.)

Store Ships.

(All with refrigerated hold space.)

ADRIA, AREQUIPA, CORDUBA, KARIN, KERSTIN, LATONA, LIOBA, MALABAR, MERAPI (1944). Displacement: 7,125 tons. Dimensions: 320 (*w.l.*), 338½ (*o.a.*) × 50 × 21 feet (*max.*). Guns: **1**—3 inch. Machinery: Nordberg Diesel. B.H.P.: 1,700 = 11 kts. (AF 30, 31, 32–38.)

GRAFFIAS (ex-*Topa Topa*, 1943). Displacement: 15,300 tons. Dimensions: 440 (*pp.*), 468 (*o.a.*) × 54 × 28 feet. Guns: **1**—5 inch, **4**—3 inch. Machinery: Geared turbines. S.H.P.: 6,000 = 15·5 kts. Boilers: 2 Babcock & Wilcox. (AF 29.)

1946, *S. C. Heal, Esq.*

HYADES (ex-*Iberville*, 1942). Displacement: 13,950 tons. Dimensions: 445 (*pp.*), 468¾ (*o.a.*) × 63 × 28 feet. Guns: **1**—5 inch, **4**—3 inch. Machinery: Geared turbines. S.H.P.: 6,000 = 15·5 kts. Boilers: 2 Babcock & Wilcox. (AF 28.)

ALDEBARAN. 1942, *U.S. Navy Official.*

ALDEBARAN (ex-*Staghound*, June 21, 1939). Displacement: 7,300 tons. Dimensions: 435 (*w.l.*), 459 (*o.a.*) × 63 × 25¾ feet. Guns: **1**—5 inch, **4**—3 inch. Machinery: Geared turbines. S.H.P.: 6,000 = 15·5 kts. Boilers: 2 Babcock & Wilcox. (AF 10.)

General Stores Issue Ships.

ACUBENS, CYBELE, GRATIA, HECUBA, HESPERIA, IOLANDA, KOCHAB, LIGURIA, LUNA (ex-*Harriet Hosmer*), **TALITA** (ex-*Jonathan Jennings*), **VOLANS** (ex-*Edward Preble*). (1941–42). 7,100 tons *gross*. Dimensions: 441½ × 57 × 27½ feet (max.) Machinery: Triple expansion. I.H.P. 2,500 = 11 kts. (AKS 5–15.)

CASTOR (ex-*Challenge*, May 20, 1939), **POLLUX** (ex-*Nancy Lykes*, 1941). 6,700 tons *gross*. Dimensions: 435 (*pp.*), 459 (*o.a.*) × 63 × 25¾ feet (max.). Guns: **4**—5 inch, etc. Machinery: Geared turbines. S.H.P. 6,000=15.5 kts. (AKS 1, 4.)

MERCURY 1946, *Mr. Wm. H. Davis.*

JUPITER (ex-*Santa Catalina*, ex-*Flying Cloud*, Sept. 30, 1939), **MERCURY** (ex-*Mormactern*, ex-*Lightning*, July 15, 1939). Displacement: 13,900 tons. Dimensions: 435 (*w.l.*), 459 (*o.a.*) × 63 × 25¾ feet (*max.*). Guns: **1**—5 inch, **4**—3 inch. Machinery: Geared turbines. S.H.P.: 6,000 = 15·5 kts. Boilers: 2 Babcock & Wilcox. (AKS 19, 20.)

JUPITER is now rated as Aviation Supply Ship (AVS 8).

Cargo Ships.

1946, *courtesy Derek Mercer, Esq.*

ALCONA, BELTRAMI, PINELLAS (all 1944). Displacement: 7,125 tons. Dimensions: 320 (*w.l.*), 338¾ (*o.a.*) × 50 × 21 feet (*max.*). Guns: **1**—3 inch d.p. Machinery: Nordberg Diesel. B.H.P.: 1,750 = 11 kts. (AK 157, 162, 202.)

1944, *U.S. Navy Official.*

Arided (ex-*Noah H. Swayne*, Oct. 28, 1942)
Ascella (ex-*Geo. C. Yount*)
Bootes (ex-*Thos. O. Larkin*)
Cheleb (ex-*Lyman J. Gage*)
Crater (ex-*John J. Audubon*)
Ganymede (ex-*James W. Nye*)
Lesuth (ex-*William M. Gwin*)
Matar (ex-*Napoleon B. Boward*)
Megrez (ex-*General Vallejo*)
Murzim (ex-*Brigham Young*)
Situla (ex-*John Whitaker*)
Sterope (ex-*James Wilson*)
Triangulum (ex-*Eugene B. Daskam*)
Venus (ex-*Wm. Williams*)

Displacement: 14,350 tons. Dimensions: 416 (*w.l.*), 441½ (*o.a.*) × 57 × 28⅓ feet (*max.*). Guns: **1**—5 inch, **4**—40 mm. AA. Machinery: Triple expansion. I.H.P.: 2,500 = 12 kts. (AK 73, 137, 99, 138, 70, 104, 125, 119, 126, 95, 140, 96, 102, 135.)

FOMALHAUT (ex-*Cape Lookout*, Jan. 25, 1941). Displacement: 11,100 tons. Dimensions: 390 (*w.l.*), 412¼ (*o.a.*) × 61 × 23½ feet. Guns: **1**—5 inch, **4**—3 inch, **2**—40 mm. AA. Machinery: Nordberg Diesel. B.H.P.: 4,000 = 14 kts. (AK 22.)

Cargo Ships, Attack type.

1946, *Mr. Wm. H. Davis.*

Achernar (Dec. 22, 1943)
Algol (ex-*James Baires*)
Alshain (Jan. 26, 1944)
Andromeda (Dec. 22, 1942)
Arneb (ex-*Mischief*)
Capricornus (ex-*Spitfire*)
Chara (March 15, 1944)
Diphda (May 11, 1944)
Leo (June 29, 1944)
Marquette (April 29, 1945)
Mathews (Dec. 29, 1944)
Merrick (Jan. 28, 1945)
Montague
Muliphen (Aug. 26, 1944)
Oglethorpe (April 15, 1945)
Ottawa
Rankin
Rolette (March 11, 1945)
Seminole
Skagit
Thuban (April 26, 1943)
Union
Uvalde (May 20, 1944)
Vermilion
Virgo (June 4, 1943)
Warrick
Washburn
Whiteside
Whitley
Winston (Nov. 30, 1944)
Wyandot
Yancey

Displacement: 14,200 tons. Dimensions: 435 (*w.l.*), 459 (*o.a.*) × 63 × 26⅓ feet (*max.*). Guns: **1**—5 inch, **8**—40 mm. AA. Machinery: Geared turbines. S.H.P.: 6,000 = 15·5 kts. Boilers: 2 Foster-Wheeler. (AKA 53–55, 15, 56–60, 95–98, 61, 73, 100, 101, 103, 99, 104, 105, 19, 106, 88, 20, 89, 108, 90, 91, 94, 92, 93.)

1945.

Artemis
Athene
Pamina
Renate
Sarita
Scania
Sylvania
Xenia
Zenobia

Displacement: 3,700 tons (*std*). Dimensions: 400 (*w.l.*), 426 (*o.a.*) × 58 × 16 feet (*max.*). Guns: **1**—5 inch, **8**—40 mm. AA. Machinery: Turbo-electric. 2 shafts. S.H.P.: 6,600 = 16·5 kts. Boilers: 2 Wickes. (AKA 21, 22, 36, 38, 40, 44, 51, 52.)

1946, *S. C. Heal, Esq.*

LIBRA (ex-*Jean Lykes*, 1941), **OBERON** (ex-*Delalba*, March 18, 1942), **TITANIA** (ex-*Harry Culbreath*, Feb. 28, 1942). Displacement: 14,225 tons. Dimensions: 435 (*w.l.*), 459 (*o.a.*) × 63 × 26½ feet (*max.*). Guns: **1**—5 inch, **8**—40 mm. AA. Machinery: Geared turbines. S.H.P.: 6,000 = 15·5 kts. Boilers: 2 Foster-Wheeler. (AKA 12, 14, 13.)

Transports.

1944, *courtesy Federal S.B. & D.D. Co.*

Gen. Alexander E. Anderson (May 2, 1943)
Gen. George M. Randall (Jan. 30, 1944)
Gen. Henry W. Butner (Sept. 10, 1943)
Gen. J. C. Breckinridge (March 18, 1945)
Gen. Wm. A. Mann (July 18, 1943)
Gen. William Mitchell (Oct. 31, 1943)

All built by Federal S.B. & D.D. Co. at Kearny. Displacement: 20,175 tons (*full load*). Dimensions: 573 (*w.l.*), 622½ (*o.a.*) × 75½ × 25½ feet (*max.*). Guns: **4**—5 inch, **8**—40 mm. AA. Machinery: De Laval geared turbines. 2 shafts. S.H.P.: 17,000 = 20 kts. Boilers: 4 Foster-Wheeler, 465 lb. working pressure. (AP 111–115, 176.)

1944, *U.S. Navy Official.*

LEJEUNE (ex-German *Windhuk*, 1936). Displacement: 19,200 tons. Dimensions: 548 (*pp.*), 573 (*o.a.*) × 72⅛ × 26 feet. Guns: **1**—5 inch, **4**—3 inch, **8**—40 mm. AA. Machinery: Geared turbines. 2 shafts. S.H.P.: 17,500 = 17·5 kts. Boilers: 3 Babcock & Wilcox. (AP 74.)

WHARTON (ex-*Southern Cross*, 1920). Displacement: 21,900 tons. Dimensions: 517 (*pp.*), 539 (*o.a.*) × 72 × 31¼ feet. Machinery: 4 sets geared turbines. 2 shafts. S.H.P.: 12,000 = 16·5 kts. Boilers: 8 Babcock & Wilcox. Oil fuel: 3,315 tons. (AP 7.)

Fleet Auxiliaries

Transports, Attack type.

OKALOOSA. 1946, *Mr. Wm. H. Davis.*

Arenac (Sept. 14, 1944)
Barnwell (Sept. 30, 1944)
Bexar
Bollinger (Nov. 19, 1944)
Botetourt (Oct. 19, 1944)
Bottineau
Bronx
Brookings
Crockett
Deuel
Edgecombe
Gage
Glynn
Grimes
Kershaw
Latimer
Lavaca
Lenawee
Logan
Lubbock
McCracken
Magoffin
Mellette
Menard
Menifee
Meriwether
Mifflin
Missoula
Montrose
Mountrail
Natrona
Navarro
Neshoba
New Kent
Noble
Okaloosa
Okanogan
Olmsted
Oneida
Pickaway
Pitt
Randall
Rawlins
Renville
Rockbridge
Rockingham
Rockwall
Rutland
St. Croix
Sanborn
Sandoval
San Saba
Sarasota
Sevier
Sherburne
Sibley
Talladega
Tazewell
Telfair

All county names. Displacement: 12,450 tons. Dimensions: 436½ (*w.l.*), 455 (*o.a.*) × 62 × 24 feet (*max.*). Guns: **1**—5 inch, **12**—40 mm. AA. Machinery: Geared turbines. S.H.P.: 8,500 = 17 kts. Boilers: 2 Babcock & Wilcox. (APA 128–239.)

1944, *U.S. Navy Official.*

Appling (April 9, 1944)
Audrain (April 21, 1944)
Berrien
Bladen
Burleson
Cleburne
Colusa
Cortland
Fergus
Fillmore
Geneva
Niagara (Feb. 10, 1945)
Presidio

All county names. Displacement: 7,080 tons. Dimensions: 400 (*w.l.*), 426 (*o.a.*) × 58 × 16 feet. Guns: **1**—5 inch, **8**—40 mm. AA. Machinery: Turbo-electric. 2 shafts. S.H.P.: 6,000 = 16·5 kts. Boilers: 2 Babcock & Wilcox. (APA 58, 59, 62, 63, 67, 73–75, 82, 83, 86–88.)

Transports, Attack type—*continued.*

Bayfield (ex-*Sea Bass*)
Cambria (ex-*Sea Swallow*)
Cavalier
Chilton (ex-*Sea Needle*, Dec. 24, 1942)
Fremont (ex-*Sea Corsair*, March 31, 1943)
Henrico (ex-*Sea Darter*)

All county names. Displacement: 16,100 tons. Dimensions: 465 (*w.l.*), 492 (*o.a.*) × 69½ × 26½ feet (*max.*). Guns: **2**—5 inch, **4**—40 mm. AA. Machinery: Geared turbines. S.H.P.: 8,500 = 18 kts. Boilers: 2 Combustion Engineering type. (APA 33, 36, 37, 38, 44, 45.)

CALVERT (ex-*Delorleans*, May 29, 1943), **CHARLES CARROLL** (ex-*Deluruguay*, 1941), **CRESCENT CITY** (ex-*Delorleans*, 1940), **MONROVIA** (ex-*Delargentino*, 1942). Displacement: 14,247 tons. Dimensions: 468 (*pp.*), 491 (*o.a.*) × 65½ × 25½ feet (*max.*). Guns: **1**—5 inch, **3**—3 inch, **4**—40 mm. AA. Machinery: Geared turbines. S.H.P.: 7,800 = 16 kts. Boilers: 2 Babcock & Wilcox. (APA 21, 28, 31, 32.)

S. CHASE. 1944, *U.S. Navy Official.*

ARTHUR MIDDLETON (ex-*African Comet*, ex-*American Banker*, 1941), **GEORGE CLYMER** (ex-*African Planet*, ex-*American Farmer*, 1941), **PRESIDENT ADAMS** (1941), **PRESIDENT HAYES** (1940), **PRESIDENT JACKSON** (1940), **SAMUEL CHASE** (ex-*African Meteor*, ex-*American Shipper*, 1941), **THOMAS JEFFERSON** (ex-*President Garfield*, 1941). Displacement: 18,000 tons. Dimensions: 465 (*w.l.*), 489 (*o.a.*) × 69½ × 27½ feet. Guns: **4**—3 inch, **4**—40 mm. AA. Machinery: Geared turbines. S.H.P.: 8,500 = 16·5 kts. (APA 25, 27, 19, 20, 18, 26, 30.)

Fast Transports.

BEVERLY W. REID. 1945, *"Ships and Aircraft"*

JOSEPH C. HUBBARD. 1946, *Mr. Wm. H. Davis.*

(*Described on following page.*)

Fast Transports—*continued.*

Alexander Diachenko (Aug. 15, 1944)
Amesbury (June 5, 1943)
Arthur L. Bristol (Feb. 19, 1944)
Balduck (Oct. 27, 1944)
Barr (Dec. 28, 1943)
Bassett (Jan. 15, 1944)
Begor (May 25, 1944)
Belet (March 3, 1944)
Beverly W. Reid (March 4, 1944)
Blessman (June 19, 1943)
Borum
Bowers (Oct. 31, 1943)
Bray (April 15, 1944)
Brock (Jan. 20, 1944)
Bull (March 25, 1943)
Bunch (May 29, 1943)
Burdo (Nov. 25, 1944)
Burke (April 3, 1943)
Carpellotti (March 10, 1945)
Cavallaro (June 15, 1944)
Charles Lawrence (Feb. 16, 1943)
Cofer (Sept. 6, 1943)
Cook (Aug. 26, 1944)
Cread (Feb. 12, 1944)
Crosley (Feb. 12, 1944)
Daniel T. Griffin (Feb. 25, 1943)
Donald W. Wolf (July 22, 1944)
Don O. Woods (Feb. 19, 1944)
Durik
Earhart (May 12, 1945)
Earle B. Hall (March 1, 1944)
Enright (May 29, 1943)
Frament (June 28, 1943)
Francovich (June 5, 1945)
Gantner (April 17, 1943)
George W. Ingram (May 8, 1943)
Gosselin (May 4, 1944)
Haines (Aug. 26, 1943)
Harry L. Corl
Hayter
Hollis (Sept. 11, 1943)
Hopping (March 10, 1943)
Horace A. Bass (Sept. 12, 1944)
Hunter Marshall (May 5, 1945)
Ira Jeffery (May 15, 1943)
Jack C. Robinson (Jan. 8, 1944)
Jenks (Sept. 11, 1943)
John P. Gray (March 18, 1944)
John Q. Roberts (Feb. 11, 1944)
Joseph C. Hubbard
Joseph E. Campbell (June 26, 1943)
Joseph M. Auman (Feb. 5, 1944)
Julius A. Raven (March 3, 1944)
Kephart (Sept. 6, 1943)
Kinzer (Dec. 9, 1943)
Kirwin (June 16, 1944)
Kleinsmith (Jan. 27, 1945)
Kline (June, 27. 1944)
Knudson (Feb. 5, 1944)
Laning (July 4, 1943)
Lee Fox (May 29, 1943)
Liddle (Aug. 9, 1943)
Lloyd (Oct. 23, 1943)
Loy (July 4, 1943)
Maloy (Aug. 18, 1943)
Myers (Feb. 15, 1944)
Newman (Aug. 9, 1943)
Odum (Jan. 19, 1944)
Pavlic (Dec. 18, 1943)
Ray K. Edwards (Feb. 19, 1944)
Raymond W. Herndon (July 15, 1944)
Rednour (Feb. 12, 1944)
Reeves (April 22, 1943)
Register (Jan. 20, 1944)
Ringness (Feb. 5, 1944)
Rogers Blood
Ruchamkin (June 15, 1944)
Runels (Sept. 4, 1943)
Schmitt (May 29, 1943)
Scott (April 3, 1943)
Scribner (Aug. 1, 1944)
Sims (Feb. 6, 1943)
Tatum (Aug. 7, 1943)
Tollberg (Feb. 12, 1944)
Truxton (March 9, 1944)
Upham (March 9, 1944)
Walsh (April 28, 1945)
Walter B. Cobb (Feb. 23, 1944)
Walter S. Gorka (May 26, 1945)
Walter X. Young (Sept. 30, 1944)
Wantuck (Sept. 25, 1944)
Weber (May 1, 1943)
Weiss (Feb. 17, 1945)
William J. Pattison (April 18, 1944)
William M. Hobby (Feb. 11, 1944)
Yokes (Nov. 27, 1943)

Ex-destroyer escorts. Displacement: 1,650 tons. Dimensions: 300 (*w.l.*), 306 (*o.a.*) × 37 × 20 feet (*max.*). Guns: **1**—5 inch, **6**—40 mm. AA. Machinery: Turbo-electric. 2 shafts. S.H.P.: 12,000 = 23 kts. Boilers: 2 Express. Complement: 204 + 162 troops. (APD 37–46, 48–136.) War loss: *Bates.*

Amphibious Force Flagships.

MOUNT MCKINLEY. 1945, *U.S. Navy Official.*

Adirondack
Appalachian (Jan. 29, 1943)
Auburn (ex-*Kathay*)
Blue Ridge (March 7, 1943)
Catoctin (ex-*Mary Whitridge*)
Eldorado (ex-*Monsoon*)
Estes (ex-*Morning Star*)
Mount McKinley (ex-*Cyclone*)
Mount Olympus (ex-*Eclipse*)
Panamint (ex-*Northern Light*)
Pocono
Rocky Mount (March 7, 1943)
Taconic
Teton (ex-*Witch of the Wave*)
Wasatch (ex-*Fleetwing*)

Displacement: 12,750 to 12,800 tons. Dimensions: 435 (*w.l.*), 459¼ (*o.a.*) × 63 × 24 feet (*max.*). Guns: **2**—5 inch, **8**—40 mm. AA. Machinery: Geared turbines. S.H.P.: 6,000 = 15·5 kts. Boilers: 2 Combustion Engineering type. (AGC 1–3, 5, 7–17.)

General Note.—Originally rated as Combined Operations Communications H.Q. Ships, these vessels are fitted as flagships for Chiefs of Combined Forces, with accommodation for Marine or Army units attached. Radar and radio equipment is exceptionally elaborate.

Miscellaneous Auxiliaries.

BURTON ISLAND (April 20, 1946), **EDISTO** (1945). Icebreakers, built by Western Pipe & Steel Co. Displacement: 5,425 tons. Dimensions: 250 (*pp.*), 269 (*o.a.*) × 63½ × 25¾ feet. Guns: **2**—5 inch, **12**—40 mm. AA. Machinery: Diesel, with electric drive. 3 shafts (1 forward, 2 aft). H.P.: 13,300 = 16 kts. Entirely welded construction, with double hull. (AG 88, 89.)

Avery Island
Baham (ex-*Elizabeth C. Bellamy*)
Basilan (ex-*J. P. Villere*)
Belle Isle
Burias (ex-*Mollie Moore Davis*)
Coasters Harbour
Cuttyhunk Island
Indian Island
Kent Island
Zaniah (ex-*Anthony F. Lucas*)

All built 1944. Displacement: 11,500 tons. Dimensions: 422¾ (*pp.*) 441½ (*o.a.*) × 57 × 23 feet. Guns: **1**—5 inch, **4**—40 mm. AA. Machinery: Triple expansion. I.H.P.: 2,500 = 11 kts. Boilers: 2 Babcock & Wilcox. Mostly, if not all, employed as Electronic Repair Ships. (AG 68–71, 73–78.)

PARRIS ISLAND (ex-*PCE* 901, 1943). Displacement: 795 tons. Dimensions: 184½ × 33 × 9½ feet. Machinery: Diesel. 2 shafts. B.H.P. 1,800 = 15 kts. (AG 72).

Landing Ships.

Note.—Attack Cargo Ships and Attack Transports, recorded on earlier pages, are in fact other species of Landing Ships.

OZARK. 1944, *U.S. Navy Official.*

CATSKILL (May 19, 1942), **OZARK** (June 15, 1942). Both built by Willamette Iron & Steel Corpn., Portland, Wash., under 1940 Programme. Designed as large Minelayers, but have been converted into Landing Ships (Vehicle). Displacement: 5,875 tons. Dimensions: 440 (*w.l.*), 455½ (*o.a.*) × 60⅙ × 20 feet. Guns: **2**—5 inch, 38 cal., **8**—40 mm. AA. Machinery: Geared turbines. 2 shafts. S.H.P.: 11,000 = 18·5 kts. Boilers: 4 Combustion Engineering type. Complement: 564. (LSV 1, 2.)

OSAGE. 1944, *U.S. Navy Official.*

MONITOR (Jan. 29, 1943), **MONTAUK** (April 14, 1943), **OSAGE** (June 30, 1943), **SAUGUS** (Sept. 4, 1943). All built by Ingall's S.B. Corpn., Pascagoula, Miss. Designed as Netlayers, but converted into Landing Ships (Vehicle). Displacement: 5,625 tons. Dimensions: 440 (*w.l.*), 451⅓ (*o.a.*) × 60¼ × 20 feet. Guns: **2**—5 inch, 38 cal., **8**—40 mm. AA. Machinery: Geared turbines. 2 shafts. S.H.P.: 11,000 = 18·5 kts. Boilers: 4 Combustion Engineering type. Complement: 564. (LSV 3–6.)

Fleet Auxiliaries

Landing Ships—*continued*

CARTER HALL. 1946, *S. C. Heal, Esq.*

Ashland (Dec. 21, 1942)
Belle Grove (Feb. 17, 1942)
Carter Hall (March 4, 1943)
Epping Forest (April 2, 1943)
Gunston Hall (May 1, 1943)
Lindenwald (June 11, 1943)
Oak Hill (June 25, 1943)
White Marsh (July 19, 1943)

All built by Moore Dry Dock Co. Displacement: 4,500 tons. Dimensions: 454 (*w.l.*), 457¾ (*o.a.*) × 72 × 18 feet. Guns: **1**—5 inch, **12**—40 mm. AA. Machinery: Skinner Unaflow reciprocating. 2 shafts. I.H.P.: 7,400 = 15 kts. Boilers: 2 of 2-drum type. (LSD 1–8.)

FT. MANDAN. 1946, *Mr. Wm. H. Davis.*

Cabildo (Dec. 28, 1944)
Casa Grande (ex-*Spear*, ex-*Portway*, April 11, 1944)
Catamount (Jan. 27, 1945)
Colonial (Feb. 28, 1945)
Comstock (April 28, 1945)
Donner (April 6, 1945)
Fort Mandan (1945)
Fort Marian (May 22, 1945)
Fort Snelling (1945)
Point Defiance (ex-*Hilton Head*, 1945)
Rushmore (ex-*Sword*, ex-*Swashway*, May 10, 1944)
San Marcos (Jan. 10, 1945)
Shadwell (ex-*Tomahawk*, ex-*Waterway*, May 24, 1944)
Tortuga (Jan. 21, 1945)
Whetstone (1945)

All built by Navy Yards. Of same type as *Ashland* class, above, but propelled by geared turbines. S.H.P.: 7,000 = 15 kts. (except *Fort Marian, Fort Snelling*, and *Point Defiance*, S.H.P.: 9,000 = 15·5 kts.). (LSD 13–27.)

Note.—These Landing Ships (Dock) serve as parent ships to landing craft and to coastal craft.

LST 1008. 1946, *S. C. Heal, Esq.*

LST 332. 1943, *U.S. Navy Official.*

L S T (Landing Ship, Tank). LSM 1–1152. (In August, 1946, 480 were still in service.) Displacement: 2,366 tons (*beaching*); 4,080 tons (*full load*). Dimensions: 316 (*w.l.*), 328 (*o.a.*). × 50 × 14 feet (*max.*). Machinery: Diesel. 2 shafts. B.H.P: 1,700 = 11 kts. Complement: 64 to 119.

Nos. 1153–1155 (building). Displacement: 6,000 tons. Dimensions: 368 (*w.l.*), 382 (*o.a.*) × 54 × 14½ feet. Machinery: Geared turbines. 2 shafts. S.H.P.: 6,000 = 14 kts.

Note.—When equipped with a portable landing strip, the LST can carry 8 reconnaissance aircraft.

Landing Ships—*continued.*

LSM (R) 188, showing rockets. 1944, *U.S. Navy Official.*

LSM 201, in operation. 1944, *U.S. Navy Official.*

L S M (Landing Ship, Medium). LSM 1–558. (In Aug. 1946 a total of 342 were left in service.) Displacement: 743 tons (*beaching*); 1,095 tons (*full load*). Dimensions: 196½ (*w.l.*), 203½ (*o.a.*) × 34½ × 7⅓ feet. Guns: **2**—40 mm. AA. Machinery: Diesel. 2 shafts. B.H.P.: 2,800 = 12 kts. Complement: 59.

Notes.—50 of these, rated as LSM(R), with full load displacements varying from 961 to 1,084 tons, and complements from 81 to 138, are armed with **1**—5 inch, **4**—4·2 inch mortars, **2**—40 mm. AA., and numerous rocket projectors. Some have been fitted with Kirsten cycloidal propellers, enabling ship to turn 360° and remain in same position.

Landing Craft.

1944, *U.S. Navy Official.*

L C T (Landing Craft, Tank). Comprised LCT (5) 1/500 (ex-*YTL* 1/500). Displacement: 285 tons, *full load.* Dimensions: 114⅙ × 32⅔ feet; LCT (6) 501/1,465. Displacement: 309 tons, *full load.* Dimensions: 119 × 32⅔ feet. Machinery: Diesel. 3 shafts. B.H.P.: 675 = 10 kts. 51 of former and 650 of latter remained in service in Aug. 1946.

L C I (Landing Craft, Infantry) and **L C S** (Landing Craft, Support). These originally comprised LCI 1–1109 and LCS 1–130, with following main particulars in common. Displacement: 387 tons *full load*. Dimensions: 159 × 23⅔ × 5⅔ feet. Machinery: Diesel. 2 shafts. B.H.P.: 1,320 = 14 kts. Complement: 29 to 78, according to employment. By August, 1946, the following remained in service:

LCFF (Flotilla flagships), 32. Guns: **5**—20 mm. AA.
LCI (G) (Gunboats), 39. Guns: **3**—40 mm. AA., **10** rocket projectors.
LCI(L) (Large), 300. Guns: **4** or **5**—20 mm. AA.

Landing Craft—*continued*

LCI(M) (Mortar), 36. Guns: **3**—4·2 inch mortars, **1**—40 mm. AA.
LCI(R) (Rocket), 3. Guns: **6**—5 inch rocket projectors, **1**—40 mm. AA.
LCS(L) (3) (Large, Mark III), 122. Guns: **6**—40 mm. AA.

1944, *U.S. Navy Official.*

Surveying Ships.

1944, *U.S. Navy Official.*

BOWDITCH (ex-*Santa Inez*), (Burmeister & Wain, Copenhagen, 1929). Purchased 1939. Displacement: 7,680 tons (*full load*). Dimensions: 370 (*w.l.*), 386 (*o.a.*) × 53 × 20 feet. Guns: **4**—3 inch. Machinery: Diesel. 2 shafts. B.H.P.: 3,500 = 12 kts. Oil fuel: 864 tons. Complement: 405. (AGS 4.)

PATHFINDER (1929). Displacement: 2,175 tons (*full load*). Dimensions: 209⅓ (*w.l.*), 229⅓ (*o.a.*) × 39 × 16 feet. Guns: **2**—3 inch. Machinery: De Laval geared turbines. S.H.P.: 2,000 = 14 kts. Boilers: 2 Babcock & Wilcox. Complement: 158. (AGS 1.)

ARMISTEAD RUST (ex-*PCS* 1404), **DERICKSON** (ex-*PCS* 1458), **HARKNESS** (ex-*YMS* 242), **JAMES M. GILLIS** (ex-*YMS* 262), **JOHN BLISH** (ex-*PCS* 1457), **LITTLEHALES** (ex-*PCS* 1388, July 17, 1943), **SIMON NEWCOMB** (ex-*YMS* 263). (1942–43.) Displacement: 245 tons. Dimensions: 136 × 23⅓ × 6 feet. Guns: **1**—3 inch. Machinery: G.M. Diesels. 2 shafts. B.H.P.: 1,000 = 13 kts. Complement: 34. (AGS 6–10, 12–14.)

Hospital Ships.

TRANQUILLITY. 1946, *U.S. Navy Official.*

BENEVOLENCE (ex-*Marine Lion*), **CONSOLATION** (ex-*Marine Walrus*), **HAVEN** (ex-*Marine Hawk*), **REPOSE** (ex-*Marine Beaver*), **SANCTUARY** (ex-*Marine Owl*), (Aug. 15, 1944), **TRANQUILLITY** (ex-*Marine Dolphin*), all built by Sun S.B. & D.D. Co. Displacement: 15,400 tons. Dimensions: 496 (*w.l.*), 520 (*o.a.*) × 71½ × 24 feet (*mean*). Machinery: Geared turbines. S.H.P.: 9,000 = 17 kts. Boilers: 2 Babcock & Wilcox. Complement: 568–574. Beds for 802 patients. Air conditioned throughout. (AH 12–17.)

Submarine Rescue Vessels.

FLORIKAN. 1943, *U.S. Navy Official.*

CHANTICLEER, COUCAL (both June, 1942), **FLORIKAN** (June 14, 1942), **GREENLET** (July 12, 1942), **KITTIWAKE** (July 10, 1945), **PETREL.** Displacement: 1,780 tons (2,141 tons *full load*). Dimensions: 251⅓ × 42 × 14¼ feet. Guns: **2**—3 inch, **2**—40 mm. AA. Machinery: Diesel-electric. B.H.P.: 3,000 = 14·5 kts. (ARS 7–10, 13, 14.)

PENGUIN (ex-tug *Chetco*, 1943). Displacement: 1,280 tons. Dimensions: 205 × 38½ × 12 feet. Guns: **1**—3 inch. Machinery: Diesel-electric. B.H.P.: 3,000 = 16 kts. (ASR 12.)

ORTOLAN. 1935, *Bear Photo Service.*

CHEWINK, MALLARD (both 1918), **ORTOLAN** (1919), **WIDGEON** (1918). Displacement: 1,060 tons (1,400 tons *full load*). Dimensions: 180 (*w.l.*), 187⅚ (*o.a.*) × 36¾ × 10½ feet *mean* draught. Guns: **2**—3 inch, 50 cal., AA. Machinery: Triple expansion. I.H.P.: 1,400 = 14 kts. Boilers: 2 Babcock & Wilcox. Oil fuel: 275 tons. Complement: 79. (ASR 1, 3, 4, 5.)

Note.—All these vessels are equipped with powerful pumps, heavy air compressors and special submarine rescue chambers.

Salvage Vessels.

BOLSTER. 1946, *U.S. Navy Official.*

Bolster (Dec. 23, 1944)
Cable (April 1, 1943)
Chain (June 3, 1943)
Clamp (ex-*Atlantic Salvor*, Oct. 24, 1942)
Conserver (Jan. 27, 1945)
Curb (April 24, 1943)
Current (Sept. 25, 1943)
Deliver (Sept. 25, 1943)
Diver (Dec. 19, 1942)
Escape (Nov. 22, 1942)
Gear (ex-*Pacific Salvor*, Oct. 24, 1942)
Grapple (Dec. 31, 1942)
Grasp (July 31, 1943)
Hoist (March 31, 1945)
Opportune (March 31, 1945)
Preserver (April 1, 1943)
Reclaimer
Recovery
Safeguard (Nov. 20, 1943)
Snatch (April 8, 1944)

Displacement: 1,360 tons. Dimensions: 207 (*w.l.*), 213½ (*o.a.*) × 39 × 13 feet. Guns: **4**—40 mm. AA. Machinery: Diesel-electric. 2 shafts. B.H.P.: 3,000 = 14 kts. Complement: 85. (ARS 5–8, 19–25, 27, 33, 34, 38–43.)

Fleet Auxiliaries

Salvage Vessels—*continued.*

1944, *U.S. Navy Official.*

ANCHOR, VALVE (May 20, 1943), **VENT.** Wood. Displacement: 800 tons. Dimensions: $183\frac{1}{4} \times 37 \times 14\frac{2}{3}$ feet. Machinery: Diesel-electric. B.H.P.: 1,200 = 12 kts. (ARS 13, 28, 29.)

GYPSY, MENDER, SALVAGER, WINDLASS (ex-*LSM* 549–552). Displacement: 1,080 tons. Dimensions: $224\frac{1}{4} \times 34 \times 7$ feet. Machinery: Diesel. 2 shafts. B.H.P.: 2,800 = 13 kts. (ARSD 1–4.) (Used as lifting vessels.)

LAYSAN ISLAND, PALMYRA (ex-*LST* 1098–1100). Displacement: 3,960 tons. Dimensions: $328 \times 50 \times 11$ feet. Machinery: Diesel. 2 shafts. B.H.P.: 1,800=11 kts. (ARST 1, 3.) (Tenders.)

DISCOVERER (ex-*Auk*), **VIKING** (ex-*Guide*, ex-*Flamingo*) (all 1918–19). Displacement: 1,060 tons. Otherwise as Submarine Rescue Vessels of similar design, above. (ARS 1, 3.)

Net Tenders (Boom Defence Vessels).

Chinaberry (July 19, 1943)
Cinnamon (ex-*Royal Palm*, June 6, 1943)
Cliffrose (Nov. 27, 1943)
Torchwood (Feb. 19, 1944)
Whitewood (April 21, 1944)

Wood (other types are steel). Displacement: 1,058 tons. Dimensions: $194\frac{1}{2} \times 37 \times 11\frac{3}{4}$ feet. Guns: 1—3 inch. Machinery: Diesel-electric. B.H.P.: 1,200 = 12 kts. Complement: 56. (AN 61, 50, 42, 55, 63.)

Cohoes (Nov. 29, 1944)
Etlah (Dec. 16, 1944)
Manayunk (March 30, 1945)
Marietta (April 27, 1945)
Nahant (June, 1945)
Naubuc (April 15, 1944)
Oneota (May 27, 1944)
Passaconaway (June 30, 1944)
Passaic (June 29, 1944)
Shakamaxon (Sept. 9, 1944)
Suncock (Feb. 16, 1945)
Tonawanda (Nov. 14, 1944)
Tunxis (Aug. 18, 1944)
Waxsaw (Sept. 15, 1944)
Yazoo (Oct. 18, 1944)

Displacement: 545 tons. Dimensions: $168\frac{1}{2} \times 33\frac{1}{2} \times 10\frac{3}{4}$ feet. Guns: 1—3 inch. Machinery: Diesel-electric. B.H.P.: 1,200 = 12 kts. Complement: 46. (AN 78–92.)

BOXWOOD. 1941, *U.S.N. Official.*

4 *American S.B. Co., Cleveland:* **LOCUST** (Feb. 1, 1941), **MANGO** (Feb. 22, 1941), **MIMOSA** (March 15, 1941), **MULBERRY** (March 26, 1941).

Net Tenders (Boom Defence Vessels)—*continued.*

6 *American S.B. Co., Lorain:* **HAZEL** (ex-*Poplar*, Feb. 15, 1941), **NUTMEG** (ex-*Sycamore*, March 13, 1941), **PALM** (Feb. 8, 1941), **REDWOOD** (Feb. 22, 1941), **ROSEWOOD** (April 1, 1941), **SANDALWOOD** (March 16, 1941).

4 *Commercial Iron Works:* **BUCKEYE** (ex-*Cottonwood*, July 26, 1941), **CATALPA** (Feb. 22, 1941), **CHESTNUT** (March 15, 1941), **CINCHONA** (July 2, 1941).

3 *General Engrg. & D.D. Co.:* **BUCKTHORN** (ex-*Dogwood*, March 27, 1941), **EBONY** (June 3, 1941), **EUCALYPTUS** (July 3, 1941).

2 *John H. Mathis Co.:* **TEABERRY** (May 24, 1941), **TEAK** (July 7, 1941).

4 *Lake Washington Shipyards:* **ALOE** (Jan. 11, 1941), **ASH** (Feb. 15, 1941), **BOXWOOD** (ex-*Birch*, March 8, 1941), **BUTTERNUT** (May 10, 1941).

4 *Marietta Mfg. Co.:* **ELDER** (ex-*Juniper*, June 19, 1941), **GUMTREE** (March 20, 1941), **HOLLY** (April 17, 1941), **LARCH** (July 2, 1941).

Displacement: 500 tons (700 tons *full load*). Dimensions: 146 (*w.l.*), 163 (*o.a.*) $\times 30\frac{1}{2} \times 10\frac{1}{2}$ feet. Guns: 1—3 inch AA., some M.G. Machinery: Diesel-electric. B.H.P.: 800 = 12 kts. Complement: 48. (AN 6–24, 26–35.)

Note.—Three of this class were transferred to the French Navy in 1944.

Fleet Tugs.

(Later units have no funnel.) 1940, *courtesy "Our Navy."*

Abnaki (April 22, 1943)
Achomawi (Sept. 10, 1944)
Alsea (May 22, 1943)
Apache (May 8, 1942)
Arapaho (ex-*Catawba*, June 22, 1942)
Arikara (June 22, 1943)
Atakapa (July 11, 1944)
Avoyel (Aug. 9, 1944)
Bannock (Jan. 7, 1943)
Cahuilla (Nov. 2, 1944)
Carib (Feb. 7, 1943)
Chawasha (Sept. 15, 1944)
Chickasaw (July 23, 1942)
Chilula (Dec. 1, 1944)
Chimariko (Dec. 30, 1944)
Chippewa (July 25, 1942)
Choctaw (Oct. 18, 1942)
Chowanoc (Aug. 20, 1943)
Cocopa (Oct. 5, 1943)
Cree (Aug. 17, 1942)
Cusabo (Feb. 26, 1945)
Hidatsa (Dec. 29, 1943)
Hitchiti (Jan. 29, 1944)
Hopi (Sept. 7, 1942)
Jicarilla (Feb. 25, 1944)
Kiowa (Nov. 5, 1942)
Lipan (Sept. 17, 1942)
Luiseno (March 17, 1945)
Mataco (Oct. 14, 1942)
Menominee (Feb. 14, 1942)
Moctobi (March 25, 1944)
Molala (Dec. 23, 1942)
Moreno (July 9, 1942)
Mosopelea
Munsee (Jan. 21, 1943)
Narragansett (Aug. 8, 1942)
Nipmuc (April 12, 1945)
Paiute
Pakana (March 3, 1943)
Papago
Pawnee (March 31, 1942)
Pinto (Jan. 5, 1943)
Potawatomi (April 3, 1943)
Quapaw (May 15, 1943)
Salinan
Sarsi (June 12, 1943)
Seneca (Feb. 2, 1943)
Serrano (July 24, 1943)
Shakori
Sioux (May 27, 1942)
Takelma (Sept. 18, 1943)
Tawakoni (Oct. 28, 1943)
Tawasa (Feb. 22, 1943)
Tekesta (March 20, 1943)
Tenino (Jan. 10, 1944)
Tolowa (May 17, 1944)
Ute (June 24, 1942)
Utina
Wenatchee (Sept. 7, 1944)
Yuma (July 17, 1943)
Yurok
Yustaga

Fleet Tugs

Displacement: 1,280 tons. Complement: 85. Dimensions: 195 (*w.l.*), 205 (*o.a.*) × 38½ × 12 feet. Guns: 1—3 inch, 2—40 mm. AA. Machinery: 4 sets Diesels with electric drive. B.H.P.: 3,000 = 16 kts. Fitted with powerful pumps and other salvage equipment. (Some are fitted as wireless controlled target ships.) (ATF 67–88, 90–94, 96–98, 100–116, 118, 148–165.)

1920.

Owl **Vireo** **Woodcock**

All built 1918–19. Displacement: 840 tons. Dimensions: 187⅚ × 35½ × 8⅚ feet (*mean*). Machinery: Triple expansion. I.H.P.: 1,400 = 14 kts. Boilers: 2 Babcock & Wilcox. Oil fuel: 275 tons. (ATO 137, 139, 141, 144, 145.)

SAGAMORE. 1946, *Mr. Wm. H. Davis.*

IUKA, KEOSANQUA, WANDANK (all 1919–20), **SAGAMORE** (ex-*Comanche*, 1917). Displacement: 795 tons, *except Sagamore* 735 tons. Dimensions: 149⅓ (*pp.*) × 30 × 12⅓ feet (*mean*) *except Sagamore* 11¾ feet. Guns: 2—3 inch AA. Machinery: Triple expansion. I.H.P.: 1,800 = 13 to 14 kts. Oil: 279 tons. (ATO 37, 38, 26, 20.)

Rescue Tugs.

47, numbered between **ATR 3** and **ATR 74** (1942–43). Wood. Displacement: 852 tons. Dimensions: 165½ × 33⅓ × 15½ feet. Guns: 1—3 inch. Machinery: Triple expansion. I.H.P.: 1,600 = 12 kts.

UNITED STATES COAST GUARD.

Notes.

Photos are official unless otherwise acknowledged.

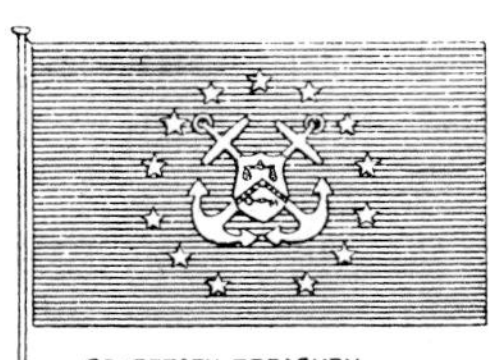

SECRETARY TREASURY

COAST GUARD STANDARD.

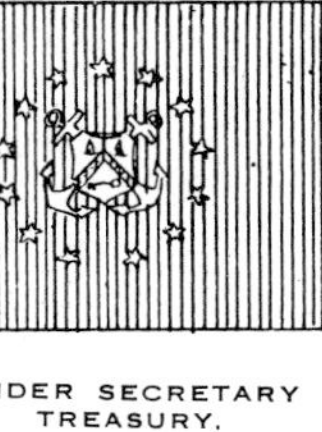

UNDER SECRETARY TREASURY.

ASST SECRETARY TREAS.

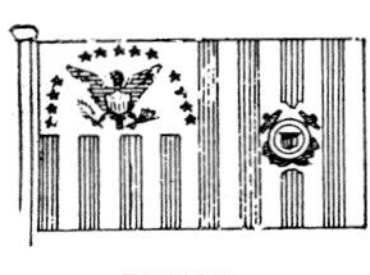

ENSIGN

COMMANDANT'S FLAG.

Red White Blue

Commandant, U.S.C.G.: Admiral Joseph F. Farley.

I.—ESTABLISHMENT.

The United States Coast Guard was established by the Act of Congress approved January 28, 1915, which consolidated the Revenue Cutter Service founded in 1790 and the Life Saving Service founded in 1878. The act of establishment provides that "the Coast Guard shall constitute a part of the military forces of the United States and shall operate as a part of the Navy, subject to the orders of the Secretary of the Navy, in time of war or when the President shall so direct". The Lighthouse Service, founded in 1789, was transferred to the Coast Guard on July 1, 1939, as a result of the President's Reorganization Plan No. II.

II.—DUTIES.

1. The peacetime duties of the Coast Guard have as their principal objective safety and security at sea through enforcement of the navigation laws, saving life and assistance to vessels in distress, and maintenance of aids to navigation.
2. Law enforcement duties, performed for all departments of the government, include those relating to customs, movements and anchorage of vessels, immigration, quarantine, neutrality, navigation and other laws governing merchant vessels and motor boats, safety of life on navigable waters during regattas, oil pollution, sponge fisheries, protection of game, seal and fisheries in Alaska, protection of bird reservations established by Executive Order and suppression of mutinies.
3. Life saving and assistance duties include maintenance of coastal stations and communication lines on the continental coasts of the United States, conduct of the International Ice Patrol, derelict destruction, winter cruising on the Atlantic coast, extension of medical aid to fishing vessels, Bering Sea Patrol and flood relief work. In its humanitarian duties the Coast Guard renders aid and assistance to vessels in distress irrespective of nationality and extends its protection, if needed, to all shipping within the scope of its operations.
4. The Coast Guard establishes and maintains navigation aids, consisting of lighthouses, lightships, radiobeacons, buoys, and unlighted beacons on the sea and lake coasts of the United States, on the rivers of the United States as authorized by law, and on the coasts of all other territory under United States jurisdiction, with the exception of the Philippine Islands and Panama.
5. In time of war the Coast Guard operates as a part of the Navy. A military organization was adopted at the time the service was established in 1790, before the establishment of the Navy Department. This organization has been continued since that date for the purpose of maintaining the general efficiency of the operation of the service in its law enforcement duties in time of peace. The executive action under which the Coast Guard operates as a part of the Navy in time of war is similar in effect to a measure of mobilization. In this respect the Coast Guard is a potential reserve force for the Navy. No personnel are normally assigned or equipped as land troops. Vessels are prepared in emergencies to equip landing forces with small arms and machine guns; stations are similarly prepared to undertake emergency police duties in a more limited sense, because of the smaller units involved, but in both cases these duties would be incidental to the primary purpose of the service, the enforcement of civil law and the saving of life and property.

III.—ORGANIZATION.

For the administration and operation of the Coast Guard, the United States, including its territories and insular possessions (except the Philippine Islands), and the waters adjacent thereto are divided into 13 districts, each under the command of a district commander operating directly under the Commandant of the Coast Guard.

Coast Guard

IV.—PERSONNEL.

Uniforms of officers and men are similar to those of U.S. Navy, but commissioned officers wear a gold shield on the sleeve instead of a star, and cap device is a gold spread-eagle, the talons grasping a horizontal foul anchor. A silver shield is mounted on the eagle's breast. Men of Coast Guard wear a shield on the sleeve.

V.—VESSELS.

Coast Guard vessels or boats more than 65 feet in length, except lightships, having a specifically designated commanding officer and standard authorized complements, are designated Coast Guard cutters. Those of tug type are detailed to the larger maritime ports to enforce Customs and Navigation laws and the regulation of the anchorage and movement of vessels.

VI.—AVIATION.

Air Stations in commission: 10. Location: Salem, Mass.; Charleston, S.C.; New York, N.Y.; Miami, Fla.; St. Petersburg, Fla.; Biloxi, Miss.; San Diego, California; Port Angeles, Washington; Elizabeth City, N.C.; San Francisco, California. (This number has doubtless been increased.)

U.S. MARITIME SERVICE.

The establishment of the U.S. Maritime Service was authorized in June, 1938, as a part of the U.S. Maritime Commission. The organization maintains training stations for unlicensed personnel at New York, N.Y., and Alameda, California. Training stations for men with no previous seagoing experience are maintained at Boston, Mass., and St. Petersburg, Florida.

The training ships *American Sailor, American Seaman, American Mariner, American Engineer, Joseph Conrad,* and *Sea Cloud* are operated by the service.

Enrolment in the Maritime Service for experienced personnel of the merchant marine is limited to licensed and unlicensed men who have served at least 12 months within the past three years in American merchant ships of 500 gross tons or over. Enrolment of inexperienced men is limited to citizens between 18 and 23 years of age.

Commandant: Rear-Admiral Telfair Knight.

Coast Guard Cutters

1944, *Official.*

MACKINAW (ex-*Manitowoc*, March 6, 1944). Built by Toledo S.B. Co. Cost over $10,000,000. Of similar type to "Wind" class below. Displacement: 5,090 tons. Dimensions: 290 × 74¼ × — feet. Guns: Only M.G. Machinery: Diesel, with electric drive. 3 shafts (1 forward and 2 aft). B.H.P. 10,000. Constructed with 1⅝" plating for service as ice-breaker on Great Lakes. Radius at cruising speed, 6,000 miles. Completed Jan. 1945.

1944, *courtesy "The Motor Ship."*

EAST WIND (Feb. 6, 1943), **NORTH WIND** (Dec. 30, 1942), **SOUTH WIND** (March 7, 1943), **WEST WIND** (March 31, 1943). All built by Western Pipe & Steel Co. Displacement: 5,350 tons. Dimensions: 250 (*pp.*), 269 (*o.a.*) × 63½ × 26½ feet. Guns: 4—3 inch (except *East Wind* 4—5 inch, etc.) Machinery: Diesel, with electric drive. 3 shafts (1 fwd. 2 aft.) Designed H.P. 10,000. Construction entirely welded, with double hull and exceptionally heavy plating, designed to crush 9 ft. ice. Cost reported as $10,000,000 each. Two were lent to Soviet Navy in 1945.

(Owasco Class.)

SEBAGO. 1946, *Lieut. R. D. Trimingham, R.N.V.R.*

ANDROSCOGGIN, CHATAUQUA, ESCANABA (ex-*Otsego*, March 25, 1945), **IROQUOIS, KLAMATH, MENDOTA** (Feb. 29, 1944), **MINNETONKA** (ex-*Sunapee*), **OWASCO, PONTCHARTRAIN** (ex-*Okeechobee*), **SEBAGO** (ex-*Wachusett*), **WACHUSETT** (ex-*Huron*, Nov. 5, 1944), **WINNEBAGO, WINONA.** All built by Western Pipe & Steel Co., Los Angeles, except *Mendota* and *Pontchartrain*, by the Coast Guard Shipyard, Curtis Bay, Md. Displacement: 2,000 tons. Dimensions: 255 (*o.a.*) × 43 × 15 feet. Machinery: Geared turbines with electric drive by Westinghouse Co. S.H.P. 4,000 = 18 kts. Cost over $2,300,000 each without armament.

Photo wanted.

STORIS (ex-*Eskimo*). Built by Toledo S.B. Co. and completed 1943. Displacement: 1,715 tons. Dimensions: 230 × 43 × 14 feet. Machinery: Diesel, with electric drive. B.H.P. 1,800 = 15 kts. Strengthened for ice navigation, and employed on Greenland service.

CAMPBELL. 1938, *Official.*

4 *Philadelphia Navy Yard:* **CAMPBELL** (ex-*George W. Campbell*), **DUANE** (ex-*William J. Duane*), **INGHAM** (ex-*Samuel D. Ingham*), **TANEY** (ex-*Roger B. Taney*). (All June 3, 1936).

1 *New York Navy Yard:* **SPENCER** (ex-*John C. Spencer*, Jan. 6, 1937).

1 *Charleston Navy Yard:* **BIBB** (ex-*George M. Bibb*, Jan. 14, 1937).

Standard displacement: 2,216 tons. Dimensions: 308 (*w.l.*), 327 (*o.a.*) × 41 × 11½ feet (*mean* draught), 12¾ feet (*max.*). Guns: 3—5 inch, 51 cal., 3—3 inch, 2 quad. M.G. AA., 2—6 pdr. (with provision for mounting a fourth 5 inch if needed). *Campbell* reported rearmed with 10—3 inch AA. 1 seaplane carried in some. Westinghouse geared turbines. 2 shafts. S.H.P.: 6,200 = 20 kts. 2 Babcock & Wilcox boilers. Fuel: 572 tons. Cruising radius: 8,000 miles at 12·5 kts., 12,300 at 11 kts. War loss: *Alexander Hamilton.*

COMANCHE. 1935, *Official.*

ALGONQUIN, COMANCHE, MOHAWK, ONONDAGA, TAHOMA (1934). All strengthened for icebreaking. First 3 built by Pusey & Jones Corpn., Wilmington, Del., other two by Defoe Works, Bay City, Mich. Displacement: 1,005 tons. Complement: 60. Dimensions: 165 (*o.a.*) × 36 × 13½ feet. Guns: 2—3 inch, 50 cal., 6 M.G. Machinery: Geared turbines. S.H.P: 1,500 = 13 kts. Oil fuel.

CHAMPLAIN (ex-H.M.S. *Sennen*, ex-*Champlain*, 1928), **ITASCA** (ex-H.M.S. *Gorleston*, ex-*Itasca*, 1930), **MOCOMA** (ex-H.M.S. *Totland*, ex-*Cayuga*, Oct. 8, 1931), **SEBEC** (ex-H.M.S. *Banff*, ex-*Saranac*, 1930). Displacement: 1,546 tons. Dimensions: 250 (*o.a.*) × 42 × 16 feet. Guns: 2—5 inch, 2—3 inch. Machinery: Turbo-electric. H.P.: 3,220 = 16 kts. Boilers: 2 Babcock & Wilcox. Fuel: 335 tons.

1944, *Official.*

NOURMAHAL (Kiel, 1928). Ex-yacht, 1969 tons *gross*. Dimensions: 260 (*w.l.*), 263¾ (*o.a.*) × 41½ × 16¾ feet. Machinery: 2 Sulzer Diesels. 2 shafts. B.H.P.: 2,300.

1938, *Official.*

SHAWNEE (1922). Steel. Displacement: 900 tons. Dimensions: 158¼ × 30 × 14 feet. Guns: 2—1 pdr. Speed as refitted: 16 kts. Oil fuel. Built by Union Con. Co., Oakland, Cal. Refitted completely, 1938.

TAMPA.

HAIDA, MODOC, MOJAVE, TAMPA. All built 1921 by Gen. Eng. & Dry Dock Co., Oakland. Steel. Displacement: 1,780 tons. Dimensions: 240 × 39 × 16½ feet. Guns: 2—5 inch, 2—3 inch AA., 6 M.G. Machinery: Turbo-electric (by General Electric Co.). S.H.P. 2,600 = 15 kts. Oil fuel.

CARRABASSET. *Photo added* 1927.

CARRABASSET (1919). Steel. Displacement: 1,133 tons. Dimensions: 155¾ × 30 × 17½ feet. Guns: 2—1 pdr. I.H.P. 1,800 = 13 kts. Oil fuel.

KICKAPOO (1919). Steel. Displacement: 840 tons. Dimensions: 157⅓ × 35 × 12 feet. Guns: 2—1 pdr. Speed: 11 kts. Strengthened for ice navigation.

1920 *Photo.*

OSSIPEE (1915). Steel. Displacement: 997 tons. Dimensions: 165⅝ × 32 × 11¾ feet. Guns: 2—3 inch, 6 M.G. I.H.P. 1,000 = 12 kts. Strengthened for ice navigation.

1920 *Photo.*

TALLAPOOSA (1915). Steel. Displacement: 964 tons. Dimensions: 165¾ × 32 × 11 feet. Guns: 2—3 inch, 50 cal., 6 M.G. I.H.P. 1,000 = 12 kts. Oil fuel.

Coast Guard Cutters

1919 *Photo, U.S. Navy Publicity Bureau.*

UNALGA (1912). Steel. Displacement : 1,181 tons. Dimensions : 190 × 32½ × 14 feet. Guns : 2—3 inch, 6 M.G. I.H.P. 1,000 = 13 kts.

PAMLICO (1907). Steel. Displacement : 451 tons. Dimensions : 158 × 30 × 5⅝ feet. Guns : 2—6 pdr. 2 shafts. I.H.P. 1,000 = 10 kts. Oil fuel.

Patrol Type.

ARGO. (AURORA, DAPHNE, PERSEUS have only one funnel.) 1933 *Photo.*

17—165 ft. steel Cutters: **ARGO, ARIADNE, ATALANTA, AURORA, CALYPSO, CYANE, DAPHNE, DIONE, GALATEA, HERMES, ICARUS, NEMESIS, NIKE, PANDORA, PERSEUS, THETIS, TRITON.** Built 1931–34. Displacement: 334–337 tons. Dimensions : 165 × 25¼ × 9½ feet. Guns: 1—3 inch, 23 cal., 2—1 pdr. Winton Diesel engines. 2 shafts. H.P.: 1,340 = 16 kts.

Note.—Electra, of this class, was renamed *Potomac* and converted into Presidential Yacht, but was discarded in 1945.

1939, *Official.*

31—125 ft. steel Cutters: **ACTIVE, AGASSIZ, ALERT, BONHAM, BOUTWELL, CAHOONE, CARTIGAN, COLFAX, CRAWFORD, CUYAHOGA, DILIGENCE, DIX, EWING, FAUNCE, FREDERICK LEE, GENERAL GREENE, HARRIET LANE, KIMBALL, LEGARE, MARION, McLANE, MORRIS, NEMAHA, PULASKI, RELIANCE, RUSH, TIGER, TRAVIS, VIGILANT, WOODBURY, YEATON** (1926-27). Displacement : 220 tons. Dimensions : 125 (*o.a.*) × 23½ × 9 feet (*max.*). Guns : 1—3 inch, 23 cal. Machinery: Diesel. 2 shafts. B.H.P. 600 = 13 kts. All re-engined in 1939–42.

Active, Colfax, Crawford, Diligence, Ewing, Harriet Lane, Legare, McLane, Vigilant and *Woodbury* recently employed as buoy tenders. *Kimball* and *Yeaton* employed on training duties.

Tender Type.

Note.—These vessels are designed mainly for duty as Lighthouse Tenders. All are armed in war time.

39 Cactus and Iris Classes.

21 *Marine Iron & S.B. Co., Duluth:* **BASSWOOD, BLACKHAW** (June 18, 1943), **BLACKTHORN** (July 20, 1943), **BUTTONWOOD** (Nov. 28, 1942), **CACTUS** (Nov. 25, 1941), **CITRUS** (Aug. 15, 1942), **CLOVER** (1942), **CONIFER** (Oct. 3, 1942), **COWSLIP** (1942), **EVERGREEN, HORNBEAM** (Aug. 15, 1943), **MESQUITE** (Nov. 14, 1942), **PAPAW, PLANETREE, REDBUD** (Sept. 11, 1943), **SASSAFRAS** (1943), **SEDGE** (1943), **SPAR** (Nov. 2, 1943), **SUNDEW** (Feb. 8, 1944), **SWEETBRIER** (Dec. 30, 1943), **SWEETGUM** (1943).

17 *Zenith Dredge Co., Duluth:* **ACACIA** (*ex-Thistle*, 1944), **BALSAM** (1942), **BITTERSWEET** (1943), **BRAMBLE** (1943), **FIREBUSH** (1943), **GENTIAN** (1942), **IRIS** (March 10, 1944), **LAUREL** (Aug. 4, 1942), **MADRONA** (Nov. 11, 1942), **MALLOW** (1943), **MARIPOSA** (Jan. 7, 1944), **SAGEBRUSH** (Sept. 30, 1943), **SALVIA** (Sept. 15, 1943), **SORREL** (Sept. 28, 1942), **TUPELO** (Nov. 28, 1942), **WOODBINE, WOODRUSH** (1944).

1 *Coast Guard Shipyard, Curtis Bay:* **IRONWOOD** (March, 1943).

Displacement: 935 tons. Dimensions: 180 (*o.a.*) × 37 × 12 feet. Machinery : Diesel, with electric drive. B.H.P.: 1,000 = 13 kts.

ALMOND, ARROWWOOD, CHAPARRAL, Length: 161 feet. **FORSYTHIA, BRIER, RAMBLER.** Type not reported, but may be additional units of foregoing class.

FERN (Nov. 6, 1942), **FOXGLOVE, SUMAC.** Displacement: 350 tons. Dimensions: 114 (*o.a.*) × 30 × 5 feet. Machinery: 3 sets Diesels. 3 shafts. B.H.P.: 600. Designed for river service and strengthened for ice navigation.

BARBERRY (Nov. 14, 1942), **COSMOS** (Nov. 11, 1942). Displacement: 328 tons. Dimensions: 110 × 26½ × 10½ feet. Machinery: Diesel, with electric drive. B.H.P.: 1,000 = 12 kts.

JUNIPER (May 18, 1940). Displacement: 790 tons. Dimensions: 177 × 32 × 8½ feet. Machinery: Diesel, with electric drive. 2 shafts. B.H.P.: 900 = 13 kts.

NETTLE (ex-*FS* 396), **SPRUCE** (ex-*FS* 222), **TRILLIUM** (ex-*FS* 397). Particulars wanted.

WALNUT. 1940, *Official.*

FIR (1939), **HOLLYHOCK** (1937), **WALNUT** (1939). Displacement: 885 tons. Dimensions : 175 × 32 × 11 feet. Machinery: Reciprocating. 2 shafts. I.H.P. : 1,000 = 12 kts.

MAPLE, NARCISSUS, ZINNIA (all 1939). Displacement: 342 tons (*Maple*, 350 tons). Dimensions: 122 × 27 × 6½ feet. Machinery: Diesel. 2 shafts. B.H.P. : 400 = 10 kts.

HEMLOCK (1934). Displacement: 1,005 tons. Dimensions: 175 × 32 × 12½ feet. Machinery: Reciprocating. 2 shafts. I.H.P.: 1,000 = 12 kts.

TAMARACK (1934). Displacement: 400 tons. Dimensions: 124 × 29 × 7½ feet. Machinery: Diesel, with electric drive. B.H.P. : 600 = 10 kts.

ARBUTUS (1933). Displacement : 960 tons. Dimensions : 175 × 32 × 12¼ feet. Machinery: Reciprocating. 2 shafts. I.H.P.: 1,000 = 11 kts.

Tender Type—*continued.*

HICKORY (1933). Displacement: 400 tons. Dimensions: 131¼ × 24½ × 9½ feet. Machinery: Reciprocating. I.H.P.: 500 = 12 kts.

LILAC (1933), **MISTLETOE** (1939). Displacement: 770 tons. Dimensions: 172 × 32 × 8½ feet. Machinery: Reciprocating. 2 shafts. I.H.P.: 1,000 = 12 kts.

COLUMBINE (1931), **LINDEN** (1931), **WISTARIA** (1933). Displacement: 323 tons. Dimensions: 121½ × 25 × 6¾ feet. Machinery: Diesel, with electric drive. B.H.P.: 240 = 9 kts.

VIOLET (1930). Displacement: 1,012 tons. Dimensions: 170 × 32 × 10½ feet. Machinery: Reciprocating. 2 shafts. I.H.P.: 1,000 = 12 kts.

WILLOW (1927). Displacement: 1,070 tons. Dimensions: 200 × 65 × 6½ feet. Machinery: Paddle. I.H.P.: 300 = 6 kts. (River Service).

WAKEROBIN (1927). Displacement: 575 tons. Dimensions: 182×43×4 feet. Machinery: Paddle. I.H.P.: 550=6 kts. (River Service.)

1934 *Photo, Official.*

PHLOX (ex-*Nansemond*). (Defoe Boat & Motor Works, Bay City, Mich., 1926). Steel. Displacement: 210 tons. Dimensions: 99⅜ × 23 × 8 feet. Guns: 1—3 inch, 23 cal. Diesel engines. 2 shafts. Speed: 10 kts.

GREENBRIER (1924). Displacement: 440 tons. Dimensions: 164 × 32 × 4 feet. Machinery: Paddle. I.H.P.: 350=8 kts. (River Service.)

HAWTHORN, OAK (1921). Displacement: 875 tons. Dimensions: 160 × 30 × 9½ feet. Machinery: Reciprocating. I.H.P.: 750 = 8 kts.

ILEX (1919). Displacement: 1,130 tons. Dimensions: 174 × 32 × 11 feet. Machinery: Reciprocating. 2 shafts. I.H.P.: 1,040 = 12 kts.

CEDAR (1917). Displacement: 1,370 tons. Dimensions: 201 × 36 × 14 feet. Machinery: Reciprocating. I.H.P.: 1,300 = 12 kts.

ROSE (1916). Displacement: 567 tons. Dimensions: 137 × 24½ × 9¼ feet. Machinery: Reciprocating. 2 shafts. I.H.P.: 450 = 10 kts.

CAMELLIA (1911). Displacement: 377 tons. Dimensions: 117 × 24 × 7½ feet. Machinery: Diesel. 2 shafts. B.H.P.: 440 = 9 kts.

ANEMONE, CYPRESS, HIBISCUS, KUKUI, MANZANITA, ORCHID, SEQUOIA, TULIP (all 1908). Displacement: 1,057 tons. Dimensions: 190 × 30 × 13 feet. Machinery: Reciprocating. 2 shafts. I.H.P.: 1,000 = 12 kts.

SUNFLOWER (1907). Displacement: 1,246 tons. Dimensions: 174 × 31 × 12 feet. Machinery: Reciprocating. 2 shafts. I.H.P.: 900 = 12 kts.

ASPEN (1906). Displacement: 415 tons. Dimensions: 126 × 25 × 8¼ feet. Machinery: Reciprocating. I.H.P.: 440= 10 kts.

CROCUS (1904). Displacement: 910 tons. Dimensions: 165 ×29×12¼ feet. Machinery: Reciprocating. 2 shafts. I.H.P.: 700 = 11 kts. (Lake Duty.)

HYACINTH (1903). Displacement: 950 tons. Dimensions: 165 × 28 × 12 feet. Machinery: Reciprocating. I.H.P.: 770 = 10 kts. (Lake Duty.)

LARKSPUR (1903). Displacement: 703 tons. Dimensions: 169 × 30 × 11 feet. Machinery: Reciprocating. 2 shafts. I.H.P.: 750 = 9 kts.

MANGROVE (1897). Displacement: 821 tons. Dimensions: 164 × 30 × 8½ feet. Machinery: Reciprocating. 2 shafts. I.H.P.: 550 = 10 kts.

AMARANTH (1892). Displacement: 975 tons. Dimensions: 166 × 28 × 12½ feet. Machinery: Reciprocating. I.H.P.: 675 = 10 kts. (Lake Duty.)

MARIGOLD (1890). Iron. Displacement: 696 tons. Dimensions: 160 × 27 × 10½ feet. Machinery: Reciprocating. I.H.P.: 600 = 10 kts. (Lake Duty.)

Smaller units of the tender type include the following:

BLUEBELL, PRIMROSE, SMILAX, VERBENA (1944), 200 tons; **CLEMATIS, OLEANDER, SHADBUSH** (1941–43), 79 tons; **DOGWOOD, SYCAMORE** (1941), 230 tons; **BIRCH** (1939), 76 tons; **BLUEBONNET, JASMINE** (1935–39), 184 tons; **GOLDENROD, POPLAR** (1938–39), 193 tons; **ELM** (1937), 69 tons; **RHODODENDRON** (1935), 114 tons; **DAHLIA** (1933), 175 tons; **CHERRY** (1932), 202 tons; **MYRTLE** (1932), 186 tons; **ALTHEA, POINCIANA** (1930), 120 tons; **BEECH** (1928), 255 tons; **PINE** (1926), 210 tons; **ASTER** (1921), 109 tons; **PALMETTO** (1916), 170 tons; **COTTONWOOD** (1915), 243 tons; **SHRUB** (1912), (wood), 356 tons; **ALDER** (wood), 80 tons.

Tug Type.

ACUSHNET (ex-*Shackle*, April 1, 1943), **YOCONA** (ex-*Seize*, April 8, 1944). Displacement: 1,360 tons. Dimensions: 207 (*w.l.*), 213½ (*o.a.*) × 39 × 13 feet. Machinery: Diesel-electric. 2 shafts. H.P.: 3,000 = 14 kts.

NAUGATUCK 1939, *Official*

ARUNDEL (June 24, 1939), **MAHONING** (July 22, 1939), **NAUGATUCK, RARITAN** (both March 23, 1939), **KAW** (1942), **MANITOU** (Sept. 29, 1942), **CHINOOK, MOHICAN** (both July, 1943), **OJIBWAY, SAUK, SNOHOMISH** (all three Aug. 10, 1943), **APALACHEE, YANKTON** (1943). First pair built by Gulfport Works, Port Arthur, Texas; second pair by Defoe Works, Bay City, Mich.; third pair by Coast Guard Yard, Curtis Bay, Md.; remaining 7 by Ira S. Bushey & Son, Brooklyn, N.Y. Displacement: 328 tons. Dimensions: 110 (*o.a.*) × 26½ × 10½ feet (*mean* draught). Machinery: Diesel-electric. S.H.P.: 1,000 = 12 kts. Strengthened for ice-breaking.

Note.—These vessels are an improvement on design of *Hudson* class. Reported to be better sea boats.

CHEROKEE (Nov. 10, 1939), **TAMAROA** (ex-*Zuni*, July 13, 1943). Displacement: 1,280 tons. Dimensions: 195 (*w.l.*), 205 (*o.a.*) × 38½ × 12 feet. Machinery: Diesel-electric. H.P.: 3,000 = 16 kts.

BEVERLY. Length: 102 feet.

TUCKAHOE. 1935, *Official.*

CALUMET, NAVESINK, TUCKAHOE (built at Charleston Navy Yard), **HUDSON** (built at Portsmouth Navy Yard). All launched 1934. Steel. Displacement: 290 tons. Dimensions: 110½ × 24 × 10½ feet. Diesel engines. 1 shaft. H.P.: 800 = 12 kts. Radius: 2,000 miles. Strengthened for icebreaking.

DAVEY (1908). Steel, 1 screw. 182 tons. Dimensions: 92½ × 19 × 10⅛ feet. Guns: *Nil.* Speed: 10·5 kts.

GOLDEN GATE (1896). Steel. Displacement: 240 tons. Dimensions: 110 × 20½ × 9 feet. H.P. 300.

GUTHRIE (1895). Iron, 1 screw. 149 tons. Dimensions: 88 × 17½ × 9 feet. Speed: 11 kts.

Coast Guard Cutters and M.T.S.

Tug Type—*continued.*

MANHATTAN. 1938, *Official.*

MANHATTAN (1918). Steel, 1 screw. Ice Breaker, Salvage Vessel, Tug and Fire Float. 406 tons. Dimensions: $120\frac{1}{4} \times 24 \times 11\frac{3}{4}$ feet. Speed: 9·5 kts. Guns: 2—1 pdr.

TIOGA. Length: 95 feet.

WINNISIMMET (1903). Steel, 1 screw. 182 tons. Dimensions: $96\frac{1}{2} \times 20\frac{1}{2} \times 9$ feet. Speed: 12 kts.

Picket Boat Type.

Note.—All now have figure of length prefixed to official number on bows for ready recognition of type, e.g., CGC 83444. Most have been renumbered.

1941

181—83 ft. Cutters numbered between Nos. 444—634 (1938–42). Wood. 45 tons. Complement: 10. Dimensions: $83 \times 16 \times 4\frac{1}{2}$ feet. Armed with 20 mm. Oerlikons and D.C. 2 petrol engines. H.P.: 1,200 = 20·5 kts. Cost $42,450 to $58,000 each.

Note.—A number of these vessels have been transferred to the Cuban, Dominican, Ecuadorian, Mexican and Peruvian Navies.

1937 *Official.*

11—81 ft. Cutters: Nos. 406—415 (1937). 47 tons. No. 490 (1931). 38 tons. Wood. Displacement: 52 tons. Dimensions: $81 \times 15\frac{5}{8} \times 4$ feet. Guns: 1—1 pdr., 2 M.G. and D.C. 4 petrol engines. 2 shafts. H.P.: 1,600 = 25 kts.

1932 *Photo.*

46—78 ft. Cutters: Nos. 400—405 and others (1931 and 1943). Wood. Displacement: 43 tons. Dimensions: $79 \times 14\frac{1}{2} \times 4$ feet. Guns: 1—1 pdr. 2 petrol engines. H.P.: 1,200 = 21 kts.

CG 182 *Photo added* 1927.

45—75 ft. Cutters: Numbered between 119—288 (1924–25). Wood. Displacement: 37 tons. Dimensions: $75 \times 13\frac{3}{4} \times 4$ feet. Petrol engine. H.P.: 400 = 13·5 kts. Guns: 1—1 pdr.

Note.—A boat of this type, *CG* 274, was sold to Nicaragua in 1938. Three more, *CG* 110, 144, 302, have been acquired by the Dominican Republic.

(There are numerous vessels of similar type but smaller size, not listed here.)

Special and Auxiliary Craft

EAGLE 1936

EAGLE (ex-*Horst Wessel*, June 13, 1936). Displacement: 1,634 tons. Dimensions: $265\frac{3}{4}$ (*pp.*), $295\frac{1}{4}$ (*o.a.*) $\times 39\frac{1}{3} \times 15\frac{3}{4}$ feet (*mean*), $16\frac{1}{2}$ (*max.*). Machinery: 2 M.A.N. auxiliary Diesels. B.H.P.: 700 = 10 kts. Fuel: 48 tons. Sail area: 21,530 sq. ft.

Note.—Sister ship *Albert Leo Schlageter* also fell into American hands, but disposal has not been reported.

SEA CLOUD (ex-*Hussar*) (1930). 2,323 tons *gross*. Dimensions: $316 \times 49 \times 25$ feet. Machinery: Diesel. 2 shafts. B.H.P. 3,000.

1938, *Official*

PEQUOT (ex-Minelayer *General Samuel M. Mills*, 1909; transferred from War Department, 1922). Displacement: 1,106 tons. Dimensions: $165\frac{1}{2} \times 32\frac{1}{2} \times 12\frac{1}{4}$ feet. Speed: 10 kts. Used as Cable Ship.

U.S. Maritime Training Service.

AMERICAN ENGINEER (ex-*Berkshire*, 1923), **AMERICAN NAVIGATOR** (ex-*City of Chattanooga*, 1923), **AMERICAN PILOT** (ex-*Empire State*, ex-*Shaume*, ex-U.S.S. *Procyon*, 1919), **AMERICAN SEAFARER** (ex-*Alleghany*, 1919). 5,486 to 5,861 tons *gross*.

AMERICAN SEAMAN. 1939, *Official.*

AMERICAN SAILOR (ex-*Edgemont*), **AMERICAN SEAMAN** (ex-*Edgemoor*), (both 1919). 6,962 and 7,000 tons *gross*, respectively. Dimensions: $409\frac{1}{2} \times 54\frac{1}{4} \times 20$ feet. Machinery: Geared turbines. S.H.P.: 2,500 = 11 kts. Oil fuel. Complement: 371, including about 300 ratings under instruction in Maritime Training Service. Each ship is fitted with distilling plant capable of producing 104,000 gallons of fresh water daily.

VEMA (ex-*Hussar*) (1923). Three-masted schooner, acquired 1941. 533 tons *gross*. Dimensions: $202\frac{1}{2} \times 33 \times 14\frac{1}{2}$ feet. Machinery: Diesel.

Added 1940, *Mr. Wm. H. Davis.*

JOSEPH CONRAD (ex-*Georg Stage*), (Copenhagen, 1882). Iron. Displacement: 500 tons. Dimensions: $100\frac{3}{4} \times 25\frac{1}{4} \times 13$ feet. Machinery: Auxiliary Diesel. B.H.P.: 160 = 5 kts.

U.S. Merchant Marine Cadet Corps.

KING'S POINTER (ex-U.S.S. *Devosa*, 1944). Displacement: 3,700 tons *std.* Dimensions: 426 (*o.a.*) $\times 58 \times 16\frac{1}{2}$ feet. Machinery: Turbo-electric. 2 shafts. H.P.: 6,600 = 16 kts.

YUGOSLAVIA

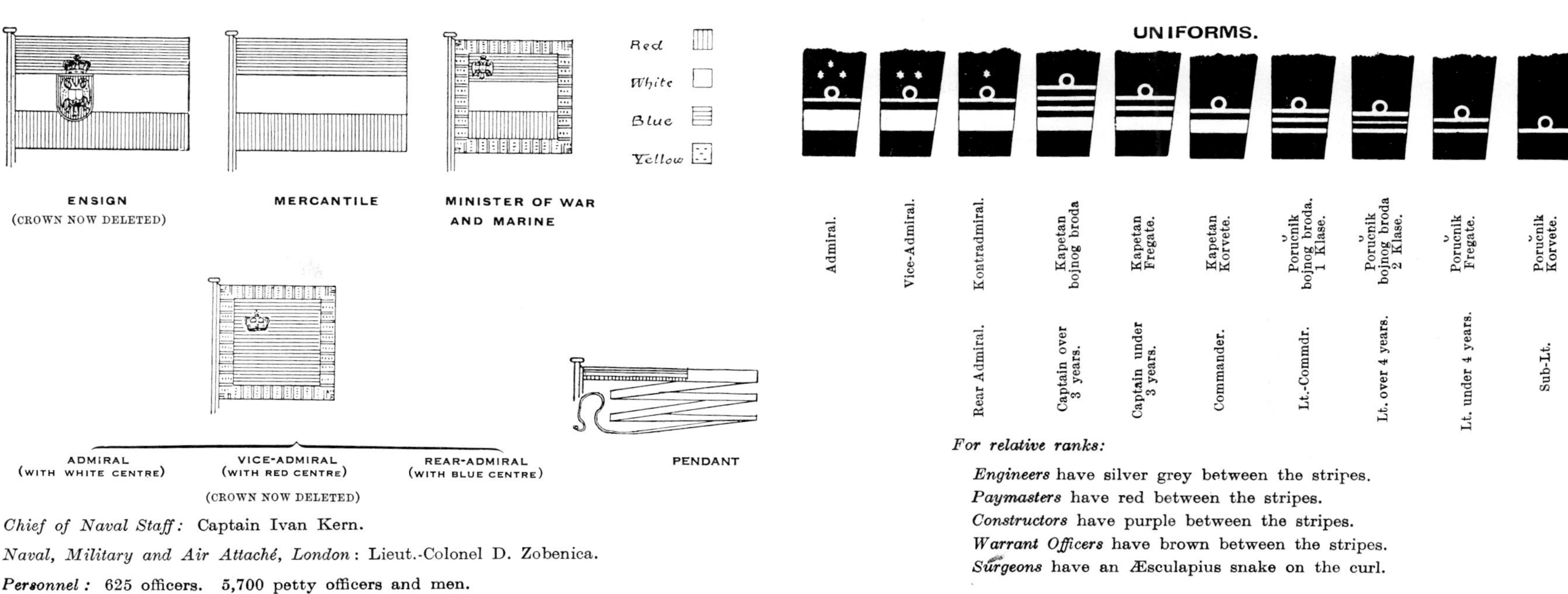

For relative ranks:

Engineers have silver grey between the stripes.
Paymasters have red between the stripes.
Constructors have purple between the stripes.
Warrant Officers have brown between the stripes.
Surgeons have an Æsculapius snake on the curl.

Chief of Naval Staff: Captain Ivan Kern.

Naval, Military and Air Attaché, London: Lieut.-Colonel D. Zobenica.

Personnel: 625 officers. 5,700 petty officers and men.

(Reserve): 400 officers. 720 petty officers and men.

Colour of Ships: Light grey.

Mercantile Marine: From "Lloyd's Register," 1939. 190 vessels of 411,384 gross tonnage.

Special Note.

It is impossible to ascertain how many of the Yugoslav warships listed here are still in service. Some of those recorded are suspected to have been lost. Displacements given are "standard."

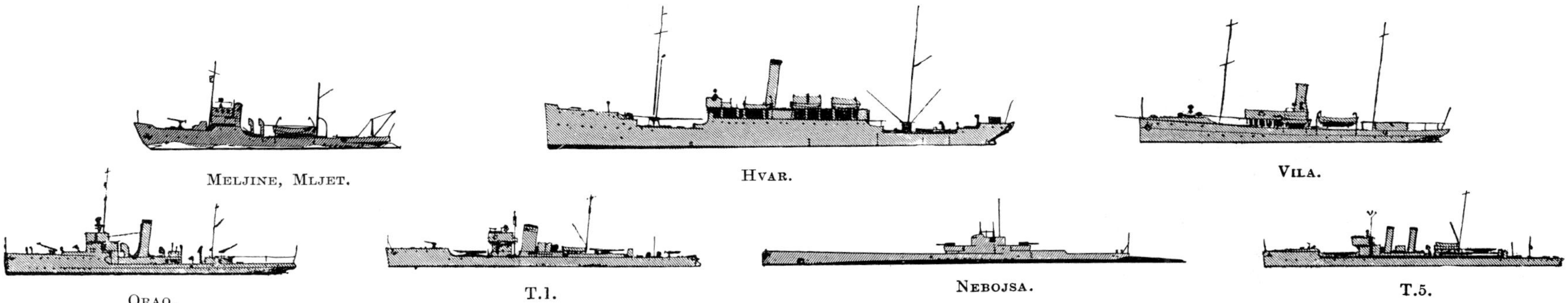

Torpedo Boats

2 Old Torpedo Boats (*Torpiljarke*) (ex-Austrian).

1931 *Photo, Official.*

T 1 (ex-76*T*, Stab. Tecnico, Trieste, 1913). Displacement: 262 tons. Fuel: 18 tons coal, 24 tons oil.

1931 *Photo, Official.*

T 5 (ex-87*F*, Ganz-Danubius Co., Porte Ré, Fiume, 1913). Displacement: 266 tons. Fuel: 20 tons coal, 34 tons oil. Other details of both boats: Dimensions: 188·3 × 18·7 × 4·9 feet. Guns: 2—66 mm. 1—M.G. Torpedo tubes: 4—18 inch (paired). Machinery: Turbine. S.H.P.: 5,000 = 20 kts. (best speed of which now capable). Yarrow boilers.

Motor Torpedo Boats (*Borbeni Čamci*).

PT 201, 204, 207–209, 211, 213, 217. Acquired from U.S. Navy on Lend-Lease terms in 1945. May have been returned.

Durmitor, Kaimakcalan (Lürssen, Vegesack, 1936–37). Displacement: 60 tons. Complement: 14. Dimensions: 92 × 14 × 5 feet. Armament: 1—47 mm. AA., 1 M.G. AA., 2—18 inch torpedo tubes. Machinery: 4 Mercedes-Benz petrol motors. H.P.: 3,000 = 34 kts.

Note.—Distinguished by numbers painted on bows. *Suvobor* was also reported to exist, but confirmation is lacking. (Old Thornycroft m.t.b. *Cetnik* may also survive, but her condition is doubtful. While in Italian hands she was numbered *ME* 43.)

1939, *Official.*

Minelayer (*Minonosci*).

1924 *Photo, by courtesy of the Navy Department.*

ORAO (ex-*M* 97, 1918). Displacement: 330 tons *standard*, 500 tons *full load*. Dimensions: 182 (*w.l.*), 192 (*o.a.*) × 23½ × 7 feet. Guns: 2—3·9 inch AA., 4—3 pdrs. Complement: 71. I.H.P.: 1,800 = 15 kts. Oil: 160 tons. This name means "Eagle".

Note.—While in Italian hands *Orao* was named *Vergada*.

Submarine Depot Ships (*Matica za Podmornice*).

HVAR. 1928 *Photo.*

HVAR (ex-*Solun*, ex-*Umtali*). Sir Jas. Laing & Sons, Ltd., Sunderland, 1896 (rebuilt 1927). 3,600 tons. Dimensions: 318¼ × 39 × 13 feet. Machinery: Triple expansion. H.P.: 1,100 = 12 kts. (This vessel was recovered intact from the Italians, who had renamed her *Quarnerolo*.)

1940, *Official.*

SITNICA (ex-*Najade*, 1891). 370 tons. Dimensions: 157½ × 23 × 6½ feet. Machinery: Triple expansion. H.P.: 500 = 9 kts. Guns: 2—3 pdr. Name means *Dew*. Italians renamed her *Curzola*.

Patrol Vessel.

1940, *Official.*

BELI ORAO (C. R. dell' Adriatico, San Marco, Trieste, June 3, 1939). Displacement: 567 tons *standard*, 660 tons *full load*. Dimensions: 197 (*pp.*), 213¾ (*o.a.*) × 26½ × 9⅓ feet. Armament: 2—40 mm. AA., 2 M.G. Machinery: 2 Sulzer Diesels. B.H.P.: 1,900 = 18 kts. Was used as Royal yacht, and is still afloat. While in Italian hands was named *Alba*.

Submarine (*Podmornice*).

1934, *Lieut.-Com. D. C. Beatty, R.N.*

Nebojsa, (Armstrong, 1927). Displacement: $\frac{975}{1164}$ tons. Complement: 45. Dimensions: 236¼ × 24 × 13 feet. Armament: 2—4 inch AA., 6—21 inch torpedo tubes. H.P.: 2,400/1,600 = $\frac{15}{10}$ kts. Radius: 5,000 miles at 9 kts.

Note—This name means "Dreadnought". Design is a modification of the British "L" type, materials having been assembled originally for *L* 68, never built.

Mining Tenders (*Tenderi minopolagaci*).

1939 *Official.*

MELJINE, MLJET (1931, Yarrow's Adriatic Yard, Kralyevica). Displacement: 130 tons. Dimensions: 174 × 26¼ × 13 feet. Machinery: Triple expansion. H.P.: 280 = 9 kts. Guns: 1—11 pdr. Identification letters painted on bows: ME, *Meljine*; MT, *Mljet*.

While in Italian hands these vessels were named *Solta* and *Meleda*, respectively.

Salvage Vessel (*Brod za Spasavanje*).

1936.

SPASILAC (1929). 740 tons. Dimensions: 174 × 26¼ × 13 feet. Machinery: Triple expansion. H.P.: 2,000 = 15 kts. Name means "Salvor." While in Italian hands she was called *Intangibile*.

Miscellaneous

Yacht (*Jahta*).

1931 *Photo, Official.*

VILA (ex-*Dalmata*) (1896). 230 tons. H.P. 325=12 kts. Name means *Nymph*. Italians called her *Fata*.

Oiler.

1940, *Official.*

PERUN (March 8, 1939). Built by Cockerill, Antwerp. Displacement: 4,500 tons (3,177 tons *gross*). Complement: 100. Dimensions: 291 (*pp.*), 311½ (*o.a.*) × 45½ × 20 feet. Guns: 4—40 mm. AA., 2—15 mm. AA. Machinery: Burmeister & Wain 2-stroke Diesels. 2 shafts. B.H.P.: 1,250 = 10 kts. *Deadweight* capacity: 3,000 tons.

Tugs (*Remorkeri*).

SNAZNI (1917). 100 tons. H.P. 300=10 kts. (Italian name, *Resistante.*)

USTRAJNI (1917). 160 tons. H.P. 250=9 kts. (Italian name, *Duraturo.*)

MARLJIVI (1898). 130 tons. H.P. 300=12 kts.

Note.—Respective meanings of above names are *Strong, Durable, Industrious.*

Training Ship (*Skolski Brodovi*).

1933 *Photo, Official.*

JADRAN (1932). Displacement: 720 tons. Dimensions: 190¼ × 29 × 13¾ feet. One Linke-Hofmann Diesel. H.P.: 375 = 8 kts. Sail area, 8,600 sq. feet. Accommodation for 150 cadets. Name means *Adriatic*. While in Italian hands this vessel was named *Marco Polo*.

Water Carrier (*Vodonosac*).

LOVĆEN (1932). Displacement: 561 tons. Complement: 20. Dimensions: 111 × 25½ × 14 feet (*max.*). Machinery: Diesel. B.H.P.: 300 = 11 kts. *light;* 8·5 kts. *loaded.*

River Patrol Vessels.

1939 *Official.*

DRAGOR (1928). Displacement: 250 tons. Dimensions: 164 × 26¼ × 3¾ feet. H.P.: 480 = 10 kts. Serves as Royal Yacht on Danube.

CER (1909). 256 tons. Dimensions: 170½ × 23 × 3 feet. 2 M.G. H.P.: 400 = 15 kts.

SISAK (ex-*Triglav*), (1915). 90 tons. Dimensions: 118 × 19½ × 6 feet. 2 M.G. H.P.: 350 = 11 kts.

SABAC (ex-*Avala*), (1914). 90 tons. Dimensions: 101¾ × 23 × 4½ feet. H.P.: 360 = 8 kts.

(Latter three vessels are converted tugs.)

Note.—Two 36-ton motor vedette boats, speed 9 kts., are maintained on Lake Ohrid. Names are *Graničar* and *Stražar*, meaning Frontier Guard and Sentinel, respectively. They were built in 1929.

River Monitors

River Flotilla (*Rečna Flotila*).

Special Note.—Though no definite reports have been received of the loss of any of them, it is doubtful whether these craft still exist.

1933 *Photo, Official.*

VARDAR (ex-Austrian *Bosna*, 1915). 530 tons. Dimensions: 200 × 34½ × 4¼ feet. Guns: 2—4·7 inch, 45 cal., 2—4·7 inch, 10 cal. howitzers, 2—66 mm. AA., 7 M.G. Armour: 1½ inch belt and bulkheads, 1 inch deck, 2 inch C.T., 2 inch turrets and cupolas. H.P. 1,600 = 13 kts. Oil: 75 tons. Complement, 100. Sister to *Basarabia*, now in Roumanian Navy.

DRAVA. 1933 *Photo, by courtesy of the Navy Dept.*

DRAVA (ex-Austrian *Enns*, 1913). 450 tons. Dimensions: 190¼ × 34½ × 4¼ feet. Guns: 2—4·7 inch + 3—4·7 inch howitzers, 2—66 mm., 7 M.G. Armour: 1½″ Belt and Bulkheads, 1″ Deck, 2″ C.T. and Turrets. Designed H.P. 1500 = 13 kts. Boilers: Yarrow. Fuel: Oil only, 70 tons. Complement, 86. Built under Austro-Hungarian 1912 Naval Programme; ceded to Yugoslavia 1920. Sister ship **Bucovina,** now in Roumanian Navy.

1933 *Photo, Official.*

SAVA (ex-Austrian *Bodrog*, Neupest, March, 1904). 380 tons. Dimensions: 183¾ × 31¼ × 4 feet. Designed H.P. 1,200=9 kts. Boilers: Yarrow. Armament: 2—4·7 inch, 35 cal., 1—4·7 inch howitzer, 1—66 mm. AA., 2 M.G., 1 or 3 machine. Armour: 1½″ Belt and Bulkheads, 1″ Deck, 3″—1½″ Turrets and Conning Tower. Complement, 79. Coal: 62 tons.

MORAVA. (Gun on superstructure since removed.) 1924 *Photo by courtesy of the Navy Dept.* Note overhanging rails at stern, for launching and hauling in boats.

MORAVA (ex-Austrian *Körös*, Budapest, 1892). 390 tons. Dimensions: 177⅙ × 29½ × 4 feet. Designed H.P. 1200=9 kts. Boilers: Yarrow. Guns: 2—4·7 inch (35 cal.), 1—66 mm. 2 M.G. Armour: 2″ Belt, ¾″ Deck, 3″ Turret, 2″ C.T. Complement, 79-80. Coal: 54 tons.

ARGENTINA

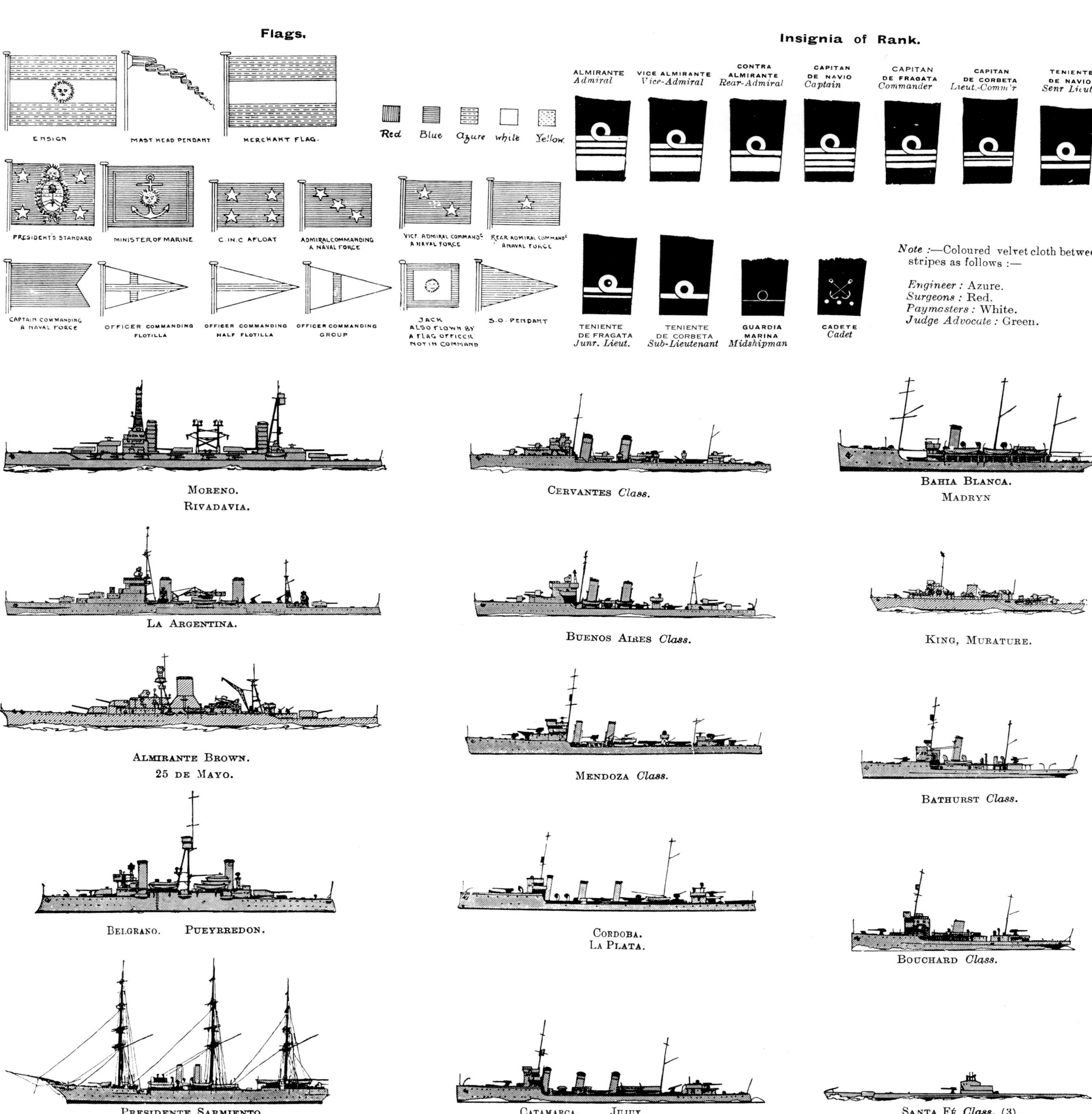

Moreno.
Rivadavia.

Cervantes *Class*.

Bahia Blanca.
Madryn

La Argentina.

Buenos Aires *Class*.

King, Murature.

Almirante Brown.
25 de Mayo.

Mendoza *Class*.

Bathurst *Class*.

Belgrano. Pueyrredon.

Cordoba.
La Plata.

Bouchard *Class*.

Presidente Sarmiento.

Catamarca. Jujuy.

Santa Fé *Class*. (3).

CHILE

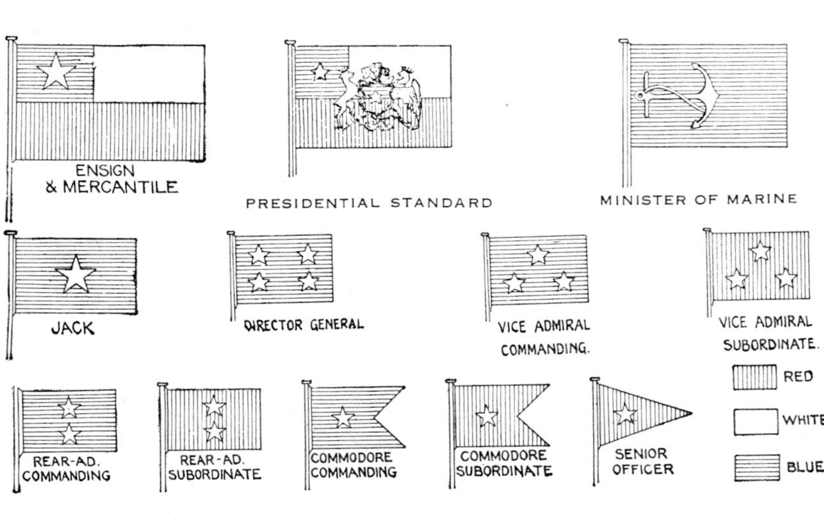

Uniforms

	Vice Almirante.	Contra-Almirante	Capitan de Navio.	Capitan de Fragata.	Capitan de Corbeta.	Teniente 1°	Teniente 2°	Guardia Marina	Aspirante
Corresponding British or U.S.	*Vice-Ad.*	*Rear-Ad.*	*Captain.*	*Commander.*	*Lieut. Comdr.*	*Lieut. (Senior).*	*Lieut. (Junior).*	*Sub.-Lieut.*	*Midshipman.*

Other Branches the same with colours as follows:— Paymasters (white), Surgeons (red), Chaplains (purple).

Minister of National Defence: Señor Manuel Bulnes Sanfuentes.
Commander-in-Chief of the Navy: Vice-Admiral Vicente Merino.
Chief of the Naval Staff: Rear-Admiral Immanuel Holger.
Naval Attaché, London: Commander Hernan Cubillos.
Personnel: About 6000, all ranks.

Naval Ordnance. (All details unofficial.)

	Type*	Calibre.		Length (cals.)	Weight of Gun. (tons.)	Weight of Proj. (lbs.)	Weight of Charge. (lbs.)	M.V. (ft.-secs.)	M.E. (ft.-tons.)	Max. R.P.M.
		Inches.	Cm.							
HEAVY	A	**14**	*35·6*	45	85	1585	324	2500	..	2
	..	..	..	..	..	..	..	..	..	..
	..	..	..	..	..	..	..	..	..	..
MEDIUM	A	**6**	*15·2*	50	$8\frac{3}{4}$	100	31	3000	6240	9
	..	..	..	..	..	..	..	..	..	..
	A	**4·7**	*12*	50	cwt. $63\frac{1}{2}$	45	$10\frac{3}{4}$	2953	2721	12
	A	**4·7**	*12*	45	53	45	8	2552	2110	10
LIGHT	A	**4**	*10·2*	..	..	..	..	..	..	..

* A = Armstrong

14 inch, 45 cal., in *Alm. Latorre.*
6 inch, 50 cal., in *Alm. Latorre* and *Chacabuco.*
4.7 inch in *Serrano* class (6).
4.7 inch in *Gen. Baquedano.*
4 inch AA. in *Alm. Latorre.*

Torpedoes: 21 inch (heater), and 18 inch. **Mines:** Similar to British pattern.

Mercantile Marine.

(From "Lloyd's Register" 1939 figures.)
106 vessels of 176,289 gross tonnage.

Naval Bases.

TALCAHUANO. Two dry docks, 614 × 87 × $30\frac{1}{2}$ feet and 800 × 116 × 36 feet respectively. One small floating dock, 216 × 42 × 15 feet. Gunnery, Torpedo, Submarine, and other Training Establishments here.

VALPARAISO. One small steel floating dock privately owned, 314 × 65 × 21 feet (4500 tons capacity). Staff College and Naval Academy for training of executive and Engineering branches here, also schools for Communications, Coast Artillery, Navigation, etc.

Almirante Latorre.

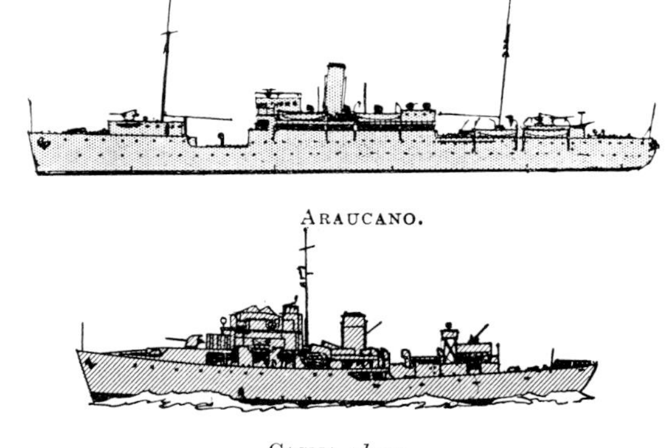

Araucano.

Yelcho.

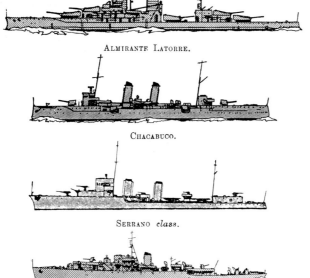

Chacabuco.

Casma *class.*

Orompello.

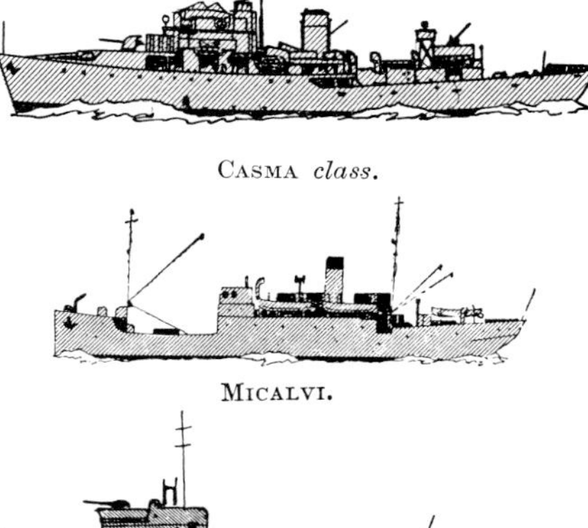

Serrano *class.*

Micalvi.

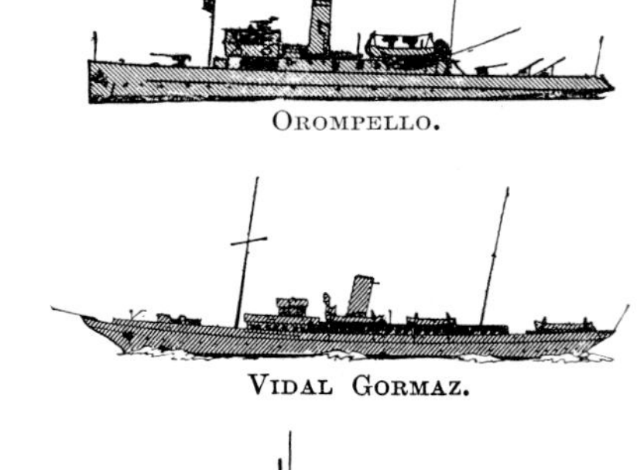

Vidal Gormaz.

Esmeralda *class.*

O'Brien *class.*

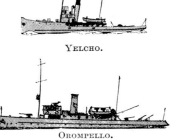

Gualcolda *class.*

PERU

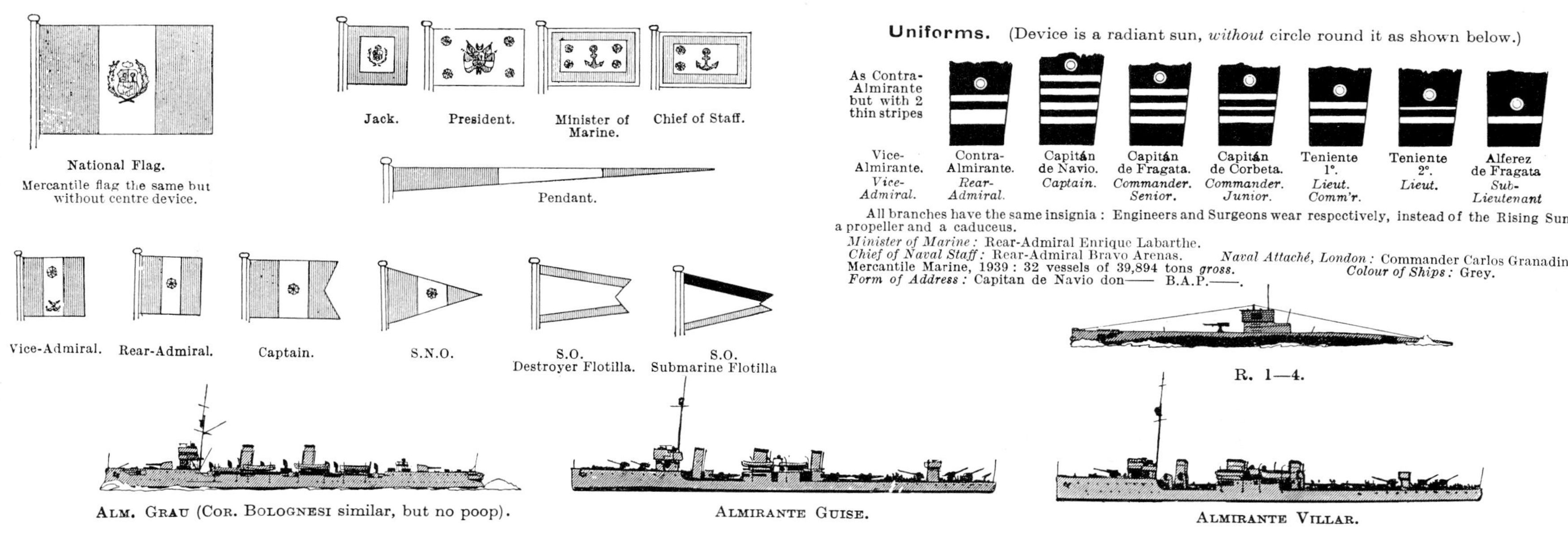

All branches have the same insignia: Engineers and Surgeons wear respectively, instead of the Rising Sun, a propeller and a caduceus.

Minister of Marine: Rear-Admiral Enrique Labarthe.
Chief of Naval Staff: Rear-Admiral Bravo Arenas. *Naval Attaché, London:* Commander Carlos Granadino.
Mercantile Marine, 1939: 32 vessels of 39,894 tons *gross.* *Colour of Ships:* Grey.
Form of Address: Capitan de Navio don—— B.A.P.——.

R. 1—4.

ALM. GRAU (COR. BOLOGNESI similar, but no poop).

ALMIRANTE GUISE.

ALMIRANTE VILLAR.

SWEDEN

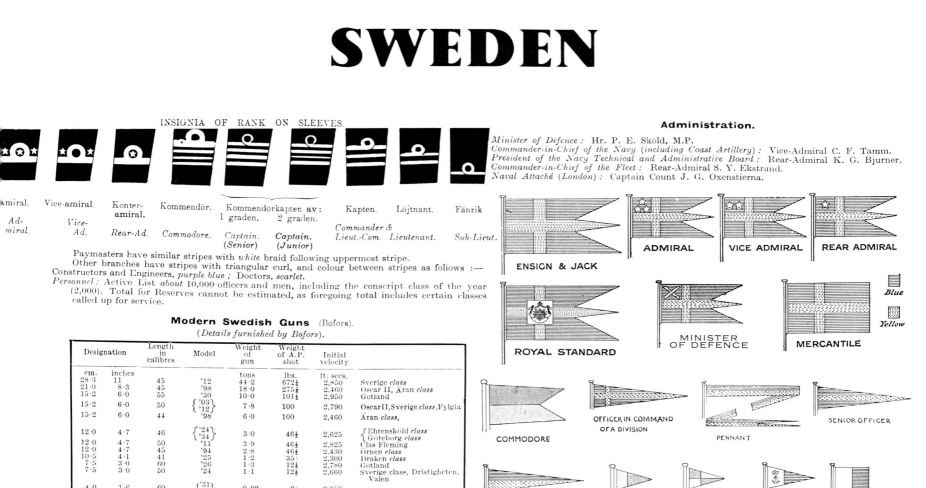

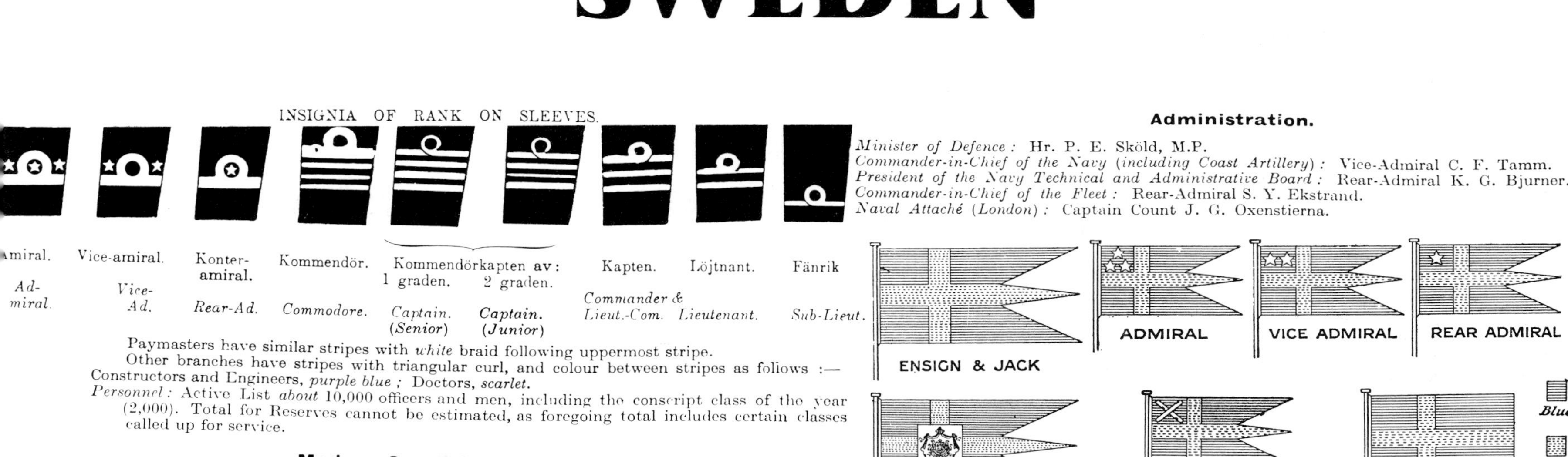

Paymasters have similar stripes with *white* braid following uppermost stripe.
Other branches have stripes with triangular curl, and colour between stripes as follows :— Constructors and Engineers, *purple blue*; Doctors, *scarlet.*

Personnel: Active List *about* 10,000 officers and men, including the conscript class of the year (2,000). Total for Reserves cannot be estimated, as foregoing total includes certain classes called up for service.

Modern Swedish Guns (Bofors).

(*Details furnished by Bofors*).

Designation (cm.)	Designation (inches)	Length in calibres	Model	Weight of gun (tons)	Weight of A.P. shot (lbs.)	Initial velocity (ft. secs.)	
28·3	11	45	'12	44·2	672¼	2,850	Sverige *class*
21·0	8·3	45	'98	18·0	275⅛	2,460	Oscar II, Äran *class*
15·2	6·0	55	'30	10·0	101¼	2,950	Gotland
15·2	6·0	50	'03, '12	7·8	100	2,790	Oscar II, Sverige *class*, Fylgia
15·2	6·0	44	'98	6·0	100	2,460	Äran *class*,
12·0	4·7	46	'24, '34	3·0	46⅓	2,625	Ehrensköld *class*, Göteborg *class*
12·0	4·7	50	'11	3·9	46⅓	2,825	Clas Fleming
12·0	4·7	45	'94	2·8	46⅓	2,430	Örnen *class*
10·5	4·1	41	'25	1·2	35[illegible]	2,300	Draken *class*
7·5	3·0	60	'26	1·3	12⅛	2,780	Gotland
7·5	3·0	50	'24	1·1	12⅛	2,660	Sverige class, Dristigheten, Valen
4·0	1·6	60	'31, '36	0·22	2[illegible]	2,950	
4·0	1·6	43	'32	0·17	2[illegible]	2,300	
2·5	1·0	64	'32	0·06	[illegible]	2,950	

Torpedoes.

21 in., and 18 in. Torpedoes manufactured at Motala.

Administration.

Minister of Defence: Hr. P. E. Sköld, M.P.
Commander-in-Chief of the Navy (including Coast Artillery): Vice-Admiral C. F. Tamm.
President of the Navy Technical and Administrative Board: Rear-Admiral K. G. Bjurner.
Commander-in-Chief of the Fleet: Rear-Admiral S. Y. Ekstrand.
Naval Attaché (London): Captain Count J. G. Oxenstierna.

ENSIGN & JACK

ADMIRAL

VICE ADMIRAL

REAR ADMIRAL

ROYAL STANDARD

MINISTER OF DEFENCE

MERCANTILE

Blue

Yellow

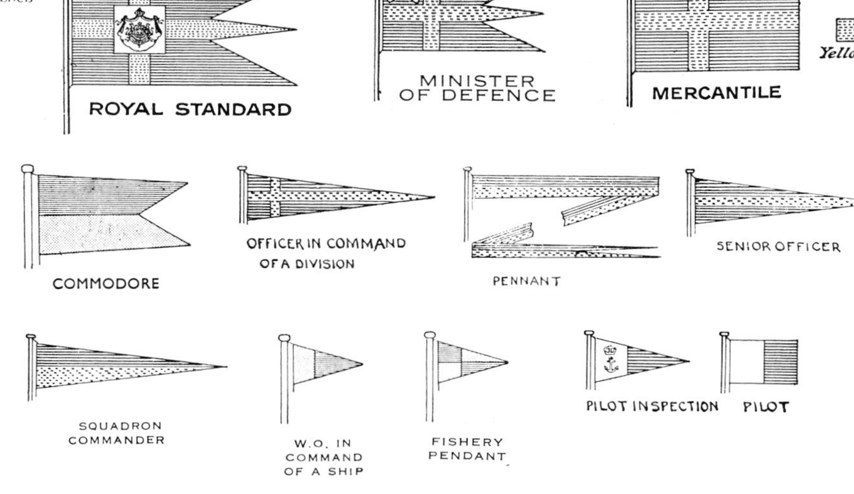

Colour of Ships.

Light Grey all over, excepting S/ms and some training ships. Displacements "Standard."

Navy Estimates.

Five-year programme, voted June 17, 1942, envisages an expenditure over that period of 725,000,000 kronor.
1942–43 : 194,600,000 kr.
1943–44 : 154,000,000 kr.

Mercantile Marine.

Official figures, 1st June, 1945 : 2,722 vessels of 1,629,780 tons gross.

Paymasters have similar stripes with *white* braid following uppermost stripe.

Other branches have stripes with triangular curl, and colour between stripes as follows :—Constructors and Engineers, *purple blue ;* Surgeons, *scarlet.*

Personnel : Active List of Navy and Coast Artillery, *about* 10,000 officers and men, including the conscript class of the year (2,000). Total for Reserves cannot be estimated, as foregoing total includes certain classes called up for service.

Note.—The blue is azure in every case but last 3 pendants.

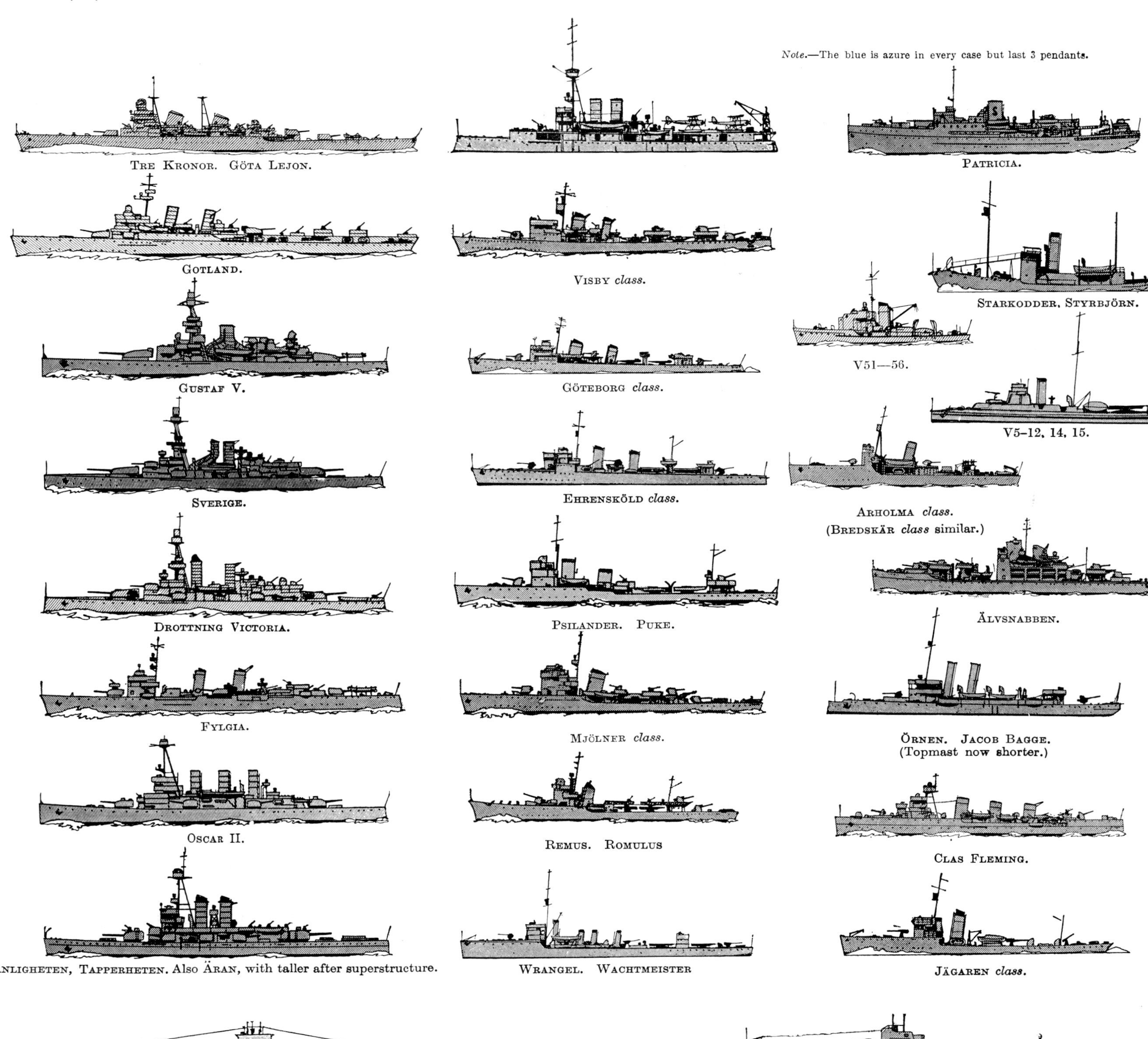

Tre Kronor. Göta Lejon.

Patricia.

Gotland.

Visby *class.*

Starkodder, Styrbjörn.

Gustaf V.

Göteborg *class.*

V51—56.

V5–12, 14, 15.

Sverige.

Ehrensköld *class.*

Arholma *class.* (Bredskär *class* similar.)

Drottning Victoria.

Psilander. Puke.

Älvsnabben.

Fylgia.

Mjölner *class.*

Örnen. Jacob Bagge. (Topmast now shorter.)

Oscar II.

Remus. Romulus

Clas Fleming.

Manligheten, Tapperheten. Also Äran, with taller after superstructure.

Wrangel. Wachtmeister

Jägaren *class.*

Draken *class.*

Delfinen *class.*

Najad *class.*

Sjölejonet *class.*

U1–9.